MindTap™

Tap into **engagement**

MindTap empowers you to produce your best work—consistently.

MindTap is designed to help you master the material. Interactive videos, animations, and activities create a learning path designed by your instructor to guide you through the course and focus on what's important.

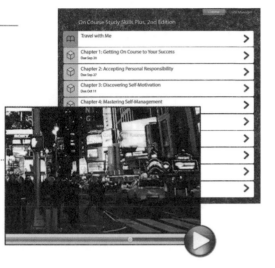

MindTap delivers real-world activities and assignments

that will help you in your academic life as well as your career.

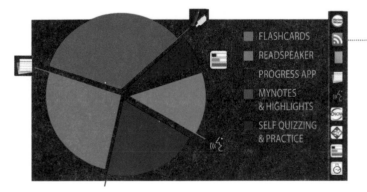

MindTap helps you stay organized and efficient

by giving you the study tools to master the material.

MindTap empowers and motivates

with information that shows where you stand at all times—both individually and compared to the highest performers in class.

"I think MindTap has helped me learn more simply in the few weeks I have used it because it has more study options and provides students with a new and interesting way to study."
— Student, Georgian College

"MindTap makes studying interesting."
— Student, York University

"[MindTap is] already one of the most visually appealing & user friendly online programs that I've used."
— Student, University of Calgary

Tap into more info at: **www.nelson.com/mindtap**

8TH
EDITION

NEW SOCIETY

8TH
EDITION

NEW SOCIETY

ROBERT BRYM
University of Toronto

New Society, Eighth Edition
by Robert Brym

VP, Product and Partnership Solutions:
Anne Williams

Publisher, Digital and Print Content:
Leanna MacLean

Marketing Manager:
Terry Fedorkiw

Content Development Manager:
Toni Chahley

Photo Researcher and Permissions Coordinator:
Marnie Lamb

Production Project Manager:
Jennifer Hare

Copy Editor:
June Trusty

Proofreader:
Linda Szostak

Indexer:
Belle Wong

Design Director:
Ken Phipps

Managing Designer:
Franca Amore

Interior Design:
Sharon Lucas

Cover Design:
Sharon Lucas

Cover Image:
Aaron Millard

Compositor:
MPS Limited

Library and Archives Canada Cataloguing in Publication Data

New society (Toronto, Ont.)
  New society / Robert Brym, University of Toronto. — 8th edition.

1st to 5th editions published under the title: New society : sociology for the 21st century.
Includes bibliographical references and index.
ISBN 978-0-17-657006-4 (bound)

  1. Sociology—Textbooks. I. Brym, Robert J., 1951-, editor II. Title.

HM586.B79 2016   301
C2015-906185-7

ISBN-13: 978-0-17-657006-4
ISBN-10: 0-17-657006-3

For my students. — *RB*

BRIEF CONTENTS

*This chapter is available online only, in the MindTap that accompanies this book.

CONTENTS

Illustrated by Aaron Millarc.

PART 3 INEQUALITY

PART 5 CHANGE AND CONFLICT

*This chapter is available online only, in the MindTap that accompanies this book.

ABOUT THE AUTHORS

ABOUT THE GENERAL EDITOR AND CONTRIBUTOR

ROBERT BRYM

Robert Brym is S. D. Clark Chair in the Department of Sociology at the University of Toronto. He is a Fellow of the Royal Society of Canada, a member of the President's Teaching Academy, and a winner of the Northrop Frye Prize for academic and teaching excellence. His introductory-level textbooks have been published in Canada, Quebec (in French), the United States, Brazil (in Portuguese), and Australia. He has published research on the sociology of intellectuals, social movements in Canada, Jews in Russia, and collective and state violence in Israel and Palestine. Currently, his research focuses on the 2010–11 Arab Spring and the ensuing Arab Winter.

ABOUT THE CONTRIBUTORS

S. HARRIS ALI

S. Harris Ali is a sociologist working in the Faculty of Environmental Studies at York University, Toronto. His research interests involve natural and technological disasters, environmental management, and the relationship of the environment to human health. He has written articles on a wide range of topics, including infectious disease outbreaks (e.g., *E. coli* O157:H7, tuberculosis, SARS, and H1N1); the political economy of disasters (e.g., a plastics recycling fire in Hamilton, Ontario; mining disasters in Nova Scotia; and heat waves in Toronto); and the environmental management of solid waste. His most recent research analyzes the disputes and controversies related to the proposed Northern Gateway and Keystone XL pipelines designed to carry oil extracted from the Alberta tar sands to British Columbia and the U.S. Gulf Coast.

REGINALD W. BIBBY

Reginald W. Bibby is one of Canada's leading experts on religious and social trends. He holds the Board of Governors Research Chair in Sociology at the University of Lethbridge. For more than three decades, he has been monitoring Canadian social trends through his *Project Canada* national surveys of adults and teenagers, recently in partnership with Angus Reid. Dr. Bibby has presented his findings in academic settings around the world. He also has taken his work well beyond the academic community through innumerable public appearances, extensive media exposure, and 13 best-selling books. They include *Fragmented Gods* (Toronto: Irwin, 1987), *Beyond the Gods & Back* (Lethbridge, AB: Project Canada Books, 2011), *Mosaic Madness* (Toronto: Stoddart, 1990), *The Boomer Factor* (Toronto: ECW Press, 2006), and *The Emerging Millennials* (Lethbridge, AB: Project Canada Books, 2009). In recognition of his contribution to the nation, the Governor General appointed him an Officer of the Order of Canada in 2006.

SONIA BOOKMAN

Sonia Bookman is Assistant Professor in the Department of Sociology at the University of Manitoba, where she teaches courses in consumer culture, media and society, and urban sociology. She is a graduate of the University of Winnipeg (B.A. Honours) and the University of Manchester (M.A. and Ph.D., 2006). Her research interests are in the sociology of brands and branding, urban culture, and consumption. Her work on these topics is published in various books and journals, including the *Journal of Consumer Culture*, *Cultural Sociology*, and *Space and Culture*.

MICHAEL BURAWOY

Michael Burawoy teaches sociology at the University of California, Berkeley. He is President of the International Sociological Association and former President of the American Sociological Association. He has authored more than 125 scholarly articles and authored or co-authored 10 books, including *Manufacturing Consent* (Chicago: University of Chicago Press, 1982), a classic study of change in the capitalist labour process, and *Global Ethnography* (Berkeley, CA: University of California Press, 2000), a pioneering work on ethnographic sociological research in the postmodern world.

NEENA J. CHAPPELL

Neena Chappell, F.R.S.C., F.C.A.H.S., Canada Research Chair in social gerontology, has been conducting research in the area of aging for more than 30 years. Throughout her career, she has sought to demonstrate the value and relevance of sociological thought and research for applied issues in aging. She believes that rigorous university-based social science research has a critical role to play in the nonuniversity community. Her interests include caregiving, health, and social policy in Canada and cross-nationally. She has established two university research centres on aging, one at the University of Manitoba and the other at the University of Victoria, where she continues to conduct research. She has published more than 300 academic articles and reports. She is past President of the Canadian Association on Gerontology and of Academy II (Social Sciences) of the Royal Society of Canada.

SANDRA COLAVECCHIA

Sandra Colavecchia received her Ph.D. from the University of Toronto and is now an Assistant Professor in the Department of Sociology at McMaster University, where she teaches introductory sociology and sociology of families. Her teaching interests include teaching technologies, active learning, and academic skill development. Her research interests are in sociology of families and family policy. Sociology is not just a job for her—it is a lens through which she understands her life and the world around her. She strives to share her excitement about sociology with her students.

SCOTT DAVIES

Scott Davies is Professor of Leadership, Higher and Adult Education, at the University of Toronto. He has studied social movements and organizations in education and is currently examining the emergence of academic inequalities from preschool to postsecondary levels. He has won awards from the American Education Research Association and the Canadian Education Research Association, and has been an associate editor and editorial board member of several journals. With Neil Guppy, he is author of three editions of *The Schooled Society*.

NEIL GUPPY

Neil Guppy is Professor of Sociology at the University of British Columbia. He is a graduate of Queen's University (B.A./B.P.H.E.) and the University of Waterloo (M.Sc./Ph.D., 1981). He has published several books, including *Education in Canada* (Ottawa: Statistics Canada, 1998, with Scott Davies), *The Schooled Society*, 3rd ed. (Toronto: Oxford University Press, 2014, with Scott Davies), and *Successful Surveys*, 4th ed. (Toronto: Thomson Nelson, 2008, with George Gray). Recently, he has published work in the *American Sociological Review*, *Canadian Public Policy*, and *International Migration Review*. At UBC, he has received both a University Killam Teaching Prize and a University Killam Research Prize.

JOHN HANNIGAN

John Hannigan is Professor of Sociology at the University of Toronto Scarborough (UTSC), where he teaches courses in urban and environmental sociology. He attended the University of Western Ontario and Ohio State University, where he received his Ph.D. in 1976. While at Ohio State, he was a Research Associate at the Disaster Research Center. He is the author of three books: *Environmental Sociology* (1995, 2006, 2014), *Fantasy City: Pleasure and Profit in the Postmodern City* (1998), both published by Routledge (New York), and *Disasters Without Borders: The International Politics of Natural Disasters* (Polity Press, U.K., 2012). *Fantasy City* was nominated for the 1999/2000 Canadian Sociology and Anthropology Association (CSAA) John Porter Award. *Environmental Sociology* has been translated into Portuguese, Japanese, Chinese, and Korean. Dr. Hannigan is a frequent contributor to media discussions of culture and urban development, having appeared on National Public Radio (United States), in *The Independent* (Britain), and in *The Globe & Mail* (Canada). He has served in a number of administrative posts including Graduate Director and Associate Chair in the Department of Sociology (1999–2002); Interim Chair, Department of Social Sciences, UTSC (2003); and Secretary, CSAA (2000–03). Polity Press (U.K.) will publish his most recent book, *The Geopolitics of Deep Oceans*, in 2015.

JOSÉE JOHNSTON

Josée Johnston is Associate Professor of Sociology at the University of Toronto. Her major interest is the sociological study of food, which is a lens for investigating questions relating to culture, politics, gender, and the environment. She co-authored (with Shyon Baumann) *Foodies: Democracy and Distinction in the Gourmet Foodscape* (New York: Routledge, 2014 [2010]), as well as *Food and Femininity* (Bloomsbury, 2015) (with Kate Cairns). She has also published articles in the *American Journal of Sociology*, *Theory and Society*, *Signs: Journal of Women in Culture and Society*, and *Gender and Society*. Her research has been supported by the Social Sciences and Humanities Research Council and the Canadian Institute for Health Research. In 2009, she was awarded the Province of Ontario's five-year Early Researcher Award. Professor Johnston teaches courses on the sociology of food and globalization with an emphasis on inequality, social justice, and sustainability.

HARVEY KRAHN

Harvey Krahn is a Professor of Sociology at the University of Alberta. His research interests include social inequality, the sociology of work, the sociology of education, immigration, environmental sociology, and political sociology. He typically uses quantitative research methods but has also participated in studies employing qualitative and historical methods. His largest research project involves interviewing a sample of 400 individuals seven times over 25 years to learn more about school–work transitions and how social inequality is reproduced across generations. He is one of three co-authors of a textbook on the sociology of work (*Work, Industry, and Canadian Society*, 7th ed. Toronto: Nelson, 2015) and has published research findings in a wide range of scholarly journals.

RHONDA L. LENTON

Rhonda Lenton is Professor, Vice-President Academic, and Provost at York University. In addition to providing strategic leadership for the university, she has oversight for institutional change management and academic resource planning. She is currently a board member of the Ontario Online Consortium and the Ontario Council on Articulation and Transfer. Her areas of teaching and research expertise include research methods and data analysis, gender, sexual harassment, and family violence. She has published peer-reviewed book chapters and articles in an array of academic journals, and she is currently working on a book based on a national study of marital conflict in Canada. She also led a team on a project recently published by the Higher Education Quality Council of Ontario assessing the impact of community-based and community-service learning on student learning, as well as opportunities for faculty development.

JOHN LIE

John Lie was born in South Korea, grew up in Japan and Hawaii, and received his A.B., A.M., and Ph.D. degrees from Harvard University. His main interests are in social theory and political economy. Currently he is the C. K. Cho Professor of Sociology at the University of California, Berkeley, where he previously served as the Dean of International and Area Studies. His recent publications include *Zainichi (Koreans in Japan)* (Berkeley, CA: University of California Press, 2008) and *Modern Peoplehood: On Race, Racism, Nationalism, Ethnicity, and Identity*, paperback ed. (Berkeley, CA: University of California Press, 2011).

MARGARET J. PENNING

Dr. Penning is interested in the sociology of health and healthcare, as well as aging. In particular, she is interested in examining issues of loneliness and social support; the impor-
tance of self, informal, and formal care for dealing with chronic illness and disability in middle and later life; the impact of structural inequalities on health and healthcare; and healthcare restructuring and reform in the Canadian context. She is currently the principal investigator of a program of research focusing on transitions and trajectories in late-life care.

LANCE W. ROBERTS

Lance Roberts was born in Calgary, grew up in Edmonton, and received his Ph.D. from the University of Alberta. He is a Fellow of St. John's College and Professor of Sociology at the University of Manitoba, where he teaches Introductory Sociology as well as research methods and statistics courses. In the last decade, he has received several teaching awards, including his university's Dr. and Mrs. H. H. Saunderson Award for Excellence in Teaching. His current research interests cover the comparative charting of social change, educational concerns, and mental health issues. In addition to publishing in research journals, Dr. Roberts recently co-authored *The Methods Coach*, *The Statistics Coach*, and *Understanding Social Statistics: A Student's Guide through the Maze* (Oxford University Press), all aimed at helping students master fundamental research techniques. He enjoys teaching Introductory Sociology and is currently developing a variety of tools to enlarge his students' sociological imaginations.

VIC SATZEWICH

Vic Satzewich is Professor of Sociology at McMaster University. He has published many books and articles on various aspects of immigration, racism, and ethnic relations in Canada. He has recently completed a major study of discretion in the immigrant selection system in Canada. His most recent books include *"Race" and Ethnicity in Canada: A Critical Introduction* (Toronto: Oxford University Press, 2013); *Racism in Canada* (Toronto: Oxford University Press, 2011);

Transnational Identities and Practices in Canada (Vancouver: University of British Columbia Press, 2006); and *The Ukrainian Diaspora* (New York: Routledge, 2002). In 2005, he received the Outstanding Contribution Award of the Canadian Sociology Association.

LISA STROHSCHEIN

Lisa Strohschein (rhymes with *sunshine*) was born in Ontario, Canada, and received her Ph.D. at McMaster University in 2002. She is currently Associate Professor and Associate Chair (Undergraduate) in the Department of Sociology at the University of Alberta. In her research, she investigates how family dynamics are related to health and well-being, with a specific focus on the impact of divorce on adults and children. Her current projects include a federally funded grant to describe and evaluate the social implications of new family forms in Canada and an international collaboration that will compare how Canadian and American youth navigated the transition to adulthood during the Great Recession.

JULIAN TANNER

Julian Tanner is a Professor of Sociology at the University of Toronto. His interest in the sociology of crime and deviance, particularly youth crime and youth culture, derives from his school days in England—as both a student in an all-boys boarding school and, later on, as a secondary-school teacher. In addition to undergraduate and graduate courses in crime and deviance, he has taught and researched in the areas of school-to-work transitions (high-school dropouts, the effects of part-time jobs, and so on), the sociology of work (the industrial and political attitudes and behaviours of male manual workers, gender and the professions), young people, and popular music. In the recent past, he has studied patterns of crime and victimization among young people in Toronto and youth gang activity, and is currently investigating youth and guns.

SANDY WELSH

Sandy Welsh is Professor of Sociology and Vice-Dean, Graduate Education and Program Reviews, in the Faculty of Arts and Science at the University of Toronto. She studies work and occupations, gender, sociology of law, and social policy. Her current research explores how changes in federal and provincial regulations affect the adoption and implementation of workplace harassment and work–family policies in Canadian corporations. Ongoing research collaborations focus on how the pending regulation of Homeopaths, Naturopaths and Traditional Chinese Medicine/Acupuncturists in Ontario is changing these occupational groups. Her research has appeared in *Gender & Society*, *Social Problems*, *Annual Review of Sociology*, *Sociology of Health and Illness*, and *Social Science and Medicine*. With Dr. Tracey Adams, she co-authored *The Organization and Experience of Work* (Nelson, 2008). She has received funding from SSHRC, CIHR, Status of Women Canada, and other foundations. Dr. Welsh provides expert testimony on sexual harassment for the Ontario and Canadian Human Rights Commissions and in other legal forums. She is a recipient of the University of Toronto Faculty of Arts and Sciences Outstanding Teaching Award.

ANTHONY WINSON

Anthony Winson's research and publications have focused on agriculture, food, and rural development issues related to Canada and the developing world. He is the author of *Coffee and Democracy in Modern Costa Rica* (London: Macmillan, 1989), *The Intimate Commodity: Food and the Development of the Agro-Industrial Complex in Canada* (Toronto: Garamond, 1993), and *Contingent Work, Disrupted Lives: Labour and Community in the New Rural Economy* (University of Toronto, 2002, with Belinda Leach). *Contingent Work* won the 2003 John Porter Tradition of Excellence Book Award of the Canadian Sociology Association. He has recently co-edited (with M. Koc and J. Sumner) *Critical Perspectives in Food Studies* (Toronto: Oxford University Press, 2012). His latest book is entitled

The Industrial Diet: The Degradation of Food and the Struggle for Healthy Eating (Vancouver: UBC Press and New York: NYU Press). See his website at www.theindustrialdiet.com and Twitter account @industrialdiet.

MARISSA YOUNG

Marisa Young is an Assistant Professor in the Department of Sociology at McMaster University. She specializes in research on the work–family interface and gender differences in paid and unpaid work. She is currently working on a series of cross-sectional and longitudinal projects in Canada and the United States examining how family and community contexts shape expectations of work and family obligations. Her recently published research examines the impact of workplace resources/demands on work–family role-blurring; gender differences in experiences and family-related consequences of work–family conflict; and the psychosocial determinants of perceived demands in the work–family interface. Her future research plans include further exploring how neighbourhood context impacts work–family relations and well-being among family members.

PREFACE

8TH EDITION

NEW SOCIETY

ROBERT BRYM

Illustrated by Aaron Millard.

The job of figuring out what to do with our lives and how to act in the world is more difficult than ever. Sociology helps by analyzing the pressing social issues of the day, showing how those issues affect all of us, and setting out options for dealing with them. Moreover, as you will learn in the following pages, sociology views social issues from a unique disciplinary perspective. All in all, it is a controversial and exciting business. Social problems are typically complex. The options for action often involve different benefits and disadvantages for different groups. Sociologists usually see things differently from other social and natural scientists. Not surprisingly, therefore, sociology, like any vibrant academic discipline, involves a lot of heated debate.

Unfortunately, most introductory sociology textbooks don't give much of a feel for the excitement of the discipline. They usually resemble encyclopedias full of definitions and presumably undeniable facts. They make sociological knowledge resemble the tablets some people say were brought down by Moses from Mount Sinai: abstract principles carved in stone, eternal truths that most people agree with but that tell us little about the way life is actually lived.

In preparing this book, I tried to overcome this deficiency in two ways. First, when I recruited authors to write chapters, I asked them to focus on social issues that are likely to be of real, everyday concern to Canadian undergraduates. Second, I asked the authors to highlight the controversies in the field, not the clichés. There is no sense keeping secret what any good scientist knows: Advances in knowledge usually result from intellectual conflict, not consensus.

WHAT'S NEW IN THE EIGHTH EDITION

With the helpful feedback of reviewers and a dedicated team of contributors, the eighth edition has been thoroughly revised and updated to include important emergent topics in the field of sociology. These topics include the following:

- Qualitative research methodologies
- New media studies, including social media and its impact on social structures, social institutions, globalization, revolutions, and government
- Intersectionality theory
- Sociology of food and the environment
- Sexuality

Beyond this comprehensive update, the chapters have undergone the following enhancements:

- **Chapter 1, Introducing Sociology**, includes two new sections, "The Cultural Turn and Poststructuralism: Gramsci and Foucault" and "Social Constructionism and Queer Theory."
- **Chapter 2, Research Methods**, has been revised to include expanded material on qualitative research. Enhanced coverage of ethics includes ethical considerations for most research methods. A new discussion of participant action research has been added, using recent Canadian data.
- **Chapter 3, Culture**, contains new material on class and clothes.
- **Chapter 4, Socialization** is a new chapter, written by Lisa Strohschein of the University of Alberta. The chapter emphasizes how societies organize the way people pass through the life course. It includes a discussion of the residential school system in Canada as an example of resocialization. Throughout, the author emphasizes the mass media as an agent of socialization.
- **Chapter 5, Gender and Sexualities**, includes new material on sexual minorities that clarifies terms such as *heteronormativity*, *transgender*, and *transsexual*. It also adds a discussion of the sex trade and information on Indigenous women and intersectionality.
- **Chapter 6, Communication and Mass Media**, is a new chapter, written by Sonia Bookman of the University of Manitoba. This chapter includes an extensive discussion of the shift from traditional to new media and the social implications of this change. There is an extensive discussion of the

functions of social media and a section on media representation that highlights the work of Stuart Hall, Indigenous television, and Canadian content. The chapter also includes an analysis of the role of social media in the 2014 pro-democracy movement in Hong Kong and the Idle No More movement.

- **Chapter 7, Social Stratification**, includes new material on Pierre Bourdieu and a discussion of why rising tuition costs and student debt are not generating protest among students in most of Canada.
- **Chapter 8, Gender Inequality**, is a new chapter, written by Marisa Young of McMaster University. The chapter contains a comparison of women's and men's participation in the Canadian paid labour force and their representation and earnings across and within occupations, using recent census data. It includes a discussion of the quantity and type of domestic work that women and men do, using the 2014 Canadian Work Stress and Health Study. The chapter also contains a discussion of the consequences of gender inequality in the workplace and domestic sphere for men's and women's mental health.
- **Chapter 9, Race and Ethnic Relations**, has been enhanced with new census and research data on ethnic demographics, ethnic discrimination, and well-being among First Nations, Inuit, and other Canadian communities. The chapter also includes a new introduction that discusses the RCMP report, *Missing and Murdered Aboriginal Women*.
- **Chapter 10, Development and Under-development**, contains a new section on post-neoliberalism in Latin America and a discussion of the value of the *Human Development Index* as a more comprehensive approach to measuring development than GDP per capita is.
- **Chapter 11, Families**, includes a new discussion of contemporary trends in marriage, fertility, and delayed home-leaving. The chapter also includes new material on child care, poverty, and inter-racial relationships.
- **Chapter 12, Work and Occupations**, contains new material on the rise of the unpaid intern and on migrant workers.
- **Chapter 13, Education**, has been enhanced with a discussion of Indigenous education and new material on change and persistence in educational attainment by gender, and the

emergence of "equity categories" in schools, illustrating how political protest gets institutionalized in school policy.

- **Chapter 14, Religion**, includes an enhanced discussion of the stereotypes that religious groups hold of one another and how these stereotypes lead to conflict and discrimination.
- **Chapter 15, Deviance and Crime**, contains new material on victimization (particularly of Indigenous women) as well as new material on surveillance, cyberbullying, and Edward Snowden. The chapter explores obesity, stigma, and stigmatization, and presents new examples of moral panic involving young people. There is also an enhanced discussion of the relationship between deviance and resistance.
- **Chapter 16, Population and Urbanization**, includes new data on urban demographics and urban and rural populations in Canada. The chapter also includes new material on the Regent Park revitalization in Toronto.
- **Chapter 17, Sociology and the Environment**, includes new material related to the muzzling of environmental scientists, the politics/sovereignty battles over Arctic Oil, the Keystone XL pipeline, and the environment and food. The chapter also includes a new section on gender and the environment, and ecofeminism.
- **Chapter 18, Health and Aging**, includes a new discussion of euthanasia and a new section on complementary and alternative medicine. The discussion of medicalization and intersectionality has also been enhanced and expanded.
- **Chapter 19, Politics and Social Movements**, includes new material on the Arab Spring, the Occupy movement, and the Idle No More movement. The chapter also includes new material on social media and social movements.
- **Chapter 20, Globalization**, has been enhanced with updated material on the corporate tax rate and a new discussion of slavery and globalization.
- **Online Chapter 21, Networks, Groups, and Bureaucracies**, includes new material on cyberbullying and how al-Qaeda and ISIS sharpened group boundaries to increase their power.

Students and instructors will also enjoy our new design, enhanced to increase visual appeal, with new part openers and chapter openers and the inclusion of new photos in every chapter.

ORGANIZATION OF THE TEXTBOOK

Chapter 1, Introducing Sociology, by Robert Brym, sets the tone for the rest of the book. Instead of sermonizing on the question "What is sociology?" as most other textbooks do, the chapter asks, in effect, "Why sociology?"—that is, why does an undergraduate in this particular time and place need to know what sociology has to offer? The chief aim of Chapter 1 is to show how sociological thinking can clarify and perhaps help to resolve the real-life social issues that confront all of us here and now. **Chapter 2**, Research Methods, concisely outlines how sociologists work. Neil Guppy's clarity, research experience, and balanced approach add much-needed lustre to a subject that first-year students often find dull. Guppy leaves the reader with the firm sense that, for all the intellectual liveliness and controversy displayed in this book, sociology can be and is disciplined by the judicious use of logic and evidence.

The remainder of the book is divided into five parts. **Part 2** could be subtitled "Becoming Human." In **Chapter 3**, Culture, Robert Brym makes a case for the view that ours is an increasingly fragmented and globalized postmodern culture that increases our freedom to fashion identities that suit our individual tastes. It also shows that, paradoxically, our increased cultural freedom develops within definite limits beyond which it is more and more difficult to move. In **Chapter 4**, Socialization, Lisa Strohschein thoroughly discusses the interactive mechanisms through which we learn beliefs, symbols, values, and self-identities throughout the life cycle and in various institutions. Rhonda Lenton then devotes **Chapter 5**, Gender and Sexualities, to an in-depth analysis of what might seem to be the most intimate and biologically determined aspects of our identity—our gender and sexuality—and demonstrates that, in fact, they have deep roots in culture and society. In **Chapter 6**, Communication and Mass Media, Sonia Bookman analyzes the impact of one of the most pervasive and influential social institutions today. In sum, the analyses of Part 2 will give the reader a solid appreciation of how we become part of society and how society becomes part of us through the transmission of culture between generations.

Part 3 is about how people become and remain unequal. Harvey Krahn shows in **Chapter 7**, Social

Stratification, that despite recent assertions of the demise of social classes, stratification persists and continues to structure our life-chances in profound ways. Indeed, inequality is increasing in many societies, including Canada. In **Chapter 8**, Gender Inequality, Marisa Young convincingly demonstrates that gender is an equally important basis of social inequality, with significant implications for economic security, family life, mental health, and much else. Vic Satzewich devotes **Chapter 9**, Race and Ethnic Relations, to highlighting the deficiencies of biological and purely cultural approaches to understanding the bases of ethnic and racial inequality. Finally, in **Chapter 10**, Development and Underdevelopment, Anthony Winson incisively criticizes modernization and other theories of economic underdevelopment and global inequality, offering a compelling argument for the analytical benefits of a modified dependency approach to the problem. The reader will complete Part 3 with a firm understanding of how people are highly differentiated and differentially rewarded, depending on their social location.

Part 4 shifts the reader's attention to some of society's fundamental institutions. Sandra Colavecchia's **Chapter 11**, Families, examines how and why families and intimate relationships have undergone change and diversification, particularly in the past several decades, and suggests where they may be headed. Sandy Welsh devotes **Chapter 12**, Work and Occupations, to tracing the development and future shape of work. In **Chapter 13**, Education, Scott Davies dissects our educational system, demonstrating that, paradoxically, it is as much a cause of the persistence of inequality as it is an avenue for upward mobility. In **Chapter 14**, Religion, Reginald Bibby assesses the social origins, consequences, and future of religion, relying heavily on his own fundamentally important survey research to argue his case for the persistence of religion in Canadian society and the growing polarization of Canadians into religious and secular camps.

Change and conflict are the subjects of **Part 5**. Here the reader is introduced to the main forces of turbulence in our society. In **Chapter 15**, Deviance and Crime, Julian Tanner elegantly analyzes one form of social conflict: deviant and criminal behaviour. He undermines several common misconceptions in the process. John Hannigan's analysis in **Chapter 16**, Population and Urbanization, is a novel and revealing look at how human populations have developed in cities from preindustrial to postmodern times. S. Harris Ali devotes **Chapter 17**, Sociology and the Environment, to one of the most pressing issues of the day—the environment. He analyzes the rise of environmental awareness and its effects on the relationship among industry, the state, and the public; the process by which environmental issues are socially constructed; how the distribution of power in society affects strategies to manage and govern the environment; and the uneven distribution of environmental risks in society. In **Chapter 18**, Health and Aging, Margaret Penning and Neena Chappell expertly discuss the aging of the Canadian population and attendant health issues. **Chapter 19**, Politics and Social Movements, Robert Brym surveys the evolution of politics and social movements, showing how various forms of conflict emerge, change our lives, and become institutionalized. Finally, globalization is the subject and title of **Chapter 20**, by Josée Johnston. She shows that culturally, politically, and economically, the world is becoming a single place and its inhabitants are developing a global consciousness. This does not imply that we are becoming one big happy family. To the contrary, conflict has persisted and even intensified in the early twenty-first century.

The book concludes with an **Epilogue**, The Future of Sociology, by Michael Burawoy, former President of the International Sociological Association. With stunning historical sweep, he argues that three waves of marketization have transformed the dominant thrust of sociology since the nineteenth century. According to Burawoy, the latest, neoliberal wave of marketization is causing many members of the discipline to become public sociologists, refusing collaboration with the market and the state, and instead engaging directly with communities, institutions, and social movements to defend society against rampant marketization.

As a bonus feature, Robert Brym, Lance Roberts, Lisa Strohschein, and John Lie prepared **online Chapter 21**, Networks, Groups, and Bureaucracies. It draws the connection between micro-level interactions, meso-level organization, and macro-level social forces and institutions. It is recommended that this chapter be assigned after Chapter 4, Socialization. This chapter is available on the Companion Website and on the MindTap that accompany this book.

FEATURES OF THIS TEXT

While the content and organization of this text have been carefully rendered, you will also find updated visual and pedagogical features in this eighth edition of *New Society*.

NEW PART OPENERS

Students and instructors alike will appreciate the unique illustrations that grace the cover and part openers. These illustrations were created by Aaron Millard, a recent graduate of OCAD University in Toronto, and were designed to engage students with the important themes in the book.

PART 2

CULTURE

Additionally, new chapter objectives presented at the beginning of each chapter prepare students to think critically and to absorb the material.

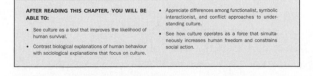

AFTER READING THIS CHAPTER, YOU WILL BE ABLE TO:

- See culture as a tool that improves the likelihood of human survival.
- Contrast biological explanations of human behaviour with sociological explanations that focus on culture.

- Appreciate differences among functionalist, symbolic interactionist, and conflict approaches to understanding culture.
- See how culture operates as a force that simultaneously increases human freedom and constrains social action.

NEW FEATURE BOXES

To further engage students and reflect the critical approach of the text, we have created three new feature boxes:

- Critical Sociology: Globalization

CRITICAL SOCIOLOGY: GLOBALIZATION   THE EDWARD SNOWDEN AFFAIR

The global scope of governmental surveillance was graphically highlighted in 2013, when Edward Snowden leaked classified information from the U.S. National Security Agency to various news agencies. The documents in question exposed details of military operations and plans. It also revealed government interest in the private activities of its own citizens, such as the online sexual activity of individuals deemed by governments to be radicals—information that could be used to discredit them.

Edward Snowden.
SOURCE: © Barton Gellman/Getty Images.

Governments were not just spying on their own citizens. The leaked documents also revealed that the United States was spying on a number of its erstwhile allies—the leaders of Britain, Germany, and Spain among them. Nor was the data gathering restricted to national security matters. The German electronics company Siemens was electronically robbed of confidential information, an act of industrial espionage.

Considerable debate has taken place concerning how Snowden's activities should be judged. Is he a traitor, as the American authorities argue? Or is he a courageous whistleblower who has legitimately drawn attention to the wrongful and harmful activities of governments? Global reaction is mixed. Were he to be apprehended, charged, and convicted by the American government, he would be liable to a 30-year prison sentence. On the other hand, he has also been awarded a number of international humanitarian awards. What do you think?

Critical Thinking Questions

1. Is Edward Snowden a hero or a villain?
2. Should governments surveil their citizens? If so, for what reasons? How intrusive should this surveillance be?

- Critical Sociology: Protest and Policy

CRITICAL SOCIOLOGY: PROTEST AND POLICY   THE RISE OF THE UNPAID INTERN

Nicholas Smith landed a job right after he graduated from the University of Toronto with an ethics degree in 2013. A year later, he was working in his second job. The trouble is that both jobs were unpaid internships. "I used to do marketing and there are a couple of marketing companies that have marketing graduates working 50-hour weeks and overtime without pay, and if you refuse to work the OT you don't get a reference," he said (Canadian Press, 2014a).

Nobody knows how many Canadian internships are unpaid, but figures from the United States (where one-third of interns are unpaid) and Western Europe (where one-half are unpaid) may give a rough indication of the likely magnitude of the problem in this country (Library of Parliament, 2013). Anecdotal evidence suggests that unpaid internships first became widespread during the Great Recession of 2008–09. Many unpaid interns work at wealthy corporations, including Bell Media and Fairmont Hotels and Resorts.

Unpaid interns tend to be young and unable to find paid employment but they need job experience on their résumés so they work for nothing. Most interns who are unpaid or are receiving less than the minimum wage are women. Some are recent immigrants who need Canadian employment experience to land a paying job. At the *Huffington Post* in the United States, a few interns actually pay to work as unpaid interns. To become an unpaid intern, you must be able to afford it; typically, unpaid interns have savings, loans, or relatives who can support them while they work for nothing. The system can provide certain advantages—useful network ties, letters of reference, job experience—but it is mainly

people from middle-class families who can afford to become unpaid interns (Cross, 2014).

In November 2014, Stephen Poloz, the governor of the Bank of Canada, was widely criticized for advising the 200 000 young Canadians who are out of work as follows: "If your parents are letting you live in the basement, you might as well go out and do something for free to put the experience on your CV" (Canadian Press, 2014b). Other outrages have sparked protests against unpaid internships. In 2011, a student DJ working for free died in a car accident after repeatedly being compelled to be on air all night at an Alberta radio station. In 2013, many Canadians were appalled when the Vancouver Fairmont Waterfront Hotel posted an ad for people to bus tables for free.

Some politicians in the New Democratic and Liberal parties are demanding laws to regulate internships fairly. The Canadian Intern Association was formed to advocate against the exploitation of interns and to improve the internship experience. People who have been abused by the system of unpaid internships have gone public with exposés of their exploitation. If such pressure persists, one may reasonably expect that, in the coming years, at least the more egregious forms of exploitation will be abolished.

Critical Thinking Questions

1. What are the potential advantages and disadvantages of unpaid internships?
2. Should internships be regulated and, if so, how? What potentially positive and negative outcomes might result from regulation?

SOURCES: Canadian Press (2014a, 2014b); Jessica Smith Cross (2014); and the Library of Parliament (2013).

- Critical Sociology: Social Inequality

CRITICAL SOCIOLOGY: SOCIAL INEQUALITY   THE PH.D. IMMIGRANT TAXI DRIVER

Evidence from a Statistics Canada study shows that a sizable proportion of immigrants who drive taxis in Canada are significantly overqualified (Xu, 2012). About half the taxi drivers in the country are immigrants. Although taxi driving normally requires a secondary school degree and/or occupation-specific training, many immigrants have bachelor's, master's, doctoral, or medical degrees. Of the 255 taxi drivers who had a Ph.D. or medical degree in Canada in 2006, nearly 80 percent were immigrants. Of the 1525 taxi drivers with a master's degree, nearly 90 percent were immigrants.

Figure 9.5 shows the differences in educational attainment of immigrant and Canadian-born

taxi drivers. These statistics provide striking evidence of the difficulties that highly educated immigrants have in making inroads in the Canadian labour market.

Critical Thinking Questions

1. Does the existence of overeducated taxi drivers among immigrants reflect racial discrimination in the broader labour market in Canada?
2. How can Canadian society improve the way it evaluates the educational credentials of immigrants to Canada?

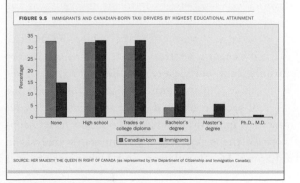

FIGURE 9.5 IMMIGRANTS AND CANADIAN-BORN TAXI DRIVERS BY HIGHEST EDUCATIONAL ATTAINMENT

SOURCE: HER MAJESTY THE QUEEN IN RIGHT OF CANADA (as represented by the Department of Citizenship and Immigration Canada);

A set of Critical Thinking Questions is provided at the end of each box.

FIGURES, TABLES, AND IN-CHAPTER LEARNING AIDS

Current census data and other up-to-date research is easily compared when presented in one of 36 tables and 96 figures integrated throughout the book to enhance student learning—55 of these figures are completely new, and *New Society*, Eighth Edition, also includes three new maps.

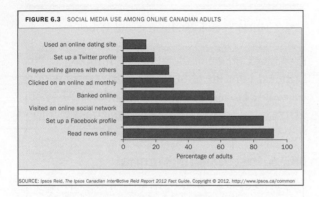

FIGURE 6.3 SOCIAL MEDIA USE AMONG ONLINE CANADIAN ADULTS

SOURCE: Ipsos Reid, *The Ipsos Canadian inter@ctive Reid Report 2012 Fact Guide*. Copyright © 2012. http://www.ipsos.ca/common

New "Time for Review" questions found at the end of important sections in each chapter balance provocative questions with factual recall.

TIME FOR REVIEW

1. What is the relationship among values, theories, and research?
2. What are the key features of the four main theoretical traditions?
3. What is the "cultural turn" in the conflict tradition?
4. What does queer theory contribute to symbolic interactionism?

END-OF-CHAPTER RESOURCES

Each chapter concludes with a set of end-of-chapter resources to help students review and apply their knowledge. A new **Summary** format covers key concepts in each chapter in question-and-answer

SUMMARY

1. **What is sociology?**
   Sociology is the systematic study of human behaviour in social context. The sociological perspective analyzes the connection between personal troubles and social structures.
2. **Where are the social relations that surround you, permeate you, and influence your behaviour?**
   Social relations exist in micro- (small-scale, face-to-face), macro- (large-scale, more impersonal),

   opportunities and close off others, they influence human behaviour.
3. **How does sociological research seek to test ideas using scientific methods and thereby improve people's lives?**
   Sociological research begins with values—ideas about what is good and bad, right and wrong. Values often motivate sociologists to define which problems are worth studying and to

QUESTIONS TO CONSIDER

1. Durkheim argued that the social solidarity of groups influences the suicide rate in those groups. How, if at all, do you think the social solidarity of groups influences the crime rate and the divorce rate in those groups? Why?
2. In what sense is sociology a science? How does sociology differ from a natural science, such as physics?
3. What kinds of sociological issues are best addressed by each of the four major theoretical traditions in sociology?

GLOSSARY

Altruistic suicide (p. 6) occurs in settings that exhibit high levels of social solidarity, according to Durkheim. Altruistic suicide results from norms very tightly governing behaviour.

Anomic suicide (p. 6) occurs in settings that exhibit low levels of social solidarity, according to Durkheim. Anomic suicide results from vaguely defined norms governing behaviour.

point where their values are universally accepted as common sense.

The **Democratic Revolution** (p. 10) began about 1750. It suggested that people are responsible for organizing society and that human intervention can therefore solve social problems.

Dysfunctional consequences (p. 14) are effects of social structures that create social instability.

format, which helps students to see the "bigger picture" and interact with concepts, not just facts. A set of **Questions to Consider** encourages readers to think critically about the material and to apply what they have learned against their own values, ideas, and experiences.

A glossary of key terms and their definitions is also provided at the end of each chapter.

ANCILLARIES

INSTRUCTOR RESOURCES

neta The Nelson Education Teaching Advantage (NETA) program delivers research-based instructor resources that promote student engagement and higher-order thinking to enable the success of Canadian students and educators. Visit Nelson Education's Inspired Instruction website at www.nelson.com/inspired to find out more about NETA.

The following instructor resources have been created for *New Society*, Eighth Edition. Access these ultimate tools for customizing lectures and presentations at www.nelson.com/instructor.

NETA Test Bank

The **NETA Test Bank** was written by **Darlene Balandin** of Western University. It includes over 1700 multiple-choice questions written according to NETA guidelines for effective construction and development of higher-order questions. Also included are over 300 true/false, 150 short-answer, and 150 essay questions.

cognero *Full-Circle Assessment* The NETA Test Bank is available in a new, cloud-based platform. **Nelson Testing Powered by Cognero®** is a secure online testing system that allows instructors to author, edit, and manage test bank content from anywhere Internet access is available. No special installations or downloads are needed, and the desktop-inspired interface, with its drop-down menus and familiar, intuitive tools, allows instructors to create and manage tests with ease. Multiple test versions can be created in an instant, and content can be imported or exported into other systems. Tests can be delivered from a learning management system, the classroom, or wherever an instructor chooses. Testing Powered by Cognero for *New Society* can also be accessed through www.nelson.com/instructor.

NETA PowerPoint

Microsoft® **PowerPoint® lecture slides** for every chapter have been created by **Rose Ricciardelli** of Memorial University. There is an average of 30 slides per chapter, many featuring key figures, tables, and photographs from *New Society*. NETA principles of clear design and engaging content have been incorporated throughout, making it simple for instructors to customize the deck for their courses.

Image Library

The **Image Library** consists of digital copies of figures, short tables, and photographs used in the book. Instructors may use these images to customize the NETA PowerPoint or create their own PowerPoint presentations.

Videos

Enhance your classroom experience with the exciting and relevant videos of *Think Outside the Book: The Nelson Sociology DVD Collection* prepared to accompany *New Society*. Designed to enrich and support chapter concepts, this set of seven 30-minute video segments was created by Robert Brym to stimulate discussion of topics raised in sociology. Produced in conjunction with Face to Face Media (Vancouver), the Jesuit Communication Project (Toronto), and the National Film Board of Canada, the selections have been edited to optimize their impact in the classroom. Many of the selections are taken from films that have won national and international awards.

NETA Instructor's Manual

The *Instructor's Manual* to accompany *New Society* was prepared by **Nikki-Marie Brown** of McMaster University. This manual contains sample lesson plans, learning objectives, suggested classroom activities, and a resource integration guide to give instructors the support they need to engage their students in the classroom.

Day One Slides

Day One—Prof InClass is a PowerPoint presentation that instructors can customize to orient students to the class and their text at the beginning of the course.

MindTap

MindTap®

Offering personalized paths of dynamic assignments and applications, **MindTap** is a digital learning solution that turns cookie-cutter into cutting-edge, apathy into engagement, and memorizers into higher-level thinkers. MindTap enables students to analyze and apply chapter concepts within relevant assignments, and allows instructors to measure skills and promote better outcomes with ease. A fully online learning solution, MindTap combines all student learning tools—readings, multimedia, activities, and assessments—into a single Learning Path that guides the student through the curriculum. Instructors personalize the experience by customizing the presentation of these learning tools to their students, even seamlessly introducing their own content into the Learning Path.

Companion Website

The **Companion Website** provides you with access to **online Chapter 21**, Networks, Groups, and Bureaucracies. Visit www.nelson.com/student to access it today.

Additional Resources

The following readers can be purchased at NelsonBrain.com in ebook or print-copy format:

- *Sociology as a Life or Death Issue*, Third Canadian Edition (0176531874), was written by Robert Brym. In seven beautifully written essays, Dr. Brym analyzes the social causes of death. Using topics such as hip-hop culture, Hurricane Katrina, and the motivations of suicide bombers, Dr. Brym reveals the powerful social forces that help to determine who lives and who dies and demonstrates the promise of a well-informed sociological understanding of the world. All essays found in the previous edition have been updated and a new chapter on gender risk, reflective of the physical vulnerability of women around the world, has been added. This is a great companion for any sociology course!

- *Society in Question*, Seventh Edition (0176509984), by Robert Brym, provides balanced coverage of the approaches and methods in current sociology as well as unique and surprising perspectives on many major sociological topics. All readings have been chosen for their ability to speak directly to contemporary Canadian students about how sociology can enable them to make sense of their lives in a rapidly changing world.

- *CourseReader for Sociology*, Canadian Edition (0176531815), by Amanda Zavitz, allows you to create a fully customized online reader in minutes. Through Nelson Education's partnership with Gale, you can access a rich collection of thousands of primary and secondary sources, readings, and audio selections from multiple disciplines. Each selection includes a descriptive introduction that puts the reading into context, and every selection is further supported by both critical thinking and multiple-choice questions, designed

to reinforce key points. This flexible, easy-to-use solution allows you to select exactly the content you need for your courses and is loaded with convenient pedagogical features such as highlighting, printing, note-taking, and downloadable MP3 audio files for each reading. *CourseReader* is the perfect complement to any class

- *Images of Society: Readings That Inspire and Inform Society*, Third Edition (0176514163), by Jerry P. White and Michael Carroll, is an exciting collection of readings designed for use in introductory sociology classes. The readings range from classic works in sociology to pieces illustrating recent sociological principles. Academic and journalistic readings have been selected by the authors to convey the distinctive way sociologists think. All readings are excerpts from longer pieces and are introduced with short prologues written by the editors.

CUSTOM PUBLISHING OPTIONS

It's your course, why compromise? Nelson Education is making it easier than ever to customize this sociology textbook to create a highly personalized and convenient course resource for your students. Learn how Custom Publishing with Nelson Education can help you teach your course, your way, by visiting www.nelsoncustom.com.

STUDENT ANCILLARIES

MindTap

MindTap®

Stay organized and efficient with *MindTap*—a single destination with all the course material and study aids you need to succeed. Built-in apps leverage social media and the latest learning technology. For example:

- ReadSpeaker will read the text to you.
- Flashcards are pre-populated to provide you with a jump start for review—or you can create your own.
- You can highlight text and make notes in your MindTap Reader. Your notes will flow into Evernote, the electronic notebook app that you can access anywhere when it's time to study for the exam.
- Self-quizzing allows you to assess your understanding.

Visit www.nelson.com/student to start using **MindTap**. Enter the online access code from the card included with your textbook. If a code card is *not* provided, you can purchase instant access at NELSONbrain.com.

ACKNOWLEDGMENTS

The eighth edition of *New Society* still bears the imprint of Heather McWhinney, Dan Brooks, Megan Mueller, Semareh Al-Hillal, Brad Lambertus, Camille Isaacs, Laura Macleod, and Maya Castle. They shepherded the book through its first editions, helping to make *New Society* distinctive and highly successful.

For the past year, I have been privileged to work closely with publishing professionals of the highest calibre, all of whom contributed heavily to the successful completion of the eighth edition. In particular, Leanna MacLean worked diligently and with good humour on this complex project, always mindful of the need to balance the diverse needs of instructors, students, and authors. Toni Chahley's energetic and meticulous approach to the project was evident from beginning to end. Visually and linguistically, this book owes much to her exemplary skill as a developmental editor. I would also like to thank Marnie Lamb (photo researcher), Jennifer Hare (production project manager), Terry Fedorkiw (marketing manager), June Trusty (copy editor), Linda Szostak (proofreader), and Daniela Glass (permissions coordinator).

New Society could not have become what it is without the authors of each chapter. They are among the very best sociologists in Canada. I believe that, although concentrating on the exposition of their own subfields, they have conveyed to the novice a real sense of the excitement and promise of sociology.

I am deeply indebted to them, as scores of thousands of introductory sociology students and their instructors inevitably have been and will be.

Finally, I would like to thank the following reviewers, whose insightful comments helped shape this edition:

Stephen F. Dumas, University of Calgary
Jenny Flagler-George, University of Waterloo
Christopher Helland, Dalhousie University
Shelly Ikebuchi, Okanagan College
Timothy MacNeill, University of Toronto Institute of Technology
Barry McClinchey, University of Waterloo
Patrick McLane, University of Alberta
Christopher Schneider, University of British Columbia
Stephanie Skourtes, University of British Columbia
E. Wilma van der Veen, Saint Mary's University

I would also like to thank the following reviewers, who provided feedback on the sixth and seventh editions:

Sonia Bookman, University of Manitoba
Jan Clarke, Algoma University
Linda Cohen, Memorial University of Newfoundland
Claudio Colaguori, York University
Lorna Doerkson, University of Saskatchewan
Stephen Dumas, University of Calgary
Morgan Holmes, Wilfrid Laurier University
Kate Krug, Cape Breton University
Guy Letts, Georgian College
Peter Landstreet, York University
Tamy Superle, Carleton University
Eric Tompkins, College of New Caledonia

R.B.
Toronto

ABOUT THE COVER IMAGE

To help students launch their careers, Nelson Education has initiated a program of contracting senior students and recent graduates of Canadian art schools to illustrate textbooks. Aaron Millard is the first illustrator hired under the terms of this program. He designed the cover and the section openers for *New Society*, Eighth Edition. A recent graduate of OCAD University in Toronto, Aaron is currently working and studying in Florence, Italy, for a postgraduate program but will be returning to Canada to continue his illustration career after he completes his studies.

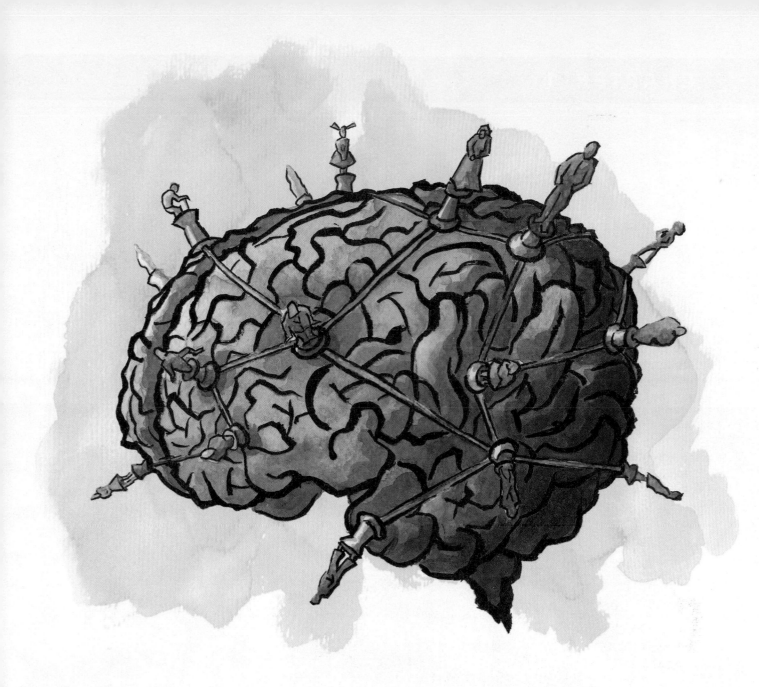

Illustrated by Aaron Millard

PART 1

INTRODUCTION

CHAPTER 1

INTRODUCING SOCIOLOGY

Robert Brym
UNIVERSITY OF TORONTO

© Aaron Huey/National Geographic Creative/Corbis

AFTER READING THIS CHAPTER, YOU WILL BE ABLE TO:

- Define sociology.

- Identify the social relationships that surround you, permeate you, and influence your behaviour.

- Describe how sociological research seeks to improve people's lives and test ideas using scientific methods.

- Summarize the main schools of sociological theory.

- Appreciate how sociology emerged out of the scientific, democratic, and industrial revolutions.

- Understand the main challenges facing society today.

INTRODUCTION

WHY I DECIDED NOT TO STUDY SOCIOLOGY

When I started university at the age of 18, I was bewildered by the wide variety of courses I could choose from. Having now taught sociology for 40 years and having met thousands of undergraduates, I am quite sure most students today feel as I did then.

One source of confusion for me was uncertainty about why I was in university in the first place. Like you, I knew higher education could improve my chance of finding good work. But, like most students, I also had a sense that higher education is supposed to provide something more than just the training necessary to embark on a career that is interesting and pays well. Several high-school teachers and guidance counsellors had told me that university was also supposed to "broaden my horizons" and teach me to "think critically." I wasn't entirely sure what they meant, but they made it sound interesting enough to make me want to know more. Consequently, I decided in my first year to take mainly "practical" courses that might prepare me for a law degree (economics, political science, and psychology). I also enrolled in a couple of other courses to indulge my "intellectual" side (philosophy, drama).

One thing I knew for sure: I didn't want to study sociology. Sociology, I came to believe, was thin soup with uncertain ingredients. When I asked a second-year student what sociology is, he told me it deals mainly with why people are unequal—why some are rich and others poor, some powerful and others weak. Coming as I did from a poor immigrant family in the Maritimes, an economically depressed region, it appeared that sociology could teach me something about my own life. But it also seemed a lot like what I imagined economics and political science to be about. What, then, was unique about sociology?

My growing sense that sociology had nothing special to offer was confirmed when another second-year student told me that sociologists try to describe the ideal society and figure out how to make the world a better place. That description appealed to my youthful sense of the world's injustice. However, it also sounded a lot like philosophy. A third-year student explained that sociology analyzes how and why people assume different roles in their lives. She made sociology appear similar to drama. Finally, one student reported that in her sociology class, she was learning why people commit suicide, homicide, and other deviant acts. That seemed like abnormal psychology to me. I concluded that sociology had no distinct flavour all its own. Accordingly, I decided to forgo it for tastier courses.

A CHANGE OF MIND

Despite the opinion I'd formed, I found myself taking no fewer than four sociology courses a year after starting university. That revolution in my life was due partly to the pull of an extraordinary professor I happened to meet just before I began my second year. He set me thinking in an altogether new way about what I could and should do with my life. He exploded some of my deepest beliefs. He started me thinking sociologically.

Specifically, he first put Yorick's dilemma to me. Yorick is a character—sort of—in *Hamlet*. Toward the end of the play, Hamlet finds two gravediggers at work. They unearth the remains of the former court jester, Yorick, who used to amuse Hamlet and carry him around on his back when Hamlet was a child. Holding high his old friend's skull, Hamlet reflects on what we must all come to. Even the remains of Alexander the Great, he says, turn to dust.

This incident implies Yorick's dilemma and, indeed, the dilemma of all thinking people. Life is finite. If we want to make the most of it, we must figure out how best to live. That is no easy task. It requires study, reflection, and the selection of values and goals. Ideally, higher education is supposed to supply students with just that opportunity. Finally, I was beginning to understand what I could expect from university apart from job training.

The professor I met also convinced me that sociology in particular could open up a new and superior way of comprehending my world. Specifically, he said it could clarify my place in society, how I might best manoeuvre through it, and even, perhaps, how I might contribute to improving it, however modestly. Before beginning my study of sociology, I had always taken for granted that things happen in the world—and to me—because physical and emotional forces cause them. Famine, I thought, is caused by drought, war by territorial greed, economic success by hard work, marriage by love, suicide by bottomless depression, rape by depraved lust. But now, this professor repeatedly threw evidence in my face that contradicted my easy formulas. If drought causes famine, why have so many famines occurred

Life is finite, and if we want to make the most of it, we must figure out how best to live. Sociology offers a useful perspective for understanding our current predicament and seeing possible ways of dealing with it.

SOURCE: M.C. Escher's "Relativity" © 2015 The M.C. Escher Company The Netherlands. All rights reserved. www.mcescher.com.

in perfectly normal weather conditions or involved some groups hoarding or destroying food so others would starve? If hard work causes prosperity, why are so many hard workers poor? If love causes marriage, why are so many families the site of violence against women and children? And so the questions multiplied.

As if it were not enough that the professor's sociological evidence upset many of my assumptions about the way the world worked, he also challenged me to understand sociology's unique way of explaining social life. He defined **sociology** as the systematic study of human behaviour in social context. He explained that

social causes are distinct from physical and emotional causes. Understanding social causes can help clarify otherwise inexplicable features of famine, marriage, and so on. In public school, my teachers had taught me that people are free to do what they want with their lives. However, my new professor taught me that the organization of the social world opens some opportunities and closes others, thus constraining our freedom and helping to make us what we are. By examining the operation of these powerful social forces, he said, sociology can help us to know ourselves, our capabilities and limitations. I was hooked. And so, of course, I hope you will be, too.

THE GOALS OF THIS CHAPTER

In this chapter I aim to achieve three goals. First, I illustrate the power of sociology to dispel foggy assumptions and help us see the operation of the social world more clearly. To that end, I examine a phenomenon that at first glance appears to be solely the outcome of breakdowns in individual functioning: suicide. You will see that, in fact, *social relations* among people powerfully influence suicide rates. This exercise introduces you to what is unique about the sociological perspective.

Second, I show that, from its origins, sociological research has been motivated by a desire to improve the social world. Thus, sociology is not just a dry, academic exercise but a means of charting a better course for society. At the same time, however, sociologists adopt scientific methods to test their ideas, thus increasing the validity of the results. I illustrate these points by briefly analyzing the work of the founders of the discipline.

Third, I suggest that sociology can help you come to grips with your century, just as it helped the founders of sociology deal with theirs. Today we are witnessing massive and disorienting social changes. Entire countries are breaking up. Women are demanding equality with men in all spheres of life. New religions are emerging and old ones reviving. People's wants are increasingly governed by the mass media. Computers are radically altering the way people work and entertain themselves. There are proportionately fewer good jobs to go around. Environmental ruin threatens us all. As was the case a hundred years ago, sociologists today try to understand social phenomena and suggest credible ways of improving their societies. By promising to make sociology relevant to you, this chapter should be viewed as an open invitation to participate in sociology's challenge.

But first things first. Before showing how sociology can help you better understand and improve the world, let us briefly examine the problem of suicide. This examination will help to illustrate how the sociological perspective can clarify and sometimes overturn commonsense beliefs.

THE SOCIOLOGICAL PERSPECTIVE

Analyzing suicide sociologically tests the claim that sociology takes a unique, surprising, and enlightening perspective on social events. After all, suicide appears to be a supremely antisocial and nonsocial act. First, it is condemned by nearly everyone in society. Second, it is typically committed in private, far from the public's intrusive glare. Third, it is comparatively rare: In 2011, there were 10.8 suicides for every 100 000 people in Canada (compared with the world average of about 16 suicides per 100 000 people; Statistics Canada, 2014a; see Figure 1.1). And, finally, when

FIGURE 1.1   SUICIDE RATE BY COUNTRY

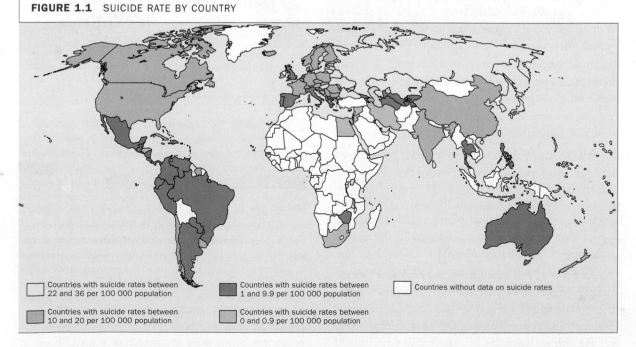

Countries with suicide rates between 22 and 36 per 100 000 population

Countries with suicide rates between 10 and 20 per 100 000 population

Countries with suicide rates between 1 and 9.9 per 100 000 population

Countries with suicide rates between 0 and 0.9 per 100 000 population

Countries without data on suicide rates

SOURCE: Reproduced, with the permission of the publisher, from "Suicide rates per 100,000 by country, year and sex (Table): Most recent year available, as of 2011," World Health Organization, 2011, (http://www.who.int/mental_health/prevention/suicide_rates/en/, accessed 20 December 2011).

you think about why people commit such acts, you are likely to focus on their individual states of mind rather than on the state of society—we are usually interested in the events that caused individuals to become depressed or angry enough to do something as awful as killing themselves. We do not usually think about the patterns of social relations that might encourage or inhibit such actions. If sociology can reveal the hidden social causes of such an apparently nonsocial and antisocial phenomenon, there must be something to it!

THE SOCIOLOGICAL EXPLANATION OF SUICIDE

At the end of the nineteenth century, French sociologist Émile Durkheim (1951 [1897]), one of the pioneers of the discipline, demonstrated that suicide is more than just an individual act of desperation resulting from psychological disorder, as was commonly believed at the time. Suicide rates, he showed, are strongly influenced by social forces.

Durkheim made his case by examining the association between rates of suicide and rates of psychological disorder for different groups. The idea that psychological disorder causes suicide is supported, he reasoned, only if suicide rates tend to be high where rates of psychological disorder are high, and low where rates of psychological disorder are low. However, his analysis of European government statistics, hospital records, and other sources revealed nothing of the kind. He discovered there were slightly more women than men in insane asylums. Yet there were four male suicides for every female suicide. Jews had the highest rate of psychological disorder among the major religious groups in France. However, they also had the lowest suicide rate. Psychological disorders occurred most frequently when a person reached maturity. Suicide rates, though, increased steadily with age.

Clearly, suicide rates and rates of psychological disorder did not vary proportionately. What then accounts for variations in suicide rates? Durkheim argued that suicide rates vary because of differences in the degree of **social solidarity** in different groups. According to Durkheim, the more a group's members share beliefs and values, and the more frequently and intensely they interact, the more social solidarity a group exhibits. In turn, the more social solidarity a group exhibits, the more firmly anchored individuals are to the social world, and the less likely they are

to take their own lives if adversity strikes. In other words, Durkheim expected groups with a high degree of solidarity to have lower suicide rates than groups with a low degree of solidarity did—at least up to a certain point (see Figure 1.2).

To support his argument, Durkheim showed that married adults are half as likely as unmarried adults are to commit suicide. That is because marriage usually creates social ties and a sort of moral cement that bind the individual to society. Similarly, he argued that women are less likely to commit suicide than men are. Why? Women are generally more involved in the intimate social relations of family life. Jews, Durkheim wrote, are less likely to commit suicide than Christians are. The reason? Centuries of persecution have turned them into a group that is more defensive and tightly knit. And seniors are more prone than the young and the middle-aged are to take their own lives in the face of misfortune. That is because they are most likely to live alone, to have lost a spouse, and to lack a job and a wide network of friends.

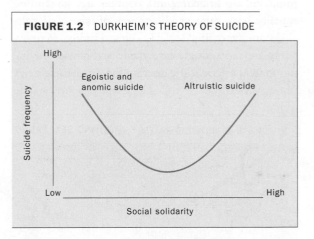

FIGURE 1.2 DURKHEIM'S THEORY OF SUICIDE

Durkheim argued that as the level of social solidarity increases, the suicide rate declines. Then, beyond a certain point, it starts to rise. Hence the U-shaped curve in this graph. Durkheim called suicides that occur in high-solidarity settings *altruistic*. *Altruism* means devotion to the interests of others. **Altruistic suicide** occurs when norms tightly govern behaviour so that individual actions are often in the group's interest. For example, when soldiers knowingly give up their lives to protect members of their unit, they commit altruistic suicide out of a deep sense of comradeship. In contrast, suicide that occurs in low-solidarity settings is egoistic or anomic, said Durkheim. **Egoistic suicide** results from a lack of integration of the individual into society because of weak social ties to others. *Anomie* means "without order." **Anomic suicide** occurs when norms governing behaviour are vaguely defined. For example, in Durkheim's view, when people live in a society that lacks a widely shared code of morality, the rate of anomic suicide is likely to be high.

In general, Durkheim wrote, "suicide varies with the degree of integration of the social groups of which the individual forms a part" (Durkheim, 1951 [1897]: 209). Note that his generalization tells us nothing about why any particular *individual* may take his or her life. That is a question for psychology. But it does tell us that a person's likelihood of committing suicide decreases with the degree to which he or she is anchored in society. And it says something surprising and uniquely sociological about how and why the suicide rate varies from group to group.

SUICIDE IN CANADA TODAY

Durkheim's theory is not just a historical curiosity. It sheds light on the factors that account for variations in suicide rates here and now. Consider Figure 1.3, which shows suicide rates by age and sex in Canada for 2011, the most recent year for which data are available as of this writing. Comparing rates for men and women, we immediately see that, as in Durkheim's France, men are much more likely than women are to commit suicide (three times more likely, to be precise). However, looking at differences between age groups, we see a striking difference between Durkheim's France and contemporary Canada. When Durkheim wrote, youth suicide was extremely rare and suicide among working-age people was uncommon. In Canada today,

suicide among people between the ages of 10 and 59 is much more common, having increased substantially since the 1960s. Suicide rates do *not* increase steadily with age in Canada today. The suicide rate is highest among people between the ages of 50 and 54. Moreover, the rate of suicide for people between the ages of 15 and 24, practically zero in Durkheim's France, stands at nearly 11 per 100 000 in Canada today.

Although the rate of suicide among young people was negligible in Durkheim's France, his theory of social solidarity helps us to understand why it has risen for this age cohort in Canada over the past half-century. In brief, shared moral principles and strong social ties have eroded since the early 1960s for Canada's youth. Consider the following facts:

- Church, synagogue, mosque, and temple attendance is down, particularly for young people. More than half of Canadians attended religious services weekly in the 1960s but today the figure is less than one-third, and it is only one-sixth for people born after 1960.
- Unemployment is up, again especially for youth. The unemployment rate was around 3 percent for most of the 1960s but rose steadily to around 10 percent for most of the 1990s; it stood at 7.0 percent in August 2015. Moreover, for Canadians between the ages of 15 and 24, the unemployment

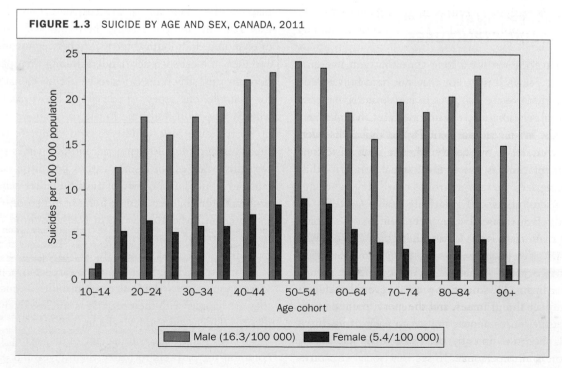

FIGURE 1.3 SUICIDE BY AGE AND SEX, CANADA, 2011

SOURCE: Adapted from Statistics Canada (2014a).

rate is nearly twice as high as it is for older Canadians (13.1 percent in August 2015).

- The rate of divorce has increased sixfold since the early 1960s. Out-of-marriage births are also much more common than they used to be. As a result, children are more often brought up in single-parent families than in the past. This fact suggests that they enjoy less frequent and intimate social interaction with parents and less adult supervision.

- Since the 1960s, an increasingly large proportion of lesbians, gays, bisexuals, and transsexuals have "come out of the closet." Most Canadians accept the lifestyles of sexual minorities, but in many Canadian schools, lesbians, gays, bisexuals, and transsexuals are prone to being bullied, terrorized, and socially excluded. Consequently, an alarmingly high proportion of youth suicides are committed by members of sexual minorities (Carole, 2011).

In sum, the figures cited above suggest that the level of social solidarity is now lower than it was just a few decades ago for young people. Less firmly rooted in society, and less likely to share moral standards, young people in Canada today are more likely than they were half a century ago to take their own lives if they find themselves in the midst of a personal crisis.

FROM PERSONAL TROUBLES TO SOCIAL STRUCTURES

You have known for a long time that you live in a society. Yet until now, you may not have fully appreciated that society also lives in you. That is, patterns of social relations affect your innermost thoughts and feelings, influence your actions, and thus help shape who you are. As we have seen, one such pattern of social relations is the level of social solidarity that characterizes the various groups to which you belong.

Sociologists call relatively stable patterns of social relations **social structures**. One of the sociologist's main tasks is to identify and explain the connection between people's personal troubles and the social structures in which people are embedded. This work is harder than it may at first seem. In everyday life, we usually see things mainly from our own point of view. Our experiences appear unique to each of us. If we think about them at all, social structures may appear remote and impersonal. To see how social structures operate inside us, we require sociological training.

An important step in broadening our sociological awareness involves recognizing that three levels of social structure surround and penetrate us: microstructures, macrostructures, and global structures. Think of these structures as concentric circles radiating out from you.

Microstructures are patterns of intimate social relations. They are formed during face-to-face interaction. Families, friendship circles, and work associations are all examples of microstructures.

Understanding the operation of microstructures can be useful. Let's say you are looking for a job. You might think you would do best to ask as many close friends and relatives as possible for leads and contacts. However, sociological research shows that people you know well are likely to know many of the same people. After asking a couple of close connections for help landing a job, you would therefore do best to ask more remote acquaintances for leads and contacts. People to whom you are weakly connected (and who are weakly connected among themselves) are more likely to know *different* groups of people. Therefore, they will give you more information about job possibilities and ensure that word about your job search spreads farther. You are more likely to find a job faster if you understand "the strength of weak ties" in microstructural settings (Granovetter, 1973).

Macrostructures are patterns of social relations that lie outside and above your circle of intimates and acquaintances. Macrostructures include class relations and **patriarchy**, the traditional system of economic and political inequality between women and men in most societies. Understanding the operation of macrostructures can also be useful. Consider, for example, one aspect of patriarchy. Most married women who work full-time in the paid labour force do more housework, child care, and eldercare than their husbands do. Governments and businesses support this arrangement insofar as they give little assistance to families in the form of nurseries, after-school programs for children, senior homes, and so on. Yet the unequal division of work in the household is a major source of dissatisfaction with marriage, especially in families that cannot afford to buy these services privately. Thus, sociological research shows that when spouses share domestic responsibilities equally, they are happier with their marriages and less likely to divorce (Hochschild and Machung, 1989).

When a marriage is in danger of dissolving, it is common for partners to blame themselves and each other for their troubles. However, it should now be clear that forces other than incompatible personalities often put stresses on families. Understanding how the macrostructure of patriarchy crops up in everyday life, and doing something to change that structure, can help people lead happier lives.

The third level of society that surrounds and permeates us comprises **global structures.** International organizations, patterns of worldwide travel and communication, and the economic relations between countries are examples of global structures. Global structures are increasingly important as inexpensive travel and communication allow all parts of the world to become interconnected culturally, economically, and politically.

Understanding the operation of global structures can be useful, too. For instance, many people are concerned about the world's poor. They donate money to charities to help with famine and disaster relief. Many people also approve of the Canadian government giving foreign aid to poor countries. However, many of these same people do not appreciate that charity and foreign aid alone do not seem able to end world poverty. That is because charity and foreign aid have been unable to overcome the structure of social relations among countries that have created, and now sustain, global inequality.

As we will see in Chapter 10, Development and Underdevelopment, Britain, France, and other imperial powers locked some countries into poverty when they colonized them between the seventeenth and nineteenth centuries. In the twentieth century, the poor (or "developing") countries borrowed money from these same rich countries and Western banks to pay for airports, roads, harbours, sanitation systems, basic healthcare, and so on. Today, poor countries pay far more to rich countries and Western banks in interest on those loans than they receive in aid and charity. Foreign aid equals about one-tenth of interest payments (Jubilee Debt Campaign, 2010: 6; Organisation for Economic Co-operation and Development, 2008: 6). It thus seems that relying exclusively on foreign aid and charity can do little to help solve the problem of world poverty. Understanding how the global structure of international relations created and helps maintain global inequality suggests new policy priorities for helping the world's poor. One such priority might involve campaigning for the cancellation of foreign debt in compensation for past injustices. Some government officials in Canada and other countries have been promoting this policy for the past decade.

As these examples illustrate, personal problems are connected to social structures at the micro-level, macro-level, and global level. Whether the personal problem involves finding a job, keeping a marriage intact, or figuring out a way to act to end world poverty, social-structural considerations broaden our understanding of the problem and suggest appropriate courses of action.

THE SOCIOLOGICAL IMAGINATION

In the 1950s, the great American sociologist C. Wright Mills (1959) called the ability to see the connection between personal troubles and social structures the **sociological imagination.** He emphasized the difficulty of developing this quality of mind. His language is sexist by today's standards, but his argument is as true and inspiring today as it was in the 1950s:

> When a society becomes industrialized, a peasant becomes a worker; a feudal lord is liquidated or becomes a businessman. When classes rise or fall, a man is employed or unemployed; when the rate of investment goes up or down, a man takes new heart or goes broke. When war happens, an insurance salesman becomes a rocket launcher; a store clerk, a radar man; a wife lives alone; a child grows up without a father. Neither the life of an individual nor the history of a society can be understood without understanding both.
>
> Yet men do not usually define the troubles they endure in terms of historical change. ... The well-being they enjoy, they do not usually impute to the big ups and downs of the society in which they live. Seldom aware of the intricate connection between the patterns of their own lives and the course of world history, ordinary men do not usually know what this connection means for the kind of men they are becoming and for the kind of history-making in which they might take part. They do not possess the quality of mind essential to grasp the interplay of men and society, of biography and history, of self and world. They cannot cope with their personal troubles in such a way as to control the structural transformations that usually lie behind them.

What they need ... is a quality of mind that will help them to [see] ... what is going on in the world and ... what may be happening within themselves. It is this quality ... that ... may be called the sociological imagination. (Mills, 1959: 3–4)

The sociological imagination is a recent addition to the human repertoire. It is only about two centuries old. True, in ancient and medieval times, some philosophers wrote about society. However, their thinking was not sociological. They believed God and nature controlled society. They spent much of their time sketching blueprints for the ideal society and urging people to follow those blueprints. They relied on speculation rather than on evidence to reach conclusions about how society works.

The sociological imagination was born when three modern revolutions pushed people to think about society in an entirely new way. First, the **Scientific Revolution** began about 1550. It encouraged the view that sound conclusions about the workings of society must be based on solid evidence, not just on speculation. Second, the **Democratic Revolution** began about 1750. It suggested that people are responsible for organizing society and that human intervention can therefore solve social problems. Third, the **Industrial Revolution** began about 1780. It created a host of new and serious social problems that attracted the attention of many social thinkers. Let us briefly consider these three sources of the sociological imagination.

ORIGINS OF THE SOCIOLOGICAL IMAGINATION

The Scientific Revolution

It is said that a group of medieval monks once wanted to know how many angels could dance on the head of a pin. They consulted the Bible and other ancient, authoritative books in Hebrew, Greek, and Latin. They thought long and hard. They employed all their intellectual skills to debate the issue. They did not, however, resolve the dispute because they never considered inspecting the head of a pin and counting. Any such suggestion would have been considered heresy. We, in contrast, would call it the beginning of a scientific approach to the subject. Scientific knowledge is based on systematic observation and the public scrutiny of evidence; the enemies of scientific knowledge are tradition, authority, and secrecy.

People often link the Scientific Revolution to specific ideas, such as Copernicus's theory that Earth revolves around the Sun and Newton's laws of motion. However, science is less a collection of ideas than a method of inquiry. For instance, in 1609, Galileo pointed his newly invented telescope at the heavens, made some careful observations, and showed that his observations fit Copernicus's theory. This is the core of the scientific method: using evidence to make a case for a particular point of view. By the mid-seventeenth century, some philosophers, such as Descartes in France and Hobbes in England, were calling for a science of society. When sociology emerged as a distinct discipline in the nineteenth century, commitment to the scientific method was one firm pillar of the sociological imagination.

The Democratic Revolution

The second pillar of the sociological imagination is the realization that people control society and can change it. Four hundred years ago, most Europeans thought otherwise. For them, God ordained the social order.

Consider the English engraving reproduced in Figure 1.4. It shows how most educated Europeans pictured the universe in Shakespeare's time. Note the cloud at the top of the circle. The Hebrew name of God is inscribed on it. God's hand extends from the cloud. It holds a chain, which is attached to a woman representing Nature. Nature also holds a chain in her hand. It is connected to "the ape of Nature," representing humankind. The symbolism is clear: God and his intermediary, Nature, control human action.

Note also that the engraving arranges everything in a linked hierarchy. The hierarchy includes the mineral, vegetable, and animal kingdoms; the elements; heavenly objects; angels; and so on. Each level of the hierarchy corresponds to and controls some aspect of the level below it. For example, people believed Archangels regulated the movements of the planet Mercury and the movements of Mercury affected human commerce. Similarly, in the medieval view, God ordained a hierarchy of people. The richest people were seen as the closest to God and therefore deserving of great privilege. Supposedly, kings and queens ruled because God wanted them to (Tillyard, 1943).

The American Revolution (1775–83) and the French Revolution (1789–99) helped to undermine these ideas. Those democratic political upheavals showed that society could experience massive change in a short period. They proved that people could

FIGURE 1.4   THE ELIZABETHAN WORLDVIEW

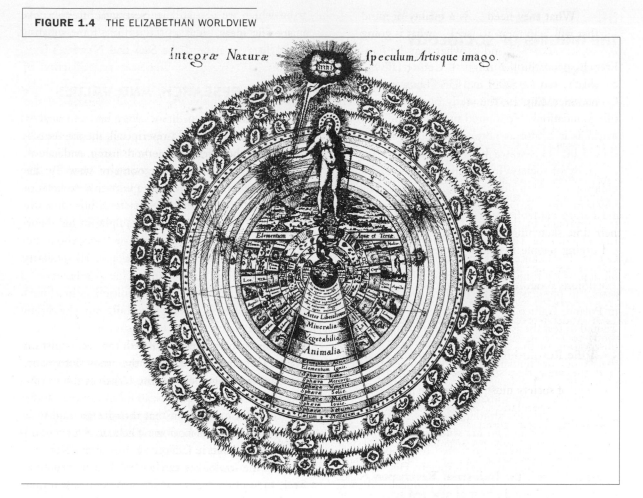

SOURCE: From Robert Fludd's *Utriusque Cosmi Historia* (1617–19). Photograph courtesy of Houghton Library, Harvard College Library.

replace unsatisfactory rulers. And they suggested that *people* control society. The implications for social thought were profound, for if it was possible to change society by human intervention, then a science of society could play a big role. The new science could help people figure out ways of overcoming various social problems, improving the welfare of all citizens, and finding the most effective way to reach given goals. Much of the justification for sociology as a science arose out of the democratic revolutions that shook Europe and North America.

The Industrial Revolution

The third pillar of the sociological imagination was the Industrial Revolution, which began in England about 1780. Because of the growth of industry, masses of people moved from countryside to city, worked agonizingly long hours in crowded and dangerous mines and factories, lost faith in their religions, confronted faceless bureaucracies, and reacted to the filth and poverty

of their existence by means of strikes, crime, revolution, and war. Scholars had never seen a sociological laboratory like this. The Scientific Revolution suggested that a science of society is possible. The Democratic Revolution suggested that people can intervene to improve society. The Industrial Revolution now presented social thinkers with a host of pressing social problems crying out for solutions. They responded by giving birth to the sociological imagination.

TIME FOR REVIEW

1. How does the sociological study of suicide show that a distinctively *social* realm influences all human behaviour, even if the behaviour seems nonsocial or antisocial?

2. What are microstructures, macrostructures, and global structures?

3. How did the Scientific Revolution, the Industrial Revolution, and the Democratic Revolution influence the emergence of sociology?

SOCIOLOGICAL THEORIES

THE ORIGINS OF SOCIOLOGY

French social thinker Auguste Comte (1798–1857) coined the term *sociology* in 1838 (Thompson, 1975). Comte tried to place the study of society on scientific foundations. He wanted to understand the social world as it is, not as he or anyone else imagined it should be. This was a highly original approach to the study of society. In ancient and medieval times, philosophers from diverse civilizations had sketched blueprints for the ideal society. We see evidence of this approach in the work of Confucius in China, Ibn Khaldun in Tunisia, and Plato and Aristotle in Greece. But Comte was swept up in the scientific revolution of his time. He was inspired by the astronomers and physicists of the modern era—Copernicus in Poland, Galileo in Italy, Newton in England. He wanted to test the validity of his ideas through careful observation of the real world rather than assuming that "God" or "human nature" determined the shape of society.

Despite Comte's breakthrough, there was a tension in his work, for although he was eager to adopt the scientific method in his study of society, he was a conservative thinker, motivated by strong opposition to rapid change in French society. His was a time not only of scientific but also of political and social revolution. Comte witnessed the democratic forces unleashed by the French Revolution, the early industrialization of society, and the rapid growth of cities. What he saw shocked and angered him because rapid social change was destroying many of the things he valued, especially respect for authority. He therefore urged slow change and the preservation of much that was traditional in social life. Thus, at its very origin, sociological research was motivated by adherence to scientific methods of research *and* a vision of the ideal society.

The same sort of tension is evident in the work of the most important early figures in the history of sociology: Karl Marx (1818–83), Émile Durkheim (1858–1917), and Max Weber (pronounced VAY-ber; 1864–1920). These three men lived in the period from 1818 to 1920. They witnessed various phases of Europe's wrenching transition to industrial capitalism, and they wanted to understand and explain it. Like Comte, they were all committed to the scientific method of research. However, they also wanted to chart a better course for their societies. The ideas they developed are therefore not just diagnostic tools from which we can still learn much, but also, like many sociological ideas, prescriptions for combating social ills.

THEORY, RESEARCH, AND VALUES

To clarify the tension in sociology between analysis and ideal, diagnosis and prescription, we can usefully distinguish three terms: theory, research, and values.

Sociological ideas are generally stated in the form of theories. A **theory** is a tentative explanation of some aspect of social life. It states how and why certain facts are related. For example, in his theory of suicide, Durkheim showed how facts about suicide rates are related to facts about social solidarity. This enabled him to explain suicide as a function of social solidarity. In this broad definition, even a hunch qualifies as a theory if it suggests how and why certain facts are related.

After theories are formulated, the sociologist can conduct research. **Research** is the process of systematically observing social reality to assess the validity of a theory. It is because research can call the validity of a theory into question that theories are said to be only "tentative" explanations. The research process is discussed in detail in Chapter 2, Research Methods.

Before sociologists can formulate a theory, however, they must decide which problems are important enough to study and how the parts of society fit together. If they are going to recommend ways of improving the operation of some aspect of society, they must even have an opinion about what the ideal society ought to look like. As we will soon see, these issues are shaped in large measure by sociologists' values. **Values** are ideas about what is right and wrong, good and bad. Inevitably, values help sociologists formulate and favour certain theories over others (Edel, 1965; Kuhn, 1970). So sociological theories may be modified and even rejected because of research, but they are often motivated by sociologists' values.

Durkheim, Marx, and Weber initiated three of the major theoretical traditions in sociology: functionalism, conflict theory, and symbolic interactionism. A fourth approach, feminism, has arisen in recent decades to correct some of the deficiencies of the three long-established traditions. It will become clear as you read this book that there are many more sociological theories than just these four. However, because these four traditions have been especially influential in the development of sociology, you will find it useful to read a thumbnail sketch of each one here at the beginning.[1]

Before delving into social research, a sociologist must first develop hypotheses—testable claims about the social world. Testing hypotheses by means of research helps determine the validity of theories.
SOURCE: © Davidian/iStockphoto.com.

FUNCTIONALISM

Durkheim's theory of suicide is an early example of what sociologists now call **functionalist theory.** Functionalist theories incorporate four features:

1. Functionalist theories stress that human behaviour is governed by relatively stable patterns of social relations, or social structures. For example, Durkheim emphasized how suicide rates are influenced by patterns of social solidarity. Usually the social structures analyzed by functionalists are macrostructures.

2. Functionalism underlines how social structures maintain or undermine social stability. Typically, Durkheim analyzed how the growth of industries and cities in nineteenth-century Europe lowered the level of social solidarity and contributed to social instability. One aspect of instability, said Durkheim, is a higher suicide rate. Another is frequent strikes by workers.

3. Functionalist theories emphasize that social structures are based mainly on shared values or preferences. Thus, when Durkheim wrote about social solidarity, he sometimes meant the frequency and intensity of social interaction, but more often he thought of social solidarity as a sort of moral cement that binds people together.

4. Functionalism suggests that reestablishing equilibrium can best solve most social problems. Thus, Durkheim said that social stability could be restored in late-nineteenth-century Europe by creating new associations of employers and workers that would lower workers' expectations about what they could expect out of life. If, said Durkheim, more people could agree on wanting less, social solidarity would rise and there would be fewer strikes, fewer suicides, and so on. Functionalism, then, was a conservative response to widespread social unrest in nineteenth-century France. (A more radical response would have been to argue that if people are expressing discontent because they are getting less out of life than they expect, discontent can be lowered by figuring out ways for them to get more out of life.)

Although functionalist thinking influenced North American sociology at the end of the nineteenth century, it was only during the continent's greatest economic crisis ever, the Great Depression of 1929–39, that functionalism took deep root here (Russett, 1966). With 30 percent of the paid labour force unemployed and labour unrest reaching unprecedented levels, it is not surprising that sociologists with a conservative frame of mind were attracted to a theory that focused on how social equilibrium could be restored. Functionalist theory remained popular in North America for 30 years. It experienced a minor revival in the early 1990s but never regained the dominance it enjoyed from the 1930s to the early 1960s.

Sociologist Talcott Parsons was the foremost proponent of functionalism. He is best known for identifying how various institutions must work to ensure the smooth operation of society as a whole. For instance, when the family successfully raises new generations, the military successfully defends society against external threats, schools are able to teach students the skills and values they need to function as productive adults, and religion creates a shared moral code among people, then, said Parsons, society is well integrated and in equilibrium (Parsons, 1951).

Parsons was criticized for exaggerating the degree to which members of society share common values and social institutions contribute to social harmony. This led North America's other leading functionalist, Robert Merton, to propose that social structures may have different consequences for different categories of people. Merton noted that some of these might be disruptive or **dysfunctional consequences** (Merton, 1968 [1949]). Moreover, said Merton, although some functions are **manifest** (visible and intended), others are **latent** (invisible and unintended). For instance, a **manifest function** of schools is to transmit skills from one generation to the next. A **latent function** of schools is to encourage the development of a separate youth culture that often conflicts with parents' values (Coleman, 1961; Hersch, 1998).

CONFLICT THEORY

The second major theoretical tradition in sociology emphasizes the centrality of conflict in social life. **Conflict theory** incorporates the following features:

1. Conflict theory generally focuses on large, macro-level structures, such as the relations between or among classes.

2. Conflict theory shows how major patterns of inequality in society produce social stability in some circumstances and social change in others.

3. Conflict theory stresses how members of privileged groups try to maintain their advantages while subordinate groups struggle to increase theirs. From this point of view, social conditions at a given time are the expression of an ongoing power struggle between privileged and subordinate groups.

4. Conflict theory typically leads to the suggestion that decreasing privilege will lower the level of conflict and increase the sum total of human welfare.

The conflict paradigm originated in the work of Karl Marx. A generation before Durkheim, Marx observed the destitution and discontent produced by the Industrial Revolution and proposed a sweeping argument about the way societies develop (Marx, 1904 [1859]; Marx and Engels, 1972 [1848]). Marx's theory was radically different from Durkheim's. Class conflict lies at the centre of his ideas.

Marx argued that owners of industry are eager to improve the way work is organized and to adopt new tools, machines, and production methods. These innovations allow them to produce more efficiently, earn higher profits, and drive inefficient competitors out of business. However, according to Marx, the drive for profits causes capitalists to concentrate workers in larger and larger establishments, keep wages as low as possible, and invest as little as possible in improving working conditions. Thus, in factories and in mines, a large and growing class of poor workers comes to oppose a small and shrinking class of wealthy owners.

Marx believed that workers would ultimately become aware of belonging to the same exploited class. Their sense of "class consciousness," he wrote, would encourage the growth of trade unions and labour parties. These organizations would eventually seek to put an end to private ownership of property, replacing it with a system in which everyone shared property and wealth. This was the "communist" society envisaged by Marx—a society in which there is no private property and everyone shares wealth in proportion to their need.

Weber

Although some of Marx's ideas have been usefully adapted to the study of contemporary society, his predictions about the inevitable collapse of capitalism have been questioned. Max Weber, a German sociologist

Max Weber wrote that the modern era is a bureaucratically organized "iron cage." Sociology promises to teach us both the dimensions of that cage and the possibilities for release.

SOURCE: Carol Wainio, *Study for a Portrait of Nietzsche*, 1985, acrylic on paper, 24" × 38". Courtesy Carol Wainio.

who wrote his major works a generation after Marx, was among the first to find flaws in Marx's argument (Weber, 1946). Weber noted the rapid growth of the "service" sector of the economy with its many non-manual workers and professionals. He argued that many members of these occupational groups stabilize society because they enjoy higher status and income than do manual workers employed in the manufacturing sector. In addition, Weber showed that class conflict is not the only driving force of history. In his view, politics and religion are also important sources of historical change (see the next section).

Other writers pointed out that Marx did not understand how investing in technology would make it possible for workers to toil fewer hours under less oppressive conditions. Nor did he foresee that higher wages, better working conditions, and government benefits, such as employment insurance and medicare, would pacify manual workers. Thus, we see that many of the particulars of Marx's theory were called into question by Weber and other sociologists. Nonetheless, Marx's insights about the fundamental importance of conflict in social life were influential then—and still are today.

Conflict Theory in North America

Conflict theory had some advocates in North America before the 1960s. Most noteworthy is C. Wright Mills, who laid the foundations for modern conflict theory in the 1950s. Mills conducted pioneering research on American politics and class structure. One of his most important books is *The Power Elite*, a study of the several hundred men who occupied the "command posts" of the American economy, military,

and government. He argued that power is highly concentrated in American society, which is therefore less of a democracy than we are often led to believe (Mills, 1956).

Exceptions like Mills notwithstanding, conflict theory did not really take hold in North America until the 1960s, a decade rocked by growing labour unrest, Quebec separatism, anti-Vietnam War protests, the rise of the black power movement, and the revival of feminism, which had fallen dormant after its first stirrings in the late nineteenth and early twentieth centuries. Strikes, demonstrations, and riots were almost daily occurrences in the 1960s and early 1970s, and therefore many sociologists of that era considered conflict among classes, nations, races, and generations to be the very essence of society.

THE CULTURAL TURN AND POSTSTRUCTURALISM: GRAMSCI AND FOUCAULT

In the 1960s and 1970s, conflict theory took what has been called a "cultural turn." Increasingly, conflict theorists directed their attention to the ways in which language, music, literature, fashion, movies, advertising, and other elements of culture express domination by the powerful and resistance by others.

The origins of a cultural approach to the study of social conflict are found in essays written in the early twentieth century by an Italian Marxist, Antonio Gramsci (pronounced GRAM-shee). In Gramsci's view, ruling classes establish their dominance partly by controlling jobs, using force, and the like. However, they also exercise power in softer ways. In particular, they fund the development, transmission, and learning of ideas that seem to embody the values of everyone but are actually biased in favour of class dominance. Gramsci wrote that **cultural hegemony** exists when these values become so deeply entrenched that the great majority of people accept them as common sense (Gramsci, 1957, 1971). Subordinate classes can resist cultural hegemony, Gramsci wrote, but only if they develop ideas and institutions that express and support their own cultural preferences. Later writers extended Gramsci's argument to include dominant, taken-for-granted ideas about race, ethnicity, sexuality, and so on.

In France from the 1950s to the 1980s, Michel Foucault (pronounced Foo-CŌ) further developed the notion that culture is the site of ongoing conflict between dominant and subordinate classes and other groups.

Foucault made his case by studying new forms of regulation that accompany capitalist industrialization. He showed that, as the goal of maximizing economic productivity grows in importance, criminals, people with physical infirmities, people with mental illness, and ordinary students and workers are subjected to new structures of control in prisons, hospitals, institutions for the mentally ill, workplaces, schools, and universities. According to Foucault (1973, 1977, 1988), modern institutions sometimes use violence to regulate behaviour but they more often rely on new technologies and the *internalization* of control mechanisms. For example, modern institutions are physically, technologically, and socially designed so that authorities can easily observe the behaviour of inmates, patients, workers, and students. Authorities may not always watch their "clientele," but when inmates and others know that they *may* be under the watchful eye of authorities, they usually act as if they *are* being observed. Before capitalist industrialization, control took place almost exclusively through force, but now more subtle and effective mechanisms of regulation are employed.

According to Foucault, power is exercised in every social interaction, but every social interaction is also subject to resistance by subordinates. Thus, the exercise of power is unstable. Dominant groups and individuals must continuously renew their power relations to maintain control but sometimes they fail, providing subordinates with the opportunity to assert their interests.

Foucault was part of a movement in French social thought known as **poststructuralism**. Earlier social thinkers had argued that social relations and cultures form structures, or stable determinants of the way people think and act. These "structuralists" typically categorized elements of social relations and of culture as binary opposites: male versus female, civilized versus uncivilized people, black versus white races, and so on (Derrida, 2004: 41). In contrast, poststructuralists, Foucault among them, denied the stability of social relations and of cultures, their capacity always to shape how people think and act, and their neat categorization of social and cultural elements as binary opposites. According to the poststructuralists, the social world is a more fluid and complex place, and people are more often the agents of their own destiny than structuralists ever imagined.

To better understand these ideas, consider that many of us casually use the term "the opposite sex" in everyday speech without giving it much thought.

Yet embedded in this term is a faulty set of assumptions based on a distribution of power that favours some categories of people at the expense of others. As you will learn in Chapter 5, Gender and Sexualities, it is factually incorrect to assume that men and women are opposites in their sexual identities, preferences, and behaviours. It is more accurate to say that men and women are arrayed along one scale with respect to their sexual identities, a second scale with respect to their sexual preferences, and a third scale with respect to their sexual behaviours, and their positions on these scales can change in different circumstances. When we perceive men as remaining clustered on one extreme of a single scale and women on the other extreme—when we view women and men as fixed "opposites"—we oversimplify the complexity of real flesh-and-blood people. We also ignore that many women and men are not so neatly pigeonholed. People who are not included in the conventional categorization are simply defined out of existence by our casual use of language and the underlying fact that some people have more power than others to name things.

As you will see in later chapters, Foucault's influence, and that of other poststructuralists, span many areas of contemporary sociology, including the study of deviance and crime, sexualities and gender, education, and social stratification.

SYMBOLIC INTERACTIONISM

Earlier it was noted that Weber criticized Marx's interpretation of the development of capitalism. Among other things, Weber argued that early capitalist development was caused not just by favourable *economic* circumstances. In addition, he wrote, certain *religious* beliefs facilitated robust capitalist growth. In particular, sixteenth- and seventeenth-century Protestants believed their religious doubts could be reduced, and a state of grace ensured, if they worked diligently and lived modestly. Weber called this belief the **Protestant ethic.** He believed it had an unintended effect: People who adhered to the Protestant ethic saved and invested more than others did. Thus, according to Weber, capitalism developed most robustly where the Protestant ethic took hold. He concluded that capitalism did not develop because of the operation of economic forces alone, as Marx argued. Instead, it depended partly on the religious meaning individuals attached to their work (Weber, 1958 [1904–05]).

In much of his research, Weber emphasized the importance of empathetically understanding people's motives and the meanings they attach to things to gain a clear sense of the significance of their actions. He called this aspect of his approach to sociological research the method of *Verstehen* (pronounced Fer-SHTAY-en, meaning "understanding" in German).

The idea that subjective meanings must be analyzed in any complete sociological analysis was only one of Weber's contributions to early sociological theory. Weber was also an important conflict theorist, as you will learn in later chapters. At present, however, it is enough to note that his emphasis on subjective meanings found rich soil in North America, for here was an idea that resonated deeply with the individualism of North American culture. A century ago, it was widely believed that individual talent and initiative could achieve just about anything on this continent of opportunity. Small wonder, then, that much of early North American sociology focused on the individual or, more precisely, on the connection between the individual and the larger society. For example, George Herbert Mead at the University of Chicago was the driving force behind the study of how individual identity is formed in the course of interaction with other people. We discuss his contribution in Chapter 4, Socialization. Here we note only that the work of Mead and his colleagues gave birth to symbolic interactionism, a distinctively North American theoretical tradition that continues to be a major force in sociology today.

Functionalists and conflict theorists assume that people's group memberships—whether they are young or old, male or female, rich or poor—influence their behaviour. This can sometimes make people seem like balls on a pool table: They get knocked around and cannot determine their destinations. We know from our everyday experience, however, that people are not like that. You often make choices, sometimes difficult ones. You sometimes change your mind. Moreover, two people with similar social characteristics may react differently to similar social circumstances because they may interpret those circumstances differently.

Recognizing these issues, some sociologists focus on the subjective side of social life. They work in the symbolic interactionist tradition. **Symbolic interactionism** incorporates these four features:

1. It focuses on face-to-face communication or interaction in micro-level social settings. This feature distinguishes it from both the functionalist and the conflict paradigms.

2. Symbolic interactionism emphasizes that an adequate explanation of social behaviour requires understanding the subjective meanings people attach to their social circumstances.

3. Symbolic interactionism stresses that people help to create their social circumstances and do not merely react to them.[2]

4. By underscoring the subjective meanings people create in small social settings, symbolic interactionism validates unpopular and nonofficial viewpoints, thus increasing our understanding and tolerance of people who may be different from us.

To understand symbolic interactionism better, let us return briefly to the problem of suicide. If a police officer discovers a dead person at the wheel of a car that has run into a tree, it may be difficult to establish with certainty whether the death was an accident or a suicide. Interviewing friends and relatives to discover the driver's state of mind just before the crash may help to rule out the possibility of suicide. But, as this example illustrates, understanding the intention or motive of the actor is critical to understanding the meaning of a social action and explaining it. Suicide, then, is not just an objective social fact but also an inferred, and therefore subjective, social fact. A state of mind must be interpreted, usually by a coroner, before the dead body becomes a suicide statistic (Douglas, 1967).

For surviving family and friends, suicide is always painful and sometimes embarrassing. Insurance companies often deny payments to beneficiaries in the case of suicide. As a result, coroners are inclined to classify deaths as accidental whenever such an interpretation is plausible. Being human, they want to minimize the family's pain after such a horrible event. Sociologists believe that, for this reason, official suicide rates are about one-third lower than actual suicide rates.

Social Constructionism and Queer Theory

Social constructionism is a variant of symbolic interactionism that has become popular in recent years. Social constructionists argue that when people interact, they typically assume things are naturally or innately what they seem to be, but in reality, apparently natural or innate features of life are sustained by *social* processes that vary historically and culturally.

For example, many people assume that differences in the way women and men behave are the result of their different biological makeup. In contrast, social constructionists show that many of the presumably natural differences between women and men depend on the way power is distributed between them and the degree to which certain ideas about women and men are shared (see Chapter 5, Gender and Sexualities; Berger and Luckmann, 1966; West and Zimmerman, 1987). Since power distributions and ideas about gender vary over time and place, social constructionists are able to show how changing social conditions produce changes in the way people act out their gender identity. They conclude that gender is more a performance shaped by social conditions than part of a person's essence. People usually do such a good job of building natural-seeming identities in their everyday interactions—not just gender but also ethnicity, race, nationality, religion, and so on—that they do not notice the materials used in the construction process. Social constructionists identify those materials and analyze how people piece them together.

Queer theory takes the social constructionist argument a step farther by denying the very existence of stable identities (Green, 2007). From the queer theorist's point of view, when we apply such labels as "male," "female," "gay," and "lesbian" to ourselves or others, we are adopting conventional labels that fail to capture the instability of sexual identities and performances that characterizes the lives of many people. Such labels impose social conventions on people, thus acting as forms of control and domination and drawing attention away from the uniqueness of each individual (for more on queer theory, see Chapter 5, Gender and Sexualities).

In sum, the study of the subjective side of social life helps to take us beyond the official picture by deepening our understanding of how society works and supplementing the insights gained from macro-level analysis. By stressing the importance and validity of subjective meanings, symbolic interactionists increase tolerance for minority and deviant viewpoints. By stressing how subjective meanings vary historically and culturally, social constructionists and queer theorists show that many seemingly natural features of social life actually require painstaking acts of social creation.

FEMINIST THEORY

Few women figured prominently in the early history of sociology, largely because the strict demands placed on women by the nineteenth-century household and the lack of opportunity outside the household prevented most of them from obtaining a higher education and finding work that could support sociological research. Not surprisingly, therefore, the women who did make their mark on the discipline in its early years had unusual social backgrounds. These exceptional people introduced into the discipline gender issues that were largely ignored by Marx, Durkheim, Weber, and Mead. Appreciation for the sociological contribution of these pioneer women has grown in recent years as concern with gender issues has come to form a substantial part of the modern sociological enterprise.

Harriet Martineau is often called the first woman sociologist. Born in England at the beginning of the nineteenth century to a prosperous family, she never married and was able to support herself comfortably from her journalistic writings. Martineau translated Comte into English. She undertook critical studies of slavery and factory laws. She also wrote about gender inequality and was a leading advocate of voting rights and higher education for women, as well as gender equality in the family. Martineau was one of the first feminists (Yates, 1985).

Despite its early stirrings, feminist thinking had little impact on sociology until the mid-1960s, when the rise of the modern women's movement drew attention to the many remaining inequalities between women and men. Since then, feminist theory has had such a big influence on sociology that it may now fairly be regarded as sociology's fourth major tradition. There are several variants of modern feminism (see Chapter 8, Gender Inequality). However, the various strands of **feminist theory** share the following four features:

1. Feminist theory focuses on various aspects of patriarchy, the system of male domination in society. Patriarchy, feminists contend, is at least as important as class inequality in determining a person's opportunities in life, and perhaps more so.
2. Feminist theory holds that male domination and female subordination are determined not by biological necessity but by structures of power and social convention. From this point of view, women are subordinate to men only because men enjoy more legal, economic, political, and cultural rights.
3. Feminist theory examines the operation of patriarchy in both micro and macro settings.

4. Feminist theory contends that existing patterns of gender inequality can and should be changed for the benefit of all members of society. The main sources of gender inequality include differences in the way boys and girls are brought up; barriers to equal opportunity in education, paid work, and politics; and the unequal division of domestic responsibilities between women and men.

The theoretical traditions outlined above are summarized in Table 1.1. As you will see in the following pages, sociologists in Canada and elsewhere have applied them to all branches of the discipline. They have elaborated and refined each of them. Some sociologists work exclusively within one tradition. Others conduct research that borrows from more than one tradition. However, all sociologists are deeply indebted to the founders of the discipline. (See The Four Paradigms in Canada box.)

TIME FOR REVIEW

1. What is the relationship among values, theories, and research?
2. What are the key features of the four main theoretical traditions?
3. What is the "cultural turn" in the conflict tradition?
4. What does queer theory contribute to symbolic interactionism?

THEIR REVOLUTION AND OURS

In the nineteenth century, the founders of the discipline devoted their lives to solving the great sociological puzzle of their time: the causes and consequences of the Industrial Revolution. However, the ideas that stirred them did not spring fully grown from their minds. Rather, their social experiences helped to shape their ideas. There is an important lesson to be learned here. In general, sociological ideas are influenced by the social settings in which they emerge.

This lesson immediately suggests two important questions. First, what are the great sociological puzzles of *our* time? Second, how are today's sociologists responding to the challenges presented by the social settings in which *they* live? We devote the rest of the book to answering these questions in depth. The remainder of this chapter offers an outline of what you can expect to learn. To provide a context for this outline, let us now consider how the Industrial Revolution of the nineteenth century was transformed into the Postindustrial Revolution of our day.

THE INDUSTRIAL REVOLUTION

The Industrial Revolution involved the application of science and technology to industrial processes, the construction of factories, and the formation of a large

---

TABLE 1.1   THE MAIN THEORETICAL TRADITIONS IN SOCIOLOGY

PARADIGM	MAIN LEVEL OF ANALYSIS	MAIN FOCUS	MAIN QUESTION	IMAGE OF IDEAL SOCIETY
Functionalism	Macro	Values	How do the institutions of society contribute to value consensus and, thus, to social stability?	A state of equilibrium
Conflict theory	Macro	Class inequality	How do privileged groups seek to maintain their advantages and subordinate groups seek to increase theirs, often causing social change in the process?	The reduction of privilege, especially class privilege
Symbolic interactionism	Micro	Meaning	How do individuals communicate so as to make their social settings meaningful?	Respect for the validity of minority views
Feminism	Micro and macro	Patriarchy	Which social structures and interaction processes maintain male dominance and female subordination?	The reduction of gender inequality

THE FOUR PARADIGMS IN CANADA

S. D. Clark
SOURCE: Photo courtesy of Ed Clark.

Each of the four major sociological paradigms has influenced research in Canada. This is evident from the following portraits of some of Canada's leading sociologists.

S. D. Clark (1910–2003) received his Ph.D. from the University of Toronto. He became the first chair of the Department of Sociology at that institution. Born in Lloydminster, Alberta, he is especially well known for his studies of Canadian social development as a process of disorganization and reorganization on a series of economic frontiers (Clark, 1968). The influence of functionalism on his work is apparent in his emphasis on the way society reestablishes equilibrium after experiencing disruptions caused by economic change.

John Porter
SOURCE: Reprinted with permission from Carleton University Archives.

John Porter (1921–79) was Canada's premier sociologist in the 1960s and 1970s. Born in Vancouver, he received his Ph.D. from the London School of Economics. He spent his academic career at Carleton University in Ottawa. There he served as chair of the Department of Sociology and Anthropology, dean of Arts and Science, and vice-president. His major work, *The Vertical Mosaic* (1965), is a study of class and power in Canada. Firmly rooted in the conflict paradigm, it influenced a generation of Canadian sociologists in their studies on social inequality, elite groups, French–English relations, and Canadian–American relations.

Erving Goffman
SOURCE: Courtesy the American Sociological Association.

Erving Goffman (1922–82) was born in Mannville, Alberta. He studied sociology and anthropology as an undergraduate at the University of Toronto and completed his Ph.D. at the University of Chicago. He pursued his academic career at the University of California, Berkeley, and the University of Pennsylvania. Goffman developed an international reputation for his "dramaturgical" approach to symbolic interactionism. This approach highlights the way people present themselves to others, managing their identities to create desired impressions on their "audience," in much the same way as actors do on stage (Goffman, 1959).

Margrit Eichler
SOURCE: Photo © Karyn Gorra. Courtesy Margrit Eichler.

Margrit Eichler (1942–) was born in Berlin, Germany. She did her Ph.D. at Duke University in the United States before beginning her academic career in Canada. She served as chair of the Department of Sociology at the Ontario Institute for Studies in Education and head of the Women's Studies Program at the University of Toronto. She is internationally known for her work on feminist methodology (Eichler, 1987). Her work on family policy in Canada has influenced students, professional sociologists, and policymakers for decades (Eichler, 1988).

class of blue-collar workers. Within about a century, it took root throughout Western Europe, North America, and Japan. A century after that, industry had begun implanting itself in most of the rest of the world.

As noted in our discussion of Marx, the industrial working class protested long workdays, low pay, and dangerous working conditions. Workers went on strike, formed unions, and joined political parties. Their protests forced governments to tax citizens to provide at least minimal protection against ill health, unemployment, and poverty. Working-class protests also forced employers to limit the length of the workweek to 40 hours, improve working conditions, and raise wages. Employers were still able to increase their profits, however, by making the organization of work more efficient and introducing new technologies.

Collecting taxes, administering social services, providing healthcare, and investing heavily in technological innovation required the growth of government and business offices, hospitals, schools, universities, and research laboratories. Thus, alongside the old manufacturing sector of the economy, the new "service" sector was born. Its employees came to be known as *white-collar workers*. Highly trained professionals stood at the peak of the service sector. Secretaries and clerks were positioned near its base. By 1980, more than half of all people working in Canada's paid labour force were in nonmanual occupations (Ornstein, 1983: 252). Sociologists call this most recent transformation of human society the **Postindustrial Revolution.** Specifically, the Postindustrial Revolution refers to the technology-driven shift from

manufacturing to service industries and the consequences of that shift for virtually all human activities (Bell, 1976; Toffler, 1990).

Especially since the early 1980s, the Postindustrial Revolution has been sped up by **globalization—** the process by which formerly separate economies, states, and cultures become tied together and people become increasingly aware of their growing interdependence (Giddens, 1990: 64; Guillén, 2001). In recent decades, rapid increases in the volume of international trade, travel, and communication have broken down the isolation and independence of most countries and people. Also contributing to globalization is the growth of many institutions that bind corporations, companies, and cultures together. These processes have caused people to depend more than ever on people in other countries for products, services, ideas, and even a sense of identity (see the Critical Sociology: Globalization box).

The causes and consequences of postindustrialism and globalization form the great sociological puzzles of our time. Much of this book is devoted to analyzing postindustrialism, globalization, and their effects. In concluding this chapter, a review of some

---

CRITICAL SOCIOLOGY: GLOBALIZATION   THE INNU OF LABRADOR

Globalization began when international trade started in the Middle East thousands of years ago. It spread at a furious pace once millions of people started using the Internet in the 1980s. But the first major burst of globalization took place in the late fifteenth century, when explorers started sailing from Europe to Asia, Africa, and the Americas in search of wealth.

The effect of globalization in the age of exploration was devastating for non-Europeans, and especially for Indigenous peoples. Military conquest, forced migration, slavery, the spread of European diseases, and the theft of gold and other valuable resources was widespread. One indicator of the devastation that globalization wrought is that, in North America, the size of the Indigenous population fell by 50 percent between 1800 and 1900.

In some cases, the full effect of globalization on Indigenous peoples was not felt until the middle of the twentieth century. The Innu of Labrador are a case in point. A nomadic people, the Innu traditionally relied on hunting and trapping for their livelihood. However, in the mid-1950s, shortly after Newfoundland and Labrador became

part of Canada, the provincial and federal governments decided to gain tighter control of Innu land to encourage economic development. Government officials reasoned that to accommodate new roads, mines, lumbering operations, hydroelectric projects, and low-level flight-training facilities for NATO air forces, the Innu would need to be concentrated in permanent settlements. Government officials also believed that, to function in these new settlements, the Innu would need to learn practical and cultural skills associated with a modern, industrial society. Consequently, governments put tremendous pressure on the Innu to give up their traditional way of life and settle in Davis Inlet and Sheshatshiu.

In the new communities, Canadian laws, schools, and churches strongly discouraged the Innu from hunting, practising their religion, and raising their children in the traditional way. Canadian hunting regulations limited access to their age-old livelihood. Priests are known to have beaten children who missed church or school to go hunting, thus introducing interpersonal violence into a culture that formerly knew none (compare Briggs, *(continued)*

(continued)

1970). Teachers transmitted North American and European skills and culture, often denigrating Innu practices. At the same time, few alternative jobs existed in the new communities. Most Innu wound up living in despair and on welfare.

In the absence of work, and lacking the stabilizing influence of their traditional culture, a people long known for their nonviolence and cooperative spirit became victims of widespread family breakdown, sexual abuse, drunkenness, and alcohol-related illness. In Sheshatshiu in 2001, at least 20 percent of the children regularly got high by sniffing gasoline. In Davis Inlet, the figure was nearly 60 percent. The Innu competed with certain Brazilian tribes for the title of the world's most suicide-prone people (Hamlin and Brym, 2006; Samson, Wilson, and Mazower, 1999). Durkheim would not have been surprised, given the destruction of traditional Innu norms and values and the elimination of stable and meaningful patterns of social interaction in the family and at work; social solidarity was abysmally low.

In 2002, the federal and provincial governments decided to move the people of Davis Inlet and create a safer community for them in Natuashish, 15 km away. The new community voted to abolish alcohol in 2008, but it is still smuggled into town, where a 1.2-litre bottle of rye has sold for $350. Some local mothers openly denounce people who supply alcohol and drugs, but substance abuse is still widespread and anti-abolitionists can still be found in the local government (Moore, 2010).

What can be done about the tragedy of the Innu? A 1984 study showed that a movement among the Innu to return to the land and to traditional hunting practices for up to seven months a year led to a dramatic improvement in health. They lived a vigorous outdoor life. Alcohol abuse stopped. Diet improved. Their emotional and social environments stabilized and became meaningful. Suicide was unknown (Samson, Wilson, and Mazower, 1999: 25).

Unfortunately, a big political obstacle stands in the way of a wide-scale return of the Innu to their traditional lifestyle. The governments of Canada

Sniffing gasoline in Davis Inlet.
SOURCE: © The Canadian Press/Ryan Remiorz

and Newfoundland and Labrador will not allow it. A widespread Innu return to the land would conflict with government and private economic development plans. For instance, the Lower Churchill Falls hydroelectric project (the second-biggest hydroelectric project in the world) and the Voisey's Bay nickel mine (the world's biggest deposit of nickel) are located in the middle of traditional Innu hunting and burial grounds. The Innu are vigorously attempting to regain control of their land. They also want to be able to decide *on their own* when and how to use Canadian health services, training facilities, and the like. Whether a compromise can be worked out between government and private plans for economic development and the viability of the Innu community is unclear.

Critical Thinking Questions

1. Why did the "return to the land" movement of the 1980s result in improved health incomes for the Innu who participated in it?

2. Why are many non-Indigenous Canadians reluctant to allow Indigenous Canadians to exercise more control over land and resources?

of the sociological issues raised by the Postindustrial Revolution and globalization is therefore in order.

POSTINDUSTRIALISM AND GLOBALIZATION: OPPORTUNITIES AND PITFALLS

At the end of the twentieth century, many observers were wildly optimistic about the benefits that postindustrialism and globalization were supposedly going to bring to humanity. One commentator proclaimed "the end of history," by which he meant that liberal capitalism had become the unrivalled socio-economic system in the world and its dominance was bound to usher in a long era of peace, freedom, and prosperity, leaving no corner of the world untouched (Fukuyama, 1992). Similarly, in a special issue of *The*

New York Times Magazine devoted to technology, one staff writer gushed:

> Individuals are acquiring more control over their lives, their minds and their bodies, even their genes, thanks to the transformations in medicine, communications, transportation and industry. At the same time, these technologies are providing social benefits and undoing some of the damage of the past. Technology helps to conserve natural resources and diminish pollution. ... The Information Revolution, besides enabling us to visit Mars at will, is fostering peaceful cooperation on Earth by decentralizing power. Political tyrants and demagogic warmongers are losing control now that their subjects have tools to communicate directly with one another. People are using the tools to do their jobs without leaving their families. They're forming new communities in cyberspace and forming new bonds with their neighbors in real space. Technology has the potential to increase individual freedom and strengthen community. (Tierney, 1997: 46–7)

This and similar outpourings of optimism were written before the stock market crash of 2000, the terrorist attacks on the United States on September 11, 2001, the second invasion of Iraq by the United States in 2003, the Great Recession of 2008-09, heightened fears about the consequences of climate change that surrounded the 2005 hurricane season, and the floods in Calgary and Toronto in the summer of 2013. However, even before these devastating shocks changed the minds of all but the most starry-eyed observers, sociologists were more realistic about the prospects of humanity. On the whole, they agreed that postindustrialism and globalization promise many exciting opportunities to enhance the quality of life and increase human freedom—but they also saw many social-structural barriers to the realization of that promise.

The unresolved social issues that confront us in the era of postindustrialism and globalization fall under three headings. Each issue is addressed in later chapters.

1. ***Autonomy versus constraint.*** One of the major themes that emerges from *New Society* is that many people are freer to construct their own identities than ever before. Almost everyone used to retain their religious, ethnic, racial, and sexual identities for a lifetime, even if they were not particularly comfortable with them. In the era of postindustrialism and globalization, however, various social developments and technological advances—ranging from international migration to the World Wide Web to greater acceptance of sexual diversity—free people from traditional constraints. The theme of increasing personal autonomy is taken up in Chapter 3, Culture; Chapter 4, Socialization; Chapter 5, Gender and Sexualities; Chapter 6, Communication and Mass Media; and Chapter 14, Religion.

Some chapters, however, point out that we experience increased freedom only within certain limits. For example, we can choose a far wider variety of consumer products than ever before, but consumerism itself increasingly seems a compulsory way of life (Chapter 3, Culture). Moreover, it is a way of life that threatens the natural environment (Chapter 17, Sociology and the Environment). Meanwhile, new technologies, such as surveillance cameras, cause us to modify our behaviour and act in more conformist ways (Chapter 15, Deviance and Crime). As these examples show, the autonomy promised by postindustrialism is only half of the story. The other half is that postindustrialism places new constraints on us.

2. ***Prosperity versus inequality.*** The second major theme that emerges from *New Society* is that postindustrialism opens up new economic, political, and educational opportunities. It makes work less onerous for many people. It raises the average standard of living. It enables women in particular to make rapid strides in all institutional spheres.

Again, however, we must face the less rosy aspects of postindustrialism. Tremendous economic and political inequality between women and men persists (Chapter 8, Gender Inequality). So does inequality between Indigenous and other Canadians (Chapter 9, Race and Ethnic Relations). Inequality between rich and poor in Canada has increased in recent decades (Chapter 7, Social Stratification). It is maintained partly by the educational system (Chapter 13, Education). By some measures, inequality between rich and poor nations has risen sharply (Chapter 10, Development and Underdevelopment). There

are more good jobs at the top of the occupational structure, but many more bad jobs at the
bottom (Chapter 12, Work and Occupations).
The quality of the Canadian healthcare system
is threatened at precisely the moment when our
population is rapidly aging and most in need
of healthcare (Chapter 18, Health and Aging).
Although elections are regularly held throughout
much of the world, it is an illusion to think that
democracy has conquered the planet (Chapter
19, Politics and Social Movements). Thus, economic and political inequality persist despite
growing prosperity and opportunity.

3. *Diversity versus uniformity.* The third major
   theme that emerges from *New Society* is that
   postindustrial society is more tolerant of diversity
   than any previous form of society was. Immigration policies no longer stipulate racial, ethnic, or
   religious criteria for entry into the country. As a
   result, our cities are more socially heterogeneous
   than ever before (Chapter 16, Population and
   Urbanization). The traditional nuclear family
   made up of mother, father, and children has
   given way to a wide variety of new family forms.
   Myriad radio stations, TV channels, newspapers,
   magazines, CD titles, books, and websites are
   now available to us.

   Yet despite growing social diversity, there
   is a strong push to conformity in many spheres
   of life. For example, most of our diverse cultural
   consumption is governed by the tastes and the
   profit motive of vast media conglomerates, most
   of them American-owned (Chapter 6, Communication and Mass Media). Powerful interests are
   trying to shore up the traditional nuclear family
   despite its inappropriateness for many people
   in postindustrial society (Chapter 11, Families).
   The globalization of economic, political, and cultural affairs may be threatening the survival of
   distinct national cultures (Chapter 20, Globalization). The push to uniformity thus counters the
   trend toward growing social diversity.

WHY SOCIOLOGY?

Renowned English sociologist Anthony Giddens
wrote that we live in an era "suspended between
extraordinary opportunity ... and global catastrophe" (Giddens, 1982: 166). Nuclear, chemical,
and biological disasters are more likely now than
they were just a couple of decades ago. A whole

range of environmental issues, deep inequalities
in the wealth of nations and of classes, racial and
ethnic violence, and unsolved problems in the relations between women and men continue to stare
us in the face and profoundly affect the quality of
daily life.

Despair and apathy are possible responses to
these complex issues. But these are not responses that
humans have often favoured. If it were our nature to
give up hope, we would still be sitting around half-
naked in the mud outside a cave.

People are more inclined to look for ways of
improving their lives, and this period of human history is full of opportunities to do so. We have, for
example, advanced to the point where for the first
time we have the means to feed and educate everyone
in the world. Similarly, it now seems possible to erode
some of the inequalities that have always been with us
and have always been the major source of human conflict. Students of sociology often pursue careers that
further such goals (see the Critical Sociology: Protest
and Policy box).

Although sociology offers no easy solutions as
to how the goal of improving society may be accomplished, it does promise a useful way of understanding
our current predicament and seeing possible ways of
dealing with it. You sampled sociology's ability to
tie personal troubles to social-structural issues when
we discussed suicide. You reviewed the major theoretical perspectives that enable sociologists to connect the personal with the social-structural. When I
outlined the half-fulfilled promises of postindustrialism and globalization, you saw sociology's ability
to provide an understanding of where we are and
where we can head.

I frankly admit that the questions raised in this
book are tough to answer. Sharp controversy surrounds them all. However, I am sure that if you grapple
with them, you will enhance your understanding of
your society's—and your own—possibilities. In brief,
sociology can help you figure out where you fit into
society and how you can make society fit you. That,
fundamentally, is sociology's goal.

TIME FOR REVIEW

1. What are some of the greatest social tensions in
   our time?
2. These tensions have emerged in a particular
   social context. What are the chief features of that
   context?

CRITICAL SOCIOLOGY: PROTEST AND POLICY   **CAREERS IN SOCIOLOGY**

Many people who want to improve the condition of humanity employ an arsenal of tactics, including voting for political parties they favour, contributing time and money to causes and organizations they support, petitioning governments and other authorities, running for office, participating in demonstrations, and so on. People with sociological training have an additional tool at their disposal. They can enjoy careers that allow them to engage in the formulation, implementation, and assessment of public policy—the laws, regulations, and programs that govern social life.

Annually in Canada, nearly 5000 people receive B.A. degrees with a major in sociology. A sociology B.A. improves one's understanding of the diverse social conditions affecting men and women, people with different sexual orientations, and people from different countries, regions, classes, races, and ethnic groups. Therefore, people with a B.A. in sociology tend to be attracted to jobs requiring good "people skills" and jobs involving the management and promotion of social change (see Table 1.2). Often, people with a B.A. in sociology go on to graduate school and obtain professional degrees in related fields, including law, urban planning, industrial relations, social work, and public policy. You will therefore find many people with bachelor's degrees in sociology working as lawyers, urban planners, city managers, statisticians, and healthcare and education administrators.

Many people with a graduate degree in sociology teach and conduct research in universities, with research being a more important component of the job in larger and more prestigious institutions. However, many sociologists do not teach. Instead, they conduct research and give policy advice in a wide range of settings outside the system of higher education. For example, in

TABLE 1.2 JOBS COMMONLY HELD BY CANADIANS WITH DEGREES IN SOCIOLOGY

Business
- actuary
- administrative assistant
- advertising officer
- computer analyst
- consumer relations
- data entry manager
- human resources specialist
- insurance agent
- journalist
- labour relations officer
- market analyst
- merchandiser/purchaser
- personnel officer
- production manager
- project manager
- public relations officer
- publishing officer
- quality control manager
- real estate agent
- sales manager
- sales representative
- technical writer

Community Affairs
- addictions counsellor
- adoption counsellor
- caseworker
- child development worker
- community organizer
- environmental organizer
- family planner
- fundraiser
- gerontologist
- group home programmer
- health outreach worker
- homeless/housing worker
- hospital administration officer
- housing coordinator
- marriage/family counsellor
- occupational/career counsellor
- public health worker
- rehabilitation worker
- residential planner
- social assistance advocate
- welfare counsellor
- youth outreach worker

Government
- affirmative action worker
- community affairs
- development aide
- foreign service worker
- human rights officer
- information officer
- legislative assistant
- personnel coordinator
- policy researcher
- urban/regional planner

Social Research
- census officer/analyst
- consumer researcher
- data analyst
- demographer
- market researcher
- social research specialist
- survey researcher
- systems analyst

Teaching/Education
- admissions counsellor
- alumni relations
- continuing studies officer
- post-secondary recruiter
- public health educator
- records & registration officer
- school counselling
- student developer
- teacher

SOURCE: Adapted from Neil Guppy, "So What Jobs Do Sociologists Have?..." *Opportunities in Sociology.* Copyright © 2014. Reprinted with permission from the Canadian Sociological Association/Société canadienne de sociologie.

(continued)

(continued)

many federal government agencies, sociologists are employed as researchers and policy consultants. Sociologists also conduct research and policy analysis in trade unions, nongovernmental organizations, and professional and public-interest associations. In the private sector, you can find sociologists practising their craft in firms specializing in public opinion polling, management consulting, market research, standardized testing, and "evaluation research," which assesses the impact of particular policies and programs before or after they go into effect.

One way of seeing the benefits of a sociological education is to compile a list of some of the famous practical idealists who studied sociology in university. That list includes several former heads of state, among them Fernando Cardoso, who was president of Brazil; Tomáš Masaryk, chief founder and first president of Czechoslovakia; Edward Seaga, fifth prime minister of Jamaica; and Ronald Reagan, who was president of the United States. The current first lady of the United States, Michelle Obama, has a sociology degree. Before she became first lady, she worked as commissioner of planning and development in Chicago City Hall and as the founding executive director of a program that prepares youth for public service. In her current role, she continues to shape public policy regarding nutrition and childhood obesity.

The former vice-president of the Liberal Party of Canada and former president and vice-chancellor of York University in Toronto, Lorna Marsden, is a sociologist. Anthony Giddens, former director of the London School of Economics and adviser to former British Prime Minister Tony Blair, earned a graduate degree in sociology. So did the heads of two of Canada's leading public opinion firms: Martin Goldfarb, chairman, president, and CEO of The Goldfarb Corporation; and Michael Adams and Donna Dasko, president and former senior vice-president, respectively, of Environics. Alex Himelfarb, former clerk of the Privy Council (Canada's highest ranking civil servant), holds a sociology Ph.D., as did Daniel Hill, the first full-time director of the Ontario Human Rights Commission and former Ontario Ombudsman. All of these people enjoyed careers that nicely answer the question, "What can you do with a sociology degree?" You can improve the world.

Critical Thinking Questions

1. How is it possible to reconcile a desire to improve the world with taking a scientific approach to studying social issues?

2. "Hard skills" include the ability to write clearly, succinctly, and convincingly; argue logically; and analyze statistically. "Soft skills" include the ability to interact effectively, empathically, and harmoniously with others. Both sets of skills are important in many types of jobs. How can sociology contribute to the learning of both skill sets?

SUMMARY

1. **What is sociology?**
   Sociology is the systematic study of human behaviour in social context. The sociological perspective analyzes the connection between personal troubles and social structures.

2. **Where are the social relations that surround you, permeate you, and influence your behaviour?**
   Social relations exist in micro- (small-scale, face-to-face), macro- (large-scale, more impersonal), and global (very large scale, cross-cultural, and cross-country) social structures. To varying degrees, people are aware of these structures, which therefore also exist in people's minds. Insofar as these social structures open up some

opportunities and close off others, they influence human behaviour.

3. **How does sociological research seek to test ideas using scientific methods and thereby improve people's lives?**
   Sociological research begins with values—ideas about what is good and bad, right and wrong. Values often motivate sociologists to define which problems are worth studying and to make initial assumptions about how to explain sociological phenomena. These explanations are theories—tentative explanations of some aspect of social life. Theories state how and why specific facts are connected. Research is

the process of systematically observing social reality to test the validity of a theory. Sociological theories may be modified and even rejected through research. Thus, sociological research uses scientific methods to evaluate ideas but the desire to improve people's lives often motivates the research.

4. **What are the main theoretical traditions in sociology?**
Sociology has four major theoretical traditions. Functionalism analyzes how social order is supported by macrostructures. The conflict approach analyzes how social inequality is maintained and challenged. Symbolic interactionism analyzes how meaning is created when people communicate in micro-level settings. Feminist theories focus on the social sources of patriarchy in both macro-level and micro-level settings.

5. **How did sociology emerge out of the Scientific Revolution, the Democratic Revolution, and the Industrial Revolution?**
The Scientific Revolution encouraged the view that sound conclusions about the workings of

society must be based on evidence, not just on speculation. The Democratic Revolution suggested that people are responsible for organizing society and that human intervention can therefore solve social problems. The Industrial Revolution created a host of new and serious social problems that attracted the attention of many social thinkers.

6. **What are the main challenges facing society today?**
The Postindustrial Revolution is the technology-driven shift from manufacturing to service industries. Globalization is the process by which formerly separate economies, states, and cultures become tied together and people become increasingly aware of their growing interdependence. The causes and consequences of postindustrialism and globalization form the great sociological puzzles of our time. The tensions between equality and inequality of opportunity, and between freedom and constraint, are among the chief interests of sociology today.

QUESTIONS TO CONSIDER

1. Durkheim argued that the social solidarity of groups influences the suicide rate in those groups. How, if at all, do you think the social solidarity of groups influences the crime rate and the divorce rate in those groups? Why?

2. In what sense is sociology a science? How does sociology differ from a natural science, such as physics?

3. What kinds of sociological issues are best addressed by each of the four major theoretical traditions in sociology?

GLOSSARY

Altruistic suicide (p. 6) occurs in settings that exhibit high levels of social solidarity, according to Durkheim. Altruistic suicide results from norms very tightly governing behaviour.

Anomic suicide (p. 6) occurs in settings that exhibit low levels of social solidarity, according to Durkheim. Anomic suicide results from vaguely defined norms governing behaviour.

Conflict theory (p. 14) generally focuses on large, macro-level structures, such as the relations between or among classes. It shows how major patterns of inequality in society produce social stability in some circumstances and social change in others. It stresses how members of privileged groups try to maintain their advantages while subordinate groups struggle to increase theirs. It typically leads to the suggestion that eliminating privilege will lower the level of conflict and increase the sum total of human welfare.

Cultural hegemony (p. 15) involves the control of a culture by dominant classes and other groups to the

point where their values are universally accepted as common sense.

The **Democratic Revolution** (p. 10) began about 1750. It suggested that people are responsible for organizing society and that human intervention can therefore solve social problems.

Dysfunctional consequences (p. 14) are effects of social structures that create social instability.

Egoistic suicide (p. 6) results from a lack of integration of the individual into society because of weak social ties to others.

Ethnomethodology (p. 29, Note 2) is the study of how people make sense of what others do and say in terms of norms that exist independently of individual social actors.

Feminist theory (p. 18) claims that patriarchy is at least as important as class inequality in determining a person's opportunities in life. It holds that male domination and female subordination are determined not by biological necessity but by structures of power and social convention. It examines the operation of patriarchy in both micro and macro settings. It contends that existing patterns of gender inequality can and should be changed for the benefit of all members of society.

Functionalist theory (p. 13) stresses that human behaviour is governed by relatively stable social structures. It underlines how social structures maintain or undermine social stability. It emphasizes that social structures are based mainly on shared values or preferences. It suggests that reestablishing equilibrium can best solve most social problems.

Global structures (p. 9) are patterns of social relations that lie outside and above the national level. They include international organizations, patterns of worldwide travel and communication, and the economic relations between and among countries.

Globalization (p. 21) is the process by which formerly separate economies, states, and cultures are becoming tied together and people are becoming increasingly aware of their growing interdependence.

The **Industrial Revolution** (p. 10) refers to the rapid economic transformation that began in Britain in the 1780s. It involved the large-scale application of science and technology to industrial processes, the creation of factories, and the formation of a working class.

A **latent function** (p. 14) is an invisible and unintended effect of social structures.

Macrostructures (p. 8) are overarching patterns of social relations that lie outside and above our circle of intimates and acquaintances. Macrostructures include classes, bureaucracies, and power systems, such as patriarchy.

A **manifest function** (p. 14) is a visible and intended effect of social structures.

Microstructures (p. 8) are the patterns of relatively intimate social relations formed during face-to-face interaction. Families, friendship circles, and work associations are all microstructures.

Patriarchy (p. 8) is the traditional system of economic and political inequality between women and men.

The **Postindustrial Revolution** (p. 21) refers to the technology-driven shift from manufacturing to service industries and the consequences of that shift for virtually all human activities.

Poststructuralism (p. 16), a school of thought that originated in mid–twentieth-century France, denies the stability of social relations and of cultures, their capacity to always shape how people think and act, and their neat categorization of social and cultural elements as binary opposites.

The **Protestant ethic** (p. 16) is the belief, originating in the sixteenth and seventeenth centuries, that religious doubts can be reduced, and a state of grace ensured, if people work diligently and live ascetically. According to Weber, the Protestant ethic had the unintended effect of increasing savings and investment and thus stimulating capitalist growth.

Queer theory (p. 18) argues that people's sexual identities and performances are so variable that such conventional labels as "male," female," "gay," and "lesbian" fail to capture the instability of sexual identities and performances that characterizes the lives of many people.

Research (p. 12) is the process of systematically observing reality to assess the validity of a theory.

The **Scientific Revolution** (p. 10) began about 1550. It encouraged the view that sound conclusions about the workings of society must be based on solid evidence, not just on speculation.

Social constructionism (p. 17) argues that apparently natural or innate features of life are often sustained by social processes that vary historically and culturally.

Social solidarity (p. 6) refers to (1) the degree to which group members share beliefs and values, and (2) the intensity and frequency of their interaction.

Social structures (p. 8) are relatively stable patterns of social relations.

The **sociological imagination** (p. 9) is the quality of mind that enables a person to see the connection between personal troubles and social structures.

Sociology (p. 4) is the systematic study of human behaviour in social context.

Symbolic interactionism (p. 17) focuses on face-to-face communication or interaction in micro-level social settings. It emphasizes that an adequate explanation of social behaviour requires understanding the subjective meanings people attach to their social circumstances. It stresses that people help to create their social circumstances and do not merely react to them. By underscoring the subjective meanings people create in small social settings, symbolic interactionism validates unpopular and nonofficial viewpoints, thus increasing our understanding and tolerance of people who may be different from us.

A **theory** (p. 12) is a tentative explanation of some aspect of social life that states how and why certain facts are related.

Values (p. 12) are ideas about what is right and wrong, good and bad.

NOTES

1. You will find more detailed discussion of these theories throughout the book. For example, on functionalism, see Chapters 13 and 14. On conflict theory, see Chapters 7, 11, 14, and 19. On symbolic interactionism, see Chapters 4 and 15. On feminism, see Chapters 5, 8, 11, and 19.

2. By emphasizing how social reality is constructed during interaction, symbolic interactionists downplay the importance of norms and understandings that precede any given interaction. **Ethnomethodology** tries to correct this shortcoming. Ethnomethodologists study how people make sense of what others do and say but stress that norms exist independently of individual social actors. Indeed, in the ethnomethodological view, everyday interactions could not take place without pre-existing shared norms. Say you pass an acquaintance on the street who offers a friendly "How are you?" If you proceed to outline in detail your financial situation, your love life, interesting developments at work, and so on, the acquaintance will quickly become annoyed. Most people expect "How are you?" to be answered with an equally brief reply. Violate the norm, and communication quickly breaks down (Garfinkel, 1967).

CHAPTER 2

RESEARCH METHODS

Neil Guppy
UNIVERSITY OF BRITISH COLUMBIA

SOURCE: © Ruslan Grumble/Shutterstock.

AFTER READING THIS CHAPTER, YOU WILL BE ABLE TO:

- Identify various sources of knowledge and know what is distinctive about each of them.

- Appreciate that, like other forms of knowledge, science can be wrong, but that science uses methods of gathering theoretically relevant evidence designed to minimize error.

- Recognize key characteristics of the research methods that sociologists use to gather evidence and test theoretical claims.

- Contrast the natural and social sciences and appreciate that what makes the social sciences unique is their study of meaningful human action.

- Compare the strengths and weaknesses of qualitative and quantitative methods.

- Know when it is more appropriate to use different sociological methods of investigation.

- Appreciate how research adds to our knowledge of the social world and how it expands opportunities and options by helping to solve social problems.

INTRODUCTION

Social research involves systematic, purposeful study. The systematic nature of sociological research comes, in part, from the methods sociologists use. Fundamental to these methods is the careful, ethical collection of evidence. However, only evidence relevant to theoretical ideas is useful. The purposeful structuring of sociological inquiry comes from asking theoretically informed questions. Systematic sociological study integrates sound theory with careful methods.

This chapter introduces you to the principles of research methods. I begin by outlining some basic assumptions involved in social science research, including assumptions about personal values or bias, the nature of facts, and the sources of knowledge. Next, I explain how the subject matter of the social sciences—people—differs from the objects of inquiry in the natural sciences (e.g., molecules). When people study people, it adds complexity to social research. This added complexity comes from people interpreting their own behaviour, and the behaviour of others, by trying to understand *meanings*. Methods of observation and questioning lie at the heart of social research, and I review the strengths and weaknesses of each of these approaches in the final section of the chapter.

SOCIAL SCIENCE AS A SOCIAL PRACTICE

James Driskell and David Milgaard were convicted of murder. In 2005, 14 years after his conviction, following new DNA tests, James Driskell had his murder charges quashed. David Milgaard had to endure prison longer, but in July 1997, after 23 years in prison, he too was exonerated. Again, DNA testing was instrumental. Courts had weighed evidence that people believed demonstrated the guilt of these men. Circumstantial evidence, filtered by personal expectations and values, had led justice astray. Subjective judgments had seriously compromised these men's lives.

Gold (1998) claimed that "good science" exonerated them, but it was "not science" that helped convict them. But what makes for "good science," the kind of science on which we can make serious decisions?

Wrongful convictions are rare. The criminal justice system minimizes such error through rules of evidence and presumptions of innocence. Likewise, science is organized to minimize error. Science is not perfect, however, and it is important not to put scientific practice on a pedestal, somehow immune to human foibles. Like all human activities, the social practice of science is influenced by subjectivity.

Science needs subjectivity but it cannot be overwhelmed by it. Subjectivity is important to certain

Sociological theories were first proposed in the nineteenth century as secular accounts of rapid social change. By the early twentieth century, systematic methods for empirically testing hypotheses were being introduced.

SOURCE: Carol Wainio, *We Can Be Certain*, 1982, acrylic on masonite, 48" × 96". Courtesy Carol Wainio.

phases of the practice of science but detrimental to other phases. Understanding the complexities of scientific methods requires distinguishing between times when subjectivity is beneficial and times when it is not. But just what is subjectivity? Most people would agree that our personal values and expectations are a core part of subjectivity. Frequently, people separate the world into facts and values; the real and objective versus the personal and subjective.

What complicates this is how our perception operates. Reality exists, certainly—it is no figment of the imagination. However, our values and expectations filter reality. While the saying "what you see is what you get" has an intuitive appeal, we know the claim is false. It exaggerates. Other things, especially our expectations and values, affect what we see.

Here is an example. The Sun is real. It is no figment of our imagination. We commonly speak about "sunsets" and "sunrises." But these terms deceive. Although we have all watched a "sunset," the Sun does not set. Our language conditions us to think of a moving Sun, but Earth rotates around the Sun. Earth's spin creates the *illusion* of a moving Sun.

Values and expectations influence our perceptions of reality, but they do not completely determine what we see. This is a critical point. The *extent* to which values and expectations influence what we see is debatable, but that is a secondary point. The key point is that *if* our perceptions of reality can be affected by our values, *then* how can scientists ever know for certain that what they "see" is true? Put another way, if observation cannot be a rock-solid foundation of scientific knowledge, then how is the practice of science to be understood?

An important claim of this chapter is that reality does not exist as some neutral scientific judge. Pure observation does not rule supreme. To think of an individual scientist as a detached, arm's-length observer of the physical or social world, making observations to test ideas, is to profoundly misunderstand science. The scientific method is not a mechanical process of collecting facts to prove things. Science is a much more complex social activity, and the methods of scientists are designed in the face of such complexity. Here is an illustration of how values and expectations may creep into scientific work.

In high-school biology classes you learned about Gregor Mendel. Mendel was the father of genetics. He cross-fertilized varieties of pea plants and noted that inherited traits followed consistent numerical ratios (i.e., the expression of dominant and recessive

genes over successive generations). R. A. Fisher, while a Cambridge University undergraduate, demonstrated that Mendel's results seemed fabricated. The likelihood that Mendel produced results conforming so closely to his hunches about heredity was, Fisher showed, in the order of 1 in 30 000.

Mendel may have been lucky, producing possible but very unlikely results. Alternatively, Mendel, or his assistant, may have unconsciously misclassified some pea plants. Classifications made by Mendel were not clear-cut, so his experimental results may have been interpreted as favouring his preconceived ideas. In this vein, Fisher (1966 [1936]: 123) claimed that Mendel's results were a "carefully planned demonstration of his conclusion."

"Observer bias" (making unconscious mistakes in classifying or selecting observations) is now commonly discussed as a danger to good methodological procedure. Mendel did not clearly and publicly describe his procedures. Although it is impossible to know exactly why his results came out as they did, his ideas about genetics have proven invaluable.

Good research methods are designed to minimize the types of errors that have been attributed to Mendel's experimental evidence. These methods do not eliminate the biasing effect that values and expectations have on scientific research. They do, however, seek to minimize their impact.

MINIMIZING BIAS IN SOCIAL SCIENCE

Sociologists apply scientific practices to the study of human society. These practices incorporate several ways of reducing bias, especially the twin pillars of public (open) scrutiny and skeptical reasoning. Scientific ideas become provisionally accepted only after scrutiny by the scientific community. Individual scientists do not just proclaim a link between family background and children's school success or between HIV and AIDS; these links must be demonstrated by presenting research findings at scientific conferences, subjecting findings to peer review, and ensuring that research results can be replicated. The scientific community is organized to promote critical scrutiny.

Scrutiny is not enough, however. If the scrutiny is not rigorous and probing, then it is of little value. Scientific practice also encourages skeptical reasoning. New ideas are accepted only after others have critically examined and questioned them. Examples of this questioning could include: Does something other than HIV cause AIDS? If HIV does cause AIDS, exactly how does the causal process work? This process of critical questioning is how good science is conducted.

Scientists are also trained to minimize the influence of their personal values and expectations on the results of their research work. They work to root out error in reasoning and observation. So, for example, scientists learn to collect and analyze information according to rules that reduce the risk that results will be affected by bias. Much of the latter part of this chapter focuses on these specific research techniques.

Science has prospered because of this healthy skepticism and public scrutiny. Both natural and social sciences have improved our world by helping to curtail malaria, improving the life chances of children with disabilities, and reducing gender inequity. Scientists are not infallible saints, however. The scientific community is not some sacred haven where only truth and enlightenment reign. Fraud and deceit are also part of science (Park, 2000).

It is also important to correct a possible misinterpretation about the role of values and expectations. I have portrayed these as "problems." This is too one-sided. Science would be substantially weaker, if not impotent, without values and expectations. Science is soaked through with individual judgments. Mendel's brilliance came from his expectation about the role of dominant and recessive genes in inheritance. Mendel provided a new way of seeing the world, a new conceptual map for understanding.

Expectations and values are in tension in science. Without them the spark of creativity and passion would be low, but with them we can be led to false conclusions (as judges and juries are occasionally misled). Put differently, objectivity and subjectivity each play an important role in science, including sociology. **Objectivity** stresses that observations should be free of the distorting effects of a person's values and expectations. Conversely, subjectivity is essential to change and innovation. Without people championing their own visions, we would have little creativity. A hallmark of science is its creativity. Mendel's was a beautiful solution to the mystery of inheritance, even if he may have been too exuberant in his experimental claims.

Science depends on both the creativity of new explanations and the assessment of whether these explanations are plausible. In sociology, this dual character resides in a division between theory (explanations of how the world works) and methods (ways of assessing the veracity of explanations).

This chapter is about assessing evidence. It explores how sociologists work within the rules of the scientific method. First, however, I contrast scientific knowledge with other forms of knowledge. The discussion moves next to the steps involved in the sociological research process. I then describe the main methods of gathering sociological data and the decisions that have to be made during the research process. Finally, I return in the conclusion to the role of subjectivity in research.

SCIENTIFIC VERSUS NONSCIENTIFIC THINKING

To differentiate good and bad science, consider what characterizes scientific thinking. Before the eighteenth century and the rise of science, our ancestors knew many things about the world. Much of this was custom or common sense—when to plant, what to plant, where to plant. Religious knowledge held centre stage. Stories of creation, of how we came to be on Earth, were powerful tales that gave coherence to people's lives. Religious doctrine and common sense remain powerful in many societies, but scientific ways of knowing have increasing authority in industrial nations.

What characterizes this scientific way of knowing? A key contribution came from Scottish philosopher David Hume (1711–76). He disputed the popular argument of his day that science begins with observation. Hume argued that no matter how many observations you make, you cannot infer your next observation. This is the *problem of induction*. Put more graphically, no matter how many white swans you see, you cannot logically infer that all swans are white. However, observing one black swan is sufficient to refute the claim that all swans are white.[1] Hume was railing against Francis Bacon's claim that observation was the bedrock of science. For Hume, the collection of "facts" is useless unless you understand how to interpret them.

Facts do not speak for themselves. Blue mould growing on spoiling food is a fact of life. It was only in 1928, however, that Alexander Fleming recognized this blue mould as a potent medical tool. Many people had seen blue mould, but only Fleming understood it as penicillin. Science is not a collection of facts. However, among other things, it is a method of collecting facts.

Facts are bits of evidence, information that we can verify using our senses. Because trillions of bits of human activity might be taken as facts, how do we select what should count as evidence? Sociological theory provides guidance for the hunting and gathering of facts. Evidence is gathered to test ideas, hunches, or theories. Only selected bits of human activity are used as evidence. Those selected bits are chosen because they relate to a sociologist's theory about how the world works.

In the twentieth century, Sir Karl Popper's (1977 [1934]) ideas about falsification improved this thinking. As he claimed, observations refuting a well-conceived idea are always more important than evidence supporting or proving a theory (e.g., observing one black swan was more important than observing yet another white swan). For Popper, science does not start by gathering facts. It starts with a question or hunch, or in his words, a well-conceived conjecture.

Recall two core ideas I noted about scientific thinking: public scrutiny and skeptical reasoning. Popper added the principles of testability and uncertainty. Testability is easy to understand. For an idea to be scientific it must have testable implications; it must be falsifiable (i.e., *if* an assertion is false, this can be demonstrated by evidence).

The principle of uncertainty may be more difficult to accept. Many people misunderstand science as a doctrine of certainty. As Park (2000: 39) puts it, "many people are uneasy standing on ... loose soil; they seek a certainty that science cannot offer." As Hume argued centuries before, observations cannot be the bedrock of science because of the problem of induction. Equally, however, science cannot proceed, as Popper correctly argued, without the possibility of observations that could refute a scientific claim. Observations based on well-reasoned methods can ferret out error and misunderstanding, although these same observations cannot guarantee universal truth or perfect certainty.

UNDERSTANDING SCIENCE SOCIOLOGICALLY

One of the most influential academic books of the twentieth century was Thomas Kuhn's (1962) *The Structure of Scientific Revolutions*. Before Kuhn, many people held a "brick-building" conception of science. They thought that individual scientists contributed to building a structure called *scientific knowledge*, one brick at a time. As scientific knowledge accumulated, the structure became taller and sturdier.

Kuhn challenged this view on several fronts. First, he held that science developed through contributions from a community of scholars who use "paradigms" as guiding tools about how the world is organized (Mendelian genetics is such a paradigm). Paradigms guide questions and answers. Evidence not fitting a paradigm is ignored. However, if significant anomalous evidence accumulates, a "scientific revolution" results. Scholars opt for a new paradigm. The transition from Newton's mechanics to Einstein's relativity illustrates a paradigm shift, or a scientific revolution (Kleppner and Jackiw, 2000).

Second, Kuhn proposed a discontinuous view of scientific progress. The community of scholars did not keep building the Newtonian structure but shifted to a new structure defined by the Einsteinian paradigm. This discontinuous view of scientific progress also influenced debates about truth. Earth as the "third rock from the Sun" we now hold as a fundamental truth. But our ancestors were equally convinced that Earth was the universe's central rock. In the future, will our "third rock" conception seem equally odd? Kuhn's view suggests that truth is contextual. A new paradigm establishes a new context, showing us that beliefs we once held to be true were naive or misleading (like a flat earth).

Finally, the argument about community was sociologically compelling. In Kuhn's hands, the practice of science was not understood as individual scientists ruthlessly questioning all ideas. To the contrary, paradigms provided a set of convictions about how the world was ordered. With faith in a paradigm, a community of scholars searched for what they were convinced existed. Paradigms had a disciplining effect, focusing attention on a delimited set of questions and answers. Notice also that Kuhn emphasized that scientific change was not gradual, but sudden (revolutionary) and that the change was organized (structured).

NATURAL VERSUS SOCIAL SCIENCE

The scientific practices of chemists and sociologists share many elements. The research methods of both disciplines help in understanding and explaining why certain patterns recur. Furthermore, values are important in this process because they underlie the creative imagination so central to scientific puzzle solving. Values also have the potential to bias or distort observations, and both the natural and the social sciences guard against distortion. If the scientific method is defined as a set of practices or procedures for testing knowledge claims, then both chemists and sociologists are doing science.

There is, however, a profound difference between the subject matter of the natural and the social sciences: Bacteria don't blush. This phrase neatly captures the key distinction. Human beings are conscious and creative; we can think, act, reason, and decide. As sociologists, we study "ourselves"—that is, our contemporaries and our ancestors. Bacteria, having no knowledge of social norms, do not blush when exposed to the beam of an electron microscope. Bacteria cannot think, act, reason, and decide.[2]

Perhaps the single most important difference is that, unlike chemists, sociologists study **meaningful action**—that is, activities that are meaningful to the people involved. For example, bacteria may not blush when studied, but people often react self-consciously when they know they are being observed. To study love, friendship, or charisma depends on learning something about the meanings people ascribe to actions. This circumstance has advantages and disadvantages. Unlike chemists, sociologists can ask questions of the people whom we study (bacteria don't talk either). But this advantage can also be a disadvantage. Interpreting people's answers is not easy.

TIME FOR REVIEW

1. How do values and expectations positively and negatively influence research?
2. How do sociologists attempt to weed out error and misinformation in the pursuit of knowledge about the social world?
3. What roles do testability, falsification, and uncertainty play in advancing sociological knowledge?
4. What does the phrase "Bacteria don't blush" illustrate by way of differentiating between the social and natural sciences?

METHODS OF SOCIAL RESEARCH

EXPLANATION

Sociologists have shown repeatedly that family background strongly influences the years of schooling people complete. Children raised in poverty tend not to go as far in school as do children from upper-class families. Although this research demonstrates a link between family background and educational attainment, this link is, as I have reported it, descriptive, not explanatory. I have offered no reason for the link. I have noted a potential cause (family background) and an effect (years of schooling), but I have failed to

provide any mechanisms through which this implied causal process might operate. An **explanation** would be judged adequate only if it could show how family background actually influences educational outcomes.

The mere association or correlation between social origin and educational destination does not prove causality. The relationship between smoking and lung cancer is a good example of the rule that *correlation does not prove causation*. Smoking has long been linked to lung cancer, but only in the past few decades have we learned more about the causal mechanisms underlying this correlation. Cigarette companies, especially, have argued that the presumed connection was a **spurious relationship**, meaning that something other than smoking caused lung cancer. Accumulated evidence and more precise understanding and observation of the underlying modes of transmission have established that the original correlation is causal.

To return to the earlier example, for a **causal relationship** to exist between social origin and educational destination, four criteria need to be satisfied: association, temporality, nonspuriousness, and the existence of mechanisms. (1) Changes in social origin have to be associated, or correlated, with changes in educational destination. (2) Social origin has to have temporally preceded educational destination. (3) To conclude the link is causal, we want to know that no other factor(s) are causing the linkage. (4) Finally, we want to know how it is that social origins are affecting educational destinations: What are the mechanisms that create this linkage? (For an expanded discussion of correlation and causation, please see the learning path for this chapter in MindTap.)

We might try to explain the mechanisms linking family and schooling in several ways (Davies and Guppy, 2014). An obvious factor is money. Although public schooling is free, costs are incurred for field trips, tutoring, postsecondary education, and a host of other events. Children living in poverty may remain in school for fewer years than their upper-class peers because of these costs (and they may seek employment sooner to help with family income).

Money seems to be a partial explanation for the link, but other factors may be at work as well. Many skills and values taught in school may be more readily grasped by children from upper-class families, not because these children are smarter than are children living in poverty, but because the home environments of the children may expose them to different skills and values. The classroom culture may be more like the culture in upper-class homes (e.g., abstract word games are valued, reading and music are prized) and these children may therefore be advantaged.

The first explanation is largely about money and material resources. The policy implications of this explanation point to eliminating or reducing the costs of schooling. This has been accomplished in large measure in Canada. However, even when the costs of postsecondary education have also been reduced (e.g., in Quebec), social-class disparities in educational attainment remain. The second explanation points to cultural factors in the home (e.g., reading) as a reason for the family–school link. This explanation has influenced policies related to compensatory education, such as Head Start and After Four, educational programs designed to help disadvantaged children by giving them educational enrichment (Guppy and Davies, 2009).

The mechanisms by which causes have effects are essential for adequate explanation (Gross, 2009). You might think of these mechanisms as the social "cogs and levers" greasing the wheels that link causes with effects. Furthermore, multiple causes are involved in social-scientific explanations; a single unitary cause rarely provides a sufficient explanation. Sociologists search for the multiple factors that can help explain some particular state of affairs. So, in the family–school example, although only two explanations for the link are mentioned here, other explanations may also be tested and refined.

UNDERSTANDING

Sociologists must not be content merely to offer explanations for why a particular relationship exists. These explanations are often sterile unless they also address the meaningfulness of human activity. People make the social world happen, and in doing so they give meaning to their actions and to the actions of others. A failure to address these meanings would leave sociology underdeveloped.

It is no simple matter, however, to understand what someone or some group means by their actions or utterances. One way to think about **understanding** is as follows. The first time I saw a cricket match, I could not fathom what was happening. To the extent that I have come to understand this complex social activity, I have learned *how to proceed with the activity*. To understand a cricket match means being able to participate fully in the activity, knowing what others mean by their actions and utterances, and knowing how others will interpret my actions and utterances.

A fundamental social process, called *taking the role of the other*, nicely captures this idea of understanding. By imagining yourself in another person's role, you come to appreciate someone else's point of view. You come to understand, to reflect on, that person's ideas and issues. I do not mean that you must become Lady Gaga to understand her; that would be impossible. Instead, sociologists focus on the web of relations in which people interact, paying attention to how people understand and interpret the views of others. They pay attention to "the definition of the situation," to the meanings of the people involved.

Erving Goffman's work in an insane asylum (as it was called then) is a good illustration of sociological understanding (Goffman, 1961). Goffman was interested in how patterns of social activity in the asylum were organized. He came to see the mental hospital from the patients' point of view. By dispensing with the medical categories and scientific labels assigned to individual patients, Goffman began to understand the ways in which patients worked cooperatively to produce a coherent social structure. He learned to appreciate how the patients defined the routine activities of the asylum and how they coped with institutional procedures that denied them privacy and stripped them of their personal identities (e.g., by issuing institutional clothing and confiscating personal objects).

Goffman (1961: 129) also learned about what he calls the "careers" of patients with mental illnesses: "Persons who become mental-hospital patients vary widely in the kind and degree of illness that a psychiatrist would impute to them. ... But once [in treatment] they are confronted by some importantly similar circumstances and respond to these in some importantly similar ways. Since these similarities do not come from mental illness, they would seem to occur in spite of it." Although social life on the "inside" might seem unique or even bizarre at first, Goffman argues that anyone, patient or researcher, would, in time, come to find it much like many other communities in which he or she has participated, possessing an identifiable social organization and rhythm of activity.

Returning to the education example, explanations of high-school dropout rates that ignore the attitudes and values of the people who drop out are one-sided. An appreciation of the experiences of people who drop out is essential to a more complete account of the schooling process. Especially important here is the resistance of students to authority, often expressed through music and clothing. Such resistance is not some idiosyncratic expression of random individuals, but represents part of a youth subculture that must be understood by anyone who wants to alter the schooling process to make it better. How young school resisters define the situation of schooling is important to a full appreciation of dropping out.

Understanding and explanation work together. Although explanations of dropping out that ignore student values are deficient, merely reporting the stories of young resisters would be equally vacuous. A full appreciation of dropping out, or of any other social activity, requires both understanding and explanation. Often, different researchers pursue these two activities and their combined results contribute to fruitful research programs leading to social change.

Is it enough to just understand and explain? Most sociologists are progressive in the sense of wanting to see a better, more just world—a world with less

Explanations of high-school dropout rates that ignore the attitudes and values of those who drop out are one-sided. An appreciation of the experiences of students who drop out is essential to a more complete account of the schooling process.

SOURCE: © iStockphoto.com/Rosmarie Gearhart.

human suffering and misery. Should sociologists be both researchers and activists? Put differently, should scholars act on their research findings to promote social change or should activism and political change be separate activities? Especially for scholars working in such areas as poverty, human rights, or racism, the urge to promote social change is pressing. Feminist scholars have been particularly adept at bridging the divide between research and social change advocacy.

Feminist research has done so by engaging in scholarship that disrupts traditional or accepted knowledge. Sociologists often ask questions from the vantage point of those on the margins of society (for example, the poor, the dispossessed, the victim). Feminist research has been pivotal in challenging traditional knowledge that excludes women, ignores discrimination, or accepts the status quo as legitimate and proper (Smith, 2005). Further, feminist methodology has stressed minimizing harm and raising ethical standards. Academic feminism pushed against traditional social science that had helped to sustain the oppression of women by focusing exclusively on men or by examining issues of interest only to men (DeVault, 1996).

ETHICS IN SOCIAL RESEARCH

Three groups share an interest in the conduct of sociological research: the sociological investigator, the people being observed or questioned, and the members of the larger society who enable, and potentially benefit from, such research. Sociologists have a self-interest in their own research, but it is imperative that proper weight also be given to the interests of research participants and the public. Although primary responsibility for the rights and welfare of both participants and the public must reside with the sociologist as researcher, the self-interest of the sociologist requires that an arm's-length body reviews research designs and procedures to ensure the protection of all interested parties (see the Critical Sociology: Social Inequality box).

The typical risks in social research are of two broad types: risks to individuals and risks to communities or social groups. Understanding individual harm is fairly straightforward. Social research can cause harm by, for example, asking people questions that remind them of trauma they once experienced. How research can cause collective harm may be less obvious. The results of social research can harm

Chemists examine molecules through scanning electron microscopes. Social scientists study people. Sometimes sociologists are able to study people unobtrusively by examining documents like court records or administrative data such as school grades. Most often, though, social scientists want evidence that requires them to question or observe people directly. Such inquiry can involve a power imbalance because researchers may have authority, education, and resources that subjects lack.

This power imbalance can be dangerous to research subjects. Consider, for example, experiments conducted on Indigenous students attending residential schools in Canada. From 1876 to 1996, about 150 000 Indigenous children were removed from their families, placed in boarding schools that were funded by the federal government and administered by Christian churches, and forced to abandon their culture. Often mistreated and neglected, some students were also used as "guinea pigs" in experiments designed to study the effect of nutritional deprivation (Mosby, 2013). The students were powerless to resist such harm.

Sadly, such abuse was not as uncommon as one might think; only in the last half-century or so has much thought been given to the rights of human subjects in research. *Studying down*—that is, researching people who lack the authority, education, and resources of the researcher—has always been far easier than *studying up*—that is, researching people in positions of power and privilege.

Research ethics have been tightened since the mid-twentieth century. All research involving human subjects must now pass through careful adjudication to ensure that research participants are not harmed and that they voluntarily consent to participate. This procedure has helped to protect research subjects, especially those who are members of disadvantaged groups. Feminist scholars have gone so far as to advocate "participatory action research" that empowers research participants by including them more directly in steering research so that it meets the needs of those being studied as well as those doing the studying (Masuda et al., 2012).

Critical Thinking Questions

1. It is often said that knowledge is power. How can knowledge acquired from research threaten to disempower some people? Provide examples.

2. Knowledge is often said to be power, but in what sense do power differences in research suggest that power is knowledge?

3. What are the pros and cons of including research participants (subjects) in designing research questions and conducting research? Do the pros outweigh the cons or vice versa?

communities or groups by, for example, reinforcing stigmas and stereotypes or supporting policies that help some groups at the expense of others. Who sponsors the sociologist's research is an important issue, especially in this latter context. Here, too, relations between political advocacy and scientific research come to the fore.

Ethically responsible research must minimize risks. Informed consent is key. Researchers must ensure that people not only consent but that they consent voluntarily after knowing what the research entails. I comment further on ethical issues in discussing a range of research projects in the remainder of the chapter (see also Haggerty, 2004).

TIME FOR REVIEW

1. What are the main differences between explanation and understanding?

2. What are the four conditions for causality that would need to be satisfied if we claimed that gender contributed causally to differences in occupational income?

3. Some research ethics boards at hospitals, schools, and universities have members of the general public as members. What are the advantages and disadvantages of such a practice?

TECHNIQUES OF SOCIAL RESEARCH

Sociologists have developed a variety of techniques for gathering evidence. I will review three of the most important: experiments, survey research, and qualitative methods. As you read my accounts of research procedures, keep asking yourself these questions: How do sociologists go about developing insights about, or knowledge of, the social world? How do they come to know what they claim to know? What methods do they use and how believable are the results generated by these methods?

EXPERIMENTS

Experiments are the hallmark of scientific research and are commonly, though inaccurately, equated with science itself. Experiments are useful because they enable researchers to isolate causes and measure their effects. By no other method can researchers determine causation so precisely. An example is the best way to illustrate the point.

The shape of families has changed recently. At one time, the family was understood as a married couple—a man and a woman—with children. No longer. Single-parent families have become more prevalent, as have common-law unions and same-sex couples. Nathan Lauster and Adam Easterbrook (2011) examined how successful people in these new types of families were in securing rental housing and, if they encountered resistance in renting, what the likely source of the resistance was.

A landlord could choose to rent to people in some types of family and not others. Landlords might judge new types of families as morally suspect or as violating the traditional family norms of existing tenants. Landlords also face the risk of damage to their premises and failure to pay rent, and they may judge people in new family types as riskier, less stable, or more likely to miss rent payments. These perceptions might vary with a landlord's previous experience with similar types of families, so there may be neighbourhood effects. That is, in neighbourhoods where people in new family forms are already renting, there might be less discrimination than in neighbourhoods where the traditional family form still dominates.

To explore these questions, Lauster and Easterbrook (2011) chose to conduct a field experiment. They compared the ability of people in different family configurations to find rental accommodation.

The field experiment worked as follows. In Vancouver, such websites as craigslist.ca and kijiji.ca carry the largest volume of rental advertisements. The researchers wrote an email inquiry in which the only information they varied was the type of family that was inquiring and the size of the unit required. The family types were as follows: male-female couple; male-male couple; female-female couple; female adult, male son; male adult, male son. Five versions of the scripted email, with appropriate variations, read as follows:

> Hi, my name is [Matt/Melissa/Kate/Kevin], and [appropriate form; e.g., my son and I] saw your listing for an apartment/suite] on [website]. We are nonsmokers and don't

have any pets [or kids, if appropriate]. I'm a teacher and [she's/he's enrolled in a professional program; or he's enrolled in third grade]. Please let us know if the [apartment/suite] is still available and if we can view it. Thanks, [names of two people].

The scripted emails were sent to landlords who had advertised a one- or two-bedroom unit for less than $1700/month. Because the family forms existing in a neighbourhood might influence responses, they targeted nine different neighbourhoods. For example, they reasoned that in neighbourhoods with higher concentrations of same-sex couples, discrimination against same-sex couples would likely be lower than in neighbourhoods where traditional male-female couples predominated. By including nine neighbourhoods, the researchers were also able to see whether such neighbourhood factors as percentage of gay couples or lone-parent families, the population under 15, and average monthly rent affected their findings.

The scripted emails ensured that all landlords received identical inquiries, save for the change in type of family. Sending emails asking about every one- or two-bedroom rental property advertised on a given day was ruled out because that would lead to a possible duplication of requests to the same landlord. Also, the experimenters wanted to code details of each advertisement, such as location, rent, and size, so they used a randomly selected set of advertisements. They also wanted to stagger their requests over two weeks to ensure that no bias crept in from differences in the day of the week they inquired.

The results showed that heterosexual couples and female couples received the most positive responses (about 62 percent each), while male couples received positive responses only about 50 percent of the time. Single parents, either mother or father, received positive responses about 54 percent of the time.

Lauster and Easterbrook (2011) also wanted to know if the likelihood of a positive response to their email varied by neighbourhood. For example, did male couples also receive significantly lower positive responses to their inquiries when the rental units were in traditionally gay neighbourhoods? The answer was no. As expected, male couples were more likely to receive positive responses when the email was directed to rental units in an area where male couples lived. While, overall, male couples experienced the greatest rental discrimination, it was lessened in neighbourhoods where many gay men already lived (although even in those neighbourhoods gay men were disadvantaged relative to heterosexual couples). Female couples did not experience rental discrimination although, as the authors note, lesbian women experience other forms of discrimination and, in that light, it is surprising that they don't experience rental discrimination.

By dissecting the Lauster and Easterbrook experiment, we can examine more carefully several key research design features. The researchers began with a **hypothesis**—an unverified but testable knowledge claim. They hypothesized that "type of family" would affect "rental discrimination," with heterosexual couples more likely to receive favourable responses than the other family types.

To test this hypothesis, Lauster and Easterbrook examined the relationship between two **variables**. A variable is a measurable concept that can have more than one value. Age is a concept we measure by years since birth (or for newborns, weeks or months). In the language of research, Lauster and Easterbrook were interested in how type of family, their **independent variable** (the hypothesized cause), influenced rental discrimination, their **dependent variable** (the hypothesized effect). Lauster and Easterbrook used five different conditions or "treatments" for their independent variable: heterosexual couple, male couple, female couple, single mother, and single father. They reasoned that the likelihood of a positive response to the email about renting depended on which type of family the email was from. The dependent variable had three values: a positive response (yes, please come and see the unit), no response, or a negative response (rented already).

How did Lauster and Easterbrook know that only type of family and not another factor, such as a household size or social class, influenced rental discrimination? They were confident in their conclusion because, by design, they know that landlords received fictitious emails where only the type of family differed. By randomly sending the email to different landlords and referencing one of the five family conditions, they could compare how landlords responded, knowing that family type was the only factor that could have systematically affected landlord responses. Household size was identical in each email. Social class was also constant since the reference was always to a teacher. It is true that rental units differed in price, and they could have been one- or two-bedroom units, but the researchers accounted for differences of this sort in their statistical analysis.

Random assignment or **randomization** lies at the heart of experimental design. Using a random procedure, such as flipping a coin or rolling a die, researchers assign people to an experimental condition based on chance. If the coin comes up heads, a person is placed in experimental condition one; if the coin comes up tails, the person is assigned to condition two. Although in Lauster and Easterbrook's case, landlords differed by sex, age, income, and so on, the emails went to an approximately equal number of women and men, people with different annual incomes, and so on. The experiment was designed to ensure that the landlords receiving each type of email constituted a randomized group. Lauster and Easterbrook used this random assignment process to ensure that the only difference among the five conditions was family type.

Sociology experiments of the type conducted by Lauster and Easterbrook are relatively rare, largely because many social processes that interest sociologists are not amenable to experimentation. Ethical and practical problems also limit the use of experiments.

Notice as well an ethical dilemma involved in this research. Landlords were duped; they didn't know they were involved in a research study. My own view is that learning about discrimination in rental housing is valuable and although some randomly selected landlords unknowingly did some extra work in dealing with the email, there was no chance of this causing harm. The ethics review board involved thought that on balance this was acceptable practice. What do you think? Was this deceit justifiable?

Laboratory experiments have been used in sociology although they have become less common recently. Martha Foschi and Jerilee Valenzuela (2008) used a lab experiment to investigate the extent to which hiring decisions for junior engineering positions were influenced by the sex of the applicant. They had university students rate application files in which there was a standard application form, a résumé, and an academic transcript. The key difference between files was the sex of the applicant.

Foschi and Valenzuela (2008) found no difference between female and male applicants. That is, they found no bias toward male applicants being preferred. They conclude that (2008: 1034) "the social climate has been changing towards equality regarding views of men's and women's competence. This is particularly the case in experiments with university students as subjects, where recent work reveals that decisions do not always favor men."

As with any research, we must be cautious in generalizing the results. The latter problem is expressed technically as the issue of **external validity**, or the degree to which research findings remain valid in different contexts. Relationships discovered in lab experiments do not always hold in more "real-life" settings. The field experiment, conducted in a natural as opposed to a laboratory setting, reduces the problem of artificiality. However, Lauster and Easterbrook in their field experiment could explore only a limited range of family types and family size, which was a complicating factor. They chose to keep family size constant at two, so an alternative explanation for some of their findings might be the presence of a child as opposed to it being a single parent that influenced their results.

As mentioned earlier, when people know they are being studied, they often become self-conscious. Being studied may influence behaviour. This was demonstrated in productivity experiments conducted first by Roethlisberger and Dickson (1939) at the Western Electric Company's Hawthorne factory. They found

One field experiment that investigated the extent of job discrimination faced by people of different ethnic backgrounds found that whites had a 3–to–1 advantage over blacks in job offers.
SOURCE: © iStockphoto.com/DWlabs Inc.

that productivity (the dependent variable) increased when they brightened the lighting but also when they dimmed the lighting. People simply worked harder whenever the research team was studying them! Social scientists have subsequently used the term **Hawthorne effect** when referring to changes in people's behaviour caused by their awareness of being studied.

SURVEY RESEARCH

The social survey is a key social science tool for gathering evidence. Survey-based knowledge is used to estimate Canadian unemployment and to calculate our rate of inflation (as measured by the Consumer Price Index). For sociologists, surveys are the main method used in collecting evidence. By asking a large, representative sample of people identical questions, survey research provides a method of systematically comparing answers. It also allows researchers to generalize the results to the larger population from which the sample was randomly chosen. Questions can be posed either on a **self-administered questionnaire** or through an **interview**. Increasingly, the Internet is used as a way to conduct surveys (Brym and Lenton, 2001).

Marjan Houshmand and her colleagues (Houshmand, Seidel, and Ma, 2014) used a survey to investigate the following research question: Does working for pay as a teenager have positive, neutral, or negative consequences for future occupational outcomes? You can imagine a set of personal benefits from paid employment, including more spending money, job experience, and skill development. But the jobs available to young workers are often part-time, boring, and low-paid. In 2013, among all 15- to 19-year-olds working for pay, 50 percent received the minimum wage (Galarneau and Fecteau, 2014: 6).

For someone who is 15, how do you adjudicate the costs and benefits of working for pay? Houshmand and her team chose to do this by examining "future occupational outcomes." They used labour market experiences in subsequent years to shed light on the research question. They measured their theoretical concept, "future occupational outcomes," in several different ways, including the likelihood of future employment and the amount of income received. Do these latter items provide good indicators of the Houshmand team's idea of future occupational outcomes? That is, are these valid indicators? **Validity** refers to accuracy or relevancy. Houshmand and her team chose to use several different indicators to help in ensuring that they were tapping the full range of occupational outcomes.

A related measurement issue is reliability. Whereas validity relates to the link between a concept (e.g., future occupational outcomes) and measures of that concept (e.g., future income), **reliability** refers to the consistency with which something can be measured. Your grade point average measures a theoretical concept, intelligence or knowledge. If your grades across several courses in a particular subject area are fairly consistent, then these marks are taken as a reliable measure of your subject knowledge. A **measurement** is reliable if it is consistent or repeatable. As we will see in moment, the Houshmand team used grade point averages as one of their measures, a measure they were fairly confident had both good reliability and validity.

The next problem that Houshmand and her colleagues faced was designing a research study that would allow them to know details about a person's employment at age 15 and their subsequent labour market outcomes. Their research question involved a claim about causality: What were the consequences of something happening at time one (employment at age 15) for something that happened later in life (future occupational outcomes)? They had to satisfy all of the claims about causality detailed earlier: association, temporality, nonspurious, and causal mechanism. They accomplished this using a survey where people were interviewed multiple times. Statistics Canada collected such information in a study called the *Youth in Transition Survey* (YITS).

As the Statistics Canada study name implies, the researchers examined transitions. One way to do this is to ask people to recall previous events and then compile a profile of how someone's life has unfolded. For example, Guppy and Beck (2015) used the *National Graduates Survey* to examine who won merit-based scholarships as undergraduates. This survey, again done by Statistics Canada, asked university graduates from 2013 to recall the number and value of scholarships they had earned. A weakness in this approach is that it requires people to accurately remember past events. Recalling precise details from previous years is prone to error. Often, however, surveys are snapshots taken at one point in time, so retrospective questions are the only way to capture previous information.

Surveys that interview the same people at several time points provide a strong alternative design. The YITS project first interviewed a sample of people in 2000 and then questioned them again every two years. Surveys always involve **sampling**. It would not have been practical for Houshmand's research team to interview all 15-year-olds in Canada (a complete enumeration of everyone would be a *census*). However, it is this larger population of 15-year-olds about which Houshmand wanted to draw conclusions. To use a different example, in doing research on urban household waste, interviewing all city dwellers is both unnecessary and impractical. Information obtained from a subset of the population, a *sample*, is used to represent the attitudes and behaviours of everyone. We use rules of chance or probability to select individuals who are representative of the larger population. Taken together, such individuals form *probability samples*.

For Houshmand's study, choosing a random sample of 15-year-olds was not easy. No listing of every 15-year-old exists. In drawing a sample, Statistics Canada chose to use a two-stage process. First, the researchers had a list of all high schools in Canada. They randomly selected 1200 schools from each of the ten provinces. Second, from each of these schools they selected a random sample of 15-year-olds.

How many students should Statistics Canada have selected? The precise answer depends mainly on the amount of variation or heterogeneity in the population and the degree of accuracy required in the study's conclusions. If you need very accurate results, you need a larger sample. Likewise, if the population is very variable, you need a larger sample to reflect that heterogeneity adequately (thankfully our blood is quite homogeneous and so only one jab is necessary to obtain a blood sample).

Selecting survey samples is not easy. How would you go about selecting a random sample of students in your faculty or program? Distributing questionnaires in classes would be one method, but many students do not attend every class. Using email addresses might seem practical, but many students do not let schools know their working addresses or they filter Internet surveys out as junk mail. Registration lists give an approximation of the student population, but these lists are never perfect. Students drop out as the term progresses, while others change their addresses and phone numbers. Even with this limitation, however, student lists maintained by the registrar might be the best alternative available. The list from which a sample is selected is called the *sampling frame*. This frame must come as close as possible to including everyone in the population.

Ethical issues are also a concern. Two key principals of **ethics** can be illustrated by the YITS study. First, participation had to be voluntary. The students who answered the survey questions had to have voluntarily agreed to participate. It would have been inappropriate to have coerced their involvement. Second, they had to have volunteered based on informed consent. That is, they had to have been informed about the nature of the study, the types of questions, the commitment of time, and especially in this case, the ongoing nature of their participation.

One of the complications of a study like the one Houshmand and her team relied on was that respondents may drop out as the years go by. Not everyone questioned in the first wave of interviewing (2000) was still available in 2010 (the final wave). People dropped out for many reasons, including having moved, not having the time, being sick, and so forth. To compensate for this, Statistics Canada ensured that they started with a large sample and they adjusted the sample in 2010 by weighting respondents differently, so that the 2010 final sample represented the initial 2000 sample as accurately as possible. For example, more men than women may have dropped out of the survey along the way. To adjust for this, weights can be used so that the final sample has proportionately the same percentage of men in 2010 as there was in 2000. Statistical tests can be run to ensure that this weighting does not introduce bias.

Remember that Houshmand and her colleagues wanted to know whether working at age 15 had any causal effects on future occupational outcomes. What she and her team found was that having a paid job at age 15 meant you were more likely to earn higher incomes in jobs, if you were working, in each of the next four interview cycles. And they found you were more likely to be working for pay in each of the subsequent cycles.

But remember that much earlier I mentioned skepticism. It might be that other explanations exist for this set of results. For example, could some other factor be accounting for these findings? Could the results be spurious? Could school grades be complicating these outcomes? It is conceivable that students who were employed at age 15 also had higher grades, and these higher grades might be causing their better occupational outcomes. It turns out that people employed at age 15 did have higher GPAs than those not employed. However, by statistically controlling for GPAs—that is, by comparing students with the same GPA— Houshmand and her team ruled out GPAs as a causal factor

explaining the results. That is, they ruled out school grades as a potentially spurious factor.

Let me introduce you to another research study to illustrate two different points. I want to describe a study by Scott Schieman and Atsushi Naridada (2014) so I can highlight their method of collecting a nationally representative sample and so I can focus on a study that examines people's attitudes as opposed to behaviours. Their research question focused on the extent to which Canadians felt they were masters of their own destiny, in control of their lives, as opposed to being pushed and pulled by external forces beyond their control. In particular, they wanted to know which groups of Canadians felt more or less of a sense of personal mastery over their life chances.

Imagine for a second trying to find a representative group of Canadians who might be asked about their sense of being in control of their own lives. How would you do this? What Schieman and Naridada did, with the help of a research firm, was to use telephone interviews where every Canadian over the age of 18 had a known probability of being selected as a sample participant. To accomplish this objective, they used a technique known as random-digit-dialing. First they established, for all regions of Canada, lists (or "banks" as they are technically known) of working telephone numbers (e.g., 604-564-25xx). Second, they let the computer randomly dial the last, or the last two, numbers. This method, used by Statistics Canada as well, provides a random sample of households. Two important refinements are used. First, some households have multiple telephone numbers. By asking respondents how many working telephone numbers there are in a house, it is possible to correct for this bias. Second, the person who is interviewed in the house must also be randomly selected (because, for example, women are more likely than men are to answer the phone). One popular strategy for obtaining a random sample of household members is to interview the person who had the most recent birthday (as Schieman and Naridada did).

Telephone surveys require that people be interviewed. An alternative to interviewing is the use of self-administered questionnaires, which can be either mailed or delivered to members of the sample. Mailing questionnaires to people and handing them out to groups (e.g., students in a classroom, patients in a clinic) are less expensive than interviewing. However, questionnaires lack the personal touch of interviewing. In an interview, misunderstandings can

Researchers collect information through surveys by asking people in a representative sample a set of identical questions. People interviewed on a downtown street corner do not constitute a representative sample of a country's adults because the sample does not include people who live outside the urban core, underestimates the number of seniors and people with disabilities, does not take into account regional diversity, and so on.
SOURCE: © Janine Wiedel Photolibrary/Alamy.

be clarified and responses can be expanded on. This cannot be done with self-administered questionnaires.

In their telephone interviews, Schieman and Naridada asked respondents about their personal beliefs, their attitudes about sense of mastery. Recall that the Houshmand team's focus was on behaviours—the work people did, the pay they received, and so forth. There is an important distinction between attitudes and behaviours, or words and deeds. I always intend to give more money to charity than I do. Most people believe that littering is irresponsible, but most people still litter sometimes. When you read research focusing on people's attitudes, remember that thought is not easily translated into action. Sociologists, and indeed social scientists more generally, focus research on both behaviour and attitudes.

Interpreting the answers that people give to researchers' questions is complicated by more than this behaviour–attitude distinction. In asking people questions, either in interviews, on questionnaires, or

by other methods of research discussed below, we must be careful about making assumptions (Guppy and Gray, 2008):

- *Do not assume that people understand what you are asking.* Language is notoriously ambiguous. How many friends did you see yesterday? This question may look simple, but people will differ in their understanding of "friends."

- *Do not assume that people know the answer to questions.* Most people do not want to appear ignorant. This was illustrated in a study of the prestige of occupations by Peter Pineo and John Porter (1967). They asked people to rate the prestige of two fictitious jobs: archaeopotrist and biologer. Most respondents cooperated and assigned these nonexistent jobs a prestige rating.

- *Do not assume that people will admit the answer, even to themselves.* Alcoholics frequently claim that they can "quit any time." They refuse to admit that they are addicted. Similarly, child abusers may define themselves as strict disciplinarians. People routinely deceive themselves, sometimes only in minor ways, but admitting the truth, even to ourselves, is a problem.

- *Do not assume that people will give valid answers.* People feel better about themselves when they are seen in a favourable light. In asking questions of people, researchers face the potential problem of "social desirability," because respondents may give only answers that reflect well on them. "What type of work do you do?" "Oh, I'm in public relations." Such a response could come from people working as telephone receptionists, tour guides, or corporate representatives.

Survey researchers do not focus only on individuals, although it is individuals who respond to survey questions. For example, it is possible to survey organizations, groups, corporations, electoral ridings, or job vacancies. In other words, the questions people answer may apply to a unit or group about which someone is knowledgeable. I am making two points here. First, surveys can focus on different units of observation (individuals, businesses, workplaces, and so on). Second, individuals can act as informants to report answers pertaining to some group or unit about which they have information.

QUALITATIVE RESEARCH

Houshmand and her team used survey methods to obtain generalizable knowledge about how working as a teenager might influence later-life employment trajectories. To generate patterns that summarized the experiences of thousands of people, they relied on many, many respondents questioned many times over several years. In contrast to creating generalizable, summary findings, a qualitative researcher might have examined a far smaller number of respondents but sought a richer and deeper understanding of how young people understood their situation.

Jade Boyd (2014) did the latter in her study of the social class anxieties of young people from East Vancouver. East Vancouver is a working-class neighbourhood, and the young people she studied worked hard to differentiate themselves from the mainstream nightlife practices of upscale youth from more affluent west-side neighbourhoods. Her "eastsiders" actively resisted the aggressive heterosexuality of the downtown nightclub scene, characterized by these youth as "hypermasculine, violently

heteronormative, and dominated by an aggressive pick-up scene" (Boyd: 11). Her work is especially lucid in showing how the social "performance" of "East Vanners" acted in complex ways to displace, erase, and reconfigure social class and social hierarchy. She takes readers inside a subculture and vividly relates how people work to make both their material and social surroundings meaningful.

How was Boyd able to do this? She relied on two principal methods. First, she spent 24 months as a participant observer, visiting an array of sites and attending a variety of events where her East Vanners congregated. During this stage of her research, she took extensive field notes about a host of topics, including emblems of East Van pride, musical tastes and dance routines, and the use of spaces and places for an alternative party culture. Second, she relied on "open-ended in-depth interviews" with 25 East Vanners. Rather than asking everyone identical questions, as a survey researcher would, she allowed her respondents the freedom to express ideas and insights in an unconstrained manner, resulting in the unstructured nature of her "open-ended" interviews.

More generally, Boyd's fieldwork is referred to as *ethnography*. Ethnographers study people in their own environment or their natural setting. Although **ethnography** includes the researcher being immersed in a group or a subculture, it also typically involves a cluster of methods, including participant observation, in-depth interviewing, and the analysis of documents. Speaking with key informants who are central to the group or the subculture is crucial (Cresswell, 1998).

In important ways, Boyd's ethnography involved a question somewhat similar to the one that Schieman and Naridada examined: How do people cope with and make sense of external pressures that confront them? In Boyd's case, these pressures were, among other things, rampant consumerism, commercialized nightlife, and heteronormative sexuality. While Schieman and Naridada wanted to know about the degree of mastery people felt over their lives, Boyd wanted to know more about how young East Vanners constructed their world to resist, complicate, and negotiate the external pressures they felt impinging on their lives.

For example, Schieman and Naridada (2014: 368) concluded that "most Canadians feel that their life chances are under their own control," a mastery that is especially pronounced among those who are better off in terms of income and education. In contrast to this overall summary of national patterns, Boyd's (2014: 4) contribution shows how her participants "create and define for themselves what it means to be from East Vancouver … and to reveal a sense of pride in a stigmatized area of the city." In the language of C. W. Mills, to whom you were introduced in Chapter 1, East Vanners, who ostensibly have less personal mastery over their life chances than people from more affluent neighbourhoods, turn their private troubles into subcultural enclaves that provide a positive sense of pride and performance as ways to affirm their identity in the face of hardship.

In qualitative studies like Boyd's, examining the intentionality of social action is especially important. Max Weber (1949 [1904]) was one of the first sociologists to address the issue of intention as a focus of social research. Weber argued that in interacting with other people, we draw on meanings. For example, the clothing we choose to wear speaks to others. We attribute meaning to bow ties, jack boots, hoodies, and silk scarves. None of this is done naively, because what we wear helps define who we are. Skateboarders, for example, dress in a particular style; they wear a uniform of sorts. Making social life intelligible is part of what Weber thought sociologists must address. To understand skateboarding, it is essential to see how skateboarders "define the situation." It is important to learn about their culture and to understand their systems of meaning. The aim of such research is not to explain the behaviour of skateboarders from an outside point of view, but to investigate their shared values and beliefs—their "worldview" (see Kelly, Pomerantz, and Currie, 2005).

Weber maintained that causal logic can be used to accomplish some of what sociologists want to explain. He thought, however, that sociology also had to make intelligible the subjective basis of social action. Weber used the German word *Verstehen*, or understanding, to refer to this mode of sociological analysis. To understand the meaning of social action requires being able, at least in principle, to fully engage in the social activity.

Let's pause to examine in more detail how Boyd sought to accomplish this in her study of youth in East Vancouver. Recall that she used two methods, **participant observation** and in-depth interviews. As a participant observer, Boyd involved herself in the daily lives of her East Vancouver participants. She visited group hangouts at 21 different sites, including "a range of formal and informal … down-market venues and pubs, makeshift art galleries, warehouse spaces, house parties, and public spaces such as alleys." For

two years, she observed the East Vanners subculture by participating in it, by being a part of the action. As a participant observer, she was able to ask many questions of different group members, gradually drawing a sociological portrait of the East Vancouver scene. In particular, she was able to contrast various interpretations: Was the subculture focused mainly on resistance, pleasure-seeking, or escapism? As her work progressed, Boyd was able to refine her understanding. She could cross-reference her observations by seeing how other group members reacted to each new insight she gained, thereby increasing both the reliability and the validity of her conclusions. In short, she came to "define the situation" as East Van participants themselves defined it.

However, Boyd did more than just participate. She also interviewed 25 East Vanners. As I noted above, she used "open-ended, in-depth interviews" (Boyd, 2014: 5). An in-depth interview means that she explored specific topics in great detail, often pursuing nuances and tangents. She allowed respondents to range widely in their replies. These were loosely structured interviews in that she had a set of general issues she wanted to discuss, but she did not ask every person exactly the same questions in exactly the same order. Her goal was to have a meaningful conversation with each person, guided by her interest in the subject but also by their knowledge, willingness, and interest in pursuing specific themes.

An obvious strength of participant observation is that sociologists can see what people actually do, as opposed to relying on reports of what people say they do, as survey researchers must. Combining this with semi-structured interviews also allows researchers to hear in respondents' own words their understanding of situations, their explanations for specific themes and interpretations.

As with experiments, the external validity of ethnography can be problematic. How confident can Boyd be that her conclusions are not dependent on the impressions she formed from a single subculture? The intensive, in-depth nature of qualitative research makes generalizability problematic. The key tradeoff is between the richly textured, "thick description" of ethnography and the insularity of detailed study of one or a few settings. Unlike survey researchers, ethnographers do not select different sets of random individuals or groups. The groups or settings they investigate are purposively chosen, sometimes because of easy access. For example, Boyd (2014) did not randomly choose East Van subcultures; she made arrangements to participate in the lives of some East Vancouver youth, and even then it was only one form of youth subculture. Imagine also the ethical issues Boyd confronted.

Boyd's research portrays a subculture from its members' points of view. There are potential pitfalls of which Boyd had to be aware. First, how much did her presence influence her findings? Did people act differently when she was not around? In principle, there is no way to answer these questions, although ethnographers have tried to account for the effect of their presence in various ways. Some researchers conceal their research role; in effect, they try to be known to the other participants as one of them, rather than as a researcher (the ethics of this are dicey). Other researchers report that, with time, participants' awareness of their presence fades and they are treated as a member, as Boyd (2014: 7) reports. Notice that this problem of presence is the Hawthorne effect in another guise. Whether in survey research, experiments, or observation studies, the researcher's presence can distort the domain of investigation. Researcher presence may undermine validity.

Beyond the potential pitfall of mere presence is the second problem: the findings of researchers may be ethnocentric. That is, researchers may impose their own values—their own worldviews—on the subject matter of their study. How do we know, for example, that Boyd depicted East Vanners' point of view and not her own? One method of reducing personal bias is known as the "member test of validity" (Douglas, 1970: 21). For example, if the subculture participants Boyd spoke with did not recognize themselves in her account—that is, if they saw Boyd's account as inauthentic—then we would worry about bias or distortion. Boyd was careful to "test" her tentative observations and insights on her informants by asking them questions and checking for observations that would falsify her impressions. Again, this is a research problem that extends well beyond ethnography. In fact, ethnography can be seen as the method that takes most seriously the task of understanding the members of a group from the members' point of view, stressing in particular their definition of the situation.

A third problem beyond presence and ethnocentrism is this: How do researchers know that the "tools" of their inquiry (e.g., questions, instructions, requests) did not in fact "create" or "generate" the resulting "findings"? For example, did Boyd (2014) create a finding by focusing attention on the East Vanners' resistance to dominant culture? Alternatively, did Schieman and Naridada (2014) invent a relationship between social class and mastery by asking questions that might be interpreted in different ways by the members of different classes? Again, this question involves issues of reliability and validity. Schieman and Naridida can be confident that they did not construct or create a pseudo-relationship between class and mastery to the extent that they show that the basic pattern of findings is repeated across different questions about life chances and mastery. Boyd distinguished between (1) East Vanners' comments made in response to her questions and (2) statements her informants volunteered or that she overheard during her fieldwork. These alternative sources of information helped her avoid the problem of "creating" meaning. If East Vanners volunteered information that corroborated Boyd's impressions, her faith in the authenticity of her account increased.

Not all qualitative research involves participation. Rik Scarce (2000) was interested in the human domination of nature. His interest was in whether we could still speak of "wild salmon" or whether, like the cow and the dog, salmon were now domesticated. He argued that the very concept of "resource

In participant observation, it is often necessary to "look" the part. Sociologist Brian Wilson participated in rave parties to study firsthand the rave subculture of Southern Ontario.

SOURCE: © Alexandru/Shutterstock.

management" speaks to the idea of humans improving on nature, of scientists enhancing nature.

In studying the "domestication of salmon," Scarce (2000) used ethnographic methods. He was especially interested in how salmon had been manipulated to serve human ends. In the modern fishery, such phrases as *fish farming, aquaculture, genetic engineering, fish stocking,* and *fish hatcheries* are commonplace. Scarce (2000) learned about the modern fishery by hanging around fish hatcheries and asking questions, by visiting fishery research centres and watching what scientists were doing in their experiments, and by talking with scientists at their conventions and at public inquiries. He came to see the fish hatchery as a biological factory and to understand how salmon were increasingly "tooled" and "engineered." Observation was his staple method. His resulting work was an ethnographic account called *Fishy Business: Salmon, Biology, and the Social Construction of Nature* (2000).

The believability of Scarce's research is enhanced by the fact that he observed events in their natural settings. He did not create a situation to see how people reacted (e.g., laboratory experiments) nor did he rely on people reporting on their own attitudes or behaviours (as in survey research). He was not a participant in the activity, so his involvement could not have distorted events (as may occur in participant observation). His presence as an observer may have influenced people, but he was often one of many observers (e.g., at scientific conferences and public inquiries).

COMPARING QUALITATIVE AND QUANTITATIVE APPROACHES

Sociology is a knowledge-seeking discipline. Evidence to support or refute theoretical knowledge claims is central. In its broadest forms, evidence is typically collected using either qualitative or quantitative methods. Each approach has strengths and weaknesses. In Table 2.1, I summarize these by pointing

TABLE 2.1 COMMONALITIES AND DIFFERENCES BETWEEN QUALITATIVE AND QUANTITATIVE METHODS

COMMON ATTRIBUTES/ISSUES	QUALITATIVE AND QUANTITATIVE METHODS	
	Both methods expand or deepen our knowledge of the social world. Validity and reliability checks are central in both methods. Veracity of evidence is cross-checked in multiple ways. In both methods, data are used to develop or test theory. Informed consent and the elimination of harm are imperative.	
DIFFERING ATTRIBUTES/ISSUES	**QUALITATIVE METHODS**	**QUANTITATIVE METHODS**
Primary focus	Social action and person-to-person interaction	Identifying and summarizing general social patterns
Purpose	Understanding context and interpreting people's points of view and the meanings they attach to different social situations	Understanding causal relationships; stress on explanation and prediction
Cases selected	Few; purposeful selection	Many; random and representative selection
Evidence collection	Detailed, in-depth; based on prolonged and persistent observation; involves journal writing	Formal, standardized; based on one or more detailed episodes of standardized questioning
Position of researcher	Immersed in, or close to, the social action/interaction	Distant; relies on respondents answering pre-scripted questions
Evidence presented	Quotations, observations, themes, nuanced interpretations	Numerical, statistical; involves tables, graphs, and the like
Examples of methods	Ethnography, participant observation, in-depth interviews	Surveys, analysis of administrative records, experiments

out what the two approaches share, and then high-lighting their principal differences. It is impossible, in a summary table, to fully capture all of the issues others have written books about (Ragin and Amoroso, 2011). But by reading the table carefully and reflecting on the examples outlined above, you should come to appreciate the similarities and differences in the two approaches.

Qualitative and quantitative approaches are central to the repertoire of methodological tools used to gather evidence in sociology. Most newly trained sociologists are skilled at both approaches and an increasing number of research projects involve both approaches.

OTHER METHODS OF RESEARCH

Historical Sociology

Many sociologists study social change. Max Weber, for example, attempted to explain the rise of capitalism by showing how Protestantism invigorated capitalist growth. Émile Durkheim was interested in how moral education helped to socially integrate a rapidly changing society. Both writers sought to answer sociological questions by examining historical change as evidence of significant social processes. Sociologists are more likely than historians are to use historical evidence to test theories of social change. Sociologists place less emphasis on history for history's sake.

Liliana Riga's (2008) work shows how sociologists make effective use of historical methods (see also Brym, 1978). Riga reexamined the nature of revolutionary Bolshevism among the leadership of the 1917–23 Russian Revolution. She wanted to understand the roots of the socialist ethic that inspired the revolution. This critical juncture in world history has often been contextualized within a framework stressing the class basis and "Russian" ethnicity of the revolutionary leadership. Riga argued that, in large measure, it was social inequalities made most visible by diverse ethnicities, and not so much by social class, that lay behind the radical mobilization. She arrived at this conclusion after systematically comparing the experiences of class and ethnicity among the revolutionary elite leaders.

Of course, these leaders have long since died, so Riga could not question or observe them. What she could do, however, was reconstruct their life histories. She used autobiographies, biographies, and memoirs, supplemented by police arrest records where ethnic backgrounds were often noted. She used sources predominantly constructed before the late 1920s. This latter refinement was essential when you recall that revolutionary leaders first had to mask their true identities in Tsarist Russia but even more importantly had to maintain social identities consistent with the *Soviet* revolutionary movement (especially problematic in the Stalinist era from 1922 to 1953).

The logic of Riga's (2008) analysis is not unlike that of other sociological research. Her key dependent variable is the revolutionary identity and politics of the Bolshevik elite. She wanted to know how important social class, ethnicity, and their intersection were to the formation of this radical group. She therefore needed to measure social class and did so by examining such indicators as landholding, occupation, education, and relations to capital of individual members of the elite (and their parents). To measure ethnicity she used a mixture of birthplace, religion, and nationality. She concluded by noting that "ethnocultural identities were often more salient dimensions to many of their social experiences—and therefore to identities and politics—than was class."

Documentary Analysis

Sociologists have also made useful contributions to knowledge through the examination of official documents. Renisa Mawani (2003) examined archival documents, including colonial maps, to demonstrate a social process whereby geographical spaces were rendered "vacant" and therefore accessible to settlement and development. By showing how Indigenous land-use was made to vanish at some points, only to have later colonial authorities redraw the maps to show their presence, Mawani demonstrates the contested nature of landscape, both then and now. She also draws on legal documents, such as cases and statutes, to understand how the rule of law was also used to displace Indigenous peoples and, again reflecting contestation, how it was later used by Indigenous peoples in resistance. As a third methodological strategy, she examined the ways in which an Indigenous presence has been commemorated (e.g., via totem poles). By a careful comparison of the evidence offered through these documented sources, she shows how Vancouver's civic identity has shifted from a settler society to a postcolonial, multicultural city. Notice that her work is also historical.

Content Analysis

Baumann and Ho (2014) studied Canadian television food advertisements to examine the relationship between race and food. They used both quantitative and qualitative approaches in their investigation. In observing 244 commercials featured on the CBC, CTV, and Global television channels, they first counted how whites, blacks, and Southeast Asians were portrayed with different food categories. One of their main findings was that whites were strongly associated with whole foods, while both blacks and Southeast Asians were linked with fast food.

In the qualitative phase of their work, they conducted a "reading of the character roles" in the advertisements to understand what qualities of the racial groups tend to be emphasized or downplayed (Baumann and Ho, 2014: 160). They found, for example, in comparison to the other racial groups, whites were often portrayed as crafting quality food products. An Oka cheese commercial stressed the historical experience of quality cheese production. In contrast, although Asians appear much less frequently than whites in commercials, they are often portrayed in ways that stress a lack of emotion and high achievement aspirations. The quantitative assessment captures numerical counts of each group across different food categories while the qualitative examination provides a richer, more nuanced sense of how these associations are developed in advertisements.

As a second example, Stoddart, Ramos, and Tindall (2014) reviewed both provincial and national print media coverage of two environmental debates in Canada: the Jumbo Pass ski resort development in British Columbia and the Tobeatic Wilderness area in Nova Scotia. They examined media coverage of these debates in *The Globe and Mail*, the National Post, Halifax's *The Chronicle Herald*, and *The Vancouver Sun*. The authors identified 132 articles discussing either the Tobeatic Wilderness or Jumbo Pass. Using a qualitative software program, NVivo, they examined each article, searching for examples of issues such as "economic development," "negative environmental impacts," and "wilderness preservation."

They next interviewed environmentalists from organizations that were mentioned in the media articles, asking questions about the participants' perception of the media reporting, the organizations' tactics, and a host of related issues. Notice again the use of both quantitative and qualitative approaches in gathering evidence pertinent to their examination of how groups make claims about and seek support for their perspectives on outdoor recreational activity.

Use of Official Statistics

Governments have a long history of collecting statistical data (see the Critical Sociology: Protest and Policy box). Government bureaucracies first began to collect statistics to help rulers determine both the size of their taxation base and the number of men they could put on the battlefield. Since then, the scope of government or official statistics has expanded and now includes information on births and deaths, unemployment rates, imports and exports, and so on. Sociologists have made good use of official statistics (see especially Haggerty, 2001).

Wortley and Tanner (2003) used official arrest records from Toronto to examine the extent of racial profiling in patterns of search and arrest practices. Detecting racial profiling requires determining that law enforcement officers use race as a significant factor in their decisions. That might sound easy, but it is incredibly complex because higher search or arrest rates among certain groups might be due to reasonable assumptions based on existing crime patterns, surveillance, or neighbourhood requests for greater police presence. Ruling out these latter factors and other possible explanations for racial differentials in police decision making must occur before conclusions about racial bias in decision making can be claimed.

Wortley and Tanner (2003) were following up on an investigative report published in the *Toronto Star* in October 2002. The *Star* analysis alleged that racial profiling did occur in Toronto, an accusation that police officials disputed. Wortley and Tanner, sociologists at the University of Toronto, examined both the *Star's* original claims and the subsequent findings put forward by the Toronto Police Service. Wortley and Tanner cautiously claimed that their analyses of both official statistics and survey research were consistent with the findings of other international studies that racial profiling is a practice used by law enforcement officers (Wortley and Tanner, 2003, 2005).

The racial profiling example illustrates a central problem with official statistics. These statistics are not objective facts on which everyone agrees. The very definition of racial profiling makes it difficult to prove. Furthermore, different interest groups have much at stake over whether such practices occur

CRITICAL SOCIOLOGY: PROTEST AND POLICY   THE POLITICS OF THE CANADIAN CENSUS

Governments routinely use a survey of the entire population, called a *census*, to monitor key indicators of a country, such as the distribution of age cohorts, marital statuses, and so on. In June 2010, the federal government decided to change a critical component of the Canadian census. It decided to make the long-form census nonmandatory, keeping only a small number of questions on a short-form census, on the grounds that in previous censuses, a few Canadians had objected to being required to answer questions about ancestry, income, or housing characteristics.

The questions previously asked on the long-form census are now included in a *voluntary* survey to which Canadians are urged, but not required, to respond. This change might seem like allowing free choice to flourish by keeping the state out of the private business of individual citizens. However, a closer look reveals that the long-form census played a pivotal role in understanding a wide array of critical issues, from housing policy, to immigrant adaptation, to unemployment. A large proportion of Canadians, 32 percent, chose not to answer the long-form census in 2011 (Brym, 2014: 8). This means that the validity of the voluntary responses is suspect.

The government uses a host of other surveys, such as the *Labour Force Survey* (LFS), to measure key social and economic indicators, such as male–female wage differences and the unemployment rate. The validity of these other surveys was always measured in relation to the long-form census, for which the response rate was close to 100 percent because it was mandatory. Now,

however, not only is the validity of the long-form census in question but so too is the validity of the LFS and every other survey that previously relied on the long-form census as a measurement standard (Green and Milligan, 2010). Furthermore, the long-form census contained questions about education, occupation, and income, along with questions about sex, ethnicity, and region. These and related questions allowed for a careful assessment of issues related to the Charter of Rights and Freedoms and other issues pertaining to social justice and fairness. Such assessments are now more difficult to achieve. And, the Canadians most likely to be undercounted are the most disadvantaged (Brym, 2014: 8). Curtailing the ability of various groups to assess issues such as discrimination, inequality, and injustice means that those in positions of power have an even easier time protecting their privileges—the status quo is reinforced.

Critical Thinking Questions

1. Businesses were once strong supporters of the mandatory long-form census but they now rely on other data to profile potential markets. What might have replaced the census as a way of tracking consumers and their spending habits?

2. Governments asking questions of citizens can be seen as an invasion of privacy. Conversely, governments are expected to serve the interests of the people. How do you weigh the invasion of privacy versus the promotion of the common good as it relates to a government census?

(Gabor, 2004). The police are charged with the difficult task of upholding the law fairly and without prejudice. Certain groups may request more police presence than do other groups and so what might appear to be racial profiling might actually reflect community requests. Official statistics require interpretation and such interpretation can be complex.

TIME FOR REVIEW

1. Using Table 2.1 as a template, compare and contrast the research studies by Jade Boyd (East Vanners) and Marjan Houshmand and her colleagues (teenage jobs), specifying the strengths and weaknesses of each study.

2. What are the most distinctive attributes of qualitative versus quantitative research methods?

3. Identify a research project you would like to conduct. Which of the methods identified above is best suited to your project?

THE ANALYSIS OF NUMERICAL DATA

Sociological evidence frequently comes in numerical form—that is, as quantifiable evidence (e.g., incomes, unemployment rates, or ethnic group membership). Finding and interpreting patterns in numerical data is a complex process, so in this section, I briefly illustrate some key aspects of the process of summarizing numerical information. I explore the following research questions: Does your family background, especially the education of one or both of your parents, continue to have lasting effects on your own success at university? Put another way, we know university access depends on family origins, but once you have been admitted to university, does parental education continue to influence the success of students? Also, since success is often influenced by gender, does this parental effect hold for both women and men? (For an expanded discussion of introducing statistical ideas about regression analysis, please see the learning path for this chapter in MindTap).

Notice the causal logic here. Family background is hypothesized to affect success in university. However, since gender is known to effect educational and occupational success, maybe the causal link between family background and university success differs by sex.

To begin, we need to examine the link between family background and university success. I do this by using data from the *National Graduates Survey* (Statistics Canada, 2015), a survey conducted by Statistics Canada of a nationally representative sample of university graduates (16 801 randomly chosen graduates, to be precise). Does family background have an effect on university success? Table 2.2, called a *contingency table* or a *cross-tabulation*, gives us an answer. I measure family background, the independent variable, by asking whether either parent of a graduate had attained a university degree. This variable, displayed across the top of the table, has two categories (low: neither parent has a university degree; and high: at least one parent has a university degree). As an indicator of university success, I ask whether a graduate did or did not receive a merit-based scholarship while attending university. This variable, the dependent

variable, has two categories (yes: did receive a merit-based scholarship; and no: did not receive a merit-based scholarship).

Notice first the table's arrangement. The title describes the two variables being related. The independent variable (parental education) is placed on the top of the table and its values are clearly delineated. The dependent variable (scholarship receipt) is arrayed on the side of the table, again with the value labels clearly shown. Beside each value of the dependent variable is a row of numbers. To illustrate, Table 2.2 shows that there are 2713 people in the top left cell, the cell defined by a low level of parental education and the receipt of a merit-based scholarship. At the intersection of each column and row is a table cell (there are four cells in Table 2.2 because row and column totals are ignored in counting the number of cells in a table).

The concept of a contingency table comes from the idea that the category into which a person falls on the dependent variable may be contingent on, or depend on, the category that a person occupies on the independent variable. If the hypothesis were true in this case, we would expect that, as we move from parents with lower education to parents with higher education, the number of people receiving merit-based scholarships ought to rise. Do the data reveal this pattern? For graduates whose parents did not attend university, 2713 received a merit scholarship. For graduates whose parents did attend university, 2928 received a merit scholarship. These figures seem, at first glance, to support our expectation. Notice, however, that because of how parental education was categorized, 8312 graduates had parents whose education I defined as low, while only 6674 had what I called high education. Comparing the actual number of people in each cell is therefore misleading, because there are different numbers of people in each column.

Rather than focusing on the raw numbers, a better understanding of the patterns comes when we standardize the data. We need to ask what *percentage* of people in each parental education category received scholarships. By expressing the numbers as percentages—that is, by standardizing the data—it is much easier to see the patterns. So, 2713 of 8312 graduates in the low parent education column received merit-based scholarships, or 33 percent (2713 divided by 8312 and then multiplied by 100). This tells us that for every 100 people with lower parental education, 33 received merit scholarships.

TABLE 2.2 THE RELATIONSHIP BETWEEN PARENTAL EDUCATION AND ACADEMIC SUCCESS AT UNIVERSITY

| | PARENTAL EDUCATION | | |
MERIT SCHOLARSHIP	LOW	HIGH	ROW TOTALS
Yes	33% (2713)	44% (928)	38% (5 641)
No	67% (5599)	56% (3747)	62% (9 345)
Column totals	100% (8312)	100% (6674)	100% (14 986)

SOURCE: Data are adapted from Statistics Canada (2015).

Making the same calculation for the high parent education column—(2928/6674) × 100—we find that 44 percent of graduates whose parents had high education received merit scholarships (or 44 of every 100 people).

If you examine Table 2.2, you will see that the percentages are entered in the table. The actual number of people in each cell appears in parentheses. Notice that the percentages are calculated separately for each column, summing to 100 percent at the bottom of each column.

So, do relatively more graduates whose parents had high education receive scholarships in comparison with graduates whose parents had less education? Yes. Of every 100 people in the high parent education column, 44 received scholarships (44 percent), compared with only 33 of every 100 in the low parent education column (33 percent). The difference between these two percentages (11 percent) is one measure of the strength of the relationship between parental education and scholarship receipt: the higher the education of your parents, the more likely you are to receive a scholarship.

In studying this table, some readers may have taken exception to my definitions of high and low parental education. Why should the lack of a university degree be considered lower education? What I defined as low and high education is arbitrary. However, when I define the lows and highs of parental education differently and produce several different tables, the basic patterns in the tables shown here do not change. This replication gives me confidence that my decisions about how to categorize parental education do not affect the results.

The evidence in Table 2.2 supports the first part of the question about the relationship between parental education and scholarship receipt. But how does gender figure into the pattern, it at all? Table 2.3 contains two contingency tables separated by a dotted vertical line. Here the question is how the link between parental education and scholarship receipt varies for women in comparison with men. Table 2.3 can be usefully thought of as Table 2.2 but with women and men separated into their own subtables. For women, the basic pattern of Table 2.2 is repeated in Table 2.3. In the subtable for women, 33 percent of women whose parents did not have a university degree received a merit scholarship, whereas 46 percent of women whose parents had a higher education received a scholarship. The difference between these two cell percentages is 13 percent.

For men, although the pattern is similar, the percentage difference is slightly smaller (and therefore the relationship between parental education and scholarship receipt is slightly weaker). Of men whose parents had a low education, 32 percent received a merit scholarship, whereas for men whose parents had more education, 41 percent have a high income. The percentage difference is only 9 percent. Contrasting the percentage differences between the two subtables in Table 2.3 gives us a way of comparing the strength of the link between parental education and scholarship receipt for women versus men.

So what do we learn from this analysis? We learn first, from Table 2.2, that graduates whose parents had more education are more likely to receive merit-based scholarships. Second, from Table 2.3 we learn that this link is perhaps a tiny bit stronger for women

TABLE 2.3   THE RELATIONSHIP BETWEEN PARENTAL EDUCATION AND ACADEMIC SUCCESS AT UNIVERSITY, BY GENDER

	WOMEN PARENTAL EDUCATION			MEN PARENTAL EDUCATION		
INCOME	LOW	HIGH	TOTAL	LOW	HIGH	TOTAL
Low	33%	46%	(3482)	32%	41%	(2158)
High	67%	54%	(5528)	68%	59%	(3817)
Totals	100% (5196)	100% (3814)	(9010)	100% (3115)	100% (2860)	(5976)

Note: Column and row totals are not equal for women because of rounding.

SOURCE: Data from Statistics Canada (2015).

than for men, although the difference is modest (the relatively large sample size of 14 986 gives us confidence that these differences are not due to chance). Notice one last thing about the tables. I initially said that 16 801 graduates were interviewed but only 14 986 observations are in the tables. Why the discrepancy? A sizable number of people either did not know or refused to answer the question about parental education, and a few people did not answer the question about receiving a scholarship. I had to exclude these respondents from the analysis. This is one of the many reasons that all research findings are provisional until we gather a large body of evidence that replicates the basic patterns, preferably using both quantitative and qualitative methodology.

TIME FOR REVIEW

1. Reflecting on the relationship between parental education and receipt (or not) of a merit-based scholarship, are the four conditions of causality identified earlier in the chapter satisfied?
2. Why are percentages calculated down the columns as opposed to across the rows in order to answer the question of whether parental education influences the likelihood of scholarship receipt?

THE FUTURE OF SOCIAL RESEARCH

Social research involves systematically studying the social world. The aim of such research activity is to develop explanations and understandings of social patterns beneficial to improving the human condition. Today, it is becoming increasingly obvious that we need to find innovative ways of organizing and running human affairs. Starvation, environmental degradation, terrorism, and social injustice are among the many social problems we must confront. Solutions require adequate explanations for, and understandings of, how these problems arise and persist.

Earlier in the chapter, I outlined several sources of knowledge: common sense, religious faith, and science. Although these forms of knowledge share certain features (e.g., they are all imperfect), scientific reason encourages a set of practices—open review and critical skepticism—that work together to reduce error.

Another way of emphasizing what is distinctive about the scientific method is to compare how social research differs from the work of other professionals who concentrate on similar social issues (e.g., the environment, gender relations). For example, what differentiates the work of documentary filmmakers, novelists, or journalists from that of social researchers? I have emphasized three features of scientific research that, in combination, separate it from the work of these other professionals:

1. Research results are subjected to the critical skepticism of other scientists.
2. Social theory guides, either directly or indirectly, the evidence gathered.
3. Evidence is systematically collected and analyzed.

Although some of these features are found in the work of other professionals, such as journalists, all three features are found in good social research. Replication and reproducibility have high currency in science as ways of encouraging skepticism. Good research contributes new ideas or evidence to our common stock of social theory. Finally, good research publicly displays the careful collection and analysis of evidence.

These principles are a feature of all good research, but the methods that sociologists use to pursue their goal of explaining and understanding the social world take many forms. This diverse array of methods, including observing, questioning, and experimenting, offers sociologists many ways of inquiring responsibly and ethically about the social world. Each method has different strengths and weaknesses, which makes the choice of research strategy dependent on the sociological question being asked.

Social science research will continue to contribute to knowledge of the world around us. Research on the environment, reproductive technology, multiculturalism, violence, and social-support networks all point to practical ways in which human problems can be influenced by research findings. Effective policy solutions that benefit all people require sound social research.

SUMMARY

1. **What is the point of research methods?**
   Basing decisions on the best available knowledge has been important to making the world more equitable and freer from coercion and deceit. Research methods are ways of gathering evidence to test suppositions about the world and how to make it a better place.

2. **What is scientific knowledge?**
   Science is one of many ways of knowing. Scientific knowledge incorporates explicit methods designed to reduce error in what is currently accepted as scientific knowledge. Evidence must be systematically and ethically collected and rigorously and publicly evaluated.

3. **What are the hallmarks of good social science?**
   Good science integrates useful theory and robust research. Theories are ideas about how the world works or claims about how to explain or understand the recurring, patterned nature of human

activity. Research allows social scientists to test the validity of theories.

4. **How do we judge the quality of a theory?**
   Evidence is crucial to developing, revising, or discarding theoretical claims. In comparison with the evidence available in the natural sciences, the evidence available to social scientists presents added complexity because of the meaningful character of human social action. People, unlike molecules, assign meaning to their actions and to the actions of others.

5. **What are the main research methods?**
   Sociologists have devised many useful methods for obtaining evidence about the social world. Qualitative and quantitative approaches are the two principal techniques. Qualitative methods include ethnographic research and participant observation. Quantitative methods include surveys and experiments.

QUESTIONS TO CONSIDER

1. The teaching effectiveness of faculty members in university and college departments could be evaluated in various ways. Suggest different sociological methods of doing such an evaluation and comment on the strengths and weaknesses of each approach.

2. Houshmand (2014) and her team used longitudinal survey evidence to evaluate whether having jobs as teenagers influences postschooling occupational careers. Suggest alternative designs for her study, commenting on the strengths and weaknesses of the various approaches, including important ethical considerations.

3. Policymakers frequently debate raising or lowering age restrictions on activities, such as driving a car, drinking alcoholic beverages, or voting. Suggest how you might design a study that could provide evidence about the possible consequences of either raising or lowering one of these age restrictions.

4. Ethical issues have been discussed alongside each of the various methods. Create a chart or a table that compares and contrasts the ethical dilemmas that are most prevalent in each type of research methodology. Are most dilemmas common to all methods or do they tend to vary by type of methodology chosen?

GLOSSARY

A **causal relationship** (p. 35) involves a relationship between two variables in which change or variation in one variable produces change or variation in a second variable. Four criteria are essential to establishing a causal relationship between two variables: association, time ordering, nonspuriousness, and theoretical rationale.

The **dependent variable** (p. 40) is a variable that is assumed to depend on or be caused by one or more other variables (independent variables); it is the variable that is the effect, or outcome, in a cause–effect relationship.

Ethics (p. 43) in research involves an individual's ability to understand what he or she is being asked to do in a research study, make a reasoned judgment about any effects research participation might have on that

person, and make a choice to participate free from coercive influence. Informed consent is central to this decision-making process. Knowledge about the funder of a research project is important to informed consent.

Ethnography (p. 45) is the detailed description of a particular culture or way of life, or the written results of a participant-observation study.

An **experiment** (p. 39) is a controlled test of the causal effects of a particular variable or set of variables on a dependent or outcome variable.

An **explanation** (p. 35) is an account of the causal logic that shows how and why variables influence one another.

External validity (p. 41) is the generalizability of a particular finding from the study group to a larger population; the relevance of conclusions for a larger population; or the ability to infer that the results of a study are representative of processes operating in a broader population.

In the **Hawthorne effect** (p. 41), people involved in a study may be influenced by the very process of being studied; the study has an impact on the subjects of the study.

A **hypothesis** (p. 40) is a knowledge claim or hunch about how the world works; it is a testable statement, derived from a theory, about the relationship between two or more variables.

The **independent variable** (p. 40) is a variable that is presumed to affect or influence another variable; it is the causal variable.

An **interview** (p. 41) is a method of collecting information by asking people questions, either in person or over the telephone. Interviews range from highly structured (preset questions in a fixed order) to loosely structured (topic guidelines, but no prescribed question wording).

Meaningful action (p. 35) occurs with specific intentions or reasons in mind. The uncontrollable tic in a person's eye is physical behaviour, which differs from that of a person who is winking at someone, where intention or purpose is central to understanding what is happening. Most human activity is meaningful action, or social action.

A **measurement** (p. 42) is reliable if it is consistent or repeatable.

Objectivity (p. 33) is the quality of minimizing the effect of personal bias on research results or the idea of impartiality, of "fair hearings." Objectivity is an ideal enhanced by research being open to the critical scrutiny of others. Objectivity as complete impartiality is a myth.

Participant observation (p. 46) involves the participation of the researcher, to varying degrees, in the activities of the group under investigation; it attempts to give an "insider's" account of a particular way of life or cultural system.

Randomization (p. 40) is a procedure used in experiments to assign test subjects to experimental conditions on the basis of chance.

Reliability (p. 42) is the consistency of measurements and the ability to reproduce the same measurements on repeated occasions.

Sampling (p. 42) is the process of selecting units from a larger population. Random sampling involves the selection of representative units (e.g., people, organizations) from a population (e.g., all Canadians, voluntary organizations in a city). Samples can be selected by probability (where every unit has a nonzero chance of selection) or nonprobability (where chance does not enter into the selection of sample units).

A **self-administered questionnaire** (p. 41) is a method of collecting information by having people record their own answers to preset questions.

A **spurious relationship** (p. 35) involves an incorrect inference about the causal relationships between variables.

Understanding (p. 36) is the ability to provide a definition of a situation that members of a culture find authentic and valid.

Validity (p. 41) is the relevance or accuracy of a measurement in relation to the theoretical concept that it is supposed to measure.

A **variable** (p. 40) is something that varies or an attribute or event that can take on more than one value (e.g., unemployment rates, age, sex).

NOTES

1. Black swans, native to Australia, were unknown to Europeans before exploration. The idea that all swans are white is thus similar to the idea that Earth is the central body in the solar system—a claim once understood to be true but now thought to be false.

2. Please do not overinterpret this claim. As a community, we have frequently treated humans as exceptional. Our theories and actions often evince a "control of nature" paradigm. Highlighting differences between the subject matter of the natural and the social sciences is complicated. For example, monkeys make friends with zoologists and, when studied, may react in ways similar to humans. It is important to consider in what ways the study of people by people may add complexity to research, and how this may in turn stimulate us to think differently about how people study nonhumans. For example, issues of animal rights and environmental ethics raise questions about our traditionally human-centric view of the world. Perhaps bacteria do blush and we are just too ignorant to notice!

Illustrated by Aaron Millard

PART 2

CULTURE

CHAPTER 3

CULTURE

Robert Brym
UNIVERSITY OF TORONTO

SOURCE: Gil.K / Shutterstock.com.

AFTER READING THIS CHAPTER, YOU WILL BE ABLE TO:

- See culture as a tool that improves the likelihood of human survival.

- Contrast biological explanations of human behaviour with sociological explanations that focus on culture.

- Appreciate differences among functionalist, symbolic interactionist, and conflict approaches to understanding culture.

- See how culture operates as a force that simultaneously increases human freedom and constrains social action.

CULTURE AS PROBLEM SOLVING

Tiger Woods wears a red shirt on the last day of every tournament in which he competes. Sidney Crosby won't sign a team jersey until he has worn it in a regular season game. When Woods and Crosby started these superstitious practices, they were taking the first step toward creating one aspect of culture, the socially transmitted ideas, practices, and material objects that people create to deal with real-life problems. Their superstitions help to reassure them and let them play better. Research shows that, in general, superstitious practices help athletes reduce anxiety and improve self-confidence and performance (Damisch, Stoberock, and Mussweiler, 2010).

Like soldiers going off to battle, university students about to write final exams and other people in high-stress situations, athletes invent routines to help them stop worrying and focus on the job at hand. Some wear a lucky piece of jewellery or item of clothing. Others say special words or a quick prayer. Still others cross themselves. And then there are people who engage in more elaborate rituals. For example, sociologists Cheryl and Daniel Albas of the University of Manitoba interviewed 300 university students about their superstitious practices before final exams. One student felt she would do well only if she ate a sausage and two eggs sunny

Sidney Crosby
SOURCE: © REUTERS/Shannon Stapleton.

side up on the morning of each exam. The sausage had to be arranged vertically on the left side of her plate and the eggs placed to the right of the sausage so they formed the "100" percent she was aiming for (Albas and Albas, 1989). Of course, the ritual had more direct influence on her cholesterol level than on her grade. Indirectly, however, it may have had the desired effect. To the degree that it helped to relieve her anxiety and relax her, she may have done better on exams.

When some people say *culture*, they refer to opera, ballet, art, and fine literature. However, for sociologists, this definition is too narrow. Sociologists define **culture** broadly as all of the socially transmitted ideas, practices, and material objects that people create to deal with real-life problems. For example, when Crosby developed his superstitions and the university student invented the ritual of preparing for exams by eating a sausage and eggs arranged just so, they were beginning to create culture in the sociological sense. These practices helped Crosby and the student deal with the real-life problem of high anxiety. Similarly, tools help people solve the problem of how to plant crops and build houses. Religion helps people face the problem of death and how to give life meaning. Tools and religion are also elements of culture because they, too, help people solve real-life problems.

Note, however, that religion, technology, and many other elements of culture differ from the superstitions of athletes and undergraduates in one important respect. Superstitions are often unique to the individuals who create them. In contrast, religion and technology are widely shared. They are passed from one generation to the next. How does cultural sharing take place? Through human interaction, communication, and learning. In other words, culture becomes shared when it is socially transmitted. A **society** involves people interacting socially and sharing culture, usually in a defined geographical area.[1] Culture, then, is the sum of the *socially transmitted* ideas, practices, and material objects that enable people to adapt to, and thrive in, their environments.

TIME FOR REVIEW

1. How do sociologists define culture?
2. How is culture socially transmitted?

THE ORIGINS AND COMPONENTS OF CULTURE

You can appreciate the importance of culture for human survival by considering the predicament of early humans about 100 000 years ago. They lived in harsh natural environments. They had poor physical endowments, being slower runners and weaker fighters than many other animals. Yet, despite these disadvantages, they survived. More than that—they prospered and came to dominate nature. This feat was possible largely because they were the smartest creatures around. Their sophisticated brains enabled them to create cultural survival kits of enormous complexity and flexibility. These cultural survival kits contained three main tools: abstraction, cooperation, and production. Each tool was a uniquely human talent. Each gave rise to a different element of culture.

ABSTRACTION: CREATING SYMBOLS

Human culture exists only because we can think abstractly. **Abstraction** is the capacity to create **symbols** or general ideas that carry particular meanings. Languages and mathematical notations are sets of symbols. They allow us to classify experience and generalize from it. For instance, we recognize that we can sit on many objects but that only some of those objects have four legs, a back, and space for one person. We distinguish the latter from other objects by giving them a name: chairs. By the time a baby reaches the end of her first year, she has heard that word repeatedly and understands that it refers to a certain class of objects. True, a few chimpanzees have been taught to make some signs with their hands. In this way, they have learned some words and how to string together some simple phrases. However, even these extraordinarily intelligent animals cannot learn any rules of grammar, teach other chimps what they know, or advance much beyond the vocabulary of a human toddler (Pinker, 1994). Abstraction at anything beyond the most rudimentary level is a uniquely human capacity. The ability to abstract

enables humans to learn and transmit knowledge in a way no other animal can.

COOPERATION: CREATING NORMS AND VALUES

The ability to cooperate is a second factor that enables human culture to exist. **Cooperation** involves creating a complex social life by establishing **norms** or generally accepted ways of doing things, and values or ideas about what is right and wrong, good and bad, beautiful and ugly. For example, family members cooperate to raise children. In the process, they develop and apply norms and values about which child-rearing practices are appropriate and desirable. Different times and places give rise to different norms and values. In our society, parents might ground children for swearing, but in pioneer days parents would typically "beat the devil out of them." By analyzing how people cooperate and produce norms and values, we can learn much about what distinguishes one culture from another.

PRODUCTION: CREATING MATERIAL AND NONMATERIAL CULTURE

Finally, culture can exist because humans can engage in **production**; we can make and use tools and techniques that improve our ability to take what we want from nature. Sociologists call such tools and techniques **material culture**. All animals take from nature to subsist, and an ape may sometimes use a rock to break another object or use a stick to keep its balance in a fast-flowing stream. However, only humans are sufficiently intelligent and dexterous to *make* tools and use them to produce everything from food to computers. Understood in this sense, production is a uniquely human activity.

Table 3.1 illustrates each of the basic human capacities and their cultural offshoots in the field of

TABLE 3.1   THE BUILDING BLOCKS OF CULTURE

THE HUMAN CAPACITY FOR ...	ABSTRACTION	COOPERATION	PRODUCTION
Gives rise to these elements of culture	Ideas	Norms and values	Material culture
In medicine, for example,	*theories* are developed about how a certain drug might cure a disease	*experiments* are conducted to test whether the drug works as expected	*treatments* are developed on the basis of the experimental results

SOURCE: Adapted from Robert Bierstedt, *The Social Order* (New York: McGraw-Hill, 1963).

medicine. As in medicine, so in all fields of human endeavour: Abstraction, cooperation, and production give rise to specific kinds of ideas, norms, and elements of material culture.

Note that people are usually rewarded when they follow cultural guidelines and punished when they do not. Taken together, these rewards and punishments, aimed at ensuring conformity, are known as **sanctions** or the system of **social control**. Rewards (or positive sanctions) include everything from praise and encouragement to money and power. Punishments (or negative sanctions) range from avoidance and contempt to arrest and physical violence.

Despite efforts to control people, we often reject elements of existing culture and create new elements of culture. Reasons for this phenomenon are discussed in Chapter 15, Deviance and Crime, and Chapter 19, Politics and Social Movements. Here it is enough to say that, just as social control is needed to ensure stable patterns of interaction, so resistance to social control is needed to ensure cultural innovation and social renewal. Stable but vibrant societies are able to find a balance between social control and cultural innovation.

CULTURE AND BIOLOGY

The Evolution of Human Behaviour

We have seen how the human capacity for abstraction, cooperation, and production enables us to create culture and makes us distinctively human. This capacity is built on a solid biological foundation. Biology, as every sociologist recognizes, sets broad human limits and potentials, including the potential to create culture.

Some biologically trained students of human behaviour go a step further. For example, evolutionary psychologists claim that genes—chemical units that carry traits from parents to children—account not just for physical characteristics but also for specific behaviours and social practices (Mealey, 2010; Neuberg, Kenrick, and Schaller, 2010). They deny the significance of culture. Such thinking is growing in popularity, and it undermines the sociological perspective. As the following example illustrates, it is also misguided.

Male Promiscuity, Female Fidelity, and Other Myths

Evolutionary psychologists employ a three-step argument for their biological explanation of human behaviour and social arrangements. First, they identify a supposedly universal human behavioural trait. Next, they offer an explanation for why this behaviour increases survival chances through reproduction. Finally, they conclude that the behaviour in question cannot easily be changed. For example, they explain alleged male promiscuity and female fidelity as follows.

1. *Universal claim*: Men are more likely than women are to want many sexual partners.
2. *Survival-value argument*: Every time a man ejaculates, he produces hundreds of millions of sperm, while fertile women typically release only one egg per month. Based on these sex differences, men and women develop different strategies to increase the chances of reproducing their genes. Because a woman produces few eggs, she improves her chance of reproducing her genes if she has a mate who stays around to help and protect her while she is pregnant, giving birth, and nursing a small infant. By contrast, because a man's sperm is plentiful, he improves his chance of reproducing his genes if he tries to impregnate as many women as possible.
3. *Conclusion*: These biologically based reproductive strategies are encoded or "hard-wired" in our genes. Therefore, male promiscuity and female fidelity are necessary.

Table 3.2 contains data from a survey of a representative sample of Americans. It shows that a minority of adult American men (21 percent) claimed having more than one sex partner in the previous year. The figure for adult American women was significantly

TABLE 3.2 NUMBER OF SEX PARTNERS BY RESPONDENT'S SEX, UNITED STATES (PERCENTAGE)

NUMBER OF SEX PARTNERS	RESPONDENT'S SEX	
	MALE	**FEMALE**
0 or 1	79	90
More than 1	21	10
Total	100	100
n (number of respondents)	1004	1233

SOURCE: Data from National Opinion Research Center, *General Social Survey, 1972–2002* (Chicago: University of Chicago, 2004).

TABLE 3.3 NUMBER OF SEX PARTNERS BY RESPON-
DENT'S SEX, UNITED STATES, MARRIED RESPONDENTS
ONLY (PERCENTAGE)

NUMBER OF SEX PARTNERS	RESPONDENT'S SEX	
	MALE	FEMALE
0 or 1	95	99
More than 1	5	1
Total	100	100
n (number of respondents)	499	534

SOURCE:Data from National Opinion Research Center, *General Social Survey, 1972–2002* (Chicago: University of Chicago, 2004).

lower (10 percent). However, if we examine just married Americans, the figures fall to 5 percent for men and 1 percent for women, a much smaller difference (see Table 3.3). These differences indicate that a *social* arrangement, the institution of marriage, accounts in substantial measure for variation in male promiscuity. There is no *universal* propensity to male promiscuity.

Still, Table 3.2 indicates that 11 percent more men than women said they had more than one sex partner in the preceding year. Among unmarried people, the male–female difference was 14 percent. Sociologists attribute these gender differences to two main factors (McConaghy, 1999: 311–14). First, on average, men are more likely than women are to have same-sex sexual relations, and gay men are more likely than lesbians are to have many sex partners. This finding contradicts the evolutionary psychologists' argument that male promiscuity reflects an adaptive reproductive strategy because, clearly, gay men do not have sex with other men to make babies. Moreover, in-depth interviews suggest that men tend to exaggerate how many sexual partners they have because our *culture* puts a premium on male sexual performance. Genes and reproductive strategies play no role in this regard. We conclude that the evolutionary psychologists' claims about male promiscuity and female fidelity are false. So are many of their other claims about so-called behavioural universals.

An additional problem with the evolutionary psychologists' argument is that little evidence links specific behaviours and social arrangements to specific genes. Finally, even if researchers discover an association between particular genes and particular behaviours, it would be wrong to conclude that variations among people are due only to their genes. Genes always develop in interaction with the environment; they *never* develop without environmental influence.

In sum, genes alone do not hard-wire your behaviour patterns. Changes in social environment produce physical change and, to an even greater degree, behavioural change. To determine the effects of the social environment on human behaviour, we need to abandon the premises of evolutionary psychology and use sociological skills to analyze the effects of social structure and culture.

LANGUAGE AND THE SAPIR-WHORF THESIS

Language is one of the most important parts of any culture. A **language** is a system of symbols strung together to communicate thought. Equipped with language, we can share understandings, pass experience and knowledge from one generation to the next, and make plans for the future. In short, language allows culture to develop. Consequently, sociologists commonly think of language as a cultural invention that distinguishes humans from other animals.

In the 1930s, Edward Sapir and Benjamin Lee Whorf proposed an influential argument about the connection among experience, thought, and language. It is now known as the **Sapir-Whorf thesis** (Whorf, 1956). It holds that we experience important things in our environment and form concepts about those things (path 1 to 2 in Figure 3.1). Then we develop language to express our concepts (path 2 to 3). Finally, language itself influences how we see the world (path 3 to 1).

FIGURE 3.1   THE SAPIR-WHORF THESIS

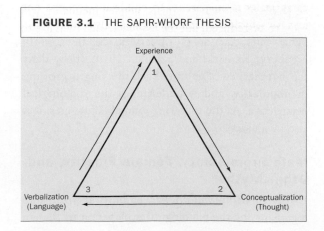

For example, different types of camels are important in the environment of nomadic Arabs, and different types of snow are important in the lives of the Inuit in Canada's Far North (path 1 to 2). Consequently, nomadic Arabs have developed many words for different types of camels and the Inuit have developed many words for different types of snow (path 2 to 3). Distinctions that these people see elude us because types of camel and snow are less important in our environment.

In turn, language obliges people to think in certain ways (path 3 to 1). If you're walking in a park, you will know whether a certain tree is in front of you, behind you, to the left, or to the right. When asked where the tree is, you will use such directions to describe its position. We think "egocentrically," locating objects relative to ourselves. However, egocentric directions have no meaning for speakers of Tzeltal in southern Mexico or of Guugu Yimithirr in Queensland, Australia. They lack concepts and words for "left," "right," and so on. They think geographically and will say that the tree is to the "north," "south, "east," or "west." Trained from infancy to attend to geographic direction, Tzeltal speakers are obliged to think in those terms. If a tree to the north is located behind them and they are asked where the tree is, they will point to themselves, as if they don't exist. Reportedly, a Tzeltal speaker can be blindfolded, put in a dark room, and spun around 20 times until he's dizzy yet still point without hesitation to the north, south, east, and west (Boroditsky, 2010; Deutscher, 2010).

Or to take an example closer to home, income and power inequality between women and men encourages some men to use terms like *fox*, *babe*, *bitch*, *ho*, and *doll* to refer to women. However, the use of such words in itself influences men to think of women simply as sexual objects. If they are ever going to think of women as equals, gender inequality will have to be reduced, but the language such men use to refer to women will also have to change.

TIME FOR REVIEW

1. What are the tools in the human "cultural survival kit?" How do they improve the survival chances of people?
2. How do evolutionary psychologists and sociologists differ in their explanations of human behaviour?
3. How does language shape the way we think? Give an example from your own experience.

CULTURE AS FREEDOM AND CONSTRAINT

A FUNCTIONALIST ANALYSIS OF CULTURE: CULTURE AND ETHNOCENTRISM

Despite culture's central importance in human life, it is often invisible. People tend to take their culture for granted. Its expression seems so sensible and natural, they rarely think about it. In contrast, people are often startled when confronted by cultures other than their own. The beliefs, norms, techniques, and practices of other cultures frequently seem odd, irrational, and even inferior.

Judging another culture exclusively by the standards of our own is known as **ethnocentrism.** Ethnocentrism impairs sociological analysis. We can illustrate this point by discussing a practice that seems bizarre to many Westerners: cow worship among Hindu peasants in India.

Hindu peasants refuse to slaughter cattle and eat beef because, for them, the cow is a religious

Taking public transportation often forces us to abandon our culturally defined personal space. However, this abandonment of personal space is itself a cultural norm.
SOURCE: Andrew Benyei, *Commuters*.

symbol of life. Pin-up calendars throughout rural India portray beautiful women with the bodies of fat white cows, milk jetting out of each teat. Cows are permitted to wander the streets, defecate on the sidewalks, and stop to chew their cud in busy intersections and on railroad tracks, causing traffic to come to a halt. In Madras, the police maintain fields where stray cows that have fallen ill can graze and be nursed back to health. The government even runs old-age homes for cows, where dry and decrepit cattle are kept free of charge. All this seems inscrutable to most Westerners, for it takes place amid poverty and hunger that could presumably be alleviated if only the peasants would slaughter their "useless" cattle for food instead of squandering scarce resources on feeding and protecting them.

According to Harris (1974), however, ethnocentrism misleads many Western observers. Cow worship, it turns out, is an economically rational practice in rural India. For one thing, Indian peasants can't afford tractors, so cows are needed to give birth to oxen, which are in high demand for plowing. For another, the cows produce hundreds of millions of kilograms of recoverable manure, about half of which is used as fertilizer and half as cooking fuel. With oil, coal, and wood in short supply, and with the peasants unable to afford chemical fertilizers, cow dung is, well, a godsend. What is more, cows in India don't cost much to maintain since they eat mostly food that isn't fit for human consumption. And they represent an important source of protein and a livelihood for members of low-ranking castes, who have the right to dispose of the bodies of dead cattle. These "untouchables" eat beef and form the workforce of India's large leather-craft industry. Thus, the protection of cows by means of cow worship is in fact a perfectly sensible and efficient economic practice. It only seems irrational when judged by the standards of Western agribusiness.

Harris's (1974) analysis of cow worship in rural India is interesting for two reasons. First, it illustrates how functionalist theory, outlined in Chapter 1, Introducing Sociology, can illuminate otherwise mysterious social practices that make social order possible. Second, we can draw an important lesson about ethnocentrism from Harris's analysis. If you refrain from taking your own culture for granted and judging other cultures by the standards of your own, you will have taken important first steps toward developing a sociological understanding of culture.

TIME FOR REVIEW

What is your favourite part of popular culture (TV, video games, movies, popular music, and so on)? Outline the elements of a functionalist interpretation of culture and apply it the element of popular culture that you selected.

CULTURE AS FREEDOM

Culture has two faces. First, culture provides us with an opportunity to exercise our freedom. We use and elaborate elements of culture in our everyday life to solve practical problems and express our needs, hopes, joy, and fears.

However, creatively using culture is just like any other act of construction in that we need raw materials to get the job done. The raw materials for the culture we create consist of cultural elements that either existed before we were born or are created by others after our birth. We may put these elements together in ways that produce something genuinely new. However, there is no other well to drink from, so existing culture puts limits on what we can think and do. In that sense, culture *constrains* us. This is culture's second face. In the rest of this chapter, we take a close look at both faces of culture.

SYMBOLIC INTERACTIONISM AND CULTURAL PRODUCTION

Until the 1960s, most sociologists argued that culture is a "reflection" of society. Harris's (1974) analysis of rural Indians certainly fits that mould. In Harris's view, the social necessity of protecting cows caused the cultural belief that cows are holy.

In recent decades, the symbolic interactionist tradition we discussed in Chapter 1, Introducing Sociology, has influenced many sociologists of culture. Symbolic interactionists are not inclined to regard society as a cause and culture as a consequence. In their view, people do not accept culture passively. We are not empty vessels into which society pours a defined assortment of beliefs, symbols, and values. Instead, we actively produce and interpret culture, creatively fashioning it and attaching meaning to it in accordance with our diverse needs.

The idea that people actively produce and interpret culture implies that, to a degree, we are at liberty to choose how culture influences us.

CULTURAL DIVERSIFICATION

This is a nice room tonight. When I look out, I see all kinds of different people. I see Black, White, Asian, everybody hangin' out, havin' a good time. ... This type of thing is not going to be able to happen about 300 years from now. You realize that? ... You realize there's not going to be any more white people? There's not going to be any more black people? Everyone's going to be beige. ... It's true, the whole world's mixing. There's nothing you can do about it. Eventually, we're all going to become some hybrid mix of Chinese and Indian. It's inevitable. They're the two largest populations in the world. So you can run from us now. But sooner or later, we're going to hump you. ... But I'm thinkin' if we're all going to mix anyway, let's start mixing people now that would never normally mix just to see what we'll get. You know, hook up a Jamaican with an Italian. They could have little Pastafarians. I'm Indian. I could hook up with a Jewish girl and we could have little Hinjews. A woman from the Philippines, a guy from Holland— little Hollapinos. A guy from Cuba, a woman from Iceland—little Ice-cubes. A French and a Greek—Freaks. A German and a Newfie— little Goofies. It's gonna happen. We might as well help it along.

—Russell Peters (2009),
Indo-Canadian comedian

Part of the reason we are increasingly able to choose how culture influences us is that a greater diversity of culture is available from which to choose. Like many societies, Canada is undergoing rapid cultural diversification. Canada used to be composed almost exclusively of Christian northern Europeans and an Indigenous minority. Then, in the 1960s, Canada eliminated overt racism from its immigration policies, and the country began to diversify culturally. In the 1970s, the Canadian government continued the trend by adopting a policy of multiculturalism, which funds the maintenance of culturally diverse communities (Fleras and Elliott, 2002).

About 95 percent of immigrants who arrived in Canada before 1961 came from Europe and the United States. In 2012, about 80 percent of immigrants came from *outside* Europe and the United States (see Table 3.4). Because of the inflow of immigrants from

Russell Peters
SOURCE: © ZUMA Press, Inc./Alamy.

TABLE 3.4 TOP SOURCE COUNTRIES OF CANADIAN IMMIGRANTS (PERMANENT RESIDENTS), 2012

COUNTRY	PERCENTAGE OF TOTAL
China	12.8
Philippines	12.7
India	11.2
Pakistan	3.9
United States	3.7
France	3.2
Iran	2.5
United Kingdom	2.5
Haiti	2.2
South Korea	2.1
Egypt	1.9
United Arab Emirates	1.6
Other	39.7
Total	100.0

SOURCE: HER MAJESTY THE QUEEN IN RIGHT OF CANADA (as represented by the Department of Citizenship and Immigration Canada).

nontraditional sources such as China, the Philippines, and India, more than a fifth of the population will be nonwhite by 2017 (excluding Indigenous Canadians). Nearly three-quarters of nonwhite Canadians will reside in Toronto, Vancouver, and Montreal, with most of the rest in Edmonton, Calgary, and Winnipeg (Brym, 2009; Cardozo and Pendakur, n.d.).

MULTICULTURALISM

Some critics argue that our immigration and multiculturalist policies weaken Canada's social fabric. For one thing, they argue that multiculturalism encourages **cultural relativism.** Cultural relativism is the opposite of ethnocentrism. It is the idea that all cultures and cultural practices have equal value. The trouble with this view is that some cultures oppose values that Canadians hold deeply. Should we respect racist and antidemocratic cultures, such as the apartheid regime that existed in South Africa from 1948 until 1992? Or female circumcision, which is still widely practised in Somalia, Sudan, and Egypt (see the Critical Sociology: Protest and Policy box)? Critics argue that by promoting cultural relativism, multiculturalism encourages respect for practices that are abhorrent to most Canadians.

CRITICAL SOCIOLOGY: PROTEST AND POLICY   FEMALE GENITAL MUTILATION: CULTURAL RELATIVISM OR ETHNOCENTRISM?

The World Health Organization defines female genital mutilation (FGM) as "procedures that intentionally alter or cause injury to the female genital organs for nonmedical reasons" (World Health Organization, 2014). FGM has no medical benefits. It usually involves partial or total removal of the clitoris and sometimes includes partial or total removal of the "lips" that surround the vagina and the surgical narrowing of the vaginal opening. It can result in severe bleeding, problems urinating, cysts, infection, infertility, and complications in childbirth, including increased risk of newborn death. Other effects include humiliation, trauma, and loss of sexual pleasure. Some 18 percent of FGM procedures are carried out by trained medical personnel, although in Egypt the figure is 77 percent (UNICEF, 2013: 2).

More than 125 million girls and women worldwide have undergone FGM, the great majority of them in Africa. However, increased international migration has brought FGM to Canada and other countries. Egypt, Ethiopia, Nigeria, and Sudan account for 83 percent of FGM cases worldwide; more than 150 000 Canadians claim to be at least partly of Egyptian, Ethiopian, Nigerian, and Sudanese ethnic origin (Statistics Canada, 2014; UNICEF, 2013:2).

Proponents of FGM often claim that women who have not experienced genital mutilation are inclined to "masculine" levels of sexual interest and activity. In contrast, women who have undergone FGM are considered more likely to remain virgins before marriage and faithful within marriage. Moreover, proponents often assert that FGM enhances fertility.

One reaction to FGM takes a human rights perspective. In this view, the practice is an aspect of gender-based oppression that women experience to varying degrees in societies worldwide. Adopting this perspective, the United Nations defines FGM as a form of violence against women. Many international, regional, and national agreements commit governments to preventing FGM, assisting women at risk of undergoing it, and punishing people who commit it. Canadian policy is clear. FGM is against the law (Ontario Human Rights Commission, 2009).

Cultural relativists regard the human rights perspective as ethnocentric. They view interference with the practice as Western attacks on African cultures. From their point of view, talk of "universal human rights" denies cultural rights to less powerful peoples. Moreover, opposition to FGM undermines tolerance and multiculturalism while reinforcing racist attitudes. Cultural relativists therefore argue that policy should affirm the right of cultures to practice FGM even if some people regard it as destructive, senseless, oppressive, and abhorrent. They assert that we should respect the fact that other cultures regard FGM as meaningful and as serving useful functions.

Critical Thinking Questions

1. Which of the policy perspectives summarized above do you find more compelling?

2. Do you believe that certain principles of human decency transcend the values of any specific culture? If so, what are those principles?

3. If you do not believe in the existence of any universal principles of human decency, then does anything go? Would you agree that, say, genocide is acceptable if most people in a society favour it? Or are there limits to your cultural relativism?

4. In a world where supposedly universal principles often clash with the principles of particular cultures, where do you draw the line? Is Canada justified in outlawing FGM?

SOURCE: Ontario Human Rights Commission (2009); Statistics Canada (2014); UNICEF (2013); World Health Organization (2014).

(Multiculturalists reply that cultural relativism need not be taken to an extreme. *Moderate* cultural relativism encourages tolerance and should be promoted.)

Critics of multiculturalism also argue that it encourages immigrants to cling to their past rather than shrug off their old self-conceptions and create a distinctive *Canadian* identity (Bissoondath, 2002). This viewpoint has two problems. First, it is by no means certain that we lack a distinctive Canadian identity. In fact, as noted below, a defining element of our distinctive Canadian identity is precisely our deep respect for diversity. Second, contrary to the claims of the critics of multiculturalism, survey research shows that support for multiculturalism is *not* correlated with traditional attitudes (such as religiosity) that keep people rooted in the past. Support for multiculturalism *is* correlated with various modern trends, such as support for equality between women and men (Adams, 1997: 173).

GLOBALIZATION

Canada's multiculturalist policies are the latest stage in a long process of cultural evolution. In general, cultures tend to become more diverse or heterogeneous as societies become more complex, with important consequences for everyday life. Thus, in preliterate or tribal societies, cultural beliefs and practices are virtually the same for all group members. For example, many tribal societies organize puberty ceremonies to mark the end of childhood and the beginning of adulthood, fertility dances to pray for good crops and healthy babies, and other rites. These rituals involve elaborate body painting, carefully orchestrated chants and movements, and so forth. They are conducted in public. No variation from prescribed practice is allowed. Culture is homogeneous (Durkheim, 1976 [1915]).

In contrast, preindustrial Western Europe and North America were rocked by artistic, religious, scientific, and political forces that fragmented culture. The Renaissance, the Protestant Reformation, the Scientific Revolution, the French and American Revolutions—between the fourteenth and eighteenth centuries, all of these movements involved people questioning old ways of seeing and doing things. Science placed skepticism of established authority at the very heart of its method. Political revolution proved there was nothing ordained about who should rule and how they should do so. Religious dissent ensured that the Catholic Church would no longer be the supreme interpreter of God's will in the eyes of all Christians. Authority and truth became divided as never before.

Globalization: Tim Hortons opened its first franchise in the United Arab Emirates in 2011.
SOURCE: © Robert Brym.

Cultural fragmentation picked up steam during industrialization, as the variety of occupational roles grew and new political and intellectual movements crystallized. Its pace is quickening again today in the postindustrial era under the impact of a variety of technological and globalizing forces.

Globalization has many roots (see Chapter 20, Globalization). International trade and investment are expanding. Members of different ethnic and racial groups are migrating and coming into sustained contact with one another. A growing number of people from these diverse groups date, court, and marry across religious, ethnic, and racial lines. Influential transnational organizations have been created, such as the International Monetary Fund, the European Union, Greenpeace, Amnesty International, and *Médecins sans frontières*. Inexpensive international travel and communication make contacts between people from diverse cultures routine. The mass media make Ryan Gosling and *Gossip Girl* as well known in Warsaw as in Winnipeg, while hip-hop is as popular in Senegal and Tunisia as it is in Chicago.

Globalization, in short, destroys political, economic, and cultural isolation, bringing people together in what Canadian communications guru Marshall McLuhan (1964) called a "global village." Because of globalization, people are less obliged to accept the culture into which they are born and freer to combine elements of culture from a wide variety of historical periods and geographical settings. Globalization is a Mumbai schoolboy listening to Bob Marley on his MP3 player as he rushes to slip into his Levis, wolfs down a bowl of Kellogg's Basmati Flakes, and says goodbye to his parents in Hindi because he's late for his English-language school (see Critical Sociology: Globalization box).

CRITICAL SOCIOLOGY: GLOBALIZATION   THE GLOBALIZATION OF ENGLISH

The spread of English is a key marker of the extent of globalization. In 1600, English was the mother tongue of between four million and seven million people. Not even all people in England spoke it. Today, about one billion people speak English worldwide, more than half as a second language. With the exception of the many varieties of Chinese, English is the most widespread language on Earth, and it is by far the most important. More than half the world's technical and scientific periodicals are written in English. English is the official language of the Olympics, of the Miss Universe contest, of navigation in the air and on the seas, and of the World Council of Churches.

English is dominant because Britain and the United States have been the world's most powerful and influential countries—economically, militarily, and culturally—for more than two centuries. (Someone once defined language as a dialect backed up by an army.) In recent decades, the global spread of capitalism, the popularity of Hollywood movies and American TV shows, and widespread access to instant communication via telephone and the Internet have increased the reach of the English language. There are now more speakers of excellent English in India than in the United Kingdom, and when a construction company jointly owned by German, French, and Italian interests undertakes a building project in Spain, the language of business is English (McCrum, Cran, and MacNeil, 1992).

Even in Japan, where relatively few people speak the language, English words are commonly used and Japanese words that are badly translated into English often become popular. The result is what is commonly known as "Japlish." Sometimes the results are unintelligible to a native English speaker. "Push to my nose! I might be changing to you?" says the catchy sign in a T-shirt store in Tokyo's Ueno district. Certain computer terms are more comprehensible to a native English speaker. For example, when you learn to open a computer file's *ai-kon* (icon) you are told to *daburu-kurikku* (double-click) the *mausu* (mouse; Kristof, 1997).

In view of the extensive use of English in Japan, *The Japanese Times,* one of Tokyo's four English daily newspapers, ran a story noting the pressures of globalization and suggesting it might be time for Japan to switch to English. However, it met with an official backlash. To limit the Anglicization of Japanese, the Ministry of Health and Welfare banned excessive use of English in its documents. The Ministry of Education has replaced many English words in official documents—such words as *sukeemu* (scheme), *eensenchibu* (incentive), *deribatibu* (derivative), and *identyityi* (identity). Whether official pronouncements will have much effect on the way English and Japlish are used in advertising and on the streets is, however, another question. As one Japanese newspaper pointed out, given the popularity of English words, it's doubtful there will be much *foro-uppu* (follow-up).

For Japanese teenagers, English and Japlish are certainly considered the height of fashion. "Japlish words are easy to pronounce. And English sounds very cool," says 11-year-old Mai Asai (quoted in Delmos, 2002). A 15-year-old girl wearing *roozu sokusu* (loose socks), might greet a friend sporting new sunglasses with a spirited *chekaraccho* (Check it out, Joe). If she likes the shades, she might say they're *cho beri gu* (ultra-good) and invite her friend *deniru* (to go to a Denny's restaurant) or *hageru* (to go to a Häagen-Dazs ice cream outlet). Of course, the girl might also *disu* (diss, or show disrespect toward) her friend. She might come right out and inform him that the new shades look *cho beri ba* (ultra-bad) or *cho beri bu* (ultra-blue, depressing, or ultra-ugly). If so, the situation that develops could be a little *denjarasu* (dangerous). Terms of affection, such as *wonchu* (I want you), might not be exchanged. The boy might decide that he has made a *misu* (mistake) and that the girl is too *hi mentay* (high maintenance) to justify pursuing. The budding relationship might go nowhere. Nonetheless, we can be pretty sure that Japanese teenagers' use of English slang will intensify under the pressures of globalization.

Less humorously, the rise of English (as well as the influence of French, Spanish, and the languages of a few other colonizing nations) is eliminating several thousand languages around the world. These endangered languages are spoken by the tribes of Papua New Guinea; the native peoples of the Americas; the national and tribal minorities of Asia, Africa, and Oceania; and marginalized European peoples, such as the Irish and the Basques. An estimated five thousand to six thousand languages spoken in the world today will be reduced to one thousand to three thousand in a century. Much of the culture of a people—its prayers, humour, conversational styles, technical vocabulary, myths, and so on—is expressed through language. Therefore, the loss of language amounts to the disappearance of tradition and perhaps even identity. These are often replaced by the traditions and identity of the colonial power, with television playing an important role in the transformation (Woodbury, 2003).

Critical Thinking Questions

1. Within a single language group, some ways of speaking are considered proper and others are considered improper. What social factors distinguish those who speak in ways that are considered proper from those who speak in ways that are considered improper?

2. How are proper ways of speaking a language imposed on people? Consider both formal (institutional) and informal (face-to-face) mechanisms.

3. In what ways is the disappearance of languages beneficial? In what ways is it harmful?

A CONFLICT ANALYSIS OF CULTURE: THE RIGHTS REVOLUTION

Underlying cultural diversification is the **rights revolution,** the process by which socially excluded groups have struggled to win equal rights under the law and in practice. After the outburst of nationalism, racism, and genocidal behaviour among the combatants in World War II, the United Nations proclaimed the Universal Declaration of Human Rights in 1948. Its preamble reads in part,

> Whereas recognition of the inherent dignity and of the equal and inalienable rights of all members of the human family is the foundation of freedom, justice and peace in the world. … Now, therefore The General Assembly proclaims this Universal Declaration of Human Rights as a common standard of achievement for all peoples and all nations, to the end that every individual and every organ of society, keeping this Declaration constantly in mind, shall strive by teaching and education to promote respect for these rights and freedoms and by progressive measures, national and international, to secure their universal and effective recognition and observance. (United Nations, 1998)

Fanned by such sentiment, the rights revolution was in full swing by the 1960s. Today, women's rights, Indigenous rights, gay and lesbian rights, the rights of people with special needs, constitutional rights, and language rights are a key part of our political discourse. As a result of the rights revolution, democracy has been widened and deepened (see Chapter 19, Politics and Social Movements). The rights revolution is by no means finished—many categories of people are still discriminated against socially, politically, and economically—but in much of the world, all categories of people now participate more fully than ever before in the life of their societies (Ignatieff, 2000).

The rights revolution raises some difficult issues. For example, groups that have suffered extraordinarily high levels of discrimination historically, such as Indigenous Canadians, Jewish Canadians, Chinese Canadians, and Japanese Canadians, have demanded reparations in the form of money, symbolic gestures, and, in the case of Indigenous Canadians, land and political autonomy.[2] Much controversy surrounds the extent of the obligation of current citizens to compensate for past injustices.

Another problem raised by the rights revolution concerns how we can achieve an acceptable balance between the right to be equal and the right to be different. For example, most residents of Quebec expect all Quebeckers to be able to compete on an equal footing for jobs, regardless of whether they are of French, English, or other origin. This is the right to equality. However, Quebeckers of French origin have also exercised their right to restrict nonfrancophones from expressing their right to be different. They have, for instance, passed laws restricting the use of English on public signs. These laws are controversial. Some English Quebeckers accept them as legitimate; others do not. Controversy therefore persists regarding the balance between the right to equality and the right to be different.

These problems notwithstanding, the rights revolution is here to stay and it affects our culture profoundly. Specifically, the rights revolution fragments Canadian culture by legitimizing the grievances of groups that were formerly excluded from full social participation and renewing pride in their identity and heritage. Our history books, our literature, our music, our use of languages, our very sense of what it means to be Canadian have diversified culturally. White male heterosexual property owners of British origin are still disproportionately influential in Canada, but our culture is no longer dominated by them in the way that it was just four or five decades ago.

POSTMODERNISM

In part because of the rights revolution, so much cultural fragmentation and reconfiguration has taken place in the last few decades that some sociologists think a new term is needed to characterize the culture of our times: **postmodernism**.

Postmodern culture has three main features. First, it involves *an eclectic mixing of elements from different times and places.* That is, in the postmodern era it is easier to create individualized belief systems and practices by blending facets of different cultures and historical periods. Consider religion. Surveys conducted by Reginald Bibby of the University of Lethbridge show that Canadians often supplement Judeo–Christian beliefs and practices with less conventional ideas about astrology, psychic powers, communication with the dead, and so forth (Bibby, 1987). People who attend church regularly are just as likely to hold such unconventional beliefs as nonattenders are. However, despite the widespread acceptance of unconventional beliefs, the overwhelming majority of Canadians still turn to established religions for **rites of passage**, or cultural ceremonies that mark the transition from one stage of life to another (e.g., baptisms, confirmations, weddings) or from life to death (funerals). Individuals thus choose their own mix of unconventional and conventional beliefs and practices. They draw on religions much like consumers shop in a mall; as Bibby says, they practise religion à la carte. Meanwhile, Canadian churches have diversified their menus to appeal to the spiritual, leisure, and social needs of religious consumers and retain their loyalties in the competitive market for congregants and parishioners. The mix-and-match approach we see when it comes to religion is evident in virtually all spheres of culture.

Second, postmodernism also involves *the erosion of authority*. Half a century ago, Canadians were more likely than they are today to defer to authority in the family, schools, politics, medicine, and religion. In fact, Canadians were often characterized as an especially deferential people, more respectful of authority than their individualistic, revolutionary, violent, and entrepreneurial cousins in the United States. In the second half of the twentieth century, however, Canadians grew skeptical about authority in many institutions, especially political institutions—even more skeptical than Americans in many respects (Brym with Fox, 1989; Nevitte, 1996). For example, voting and other forms of conventional politics are less popular than they used to be, while nonconventional political action, such as participating in demonstrations, is more popular (see Figure 3.2).

Finally, postmodernism is characterized by *the decline of consensus around core values*. Half a century ago, people's values remained quite stable over the course of their adult lives and many values were widely accepted. Today, value shifts are more rapid

FIGURE 3.2 CANADA: VOTING DOWN, DEMONSTRATING UP

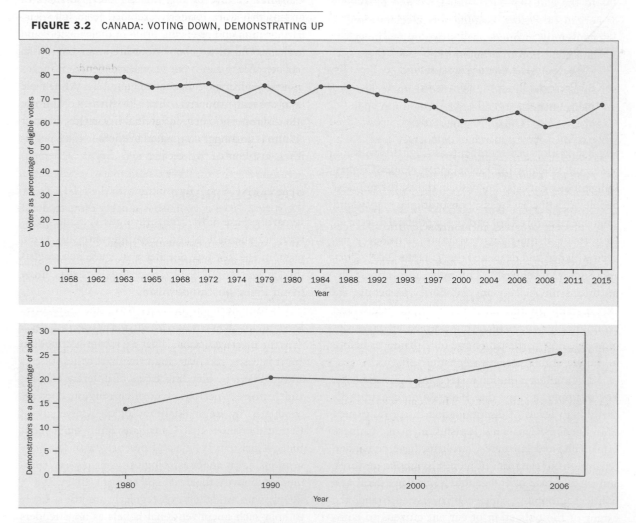

SOURCES: (Top) Elections Canada (2013); Harris (2015). This is an adaptation of the version available at www.elections.ca. Reproduced with the permission of Elections Canada; (bottom) *World Values Survey* (2012).

and consensus has broken down on many issues. For instance, half a century ago, the great majority of adults remained loyal to one political party from one election to the next. Today, people are more likely to vote for different parties in succeeding elections (Clarke et al., 1996: 139–46).

The decline of consensus can also be illustrated by considering the fate of Big Historical Projects. For most of the past two hundred years, consensus throughout the world was built around Big Historical Projects. Various social movements convinced people they could take history into their own hands and create a glorious future just by signing up. German Nazism was a Big Historical Project. Its followers expected the Reich to enjoy a thousand years of power. Communism was an even bigger Big Historical Project, mobilizing hundreds of millions of people for a future that promised to end inequality and injustice for all time. However, the biggest and most successful Big Historical Project was not so much a social movement as a powerful idea—the belief that progress is inevitable, that life will always improve, mainly because of the spread of democracy and scientific innovation.

The twentieth century was unkind to Big Historical Projects. Russian communism lasted 74 years, German Nazism a mere 12. The idea of progress fell on hard times as 100 million soldiers and civilians died in wars; the forward march of democracy took wrong turns into fascism, communism, and regimes based on religious fanaticism; and pollution from urbanization and industrialization threatened the planet. In the postmodern era, more and more people recognize that apparent progress, including scientific advances, often has negative consequences (Scott, 1998).

The aspects of postmodernism listed previously—the eclectic mixing of cultural elements from different times and places, the erosion of authority, and the decline of consensus around core values—have many parents, teachers, politicians, religious leaders, and not a few university professors worried. How can we make binding decisions? How can we govern? How can we teach children and adolescents the difference between right and wrong? How can we transmit accepted literary tastes and artistic standards from one generation to the next? These are the kinds of issues that plague people in positions of authority today. Although their concerns are legitimate, many of them seem not to have considered the other side of the coin: The postmodern condition, as described above, empowers ordinary people and makes them more responsible for their own fate. It renders them

more tolerant and appreciative of ethnic, racial, religious, and sexual groups other than their own—no small matter in a world torn by group conflict. The postmodern attitude encourages a healthy skepticism about rosy and naive scientific and political promises. And it frees people to adopt religious, ethnic, and other identities they are comfortable with, as opposed to identities imposed on them by others.

IS CANADA THE FIRST THOROUGHLY MODERN POSTMODERN COUNTRY?

Until the mid-1960s, the image of Canadians among most sociologists was that of a stodgy people: peaceful, conservative, respectful of authority, and therefore quite unlike our American cousins.

According to conventional wisdom, the United States was born in open rebellion against the British motherland. Its Western frontier was lawless. Vast opportunities for striking it rich bred a spirit of individualism. Thus, American culture became an anti-authoritarian culture.

Canada developed differently according to the conventional view. It became an independent country not through a revolutionary upheaval but in a gradual, evolutionary manner. The Northwest Mounted Police and two very hierarchical churches (Roman Catholic and Anglican) established themselves on the Western frontier before the era of mass settlement, allowing for the creation of an orderly society rather than a "wild West." Beginning with the Hudson's Bay Company, large corporations quickly came to dominate the Canadian economy, hampering individualism and the entrepreneurial spirit. Thus, Canadian culture became a culture of deference to authority. That, at least, was the common view until the 1960s (Lipset, 1963).

Although the contrast between deferential Canadian culture and anti-authoritarian American culture may have had some validity 40 or 50 years ago, it is an inaccurate characterization today (Adams, 1997: 62–95). As we have seen, the questioning of authority spread throughout the Western world beginning in the 1960s. Nowhere, however, did it spread as quickly and thoroughly as in Canada. Canadians used to express more confidence in big business than Americans did, but surveys now show the opposite. Canadians used to be more religious than Americans were, but that is no longer the case. Fewer Canadians (in percentage terms) say they believe in God and fewer attend weekly religious services.

Confidence in government has eroded more quickly in Canada than in the United States. Americans are more patriotic than Canadians are, according more respect to the state. Finally, Americans are more likely than Canadians are to regard the traditional nuclear family as the ideal family form and to think of deviations from tradition—same-sex couples, single-parent families, cohabitation without marriage—as the source of a whole range of social problems. Thus, whether sociologists examine attitudes toward the family, the state, government, religion, or big business, they now find that Americans are more deferential to traditional institutional authority than Canadians are.

Because Canadians are less deferential to traditional institutional authority than Americans are, some commentators say that Canadians lack a distinct culture. For example, American patriotism sparks awareness of great national accomplishments in art, war, sports, science, and, indeed, all fields of human endeavour. Anthems, rituals, myths, and celebrations recognize these accomplishments and give Americans a keen sense of who they are and how they differ from non-Americans. Not surprisingly, therefore, a larger percentage of Americans than of Canadians think of themselves as "Americans" plain and simple rather than, say, Italian-Americans. In Canada, a larger percentage of the population thinks of itself in hyphenated terms; compared with the Americans, our identity is qualified, even tentative.

Does this mean that Canadians lack a distinct national culture? Hardly. It means that although American culture is characterized by a relatively high degree of deference to dominant institutions, Canadian culture is characterized by a relatively high degree of tolerance and respect for diversity. We are more likely than Americans are to favour gender equality, accept gay and lesbian relationships, encourage bilingualism and multiculturalism, and accept the right of Indigenous peoples to political autonomy. Characteristically, a large international survey by a condom manufacturer found that Americans have sex more often than Canadians do but Canadians are most likely to say that the pleasure of their partner is very important. As public opinion pollster Michael Adams writes,

> Twenty-five years of public-opinion polling in Canada has taught me a seemingly paradoxical truth. Canadians feel strongly about their weak attachments to Canada, its political institutions and their fellow citizens. In other words, they feel strongly about the right to live in a society that allows its citizens to be detached from ideology and critical of organizations, and not to feel obliged to be jingoistic or sentimentally patriotic. Canadians' lack of nationalism is, in many ways, a distinguishing feature of the country. (1997: 171)

In short, Canadian culture is distinctive, and its chief distinction may be that it qualifies us as the first thoroughly postmodern country.

TIME FOR REVIEW

1. Contrast ethnocentrism and cultural relativism. How is it possible to avoid both extremes?
2. What are the major forces that have led to cultural diversification and greater freedom to make cultural choices since World War II?
3. In what sense is Canada the first truly postmodern country?

CULTURE AS CONSTRAINT

We noted previously that culture has two faces. One we labelled "freedom," the other "constraint." Diversity, globalization, and postmodernism are all aspects of the new freedoms that culture allows us today. We now turn to an examination of two contemporary aspects of culture that act as constraining forces on our lives: rationalization and consumerism.

RATIONALIZATION

In fourteenth-century Europe, an upsurge in demand for textiles caused loom owners to look for ways to increase productivity. To that end, they imposed longer hours on loom workers and installed the first public clocks. The clocks, known as *Werkglocken* ("work clocks") in German, signalled the beginning of the workday, the timing of meals, and quitting time. Workers were accustomed to enjoying many holidays and a flexible and vague work schedule regulated only approximately by the seasons and the rising and setting of the Sun. The regimentation imposed by the work clocks made life harder. Therefore, the workers staged uprisings to silence the clocks—but to no avail. City officials sided with the employers and imposed fines for ignoring the *Werkglocken*. Harsher penalties, including death, were imposed on anyone trying to use the clocks' bells to signal a revolt (Thompson, 1967).

Now, more than six hundred years later, many people in the world's rich countries—especially big-city couples who are employed full-time in the paid labour force and have preteen children—are, in effect, slaves of the *Werkglocke*. Life often seems an endless round of waking up at 6:30 a.m., getting everyone washed and dressed, preparing the kids' lunches, getting them out the door in time for the school bus or the car pool, driving to work through rush-hour traffic, facing the speed-up at work that resulted from the recent downsizing, driving back home through rush-hour traffic, preparing dinner, taking the kids to their soccer game, returning home to clean up the dishes and help with homework, getting the kids washed, brushed, and into bed, and (if you haven't brought some office work home) grabbing an hour of TV before collapsing, exhausted, for six-and-a-half hours before the story repeats itself.

Life is generally less hectic for residents of small cities and towns, unmarried people, couples without small children, retirees, and the unemployed. However, the lives of many people are so packed with activities that time must be carefully regulated, each moment precisely parcelled out so we may tick off item after item from an ever-growing list of tasks that need to be completed on schedule (Schor, 1992). Women in particular are working more hours per week for pay, and overtime work is increasing, especially for senior managers (Statistics Canada, 2012).

After more than six hundred years of conditioning, it is unusual for people to rebel against the clock in the town square anymore. In fact, we now wear a watch on our wrist without giving it a second thought. This signifies that we have accepted and internalized the regime of the work clock. Allowing clocks to regulate our activities precisely seems the most natural thing in the world—which is a pretty good sign that the internalized *Werkglocke* is, in fact, a product of culture.

Is the precise regulation of time rational? It certainly is rational as a means of ensuring efficiency, that is, maximizing how much work you get done in a day. But is it rational as an end in itself? For many people, it is not. The precise regulation of time has gotten out of hand. Life has simply become too hectic for many people to enjoy fully. In this sense, rationality of means has led to irrationality of ends.

For sociologist George Ritzer, the McDonald's fast-food restaurant epitomizes the rationalization process. Ritzer speaks of the "McDonaldization" of the world, by which he means that the organizational

principles of the fast-food restaurant are coming to dominate everywhere (Ritzer, 1993, 1996).

At McDonald's, a set list of carefully weighed food portions with identical ingredients are cooked according to a uniform and precisely timed process. But, says Ritzer, the application of assembly-line procedures to meal preparation is dehumanizing for both employees and customers. Thus, the work is done by mainly nonunionized, uniformed, teenaged workers who receive minimum wage. To boost sales, they are required to smile as they recite fixed scripts ("Would you like some fries or a drink with your burger?"). Nearly half of all McDonald's employees are so dissatisfied with their work, they quit after a year or less. To deal with this problem, McDonald's is field-testing self-service kiosks in which an automated machine cooks and bags French fries while a vertical grill takes patties from the freezer and grills them to your liking (Carpenter, 2003). Meanwhile, customers are expected to spend as little time as possible eating the food—hence the drive-through window, chairs designed to be comfortable for only about 20 minutes, and small express outlets in subways and department stores where customers eat standing up or on the run. In short, McDonald's executives have carefully thought through every aspect of your lunch. With the goal of making profits, they have rationalized food preparation, making it as inexpensive and as fast as possible.

Taking McDonaldization to a new extreme, one restaurant in Japan has even installed a punch-clock

BlackBerrys and iPhones allow people to stay in touch with friends and work every waking moment. Many people have mixed feelings about these devices. Sometimes they seem pleasurable and efficient. At other times, they prevent relaxation and intimacy. As such, they typify the two faces of culture.
SOURCE: © Dave Murray.

for its customers. The restaurant offers all you can eat for 35 yen per minute. As a result, "the diners rush in, punch the clock, load their trays from the buffet table, and concentrate intensely on efficient chewing and swallowing, trying not to waste time talking to their companions before rushing back to punch out. This version of fast food is so popular that, as the restaurant prepares to open at lunchtime, Tokyo residents *wait in line*" (Gleick, 2000: 244; emphasis in the original). Meanwhile, in New York and Los Angeles, some upscale restaurants have gotten in on the act. An increasingly large number of business clients are so pressed for time, they feel the need to pack in *two* half-hour lunches with successive guests. The restaurants oblige, making the resetting of tables "resemble the pit-stop activity at the Indianapolis 500" (Gleick, 2000: 155).

As the examples of the *Werkglocke* and fast food show, rationalization enables us to do just about everything more efficiently, but at a steep cost. In fact, because it is so widespread, rationalization is one of the most constraining aspects of culture today. In Weber's view, it makes life in the modern world akin to living inside an "iron cage." (Weber, 1958 [1904–05]).

CONSUMERISM

The second constraining aspect of culture is consumerism. **Consumerism** is the tendency to define ourselves in terms of the goods and services we purchase. As conceptual/pop artist Barbara Kruger put it in one of her works: "I shop, therefore I am" (Art History Archive).

Consumerism ties identities to purchases.
SOURCE: © Barbara Kruger. Courtesy: Mary Boone Gallery, New York.

Advertising works by making it seem as if buying commodities will ensure that you gain desirable characteristics. For example, some years ago, the Gap hired Hollywood talent to create a slick and highly effective series of TV ads for khaki pants. According to the promotional material for the ad campaign, the purpose of the ads was to "reinvent khakis," that is, to stimulate demand for the pants. In *Khakis rock*, "skateboarders and in-line skaters dance, glide, and fly to music by the Crystal Method." In *Khakis groove*, "hip-hop dancers throw radical moves to the funky beat of Bill Mason." In *Khakis swing*, "two couples break away from a crowd to demonstrate swing techniques to the vintage sounds of Louis Prima" (Gap.com, 1999).

About 55 seconds of each ad featured the dancers. During the last 5 seconds, the words "GAP khakis" appeared on the screen. The Gap followed a similar approach in another ad campaign a couple of years later. Inspired by the musical *West Side Story*, the 30-second spots replaced the play's warring street gangs, the Jets and the Sharks, with fashion factions of their own, the Khakis and the Jeans. Again, most of the ad was devoted to the riveting dance number. The pants were mentioned for only a few seconds at the end.

As the imbalance between stylish come-on and mere information suggests, the people who created the ads understood that it was really the appeal of the dancers that would sell the pants. They knew that to stimulate demand for their product, they had to associate the khakis with desirable properties, such as youth, good health, coolness, popularity, beauty, and sex. As an advertising executive said in the 1940s: "It's not the steak we sell. It's the sizzle."

Because advertising stimulates sales, business has a tendency to spend more on advertising over time. And because advertising is widespread, most people unquestioningly accept it as part of their lives. In fact, many people have *become* ads. When your father was a child and quickly threw on a shirt, allowing a label to hang out, your grandmother might have admonished him to "tuck in that label." Today, in contrast, many people proudly display consumer labels as marks of status and identity. Advertisers teach us to associate the words "Gucci" and "Nike" with different kinds of people, and when people display these labels on their clothes, they are telling us something about the kind of people they are and whom they associate with. Advertising becomes us (see the Critical Sociology: Social Inequality box).

Recent innovations in advertising take full advantage of our tendency to define ourselves in terms of

Thorstein Veblen (1899) coined the term "conspicuous consumption" more than a century ago. He argued that rich people (Veblen called them members of the "leisure class") normally engage in ostentatious and wasteful displays of buying power. According to Veblen, they do so to show the world that they are rich and that they enjoy good taste and therefore good character. However, the relationship between class and clothes has taken different forms in different historical periods.

Until about 1700, laws regulated the kinds of clothing people could wear (Lurie, 1981). For example, in ancient Egypt, only people in high positions were allowed to wear sandals. The ancient Greeks and Romans passed laws controlling the type, number, and colour of garments people could don and the type of embroidery with which their clothes could be trimmed. In medieval Europe, too, various aspects of dress were regulated to ensure that certain styles were specific to certain groups.

European laws governing dress styles fell into disuse after about 1700 with the emergence of a new method of distinguishing rank by the clothes one wore. As Europe became wealthier, the *cost* of clothing came to designate a person's rank. Expensive materials, styles that were difficult to care for, heavy jewellery, and superfluous trimmings became all the rage. It was not for comfort or utility that

rich people wore elaborate powdered wigs, heavy damasked satins, the furs of rare animals, diamond tiaras, and patterned brocades and velvets. Such getups were hot, stiff, heavy, and itchy. People could scarcely move in them. And that was just their point—to prove not only that the wearer could afford enormous sums for handmade finery but also that he or she could not possibly work in them and therefore did not have to work to pay for them.

Today, we have different ways of using clothes to signal status. Designer labels loudly proclaim the dollar value of garments and signify the wearer's good taste. However, modern production techniques allow new fashions to be copied quickly and relatively inexpensively, and cheap knock-offs of luxury goods are widely available. This means that designers of luxury goods have had to increase the pace with which they introduce new fashions into the marketplace, while consumers have had to buy more stuff to maintain the appearance of rank–even when they can scarcely afford to do so.

Critical Thinking Questions

1. What are the manifest and latent functions of clothes?

2. Are clothing styles more "democratic" now than they were in ancient, medieval, or early modern times? If not, why not? If so, how and why?

the goods we purchase. For example, when channel surfing and the use of personal video recorders spread, advertisers realized they had a problem on their hands. Viewers started skipping TV ads that cost millions of dollars and untold hours of creative effort to produce. As a result, advertisers had to think up new ways of drawing products to the attention of consumers. One idea they hit on was paying to place their products in TV shows and movies. They realized that when Brad Pitt or some other big star drinks a can of Coke or lights up a Marlboro, members of the audience tend to associate the product with the star. Wanting to be like the star, they are more likely to buy the product. Typically, sales of Travelpro luggage spiked in 2009, when the Oscar-nominated movie *Up in the Air* featured several travel scenes focusing on George Clooney's efficient and elegant suitcase. The product became part of who many audience members wanted to be.

Since the 1980s, there has been an explosion of advertising directed at children. Here, advertisers recognized, was a vast untapped market; children

could be used to nag their parents to buy more products. The manipulation of children by advertisers soon became a sort of quasi-science. One advertising expert said seven basic types of nagging tactics can be unleashed by effective child-directed advertising:

A *pleading* nag is one accompanied by repetitions of words like "please" or "Mom, Mom, Mom." A *persistent* nag involves constant requests for the coveted product and may include the phrase "I'm gonna ask just one more time." *Forceful* nags are extremely pushy and may include subtle threats, like "Well, then, I'll go and ask Dad." *Demonstrative* nags are the most high-risk, often characterized by full-blown tantrums in public places, breath-holding, tears, a refusal to leave the store. *Sugar-coated* nags promise affection in return for a purchase and may rely on seemingly heartfelt declarations like "You're the best dad in the world." *Threatening* nags are youthful forms of blackmail, vows of eternal hatred and of running away if something isn't bought. *Pity* nags claim the child will be heartbroken, teased, or socially stunted if the parent refuses to buy a certain product. (Schlosser, 2002: 44)

Note that getting children to nag their parents to buy more products is only one aim of child-directed advertising. In addition, advertisers recognize that ads directed at children can be used to develop brand loyalty that will, in the ideal case, last a lifetime. A few years ago, executives at one large brewery must have been delighted to read the results of a consumer survey that found that the most popular ads among American children were a Taco Bell commercial featuring a talking Chihuahua and an ad for Budweiser beer.

The rationalization process enables us to produce more efficiently, to have more of just about everything than our parents did. However, it is consumerism, the tendency to define ourselves in terms of the goods we purchase, that ensures the goods will be bought. Of course, people living in the world's rich countries have lots of choice. We can select from dozens of styles of running shoes, cars, and all the rest. We can also choose to buy items that help define us as members of a particular **subculture**, adherents of a set of distinctive values, norms, and practices within a larger culture. But, regardless of individual tastes and inclinations, nearly all of us have one thing in common: We tend to be good consumers. We are motivated by advertising, which is based on the accurate insight that people will likely be considered social outcasts if they fail to conform to stylish trends. By creating those trends, advertisers push us to buy. That is why North Americans' "shop-till-you-drop" lifestyle prompted French sociologist Jean Baudrillard to remark pointedly that even what is best in North America is compulsory (Baudrillard, 1988 [1986]).

FROM COUNTERCULTURE TO SUBCULTURE

In concluding my discussion of culture as a constraining force, I want to note that consumerism is remarkably effective at taming countercultures. **Countercultures** are subversive subcultures. They oppose dominant values and seek to replace them. The hippies of the 1960s formed a counterculture and so do environmentalists today.

Countercultures rarely pose a serious threat to social stability. Most often, the system of social control, of rewards and punishments, keeps countercultures at bay. In our society, consumerism acts as a social control

mechanism that normally prevents countercultures from disrupting the social order. It does that by transforming deviations from mainstream culture into means of making money and by enticing rebels to become entrepreneurs (Frank and Weiland, 1997). The development of hip-hop helps to illustrate the point (Brym, 2014).

Hip-hop originated in the American inner city in the 1970s. At the time, manufacturing industries were leaving the inner city for suburban or foreign locales, where land values were lower and labour was less expensive. Unemployment among African American youth rose to more than 40 percent. At the same time, many middle-class blacks left the inner city for the suburbs. Their migration robbed the remaining young people of successful role models. It also eroded the taxing capacity of municipal governments, leading to a decline in public services. Meanwhile, the American public elected conservative governments at the state and federal levels. They cut school and welfare budgets, thus deepening the destitution of ghetto life (Piven and Cloward, 1977: 264–361; Wilson, 1987).

With few legitimate prospects for advancement, poor African American youth in the inner city turned increasingly to crime and, in particular, the drug trade. In the late 1970s, cocaine was expensive and demand for the drug was flat. Consequently, in the early 1980s, Colombia's Medellin drug cartel introduced a less expensive form of cocaine called *rock* or *crack*. Crack was inexpensive, it offered a quick and intense high, and it was highly addictive. It offered many people a temporary escape from hopelessness and soon became wildly popular in the inner city. Turf wars spread as gangs tried to outgun each other for control of the local traffic. The sale and use of crack became so widespread, it corroded much of what was left of the inner-city African American community (Davis, 1990).

The shocking conditions described above gave rise to a shocking musical form: hip-hop. Stridently at odds with the values and tastes of both whites and middle-class African Americans, hip-hop described and glorified the mean streets of the inner city while holding the police, the mass media, and other pillars of society in utter contempt. Furthermore, hip-hop tried to offend middle-class sensibilities, black and white, by using highly offensive language.

In 1988, more than a decade after its first stirrings, hip-hop reached its political high point with the release of the album *It Takes a Nation of Millions to Hold Us Back* by Chuck D and Public Enemy. In "Don't Believe the Hype," Chuck D accused the mass media of maliciously distributing lies. In "Black Steel in the Hour of Chaos," he charged the FBI and the CIA with assassinating the two great leaders of the African American community in the 1960s: Martin Luther King and Malcolm X. In "Party for Your Right to Fight," he blamed the federal government for organizing the fall of the Black Panthers, the radical black nationalist party of the 1960s. Here, it seemed, was an angry expression of subcultural revolt that could not be tamed.

However, the seduction of big money did much to mute the political force of hip-hop. As early as 1982, with the release of Grandmaster Flash and the Furious Five's "The Message," hip-hop began to win acclaim from mainstream rock music critics. With the success of Run-D.M.C. and Public Enemy in the late 1980s, it became clear there was a big audience for hip-hop. Significantly, much of that audience was composed of white youths. As one music critic wrote, they "relished ... the subversive 'otherness' that the music and its purveyors represented" (Neal, 1999: 144). Sensing the opportunity for profit, major media corporations, such as Time/Warner, Sony, CBS/Columbia, and BMG Entertainment, signed distribution deals with the small independent recording labels that had formerly been the exclusive distributors of hip-hop CDs. In 1988, *Yo! MTV Raps* debuted on MTV. The program brought hip-hop to middle America.

Most hip-hop recording artists proved they were eager to forgo political relevancy for commerce. For instance, WU-Tang Clan started a line of clothing called WU Wear, and, with the help of major hip-hop recording artists, companies as diverse as Tommy Hilfiger, Timberland, Starter, and Versace began to market clothing influenced by ghetto styles. Independent labels, such as Phat Farm and Fubu, also prospered. Puff Daddy reminded his audience in his 1999 CD, *Forever*: "N——get money, that's simply the plan." According to *Forbes* magazine, he became one of the country's 40 richest men under 40. By 2005, having renamed himself Diddy, he had his own line of popular clothing. The members of Run-D.M.C. once said that they "don't want nobody's name on my behind," but those days were long past by the early 1990s. Hip-hop was no longer just a musical form but a commodity with spin-offs. Rebellion had been turned into mass consumption. Hip-hop's radicalism had given way to the lures of commerce. A counterculture had become a subculture.

Radical political currents in hip-hop still exist. For example, in 2012, Macklemore and Lewis's first hit, "Same Love," criticized homophobia in hip-hop and promoted gay rights. Their single, "Thrift Store," which topped the *Billboard* "Hot 100" for six weeks and

Diddy marketing "rebellion."
SOURCE: © REUTERS/Mike Blake.

won a Grammy award for best rap song in 2014, is a critique of mindless consumerism. Nonetheless, such currents seem to be less common in English-speaking countries than elsewhere. In Senegal, the playing of hip-hop that is highly critical of the government is widely believed to have helped topple the ruling party in the 2000 election. In France, North African youth living in impoverished and segregated slums use hip-hop to express their political discontent, and some analysts say the genre helped mobilize youth for anti-government rioting in 2005 (Akwagyiram, 2009). "*Rais Lebled* [Mr. President]," a song by a Tunisian rapper, became the anthem of young people participating in the democratic uprisings in Tunisia, Egypt, and Bahrain in 2011: "Mr. President, your people are dying/People are eating rubbish/Look at what is happening/Miseries everywhere, Mr. President/I talk with no fear/Although I know I will get only trouble/I see injustice everywhere" (Ghosh, 2011).

However, in the United States and Canada, hip-hop has become, for the most part, an apolitical commodity that increasingly appeals to a racially heterogeneous, middle-class audience. As one of hip-hop's leading analysts and academic sympathizers writes, "the discourse of ghetto reality or 'hood authenticity remains largely devoid of political insight or progressive intent" (Forman, 2001: 121). The fate of hip-hop is testimony to the capacity of consumerism to change countercultures into mere subcultures, thus constraining dissent and rebellion.

TIME FOR REVIEW

1. What are the causes of rationalization and consumerism? How do they constrain cultural choices?
2. Distinguish subculture from counterculture.

SUMMARY

1. **In what sense does culture increase the likelihood that humans will survive?**
   Culture increases the chance of human survival insofar as it enables people to adapt to their environments. In particular, the ability to create symbols, cooperate, and make tools has enabled humans to thrive.

2. **What is the best vantage point for analyzing culture?**
   Culture can be invisible if we are too deeply immersed in it. The cultures of others can seem inscrutable if we view them exclusively from the perspective of our own culture. Therefore, the best vantage point for analyzing culture is on the margins—neither too deeply immersed in it nor too much removed from it.

3. **How does the increasing complexity of society affect cultural freedom?**
   As societies become more complex, culture becomes more diversified and consensus declines in many areas of life. These processes increase human freedom, giving people more choice in their ethnic, religious, sexual, and other identities. So much cultural diversification and reconfiguration have taken place in recent decades that some sociologists characterize the culture of our times as postmodern. Postmodernism involves an eclectic mixing of cultural elements from different times and places, the erosion of authority, and the decline of consensus around core values. The rights revolution—the process by which socially excluded groups have struggled to win equal rights under the law and in practice—also underlies cultural diversification.

4. **How does the increasing complexity of society affect cultural constraint?**
   The growth of complex societies establishes limits within which diversification may occur. This fact is illustrated by increasing rationalization (the optimization of means to achieve given ends) and the growth of consumerism (which involves defining one's self in terms of the goods one purchases). Both of these processes are especially evident in advanced capitalist societies.

QUESTIONS TO CONSIDER

1. We imbibe culture but also create it. What elements of culture have you created? Under what conditions were you prompted to do so? Was your cultural contribution strictly personal or was it shared with others? Why?

2. Do you think of yourself in a fundamentally different way from the way your parents (or other close relatives or friends at least 20 years older than you) thought of themselves when they were your age? Are your attitudes toward authority different? Interview your parents, relatives, or friends to find out. Pay particular attention to the way in which the forces of globalization have altered ethnic, racial, and religious self-conceptions, and how your attitudes to authority differ from those of your elders.

3. One of the main themes of this chapter is that rationality of means sometimes results in irrationality of ends. Select a sphere of culture (religion, education, the mass media, etc.) and illustrate the point.

GLOSSARY

Abstraction (p. 60) is the human capacity to create complex symbols, including languages, mathematical notations, and signs, in order to classify experience and generalize from it.

Consumerism (p. 74) involves defining ourselves in terms of the goods we purchase.

Cooperation (p. 60) is the human capacity to create a complex social life by establishing norms.

Countercultures (p. 76) are subversive subcultures. They oppose dominant values and seek to replace them.

Cultural relativism (p. 66) is the opposite of ethnocentrism. It is the idea that all cultures and all cultural practices have equal value.

Culture (p. 59) is the sum of socially transmitted practices, languages, symbols, beliefs, values, ideologies, and material objects that people create to deal with real-life problems. Cultures enable people to adapt to, and thrive in, their environments.

Ethnocentrism (p. 63) is the tendency to judge other cultures exclusively by the standards of our own.

A **language** (p. 62) is a system of symbols strung together to communicate thought.

Material culture (p. 60) comprises the tools and techniques that improve our ability to take what we want from nature.

Norms (p. 60) are standards of behaviour or generally accepted ways of doing things.

Postmodernism (p. 69) is characterized by an eclectic mixing of cultural elements, the erosion of authority, and the decline of consensus around core values.

Production (p. 60) is the human capacity to make and use tools. It improves our ability to take what we want from nature.

The **rights revolution** (p. 69) is the process by which excluded groups have obtained equal rights under the law and in practice.

Rites of passage (p. 70) are cultural ceremonies that mark transitions from one stage of life to another or from life to death.

Sanctions (p. 61) are rewards and punishments intended to ensure conformity to cultural guidelines.

The **Sapir-Whorf thesis** (p. 62) holds that we experience certain things in our environment and form concepts about those things. We then develop language to express our concepts. Finally, language itself influences how we see the world.

The system of **social control** (p. 61) is the means by which members of society ensure that people conform to cultural guidelines.

A **society** (p. 59) involves people interacting socially and sharing culture, usually in a defined geographical area.

A **subculture** (p. 76) is a distinctive set of values, norms, and practices within a larger culture.

A **symbol** (p. 60) is anything that carries a particular meaning, including the components of language, mathematical notations, and signs. Symbols allow us to engage in abstraction.

NOTES

1. New forms of society on the Internet ("virtual communities") show that physical proximity is not always a necessary part of the definition.

2. Many children of Indigenous Canadians were put into residential schools in the twentieth century, and many of them were physically and sexually abused by the ministers, priests, and nuns who ran these schools. Many Indigenous Canadians also claim that much land was taken from them illegally. Some 21 000 Japanese Canadians living within 160 kilometres of the Pacific Coast, three-quarters of them Canadian citizens, were forcibly moved to prisoner-of-war, internment, and work camps in 1942. They lost most of their property. Descendants of many Chinese Canadians were forced to pay an exorbitant "head tax" in the late nineteenth and early twentieth centuries, the purpose of which was to encourage them to leave the country. The Nazis enslaved and slaughtered millions of European Jews in World War II and stole their property. Survivors, a considerable number of them residing in Canada, later sought and received reparations from the German and Swiss governments.

CHAPTER 4

SOCIALIZATION

Lisa Strohschein
UNIVERSITY OF ALBERTA

SOURCE: © HeardInLondon/Demotix/Corbis.

AFTER READING THIS CHAPTER, YOU WILL BE ABLE TO:

- Appreciate the degree to which social interaction unleashes human abilities, including the ability to see oneself as different from others.

- Evaluate how stages in life are influenced by the historical period in which people live.

- Contrast the declining socializing influence of the family with the rising socializing influence of schools, peer groups, and the mass media over the past century.

- Compare the greater speed, frequency, and comprehensiveness of identity change today with the lower speed, frequency, and comprehensiveness of identity change just a few decades ago.

THE CONSEQUENCES OF SOCIAL ISOLATION IN CHILDHOOD

One day in 1800, a 10- or 11-year-old boy was captured in the woods in southern France. He was filthy, naked, unable to speak, and had not been toilet trained. The boy was brought to Paris to be scrutinized by medical experts. How had he come to be living in the forest? A scar on his neck suggested a horrific past. Was the boy an unwanted child, left to die in the woods after an unknown person slit his throat? No one knew.

Equally challenging was determining what was wrong with the boy, who came to be known as "the savage of Aveyron." Some experts said the boy was mentally retarded, others that he was a deaf-mute. One ambitious young doctor, Jean-Marc Itard, expressed a different view. He hypothesized that the boy's strangeness might be due to the effects of being raised in extreme isolation. Intrigued by the mysterious boy, Itard took over his care, called him Victor, and conducted an initial assessment of his capabilities. Next, Itard tried to teach Victor a few basic skills. The task was daunting. As he began his work, Itard recorded in his journal that this was a "disgustingly dirty child affected with spasmodic movements, and often convulsions, who swayed back and forth ceaselessly like certain animals in a zoo, who bit and scratched those who opposed him, who showed no affection for those who took care of him, and who was, in short, indifferent to everything and attentive to nothing" (Lane, 1976: 4, quoting from Itard's journal).

Itard's efforts to train Victor led to great fame for the doctor but little success with Victor. After a few years of trying to teach Victor how to read and communicate with others, Itard gave up. He wrote up his findings in a formal report, concluding that the project to educate and civilize Victor had been a total failure. Despite intensive training, Victor never mastered speech, displayed limited intellectual engagement, and failed to develop emotional attachments to people (Benzaquen, 2006).

Sadly, other cases of children lacking human contact at a critical stage in their development have emerged over the years. An especially shocking case, because of its mass scale, became known in 1989. That year, on Christmas Day, the rule of a corrupt Romanian dictator came to an abrupt end when he and his wife were executed by their own people.

In the following months, the world learned the chilling details of how children had been treated by the regime. Because of harsh economic conditions, nearly 100 000 children had been abandoned by their families. Left in the hands of the state, the children were warehoused in orphanages that provided little food and even less love. The toll appeared greatest for those who had been abandoned at birth. Starving and listless, many babies were also strangely cross-eyed. Had they developed a strange illness? No. Because they had spent their short lives lying on their backs and staring at the blank ceiling overhead, these infants never had the opportunity to focus on objects, an activity that would have allowed them to develop their vision properly.

Stunned by the deplorable conditions of the orphanages, families around the world descended on Romania to adopt the children. Approximately 600 of them were adopted by Canadians. Seizing the opportunity to learn more about the long-term effects of early life deprivation, researchers in Canada and elsewhere began to study some of these children. The researchers wondered whether the children could overcome their early neglect and grow up to become normal adults.

The results were mixed. A decade later, Romanian orphans who had been adopted by Canadians had caught up to Canadian children in weight and height (Le Mare and Audet, 2006). However, as in Victor's case, researchers discovered that the emotional scars of neglect run deep. The brains of the adopted Romanian children were smaller and less developed than they should have been, resulting in a wide array of emotional and intellectual deficits. As young adults, many reported struggling to fit in and some had been convicted of crimes.

The lesson seems clear. During the first few months of life, children must be exposed to other humans who will care for and love them. Otherwise, the neural structures that are responsible for emotional and intellectual development wither and die (Nelson, Fox, and Zeanah, 2014).

The examples of Victor and the Romanian orphans suggest that the ability to become human is only a potential. To be actualized, **socialization** must unleash the potential. Socialization is the process by which people learn to function in their culture. They do so by (1) entering and disengaging from a succession of roles and (2) becoming aware of themselves as they interact with others. A **role** is the behaviour expected of a person occupying a particular position in society.

1. What evidence suggests that children require contact with others to realize their human potential?
2. How and why do you think prolonged social isolation might affect adults differently from the way it affects young children?

FORMATION OF THE SELF

To paint a picture of the socialization process, we first review the main theories of how a sense of self develops during childhood, during which the contours of the self are first formed.

Driven by elemental needs, infants cry out. Those who hear their cries, usually their parents, respond by providing the infant with food, comfort, and affection. At first, infants do not seem able to distinguish themselves from their main caregivers. However, continued social interaction enables infants to begin developing a self-image or sense of **self**—a set of ideas and attitudes about who they are as independent beings.

SIGMUND FREUD

Austrian psychoanalyst Sigmund Freud proposed the first social-scientific interpretation of the process by which the self emerges (Freud, 1962 [1930]), 1973 [1915–17]). He noted that infants demand immediate gratification but begin to form a self-image when their demands are denied—when, for example, parents decide not to feed and comfort them every time they wake up in the middle of the night. The parents' refusal at first incites howls of protest. However, infants soon learn to eat more before going to bed, sleep for longer periods, and go back to sleep if they wake up. Equally important, the infant begins to sense that its needs differ from those of its parents, it has an existence independent of others, and it must somehow balance its needs with the realities of life.

Because of many such lessons in self-control, the child eventually develops a sense of what constitutes appropriate behaviour and a moral sense of right and wrong. Soon a personal conscience crystallizes. It is a storehouse of cultural standards. In addition, a psychological mechanism develops that normally balances the pleasure-seeking and restraining components of the self. Earlier thinkers believed that the self emerges naturally, the way a seed germinates. In a revolutionary departure from previous thinking on the subject, Freud argued that only social interaction allows the self to emerge.

CHARLES HORTON COOLEY

American scholars took ideas about the emergence of the self in a still more sociological direction. Notably, Charles Horton Cooley introduced the idea of the "looking-glass self," making him a founder of the symbolic interactionist tradition and an early contributor to the sociological study of socialization.

Cooley observed that when we interact with others, they gesture and react to us. This allows us to imagine how we appear to them. We then judge how others evaluate us. Finally, from these judgments we develop a self-concept or a set of feelings or ideas about who we are. In other words, our feelings about who we are depend largely on how we see ourselves evaluated by others. Just as we see our physical body reflected in a mirror, so we see our social selves reflected in people's gestures and reactions to us (Cooley, 1902).

For instance, when teachers evaluate students negatively, students may develop a negative self-concept that causes them to do poorly in school. Poor performance may have as much to do with teachers' negative evaluations as with students' innate abilities (Sanchez and Roda, 2003). Here we have the hallmarks of what came to be known as *symbolic interactionism*—the idea that in the course of face-to-face communication, people engage in a creative process of attaching meaning to things.

GEORGE HERBERT MEAD

George Herbert Mead (1934) further developed Cooley's idea of the looking-glass self. Like Freud, Mead noted that a subjective and impulsive aspect of the self is present from birth. Mead called it simply the **I**. Again like Freud, Mead argued that a repository of culturally approved standards emerges as part of the self during social interaction. Mead called this objective, social component of the self the **me**. However, while Freud focused on the denial of the impulsive side of the self as the mechanism that generates the self's objective side, Mead drew attention to the unique human capacity to "take the role of the other" as the source of the me.

Mead's Stages of Development: Role-Taking

Mead argued that the self develops in four stages of role-taking:

1. At first, children learn to use language and other symbols by imitating important people in their

lives, such as their mother and father. Mead called such people **significant others**.

2. Next, children pretend to be other people. That is, they use their imaginations to role-play in games such as "house," "school," and "doctor."

3. Then, about the time they reach the age of seven, children learn to play complex games that require them to take the role of several other people simultaneously. In baseball, for example, the infielders have to be aware of the expectations of everyone in the infield. A shortstop may catch a line drive. If she wants to make a double play, she must almost instantly be aware that a runner is trying to reach second base and that the person playing second base expects her to throw there. If she hesitates, she probably cannot execute the double play.

4. Once a child can think in this complex way, she can begin the fourth stage in the development of the self, which involves taking the role of what Mead called the **generalized other**. Years of experience may teach an individual that other people, employing the cultural standards of their society, usually regard her as funny, temperamental, or intelligent. A person's image of these cultural standards and how they are applied to her is what Mead meant by the generalized other.

PAUL WILLIS

Mead focused on childhood socialization. More recently, British sociologist Paul Willis (1990) usefully emphasized the degree to which identity formation continues among teens and young adults. He also paid more attention than Mead did to variations in the social contexts within which teens and young adults forge, maintain, and transform their identities.

For Willis, class, racial, ethnic, gender, and regional differences are associated with differences in socialization patterns. In addition, the institutions to which people belong provide them with symbolic resources that influence how they can express themselves and how others see them. These facts do not mean that people automatically learn the norms and values of the social contexts in which they happen to find themselves. They learn norms and values but also experiment and make choices from the variety of socialization opportunities they confront. Moreover, they are often helped by cultural industries, which seek to profit from the desire of young people to have fun, express themselves, and be stylish. Mass

Abby, a character on the popular TV show *NCIS*, represents the Goth subculture to her many fans.
SOURCE: © CBS Photo Archive / Darren Michaels via Getty Images.

consumption of music, movies, and clothing are the accepted means by which youth experiment with identity and find their authentic selves.

Consider the goth subculture, which has been around since the 1980s and remains popular today. Fascinated by freakishness, death, and all things macabre, goths have a taste for sinister music and horror films. They dress in dark clothing, dye their hair black (sometimes streaked with red or purple highlights), ring their eyes with dark eyeliner, paint their fingernails with black nail polish, and may adorn their bodies with piercings. Goths are inspired by the role models they see on TV. Tina from *Glee* and Abby from *NCIS* are just two of the goth characters youth may try to emulate. The positive depiction of goths in the mass media sends youth the message that a goth is a desirable identity, one of a host of identities they may choose from.

By stressing the links among creativity, identity, and social context, Willis suggests that young people take advantage of every opportunity to make the everyday world around them meaningful and enjoyable. Like Mead, he reminds us that human beings are creative and strategic social actors, not pawns of vast, impersonal forces. Still, Willis acknowledges that social categories make a difference. The character of your socialization depends on the groups and institutions to which you belong and your statuses within those groups and institutions.

Until now, we have focused on how the self is shaped by social interaction and social institutions. Such reflections help us to see that we are a product of the society into which we are born. However, we must also recognize that society and its institutions are not static entities. They are always changing. The world that you were born into is not the same as the world into which your parents were born, and the world will be different yet again a generation from now. So when we say that society lives in us and makes us who we are (see Chapter 1), we are also saying society aims to create the type of people it needs to perpetuate its own existence.

Of course, the fit between a given society and the people it creates may not be tight. When enough people perceive that society does not work as it needs to, they protest. The outcry can lead society to adapt its institutions to accommodate their demands. For sociologists, then, thinking about how lives reflect the imprint of society, even as society itself is changing, reveals the full dynamic of the socialization process.

TIME FOR REVIEW

1. What makes Cooley's depiction of the "looking glass self" a *sociological* insight?
2. According to Mead, what is the distinction between the me and the I?
3. Why is it important to view youth as individuals who experiment with and choose among different identities?

AT THE INTERSECTION OF BIOGRAPHY AND HISTORY

Mead highlighted how the self emerges in stages. Yet the formation of the self is more than a developmental process. A person's potential is also shaped by the unique slice of history through which he or she lives. Said differently, success and failure in life occur in part because of circumstances beyond our control. We tend to think that we are masters of our destiny but we are equally a product of our society: What we can become is made possible (or not) by the historical circumstances in which we live.

To illustrate this point, let us draw on the work of sociologist Norbert Elias, who compared the biographies of Mozart and Beethoven, two of the most well-known composers of all time. Although their musical legacy is undeniable today, their life stories are quite different.

Mozart was born fewer than 20 years before Beethoven but enjoyed far less financial success. The reason, according to Elias, was that Mozart lived during a time when musicians had few options to support themselves outside of a patronage system in which wealthy individuals sponsored a few lucky musicians for pleasure and prestige. Mozart, who resented being treated as an inferior, broke away from his patron, and tried instead to support himself by selling his music. However, times were tough and few people could afford to pay him for his work. Mozart was often in debt and struggled to keep his household afloat.

In contrast, Beethoven's career took off when economic conditions were on the upswing and many people were willing to pay for musical compositions. Consequently, when Beethoven too decided to leave the comfort of his patron, he was flooded with requests for his music from wealthy people. He thrived in this environment, never having to worry about where his next meal might come from. Had Beethoven been born within a year or two of Mozart, his life would have more closely resembled that of Mozart. Their contrasting fortunes depended less on their own actions and more on their differing historical circumstances.

What is true in this regard for individuals is true for the characteristic way that entire civilizations develop: Identifiable social circumstances in specific historical situations leave their imprint on individuals' socialization processes and on the cultures of entire civilizations.

Contrast ancient China with ancient Greece. In large part because of complex irrigation needs, the rice agriculture of ancient southern China required substantial cooperation among neighbours. It had to be centrally organized in an elaborate hierarchy within a large state. Harmony and social order were therefore central to ancient Chinese life. Ancient Chinese thinking, in turn, tended to stress the importance of mutual social obligation and consensus rather than debate. Ancient Chinese philosophy focused on the way whole systems, not discrete analytical categories, cause processes and events.

In contrast, the hills and seashores of ancient Greece were suited to small-scale herding and fishing, so ancient Greece was less socially complex than ancient China was and it was more politically decentralized. It gave its citizens more personal freedom. Consequently, philosophies tended to be analytical, which means, among other things, that processes and events were viewed as the result of discrete categories rather than whole systems. Markedly different cultures—patterns of behaviour and styles of thinking—grew up on these different cognitive foundations. Civilizational differences depended less on the innate characteristics of the ancient Chinese and Greek "mind" than on the structure of their societies in their formative years.

Sociologists who study socialization focus on the following questions: How does society shape identities, attitudes, and behaviour as individuals move through life? How do societies differ in the ways they organize life transitions, life stages, and life trajectories? How are changing societies, changing biographical patterns, and the subjective experiences of individuals related to one another? In the next sections of this chapter, we touch on each of these questions (Shanahan and MacMillan, 2008).

SOCIOLOGY OF THE LIFE COURSE

All individuals pass through distinct stages of life, which, taken in its entirety, sociologists call the **life course**. As individuals sequentially move through the stages of life on the path from birth to death, they experience a predictable pattern of age-graded roles and responsibilities. In that sense, the life course can be thought of as a social structure: Our life courses have been organized for us by the society we live in.

Sometimes the stages of life are marked by **rites of passage**, or rituals signifying the transition from one life stage to another (Fried and Fried, 1980). Baptism, confirmation, the bar mitzvah and bat mitzvah, high-school graduation, college or university convocation, the wedding ceremony, and the funeral are among the best-known rites of passage in Canada.

Rituals do not mark all transitions in the life course, however. For example, in Canada, people often complain about the "terrible twos," when toddlers first begin to defy parental demands in their attempt to gain autonomy. Similarly, when some Canadian men reach the age of about 40, they experience a "midlife crisis," in which they attempt to defy the passage of time and regain their youth. (It never works.)

The age-graded roles and expectations that define each stage of life vary from one society and historical period to the next. For example, most societies have laws that stipulate the minimum age for purchasing tobacco products, drinking alcohol, driving a vehicle, and voting. As the public became more disapproving of cigarette smoking over the past half century, there was a gradual increase in the legal age at which one could buy tobacco products in Canada. Today, depending on what province you live in, the minimum age one can purchase cigarettes may be 18 or 19. Similarly, most modern societies used to treat 65 as the age at which one became eligible for a pension but longer life expectancy meant that a growing number of retirees were likely to exhaust their savings

before they died. To avoid this problem, several countries around the world, including Canada, have delayed eligibility for the receipt of pension benefits.

In the same way, each society sets its own rules about when a person becomes an adult. In preindustrial societies, adulthood arrived soon after puberty. In Japan, a person becomes an adult at 20. In Canada, adulthood arrives at 18 (the legal voting age and the legal drinking age in some provinces) or 19 (the legal drinking age in other provinces). The Critical Sociology: Protest and Policy box describes shifting Canadian attitudes and behaviours toward the age at which one should marry. It reminds us that age-graded roles are embedded in institutions in ways that serve the interests of society and facilitate the journey of its members through the life course. Because societies change over time, no society structures the life course the same way for very long.

Childhood and Adolescence

Did you know that the *number* of stages in the life course varies historically and across societies? For instance, childhood was a brief stage of development in medieval Europe (Ariès, 1962 [1960]). In contrast, childhood is a prolonged stage of development in rich societies today, and adolescence is a new phase of development that was virtually unknown just a few hundred years ago (Gillis, 1981).

How did childhood and adolescence come to be recognized as distinct stages of life? In preindustrial societies, children were considered small adults. From a young age, they were expected to conform as much as possible to the norms of the adult world. They were put to work as soon as they could contribute to the welfare of their families. This often meant doing chores by the age of 5 and working full-time by the age of 10 or 12. Marriage, and thus the achievement of full adulthood, was common by the age of 15 or 16.

Children in Europe and North America fit this pattern until the late seventeenth century, when the idea of childhood as a distinct stage of life emerged. At that time, the feeling grew among well-to-do Europeans and North Americans that boys should be permitted to play games and receive an education that would allow them to develop the emotional, physical, and intellectual skills they would need as adults. Girls continued to be treated as "little women" (the title of Louisa May Alcott's 1869 novel) until the nineteenth century. Most working-class boys did not enjoy much of a childhood until the twentieth century. Only in the last century or

CRITICAL SOCIOLOGY: PROTEST AND POLICY   THE MODERN EFFORT TO BAN CHILD MARRIAGE

Between 1663 and 1673, France paid about 800 young women, known as *filles de roi* ("the King's girls"), to migrate to New France and provided them with a dowry so they could be married off to single male settlers. It was a policy intended to solve a pressing social problem. A harsh climate and difficult living conditions had created a massive gender imbalance, with men far outnumbering women. To strengthen France's claim on the land, young families were needed to ensure the survival and future growth of the population. *Filles de roi*, some of whom were as young as 12, were put on boats headed for Canada. Besieged by desperate bachelors, many were married the moment they landed. Children followed in short order.

Today, the average age at first marriage in Canada is around 29 years for women and 31 years for men (Statistics Canada, 2011; see Figure 4.1). To be married at an early age is not only seen as undesirable by most Canadians, it is against the law. Those under the age of 18 cannot marry except when they are pregnant or if their parents consent to the marriage.

These legal exceptions may soon be a thing of the past, however. In 2014, the federal government proposed new legislation that would prevent those under the age of 18 from getting married for any reason. Called the Zero Tolerance for Barbaric Cultural Practices Act, the legislation aims to curb the behaviour of newcomers to Canada, particularly those who come from cultures that condone and even encourage marriage at an early age.

What makes child marriage a focus of government attention and policymaking is that regulating the age at which citizens marry can help a society accomplish its goals. Given that child marriage almost always correlates with a higher number of births, encouraging young girls to marry settlers in the New World was an easy way for France to boost its population and expand its hold on the land. Contrast this situation with contemporary Canada, where child marriage is seen as a threat to Canada's economic well-being. To maintain a competitive edge in the global economy, Canada must encourage its citizens to acquire advanced skills. Because child marriage often puts an abrupt end to schooling, thus limiting children from reaching their full potential as adults, Canada cannot afford to let child marriage become widespread.

Critical Thinking Questions

1. Do you think a law banning child marriage can work? Why, or why not?

2. Do you think a law banning child marriage would violate Canada's multiculturalism policy, which advocates respect for cultural differences?

FIGURE 4.1   AVERAGE AGE AT FIRST MARRIAGE, BY GENDER, 1921–2008

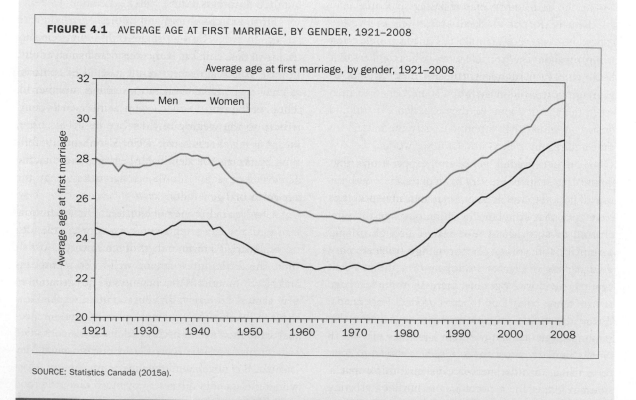

SOURCE: Statistics Canada (2015a).

so has the idea of childhood as a distinct and prolonged period of life became universal in the West.

The idea of childhood emerged when and where it did because of social necessity and social possibility. Prolonged childhood was necessary in societies that required better-educated adults to do increasingly complex work because childhood gave young people a chance to prepare for adult life. Prolonged childhood was possible in societies where improved hygiene and nutrition allowed most people to live more than 35 years, the average lifespan in Europe in the early seventeenth century. In other words, before the late seventeenth century, most people did not live long enough to permit the luxury of childhood. Moreover, young people faced no social need for a period of extended training and development before the comparatively simple demands of adulthood were thrust upon them.

In general, wealthier and more complex societies whose populations enjoy a long average life expectancy stretch out the pre-adult period of life. For example, we saw that in seventeenth-century Europe, most people reached mature adulthood by the age of about 16. In contrast, in Canada and other postmodern countries, most people are considered to reach mature adulthood only in their early 30s, by which time they have completed their formal education, married, and "settled down." Once teenagers were relieved of adult responsibilities, people had to coin a new term to describe the teenage years: *adolescence*. Subsequently, the term *young adulthood* entered popular usage as an increasingly large number of people in their late teens, 20s, and early 30s delayed marriage to attend university.

AGE COHORT

As you pass through the life course, you learn new patterns of behaviour that are common to people about the same age as you. Sociologically speaking, a category of people born in the same range of years is called an **age cohort**. For example, all Canadians born in 1998 form an age cohort. **Age roles** are patterns of behaviour that we expect of people in different age cohorts. Age roles form an important part of our sense of self and others (Riley, Foner, and Waring, 1988). As we pass through the stages of the life course, we assume different age roles. To put it simply, a child is supposed to act like a child, an older person like an older person. We may think that a 5-year-old dressed in a suit is cute but look askance at a lone 50-year-old on a merry-go-round. "Act your age" is a demand that we make when people of any age do not conform to their age roles. Many age roles are informally known by character types, such as the "rebellious teenager" and the "wise old woman."

We find it natural that children in the same age cohort, such as preschoolers in a park, should play together or that people of similar age cluster together at parties. Conversely, many people find romance and marriage between people widely separated by age problematic and even repulsive.

At the same time, no two cohorts have the same experience as they pass through the age structure. As each cohort confronts its own sequence of social events and circumstances, its members both change and are changed by their experiences.

GENERATION

A **generation** is a special type of age cohort. Many people think of a generation as people born within a 15- to 30-year span. Sociologists, however, usually define *generation* more narrowly. From a sociological point of view, a generation comprises members of an age cohort who have unique and formative experiences during youth. Age cohorts are statistically convenient categories, but members of a generation form a group with a collective identity and shared values.

Not all cohorts can become a generation. Generations are most likely to form during times of rapid social change. When society is in upheaval, young people seeking to find their way in the world can no longer rely on the predictable patterns of the past but must carve out new trails. Revolutionary movements, whether in politics or the arts, are often led by members of a young generation who aggressively displace the ideas of the older generation (Eisenstadt, 1956; Mannheim, 1952).

Canada has five identifiable generations (Statistics Canada, 2012; see Table 4.1). In describing them, we recognize that generations tend to be clearest at their centre and fuzzier at their boundaries. The generation that is currently passing away and whose experiences are increasingly known only through history books is often called "the greatest generation." Born between the early 1900s and 1928, members of this generation were at least 88 years old in 2016. They are called the greatest generation because they came of age during the Great Depression (1929–1939) and then went on to endure World War II (1939–1945). By rising to the formidable challenges of these two events, the greatest generation laid the groundwork for economic prosperity and stability in the decades ahead.

TABLE 4.1   FIVE CANADIAN GENERATIONS

GENERATION	AGE IN 2016	IN THEIR PRIME
The greatest generation (born between the early 1900s and 1928)	88+	 Soldiers who took part in the raid on Dieppe during World War II (1939–45) disembarking from a Royal Navy destroyer in England in 1942. Members of this generation also had to face the Great Depression. SOURCE: Army [Numerical] (R112) Collection, Library and Archives Canada, accession number 1967-052 NPC, item 8243, PA-183765.
The silent generation (born between 1929 and 1945)	71–87	 Sometimes called the *traditionalist generation* because of their shared values of hard work, thriftiness, and conformity. Craving security, they are often characterized as risk-averse, patriotic, and community-minded, but not especially innovative. SOURCE: © ClassicStock / Masterfile.
Baby boomers (born between 1946 and 1964)	51–70	 The Woodstock festival in the summer of 1969 was one of the markers of the baby boomers' cultural revolution. They have been characterized as idealistic, tolerant, and creative, and, at work, as highly competitive, independent, and innovative. SOURCE: © Ralph Ackerman/Getty Images.

(continued)

TABLE 4.1 *(CONTINUED)*

GENERATION	AGE IN 2016	IN THEIR PRIME
Generation X (born between 1965 and 1981)	35–51	

Members of this generation faced a period of relatively slow economic growth and a job market glutted by baby boomers. Fortunately, the lives of Generation Xers eventually improved as they settled into careers. They are sometimes described as skeptical, individualistic, adept with technology, and conservative with money.

SOURCE: © Pictorial Press Ltd / Alamy.

| Millennials (born between about 1982 and 1995) | 21–34 | |

Are called "Millennials" because they came of age in the early twenty-first century. Due to increased immigration, they are more ethnically diverse than previous generations of Canadians and are also on track to becoming the most educated generation in history. Although the Great Recession of 2008–09 put a damper on the career aspirations of some, Millennials are environmentally conscious, have an unshakable faith that they can make a positive difference in their world, and are always searching for new experiences.

SOURCE: © Ridofranz/iStock/Getty Images Plus.

The greatest generation was followed by "the silent generation," members of whom became the parents of Canada's most well-known generation, the "baby-boomers." Members of the silent generation were born between 1929 and 1945; in 2016, they were between the ages of 71 and 87. The silent generation is sometimes called the *traditionalist generation* because of their shared values of hard work, thriftiness, and conformity. Occasionally, they are referred to as the *lucky generation* because they were old enough to be shaped by the events of World War II, but too young to have experienced combat. Craving security, the silent generation is risk-averse, patriotic, and community-minded. As a generation, its chief shortcoming is that it was not especially innovative. Its members often felt threatened by change.

As soldiers returned home after World War II and wanted to settle down to family life, Canada experienced a baby boom that lasted until the mid-1960s. During this period, approximately 400 000 children were born each year. In 2016, baby boomers between the ages of 52 and 70 will make up approximately one-third of Canada's population. When this cohort came of age in the 1960s and 1970s, they turned the stolid, comfortable world of their parents upside down. Baby boomers were the leading edge of a cultural revolution. The war in Vietnam, Trudeaumania, Canada's centenary, and popular music (the songs of the Beatles, the Rolling Stones, and the Guess Who) bound them together. Baby boomers have been characterized as idealistic, tolerant, and creative. In the workplace, they are highly competitive, independent, and innovative. Their main weakness is the need for instant gratification. Because of their relative greed and self-absorption, baby boomers are often vilified for leaving massive debt for future generations (Higgs and Gilleard, 2010).

"Generation X" followed the baby boomers. Born between 1965 and 1981, they were between 35 and 51 years old in 2016. Members of Generation X faced a period of relatively slow economic growth and a job market glutted by the baby boomers. Consequently, many of them resented having to take so-called McJobs when they entered the labour force. Douglas Coupland, the Vancouver novelist who invented the term *Generation X*, cuttingly defined a McJob as a "low pay, low-prestige, low-dignity, low-benefit, no-future job in the service sector. Frequently considered a satisfying career choice by people who have never held one" (Coupland, 1991: 5). Fortunately, the lives of Generation Xers eventually improved as they settled into careers.

As a group, Gen Xers tend to be skeptical, individualistic, adept with technology, and conservative with money (Gordinier, 2008; Watson, 2013). They are entrepreneurial but desire work–life balance. Moreover, they have little loyalty to their employer: If they see a better job, they will switch. Their lack of loyalty is sometimes seen as a liability, as is their difficulty in working collaboratively.

Finally, the "Millennials," born between about 1982 and 1995, are so named because they came of age in the early twenty-first century (Howe and Strauss, 2009). They are also sometimes referred to as *Generation Y, Generation Next,* or *Generation Me*. Because of the growing number of immigrants to Canada who come from around the world, Millennials are more ethnically diverse than are previous generations of Canadians. They are also on track to becoming the most educated generation in history. But don't be misled into thinking that being well educated has helped them get ahead. The Great Recession (2008–09) put a damper on many of their career aspirations. Today, Millennials are likely to be struggling to fit into the labour market. Many of them live with their parents and are uncertain when they will finally be able to make it on their own.

Although their parents were sometimes overly involved in their lives, Millennials are in general emotionally close to their parents (Winograd and Hais, 2011). Millennials are environmentally conscious, have an unshakable faith that they can make a positive difference in their world, and are always searching for new experiences (Pew Research Center, 2014). They are passionate and open with their opinions. They value teamwork and they take technological advances such as the Internet for granted.

Do you consider yourself a Millennial? You may find that you share some of the values that define Millennials, but it is equally likely that a new generation is on the verge of forming. If so, what values and experiences do you think this new generation will share?

TIME FOR REVIEW

1. In what ways do the number and duration of life stages vary across societies and historical periods?
2. What transforms a cohort into a generation?

HOW SOCIALIZATION WORKS

Why is it that people turn out the way they do? A detailed answer to this question is complex, but the basic principles are not: People are surrounded and influenced by real or imagined others, who constitute a person's **social environment**. To satisfy individual needs and interests, every person needs to adapt to his or her environment. **Adaptation** involves arranging one's actions to maximize the degree to which an environment satisfies one's needs and interests.

The challenge of learning to ride a bicycle illustrates these concepts. If a girl wants to ride a bicycle, she cannot act any way she likes. To be successful, she must adjust her behaviour to satisfy the characteristics of the physical environment. In this case, the dominant environmental characteristic is gravity. On her first attempt, the novice cyclist will do her best, but her adaptive behaviour will likely be imperfect. As a result, the environment provides feedback in the form of skinned knees, scraped hands, and bruised legs. These are all signals that the environment is not cooperating. To gain cooperation, and satisfy her bike-riding interests, the girl must learn how to balance herself on the bicycle. As she acquires the necessary skills, she can pay less attention to the motions she uses to stay on the bike and focus instead on arriving at her chosen destination.

The same process occurs in social environments, each of which has distinctive requirements. Different types of families make different kinds of demands on their children. Different kinds of schools have distinctive expectations of students. Neighbourhood environments differ, and so do friendship groups and every other social setting. Each of these environments shapes its participants through socialization. In an abusive family, the adaptive strategies children learn, and the kind of people they become, are very different from what they learn and become in a warm, supportive family.

Prolonged exposure to a given social environment mimics what happens for the experienced cyclist. One no longer needs to maintain awareness of the social forces that have made us who we are. Through habit and repetition, the social structures surrounding us become invisible. This is why it is so difficult to stand outside of our own experiences: We see the world through the lens of our own learning, forgetting that the lessons taught to others are not necessarily the same as our own.

As these examples make clear, socialization is fundamentally an evolutionary process. Simply stated, the steps in the process are as follows: (1) In any environment, a person acts on the basis of his or her existing personal characteristics and interests. (2) The environment responds to the person's actions more or less cooperatively. (3) The environmental response shapes the individual's conduct by either reinforcing existing patterns (cooperation) or encouraging change (resistance). In short, individual character leads to actions to which environments respond selectively. When environments respond cooperatively—when they satisfy individual needs—the rewards reinforce existing individual characteristics. When environments frustrate individual needs, change (learning) is encouraged.

AGENTS OF SOCIALIZATION

Each society has a range of different institutions that prepare and guide successive cohorts through each stage of life. In the following sections, we discuss in turn families, schools, peer groups, and the mass media as "agents of socialization."

FAMILIES

The family is the most important agent of **primary socialization**, the process of mastering the basic skills required to function in society during childhood. The family is well suited to providing the kind of careful, intimate attention required for primary socialization.

As the first major agent of socialization, families help children to learn basic skills and internalize the values of their society.
SOURCE: © Meiko Arquillos/Getty Images.

It is a small group, its members are in frequent face-to-face contact, and most parents love their children and are highly motivated to care for them. These characteristics make most families ideal for teaching small children everything from language to their place in the world.

The family into which you are born also exerts an *enduring* influence over the course of your life (see the Critical Sociology: Social Inequality box). Consider the long-term effect of the family's religious atmosphere.

Research shows that the main way religious groups grow is by recruiting and retaining children whose parents already belong to the group (Bibby, 2001: 115). Parents are the key source of their children's religious identification throughout life. Even Canadians who say they have abandoned the religious faith of their parents—or claim to have no religious identification—typically readopt the religious identities of their parents when they participate in rites of passage, such as marriage and baptism (Bibby, 2001: 200).

CRITICAL SOCIOLOGY: SOCIAL INEQUALITY   INEQUALITY ACROSS THE LIFE COURSE

In the Scandinavian countries (Finland, Norway, Sweden, and Denmark), one's economic status in childhood does not strongly determine one's status in adulthood (Torche, 2015). These countries tend to offset inherited disadvantages by providing pathways out of poverty for those who are motivated to succeed. In contrast, in the United States, Italy, and South Africa, if you are the child of wealthy parents then chances are good that you will be wealthy as an adult. If your parents are poor, you will find it difficult to escape poverty as an adult. There are simply too few ways in which one can break the cycle of disadvantage, no matter how hard one tries.

In every country, the resources parents have at their disposal are factors that shape how their children turn out. In Canada, only wealthier households can afford to send their children to the best schools, hire tutors for extra lessons, and purchase educational materials that foster learning. Consequently, wealthier children are primed to excel academically and so are more likely than are poor children to attain high levels of education and find financially rewarding jobs.

What wealthier parents can buy for their children represents only part of the advantage they give their children. Sociologist Annette Lareau (2003) described a profound difference between the ways in which middle-class parents socialize their children and how working-class parents interact with their children. Middle-class parents engaged in what Lareau called *concerted cultivation*, meaning that these parents felt it their duty to help their children develop to their fullest potential. They saw their children as "projects," and put the children into many different kinds of organized activities, including arts and team sports. It wasn't just that they could afford to do this; from their perspective, they couldn't afford *not* to expose their children to all that life had to offer. Middle-class parents also closely supervised what their children did and frequently sought their children's input on day-to-day affairs. They expected their children to negotiate with them.

Working-class parents wanted their children to succeed too, but they were more likely to believe that child development is spontaneous, so they took a more hands-off approach to parenting. The result was that children in working-class households had a lot of unstructured time. Mostly they watched television or hung out with friends. In addition, working-class parents spoke less frequently to their children than did middle-class parents, and instead of negotiating with their children, working-class parents almost always expected their children to obey them without question.

Other research shows that middle-class parents also approach their child's teacher differently than do working-class parents (Gillies, 2005). Middle-class parents are vocal advocates for their children. They insist that their children are bright and deserving of the best education they can get. On the other hand, working-class parents approach the parent–teacher interview through the lens of their own difficult experiences in school as a child, so they often limit the time they spend with the teacher. When they do talk to the teacher, it is the teacher who generally leads the conversation. Consequently, it is the concerns of the teacher that drives the exchange, not the interests of the parents. No wonder middle-class children tend to perform better in school than do working-class children. Their parents have the resources to support their success and they socialize their children accordingly.

Critical Thinking Questions

1. As of 2015, the Children's Fitness Tax Credit allows parents to claim up to $1000 for each child registered in a program that involves physical activity. Who would be more likely to benefit from the Children's Fitness Tax Credit—middle-class families or working-class families? Does the tax credit narrow the differences between social classes or potentially increase the differences?

2. In what ways might living in a socioeconomically deprived neighbourhood magnify the effects of growing up in a poor household?

Do not think, however, that socialization within the family is solely a top-down transmission of values, where parents wield all the power in shaping who their children become. Children are not passive recipients of social processes. Rather, they give meaning to their experiences and actively participate in their own socialization. This means that the relationship between parents and children is bidirectional. Each influences the other.

Consider the experience of first-time parents. No instruction manual accompanies children when they are born. It is only through growing familiarity with their child's temperament and needs that parents learn which parenting strategies work. When a second child is born, parents must learn again. Some tasks may be easier the second time around, but because each child is different, parents often invest as much time getting to know their newborn child as they did for their first child. With only so many hours in a day, parents typically change how they interact with their older children when a new sibling enters the household—they spend less time with them but expect more from them (Strohschein et al., 2008). The lesson here is that because no two children are alike and every family has changing needs, the child socialization process is not the same for each child in the household, nor is it the same for any one child over time.

Note too that the socialization function of the family was more pronounced a century ago, partly because adult family members were more readily available for child care than they are today. As industry grew, families left farming for city work in factories and offices. Especially after the 1950s, many women had to work outside the home for a wage to maintain an adequate standard of living for their families. Fathers partially compensated by spending more time with their children.

As divorce rates began to rise, family life underwent another massive shift. Today, families are less stable and more complex than they were even a few decades ago (Tach, 2015; see Chapter 11, Families). As Canadian children spend less of their childhoods living in a household with both of their parents, contact with fathers in particular has dwindled. Because of these developments, child care—and therefore child socialization—has become a big social problem.

SCHOOLS: FUNCTIONS AND CONFLICTS

For children over the age of five, the child-care problem was partly resolved by the growth of the public school system, which was increasingly responsible for **secondary socialization**, or socialization outside the family after childhood. Industry needed better-trained and better-educated employees. In response, by the early twentieth century, provinces passed laws prescribing school attendance. In 2014, 85 percent of Canadians over the age of 25 had completed high school, and 65 percent had postsecondary qualifications (Statistics Canada, 2015b). Canadians are among the most highly educated people in the world.

Instructing students in academic and vocational subjects is just one part of the school's job. In addition, a **hidden curriculum** teaches students what will be expected of them in the larger society once they graduate. It teaches them how to be conventionally "good citizens" (Jackson, 1990 [1968]).

What is the content of the hidden curriculum? In the family, children tend to be evaluated on the basis of personal and emotional criteria. As students, however, they are led to believe that they are evaluated solely on the basis of their performance on impersonal tests. They are told that similar criteria will be used to evaluate them in the work world. The lesson is only partly true. As you will learn in the following chapters, it is not just performance but also class, gender, sexual orientation, and racial criteria that help determine success in school and in the work world. But the accuracy of the lesson is not the issue here. The important point is that the hidden curriculum has done its job if it convinces students that they are judged on the basis of performance alone. Similarly, a successful hidden curriculum teaches students punctuality, respect for authority, the importance of competition in leading to excellent performance, and other conformist behaviours and beliefs that are expected of good citizens, conventionally defined.

SYMBOLIC INTERACTIONISM AND THE SELF-FULFILLING PROPHECY

The hidden curriculum applies to all students. However, some working-class and minority-group children reject it. They learn from their own experience and the experience of their parents that, because they have limited resources and face discrimination, they are less likely than middle-class and wealthy students are to achieve much even if they play by the rules of the hidden curriculum. They may therefore disrespect authority, perform poorly academically, or drop out. Such actions ensure that they will experience limited upward mobility and economic success.

Learning disciplined work habits is an important part of the socialization that takes place in schools.
SOURCE: Photos.com.

Early in the twentieth century, symbolic interactionists proposed the **Thomas theorem**, which describes the plight of many working-class and minority-group students. The Thomas theorem holds that "situations we define as real become real in their consequences" (Thomas, 1966 [1931]: 301). Symbolic interactionists also developed the closely related idea of the **self-fulfilling prophecy**, an expectation that helps to cause what it predicts.

Self-fulfilling prophecies can affect teachers as well. In one famous study, researchers informed teachers in a primary school that they were going to administer a special test to the pupils to predict intellectual "blooming." In fact, the test was just a standard IQ test. After the test, they told teachers which students they could expect to become high achievers and which they could expect to become low achievers. In fact, the researchers randomly assigned pupils to the two groups. At the end of the year, the researchers repeated the IQ test. They found that the students singled out as high achievers scored significantly higher than those singled out as low achievers. Since the only difference between the two groups of students was that teachers expected one group to do well and the other to do poorly, the researchers concluded that teachers' expectations alone influenced students' performance (Rosenthal and Jacobson, 1968). The clear implication of this research is that if a teacher believes that poor children or children from minority groups are likely to do poorly in school, chances are they will. Subsequent research bears out this finding (Becker, 2013; Rubie-Davis, Hattie, and Hamilton, 2006).

PEER GROUPS

Like schools, **peer groups** are agents of socialization whose importance grew in the twentieth century. Peer groups consist of people who are not necessarily friends but who are about the same age and of similar status. (**Status** refers to a recognized social position that a person can occupy.) Peer groups help children and adolescents separate from their families and develop independent sources of identity. They are especially influential over such lifestyle issues as appearance, social activities, and dating. In fact, from middle childhood through adolescence, the peer group is often the dominant socializing agent.

As you have probably learned from experience, conflict often erupts between the values promoted by the family and those promoted by the adolescent peer group. Adolescent peer groups are controlled by youth, and through them young people begin to develop their own identities. They do this by rejecting some parental values, experimenting with new elements of culture, and engaging in various forms of rebellious behaviour. In contrast, families are controlled by parents. They represent the values of childhood. Under these circumstances, such issues as hair and dress styles; music; curfews; tobacco, drug, and alcohol use; and political views are likely to become points of conflict between the generations.

We should not, however, overstate the significance of adolescent–parent conflict. For one thing, the conflict is usually temporary. Once adolescents mature, their families exert a more enduring influence on many important issues. Research shows that families have more influence than peer groups do on the educational aspirations and the political, social, and religious preferences of adolescents and university students (Crosnoe and Johnson, 2011).

A second reason not to exaggerate the extent of adolescent–parent discord is that peer groups are not just sources of conflict. They also help *integrate* young people into the larger society. A study of preadolescent children in a small North American city illustrates the point. Over eight years, sociologists Patricia and Peter Adler conducted in-depth interviews with school children between the ages of 8 and 11. They lived in a well-to-do community comprising about 80 000 whites and 10 000 racial minority-group members (Adler and Adler, 1998).

In each school they visited, they found a system of cliques arranged in a strict hierarchy, much like the arrangement of classes and racial groups in adult society. In schools with a substantial number of visible-minority students, cliques were divided by race. Visible minority cliques were usually less popular than white cliques were. In all schools, the most popular boys were highly successful in competitive and aggressive, achievement-oriented activities, especially athletics. The most popular girls came from well-to-do and permissive families. One of the main bases of their popularity was that they had the means and the opportunity to participate in the most interesting social activities, ranging from skiing to late-night parties. Physical attractiveness was also an important basis of girls' popularity. Thus, elementary-school peer groups prepared these youngsters for the class and racial inequalities of the adult world and the gender-specific criteria that would often be used to evaluate them as adults, such as competitiveness in the case of boys and physical attractiveness in the case of girls. What we learn from this research is that peer groups function not only to help adolescents form an independent identity by separating them from their families but also to teach them how to adapt to the ways of the larger society.

THE MASS MEDIA

Like the school and the peer group, the mass media have become increasingly important socializing agents in the twenty-first century. The mass media include television, radio, movies, videos, audio recordings, the Internet, newspapers, magazines, and books. The fastest-growing mass medium is the Internet. Worldwide, the number of Internet users jumped from just 36 million in 1996 to more than 3 billion in 2015 (Internet World Stats, 2015). The Internet has replaced television as the medium that young Canadians spend the most amount of time using on a daily basis. However, this fact overlooks a profound change in user behaviour. Canadians multi-task: increasingly, they surf the Internet and chat online while they watch TV. Young people, in particular, use social media sites such as Facebook and Twitter to exchange comments on shows they watch. These changing habits force advertisers to find new ways of engaging their increasingly distracted audience. One strategy is to invite television viewers to access additional content online, blurring the boundaries between these two forms of media.

On average, Canadian adults watched about 4.2 hours of television daily in 2014 (see Figure 4.2). They also spent about 2.5 hours listening to the radio and 2.4 hours on the Internet. They spent less than half an hour reading newspapers and less than five minutes reading magazines. However, these averages mask differences between age cohorts, between classes, between gender categories, and between regions. For example, television was by far the most popular mass medium for Canadians over the age of 55, who spent nearly six hours a day watching it in 2014. In contrast, the Internet was the number one mass medium for Canadians between the ages of 18 and 34. They spent about 3.3 hours a day using it. Low-income Canadians watch more TV than high-income earners do, men watch more than women do, and those living in the North watch more than those in other regions do (Television Bureau of Canada, 2014).

FIGURE 4.2 CANADIAN ADULT MEDIA USAGE, MINUTES PER DAY, 2001 AND 2014

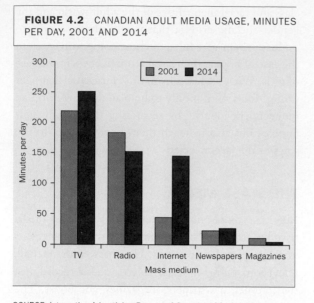

SOURCE: Interactive Advertising Bureau of Canada, "2014: Internet in the Media Garden." http://iabcanada.com/wp-content/uploads/2014/12/V2-Total-Canada-2014-CMUST-Exec-Summary-Nov-18-2014.pdf (accessed Sept. 21, 2015). Copyright © 2014.

The fastest-growing mass medium by far is the Internet. Canadians increasingly live in a world of continuous connectivity (Turkle, 2011). There are benefits, to be sure. Parents can better keep track of their children's whereabouts. One can share pictures of a vacation with others while still on vacation. And if you've ever wondered what song was playing on the mall audio system, an app will identify it after just a few phrases and send you to a website where you can buy it. However, researchers wonder whether continuous connectivity comes at a cost. What does it mean that there is almost no possibility of being truly alone or unavailable? How does one take back a comment or a picture that was posted in haste but that can be seen immediately by others and reposted many times over?

THE MASS MEDIA AND THE FEMINIST APPROACH TO SOCIALIZATION

The mass media expose people to influences that shape their ideas, attitudes, expectations, values, and behaviour. This is especially true for children and adolescents. Although people are to some extent free to choose socialization influences from the mass media, they choose some influences more often than others. Specifically, they tend to choose influences that are more pervasive, fit existing cultural standards, and are made especially appealing by those who control the mass media. We can illustrate this fact by considering how feminist sociologists analyze gender roles.

Gender roles are widely shared expectations about how males and females are supposed to act. They are of special interest to feminist sociologists, who claim that people are not born knowing how to express masculinity and femininity in conventional ways. Instead, say feminist sociologists, people *learn* gender roles, partly through the mass media.

Although recent exceptions exist, most movies, popular fiction, ads, music, and video games reinforce the notion that women should be passive and men potent. For example, a central theme in Harlequin romance novels (the world's top sellers in this genre, based in Toronto), is the transformation of women's bodies into objects for men's pleasure. In the typical Harlequin romance, men are the sexual aggressors. They are typically more experienced and promiscuous than the women are. Similarly, *Fifty Shades of Grey* features a young college graduate who enters into a sexual relationship with a wealthy young man in which he dominates sexually and in all other respects. The best-selling *Twilight* trilogy starts with a teenage girl who meets and falls under the spell of a mysterious boy, who is actually a 104-year-old vampire. The common theme in all of these novels is that females are sexually inexperienced and need strong, skillful men to fulfill them sexually.

People do not passively accept messages about appropriate gender roles. They often interpret them in unique ways and sometimes resist them. For the most part, however, people try to develop skills that will help them perform conventional gender roles (Eagley and Wood, 1999: 412–13). Of course, conventions change. It is important to note in this regard that what children learn about femininity and masculinity today is less sexist than what they learned just a few generations ago. For example, comparing *Snow White and the Seven Dwarfs* (1937) and *Cinderella* (1950) with *Tangled* (2010), *Brave* (2012), and *Frozen* (2013), we see immediately that children going to Disney movies today are sometimes presented with more assertive and heroic female role models than the passive heroines of previous generations. However, the amount of change in gender socialization should not be exaggerated. *Cinderella* and *Snow White* are still popular movies. Moreover, for every *Frozen* there is a *Monsters University* (2012), *Planes* (2013), or *SpongeBob Movie: Sponge Out of Water* (2015), where females occupy subordinate positions and males dominate.

As the learning of gender roles through the mass media suggests, not all media influences are created equal. We may be free to choose which media messages influence us, but most people are inclined to choose

"Well hello, ladies. You ready to lose?" So begins the 2013 animated hit movie, *Planes*, when an upstart single-engine turboprop challenges other aircraft to a race. The clear implication is that femininity is associated with inferior characteristics. What do you think? Is the film relaying the message to young children that it is better to be male than female?

SOURCE: © Walt Disney Studios Motion Pictures/Courtesy Everett Collection/The Canadian Press.

the messages that are most widespread, most closely aligned with existing cultural standards, and made most enticing by the mass media. In the case of gender roles, these messages usually support conventional expectations about how males and females are supposed to act.

RESOCIALIZATION AND TOTAL INSTITUTIONS

In concluding our discussion of socialization agents, we must underline the importance of **resocialization** in contributing to the lifelong process of social learning. Resocialization takes place when powerful socializing agents deliberately cause rapid change in people's values, roles, and self-conception, sometimes against their will.

You can see resocialization at work in the ceremonies that are staged when someone joins a fraternity, a sorority, a sports team, or a religious order. Such a ceremony, or **initiation rite**, signifies the transition of the individual from one group to another and ensures his or her loyalty to the new group. Initiation rites require new recruits to abandon old self-perceptions and assume new identities. Typically, they comprise a three-stage ceremony involving (1) separation from the old status and identity (ritual rejection); (2) degradation, disorientation, and stress (ritual death); and (3) acceptance of the new group culture and status (ritual rebirth).

Much resocialization takes place in what Erving Goffman (1961) called **total institutions**. Total institutions are settings in which people are isolated from the larger society and under the strict control and constant supervision of a specialized staff. Asylums and prisons are examples of total institutions. Because of the "pressure cooker" atmosphere in such institutions, resocialization in total institutions is often rapid and thorough, even in the absence of initiation rites.

A famous failed experiment illustrates the immense resocializing capacity of total institutions (Haney, Banks, and Zimbardo, 1973; Zimbardo, 1971). In the early 1970s, a group of researchers created their own mock prison in what is known as the Stanford prison experiment; 2008. They paid about two dozen male volunteers to act as guards and inmates. The volunteers were mature, emotionally stable, intelligent university students from middle-class homes in the United States and Canada. None had a criminal record. By the flip of a coin, half the volunteers were designated prisoners, the other half guards. The guards made up their own rules for maintaining law and order in the mock prison. The prisoners were picked up by city police officers in a squad car, searched, handcuffed, fingerprinted, booked at the police station, and taken blindfolded to the mock prison. At the mock prison, each prisoner was stripped, deloused, put into a uniform, given a number, and placed in a cell with two other inmates.

To better understand what it means to be a prisoner or a prison guard, the researchers wanted to observe and record social interaction in the mock prison for two weeks. However, they were forced to end the experiment abruptly after only six days because what they witnessed frightened them. In less than a week, the prisoners and prison guards could no longer tell the difference between the roles they were playing and their "real" selves. Much of the socialization these young men had undergone over a period of about 20 years was quickly suspended.

About a third of the guards began to treat the prisoners like despicable animals, taking pleasure in cruelty. Even the guards who were regarded by the prisoners as tough but fair stopped short of interfering in the tyrannical and arbitrary use of power by the most sadistic guards.

All of the prisoners became servile and dehumanized, thinking only about survival, escape, and their growing hatred of the guards. Had they been thinking as university students, they could have walked out of the experiment at any time. Some of the prisoners did, in fact, beg for parole. However, by the fifth day of the experiment they were so programmed to think of themselves as prisoners that they returned docilely to their cells when their request for parole was denied.

A particularly shameful example of how total institutions function can be found in the experience of Canadian Indigenous peoples in residential schools. From the 1870s to 1996, the Canadian government snatched about 150 000 Indigenous children from their families and placed them in residential schools. The primary purpose of the residential school system was to isolate children from the influence of their families, communities, and traditions so that they could be assimilated into the dominant European culture. Such actions were sustained by the unwavering belief of European settlers that Indigenous cultures and spiritual beliefs were inferior and unequal.

In the residential school system, Indigenous children were forced to abandon their cultural practices. Harsh punishments, including beatings and the withholding of food, were meted out to children who attempted to communicate in their own language or to follow their own customs. Children who ran away were tracked down and brought back to the school. Their only option was to adopt European ways. As a result of resocialization, many Indigenous children came to believe that their culture was inferior. Any reminder of their heritage and who they were often elicited feelings of shame and self-loathing.

The message on the blackboard of this Anglican-run school in Lac la Ronge, Saskatchewan, in 1945, is "Thou Shalt Not Tell Lies."
SOURCE: Library and Archives Canada, PA-134110.

The effects of the residential school system are still with us because the institution failed to equip Indigenous children to successfully take on adult roles in the outside world. Without proper role models, Indigenous children who left the school as young adults had no concept of what it meant to be a parent. Not surprisingly, many resorted to what they knew, neglecting and abusing their children in ways that mimicked what had happened to them in the school system. Such patterns, repeated across the generations, have made entire communities vulnerable to devastating social problems. High rates of substance abuse, depression, violence, and suicide in Indigenous communities today are just some of the ripple effects caused by the residential school system.

TIME FOR REVIEW

1. What is the role of children in their own socialization?
2. How does the hidden curriculum influence successful school performance?
3. What messages do the mass media send about appropriate roles for men and women?
4. Why are total institutions ideal for resocialization?

SOCIALIZATION AND THE FLEXIBLE SELF

The development of the self is a lifelong process. When young adults enter a profession or get married, they must learn new occupational and family roles. Retirement and old age present an entirely new set of challenges. Giving up a job, seeing children leave home and start their own families, and losing a spouse and close friends—all of these changes later in life require that people think of themselves in new ways and redefine who they are. Many new roles are predictable. To help us learn them we often engage in **anticipatory socialization**, which involves beginning to take on the norms and behaviours of the roles to which we aspire. (Think of 15-year-old fans of *Girls* learning from the TV show what it might mean to be a young adult.) Other new roles are unpredictable. You might unexpectedly fall in love and marry someone from a different ethnic, racial, or religious group. You might experience a sudden and difficult transition from peace to war. If so, you will have to learn new roles and adopt new cultural values or at least modify old ones. Even in adulthood, then, the self remains flexible.

Today, people's identities change faster, more often, and more completely than they did just a few decades ago. One factor contributing to the growing flexibility of the self is globalization. As we saw in Chapter 3, Culture, people are now less obliged to accept the culture into which they are born. Because of globalization, they are freer to combine elements of culture from a wide variety of historical periods and geographical settings.

A second factor increasing our freedom to design our selves is our growing ability to fashion new bodies from old. People have always defined themselves partly in terms of their bodies—your self-conception is influenced by whether you're a man or a woman, tall or short, healthy or ill, conventionally attractive or plain. However, our bodies used to be fixed by nature. People could do nothing to change the fact that they were born with certain features and grew older at a certain rate.

Now, however, you can change your body and, therefore, your self-conception, radically and virtually at will—if, that is, you can afford it. Bodybuilding, aerobic exercise, and weight reduction regimens are more popular than ever. Plastic surgery allows people to buy new breasts, noses, lips, eyelids, and hair—and to remove unwanted fat, skin, and hair from various parts of their bodies. Other body-altering procedures include sex-change operations and organ transplants. At any given time, more than 50 000 North Americans are waiting for a replacement organ. Brisk, illegal international trade in human hearts, lungs, kidneys, livers, and eyes enables well-to-do people to enhance and extend their lives (Cohen, 2013). Modern bionics makes it possible to wire realistic prosthetic limbs into brain circuitry that, with practice, can function almost like the original limbs. Technologies are also being developed that can restore vision and hearing using cameras, microphones, and microscopic electrodes. As these examples illustrate, many exciting opportunities for changing our bodies, and therefore our self-conception, have been introduced in recent decades.

SELF-IDENTITY AND THE INTERNET

Further complicating the process of identity formation today is the growth of the Internet. In the 1980s and early 1990s, most observers believed that social interaction by means of computer would involve only the exchange of information between individuals. They were wrong. Computer-assisted social interaction can profoundly affect how people think of themselves (Brym and Lenton, 2001; Haythornthwaite and Wellman, 2002).

Internet users interact socially by exchanging text, images, and sound via email, instant messaging, Internet phone, Facebook, Twitter, videoconferencing, computer-assisted work groups, online dating services, and so on. In the process, they often form **virtual communities**. Virtual communities are associations of people, scattered across the country or the planet, who communicate via computer about subjects of common interest.

Because virtual communities allow interaction using concealed identities, people are free to assume new identities and encouraged to discover parts of themselves they were formerly unaware of. In virtual communities, shy people can become bold, normally assertive people can become voyeurs, old people can become young, straight people can become gay, women can become men, and vice versa (Turkle, 1995). Experience on the Internet thus reinforces our main point: In recent decades, the self has become increasingly flexible, and people are freer than ever to shape their selves as they choose.

TIME FOR REVIEW

1. What is meant by "the flexible self?"
2. How have globalization, various medical advances, and the pervasiveness of the Internet produced more flexible selves?

SUMMARY

1. **Why is social interaction necessary to unleash human potential?**
Studies show that children raised in extreme isolation do not develop normally. They often lack the intellectual and emotional capacity of children raised in normal environments. Various theories suggest that socialization leads to the formation of self. Freud argued that a self-image begins to emerge when a baby's impulsive demands are denied. Because of many lessons in self-control, a child eventually develops a sense of what constitutes appropriate behaviour, a moral sense of right and wrong, and a personal conscience. Ongoing social interaction is thus necessary for the self to emerge. Like Freud, Mead noted that an impulsive aspect of the self (the "I") is present from birth. Developing Cooley's idea of the "looking-glass self," Mead also argued that a repository of culturally approved standards emerges as part of the self during social interaction. Mead drew attention to the unique human capacity to take the role of the other as the source of the "me." People develop, he wrote, by first imitating and pretending to be their significant others, then learning to play complex games that require understanding several roles simultaneously, and finally developing a sense of cultural standards and how they apply.

2. **How are stages in the life course influenced by the historical period in which people live?**
The stages of the life course have been structured differently across history. For example, in the past, childhood and adolescence were not recognized as distinct life stages, with the consequence that children were expected to live in much the same way that adults did. Accordingly, children would start working as soon as they were able to perform work tasks. A new view of childhood, which emerged more than two centuries ago, began to treat children as unsocialized people who needed instruction and training to develop properly. In response, school attendance became mandatory and labour laws prohibited children from working in the paid labour market. In each historical period then, we can see that socialization prepares individuals to become the people society needs them to be.

3. **In what ways has the socializing influence of the family decreased in the twentieth century, while the influence of schools, peer groups, and the mass media has increased?**
Families remain an important and enduring agent of socialization. However, their influence has dwindled as the reach of other institutions and social forces has grown. The transfer of knowledge and skills that, in the past, would have been the primary if not sole responsibility of families increasingly occurs outside of the family system. Thus, what parents teach their children may be offset by what the children learn in other settings. For example, sex education in the curriculum in Canadian schools may reflect values that conflict with what children learn in the home. Similarly, peers and the mass media may introduce children to perspectives that differ from what they are typically exposed to through their families.

4. **In what sense is the self more flexible than it used to be?**
People's self-conceptions are subject to more flux now than they were even a few decades ago. Cultural globalization, medical advances, and computer-assisted communication are among the factors that have made the self more flexible.

QUESTIONS TO CONSIDER

1. Consider the significant people in your life. Have they always been important to you? How have they shaped and influenced your sense of self?

2. Prisons are socialization institutions organized to rehabilitate or "correct" deviant behaviour. How effective are these institutions and why are they not more successful in meeting their goals?

3. What is the self that you project to the world when you use social media (e.g., Facebook, Twitter, Pinterest, Snapchat)? Does this self differ from how your significant others see you? To what extent might participation in these virtual communities exert an influence on your relationships with your significant others?

GLOSSARY

Adaptation (p. 91) is the process of arranging one's actions to maximize the degree to which an environment satisfies one's needs and interests.

An **age cohort** (p. 87) is a category of people born in the same range of years.

Age roles (p. 87) are norms and expectations about the behaviour of people in different age cohorts.

Anticipatory socialization (p. 99) involves taking on the norms and behaviours of the role to which we aspire.

A **gender role** (p. 96) is the set of behaviours associated with widely shared expectations about how males and females are supposed to act.

A **generation** (p. 87) is an age cohort that shares unique formative experiences during the first few decades of life, which help to shape a collective identity and set of values.

The **generalized other** (p. 83), according to Mead, is a person's image of cultural standards and how they apply to him or her.

The **hidden curriculum** (p. 93) in school involves teaching obedience to authority and conformity to cultural norms.

The **I** (p. 82) is the subjective and impulsive aspect of the self that is present from birth, according to Mead.

An **initiation rite** (p. 97) is a ritual that signifies a person's transition from one group to another and ensures his or her loyalty to the new group.

Life course (p. 85) refers to the distinct phases of life through which people pass. These stages vary from one society and historical period to another.

The **me** (p. 82) is the objective component of the self that emerges as people communicate symbolically and learn to take the role of the other, according to Mead.

A person's **peer group** (p. 94) comprises people who are about the same age and of similar status as the individual. The peer group acts as an agent of socialization.

Primary socialization (p. 91) is the process of acquiring the basic skills needed to function in society during childhood. Primary socialization usually takes place in a family.

Resocialization (p. 97) occurs when powerful socializing agents deliberately cause rapid change in a person's values, roles, and self-conception, sometimes against a person's will.

Rites of passage (p. 85) are cultural ceremonies that mark the transition from one stage of life to another (e.g., baptisms, confirmations, weddings) or from life to death (funerals).

A **role** (p. 81) is the behaviour expected of a person occupying a particular position in society.

Secondary socialization (p. 93) is socialization outside the family after childhood.

The **self** (p. 82) consists of your ideas and attitudes about who you are.

A **self-fulfilling prophecy** (p. 94) is an expectation that helps bring about what it predicts.

Significant others (p. 83) are people who play important roles in the early socialization experiences of children.

The **social environment** (p. 91) is composed of the real or imagined others to whom individuals must adapt to satisfy their own needs and interests.

Socialization (p. 81) is the process by which people learn to function in their own culture.

Status (p. 94) refers to a recognized social position that a person can occupy.

The **Thomas theorem** (p. 94) states, "Situations we define as real become real in their consequences."

Total institutions (p. 97) are settings in which people are isolated from the larger society and under the strict control and constant supervision of a specialized staff.

A **virtual community** (p. 99) is an association of people, scattered across the country, continent, or planet, who communicate via computer about a subject of common interest.

CHAPTER 5

GENDER AND SEXUALITIES

Rhonda L. Lenton
YORK UNIVERSITY

SOURCE: © Kurt Krieger/Corbis.

AFTER READING THIS CHAPTER, YOU WILL BE ABLE TO:

- Distinguish sex from gender.

- Describe the cultural "scripts" that define our sexuality by telling us whom we should find sexually attractive, when and where it is appropriate to be sexually aroused, and when it is permissible to have sex.

- Compare and contrast two major perspectives on the relationship among sex, gender, and sexuality—one claiming that gender roles and sexual scripts develop naturally from biological differences between the sexes, the other claiming that gender roles and sexual scripts emerge in response to the different social positions women and men occupy.

- See how the current structuring of gender and sexuality produces intolerance against sexual minorities and male violence against women, and how redefining sexuality can help to overcome these problems.

THE CASE OF DAVID/BRENDA

In April 1966, identical eight-month-old twin boys were brought to St. Boniface hospital in Winnipeg to be circumcised. They had developed a condition called *phimosis*, or closing of the foreskin. However, because of mechanical malfunction or doctor error, the electric cauterizing needle used for the procedure released a surge of heat. It burnt off the entire penis of one baby.

The parents sought expert medical advice but were given little hope. One psychiatrist summarized the baby's future as follows: "[H]e will be unable to consummate marriage or have normal heterosexual relations ... he will have to recognize that he is incomplete, physically defective, and that he must live apart" (quoted in Colapinto, 2001: 16). The baby's name was David Reimer.

Seven months later, David Reimer's parents happened to be watching a CBC television program featuring Dr. John Money of Johns Hopkins University in Baltimore. He was discussing how he had successfully assigned a male or female identity to children whose external sex organs and internal reproductive system were not clearly male or female. The main criterion he used for deciding the child's sex was expected "erotic functioning" as an adult. He recommended boys born with a penis shorter than 2.5 centimetres and girls born with a clitoris longer than 1 centimetre for sex reassignment, preferably within weeks of birth. According to Money, it was imperative, once the child's sex was decided, that doctors and parents never waver in their decision and never tell the child about his or her condition at birth.

Until David Reimer, Dr. Money had never had the opportunity to test his idea on a child born unequivocally a boy or girl. Therefore, when David's mother wrote to Dr. Money shortly after the television show, he urged her to bring the baby to his office in Baltimore. He considered it a bonus that David was a twin. This would allow him to compare the development of the two siblings. Dr. Money was eager to proceed. He believed that the "gender identity gate"—the time after which a child is "locked" into an identity as a male or a female—closes at two years of age. The parents nevertheless took several months to deliberate and consult with family and friends before giving the go-ahead. On July 3, 1967, David, now 22 months old, underwent surgical castration and reconstructive surgery. He became Brenda Reimer.

As the years passed, the parents followed Dr. Money's instructions. Brenda was given dresses to wear, skipping ropes and dolls for presents, and regular doses of the female hormone estrogen at puberty.

In 1972, at a meeting of the American Association for the Advancement of Science, Dr. Money unveiled the story of David/Brenda Reimer. He claimed that the experiment was an unqualified success. In a co-authored book intended for the general public, he described David's sex reassignment as "dramatic proof that the gender-identity option is open at birth for normal infants." Money was equally optimistic in a 1978 journal article, where he reported that "[n]ow prepubertal in age, [Brenda Reimer] has ... a feminine gender identity and role, distinctly different from that of her brother" (quoted in Colapinto, 1997: 72).

Then, in March 1997, a bombshell: Dr. Money, it emerged, had doctored his reports. A biologist from the University of Hawaii and a psychiatrist from the Canadian Ministry of Health started a scientific scandal when they published an article in the *Archives of Adolescent and Pediatric Medicine* showing that David/Brenda had, in fact, struggled against his/her imposed girlhood from the start.

The authors documented Brenda's resistance to being a girl, including everything from tearing off her first dress to insisting on standing to urinate. According to her brother, Kevin, there was "nothing feminine about Brenda. ... She walked like a guy. Sat with her legs apart. She talked about guy things, didn't give a crap about cleaning house, getting married, wearing makeup. We both wanted to play with guys, build forts and have snowball fights and play army" (quoted in Colapinto, 2001: 57).

By the age of seven, Brenda announced she wanted to be a boy, and she refused to have further vaginal surgery because it would make her look more like a girl. She took estrogen only after being told that failure to do so would result in her limbs being disproportionate to her body. She refused to see Dr. Money after 1978. In 1979, Brenda made the decision to stop living as a girl.

In 1980, her father finally told Brenda what had happened to her. Brenda's first reaction was relief. She then resolved to become David again. By the age of 16, she started taking male hormone treatments and had her breasts removed and a penis surgically constructed. Subsequent surgeries allowed David to have sex with a woman at the age of 23. He married the woman two years later, in 1990, and adopted her three children. That did not, however, end his ordeal. In May 2004, at the age of 38, David Reimer committed suicide.

David Reimer, February 2001.
SOURCE: © Reuters/CORBIS.

The story of David/Brenda introduces many of the issues raised in this chapter. How do we define *female* and *male?* What is the relationship between biological sex and the attitudes and behaviours that we associate with being male or female? What are the implications of this relationship for our sexual identity and sexual relations? I will touch on all these questions here. The answers, it will emerge, are not as obvious as they may at first appear.

SEX AND GENDER
DEFINING MALE AND FEMALE

While preparing to write this chapter, I asked my then six-year-old the difference between boys and girls. She answered: "Boys have a penis, girls have a vagina." Like most people, she distinguished men and women based on biological **sex.** Your sex depends on whether you were born with distinct male or female genitalia and a genetic program that released male

or female hormones to stimulate the development of your reproductive system. Table 5.1 gives a more complete version of this common view by summarizing four key sex differences.

At the point of conception, a newly formed zygote has 46 chromosomes. If the last chromosome has an XX pattern, the zygote becomes a female. If it has an XY pattern, it becomes a male. About 1 in 400 children is born with an unusual 46th chromosome pattern caused by the failure of the sperm to divide properly (Berch and Bender, 1987). Most of these combinations are never diagnosed.

Around the sixth or seventh week of gestation, the gonads or sex glands begin to develop—testes in the case of a male, ovaries in the case of a female. The testes and ovaries subsequently produce various hormones in varying amounts. These hormones contribute to the development of the sex organs. Differences between the sex organs are noticeable by the fourteenth week after conception. The scientific community appears to agree about only one sex difference in the brain (Blum, 1997): The part of the brain known as the hypothalamus makes the female brain sensitive to estrogen and is responsible for creating menstrual cycles in women.

Being male or female involves more than just biological sex differences, however, as the case of David/Brenda shows. Recalling his life as Brenda, David said, "[E]veryone is telling you that you're a girl. But you say to yourself, 'I don't *feel* like a girl.' You think girls are supposed to be delicate and *like* girl things—tea parties, things like that. But I like to *do* guy stuff. It doesn't match" (quoted in Colapinto, 1997: 66; author's emphasis). As this quotation shows, being male or female involves not just biology but also

TABLE 5.1   SUMMARIES OF BIOLOGICAL SEX DIFFERENCES DURING TYPICAL FETAL DEVELOPMENT

VARIABLE	FEMALE	MALE
Chromosomal pattern	XX	XY
Gonadal	Ovaries	Testes
Hormonal	More estrogens than androgens	More androgens than estrogens + MIH
Sex organs	Uterus, fallopian tubes, vagina, clitoris, labia	Epididymis, vas deferens, seminal vesicles, prostate, penis, scrotum

SOURCE: Adapted from E. D. Nelson and Barrie W. Robinson, *Gender in Canada* (Toronto: Pearson Education, 1999), p. 48. Reprinted with permission by Pearson Canada Inc.

certain "masculine" and "feminine" feelings, attitudes, and behaviours. Accordingly, biological sex must be distinguished from sociological gender. **Gender** comprises the feelings, attitudes, and behaviours associated with being male or female. Identification with, or sense of belonging to, a particular sex—biologically, psychologically, and socially—is known as **gender identity**. When people behave according to widely shared expectations about how males or females are supposed to act, they adopt a **gender role**.

The fact that David Reimer learned a conventional male gender role for the first 22 months of his life probably contributed to the failure of his first sex-change operation. David was raised as a boy for nearly two years. He had seen boys treated differently from girls on television and in storybooks. He had played only with stereotypical boys' toys. After his sex reassignment, he received new, conventionally feminine clothes and toys. He was instructed on how to behave like a girl. Yet the constant presence of his twin brother must have reinforced David's early understanding of how boys ought to behave. Evidence suggests that if gender reassignment takes place before the age of 18 months, it tends to be "successful" (Creighton and Minto, 2001; Lightfoot-Klein et al., 2000).

SEXUAL MINORITIES

Research shows that North Americans' expectations about how males and females are supposed to act have changed only somewhat since the 1960s, when David Reimer was born (Bergen and Williams, 1991; Carrigan, Connell, and Lee, 1985; Kimmel and Bridges, 2011; Schrock and Schwalbe, 2009). This is true despite significant changes in women's lives in particular. For example, in the 1960s, males were expected to act tough and hide their emotions, and they still are today, albeit to a lesser extent. Boys still tend to learn at a young age that crying or displaying their feelings in public is likely to result in taunts and accusations of being a "sissy." As a result, they curb their nurturing abilities, thus fulfilling gender expectations.

Great pressure can be brought to bear on individuals who do not conform to gender expectations. Brenda Reimer is a case in point. She was ostracized and tormented by her peers for not acting sufficiently feminine, as conventionally understood. All sexual minority groups report similar experiences of rejection. They suffer from the fact that most people are "heteronormative." **Heteronormativity** is the belief that one's biological sex should be perfectly aligned with one's sexual preferences, gender identity, and

gender role. When such alignment does not exist, most people seek to enforce it. Making David Reimer undergo a sex change operation and treating him like a girl is an example of heteronormativity in practice.

As noted earlier, the overwhelming majority of people are born with 23 pairs of chromosomes, one pair of which determines their sex. If a person's sex chromosome is of the XX variety, she will be a woman. If a person's sex chromosome is of the XY variety, he will be a man. However, other sex chromosome types occur naturally—X, XXY, XXYY, and so on. Such combinations often result in people who are **intersex**, that is, they do not fit the conventional male or female sex categories. Their genitals, reproductive system, and secondary sexual characteristics such as breasts and body hair may not be distinctly male or female in the conventional sense of the terms. It is estimated that roughly 1.7 percent of people lie somewhere between male and female as conventionally understood (Fausto-Sterling, 2000; Hird, 2005).

Some people who are not intersex have a gender identity that does not correspond with his or her sex. Consider the well-known case of Caitlyn Jenner (formerly Bruce Jenner). Caitlyn Jenner is a woman in terms of gender identity. People like her, who are uncomfortable with the gender assigned to them at birth or who do not fit neatly into conventional male or female gender categories, are considered **transgender**. There are no survey-based estimates of the percentage of Canadians who identify as transgender, but the best estimate from the United States is 0.3 percent (Gates, 2011).

Neither biologists nor social scientists have yet developed convincing explanations for why sex and gender identity may not correspond (Lips, 2014: 18). However, we do know that, unlike sex, gender is not determined solely by biology.

People who identify as **homosexuals** prefer sexual partners of the same sex, and those who identify as **bisexuals** are attracted to sexual partners of either sex. People usually call homosexual men *gay* and homosexual women *lesbians*. While fewer than 2 percent of Canadians identify as homosexual or bisexual, the percentage is higher on university campuses and in large urban centres (Kinkartz, Wells, and Hillyard, 2013; Tjepkema, 2008).

The picture becomes still more complicated when we consider sexual behaviour. For example, as you will soon learn, many people who consider themselves heterosexual have some same-sex sexual experience or desire. Expectations about sexual behaviour are arguably among the most rigid of our gender

Being male or female involves not just biology but also certain "masculine" or "feminine" feelings, attitudes, and behaviours.
SOURCE: Susan G. Scott, *The Princess*. Courtesy Susan G. Scott.

norms, yet sexual behaviour often departs from biological sex and sociological gender.

TIME FOR REVIEW

1. What is the difference between sex and gender?
2. How is gender learned?
3. What is heteronormativity and how does it affect the treatment of sexual minorities?

SEXUALITIES, SEXUAL ATTITUDES, AND SEXUAL BEHAVIOUR

Sexuality refers to activities that are intended "to lead to erotic arousal and produce genital response" (Reiss, 1986: 20). Sexual behaviour is guided by a set of **sexual scripts** that tell us whom we should find attractive, when and where it is appropriate to be aroused, what is permissible, and how to behave sexually. These scripts are linked to gender roles. Men are usually expected to be the sexual aggressors, typically more experienced and promiscuous than women are. Women are usually expected to desire love, or at least deep affection, before intimacy. They are generally assumed to be relatively sexually passive, giving only subtle cues to indicate their interest in male overtures. Presumably lacking the urgent sex drive that preoccupies men, women are often held accountable for moral standards and contraception (Jensen, 1984).

Traditional sexual scripts expect each of us to meet a member of the "opposite" sex, fall in love, get married, and then have intercourse with our spouse. However, surveys reveal considerable departure from tradition and considerable diversity in sexual attitudes and behaviour. For example, only 20 percent of Canadians disapprove of premarital sex and just 25 percent disapprove of an unmarried couple living together (Bibby with Russell and Rolheiser, 2009: 44, 146). By the time they are 15 years old, half of Canadian males and a third of Canadian females say they have had sexual intercourse at least once. By the time they are 19 years old, the figure for both males and females rises to more than 80 percent (Bibby with Russell and Rolheiser, 2009: 52; Hobart, 1996: 150; Rotermann, 2008).

Figure 5.1 shows the frequency of sexual activity by gender and age in Canada. Not surprisingly, sexual activity declines with age. However, a considerable percentage of people over the age of 69 say they

FIGURE 5.1 FREQUENCY OF SEXUAL INTERCOURSE, CANADIANS, BY AGE AND SEX

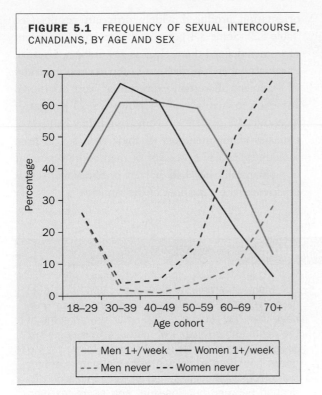

SOURCE: Adapted from Reginald W. Bibby, *Project Canada 2005 National Survey Data.* Reprinted with permission of the author.

engage in sexual activity. This finding challenges the myth that seniors are asexual.

Interestingly, in most age cohorts, men are more likely to report having sexual intercourse than women are, while women are more likely to report never having sexual intercourse. The gap in the percentage of women and men who say they never have sex grows rapidly after the age of 49. One interpretation of this pattern is that men exaggerate their virility to conform to conventional gender stereotypes, and they are more inclined to do so as they age.

Men and women differ in terms of the standards they use to justify sexual activity. Women are more likely to endorse the "love standard," which holds that sexual activity is acceptable as long as the partners have a strong emotional attachment. Men are more likely to accept the "fun standard," which holds that sexual activity is acceptable as long as both partners want it (Hobart, 1996: 148). Much research corroborates the existence of this difference. For instance:

- One American survey showed that women are more likely to cite "affection for partner" as the major reason for their first intercourse experience (48 percent), followed by "curiosity/readiness for sex" (24 percent). In contrast, men most often mention "curiosity/readiness for sex" (51 percent), followed by "affection for partner" (25 percent). Four times more men than women report having their first sexual experience for the sake of physical pleasure (12 percent versus 3 percent; Michael et al., 1994: 93–94).
- An analysis of 52 million Internet searchers on sexual topics in 2009 and 2010 found that men tend to search for films of graphic sex while women tend to search for romance stories (Vasey and Abild, 2013: 1101).
- One survey of 1479 Canadians over the age of 18 found that men have sexual thoughts more often than women do, have first intercourse at a younger age, have more lifetime sexual partners, are more likely to have oral sex, and are more in favour of casual sex (Fischtein, Herold, and Desmarais, 2007).

Attitudes about extramarital affairs are quite conservative, and they are becoming more so over time. Between 1975 and 2000, adult endorsement of extramarital sex fell from 21 percent to 14 percent, while among teenagers, the drop was from 12 percent to 9 percent (Bibby with Russell and Rolheiser, 2009: 47). Disapproval is one thing, behaviour another. In one survey of 13 countries, 30–39 percent of Canadians between the ages of 16 and 45 admitted to sexual infidelity. That put Canadians in the same league as South Africans, Australians, French, Italians, and Thais. By comparison, 40 percent or more of Americans, Russians, British, and Germans between the ages of 16 and 45 admitted to sexual infidelity. For Spaniards, Poles, and residents of Hong Kong, the comparable figure was in the 20–29 percent range (Mackay, 2000: 36–7).

Despite the spread of sexually transmitted infections since about 1980, about half of Canadians have unprotected sex without knowing their partner's sexual history (Durex, 2005). Condom use is increasing slightly over time but declines with age (see Figure 5.2).

Finally, we note that Canadians are becoming more tolerant of homosexuality and same-sex marriage over time. For example, in 1975 fewer than 3 in 10 Canadians agreed that sexual relations between two adults of the same sex were "not wrong at all" or only "sometimes wrong." Today, that figure is more than 6 out of 10. Acceptance of homosexuality is correlated with age, gender, and region. Young adults, women, and residents of Quebec and, to a lesser degree, British Columbia, are more accepting of homosexuality than are other Canadians (Bibby, 2006: 21–22;

Bibby with Russell and Rolheiser, 2009: 46–7; see the Critical Sociology: Protest and Policy box).

SEXUAL ORIENTATION AND QUEER THEORY

People sometimes assert that 1 in 10 North Americans is gay or lesbian. Research shows that this view is an oversimplification. Based on a sample of nearly 8000 university students in Canada and the United States, researchers found that different measures of sexual orientation produced widely different results (see Table 5.2). Some 3.4 percent of men and 2.4 percent of women defined themselves as gay, lesbian, bisexual, or other nonheterosexual, but 12.0 percent of men and 13.4 percent of women expressed at least occasional attraction to members of their own sex, 21 percent of men and 25.8 percent of women said they had sexual fantasies about members of their own sex at least sometimes, and 12.5 percent of men and 8.0 percent of women said they had at least one intimate sexual experience with a member of the same sex.

CRITICAL SOCIOLOGY: PROTEST AND POLICY   SAME-SEX MARRIAGE

Two factors are chiefly responsible for the increase in acceptance of homosexuality, one scientific, the other political. In the twentieth century, sexologists—psychologists and physicians who study sexual practices scientifically—first recognized and stressed the wide diversity of existing sexual practices. Alfred Kinsey was among the pioneers in this field. He and his colleagues interviewed thousands of men and women. In the 1940s, they concluded that homosexual practices were so widespread that homosexuality could hardly be considered an illness affecting a tiny minority (Kinsey, Pomeroy, and Martin, 1948; Kinsey et al., 1953).

If sexologists provided a scientific rationale for belief in the normality of sexual diversity, sexual minorities themselves provided the social and political energy needed to legitimize sexual diversity among an increasingly large section of the public. Especially since the 1970s, gays and lesbians have built large communities and subcultures, particularly in major urban areas and have gone public with their lifestyles. They have organized demonstrations, parades, and political pressure groups to express their self-confidence and demand equal rights with the heterosexual majority (Goldie, 2001). These activities have done much to legitimize homosexuality and sexual diversity in general.

Largely because of such efforts, in 2005 Canada became the third country, after the Netherlands and Belgium, to legalize same-sex marriage. Thirteen other countries have since followed suit. By 2011, 21 015 same-sex couples had tied the knot in Canada—just under 1 percent of all Canadian couples. Nearly 46 percent had children under the age of 25 living with them. Eighty percent of such families were headed by women. In addition, 43 560 same-sex couples were living common-law. More than 54 percent of same-sex couples were male and more than 44 percent were female (Statistics Canada, 2014).

Many governments deal with public disagreement over same-sex marriage by distinguishing marriage from "civil union." A civil union grants some of the rights and privileges of marriage to a same-sex couple. At least some jurisdictions in more than a dozen countries allow same-sex couples to enter civil unions. Although Canadian law makes no distinction between heterosexual and same-sex marriage, it respects the right of religious organizations to discriminate against gays and lesbians who want to marry insofar as no religious organization is required by law to marry a same-sex couple.

In 2005, Canada became the third country, after the Netherlands and Belgium, to legalize same-sex marriage.
SOURCE: Annette Shaff/Shutterstock.

Critical Thinking Questions

1. What are the advantages and disadvantages of allowing civil unions but declaring same-sex marriage illegal?

2. Which categories of the Canadian population do you think are most in favour of, and most opposed to, same-sex marriage. Why?

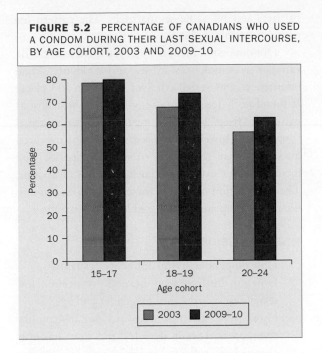

FIGURE 5.2 PERCENTAGE OF CANADIANS WHO USED A CONDOM DURING THEIR LAST SEXUAL INTERCOURSE, BY AGE COHORT, 2003 AND 2009–10

SOURCE: Statistics Canada (2013a).

These findings suggest that estimates of the prevalence of homosexuality depend on how homosexuality is measured. An estimate based on sexual identity results in a lower percentage than does an

estimate focusing on **sexual orientation**. (*Sexual orientation* refers to the way a person derives sexual pleasure, including whether desirable partners are of the same or a different sex.) Thus, it is inaccurate to think about sexuality in terms of a strict dichotomy between heterosexuality and homosexuality. It is more appropriate to conceptualize sexuality as comprising four somewhat independent continua: sexual attraction, sexual desire, sexual behaviour, and sexual identity (Michael et al., 1994: 174–79).

Research not only confirms that sexuality is multidimensional but also calls into question whether the conventional characterization of people as heterosexual, bisexual, or gay or lesbian adequately captures the range of sexual orientations in human populations. The provocatively labelled stream of thought known as **queer theory** denies the existence of stable sexual orientations altogether (Green, 2007). From the queer theorist's point of view, when we apply labels like heterosexual, bisexual, gay, and lesbian to ourselves or others, we are adopting official or at least socially accepted labels that fail to capture the fluidity and variability of people's actual identities and performances. According to this school of thought, such labels impose social conventions on people, thus acting as forms of control and domination, and drawing attention away

TABLE 5.2 MEASURES OF SEXUAL ORIENTATION AMONG CANADIAN AND AMERICAN UNIVERSITY STUDENTS

	MEN	WOMEN
Self-reported sexual orientation		
Heterosexual	96.6	97.6
Homosexual, bisexual, other nonheterosexual	3.4	2.4
Total	100.0	100.0
Attraction		
Only to the opposite sex	88.0	86.6
At least partly to one's own sex	12.0	13.4
Total	100.0	100.0
Sexual fantasies		
Always involving only the other sex	79.0	74.2
Sometimes involving the same sex	21.0	25.8
Total	100.0	100.0
Same-sex intimate sexual experiences (for those with intimate experiences)		
Only with other sex	87.5	92.0
At least once with same sex	12.5	8.0
Total	100.0	100.0

SOURCE: With kind permission from Springer Science and Business Media: *Archives of Sexual Behavior,* Volume 34(5), 2005, pp. 569–581, "Sexual Orientation in United States and Canadian College Students," Lee Ellis, Brian Robb, and Donald Burke.

from the uniqueness of each individual and the way in which the sexual preferences of many people fluctuate over time and in different social settings.

Supporting these assertions, researchers asked a sample of 1784 Americans, half women and half men, to choose among various labels to define their sexuality, including heterosexual, mostly heterosexual, bisexual, mostly gay/lesbian, and gay/lesbian (Vrangalova and Savin-Williams, 2012; see also Knight and Hope, 2012). To understand better the differences among the various sexual orientations, the researchers also asked respondents to situate themselves along two dimensions: sexual attraction to men and women, and lifetime number of male and female sexual partners. They measured sexual attraction by asking respondents to indicate on a scale of 1 to 5 how sexually attracted they are to men and to women. They measured the number of sexual partners by asking respondents the total number of male and female partners with whom they have had a genital sexual experience. Figure 5.3 illustrates the results for women. It shows that, for all five sexual orientations, women are on average *simultaneously* attracted to same-sex and other-sex partners, albeit to varying degrees. For example, women who define themselves as heterosexual (signified by green squares) scored 4.86 out of 5 on other-sex attraction and 1.49 out of 5 on same-sex attraction. It also shows that, for all five sexual orientations, women have had on average more than one male *and* at least one female sexual partner. For example, heterosexual women (signified by green squares) had on average 10.2 other-sex

partners and 1.7 same-sex partners. The pattern for men differs only in detail.

Our discussion demonstrates the existence of wide variation in attitudes toward sex, sexual identity, sexual orientation, and sexual conduct over time and place. It therefore helps to dispel myths about sexuality as natural or "fixed" and about men and women as sexual "opposites." However, our discussion has not answered questions about the *origins* of sexual scripts or why inconsistencies exist between norms and behaviour. The next section addresses these issues by examining the relationship among sex, gender, and sexuality.

TIME FOR REVIEW

1. How do gender scripts influence sexuality?
2. How do the frequency of, and justification for, sexual intercourse vary by gender and age?
3. How have attitudes toward homosexuality changed in recent decades and how has this change been reflected in law?
4. What are the main arguments of queer theory?

DOES SEX DETERMINE DESTINY?

ESSENTIALISM

Most arguments about the origins of gender differences in human behaviour adopt one of two perspectives. Some analysts see gender as a reflection of naturally evolved dispositions. Others see gender as a

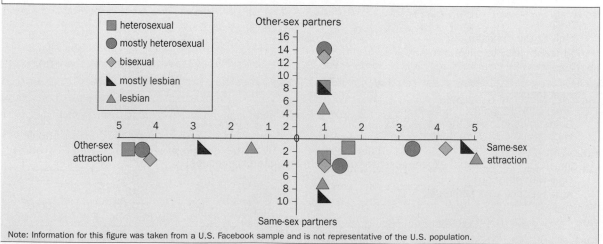

FIGURE 5.3 SAME/OTHER SEXUAL ATTRACTION AND NUMBER OF SAME/OTHER SEX PARTNERS FOR WOMEN OF FIVE SEXUAL IDENTITIES

Note: Information for this figure was taken from a U.S. Facebook sample and is not representative of the U.S. population.

SOURCE: With kind permission from Springer Science and Business Media: *Archives of Sexual Behavior*, Volume 41(1), 2012, pp. 7 and 9, "Mostly Heterosexual and Mostly Gay/Lesbian: Evidence for New Sexual Orientation Identities," Zhana Vrangalova and Ritch C. Savin-Williams.

reflection of the different social positions occupied by women and men. Sociologists call these two perspectives, respectively, *essentialism* and *social constructionism*.

Essentialists first observe male–female differences in sexual scripts, the division of labour at home and in the workplace, mate selection, sexual aggression, jealousy, promiscuity, fidelity, and so forth. They then interpret these differences as natural and universal. According to essentialists, child rearing may reinforce differences between men and women, but nature is the ultimate force at work in shaping them.

Essentialism has many variants, most of which originate in biology and psychology. I will now briefly consider three of the most popular variants: brain studies, sociobiology, and Freudian theory.

Brain Studies

Male–female differences in brain structure are sometimes said to account for male–female differences in behaviour and achievement. The brain comprises two hemispheres of about equal size, connected by a bundle of fibres. The left hemisphere is generally associated with language abilities, the right with nonverbal perception and visual and spatial skills. About this, little controversy exists in the scientific community. However, some brain researchers argue that the two hemispheres develop differently in boys and girls, as do the fibres connecting the hemispheres. Specifically, they claim that when the male fetus starts to secrete testosterone (the hormone responsible for furthering the sexual development of the male), it washes over the brain and briefly inhibits the growth of the left hemisphere. As a result, use of the *right* hemisphere becomes dominant in men. This outcome supposedly allows men to excel in mathematical, artistic, musical, and visual-spatial abilities. Meanwhile (the theory continues), the bundle of fibres connecting the left and right hemispheres is bigger in women. This supposedly allows women to use the hemispheres more symmetrically, giving them an edge in feelings, intuition, language skills, and quick judgments (Bleier, 1984: 92; Blum, 1997: 36–63; Tavris, 1992: 45–46).

Such presumably innate differences in brain structure allegedly give rise to male–female differences in behaviour and achievement. For example, some proponents of this line of thought claim that men are best at jobs requiring logic and visual-spatial manipulation. Hence, the disproportionately large number of men who work as scientists, mechanics, pilots, and so forth. For their part, women are presumably best at jobs requiring empathy, intuition, and language skills.

Hence, the disproportionately large number of women who stay home to raise children and who work outside the home as teachers, secretaries, social workers, and nurses. It follows from this line of reasoning that the gender division of labour is perfectly natural, structured by our brains rather than by society.

Sociobiology

Sociobiology is a second variant of essentialism, and E. O. Wilson (1975) is its leading exponent. Wilson argues that all human beings instinctually want to ensure that their genes get passed on to future generations. However, the different reproductive status of men and women means they have had to overcome different adaptive problems and develop different adaptive strategies. This apparent requirement supposedly gave rise to patterns of behaviour we now call "masculine" and "feminine." Individuals who possessed the characteristics that best resolved these problems—the most feminine women and the most masculine men—had a better chance of surviving and passing their genes to their offspring. Thus, over time, masculine and feminine behaviours became genetically encoded. According to sociobiology, genetic factors also trigger biochemical processes that further enhance sex differences through varying levels of hormone production in women and men.

David Buss, a well-known evolutionary psychologist, argues that four adaptive strategies or "universal features of our evolved selves" govern the relations between the sexes and contribute to the preservation of the human species (Buss, 1994: 211; see also Buss, 1995a, 1995b, 1998; Dawkins, 1976; Wilson, 1978). First, men want casual sex with women. Second, men treat women's bodies as men's property. Third, men beat or kill women who incite male sexual jealousy. And fourth, women are greedy for money.

Buss bases his argument on the claim that a woman has a bigger investment than a man in ensuring the survival of their offspring. That is because a woman produces only a small number of eggs during her reproductive life. Specifically, she releases fewer than 400 eggs during her reproductive years. At most, she can give birth to about 20 children. Men, however, typically release between 200 million and 500 million sperm every time they ejaculate. This number of sperm can typically be produced every 24 to 48 hours (Saxton, 1990: 94–95). It is thus adaptive in an evolutionary sense for a man to be promiscuous yet jealously possessive of his partners (Wilson and Daly, 1998) insofar as a promiscuous yet jealous man maximizes the chance that his, and only his, off-spring will be produced.

Moreover, since men compete with other men for sexual access to women, men evolve competitive and aggressive dispositions that include physical violence. In contrast, Buss says, it is in a woman's best interest to maintain primary responsibility for her genetic child and to look around for the best mate with whom to intermix her genes. He is the man who can best help support the child after birth. Hence, women's alleged greed for money in contemporary society.

Research certainly supports the view that men and women emphasize different characteristics in selecting a mate. Simon Davis, for example, conducted a content analysis of personal advertisements in *The Vancouver Sun*. He discovered that attractive physical features were the most frequently mentioned desirable characteristic in a partner for both men and women. However, women were more likely than men were to list professional status, employment status, financial considerations, intelligence, commitment, and emotion. Men, conversely, were more likely to list attractiveness, physique, and sexiness, and to require a picture (Davis, 1990: 43–50). These results do not, however, establish that sex-typed mating preferences are *genetically* determined. As we will see, the results are also consistent with differences in how we assign status to masculine and feminine gender roles.

Freud

Freud (1977 [1905]) offered a third influential essentialist explanation of male–female differences. He believed that sexuality is the main human instinct. In his view, it motivates human behaviour and accounts for the development of distinct masculine and feminine gender roles.

According to Freud, children around the age of three to five begin to pay attention to their genitals. As a young boy becomes preoccupied with his penis, he unconsciously develops a fantasy of sexually possessing his mother. He begins to resent his father because only his father is allowed to sexually possess the mother. Freud called these unconscious sentiments the "Oedipus complex." However, because he has seen his mother or another girl naked, the boy also develops anxiety that he will be castrated by his father for desiring his mother. To resolve this fear, the boy represses his feelings for his mother. That is, he stores them in the unconscious part of his personality. In due course, this repression allows him to begin identifying with his father. This leads to the development of a strong, masculine personality.

In contrast, the young girl begins to develop a feminine personality when she realizes she lacks a penis. According to Freud,

> [girls] notice the penis of a brother or playmate, strikingly visible and of large proportions, at once recognize it as the superior counterpart of their own small and inconspicuous organ, and from that time forward fall victim to envy for the penis. ... She has seen it and knows that she is without it and wants to have it. (Quoted in Steinem, 1994: 50)

Because of her "penis envy," the young girl soon develops a sense of inferiority, according to Freud. She also grows angry with her mother, who, she naively thinks, is responsible for cutting off the penis the girl must have once had. She rejects her mother and develops an unconscious sexual desire for her father. Eventually, however, realizing she will never have a penis, the girl comes to identify with her mother. This is a way of vicariously acquiring her father's penis in Freud's view. In the "normal" development of a mature woman, the girl's wish to have a penis is transformed into a desire to have children. However, says Freud, since women are never able to completely resolve their penis envy, the feminine gender identity is normally immature and dependent on men. This dependence is evident from the "fact" that women can be fully sexually satisfied only by vaginally induced orgasm. Thus, a host of gender differences in personality and behaviour follow from the anatomical sex differences that children first observe around the age of three.

A Critique of Essentialism

Six main problems are associated with essentialist arguments, such as those just described. First, *essentialists ignore the historical and cultural variability of gender and sexuality*. In some cultures, men are socialized to be nurturing and sensitive. Rape is incomprehensible. For example, anthropologist Margaret Mead reports that the Arapesh, a preliterate people in New Guinea, "know nothing of rape beyond the fact that it is the unpleasant custom of the Nugum people to the southeast of them" (Mead, 1935: 110). More generally, rates of rape vary widely across cultures (Sanday, 1981). This variability deflates the idea that biological constants account for innate behavioural differences between women and men, such as male aggressiveness and violence. Moreover, societies and cultures sometimes change rapidly without any apparent genetic change taking place. Essentialist arguments have a difficult time explaining, for example, recent changes in child-care arrangements, women's increased participation in the paid labour force, and other aspects of women's lives, given the absence of any documented shift in male or female genetic structure that might account for such change.

Second, *essentialists ignore the fact that gender differences are declining and in some cases have disappeared* (Caplan and Caplan, 1999). Hundreds of studies have shown that women are developing traits that were traditionally considered masculine. For example, research shows that women have become more assertive, competitive, independent, and analytical since the early 1970s. They play more aggressive sports, choose more mathematics and science courses, perform better in standardized tests, take more nontraditional jobs, and earn more money than they used to (Twenge, 1997). In what must be considered a serious blow to brain research on alleged male–female differences, a review of 165 studies of verbal ability representing tests of more than 1.4 million people found no gender differences in verbal skills. A review of 100 studies of mathematics performance representing tests of nearly 4 million students showed small differences favouring *females* in the general population. (Differences favouring males exist in samples of high-achieving individuals but these differences seem to result from socialization differences; see Campbell and Beaudry, 1998). A review of dozens of studies on spatial ability reported that some studies found no gender differences, while other studies found only small differences in favour of men (Tavris, 1992: 52). Taken as a whole, this body of research suggests that few gender differences in cognitive ability remain to be explained, the few remaining differences are small, and those few small differences are disappearing.

Third, the research evidence employed by essentialists is often deeply flawed. Consider the sociobiologists' observation that men are more independent than women are. Research shows that, in fact, girls are more dependent than boys are *only at certain ages*. So although infant girls seem to behave in a more dependent fashion than infant boys do, girls at the age of two are more independent than boys are (Feiring and Lewis, 1979; Goldberg and Lewis, 1969). More generally, sociobiologists and evolutionary psychologists have not been able to identify *any* of the genes that, they claim, cause male jealousy, female nurturance, or the unequal division of labour between men and women.

Meanwhile, brain researchers have had great difficulty showing how observed physical differences between male and female brains might be related to (nonexistent or small and shrinking) differences in male and female abilities. That is one reason several brain theories make contradictory arguments. For example, the theory reviewed previously says that men have greater right hemisphere specialization. However, a second theory holds that men have greater *left* hemisphere specialization, which gives them an intellectual advantage over women. Meanwhile, a third theory agrees that men have greater right brain specialization but insists that this gives men superior artistic and musical abilities; yet this contradicts the first theory, which says that women have the edge in musical and artistic skills, which rely on intuition and empathy (Tavris, 1992: 45–49). Lack of hard evidence encourages such unsubstantiated speculation.

Fourth, *essentialists tend to generalize from the average, ignoring variations within gender groups.* On average, women and men do, of course, differ in some respects. For example, one of the best-documented average differences between women and men concerns aggressiveness. Men are on average more verbally and physically aggressive than women are. However, when sociobiologists say men are *inherently* more aggressive than women are, they make it seem as if this is true of all men and all women. As Figure 5.4 shows, however, it is not. When verbal or physical aggressiveness is measured by trained researchers, scores vary widely within gender groups. Aggressiveness is distributed so that considerable overlap occurs between men and women. Many women are more aggressive than the average man, and many men are less aggressive than the average woman.

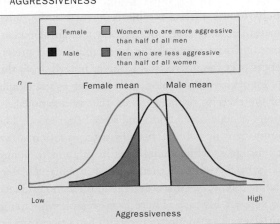

FIGURE 5.4   THE DISTRIBUTION OF MALE AND FEMALE AGGRESSIVENESS

Fifth, *essentialists exaggerate the degree to which gender differences are unchangeable.* For example, David Buss and his colleagues (1990) used data from 37 cultures to show that women consistently prefer older men with high earning capacity as partners. In contrast, men prefer women with good domestic capabilities. Buss claims that this demonstrates a genetic basis for mate selection. However, a reexamination of his data showed that women's tendency to stress the "good provider" role in selecting male partners and men's tendency to stress women's domestic skills decrease in societies that have more gender equality (Eagley and Wood, 1999). Similarly, women express less preference for older men, and men less preference for younger women, in more gender-egalitarian societies. As this example shows, gender differences vary with social conditions, a fact that essentialists ignore.

Another example of how social conditions affect gender differences: The "male" hormone testosterone is associated with greater aggressiveness. However, social situations involving competition and threat stimulate production of testosterone in *women* and cause them to act more aggressively (Blum, 1997: 158–88; Caplan and Caplan, 1999). For example, when women take jobs that maximize competition and threat—when they become, say, corporate lawyers or police officers—they undergo hormonal and behavioural changes, thus decreasing behavioural differences between men and women.

Finally, *essentialists offer explanations for gender differences that ignore the role of power.* Sociobiologists assume that existing behaviour patterns help ensure the survival of the species because they are the patterns that endured as humans evolved. However, their assumption overlooks the fact that some groups (such as men) are in a position of greater power and authority than are other groups (such as women). Behavioural differences between men and women may, therefore, result not from any biological imperative but from men's ability to establish their preferences over the interests of women. Indeed, from this point of view, sociobiology may be seen as an example of the exercise of male power, that is, a rationalization for male domination and sexual aggression. The same may be said of Freud's interpretation. *Must* young girls define themselves in relation to young boys by focusing on their lack of a penis? *Do* they define themselves that way? Freud offers no evidence to support his case. There is no reason why young girls' sexual self-definitions cannot focus positively on their own reproductive organs, including their unique ability to bear children. Freud simply assumed that men are superior to women and then created a speculative theory that justifies gender differences.

SOCIAL CONSTRUCTIONISM

Social constructionism is the main alternative to essentialism. Social constructionists argue that gender differences are not the product of biological properties, whether chromosomal, gonadal, or hormonal. Instead, gender and sexuality are products of social structure and culture. *Culture* is composed of shared systems of meaning. It incorporates people's values and beliefs. Although many systems of meaning coexist and compete at any one time, patriarchy, or male domination and belief in its validity, is widely accepted in nearly all societies today. *Social structure* refers to the way major institutions, such as families, the economy, and the political system, are organized. Social structures in most societies today are patriarchal in that they reinforce inequalities between women and men.

Social constructionists stress three main sociohistorical changes that led to the development of gender inequality. The first was *long-distance warfare and conquest.* Anthropologists have shown that a high level of gender equality existed in foraging or hunting-and-gathering societies, the dominant form of society for 90 percent of human history. Rough equality between women and men was based on the fact that women produced a substantial amount of the band's food, up to 80 percent in some cases. Archaeological evidence from "Old Europe" tells a similar story. Old Europe is a region stretching roughly from Poland in the north to the Mediterranean island of Crete in the south, and from Switzerland in the west to Bulgaria in the east (see Figure 5.5). Between 7000 and 3500 BCE, men and women enjoyed rough equality throughout the region. The religions of the region gave primacy to fertility and creator goddesses. Kinship was traced through the mother's side of the family. Then, sometime between 4300 and 4200 BCE, all this began to change. Old Europe was invaded by successive waves of warring peoples from the Asiatic and European northeast (the Kurgans) and the deserts to the south (the Semites). Both the Kurgan and Semitic civilizations were based on a steeply hierarchical and patriarchal social structure. Their religions gave primacy to male warrior gods. They acquired property and slaves by conquering other peoples and imposed their religions on the vanquished. They eliminated, or at

FIGURE 5.5 APPROXIMATE AREA FOR EARLY CIVILIZATION OF OLD EUROPE

SOURCE: Adapted from Marija Gimbutas, *The Goddesses and Gods of Old Europe: 6500–3500 B.C.: Myths and Cult Images* (Oakland: University of California Press, 1982). Reprinted with permission of the Estate of Marija Gimbutas and the University of California Press.

least downgraded, goddesses as divine powers. God became a male who willed that women should be ruled by men. Laws reinforced women's sexual, economic, and political subjugation to men. Traditional Judaism, Christianity, and Islam all embody ideas of male dominance, and they all derive from the tribes who conquered Old Europe in the fifth millennium BCE (Eisler, 1987).

The second change was the development of *plow agriculture*. Long-distance warfare and conquest catered to men's strengths and so greatly enhanced male power and authority. Large-scale farming with plows harnessed to animals had much the same effect. Plow agriculture originated in the Middle East around five thousand years ago. It required that strong adults remain in the fields all day for much of the year. It also reinforced the principle of private ownership of land. Since men were on average stronger than women, and since women were restricted in their activities by pregnancy, nursing, and childbirth, plow agriculture made men more powerful socially. Thus, land was owned by men and ownership was typically passed from father to son (Coontz and Henderson, 1986).

Third came *the separation of public and private spheres*. In the agricultural era, economic production was organized around the household. Men may have worked apart from women in the fields, but the fields were still part of the *family* farm. In contrast, during the early phase of industrialization, men's work was moved out of the household and into the factory and the office. Most men became wage or salary workers. Some assumed decision-making roles in economic and political institutions. But while men went public, most women remained in the domestic or private sphere.

The idea soon developed that this was a "natural" division of labour. This idea persisted until the second half of the twentieth century, when a variety of social circumstances, ranging from the introduction of the birth control pill to women's demands for entry into university, finally allowed women to enter the public sphere in large numbers.

So we see that, according to social constructionists, gender inequality derives historically from three main circumstances: the advent of long-distance warfare and conquest, the development of plow agriculture, and the assignment of women to the domestic sphere and men to the public sphere during the early industrial era.

Although gender inequality is decreasing somewhat in many societies today, it still persists. It is supported by a variety of economic and political arrangements discussed elsewhere in this book (see especially Chapter 8, Gender Inequality). In what follows, I fill out the social constructionist perspective by outlining just two dimensions of contemporary gender inequality. First, I show how socialization still pushes girls to act in stereotypically feminine ways and boys to act in stereotypically masculine ways. I then discuss eating disorders and male violence against women to show that the social construction of gender has far-reaching implications for women, men, and the relations between them.

TIME FOR REVIEW

1. What are the main arguments and criticisms of essentialist approaches to gender differences?
2. What are the main arguments of social constructionist approaches to gender differences?

CONSTRUCTING GENDER THROUGH SOCIALIZATION
PRIMARY SOCIALIZATION

Parents apparently talk differently to boys and girls even before they are born; at least one study found that a mother's voice became sharper and stronger once her baby was identified as a male by a sex-identifying ultrasound (Smith, 2005). Much research shows that, from the moment of birth, infant boys and girls are treated differently by parents, particularly fathers, and especially if the parents are heterosexuals. Girls are more likely to be characterized as delicate, weak, beautiful, and cute; boys as strong, alert, and well-coordinated (Rubin, Provenzano, and Lurra, 1974; Sutfin et al., 2008).

Interpretations of behaviour also vary by the sex of the child. For example, when viewing a videotape of a nine-month-old infant, experimental subjects tend to label startled reactions to a stimulus as "anger" if the baby has been previously identified as a boy, and as "fear" if the baby is identified as a girl, *regardless of the baby's actual sex* (Condry and Condry, 1976). Parents also tend to encourage their sons to engage in boisterous behaviour and competitive play. They tend to encourage their daughters to engage in cooperative play (MacDonald and Parke, 1986). Boys are more likely than girls are to be praised for assertiveness, and girls are more likely than boys to be rewarded for compliance (Kerig, Cowan, and Cowan, 1993).

Parents reinforce gender-specific behaviour by the design of the child's room, the clothes they buy, and the toys they provide. Boys' toys, for example, are more likely to emphasize aggressive competition and spatial manipulation. Girls' toys tend to be more passive and oriented toward the home (for example, dolls, kitchen sets, washers and dryers; Hughes, 1995). Most parents encourage their children to play with gender-stereotyped toys. Preschool boys are just as likely to play with a dish set as a tool set if given a choice—unless they are told that the dish set is a girl's toy and they think their fathers will view playing with it as "bad" (Raag and Rackliff, 1998).

SECONDARY SOCIALIZATION

The process of channelling girls into roles culturally defined as appropriately feminine and boys into roles culturally defined as appropriately masculine continues in school. In most schools, teachers still tend to assume that boys will do better in the sciences and mathematics, girls in languages. Most parents tend to reinforce these expectations at home (Eccles, Jacobs, and Harold, 1990; Gunderson et al., 2012).

By the age of about 14, interaction with peers becomes an important factor in reinforcing gender-typed attitudes and behaviours because the subcultures of male and female peer groups emphasize gender-stereotypical values. Boys tend to establish less intimate friendships than girls do. Moreover, boys' friendships tend to be based on such activities as team sports, which focus on independence, emotional control, and conquest. Girls tend to form less extensive friendship networks than boys do and focus on sociability, popularity, and attractiveness (Elkin and Handel, 1989; Udry, 1971: 76, 82).

THE MASS MEDIA

The symbolic representation of gender in the mass media also creates and reinforces gender stereotypes. It begins when small children learn that only a kiss from Snow White's Prince Charming will save her from eternal sleep and it continues for a lifetime. In popular, general-audience movies, there are about 2.5 times more male than female characters (Smith, 1990). Women perform domestic tasks and attend to their physical attractiveness much more often than men do, while men spend a lot more time than women do engaging in paid work, adventures, and sexual conquests (Paek, Nelson, and Vilela, 2010; Smith, 2012; Zayer et al., 2012). Among couples in romantic movies, the men are often considerably older than the women are (see Figure 5.6).

These characteristics of movies are only tendencies. There are plenty of exceptions to the general pattern. However, the dominant tendencies indicate the features of gender roles that movies reinforce most strongly. Moreover, although movies are only one mass medium, the gendered landscape of popular books, music videos, TV, and video games is similar.

It can be dangerous to challenge the status quo. In 2014, Canadian media critic Anita Sarkeesian spoke out publicly about the fact that women tend to be stereotyped as sex objects in most video games. She received death, bomb, and rape threats for her efforts. Someone created a game on the Web that allowed players to click their mouse to punch an image of her face. Her lecture scheduled for the University of Utah had to be cancelled when the university received an email threatening that, if the talk went ahead, "this will be the deadliest school shooting in American history." It was signed Marc Lépine, the name of the shooter who killed 14 women at l'École Polytechnique de Montréal in 1989. To be sure, the gaming world is changing as women like Anita Sarkeesian speak up and as more women play video games and become game developers (about a fifth of developers are now women). For the time being, it is a highly gendered and sexist world (Wingfield, 2014).

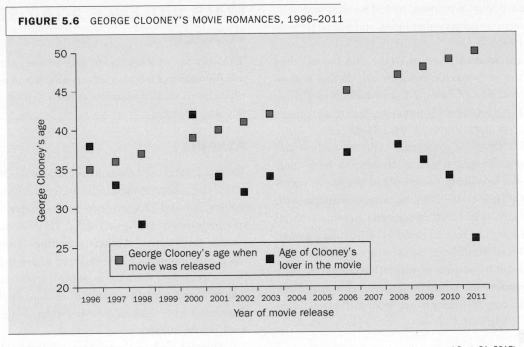

FIGURE 5.6   GEORGE CLOONEY'S MOVIE ROMANCES, 1996–2011

SOURCE: Compiled from *Internet Movie Database* (http://www.imdb.com/name/nm0000123/?ref_=fn_al_nm_1, accessed Sept. 21, 2015).

BODY IMAGE AND EATING DISORDERS

The social construction of gender involves defining standards of physical attractiveness for women and men. Physical attractiveness is especially important for women because they are judged based on appearance more often than men are; men are more likely to be assessed in terms of status and power. What then does the ideal woman look like in our culture? One way of answering this question is to assume that *Playboy* centrefolds represent the cultural ideal and see how their body mass index (BMI) has changed over the years. BMI is equal to body mass in kilograms divided by the square of body height in metres. Most centrefold descriptions conveniently list the woman's height and weight, allowing the calculation of BMI for each "Playmate of the Month."

The spiked blue line in Figure 5.7 plots the BMI of the 609 Playboy centrefolds for whom data were available between 1953 and 2009. The straight red line shows the trend in these data. The average BMI of *Playboy* centrefolds fell 7 percent from 1953 to 2009. The straight black line represents a BMI of 18.5. Physicians say that a BMI of less than 18.5 indicates underweight. By this measure, the average *Playboy* centrefold has been underweight since about 1986. By way of comparison, the average BMI of

Canadian women was 25.2 in 1978–79 and 26.7 in 2004—a rise of 6 percent. Physicians say that a BMI of 25.0 indicates overweight. One may conclude that as the ideal North American woman's body has grown thinner and become underweight, the average North American woman's body has grown heavier and become overweight.

Given the growing discrepancy between ideal and reality, it is not surprising that nine out of ten North American women want to lose weight (Garner, 1997; Walters, 1992). The "cult of thinness" has

FIGURE 5.7   BODY MASS INDEX (BMI) OF 609 PLAYBOY CENTREFOLDS, DEC. 1953–JAN. 2009

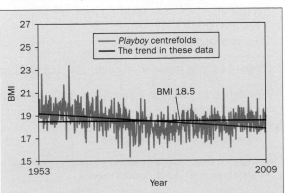

SOURCES: Gammon (2009); Tjepkema (n.d.).

spawned major industries, including diet and self-help, cosmetic surgery, diet foods, and fitness (Hesse-Biber, 1996).

Many women resent the rake-thin models they see in the mass media. Nonetheless, dieting to lose weight and fear of being fat are common in girls as young as nine. One study found that half of all teenage girls are on diets (Pipher, 1994: 184–85).

Body image is associated with self-esteem and behaviour. People who are dissatisfied with their bodies are less likely to desire and engage in sexual activity. (Garner, 1997). At the extreme, concern with body image may result in anorexia nervosa (refusal to eat enough to remain healthy) or bulimia (regular, self-induced vomiting). Some women change their body shape by means of surgical procedures, such as liposuction and cosmetic surgery. Nine out of ten cosmetic surgery patients are women (Hesse-Biber, 1996: 51, 53).

TIME FOR REVIEW

1. How do various agents of socialization help to socially construct gender?
2. Both men and women learn about culturally appropriate body images. For whom does this learning have more negative effects? Why?

MALE VIOLENCE AGAINST WOMEN

The way in which gender and sexual scripts are socially constructed also affects the frequency with which men assault and harass women. Let us consider this issue in detail.

ASSAULT

About 2.5 percent of Canadians are sexually assaulted every year. Approximately 70 percent of them are women. Around 75 Canadians are murdered by their spouses every year. Again, about 70 percent of the victims are women. Women reporting spousal violence to the police are about three-and-a-half times more likely than men are to report severe violence, that is, being sexually assaulted, beaten, choked, or threatened with a gun or a knife (Sinha, 2013; Statistics Canada, 2013b).

Spousal violence and spousal homicide have declined over the past two decades (see Table 5.3), but dating violence seems to be on the rise, and more than 80 percent of victims of dating violence are women. One survey found that even back in the 1990s, a fifth of men in Canadian colleges and universities said they had forced a woman to engage in sexual activities

TABLE 5.3   INTIMATE VIOLENCE IN CANADA, 1993–2011

	1993	1999	2004	2009	2011
Prevalence of self-reported spousal assault, preceding five years (percentage)					
Male victims	n.a.	7	6	6	n.a.
Female victims	12	8	7	6	n.a.
Spousal homicide (per 100 000 men and women)					
Male victims	0.3	0.1	0.1	0.2	0.1
Female victims	0.8	0.7	0.7	0.5	0.5
Sexual assaults reported to police (per 100 000 pop.)	120	78	70	71	63
Prevalence of criminal harassment (stalking) reported to police					
By current or ex-husband or boyfriend	n.a.	1300	2125	7755	6786
By current or ex-wife or girlfriend	n.a.	100	200	1242	n.a.

Note: Some of these figures are approximate because they were read from graphs. The enormous increase in the prevalence of stalking between 1999 and 2009 is largely a result of increased reporting.

SOURCES: Milligan (2011); Sinha (2013); Statistics Canada (2006, 2011a, 2013b).

with them at least once since high school. A recent estimate puts the figure at closer to 50 percent (Anderssen, 2014; Brym, 2014: 124-5; DeKeseredy and Schwartz, 1998).

Of course, men are the victims of violence, too. Like women, they are far more likely to be assaulted by men than by women. Some studies show that female partners are as likely as male partners are to participate in abusive acts—with the exception of sexual assault, which is almost exclusively a male domain (Straus, 1995). Note, however, that women are more likely to use violence as a response to their own powerlessness, attacking partners out of self-defence. Conversely, men are more likely to use force to retain control and power over their partners. Moreover, abusive men are far more likely to cause serious physical injury than abusive women are (see Figure 5.8).

Only about 60 percent of Canadian women whose husbands beat, choke, or threaten them with a gun or a knife report the incident to the police. The figure is even lower—around 52 percent—for women who are sexually assaulted by their husbands. When asked why they do not report instances of spousal or nonspousal violence more often, women typically say they want to deal with the matter privately, they believe the police would not do anything anyway, and they fear publicity and retaliation from the perpetrator (Sinha,

2013: 96, 98–99). In short, shame, fear, and lack of confidence in the criminal justice system combine to prevent many women from reporting assaults against them, even in their most severe forms, including rape.

Research shows that some rapists are men who were physically or sexually abused in their youth. They develop a deep-seated need to feel powerful as emotional compensation for their early powerlessness. Other rapists are men who, as children, saw their mothers as potentially hostile figures who needed to be controlled, or as mere objects available for male gratification, and saw their fathers as emotionally cold and distant. Raised in such a family atmosphere, rapists learn not to empathize with women. Instead, they learn to want to dominate them (Lisak, 1992).

Significantly, rates of rape are especially high during wars, when conquering male soldiers feel justified in wanting to humiliate the vanquished, who are powerless to stop them (Human Rights Watch, 1995). This fact suggests that, in general, rape involves using sex to establish dominance.

In short, the incidence of rape is highest in situations where early socialization experiences predispose men to want to control women, where norms justify the domination of women, and where a large power imbalance between men and women exists (see Critical Sociology: Globalization box).

FIGURE 5.8 SEVERITY OF SPOUSAL VIOLENCE BY SEX OF VICTIM, CANADA, 2009

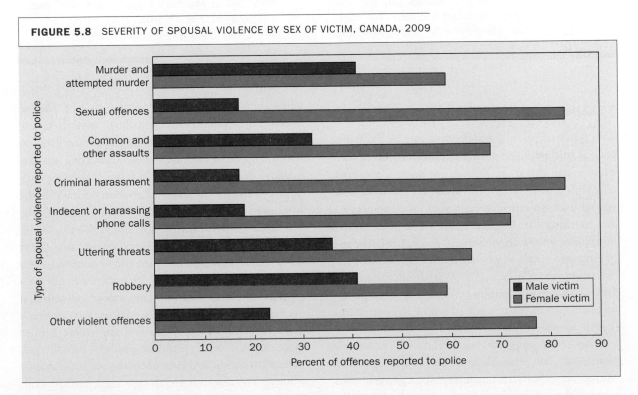

SOURCE: Statistics Canada (2011).

CRITICAL SOCIOLOGY: GLOBALIZATION   THE INTERNATIONALIZATION OF SEX WORK

The sex trade thrives on power imbalances. In Canada and the United States, working as an adult prostitute is associated with certain childhood experiences: growing up in a family that needed social assistance, having a parent or parents with low educational attainment, living in a family or families with a succession of different parents or guardians, living in a foster home or a group home, and experiencing physical and sexual abuse as a child. Working as an adult prostitute is also correlated with adult experiences indicating relative powerlessness, including low educational attainment, enjoying few employment opportunities outside the sex trade, and having an unemployed romantic partner (McCarthy, Benoit, and Jansson, 2014). Especially in Canada's west, a disproportionately large number of sex workers are Indigenous women.

The sex trade has become increasingly globalized in recent decades, as millions of women and girls have been recruited from abroad to work in rich countries. Victims of the sex trade who are recruited from abroad are generally *not* the poorest of the poor. While some victims are deeply impoverished women and girls who are intimidated and kidnapped by traffickers, the great majority of them are potential economic migrants who are not well off but have some money and are eager to find better economic opportunities. Traffickers typically promise them employment, education, or husbands in rich countries, and the victims pay the traffickers for the supposed opportunities. Moreover, victims must typically adhere to norms of beauty,

cleanliness, and politeness that are expected in rich countries. Most victims of sex trafficking have at least gone to high school. Given such requirements, it is not surprising that Eastern European women form a large percentage of sex trafficking victims in North America and Western Europe (Rao and Presenti, 2012).

Once trafficked women arrive in a rich country, they are coerced into working as sex workers. Drugs, beatings, gang rape, and other abusive tactics may be used to get them to comply. Escape is difficult and dangerous.

The first international convention against sex trafficking dates back to 1949. Today, international laws and the laws of 134 countries criminalize it. Nonetheless, the problem continues to grow rapidly. Nearly 21 million adults and children worldwide have been bought and sold as slaves. More than 12.5 million of them are part of the sex trade. Ninety-eight percent of those 12.5 million are women and girls (Equality Now, 2014).

Critical Thinking Questions

1. How does the social profile of sex workers born in Canada differ from the social profile of sex trade workers in Canada who come from abroad? Why do these differences exist?

2. Should laws ban the sex trade or limit it in some way? Why or why not? If you believe such laws should exist, exactly what should they ban or limit? How could they be enforced?

SEXUAL HARASSMENT

Two types of sexual harassment occur in the workplace. **Quid pro quo sexual harassment** takes place when sexual threats or bribery are made a condition of employment decisions. **Hostile environment sexual harassment** involves sexual jokes, comments, and touching that interferes with work or creates an unfriendly work setting. Surveys show that between a quarter and a half of women are sexually harassed in the workplace (Gruber, 1997; Welsh and Nierobisz, 1997). When semipublic and public settings are included, up to 87 percent of women report being sexually harassed (Lenton et al., 1999).

Research suggests that relatively powerless women are the most likely to be sexually harassed. Moreover, sexual harassment is most common in work settings that exhibit high levels of gender inequality

and a culture justifying male domination of women. Specifically, women who are young, unmarried, and employed in nonprofessional jobs are most likely to become objects of sexual harassment. They are particularly likely to be sexually harassed if they are temporary workers, the ratio of women to men in the workplace is low, and the organizational culture of the workplace tolerates sexual harassment (Welsh, 1999).

As the foregoing discussion makes clear, large power imbalances between men and women and a culture that supports patriarchy are associated with high rates of sexual assault and harassment (see Critical Sociology: Social Inequality box). Where men are much more powerful than women are, and where gender inequality is justified culturally, gender is socially constructed to permit and even encourage violence against women. The research literature is clear on this point. It shows, for example, that men who most enjoy sexist

CRITICAL SOCIOLOGY: SOCIAL INEQUALITY INDIGENOUS WOMEN AND INTERSECTIONALITY

Violence against women tends to be more prevalent in lower classes than in higher classes. It also tends to be more prevalent in disadvantaged ethnic and racial groups than in advantaged ethnic and racial groups. Where low class and ethnic/racial status intersect, violence against women is especially widespread. This phenomenon is known as **intersectionality**, the tendency for class location and ethnic or racial group membership to amplify the effect of gender on a range of behaviours, including violence.

Indigenous women in Canada are a case in point. Like Indigenous men, they are victims of conquest, punishing government policy, and widespread discrimination (see Chapter 9, Race and Ethnic Relations). Consequently, they are on average about three times more likely than non-Indigenous women are to live in a dwelling requiring major repairs and about twice as likely to lack a high-school diploma and to be unemployed. They earn about a quarter less than non-Indigenous women do.

Their predicament has pushed them into high-risk situations, including living in communities marked by overcrowded dwellings and widespread alcohol abuse, and disproportionate involvement in prostitution. Not surprisingly, therefore, Indigenous women experience five times the homicide rate of non-Indigenous women and two-and-a-half times the rate of spousal violence. Those who suffer spousal violence are 41 percent more likely than non-Indigenous women are to sustain an injury (Brym, 2014; O'Donnell and Wallace, 2011).

Critical Thinking Questions

1. What non-Indigenous categories of women in Canada suffer from intersectionality?

2. What categories of women in Canada benefit from intersectionality?

Jian Ghomeshi (pictured here) and Members of Parliament Scott Andrews and Massimo Pacetti were among the high-profile, alleged perpetrators of sexual harassment and sexual violence who attracted public notice in 2014. Late in the year, it was discovered that 13 male students in fourth-year dentistry at Dalhousie University had created a Facebook group that, among other things, joked about using chloroform to subdue women and polled members on which female dentistry students they would like to "hate fuck." Meanwhile, at the University of Manitoba, a female dental resident reported receiving a text from a male classmate asking where he could find girls like her. When she asked what he was talking about, he wrote, "oh, because you're a whore." In another text message, the same male resident referred to female dentistry residents as "psycho bitches" and noted that "all females are good for are cooking eggs and sucking cock."

SOURCES: *CBC News* (2014); Coubrough (2014). Photo: © The Canadian Press/Nathan Denette.

jokes are most likely to report engaging in acts of sexual aggression against women and that men who link sexuality with social dominance are more likely to sexually harass women (Pryor, Giedd, and Williams, 1995; Ryan and Kanjorski, 1998).

TIME FOR REVIEW

1. Why does male assault against women tend to be more harmful than female assault against men?

2. Why do women tend not to report sexual assault to the police?

3. What is intersectionality and how does it influence rates of assault against women?

LOOKING AHEAD: TOWARD A NEW SEXUAL ETHIC

For the past 50 years, most sociologists of gender have criticized the essentialist view that sexual scripts are part of "human nature." Rather than seeing sexuality as natural, they have examined how it is socially constructed. They do not deny the biological basis of sexuality. They simply appreciate that the form sexual expression takes is not binary, inevitable and immutable. In the preceding pages, I illustrated the social constructionist case by examining the historical factors that shaped the emergence of sexual scripts, the relationship between gender socialization and sexuality, the ways in which sexual relations reflect and reinforce power differentials, the privileging of heterosexuality, the marginalization of other sexual identities, and the implications of gender roles for the sexual assault and harassment of women by men. There remains the task of discussing the implications of these insights for the new sexual ethic that is emerging in much of the world and the role that feminism has played in advancing it.

FEMINISM AND SEXUALITY

Feminism has been chiefly responsible for the social constructionist turn in the study of gender and sexuality. Its influence has been multifaceted.

In the 1970s and 1980s, some feminists took what many scholars now regard as an extreme position on the question of sexuality. For example, Catherine Mackinnon argued that heterosexual sex, even when it is consensual, necessarily involves a man *dominating* a woman. Why? Because, according to Mackinnon, men enjoy the power to define the meaning of sexuality, even for women. By sexualizing hierarchy and defining domination as pleasure, they limit the way women are allowed to experience and express their sexuality (Mackinnon, 1997: 158, 167; see also Jeffreys, 1990; Kitzinger and Wilkinson, 1994).

Mackinnon and others found abundant evidence of this process in the male-controlled pornography industry. Some estimates peg annual revenue from the global porn industry at about US$100 billion a year, making it as big as IBM or BMW and bigger than Microsoft. According to Andrea Dworkin, pornography oppresses women in three ways (Dworkin, 1981, 1987). First, it exploits women who work in the pornography industry by paying them low wages and requiring that they engage in demeaning acts of submission and abuse. Second, it teaches men how to treat women sexually. Specifically, by eroticizing and normalizing the degradation of women, pornography contributes to sexual harassment and the sexual and physical abuse of women, including rape. Third, pornography teaches women what men supposedly want—how they should dress, act, and have intercourse in ways that please men. In all these ways, then, pornography helps to turn heterosexual sex into male domination. The Internet intensifies the problem, not just because it makes pornography easily accessible but because it makes pornography easily accessible to *children*. As one sex educator claims, "the porn industry is the country's main sex educator of our boys and girls" (Schwartz, 2014).

Some feminists have criticized the view that men control the meaning of sexuality and have turned heterosexual sex into a form of male domination. They point out that while *gender* inequality tends to favour male domination of women, *sexual* inequality tends to favour heterosexuality over homosexuality (Rubin, 1993: 33). Lesbians are discriminated against and oppressed as women *and* as members of a sexual minority; gays, male transvestites, and other male sexual minority group members are discriminated against and oppressed despite the fact that they are men. Sexuality, the critics conclude, is rooted not just in gender stratification but also in sexual stratification.

A second feminist criticism of Mackinnon's view that men control the meaning of sexuality and have turned heterosexual sex into a form of male domination cites contradictory data. It is a matter of historical fact that pornography has not always involved male domination of women. For example, between the 1910s and 1950s, many pornographic films were playful, even silly depictions of a wide variety of sexual acts involving laughter, sweet expressions, and moments of shared affection (Power, 2009: 52–53). They were not the humiliating and often sadistic medium of women's oppression we know today so much as attempts to encourage sexual freedom. They support the idea that pornography and, more generally, sexuality, have not always expressed, and do not necessarily express, gender and sexual inequality. Pornography and, more generally, sexuality can be a means for women and men to create and disseminate their own sexual scripts based on female and male sexual fantasies, both heterosexual and nonheterosexual (Matrix, 1996).

Sexual Pluralism

In reality, more and more people accept that sexuality does not have to be expressed in traditionally feminine or masculine ways. An attitude of **sexual pluralism** is growing (Weeks, 1986). For most people, sexual pluralism does *not* mean "anything goes." Most sexual pluralists recognize that there will always be a need to regulate sexual behaviour. For example, they oppose the abuse of power in sexual relations and see the need for the state to punish, and help prevent, incest, rape, and other forms of sexual abuse. Sexual pluralism *does* mean judging sexual acts only by their meaning for the participants. Are power relations at play? If so, are they harmful to the participants? These are the sorts of questions that sexual pluralists use in evaluating the validity of sexual acts. They do not automatically condemn a sexual practice because it is, say, "homosexual" or "heterosexual." From a sexual pluralist perspective, heterosexuality is not inherently about men dominating women any more than it is inherently about strict adherence to traditional masculine and feminine sexual scripts. The sexual expression of heterosexuality may involve the perpetuation of harmful relations of domination or it may not. Sexual pluralists would judge only the former negatively. Sexual pluralism, then, fosters a view of sexuality as something more than a form of victimization because of unequal power relations. It also encourages people to see sexuality positively, as a means of achieving greater pleasure, freedom of expression, and self-realization.

Riane Eisler (1987) convincingly argues that, for the first time in 7000 years, social conditions now make it possible for humanity to return to the state of rough gender equality that existed before the invasion of Old Europe by conquering hordes from the north, east, and south. At least in the world's rich countries, nothing prevents us from adopting social policies that would create gender equality in the workplace, the home, and other spheres of life (see Chapter 8, Gender Inequality). As this chapter demonstrates, the examination and redefinition of sexuality is an important step in the process of achieving gender equality.

TIME FOR REVIEW

1. In your opinion, is heterosexual sex a form of male domination?
2. What is sexual pluralism?

SUMMARY

1. **What is the difference between sex and gender?**
   Sex refers to biological differences between males and females while *gender* refers to the attitudes, beliefs, and behaviours that we commonly associate with each sex.

2. **What does the sociological study of sexuality teach us about the notion that men and women are "opposites" and, more generally, about variation in sexual preferences within human populations?**
   The sociological study of sexuality demonstrates that the notion of men and women as sexual opposites is invalid and, more generally, that tremendous variation exists in sexual preferences within human populations. Specifically, lesbians, gays, bisexuals, people who are intersex, and people who are transgender form substantial parts of all human populations; the sexual orientations of people may fluctuate over time and in different settings; and the sexual behaviour and preferences of all sexual groups, including heterosexuals, often do not conform to stereotypes.

3. **What is the difference between essentialist and social constructionist explanations of gender differences?**
   Essentialism holds that gender differences are the result of dissimilarity in the genetic composition of women and men, the structure of the male and female brain, and/or the psychological makeup of the two sexes. Social constructionism holds that gender differences widened under identifiable sociohistorical circumstances and are sustained by social and cultural institutions that accord men and women different amounts of power and teach men and women different gender roles.

4. **What are the main criticisms of essentialism?**
   Essentialism ignores the historical and cultural variability of gender and sexuality. It deflects attention from the fact that gender differences are declining and, in some cases, have disappeared. It employs deeply flawed research evidence. It tends to generalize from the average, ignoring variations within gender groups. It exaggerates the degree to which gender differences are unchangeable. It offers explanations for gender differences that ignore the important role of power.

5. **What are the main agents of gender socialization?**
   The main agents of gender socialization are families, schools, and the mass media.

6. **What are the main social causes of male violence against women?**
   Where men are much more socially powerful than women are, and where gender inequality is justified culturally, gender is socially constructed to permit and even encourage violence against women.

QUESTIONS TO CONSIDER

1. Do you think sexual orientation is genetically programmed or a function of social experience? On what do you base your opinion? What type of evidence would persuade you one way or the other?

2. Design a study to test whether gender roles are inherent or socially constructed.

3. What policy recommendations would you make to lower the level of sexual assault and sexual harassment? Why do you think these policies would be effective?

GLOSSARY

Bisexuals (p. 105) are attracted to sexual partners of either sex.

Essentialists (p. 111) observe male–female differences in sexual scripts, the division of labour at home and in the workplace, mate selection, sexual aggression, jealousy, promiscuity, fidelity, and so on. They then interpret these differences as natural and universal.

Gender (p. 105) encompasses the feelings, attitudes, and behaviours that are associated with being male or female, as conventionally understood.

Gender identity (p. 105) refers to identification with, or a sense of belonging to, a particular sex, biologically, psychologically, and socially.

A **gender role** (p. 105) comprises the repertoire of behaviours that match widely shared expectations about how males and females are supposed to act.

Heteronormativity (p. 105) is the belief that one's biological sex should be perfectly aligned with one's sexual preferences, gender identity, and gender role.

Homosexuals (p. 105) prefer sexual partners of the same sex.

Hostile environment sexual harassment (p. 120) involves sexual jokes, comments, and touching that interfere with work or create an unfriendly work setting.

Intersectionality (p. 121) is the tendency for class location and ethnic or racial group membership to amplify the effect of gender on a range of behaviours, including violence.

Intersex people (p. 105) do not fit conventional male or female sex categories. Often, intersex people do not have a sex chromosome that is XX or XY, and their genitals, reproductive system, and secondary sexual characteristics (such as breasts and body hair) are not distinctly male or female in the conventional sense of the term.

Queer theory (p. 109) denies the existence of stable sexual orientations and argues that when we use terms like "heterosexual," "gay," lesbian," and so on, we are adopting official or at least socially acceptable labels that fail to capture the fluidity and variability of people's actual identities and performances.

Quid pro quo sexual harassment (p. 120) involves sexual threats or bribery used to extract sexual favours as a condition of employment decisions.

Sex (p. 104) refers to being born with distinct male or female genitalia and a genetic program that releases either male or female hormones to stimulate the development of one's reproductive system.

Sexuality (p. 106) involves actions that are intended to produce erotic arousal and genital response.

Sexual orientation (p. 109) refers to the way a person derives sexual pleasure, including whether desirable partners are of the same or a different sex.

Sexual pluralism (p. 122) assesses sexual acts only by their meaning for the participants.

Sexual scripts (p. 106) are assumptions that guide sexual behaviour by telling us whom we should find attractive, when and where it is appropriate to be aroused, what is sexually permissible, and so on.

Social constructionism (p. 114) is the main alternative to essentialism. Social constructionists argue that gender differences are not the product of biological properties, whether chromosomal, gonadal, or hormonal. Instead, gender and sexuality are products of social structure and culture.

Sociobiology (p. 111) is a variant of essentialism. It holds that all human beings instinctually want to ensure that their genes get passed on to future generations. However, the different reproductive status of men and women means that they have had to develop different adaptive strategies. This gave rise to "masculine" and "feminine" patterns of behaviour that presumably became genetically encoded because of their adaptive value.

Transgender (p. 105) People who are transgender are uncomfortable with the gender assigned to them at birth or do not fit neatly into male or female gender categories.

CHAPTER 6

COMMUNICATION AND MASS MEDIA

Sonia Bookman
UNIVERSITY OF MANITOBA

SOURCE: © Richard Baker/In Pictures/Corbis.

AFTER READING THIS CHAPTER, YOU WILL BE ABLE TO:

- Identify the social significance and key characteristics of the mass media.

- Summarize the main sociological explanations of mass media influence.

- Distinguish different types of mass media.

- Outline the potential of social media to contribute to, and limit, the democratization of communications and culture.

WHY STUDY THE MASS MEDIA?

On a sunny day in August, 2014, Leonardo DiCaprio, two First Nations Chiefs, and the president of the Sierra Club, an environmental organization, took the "'Ice Bucket Challenge" at Lake Athabasca. DiCaprio had been visiting the tar sands in northern Alberta to conduct research for an environmental documentary (Canadian Press, 2014a). A video recording of the event was posted on DiCaprio's Facebook page, accompanied by a statement. The statement said that two First Nations chiefs, the president of an environmental group and DiCaprio himself were challenging the president of the Canadian Association of Petroleum Producers, two executives of major Canadian tar sands firms, and Prime Minister Stephen Harper to take the ice bucket challenge (DiCaprio, 2014).

The Ice Bucket Challenge involved people getting drenched with a bucket of ice water on video and nominating others to do the same thing to raise awareness of ALS (Lou Gehrig's disease). The videos were posted on Facebook and Twitter. Nominees either accepted the challenge or made a donation to an ALS charity—or both. Harper opted to make a donation to ALS Canada. Some, like DiCaprio, used their videos to promote awareness of other social concerns. Harnessing his star power and the viral nature of the campaign, DiCaprio made sure his video raised funds for ALS and created awareness of the detrimental effects of Canadian tar sands development on the environment and on the people of northern Alberta in particular.

Overall, the Ice Bucket Challenge was heralded as a success, raising both awareness and considerable funds for ALS charities (ALS Association, 2014). Described as "one of the most viral philanthropic social media campaigns in history" (Canadian Press, 2014b), videos of people being doused with ice water spread rapidly through social media networks. DiCaprio's video alone received 50 000 "shares" and a quarter of a million "likes" within weeks of its Facebook launch. The campaign was also far-reaching, attracting participants from the United States, Canada, Australia, India, Brazil, and elsewhere. Newspaper and TV reports on the campaign spread the news even farther afield.

The Ice Bucket Challenge illustrates the growing importance of social media in mobilizing social activists. As I discuss later, social media not only enable campaign messages to spread quickly through people's online networks, they also create opportunities on a global scale for participating in movements that aim to change society. They allow social movements—collective attempts to change aspects of society—to go viral, making them a cultural sensation.

Of course, social media represent just one (albeit a very important) segment of the mass media, which include TV, the movies, newspapers, radio, and so on. Nonetheless, the use of social media typified by The Ice Bucket Challenge raises several questions that sociologists ask when analyzing the mass media in general: How do the mass media affect individuals, institutions, and collective processes such as the growth of social movements? In turn, how does society shape media images, institutions, and industries? How can we explain the influence of the media, its institutions, and its relationship to society?

In this chapter, I address each of these questions. I outline key approaches to understanding the mass media, focusing on different aspects of media production, messaging, and consumption. I also explore contemporary media developments and trends, notably the rise of social media and their impact on communications and culture. First, however, it is important

The Ice Bucket Challenge: A viral social movement and cultural phenomenon that celebrities and ordinary people popularized in 2014.
SOURCE: Debby Wong/Shutterstock.com.

to discuss exactly what sociologists mean by the term *mass media*.

WHAT ARE THE MASS MEDIA?

What comes to mind when you think of the mass media? Mobile phones? Video games? Advertising agencies? The Walt Disney Company? The mass media encompass all of these technologies, institutions, and processes. However, it is less useful to define the mass media by listing examples than by discussing their chief characteristics. The **mass media** are technology-driven and usually profit-driven methods of communicating meaningful information between one source and many recipients or between many sources and many recipients (O'Shaughnessy and Stadler, 2012). Let us consider the features of this definition in detail:

- *The mass media are technology-driven means of communication.* All **communication** involves people exchanging meaningful information using signs or representations of things, people, events, and ideas. The mass media are one means of communication. They differ from talking face to face insofar as they employ technology to send and receive messages across time and/or space. So the first characteristic of the mass media is that they are means of communication driven by technologies located between senders and receivers.

- *The mass media link many people.* Two tin cans joined by a taut piece of string are a technology that links a sender and a receiver, allowing them to communicate meaningful information. However, such a device is not a *mass* medium because it links only two people. The mass media link many people. Newspapers, books, magazines, radio, the movies, television, and various Internet and mobile phone applications, including YouTube, Facebook, and Twitter, qualify as mass media.

- *Traditional mass media involved one-to-many communication.* From the mid-fifteenth century until the latter half of the twentieth century, the mass media transmitted` messages from single, fixed sources to large audiences. The first truly mass medium, the printing press, was developed by Johannes Gutenberg in 1455 and was powered by human muscle (Lorimer, Gasher and Skinner, 2008). Steam and other technologies were adapted to printing in the eighteenth and nineteenth centuries, allowing the mass production of books, newspapers, and print advertisements (McFall, 2004).

The late nineteenth and early twentieth centuries witnessed the introduction of film, radio, and television, but even these electronic media involved communication from single sources to many audience members. True, in recent decades,

"Modern Advertising: A Railway Station, 1874," by Alfred Concanen. In the nineteenth century, industrialized print technologies were first used to make advertising posters, which were posted in an increasingly organized manner in public spaces such as railway stations.

SOURCE: National Railway Museum/Science & Society Picture Library.

audiences have become more fragmented. For example, the introduction of cable, satellite, and digital television has allowed television channels to multiply. Compared to the early days of television, when audiences could choose from, at most, only a few channels, telecommunications providers now offer hundreds of specialty channels, packaged and targeted to niche audiences. Still, audiences for each source number from the hundreds of thousands to many millions.

• *New media involve many-to-many communication.* By 1977, personal computers were being mass-produced. Engineers had already invented hypertext—a way for a computer monitor to display text containing links to other text that a user could access immediately. Then, in 1989, Tim Berners-Lee developed an implementation of hypertext on a computer network via the Internet, giving birth to what became known as the World Wide Web. It was now possible for anyone with the appropriate technology to communicate with many other people, a process that was greatly aided by the introduction of the first graphical browser and the first smart phone in 1993. The Internet thus initiated a process of media "demassification," allowing ordinary individuals to create and circulate their own messages to many other people, and media fragmentation, allowing the creation of many niche audiences.

The new media that have emerged since the early 1990s and that we use every day when we fire up our smart phones, laptops, and tablets integrate digitized data, text, sound, and images. The new media enable people like you and me to create content and broadcast it. The new media are wireless and mobile, allowing us to produce content on the fly. Audience members can interact with the content and recirculate it to others. So, while traditional mass media involved "one-to-many" communication, the new media make "many-to-many" communication possible (see Table 6.1).

• *Commercial interests strongly influence the mass media.* Most mass media, traditional and new, are dominated by large corporations whose main goal is to satisfy advertisers and earn profits for shareholders. For instance, the market value of Google was US$366.4 billion in late November 2014. Google is primarily a search engine, dominating Internet search globally with an over 83 percent market share, but it also operates a variety of other Internet services, including email, cloud storage, mapping, social networking, and online advertising (Hesmondalgh, 2013: 329). The company is also working on all manner of experimental projects, including self-driving cars, drone delivery, wind power, electronic eyewear, and even a tremor-cancelling

TABLE 6.1   TRADITIONAL MEDIA AND NEW MEDIA COMPARED

TRADITIONAL MEDIA ...	NEW MEDIA ...
Use analogue information (recordings of sound and light waves)	Use digital information (translations of sound and light waves into digits—0s and 1s—thus removing noise, compressing bandwidth, and increasing security, among other advantages)
Employ a broadcast (one-to-many) model of communication	Employ a network (many-to-many) model of communication
Reach a mass audience	Reach a more fragmented audience
Use immobile, centralized production facilities	Decentralize production and render it more mobile
Allow communication from sender to receiver	Allow interaction between sender and receiver
Separate means of communication into different devices (telephone, television, radio, book, stereo system, and so on)	Converge types of media into one device (for example, a smart phone combines the functions of a telephone, a television, a radio, a book reader, a music player, a Web browser, and a GPS device)

SOURCES: Based on T. Flew and T. Smith, *New Media: An Introduction, Canadian Edition* (Toronto: Oxford University Press, 2011); M. O'Shaughnessy and J. Stadler, *Media and Society, Fifth Edition* (South Melbourne, Australia: Oxford University Press, 2012).

spoon for Parkinson's patients. It has grown rapidly, in part by acquiring related companies and websites, including YouTube and Blogger.

The foregoing considerations clarify why I define the mass media as technology-driven and usually profit-driven methods of communicating meaningful information between one source and many recipients or between many sources and many recipients. Bearing this definition in mind, we can now consider how the mass media influence us.

MASS MEDIA AND SOCIETY

Think of the mass media that you encounter in a typical day. You might wake up to hip-hop streaming from an app on your mobile phone, chuckle at an amusing ad in a bus shelter, text friends to arrange an afternoon coffee break, watch a sociology lecture on YouTube because you missed it on Monday when you were home with a cold, catch an episode of *Orange Is the New Black* on Netflix, and upload a photo of a delicious salad on Instagram. The mass media are not just an important part of everyday life—they are by some measures the most important part. They offer information, entertainment, a means of staying connected to family and friends, and a way to meet new people. If you are like most North Americans,

you spend more time interacting with the mass media than engaging in any other single activity, including working and sleeping. So exactly how do the mass media influence us?

The easy answer is that the mass media help us to define who we are as individuals and as members of a range of collectivities, including our local community, ethnic group, religious group, and country. (We'll get to the hard answer later.) Where do you get your ideas about the clothes that are cool or fashionable this season? About the music that moves you? About what is worth reading? About the movie you're dying to see this weekend? About which careers are worth pursuing? About what you want in a life partner? About how to treat others and how others should treat you? About the people you should associate with and the people you should avoid? About where you feel at home and where you feel like a stranger? Certainly, you learn some of these things directly from your family, friends, school, religious institution, and so on. However, insofar as the mass media create "imagined communities" and entice you to join them, they contribute heavily to your socialization, your culture, and therefore your sense of self.

An **imagined community** is a social world composed of members who do not necessarily know each other or meet in person yet consider themselves part of that social world (Anderson, 1989). There are

Members of an imagined community called "Canada" congregate at the Maple Leaf pub in London, United Kingdom, to watch the men's hockey final of the 2014 Winter Olympics on satellite TV, enabling them to reinforce their citizenship ties and sense of national identity.
SOURCE: © Robert J. Brym.

about 35 million Canadians. You may know a couple hundred of them personally. What links you to the other 34 999 800? The crowd that flowed into the streets outside the Maple Leaf pub in Covent Garden (London, United Kingdom) during the men's hockey final of the 2014 Winter Olympics could have told you. Passersby looked askance when our boys in red and white scored and the throng burst into a rousing chorus of *O Canada*, but at that moment, the bond between each person at the pub and the more than 15 million other Canadians watching the game everywhere from Afghanistan to Alberta could not have been stronger. Signals communicated by satellite to televisions, computers, and cellphones around the world helped to reinforce the sense that they were proud citizens of a community that was in part imagined: Canada. Some people say you're not a true Canadian unless you know the meaning of three numerical expressions: 99, two-four, and double-double. Chances are you learned the meaning of these terms from the mass media.

Modern mass media untether imagined communities from single, fixed locations. As late as the 1970s, Canadian immigrants were largely cut off from their countries of origin apart from occasional letters and perhaps a rare trip to the homeland for a special occasion. Today, immigrants from India, Pakistan, the Philippines, Egypt, China, Russia, and elsewhere think nothing of watching programs from their country of origin on satellite TV and participating in video calls with friends and relatives back home using Skype. Doing so enables them to maintain their ethnic ties and identity in a way that was impossible before the era of inexpensive global communication. Moreover, social media allow new kinds of imagined social communities to form—communities based not on kinship, geographical origin, or physical proximity but **virtual communities** based on shared interests, existing on the Internet and in the minds of their members (Rheingold, 1993). If you are an iRobot fan you can swap photos and share stories on iRobot's Facebook page, and if you are looking for a dating site that caters to zombie lovers or people who want to live gluten-free or female prisoners or people who like to dress up as cartoon characters, well, you can become a member of those imagined communities, too.

Earlier I asked, "So exactly how do the mass media influence us?" I replied, "The easy answer is that the mass media help us to define who we are as individuals and as members of a range of collectivities." That much should now be clear. But what then is the hard answer? Arriving at the hard answer first requires recognizing that expressions like "the mass media help us to define who we are" are pretty vague statements of cause and effect, insofar as they give no indication of *how* the mass media help us to define who we are or *how much* they help us to do so. Scholars disagree about these issues (Hjarvard, 2013). We need to understand their analyses to sort out the hard answer for ourselves.

At one extreme, some analysts make it seem as if people are just complex iRobots. I refer to this school of thought as **media determinism**. From the point of view of some media determinists, we are programmed to buy, aspire, envy, vote, eat, dress, dance, protest, and love in ways that suit those who control the mass media and entice us with their ideals of the good life. Others emphasize the role of media technologies, suggesting that they shape communications and culture more broadly. At the other extreme are analysts who hold that we are free to choose the media messages that suit us. I refer to this school of thought as **media voluntarism**. From the point of view of media voluntarists, *we* decide who we are and which imagined communities we will join, the mass media merely offering us an inviting menu of options almost without end. As you will see, the truth lies somewhere between these two extremes.

TIME FOR REVIEW

1. What are the key characteristics of the mass media?
2. What is new about new media?
3. What are imagined communities? How do the mass media help to create the imagined communities you participate in?

DETERMINISTIC THEORIES OF MEDIA INFLUENCE

INNIS AND McLUHAN

Harold Innis (1894–1952) and his student, Marshall McLuhan (1911–1980) were early pioneers in the study of the mass media. Both were Canadians, and both were media determinists. Innis (1951) distinguished time-based media that are characterized by endurance and relative immobility (such as writing on stone tablets) from space-based media that are relatively short-lived but can easily traverse great distances (such as radio signals). He sought to demonstrate that different types of media create different kinds of social institutions and values. Specifically, time-based media foster traditionalism and established religion. Space-based media encourage colonization, empire-building, and the growth of secular states and armies.

McLuhan (1964) added that when new mass media are introduced, the very way we perceive and think changes. For example, printing undermined oral communication and, therefore, pre-literate cultures based on talk. Print media encouraged the development of cultures that are more visually oriented, abstract, individualistic, and rational than pre-literate cultures are. In the twentieth century, electronic media undermined print-based cultures. For instance, television affects its audience more deeply than print does because it combines hearing with seeing. It is also more socially inclusive than print is because watching television requires less training and effort than reading does and so is accessible to more people. Finally, television allows communication to occur at the speed of light. It shrinks the world, creating what McLuhan called a "global village." In a way that no preceding mass medium did, television holds out the hope that people can begin to identify with a collectivity that had previously been conceived only in theoretical terms: humanity as a whole. If McLuhan were alive today, he would no doubt see the Internet as an additional step along that path.

THE POLITICAL-ECONOMY PERSPECTIVE

Today, the **political-economy perspective** is the dominant form of media determinism. Proponents of the political-economy perspective are chiefly concerned with how power relations and the pursuit of profit shape (1) media ownership, production, and distribution, and (2) media influence (Mosco, 2009). Let us consider each of these issues in turn.

Concentration of Ownership and Control

In a complex society like ours, members of various classes, ethnic groups, genders, and regions inevitably

Harold Innis (1894–1952).
SOURCE: UTA, H.A. Innis, B1972-0003/034(57).

Marshall McLuhan (1911–1980).
SOURCE: Josephine Smith, Marshall McLuhan fonds, Library and Archives Canada, accession number 1988-022 NPC, PA-172791.

have somewhat different cultural tastes and definitions of how they can best promote the well-being of themselves and their society. In a truly democratic society, one would expect the mass media to reflect diverse interests in news reporting and entertainment programming. If news and entertainment programs were all about issues and features that interested only, say, well-to-do, middle-aged, white men, other categories of the population might be excused for failing to see themselves and their interests reflected in the mass media. They might not regard their interests as well served. They might consider news and entertainment programming biased and undemocratic.

From this point of view, too much media concentration is a danger signal. **Media concentration** refers to the process by which fewer and fewer companies control the mass media over time as smaller and less efficient companies go out of business or get bought up by bigger and more efficient companies (Straw, Gabriele, and Wagman, 2011). Media concentration can be limited by government policy that supports a large, publicly funded broadcaster such as the CBC and sets rules ensuring that the mass media express a wide diversity of viewpoints and do not become concentrated beyond a certain level. However, the opposite tendency has been evident in Canadian government policy since the 1980s. Successive federal governments have loosened media regulation and cut funding to the CBC. They have thus contributed to mergers and acquisitions though which privately owned media companies have expanded in size and shrunk in number. The Canadian story is different only in scale from the global scene, where a handful of global multimedia titans have emerged in recent decades (Hesmondalgh, 2013).

Forbes business magazine lists the top 10 global media companies every year, ranked by an index that combines profits, market value, assets, and sales (see Figure 6.1). In 2014, nine of the ten biggest media companies were American. These megacorporations own and control multiple media industries. For example, 21st Century Fox, headquartered in New York, enjoys annual revenue of more than US$30 billion and is the 152nd-largest corporation in the world. It operates broadcast television stations and produces and licenses television programming in the United States, Canada, Europe, Asia, and Latin America. It also produces, acquires, and distributes motion pictures worldwide. Through News Corp, it publishes newspapers and books, provides information services, and operates the Fox News Channel. Its main shareholder is billionaire Rupert Murdoch. Many media scholars have criticized Fox News for failing to live up to its claim of being "fair

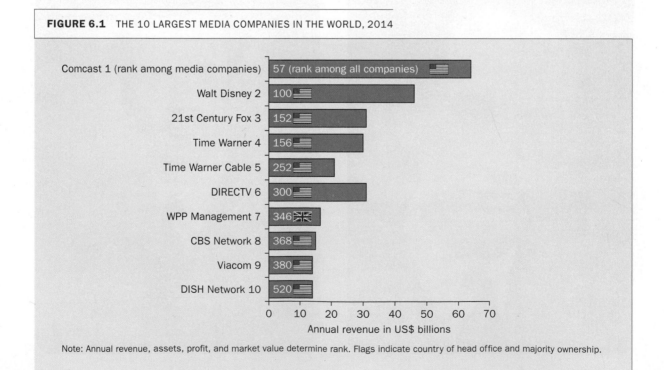

FIGURE 6.1 THE 10 LARGEST MEDIA COMPANIES IN THE WORLD, 2014

Note: Annual revenue, assets, profit, and market value determine rank. Flags indicate country of head office and majority ownership.

and balanced." They claim that Fox News promotes a right-wing political agenda in its news coverage and commentary that strongly favours white, well-to-do Americans at the expense of everyone else (Straw, Gabriele, and Wagman, 2011).

In most countries, a second tier of national companies controls a large part of media production and distribution (Herman and McChesney, 1997: 53). Canada is a case in point. Control of newspapers, television, radio, telephony, and the Internet is concentrated in just eight companies, including Rogers Communications, Telus, Shaw, Quebecor, and Bell Media. Only one of Canada's eight big media companies—the CBC—is publicly owned and funded, and it stands in seventh place, with annual revenue totalling less than 2 percent of the revenue earned by the other seven media giants (see Figure 6.2). Again, we find quite a remarkable degree of media concentration and a tendency toward more of the same.

Of particular concern, three media conglomerates—Rogers Communications, Bell Media, and Telus—dominate Canada's wireless market, and along with Shaw and Videotron, they also dominate the Internet market. As a report on media concentration in Canada maintained, "[T]he dominance by a small number of firms in these markets becomes a greater concern as the Internet becomes more important to Canadians, with a handful of firms having potential gatekeeping power over the content Canadians wish to access" (Theckedath and Thomas, 2012). A main

concern has to do with the issue of **net neutrality**—the principle that networks remain unbiased in terms of content transmission, regardless of source, ownership, data size, or destination (Flew and Smith, 2011). The fear is that telecommunications carriers who control the Internet market will develop discriminatory practices such as limiting the amount of bandwidth available for certain activities (such as downloading movies) or giving preferential access to services within their own corporate family (Flew and Smith, 2011).

Corporate Integration

In their quest to dominate markets, large media companies engage in corporate integration (Hesmondalgh, 2013). **Corporate integration** involves the acquisition by one company of other companies in similar or related fields. Such acquisitions afford opportunities for cross-promotion of media products. For example, in Canada, Rogers owns the Rogers Centre and the Toronto Blue Jays. It promotes the Blue Jays on its sports radio stations and television channels. Recently, Rogers acquired a controlling stake in the rights to broadcast NHL games in Canada. It also developed an app that streams NHL games to smart phones and other wireless devices. It sells smart phones online and in its retail outlets. It owns *Maclean's*, *Chatelaine*, and about seven dozen other magazines, where it advertises its new capability under the slogan, "Hockey's New Home"—placing Rogers at the centre of Canadian culture and life.

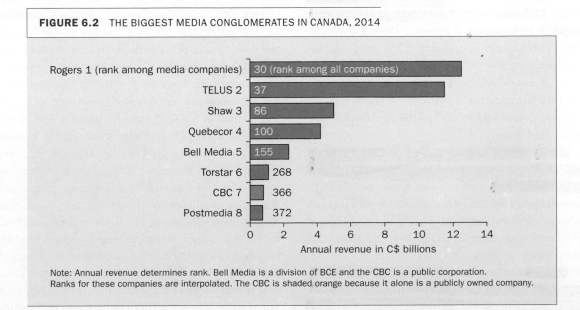

FIGURE 6.2 THE BIGGEST MEDIA CONGLOMERATES IN CANADA, 2014

Note: Annual revenue determines rank. Bell Media is a division of BCE and the CBC is a public corporation. Ranks for these companies are interpolated. The CBC is shaded orange because it alone is a publicly owned company.

SOURCES: Adapted from BCE (2014: 15); CBC (2014); FP500: 2014. (2014).

Rogers magnifies its ability to sell its products by integrating a wide range of companies across many related industries, including professional sports, cable television, cellular telecommunication, retailing, and print media. Each branch promotes the others, making the whole richer than its parts would be under separate ownership.

Cultural Imperialism or Globalization?

According to some researchers working in the political-economy tradition of media research, the global domination of the mass media by large, "top-tier," mainly United States-based companies amounts to **cultural imperialism**—the imposition of American culture and values on almost everyone worldwide (Schiller, 1976; see also Herman and McChesney, 1997). In Canada, for example, television programming, popular music, movies, and video games are saturated with American product.

While American media products are undoubtedly popular worldwide, critics of the cultural imperialism thesis emphasize four countertrends. First, non-American competitors abound. For instance, "Bollywood"—the Indian film industry based in Mumbai—produces more films per year than Hollywood does and distributes its products throughout Asia and to Indian communities in North America and Europe (Sturken and Cartwright, 2009). Films produced in "Nollywood"—the Nigerian film industry—are popular throughout Africa.

A second countertrend involves the degree to which countries outside the United States adapt and change American cultural products to reflect local conditions and cultures (Gillespie, 1995; Robertson, 1995). This process, sometimes called *indigenization* or *glocalization*, is especially evident in the transformation of inner-city American hip-hop into a musical form that expresses the anger of First Nations youth in Canada, pro-democracy youth in Senegal and Tunisia, and so on.

Third, foreign sources influence American mass media, reversing the process identified by the cultural imperialism thesis. The popular television series *In Treatment* and *Homeland* were adapted from Hebrew-language television series originating in Israel (*Betipul* and *Khatufim*, respectively). *Ugly Betty* is a remake of Colombian soap opera, *Yo soy Betty, la fea*.

Fourth, we should note that governments, particularly in France and Canada, have sought with some success to constrain the influence of the American mass media through the regulation of local media industries (see the Critical Sociology: Protest and Policy box).

Mention of official policy ought to remind us that the governments of some countries control the mass media so tightly that cultural imperialism on the part of giant transnational capitalist enterprises is barely noticeable. Strong state control of television and the Internet in Russia, China, Cuba, and Iran, for example, make the Canadian and American media markets seem like the Wild West in terms of diversity and competitiveness. All five of the factors just listed lead one to question the force with which proponents of the cultural imperialism thesis make their case.

The Newspaper Industry

Concentration of the newspaper industry is an area of special concern for media analysts because newspapers, including their digital editions, provide important information about current events, politics, the economy, education, and other issues that concern the public. A healthy democracy requires that newspapers vigorously express diverse viewpoints, not homogenize public opinion. Yet Canada's news industry became highly concentrated in the 1970s, and concentration intensified in the 1990s and 2000s with a series of mergers, takeovers, and closures (Skinner and Gasher, 2005).

By 2014, there were just 111 daily newspapers in the country—about 1 for every 320 000 people—owned by a mere 15 companies. The lion's share of circulation was controlled by a few large media corporations. Quebecor Media owned 38 dailies, including *Le Journal de Montréal*, *Le Journal de Québec*, and the *Sun* newspaper chain. Torstar owned 13 dailies, including the *Toronto Star* and *Metro* papers in cities across the country. Postmedia owned 10 dailies, including the *National Post* (Newspapers Canada, 2014). Late in 2014, Postmedia struck a deal to buy Quebecor's English-language news media, encompassing *Sun* dailies in Ottawa, Toronto, Calgary, Edmonton, and Winnipeg, *The London Free Press*, and more than 160 community newspapers, magazines, and trade publications. The price tag: more than $300 million (Bradshaw, 2014). Once finalized, Postmedia will enjoy a virtual monopoly of the English-language newspaper market in many of the country's major cities. New Brunswickers know what that's like. The province's three dailies are all owned by one man: James Irving. He is the 106th richest man in the world and the province's biggest employer. Little wonder

CRITICAL SOCIOLOGY: PROTEST AND POLICY   GOVERNMENT INTERVENTION IN CANADIAN MEDIA INDUSTRIES

The Canadian government has established policies, regulatory bodies, and organizations to promote Canadian mass media. The Broadcasting Act is based on the idea that broadcasting is "a public service essential to the maintenance and enhancement of national identity and cultural sovereignty." It mandates the Canadian broadcasting system to

> safeguard, enrich and strengthen the cultural, political, social and economic fabric of Canada ... [and,] through its programming and the employment opportunities arising out of its operations, serve the needs and interests, and reflect the circumstances and aspirations, of Canadian men, women and children, including equal rights, the linguistic duality and multicultural and multiracial nature of Canadian society and the special place of aboriginal peoples within that society. (Government of Canada, Broadcasting Act, s. 3d)

The Broadcasting Act is implemented in part by the Canadian Radio-television and Telecommunications Commission (CRTC). The CRTC is an independent public authority responsible for regulating and licensing the broadcasting and telecommunications industry. It also ensures the development of Canadian programming, talent, and perspectives through the establishment of Canadian content guidelines. In television, for example, the guidelines require that private broadcasters maintain a Canadian content level of 55 percent overall, with 50 percent of prime-time programming (6 p.m. to midnight) dedicated to Canadian shows. Various incentives are offered to promote Canadian drama, music, dance, variety programs, regionally produced programs, and documentaries (CRTC, 1999, 2011).

Private broadcasters have been able to fill Canadian content requirements with news programming, low-budget dramas, and, more recently, reality television shows, especially in off-peak viewing hours. However, the CBC is mandated by the Broadcasting Act to offer a wide range of mainly Canadian programming that is educational, informational, and entertaining. The public broadcaster operates two major television and radio networks in English and French, as well as online services. It provides programming in several Indigenous languages and offers service in the Canadian North. The CBC is thus the main stage for original Canadian radio and television programs (Raboy and Taras, 2007: 86). Because much of its budget comes directly from the federal government, it is not driven solely by commercial imperatives. Designed to serve the public interest, it provides programs that seek to meet the needs of diverse groups of Canadians. Some observers contend that it is one of the few channels through which citizens can communicate effectively among themselves (Raboy and Taras, 2007).

The CBC's ability to meet the needs and interests of Canadians has eroded in recent decades because it has suffered several rounds of funding cuts. Station closures, programming changes, and dwindling audiences have followed each cutback. Some analysts believe the CBC is on the verge of extinction (Raboy and Taras, 2007: 85).

Critical Thinking Questions

1. Do you think that the influence of the American mass media in Canada amounts to cultural imperialism? Why or why not?

2. Doesn't the CBC uses tax dollars to create programming that few Canadians want? Shouldn't Canadians be free to buy the media products they want and shouldn't media companies be free to sell whatever products the public will buy?

---

that New Brunswick newspapers rarely if ever print a critical word about the many Irving companies, a telling example of how extreme concentration in the newspaper industry works in practice.

Criticisms of the Political-Economy Tradition

Proponents of the political-economy tradition identify various mechanisms that enable "money and power ... to filter out the news [that is not] fit to print, marginalize dissent, and allow the government and dominant private interests to get their messages

across to the public" (Herman and Chomsky, 2006: 257). For example, Chomsky and Herman's "propaganda model" of the media argues that

- In the highly competitive mass media environment, noncorporate media that could provide alternative views of the world are marginalized or driven out of business by giant corporations.
- Advertising constitutes by far the biggest share of news industry revenue, and advertisers support mostly mainstream media whose audiences enjoy substantial buying power and whose messages reinforce business interests. On occasion,

news media can be kept in line by advertisers threatening to pull their business if unflattering or damaging reports are circulated.

- Information sourcing tends to filter out minority viewpoints. Journalists rely heavily on government and corporate public relations offices for information, producing news bias.
- Governments and corporations often influence public opinion by responding forcefully and negatively to news reports that criticize them.
- News often conforms to the dominant ideals and beliefs of a society, limiting what can be said about topics such as terrorism.

Do such mechanisms entirely homogenize the news and render it consistently pro-business and pro-government? Certainly not in all respects. Pick up a major newspaper or listen to the nightly television news and you will find plenty of stories about government corruption, ineffective public policy, and corporate wrongdoing. Journalists and other media workers influence what gets published, and they are often critical of authority. In recent years, the Canadian public has not exactly been kept in the dark about the Senate spending scandal, the environmental dangers of the tar sands and of transcontinental oil pipelines, the poor record of the Conservative government in supporting independent scientific and social scientific research, the shocking behaviour of ex-Toronto mayor, Rob Ford, problems with the food industry failing to deliver safe and sufficiently nutritious food to our tables, the controversial involvement of the Canadian military in Afghanistan and Iraq, and myriad other issues. It is true, as proponents of the political-economy tradition say, that news reports almost never question Canadians' core beliefs in the virtues of capitalism, democracy, and consumerism as a way of life. But short of consensus on such core values, there is plenty of controversy and much criticism of the status quo in the mass media.

A second important criticism of the political-economy perspective concerns its view of the typical audience member as something like an automaton passively absorbing whatever information governments and corporations feed it and adjusting its behaviour accordingly in support of the status quo (Horkheimer and Adorno, 2006). I know few people who uncritically accept everything they see and hear in the mass media, and I bet you don't know many such people either. In general, audience members are a lot more independent-minded than proponents of

the political-economy tradition make them appear. To fully appreciate this fact, we next investigate interpretations of media influence that are more voluntaristic than the political-economy approach is.

VOLUNTARISTIC THEORIES OF MEDIA INFLUENCE

CULTURAL STUDIES

Cultural studies constitute an interdisciplinary field of study, the main goal of which is to analyze culture's relationship to social power (Hesmondalgh, 2013: 51). Parallels exist between cultural studies and the symbolic interactionist perspective discussed in Chapter 1, insofar as both are concerned with how people create cultural meaning.

Media Representation

The central concept in cultural studies is **representation**, the use of signs for the purpose of conveying meaning. According to analysts working in this school of thought, people produce meaningful communication by employing signs to represent objects, people, events, and ideas (Hall, 2013: 14). Media representations are selective and evaluative; they include and emphasize some objects, people, events, and ideas while excluding and de-emphasizing others. They thus form "interpretive frames" that allow us to make sense of the world, including the way we understand our place and the place of others in it (Hjarvard, 2013: 37).

For example, media representations help us to make sense of masculinity and femininity, gender relations, and sexuality. Films, television shows, and advertisements depict men and women in particular roles and associate masculinity and femininity with specific characteristics. Think of how Axe deodorant commercials convey masculinity: heterosexual, young, white, cool, irresistible to beautiful women, and always in control. The "Axe Effect" advertising campaign features women in meagre attire seduced by the power of Axe and the men who use it. The campaign thus reinforces norms surrounding gender and sexual relations. In general, ads perpetuate commonsense ideas about the way things are and the way they should be—concerning not just gender, but also class, race, family, and so on.

Cultural studies analysts pay much attention to dominant ideologies, that is, the widely shared values and beliefs that support the interests and social position of powerful categories of the population (O'Shaughnessy and Stadler, 2005: 172). They argue that social inequalities are maintained partly through the production and circulation of values and beliefs that make unequal power relations appear perfectly natural, not socially constructed. For instance, some media scholars argue that widespread media depictions of women as sex objects, domestic and maternal service providers, and damsels in distress help to maintain women's subordinate position in society. The former representation is certainly evident in the "Axe Effect" ads, where women play secondary roles as sex objects for male pleasure while men activate women's desires and thus control them by dousing themselves in Axe body spray.

Conflicting Frames

Significantly, cultural studies analysts argue that the mass media provides audiences with dominant interpretive frames *and* interpretive frames that are at odds with dominant representations. In admitting the existence of competing frames, they are less deterministic than are researchers operating in the political-economy tradition; they allow that audience members have the capacity to choose interpretive frames that do not support existing power relations.

Consider in this connection the role of Leslie Knope (played by Amy Poehler) in the television comedy series, *Parks and Recreation*. She often challenges dominant conceptions of gender roles by associating women with intelligence, prestigious occupations, and political clout. In one episode, Knope is elected to city council, whereupon she promptly installs in her office a gallery of photos of smart, powerful women—including herself. She calls it her "wall of inspirational women" (Madrid, 2014). As this example suggests, and as cultural studies analysts emphasize, the mass media are properly understood as sites of struggle over cultural meanings.

Contested notions of what constitutes "Canadianness" further illustrate this struggle. Media representations often portray members of dominant ethnic groups (white people of British or French origin) as true Canadians, while rendering members of minority groups as somehow less Canadian and therefore socially inferior. Thus, sociologists analyzing Canadian television programming have found that minority-group members are underrepresented as winners in reality television contests and in lead roles in prime-time dramas, and are typically portrayed in

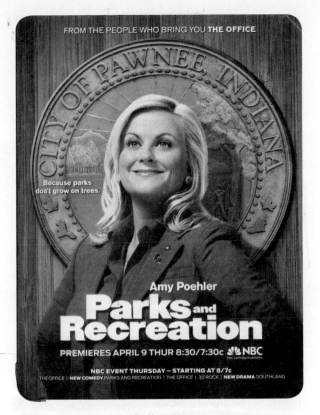

Parks and Recreation's Leslie Knope.
SOURCE: © AF archive/Alamy.

stereotypical ways (Byers, 2008; Fleras, 2003; Fleras and Kunz, 2001).

Nonetheless, such media depictions of Canadian minority groups are increasingly challenged by a growing diversity of media representations and the emergence of minority-group media outlets. It is no longer unusual to see the news read by black, Chinese, or Indo-Canadians. Programs like *Little Mosque on the Prairie* and *Modern Family* portray Muslims and Latinos (not to mention homosexuals) in leading roles. Meanwhile, media outlets catering to ethnic minority groups are on the rise. As early as 1981, the Inuit Broadcasting Corporation was established to serve audiences in Inuktitut. The Indigenous Peoples Television Network was founded in 1999. Based in Winnipeg, it broadcasts and co-produces programs in multiple languages for, by, and about Indigenous peoples: news broadcasts, dramas, documentaries, and children's programs. It serves as a showcase for Indigenous media, culture, and talent (Roth, 2014). OMNI Television has been in existence since 2002 and broadcasts programs in 20 languages spoken mainly by immigrant groups. The growth of minority-group media outlets and the increasing representation of minority-group members in important roles in the mainstream media reinforce minority-group identities and elevate their status in the public's mind.

RECEPTION ANALYSIS

One of the key ideas in cultural studies is that media representations give audiences the opportunity to choose between dominant and nondominant interpretations of various aspects of the social world. Reception analysis, an offshoot of cultural studies, is even more voluntaristic. Its proponents hold that audience members interact with the mass media creatively, giving rise to all manner of interpretations of media messages.

In this view, producers encode media messages with an intended meaning. Then audience members decode media messages in various ways, many of them unintended (Hall, 1980). Such variety notwithstanding, decoding takes three main forms. First, audience members may accept the intended meaning. Second, they may negotiate an interpretation of the media message, accepting part of what is intended but adding their own interpretive twist. Third, they may resist or reject the intended meaning altogether. In all cases, audience members bring their own identities, experiences, and cultural associations to their interpretation of the media message. These background factors influence how they make sense of it.

Recent media analysis focuses on the interactive nature of audience engagement with new media, particularly social media. With new media, audience members do not simply receive and interpret media messages that are produced and circulated by media industries. Rather, they modify, create, and recirculate those messages. Online news articles invite reader comments. YouTube users don't just watch videos. They modify them and create new videos for others to watch. Facebook relies on each member to generate content by creating a user profile, uploading photos, and circulating messages to relatives, friends, and acquaintances. Audience members thus become consumers and producers of media messages, blurring the distinction between these two previously divorced roles (Ritzer, Dean, and Jurgenson, 2012). This idea is captured in the notion of the "prosumer." Some analysts contend that media companies exploit audience members by encouraging them to produce media messages for free (Arvidsson, 2006). However, their work is by no means completely controlled by media companies. Instead, social media give audience members the opportunity to become creatively involved in production in a way that was simply impossible before the twenty-first century (Hesmondalgh, 2013).

TIME FOR REVIEW

1. What is media concentration? Why is it a major concern according to media analysts operating in the political-economy tradition?
2. According to the propaganda model, what are the main mechanisms that allow rich and powerful interests to shape the news in ways that suit them?
3. What are media representations and how do they operate?
4. According to reception studies, how do audiences engage with media texts?
5. In what sense do social media blur the distinction between producer and consumer of media messages?
6. In what sense are the various theories of media influence deterministic or voluntaristic?

SOCIAL MEDIA

The past decade has witnessed tremendous growth in social media. Facebook, Twitter, and Instagram are now integrated into our daily lives and routines, shaping how we connect with others, share information, and make plans. We mark our movements and follow friends on Facebook Places, find dates using online dating services, and post photos of our dogs on pet sharing sites. We play in virtual worlds, run blogs, work on group projects, videoconference, and join online communities (Dewing, 2010a; Kaplan and Haenlein, 2010). The Internet used to allow people to "surf" and consume media content produced by others. Now it encourages people to create media content, interact, learn collaboratively, network, and harness collective intelligence (Flew and Smith, 2011: 20). Figure 6.3 shows just how actively engaged Canadians are with the Internet and social media in particular.

Much optimism has greeted the rise of social media because they multiply our capabilities and shift control over the production and circulation of media messages away from large corporations and into the hands of the masses. However, social media are paradoxical. While they facilitate new ways of connecting, communicating, and creating, they are

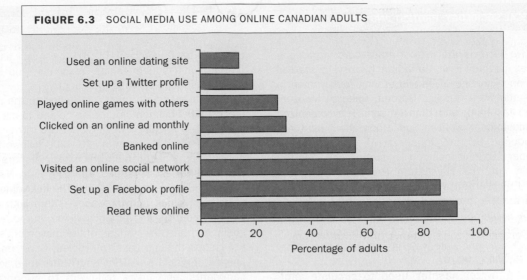

FIGURE 6.3   SOCIAL MEDIA USE AMONG ONLINE CANADIAN ADULTS

SOURCE: Ipsos Reid, *The Ipsos Canadian inter@ctive Reid Report 2012 Fact Guide.* Copyright © 2012. http://www.ipsos.ca/common/dl/pdf/Ipsos_InteractiveReidReport_FactGuide_2012.pdf (accessed Sept. 22, 2015).

also bound up with new forms of commodification, surveillance, and control (Werbin, 2014). In what follows, we explore both the potential and the limitations of social media.

SOCIAL MEDIA'S POTENTIAL

Democratization is one important benefit of social media. It is a consequence of their interactive, decentralized nature. Consider blogs, which allow just about anyone to write entries on any subject for others to read and comment on in a sort of informal journal. Blogs usually contain links to articles, videos, and photos, and are featured on websites such as Facebook and Buzzflash. The startup and maintenance costs of a blog are negligible compared to the cost of starting and running a newspaper. Blogs thus allow many people to publish information on a wide range of topics that reflect diverse viewpoints that are unlikely to be published by companies or mainstream news media. Travel blogs offer frank reviews of hotels by people who have stayed in them. Local news blogs report on issues that mainstream newspapers might not consider newsworthy. Political blogs espouse opinions too radical (either conservative or left-wing) for mainstream mass media to touch (Greenberg and Gilberds, 2011; Lievrouw, 2011).

A second benefit of social media is that they afford new ways of connecting to other people. They encourage the strengthening of existing social networks and the development of new ties that may bridge otherwise unconnected networks (Hampton,

2010). Such bridging ties provide access to information such as job postings on LinkedIn; funding for independent films via crowdsourcing campaigns; participation in virtual communities; and so on.

Third, social media play an important role in contemporary social activism by creating awareness of various causes and helping to mobilize support for political action (Harlow, 2011; Vegh, 2003). Awareness is generated through the creation and circulation of information on social media by organizations like Greenpeace and individuals like Leonardo DiCaprio, whose Ice Bucket Challenge promoted two major social causes, as noted in this chapter's opening vignette. Information can spread quickly and extensively through interlinked online networks. Many social movements therefore maintain Twitter accounts and Facebook pages to share information and mobilize followers for online and offline collective action. Smart phone apps are also important in this regard. For instance, in the 2014 pro-democracy movement in Hong Kong, messaging applications like WhatsApp, BBM, and FireChat were used extensively to send information and coordinate demonstrations. BBM and FireChat, which do not rely on the phone system, were especially useful when the authorities started jamming phone signals (Chen, Law, and Purnell, 2014) (see also the Critical Sociology: Protest and Policy box).

THE DOWNSIDE OF SOCIAL MEDIA

Despite its many benefits, the democratic potential of social media is limited in a number of ways.

Idle No More is the largest grassroots indigenous social movement in Canadian history. It started with an exchange of emails among four women in Saskatchewan—Jessica Gordon, Sheelah McLean, Sylvia McAdam, and Nina Wilson. They organized an educational event in Saskatoon about Bill C-45, introduced by the Conservative government in October 2012. It included legislation changing the Indian Act, the Navigation Protection Act, and the Environmental Assessment Act, among others. The proposed changes threatened to erode indigenous sovereignty and environmental protections by accelerating oil pipeline construction through land and waterways in First Nations territory (Idle No More, 2014a).

The Twitter hashtag used to circulate information about the movement started with a single tweet: "@shawnatleao wuts being done w #billc45 every1 wasting time talking about Gwen Stefani wth!? #indianact #wheresthedemocracy #IdleNoMore" (*CBC News*, 2013). A Saskatoon teach-in was promoted on the Idle No More Facebook page. Similar events followed, and the movement quickly grew to encompass a broader range of issues, including the demand for adherence to traditional treaties, a call for increased consultation regarding development projects, and resistance to violence against indigenous women (Idle No More, 2014b). After capturing the attention of the mainstream media, thousands participated in the movement's National Day of Action on December 10, 2012, as well as hundreds of subsequent rallies, teach-ins, and round dance flash mobs across the country.

Social media not only contributed to the movement's initial momentum, it also helped to maintain interest and ongoing involvement. The movement's Facebook site has more than 134 000 followers and operates as a platform on which people share links and material about issues affecting First Nations people in Canada and worldwide. The IdleNoMore.ca website provides activists and visitors with information about the movement's vision, purpose, and goals. It creates awareness of the movement's central issues through links to articles, webinars, and images. It displays a streaming Twitter feed, invites comments, and urges followers to support the movement by volunteering, endorsing, and donating. Social media have been harnessed to propel the growth of Idle No More and other social movements throughout the world.

Critical Thinking

1. To what extent do you think social media is transforming social activism?

2. Some critics argue that the use of social media by social movements contributes to "slacktivism," which reduces activism to the click of a mouse. Do you agree with this critique? Why, or why not?

Foremost among them is the so-called *digital divide*. Although it may seem like everyone uses some form of social media, access is far from universal. Young people living in cities are most likely to have access to social media, especially if they enjoy higher education and high income (Brodock, 2010). From this point of view, and to the degree that being disconnected means being disenfranchised, some people—those who are less educated, poorer, older, and living in rural areas—are deprived of their democratic rights (see the Critical Sociology: Social Inequality box).

A second downside of social media is that they are subject to concentration and commercialization. Like the traditional media, social media are dominated by large corporations such as Google and Facebook. Much of the revenue for both companies derives from online advertising.

Social media generate tremendous amounts of user data that are mined, organized, packaged, and sold to advertising and marketing companies.

Some of this information comes from user profiles, some from user behaviour—online buying habits, site visits, ad views, and so on. This information yields a snapshot (more accurately, a movie) of our tastes and interests that social media giants turn into a commodity and sell to advertisers and marketers who use it to target audiences with their messages. The ads that run alongside your Facebook page represent the cost of your seemingly free use of Facebook. People consent to supplying such information when they sign up to use a social media service but they rarely read the company's privacy policy to find out exactly what information is being handed over and how it is used. People can limit the amount of information they supply, but doing so can be a complex and time-consuming process, so they often do not bother to specify limits (de Souza e Silva and Frith, 2012).

The involvement of social media in the capture and commodification of user data raises a surveillance issue, too. **Surveillance** involves authorities,

CRITICAL SOCIOLOGY: SOCIAL INEQUALITY   THE DIGITAL DIVIDE

The **digital divide** refers to inequalities in knowledge about how to use the Internet and social media, access to online technology, and the rate of using such technology (Hesmondalgh, 2013). Such divisions are certainly evident at the global scale (see Figure 6.4). In brief, high-income continents, countries, and regions enjoy the highest rates of Internet access.

Beyond Internet access, it is useful to consider emerging trends in mobile phone use worldwide, since mobile phones allow people to use social media without Internet access. For example, it is possible to send and receive text messages, use BBM and Google Talk, and send and receive Twitter feeds with entry-level mobile phones that lack Internet access (Ramakrishnan, 2013). Mobile phone use has expanded quickly around the world. In 2014, there were 6.9 billion mobile subscriptions

worldwide (ITU, 2014). Even middle- and low-income countries enjoy high subscription rates, although smart phone ownership tends to be considerably more widespread in high-income countries than elsewhere (Pew Research Center, 2014). Access to the Internet and social media is unequal within countries, too. Thus, the same factors responsible for the digital divide globally—income, education, age, and urban vs. rural residence—operate in Canada (Dewing, 2010b; Statistics Canada, 2011).

Critical Thinking

1. Do you think the digital divide will continue to grow, remain the same, or shrink? What factors will cause the outcome you predict?

2. What measures can be taken to bridge the digital divide in Canada?

FIGURE 6.4   THE DIGITAL DIVIDE, 2000 AND 2015

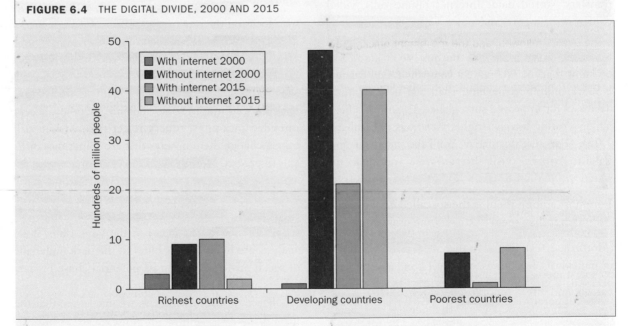

SOURCE: International Telecommunication Union. "ICT Facts and Figures – The World in 2015." Copyright © 2015. http://www.itu.int/en/ITU-D/Statistics/Pages/facts/default.aspx (retrieved Sept. 10, 2015).

organizations, businesses, and individuals paying sustained and often systematic attention to people's personal details and behaviour, typically to influence, manage, protect, or suppress them (Flew and Smith, 2011: 231).

Social media permit top-down and bottom-up surveillance. Bottom-up surveillance involves friends, acquaintances, or strangers observing us on social media. For example, our Facebook "friends" and Twitter followers can see our status updates, photos,

and the information on our profiles, which we tailor to present particular versions of our selves (Utz, 2010). Members of our social network comment and provide feedback on our posts, links, and "likes." Knowing that we are constantly watched, we monitor ourselves; we manage our online presence with a view to the norms and expectations of friends, family, and others who might see us (Turkle, 2011).

Top-down surveillance involves businesses and other powerful social institutions recording our activities and characteristics for commercial or political purposes. Mobile social media take this a step farther by using the global positioning system (GPS) to track people's movements and activities offline (Kaplan 2012: 131). For example, Foursquare allows users to notify others of their location. The company collects the location data and sells them to advertisers who use it to send out location-based advertising. That is why a Foursquare user might suddenly receive an offer for a free coffee from a nearby café (de Souza e Silva and Frith, 2012).

The police access videos on YouTube to conduct criminal investigations. Employers access profiles on Facebook to screen potential candidates and track the behaviour of employees. In the United States, the National Security Agency uses a surveillance system called PRISM to collect user data in real time from Google, Apple, Facebook, Yahoo!, Microsoft, and other social media companies. These data—including information on emails, video and voice chats, file transfers, stored data, Internet phone calls, video conferences, logins, and more—are used to identify potential threats to the United States and may be used for other, secret purposes. We just don't know. We do know that the CIA gave a company called Palantir US$5.1 billion to develop methods of combining databases for improved surveillance. Palantir has been under scrutiny for civil rights violations (Greenberg, 2013). (For an informative YouTube video on how Palantir works, visit https://www.youtube.com/watch?v=f86VKjFSMJE.). In Egypt, Syria, Iran, and other Middle Eastern countries, authoritarian governments have used surveillance software to track—and track down—pro-democracy activists (Morozov, 2011). The idea that we are being watched by individuals, businesses, employers, and governments necessarily influences what we say and do on social media. Therefore, surveillance can have the effect of limiting our freedom of action and of expression (Werbin, 2014: 272).

THE HARD ANSWER

Proponents of the political-economy approach make a valid point when they claim that large media enterprises tend strongly to support core societal values. The media giants do so by marginalizing alternative voices, respecting the interests of big advertisers, and relying heavily on official news sources. By responding forcefully to critical news reports, governments and corporations reinforce the core societal values propounded by the media giants.

Political-economy analysts are on shakier ground when it comes to the mass media's treatment of non-core issues, where we find lively controversy and debate. Moreover, the political-economy tradition tends to be overly deterministic in its assessment of audiences, which it regards as little more than assemblies of puppets responding to jerks of the puppet-master's strings.

The field of cultural studies provides a more realistic assessment of the interaction between the mass media and their audiences. Cultural studies analysts agree that media representations tend to be biased in favour of dominant economic, political, ethnic, racial, and gender groups. But, importantly, they allow that alternative representations also exist, competing with dominant representations for the attention of audience members. From their point of view, the mass media are sites of negotiated meaning, and audience members are constantly engaged in the negotiations.

Still more voluntaristic are reception analysts, who focus on the way media producers encode media messages with intended meaning, only to have audience members, influenced by the idiosyncrasies of their identity, experience, and culture, decode those messages in various ways, many of them unintended. Accordingly, some audience members accept intended meanings, others reject them, while still others change them in ways that are sometimes difficult to predict. Media analysts strengthen the case for audience autonomy by paying careful attention to the interactive and creative opportunities introduced by social media, which blur the line between media consumer and media producer. At the same time, these analysts are by no means blind to the dark underside of social media, including its potential abuse by data miners and surveillance experts.

Based on this assessment, we may agree that the mass media help us to define who we are as individuals and as members of a range of collectivities. But we must quickly add that ordinary people like you and me play an increasingly active and creative role in generating meaning, modifying and resisting the messages delivered by powerful media interests in a complex interactive process that sociologists continue eagerly to explore.

TIME FOR REVIEW

1. What are social media?
2. What are the main benefits of social media?
3. What are the main disadvantages of social media?

SUMMARY

1. **What are the mass media and why do they matter?**
The mass media use industrial technologies to enable communication between media companies and large audiences, and among individuals. They are industries that are influenced by commercial interests and the profit motive. In their communications and business roles, the mass media help to shape beliefs, values, and culture.

2. **What is the difference between traditional mass media and new media?**
Traditional mass media include newspapers, radio, and television. They were designed to reach mass audiences using a broadcast model of communication, which transmits standardized information from single sources to many audience members. New media include the Internet and Internet-based technologies and platforms, including social media. New media are based on a "many-to-many" model of communications. They circulate digitized, niche content to fragmented audiences. They are interactive insofar as they invite audience members to participate in their creation, modification, and retransmission. They thus blur the line between producers and consumers of mass media products.

3. **What are the main approaches to understanding the influence of the mass media?**
Three main approaches to understanding the mass media exist. In order from the most deterministic to the most voluntaristic, they are (a) the political-economy approach (which analyzes how large media corporations use their power to shape people's ideas in support of the core values of capitalism, democracy, and consumerism); (b) the cultural studies approach (which analyzes the effects of media representations on audience members and recognizes that dominant and alternative representations compete for audience attention); and (c) the reception analysis approach (which analyzes audience interaction with media messages and emphasizes the creativity of audience members in interpreting media messages).

4. **What is the democratic potential of social media, and how is this potential limited?**
Optimists argue that social media hold tremendous democratic potential insofar as they are interactive and networked. Interactivity allows ordinary people to be involved in the production and circulation of media, shifting control away from large corporations and into the hands of the masses. Networking enables people to share information, collaborate in media production, and engage in social activism. However, the democratic potential of social media is limited by the digital divide, commercialization, and surveillance.

QUESTIONS TO CONSIDER

1. Apply what you have learned about media representation to a gender analysis of a reality television show. How does the show represent masculinity and femininity? In what ways does it challenge or reproduce dominant or alternative gender ideologies?

2. How do individuals contribute to the creation of new media content? To what degree are they creative and autonomous producers of media? To what degree are they doing free labour for the benefit of new media companies?

3. Social media use involves a tradeoff whereby we supply information to companies in exchange for the free use of social media platforms. Do you think this tradeoff is acceptable? Why, or why not?

GLOSSARY

Communication (p. 127) involves people exchanging meaningful information using signs or representations of things, people, events, and ideas.

Corporate integration (p. 133) involves the acquisition by one company of other companies in related fields.

Cultural imperialism (p. 134) involves the process whereby Western (mainly American) media conglomerates circulate and impose Western culture and values throughout the world via media products and texts.

The **digital divide** (p. 141) refers to inequalities in access to the Internet and new media. It encompasses divisions in terms of access, activity, and know-how.

An **imagined community** (p. 129) is a social world composed of members who do not necessarily know each other or meet in person yet consider themselves part of that social world.

Mass media (p. 127) are technology-driven and usually profit-driven methods of communicating meaningful information between one source and many recipients or between many sources and many recipients.

Media concentration (p. 132) denotes the process whereby the ownership and control of media becomes more centralized.

Media determinism (p. 130) is a school of thought which holds that people are programmed to buy, aspire, envy, vote, eat, dress, dance, protest, and love in ways that suit those who control the mass media and entice us with their ideals of the good life.

Media voluntarism (p. 130) is a school of thought which holds that ordinary people decide who we are and which imagined communities we will join, the mass media merely offering us an inviting menu of options almost without end.

Net neutrality (p. 133) is the principle that the Internet should treat all transmissions the same way, regardless of source, ownership, data size, or destination.

Proponents of the **political-economy perspective** (p. 131) are chiefly concerned with how power relations and the pursuit of profit shape (1) media ownership, production, and distribution, and (2) media influence.

Proponents of **reception analysis** (p. 138) hold that audience members interact with the mass media creatively, giving rise to all manner of interpretations of media messages.

In media studies, **representation** (p. 136) involves the use of signs that refer to objects, people, and events in the material world; imaginary objects, people, and events; and abstract ideas.

Surveillance (p. 140) involves authorities, organizations, businesses, or individuals paying sustained and often systematic attention to people's personal details and behaviour, typically to influence, manage, protect, or suppress them.

Virtual communities (p. 130) are communities based on shared interests, existing on the Internet and in the minds of their members.

Illustrated by Aaron Millard

PART 3

INEQUALITY

CHAPTER 7

SOCIAL STRATIFICATION

Harvey Krahn
UNIVERSITY OF ALBERTA

SOURCE: rmnoa357/Shutterstock.com.

AFTER READING THIS CHAPTER, YOU WILL BE ABLE TO:

- Explain how persistent patterns of social inequality arise and are maintained in different types of societies.

- Compare and contrast different explanations of the origins and impact of social stratification systems.

- Explain the extent to which income and wealth are unequally distributed in Canada and the factors that underlie the trend toward increased inequality.

- Understand how a person's position in society's stratification system has important consequences for lifestyle and the quality of life.

INTRODUCTION

While bundling up copies of the *Edmonton Journal* for recycling, I flip through them quickly. Although the news writers don't use the term, I find myself reading about **social stratification**—that is, persistent patterns of social inequality.

A headline catches my attention: "Rate of Kids in Poverty Still High." The reporter writes that, between 1989 and 2012, the percentage of Alberta children living below the poverty line (a measurement discussed later in this chapter) remained at 16 percent (Pratt, 2014). That translates into 143 200 Alberta children living below the poverty line in 2012. Another headline—"Alberta Home to Top Earners"—appears above a story reporting that, in 2012, Alberta (with 11 percent of Canada's population) was home to 23 percent of Canada's top one-percent earners (Toneguzzi, 2014). How is it possible for so many children to be living in poverty in a province with the highest average incomes in Canada? Perhaps these children's parents are unemployed or unable to work? The writer of the first story notes, however, that more than 60 percent of the children living in poverty have at least one parent who is employed full-time. The reporter also observes that Alberta (along with Saskatchewan) has the lowest minimum wage in Canada. Perhaps that is part of the explanation for this poverty paradox?

A third article discusses a judicial inquest into why Brian Sinclair, a 45-year-old Indigenous Canadian who had previously had both legs amputated, waited for 34 hours in a Winnipeg hospital for help with a treatable infection. He died before receiving medical assistance (Canadian Press, 2014). The judge heading up the inquest made 63 recommendations about how emergency treatment in hospitals should be organized but concluded that an enquiry into racism in the health care system—something Sinclair's family wanted—was not required. I wonder how someone like me—white, employed, well-paid, and not disabled—would be treated in my local hospital.

Another newspaper story discusses how "an underclass of disposable workers" is being created in Canada (Byl and Foster, 2014). The story writers document the plight of well-educated "temporary foreign workers" who are willing to labour in poorly paid, unskilled jobs in return for the possibility of Canadian citizenship. They have recently been made ineligible for future Canadian citizenship. Why? Some Canadian employers were found to be denying jobs to unemployed Canadian citizens because temporary foreign workers could be hired more cheaply. Canadian citizens protested, so citizenship eligibility for temporary workers was changed. The Canadian social stratification story is clearly complicated.

Although the unemployed and very poor catch my attention, so do the very rich. A news item reminds me of just how rich some people are. In 2013, the 100 most highly paid chief executive officers (CEOs) of companies operating in Canada earned an average of $9.2 million dollars, compared to the $47 358 average earnings of all Canadian workers (Blatchford, 2015). The article also notes that, over the previous five years, top CEO incomes rose by 25 percent, compared to only 12 percent for the average Canadian worker. In other words, income inequality in Canada is high and continues to rise. A quick Internet search for the statistical report on which the news item is based further highlights the extent of income inequality. In 2013, Canada's top CEOs earned 195 times as much as the average Canadian worker (Canadian Centre for Policy Alternatives, 2015). This means that, by noon on the first working day of 2015, Canada's top CEOs had already earned more than the typical Canadian worker will earn all year!

It's time to take the newspapers out to the curb, but two more headlines can't be ignored: "On Giving Tuesday, Think of the Needy" (*Edmonton Journal*, 2014), and "Fighting Inequality Is Not a Job for Toronto's New Mayor" (Yakabuski, 2014). The first story suggests that, after most Canadians have spent extravagantly on gifts for family and friends on Black Friday (the first shopping day after Thanksgiving) and Cyber Monday (the Monday after Black Friday, when consumers are encouraged to shop online), perhaps they should think about making donations to the needy. The second news item argues that it is not the role of Toronto's new mayor to worry about social inequality, in particular, the financial problems experienced by many recent immigrants. Newcomers to Canada always start out poor, the writer argues, and then their children come to be better off. So the mayor should focus on things like safe neighbourhoods and public transit.

I'm surprised that the newspaper columnist is not aware of how much more economic difficulty immigrants to Canada are facing today compared to several decades earlier (more about this later in this chapter). I'm also frustrated by the underlying assumption of the two articles, that poverty and inequality need be addressed only by individual acts of charity and that public policy is not part of the solution. If charity were sufficient, you would think we would have solved the problem long ago.

The common theme in these different news stories is the existence of groups—the unemployed and low-income workers, First Nations, and immigrants, for example—that rank lower than others in the social stratification system. A low position in this ranking typically means having little wealth, **power** (the ability to impose one's will on others), and prestige (or esteem). A higher position generally implies the opposite. In this chapter, I begin by discussing how sociologists study social stratification. I then examine theories of social stratification that attempt to explain its origins and impacts. The next section focuses on occupational and class structures and material inequality in Canada, and asks whether social inequality has been increasing. The chapter ends with a discussion of some of the consequences of social inequality and what might be done about it.

STRATIFICATION: A CORNERSTONE OF SOCIOLOGY

Sociologists have four basic areas of inquiry. We study social structure, or the way in which society is organized, both formally and informally. We ask questions about social order. What is it that holds together a society comprising individuals with different interests, and when and why does social order break down? Inquiries about social change form a third key area in the discipline. How and why do societies, the institutions and power structures within them, and the values and beliefs held by individual members change? Finally, sociologists spend a lot of time studying social stratification, the manner in which valued resources—that is, wealth, power, and prestige—are distributed, and the way in which advantages are passed from generation to generation.

It could easily be argued that the study of social stratification is the cornerstone of sociology. Descriptions of social structure that ignore the stratification system are clearly inadequate. Imagine describing Canadian society to someone from another country without referring to some features of stratification. Would the listener really understand our society if

she or he did not know that most large corporations are run by men, that the working poor continue to struggle to make ends meet even though the majority of employed Canadians earn a decent living, that First Nations are much more likely than most others to be living in poverty, and that immigrants are doing less well today than they were several decades ago, even though they are better educated?

Furthermore, inequalities in wealth can threaten social stability (the poor resenting the wealthy, for example, and demanding more equality), and inequalities in power can be used to maintain social order. For example, powerful corporations might lobby provincial or territorial governments for changes in the labour laws that would make it more difficult for unions to organize company employees. In less democratic countries, high levels of inequality and direct control of the police and military by a powerful political minority can lead to the quick and violent suppression of unrest among the masses (Ortiz, 2007).

An understanding of social stratification is also essential for studying social change since, frequently, it is the stratification system that is undergoing change. For example, changing gender roles and the slow movement of women into positions of power and authority in North America in the past few decades are really features of a changing stratification system. The massive social, economic, and political changes that began in the former Soviet Union in the late 1980s and in China a decade earlier are, among other things, changes in stratification systems, as the main sources of power come to include both the political system and the emerging capitalist economy.

SOCIAL HIERARCHIES IN STRATIFIED SOCIETIES

Imagine a society in which stratification did not exist, in which all things of value were distributed equally. Even if you picture a very small group, perhaps a pre-industrial society with only a few hundred members, living on some isolated island where the necessities of life are easily obtained, it is still difficult to imagine a nonstratified society. A social hierarchy might emerge as a result of skill differences in fishing, in nursing the ill back to health, or in communicating with the spirits, for example. Inequalities in wealth might develop simply because some families were fortunate enough to have a larger number of children, providing more of the labour needed to accumulate valued possessions. And once accumulations of wealth began to be passed from generation to generation, a structured and relatively permanent pattern of inequality would emerge.

Perhaps you imagined some contemporary society comprising adults who, believing strongly in equality, decided to live and work together in some kind of urban or rural commune, sharing all their possessions. Again, it is easy to imagine how a social hierarchy could emerge, as those with more useful skills found themselves playing a more central role in this small-scale society. No doubt, when important decisions needed to be made, these individuals would be more likely to influence the outcome.

We do not need to repeat this mental exercise too many times before we see that social stratification in one form or another exists in all societies. However, our hypothetical examples are far from typical. In most societies, stratification is much more pronounced, and basic skills are seldom the foundation of primary social hierarchies. Nevertheless, cross-cultural variations exist in the criteria by which individuals and groups are ranked, the degree to which they can move from one position to another within the hierarchy, and the extent of inequality in wealth and power that exists within the hierarchy.

ASCRIBED AND ACHIEVED STATUS

Let's begin by defining the rank or position that a person has within a social hierarchy as that person's **status**. We can further distinguish between an **ascribed status** and an **achieved status**. The former is assigned to individuals, typically at birth. An ascribed status can be a function of race, gender, age, and other factors that are not chosen or earned and that cannot be changed (a few people do choose their gender status, but they are rare exceptions). In contrast, an achieved status is precisely that—a position in a hierarchy that has been achieved by virtue of how well someone performs in some role. The most obvious example is that of occupational status—for instance, individuals who have performed well in law school are entitled to become lawyers, and high-performance athletes strive to achieve the status of "professional athlete." By the same logic, someone could achieve the status of "bum" by performing poorly in educational, employment, family, and other social roles.

Although we may accept that a completely non-stratified society is impossible, most of us would probably agree that a stratification system in which higher positions were achieved, not ascribed, would be preferable. In a **meritocracy**, everyone would have equal chances to compete for higher status positions and, presumably, those most capable would be awarded the highest rank. Such a society would exhibit a considerable degree of **social mobility**, as those who were more qualified moved up the social hierarchy to replace those who were less competent and who were consequently compelled to move down.

OPEN AND CLOSED STRATIFICATION SYSTEMS

When we compare Canada with other societies, or look back at our history, we find that this country has what appears to be a fairly **open stratification system**, in which merit, rather than inheritance (or ascribed characteristics), determines social rank and in which social change is therefore possible. For example, dramatic changes in the status of various groups have occurred in this country over time. Although the practice was not nearly as widespread in Canada as in the United States, slaves (most of them black people from Africa but also some First Nations) were bought and sold in Canada from the 1630s till the 1830s (Milan and Tran, 2004). Chinese labourers, brought into the country to help build the railways, were kept out of most "white" jobs by law until well into the twentieth century (Li, 1982). Similarly, it was not until the 1960s that black Canadians were allowed to compete for much more than the lowest-level positions in the Canadian railway industry (Calliste, 1987). However, by the 1830s, slavery had disappeared in Canada, and we now have laws against racial discrimination.

Comparing ourselves with other contemporary societies, we note that Canada does not have an aristocracy, such as the one that exists in Britain, where children of wealthy and powerful families of long standing inherit positions and titles. The degree to which Canadians compete for higher status occupations (in the education system and, later, in the workplace) stands in clear contrast to the situation in India, for example, where the caste into which an individual is born largely determines the type of work that he or she will be allowed to do. Although discrimination on the basis of caste membership has been illegal in India for many decades, the **caste system** continues to underpin a relatively **closed stratification system**. Compared with India, Canada offers many more chances for upward social mobility, an indication of a more open stratification system.

Ascribed and achieved statuses.

SOURCES: © Gouhier-Guibbaud-JMP/ABACAPRESS.COM/Newscom (left); © Ronald Martinez/Getty Images (right).

It is all too easy, however, to overlook the extent to which ascribed statuses continue to limit opportunities for many Canadians as well. Discrimination against members of First Nations and visible minority groups continues to occur in Canada today. So, too, does discrimination against members of the gay community, against seniors and people with disabilities, and against women. These people are in lower status positions not because they competed poorly for some higher ranking in the social hierarchy, but because they are gay, are old, have disabilities, or are female.

These are fairly obvious examples of the ways in which ascribed statuses continue to play a prominent role in Canada's social stratification system. But what about the child from a wealthy family who graduates from an excellent high school in a wealthy neighbourhood, completes a degree or two in a prestigious and costly university, and then begins a career in a high-status, well-paying profession? Is this simply an example of someone achieving a deserved high-status position, or did the advantages of birth (ascribed status) play some part in this success story? Similarly, when we hear of large companies laying off hundreds of workers, does their sudden downward mobility reflect their failure to compete in an open, merit-based stratification system, or were they simply unfortunate enough to be employed in a corporation that was being downsized?

As these examples illustrate, the social stratification system consists of a number of different hierarchies, some based on ascribed characteristics, others on achievement. Elsewhere in this book, you will read chapters devoted to various dimensions of stratification, such as gender, race, and ethnicity, and their "intersectionality," or how they sometimes overlap. Other chapters address activities (for example, work) and institutions (for example, education) in which stratification processes are extremely important, and still others focus on inequalities among regions and countries. Once you have read all these chapters, you will, I expect, be convinced of the central importance of social stratification in the discipline of sociology.

SOCIAL CLASS

You will also notice that, even though studies of gender, race, ethnicity, and work take you in quite different directions, all frequently share an emphasis on inequalities in income, wealth, or property, and on resulting inequalities in power. On average, for the past two decades, women have been earning less than 75 percent of what men earn (Krahn, Hughes, and Lowe, 2015: Ch. 6). Older women are much more likely than are older men to be living in poverty. Immigrants and, particularly, First Nations are more likely to be unemployed or, if they are employed, to be in low-paying jobs. Owners of large workplaces are wealthier than are most other members of society, and employees in professional and managerial occupations typically earn much more than lower-level employees do. Recognizing, then, the extent to which such material inequality (that is, differences in income and wealth or property) parallels and overlaps with other social hierarchies, the rest of this chapter will focus primarily on material inequality or, after we define the terms, on social class and class structure.

Definitions of the concept of **social class** vary considerably, as we will see in the next section, which outlines different theories of social stratification. I prefer to use the term in a general sense to indicate the position of an individual or a family within an economic hierarchy, along with others who have roughly the same amount of control over or access to economic or material resources. For example, an individual can be said to be a member of a class of large landowners, a class of wage-labourers and salaried workers (that is, the "working class"), or a "professional/managerial class." It is their similar economic situation and opportunities, a result of their shared position within a society's system of economic production, that makes these individuals members of the same class. In turn, we can use the term **class structure** to refer to the overall economic hierarchy comprising all such classes, choosing the word *structure* deliberately to indicate the relative stability and permanence of this social ranking.

Do you think of yourself as a member of a specific social class? Probably not. Like most North Americans, you probably have a reasonably good idea of how well off you are compared with others in your community. You probably have some sense of where your education, occupation, and income (or your parents' education, occupation, and income) fit in some general hierarchy of socioeconomic status. "Class," however, is unlikely to be part of your everyday vocabulary. Nor is it typically part of the media's vocabulary. The newspaper stories I discussed earlier, for example, identified a number of different dimensions of stratification, but social class was not among them.

This, however, does not make class a useless concept. As I have already suggested, pronounced patterns of material inequality exist in our society and overlap with most other dimensions of social stratification. The economic hierarchy is obviously not completely closed, but it is relatively stable and permanent, and it comprises some fairly distinct categories of individuals with similar amounts of control over material resources. Hence, it is useful to try to identify the classes that make up the stratification system (or class structure), to seek to understand their origin, and to examine the effects of membership in them on individuals and families. Rather than discarding the concept of class because few people think in these

terms, we should perhaps ask why few people think about social classes despite their prominence. This is one of the topics discussed in the next section.

TIME FOR REVIEW

1. Why is the study of social stratification a cornerstone of sociology?
2. Would be possible to have a society in which no stratification exists? Why, or why not?
3. What do we mean by "meritocracy," "open and closed societies," and "social mobility?"

EXPLANATIONS OF SOCIAL STRATIFICATION

Now that you have considered some examples of social stratification and learned some new concepts, it is time to examine theories (or explanations) of social stratification elaborated by a number of important social thinkers, including some who were analyzing society many decades ago and others who have written about it more recently. It is important to take into account the time and place in which a social theory was developed, since theorists construct their social explanations on the basis of what they see around them and expect to see in the future.

KARL MARX: CAPITALISM, EXPLOITATION, AND CLASS CONFLICT

Karl Marx had an immense impact on how we think about social stratification (Marx, 1904 [1859], 1972 [1848]). He was born in Germany in 1818 but lived in England from 1849 until he died in 1883. His writings about the social and economic forces that brought about economic change look back over history but focus particularly on the rapidly changing European world that he observed during his lifetime. This was a time when industrial capitalism was transforming the economy and society. Large, mechanized, factory-based systems of production were emerging; cities were growing rapidly as peasants were being forced off the land or attracted to the city by the possibility of jobs in factories; and material inequality was extreme, as factory owners and merchants made huge profits while labourers lived in poverty. Trade unions and labour laws that offer some protection to workers did not yet exist. Thus, as Marx observed, the Industrial Revolution was a time when both the level of economic production and the degree of inequality in society increased tremendously.

Modes of Production and Social Classes

Marx called the system of economic activity in a society its **mode of production**. In turn, its major components were the **means of production** (technology, capital investments, and raw materials) and the **social relations of production** (the relationships between the main classes involved in production). Slavery had been the primary mode of production in some societies in earlier times, and feudalism, an economic system in which peasants worked for landowners, not for a wage but for some share of the produce, was the mode of production that gave way to industrial capitalism in Europe.

Within industrial capitalism, Marx identified two major classes: the capitalist class, or **bourgeoisie**, which owned the means of production; and the **proletariat**, or working class, which exchanged its labour for wages. He also described a middle class—the **petite bourgeoisie**—comprising independent owners/producers (farmers, for example) and small-business owners. Marx expected this middle class largely to disappear as capitalism matured and drew some of its members up into the bourgeoisie but pushed most down into the proletariat. Of much greater importance in his theory of class inequality and social change was the relationship between workers and owners.

Marx reasoned that the value of a sold product was directly proportional to the average amount of labour needed to produce it. Thus, for example, an elegant piece of furniture was more valuable than its component pieces mainly because of the labour invested in it by the worker(s) who built it. Marx argued that the value of goods produced by wage-labourers far exceeded the amount needed to pay their wages and the cost of raw materials, technology, and other factors of production. Marx referred to this excess as **surplus value**. According to Marx, when commodities were sold, their surplus value was turned into profits for the owner. Marx viewed this as an exploitive relationship but one that differed from the exploitive relationships that characterized slavery or feudalism. After all, factory workers were paid a wage for their labour and were not legally forced to stay with the job. However, because most workers had few other options for making a living, and because owners controlled all aspects of the work, the legal freedom of wage-labourers to change jobs was, in practical terms, an illusion.

Class Conflict and Class Consciousness

The idea of **class conflict** among the major classes in a society was the driving force behind Marx's theory of social change. He argued that previous modes of production had collapsed and been replaced because of class conflict. Feudalism in Europe had given way to capitalism as a result of the growing power of the merchant class relative to the traditional alliance of landowners and the aristocracy, and the deteriorating relationship between landowners and peasants. Furthermore, Marx argued, capitalism would eventually be replaced by a socialist mode of production, in which private ownership of property would disappear, along with the exploitation and inequality it produced. The impetus for this massive change would again be widespread class conflict, this time between wage-labourers and the owners of the means of production, as inequality between these two classes became more pronounced.

Marx stated that this revolution would take place only when members of the working class began to recognize that they were being exploited. Marx did not take it for granted that members of a class would see how their interests were similar. Whereas capitalists might be conscious of their group interests, wage-labourers needed to become personally aware of their common enemy. They needed to be transformed from a "class in itself" to a "class for itself." Thus, **class consciousness** was an important social-psychological component of Marx's theory of social inequality and social change. His vision of the future was that of a revolutionary upheaval in which the oppressed working class would recognize its enemy, destroy the institutions of capitalism, and replace them with a classless society based on collective ownership of the means of production.

Responses to Marx

During much of the twentieth century, critics of Marx's ideas pointed to the communist countries, with their apparently socialist system of government and absence of private property, and noted that inequality had not disappeared there. Instead, a new hierarchy had emerged, in which control of the political and bureaucratic apparatus was the main basis of power. These observations were largely correct. As a Russian quip from the 1970s noted, under capitalism man exploits man, but under communism it is the other way around.

I expect that Marx himself would have been highly critical of the Soviet communist system, given the degree to which individual citizens were exploited and harshly treated by a powerful minority. However, it is slowly becoming apparent that the emergence of a capitalist economy in Eastern Europe over the past two decades is leading to increased material inequality but from a different source (Remington, 2011). Today, individuals with control over some form of production or access to some marketing system are accumulating wealth while the majority of citizens appear to be no better off than before—indeed, many are worse off. The same pattern of growing social inequality has been observed in China where, despite the continued control of the economy by the Communist Party, some forms of free enterprise have been encouraged (Whyte, 2010). While Marx's predictions about the inevitable emergence of a classless society have not been borne out, his type of class analysis still has considerable relevance for understanding the changing stratification system in North America, Eastern Europe, and even communist China.

Most theories of social stratification developed after Marx's were essentially a "debate with Marx's ghost" (Zeitlin with Brym, 1991: 117). Some social philosophers and sociologists elaborated on Marx's ideas, while others attempted to refute them. Among the critics, some focused on the absence of widespread class conflict, the growth of the middle class, and the relative decline in material inequality in Western Europe and North America in the twentieth century. I will examine some of these theories below, along with others that tried to develop more complex models of the contemporary class structure while basically following Marx's class-based analysis.

MAX WEBER: CLASS AND OTHER DIMENSIONS OF INEQUALITY

Max Weber was born in Germany half a century after Marx—in 1864. Like Marx, he built his analysis of social stratification on a careful reading of history and a thorough analysis of the economic and political events of his day. But because he was only beginning his university studies about the time Marx died, Weber had the advantage of seeing the direction in which a more mature industrial capitalism was taking European society. He continued to write about many aspects of social stratification and social change until his death in 1920.

Class, Status, and Party

Weber shared with Marx a belief that economic inequalities were central to the social stratification system and that the ownership of property was a primary determinant of **power,** or the ability to get others to do what you want them to do. However, he argued that power could lie in controlling other types of resources as well (Weber, 1948 [1922]). Specifically, he proposed that structures of social stratification could be better understood by looking at economic inequalities, hierarchies of prestige (or social honour), and political inequalities (control of power blocs, such as political parties or other organizations)—or, in his words (in translation), at "class, status, and party." Although these different hierarchies often overlap, they need not. For example, suddenly wealthy individuals might not enjoy the prestige they desire, being rejected in "high society" by those with "old money." Similarly, a politician might have considerable power through control of government resources, but might not be very wealthy or, for that matter, enjoy much prestige.

Since Weber lived to see the emergence of white-collar workers, the growth of large private- and public-sector bureaucracies, and the growing power of trade unions, he was able to write about these alternative sources of power in a stratified capitalist society. He provided an insightful analysis of how power resided in the control of top positions in large bureaucratic organizations, even if the officeholder was not an owner of the organization. He recognized that well-educated wage-labourers might not be as powerless as were the factory workers of an earlier era. He also saw that a new class of middle-level, educated workers might not necessarily align themselves with blue-collar workers, and he was less inclined to conclude, as had Marx, that the middle class would disappear (Zeitlin with Brym, 1991: 118–19). In fact, he expected that the number of educated technical and professional workers in bureaucratic capitalist society would increase.

What Weber saw, compared with what Marx saw, was considerably more complexity in the social stratification system because of the growing diversity of the occupational structure and of capitalist enterprises. And although Weber was sometimes pessimistic in his writings about the future of democracy in a bureaucratic capitalist society, he did not link inequality and class conflict to the ultimate demise of capitalism itself, as did Marx. Similarly, although Weber, like

Marx, commented on how members of a class might or might not recognize their shared interests, he did not conclude that it was the inevitable destiny of the working class to become a "class for itself."

Social Class and Life-Chances

Despite these divergences in their thinking, Weber, like Marx, placed primary emphasis on the economic underpinnings of social stratification. However, he defined class more broadly than Marx did. Rather than insisting that a limited number of class positions were based on an individual's relationship to the means of production, Weber saw a larger variety of class positions based both on ownership of property and on other labour-market statuses, such as occupation and education. Furthermore, he emphasized the **life-chances** that class positions offer, noting that a higher position in the economic hierarchy, however obtained, provides more power and allows an individual and his or her family to enjoy more of the good things in life.

Thus, the general approach to studying stratification that I outlined earlier, one that recognizes the central importance of class while acknowledging that gender, race, and other possibly intersecting dimensions of social inequality can also be very important, is in the Weberian tradition. Similarly, my general definition of class as a relatively stable position within an economic hierarchy held by an individual or a family, along with others with roughly the same amount of control over or access to material resources, follows Weber's use of the term.

DAVIS AND MOORE: A FUNCTIONAL THEORY OF STRATIFICATION

Twentieth-Century Affluence and Functionalist Theory

Although other social theorists in Europe and North America also wrote about social stratification in the early decades of the twentieth century, I will skip ahead to 1945, when Kingsley Davis and Wilbert Moore published their brief but much-debated article, "Some Principles of Stratification." In Chapter 1, Introducing Sociology, you read about functionalist theory, which emphasizes consensus over conflict and seeks to explain the function for society as a whole of social institutions and various aspects of social structure. Davis and Moore were part of this intellectual tradition, which arose in reaction to the conflict-oriented and socially radical theories of Marx (and, to a lesser extent, of Weber).

The emergence of functionalism can be better understood if we view it as reflecting the highly optimistic view in mid-twentieth-century North America that, because World War II was over and the economy was expanding rapidly, affluence was increasing, social conflict was decreasing, and a harmonious future for society was dawning. Thus, during the several decades following World War II, an era some describe as the golden era of North American capitalism (Marglin and Schor, 1990), many social scientists were attracted to theories that downplayed conflict and emphasized the benefits to all of what seemed like an ever-expanding economy.

The Functional Necessity of Stratification

Davis and Moore (1945) argued that, because inequality exists in all societies, it must be a necessary part of society. All societies, they noted, have a variety of occupational roles that need to be filled, some requiring more training than do others, some having more functional importance, and some being less pleasant and more difficult to perform. To get people to fill important roles and to perform critical tasks well, and to spend time training for high-skill occupations, societies must ensure that the rewards for performance are greater. So, for example, doctors and schoolteachers need to be paid more than factory workers and secretaries need to be paid, and they also rank higher than the latter in terms of social honour and prestige.

In short, according to Davis and Moore, social inequality is both inevitable and functionally necessary for society. Davis and Moore were not describing a class-based and conflict-prone stratification system. Rather, they saw a much more fluid socioeconomic hierarchy, with many different occupational statuses into which individuals are slotted on the basis of their effort and ability. This system is supposedly held together by consensus and shared values (not torn apart by conflict, as Marx theorized) because members of society generally agree that the hierarchy is fair and just. It follows from their reasoning that efforts to reduce social inequality will be ineffective and might even be harmful to society.

Criticisms of Davis and Moore

Many criticisms have been levelled against Davis and Moore's theory. For example, although some differences in pay might be justified to reimburse those who spend more years in school preparing for a specific occupation, are the huge income and wealth inequalities we see in our society really necessary? Are movie stars, professional athletes, and chief executive officers with multimillion-dollar annual incomes really so much more important to society than are nurses, daycare workers, prison guards, and most other low-paid workers? And how does a theory like this account for inherited wealth and for the fact that wealth leads to power and the ability to accumulate still more wealth?

Given these criticisms, what accounts for the appeal of this theory? Perhaps it is the kernel of truth at its core that is so attractive—namely, the recognition that, to some extent, differences in income and prestige are based on different amounts of effort and ability. After all, we can easily find examples of better-paying occupations that require long years of education and training. Nevertheless, this is far from the complete story about inequality in our society, which is much more pronounced than what such differences in effort and ability might lead us to expect. In fact, the theory's appeal probably lies more in its apparent justification of these large inequalities. You might test this hypothesis by explaining the theory, first to someone with a high income or inherited wealth, and then to someone who is unemployed or earning very little. Chances are that the functionalist explanation of stratification would sound much more plausible to the wealthier person.

GERHARD LENSKI: TECHNOLOGY AND STRATIFICATION SYSTEMS

Writing in the 1960s, a time of growing prosperity in North America, Gerhard Lenski (1966) developed a theory of "power and privilege" to explain the extent of material inequality in both contemporary and past societies. Lenski's explanation recognized power and conflict much more explicitly than had Davis and Moore's functionalist explanation. Like Weber, he identified different dimensions of social stratification, such as education and ethnicity, while emphasizing the centrality of economic inequalities. Although he used the term *class*, Lenski did not define it precisely, choosing instead to talk about the ruling elites in society in general terms and about how they managed to maintain their wealth and power.

Lenski reasoned that a society's technological base largely determines the degree of inequality within it. In simple hunting-and-gathering societies,

he argued, the society's few resources were distributed primarily on the basis of need. But as societies became more technologically complex, resources in excess of those required to fulfill basic needs were produced. Control of those surplus resources, or privilege, came to be based on power, allowing ruling elites to keep a much larger share of these resources. Thus, more complex agricultural societies, such as that of precolonial India, developed highly structured governing and tax-collecting systems, through which the privileged ruling elites accumulated immense amounts of wealth, while the masses lived in poverty.

As a result of industrialization and the complexity of modern technology, this "age-old evolutionary trend toward ever-increasing inequality" (Lenski, 1966: 308) was reversed. Owners of the means of production could no longer control the production process directly and had to rely instead on educated managerial and technical workers to keep the complex system operating. Education broadened the horizons of these middle-level employees, introducing them to ideas of democracy, encouraging them to demand a larger share of the profits, and making them more articulate in their demands for equality.

Thus, Lenski's theory proposed a causal link among complex industrial technology, increased education of workers, and their insistence on sharing the growing wealth of an industrial society. But why would employers give in to such demands? Because, argued Lenski, the industrial elite needed educated workers—they could not produce wealth without them. Equally important, the much greater productivity of industrial societies meant that the elite could "make economic concessions in relative terms without necessarily suffering any loss in absolute terms" (Lenski, 1966: 314). Because the economic pie was so much bigger, everyone could have a larger slice.

In one obvious sense, Lenski's theory resembled the functional theory of stratification—both noted that better-educated and more highly skilled workers are paid more. However, unlike the functionalist approach, Lenski's theory clearly took power differences into account, emphasizing how the extent of accumulation of wealth by elites, or the degree of material inequality, depends on the power and bargaining ability of middle-level workers. But in contrast to Marx's nineteenth-century predictions of growing inequality as industrial capitalism matured, Lenski, writing in the middle of the twentieth century, believed that inequality was decreasing.

ERIK OLIN WRIGHT: A NEO-MARXIST APPROACH

In reaction against functionalism, Lenski (1966) brought power and conflict back into his explanation of social inequality, coming closer to the approach taken by Marx and Weber. But he did not employ a traditional Marxist analysis of the relationships of different classes to the means of production. In contrast, a number of neo-Marxist scholars, writing in the 1970s and 1980s, attempted to update the original Marxist model to the late twentieth century. One of them was Erik Olin Wright.

Although Marx acknowledged the existence of a middle class comprising several distinct groups, including independent producers and small-business owners, he predicted that this middle class would disappear. Wright's contribution lies in recognizing that, as industrial capitalism matured, the middle class had grown and become more diverse, and in trying to understand the class dynamics of our more complex capitalist system of production. Of particular importance is Wright's notion of **contradictory class locations**—that is, occupational groupings that have divided loyalties within a class structure. For example, although managers work for capitalists, supervising and trying to motivate lower-level employees to produce as much as possible, managers are themselves employees, potentially exploited by owners. Considering the substantial numbers of people in such contradictory locations, we can begin to understand why the widespread class conflict envisioned by Marx seldom emerged.

Wright (1985) also argued that exploitation of one class by another can occur through control of property or the means of production (as Marx had insisted), as well as through ownership of skill or credential assets and control of high positions within organizations. Thus, he identified three classes of owners (the bourgeoisie, small employers, and the petite bourgeoisie with no employees), and nine classes of wage-labourers (nonowners), differentiated on two dimensions: the possession of organizational assets and of skill/credential assets (Wright, 1985: 88). For example, "expert managers" (such as engineers or lawyers in senior management positions in large companies) fill a class location characterized by extensive organizational assets and high skill/credential assets, in contrast to "proletarians," who have no specific skill/credential assets and no management or supervisory responsibilities (see Figure 7.1).

FIGURE 7.1 ERIC OLIN WRIGHT'S TYPOLOGY OF CLASS LOCATION IN CAPITALIST SOCIETY

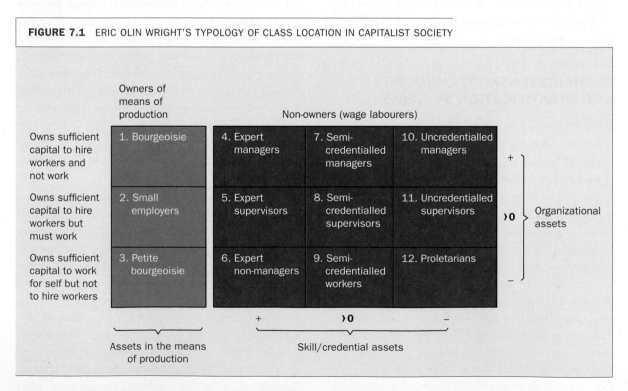

SOURCE: From Erik Olin Wright, *Classes*. 1985, p. 88. Reprinted with permission from Verso Books.

FRANK PARKIN: A NEO-WEBERIAN APPROACH

With his emphasis on organizational and skill/credential assets and contradictory class locations, Wright attempted to bring Marx's class analysis back into the discussion of contemporary forms of social stratification. Frank Parkin (1972, 1979) was equally explicit in stating his intellectual debts to Max Weber's discussions of power, class, and social stratification (Grabb, 2007). As a neo-Weberian, Parkin criticized traditional Marxist and contemporary neo-Marxist analyses for failing to take into account gender, race, religious, and other forms of social stratification that do not grow out of the relations of production in capitalist society but clearly have an origin and a permanency all their own (1979: 4–5). Nevertheless, like both Weber and Marx before him, Parkin continued to emphasize the importance of property relations in contemporary stratification systems (Grabb, 2007).

Among Parkin's most useful contributions to stratification theory is his explanation of how structured inequality, whether based on class, gender, race, or some other ascribed or achieved status, is maintained or changed. To do so, Parkin returned to a concept introduced by Weber, that of **social closure**. Parkin defines this term as "the process by which social collectivities seek to maximize rewards by restricting access to resources and opportunities to a limited circle of eligibles" (1979: 44). He then identifies two types of closure strategies that help explain how patterns of social inequality are maintained but also sometimes altered.

Exclusion refers to the organized efforts of privileged, powerful groups to maintain their advantaged position. Processes of exclusion can range from centuries-old caste systems in closed societies to the use, in contemporary open societies, of educational credentials to maintain power and privilege. For example, lawyers and other professional groups have managed to ensure, via legal restrictions, that only they can perform certain types of work in our society. By excluding others from engaging in such work, it is possible to maintain high income, enjoy a high standard of living, and exercise a great deal of power. Similarly, members of trade unions can use legal sanctions to keep nonmembers, who might have similar skills, from taking on well-paying jobs.

In contrast, **usurpation** refers to the efforts of excluded groups in a stratification system to gain advantages and power. As Parkin put it, all such actions have as their goal "biting into the resources and benefits accruing to dominant groups in society" (1979: 74). Usurpation efforts can range from lobbying and voting for social change to outright revolt against groups in power. Thus, over the past several decades, we have seen successful efforts by women's groups, First Nations groups, and other disadvantaged groups to change the balance of power and privilege in Canada. Going back further, labour unions took even stronger, sometimes illegal, actions to gain new powers and a more equitable distribution of resources for their members.

Parkin, like Lenski, took a keen interest in the power struggles in society between groups with more and less power. However, Parkin's neo-Weberian theory does not contain a premise of inevitability, either one of increased inequality and eventual social revolution as Marx predicted, or one of reduced inequality resulting from technological change and economic growth as Lenski predicted. Parkin, however, did see a clear trend with respect to processes of social closure. With the growing emphasis on education in modern society, the use of educational credentials to maintain power and privilege has become more widespread. As a result, well-educated professionals have become a powerful class grouping, sometimes almost as powerful as wealthy capitalists who control the means of production (Grabb, 2007). Beneath these two powerful groups are a range of other groups with varying amounts of power, trying, when possible, to usurp more power from those above.

PIERRE BOURDIEU: DIFFERENT FORMS OF CAPITAL

French anthropologist and sociologist Pierre Bourdieu also analyzed patterns of social stratification in modern societies through what might be seen as a neo-Weberian lens. Bourdieu developed the concepts of field, habitus, social capital, cultural capital, and symbolic capital, using them extensively in his explanation of how social hierarchies are reproduced across generations (Bourdieu, 1986; Grenfell, 2008).

A field of power, according to Bourdieu, is a social space (work organization, religious institution or community, for example) where individuals or groups with varying degrees of access to societal resources compete for power, more prominent positions, and even more resources (Everett, 2002). Bourdieu used the term *habitus* to describe people's sense of how to cope or compete and succeed in a particular field of power. Habitus is acquired through extended social relationships in social groups and the learning of shared values and lifestyles. A habitus that can lead to success in a particular field of power is one that involves knowledge of how different forms of capital can be used to get ahead and skill in acquiring such capital.

Economic capital (money, property, and other material assets) is the core form of capital in contemporary society, according to Bourdieu. This view put him in the same general theoretical camp as Marx and Weber, who argued that the economic dimension is the most important determinant of inequality. However, economic capital can be converted into other forms of capital, and individuals born into families with more economic capital are likely to acquire a habitus that involves familiarity with and skill in using these different forms of capital.

Social capital is comprised of social relationships, including networks of relationships, that can help people get ahead in life. An example would be the ability to ask your father to ask another lawyer in his firm to write a reference letter to support your application to law school. **Cultural capital** refers to knowledge and skill in navigating the social world of those who are most advantaged in society. If you were raised in a wealthy family, for example, you would be more likely to have received music lessons, visited art galleries, and travelled in Europe. You would likely know how to ski and play golf and you would probably be comfortable meeting others and making "small talk" in a social gathering involving wealthy and powerful people.

Symbolic capital is obtained through social recognition. Such recognition might involve being elected president of a community organization, being featured as a trendsetter for clothing or music in a magazine, or receiving an honour for an accomplishment in acting or sports. It is not difficult to imagine how greater access to economic, social, and cultural capital might also increase one's chances of acquiring symbolic capital.

Bourdieu's main point is that a person's habitus is not built just on economic foundations. Economic capital enables the acquisition of social capital that, in turn, increases the likelihood of acquiring cultural and symbolic capital. A complete sociological analysis of how stratification systems are maintained requires understanding how people acquire each type of capital. It is possible although not common for a person to acquire, say, cultural capital without economic capital and so improve his or her position in the stratification system. However, all forms of capital are correlated—economic advantage tends to breed social, cultural, and symbolic advantage. Altogether, knowledge about how to use these various forms of capital forms the habitus of each one of us and helps to explain how social stratification systems persist.

EXPLANATIONS OF SOCIAL STRATIFICATION: SUMMING UP

The theories we have reviewed differ in the assumptions they make and the conclusions they draw about the future of material inequality. Marx clearly saw inequality and exploitation of the working class increasing, and he predicted that class conflict would lead to the death of capitalism. Weber was not convinced that a socialist society would eventually emerge, nor did he argue that inequalities would gradually decrease (Grabb, 2007). Neo-Weberians like Parkin and Bourdieu took a similar stance. Wright's neo-Marixist analysis of the growing number of middle-class locations also does not suggest an increasing level of material inequality, but neither does it imply the opposite. However, the functionalists and Lenski, writing in an era of economic growth and widespread optimism about the ability of capitalism to raise the overall standard of living, clearly felt that material inequalities were shrinking in Western industrial societies.

The various explanations also differ in the degree to which they emphasize class differences in access to and control of material resources. For Marx, class was the primary determining factor in this regard. Weber, using the term *class* somewhat more broadly, emphasized its central role but recognized other important dimensions of social stratification. So, too, did Parkin, who explicitly discussed the independent effects of gender, race, and religion, and Bourdieu, who encouraged us to examine different forms of capital. Davis and Moore basically ignored the concept of class. Although Lenski focused more directly on economic inequality, he did not really describe society in terms of distinct classes, as Wright, in his neo-Marxist approach, did.

In the following section, we turn from theories of social inequality to data on occupations and material inequality in Canada to see if the concept of social class still has relevance in contemporary society.

TIME FOR REVIEW

1. What is the key difference between the functionalist theory of stratification and conflict-oriented explanations?
2. How are theories of social stratification shaped by the historical period during which the theorist lived? Provide examples.
3. How did Weber's analysis of social stratification differ from Marx's?
4. What are the unique insights that Frank Parkin and Pierre Bourdieu brought to our understanding of contemporary patterns of social stratification?

OCCUPATIONS, SOCIAL CLASS, AND INEQUALITY IN CANADA
OCCUPATIONAL SHIFTS OVER TIME

Some of the explanations of social stratification we reviewed above, such as Lenski's, focus directly on occupations while others, such as Wright's, rely on occupational data to discuss social class. Consequently, it would be useful to begin this section by examining occupational shifts in Canada over the past century. Table 7.1 displays the types of occupations most common near the beginning (1911) and in the middle (1951) of the last century, and recently (2011). The biggest change was the decline in agricultural occupations, from 34 percent of all labour force participants in 1911 to only 1 percent in 2011. Other natural resource-based occupations (forestry, fishing, mining) also declined, but not quite as steeply. Manufacturing occupations increased in relative terms (from 14 to 17 percent) between the beginning and middle of the last century, but by 2011 had dropped to only 5 percent of the employed labour force.

Manufacturing, construction, transportation, and resource-based occupations are typically called *blue-collar occupations*, in contrast to *white-collar occupations* in the managerial, professional, clerical, sales, and service categories. Table 7.1 shows that white-collar occupations have come to greatly outnumber blue-collar occupations as industrial capitalism has matured. In 2011, 12 percent of Canadian labour force participants were in managerial/administrative occupations, up from only 5 percent a century earlier.

Professional/technical occupations had multiplied by seven times in relative terms, from 4 to 28 percent.

TABLE 7.1 OCCUPATIONAL DISTRIBUTION OF LABOUR FORCE PARTICIPANTS,* CANADA, PERCENTAGE, 1911, 1951, 2011

OCCUPATION TYPE	1911 %	1951 %	2011 %
Managerial/ administrative	5	8	12
Professional/ technical	4	7	28
Clerical	4	11	13
Sales	5	7	10
Service	8	10	16
Manufacturing	14	17	5
Transportation	6	8	8
Construction	5	6	6
Agriculture	34	16	1
Forestry/ fishing/mining	5	4	1
Other occupations	10	6	—
Total	**100**	**100**	**100**

*1911 and 1951 data describe all labour force participants (the employed and the unemployed); 2011 data are for employed labour force participants only. All three percentage distributions are based on the population aged 15 and older.

SOURCES: 1911 and 1951 data adapted from 1911 and 1951 Census results, presented by O'Neill (1991); 2011 data adapted from 2011 *National Household Survey* results, Statistics Canada (2013).

Clerical, sales, and service occupations also had become much more common, from a total of only 17 percent in 1911 to 39 percent of all occupations in 2011.

What do these occupational changes tell us with respect to our previous discussion of the bases of social stratification? First, as various theories stipulate, the proportion of occupations requiring higher education has increased while the proportion of traditional blue-collar, "working-class" occupations has declined. With the expansion in white-collar occupations, average incomes rose, at least until the early 1980s. Thus, to the extent that occupational data can inform us about class structure in the Weberian sense, occupational shifts over the past century suggest greater class diversity, rather than a polarization of classes, as a strict reading of Marx's theory would predict, and a rising standard of living for Canadian workers, rather than increasing poverty and exploitation.

And what do the numbers in Table 7.1 not tell us? First, they do not distinguish between the occupations typically held by women and those typically held by men. Since the middle of the last century, a rising proportion of women have been entering the labour force and moving into better jobs. But, as you will see (Chapter 8, Gender Inequality), women are still more likely to be employed in clerical, sales, and service occupations (what might be called a "pink-collar sector") than in blue-collar occupations or in higher-status and better-paying managerial and professional occupations. Thus, gender-based labour market stratification continues to exist, intersecting with class-based stratification.

Second, the over-time data in Table 7.1 do not directly describe workers' relationships to the means of production. Unfortunately, Statistics Canada has never collected and categorized national data in a manner that would allow us to examine changes in Canada's class structure, either as Marx would have conceptualized it or as Erik Olin Wright updated it (refer back to Figure 7.1). Even so, we can learn something from data on self-employment. Between 1946 and 1981, a period of significant decline in the number of people employed in agriculture, the proportion of self-employed Canadians dropped dramatically, from 33 percent to 10 percent. However, beginning in the 1980s, a slow reversal of the trend began in Canada, the United States, and other Western industrialized countries. By 2012, 11 percent of employed Canadians were own-account self-employed (without any employees) and 4 percent employed others (Krahn, Hughes, and Lowe, 2015: Ch. 4). Researchers are uncertain whether more Canadians are voluntarily choosing self-employment or are being pushed into it as a result of higher levels of unemployment and growing corporate and public-sector downsizing. Nevertheless, the reversal of the decline in self-employment—the increase in the size of the petite bourgeoisie—is something theorists are trying to explain as they attempt to further update Marx's ideas of class-based stratification (Myles and Turegun, 1994).

Finally, the data in Table 7.1 do not reflect some of the dramatic changes in employment opportunities and outcomes that have been occurring in the past four decades. I will return to this topic later, but for now I will simply note that unemployment rates have risen and fallen, but never fallen to the level of the mid-twentieth century; part-time and temporary work have become much more common; and income growth appears to have stopped, while income and wealth inequality have increased. Consequently, the higher standard of living that accompanied occupational changes in the second half of the twentieth century is no longer guaranteed for all those in middle-status occupations. Thus we need to look carefully at the distributional side of the occupation and class structures, at "who gets what" in return for their employment (Westergaard, 1995). But before examining changing patterns of material inequality in Canada, I will first discuss another important feature of stratification systems in modern societies—opportunities for occupational mobility and status attainment.

OCCUPATIONAL MOBILITY AND STATUS ATTAINMENT

Many people move up the occupational and income ladders during their careers, frequently after investing in higher education of some kind. Some move down, often because of economic circumstances beyond their control. Sociologists have conducted a great deal of research on such **intragenerational occupational mobility** (mobility within an individual's lifetime) and on **intergenerational occupational mobility**, the process of reaching an occupational location higher or lower than the location your parents held. Such research is interesting in itself, since we all like to compare how well we have done relative to others. It is also theoretically important since it tests hypotheses derived from explanations of inequality (the functionalist perspective, for example) that propose that higher positions in society are generally filled by those most qualified.

If the only intergenerational occupational mobility we observed was a result of better-qualified people moving up to replace those who were less qualified, we should also see an equivalent amount of downward mobility. Such a scenario of "musical jobs" or, to use the technical term, **circulatory mobility**, does not really describe the Canadian situation over the past 70 years, however, because of the pronounced parallel process of **structural mobility** resulting from a significant change in the shape of Canada's overall occupational structure. As noted earlier, since the middle of the twentieth century, industrial societies, including Canada, experienced a great deal of growth in white-collar occupations (clerical, managerial, and professional positions) as traditional agricultural and blue-collar industrial jobs declined in relative importance. Hence, with an increase in the number of higher-status jobs, each generation had more chances than the preceding one to improve the status of their jobs.

Even so, Canadian studies conducted over the past several decades indicate that Canada, like the United States, has a relatively open stratification system, more so than countries like Sweden, the United Kingdom, France, and the Netherlands (Wanner, 2009). In other words, in Canada relatively more people have been able to move up the occupational ladder relative to their parents. During the second half of the last century, the Canadian occupational structure opened up for women and men in different ways. The steep decline in agricultural employment meant that many men moved out of the agricultural occupations held by their fathers. For women, the major shift was away from the housework that had been the main female occupation for their mothers' generation. For both sexes, expansion of postsecondary educational opportunities, leading to higher status occupations, played an important role (Wanner, 2009). However, most of this opening of the stratification system occurred between 1973 and 1986. Little changed in terms of mobility opportunities in the following decades.

Thus, overall, Canadian mobility studies find only a limited amount of direct occupational inheritance across generations. Yet those at or near the top of the occupational hierarchy are still more likely to pass their advantages on to their children. As Richard Wanner (2009: 129) concludes, "Canada is still a stratified society characterized by a considerable amount of inheritance of privilege." This intergenerational transfer of advantage takes place primarily through different levels of access to the postsecondary education system.

Research in Canada and other Western countries examining the process of occupational status attainment has shown, not surprisingly, that the most important influence on the status of an individual's current job is the status of that person's first job. Individuals who enter the labour market as articling lawyers, for example, typically make their way higher up the occupational ladder than do those who began as unskilled labourers. In turn, the status of that first job is heavily influenced by the level of education completed. Such findings obviously lend some support to theories suggesting that more-qualified people, as indicated by higher education, end up in higher-status and better-paying occupations.

However, many studies have also traced education-job linkages back to the previous generation, showing that those who obtain more education and hence better jobs are more likely to come from families with better-educated parents. For example, a 2009 study divided Canadians between the ages of 25 and 39 into two categories—those whose parents had no university degree and those whose parents had at least one university degree. Fifty-six percent of 25- to 39-year-olds in the former category but just 23 percent of 25- to 39-year-olds in the latter category had completed university themselves (Turcotte 2011). For a variety of reasons, including, in Pierre Bourdieu's language, access to more economic, social, and cultural capital, children from more advantaged backgrounds can build on their initial advantages.

THE DISTRIBUTION OF WEALTH

Evidence from various sources demonstrates that a small number of people continue to own or control a very large portion of the wealth in Canada. For example, in 2014, 57-year-old David Thomson and his family were estimated to be worth $25.3 billion. While only number 21 on the *Forbes* list of "The World's Billionaires" (2014), they were Canada's wealthiest family. In contrast, in 2011, the average wealth, or net worth (the difference between the total assets owned by a family, including a home, and its debt), for Canadian households was $465 000 (Sauvé and Battams, 2013), less than 0.002 percent of the Thomson family's net worth. This is a huge difference, but we should remember that, included in the Canadian average are the extremely rich, including the Thomson family. A 2012 survey revealed that almost 29 percent of Canadians reported that they had no wealth at all (Sauvé and Battams, 2013).

These statistics highlight the wealth gap between low-income and very rich Canadian families, such as the Thomsons, the Westons, and the Irvings, who have business holdings spread around the globe as well as in Canada. Together with highly paid CEOs and corporate directors, these wealthy families clearly form a distinct upper class, the haute (or high) bourgeoisie in Marx's terms. By way of example, it would take the average Canadian worker (employed full-time and year-round) nearly 200 *years* to earn as much as the average annual income of the top 100 CEOs in the country.

At the other end of the wealth scale are the 7 percent of Canadian families (excluding seniors) with low income and no-wage earners who reported a median net worth in 2009 of only $1000. These families, about 1.2 million people in total, typically relied on government transfer payments (for example, employment, welfare, or disability support payments) and had trouble making ends meet. Three out of 10 (29 percent) were at least two months behind in paying bills, and almost one in 10 (8 percent) was at least two months behind on loan payments (Luong, 2011).

Over the long term, the economic growth experienced in Western industrialized countries, along with some income redistribution efforts by governments, have had an equalizing effect on the distribution of household wealth. Wolff (1991), for example, showed that inequality in household wealth decreased between 1920 and the 1970s in Sweden, Britain, and the United States. Although comparable data are not available for Canada for the same period, it is likely that a similar decline occurred here as well. However, Wolff also noted that, in the mid-1970s, wealth inequality began to increase again in the United States and Sweden (it remained constant in Britain). What about Canada?

A recent study reveals that, on average, Canadian families were considerably wealthier in 2005 than they were in 1970 (Morissette and Zhang, 2007). However, there is more to this story. Wealth inequality declined between 1970 and 1977, remained steady until 1984, and then increased considerably in the next 20 years. Thus, back in 1984, the top 10 percent of Canadian families owned 51.8 percent of total family wealth.

By 2005, this figure had increased to 58.2 percent (Morissette and Zhang, 2007). In other words, the wealth gap between rich and poor families has been growing over the past several decades in Canada. In fact, as of 2012, Canada's wealthiest 86 families owned more than the 11 million people at the bottom of the country's wealth distribution (Macdonald, 2014).

INCOME DISTRIBUTION

High-Paying and Low-Paying Occupations

Although most people have no contact with the wealthiest families in Canada, we are much more aware of, or perhaps are even members of, a larger, not quite as wealthy but still very affluent group of households containing one or more individuals in high-paying occupations. For example, *the 2011 National Household Survey* reported that Canadian dentists earned a median income of $105 104 in 2010, while medical specialists earned considerably more ($126 119). Judges earned even more ($228 104), while lawyers had to be content with average yearly earnings of $92 356 (Statistics Canada, 2014a). In contrast, cashiers earned only a fraction of this ($8965), as did hotel clerks ($19 109), hair stylists and barbers ($15 163), and pet groomers and other animal-care workers ($10 871). The very low incomes of these service sector workers reflect, in part, the fact that many are employed part-time.

Using the term *class* in the Weberian sense, you could label individuals in well-paid managerial and professional occupations as members of an upper-middle class, given their high incomes and their access to and control of material resources through their employment positions. In contrast, retail workers and those employed in some service occupations (for example, food and beverage services, child-care and home-support services) work in the low-paying, insecure occupations that we might describe as the lower working class.

These occupational earning patterns hide large gender differences. Among people working full-time and full-year, women's earnings were 72 percent of men's earnings in 2011, a figure that has not changed significantly since 1995 (Krahn, Hughes, and Lowe, 2015: Ch. 6). Female dentists' median earnings were 74 percent of their male counterparts' median earnings in 2010. Among senior managers in finance and communications, women earned 87 percent of what men earned. In the higher education sector, the female–male median earnings ratio was 86 percent. Among

SOURCE: Malcolm Mayes/Artizans.com.

lower-paid occupations, female salesclerks earned only 68 percent of what male salesclerks earned, while female general farm workers earned 64 percent of their male counterparts' earnings (Statistics Canada, 2011). As these examples demonstrate, the female–male earnings ratio varies considerably by occupation, and tends to be lower in higher status and better paying occupations.

Income Inequality

The *2011 National Household Survey* data discussed above give some indication of the distribution in Canada of employment earnings, the largest component of total income, which also includes income from investments, government assistance, and all other sources. Studies of income tax data show that the level of total income inequality in Canada has increased dramatically over the past seven decades.

In 1945, at the end of World War II, the most advantaged 10 percent of Canadians (the top decile) received 37 percent of all income (Yalnizyan, 2010). While this figure fluctuated over the next four decades, income inequality in Canada slowly declined. In 1985, the top decile received 35 percent of all income. However, the long-term trend then reversed, and income inequality increased steadily during the next two decades—in 2007, the top 10 percent received 41 percent of all income. In fact, by 2007, the top 1 percent of Canadian income earners were receiving 13.8 percent of all income, up from 7.9 percent 25 years earlier (Yalnizyan, 2010; see Figure 7.2). A more recent study (Wolfson, Veall, and Brooks, 2014) demonstrates that, when income from privately owned corporations (frequently set up by high earners to reduce their taxes) is taken into account, income inequality is even higher.

THE POOR

Defining and Measuring Poverty

Poverty can be defined in different ways. We could talk about **absolute poverty**, arguing that the poor are those who have barely enough to stay alive, like many of the inhabitants of poor countries. Or we could conclude, as most Canadians do, that **relative poverty** is really what matters. If your neighbours own their homes and one or more cars, eat in nice restaurants, put money into pension plans, and take foreign vacations, while you rent a small apartment, ride the bus, look forward to a meal at McDonald's, have no savings, and watch travel shows on TV, you probably consider yourself poor. According to this definition, Canada does have a considerable number of poor people.

Most discussions of poverty in Canada rely on the **low-income cutoff** (**LICO**; commonly, although unofficially, known as the "poverty line") estimated by Statistics Canada on the basis of data obtained from its ongoing *Family Expenditure Survey*. According to this survey, the average Canadian spends about 43 percent of after-tax income on the basic necessities (food, shelter, and clothing). To establish the LICO, Statistics Canada adds 20 percent to this figure (Statistics Canada, 2014b). Hence, anyone spending more than 63 percent of after-tax income on the basic necessities is considered a low-income earner. Obviously, some people budget better than others do, so these are average cost estimates. However, there is no denying that the cost of living is higher in larger urban centres and that it takes more money to feed and clothe additional people, so different LICOs are calculated for communities of various sizes and for families of various sizes within those communities (Statistics Canada, 2014b). For example, based on 2013 income data, Statistics Canada sets the after-tax

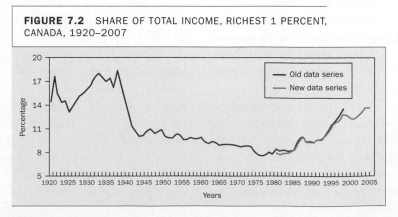

FIGURE 7.2 SHARE OF TOTAL INCOME, RICHEST 1 PERCENT, CANADA, 1920–2007

SOURCE: Yalnizyan, Armine. (2010). *The Rise of Canada's Richest 1%*. Ottawa: Canadian Centre for Policy Alternatives, pp. 11–12.

LICO for a single person living in a city with more than half a million residents at $19 774, compared with $12 935 for a single person living in a rural area. The after-tax low-income line for a family of four in a large city was $37 387, substantially higher than that for a similar-sized family in a rural area ($24 456).

Who Are the Poor?

Rising unemployment causes the number and proportion of people living below the poverty line to increase. In 1980, for example, 11.6 percent of all Canadians were below the after-tax poverty line but, with the recession of the early 1980s, that figure climbed to 13.7 percent by 1984. As the economy recovered, the proportion of poor Canadians dropped again to 10.2 percent in 1989 but then rose steeply to 15.2 percent in 1996 following the recession in the early 1990s. Over the next decade, the proportion of poor Canadians rose and fell again. In 2011, the most recent year for which data are available, 8.8 percent of Canadians were living below the after-tax LICO (Sauvé and Battams, 2013).

Although poverty rates tend to follow unemployment rates, not all of Canada's poor are unemployed or out of the labour force. Using a measure of low income, based on the cost of a basket of necessary household goods and services, more than 1.2 million Canadians (32 percent of all low-income Canadians) were living in working poor households, where the main earner had been paid for at least 910 hours of work in 2011 (Employment and Social Development Canada, 2015). These families were poor, not because no one was working for pay but because they earned so little. Overall, as part-time and temporary work have become more common in Canada, the working poor have come to make up a larger proportion of Canada's poor (Krahn, Hughes and Lowe, 2015: Ch. 4).

First Nations are among the poorest citizens of our country. In 2011, the unemployment rate among 25- to 64-year-old Indigenous Canadians (13 percent) was more than twice as high as among non-Indigenous in the same age category (6 percent) (Indigenous Affairs and Northern Development Canada, 2013). First Nations living on reserves have the highest unemployment rates (23 percent in 2006). The poverty rate (LICO) for First Nations living off-reserve in 2011 was 17.3 percent, compared with 8.8 percent for all Canadians (Employment and Social Development Canada, 2015). The comparable rate for First Nations living on reserves, if available, would be much higher.

On average, recent immigrants are younger and more educated than are native-born Canadians (see Chapter 9, Race and Ethnic Relations). Even so, in 2011, 16.4 percent of immigrants who had arrived in Canada in the previous decade were living below the LICO (Employment and Social Development Canada, 2015). Thus, despite their high level of education over the past several decades, recent immigrants have come to be significantly overrepresented among Canada's working poor (Wallis and Kwok, 2008).

Several decades ago, senior citizens were more likely than younger Canadians were to be living below the poverty line. However, higher proportions of recent cohorts of retirees have had employer-provided pensions and personal retirement funds (Gougeon, 2009), and the federal government has maintained old-age pension levels, even though they are quite small. Consequently, in contrast to the working poor, among whom poverty rates have risen, the poverty rate for seniors has declined. In 2011, only 5.2 percent of seniors were living below the LICO, compared with 8.8 percent of the total Canadian population (Employment and Social Development Canada, 2015). In contrast, 19.7 percent of Canadian single parents were living below the LICO in 2011. Ninety percent of these single parents were women. Many of these young women were completely dependent on social assistance, since it is almost impossible for a single young mother to look after children and hold down a job.

Social Assistance for the Poor

Many people believe that "welfare" (social assistance) and employment insurance are too easy to obtain and that the amount of money received is enough to encourage people to avoid seeking work (Swanson, 2001). Is this true? Because welfare regulations vary across provinces and territories, we will examine data from Ontario, the largest province and among the provinces with the highest welfare incomes, for 1992 and 2011.

Figure 7.3 shows that, in 1992, a single, employable adult (an adult who did not have a disability, was not a senior, and was not considered unable to seek work because of family responsibilities) who was eligible for Ontario social assistance received 62 percent of the after-tax low-income cut-off (LICO). Two decades later, in 2012, the same type of person receiving welfare received only 41 percent of LICO. Single people with disabilities who are receiving welfare have generally been treated a bit more generously Thus, in 1992,

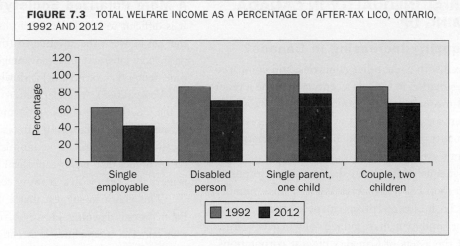

FIGURE 7.3 TOTAL WELFARE INCOME AS A PERCENTAGE OF AFTER-TAX LICO, ONTARIO, 1992 AND 2012

SOURCES: 1992 data from National Council of Welfare, *Welfare Incomes 2009* (Ottawa: 2010), Table 13; 2012 data from Anne Tweddle, Ken Battle, and Sherri Torjman, *Welfare in Canada 2012* (Ottawa: The Caledon Institute of Social Policy, 2013), Tables 3 and 6.

such an individual would have received total annual transfer payments that were 86 percent of the LICO. In 2012, the $13 772 that a person with a disability received from the provincial government was only 70 percent of the LICO and only 47 percent of the median income for all single adults in Ontario.

Single parents and couples with children, like adults with disabilities, have also been treated somewhat better by the welfare system, compared to single, employable adults. However, for both groups, we see in Figure 7.3 that their total annual welfare payments, as a percentage of the appropriate low-income line for their family type, declined over the past two decades. In fact, in 2012, a single parent with one child would have received $18 598, only 44 percent of the median income for a two-person family in Ontario that year. The $24 944 that a couple with two children would have received from welfare that year was only 29 percent of the Ontario median income for four-person families (Tweddle, Battle, and Torjman, 2013).

Summing up, in Ontario, and also across Canada, the amount of welfare assistance is very low. Furthermore, in almost every province and territory, welfare incomes have been cut over the past several decades, sometimes substantially, for almost all types of recipients. Newfoundland and Labrador is the exception, having raised its welfare assistance rates somewhat in the past several years (Tweddle, Battle, and Torjman, 2013). Consequently, it is difficult to accept the argument that overly generous welfare systems discourage people from looking for work.

Many of those who receive assistance cannot work outside the home, and the money provided keeps the poor who receive it well below the poverty line.

Moving Into and Out of Poverty

Discussions of poverty can leave the impression that the poor and the nonpoor are separate groups and that there is little mobility from one status to the other. While the proportion of Canadians living below the after-tax LICO has varied between 9 and 15 percent over the past several decades, Statistics Canada data show that, between 1996 and 2001, 25 percent of all Canadians lived below the after-tax LICO for at least one year (Statistics Canada, 2005: 122).

Another study revealed that, for a single year (2003–04), about 4 percent of all Canadians slid below the after-tax LICO, while a similar proportion moved above it (National Council of Welfare, 2008). Thus, poverty is not a static status. Individuals and families move into and out of poverty each year. Nevertheless, a sizable minority remain stuck in poverty year after year. Losing a job, having to take a lower-paying job, becoming a single parent, or being widowed can drastically increase the chance of falling into, and remaining stuck in, poverty. In addition, welfare regulations in many provinces "claw back" social assistance benefits as soon as welfare recipients start earning even a small income (Tweddle, Battle, and Torjman, 2013). This predicament creates a "welfare trap" that further increases the chances of poor Canadians, particularly single-parent families, remaining poor.

MATERIAL INEQUALITY IN CANADA: SUMMING UP

Is Inequality Increasing in Canada?

Compared with some other countries, and compared with the situation in Canada a century ago, the level of material inequality in this country today is relatively low. Even so, you have seen evidence of a great deal of inequality in wealth and income. Furthermore, indications are that, for at least several decades, the level of inequality has been slowly rising. Corporate concentration has been increasing as a small number of huge business enterprises, many of them family-owned or family-run, have gained control over a larger share of the assets of Canada's biggest corporations. Wealth inequality in general appears to be increasing, income inequality has risen, and the number of working poor has increased.

Looking more closely at the labour market, we see that unemployment rates have been rising slowly but steadily for several decades. Although these rates have gone up and down a number of times, and are lower now than they were in the 1990s, the long-term trend since the mid-twentieth century has been upward. In 2013, the average annual unemployment rate was 7.1 percent, representing 1.35 million unemployed Canadians (Statistics Canada, 2015), a number almost equal to the populations of Manitoba and Prince Edward Island combined. With increasing global financial and economic uncertainty, we can expect the national unemployment rate to stay at least at this level over the next several years. Comparisons across provinces in 2013 reveal the extent of regional inequality in Canada, with unemployment rates of 11.4 percent in Newfoundland and Labrador, 10.4 percent in New Brunswick, 7.5 percent in Ontario, and only 4.0 percent in Saskatchewan.

Part-time employment rates have also been rising over the past few decades. Back in 1953, fewer than 4 percent of employed Canadians worked part-time. In 2012, 18.8 percent had a part-time job. Employers do not have to pay pension and other benefits to part-time employees, so they have been hiring more part-time employees since the 1980s, thus cutting costs. By 2012, 13.6 percent of working Canadians had a job with a specific end date (Krahn, Hughes, and Lowe, 2015: Ch. 4). Real wages are no longer increasing, and inequality in earnings has been rising as a result of these part-time and temporary employment trends, as well as declines in employment in traditionally higher-paying industries and occupations.

A More Polarized Society?

It is difficult to avoid the conclusion that, in Canada, the gap between the advantaged (those with full-time, permanent jobs) and the disadvantaged (those with part-time, temporary, or no jobs) is slowly increasing (Fuller and Vosko, 2008). A similar pattern has been observed in the UK (Dorling et al., 2007) and the United States (Cavanagh and Collins, 2008). In fact, a widely discussed recent book by French economist Thomas Piketty (2014) argues that, under capitalism, growing inequality is inevitable, even with a growing economy.

This is not to suggest that a new era of massive inequalities is dawning. However, the evidence is clear that material inequalities are rising, and that society is becoming more polarized in terms of access to and control over economic resources (OECD, 2011; Sharpe and Capeluck, 2012; Yalnizyan, 2010). Using Weber's definition of *class*, we can conclude that class differences in Canada and many other countries are becoming more pronounced.

Obviously, many interrelated factors have contributed to the growth in material inequality. In North America, layoffs and downsizing have been a frequent response to economic downturns. So has the replacement of full-time permanent jobs with part-time and temporary positions. Globalization, the process whereby goods and services are produced by business enterprises operating in many different countries, has led to a more competitive and cost-cutting economic environment (see the Critical Sociology: Globalization box). Business enterprises have responded by shifting many of their activities to countries in which lower wages and less rigorous environmental and labour laws allow them to earn higher profits.

Labour unions, which traditionally have resisted attempts to cut wages and jobs, have lost some of their power. At the political level, an ideology emphasizing that "the market knows best," and that people need less rather than more government intervention in the economy and the labour market, has led to fewer government efforts to reduce material inequalities and reduced transfer payments to the poor (Sharpe and Capeluck, 2012). Tax cuts for the highest income groups have exacerbated patterns of income and wealth inequality (OECD, 2011; Yalnizyan, 2010).

CONSEQUENCES OF MATERIAL INEQUALITY

Other chapters in this textbook will go into more detail about the many consequences of material

CRITICAL SOCIOLOGY: GLOBALIZATION   HOW GLOBALIZATION CONTRIBUTES TO INEQUALITY IN CANADA

Unlike sociologists, the owners and managers of large business organizations don't usually spend much time thinking about social stratification. Instead of worrying about the effects of inequality on the life chances of the poor, or on the social cohesion of society, they are preoccupied with making profits.

However, such organizations have begun to express concerns with growing inequality, seeing it as "a threat to economic growth and long-term prosperity," as a recent TD Bank report observed (Alexander and Fong, 2014: 1). The report argues that technological change and globalization are the primary factors contributing to higher inequality. New technologies have "either replaced many middle-income, middle-skill workers, or deeply eroded their bargaining power" while with globalization "[b]usinesses (and supply chains) can now operate and coordinate activities anywhere in the world almost seamlessly. As a result, the production of goods and services has been transferred to lower cost regions" (Alexander and Fong, 2014: 3).

The Conference Board of Canada released a similar report, asking whether the income gap between rich and poor countries has widened (Conference Board of Canada, 2011). It found that the gap had been growing for the past three decades, with the exception of the period between 2007 and 2010. Moreover, it found that income inequality in Canada has also increased, as it has in most other wealthy countries. It, too, concluded that growing inequality between countries and within countries is being fuelled by globalization, in particular the importing of cheaply produced products from poorer countries to wealthier countries and the loss of highly skilled jobs from the former to the latter.

The Conference Board of Canada suggested that globalization leading to growing inequality is largely the inevitable result of the operation of market forces (for a contrary view, see Chapter 20, Globalization). However, it also acknowledged that declining unionization rates, stagnating minimum wage levels, economic deregulation, and national policies favouring the wealthy might be contributing factors.

Historically, banks and pro-business think tanks have been reluctant to advise interfering with market forces. When such organizations start acknowledging that governments might be able to help slow down or reverse the trend toward growing inequality, we should pay particular attention.

Critical Thinking Questions

1. Why do some banks and pro-business think tanks think that high inequality could interfere with economic growth in Canada?

2. Identify Canadian examples of globalization leading to higher inequality.

inequality for individuals and families. You will see that position in the class structure has an effect on behaviours, and that the poor, the middle classes, and the very wealthy frequently hold different opinions on various subjects, may vote differently, and certainly enjoy different lifestyles. In short, people in different positions in society's economic hierarchy experience different life-chances, to use Weber's term.

Consequences for Individuals and Families

Children from poorer families typically do not do as well in school as children from more affluent families do (Davies and Guppy, 2006). They are more likely to drop out before completing high school (Tanner, Krahn, and Hartnagel, 1995) and to be enrolled in nonuniversity academic streams if they stay in school (Taylor and Krahn, 2009). They are also much less likely to go to university and to experience more difficulties if they do go (Lehmann, 2013). As noted earlier in the discussion of occupational mobility,

such effects of poverty are largely responsible for the perpetuation of class inequalities from one generation to the next.

For a variety of reasons, including better nutrition, access to better health care, and less hazardous working conditions, those who are situated higher in the economic hierarchy are typically healthier than are poor people (Raphael, 2011). Consequently, on average, the poor do not live as long as those who are better off (Wilkinson and Pickett, 2010). Similarly, when dealing with the criminal justice system, those with greater access to and control over economic resources tend to fare better (King and Winterdyk, 2010). As a result, the poor are overrepresented in jails. First Nations and visible minority Canadians with low incomes are particularly disadvantaged when dealing with the criminal justice system (Fitzgerald and Carrington, 2008). I could go on, but these examples are probably sufficient to make the point that life-chances are a function of position in the class structure and that those higher up in the economic hierarchy enjoy a better quality of life and, often, a longer life.

Consequences for Society

In addition to these substantial consequences for individuals and families, can material inequality have other broader social outcomes? Specifically, given the relatively high and increasing level of inequality in Canada, can we expect more social unrest? Will conflict between the "haves" and the "have-nots" increase? Those committed to a classical Marxist theory of social change might welcome such conflict; for them, it would indicate that capitalism was finally beginning to give way to a socialist society. Others might view such conflict more negatively. Whatever the response to such a possibility, it is clear that values and beliefs directly influence the way that people respond to evidence of inequality and its consequences.

But returning to the question, can we expect an increase in social unrest and conflict as a result of higher levels of inequality? During the early 1980s, for example, the solidarity movement in British Columbia brought together members of trade unions, social-welfare organizations, and various community-based groups in opposition to the Social Credit government's cutbacks in government programs and attempts to change labour legislation. Bryan Palmer (1986) described the protests and rallies that took place as evidence of growing class conflict. However, these events were exceptional. Much more often, the poor and the near-poor put up with their less advantaged position because they have few of the resources (for example, money, education, organizations) that make it possible to fight for social change (Brym, 1979). In fact, in the past decade, we have seen more opposition from a better-organized middle class in response to government cutbacks in health and education funding, and in support for seniors, than from the poor in response to welfare cutbacks. And we have witnessed intensified negative stereotyping of the poor and those on welfare, a process that Jean Swanson (2001) calls "poor-bashing."

Several years ago, however, we saw the emergence of a remarkable new social movement, Occupy Wall Street, that brought together a wide range of individuals and groups, including middle-class, university-educated social activists and the homeless, all concerned about the growing level of social inequality in North America. The movement attracted a great deal of public attention, but after some time died down as other social, political, and environmental issues took centre stage (see the Critical Sociology: Protest And Policy box). It remains to be seen whether this movement will have an impact on patterns of social inequality in Canada and elsewhere.

It is unlikely that growing social inequality and fewer opportunities for upward mobility will translate into widespread social unrest in Canada. However, at least one study shows that some workers are digging in for long struggles against the threat of job cuts (Brym, Birdsell Bauer, and McIvor, 2013). Moreover, it remains possible that coalitions of concerned citizens will have an impact on the long-term trend toward growing inequality and declining opportunities. For example, despite the declining strength of unions in North America, we are beginning to see some responses to social inequality from the "social unionism" movement (Camfield, 2011; Krahn, Hughes, and Lowe, 2015: Ch. 11). Rather than focusing only on the needs of their members, some activist unions have begun making alliances with community groups and social justice organizations to implement social reforms in the broader community.

As for the long-term consequences for global peace and security as a result of a growing gap between rich and poor countries, they are difficult to predict. Even so, as Paul Krugman, an influential American economist, noted some years ago, "The ultimate effects of growing economic disparities on our social and political health may be hard to predict, but they are unlikely to be pleasant" (Krugman, 1994: F9).

TIME FOR REVIEW

1. What do occupational, income, and unemployment trends in Canada over the past several decades tell us about Canada's social stratification system?
2. Are any of the theories of stratification discussed earlier in this chapter clearly supported or refuted by these trends? If yes, which theories, and how?
3. Why do you think most poor people are poor?
4. Does it really matter if material inequality increases in Canadian society? Why, or why not?

CRITICAL SOCIOLOGY: PROTEST AND POLICY | **DIFFERENT REACTIONS TO RISING TUITION FEES IN QUEBEC AND THE REST OF CANADA**

Compared to half a century ago, access to high-paying, high-status, secure jobs depends more on completing university or college (see Chapter 13, Education). However, tuition rates have risen rapidly in most Canadian provinces and students are graduating with much higher debt (Mason, 2013; Shaker and Macdonald with Wodrich, 2013). Consequently, it is increasingly difficult for young people from poorer families to acquire a college diploma or a university degree. In 2013, Quebec university students protested in the streets for weeks about proposed tuition increases that, if they had been implemented, would still have left Quebec tuition rates considerably lower than in any other province. Léo Charbonneau (2013) describes how

> the conflict began as a protest against the then Liberal government's plan to raise tuition fees by $325 a year for five years, which would have brought tuition to $3,800 a year when fully implemented by fall 2016—a rise of roughly 75 percent. ... The protests garnered international attention, yet most Canadians outside Quebec remained essentially bystanders to the action. ...

> Why has there been so little echo of the Quebec protests among students in the rest of Canada? It's an interesting question, and one which Laura Pin, a PhD student in political science at York University, valiantly tried to answer at the "Academia in the Age of Austerity" conference held earlier this month in Toronto. ...

> Ms. Pin suggested four factors accounting for a lack of action outside Quebec. The first involves what she called the "political opportunity" structure. There was a "clear initiating event"—the Charest government's planned tuition hikes—which spurred students to action. Speaking of Ontario, Ms. Pin noted that tuition increases have been persistent but incremental, so students haven't quite faced the same "sticker shock" as those in Quebec. ...

> Second, the Charest government was in its third mandate and was seen by many as tired and past its prime. Ms. Pin noted that the Liberals were sitting low in the opinion polls and reaching the end of their current mandate, and many wanted simply to see them go. The student protests were a great opportunity for opposition groups, in general, to oppose and weaken the government.

> Third, there is a long history of social action in Quebec regarding postsecondary education going back to the Quiet Revolution of the 1960s, resulting in major student mobilizations every few years. As well, the tuition hikes were seen in Quebec as being part of broader social issues on equality and opportunity that were raised by the conflict. By contrast, in Ontario, Ms. Pin said there has been 'lots of austerity rhetoric' for years. ... Plus, university education is increasingly being seen in Canada as a private benefit accruing to the individual, so tuition fees and student debt become more of a personal than a societal issue, she said.

> Fourth, and finally, Ms. Pin hypothesized that high tuition in Ontario (and much of the rest of Canada) may in itself stifle protest because there is "more to lose"—i.e., the opportunity cost of protest is higher. Additionally, a high debt load and the necessity for many students to work part-time while studying can impede collective action, she said; it is harder for students with heavy workloads "to engage" with the issues. ...

Critical Thinking Questions

1. In terms of their importance, rank the four factors that Pin uses to explain differences in student protest. Justify your ranking.

2. What other sociological explanations can you propose for differences in students' reactions to rising tuition fees? How would a sociologist find evidence to test your explanations?

RESPONDING TO INEQUALITY

Some people believe that more equal distribution of society's resources would be preferable to the current level of inequality. They believe that existing differences in life-chances are unjust and look for ways in which social institutions, laws, and tax systems might be changed to reduce material inequality. Others, equally offended by inequality and its consequences, reject this reformist approach in favour of a more radical position, advocating the replacement of capitalist society by some kind of socialist or social-democratic alternative. Still others respond to evidence of extensive inequality

Protesters in the Occupy Movement.
SOURCE: © Tomas Abad/Alamy.

with little ambition to change it, believing, simply, that this is "the way things are." Although perhaps bothered by its consequences, members of this group might still conclude that the existing level of inequality is inevitable and that well-intentioned efforts to reduce it will, in the long run, have little effect. They might even conclude that inequality is functional, as Davis and Moore (1945) argued 70 years ago, and that efforts to reduce it will be counterproductive. In short, reactions to inequality, and recommendations about what, if anything, should be done about it, reflect personal values and political orientations.

Assuming that a lower level of inequality is a goal worth striving for, it is clear that the government has a role to play in trying to reach that goal. The Canadian state has a significant impact on the distribution of wealth and income through tax systems that redistribute wealth from the rich to the poor (Yalnizyan, 2010); through minimum-wage and other types of legislation; and through transfer payments, such as pensions for seniors and those with disabilities, social assistance for low-income individuals and families, and employment insurance. Even so, compared with some other industrialized countries, Canada spends considerably less on attempts to reduce poverty and inequality. Analysts estimate that nearly two-thirds of the increase in after-tax inequality that has occurred in Canada since 1981 would be eliminated if our tax and redistribution system was like that of Western European countries (Sharpe and Capeluck, 2012: 22).

However, Canada's welfare policies appear to be based on the belief that a relatively unregulated labour market will produce wealth and jobs that should, in time, trickle down to the poor (Esping-Andersen, 1990). Unfortunately, as my review of labour market trends indicates, there is little evidence that the free market has performed successfully in this regard. Instead, unemployment rates have risen, precarious employment has become more common, and social inequality has increased.

Furthermore, during the past several decades, the political mood has changed, and concerns about reducing government deficits, streamlining government, and making Canada more competitive in the global marketplace appear to have been influencing government policy more than concerns about reducing inequality. In fact, some deficit-reducing initiatives (for example, reductions in social-assistance payments) have led to increases in material inequality in Canada, as have tax reform initiatives that have favoured the very rich.

But twenty-first-century government policies do not necessarily require this tradeoff. For example, government-funded job-creation strategies may continue to be useful in the future, as they were during the aftermath of the global financial crisis of 2008–09. Revised tax policies that would raise corporate income taxes, increase the marginal tax rate for Canada's highest paid citizens, and eliminate some of the tax writeoffs enjoyed by the upper and middle classes could also be useful.

A large part of the problem lies, of course, in the fact that any serious effort to redistribute the wealth and income from the well-off to the poor would probably be opposed by the former. If we really want to do something about material inequality in Canada, and globally, if we want a different kind of society and a different kind of world, many of us—and that would include me—have to be willing to accept less so that others can have more.

SUMMARY

1. **What is social stratification?**
   Social stratification refers to persistent patterns of social inequality. Some social hierarchies are based on ascribed statuses, such as gender, race, and age, which are typically assigned to an individual at birth. Other social hierarchies are based on achieved status, which indexes how well an individual has performed in some role.

2. **What are the main sociological theories that explain social stratification systems?**
   In his class-based theory of social stratification, Karl Marx emphasized the exploitation of the working class by the owners of the means of production and the potential for class conflict to generate social change. Max Weber also put considerable emphasis on the power that resides in ownership of property but argued that hierarchies of prestige and political power are influential as well.

3. **Do any sociological theories argue that social stratification is useful?**
   The functional theory of social stratification suggests that inequality is both inevitable and necessary insofar as it ensures that the most qualified individuals are selected to fill the most important and rewarding roles. This theory downplays power differences and conflict between social classes.

4. **How do sociological theorists account for how society and the economy have changed over the past century?**
   Erik Olin Wright developed a class-based theory of stratification that adapts many of Marx's ideas to today's circumstances. Frank Parkin's approach follows in the footsteps of Weber by focusing on how some social groups exclude others from power. Pierre Bourdieu's explanation of how social inequality is reproduced across generations emphasized different forms of capital: economic, social, cultural, and symbolic.

5. **What can we learn about Canada's social stratification system by examining relevant data?**
   While studies of occupational mobility show that Canada is a relatively open society, strong evidence exists that class-based advantages are often passed from one generation to the next. Ownership of wealth and property in Canada remains highly concentrated, and income inequality is also relatively high. There is considerable evidence that the poor and others near the bottom of the social hierarchies in our society enjoy fewer life-chances than do the well-off. Because of their limited access to social and material resources, the poor have seldom become an active force for social change.

6. **Is social inequality decreasing, staying the same, or increasing?**
   Some theories of social stratification developed in the middle of the twentieth century suggested that material inequality was declining as the North American economy expanded. However, the period of rapid economic growth that characterized the middle decades of that century appears to have ended. As unemployment rates have risen, as part-time and temporary jobs become more common, and as governments cut back on social-assistance programs while reducing taxes for the very wealthy, evidence accumulates that material inequality is slowly increasing in Canada and also in other Western industrialized countries.

QUESTIONS TO CONSIDER

1. Does social class play a more or less significant role than do ascribed statuses (such as race, gender, and age) in determining patterns of inequality in Canada?

2. Use information provided in this chapter, as well as your own experience, to explain how social and material advantages are passed from one generation to the next, resulting in persistent patterns of social inequality.

3. Present arguments for and against why governments should play a significant role in addressing persistent patterns of social inequality.

4. What is poverty and how can it best be measured?

GLOSSARY

Absolute poverty (p. 163) is the state of existence of those who have so little income that they can barely stay alive.

Achieved status (p. 149) is a changeable status that is acquired on the basis of how well an individual performs a particular role.

Ascribed status (p. 149) is a status such as age, gender, or race, that is assigned to an individual, typically at birth

The **bourgeoisie** (p. 152), according to Marx, is one of the two main classes in the capitalist mode of production. It comprises the owners of the means of production.

A **caste system** (p. 149) is a closed stratification system, like India's, with strict rules regarding the type of work that members of different castes (the strata of Indian society into which people are born) can do.

Circulatory mobility (p. 160) is the occupational mobility that occurs in a society when better-qualified individuals move upward to replace those who are less qualified and who must consequently move downward.

Class conflict (p. 152), according to Marx, is conflict between major classes in a mode of production. It eventually leads to the evolution of a new mode of production.

Class consciousness (p. 152), according to Marx, is the recognition by members of a class of their shared interests in opposing members of another class.

Class structure (p. 151) is the relatively permanent economic hierarchy comprising different social classes.

In a **closed stratification system** (p. 149), little or no social mobility occurs because most or all statuses are ascribed.

Contradictory class locations (p. 156), according to Erik Olin Wright, are the locations within a class structure populated by occupational groupings with divided loyalties (for example, managers who supervise others yet report to owners).

Cultural capital (p. 158) refers to the knowledge and skill required to navigate the social world of the more advantaged people in society.

Economic capital (p. 158) consists of money, property, and other material assets. It is the core form of capital in contemporary society.

Exclusion (p. 157), according to Frank Parkin, is the organized effort by privileged, powerful groups to maintain their advantaged position.

Intergenerational occupational mobility (p. 160) refers to an individual's occupational mobility, either upward or downward, in relation to her or his parents' occupational status.

Intragenerational occupational mobility (p. 160) refers to an individual's occupational mobility, either upward or downward, within his or her own lifetime.

Life-chances (p. 154), according to Weber, are the opportunities (or lack thereof) for a higher standard of living and a better quality of life that are available to members of a given class.

The **low-income cutoff (LICO)** (p. 163), known unofficially as the "poverty line," is an estimate of the income level below which a person or family might be considered to be living in relative poverty. It is defined by Statistics Canada as the level of income at which more than 63 percent of income is spent on basic necessities.

The **means of production** (p. 152), according to Marx, constitute one of the main components of a mode of production, consisting of the technology, capital investments, and raw materials used in production.

A **meritocracy** (p. 149) is a society in which most or all statuses are achieved on the basis of merit (how well a person performs in a given role).

The **mode of production** (p. 152), according to Marx, is the system of economic activity in a society, comprising the means of production and the social relations of production (the class system).

In an **open stratification system** (p. 149), merit, rather than inheritance (or ascribed characteristics), determines social rank.

The **petite bourgeoisie** (p. 152), according to Marx, is a secondary class within the capitalist mode of production, including independent owners/producers (for example, farmers) and small-business owners.

Power (p. 148) is the ability to impose one's will on others.

The **proletariat** (p. 152), according to Marx, is one of the two main classes in a capitalist mode of production, comprising workers who exchange their labour for a wage.

Relative poverty (p. 163) is a state of existence in which individuals have significantly less income than do most others in their society, causing their lifestyle to be more restricted and their life-chances to be substantially curtailed.

Social capital (p. 158), according to Pierre Bourdieu, is comprised of relationships with other individuals and groups that can help someone get ahead in life.

Social class (p. 151) is a position in an economic hierarchy occupied by individuals or families with similar access to, or control over, material resources.

Social closure (p. 157), according to Max Weber and Frank Parkin, refers to the methods used by relatively powerful groups to maintain their unequal access to status and resources, and to exclude others from such access.

Social mobility (p. 149) is the process whereby individuals, families, or other groups move up or down a status hierarchy.

Social relations of production (p. 152), according to Marx, are one of the main components of a given mode of production—specifically, the relationships between the main classes involved in production.

Social stratification (p. 147) refers to persistent patterns of social inequality perpetuated by the way wealth, power, and prestige are distributed and passed from one generation to the next.

Status (p. 149) is a culturally and socially defined position that a person occupies in a group.

Structural mobility (p. 160) refers to the occupational mobility in a society resulting from changes in the occupational structure (for example, the upward mobility of many individuals resulting from the creation of more middle- and upper-level jobs).

Surplus value (p. 152), according to Marx, is the value of goods in excess of the cost of production, which takes the form of profit when the product is sold.

Symbolic capital (p. 158), including honours and prizes, involves social recognition by advantaged people.

Usurpation (p. 157), according to Frank Parkin, is the effort of excluded groups within a stratification system to gain advantages and power at the expense of more powerful groups.

CHAPTER 8

GENDER INEQUALITY

Marisa Young
McMASTER UNIVERSITY

SOURCE: John Lund/Drew Kelly/Getty Images.

AFTER READING THIS CHAPTER, YOU WILL BE ABLE TO:

- Compare women and men in terms of their participation in the Canadian paid labour force and their representation and earnings across and within occupations.

- Describe persistence and change in the quantity and type of domestic work that women and men do.

- Analyze the consequences of gender inequality in the workplace and the domestic sphere for people's mental health.

- Outline and contrast a variety of sociological explanations for gender differences in work and family responsibilities.

- Appreciate that we can achieve a higher level of gender equality by implementing certain policy initiatives and challenging persistent ideas about appropriate work roles for women and men.

INTRODUCTION

When my partner and I first discussed having a child, my reaction surprised me. Unlike many women, I didn't immediately feel excited at the prospect of becoming a new mother. I didn't wonder how the baby might look. I didn't speculate about what occupation she or he might enter as an adult, nor did I start thinking about names for my new bundle of joy. Instead, as a 31-year-old career woman, my first thought was "How am I possibly going to meet my career expectations while raising a child?" Soon, other questions flooded my mind: How could I put in the hours necessary to get ahead in my job? How could I meet deadlines that my supervisors imposed on me or that I placed on myself? Would I face negative career consequences because of additional family obligations? Would I resent myself for jeopardizing all the work I had done trying to get ahead? Worst of all, would I resent my partner for pushing his career forward while I was at home tending to our child's needs?

I'd seen other women face this dilemma. After working hard to succeed in their careers, they were torn between the decision to have children or continue focusing on their jobs. For example, my oldest sister had become chief probation officer for the Government of Alberta at 32. She worked almost around the clock and was seen as the "top dog" when it came to decision-making authority in the district. Her job was her life, and she was proud of what she did. When she was 36, she decided to have her first child. She started taking more time off work to be with her son. However, she soon fell behind in her paid work and was overlooked when it came to important assignments and career opportunities. Attempting to balance her obligations, she hired a nanny. She caught up on paid work and restored her reputation. Life again seemed manageable—until she came home one night to the news that she had missed hearing her son say his first words. She was crushed. It was then that she realized a sacrifice was necessary. She could remain a high-powered government worker and continue missing important parts of her child's life or she could settle for being a lower-level employee to ensure that she was home more often. My sister decided to take a less demanding job but I know she has regrets to this day.

Women today still have to make compromises when they are torn between pursuing a career and having children because work and family institutions have not adequately adapted to changes in women's level of education, participation in the paid labour force, and desire to have children. Typically, women are still perceived as primarily responsible for the domestic sphere, regardless of their economic responsibilities, while men are usually seen as the primary breadwinners whose proper place is outside the home, in the world of paid work.

In this chapter, I examine various aspects of this dilemma in depth. Specifically, I analyze patterns of gender inequality in paid and unpaid (domestic) work. I assess competing sociological explanations of gender inequality. I highlight the progress we have made toward achieving gender equality in the home and in the paid labour force. Finally, I discuss how trends in gender inequality influence work–family conflict and the mental health of Canadian women and men. To set the stage, I first offer some historical background.

A BRIEF HISTORY OF GENDER DIFFERENCES IN PAID AND DOMESTIC WORK

During the first 90 percent of human history, when people lived in tribes of no more than about 100 people each, most men hunted animals and most women gathered wild, edible plants and did most of the child care. However, this gender division of labour was not associated with large differences in power and authority because women produced up to 80 percent of the tribe's food. Men had few privileges that women didn't also enjoy.

Gender differences in power and authority became significant only when people settled down and men came to control private property. Gender differences were highly pronounced in agrarian (farming) societies and during the Industrial Revolution, which began in England in the 1770s, spreading to continental Europe and North America in the 1800s.

On the family farm, workplace and home were one and the same, but during the Industrial Revolution, the mill, the mine, the factory, and the office separated themselves from the home. The family now came to depend on one adult member doing paid work outside the home and another doing domestic work in the home. Gender roles became more apparent. The ideal woman was no longer seen as a hardy and productive member of the family responsible for gathering food or tending animals, but as a "feminine" creature better suited to unpaid housework and managing the social and emotional affairs of the family. In contrast, men came to be regarded as better suited to managing the rough-and-tumble, "masculine" world of paid work.

A more or less strict **gendered division of labour** was institutionalized as work tasks were based on sex differences (Nash and Fernandez-Kelly, 1983).

Women were not completely shut out of the public sphere. They started entering the paid labour force during the Industrial Revolution, in most cases taking jobs that men did not want, including low-paying work in domestic service and textile factories. Their presence in the paid workforce began to increase in the early to mid-1900s because of labour shortages during World Wars I and II (see Figure 8.1). While men were off fighting on the front lines, women assumed a more central role in the workplace to help sustain the economy. When men returned from war, women were expected to return to their traditional roles in the home. Most did, but others had grown accustomed to the rewards of paid work. They sought new employment opportunities just as the nonmanual, "service" sector of the economy started to expand quickly (Pinchbeck, 1930). In Canada today, the paid labour force comprises about 60 percent men and 40 percent women (Statistics Canada, 2011).

Despite near-equality in overall numbers, the representation and rewards of men and women still vary greatly within and across occupations, as you will soon learn (Ferrao, 2010). Moreover, although men now do more domestic work than they used to, women—even women who work full-time—still do considerably more domestic work than men do (Beaujot and Andersen, 2007; Statistics Canada, 2011; Young,

Schieman, and Milkie, 2014). Women's unequal access to rewards in the workplace, coupled with their over-representation in domestic work, has negative implications for their psychological well-being—a topic I discuss in detail later.

GENDER INEQUALITY AND THE DIVISION OF LABOUR

What do sociologists mean by gender inequality? *Social inequality* refers to significant differences across social categories in access to valued goods, services, rights, and experiences. For purposes of analyzing inequality between men and women in the public and domestic spheres—a key part of gender inequality—we may usefully focus on differences in (1) power and resources, (2) several dimensions of self-conception, and (3) responsibilities. Let us consider each of these terms in turn.

Power is the ability to impose one's will on others despite resistance. The exercise of power influences behaviours, attitudes, and experiences, both those of the relatively powerful and those of the relatively powerless. Power is not always exercised by individuals. Groups, organizations, and institutions can impose it. However, when individuals exercise power, it derives from a person's social position. Your professor holds power over you by determining what you need to read, your test schedule, and your course grade, just as your boss has power over your job schedule and earnings.

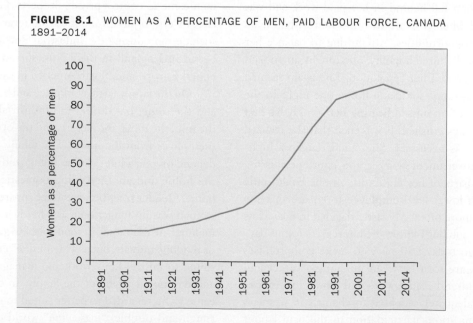

FIGURE 8.1   WOMEN AS A PERCENTAGE OF MEN, PAID LABOUR FORCE, CANADA 1891–2014

SOURCES: Statistics Canada (2014a, 2014b).

Resources are valued assets that individuals can draw on to contribute to the achievement of their goals. Resources include money and material goods that help sustain one's self and one's family, education, the high prestige that accompanies some occupations, and the good work conditions that accompany some jobs.

Yet another resource is composed of the psychological coping mechanisms that some people have in abundance. Such **dimensions of self** include self-esteem and a sense of personal control or mastery over one's life circumstances.

Finally, **responsibilities** are the obligations that people are expected to meet. Examples include job demands, work hours, domestic chores, child care, and emotional support of friends and family. *Conflicting responsibilities* are incompatible expectations or demands that may exist, for example, between family life and paid work. The consequences of conflicting responsibilities tend to be worse among the most disadvantaged people in society, such as single mothers living in poverty (see the Critical Sociology: Social Inequality box).

Bearing these definitions in mind, we now consider how gender inequality in paid and unpaid work varies across power and resources, dimensions of self, and responsibilities.

PATTERNS OF INEQUALITY IN PAID WORK

People need paid work to support themselves and their family members. Paid work is associated with intrinsic rewards such as job satisfaction and extrinsic rewards,

---

CRITICAL SOCIOLOGY: SOCIAL INEQUALITY   CONFLICTING RESPONSIBILITIES AMONG SINGLE MOTHERS

Income inequality is a growing concern, and people who earn high incomes experience the balancing act between work and family differently than do people who earn low incomes. Single mothers face the biggest challenge, as a recent tragedy reminds us:

> Kim Braithwaite was making progress. She was working two jobs to support her two children, 9-year-old Justina and 1-year-old Justin. But on October 12, 2003, she faced a dilemma: Her babysitter was late. Kim would be tardy for her shift at McDonald's if she delayed and she worried that she would be fired. The sitter would arrive in a few minutes, Kim reasoned, and she left for work.
>
> The next she heard was from the police. Her children were found dead in her front room; her apartment had caught fire before the babysitter arrived. Kim was arrested for child neglect. Said a neighbour, "It's hard when a single mother has two or three kids and has to work a lot. But I never hear her kids crying, never see her yelling at them. She is a good mom." (Williams and Boushey, 2010: ii)

Single parents head about one out of seven Canadian families, and women head around eight out of ten single-parent households. More than a fifth of those women are poor (Women in Canada, 2000). Like Kim Braithwaite, they have few resources to help them balance work and family demands. Child care is an especially big problem. In one mother's painful words:

> I compromised my, my integrity or my, you know, self-worth to bring a paycheck home for my kids ... I'm sure I compromised. [long pause] I'm trying to think how to put this ... I think I've compromised my kids, on not a real high level, but more than one time, and taken them to day cares that maybe they shouldn't have been at ... You know, because I had to go to work. (Quoted in Williams and Boushey, 2010: 11)

The lack of child-care options for poor, single mothers can lead them to compromise their children's safety and overall well-being because missing work is simply not an option. Women in these precarious circumstances experience a much different type of work–family conflict than do employed, middle-class mothers who can afford good child care.

Critical Thinking Questions

1. Imagine you were telling a fellow student about Kim Braithwaite's unfortunate situation and she responded, "Well, it's her fault her children died. She's a bad mother leaving her children unattended." While admitting that Kim Braithwaite's decision was a bad one, use your sociological imagination to convince your friend that social forces influenced Ms. Braithwaite's actions and that such bad decisions would be less frequent under different social circumstances.

2. Work–family conflict is experienced differently in different social classes and among people with different marital status. Comparing poor and middle-class single-parent and two-parent families, list the main differences in the experience of work–family conflict.

notably a salary or wage. Although women have made rapid strides in paid labour force participation in recent decades, they still face inequalities insofar as they are segregated in particular kinds of jobs that tend to pay relatively little and are often part-time or "precarious" workers in other ways that we will examine.

Occupational Segregation

Think about the following occupations: Doctor, nurse, engineer, teacher. In which occupations are you more likely to find a man? In which are you more likely to find a woman? If you're like most people, you believe (correctly) that men are more likely to be doctors and engineers, while women are more likely to be nurses and teachers. Sociologists say that men and women tend to be "horizontally and vertically segregated" across and within occupations and job sectors.

Horizontal segregation refers to an unequal gender distribution across occupations. Women are overrepresented in relatively low-skill, low-paid, service occupations such as clerical work and teaching. Men are overrepresented in relatively high-skill, high-paid occupations like medicine and law (Statistics Canada, 2011).

Figure 8.2 breaks down the representation of women across types of occupation in Canada in, 2011.

Men and women in Canada's paid workforce are also vertically segregated. **Vertical segregation** refers to the domination of one gender (typically men) in positions of high authority and power in each occupation. It is difficult to compare the degree of vertical segregation between occupations because of the wide scope and variation in job titles within each occupation; job titles don't easily translate from one occupation to another (Fortin and Huberman, 2002). However, research shows that, within occupations, men generally tend to hold job titles associated with more authority, prestige, and pay. What is more, where women hold positions of high authority, their subordinates tend to be other women, not men (Clement and Myles, 1994; Fortin and Huberman, 2002; Jarman, Blackburn, and Racko, 2012).

Job Resources and Rewards

Horizontal and vertical segregation have negative consequences for women's access to job resources and rewards, especially when it comes to earnings. On

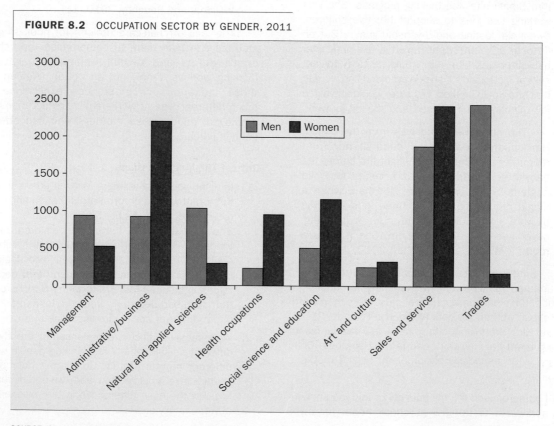

FIGURE 8.2 OCCUPATION SECTOR BY GENDER, 2011

SOURCE: Statistics Canada (2011).

While the gender wage gap is decreasing in Canada, there is still a 9 percent discrepancy between men's and women's median annual earnings for women and men of the same age and with the same work experience who work the same number of hours, have the same type of job, and are unionized.

SOURCE: © Michele Paccione/Shutterstock.

average, women tend to make less than men do. The **gender wage gap** is the difference between men's and women's earnings. Since 1992, the gender wage gap in Canada has hovered around 30 percent, meaning that women make only about 70 percent of men's annual earnings. This figure, however, masks gender differences in work hours, union representation, age, and type of job—factors that might explain at least part of the noted discrepancy. For instance, women tend to work fewer hours than men do; 23 percent of women work fewer than 30 hours per week, compared to only 12 percent of men (Ferrao, 2010).

Even if we compare women and men of the same age and with the same work experience who work the same number of hours, have the same type of job, and are unionized, women make only 91 cents for every dollar that men earn (Blau and DeVaro, 2007). This means that if you compare a man making $100 000 a year with a woman having exactly the same qualifications, experience, and so on, she will make just $91 000 a year. Figure 8.3 provides a sense of these discrepancies in Canada. Panel A of Figure 8.3 shows the median hourly wage for men and women from 1981 to 2011. The gap between median hourly wages has decreased over the years but persists. Panel B of Figure 8.3 shows the change in the ratio of men's and women's

median hourly earnings. In a perfect world, that ratio would equal one. However, as you can see, this is not the case. Despite progress since 1981, women still make about 90 cents for every dollar that men make according to 2011 statistics (Morissette, Picot, and Lu, 2013). Presumably, that gap is an indicator of gender discrimination against women.

Gender inequality in the paid workforce is even more striking when we compare Canada with some other countries. In a recent report, Canada ranked 20th of 136 countries in gender wage equality (World Economic Forum, 2013). Not only did we place lower than most Western European countries, we also fell short of Nicaragua, Cuba, and South Africa. Canada is highly developed economically and socially, but it exhibits relatively high and enduring inequality between men's and women's wages.

Women also fall short when it comes to other types of workplace rewards aside from earnings, including job autonomy, authority, and promotion opportunities. A recent study of 6000 Canadians found that women were less likely to report autonomy and authority than men were across a wide variety of occupations (Schieman, Young, and Glavin, 2014).

Other studies show that women are also less likely to be promoted than men are even if their on-the-job performance is the same as that of men (Blau and DeVaro, 2007; Kay and Brockman, 2000). One study of Ontario lawyers found clear evidence that women are held to different standards than men are when facing promotion in law firms. Women must exhibit stronger adherence to law firm culture than men do, bring in more corporate clients, and show more often that they are prioritizing work over family obligations to be promoted to the rank of partner (Kay and Hagan, 1998).

Precarious Employment

Women are also overrepresented in precarious or nonstandard work, which may be part-time, seasonal, contract-based, or held in conjunction with one or more other, similar jobs (Young, 2010). Precarious work is characterized by low pay, instability of employment, and lack of benefits such as employer pension and dental plans (see Chapter 12 for a detailed discussion of nonstandard work). In the study of 6000 Canadians mentioned earlier, men were found to be significantly more likely than women were to work 40 or more hours per week and to work overtime (Schieman, Schafer, and McIvor, 2013).

FIGURE 8.3   GENDER WAGE GAP, 2011

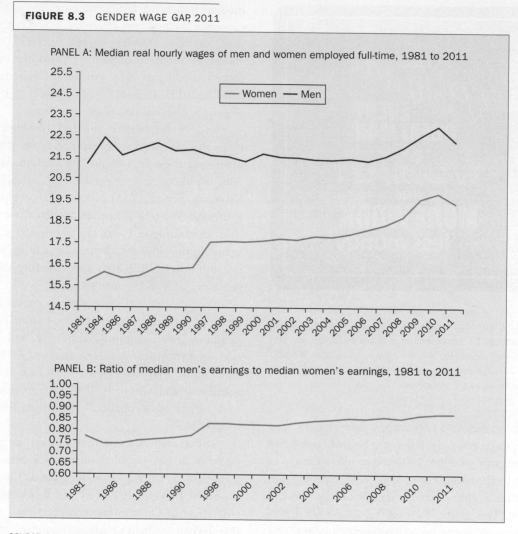

PANEL A: Median real hourly wages of men and women employed full-time, 1981 to 2011

PANEL B: Ratio of median men's earnings to median women's earnings, 1981 to 2011

SOURCE: Adapted from Morissette, Picot, and Lu (2013).

Some women undoubtedly prefer part-time jobs so they can more easily take care of their children. However, sociological research repeatedly shows that many women do not share this preference (Bianchi, Robinson, and Milkie, 2006; Duffy and Pupo, 1992; Stone, 2007). Nearly 30 percent of Canadian women working part-time prefer to work more hours and make more money (Statistics Canada, 2008).

Women used to be less likely than men were to be union members. However, the unionization gender gap has closed in the past few decades; the unionization rate for women now exceeds that for men. That is largely because unionization rates in the private sector of the economy have declined while unionization rates in the public (government) sector have increased—and most public-sector employees are women (think of teachers and nurses, for example) (Morissette, Picot, and Lu, 2013).

TIME FOR REVIEW

1. What are the main reasons for the gendered division of labour?
2. What is the difference between horizontal and vertical occupational gender segregation?
3. How do you explain the persistent gender wage gap we see in Canada today?

EXPLAINING GENDER INEQUALITY IN PAID WORK

Now that we know that gender inequalities in paid work exist, how can we explain them? Explanations for gender patterns in paid work come in two main varieties. *Supply-side* arguments hold that men invest more time, energy, and education in work, so they are rewarded more highly than women are. Men

Individual-based explanations of gender differences in paid and unpaid work are often rooted in traditional cultural understandings of what constitutes appropriate behaviour for men and women.

SOURCE: © Barry Deutsch.

supply more, so they are paid more. *Demand-side* arguments emphasize the institutional and structural barriers that constrain women's participation in paid work. These constraints supposedly limit demand for female workers.

SUPPLY-SIDE EXPLANATIONS

Human Capital Theory

Researchers have examined two main supply-side forces: human capital and the personal preferences that derive from sex-role socialization.

Human capital theory proposes that a person's location in the labour market depends largely on his or her rationally chosen investment in education and skills, which constitute that person's human capital (see Chapter 13 for more discussion of this subject). In this view, the more you invest in human capital, the more valuable you will be to the labour market and the more likely you will be rewarded with a stable, high-status, well-paying job (Becker, 1993; Mincer and Polachek, 1974).

Human capital theory could be considered gender-neutral insofar as it does not discriminate between men and women, who are seen as enjoying equal opportunity to invest in human capital. From this point of view, they just choose different types of investment. Presumably, men choose to pursue education and other means of labour market knowledge to a greater degree than women do. Women choose to invest more energy in their families. Presumably, they also have to opt out of the workforce during and after childbirth, which makes them less reliable and experienced on average. Employers therefore prefer male workers. It follows that men's greater investment in human capital leads them to be overrepresented in more lucrative jobs.

Could the explanation really be that simple? Think about your high school graduating class. Did it have more boys than girls? Probably not, unless you went to an all-boys school. What about the postsecondary level? In Canada and other highly developed countries in recent decades, more women than men have graduated from university (Statistics Canada, 2006). Even in all professional and graduate programs combined, most graduates are now women (Canadian Medical Association, 2012; England, 2005; Ornstein, 2010). Yet, despite these facts, men tend to substantially outnumber women in higher-paying and more prestigious fields such as those requiring science or engineering degrees. For example, in 2011, just 23 percent of engineering graduates in Canada were women, and among employed engineers, a mere 7 percent were women (Statistics Canada, 2011).

The most lucrative working-class jobs are those for skilled manual workers in the trades and construction. In such jobs, men predominate by a wide margin. In fields such as medicine and law, where, as we have seen, the number of women has surged, men still tend to earn more and have more authority than women do (Cohen and Huffman, 2003; Ferrao, 2010). Recall also our discussion of lawyers in Ontario: Female lawyers are promoted less frequently than men are even if they have the same qualifications. This pattern holds universally. Such findings from sociological research suggest that human capital theory cannot adequately explain gender differences in representation and rewards in the paid labour force.

Sex-Role Socialization

A second supply-side theory is that women prefer domestic work to paid work, while men prefer paid work to domestic work, largely because women and men are socialized to have different work preferences (Reskin, 2002; Reskin and Roos, 1990). From this point of view, sex-specific work preferences are part of our culture. People learn their job preferences in families, during their school years, and through the mass media.

Many women may not be inclined to pursue some occupations because they are taught that they should focus on family obligations more than men should (Reskin and Hartmann, 1986; see Chapter 5, Gender and Sexualities, for a review of gender socialization).

In fact, research shows show that most girls and young women tend to select courses of study that lead to relatively low-paying jobs with little prestige, authority, and autonomy because they expect to devote much of their lives to child rearing and housework (Eccles et al., 1999; Schroeder, Blood, and Maluso, 1993). So the sex-role socialization theory is not wrong. It is, however, incomplete.

Specifically, many sociologists criticize sex-role socialization theory because it is overly deterministic. It makes it seem as if cultures and social institutions never change and *inevitably* socialize women and men to take particular kinds of domestic and labour market roles. However, much historical and sociological research demonstrates that cultures and social institutions do change in ways that alter work roles. Some of this research is summarized in Chapter 5, Gender and Sexualities. The very fact that 14 percent of women worked in the paid labour force in the early twentieth century while 62 percent of women do so today suggests that change, not stability, is inevitable (Boyd, 2014: 163).

To achieve a well-rounded understanding of gender differences in paid work, we must also consider demand-side explanations, to which we now turn.

DEMAND-SIDE EXPLANATIONS

Two main demand-side explanations exist. One focuses on employer preferences, the other on discrimination.

Employer Preferences

Employers may prefer hiring men to women. Consequently, women are underrepresented and underrewarded in the workplace (Becker, 1993; Gorman, 2005; Kay and Hagan, 1998; Reskin, 2002). From this point of view, most workplaces are "gendered" insofar as they are built on the ideal image of a male worker—fully committed to his job without the distractions of family obligations. From this perspective, the gendered workplace influences hiring decisions and reward allocations to the detriment of female employees (Acker, 1990; Williams, 2000). We see the operation of this principle in the results of one study of 1547 Canadian MBAs who graduated between 1996 and 2007. It found that the starting pay for women was $8167 less per year than the starting pay for men even though they were equally qualified. Employers seem to have anticipated that the women would likely experience more career disruptions due to pregnancy and childcare responsibilities, and so paid equally qualified women less for the same work done by men (McFarland, 2013).

Discrimination

Closely related to employer preference theory is the idea of discrimination. Discrimination occurs when employers use stereotypes to focus on visible characteristics of people and, on that basis, decide that some people will be more productive workers than others will be (Bielby and Baron, 1986; England, 2005; Padavic and Reskin, 2002). For example, an employer may consider a woman more suitable than a man for a nursing job, assuming that the woman had more caregiving responsibilities at home from childhood to adulthood and is therefore more familiar with, and adept at, the kind of work a nurse is expected to do. Male and female applicants for a nursing job may be equally qualified, but the woman is likely to get the job if such discrimination takes place.

Queuing Theory: Combining Supply-Side and Demand-Side Theories

Could supply *and* demand be at play when it comes to gender inequality in paid work? Cultural expectations might inform personal preferences. Men may prefer to hire other men to maintain the masculine culture of a given organization or firm. Employers might avoid hiring women of childbearing age because they don't want to pay for work disruptions and the training of new personnel. Women may choose less demanding jobs to balance work and family obligations. In other

Would you hire this woman? Employers may discriminate against hiring women because of their current or expected family obligations.
SOURCE: Zurijeta/iStock.

words, supply and demand forces may interact to ensure that patterns of gender inequality in paid work endure.

Queuing theory offers one explanation of how all of these social processes are related (Reskin and Roos, 1990). Like discrimination theory, **queuing theory** assumes that employers rank prospective employees from most to least suitable and reward them accordingly. However, queuing theory goes beyond the idea of employer discrimination by bridging workers' and employers' preferences. It does so by distinguishing *job queues* (workers' preference rankings of jobs) from *labour queues* (employers' preference rankings of workers). The two queues influence each other. Employers' stereotypes of what constitutes appropriate work for women and men affect the kind of education and training women and men pursue. In turn, the kind of education and training women and men pursue affects employers' use of stereotypes to hire and reward workers. This interaction helps gender segregation in the workplace to endure. Studies testing the theory find that the queuing practices of both employers and employees as they relate to gender (and ethnicity) predict the occupational position of workers better than any other set of variables do (Kaufman, 2002; Young, 2010). Thus, queuing theory provides researchers with a theoretical tool that explains employee supply and employer demand practices, along with the interaction between the two.

TIME FOR REVIEW

1. Why do many sociologists consider human capital theory, sex-role socialization theory, employer preference theory, and discrimination theory incomplete?
2. How does queuing theory relate to supply-side and demand-side theories of gender inequality in paid work?

GENDER DIFFERENCES IN UNPAID WORK
DOMESTIC RESPONSIBILITIES

You can't fully understand inequality in *paid* work without considering gender inequality in *unpaid* work because one influences the other. If people expect you to spend most of your work time taking care of the household, you can't devote as much time as you might like to working in the paid workforce. Conversely, if they expect you to be the main breadwinner for your family, you may not be able to spend much time on child care and housework.

Do gendered work stereotypes resonate with your personal experience? Think back to when you were a child. Who packed your lunch for school, cleaned the house, and made dinner? Mom, Dad, or someone else? Your answer may differ from others, depending on your parents' work arrangements and the climate of your household.

I grew up in a single-parent family, so my father did most of the domestic work. I was about nine years old when I realized that my situation was not the norm. I observed a common pattern among my friends' parents: Most of their mothers were responsible for cleaning, cooking, and caring for children. I thought fathers were expected to take care of all household duties until I started noticing these differences among my friends' parents.

In most Canadian households, domestic tasks are still disproportionately delegated to women, including housework and child care. On average, women report spending 4.5 hours a day on housework, while men report 3.25 hours. The number of hours spent caring for children depends on the age of the children, since young children require more care. However, looking just at time spent caring for children under the age of four, women report approximately 6.5 hours of care per day, while men report just over 3.5 hours (Statistics Canada, 2011).

The types of tasks that men and women perform also differ. Women are more likely to perform mundane, repetitive, less attractive, daily tasks, such as meal preparation, household cleaning, dishwashing, and laundry. Men are often responsible for tasks that are less frequent or mandatory, such as lawn maintenance, car repairs, and house repairs. Given the difference in the types of domestic tasks performed by women and men, it is not surprising that men are more likely than women are to report enjoying household chores (Bianchi et al., 2000; Young, Wallace, and Polachek, 2013).

The division of tasks associated with childcare also tend to be gendered. Usually, mothers are responsible for the hygienic and emotional care of the child, including bathing, clothing, and school- and health-related concerns. Fathers are likely to spend more time with their children in interactive activities—playing with them and talking and reading to them (Bianchi, Robinson, and Milkie, 2006). For example, a mother might be responsible for packing her daughter's lunch and picking her up after school, while a father might be responsible for reading his daughter bedtime stories and coaching her hockey team.

THE PARADOX OF PREFERENCES

Despite inequality in the domestic division of labour, studies report that more than half of husbands and wives perceive existing arrangements to be fair (Baxter, 2000; Lennon and Rosenfield, 1994; Young, Schieman, and Milkie, 2014). In fact, among a representative sample of married Canadians, about 70 percent of respondents recently agreed that the distribution of household chores and child care was fair (Schieman, Young, and Glavin, 2014).

Such findings have prompted researchers to ask, "Why do men and women accede to such an unequal arrangement?" (Lennon and Rosenfield, 1994: 507). Explanations focus on the extent to which each partner contributes financially to the household, the time constraints on each spouse, and the gendered expectations of men and women in the household.

Figure 8.4 illustrates the disconnect between time spent on chores and perceived fairness. The data come from a survey of a representative sample

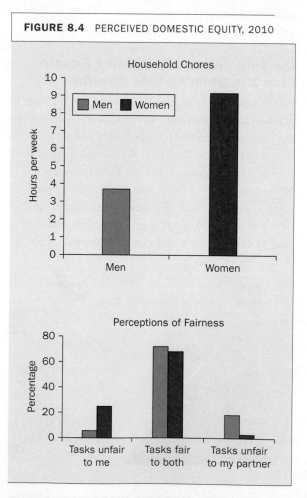

FIGURE 8.4 PERCEIVED DOMESTIC EQUITY, 2010

SOURCE: Data from Patricia O'Campo and Blair Wheaton, *Neighbourhood Effects on Health and Well-Being* (2011).

of 2000 Torontonians. Panel A shows that women perform far more hours of housework per week than men do. Panel B shows that, like men, most women find that the distribution of tasks is fair to both themselves and their spouse. The disconnect between the real and perceived distribution of tasks among couples is something researchers continue to explore.

EXPLAINING GENDER DIFFERENCES IN UNPAID WORK

How can we explain gender differences in unpaid work? Theories range from those that focus on the characteristic of individuals to those that emphasize the social structures and cultures in which people are embedded. Two popular individual-centred explanations are relative resource theory and time availability theory.

INDIVIDUAL-CENTRED THEORIES

Relative Resources

According to relative resource theory, the quantity of financial resources each partner brings to the household determines the quantity and type of domestic tasks he or she performs. From this point of view, since men usually earn more than women do, it makes perfect sense that they spend more of their time doing paid work and less time doing unpaid work. In general, the spouse with lower earnings tends to do more household chores and child care. Moreover, when each partner specializes in paid or unpaid labour, it supposedly maximizes the family's sustainability.

Relative resource theory assumes that power in the household operates in a gender-neutral way. This means that if the quantity of resources that one spouse brings in changes, paid and domestic tasks should rebalance accordingly. For example, if a woman starts contributing more financial resources to the family by taking a paying job, her time performing domestic duties should decrease and her husband's time should increase proportionately. Yet research shows that this doesn't often happen. Typically, when a wife contributes more financially to the family, her husband does more domestic work but the increase is not proportional to the wife's increased contribution to household finances (Bianchi et al., 2012; Lennon and Rosenfield, 1994; Young, Schieman, and Milkie. 2014).

Change in time devoted to child care changes even less (Brines, 1994). Some studies even show that highly educated women with high earnings average more child-care hours than do less highly educated women with low earnings (Craig, 2006).

Time Availability

A second individual-level explanation of gender differences in unpaid work is time availability theory, which holds that time spent in paid work limits the amount of time spent on domestic chores (Bianchi et al., 2012). Here, researchers treat time as a finite resource; there are only 24 hours in a day, and we can work only a fixed number of waking hours. From this perspective, men are less involved in domestic work simply because they spend more time doing paid work.

If the time-availability theory were fully valid, a woman's time spent doing domestic work should fall proportionately with an increase in her time doing paid work. Yet this is not necessarily the case. Most women do most of the housework even if they work full-time. As a woman's time doing paid work increases, the time she spends on domestic tasks does not usually decrease at a comparable rate (Young, Schieman, and Milkie, 2014). This is especially true of child care. When they start working in the paid labour force, women tend to cut back on leisure, personal, and sleep time, not on taking care of their children (Wallace and Young, 2008). Findings such as these lead us to question whether couples employ economically rational rules to allocate domestic chores. It seems more likely that they rely on culturally prescribed gender expectations to assign paid and unpaid work (Baxter, 2000; Carriero, 2011). To explore this possibility, we need to move from individual-centred explanations to cultural explanations of gender differences in unpaid work.

CULTURAL THEORY

The cultural theory of gender differences in unpaid work challenges the assumption that people allocate domestic work in a gender-neutral and economically efficient manner (Ferree, 1991). It highlights the way cultural ideologies of motherhood and fatherhood influence men's and women's behaviour (Berk, 1985; Bianchi et al., 2000). Its proponents argue that, to varying degrees, most women internalize the traditional idea that domestic work is primarily women's work. Consequently, women try to demonstrate that they are good wives by performing household and child-care tasks (Ferree, 1991; Hays, 1996). Thus, when it comes to housework, women often report preference for a clean home as an appropriate enactment of femininity and a reflection of their competence (Bianchi et al., 2000: 195).

Gender socialization and the ideology of what constitutes a "good woman" are closely linked to the cultural ideal of **intensive motherhood** (Hays, 1996). Intensive motherhood refers to the predominant cultural model of the loving, maternal figure selflessly devoting most of her time and energy to her children. This ideal defines the quality of a woman in many societies, where performing the motherhood role in a way that encompasses an enormous part of a woman's life is, to a considerably degree, precisely what defines her gender.

Women who embrace the expectations of intensive motherhood often find housework and child care rewarding (Bianchi and Milkie, 2010; Young, Schieman, and Milkie, 2014). However, many women have qualms about intensive motherhood and so find themselves torn between culturally imposed expectations and their desire for a different way of living (Blair-Loy, 2003; Ceci and Williams, 2010; Hays, 1996).

TIME FOR REVIEW

1. What are some key differences in the types of domestic tasks performed by men and women?

2. Can you think of alternative reasons for why men and women might agree to an unequal distribution of domestic chores?

3. Which theory resonates most with the distribution of domestic tasks in your own household? Why?

CHANGING PATTERNS OF GENDER INEQUALITY

The gendered division of labour and its associated inequality are fading, although insufficiently and too slowly in the eyes of many people. Consider only that, in Canada, the employment rate for women with children under the age of six more than doubled between 1976 and 2012, growing from 31.4 percent to 67.8 percent (Statistics Canada, 2011). A remarkable shift in just a third of a century! Figure 8.5 displays the rise in women's labour force participation rate for women without children and those with children in different age cohorts.

Recent decades have witnessed gains for women in terms of power and resources, too. The gender gap in paid work hours and wages has shortened over the past few decades, and the representation of women has increased in prestigious, traditionally male-dominated occupations in science, engineering, technology, accounting, law, politics, and senior management (Ferrao, 2010; Morissette, Picot, and Lu, 2013).

FIGURE 8.5 WOMEN'S LABOUR FORCE PARTICIPATION, 2011

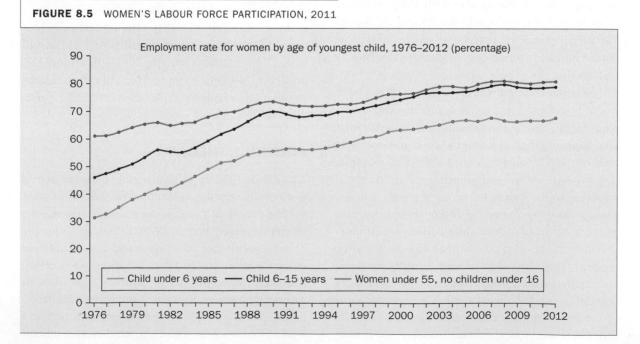

SOURCE: Statistics Canada (2012).

Researchers have also observed greater equality in domestic work in recent decades. While the total amount of time people spend cooking, cleaning, grocery shopping, and doing laundry has fallen by about 20 percent since 1986, a larger proportion of men are performing core housework tasks, including meal preparation, meal cleanup, indoor cleaning, and laundry (Marshall, 2009).

A dramatic shift in the gendered distribution of child care has also occurred. Men spend a lot more time taking care of their children than they used to. Some studies suggest that the time fathers spend with children has doubled over the last half-century. Married fathers now spend approximately 6.5 hours a week on child care, which is approximately three hours more than reported in the 1960s (Livingston and Parker, 2011). In a recent study of 6000 Canadians, my colleagues and I found that about a fifth of fathers reported that they were *primarily* responsible for several child-care tasks related to getting children ready for school and helping them with their homework (Young, Schieman, and Milkie. 2014; see also Marshall, 2011). Gender shifts in child care might result from growing options for fathers to take paternity leave after the birth of a child. However, among some employers this issue is still controversial. The Critical Sociology: Protest and Policy box discusses the movement toward, and resistance against, paternity leave options among men in North America.

Changing social patterns in the domestic sphere have led scholars to explore the meaning of child care. For example, when caring for children, do men exhibit "mothering" characteristics similar to those exhibited by women or do men redefine fatherhood to include care-related behaviours? One Canadian researcher conducted interviews with stay-at-home and single fathers and found that men perform child care differently than mothers do. Their care techniques tried to reconstruct traditional images of what it means to be a "good man." Many fathers in her study adopted traditionally masculine roles in the family and community, including sports activities and leadership positions, to help compensate for assuming a more central, traditionally feminine role in child care (Doucet, 2006).

Other scholars question whether men are actually doing more child care or just engaging in more play with children. Recall that men are still less likely to perform custodial types of child care and more

Men are becoming increasingly involved in child care. However, fathers have yet to receive appropriate paternity leave from their employers.
SOURCE: Fuse/Thinkstock.

likely to spend time in interactive activities with their children. Persistent variation in types of child care performed by women and men raise the question of whether the gender gap in child care is closing or just changing.

GENDER DIFFERENCES IN INFORMAL CAREGIVING

The definition of domestic work has expanded in recent decades beyond housework and child care to consider caregiving efforts to loved ones other than children. More and more parents are responsible for taking care of their ageing parents as well as their own children.

In the past, women reported higher levels of informal caregiving obligations compared to men. According to a 1996 Statistics Canada survey of 13 000 Canadians, 19 percent of women compared to just 11 percent of men reported providing informal care (Fast and Keating, 2000).

Today, however, the gender gap in informal caregiving is decreasing. Out of 8.1 million Canadians who reported providing care to a friend or family member with a health issue, 45 percent were men and 55 percent were women (Statistics Canada, 2011). These patterns reflect growing equality in men's and women's caregiving obligations.

CRITICAL SOCIOLOGY: PROTEST AND POLICY   PERSPECTIVES ON PATERNITY LEAVE

Edward was at a work dinner with his boss when he first decided to broach the idea of paternity leave. His wife had just given birth to a baby girl—their first child—and he knew he wanted to take a few months off from his job as an IT manager to spend some time at home. His proposal didn't go over well. "My boss dead-eyed me," Edward says, "and said he would kick me in the balls if I applied." (Balkissoon, 2013)

Edward is not alone in his experience. Many bosses frown on paternity leave. Most male workers don't expect it. In 2011, just 30 percent of Canadian fathers took leave when their children were born, compared to 90 percent of women who took maternity leave. The limited availability of paternity leave is not the only challenge. It is difficult to get many men to take advantage of available leave opportunities (Berdahl and Moon, 2013).

So what's the solution? Jennifer Berdahl recommends legislation *enforcing* paternity leave. She says:

One of the most effective ways to encourage men to take paternity leave is through legislation—most of the increase in Canada's dad-leave stats is thanks to Quebec, which introduced five weeks of leave available only to fathers in 2005. Since then, the number of

Québécois men taking leave has jumped to 76 percent, compared to 11 percent in the rest of the country. (Quoted in O'Kane, 2013)

Despite the benefits of legislated paternity leave, it may still be some time before we see it enforced in other parts of Canada and the United States. Resistance to changing family forms can lead to stigmatizing and discriminatory reactions from workers and employers. One of the founders and co-organizers of New York City's Dads Group summarizes this point well in a recent interview: "I don't see the problem as being a lack of incentive. When men start to see their peers, mentors and leaders take paternity leave, they'll be more likely to take the opportunity themselves" (Eichler, 2013a, 2013b). This comment suggests that successful implementation and use of paternity leave requires a transformation in cultural values and behaviours in addition to the introduction of formalized policies.

Critical Thinking Questions

1. Do you agree that men should be forced by the state to take paternity leave? Why or why not?

2. Why do you think employers might resist paternity leave policies?

WHY SHOULD WE CARE ABOUT GENDER DIFFERENCES?

Now that we've discussed the general patterns, explanations, and changing nature of gender inequalities in paid and unpaid work, it's worth considering the big question: Why should we care? Does it really matter whether women perform certain roles and men perform others? The short answer is "yes." Aside from the fact that sociologists generally care about social injustice, men's and women's roles in economic and domestic spheres have implications for exposure to work–family conflict and psychological well-being.

CONFLICTING WORK AND FAMILY RESPONSIBILITIES

Gendered patterns of paid and unpaid work contribute to gendered patterns of exposure to work–family conflict, a particularly modern mental health risk (Bellavia and Frone, 2005; Frone, Yardley, and Markel, 1997;

Studies report no gender differences in levels of work–family conflict, but these patterns may neglect the distinct meanings men and women attribute to work and family roles.

SOURCE: © Photoeuphoria | Dreamstime.com — Baby Businessman In Briefcase Photo.

Greenhaus and Beutell, 1987; Young and Wheaton, 2013). Wives entering the paid labour force may find that they lack the time to do the kind and amount of housework and child care they desire and may put more pressure on their husbands to pitch in. Husbands who work full-time and are unaccustomed to doing housework and child care may resist. The strain is likely to reverberate throughout the family. It often causes unhappiness, anxiety, and depression.

Some studies suggest that men and women now experience similar levels of work–family conflict because men are more likely to report the problem than in the past (Aumann, Galinsky, and Matos, 2011). The situation may reflect men's increased participation in the domestic sphere; many men are starting to experience what women have endured for years. Other researchers are skeptical of this finding because women still do the lion's share of housework and child care while facing new demands in paid work. Is it possible that studies suggesting the existence of gender equality in work–family conflict are overlooking something? Let's consider this possibility.

EXPLAINING GENDER EQUALITY IN WORK–FAMILY CONFLICT

Do Some Women Opt Out?

A possible reason for the finding of comparable levels of work–family conflict among women and men is that studies of the subject include only women who do domestic and paid labour. Women who experience high levels of work–family conflict are more likely than men are to leave the workforce to attend to child-care demands, so researchers exclude them from such studies. This tendency biases findings in favour of finding gender inequality in work–family conflict (Belkin, 2003; Stone, 2007).

The existence of high levels of work–family conflict that lead some women to opt out of paid work or at least cut back on their obligations in the paid labour force leads to the question of whether women can "have it all"—a great job with good pay and status as well as a healthy and rewarding family life. As one might expect, there are competing perspectives on this issue.

Anne-Marie Slaughter, the first woman director of policy planning at the U.S. State Department, brought the debate into the spotlight in a 2012 magazine article. Ms. Slaughter justified leaving her top government position as follows:

> On a Wednesday evening, President and Mrs. Obama hosted a glamorous reception at the American Museum of Natural History. I sipped champagne, greeted foreign dignitaries, and mingled. But I could not stop thinking about my 14-year-old son, who had started eighth grade three weeks earlier and was already resuming what had become his pattern of skipping homework, disrupting classes, failing math, and tuning out any adult who tried to reach him. Over the summer, we had barely spoken to each other—or, more accurately, he had barely spoken to me. And the previous spring I had received several urgent phone calls—invariably on the day of an important meeting—that required me to take the first train from Washington, D.C., where I worked, back to Princeton, New Jersey, where he lived. My husband, who has always done everything possible to support my career, took care of him and his 12-year-old brother during the week; outside of those midweek emergencies, I came home only on weekends. (Slaughter, 2012)

Ms. Slaughter concludes that women can't have it all. From her perspective, women can have either a high-powered career or a successful home life, but society does not allow both. The demands of the modern workplace cannot accommodate women's family obligations. In January 2011, Ms. Slaughter quit her career to be closer to her family.

Many women criticized Ms. Slaughter's comments, arguing that she should reflect on her own parenting practices before generalizing her situation to other high-powered, professional mothers. The backlash against Ms. Slaughter's article suggests that many people believe that women *can* have it all. From this point of view, women who opt out of paid work are personally responsible for their inability to cope.

Even if they can't have it all, many women try to. In fact, few women opt out of paid work to cope with work–family conflict (Young and Schieman, 2014). The assumption that women will opt out of the paid labour force to attend to family obligations is part of a perpetual stereotype that may influence discriminatory practices among employers. While approximately 40 percent of women are likely to take leave from paid work throughout their lifetime, the reasons for doing so vary, work–family conflict being only one of the possible reasons. Nonetheless, because women who experience a high level of work–family conflict may be more likely to opt out of the workforce, it is difficult to know whether women experience higher levels of work–family conflict compared to men, as we might expect.

An important question remains: Why is the level of work–family conflict similar among mothers who remain in the workforce and fathers in the same types of jobs? This question has led researchers to explore the different meanings and experiences of work and family for women and men.

Gendered Experiences of Work–Family Conflict

Research on the way men and women experience work–family conflict demonstrates the following facts (Simon 1995):

1. Men and women tend to hold different beliefs about their respective economic and domestic roles. Most people expect men to provide mainly financial support to the family while they expect women to provide mainly emotional support.

2. Men and women tend to feel differently about combining work and family roles. Women often feel guilty about combining roles. Men usually don't.

3. Men and women tend to report different experiences of work–family conflict. Men experience conflict as specific and delimited—at a particular time and around a certain event. In contrast, women experience conflict as diffuse and nonspecific—all- consuming and unrelated to particular events.

4. Men and women tend to report different self-evaluations of role performance. Most women have negative self-evaluations. Most men have positive self-evaluations.

These findings lead us to discuss yet another realm of gender inequality, concerning dimensions of self.

TIME FOR REVIEW

1. How has gender inequality in domestic work changed in the past few decades?

2. Why are sociologists skeptical about men's and women's comparable reports of work–family conflict?

3. How would you characterize differences in men's and women's experiences in work–family conflict?

4. Think about your own experience of work–family conflict. Does your situation resonate with the patterns discussed in this chapter? If not, why not?

GENDER INEQUALITY AND DIMENSIONS OF SELF

Gender inequality in the paid labour force and at home typically results in men and women evaluating various dimensions of their selves differently. The four dimensions of self that are relevant in this context are one's sense of (1) control, (2) trust in others, (3) connection to others, and (4) self/other salience (importance of one's own needs versus others' needs).

Each of these dimensions influence mental health. High levels of control, trust, connection with others, and self-salience help people avoid exposure to stress and cope with stress when they confront it. In general, people who can avoid stress are better off than those who can't because chronic stress often leads to anxiety, depression, and a variety of physical ailments. In the short term, these ailments may include headaches, upset stomach, loss of sexual desire and ability, and insomnia. In the long term, persistent anxiety may results in heart disease, obesity and other eating disorders, and gastrointestinal problems. Thus, having relatively little power and access to resources in paid work and relatively burdensome responsibilities in unpaid domestic work can have a big, negative health impact on women (Bird and Rieker, 2008; Rosenfield, 1999).

To the degree that women focus on the domestic sphere and men on the world of paid work, their ties to others differ. Women are often closer and more dependent on other family members than men are. Men tend to be connected to more people outside the family. This circumstance cuts two ways. On the one hand, women may be better off emotionally than men are insofar as they tend to have closer relationships with significant others than their husbands do. On the other hand, some women become overly involved with troubles experienced by relatives, taking them on as their own. Close relationships also have the potential to generate high levels of conflict. Women endure more disputes with loved ones than men do and thus experience more negative emotions from these encounters. These are the costs of having stronger "other-salience" than "self-salience" (Rosenfield, 1999).

THE INTERSECTING BASES OF SOCIAL INEQUALITY

When gender combines with other bases of inequality—age, ethnicity, race, sexuality, socioeconomic status, and immigration status—the problems just mentioned are compounded (Browne and Misra, 2003; Creese and Stasiulis, 1996; King, 1988). For instance, a 50-year-old Filipina lacking higher education and Canadian citizenship is likely to work long hours near the bottom of the socioeconomic hierarchy as a nanny or a chambermaid. Her circumstances will make it especially difficult for her to meet the demands of domestic work in her own family. The resulting work–family conflict may result in acute mental health issues. As this example suggests, intersecting low statuses do not just add to women's woes, they multiply them (see the Critical Sociology: Globalization box).

Our discussion highlights the fact that women tend to be more vulnerable psychologically than men are because they typically have access to fewer resources needed to combat the stress that is usually associated with disadvantaged circumstances. Rectifying gender inequality in paid and unpaid work may therefore profoundly benefit women's psychological well-being.

CLOSING THE GAP: INITIATIVES TO EQUALIZE MEN'S AND WOMEN'S STATUSES

As noted earlier, gender inequality in paid and unpaid work is declining. However, much inequality remains. To continue reducing gender inequality, political, cultural, and individual initiatives are required.

CRITICAL SOCIOLOGY: GLOBALIZATION   GLOBALIZATION AND MIGRANT CAREGIVERS

A big market for migrant domestic workers now exists in Canada. Almost all migrant domestic workers in Canada are women. Most are from the Philippines (Gorodzeisky and Semyonov, 2005). Typically, employment agencies hire these women from overseas and match them to families that need their services. The women often live with the families that employ them and work for minimum wage.

Domestic migrant workers help to reproduce the workforces of host countries by providing child care and domestic work. They help parents balance competing work and family demands and, potentially, equalize gender inequalities in paid and unpaid work. By freeing women in host countries to work in the paid labour force, they boost household income and stimulate economic growth. At the same time, domestic migrant workers typically transfer part of their earnings back to their home countries to help their own families (Licuanan, 1994; Meerman, 2001; Parreñas, 2000).

The globalized flow of domestic labour also has more than one downside. Many children in less developed countries are forced to grow up in the absence of their mothers. The ready availability of poorly paid female domestic workers reinforces the notion that domestic work is women's work and that women's work is worth comparatively little. Finally, more than a few foreign domestic workers are subjected to long hours of work at low pay and other forms of abuse by their employers.

To care for their own children financially, Filipina domestic workers must often care for someone else's children in another country.
SOURCE: © Kevin Dodge/Masterfile.

Critical Thinking Questions

1. Compare work–family conflict among women who hire foreign domestic workers with work–family conflict among foreign domestic workers. How does work–family conflict differ in these two groups?

2. Overall, do you think that the presence of migrant domestic caregivers helps to increase or decrease gender inequality? How does it do so? In what countries and spheres of life does it do so?

POLITICAL SOLUTIONS

Political solutions are government regulations that help reduce the gendered division of labour. Such regulations could reduce discriminatory practices among employers and help mothers balance work and family demands by providing convenient, affordable, high-quality daycare.

Employment Policies

The 1995 Employment Equity Act (EEA) is a good example of a policy aimed at increasing women's representation (and the representation of other disadvantaged groups) in Canada's paid labour force. The purpose of the Act is "to achieve equality in the workplace so that no person shall be denied employment opportunities or benefits for reasons unrelated to ability" (Employment Equity Act (1995, c. 44), Act current to April 16, 2010).

While encouraging, researchers and policy analysts question the Act's effectiveness in practice. One study covering the period 1997-2004 found that employment equity is increasing but the rate of increase is slowing (Jain et al., 2010). Some analysts argue that hiring more women and members of other disadvantaged groups is so slow that it amounts to little more than **tokenism**, a symbolic gesture that makes it seem progress has been made when in reality it doesn't amount to much. This argument gains credibility from another finding: Increased equity is more a result of hiring of members of racial minority groups and people with disabilities than of women. While some scholars forecast that the EEA might eventually have a big impact, others argue that women's representation will increase substantially only when the organizational culture of the workplace changes—when deeply embedded and persistent norms and values that govern hiring are no longer biased against women (Stichman, Hassell, and Archbold, 2010).

Regulations concerning labour standards seek to equalize men's and women's treatment in paid work. For instance, Ontario passed the Employment Standards Act (ESA) in 2000. It guarantees that men and women receive equal pay for equivalent work. Legislation defines jobs as equivalent if they are equally demanding, require the same amount of skill and responsibility, and are performed in similar contexts and work conditions (Ontario Ministry of Labour, 2013).

Policies such as ESA help to reduce gender inequality in labour force rewards but do not eliminate them. Employers routinely argue that different job titles imply different skill levels and functions. Therefore, even if their work tasks are similar to those of men, many women at a lower rank or with a different job title are still paid less (Fortin and Huberman, 2002).

Family-Friendly Policies in the Workplace

Workplace policies have also encouraged greater equality between men's and women's paid and unpaid work. Many reputable organizations now have work–family balance programs (see "Canada's Top 100 Employers," 2014, for an overview of the most family-friendly workplaces in Canada). These programs involve on-site daycare and flexible work schedules to accommodate family commitments.

Employers have also started introducing paternity leave for families with newborns. The benefits of paternity leave are twofold. It allows men to play a more important role in the domestic sphere and alleviates some of the burden faced by new moms. It also helps to reshape ideas governing men's and women's appropriate work roles by normalizing men's absence from paid work and dedication to domestic responsibilities.

CULTURAL CONVENTIONS

While the policies discussed earlier are steps in the right direction, they do not affect traditional stereotypes of men's and women's roles in paid and unpaid work. When was the last time you saw a commercial featuring a man mopping a kitchen floor or a woman hard at work fixing the underside of a car? Probably never. Gendered images perpetuate work stereotypes in commercials, TV programs, movies, popular literature, and video games. During my recent move from Toronto to Hamilton, I noticed the blatantly obvious stereotypes even embedded in the names of companies performing various tasks. The name of the moving company we hired: "Two Men and a Truck" (even though several women helped with the move). The name of the cleaning company we hired: "Molly Maids" (Molly, of course, being a woman's name, and the company hires only women). It is difficult to imagine that we can achieve substantially greater equality in paid and unpaid work until images of what it means to be an ideal mother, father, and worker change at a broad, societal level (Acker, 1990; Blair-Loy, 2003; Hays, 1996).

Household cleaning is often seen as women's work, while outdoor work, like barbequing or fixing cars, is seen as men's work. These stereotypes are apparent in everyday advertising, and often go unnoticed by the public.

SOURCES: Photographee.eu/Shutterstock (top); nandyphotos/iStock (bottom).

Surveys show that younger people are on average more gender-egalitarian than older people are. Younger people are more exposed to women in nontraditional roles. That circumstance helps to shape their conception of gender-appropriate norms (Pampel, 2010). However, traditional views are still deeply entrenched. One example comes from a recent male WestJet passenger, who left a note for the pilot after discovering that she was a woman. Here is what happened:

> Female WestJet pilot Carey Smith Steacy captained a flight from Calgary to Victoria on Sunday. After landing with no issue and seeing all passengers off the plane, the crew discovered a note left behind on a napkin that stated "the cockpit of an airline is no place for a woman."
>
> Signing the note "David," the passenger stated "a woman being a mother is the most honor, not as 'captain.' Sorry not PC (politically correct)." He went on to list a Bible verse and say, "I wish WestJet could tell me a fair lady is at the helm so I can book another flight." Smith Steacy said David also asked flight attendants if she had enough flying hours under her belt before they even took off. (Feenstra, 2014: 20)

The disparaging views expressed by this passenger exemplify the stereotypes that some people still hold. The idea that a woman's proper place is in the home and that only men are fit to hold prestigious jobs reflects antiquated gender roles. The truth is that women are entering all types of occupations. Most people now expect that both parents will work for pay. The time fathers spend with their children is on the rise, and access to paternity leave is growing. The passage of progressive legislation preventing gender inequality is beginning. The roles of men and women in work and family have changed dramatically over the past century. It is now time that the institutions and ideologies of society mirror that change.

TIME FOR REVIEW

1. What are the dimensions of self that are relevant in the study of work–family balance? How do the dimensions differ for men and women?
2. Suppose you were asked by a policymaker working for the Canadian government, "What is the most effective strategy for reducing gender inequality in paid and unpaid work?" How would you answer this question?
3. How can employment equity policies result in tokenism?

SUMMARY

1. **Are men and women equally represented and rewarded in the labour market?**
No. Women are segregated across and within occupations. They tend to hold jobs characterized by less power and fewer rewards than jobs held by men. On average, compared to men, women receive less pay, are promoted less often, and hold less authority over others. However, women are making progress in achieving equality in the workplace.

2. **How do sociologists explain gender differences in paid work?**
Common explanations for gender inequality in paid work include supply-side and demand-side theories. Supply-side theories emphasize characteristics of the worker. Demand-side theories emphasize characteristics of the labour market and employers.

3. **How does gender shape the performance of unpaid domestic work, and how do sociologists explain those patterns?**
Women tend to perform the lion's share of domestic work. However, men are increasing their time spent in child care and informal caregiving. Explanations for gender differences in unpaid work focus on relative resources, time constraints, and cultural constraints.

4. **Do men and women report differences in work–family conflict because of inequalities in paid and unpaid work?**
Men and women report similar work–family conflict levels despite inequalities in paid and unpaid work. They may do so because women with high levels of work–family conflict may be more likely to opt out of paid work. It may also be that men and women assign different meanings to work and family, leading to different experiences of conflict.

5. **What are some of the psychological and physical consequences of gender inequality in paid and unpaid work?**
Gender inequality in paid and unpaid work may damage women's psychological and physical well-being because gender inequality negatively affects psychological resources that help individuals fight undesirable situations and stressors. Psychological consequences of stress include anxiety and depression. Physical consequences range from headaches, upset stomach, loss of sexual desire and ability, and insomnia to heart disease, obesity and other eating disorders, and gastrointestinal problems.

6. **How can we increase gender equality in work and the domestic sphere?**
We can help equalize gender differences in paid and unpaid work through government and workplace policies as well as by transforming cultural notions of gender roles at institutional and individual levels.

QUESTIONS TO CONSIDER

1. You now know that traditional notions of gender roles strongly influence inequality in paid and unpaid work, at least in heterosexual households. How do you think the division of labour works in same-sex households, where there are two mothers or two fathers? Do you think traditional notions of gender apply to these sorts of situations? How might individuals in same-sex households negotiate the distribution of household chores?

2. Andrea Doucet's research finds that men and women "mother" differently, meaning that they "do" child care in gender-specific ways. Can you relate these ideas to your own experiences growing up? Were there differences in the ways that your Mom and Dad provided care for you?

3. Common explanations for inequality focus on individual choice or structural constraint. Can you think of an example to illustrate how both choice and constraint have influenced your current or previous experience in paid or unpaid work?

GLOSSARY

Dimensions of self (p. 177) include the basic assumptions of the world that individuals develop based on current and past experience to help make sense of their situation. Dimensions of the self affect internalized personal resources, such as self-esteem, sense of control, and levels of self- and other-salience.

The **gender wage gap** (p. 179) is the discrepancy between men's and women's earnings.

The **gendered division of labour** (p. 176) is the allocation of tasks to people in the public or private realm based on sex differences.

Horizontal segregation (p. 178) reflects the unequal distribution of men and women across occupations.

Human capital theory (p. 181) argues that one's location in the labour market depends largely on one's rationally chosen investment in education and skills.

Intensive motherhood (p. 186) refers to the predominant cultural model of the caring, loving maternal figure that comes to define the overall quality of a woman.

Power (p. 176) is the ability to impose one's will on others despite resistance.

Queuing theory (p. 183) assumes that employers rank prospective employees from most to least suitable and reward them accordingly. It also assumes that workers rank jobs from most to least preferable. From this point of view, hiring practices are the outcome of the interaction between employee (supply) and employer (demand) preferences.

Resources (p. 177) are extrinsic or intrinsic assets that individuals can draw on to aid or contribute to short- or long-term endeavours.

Responsibilities (p. 177) are the obligations that people are expected to meet.

Tokenism (p. 192) involves employers making largely symbolic gestures to demonstrate increased minority representation in the workplace.

Vertical segregation (p. 178) is the unequal distribution of men and women within occupations.

CHAPTER 9

RACE AND ETHNIC RELATIONS

Vic Satzewich
McMASTER UNIVERSITY

SOURCE: © Karen Moskowitz/Getty Images.

AFTER READING THIS CHAPTER YOU WILL BE ABLE TO:

- Compare and apply various theoretical approaches to understanding race and ethnic relations.

- Recognize race as a sociological construct, not a meaningful biological category.

- Contrast the main sociological interpretations of Indigenous people's socioeconomic status.

- Identify the social and historical roots of Quebec nationalism.

- Understand immigration's central role in Canadian social development.

- Describe what sociologists mean when they describe Canada as a vertical mosaic and outline how the vertical mosaic is being recast along racial lines.

INTRODUCTION

The May 2014 RCMP report *Missing and Murdered Aboriginal Women* is disturbing reading. The report notes that between 1980 and 2012, 1181 Indigenous women were homicide victims. Making up about 4 percent of Canada's female population, they comprised 16 percent of all murdered Canadian women over that period. Moreover, the situation seems to be getting worse. In 1984, Indigenous women were 8 percent of female homicide victims but by 2012 that figure had climbed to 23 percent (Royal Canadian Mounted Police, 2014: 7–10). The report also shows that there are currently 164 Indigenous women who are considered "missing," constituting about 11 percent of all missing women in the country today (Royal Canadian Mounted Police, 2014: 8).

The causes of crime are complex, as are the reasons why some people go missing. The RCMP report identifies three "risk factors" that contribute to the high rate of victimization of Indigenous women: poor employment conditions and opportunities; the consumption of drugs, alcohol, or other intoxicants prior to the incident; and involvement in the sex trade (Royal Canadian Mounted Police, 2014).

The RCMP report followed on the heels of another report by the Special Parliamentary Committee on Violence against Indigenous Women. The Committee report tried to put the problem into a larger context. It argued that the "root causes" of violence against Indigenous women include the legacy of Indigenous children being removed from their families and their culture by the government and placed in church-run boarding schools; persistent poverty and poor housing conditions; and widespread racism in Canadian (House of Commons, 2014).

Not everyone was pleased with the RCMP report because it was silent on the larger context contributing to violence against Indigenous women. Some people called the Special Committee's report a whitewash because of its timid recommendations for improving the situation; rather than demanding a national inquiry and a comprehensive national action plan, the committee merely recommended that the federal government "learn from the stories of missing and murdered Indigenous girls and work … to create a public awareness and prevention campaign focusing on violence against Indigenous women and girls in Canada" (Special Committee on Violence Against Indigenous Women, 2014: 43). According to Human Rights Watch, a nongovernmental agency

that monitors human rights abuses around the world, one of the glaring silences in both reports concerns the role that the police may play in the victimization of Indigenous women. Human Rights Watch (2013) argues that a big part of the problem is that police do not take the issue of violence against Indigenous women seriously. To support their claim, they document cases in which Indigenous women are sexually and racially abused at the hands of the police.

Other kinds of ethnic and racial problems also exist in Canada. In Ontario, the Safe Schools Act, which mandates a policy of "zero tolerance" for violent and disruptive behaviour in schools, is alleged by some to work to the disadvantage of black students (Henry and Tator, 2006: 211). In 2008, Toronto school trustees voted to establish a black-focused elementary school in the city. Critics argued that this was a step backward to racial segregation (Brown and Popplewell, 2008). The same debate rekindled in Toronto in 2011 with a proposal to establish a black-focused high school. As of 2007, there were 800 outstanding land claims filed by First Nations against the federal government. At the current pace of resolution, it will be 2100 before most of them are dealt with (Frideres and Gadacz, 2012: 226).

Arab Canadians complain that they have faced increased stereotyping and discrimination in Canada and at the Canada–U.S. border since September 11, 2001 (Li, 2003). In 1995, the country was on the verge of collapse after nearly half the voters in Quebec voted in favour of separation. Some observers claim that the federal government's policy of multiculturalism undermines the unity of our country (Bissondath, 1994), creates disloyalty to Canada, undermines foreign policy (Granatstein, 2007), and causes "more overt hostility in Canada to those of European ancestry … than to the nonwhite minority" (Stoffman, 2002: 126).

These examples say something about the distribution of power and resources in Canada. The sociology of ethnic and racial relations concerns primarily the study of how power and resources are unequally distributed among ethnic and racial groups. Sociologists who are interested in race and ethnic relations ask a number of interrelated questions: What are the conditions under which ethnic and racial groups come into contact? Which ethnic and racial groups hold most of the power in a society? How do they exercise power? Are there social and economic advantages associated with particular ethnic or racial backgrounds? What are the social consequences of the unequal distribution of power and resources? How have ethnic and racial groups challenged inequality and power imbalances? How have governments tried to manage and contain ethnic and racial conflict?

My aim in this chapter is to provide sociological answers to these questions. I begin by examining what sociologists mean by ethnicity, race, and racism, and then discuss various theoretical approaches to the study of ethnic and racial relations. Next, I examine the three main forms of ethnic and racial relations in Canada: Indigenous/non-Indigenous relations, French/English relations, and immigrant/nonimmigrant relations. In each case, you will see how power and resource imbalances play important roles in structuring relationships among groups.

THE SOCIAL CONSTRUCTION OF DIFFERENCE

We use the terms *race*, *racial*, *ethnic*, and *ethnicity* in a variety of ways in our everyday lives. Some students in my classes talk about how they are under pressure from their parents to marry someone of the same "race" or "ethnicity." Others are concerned that "race relations" in Canada seem to be getting worse. Yet others describe the joys of living in a "multiethnic" country, of eating meals in a variety of "ethnic" restaurants, and of observing and participating in the rituals and festivals of "ethnic" groups from around the world.

The assumption underlying our commonsense understandings of these terms is that race and ethnicity are *ascribed* characteristics. That is, we assume that we are born with a certain race or ethnicity that cannot be changed. Sociologists, however, recognize that, although we cannot change our birth parents and generally cannot change our skin colour, we do not necessarily have fixed and unalterable ethnic and racial characteristics or identities. Instead, sociologists believe it is more useful to see race and ethnicity as *achieved* statuses—statuses that are acquired by virtue of social definition.

ETHNICITY

Sociologists do not agree on how to define and measure ethnicity. *Objective definitions of ethnicity* assume that ethnic groups exist because of people's social attachments (Isajiw, 1999). From this point of view, ethnicity is something that people possess because of differences in language, culture, customs, national origin, and ancestry. *Subjective approaches to ethnicity* focus on the process of ethnic identification. Sociologists who emphasize the socially constructed nature of perceived reality insist that ethnicity is a "transactional" process. Ethnic groups are made up of people who identify themselves, or who are identified by others, as belonging to the same ancestral or cultural group. Whether they display any of the cultural characteristics of the group with which they identify, or whether they are merely born into that group, is largely irrelevant. When subjective definitions are used, then, "ethnicity" is self-defined and reflects "a shared 'we-feeling' within a collectivity (groupness) whose symbolic components can vary [over] time and place" (Fleras and Elliot, 1996). From this perspective, ethnic identities and boundaries are situational, variable, and flexible.

Most of the ethnic categories that we take for granted are actually recent historical creations. The ethnic category "English" would have been unthinkable to a person who lived in the British Isles 800 years ago. People defined themselves, and were defined by others, as Celts, Saxons, Normans, and so on. Only some of those people came to be known as "the English" (Lieberson, 1991). Similarly, the people whom we now think of as "Germans" did not exist 150 years ago. As these examples suggest, the way in which people define themselves, and are defined by others, is in constant flux (Lieberson, 1991: 444). If we take a long view, it is common for ethnic categories and identities to be recast and created anew.

This is what seems to be happening in Canada now. A feeling of commonality has crystallized that is the basis for a common ethnic identification. In preparing for the 1991 census, Statistics Canada held meetings, organized focus groups, and tested different ways of posing questions that tried to measure the ethnicity of our population. One thing that Statistics Canada found "was a strong tendency [for respondents] to report Canadian as their ethnic origin and as their ethnic identity" (White, 1992: 166). Largely because of political pressure, "Canadian" was included as a response category in the ethnicity question for the next census. "Canadians" are now the numerically largest ethnic group in Canada (see Figure 9.1).

Why do some of us define our ethnic roots or ethnic identity as "Canadian"? Some of us may simply be unaware of or uninterested in our ancestral roots and, hence, by default define ourselves as Canadian. For others, defining ourselves as Canadian is a political act used to express our dissatisfaction with the government's policy of multiculturalism

FIGURE 9.1   THE 25 LARGEST ETHNIC GROUPS IN CANADA, 2011 (IN MILLIONS)

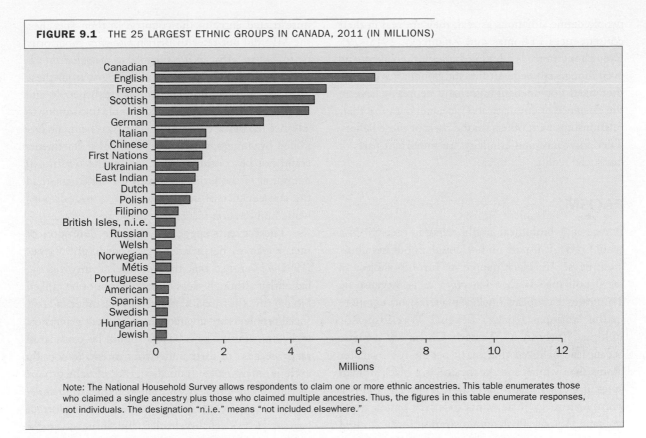

Note: The National Household Survey allows respondents to claim one or more ethnic ancestries. This table enumerates those who claimed a single ancestry plus those who claimed multiple ancestries. Thus, the figures in this table enumerate responses, not individuals. The designation "n.i.e." means "not included elsewhere."

SOURCE: Statistics Canada (2014a).

(White, 1992: 168–69). At the same time, though, many of us insist that we are Canadian because that is simply the group with which we identify and with which we share a sense of belonging (Angus Reid Group, 1991; Howard, 1998). The emergence of this sense of community means that "the ethnic English-Canadian is a new social creation" (Howard-Hassmann, 1999: 528).

RACE

For much of the twentieth century, there was little difference between commonsense understandings of **race** and the way that race was analyzed in the social and natural sciences. Most scientists believed that races were real and objective subdivisions of *Homo sapiens.* These divisions were supposedly based on a combination of unalterable physical and genetic characteristics. Features, such as skin colour, hair texture, body and facial shape, genetic diseases, metabolic rates, and distribution of blood groups, were used to construct various racial typologies. The most common typology was the division of humanity into "Caucasoid," "mongoloid," and "negroid" races (Montagu, 1972).

During the 1930s, scientists began to raise doubts about the scientific validity of the concept of race (Barkan, 1992). Since the 1950s, the scientific consensus has been that racial classifications of humanity are arbitrary, that genetic differences between groups are tiny, and that genetic differences are behaviourally insignificant (Montagu, 1972). Racial classifications based on a characteristic such as skin colour are as illogical as racial classifications based on the length of index fingers (Miles, 1982). Moreover, only a fraction of 1 percent of all human genes are necessarily shared by members of the same race, genetically defined. Thus, from a strictly genetic point of view, Prime Minister Stephen Harper may have more in common with black hockey star P. K. Subban of the Montreal Canadiens than with white businessman David Thomson, the richest person in Canada.

In sum, genetic differences between races are arbitrary, extremely small, and without behavioural consequences. Ethnic boundaries and identities are flexible, negotiated, and historically variable. We should not conclude, however, that race and ethnicity are unimportant aspects of modern society. According to W. I. Thomas's famous sociological dictum, if people define situations as real, they are real in their consequences (Thomas and Znaniecki, 1918: 79). Even though race is a hollow biological concept, and even though ethnic identities and boundaries are neither fixed nor unchanging, many people believe in the existence of ethnicity and race, and organize their relationships with others on the basis of those beliefs. Therefore, race and ethnicity are important parts of our social reality.

RACISM

If race is a biological myth, what is racism? Is a school racist if it puts on hot dog days but not chow mein days? Are black people in Toronto subject to racist policing? Is Don Cherry a racist because he denigrates European hockey players who compete in the National Hockey League? Was Professor Philippe Rushton of Western University a racist because he believed that black people have smaller brains than whites and Asians do? Is a black woman racist if she wants to marry only a black man? Is a white man racist if he wants to marry only a white woman? Was the Bush administration in the United States racist for the way that it managed the aftermath of Hurricane Katrina in New Orleans in September 2005?

Before we can begin to answer these kinds of questions, we need to define racism. Sociologists define racism as both a certain kind of idea and a certain kind of institutional practice. I will consider each of these definitions in turn.

Traditionally, sociologists defined racism as "the belief that humans are subdivided into distinct hereditary groups that are innately different in their social behaviour and mental capacities and that can therefore be ranked as superior or inferior" (Marger, 1997: 27). Some scholars have suggested that because ideas about the inherent superiority and inferiority of groups have been so thoroughly discredited, racism has taken new forms (Omi and Winant, 1986). Biological versions of racism may be dead, but researchers have developed the concept of new racism as a way of analyzing its changing manifestations (Adeyanju, 2010).

The concept of **new racism** was developed by Martin Barker (1981) to analyze the way that racist ideas were being expressed in the 1970s by some British members of Parliament (MPs) when they were speaking out against British immigration policy. That policy permitted people from former British colonies in Asia, Africa, and the Caribbean unrestricted entry to the country. In their speeches, the MPs did not refer to British *biological* superiority or to Indian, African, or Caribbean *biological* inferiority. Instead, they regarded immigrants from these areas as *culturally* different from British people and alleged that the ability of British people to continue to advance the moral level of humanity was being undermined by immigration policy. The MPs' statements could not be considered "racist" by the traditional definition of the term. However, the statements had the consequence of helping to stop almost all nonwhite immigration from those countries.

These events suggested that the definition of racism had to be broadened. Accordingly, Barker (1981: 21) argued that the new racism involves the belief that although races of people cannot be ranked biologically, they are different from each other and that social problems are created when different groups try to live together. These beliefs should be considered racist because of their underlying intent: to socially exclude, marginalize, and denigrate certain groups of people but to do so without reference to unalterable biology. People may even believe in abstract virtues, such as equality, justice, and fairness, yet still hold negative attitudes, and engage in discriminatory behaviour, toward minority group members (Henry and Tator, 2006: 19).

How widespread is racism? One survey (Leger Marketing, 2007) found the following:

- 9 percent of Canadians considered themselves strongly or moderately racist.
- Men are more likely than women are to describe themselves as moderately racist (10 percent versus 6 percent of women).
- 21 percent of Canadians believed that some races are more gifted than others are.
- 9 percent of Canadians would react negatively if their child married someone of a different race.
- 92 percent of Canadians have witnessed comments or behaviours that they regard as racist.
- 17 percent of respondents believe that their city is more racist than it was 10 years ago.

A different indicator of the scope of racism in Canada is given in Figure 9.2, which focuses on *perceived* discrimination. This figure shows that Canadians perceive that discrimination against various ethnocultural groups increased between 2006 and 2010. It also shows that, in 2010, Muslims were seen as the group that was most discriminated against, with 44 percent of respondents saying that Muslims

FIGURE 9.2   PERCEPTIONS OF DISCRIMINATION IN CANADA, 2006 AND 2010

Survey question asked:

For each of the following groups, please tell me whether you think they are often, sometimes, rarely, or never the subject of discrimination in Canadian society today.

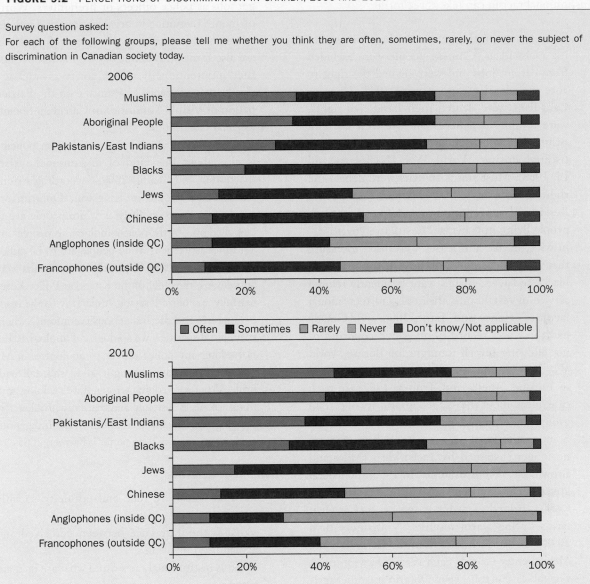

SOURCE: HER MAJESTY THE QUEEN IN RIGHT OF CANADA (as represented by the Department of Citizenship and Immigration Canada).

"often" face discrimination. Indigenous people were not far behind (42 percent), followed by Pakistanis/East Indians (36 percent), blacks (32 percent), Jews (17 percent), and Chinese (13 percent).

One must be careful to distinguish perceptions of discrimination from actual discrimination. An individual may overestimate or underestimate the actual level of discrimination against a particular group because of his or her level of education, the degree to which the mass media bias his or her perceptions, and other factors. Sociologists measure the *actual* level of discrimination against a group using objective factors. For example, do people from different ethnic or racial groups earn different average annual incomes? If so, how much of the difference is *not* the result of their average level of education, years of work experience, and other factors that generally explain earnings? The unexplained difference is arguably a measure of actual discrimination. To what degree does this difference persist beyond the immigrant generation? The degree of persistence indicates how deeply rooted discrimination is. Later, we analyze such objective measures of discrimination in Canada.

An important type of actual discrimination is **institutional racism**, or "discriminatory racial practices built into such prominent structures as the political, economic and education systems" (Doob, 1996: 6). Institutional racism can take three forms:

1. Some institutional practices are based on explicitly racist ideas. Chinese people were excluded from certain jobs and were denied the right to vote in federal elections until 1947. Japanese Canadians were denied their basic civil rights, were forcibly expelled from the west coast of British Columbia, and had their property confiscated during World War II (Bolaria and Li, 1988). Most status Indians were denied the right to vote in federal elections until 1960. Residential segregation was widespread for black people living in Canada. "Restrictive covenants" in wills, deeds, and leases were used to ensure that property could not be sold or leased to blacks and Jews. Blacks were frequently refused service in restaurants, theatres, and recreational facilities (Henry and Tator, 2006: 69). Canada had the worst record of all Allied countries of not allowing Jewish immigration during World War II, when millions of Jews were being gassed in Europe (Abella and Troper, 1982). In each case, ideas about the alleged inferiority of certain groups underpinned institutional practices.

2. Some institutional practices arose from, but are no longer sustained by, racist ideas (Miles and Brown, 2003). For example, in 1966, the federal government admitted a small number of black workers from the Caribbean to work on Canadian farms during warm months. Now, more than 20 000 migrant workers from the Caribbean and Mexico enter Canada each year to harvest fruits, vegetables, and tobacco in Ontario and other agricultural areas. Canadian government officials originally justified this practice partly by arguing that black workers are racially suited to back-breaking labour under the hot sun but racially unsuited to cold Canadian winters (Satzewich, 1991). The present migrant-labour policy had its origins in racist thinking, but racist ideas are no longer used to justify this migration stream.

3. Institutions sometimes unintentionally restrict the life-chances of certain groups through a variety of seemingly neutral rules, regulations, and procedures. This is sometimes referred to as *systemic discrimination*. For example, height and weight requirements for jobs with police forces and fire departments did not necessarily originate in racist ideas, but these requirements meant that

for many years, certain Asian groups could not get jobs as police officers or firefighters. Word-of-mouth recruiting in organizations and inflated educational requirements for nontechnical jobs are also forms of systemic discrimination because they unintentionally put minority groups at a disadvantage (Special Committee on the Participation of Visible Minorities in Canadian Society [Special Committee], 1984).

The debate about racial profiling in policing is also about this kind of institutional racism (Satzewich and Shaffir, 2009). According to one study, black people in Kingston, Ontario, are nearly four times as likely as white people are to be pulled over by the police. Indigenous peoples are 1.4 times as likely as white people are to be pulled over (Wortley, 2005). When the study results were announced, the chief of the Kingston Police Force tearfully apologized, saying "especially to the black community and the Indigenous community where there are disparities, we apologize. I apologize. I'm not asking any police officer to apologize. ... My police officers have the right to ... walk tall with pride. What we're doing wrong, if we're doing anything wrong, is systemic and that's my problem. So I apologize to the black community, the Indigenous community and we'll do better" (Farmer, 2005).

TIME FOR REVIEW

1. In what sense are race and ethnicity socially constructed?
2. What is the difference between perceived and actual discrimination?
3. What is institutional racism and what are its main forms?

THEORIES OF RACE AND ETHNIC RELATIONS

There are numerous sociological interpretations of race and ethnic relations (Rex and Mason, 1986). In this section, I discuss four approaches that seek to explain various forms of ethnic and racial hostility. Such hostility is multifaceted and, depending on the circumstances, is described as racism, prejudice, ethnocentrism, or xenophobia.

SOCIAL PSYCHOLOGY

Social-psychological theories of race and ethnic relations focus on how **prejudice**—an unfavourable, generalized, and rigid belief that is applied to all members of a group—and racism satisfy the psychic needs of certain people. The *frustration-aggression thesis* is a popular variant of social-psychological theory. It explains prejudice and racism as forms of hostility that arise from frustration. The theory suggests that people who are frustrated in their efforts to achieve a desired goal—a better-paying job, for example, or entry to a university—respond with aggression (Marger, 1997). Since the real source of frustration is usually too powerful to confront directly, or may not be known, people take out their frustrations on the less powerful. From this perspective, minority ethnic and racial groups are convenient and safe targets of displaced aggression. This displacement is also referred to as *scapegoating*. The concept of scapegoating is sometimes used to explain anti-Semitism—negative attitudes and everyday discrimination directed against Jews (Brym and Lenton, 1993).

This kind of explanation has a commonsense appeal. We all have bad days at work or at school, and when we get home, we sometimes lash out at the people close to us. However, the theory has limitations. First, people respond to frustrating circumstances in a variety of ways. Displaced aggression does not always follow frustration. We sometimes internalize frustrations and end up giving ourselves an ulcer, or we may direct our frustrations at the real source of our problems. The theory does not say why we respond to frustrating circumstances in different ways. Second, the theory does not explain why some groups, and not others, are chosen as scapegoats.

PRIMORDIALISM

Primordialist theory argues that ethnic and racial attachments reflect an innate tendency for people to seek out, and associate with, others who are similar in terms of language, culture, beliefs, ancestry, and appearance (Scott, 1990). From this point of view, ethnic prejudice and racism are ways of maintaining social boundaries.

Sociobiologists offer a popular form of primordial theory. They suggest that prejudice and **discrimination**—practices that deny members of particular groups equal access to societal rewards—stem from our supposedly biologically grounded tendency to be nepotistic. Sociobiologists argue that the process of natural selection does not operate at the level of individuals, but rather at the level of kin groups. Clusters of genes are assumed to be passed on through kin selection (Wilson, 1978). Ethnic and racial groups are seen to be nothing more than large extended families. Since people have a "natural" tendency to want to pass on their genes, they favour their own "families." Thus, people are inherently both altruistic (prepared to sacrifice their own individual interests for the sake of the group) and ethnocentric because they want to pass on their genes only to their own group. Humans, therefore, naturally favour members of their own ethnic or racial group—their "relatives"—and have a natural distrust and dislike of "nonfamily" members (van den Berghe, 1986: 255).

Are racism, prejudice, and discrimination programmed by our genes? It seems unlikely. The first problem with sociobiology is that shared ethnicity or race does not prevent conflict from erupting. White workers have struck against white-owned factories, and people have killed members of their own ethnic or racial group without concern for common ethnicity or race (Bonacich, 1980). Second, sociobiology is not able to explain how and why we frequently break out of our supposed genetically programmed nepotism. For example, Canadians of diverse ethnic and racial origins participate together in various kinds of anti-racist social movements (Henry and Tator, 2006). Ethnic and racial relations, therefore, are not necessarily zero-sum games in which one group wins at the expense of another.

NORMATIVE THEORIES

Normative theories of ethnic and racial prejudice concentrate on the way in which prejudice is transmitted through socialization and the social circumstances that encourage discriminatory behaviour (Marger, 1997). For example, the *socialization approach* focuses on how we are taught ethnic and racial stereotypes, prejudices, and attitudes by our families, peer groups, and the mass media. For instance, as a teenager in Saskatchewan in the 1970s, I remember watching the TV show *All in the Family*. People in Saskatchewan at the time held many prejudicial attitudes, particularly toward Indigenous peoples. However, the television program *All in the Family* exposed my generation to a repertoire of ethnic and racial slang and stereotypes that we had not heard before. Archie Bunker, the show's central character, was supposed to be a caricature of an American "bigot," but he also taught us terms like "wop," "dago," "spic," and "nigger," and the corresponding stereotypes.

Socialization theories are superior to social-psychological and primordialist approaches because they emphasize the way in which ethnic and racial prejudices and attitudes are learned through social interaction. **Power-conflict theories of ethnic and racial prejudice** go a step farther by explaining how prejudicial ideas, attitudes, and practices arise in the first place.

POWER-CONFLICT THEORIES

Karl Marx (1967 [1867]: 751) wrote that "the turning of Africa into a warren for the commercial hunting of black-skins signaled the rosy dawn of the era of capitalist production." Marx did not take his analysis of slavery and racism much further than that. Later generations of Marxist scholars, however, have sought to link racism to the structure of capitalist societies.

Orthodox Marxists argue that racism is an *ideology*—a set of ideas shaped by economic interests about the way the social world works. Racism is ideological insofar as it is used by capitalists to mystify social reality and justify the exploitation and the unequal treatment of groups of people.

This justification can take many forms. For example, in the seventeenth century, American and Caribbean plantation owners justified the use of Africans as slaves by denying the humanity of Africans (Williams, 1964). In Marxist terms, the existence of racist ideas did not cause slavery; rather, slavery was a particular system of labour control that was justified by racist ideology.

In the case of advanced capitalism, racism is viewed by Marxists as an ideology that justifies the especially intense exploitation of racial minority and immigrant workers (Bolaria and Li, 1988; Castles and Kosack, 1984). From this point of view, racist ideas are used by employers as a means of creating artificial divisions in the working class so as to prevent the formation of a class consciousness that would threaten the social and economic order (Bolaria and Li, 1988; Castles and Kosack, 1984; Nikolinakos, 1973). Racist ideas can also help to justify the allocation of certain groups to low-wage, socially marginal jobs.

RACE AND THE SPLIT LABOUR MARKET

Split labour market theory was developed by Edna Bonacich (1972, 1979) because of the limitations of orthodox Marxism in analyzing racism. She argues that orthodox Marxism tends to assume that the capitalist class is all-powerful and that other classes play no role in the development of racist thinking. This is inaccurate; racism is found in all classes to varying degrees. Second, orthodox Marxism portrays racism in overly conspiratorial terms. Little evidence demonstrates that capitalists sit around plotting new and devious ways of using racism to stop workers from developing class consciousness. Third, orthodox Marxism has trouble explaining why racialized conflict so often results in *exclusionary practices*—practices that deny employers access to cheaper, more exploitable labour. In 1885, for example, the Canadian government instituted a "head tax" on new immigrants from China. Chinese immigrants had to pay $50 to the federal government. In 1900, the tax was raised to $100, and in 1903 to $500. The Chinese Immigration Act of 1923 completely barred Chinese immigration and was in force until 1947 (Li, 1988: 30). If racism is developed by capitalists to justify exploitation, then why does it so often result in efforts to block the entry of new immigrants and limit the job opportunities of those already in the country? Bonacich feels that more attention has to be paid to the way in which the competition for jobs and other scarce resources within the working class creates and sustains racism.

Split labour market theory suggests that racial and ethnic conflict is rooted in differences in the price of labour. For historical reasons—mainly involving military conquest—nonwhite workers have often received low wages and white workers high wages. Employers try to replace high-paid white workers with low-paid nonwhite workers. Meanwhile, high-paid workers, faced with displacement or the threat of displacement, try to protect their own interests by limiting capitalists' access to cheaper nonwhite workers. Thus, cheaper nonwhite workers are the victims of a complicated process of class struggle between expensive labour, cheap labour, and capitalists.

The theory applies well to Canada. During the late nineteenth and early twentieth centuries, the presence of Chinese workers and merchants in British Columbia provoked a negative response on the part of various segments of the white working class and white shop owners. As split labour market theory predicts, the hostility of whites was rooted in differences in the price of labour. According to evidence presented at the Royal Commission on Chinese and Japanese Immigration in 1903, Chinese workers earned about one-half of the wages that white workers earned in the same jobs (Li, 1988: 44). A number of racist organizations emerged whose aim was to limit the number of places where Chinese people could work, which helped stop additional Chinese immigration (Roy, 1989).

Split labour market theory makes three other points that are relevant to the analysis of ethnic and race relations in general. First, it argues that individual racism, ethnic prejudice, and institutional racism emerge from intergroup conflict. Second, the theory maintains that prejudicial ideas and discriminatory behaviour are ways of socially marginalizing minority groups that the dominant group sees as threats to their position of power and privilege. Third, the theory suggests that to understand ethnic and racial relations, we need to look beyond individual personalities and sociobiological processes and analyze processes of economic, social, and political competition among groups (Marger, 1997: 98).

Keeping these three observations in mind will help you understand the three main patterns of ethnic and racial relations in Canada: Indigenous/non-Indigenous relations, French/English relations, and immigrant/nonimmigrant relations. These are the topics that we turn to next.

TIME FOR REVIEW

1. How do the main theories of race and ethnic relations differ from one another?
2. Which theory best explains patterns of race and ethnic relations? Why?

INDIGENOUS PEOPLES

Have you ever fumbled trying to find the right way to refer to someone who is ethnically or racially different from you? Are we supposed to say that a person is a "Native," an "Indian," an "Indigenous" person, or a member of the "First Nations"? Are you sensitive about how you want others to refer to your ethnic or racial origins? You may think that this sensitivity is an indication that political correctness has run amok. However, you should not dismiss the issue of labels and names easily.

Ethnic and racial labels are about power. Take the term *Indian*. A hopelessly lost Christopher Columbus thought he had found a sea route to India when he was discovered in 1492 by people indigenous to this part of the world. He mislabelled them "Indians." Britain's military, political, and economic domination of North America in the eighteenth century meant that it had the power to ignore the linguistic and cultural differences among indigenous groups and define them in any way they saw fit. They chose the term *Indian*.

As Indigenous people have acquired more power, they have begun to challenge externally imposed labels. In the 1980s, for example, the National Indian Brotherhood renamed itself the Assembly of First Nations, and people in Alberta who were called Sarcee Indians by Europeans for most of the twentieth century now refer to themselves as Tsuu T'ina, which means "Earth People" in English (Steckley 2003: 7). Groups have rejected externally imposed labels as part of a search for forms of consciousness, identity, and culture that are untainted by the colonizing power's definition of the situation (Jenson, 1993).

One, albeit imperfect, way to navigate through the complex issue of naming is to use the definition of "Indigenous peoples" in the 1982 Canadian Charter of Rights and Freedoms. In the Charter, the "Indigenous peoples" of Canada include Indians, Inuit, and Métis. According to the *2011 National Household Survey*, in 2011 there were 697 510 registered Indians, 418 380 Métis, and 59 115 Inuit, and 213 900 non-status Indians in Canada, who together made up 4.3 percent of the total population (Indigenous and Northern Affairs Canada, 2013).

At its simplest level, the term *Indian* (or *status* or *registered Indian*) refers to people who are recognized as "Indians" by virtue of the federal government's Indian Act. Many people now use the term "First Nations" to refer to Indians. But deciding who is an Indian under the Indian Act is a much more complicated question. Until 1985, Indian women who married non-Indian men, along with their children, lost their federally recognized Indian status; they became *non-status Indians*. In 1985, Bill C-31 was passed. It allowed these women and their dependent children to regain their Indian status. Indian bands, however, now have the power to develop their own membership codes. This means that not all individuals who have had their Indian status reinstated are members of an Indian band (Frideres and Gadacz, 2012).

There are two definitions of *Métis*. Métis organizations in western Canada tend to focus on a person's objective "roots" as the condition for being considered Métis. Thus, the Métis National Council defines the Métis as "descendants of the historic Métis who evolved in what is now western Canada as a people with a common political will" (Métis National Council, 1983). The Congress of Indigenous Peoples uses a broader definition, suggesting that the Métis should include descendants of the historic Métis in western Canada *and* anyone of mixed European-Indian ancestry who defines himself or herself as Métis (Congress of Indigenous Peoples, 2008). Thus, subjective definitions of ethnic group membership are more important for groups like the Congress of Indigenous Peoples.

Finally, *Inuit* are part of a diverse group of people who have lived for many centuries north of the tree line. In Canada, the name *Inuit* has replaced the earlier name *Eskimo*. The language of the Inuit is Inuktitut (McMillan, 1988: 240).

EXPLANATIONS OF INDIGENOUS CONDITIONS

The socioeconomic conditions of Canada's Indigenous peoples are a national tragedy (Royal Commission on Indigenous Peoples, 1996). Canada has made admirable efforts to condemn social inequality and the denial of human rights in other countries, such as South Africa when apartheid—the policy of legalized racial separation and inequality—was still in force. Ironically, though, the commitment to social justice for Indigenous peoples in our own country has not been as strong, which is why, in the 1980s, the South African government routinely defended itself against our criticisms by saying that we should first clean up our own backyard (Bourgeault, 1988; York, 1989).

Statistical evidence shows that Indigenous peoples are the most socially and economically disadvantaged groups in the country. One way to measure the differences in living and socioeconomic conditions between First Nations and Inuit communities and the rest of Canada is through the *Community Well-Being (CWB) Index*. The Index uses four indicators—level of education, labour force activity, income, and housing conditions—to measure the well-being of communities in Canada. Figure 9.3 indicates that while significant improvements in overall well-being were achieved in First Nation and Inuit communities in the 1980s and 1990s, the degree of improvement levelled off in the 2000s. Moreover, First Nations and Inuit communities continue to lag far behind other Canadian communities.

For many years, Canadian politicians, bureaucrats, and social scientists have debated how inequalities between Indigenous peoples and other Canadians originated, why they persist, and what can be done to lessen them. Indeed, when the federal government announced in 1991 the establishment of the Royal Commission on Indigenous Peoples, Ovide Mercredi, then chief of the Assembly of First Nations, caustically commented that "Indians have been studied to death." I want first to consider the federal government's historical explanation of these conditions. Then I will examine two sociological explanations: the culture of poverty thesis and conflict theory.

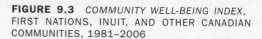

FIGURE 9.3 *COMMUNITY WELL-BEING INDEX, FIRST NATIONS, INUIT, AND OTHER CANADIAN COMMUNITIES, 1981–2006*

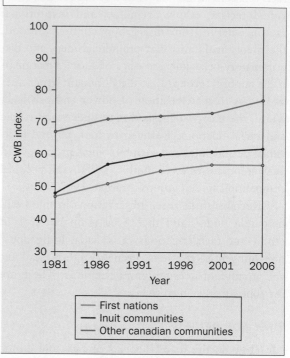

SOURCE: Statistics Canada, 1981 to 2006 Census of Population, Aboriginal Affairs and Northern Development Canada tabulations.

The Government's View

Throughout the first half of the twentieth century, government Indian policy was premised on the belief that Indigenous culture was both different from and inferior to European culture. Armed with this ethnocentric attitude, the federal government sought to assimilate Indigenous people into mainstream Canadian society (Gibbins and Ponting, 1986). In 1920, this approach was summed up as follows by Duncan Campbell Scott, the deputy minister of the federal government's Department of Indian Affairs: "[O]ur object is to continue until there is not a single Indian ... that has not been absorbed into the body politic and there is no [longer an] Indian question" (quoted in Titley, 1986).

The government, therefore, forcibly tried to Europeanize Indigenous people and culture. Traditional cultural practices, such as the potlatch, a winter exchange of gifts and property on the British Columbia coast, and the sun dance, a summer solstice religious ceremony on the Prairies, were outlawed. Such practices were regarded as pagan, anti-capitalist rituals that inhibited the development of both Christianity and a capitalistic work ethic (Cole and Chaikin, 1990; Pettipas, 1995).

The federal government also tried to assimilate and Christianize Indigenous children by establishing a series of residential schools. These boarding schools were located far from the children's families and home communities. While in school, the children were forbidden to speak in their mother tongue and to speak with siblings of the opposite sex, and they had their hair shorn. Boys were given extensive training in manual labour and girls were taught domestic labour skills. The goal of this schooling was to resocialize Indigenous children and to instill in them a new European identity (Titley, 1986). The government's legislative, regulatory, and educational approach to Indigenous people reflected the view that inequality, poverty, and poor social conditions were rooted in Indigenous cultural and racial inferiority.

The Culture of Poverty Thesis

In the 1960s and 1970s, many sociologists also saw Indigenous culture as the source of the "Indian problem." To account for the origins and persistence of the problem, some sociologists proposed a variant of the **culture of poverty thesis.** The concept of a culture of poverty was first developed by Oscar Lewis (1961), an American anthropologist interested in explaining the slow pace at which Mexican Americans and Puerto Ricans were being assimilated into U.S. society. He suggested that some ethnic groups do not readily assimilate, and hence are poor because their culture does not value economic success, hard work, and achievement.

Kazemipur and Halli (2000) have applied Lewis's framework to the issue of ethnic poverty in Canada, and Nagler (1972) has applied it to the conditions of Indigenous people. More recently, Frances Widdowson and Albert Howard (2008) have argued that because many Indigenous peoples participate in modern society as consumers rather than producers, they remain stuck at an earlier, "Neolithic" stage of human development:

> Isolation from economic processes has meant that a number of Neolithic cultural features, including undisciplined work habits, tribal forms of political identification, animistic beliefs, and difficulties in developing abstract reasoning, persist despite hundreds of years of contact. (Widdowson and Howard, 2008: 13)

They argue that the cultural gap between Indigenous peoples and the rest of the Canadian population prevents the integration of Indigenous peoples and is responsible for many of the social problems and pathologies in their communities.

Some sociologists, such as Stephen Steinberg (1981), criticize culture of poverty explanations by arguing that groups generally do not get ahead or lag behind because of their cultural values. Instead, they are born into certain stations in life and adopt the values and attitudes that are consistent with their life-chances. If Indigenous peoples have low aspirations, it is likely the result of a realistic assessment of their dismal job prospects and a resignation born out of bitter personal experience. For Steinberg, the culture of poverty is the consequence, not the cause, of poverty.

Conflict Theory

Since the 1970s, sociologists have focused on blocked opportunities rather than culture as the explanation for inequalities between Indigenous and non-Indigenous peoples. The *colonization model* is the most popular variant of the conflict approach (Frideres and Gadacz, 2012). The colonization model analyzes the problem of inequality in terms of power imbalances and the exploitation of Indigenous peoples and lands by white society.

Theorists of colonization argue that the Indian Act, which outlines the federal government's policies and procedures for dealing with Indian issues, is a paternalistic document that disempowers Indian people (Frideres and Gadacz, 2012). It places limits on the actions of both individual Indians and their band councils. When Indians from Brantford, Ontario, wanted to sue the federal government over unfulfilled treaty promises in the 1920s, the government passed a law making it illegal for them to use band funds to hire lawyers to pursue their claims (Titley, 1986). Indians did not get much help from federal or provincial/territorial politicians either. Since most Indians could not vote in federal or provincial/territorial elections until the 1960s, politicians had no need to stand up for the interests of Indians who lived in their constituencies. Chiefs who failed to cooperate with the government's designs were routinely removed from their positions (Satzewich and Mahood, 1994). Band councils are still required to have their decisions approved by the federal minister of Indian Affairs. Thus, rather than helping to create the social conditions that would afford Indian people greater autonomy over their lives, government policy has fostered social marginality and dependence. This is why many Indian leaders have called for the abolition of the Indian Act.

Furthermore, most present-day conflicts between Indigenous peoples and various levels of government originated in the past misuse of power by government officials. Present-day land-claim disputes sometimes go back a hundred years, when government officials could arbitrarily lop off chunks of Indian reserve land and sell it to whites (Frideres and Gadacz, 2012). The Canadian government and private business have derived tremendous economic benefits from the exploitation of land appropriated from Indigenous communities (see the Critical Sociology: Protest and Policy box).

CLASS AND GENDER DIVERSITY

Criticisms of the internal colonial model have focused on its tendency to overgeneralize about the conditions of Indigenous people in Canada. As significant as inequalities between Indigenous and non-Indigenous peoples are, conflict and feminist sociologists argue that it is worth remembering that socioeconomic diversity also exists within Indigenous communities. These sociologists analyze class and gender differentiation within Indigenous communities and the implications of such differences for both individual life-chances and wider community life (Satzewich and Wotherspoon, 2001; Voyageur, 2008).

Feminist sociologists have been interested in the role of gender in recent debates about the inclusion of the right to self-government in the Canadian Constitution. During the debate over the Charlottetown Accord in 1992, many Indigenous women were concerned that the proposal for self-government, which was advanced by the predominantly male leadership of Indigenous organizations, did not contain any guarantees of gender equality (Fiske, 1996; Krosenbrink-Gelissen, 1994: 357–60). The Native Women's Association of Canada, therefore, fought against the accord in the months leading up to the referendum.

CRITICAL SOCIOLOGY: PROTEST AND POLICY   IDLE NO MORE

The Idle No More movement began in October 2012 when four Saskatchewan women were trying to figure out how they could oppose a new federal government bill that threatened to erode Indigenous land rights. To help publicize an event in Saskatoon, they turned to Facebook and called their page "Idle No More." Soon after, other Canadians began organizing similar events across the country.

Today, Idle No More is a broad-based social movement that is organized around honouring Indigenous sovereignty and protecting the land and water from environmental degradation. Idle No More's manifesto proclaims that treaties enacted between First Nations and the British Crown are agreements between sovereign nations that cannot be changed by one side. They are based on the principle that the land and its resources should be shared. In practice, however, First Nations lost control of most of the land and its resources. While white settlers prospered, First Nations were impoverished and often forced to live in areas where land and water became badly polluted because of industrial development. Accordingly, Idle No More's manifesto asserts the inherent right of First Nations to their land and resources and it demands equitable, sustainable, and healthy development:

Idle No More demands that today's non-Indigenous Canadians confront a difficult question: To what degree should they be held responsible for injustices whose roots go back 50, 100, or 200 years? New immigrants in particular may ask why they should be expected to pay for such historic wrongs. Part of the answer is that the high standard of living and abundant opportunities that most Canadians enjoy derive ultimately from resources that were alienated from the Indigenous population with little or no compensation. Another part is that when you get married, invest in a business, or become a citizen of a country, you are entitled to enjoy the benefits of the new relationship but you must also assume some responsibility for the debts and obligations of your new partner. Idle No More asks all Canadians to live up to this simple fact of life.

Critical Thinking Questions

1. What role do social media play in mobilizing people to protest government policy?

2. Why did Idle No More capture the attention, and gain support, from many non-Indigenous Canadians?

SOURCE: Idle No More (2013).

Other conflict theorists are interested in the political and economic implications of socioeconomic differentiation within Indigenous communities. Researchers challenge the stereotype that all Indigenous people are either poor, unemployed, living on welfare, or working in low-skill, dead-end jobs. In fact, a small but significant and growing proportion of Indigenous men and women work in skilled professional and technical occupations, and others are owners or managers of small and large businesses (Gerber, 1990). Menno Boldt (1993: 124) argues that most Indian reserves are characterized by a two-class social order (see also Alfred, 1999). One class consists of "a small, virtually closed élite class comprising influential landowners, politicians, bureaucrats, and a few entrepreneurs," while the second consists of "a large lower class comprising destitute, dependent, powerless [and wage-earning] people" (Boldt, 1993: 124). Boldt argues (1993: 125) that this two-class structure has important consequences for community life and politics:

> With the élite class controlling the political agenda, lower-class interests get neglected. Elite class interests tend to be primarily "power" not "problem" oriented; that is, such interests are related to expanding their jurisdiction and control over band/tribal political and administrative structures. ... [These] are given preference over the problems that afflict the Indian lower class: high unemployment; excessive rates of family disintegration; alcohol and substance abuse; extraordinary levels of violence, suicide, incarceration, and so on.

Land-claim settlements and rising educational levels explain the growth not just of Indigenous elites but of an Indigenous middle class, too (Mitchell, 1996; Wotherspoon, 2012). In 2011, 48 percent of Indigenous Canadians between the ages of 25 and 64 had a postsecondary qualification and 10 percent had earned a university degree (Statistics Canada, 2014b). Women were nearly twice as likely as men were to have attained a university degree. These figures represent enormous progress compared to even two or three decades ago. On the other hand, 65 percent of non-Indigenous Canadians between the ages of 25 and 64 had a postsecondary qualification and 27 percent had a university degree in 2011, highlighting the long road toward equality that must yet be traversed.

TIME FOR REVIEW

1. Describe the different groups that make up Canada's Indigenous population.
2. Does the culture of poverty thesis offer a credible explanation of the socioeconomic differences between Indigenous and non-Indigenous peoples in Canada?
3. Describe class and gender differences in Indigenous communities.

QUEBEC: NATIONALISM AND IDENTITY

On the evening of October 30, 1995, many adult Canadians were tuned to TV or radio coverage of the Quebec referendum on separation. I followed the results that night with mixed emotions. On the one hand, as a second-generation Canadian with no ethnic roots in the old British Empire, I could empathize with people in Quebec. On the other hand, as a child of the Trudeau years, I was socialized to believe in a vision of Canadian unity. Many on the "no" side believed that a lot of Quebeckers were just bluffing in the pre-referendum rhetoric; when it came to the crunch, they would vote in favour of staying in Canada. Then the results came in. In some parts of Quebec, 90 percent of voters were in favour of separation. As the results from around Montreal were tabulated, the "no" side gained ground. When the final count was tallied, 49.6 percent of Quebeckers voted for separation. Across Canada, people were both exhilarated and downcast because Canada had "won."

Will the issue of separation go away? Despite the ebb and flow in support for separation, the answer is clearly "no." As with other areas of ethnic relations in Canada, an understanding of the contemporary scene must begin with an appreciation of history and of power relations. In this section, I examine three main sociological questions: (1) What is the historical basis for the emergence of Québécois nationalism? (2) Who is a Québécois? (3) What does the close 1995 vote mean for ethnic relations in Quebec and the country?

THE SOCIAL BASIS OF QUÉBÉCOIS NATIONALISM

Even though the 1867 British North America Act asserted that there were two founding peoples of Canada, the English and the French, and that they had equal places in Canadian Confederation, *les Québécois* are one of the oldest colonized peoples in the world (Milner and Milner, 1973). The French government controlled the colony of New France from the early 1600s to 1763. The inhabitants of New France were expected to serve the interests of France. The colony was established in part to pursue the fur trade and to transfer economic resources to the mother country. Much of the French commercial and political elite left the colony following the British victory over France in 1763. When New France was transferred to British control—what the Québécois refer to as "The Conquest"—a new colonizing power came to dominate the society.

An anglophone—unilingual, English-speaking—elite gradually took over the economic and political affairs of the province. Most French Canadian peasants (*habitants*) remained subsistence farmers. During the nineteenth century, some of them immigrated to the northeastern United States to work in the expanding cotton and linen mills; others moved to other provinces in Canada; and still others became part of the urban industrial working class in the province (Ramirez, 1991). By the late nineteenth century, Quebec was a province where "capital speaks English and labour speaks French" (Whitaker, 1993: 22)—a telling description of the way in which linguistic and class structures overlapped. The French Canadians in Quebec, who formed a numerical majority, were worse off than the anglophone minority in virtually every material way (Whitaker, 1993: 22).

The Catholic Church occupied a unique position as a social, political, and religious intermediary between the two groups. In addition to attending to the religious needs of its French-speaking parishioners, the Catholic Church acted as an agent of social control over French Canadian workers and farmers. The church promoted ideologies that were conservative and anti-modern. It devalued the importance of formal education for the masses, discouraged workers from forming and joining secular trade unions, encouraged married couples to have large families, and vigorously discouraged French Canadians from taking up professions or establishing businesses of their own. These ideas were not in the best material interests of French Canadian workers and farmers, but they helped ensure the survival of French Canadian culture (Latouche, 1993).

Quebec's social structure began to change quickly during the rapid industrialization stimulated by World War I. The industrial working class became a significant player on the political scene. One of the biggest changes in the 1940s and 1950s was the rise of a new francophone middle class of technical workers and professionals. The upper echelons of the corporate world, still under the control of anglophones, remained hostile to the advancement of francophones, even if they were bilingual. The new francophone middle class, therefore, faced a situation of blocked social mobility, which was partly responsible for the Quiet Revolution in Quebec.

The **Quiet Revolution** was the social, political, and cultural transformation of Quebec in the 1960s, in part because of the initiatives of this new middle class. These changes included the secularization of the educational system, reform of the civil service, growth in the provincially controlled public sector, greater involvement of the Quebec provincial government in the economic affairs of the province, and questioning of the Catholic Church's authority in all areas of life. Facing blocked mobility in the corporate world, francophones created their own economic opportunities by expanding the power of the provincial government.

Social scientists and political pundits have pored over referendum and federal and provincial election results over the past 30 years in an effort to determine which social forces are responsible for sustaining the push for sovereignty. Some see the present-day sovereignty movement as an expression of middle-class nationalism that is a continuation of the Quiet Revolution. From this perspective, separation is promoted by middle-class professionals as a way of furthering their material interests. Emboldened by the success at expanding the activities of the provincial government during the Quiet Revolution, they desire even more control over their affairs (Whitaker, 1993).

However, likening the sovereignty movement to a massive job-creation project is too simplistic. First, francophone professionals are no longer shut out of the corporate sector in Quebec. Over the past 30 years, middle-class francophones have achieved upward mobility in both the public and private sectors. Second, a diversity of class interests exists within the sovereignty movement. Many francophone professionals support sovereignty, but there is also a social democratic tradition within the movement that is trying to mobilize working people against foreign (anglophone and U.S.) capitalist domination. Their vision of a sovereign Quebec involves a reorganization of power relations between francophones and non-francophones, and between workers and capitalists. Some francophone capitalists also support the sovereignty movement (Whitaker, 1993).

Clearly, the contemporary sovereignty movement is not based on the support of only one social class. According to Fleras (2012), the nationalist movement is sustained by a broadly based desire among most francophone Quebeckers to achieve a common goal—to create the conditions that will allow them to preserve the French language and culture and *"voler de ses propres ailes"* (fly using their own wings) by acquiring the freedom to make their own decisions on everything from cultural policy to social development" (Turp, 2005: A25). Fleras argues that, rather than defining support for the sovereignty movement in class terms, it is more useful to conceptualize the movement as made up of groups who have differing views about how best to maintain their language and culture. Thus, the present-day sovereignty movement consists in part of moderates who want to strengthen Quebec's position within the federal system. This involves a new constitutional division of powers that has yet to be settled. Radical supporters, however, argue that the best way for the French language and culture to survive is for the people of Quebec to have their own state. They argue that they will always be a minority if they stay in Canada and that they will always be subject to the tyranny of the majority. As Louise Beaudoin of the Parti Québécois put it, "I want to be a majority in my own country" (Fleras, 2012: 242).

WHO IS QUÉBÉCOIS?

The population of Quebec is ethnically and linguistically heterogeneous, with 20.5 percent of the population made up of people whose mother tongue is not French: Jews, anglophones, allophones (people whose mother tongue is neither French nor English), visible minority immigrants, and Indigenous peoples (Fournier, Rosenberg, and White, 1997: 282). One of the central issues facing the nationalist movement in Quebec is the definition of a Québécois. This question cuts to the heart of ethnic relations in the province.

Benedict Anderson (1983) regards nations as "imagined communities." They are imagined in the sense that, even though members of the smallest nation can never know everyone in the community, there is still a common feeling of fellowship with others in the nation. People in Shawinigan do not know all other Quebeckers, but they have a comradeship that

extends beyond personal relationships. Nations also possess physical and symbolic boundaries that define who is a member and who is not. Sociologists interested in nationalism want to identify the symbolic boundaries of the nation. In the case of the nationalist movement in Quebec, this issue is translated into the question of who is "in" and who is "outside" the imagined community. And if some groups are "out," will they ever be accepted as Québécois?

Most nationalists define the imagined community as all people who now live in the province of Quebec. For them, the social and symbolic boundaries of the nation correspond to present-day provincial boundaries. Sociologists call this a form of **civic nationalism** (Balthazar, 1993).

A minority of nationalists reject civic nationalism in favour of cultural and linguistic criteria for membership in the nation. *Ethnic nationalists* define the Québécois as people who share a common history, culture, ancestry, or language. This is where the concept of *pure laine* ("pure wool") Québécois becomes important. Some nationalists regard the true Québécois as only those who are the direct descendants of the French people who settled in the colony of New France before the conquest of 1763. Other groups in the province are regarded as "cultural communities" (Groupe de recherche ethnicité et societé, 1997: 107). According to the province's policy of interculturalism, these cultural communities must learn to accommodate themselves to the dominant francophone culture and language.

The debate about how to define a nation is not academic hairsplitting. Then-premier Jacques Parizeau commented on referendum night in 1995 that the pro-sovereignty forces were defeated by "money and the ethnic vote." After his resignation, Parizeau commented further that it was the first time in Canadian history that the majority (60 percent) of francophone Quebeckers voted in favour of sovereignty. These statements implied that ethnic minorities were not really part of the nation and that *pure laine* votes should be worth more than the votes of others. At the time, Parizeau's remarks also confirmed the worst fears of ethnic minorities—namely, that sovereigntists are not civic nationalists but rather ethnic nationalists at heart and that ethnic minorities will never be considered full and equal citizens in a sovereign Quebec (Ha, 1995).

Many people in the sovereignty movement distanced themselves from Parizeau's comments, and the movement has sought to repair the damage that they caused to ethnic relations. Yet a poll conducted in 2015 indicated that just more than a third of Quebeckers would vote in favour of sovereignty in a new referendum (Presse Canadienne, 2015). A possible reason for the persistent, substantial support for sovereignty is that the "children of Bill 101" are coming of age. Bill 101 was enacted in 1977 and requires that the children of immigrants attend francophone schools. Immigrant children educated in francophone schools are now entering the political arena and many believe that their interests would be better served in an independent Quebec (Laforest, 2005: A25; Turp, 2005: A25).

Even though some of the children of immigrants may be buying into the sovereignty movement, the nature of Quebec identity continues to be hotly debated. In 2007, the government of Quebec established the Consultation Commission on Accommodation Practices Related to Cultural Differences to investigate public discontent over the nature of change in Quebec society occurring as a result of immigration and increasing cultural and religious diversity. The "Reasonable Accommodation Commission," as it came to be known, held public forums around the province. Quebeckers from all walks of life participated in these forums. Some embraced the new diversity and called for renewed effort to welcome newcomers and ethno-religious communities. Others expressed anxiety over the future of Quebec's core secular values and the status of the French language and French culture in North America (Bouchard and Taylor, 2008: 37). As Commissioners Gerard Bouchard and Charles Taylor suggested:

> The main danger we are facing is that the groups that make up our society combine their mistrust and (largely unfounded) reciprocal fears and thus jeopardize the *rapprochement* process now under way. In other words, there is a risk that our imaginary fears will engender a genuine danger. We are thinking, in particular, of the still fragile Quebec identity that has taken shape in recent decades and continues to grow despite our differences, or more precisely, from our differences. Moreover, and quite rightly, it is abundantly but freely sustained by the French-Canadian heritage, a very rich heritage that is thus enjoying a new life not by closing in on itself but by opening up the creative, fruitful contribution of the Other. This is precisely what it has done repeatedly in the past. In short, it is the future of the Quebec nation that is at stake here. (Bouchard and Taylor, 2008: 242)

Quebeckers, and Canadians more generally, intently followed the work of the Reasonable Accommodation Commission. In 2014, the debate about Quebec's identity was rekindled when the governing Parti Québécois pushed for the establishment of a "Charter of Quebec Values," which advocated, among other things, a ban on wearing "conspicuous" religious symbols, such as headscarves, by government employees. The PQ lost the 2014 election and the Charter issue has been dropped. However, as Augie Fleras (2012: 234) puts it, "Quebec must strike a balance between securing its future identity as a francophone and secular-liberal society with remaining a welcoming community for ethno-religious minorities." Although less politicized, the rest of Canada also faces a balancing act between maintaining "Canadian" values and identity and becoming a more hospitable place for newcomers.

TIME FOR REVIEW

1. What was the Quiet Revolution in Quebec?
2. Is the sovereignty movement in Quebec based on ethnic or civic nationalism?
3. How can Quebecers strike a balance between (a) protecting their unique French language and culture and (b) creating a welcoming society for immigrants and ethno-religious communities?

IMMIGRATION: STATE FORMATION AND ECONOMIC DEVELOPMENT

The third aspect of ethnic and racial relations in Canada that I consider is immigrant/nonimmigrant relations. In 2011, 6.8 million immigrants were living in Canada, representing 20.6 percent of the population. In large cities, the impact of immigration is even greater. In 2011, immigrants made up 22.6 percent of the population of Montreal, 26.2 percent of the population of Calgary, 39.6 percent of the population of Vancouver, and 46 percent of the population of Toronto (Statistics Canada, 2011). Canada accepts more immigrants and refugees in proportion to our population than any other country in the world apart from Australia and Israel (Li, 2003).

Migration has been a feature of our history for more than 300 years. However, the nature, sources, determinants, and consequences of immigration have varied through history. In the nineteenth century, immigrants contributed to the processes of capitalist state formation—the process of creating a capitalist system of production and governance. They did this in a number of ways. The early working class in Canada was made up largely of immigrants (Avery, 1995; Pentland, 1981). Immigrant workers helped build the canals, railways, and roads that became part of our economic infrastructure. Many nineteenth-century immigrants were farmers. Their crops were used to feed Canadian workers and, as productivity increased, were exported to feed people in other countries. Those farmers helped to stimulate capitalist industry through their roles as consumers of goods. A significant proportion of the corporate elite in nineteenth-century Canada was made up of immigrants (Clement, 1975; Macmillan, 1985), as was a large segment of the early political elite. Canada's first prime minister, Sir John A. Macdonald, was an immigrant from Glasgow, Scotland.

Immigrants continue to make important contributions to Canadian society. Demographers note that, after 1991, without new immigrants, the population of Canada would have begun to decline in 2015. Without new immigrants to replenish our population, the next generation of taxpayers would have to pay far more in taxes and Canada Pension Plan contributions. Retiring at the age of 55, or even 65, would become a pipe dream for many older workers, as employers and governments would need to take steps to retain enough workers. Employers would face serious shortages of workers, and manufacturers would face a smaller consumer market in which to sell their goods (Economic Council of Canada, 1991).

FACTORS THAT SHAPE CANADIAN IMMIGRATION

No single variable can explain the complex pattern of immigration to Canada. Over the past 100 years, six main variables have influenced which groups of people have been let into the country as immigrants.

The most important factor is the perceived economic value of certain occupational groups of immigrants. Most immigrants are admitted to Canada because they fill job vacancies, have certain skills that are in demand, or because they create jobs for other Canadians. Indeed, one of the central objectives of Canadian immigration policy is to contribute to the country's prosperity. As such, the flow of immigrants to Canada has been closely linked to the structure of the Canadian economy. Between 1947 and the early 1960s, for example, immigrants

were regarded by the Canadian government as "factory fodder" (Collins, 1988). Immigrants were recruited to fill unskilled and semiskilled manual jobs in agriculture, construction, mining, logging, the garment industry, and heavy manufacturing. During this time, it was common for individual employers to demand that the government recruit as many as 300 immigrant workers at a time to fill job openings (Avery, 1995).

In the early 1960s, immigration policy began to place more emphasis on the recruitment of highly skilled professional and technical workers, and on immigrants with large amounts of investment capital. Canada still wants highly skilled workers, but it also admits large numbers of unskilled workers for jobs that Canadians do not want to do.

The second determinant of immigration is ethnic and racial **stereotypes**—exaggerated, oversimplified images of the characteristics of social groups. Before 1962, Canadian immigration policy had a racialized hierarchy of desirability. Immigration policy was based on the assumption that European immigrants were racially and culturally superior to all other potential immigrants. Non-Europeans were stereotyped as racially and culturally inferior and, therefore, were not welcome. In the 1950s, for example, immigration officials could bar groups from entering Canada on the grounds that the groups were "unsuited to climatic and economic conditions" or that they were "unable to assimilate" (Bolaria and Li, 1988). These phrases were thinly veiled excuses for racial preferences in the selection of immigrants.

Since 1962, ethnic and racial stereotyping in selecting new immigrants has become less important. Canadian immigration policy is now more open in terms of the ethnic and racial origins of immigrants (see Table 9.1). Thus, until 1962, Europeans made up more than 90 percent of immigrants to Canada. Now, immigrants from Europe make up about 14 percent of the yearly intake.

The third variable that shapes immigrant selection consists of a variety of geopolitical considerations stemming from Canada's relationships with other countries. Racist selection criteria were taken out of immigration regulations in the 1960s, in part because they interfered with Canadian international diplomacy. In the early 1960s, Canada began to assert itself as a middle power in world politics that could mediate social conflicts in and between other countries. Outside of Europe, though, our

TABLE 9.1 TOP 10 SOURCE COUNTRIES OF CANADIAN IMMIGRANTS, 1966 AND 2013

1966		2013	
COUNTRY	NUMBER	COUNTRY	NUMBER
United Kingdom	63 291	China	33 908
Italy	31 625	India	30 576
United States	17 514	Philippines	27 292
Germany	9 263	Pakistan	11 354
Portugal	7 930	United States	10 625
France	7 872	Iran	10 035
Greece	7 174	France	7 148
The Netherlands	3 749	United Kingdom	5 935
Australia	3 329	South Korea	4 450
Switzerland	2 982	United Arab Emirates	4 093

SOURCES: Manpower and Immigration. (1967: 5); HER MAJESTY THE QUEEN IN RIGHT OF CANADA (as represented by the Department of Citizenship and Immigration Canada).

diplomats did not have much credibility because our immigration policy implied that certain groups were inferior and therefore not suited to life in Canada (Hawkins, 1989).

In the 1980s, the Cold War also played a role in shaping who was let in. According to Whitaker (1987), a double standard was at work in the admission of refugees. People who managed to escape from the Soviet Union or other Eastern Bloc countries were routinely granted refugee status in Canada. In 1985, for example, it took a day for the brother of a Czech hockey star who played for the Toronto Maple Leafs to be granted refugee status. Canadian immigration bureaucrats were much more cautious, however, about admitting "socialist" refugees who were fleeing right-wing dictatorships in various Central American countries. More recently, in the context of the U.S.-led war in Iraq, Canada agreed to accept several thousand Iraqi refugees as a way of helping the American government manage tensions in the Middle East.

The fourth variable affecting immigrant selection is humanitarianism. Canada accepts immigrants and refugees partly on humanitarian and compassionate grounds. In 1986, Canada was the first country to be awarded the Nansen Medal by the United Nations for its generosity and commitment to international refugee programs (Fleras, 2012).

The influence of the fifth variable, public opinion, is more difficult to determine, in part because Canadians do not speak with one voice regarding immigration (Wilkes, Guppy, and Farris, 2008). A 1991 poll found five distinct segments of opinion regarding immigration. Twenty-three percent were "protagonists" who supported increased levels of immigration and believed that immigrants made important contributions to the betterment of Canadian society; 22 percent were "concerned supporters" who approved of current levels of immigration but who were concerned that immigration had certain negative effects on Canadian institutions; 21 percent were "indifferent" in their attitudes toward immigration and ambivalent about the contributions that immigrants make; and 19 percent were "reactionaries" who felt that the government has lost control over immigration and that immigration was largely negative for Canada. The size of the last segment seems to increase when cases of people who appear to be abusing the immigration system come to light. This happened during the summer of 1999, when four boatloads of what appeared to be economic migrants from China were dumped on the Vancouver Island coastline. The remaining 15 percent of Canadians in the poll had no opinion on immigration (Holton and Lanphier, 1994).

The sixth variable, security considerations, has become more important since the terrorist attacks on the United States on September 11, 2001. In the aftermath of the attacks, Canada introduced a new Permanent Resident Card and a number of new measures to increase security at Canadian borders. In addition, Canada and the United States are increasingly discussing the harmonization of immigration policies, particularly in the area of security screening of immigrants and refugees. Some commentators refer to this harmonization as a move toward a "Fortress North America" (Satzewich and Wong, 2003).

CONTEMPORARY IMMIGRATION CATEGORIES

Immigrants in Canada fit into one of three main categories: refugees, family class, and economic immigrants. Altogether, 258 953 immigrants entered Canada in 2013.

Refugees

More than 28 000 refugees and their dependants were admitted to Canada in 2013. There are three categories of refugees that Canada accepts through its immigration program. *Convention refugees* are people who are defined as refugees by the 1951 Geneva Convention Relating to the Status of Refugees and its 1967 protocol. They are people who, by reason of their race, religion, nationality, membership in a particular social group, or political opinion, live outside of their country of nationality or their country of habitual residence and who are unable or unwilling, because of fear of persecution, to return to their country of origin (Citizenship and Immigration Canada, 1996: 28).

Country of asylum class refugees are people who are outside their country of citizenship or residence who are seriously and personally affected by civil war, armed conflict, or massive violations of human rights. Finally, *source country class* refugees include people who would meet the definition of a Convention refugee but who are still in their country of citizenship or residence. This category also includes people who have been detained or imprisoned and are suffering serious deprivations of the right of freedom of expression, the right of dissent, or the right to engage in trade union activity.

Family Class Immigrants

Nearly 82 000 *family class immigrants* arrived in Canada in 2013. Family class immigrants have close family members already living in Canada who are willing and able to support them. A sponsor must be a Canadian citizen or a permanent resident who is over 18 years of age and who is living in Canada. Depending on the circumstances, a sponsor must be able to provide for the lodging, care, maintenance, and normal settlement needs of the family member(s) for between three and ten years (Citizenship and Immigration Canada, 2002).

Economic Immigrants

Economic immigrants numbered about 148 000 in 2013. The government recently increased the size of this category in total immigration flows and decreased the number of family class immigrants because it believes that the former are of greater economic benefit to Canada. There are six subcategories of independent immigrants. *Skilled workers* have to either have an offer of employment from an employer in Canada or be a skilled worker with one year of continuous full-time paid work experience in an occupation that is deemed to be short of Canadian-born workers by the Minister of Citizenship and Immigration. The occupations on the list of eligible occupations included architects, dentists, dental hygienists, nurses, cooks, plumbers, and crane operators. Skilled workers are also assessed on the basis of merit as measured by the **points system**.

As Table 9.2 shows, applicants are awarded points for various attributes that the Canadian government deems important in determining an immigrant's economic and settlement prospects. An applicant has to earn a minimum of 67 out of 100 points to "pass" and potentially gain

TABLE 9.2 THE POINTS SYSTEM FOR THE SELECTION OF SKILLED WORKERS AND PROFESSIONALS, CANADA, 2015

CRITERIA	MAXIMUM POINTS
Proficiency in English and/ or French	28 points
Education	25 points
Work experience	15 points
Age	12 points
Arranged employment in Canada	10 points
Adaptability	10 points
Pass Mark	**67 points**

SOURCE: HER MAJESTY THE QUEEN IN RIGHT OF CANADA (as represented by the Department of Citizenship and Immigration Canada).

CRITICAL SOCIOLOGY: GLOBALIZATION   TRANSNATIONAL ETHNICITY

Sociological research demonstrates that second-generation Indo-Canadians are strongly attached to Canada while maintaining contact with, and loyalty to, India (Somerville, 2008). Their ethnic identity is "transnational" in the sense that it spans two countries.

Even 50 years ago, immigrants were more or less cut off from their homeland apart from occasional letters, infrequent and expensive phone calls, and rare and costly trips back home for special family occasions. Lack of contact encouraged ethnic assimilation in the second generation. In contrast, transnational ethnic identity—not just among Indo-Canadians, but among all immigrant groups—is made possible today by the Internet, cellphones, cable TV, and international travel, all of which have become widely affordable. These technologies allow second-generation Canadians to interact almost daily with relatives in their parents' homeland and to gain easy access to its living and breathing language and culture. These connections influence the ethnic identity of second-generation immigrants and are reflected in their emotional attachments, clothing choices, language use, and much else. One

respondent from the Toronto research on Indo-Canadians put it this way:

> Anything that makes me feel more Canadian is kind of Canadian cultural things like ... hockey and watching hockey with other Canadians. ... But there are definitely times I feel more Indian, like ... if I am in a temple I would absolutely feel more Indian. ... But there are times I feel a blend of [Indian and Canadian], like when I am at home with my family I feel a blend because at the end of the day I am both, and I don't think you have to be one or the other.

Critical Thinking Questions

1. Do ties to their country of origin deter newcomers from integrating into Canadian society?

2. How might transnational ties facilitate social integration into Canada?

3. How does multicultural policy encourage immigrants and their children to maintain ties to their ancestral homeland?

SOURCE: Based on Kara Somerville, "Transnational Belonging among Second Generation Youth: Identity in a Globalized World," *Journal of Social Sciences,* Special Volume, no. 10: 23–33. 2008.

admission to Canada as a skilled worker. The amount of money immigrants need to have when they arrive in Canada depends on the number of people in their family. For example, an immigrant who brings three family members to Canada needs to have $20 654.

Immigrant investors are capitalists who have a personal net worth of at least $1.6 million and who plan to invest at least $800 000 in Canada. *Self-employed immigrants* must have the intention and ability to create their own employment. They are expected to contribute to the cultural or artistic life of the country. They can also qualify under this program if they purchase and manage a farm in Canada.

Provincial Nominees and the Canadian Experience Class

Provincial nominees and the *Canadian experience class* are recently established fourth and fifth categories. Provinces may fast-track individuals for admission to Canada based on specific provincial labour shortages. The Canadian experience class allows temporary workers and international students who have studied in Canada to apply for permanent

residency. *Live-in caregivers*, the sixth category, are admitted as housekeepers and nannies, mainly for upper-middle-class and wealthy families.

TIME FOR REVIEW

1. To what extent did ethnic and racial stereotypes shape Canadian immigration policy? To what degree do they continue to do so today?

2. What are the main features of Canadian immigration policy?

3. What characteristics does the points system emphasize? Why?

ETHNIC INEQUALITY AND THE CANADIAN LABOUR MARKET
JOHN PORTER AND THE VERTICAL MOSAIC

What happens to immigrants after they come to Canada? How are they sorted and placed in the socioeconomic structure? John Porter's answers to these questions in *The Vertical Mosaic* (1965) have had a profound impact on Canadian sociology. Since the book's publication, Canadian sociologists have been interested in whether ethnicity and race affect the operation of the labour market, social mobility, and the composition of elites.

Porter argued that Canada is a **vertical mosaic,** a society in which ethnic groups tend to occupy different and unequal positions in the stratification system. He called the first ethnic group to take control of a previously unoccupied or newly conquered territory the *charter group* of that society. One prerogative that goes to a charter group is the ability to decide "what other groups are to be let in and what they will be permitted to do" (Porter, 1965: 62). Canada has two charter groups, the English and the French. Although their power was, and is, unequal, Porter argued that the two charter groups have been able to set the terms by which other immigrants are admitted to Canada. These charter groups reserved for themselves the top positions in the occupational hierarchy. They also made up the upper ranks of the labour, political, bureaucratic, religious, and media elites.

Immigrants who arrived after these charter groups were assigned to less preferred positions. Non-English and non-French immigrants were assigned an entrance status that was linked in part to the social evaluation of their cultural and racial capacities. Groups from Northern and Western Europe were considered more racially and culturally like the English and French, and were accorded a higher entrance status than Southern and Eastern European immigrants were. The latter were regarded as culturally, if not racially, inferior to the charter groups and were therefore placed in lower levels of the occupational hierarchy and excluded from elite positions. Non-Europeans were defined as unable to assimilate and were virtually barred from entry (Woodsworth, 1972).

Porter argued that once the vertical mosaic was established, it took on a life of its own. Immigrants and their descendants who were initially allocated a subordinate entrance status faced limited prospects for upward social mobility. He thought two factors accounted for the rigidity of the vertical mosaic. One was blatant prejudice and discrimination by charter groups. The other was the retention by ethnic groups of cultural practices that were incompatible with economic success in modern, industrialized societies. In other words, certain immigrants and their descendants were caught in an *ethnic mobility*

trap because of their continued identification with a subordinated and marginalized ethnic group (Wiley, 1967).

In the context of its time, Porter's analysis was powerful and insightful. As we have seen, before 1962, the selection of new immigrants was based on ethnic and racial stereotypes. These stereotypes also shaped charter group perceptions of what kinds of jobs immigrants were fit to do. In the 1950s, for example, Italian immigrant men were regarded by immigration bureaucrats and members of the economic elite as culturally willing and able to "tolerate irregular employment, low wages and physically demanding work." They were recruited specifically for work in agriculture, mining, domestic service, the metal trades, and logging (Iacovetta, 1992: 28). Black women from the Caribbean were recruited specifically as housekeepers and nannies for middle-class families in the 1950s and 1960s, in part because they were believed to be nurturing and passive (Daenzer, 1993).

THE DECLINING SIGNIFICANCE OF THE VERTICAL MOSAIC

Does the vertical mosaic still exist? Is the distribution of economic rewards still based on ethnicity? Since the 1970s, debates have raged among Canadian sociologists about whether race and ethnicity continue to shape our stratification system (Brym with Fox, 1989). Gordon Darroch (1979) and Edward Herberg (1990) argue that the vertical mosaic is no longer a useful way of describing our society. Later in his life, John Porter also had doubts about its relevance (Pineo and Porter, 1985). Other scholars argue that, although we may be moving in the direction of greater equality, the vertical mosaic is still a useful metaphor for describing our society. Some analysts suggest that the vertical mosaic has been recast along racial lines (Fleras, 2012); others argue that immigration status is the key to understanding patterns of inequality within the "new vertical mosaic" (Nakhaie, 2006).

What is the evidence for the view that "race" (visible minority status) and/or immigration status constitute fundamental dividing lines in Canadian society? One way to answer this question is to compare the earnings of visible minorities with the earnings of those who are not visible minorities.

One sociologist analyzed census data to determine whether race made a difference in how much university

FIGURE 9.4 ANNUAL EARNINGS OF CANADIAN MALE UNIVERSITY PROFESSORS BY RACE

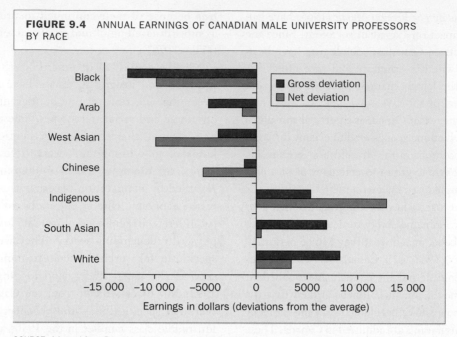

Earnings in dollars (deviations from the average)

SOURCE: Adapted from Peter Li, "Differences in Employment Income of University Professors," *Canadian Ethnic Studies* 44 (2): 39–48. 2012.

professors earned in 2006 (Li, 2012). Figure 9.4 summarizes some of his findings. Pay attention first to the red bars, which show the amount by which group earnings deviated from the average earnings of all male professors. Black professors earned $12 712 less than the average. Arab professors earned $4723 less. White professors earned $8243 *more* than the average. Surprisingly, Indigenous professors earned $5340 more.

Many factors other than race may account for deviations from average earnings. Earnings are correlated with age, and some groups may be older than others on average. Earnings are also correlated with province of residence, holding a Ph.D., field of study, and immigrant status, and some groups may be distributed among these variables in a way that gives them higher or lower earnings. What happens to earnings when groups are statistically matched in terms of all these variables—when, for example, we compare white and black male professors of the same age, residing in the same province, specializing in the same field of study, and so on? The answer lies in the blue bars in Figure 9.4. They depict "net differences" in earnings, or differences that remain after groups are matched by all of the variables just listed.

Focusing on net differences, we see that West Asian and black professors still earn nearly

$10 000 a year less than the average. White professors earn $3431 *above* the average. Again surprisingly, Indigenous professors earn fully $12 861 above the average. Arguably, the net differences indicate the level of discrimination or of advantage associated with membership in various racial groups for male Canadian professors.

Two words of caution are in order. First, earnings of university professors are based partly on their productivity as measured by the quantity and quality of their publications, teaching, and administrative contributions. Census data for these characteristics do not exist, yet they may account in part for remaining group differences. Second, and more importantly, many people face enormous barriers on the road to attaining a higher education. They drop out before obtaining a postgraduate degree and becoming a university professor. Analyzing earnings of university professors ignores members of racial groups who faced poverty, discrimination, and other impediments that prevented them from making it into the ivory tower in the first place. Indigenous Canadians comprise more than 4 percent of male Canadians but just 0.6 percent of male Canadian professors. Those who become professors earn exceptionally high incomes, but very few of them become professors because of poverty, discrimination, and so on. Clearly, we need a lot more research on different occupations, on the labour force as a whole, on specific racial groups, and on men and women separately before we gain a clear picture of racial stratification in Canada.

Unfortunately, much of the research conducted on racial stratification to date deals with broad racial categories like "visible minority" and "white," which are actually made up of diverse groups of people. "Visible minority" Canadians have different immigration histories, histories of settlement, and times of arrival in Canada, so some do better economically in Canada than others do. Furthermore, when looking only at those born in Canada, some "visible minority" groups do as well as, or better than, their white counterparts. For example, Canadian-born Chinese and South Asian-origin men and women in the public sector, and South Asian and Chinese women in the private sector, do as well as or better than comparable Canadian-born white men and women (Hou and Coulombe, 2010).

Notwithstanding these cautions, the vertical mosaic metaphor seems to describe accurately the position of many visible minority immigrants, who are struggling with higher rates of poverty and unemployment, and lower earnings, than their white immigrant counterparts and Canadian-born members of visible minority groups (Fleras, 2012: 139–44).

Some sociologists have explained overall earnings differences between visible minority and white immigrants by examining immigrant credentials. They suggest that the education credentials of visible minority immigrants are often devalued by the labour market and certification authorities. In one celebrated case, an evaluation officer of the Ontario Ministry of Education wrote to a Jamaican immigrant that his honours degree from Harvard University and his Ph.D. from Stanford were equivalent to "at least Grade Thirteen in the Ontario school system" (Special Committee, 1984). Although this case may have been a bureaucratic error, evidence shows that many immigrant teachers, doctors, nurses, and engineers find that their non-Western university degrees and diplomas are of little value in Canada (see the Critical Sociology: Social Inequality box). Some analysts say that the devaluation of credentials is a reflection of racism in Canadian society. Others emphasize the lack of adequate certification authorities in the country. Both groups hope that, as visible minority immigrants spend more time in the country, their economic success will increase (Basran and Zong, 1998; Henry and Tator, 2006; Reitz, 2011).

Other research on hiring practices documents the influence of racial discrimination. Henry and Ginsberg (1985) sent two groups of actors with virtually identical résumés to apply for various jobs. The only difference between members of the two groups was the colour of their skin or their accent: One group consisted of actors who were white and who had Anglo-Canadian accents, and the other group consisted of visible minority group members, some of whom had non-Anglo-Canadian accents. The researchers found that, in both face-to-face interviews and approaches over the telephone, whites received three job offers for every job offered to applicants from visible minority groups. Applicants from visible minority groups were five times as likely to be told that the job had been filled when a subsequent white applicant was invited for an interview (Henry and Ginsberg, 1985).

A follow-up study showed no racial discrimination in job offers following face-to-face contacts between applicants and employers. Blacks and whites received equal numbers of job offers. When it came to approaches over the telephone, however, callers with foreign accents were less likely to be invited for an interview and more likely to be told that the job was filled when, in fact, it was not (Henry, 1989). A more recent study suggests that having an "ethnic-sounding" name affects the hunt for jobs. Employers in Toronto, Montreal, and Vancouver are about 40 percent more likely to interview applicants for jobs with English-sounding names than someone with a "foreign-sounding" name, even when they have the same credentials (Immen, 2011: B12; Oreopoulos and Dechief, 2011).

TIME FOR REVIEW

1. What is the difference between John Porter's concepts of "charter group" status and "entrance group" status?
2. Are some immigrant groups in Canada today caught in an "ethnic mobility trap"?
3. Does discrimination by mainstream society or the different cultures and values that immigrants bring with them explain why some groups do better economically in Canadian society than others do?

Evidence from a Statistics Canada study shows that a sizable proportion of immigrants who drive taxis in Canada are significantly overqualified (Xu, 2012). About half the taxi drivers in the country are immigrants. Although taxi driving normally requires a secondary school degree and/or occupation-specific training, many immigrants have bachelor's, master's, doctoral, or medical degrees. Of the 255 taxi drivers who had a Ph.D. or medical degree in Canada in 2006, nearly 80 percent were immigrants. Of the 1525 taxi drivers with a master's degree, nearly 90 percent were immigrants.

Figure 9.5 shows the differences in educational attainment of immigrant and Canadian-born taxi drivers. These statistics provide striking evidence of the difficulties that highly educated immigrants have in making inroads in the Canadian labour market.

Critical Thinking Questions

1. Does the existence of overeducated taxi drivers among immigrants reflect racial discrimination in the broader labour market in Canada?

2. How can Canadian society improve the way it evaluates the educational credentials of immigrants to Canada?

FIGURE 9.5 IMMIGRANTS AND CANADIAN-BORN TAXI DRIVERS BY HIGHEST EDUCATIONAL ATTAINMENT

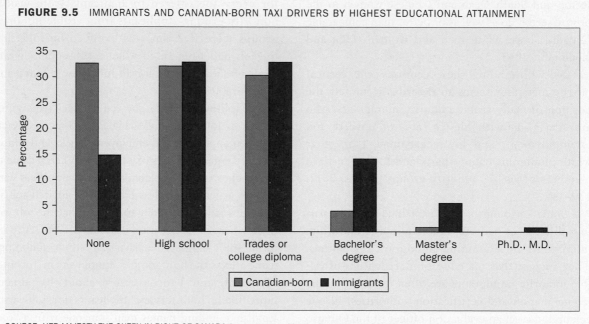

SOURCE: HER MAJESTY THE QUEEN IN RIGHT OF CANADA (as represented by the Department of Citizenship and Immigration Canada);

SUMMARY

1. **What is racism?**
   Racism involves ideas and practices that discriminate against members of groups that are perceived as racially distinct. *Institutional racism* refers to circumstances in which social institutions operate, intentionally or otherwise, based on racist ideas.

2. **What are the main sociological perspectives that explain patterns of race and ethnic relations?**
   Social-psychological theories focus on how prejudice—an unfavourable, generalized, and rigid belief that is applied to all members of a group—and racism satisfy the psychic needs of certain people. Primordialism argues that ethnic and racial attachments reflect an innate tendency for people to seek out, and associate with, others who are similar in terms of language, culture, beliefs, ancestry, and appearance. Normative theories concentrate on the way in which prejudices are transmitted through socialization and the social circumstances that encourage discriminatory behaviour. Power-conflict theories explain how prejudicial ideas, attitudes, and practices arise in the first place—due to split labour markets, for example.

3. **Who makes up Canada's Indigenous population?**
The term "Indigenous peoples" includes people who are defined by the Constitution as "Indian," "Métis," and "Inuit." The terms used to describe Indigenous peoples are socially negotiated; they change because of shifts in power relations among groups.

4. **What are the sociological perspectives used to explain socioeconomic inequalities between Indigenous and non-Indigenous Canadians?**
The culture of poverty thesis explains the disadvantaged socioeconomic conditions of Indigenous people as the product of their values. Because sociologists came to recognize that values were typically a product of socioeconomic conditions rather than vice versa, they developed the internal colonial theory, which is a variant of conflict theory. Increasingly, conflict and feminist sociologists are interested in class and gender diversity within the Indigenous population.

5. **What is the difference between civic and ethnic nationalism and how is this distinction relevant to understanding contemporary Quebec?**
Economic inequalities between French and English in Quebec formed the historical basis for the emergence of Quebec nationalism. Since the mid-1960s, tension has developed between nationalists who imagine Quebec as a homogeneous ethnic community (ethnic nationalists) and nationalists who include everyone living in Quebec, regardless of ethnicity or language, as a member of the Québécois nation (civic nationalists).

6. **What are the main social forces that have shaped Canadian immigration policy?**
Immigrants contributed significantly to the formation of Canada and continue to do so. Sociologists have identified six main factors that have shaped immigrant selection in Canada: the perceived economic value of certain occupational groups of immigrants, the application of ethnic and racial stereotypes, geopolitical considerations, humanitarianism, public opinion, and security considerations. Most sociologists agree that ethnic and racial stereotypes now play less of a role in shaping immigration policy than they did before the early 1960s.

7. **What did John Porter mean when he argued that Canada was a vertical mosaic?**
John Porter described Canada as a social structure in which ethnic groups occupy different positions within the stratification system. Evidence suggests that the vertical mosaic is declining in importance, at least for European immigrants and people born in Canada. However, many sociologists argue that it has been replaced by a vertical mosaic based on race.

QUESTIONS TO CONSIDER

1. To what extent do racist attitudes and behaviour affect the life-chances of different groups of Canadians?

2. What obligations, if any, do societies have to accommodate themselves to ethno-religious diversity?

3. Do you think that the importance of class and gender diversity within Indigenous communities will increase or decrease in the future? Why?

GLOSSARY

Civic nationalism (p. 211) is a form of nationalism in which the social boundaries of the nation are defined in territorial and geographic terms.

The **culture of poverty thesis** (p. 207) holds that some ethnic groups do not readily assimilate and hence are poor because their cultures do not value economic success, hard work, and achievement.

Discrimination (p. 203) refers to practices that deny members of particular groups equal access to societal rewards.

Institutional racism (p. 201) refers to discriminatory racial practices built into the political, economic, and education systems.

New racism (p. 200) is a theory that suggests that it is natural for groups to form bounded communities. One group is neither better nor worse than another, but feelings of antagonism will arise if outsiders are admitted into a group.

Normative theories of ethnic and racial prejudice (p. 203) focus on the way in which prejudices are transmitted through socialization and the social circumstances that encourage discriminatory behaviour.

The **points system** (p. 215) is used by the Canadian government to select independent immigrants. Applicants are awarded points for various attributes that the Canadian government deems important in determining an immigrant's potential economic contribution to Canada.

Power-conflict theories of ethnic and racial prejudice (p. 204) explain how prejudicial ideas, attitudes, and practices originate.

Prejudice (p. 202) is an unfavourable, generalized, and rigid belief applied to all members of a group.

Primordialist theory (p. 203) argues that ethnic attachments reflect a basic tendency of people to seek out, and associate with, their "own kind."

The **Quiet Revolution** (p. 210) refers to the social, political, and cultural modernization of Quebec in the 1960s, in part because of the emergence of a large francophone middle class.

Race (p. 199) is a socially constructed label that has been used to describe certain kinds of physical differences between people.

Social-psychological theories of race and ethnic relations (p. 202) focus on how prejudice and racism satisfy the psychic needs of certain people.

The **split labour market theory** (p. 204) holds that racial and ethnic conflicts are rooted in differences in the price of labour.

Stereotypes (p. 213) are exaggerated, oversimplified images of the characteristics of social categories.

The **vertical mosaic** (p. 217) is a social structure in which ethnic groups occupy different and unequal positions in the stratification system.

CHAPTER 10

DEVELOPMENT AND UNDERDEVELOPMENT

Anthony Winson
UNIVERSITY OF GUELPH

HAIL, BRITANNIA!
(OPENING OF THE COLONIAL EXHIBITION, MAY 4.)

SOURCE: Reproduced with permission of Punch Ltd., www.punch.co.uk.

AFTER READING THIS CHAPTER, YOU WILL BE ABLE TO:

- Identify different meanings of *development* and *underdevelopment*.

- Appreciate that global inequalities are staggering and are wider than once believed.

- Compare and contrast different explanations for why countries are more or less developed.

- List the factors that have allowed the rapid development of a few formerly poor countries and the reasons why such development is typically accompanied by steep social and environmental costs.

- Explain how military aggression, often sponsored by developed countries, has negatively influenced development in many poor countries.

COMMONSENSE THEORIES OF DEVELOPMENT

Many people entertain pet theories or working hypotheses about why some parts of the world are poor and others are rich. A personal example may help illustrate this point. My parents lived for several years in countries that were poor by Canadian standards, and my mother held a theory that was popular at the time. She told me about living in a small South American jungle mining camp in what was then the colony of British Guiana and commented that "if you had lived in that heat and humidity you would know why they are so poor." It was perhaps not surprising that a young woman who had lived through 20 Saskatchewan winters would find the tropics an obstacle to productive activity. It was just common sense to her that the climate explained why British Guiana was underdeveloped.

Decades later, my experiences and observations in Mexico and Central America challenged my mother's views. I confronted the architectural evidence of a wealthy colonial past and the archaeological wealth of complex indigenous civilizations that predated the invasion of Europeans. Excavations in Mexico City had just unearthed evidence of the rich city–state of Tenotitchlán that existed when Hernán Cortés and his Spanish soldier adventurers arrived on horseback from the Atlantic Coast in 1519. Just to the north lay the pyramids of Teotihuacán, structures that dwarf the fabled pyramids of Egypt. This city–state reached its peak between 500 and 600 CE, encompassed 21 square kilometres, and had a population 10 times larger than that of contemporary London (Waldman, 2005).

To the south, I encountered the imposing ancient hilltop city of Monte Alban near present-day Oaxaca City and evidence of several other precolonial settlements of considerable size and development along the highway leading farther south into the mountains of the mist-shrouded Lacandon forest in the Mexican state of Chiapas that borders Guatemala. In the lowland regions of this zone, I came across some of the most impressive archaeological finds in the Western Hemisphere, relics of the extensive Mayan civilizations that existed from approximately 50 BCE to 1000 CE. Over time, the Mayans constructed a series of cities that boasted ornate architecture, elaborate irrigation infrastructure and palatial structures for their nobility, and massive platforms to accommodate elaborate religious rituals. Between 600 and 800 CE, this civilization reached the highest development of its arts and sciences. By then, the Mayans had invented an elaborate system of hieroglyphic writing, a complex calendar for predicting the seasons, accurate computations of time, and detailed astronomical observations. All of this 1500 years ago in the midst of a part of the world notable for its heat and humidity. So much for my mother's climate theory of development.

Climate is not completely insignificant in understanding the origins and development of human civilizations. Regions with year-round permafrost or great deserts do not allow dense human settlement and the agriculture it depends on, let alone the accumulation of wealth. Or at least they did not in the past. Today, as the example of the desert kingdom of Dubai shows, oil wealth can help spur impressive development in formerly inhospitable places. The key word here is *can*; other oil-rich countries, such as Nigeria, have failed to mobilize their wealth to realize development goals. They remain mired in poverty. Why? With this question we enter ongoing debates that animate the study of development and the explanations for global inequalities that flow from these debates. One of the goals of this chapter is to introduce you to key explanations or theories of development and the controversies they have engendered.

But why study development at all, you might ask? What relevance does it have for my life? What *is* development anyway? It makes sense to address these questions before we examine key debates in the field.

WHAT IS DEVELOPMENT?

The idea of development dates from the eighteenth century, when scholars in Scotland and France formulated the idea of progress. They promoted the industrialization and democratization of society based on the equal rights and freedoms of its citizens.

At first, development was just an idea. It was not until after World War II that the idea crystallized into a full-blown project or, more accurately, a series of projects that became part of state policy and the policy of some non-state organizations (Parpart and Veltmeyer, 2003). After World War II, development came increasingly to mean a process that generated economic growth, industrialization, and modernization in regions and countries perceived to be poor, traditional, and undeveloped. More recently, development has had a broader, more complex meaning, incorporating such notions as progress for women, empowerment of the underprivileged, and environmental sustainability.

Two main factors motivated interest in development after World War II. First, the Cold War broke out between the developed capitalist countries led by the United States and the communist countries led by the Soviet Union. Among other things, the Cold War involved intense competition between the two rival blocs to amass power by gaining influence and control over less developed countries. Second, businesses in the developed West, particularly the United States, were interested in new markets outside their traditional spheres of operation. Latin America, Africa, and Asia were thus of great interest to the Western powers for geopolitical and economic reasons.

Given the context just described, it may not surprise you to learn that some analysts have argued that development, and the study of development, have served to support world **capitalism,** an economic system based on competitive enterprises seeking to maximize profits by using wage labour. However, as we will see, other analysts deny that that genuine development can occur within the confines of capitalism. They have promoted a non-capitalist road to development.

THE RELEVANCE OF DEVELOPMENT AND GLOBAL INEQUALITIES: SOCIAL JUSTICE AND SECURITY

Earlier I asked why you should care about development. We can look at this question from two perspectives, one involving morality and social justice, the other involving self-interest and the need for security.

Development is an important issue for many people because they find it morally repugnant that more than a billion people earn US$1.25 or less a day (see Table 10.1). They consider it a matter of social justice that the world's desperately poor be lifted out of a life of illiteracy, disease, and hopelessness. They regard it as unacceptable that a Canadian student buys a coffee at Starbucks for three times the average daily wage of more than a billion people, or spends more on a laptop computer than the per capita gross domestic product of the world's 51 poorest countries—less than US$1000 (Milanovic, 2009; United Nations, 2009). (**Gross domestic product** is the dollar value of all goods and services produced in a country in a year. "Per capita" gross domestic product is gross domestic product divided by the number of people living in the country. It is one measure of a country's wealth per person.)

Other people are more concerned with the practical implications of having so many people in the world with so little to sustain them. Few of us

would feel comfortable living in a luxurious house with expensive furnishings and two luxury cars in the driveway if several of our immediate neighbours lived in a one-room shanty with a tin roof, owned virtually nothing, lacked regular employment, and spent much of their time staring enviously at our lifestyle and property. Eventually, our neighbours' poverty would have unpleasant implications for us.

The higher levels of violence and unrest that accompany poverty would likely wash over to our side of the street. We would have to pay higher taxes to bolster police forces to maintain order and deal with those who decide that it's not fair for us alone to have all the nice things in life. We would soon come to realize that our personal security cannot be divorced from the living conditions of our neighbours, and our failure to help raise their living standard must inevitably have serious, negative implications for us.

Life today is like the scenario painted above, but with added complications. Our poor neighbours might, for example, be living on land we own or land we took from them by using to our advantage property laws and the fact that our neighbours didn't have formal title to the land they had been living on for generations. We might allow our poor neighbours to grow crops, but they would have to give us most of their harvest for the privilege of living on our land. We might select a few of the poor neighbours to supervise the land and reward them with a disproportionate amount of the crop and some extra money under the table. We might also provide the chosen few with firearms and training so they could protect the property and especially the production of fruits and vegetables, dealing appropriately with anyone who might want to challenge existing property rights.

Challenges would likely arise because most households enjoy only a bare subsistence and grow rapidly, making less food per person available over time. Unrest would mount. We would therefore be forced to send some of our family members to help our managers keep order, and some of them would come back with injuries from the skirmishes. Before long, it would be necessary to lock up and occasionally kill people in the poorer households to maintain the status quo, and some of our own family members would undoubtedly get killed trying to police the growing violence.

When we add these complications to our fictitious neighbourhood economy, we have a model that better mirrors the world as it has existed for some time. It is a model that not only describes huge differences in income between our neighbours and us but

TABLE 10.1   COUNTRIES WITH MORE THAN 10 PERCENT OF THEIR POPULATION LIVING ON US$1.25/DAY OR LESS

COUNTRY	REGION	% OF POPULATION LIVING ON US$1.25 OR LESS/DAY
Bangladesh	South Asia	43.3
Benin	Sub-Saharan Africa	51.6
Cambodia	Sub-Saharan Africa	10.1
Chad	Sub-Saharan Africa	36.5
Congo, Republic	Sub-Saharan Africa	32.8
Ethiopia	Sub-Saharan Africa	36.8
Georgia	Eurasia	14.1
Guatemala	Central America	13.7
Guinea	Sub-Saharan Africa	40.9
Honduras	Central America	16.5
India	South Asia	23.6
Laos	Southeast Asia	30.3
Madagascar	Sub-Saharan Africa	87.7
Malawi	Sub-Saharan Africa	72.2
Mali	Sub-Saharan Africa	50.6
Namibia	Sub-Saharan Africa	23.5
Nepal	South Asia	23.7
Niger	Sub-Saharan Africa	40.8
Pakistan	South Asia	12.7
Philippines	Southeast Asia	20.0
Rwanda	Sub-Saharan Africa	63.0
Sao Tome and Principe	Sub-Saharan Africa	43.5
Senegal	Sub-Saharan Africa	34.1
Sierra Leone	Sub-Saharan Africa	56.6
Swaziland	Sub-Saharan Africa	39.3
Tanzania	Sub-Saharan Africa	43.5
Togo	Sub-Saharan Africa	52.5
Uganda	Sub-Saharan Africa	37.8
Zambia	Sub-Saharan Africa	74.3

Notes: (1) Data are for the most recent year available, in most cases 2010. (2) Data are unavailable on some of the world's poorest countries, such as Haiti. (3) The table uses the number of units of a country's currency needed to buy the same amount of goods and services in the domestic market as US$1.25 would buy in the United States.

SOURCE: World Bank (2015).

also points out the inequality that exists *within* poor neighbourhoods. Importantly, the model also establishes that the neighbourhood economy is maintained by a system of power relations backed up by disproportionate wealth and, ultimately, our willingness to exercise violence when all else fails.

Social scientists who study development have proposed radically different theories to explain development and lack of development. It is now time to outline some of the most important of them. I begin with a brief discussion of approaches that dominated the social sciences in the 1960s.

EARLY THEORIES OF DEVELOPMENT

DEVELOPMENT IN STAGES

The social sciences emerged in the nineteenth century in the context of lively debate in the biological sciences around theories of evolution propounded by Charles Darwin and others. Debates in the natural sciences, especially concerning evolution, deeply influenced social thinkers. Human societies were like biological organisms, they reasoned. Just as animals and plants pass through stages of development, so do societies; and like animals and plants, societies are susceptible to pathologies or diseases.

Such ideas were still influential in the 1960s, when W. W. Rostow argued that societal development follows several necessary **stages of development** (Rostow, 1960). According to Rostow, in the beginning, a society might be traditional, undifferentiated, and undeveloped. When it comes into contact with a developed society, however, science and technology spread, and the traditional society enters a stage of possible "takeoff." Takeoff occurs when and if an increase in market transactions, manufacturing, and trade takes place. The faster society moves along the path to development, the more quickly barriers to the spread of market relations are removed and the more efficiently scientific and technological diffusion occurs.

DEVELOPMENT AS A STATE OF MIND

Another popular approach in the 1960s was **modernization theory**, which emphasizes the importance of values and norms as drivers of development. David McClelland (1961), for example, argued for the importance of entrepreneurship and what he called the "need for achievement," the desire for feelings of accomplishment and personal satisfaction. People who enjoy a high need for achievement are more likely to become successful entrepreneurs, McClelland argued, and societies that encourage entrepreneurial behaviour and competitiveness are the most likely to develop economically and socially.

Other writers in this tradition emphasized the importance of other values in the development process—the need for savings, investment, innovation, education, high achievement, self-control in having children, and so on. Still others recognized that poor societies also lack capital, stable governments, and business techniques (Inkeles and Smith, 1976). But what all modernization theories had in common was their assumption that most of the responsibility for economic backwardness lies with the societies of the "Third World" or "Global South" themselves. According to modernization theorists, development happens when the citizens of the poor countries adopt the virtues of the developed North. If they fail to do so, they remain in a pathological, undeveloped state.

DEVELOPMENT AS DEPENDENCY

Dependency theory sharply challenged the notion that lack of development is due to the deficiencies of less developed countries. It did so by taking a holistic view—recognizing that each part of the world is shaped by, and helps to shape, a wider, global reality—and attending to the history and structure of relations between countries.

Dependency theorists produced abundant evidence of strong and enduring economic and social relationships between "metropolitan powers," such as Spain, Portugal, Britain, and France, and "satellite regions" of the Global South. First focusing on Latin America and the Caribbean (Cardoso and Faletto, 1979; Frank, 1966), they established that it was precisely the nature of the relationship between metropolitan powers and satellite regions that blocked economic progress in the Global South. Let us consider the implications of this argument in detail.

FROM CONTACT TO CONQUEST

Evidence contradicts the notion that the societies of the Global South existed in an undeveloped state, as stage and modernization theories suggest. From China through the Middle East and the Mediterranean to Central and South America, great civilizations rose and fell. For example, between 1200 and 200 BCE, Carthage flourished on the northern shores of Africa, while the later naval, military, commercial, and cultural advances of the Muslim people of the Maghreb region of northwestern Africa allowed them to invade and dominate Spain and Portugal until the twelfth century. In the area of east Africa now known as Zimbabwe, we find great stone constructions and evidence of extensive metallurgical development and trade across vast distances. Africans had developed a great deal on their own before Europe began asserting its dominance over the continent (Rodney, 1972).

Initial contact between Europe and the societies of the Global South took place around 1500. For the next several hundred years, the Europeans engaged in wholesale pillage and plunder, causing massive death, migration, and economic upheaval—unpleasant facts that stage and modernization theories ignore. Before Europeans could exploit the Global South for its riches, they had to conquer existing civilizations. Superior technology in the form of gunpowder and firearms helped to secure the conquest, as did diseases borne by the Europeans. Europeans had evolved resistance to smallpox, influenza, and other diseases that they introduced into the Global South. In Mexico alone, the population was reduced from 20 million to 2 million in the first century of contact with Europe. A population collapse of similar magnitude occurred in North America and among the Inca of Peru. Overall, some 95 percent of the New World's population was wiped out in a fairly short period after European contact (Diamond, 1999: 210–11).

Following their conquest of the New World, the Spanish established a feudalistic landholding system based on hierarchical relationships imported from Europe and subordinated to the power of the Spanish Crown. Its purpose was to support a local European landed elite and funnel valuable minerals, principally gold and silver, and agricultural commodities to the mother country. The Spanish monarchy appropriated much of the profit.

THE SLAVE TRADE

Another disruptive aspect of the relationship between Europe and the Global South involved the West African slave trade. It undermined traditional state structures and forms of governance in West Africa and created deep-seated ethnic animosities.

Forced labour had existed for centuries in Europe. Muslim pirates from North Africa had undertaken raids as far afield as southern England to enslave people. However, the trans-Atlantic slave trade, initiated by Europeans after 1500, established slave economies of unprecedented size, with dire consequences for West Africa in particular.

African slaves taken on board *HMS Daphne*, November 1, 1868.
SOURCE: The National Archives of the UK, ref. 84/1310.

The Portuguese initiated the trans-Atlantic slave trade near the mouth of the Congo River around 1500. Taking advantage of the custom of local African chiefs to buy household slaves, the Portuguese began trading European merchandise for human lives and shipping enslaved Africans across the Atlantic to work in the vibrant Portuguese colony of Brazil, where they produced first sugar, then coffee. By 1530, five thousand slaves a year were being removed from their homelands for shipment to Brazil (Hochschild, 1999: 12).

Slavery soon became a major disruptive force in West Africa. The ruler of the Kingdom of the Congo, Nzinga Mbemba Alfonso, a convert to Christianity who learned Portuguese, wrote to the King of Portugal to protest what was happening to his people:

> Each day the traders are capturing our people—children of this country, sons of our nobles and vassals, even people of our own family. ... Corruption and depravity are so widespread that our land is entirely depopulated. ... We need in this kingdom only priests and schoolteachers, and no merchandise, unless it is wine and flour for Mass. ... It is our wish that this kingdom not be a place for the trade or transport of slaves. (Quoted in Hochschild, 1999: 13)

The King of Portugal was unmoved. Slave trading accelerated, and before long, Dutch merchant traders began introducing slavery to the English Caribbean, initially on the island of Barbados. Later, the English established a major Caribbean sugar colony in Jamaica and the Spanish followed suit in Cuba. Later still, American rice and cotton plantations stimulated demand for still more slave labour. By the early nineteenth century, some 12 million Africans and their descendants worked on the plantations of the Caribbean and the United States.

The societies of entire regions of Africa were thus ruined, and the foundation was set for the deep, enduring impoverishment of Africa. Matters worsened when, in the nineteenth century, England, Belgium, France, and Germany carved up much of Africa for its resource wealth. They established artificial boundaries that ignored traditional ethnic spheres of influence, thereby increasing ethnic antagonism and warfare. In some areas, such as the territory that the British named Rhodesia, the colonizers imposed heavy taxes on peasant farmers, forcing them off the best agricultural lands and into wage labour for white farmers (Arrighi, 1970). Later, some dispossessed Africans began a mass migration to South Africa for work in the expanding gold and diamond mines.

Meanwhile, across the Atlantic, the slave economies of the Caribbean and the United States flourished, generating unheard of wealth for slave traders, slave owners, and the European aristocracy and royalty. Slavery enabled capital to accumulate—capital that industrialists would later use to spur European development.

THE STRUCTURAL ROOTS OF UNDERDEVELOPMENT

Dependency theory shows how social and economic structures established by European colonizing powers since about 1500 distorted local societies for the benefit of European traders and merchants, and later blocked the emergence of industrial capitalism in the Global South. In the words of Andre Gundar Frank, a leading dependency theorist, "the historical development of the capitalist system generated **underdevelopment** in the peripheral satellites" (Frank, 1966: 3). At the same time, the extraction of resources from the Global South propelled the rapid development of industry in Western Europe and, later, North America. What remains unclear is whether European *countries* or *classes* were responsible for underdevelopment in the Global South.

Slave labour on a Caribbean sugar plantation in the 1830s.

SOURCE: © British Library Board/Robana/Art Resource, NY.

COUNTRIES VERSUS CLASSES AS CAUSES OF UNDERDEVELOPMENT

During the 1970s, debates on development and underdevelopment focused on the *mechanisms* through which metropolitan powers exploited the Global South. Originally, dependency theorists conceived of underdevelopment as a process involving one area—Western Europe—extracting surplus from other areas—Latin America, Africa, and Asia. Some scholars argued that, in recent times, it was primarily through unfavourable **terms of trade** that exploitation took place. They held that prices of agricultural exports primarily from the underdeveloped south declined over time relative to prices of industrial goods made in the developed countries and imported by the poor countries. However, they still imagined that one *area* was exploiting another.

Robert Brenner (1977) challenged the geographical version of dependency theory and revived interest in a Marxist approach that emphasized class relationships. He argued that dependency theory ought to focus on exploitation occurring at the level of *class relationships*. In his view, by analyzing the nature of the class interests that shape underdevelopment and the types of class conflict that underdevelopment engenders, we can gain a fuller and more precise understanding of the process of underdevelopment.

Following Marx, Brenner argued that the struggle among classes to achieve dominance is the prime mover of social change. Accordingly, identifiable classes in the metropolitan countries—merchants, traders, shippers, and the aristocracies and monarchies of Spain, Portugal, Holland, Belgium, France, and England—orchestrated the plunder of the Global South. Moreover, these social actors counted on elites in the Global South to establish mechanisms for extracting valuable commodities by using the forced labour of indigenous peoples and imported slaves. Brenner further argued that, in more recent times, the mechanisms of underdevelopment changed as England and then the rest of Western Europe began to industrialize under the direction of a new class of industrial capitalists. As industrialization occurred, so too did the nature of demands on the Global South (for example, see the Critical Sociology: Globalization box).

NOT ALL COUNTRIES ARE ALIKE: CLASS ALLIANCES AND STATE CONTROL

The Global South is not homogeneous. Each country has a unique history. In particular, different class alliances came to control the states of the Global South, with widely different consequences for the pattern of underdevelopment that ensued (Cardoso and Faletto, 1979). For example, in Argentina and Brazil, the large export-oriented economy that developed under the control of foreign capitalists allowed local elites and a sizable middle and industrial working class to emerge by the late nineteenth century (Murmis and Portantiero, 1969). Especially in periods when foreign influence was weakest (during global recessions, for instance), internal elites and their allies were able to establish local industrial enterprises and internal markets that deepened the process of development and strengthened local economies. In contrast, foreign capital was so dominant in small countries, such as Honduras, Costa Rica, and Guatemala, that middle and industrial working classes of much political significance failed to develop, and the economy was based almost exclusively on the exports of just a few commodities, such as bananas and coffee (Ellis, 1983; Handy, 1985; Stone, 1975; Winson, 1983, 1989).

BEYOND DEPENDENCY: AGRARIAN CLASS STRUCTURE AND UNDERDEVELOPMENT

In the 1980s and 1990s, researchers focused increasingly on the role of class structures, class alliances, and state policies to better understand the processes of development and underdevelopment. Consider, for example, research on estates—large, privately owned agricultural enterprises employing many agricultural workers to produce export crops, such as coffee, wheat, and cotton, in societies as diverse as Chile, Brazil, and Egypt. Analysts found that, for three reasons, estate agriculture was more of an impediment to development than were agrarian structures dominated by small family farms (the North American model in the nineteenth and early twentieth centuries). First, estate owners tended to compensate their workers with small plots of land rather than substantial money wages. This greatly restricted the purchasing power of rural workers and therefore the demand for goods that small manufacturers could have produced locally.

Second, with a ready supply of cheap labour at hand, estate owners had little incentive to employ advanced agricultural machinery on their estates. This limited the local market for manufacturers of agricultural machinery, who in North America were central to early industrialization. Third, estate owners exercised enormous political power. They influenced

Before the Industrial Revolution began in England in the late eighteenth century, many goods other than foodstuffs were produced in both Europe and the Global South by traditional industry. Small workshops produced a huge variety of metal goods and wooden implements, and all manner of luxury goods made from glass, silver, gold, and so on. Grain was ground in stone grinding mills powered by water or animals. People wove textiles at home on looms from yarn or thread spun on hand-operated spinning wheels. While productivity was low, many people worked in these ways, so output was considerable. Paul Bairoch (1982) estimates that in 1830, the Global South (including Japan) accounted for 63 percent of world manufacturing, compared with just 37 percent for Europe and North America. Levels of productivity differed little by region. This would soon change, however.

In England, the rising influence of modern industrialists challenged the longstanding dominance of old merchant families whose fortunes relied on trade. By the early nineteenth century, industrialists sought to extend markets for their products beyond England, inaugurating the globalization of trade in English-manufactured goods. The old "mercantilist" system relied on protected markets and trade monopolies within them. For example, the British East India Company was allowed to block the import of European-manufactured goods into India, which was good for traders but bad for industrialists. In 1813, however, the monopoly of the British East India Company was ended by the British Parliament. Now, Birmingham textile manufacturers could export cheap textiles produced by modern machinery and the new factory system to India. This devastated millions of Indian domestic textile producers. Similar events took place elsewhere.

The English factory system integral to industrial capitalism, together with actions by the British government to tear down obstacles to trade in English industrial goods, dramatically reorganized the distribution of industry globally. As Bairoch argued, it was "in the years 1830 to 1860 that this division between the future developed world and the Third World ... began to take shape. The industrialization of the former led to the deindustrialization of the latter, and the proportional contribution of each region to the total [world] output of manufacturing production was almost exactly reversed" (Bairoch, 1982: 274).

Even relatively wealthy countries are not immune to the distortions of capitalist development. For example, the Maritime Provinces were the first locus of industrial development in Canada, with a thriving shipbuilding and steel industry (Alexander, 1978). By the 1890s, the proportion of people employed in manufacturing was about the same in Nova Scotia, New Brunswick, and Ontario (Winson, 1985: Table 1).

Despite this promising early start, and in some ways reminiscent of the impact of British manufacturers on Third World industry described by Bairoch, Maritime industries were disadvantaged by federal policies and the actions of central Canadian financial institutions that control Canadian industry. Maritime industry went into decline, negatively affecting the regional farming economy and resulting in a long-term legacy of high unemployment, underemployment, and lower average income for the Maritime population (Acheson, 1972; Winson, 1985).

Critical Thinking Questions

1. History tells us that manufacturing was not always predominantly located in what are today the rich countries. What do you think ultimately prevented India from protecting its own manufacturing industry from being destroyed by Britain's lower-cost manufactured goods?

2. The history of manufacturing in Canada's Maritime provinces also provides a valuable lesson regarding the notion that the dominance of industry in a given region or country is simply a "natural" evolution of the economy. Discuss.

governments to maintain free trade policies so they could export agricultural products and import whatever machinery they needed, unhindered by tariffs. This made it difficult for local industry to develop. In contrast, in Canada and the United States, tariffs protected local manufacturing in the early stage of industrialization (Richards, 1976; Winson, 1989).

DEVELOPMENT IN CANADA

Canada achieved independence in 1867. Before then, it consisted of a number of British colonies and a vast western and northern territory controlled by the Hudson's Bay Company, which was incorporated by British charter in 1670. How did Canada become a prosperous country despite its colonial past?

First, like Australia, New Zealand, and the United States, Canada was settled by large numbers of Europeans who soon overwhelmed the Indigenous population. The European settlers were determined to reproduce or improve the standard of living they enjoyed in the old country. Much of the wealth they produced was therefore reinvested locally.

In contrast, when the European powers colonized most of Africa, they set up only small enclaves of white settlers. Their main aim was to exploit local resources and populations, sending nearly all of the wealth back to Europe.

Second, Canada's geopolitical position helped it overcome its colonial past and develop economically. Canada served as a major supplier not just of raw materials but also of manufactured goods, such as airplanes, to the Allies during World War II. Canada's favourable geopolitical position gave its industry a major boost.

Third, Canadian state policy sometimes protected and stimulated Canadian industrial growth. For example, the 1879 National Policy established a duty on imported manufactured goods. The National Policy sheltered the growth of Canadian industry, then in its infancy, by making foreign-made manufactured goods more expensive. Similarly, the 1965 Auto Pact required that foreign automobile companies wanting to sell cars in Canada duty-free manufacture cars in Canada and use a certain proportion of Canadian-made components. The Auto Pact stimulated the growth of an industry that, directly or indirectly, was responsible at its height for the employment of one-sixth of Ontario's labour force (Brym et al., 2012: 232).

TIME FOR REVIEW

1. How did European influence in much of the Global South since the fifteenth century create underdevelopment and dependency?
2. What three factors hindered development in countries where large landholdings were the predominant form of settlement?
3. Why was industrialization in the European colonies that became Canada successful?

GEOGRAPHY AND BIOLOGICAL RESOURCES

A recent, provocative contribution to the study of development and underdevelopment is Jared Diamond's examination of the early history of human civilization. Diamond set out to understand why wealth and power are distributed as they now are rather than in some other way. For Diamond, the answer is complex but boils down to the following idea: "History followed different courses for different peoples because of differences among peoples' environments" (Diamond, 1999: 25).

To make his case, Diamond distinguished between proximate (or immediate) and ultimate (or fundamental) causes of development. He found that the development of firearms and modern metallurgy by Europeans, along with lack of resistance to deadly diseases in the peoples of the Americas, were the *proximate* causes of the defeat of established, complex civilizations by the marauding Spanish army in Latin America in 1520. The conquest set the stage for the emergence of commercial, administrative, military, and industrial structures over the next several hundred years—structures that helped to enrich Europe while retarding progress in the Americas, Australia, Africa, and much of Asia.

Why did the Europeans alone enjoy such early advantages as firearms, modern metallurgy, and resistance to diseases that proved deadly to the peoples they subjugated? What, in other words, were the *ultimate* causes of European development? Diamond argues that the geographical features of different continents and the biological resources available to early peoples were fundamentally important. Europe (and the adjacent Middle East) was especially rich in plants and animals that could be domesticated. Moreover, their east–west axis facilitated the intermingling and dissemination of a wide variety of species because geographical barriers were few and climate was roughly similar across the region. In contrast, relatively few animals were available for domestication in the Americas. Moreover, the Americas, Africa, and most of Asia ran along a north–south axis with physical barriers and climatic differences that made the dissemination of species difficult. Australia was isolated and had no animal species that could be domesticated.

The wealth of species available for domestication in Europe and the Middle East allowed for the accumulation and storage of large food surpluses, which in turn enabled the growth of large, complex, hierarchical societies. The first cities emerged in the Middle East and so did technological advances beyond the stone tools of the pre-agricultural period, including the refinement of metal, the manufacture of implements and arms, and the construction of ocean-going vessels. These advances spread to Europe relatively easily. Dense population centres and proximity to domesticated animals also allowed germs to spread and cause the first mass epidemics. However, the survivors developed resistance to these germs. For Diamond, then, the early domestication of plants and animals made agriculture possible and was a prerequisite for the development of the guns, germs, and steel that eventually ensured the dominance of

European colonizers in the Americas and later in Asia and Africa.

CRITICISMS OF DIAMOND'S THESIS

Diamond's thesis has sparked much debate. Some critics argue that he ignores the mountain ranges and deserts that surely impeded the diffusion of domesticated plants and animals across Europe. Others point out that corn, a major staple, *was* disseminated from Central to South America (Blaut, 2000). Still others note that Diamond ignores crucial political factors. For example, the Ottoman Empire cut off Europe's trade with Asia in the fifteenth century, so European merchants were encouraged to develop marine transportation technology and navigational and cartographic knowledge to reach the East by travelling around the southern African coast. Their technological advantage later allowed them to dominate the seas, exploring and exploiting much of the rest of the globe (Pickover, 1997). Despite the criticisms of Diamond's work, the broad scope of his argument and the eloquence with which he makes it have proven attractive to a wide audience.

THE NEOLIBERAL ERA: DEBT, STRUCTURAL ADJUSTMENT, AND UPHEAVAL IN THE SOUTH
THE RISE OF NEOLIBERALISM

In recent years, the **neoliberal theory** of economic development has become influential in the highest policy circles. It is worth analyzing because the most important institutions affecting development policies in the Global South adopted it and still apply it today. A central idea of neoliberal theory is that only in societies where markets are free of government interference can competitive entrepreneurs maximize economic growth for the benefit of themselves and the rest of society. This idea was not always popular. A "hands-off" approach by governments contributed to the severity of the Great Depression of the 1930s, when the North American unemployment rate reached 30 percent. Thereafter, desperation brought a strong desire for a new approach to economic thinking. In the United States, the Democratic Party under Franklin Delano Roosevelt, inspired by the economic thinking of the British economist John Maynard Keynes, took the view that government *should* intervene in the market. Its policies, and those of like-minded governments in Canada, Britain, and elsewhere, favoured massive government spending to stimulate the economy and the establishment of public enterprises where the market had failed to provide viable alternatives.

The "Keynesian" approach to economic development worked well for four decades. Then, in the 1970s, it too began to run into difficulties—specifically, high inflation coupled with low or stagnant economic growth. This situation provided the context for American economist Milton Friedman and his followers to advocate a return to policies that would drastically restrict the role of government in the economy in favour of private market solutions.

What implications did the spread of Freidman's ideas have for the Global South? In the 1970s, international banks and lending institutions had gone on a lending spree. Many governments in the Global South were eager to accept low-interest loans to assist in the industrialization of their nations. The election of Republican president Ronald Reagan in 1981 brought a dramatic change in monetary policy along the lines advocated by Friedman. Among other things, the change entailed a drastic increase in interest rates to deal with inflationary tendencies in the economy. This policy had a global impact.

Interest payments on loans made by the countries of the Global South soared, and a debt crisis, especially acute in South America, ensued. As governments faced defaulting on their loans, international lending agencies put in place a new set of policies that poor debtor countries would have to follow to be bailed out of their dilemma. These policies reflected Friedman's neoliberalism.

The new policy, often called the **Washington consensus**, united the International Monetary Fund (IMF), the World Bank, and the U.S. Treasury around Freidman's neoliberalism. The chief economist at the World Bank, Joseph Stiglitz, wrote that the three pillars of this consensus are austerity, privatization, and market liberalization (Stiglitz, 2003: 53).

In practice, **structural adjustment programs (SAPs)** became the basis of the bailout of the countries of the Global South facing a debt crisis. The IMF and the World Bank offered to help the debtor countries financially if they met a set of harsh conditions: Privatize state-owned enterprises, such as telephone and oil companies and national banks; let in international corporations and goods produced in the developed countries; end tariff protection of local industry and agriculture; radically curtail social welfare programs; encourage new lines of agricultural exports—these were key aspects of SAPs. Proponents of SAPs claimed they were necessary to provide needed economic discipline and achieve economic growth. Critics argued that SAPs would cause social upheaval and misery. As we will see, the critics were right.

Neoliberals assumed that markets work perfectly if left free to do so. Demand for labour, capital, and commodities will equal supply. There will be no unemployment. The only thing that could prevent this ideal outcome is market interference. They argue that if greedy unions constrain the workings of free markets by demanding and receiving excessively high wages, or if meddling politicians encourage the growth of social policies (employment insurance, welfare, universal health insurance, and so on), then the market will not be able to work its magic. By implication, if economic problems exist, markets must be unleashed. By this logic, the solution to unemployment, for example, is a reduction in wages.

NEOLIBERALISM AND SAPS AS SOLUTIONS TO POVERTY

Proponents of neoliberal reforms in developing countries argue that they have raised incomes in poor countries and lifted millions of people out of poverty (Neilsen, 2007). Critics have argued that

neoliberalism has produced a dramatic increase in global income inequality, widespread misery, and social dislocation. Who is right? Let us consider the conflicting evidence.

Clearly, there have been winners in the neoliberal global economy. For example, after Mexico opened its economy to foreign capital and free trade, and privatized publically owned companies, a new class of billionaires emerged. Some benefited from the sale of public sector enterprises at low prices. Others managed to monopolize lucrative new markets. Notably, the Mexican entrepreneur Carlos Slim became the richest man in the world in 2007—richer than Bill Gates (although Gates has since retaken the number one spot). Large commercial agricultural producers also benefited from the development of new agro-export industries oriented to the U.S. market.

Brazil, India and China also opened their economies to foreign corporations and trade, helping them realize exceptional rates of economic growth (see Figure 10.1). New industries have rapidly expanded to serve overseas and domestic markets. New entrepreneurial and professional middle classes have arisen in these countries, while masses of rural poor flood into cities to take up work in new factories that provide incomes considerably higher than those available in rural areas.

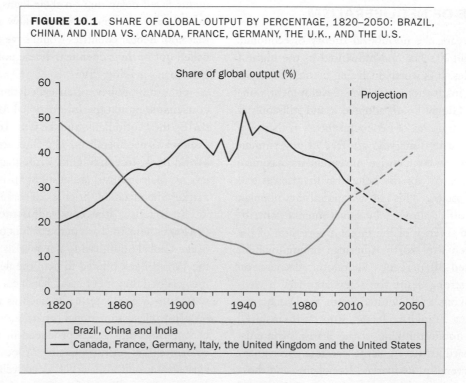

FIGURE 10.1 SHARE OF GLOBAL OUTPUT BY PERCENTAGE, 1820–2050: BRAZIL, CHINA, AND INDIA VS. CANADA, FRANCE, GERMANY, THE U.K., AND THE U.S.

Share of global output (%)

Projection

— Brazil, China and India
— Canada, France, Germany, Italy, the United Kingdom and the United States

SOURCE: Human Development Report 2013. "The Rise of the South: Human progress in a Diverse World." Human Development Report Office, United Nations Development Programme. hdr.undp.org.

Do these examples not prove the success of the neoliberal economic model? The answer depends partly on how we define success. In narrow economic terms, policies associated with neoliberalism have succeeded in some places. The wealth of some countries has increased, as has the standard of living. New infrastructure, including hydroelectric stations, rail networks, highway systems, and air transportation facilities, has been built. These facts suggest development is indeed taking place.

Nevertheless, even among the success stories, glaring problems have emerged. And then there are the many countries that have benefited little or not at all from neoliberalism or have suffered because of it. Let us consider these issues in detail.

Level of Consumption versus Quality of Life and the Environment

An increase in monetary income in India and China does not mean that the average quality of life has necessarily improved in those countries. Life in rural areas often provides nonmonetary benefits—personal security, tranquility, better air quality, the benefits of having family close, and so on—that are not captured by economic indicators of well-being. Life in the city for new immigrants often brings increased personal insecurity with dramatic increases in crime and violence, negative health outcomes associated with heavily polluted air and water, dangerous work environments, and deterioration in diet associated with the consumption of fast food and low-quality street foods.

The kind of unregulated development seen in India and China in recent years has also brought with it massive environmental destruction. For example, to power its expansion, China constructed the massive Three Gorges electric dam project on the Yangtze River. The lake it created has displaced more than a million people and destroyed 13 cities and 140 towns, including historical sites and valuable agricultural land. Lack of regulation means that dangerous and environmentally destructive industries, such as the scavenging of waste from electronic devices and the breaking up of decommissioned ships in vulnerable marine environments, are commonplace.

Agricultural expansion has denuded vast territories and resulted in the rapid spread of deserts. China is rapidly exceeding the carrying capacity of its ecosystem. Winds carry soil from highly eroded land in the northwest as far away as South Korea and Japan, while air and water pollution affect the health of hundreds of millions of families. At the same time, industrial development has claimed tremendous water resources previously devoted to agriculture. The Yellow River no longer reaches the sea for part of the year or even the downstream agricultural province of Shandong. This situation has imperilled agriculture in an important food-producing region. As renowned environmentalist Lester Brown concluded, "China is on the verge of a massive ecological meltdown" (2003: 11, 37).

Absolute Poverty and Global Income Inequality

Many parts of the world have not witnessed the kind of income growth that China and India have enjoyed. In fact, as Stiglitz noted, in the last decade of the

Workers stretch as far as the eye can see in the Cankun Factory, Xiamen City, China.

SOURCE: © Edward Burtynsky, courtesy Nicholas Metivier, Toronto/Howard Greenberg & Bryce Wolkowitz, New York.

twentieth century, "the number of people living in poverty has actually increased by almost 100 million. This occurred at the same time that total world income increased by an average of 2.5 percent annually" (Stiglitz, 2003: 5).

Measuring the gap at the global level between people with high and low income is difficult. Various experts use different methods and come up with different results. Nevertheless, as a leading researcher states, "the most basic fact about world inequality is that it is monstrously large; that result is inescapable, whatever the method or definition" (Sutcliffe, 2005; see the Critical Sociology: Social Inequality box).

Branko Milanovic, a leading economist with the World Bank, notes that the top 5 percent of individuals in the world receive about one-third of total world income, while the top 10 percent get one-half. On the other hand, the bottom 5 and 10 percent of people in the world get just 0.2 and 0.7 percent of world income, respectively. Looked at another way, the ratio of the richest 5 percent compared with the poorest 5 percent of world citizens is 165 to 1. The richest 5 percent earn in 48 hours about what the poorest 5 percent earn in an entire year (Milanovic, 2005: 15; see Figure 10.2 and Figure 10.3).

A recent international project to measure the direction of change in global inequalities provides us with a more accurate estimate of global inequalities than we have had up to now. The International Comparison Program includes data from 146 national statistical agencies and major financial and development organizations, including the United Nations, the World Bank, and the International Monetary Fund. A key finding of the project is that price levels in most Asian countries, notably China, India, Indonesia, and the Philippines—countries with about 38 percent of the

---

CRITICAL SOCIOLOGY: SOCIAL INEQUALITY	HOW SHOULD WE MEASURE THE DEVELOPMENT GAP BETWEEN COUNTRIES?

Today, many analysts believe we need better measures of development because GDP per capita does not give us a complete picture of how developed a country is. If we compare, say, the United States with Costa Rica on GDP per capita, we might be inclined to conclude that the United States is far more developed because its GDP per capita is 5.7 times higher than Costa Rica's (World Bank, 2013). However, if we include good health as a measure of development, and examine life expectancy, we find no difference between the United States and Costa Rica. Life expectancy in both countries is 79 years. If we take happiness as a measure of development, the results change again. According to one recent index, Costa Ricans are the happiest people in the world. Americans rank 104th (Happy Planet Index, 2015).

How did Costa Rica achieve this feat? In the 1950s, it overcame the domination of its coffee oligarchy, causing economic inequality in the country to plummet. The government funded the development of free public health institutions benefiting the citizenry as a whole, something that the United States lacks. It helps, of course, to live in an environmental paradise like Costa Rica, but the economic and social policies adopted by the Costa Rican people are surely the principal factors accounting for their relatively high life expectancy and level of happiness.

Efforts to create a comprehensive indicator of development have been advanced by the work of United Nations economist Mahbub ul Haq, who worked with a group of prominent development economists to produce the *Human Development Index* (HDI). The HDI incorporates data on life expectancy, educational attainment, and gross national income per capita. The HDI has been criticized on the grounds that it fails to incorporate an indicator of the health of the environment. This is a serious failing, given that many countries pursuing rapid economic growth have seriously compromised the integrity of their air and water, thus endangering human health. Nonetheless, the introduction of the HDI has stimulated useful debate about what development really means, which countries are truly rich and which are truly poor, and what government development priorities ought to be.

Critical Thinking Questions

1. Gauging a country's development solely on the basis of its per capita gross domestic product in increasingly recognized as inadequate. What would a comprehensive measure of development ideally take into account?

2. What sectors of society benefit most from an approach to development that prioritizes economic growth?

SOURCE: Happy Planet Index (2015); United Nations (2013); United Nations Development Programme (2014); World Bank (2013).

FIGURE 10.2   GLOBAL INCOME INEQUALITY, 2014

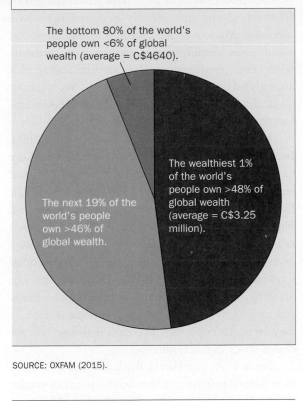

The bottom 80% of the world's people own <6% of global wealth (average = C$4640).

The wealthiest 1% of the world's people own >48% of global wealth (average = C$3.25 million).

The next 19% of the world's people own >46% of global wealth.

SOURCE: OXFAM (2015).

FIGURE 10.3   WHERE DO THE WEALTHIEST 1 PERCENT OF PEOPLE LIVE? (BY PERCENTAGE)

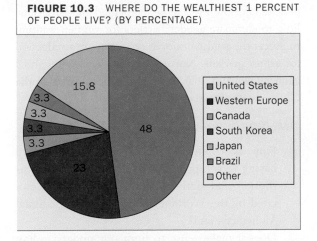

15.8 3.3 3.3 3.3 3.3 23 48

■ United States
■ Western Europe
□ Canada
■ South Korea
□ Japan
■ Brazil
□ Other

SOURCE: Milanovic (2012).

world's population—are much higher than was formerly assumed. This means that they have many more poor people than previously thought, with new estimates bringing incomes down some 40 percent in China and India, 17 percent in Indonesia, 41 percent in the Philippines, 32 percent in South Africa, and 24 percent in Argentina. Average incomes did not decline in all of the poorer economies, but increases in Russia, Egypt, Nigeria, and Lebanon were more modest than declines in the Asian countries. Milanovic (2008) concludes that

global inequality is much greater than even the most pessimistic analysts thought.

Trends in Inequality within and between Countries

What is the *trend* in global income inequality? Is it decreasing or increasing, and if so, for what time period? Scholars have marshalled evidence that gives us a good idea of inequality trends since the 1930s. The data are better for the developed countries, but trends are apparent for the Global South, too.

Considering inequality within developed countries, the gap between the rich and poor decreased from the 1930s to the 1960s. This was the period when the welfare state was being constructed and Keynesian economic policies were being implemented (Bornschier, 2002: 102). For the Global South, the same trend is apparent for only some countries. Brazil and Mexico saw increased gaps between rich and poor between 1950 and 1970. The gap between rich and poor countries was quite stable during these decades.

After the 1970s, when neoliberal policies were implemented, the picture becomes less rosy. Inequalities within countries substantially increased. Between countries, the gap also increased, especially during the 1980s (Bornschier, 2002: 108–10; Braun, 1997). Neoliberal policies were probably not the only factor contributing to this outcome. Other causes of the growing gap between rich and poor include the increasing penetration and integration of national economies by transnational corporations and the ongoing massive technological shift away from industrial production to the digital information economy, especially in the developed countries. Nevertheless, neoliberalism helped to widen the gap between rich and poor.

Growth Needs Strong States

Neoliberal policies have not stimulated growth in the Global South. To the contrary, growth rates were higher in the decade before the introduction of SAPs (an average of 2.5 percent between 1960 and 1979) than in the era when SAPs were imposed by international lending agencies (0.0 percent between 1980 and 1998; Brym et al., 2005: 1). But what does history teach us about the policies the *rich* countries followed to encourage industrialization? Did they follow the tenets of neoliberalism? Aside from Britain, the first industrializing country, they did not. As French political economist François Chesnais (2004) notes, "the United States, France, Germany and the other industrialised countries [including Japan] benefited from selective *protection* of their home market for over a century or more" (my emphasis). This gave them time to grow until they could compete with Britain in world markets. Only the countries of the Global South that fell under the sway of neoliberalism have lacked the opportunity to nurture their industrial and technological base. "Time has been denied to them," writes Chesnais.

Contrary to neoliberal theory, minimal state involvement is about the last thing industrializing countries need. In recent decades, the rapid industrialization of the "Asian tigers"—South Korea, Taiwan, Singapore, and, later, China and India—depended on strong states and considerable state involvement in the economy. For example, governments in South Korea and Taiwan after World War II were highly centralized and authoritarian. They succeeded in carrying out sweeping land reforms that eliminated the class of powerful landowners—the same class that opposed protectionist policies in Latin America. The governments of these two countries opted for a strong industrial policy that marshalled the resources of the state to develop infrastructure and use state credit to fund investment in key industrial sectors. They kept control of industrial development by preventing foreign corporations from taking over their expanding industries. They also used their power to repress labour movements, which kept wages down and made emerging industry highly competitive in the world market.

China followed suit. The all-powerful Communist Party organized a top–down transformation of the economy to encourage foreign investment—but on their terms rather than terms dictated by neoliberal institutions. The Communist Party organized massive infrastructure projects that encouraged industrial investment. It kept wages low and used violence to prevent the formation of independent labour organizations.[1]

Women under Neoliberalism

Other signs exist that neoliberalism has failed to produce the results claimed by its advocates. The dismantling of many national banks by IMF policy prescription undermined cheap credit to small farmers and imperilled rural incomes in many poor countries (Rodriguez Gomez and Torres, 1996: 157–58). Trade liberalization encouraged the import of heavily subsidized agricultural commodities from the developed countries. They undermined rural incomes, as prices for food produced by small farmers plummeted in the

face of an incoming tide of low-cost food. Because of such policies, millions of rural poor have been forced off the land and into already overcrowded towns and cities. Millions more migrated to the developed world, some illegally and at great danger to themselves. Such migrants have become the source of a huge global economy in recent years. They typically do menial work and send money back to family members in Mexico, the Philippines, and elsewhere.

In some parts of the Global South, such as India and Thailand, neoliberal policies have been especially hard on women, partly because women form the bulk of the agricultural workforce (Shiva, 1993: 232). Elsewhere, in countries as diverse as Nicaragua and Nigeria, women have had to raise families on their own as their husbands are forced to migrate to the cities or to the developed world in search of cash income. Evidence suggests that these circumstances are breaking down long-standing patriarchal structures and forging new ties of solidarity among women as they strive to cope with the new realities, but the change involves much suffering.

Since 1999, the World Bank and the IMF have implemented policies that they believe promote gender equity. However, critics point out that these new policies have been weakly implemented and have done little to eliminate gender barriers for women wanting to access the paid workforce or engage in production for export markets. Nor do they tackle the substantial gender inequality that exists in the households of the Global South (Brym et al., 2005).

TIME FOR REVIEW

1. How did countries in the Global South end up having to accept the policies of austerity, privatization, and market liberalization that were dictated by the World Bank and the International Monetary Fund?

2. Does it make sense to limit our understanding of "development" to an increase in the gross national product?

3. While measuring inequality is a difficult task, what can we conclude about the level of world inequality today?

STATE VIOLENCE, WAR, AND THE PRODUCTION OF POVERTY

Military aggression and war have helped undermine development in much of the post-World War II era, and they therefore deserve to be discussed at some length. During the Cold War, mutually assured destruction by nuclear weapons made military confrontation between the Soviet Union and the United States out of the question. Nevertheless, both countries used their economic and military might to reshape the world during this period.

Under the guise of making the world "safe for democracy" and "fighting communism," the United States was directly or indirectly involved in a series of military *coups d'état* in Latin America and elsewhere from the 1950s to the late 1970s, beginning with the CIA-organized overthrow of the Iranian government in 1953 and the invasion of Guatemala in 1954. The government it installed in Guatemala prepared the ground for a series of pro-American regimes that have carried on continual campaigns of **state terrorism** that have killed many tens of thousands of Guatemalans, often with unspeakable brutality (Falla, 1994). More than a million citizens have been forced to flee the violence. For most of the decades that followed, Washington provided military aid, training, and diplomatic support for these regimes (Gareau, 2004: 63). When it became politically impossible for Washington to provide such assistance because of the Guatemalan military's gross human rights abuses, the Israeli government stepped in to provide military aid and training (Marshall, Scott, and Hunter, 1987).

The "domino theory" held that if one country fell under communist influence, its neighbours would soon follow suit. Operating with the domino theory in mind, the United States began a decade-long military intervention in Vietnam in the 1960s. This intervention followed years of French colonial domination. America's undeclared war killed more than a million North Vietnamese military personnel, between 500 000 and two million civilians, and more than 58 000 American military personnel. The war destroyed Vietnam's economic infrastructure; the country has only recently shown signs of recovery and economic expansion.

The main American rival on the world stage at this time was the Soviet Union, which also sought to extend its influence and promote the economic model it favoured. In so doing, it used military force to block efforts to democratize and liberalize authoritarian communist regimes within its sphere of influence (Hungary in 1956, Czechoslovakia in 1968) while lending its support to pro-Soviet governments elsewhere in Eastern Europe with strong authoritarian tendencies. Throughout the Cold War, the Soviet Union provided military equipment, training,

and advisers to various authoritarian regimes in the Middle East, notably Syria, Algeria, and Iraq under Saddam Hussein, as it competed with the United States for influence in the region. It refrained from supplying the most advanced weaponry to these states, however, for fear that doing so would drag it into direct military confrontation with the Americans (Antonenko, 2001).

Soviet economic and military aid also assisted the struggles of different movements around the globe to remove colonial and neocolonial domination. It bolstered the Vietnamese war effort against the United States, helped the Cubans resist the American economic blockade of that country, and provided arms and materiel to Angola, Mozambique, and Nicaragua in their war against "contra" mercenary armies and the apartheid South African government. Such countries as Cuba and Nicaragua turned to the Soviet Union for military aid only after the United States had fostered economic destabilization and engaged in covert military operations with the intention of bringing down their governments.

In the 1970s, the United States, with the help of allies such as France, provided military equipment, extensive training, and expertise to help install military governments in Brazil, Uruguay, Chile, Argentina, and the Dominican Republic. When these oppressive military regimes came to power, they typically forged strong ties with multinational corporations while suppressing trade unions and popular organizations and groups that opposed them. The oppression they unleashed was brutal. In Argentina, the number of citizens killed by the pro-American dictatorships exceeded 30 000 people, with members of the younger generation being the principal victims (Marchak, 1999). Increasingly, the tactics of repression developed by these dictatorships in Latin America are being used in other part of the world to stamp out dissent.

In the 1970s, popular struggles against a staunchly pro-American dictatorship in Nicaragua, and European colonial regimes in Angola and Mozambique, were successful in establishing governments that sought to redistribute land and wealth, and establish more democratic forms of popular participation. In their first years in power, they made dramatic strides in combating illiteracy and expanding healthcare (Vilas, 1986).

In the 1980s, the U.S. government sponsored illegal arms deals to covert armies to fight the revolutionary government in Nicaragua and support the

South African government in its campaign to destabilize Mozambique and Angola (Gareau, 2004; Marshall, Scott, and Hunter, 1987). In Mozambique, the South African strategy of destabilization was responsible for destroying 718 health facilities and schools accommodating 300 000 students between 1981 and 1986 (Gareau, 2004: 139–40). In Nicaragua, more than 50 000 people were killed or wounded in what was called the "contra war." In southern Africa, a task force appointed by the secretary general of the United Nations estimated that damage to Mozambique, Angola, and Zimbabwe from South Africa's destabilization campaign amounted to $60 billion (1988 prices) between 1981 and 1988, an immense sum for such desperately poor countries. Moreover, 1.5 million people died from violence or violence-related disease and famine, and half the population of Mozambique and Angola was displaced (Gareau, 2004: 141).

In the twenty-first century, war has continued to plague parts of the Global South, particularly sub-Saharan Africa and the Middle East, and has undermined the benefits that might come from development assistance. Post-communist Russia has become a major arms vendor. The Russian defence industry now depends on arms exports for its survival, and private interests in Russia increasingly act without government support to penetrate the lucrative Middle East arms market (Antonenko, 2001).

New actors have also emerged to pursue self-serving policies that fuel war, economic turmoil, and social disruption and dislocation, China chief among them. For example, China's pursuit of oil in Sudan has led it to support the Sudanese regime, which is responsible for the ongoing genocide in Darfur.

RESISTANCE TO THE NEOLIBERAL NEW WORLD ORDER
GOVERNMENT RESISTANCE

We end our discussion by considering how governments and people in the Global South, and most recently in the developed north as well, have resisted neoliberal policies.

Such resistance has been particularly acute in Latin America. Since 2000, Argentina, Brazil, Bolivia, Ecuador, and Venezuela have elected governments that oppose neoliberalism. These governments have been deeply concerned with the increasing concentration of land ownership, the concomitant spread of landlessness, and skyrocketing urban poverty in recent decades. They have sought to aid the landless and the urban poor, and in some cases to nationalize key resource industries and capture the profits that for decades went largely to transnational companies

Women members of the Movimento Sem Terra (MST), Brazil's Landless Workers Movement, protest against then United States president George W. Bush's visit to Brazil. The march also marked support of International Women's Day.
SOURCE: © Carlos Cazalis/Corbis.

with little local benefit. The Chavez government in Venezuela has used its oil wealth to provide substantial aid to other poor countries in Latin America. In fact, it has provided more aid than has the United States, which has an economy 90 times the size of Venezuela's ("Chavez," 2007).

POST-NEOLIBERALISM

The rejection of the neoliberal idea that free markets ensure development has inaugurated what some observers call the "post-neoliberal era" in the Global South. In the post-neoliberal era, alternative development strategies have been proposed. For example, in Latin America, **import substitution** has been widely recommended over neoliberalism as a superior development model. Import substitution involves replacing foreign-produced manufactured goods with domestically produced manufactured goods. Various forms of state intervention are deemed necessary for a successful import substitution strategy. They include government support for local technical innovation, labour force training, public–private sector partnerships, programs aimed at increasing social cohesion among the population, and so on.

It is, however, questionable whether import substitution is a serious challenge to the neoliberal model and the social inequities it spawned (Leiva, 2008). Critics of the import substitution strategy acknowledge that it may improve the competitive advantage of some countries in the global economy. It may also blunt some of the social damage caused by neoliberalism. However, they insist that import substitution does not challenge either the power of transnational corporations that have come to occupy a privileged position in many underdeveloped countries or the inequitable power relations that their dominance implies. Critics conclude that import substitution is more of a painkiller than a cure for the problem of underdevelopment.

POPULAR RESISTANCE

Social movements started challenging the neoliberal development model in 1999, when the World Trade Organization met in Seattle to start a round of trade talks that would open up markets around the world. Around 40 000 protesters gathered to demonstrate against the meeting, fearing the consequences of the new policies for Indigenous peoples, the environment, and global inequality. The violent police response and the resistance of the protesters were dubbed the "Battle of Seattle."

To formulate alternatives to the neoliberal agenda, the World Social Forum held its first meeting in 2001. It brought together activists, intellectuals, and members of nongovernmental organizations from around the world in Porto Alegre, Brazil, in 2001. Their statement of principles set out their aims as follows:

> The alternatives proposed at the World Social Forum stand in opposition to a process of globalisation commanded by the large multinational corporations and by the governments and international institutions at the service of those corporations' interests, with the complicity of national governments. They are designed to ensure that globalisation in solidarity will prevail as a new stage in world history. This will respect universal human rights, and those of all citizens—men and women—of all nations and the environment and will rest on democratic international systems and institutions at the service of social justice, equality and the sovereignty of peoples. (World Social Forum, 2009)

Since then, the World Social Forum has met annually in different places in the Global South.

Another important example of popular resistance to neoliberalism in the Global South is *Via Campesina*, an international organization of peasant farmers, rural women, and landless workers that seeks to achieve social justice and gender parity in the context of sustainable agricultural production (Borras, 2008). This movement has called for the establishment of "food sovereignty" that challenges the increasing dominance of global seed companies and food transnationals. It calls for the right of millions of small holders in the developing world to control their own food systems (Witmann, Desmarais and Wiebe, 2010: 2).

The Occupy Movement erupted in more than 80 countries around the world in 2008, a reaction to growing income inequality during the Great Recession of 2008-09. In the United States, many people were disgusted by the failure of governments to prosecute any of the wealthy people believed to be at the heart of decisions that brought on the financial crisis of 2008, while millions of ordinary Americans lost their jobs and their houses. In Europe, government austerity measures in the face of economic slowdown and skyrocketing unemployment were the

About 310 000 demonstrators gathered in New York City on September 21, 2014, to advocate global action on climate change. It was the largest climate change march in history.

SOURCE: © Stelya | Dreamstime.com - People\'s Climate March NYC Photo.

most prominent motivators. Everywhere, stark economic inequalities brought on by three decades of neoliberal policies provoked anger and spurred tens of thousands to demonstrate in the streets. We can probably expect other, similar social movements to erupt in coming years, especially movements linked to the growing threats of climate change and environmental ruin.

SUMMARY

1. **What are the stage and modernization theories of development and why are they problematic?**
   The stage theory of economic development holds that societies proceed through various phases of development much as biological organisms do. Contemporary American market society is considered the ultimate stage. Modernization theory argues that value orientations strongly influence how successfully countries develop. In this view, countries in which people have a high need for achievement and value competitive behaviour are more likely to develop successfully. Both theories ignore the history of exploitative relationships between rich and poor countries and the degree to which rich countries undermined the economic, social, and political structures of the Global South, thus condemning them to underdevelopment for centuries.

2. **What is dependency theory and why is it problematic?**
   Dependency theory holds that the most important mechanism blocking the development of poor countries is their exploitation by rich countries. While more historically accurate than stage and modernization theories, dependency theory is problematic insofar as it implies that certain geographical *regions* exploiting other geographical *regions* led to the underdevelopment of the latter. A more accurate rendering of the process of underdevelopment examines how certain *classes* in metropolitan countries, with their allies in the

colonies, acted to undermine colonial economies in the pursuit of profit over several centuries.

3. **According to Jared Diamond, how are geography and biological resources related to development prospects?**
Diamond argues that the Middle East and Europe enjoyed a friendly climate and numerous plant and animal species suitable for domestication. Coupled with their location on an east–west axis, these circumstances allowed for the spread of domestication, the rise of agriculture, the development of elaborate civilizations, and, eventually, technological innovation and resistance to disease. In contrast, societies in the New World existed on a north–south axis that impeded the spread of the few domestic species available to them and subsequent technological advantages and resistance to disease.

4. **What is problematic about using gross national product per capita as the sole indicator of development?**
The gross national product per capita of a country ignores other factors that influence human well-being, such as education, health, and environmental health. For this reason, social scientists increasingly use more comprehensive

development indicators, such as the United Nations' *Human Development Index*, as a measure of development.

5. **Haven't certain poor countries been able to escape from poverty in recent decades?**
China, Brazil, and other countries are experiencing rapid increases in gross domestic product per capita. However, the associated costs for society and the environment have often been high. Moreover, global inequalities remain staggering, and new evidence indicates that the gap between rich and poor countries is wider than earlier believed.

6. **Why is resistance to neoliberalism increasing?**
Policies of austerity, privatization, and free trade promoted by the World Bank and the International Monetary fund did not generally stimulate economic growth. Moreover, these policies created considerable social disruption and suffering. In Latin America in particular, several governments have resisted the worst aspects of these policies and opted for more government intervention with increased social welfare provisions. In recent years, growing income inequality and environmental degradation have stimulated opposition to neoliberalism in the world's rich countries, too.

QUESTIONS TO CONSIDER

1. Do you think global inequality will change over the next 25 years? In what ways? Why do you think these changes will occur? If you think global inequality will remain the same, explain why.

2. Should Canadians do anything to help alleviate global poverty? Why, or why not? If you think

Canadians should help end global poverty, then what should we do?

3. What circumstances allowed some countries to escape underdevelopment in the late twentieth and early twenty-first centuries?

GLOSSARY

Capitalism (p. 225) is an economic system based on profit-seeking in competitive markets. It is associated with dynamic technological development, the development of class inequality, and accelerating environmental destruction.

Deindustrialization (Note: p. 244) is a process, linked to neoliberal policies, that facilitates businesses moving to the lowest wage jurisdictions nationally or abroad, resulting in social dislocation and economic decline in older industrial regions.

Dependency theory (p. 227) is an explanation of uneven global development that stresses the exploitative relationships that have existed between Europe and the Global South, to the detriment of the latter (see the definition for *underdevelopment*).

Gross domestic product (GDP) (p. 225) is the dollar value of all goods and services produced in a country in a year. "Per capita" GDP is GDP divided by the

number of people living in the country. It is a measure of a country's wealth per person.

The **Human Development Index** (HDI) (p. 236) is a more comprehensive indicator of progress in development than is gross domestic product per capita. HDI incorporates measures of educational attainment and literacy and health outcomes.

Import substitution (p. 241) involves replacing foreign-produced manufactured goods with domestically produced manufactured goods. Various forms of state intervention are deemed necessary for a successful import substitution strategy.

Modernization theory (p. 227) argues that economic growth and development can best be achieved if the values underlying market capitalism are aggressively fostered.

Neoliberal theory (p. 233) calls for the elimination of government involvement in the economy, which presumably allows free markets to achieve economic growth and development.

Stages of development (p. 227) in W. W. Rostow's theory are the developmental phases through which societies supposedly pass. Rostow believed that modern American capitalism represents a final developmental stage characterized by sustained economic growth.

State terrorism (p. 239) is a deliberate act of physical or psychological violence perpetrated by state organizations (the army, secret police, etc.) to intimidate and coerce certain groups by causing fear, anxiety, panic, and horror.

Structural adjustment programs (SAPs) (p. 233) are policies imposed on debtor countries by the World Bank that entail privatizing of state enterprises, opening of debtor economies to imports

and capital from developed countries, eliminating social welfare and poverty reduction programs, and meeting debt obligations to the financial institutions of the rich countries.

Terms of trade (p. 230) refers to the ratio of the price of exports to the price of imports.

Underdevelopment (p. 229) is the idea that the development of Europe required the exploitation of the Global South and undermined its economic development.

The **Washington consensus** (p. 233) is the shared view of the International Monetary Fund, the World Bank, and the U.S. Treasury Department that emerged in the late 1970s, promoting a neoliberal approach to economic development and stabilization in the Global South.

NOTE

1. As transnational manufacturing firms shifted investment to low-cost labour markets, the **deindustrialization** of many developed countries took place, devastating communities in the north of England and the north-central United States (Bluestone and Harrison, 1982, 1988). Canadian workers and communities in Ontario and Quebec have not been immune to these forces (Winson and Leach, 2002). Investment has not shifted to all low-wage countries, however, because few can offer the massive infrastructure, disciplined low-cost labour force, and political stability that China can.

Illustrated by Aaron Millard.

PART 4

INSTITUTIONS

CHAPTER 11

FAMILIES

Sandra Colavecchia
McMASTER UNIVERSITY

SOURCE: Bob D'Amico/ABC via Getty Images.

AFTER READING THIS CHAPTER, YOU WILL BE ABLE TO:

- Understand how definitions of family and marriage are embedded in social policies and how these definitions influence our personal decisions about intimate relationships.

- Summarize how functionalist, conflict, symbolic interactionist, and feminist theorists view families.

- Explain how family forms have changed over time.

- Describe how industrialization changed family life and redefined men's and women's roles.

- Outline how social, economic, political, and ideological factors have led to contemporary trends in divorce, cohabitation, lone-parent families, delayed home-leaving, same-sex families, transnational families, and one-person households.

- Evaluate Canadian family policy in international context.

INTRODUCTION

Whether you are male or female, single or in a relationship, childless or a parent, living on your own or still living with your parents, heterosexual, lesbian, gay, bisexual, or transgendered, the choices you make about your intimate relationships are probably markedly different from those your parents and grandparents faced. Like an increasing number of young Canadians, you may have decided to delay marriage and family and live with your parents while pursuing your education and career goals. You may be in a same-sex relationship or living with a girlfriend or boyfriend or raising a child as a single parent. You may have made decisions for or against premarital cohabitation; getting involved with someone of a different race, culture, or faith; or balancing full-time employment and parenthood.

If you've delved into the life histories of your parents or grandparents, you may have concluded that, when they were young, they faced a much narrower range of choices about how their lives would unfold. Two sets of statistics illustrate the magnitude of the change. First, divorce rates have shot up in the past century. In 1925, fewer than 1 percent of marriages ended in marital dissolution, but the divorce rate rose steadily until 1987 and then levelled off. Today, 38 percent of Canadian couples divorce by their thirtieth anniversary and 30 percent of Canadian children experience a parental separation or divorce before the

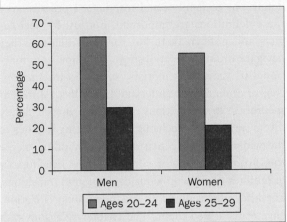

FIGURE 11.1 YOUNG ADULTS RESIDING IN THEIR PARENTS' HOME, CANADA, 2011

SOURCE: Statistics Canada (2014).

age of 16 (Ambert, 2012; Juby, Marcil-Gratton, and Le Bourdais, 2004; Sev'er, 1992; Wu and Schimmele, 2009). Second, an increasing number of young adults in their twenties are remaining in the parental home. In 2011, almost 60 percent of Canadians between the ages of 20 and 24 were living with their parents (see Figure 11.1).

This chapter examines how and why families and intimate relationships have undergone change and diversification, particularly in the past several decades. The main goal of this chapter is to advance a

The 1950s TV classic *Father Knows Best* (left) portrayed smoothly functioning, happy, white, middle-class, mother-homemaker, father-breadwinner families. *Modern Family* (right) reached the TV screen in 2009. Jay, a white Anglo-Saxon man in his 60s, is divorced and married to Gloria, who is Colombian, divorced, and in her 30s, and has a young son (Manny) from her first marriage. Jay has two adult children—Claire (married with three children) and Mitch (who, together with his male partner, have adopted a Vietnamese baby). Comparing sitcoms from the 1950s with today's sitcoms, we see that age, ethnicity, race, sexual orientation, and marital status have been transformed from constants into variables.

SOURCE: © John Springer Collection/CORBIS (l); © ABC/Photofest (r).

sociological perspective on families and to show how families are socially constructed. I begin by discussing definitions of families and marriage. I describe why these definitions are important, not just for sociologists and policymakers but for individuals as they navigate intimate relationships. I outline how functionalists, conflict theorists, symbolic interactionists, and feminists understand families. Different theoretical interpretations of family structure, family diversity, and the mechanisms connecting families to the wider society deepen our understanding of the social roots of family life. Next, I offer a brief history of families to show how major economic transitions, notably industrialization and postindustrialization, have transformed them. The chapter wraps up with an analysis of contemporary social policy, situating Canadian family policy in international context. This discussion highlights how policy is informed by political ideology and how, in turn, family policy constrains the personal decision making of Canadians, particularly working parents.

DEFINING FAMILIES

Just a half a century ago, most sociologists and nonsociologists defined *the* family as Mom, Dad, and their children—as if only one family form existed. The standard sociological definition of the family was something like "a cohabiting man and woman who maintain a socially approved sexual relationship and have at least one child." Today, we define families (now in the plural) more broadly to capture a wide range of family structures. Many sociologists now define **families** as sets of intimate social relationships that people create to share resources to ensure their welfare and that of their dependants. Social scientists prefer the broader definition partly because they recognize that definitions have significant implications for government social policy and inform the decisions we make about how to live. Governments deny some people certain rights, services, and benefits if they fall outside the definition of what constitutes a family, and people may make marital or other choices partly because of such exclusions. The traditional, narrow definition of family harms many people.

Implications for Social Policy

To understand the importance of definitions, consider the Compassionate Care benefits established as part of the Employment Insurance program in 2004. Compassionate Care benefits are paid to Canadians

to help them care for a gravely ill family member. Initially, the government provided a definition that excluded the following family members: grandparents; siblings; in-laws; same-sex partners and their extended family; other extended family members, such as aunts and uncles; and people who live in other kinds of unconventional families. Because of public criticism, the government has since expanded the criteria so that all Canadians can apply for benefits as long as they can make the case that the person who is gravely ill is someone they consider a family member, even if he or she is a close friend or neighbour. The expanded definition of family thus had far-reaching consequences for the care of gravely ill Canadians.

Government policies do not rely on just *explicit* definitions. They depend on *implicit* expectations of the kind of support that individuals receive from family members. One example is loan programs for postsecondary students. Eligibility criteria for student loans are based on parental income. It is assumed that parents support their children financially. Children whose parents' incomes are above a certain threshold are ineligible for loans even if they are in a situation where their parents do not provide financial support. Many of my students have been in this position or have friends in this situation. They must rely on part-time employment or other means of support.

People receiving government assistance in the form of welfare or disability payments are also constrained by government policy insofar as they may have their assistance reduced or taken away if they are found to be cohabiting. Typically, rules governing welfare assume that a man living with a woman on social assistance automatically provides financial support to the woman and her children. However, research shows that this assumption is false. Many such relationships involve men who are not the biological fathers of children. In **blended families**—two parents and the child or children from their former marriages or intimate unions—partners are less likely to pool resources than they are in other family types (Burgoyne and Morison, 1997; Colavecchia, 2009). Thus, welfare eligibility rules deter relationship formation because some women are reluctant to get involved with a man for fear of losing government benefits.

It follows that the high frequency of single-parent households among black families in North America may be at least partly the result of government policy (Calliste, 2001; Sudarkasa, 1993; Wilson, 1987). Welfare rules have effectively dissuaded single mothers from living with and receiving financial and nonmaterial support from parents, extended kin, friends, and unemployed male partners, thus weakening black families and communities. This example, too, illustrates how definitions of the family strongly influence families and the provision of government services.

DEFINING MARRIAGE

Traditionally, sociologists defined **marriage** as a socially approved, presumably long-term sexual and economic relationship between a man and a woman, involving reciprocal rights and obligations between spouses and between parents and children (Murdock, 1949: 2). Government definitions of marriage were similarly restrictive, excluding, for example, long-term, intimate, same-sex relationships. Many countries prohibited interfaith and interracial marriages, and even when they did not, citizens often disapproved of them.

Another example of how government definitions of marriage can exclude certain relationships is that of cohabiting or common-law marriages, in which a couple lives together but is not legally married. In the past, governments did not recognize such relationships. Consequently, many cohabiting spouses were denied access to government benefits. Today, many cohabiting couples consider themselves no different from married couples, and they have access to the same medical and pension benefits as formally married spouses. However, unlike married couples, cohabiting couples often face a one-year probationary period before they can gain access to a partner's benefits.

While many view common-law and marital relationships as indistinguishable, they are distinguishable in laws related to relationship dissolution. While married couples are entitled to an equal division of assets upon divorce, this does not apply to common-law couples. Nationally there have been many court challenges to these laws and it has been argued that women and children are particularly financially vulnerable in the event of common-law relationship dissolution. In 2013, the courts in British Columbia decided that common-law couples who have lived together for at least two years should have an equal division of assets if the relationship ends. Whether other provinces will follow British Columbia's lead remains to be seen. However, this legislative change underscores how government legislation defines the rights of individuals within intimate relationships.

Definitions have become a matter of heated debate with respect to same-sex marriage. In 2001, the Netherlands became the first country in the world to legalize same-sex marriage. Belgium, Spain, Canada (in 2005), South Africa, Norway, Iceland, Sweden, Argentina, and the United States (in 2015) followed suit. Other countries do not recognize same-sex marriage, although many Western European countries allow same-sex couples to register their partnerships under the law in so-called civil unions. Civil unions recognize the partnerships as having some or all of the legal rights of marriage.

Groups favouring same-sex marriage argue that it is a civil and human right, and that religious gay men and lesbians have the right to make a religious commitment in a place of worship that permits same-sex blessings (Abbott, 2010). Same-sex marriage helps to challenge systemic, institutionalized homophobia and affords gays and lesbians legal protection and greater social legitimacy (Green, 2011). Pragmatically, it ensures equal access to pensions and medical benefits, and extends other legal rights, such as the right to make medical decisions for a partner. Other groups oppose same-sex marriage, usually on the religious grounds that it is "unnatural" or "immoral." In the United States, before the U.S. Supreme Court's decision that legalized same-sex marriage, opposition was fuelled by the Christian evangelical right, which used vast economic resources, including ownership of important media outlets, to raise funds and mobilize opposition to same sex-marriage (Fetner, 2008).

Questions about how to define marriage have also surfaced in recent debates over polygamy (the marriage of a man to more than one wife) as Mormons in British Columbia and Utah face state prosecution for the practice (Javed, 2008).

Implications for Personal Decision Making

The choices we make about our living arrangements are shaped by our social context. For example, delaying or forgoing marriage and living independently are possible choices for many young people today. However, some young people are constrained from making these choices by the norms of their ethnic or religious group, which require that people remain in the parental home until marriage. Living on one's own is widely acceptable today, but not so for earlier generations, particularly earlier generations of women. Prior to the 1960s, most women did not have the means to live independently and even if they had the means, there was widespread social pressure for women to marry. Our social context moulds the decisions we make about where and with whom we will live.

I once had a conversation with Lucy, a woman in her nineties. Lucy told me that when she was growing up in the early 1900s, only two real options were available to her—getting married or joining a convent. Lucy got married. Her younger sister, Catherine, joined the convent. At the time, people considered it odd if adult women lived independently, with roommates, or in any kind of arrangement outside marriage for more than a few years.

My mother's history resembles Lucy's. She, too, faced few choices when she married my father in the 1960s. Lucy and my mother were constrained not just by government definitions and policies but also by cultural and religious norms and expectations. As a Roman Catholic Italian immigrant, my mother could not even dream of remaining single and living independently—even though she had the financial resources to do so because she had worked full-time ever since coming to Canada as a young teen. Similar constraints exist today for some young Canadians, particularly women, who are discouraged from living independently because of the religious or cultural norms of their communities. These examples illustrate how the social context in which people find themselves, not just political regulations, mould individual destinies.

Beginning in the late 1960s, women and men started to enjoy more options. Increasing secularism meant that support for the institution of marriage and traditional gender roles that underpinned religious doctrine started to erode. The women's movement of the 1960s gave women a political voice to challenge the idea that women belonged in the domestic sphere. The women's movement advanced exclusively the sexual revolution for women. It supported sex and living arrangements outside of marriage and women's right to contraception and abortion. The expansion of postsecondary institutions and the service sector provided women with the economic resources needed to live independently.

TIME FOR REVIEW

1. Why do definitions of families and marriage matter?

2. How have historical definitions of families and marriage excluded certain individuals or groups?

3. How might definitions influence decisions that people make about their intimate relationships?

SOCIOLOGICAL PERSPECTIVES ON FAMILIES

As new family types flourished beginning in the late 1960s, so did sociological definitions of families. They became more inclusive, acknowledging that many different types of family structure exist. Increasingly, sociologists rejected definitions that focused on clearly defined gender roles and specific types of family structure. Instead, they came to define families as sets of enduring social relationships responsible for **social reproduction**, that is, the physical and emotional work of bringing new generations into existence and nurturing and caring for both new and older generations (Fox and Luxton, 2001).

More inclusive definitions deflect our attention from fixed roles and structures, and toward the activities within families. When sociologists describe families as socially constructed, we convey the idea that families are neither static, universal, nor biologically determined (Baker, 2009a; Eichler, 1983). Although change in family structures and roles has been especially rapid since the late 1960s, families have *always* evolved along with, and in response to, broader economic and political change.

For instance, the transition from agriculture to industry in Western Europe in the late eighteenth and nineteenth centuries redefined women's relationship to production and their role in the family. In the agricultural and artisanal households of the preindustrial era, women's productive labour was valued because it was visible and central to daily subsistence. Under this system, husbands and wives were economic partners and women's caregiving was bound up with their daily productive work. In contrast, industrialization entailed mass production in factories, the disappearance of households as units of production, and the necessity of working for a wage to support a family. The public sphere of work became separated from the private sphere of the family. Among the poor and members of the working class, wives also worked for a wage. However, in the more affluent classes, women were relegated to the domestic sphere alone. Here they became financially dependent on breadwinning husbands. Their unpaid housework and caregiving became less visible and less socially valuable. Thus, the separation of the public and private spheres that accompanied industrialization increased the level of gender inequality.

Historical information on family change has been useful to sociologists interested in developing theories of the family. In the next section, I describe four theoretical perspectives that elucidate the inner workings of families and how families relate to the wider society. Each theory has its own point of emphasis, and while each theory is not entirely satisfactory in its explanatory power, each contributes to our understanding of the way families operate and change.

FUNCTIONALISM

Functionalists draw an analogy between the human body and society. The human body comprises different parts, each with a unique function, and these parts depend on one another to maintain a state of equilibrium and well-being for the entire body. Similarly, functionalists view society as consisting of interdependent parts. The family is one part that is central to the well-being of the entire society.

Talcott Parsons held that the **nuclear heterosexual family** is optimally functional for society and the ideal social unit in which to raise children. He premised his argument on the supposed efficiency of a strict sexual division of labour between husbands and wives, where husbands take on the "instrumental" role of breadwinner and wives take on the "expressive" role of caregiving (Parsons, 1951). According to Parsons, this division of labour holds families together because it makes men and women interdependent. Without such interdependence, marriages would dissolve and society would be destabilized.

Apart from providing a stable structure for economic cooperation, emotional support, and the socialization of children, Parsons identified two other functions that families perform—they provide a framework for reproduction and sexual activity. In Parsons's view, the biological requirements of reproduction necessitate heterosexuality, and marriage norms regulate heterosexual sex. Parsons believed that, over time, the family performed fewer functions because schools, nursing homes, the medical profession, and other institutions took on more of the work that was once done exclusively by the family.

By defining the heterosexual nuclear family as ideal, Parsons implicitly criticized families that diverge from the ideal, such as dual-earner families, single-parent families, and nonheterosexual families. Like other functionalists, he emphasized husbands' and wives' presumably shared interests. He did not address the possibility that their interests might not always coincide and that men's breadwinning enhances men's power in the family and creates economic inequality between men and women. By advocating a traditional

gender division of labour and women's financial dependence, functionalists in effect promote gender-based inequality in families. They do not address how women's financial dependence reduces women's leverage in marital decision making and prevents women from leaving marriages that are conflict-ridden and harmful to them and their children. They fail to see that the financially coercive nature of traditional nuclear families can compromise the successful socialization of children and the provision of emotional support.

Functionalism also promotes an historical view of families. The traditional nuclear family with a male breadwinner and a female homemaker was an historical anomaly, especially popular in the 1950s among North American families in which husbands earned a wage that was generous enough to support a family—a so-called **family wage**. Functionalists do not examine how historically specific factors, notably relatively generous state support for families, including "baby bonuses," and the expansion of the manufacturing sector that provided relatively high wages, reinforced the nuclear family. The nuclear family was also supported by ideal housing conditions: Homes in the suburbs were affordable partly because of massive government-funded road construction projects. Apart from these economic factors, nuclear families were pursued as an emotional response to the economic challenges of the Great Depression and the trauma and losses of World War II.

A less well-known example of state involvement to support heterosexual nuclear families occurred in the late 1940s and 1950s. During this period, fear of communism in North America led to political and educational campaigns promoting heterosexuality, marriage, and childbearing (Adams, 1997). Conforming to traditional nuclear family ideals became a show of patriotism and support for democracy. Difference was equated with dissent; nonconformists were regarded as potential security threats. Consequently, the RCMP subjected some gays and lesbians and childless married couples to surveillance because they were regarded as potentially sympathetic to communism and a threat to national security (Adams, 1997). Gays, lesbians, and others who did not conform to the traditional roles of the nuclear family, had their employment in the civil service terminated on the grounds that they were security threats.

CONFLICT THEORY

Conflict theory corrects functionalism's historical bias by underscoring how changing economic forces structure family life. Notably, Karl Marx and his friend, Friedrich Engels, examined how "modes of production" shape family life and living arrangements. (A mode of production, you will recall from Chapter 7, Social Stratification, consists of the form of labour and tools that characterizes an entire historical era and the type of class structure that is associated with it.)

Engels (1972) observed that in preindustrial times, families were "units of production" in the sense that they produced most of the goods and services needed for daily survival. Agricultural and artisanal families worked and lived in their homes, where no clear distinction existed between the private sphere of the family and the public sphere of work and citizenship. Accordingly, productive labour and caregiving were easily combined because they were accomplished in the same physical space.

With industrialization, production moved outside the family. Working-class families came to depend on wages earned by factory workers, male and female adults and children. A clear distinction emerged between the public sphere of work and the private realm of family relations. Households were no longer units of production. Among the middle class and the affluent, women did not need to work for wages, and the view emerged that the home was a haven from the horrors of the industrial workplace. Middle-class and affluent people increasingly saw women as the guardians of this new sanctuary. The notion emerged that "a woman's place is in the home" (Cott, 2009; Margolis, 2009).

Engels argued that in foraging societies, there was no private property, but as people began to settle in villages, economic surpluses accumulated. Social classes formed as some individuals were able to claim surplus production as their own property. However, a problem then emerged, Engels wrote—the problem of how to transmit wealth to offspring. The problem was solved by requiring female fidelity and male control of property. If men control property, they can ensure it is not squandered. If they enforce the fidelity of their wives, they increase the probability that their sons, who will inherit their property, are in fact *their* sons. These two principles—male control of property and female fidelity—are the foundations of the nuclear family, according to Engels.

If, for Marx and Engels, private property gave rise to the nuclear family, then the nuclear family in turn supported capitalism insofar as it produced, nurtured, socialized, fed, clothed, and housed people who would become workers. However, Marx and Engels paid little attention to social processes within families, such as the social relations that structure unpaid work in the home. In prioritizing class relations, Marx and Engels largely ignored gender relations and gender-based inequalities—precisely the topics that are of principal interest to feminists.

FEMINISM

In the 1960s, some feminist researchers attempted to extend Marxist theory by studying gender relations in families and how women's unpaid labour in the home is essential for the smooth functioning of capitalism (Luxton, 1980). While the term feminist scholarship is an umbrella encompassing many specialized theories, there are some recurring themes across all feminist scholarship. The goal of much feminist research is to render visible women's "hidden" experiences—experiences that, despite their significance in family life, are commonly ignored by nonfeminist researchers (DeVault, 1999). These experiences include housework, meal preparation, and the transition to parenthood (DeVault, 1991; Fox, 2009; Oakley, 1975; Walzer, 1998).

In their examination of such subjects, feminists introduced the concept of patriarchy, the social system by which men control women, and identified the consequences of men having more power than women do in families. Unlike functionalists, who argue that the gendered division of labour produces family stability, feminists see the gendered division of labour as hierarchical, coercive, nonfunctional, and a potential source of conflict. For feminists, the division of labour between women and men in the family crystallized when men started to exercise economic and political dominance and developed a patriarchal ideology justifying their authority. At its most extreme, it results in male violence against women; in the feminist view, when men engage in physical, emotional, psychological, and financial abuse, their aim is to control women (Ambert, 2012; Cory and McAndless-Davis, 2008; Gartner, Dawson, and Crawford, 2001).

A second important difference between functionalism and feminism concerns the issue of the uniformity or diversity of family forms. Functionalists regard the traditional nuclear family as universal. In contrast, feminists recognize that diverse family structures have always existed to satisfy a wide range of human needs that are influenced by the social environment (Stacey, 2011). For instance, women tend to become more domestic when opportunities for work in the paid labour force are relatively scarce and less domestic when such opportunities are abundant (Gerson, 1985; Luxton, 1980). By the same logic, cultural norms of femininity and masculinity change over time and differ from place to place, influencing the diverse ways in which people enact gender roles (West and Zimmerman, 1987).

Late-nineteenth- and early-twentieth-century feminists, and "second-wave" feminists from the 1960s and 1970s, have been criticized in recent decades for focusing too much on the concerns of young, professional, affluent, white, heterosexual, able-bodied women and ignoring the experiences and interests of marginalized women, including Indigenous women, women of colour, immigrant women, poor and working-class women, older women, women with disabilities, and lesbians. Recent feminist scholarship has sought to correct this imbalance by paying more attention to the unique issues and experiences affecting less privileged women (Nelson, 1996).

SYMBOLIC INTERACTIONISM

The theories I examined earlier offer mainly macro-level analyses of the family. In contrast, symbolic interactionists focus on families at the micro-level, exploring how people fashion a meaningful family life out of their everyday interactions. It analyzes how our sense of self develops in interaction with others, particularly parents and other family members. For symbolic interactionists, it is above all the use of symbols and rituals, such as the rings, houses of worship, and ceremonies associated with weddings, that create the meaningful experiences that hold families together (Ambert, 2012: 14).

As noted in Chapter 4, Socialization, the development of the self extends beyond childhood and primary socialization. With respect to the family, research has found, for example, that the birth of a baby changes a new mother's sense of self in ways that are different from the changes new fathers experience. In a study of first-time parents, Walzer (1998) found that mothers spent more time than their husbands did taking care of the baby's physical needs and also thinking about, and being preoccupied with, the newborn. Moreover, women's worries were different from those of their husbands. For instance, while mothers worried that maternal absence might deprive the baby of something important, men viewed

paternal absence as more of a loss for themselves, in that they might miss an important milestone, such as the first time the baby crawls. In a study I conducted on family finances, I found that husbands and wives reported that wives experienced more worry, anxiety, and guilt over personal spending, and were more focused on the family in their spending, and that these differences emerged during the transition to motherhood (Colavecchia, 2009).

The main criticism levelled against symbolic interactionism is that by emphasizing micro-level interactions, it neglects how larger structures influence families. Consider the emergence since the 1970s of neoliberal government economic policy as it relates to the family. By emphasizing the need to privatize child care and eldercare, neoliberalism seeks to place the burden of responsibility for the care of children and seniors on individual families rather than on the state (Baker, 2009b). Doing so increases the burden on women since they do a disproportionate amount of child care and eldercare.

TIME FOR REVIEW

1. How do functionalist, conflict, symbolic interactionist, and feminist theories of the family differ (see Table 11.1)?
2. What are the limitations of each theory in helping us understand the structure and purposes of families?

HISTORICAL AND CROSS-CULTURAL VARIATION
EARLY HUNTING AND GATHERING SOCIETIES

The influence of the social environment on families has been evident ever since foraging societies first emerged. Foraging societies were nomadic bands or tribes of up to about a hundred people who roamed the countryside to harvest edible wild plants and hunt animals.

The nuclear heterosexual family living in a privatized household with specialized gender roles is a new creation. It was not the norm for most of human history and prehistory. Humans have been around for about 100 000 years, and foraging societies predominated during the first 90 000. Because women spent much of their time gathering the food that constituted a large part of the band's needs, the care of children in foraging societies was not the responsibility

TABLE 11.1   FOUR THEORIES OF FAMILIES

THEORETICAL TRADITION	MAIN LEVEL OF ANALYSIS	VIEW OF FAMILIES	INTERPRETATION OF CONTEMPORARY TRENDS	EXAMPLES OF RESEARCH TOPICS SUGGESTED BY THE THEORY
Functionalism	Macro	Examines how families promote social order and social solidarity. The heterosexual nuclear family is seen as the ideal family structure. Families function to reproduce and socialize children, regulate sexuality, and provide economic and emotional support.	As the traditional heterosexual family declines, diversity of family forms will undermine social cohesion and social stability.	How does the family function to socialize children? How does family structure predict outcomes for children?
Conflict theory	Macro	Examines how changing economic forces structure family life. For example, industrialization led to the separation of the public sphere of work from the private sphere of the family with wide-ranging consequences for the roles played by different family members.	Fertility decline is linked to changes in the economic costs of children and to women's entry into paid employment. Delayed home-leaving prolongs children's dependence on parents.	How did the 2008–09 recession and its aftermath affect families? How do economic changes such as the expanding service sector influence family life?
Symbolic interactionism	Micro	Examines the way families are created through micro-level interactions among family members.	Family members create meaningful and intensely emotional relationships as they interact. For example, cohabiting adults may understand living together as a trial phase before marriage or an alternative to marriage; they negotiate the meaning of their relationship before and while living together.	How do family government policies influence personal decision making about relationships? What meanings do people attach to marriage, cohabitation, and so on?
Feminism	Micro and macro	Examines the causes and consequences of men's power and privilege, and women's disadvantages, in families and intimate relationships.	More so in the past than today, family life and intimate relationships reinforced gender-based inequalities. Families that did not conform to the nuclear ideal faced social stigma and lack of support. Today, gender inequalities persist, but women enjoy expanded educational and economic opportunities. Family forms are more diverse, and it has become necessary to figure out how state policies can better support diverse family forms.	Have gender-based inequalities in unpaid labour narrowed? What policies are needed to address gender inequality, violence, and abuse in families and intimate relationships?

of an individual household but of a wider group that included men. Men hunted more than women did, but the unpredictability of hunting meant that women's economic contributions were highly valued.

PREINDUSTRIAL SOCIETY

When nomadic tribes finally settled in permanent communities, they turned to agriculture and the domestication of animals. Family households were premised on assumptions and practices quite different from those that are now familiar to us. Today, families are based on ideas of love and caring, and of the special bonds and expectations of support between spouses and between parents and children. Love as a prerequisite or main motivator of marriage is a relatively recent social development. For millennia, marriage was a social contract that served to join two families and advance their mutual economic and political interests (Coontz, 2005).

In the preindustrial era, throughout Europe and North America, the composition and size of households were based almost exclusively on economic and labour needs. Husbands and wives were economic partners. Women did not focus exclusively on caregiving. Spouses continually made economic calculations about how much labour was required to run the farmstead or artisan shop. Household size fluctuated, depending on labour needs. For instance, more people would typically live in the home during harvest season as people were brought in to help with the harvest. A sharp line of demarcation between the public and private spheres did not exist because productive labour and caregiving were done in the same space.

There was no expectation that children would live with their parents until adulthood. Parents often saw children as an economic liability—another mouth to feed—if their labour was not required. Households could not afford to sustain many nonproductive members, so children as young as six or seven were expected to do chores, and they were routinely sent to live and work in other households if their labour was not required at home. Given today's ideas about the special bond between parents and children, it is hard to imagine the practice of sending young children to live with others, yet the economic structure and ideology of the day supported this arrangement. Moreover, since husband–wife partnerships were essential for the economic survival of a household, widowhood was sometimes followed by immediate remarriage if children were young and the labour of a spouse was needed.

INDUSTRIALIZATION

Industrialization began in the late eighteenth century in England. A hundred years later, North America, Western Europe, and Japan had followed suit. Industrialization had a profound effect on family life. Production by individual family households was replaced by large-scale factory production. As wage labour in factories and offices supplanted labour on farms and in small workshops, households shrank and increasingly contained just parents and their children, while the separation of public and private spheres transformed men's and women's family roles.

Among the poor and the working class, it was generally necessary for all family members, some as young as six or seven, to work for a wage. Things were not as jolly as the young chimney sweeps dancing on the rooftops in *Mary Poppins* make it seem. Young boys in the early industrial era were recruited to crawl up narrow chimney flues and clean out the soot. They would have to strip off their clothes to be able to wriggle up and down the chimneys, scraping their knees, elbows, and other protruding body parts against the sooty chimney walls in the process. The first recorded cases of industrial cancer (known at the time as "soot wart") date from this era. Similarly, Charles Dickens's story was not in the least unusual. When the police arrested his father in 1824 for failure to pay a debt, Dickens was set to work in a shoe polish factory, a dreadful ordeal that coloured much of his writing. He was 12 at the time.

Preindustrial families were the economic units of production. This scene shows a husband weaving at his loom and the wife spinning yarn.

SOURCE: © Culver Pictures/The Art Archive at Art Resource, NY.

For four reasons, the preference was to keep women at home if possible. First, domestic labour—preparing meals, washing clothes, cleaning, and so on—was time-intensive because households did not have modern conveniences, such as running water and electricity. Second, factory work was often dirty and dangerous, and workers were often subject to physical (and, in the case of women, sexual) abuse. Parents, worried about their daughters' safety, preferred to send sons out to the factories. Third, men's wages were generally higher than women's wages were. Fourth, some opportunities existed for women to earn money in the home, for instance, by taking in other people's laundry or doing sewing in the home for textile factories (Bradbury, 1993).

Among the middle and upper classes, women focused exclusively on homemaking and caregiving. New ideologies about femininity, motherhood, and children emerged to support the relegation of more affluent women to the private sphere, including the idea that women are biologically and uniquely predisposed to caregiving because of their "maternal instinct." Burgeoning medical and scientific literature and religious doctrine supported such notions. New psychological and child development theories promoted "intensive mothering," asserting that children need intensive and exclusive maternal care to ensure their long-term psychological well-being and avoid delinquency (Margolis, 2009). This literature stirred up women's fears and guilt, helping to keep them away from the public realm of wage labour and politics.

Under the new industrial regime, children required substantial economic investment for education and training. As a result, families became smaller, particularly in the more affluent classes, as parents, largely mothers, poured time, energy, and resources into ensuring that their children would succeed in the new economic order. Thus, the economic transformation of society gave rise to a new set of ideas about the socialization of children and the responsibilities that parents, and mothers in particular, needed to undertake.

THE 1950s AND BEYOND
ECONOMIC PROSPERITY AND THE TRADITIONAL NUCLEAR FAMILY

Today, when politicians, writers, and others argue that the modern family is in crisis and give us an idealized image of the family, they use the 1950s as their point of comparison (Popenoe, 1993). However, marital and fertility trends were anomalous in that decade compared with the decades leading up to and following the 1950s. Moreover, considerable evidence shows that observers who idealize the 1950s ignore the dark underside of family life (Coontz, 1992; Luxton, 1980). Many people were trapped in unhappy and abusive marriages. Some marriages resulted in divorce, and divorce rates would undoubtedly have been higher if women had been less economically dependent on their husbands and divorce laws had been more liberal.

ECONOMIC CRISES AND THE EMERGENCE OF THE DUAL-EARNER FAMILY

The tide quickly turned as economic affluence gave way to repeated recessions in the period from 1973 to, most recently, 2008–09. During this period, the growth of low-wage manufacturing in China and other countries caused the Canadian manufacturing sector to shrink. Unionized jobs that at one time paid a family wage became scarcer. More wives found it necessary to take jobs in the paid labour force to make up for the declining wages of their husbands. The great majority of these jobs were in the service sector. Although many were part-time, and therefore associated with relatively low pay and few benefits, they helped to alleviate the economic squeeze that families experienced. Today, there are nearly as many women in the paid labour force as there are men, and most women with preschool-aged children are in paid employment.

Some people urge a return to the male-breadwinner/female-homemaker nuclear family, ignoring that this model fails to address the economic needs of most families and the widespread desire of women to become educated, hold jobs, and pursue careers. Such critics find it acceptable that caregiving is a privatized responsibility assumed disproportionately by women. They criticize the alternative: new social policies, including support for high-quality, affordable, and universally accessible child care that would enhance the ability of parents to juggle paid employment and caregiving.

In sum, much of what we take for granted about families—how they are organized, the views we hold about children and marriage, and what we deem to be appropriate roles for men and women—is a consequence of change in the larger society. Contemporary trends in family life, outlined in the next section, further demonstrate this important fact.

TIME FOR REVIEW

1. Compare family structure and gender roles in hunting-and-gathering societies with family structure and gender roles in preindustrial societies.
2. What impact did industrialization have on men's and women's roles?

CONTEMPORARY TRENDS

I now want to outline major trends in contemporary families and some of the economic, social, political, and ideological factors underlying them. Specifically, I examine marriage, divorce, cohabitation, fertility, single-person households, delayed home-leaving, and transnational and multifamily households.

MARRIAGE

Most people marry but the rate of first marriages (the number of first marriages per 1000 Canadians per year) is declining as a growing number of Canadians cohabit and have children within a cohabiting context. Following divorce, most Canadians pursue another conjugal relationship, with cohabitation being more popular than remarriage. Divorced men are more likely to remarry or cohabit than are divorced women. Recent evidence suggests an increase in the number of divorced people who choose not to remarry or cohabit and this is

particularly true of divorced women with children (Vanier Institute of the Family, 2010). Married-couple families, although declining as a proportion of all households, remain the most common family form in Canada (see Figure 11.2).

The major changes we have seen in marriage include a growing number of Canadians deciding to forgo marriage altogether to remain single and live alone; people opting to cohabit rather than marry formally; commuter marriages where couples live apart, often to pursue jobs in different cities; the legalization of same-sex marriages; and the growth of single-parent households. Canadians are also delaying marriage, as evidenced by a higher age at first marriage for males and females (now more than 30 for men and more than 28 for women). The pursuit of educational and career goals leads to the postponement of marriage, and the attainment of economic security allows women to forgo marriage and live independently.

DIVORCE

Today, most Canadians choose a marriage partner based on love and romance. Yet for most of human history, people married to advance the economic and political interests of two families (Abbott, 2010; Coontz, 2005). Since love requires work and

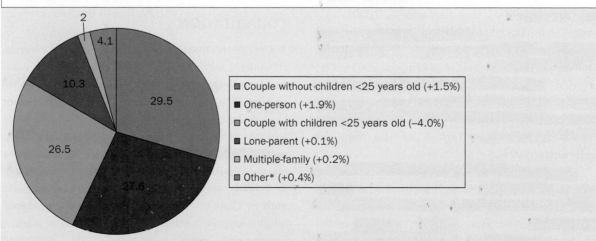

FIGURE 11.2 HOUSEHOLD TYPES, CANADA, PERCENTAGE, 2011 (CHANGE SINCE 2001 IN PARENTHESES)

- Couple without children <25 years old (+1.5%)
- One-person (+1.9%)
- Couple with children <25 years old (−4.0%)
- Lone-parent (+0.1%)
- Multiple-family (+0.2%)
- Other* (+0.4%)

*Two or more people who share a private dwelling, but who do not constitute a census family.

Note: As recently as 2001, couples with children under the age of 25 were the most common household type in Canada. Now they rank third (26.5 percent of the total) behind one-person households (27.6 percent) and couples without children under the age of 25 (29.5 percent). The figures in parentheses in the legend accompanying this graph indicate the percentage change in each household type since 2001. The prevalence of all household types except for couples with children is growing.

SOURCE: Adapted from Statistics Canada (2013).

commitment if it is to endure, we can understand how marriages based on love might be more fragile than those based on economic, political, and family obligations.

Many scholars link rising divorce rates to legal reforms that have made divorce easier. Historically, the Canadian divorce rate was suppressed until legislation was liberalized in 1925, 1968, and 1985. It was not until 1925 that Canadian women could petition for divorce on the grounds of adultery (Sev'er, 1992). Before 1968, however, divorce was inaccessible to most Canadians because a person wanting a divorce had to apply to the Canadian Senate to have the divorce granted by an Act of Parliament (Wu and Schimmele, 2009). The Divorce Act of 1968 introduced the concept of marriage breakdown as a ground for divorce, meaning that spouses who were separated for three years could now seek a divorce. Consequently, the 1968 divorce rate was almost 10 times higher than the 1925 rate. The 1968 law retained fault-based grounds for divorce, including adultery, cruelty, and desertion, but the divorce rate soared to 124 out of 1000 marriages in 1969.

The Divorce Act of 1985 instituted no-fault divorce, meaning that a person wanting a divorce no longer needed to show any wrongdoing, such as adultery or cruelty, on the part of their spouse. The 1985 legislation shortened the period of separation from three years to one year. Changes in legislation reflected changes in social demand. The divorce rate continued to increase, by 1980 reaching 260 out of 1000 marriages (Wu and Schimmele, 2009). The divorce rate peaked in 1987 and then levelled off. Recent marriages have a nearly 40 percent chance of ending in divorce (Statistics Canada, 2005). The fact that 30 percent of children will experience a parental separation or divorce before reaching the age of 16 means that family change is normative for many young Canadians (Juby, Marcil-Gratton, and Le Bourdais, 2004).

Higher divorce rates were also a by-product of shifts in the economy. As we have seen, the decline of the manufacturing sector squeezed many families economically, motivating women to take jobs in the expanding service sector. Increased participation of women in the paid labour force gave them the financial means to leave unhappy or abusive marriages. In addition, with too few daycare spaces to satisfy demand, married women's entry into the paid labour force often created marital stress as couples struggled with the competing demands of domestic and paid work. Such stress was often resolved through divorce.

Divorce has led to an increase in single-parent families, 82 percent of which are headed by women, many of whom must cope with low income and poverty (Richards, 2010). Divorce has also resulted in an increase in blended families. While second marriages have higher divorce rates than first marriages do, and some children in blended families have problems adjusting, in many blended families parents meet the challenge of bringing together adults and children from different families and creating a harmonious home environment.

The effect of divorce on children's well-being has been the focus of much public concern. Social science research offers two important conclusions about how children are affected by parental divorce. First, children are most adversely affected by divorce when there is a high degree of conflict between parents. In fact, children suffer more in high-conflict *intact* families than in low-conflict divorced families. Divorce provides a solution to the problem of high parental conflict. Second, it is not divorce per se, but the disruption in children's daily routines following divorce that more adversely affects children. Since most single parents are women and most experience a decline in their incomes post-divorce, divorce often means moving house, changing schools, and disrupting children's friendship networks. Such change undermines children's need for routine (Furstenberg and Cherlin, 1991).

COHABITATION

A growing number of couples, particularly younger Canadians, are deciding to cohabit, and an increasing number of children are being born to cohabiting couples. The fact that most cohabiters have never been married and half of cohabiters marry their partners supports the claim that cohabitation is often a trial phase before marriage (Wilson, 2009). For others, cohabitation is an alternative to marriage. In Canada, rates of cohabitation are exceptionally high in Quebec, which enjoys relatively generous family support policies (notably, widely available, inexpensive, government-funded daycare), and where many people reject Catholic traditions. Cohabiting relationships tend to be less stable than marital relationships are, partly because cohabiters tend to hold less traditional ideas about family life and are less likely to believe in marital permanence (Wilson, 2009).

FERTILITY

Long-term fertility decline is associated with the economic, social, and ideological changes that accompanied industrialization. Every year, I poll my students to find out how many siblings they have to illustrate the trend toward smaller family sizes. Most of my students are only children or have one sibling, which mirrors what we see among Canadian families generally. The number of live births in Canada per 1000 people dropped from 45 in 1851 to 10.5 in 2004 (Baker, 2009a).

How can we explain the trend toward small families? The decriminalization of contraception, the availability of the birth control pill, and the legalization of abortion certainly gave women more control over childbearing. Yet historical evidence shows that women have always attempted to prevent pregnancy and limit childbearing by means of withdrawal and self-induced abortions. Declining fertility in the past several decades is also a consequence of women's rising level of education, which leads to the postponement of marriage and childbearing, and shortens the reproductive years.

Marriage and fertility are becoming increasingly uncoupled. More people have children outside of marriage, either as single parents or in a cohabiting relationship, and some married couples are voluntarily childless. Reproductive technologies, such as in vitro fertilization, offer new possibilities for creating life and in the process transform how we define and understand parenthood. Increasingly, parenthood is becoming detached from biology as individuals and couples who cannot reproduce biologically use adoption, sperm and egg donors, and surrogates to become parents (Baker, 2009a).

People who have no biological connection to a child, either because they are stepparents or adoptive parents, can still define themselves as parents. For instance, among lesbian couples who have children, both the woman who carried the baby and the woman who did not are considered mothers. A male friend may donate sperm to a lesbian couple, and sometimes he may play an active role in raising the child (Dunne, 2000). A different pattern is exemplified by actors Neil Patrick Harris and David Burtka. Harris and Burtka hired a surrogate and had eggs fertilized with their sperm. One of their twins is biologically Harris's child while the other is biologically Burtka's child. They have chosen not to know the paternity of each twin.

SAME-SEX MARRIAGE AND SAME-SEX COUPLES RAISING CHILDREN

Same-sex cohabitation and marriage, with and without children, have increased in Canada (see Figure 11.3). The raising of children by same-sex parents predates same-sex marriage legislation in 2005, but it has only been recently that same-sex parents have been able to foster and adopt children through the Children's Aid Society. The question of how children raised by lesbian and gay parents fare compared with children

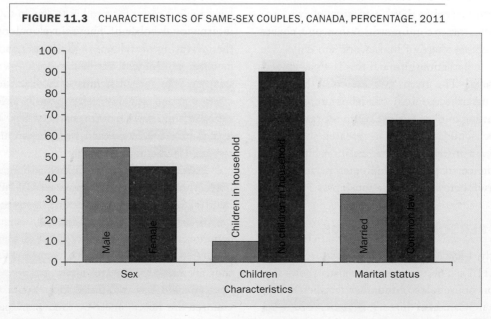

FIGURE 11.3 CHARACTERISTICS OF SAME-SEX COUPLES, CANADA, PERCENTAGE, 2011

SOURCE: Statistics Canada (2013).

raised by heterosexual parents has been important for family law, specifically judicial decision making in post-divorce litigation involving disputes over child custody.

Opponents of same-sex marriage have often argued that children are adversely affected by being raised by same-sex parents and have argued that the sexual orientation of parents should be considered in child custody cases. However, research comparing children raised by lesbian and gay parents and by heterosexual parents finds no differences that would warrant discrimination against a parent based on sexual orientation. Children raised by lesbian and gay parents are similar to children raised by heterosexual parents in terms of various outcomes, such as mental health, academic achievement, behavioural issues, and quality of parent–child relationships (Stacey and Biblarz, 2001).

The fact that children raised by gay and lesbian parents have done so well despite the social stigma and discrimination they often face is a testament to the quality of parenting by gays and lesbians. Much of the explanation for why children of lesbian and gay parents do well is related to the fact that same-sex parents tend to differ from heterosexual parents in ways other than sexual orientation that make them good parents. Children born to heterosexual parents are more likely to have been unplanned. Heterosexual parents are also likely to be younger and have fewer economic resources than do gay and lesbian parents.

Research shows that gay and lesbian parents are more successful in sharing housework and child care than heterosexual parents are (Dunne, 2000; Nelson, 1996). Despite their increasing labour-force participation, women continue to do a disproportionate (albeit declining) share of housework and child care in heterosexual relationships and this leads to marital dissatisfaction. The term "second shift" has been coined to describe the domestic labour that women do after putting in their "first shift" in the paid labour force (Hochschild, 1989). The greater sharing of unpaid labour in gay and lesbian relationships points to the salience of gender ideologies in sustaining inequalities in heterosexual relationships.

SINGLE-PERSON HOUSEHOLDS

Increasingly, Canadians are living alone (refer back to Figure 11.2). The most recent census shows that lone-person households outnumber families for the first time in Canadian history. Some people who live alone were once married or cohabiting. Higher divorce rates, greater financial stability, and improved health for older widows and widowers helps to explain this trend. In addition, more people are remaining single. This trend is largely the result of increased financial independence for women and the weakening of the stigma once associated with remaining single.

DELAYED HOME-LEAVING

In attempting to reach their educational and career goals, young adults are remaining in their parents' home longer than they used to. In 1981, about 27 percent of young adults between the ages of 20 and 29 lived with their parents. By 2011, that figure had risen to more than 42 percent (Statistics Canada, 2011: 2). In addition, some young adults return to their parents' home after living independently for a time. Young adults may return after divorce or separation to receive emotional support or assistance with child care, or because they want to upgrade their educational qualifications and need their parents' financial support. Cultural and gender factors influence these patterns. Some ethnic groups place a strong emphasis on adult children, particularly daughters, remaining in the parental home. Overall, men in their twenties are more likely than women of the same age are to reside in the parental home.

TRANSNATIONAL AND MULTI-FAMILY HOUSEHOLDS

Since the 1980s, the world has witnessed unprecedented levels of international migration and travel. At the same time, new communications technologies have made it easier for families to stay in touch across international borders. These developments explain the increasing prevalence of **transnational families**, in which family members reside in different countries. In some cases, family members lead lives and work in one country while the remaining family members live in another country. In other cases, young adult children reside in a host country while parents work in the family's country of origin.

Multifamily households include more than one nuclear family, while **intergenerational households** include multiple generations, such as grandparents, parents, and children, living together. Such families are common among immigrants. Often financial pressures necessitate these arrangements. Sometimes, however, they are based on an interest in preserving cultural heritage, language, and religion. Some Canadian children are raised solely by their grandparents and these families are referred to as *skip generation families*.

SOCIAL MOVEMENTS AND IDEOLOGICAL CHANGE

Since the 1960s, social movements—collective attempts to change the social order—have changed people's attitudes about families significantly. For example, in the United States, the civil rights movement extended political, social, and economic rights to people of colour, and the movement positively affected race and ethnic relations in Canada, too. One upshot was that interracial and interethnic marriage became more socially acceptable (see the Critical Sociology: Globalization box). The gay and lesbian social movement successfully promoted the

---

CRITICAL SOCIOLOGY: GLOBALIZATION **CANADA IS LEADING THE PACK IN MIXED UNIONS**

The following is an editorial that ran on the website Macleans.ca in July 2014, based on the release of Statistic Canada's *2011 National Household Survey* (Editorial, 2014).

Canada has always been something of a mashup. Whether by necessity or choice, our history is marked by the coming together of different groups and races to produce something new: European and Aboriginal, English and French, old stock and immigrant ...

Last month [June 2014], Statistics Canada released its latest numbers on couples who cross racial or ethnic lines, revealing surprising and continued growth. Mixed unions are no longer unusual, nor an excuse for cultural conflict or bigotry; today, they've become a commonplace feature of life as it is lived in Canada. As such, we're setting the global standard for multicultural acceptance and integration.

According to the most recent National Household Survey, there were more than 360,000 mixed-race couples, either married or common-law, in Canada in 2011. This comprises 4.6 per cent of all couples in private households. While still a small share of the country's nearly eight million couples, the rate of growth for mixed unions is accelerating—having leapt from 3.1 per cent in the 2001 census and 2.6 per cent in 1991. In the past five years alone, the number of mixed unions is up by nearly one-quarter, far outpacing the 5.1 per cent growth for all legal couples over the same time period. All this suggests Canadians are no longer bound by outdated cultural mores or strictures when picking a partner. ...

A mixed union is defined by Statistics Canada as a conjugal relationship between two people who belong to different visible minority groups, or between one visible minority and one white. Within such groupings, however, there's considerable diversity. Nearly 80 per cent of Japanese "marry out," as sociologists put it. Latin Americans and blacks are also proportionately overrepresented within mixed unions. Groups least likely to marry out include Chinese and South Asians.

A couple of trends suggest the overall growth rate will move up in future, regardless of ethnicities involved. First, mixed unions tend to track the percentage of visible minorities in the greater Canadian populace. With visible minorities predicted to account for up to a third of the population by 2031, further growth will no doubt occur as the dating pool changes. Mixed unions are more common within younger age groups, as well, suggesting a gradual progression through society. Higher education is also correlated with mixed unions, as is urban living. Vancouver boasts the highest percentage of mixed unions, at nearly 10 per cent, followed by Toronto, Victoria, Ottawa and Calgary. As the number of mixed unions grows, so, too, will the offspring from these relationships. Whatever taboos may have existed for these children in the past, they're being erased by sheer numbers. ...

Critical Thinking Questions

1. Why is higher education correlated with interracial and interethnic unions?
2. The editorial in this boxed feature suggests that, for several reasons, stigma surrounding interracial unions will decline as interracial unions increase. What social factors other than those mentioned in this editorial might challenge such stigma?

SOURCE: Reproduced by permission of Peter Taylor.

extension of economic and political rights to people involved in same-sex relationships, paving the way for the legalization of civil unions and same-sex marriage (Fetner, 2008). The women's movement helped enormously in women's struggle for the right to higher education, paid employment, equal pay for doing the same work as men, and so on. As women's education, income, and independence increased, the fertility rate fell and the divorce rate rose because women now had the capacity to limit childbirth and leave unsatisfying marriages. Radical feminism in particular embraced the rights of gays and lesbians and brought attention to the problem of violence in intimate relationships.

Long-term trends, such as increasing secularism and individualism, had implications for family life too. Growing secularism eased religious strictures against divorce, cohabitation, and same-sex relationships. Individualism involves prioritizing personal happiness over social obligation, including the responsibilities bound up with marriage and family. One consequence of growing individualism is that we have higher expectations of our partners than our parents or grandparents had of theirs. Our higher expectations create more fulfilling relationships as we seek compatible partners and are less likely to remain in unsatisfying relationships. However, our higher expectations also lead to higher rates of relationship dissolution and people deciding to live alone when partners or spouses fall short of our expectations. These cultural shifts partly explain the increasing number of voluntarily childless married couples. While the stigma surrounding voluntarily childless couples has not disappeared, voluntarily childless couples challenge the conventional view that children are a prerequisite to personal happiness and fulfillment (Basten, 2009; Carroll, 2000).

Sociologists, politicians, religious leaders, and others differ in their evaluations of the changes I have just reviewed. Social conservatives assert that the family is in crisis and is undermined by feminism, secularism, and individualism (Popenoe, 1993).

Social liberals contend that these changes are not harmful. Rather, they promote equality and choice, thus leading to happier and more fulfilling lives. The following discussion of family policies shows that such ideologies and assumptions about family life are important as they become concretized in family policy.

TIME FOR REVIEW

1. Why did divorce increase between the 1960s and the 1980s?
2. Why are an increasing number of young adults "delayed home-leavers?"
3. What connections exist between declining fertility, increasing divorce, increasing cohabitation, and increasing single-person households?

SOCIAL POLICY

Family policies encompass marriage and divorce laws; income security programs, such as maternity and parental leave; child welfare programs; and child-care services. Given Canada's universal healthcare system and high standard of living, we might assume that the state generously supports families in this country. However, in many ways, Canadian family policies fall short of those in Western Europe. Imagine a family policy continuum, one pole of which signifies that families are a *collective* responsibility and the other of which signifies they are an *individual* responsibility. Canada and Western Europe lie close to the opposite poles (although the United States lies even closer to the ideal of individual responsibility; see Figure 11.4).

INCOME SUPPORT POLICIES

Some of the shortcomings of Canadian family policy are evident if we compare income support plans in Canada with those in Western Europe. Income support payments include cash transfers to families in the form of direct payments and tax

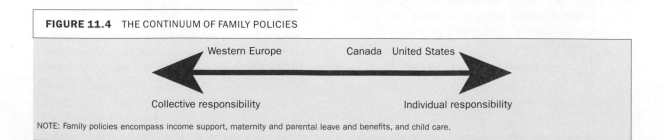

FIGURE 11.4   THE CONTINUUM OF FAMILY POLICIES

Western Europe   Canada   United States

Collective responsibility   Individual responsibility

NOTE: Family policies encompass income support, maternity and parental leave and benefits, and child care.

deductions, maternity and parental leave benefits, and maintenance payments, which involve child support for children whose parents have divorced.

In Canada, the main forms of support include the Universal Child Care Benefit, the Canada Child Tax Benefit, the Family Supplement (paid when one parent is receiving employment insurance), and the Maternal and Parental Benefits. Benefit levels in Canada are lower than levels in Sweden, Denmark, Germany, and Norway, among other Western European countries (Phipps, 2009). In fact, they are even lower than levels in some poorer Eastern European countries, such as Romania, Lithuania, and Slovenia (McGill Institute for Health and Social Policy, 2012). Moreover, Canadian policy uses stricter eligibility criteria, making it more difficult for families to qualify for support (Phipps, 2009). Unlike our Universal Child Care Benefit, which the government considers to be taxable income, many European programs offer tax-free income support programs.

Western European countries, including Finland, Sweden, Germany, and France, have implemented advanced maintenance payments that provide economic support to children of divorced parents where the absent parent does not pay child support (Phipps, 2009). This system does not exist in Canada. Instead, we require that noncustodial parents pay child support and put measures in place to try to enforce it when a parent is not voluntarily providing the support. Often these measures are insufficient to meet the economic needs of children.

MATERNITY AND PARENTAL LEAVE AND BENEFITS

Leave

Maternity and parental leave provide job protection for Canadians while parents care for their newborns. In Canada, we distinguish maternity from parental leave and allow provincial and territorial differences in the length of leave. Maternity leave varies from 15 to 18 weeks depending on the jurisdiction. Only biological and surrogate mothers are eligible for such leave. Parental leave varies from 35 to 52 weeks, depending on the province or territory. It is available to mothers and fathers, including adoptive parents. Many European countries offer longer leave, paid and unpaid. For instance, the Netherlands provides unpaid leave for parents with children under the age of eight, and Spain offers three-year unpaid leave (Organisation for Economic Co-operation and Development, 2011).

Our system offers fathers parental leave, but it is mostly mothers who take it. In other countries, fathers are more strongly encouraged to take parental leave. In addition to parental leave for mothers, such countries offer "take it or lose it" leave for fathers only. The fact that so few men take parental leave stems from societal attitudes about men's and women's appropriate roles, and also from the fact that women on average earn less than men do; gender disparities in the labour market channel the lower-earning spouse, typically the woman, into parental leave. For most couples, the decision about who should take parental leave is made on a purely economic basis rather than taking into consideration the aptitudes, dispositions, and desires of individuals.

Benefits

Benefits refer to the money parents receive from employment insurance and sometimes from employers during their leave. Residents of Quebec enjoy higher benefit levels than other Canadians do and there are other provincial and territorial variations as well. Some Canadians receive a "top-up" of their benefits from their employer. Some observers therefore suggest we have a two-tier system, with higher benefits going to employees who are already the most advantaged in the labour market.

One of the main criticisms of how Canadian maternity and parental benefits are determined is that we require recent labour-force participation and link benefits to earnings in the previous year only. Our laws preclude women from receiving benefits for second and third children if they have not been working in the year before giving birth. This eligibility requirement forces many women to decide between (1) returning to work sooner than they would like to so they can qualify for benefits for a subsequent child, or (2) forgoing benefits altogether so they can stay at home with their children.

In France and Germany, the state allocates leave benefits to new parents even if they lack a recent history of paid employment. This approach results in more families qualifying for benefits. Other family-friendly policies that exist in some Western European countries but not in Canada include the option of parents working shorter work days and taking paid sick days to care for sick children at home. These cross-national differences underscore how the larger social context shapes ostensibly private decisions, such as the decision whether to stay at home to take care of a sick child.

CHILD CARE

Canada lacks a country-wide system of universally accessible, affordable, high-quality, regulated daycare (see the Critical Sociology: Protest and Policy box).

Some analysts argue that universal child care would provide short- and long-term benefits to our economy; others say that the costs are prohibitive. Our government's willingness to provide daycare during World

---

CRITICAL SOCIOLOGY: PROTEST AND POLICY   **CHILD-CARE COSTS HIGHEST IN TORONTO AREA, LOWEST IN QUEBEC BECAUSE OF PROVINCIAL POLICIES**

The following article appeared in the *Toronto Star* in November 2014.

For Eitan Grinspun, daycare debt is the new student loan.

"It's just the most important thing I can give my child," says the father of 3-year-old twins.

"It's not about the college fund. It's about giving them the right start."

But for the Toronto dad and his partner, the right start for their kids costs $3,000 a month. That reality has recently forced the couple to take out a loan to cover the expense, in a city where spaces are scarce and wait-lists long.

"I see parents all the time when we go outside to play in the playground. And you see the desperation—like, how did you get there, what did you do?" says Grinspun.

Sky-high daycare costs are no secret to GTA parents, but a new study reveals for the first time how their fees fare in comparison to other Canadian cities.

Research by the Canadian Centre for Policy Alternatives shows Brampton, Toronto, Mississauga and London to be the least affordable in the country.

In Toronto, parents with kids under age 2 can expect to pay $1,676 a month for the service. In contrast, that cost is $152 for parents in cities across Quebec. In Winnipeg, the next cheapest city, families spend about $650.

"Quebec has $7-a-day child care* which is very different to the situation you find everywhere else in the country," says David Macdonald, senior economist at the think-tank and a co-author of the report.

"The other province that has capped fees is Manitoba, and therefore you see Winnipeg, in every one of the other measures, as the next most affordable place to put your children. And this is due to a substantial subsidy program both in Quebec as well as in Manitoba."

"What this report makes clear is that provincial policy really makes a difference," says Carolyn Ferns, of the Ontario Coalition for Better Child Care.

"Four of the five highest fees are in Ontario, and that should be a wake-up call."

Ferns says addressing affordability should be "key" to the Ontario government's renewed efforts to modernize child care in the province.

In July [2014], the government introduced a new bill aiming to increase the number of available spaces in licensed care in Ontario, and to improve regulation of unlicensed daycare. Currently only around 20 per cent of children in the province are in regulated care settings.

Provincial NDP education critic Peter Tabuns responded to the Canadian Centre for Policy Alternatives report by saying that the Liberals "need to stop paying lip service and make the expansion of licensed child-care spaces a top priority."

"Families can't afford to wait any longer," he added.

Critical Thinking Questions

1. What are the advantages and disadvantages of low-cost daycare such as provided by the provincial government in Quebec?

2. Do barriers other than cost limit the provision of affordable, universal child care in Canada?

SOURCE: Sara Mojtehedzadeh (2014). Reprinted with permission – Torstar Syndication Services.

*On 22 April 2015, the daily rate rose to $7.30 for families with incomes under $50 000. The rate became $8 a day for families earning between $50 000 and $74 999. On family incomes of $75 000 or more, the daily rate is now on a scale, increased gradually to $20 on family incomes of about $155 000.

War II to entice women to work in munitions factories and take other jobs to help the war effort suggests that universal child care can be implemented if there is sufficient political will. This is most evident when we consider how Quebec has made child care a political priority. In Quebec, parents have access to regulated, licensed, and affordable childcare for as little as $7.30 a day. In the rest of the country, child care in licensed, regulated daycare centres is expensive, scarce, and often involves long waiting lists. Consequently, most Canadian children are cared for in informal and unregulated settings—by relatives, by friends, in home daycares, and by nannies.

In the absence of a universal child-care system, Canadians have relied on the Temporary Live-in Caregiver program as a way of offering affordable child care to working Canadians. This program allows women from foreign countries to work as nannies, with the objective of receiving permanent resident status after two years of such work. Faced with dire economic need in their countries of origin, many women who come to Canada under this program have left their own children to care for Canadian children. Some of these women are exploited and abused by their employers but unable to do anything about their situation because of their immigration and economic status (Arat-Koc, 2001). Some have argued that the requirement that foreign workers live with their employers is problematic because it increases their vulnerability to exploitation.

IMPLICATIONS OF SOCIAL POLICY

Family policies strongly influence the economic security of families. In many European countries, poverty rates are substantially lower than in Canada (see the Critical Sociology: Social Inequality box). The lack of policy support for working parents

---

CRITICAL SOCIOLOGY: SOCIAL INEQUALITY | CHILD POVERTY

This article appeared in the *Toronto Star* in November 2014.

One in five Ontario children still faces life in poverty, according to a new study.

This remains true despite a pledge in Ottawa, made exactly 25 years ago today, to eliminate child poverty by 2000 and the province's promise in 2008 to reduce poverty by 25 per cent by 2013.

The national problem has not just lingered. It is worse than it was in 1989.

More than 1.3 million children across the country—550,000 of them in Ontario—live this way, according to authors of the 2014 report card on child and family poverty.

The odds only get worse for single-parent homes with one child, where the rate of poverty is 44 per cent in Ontario. The numbers are also bleak for First Nations children living on reserves, those with disabilities and children of colour. According to one calculation, half of all Ontario children born to immigrant parents live in poverty.

For all these children, poverty can mean a lack of access to healthy food, affordable shelter and other basic necessities.

It means more than half a million Ontario children start life on unequal footing.

And as the wealth of the nation has more than doubled, the report points out that income for the country's poorest families has essentially flatlined.

"The numbers evoke for me a serious concern about whether our leaders and our policies are reflecting what I think Canadians still value, which is a sense of fairness, and of value in sharing and collective solutions," said Laurel Rothman, who works with Family Service Toronto and is the national co-ordinator of Campaign 2000, authors of the report.

"We can fix this. You're not looking for a cure for cancer. We're looking for the will to use the tools that exist."

Critical Thinking Questions

1. What tools exist to improve child poverty in Canada?
2. What are the social and economic causes of increasing child poverty in Canada?

SOURCE: Jennifer Pagliaro (2014). Reprinted with permission – Torstar Syndication Services.

in Canada means that women—single mothers in particular—are less likely than their Western European counterparts are to work in the paid labour force. Apart from economic security, family policies influence the quality of care that children receive. In the absence of sufficient government support, families must navigate the daily dilemmas of juggling paid labour and caregiving by relying on individual rather than collective solutions.

TIME FOR REVIEW

1. What supports are in place for families and parents in Canada?
2. How does family policy in Canada compare to family policy in other countries?

CONCLUSION

Sociology helps us appreciate how social forces influence our intimate relationships and family life. The chapter began with a discussion of why definitions of family and marriage matter. We saw that the definitions embedded in policies include some categories of people and exclude others from various forms of support. We also saw how definitions provide a framework for individual decision making about the kinds of relationships and families we might pursue. Most sociologists argue for a more inclusive definition of family than currently exists in Canadian legislation. This inclusive definition emphasizes that social reproduction—the caring work of families—lies at the basis of family life.

We also saw that each of the four main sociological perspectives offers a different interpretation of families. The most diametrically opposed are the functionalist and feminist perspectives. Functionalists regard the traditional heterosexual nuclear family, consisting of a male breadwinner and female homemaker, as the ideal family form. Feminists seek to demonstrate that this type of family is by no means universal and is characterized by a high level of gender inequality and frequent failure to satisfy the needs of all family members. Our overview of the social history of families from foraging societies to the present revealed enormous variation in family structure, men's and women's roles, and changing ideologies surrounding marital and parent–child relationships. The interplay between economic forces and family life continues. Many contemporary trends in family life, including delayed marriage, fertility, and home-leaving, reflect broad economic shifts.

What might Canadian families look like in a hundred years? Will our children and grandchildren face life options similar to ours or will their futures look entirely different? Imagining the future reminds us of the plasticity of families and the need to implement social policies that address the needs of diverse Canadian families. While the term *policy* may seem remote and complex, in fact what we are talking about is finding ways to ensure that children whose parents are working in the paid labour force enjoy high-quality child care and that policies are set up to minimize child poverty. These are not lofty goals or a luxury we cannot afford. The examples of many other countries, and the province of Quebec, provide clear evidence that thoughtful family policy is essential for children and their families, whatever form the family might take.

SUMMARY

1. **Why are definitions of family important for government policy making and personal decision making?**
   The government uses definitions of family and marriage to formulate social policy. Historically, these definitions have excluded many types of families, denying them government services and benefits. In formulating social policy, governments also make assumptions about the kinds of support that should exist within families, so social policy has repercussions for many aspects of families, including relationship formation and dissolution. Definitions of family and marriage shape personal decision making. As definitions broaden, people have more choice in how they want to organize their family life.

2. **How do functionalists, conflict theorists, feminists, and symbolic interactionists understand families?**
   Functionalists view the traditional nuclear family as the ideal unit within which to raise children. Conflict theorists focus on how family life is shaped by larger economic structures. Feminist approaches systematically examine women's experiences and the consequences of gender-based inequality in families. Symbolic

interactionism advances a micro-level perspective by examining how families are produced and reproduced through everyday interactions.

3. **How do comparisons of family life in different historical periods illustrate the sociological insight that families are socially constructed?**
Family forms vary over time and place. The traditional nuclear family living in a privatized household is a relatively recent phenomenon. In foraging societies, families were embedded in the larger group and privatized households did not exist. In preindustrial societies, households were economic enterprises and household composition was determined by labour requirements. Industrialization and the need for wage work brought about a separation of public and private spheres that led to the emergence of the nuclear family living in a privatized household.

4. **What are some of the contemporary trends in family life?**
Some of the most significant trends in family life include delayed marriage and home-leaving, lower fertility, and higher rates of same-sex marriage,

cohabitation, divorce, lone-parent families, single-person households, transnational and multi-family households, and unconventional families.

5. **What are the causes of contemporary trends in family life?**
Myriad social, economic, political, and ideological factors explain recent change in family forms. They include the influence of the civil rights movement, the women's movement, and the gay and lesbian social movement. Family trends have also been influenced by increasing secularism, individualism, and declining social stigma for nontraditional family choices.

6. **How does family policy in Canada compare to family policy in Western Europe?**
Compared with family policy in Western Europe, Canadian family policy does not provide sufficient family support, particularly for working parents in need of high-quality child care. Family policies provide inadequate economic security to Canadian families, which accounts for the relatively high rate of child poverty and of single-parent families living in poverty in this country.

QUESTIONS TO CONSIDER

1. In what ways were the family-life options available to your grandparents and your parents different from the options available to you?

2. Imagine that you have been elected to public office and have influence over family policy. What social programs would you reform or establish to best support Canadian families?

3. Speculate on what marriage, divorce, cohabitation, and fertility will look like 100 years from now based on contemporary trends and likely developments.

GLOSSARY

Blended families (p. 248) include two parents and the child or children from their former marriages or intimate unions.

Families (p. 248) today are defined by many sociologists as sets of intimate social relationships that people create to share resources to ensure their welfare and that of their dependants.

The **family wage** (p. 251) refers to the wage men traditionally received that was sufficient to support a family.

Income support payments (p. 262) include cash transfers in the form of direct payments or tax deductions, and maternity and parental leave benefits. In Canada, the main forms of support include the Universal Child Care Benefit, the Canada Child Tax Benefit, the Family Supplement (paid when one parent is receiving employment insurance), and Maternity and Parental Benefits.

Intergenerational households (p. 260) are families that include multiple generations such as grandparents, parents, and children living together.

Marriage (p. 249) was traditionally defined as a socially approved, presumably long-term, sexual and economic relationship between a man and a woman involving reciprocal rights and obligations between spouses and between parents and children. Today, many countries recognize common-law marriage and some, including Canada and the United States, allow marriage between people of the same sex.

Multifamily households (p. 260) include more than one nuclear family.

A **nuclear heterosexual family** (p. 251) includes a father, mother, and children living in a privatized household.

Social reproduction (p. 250) involves the physical and emotional work of bringing new generations into existence and nurturing and caring for both new and older generations in families.

Transnational families (p. 260) are families whose members are geographically separated for extended periods.

CHAPTER 12

WORK AND OCCUPATIONS

Sandy Welsh
UNIVERSITY OF TORONTO

SOURCE: Andrey Pavlov/Shutterstock.

AFTER READING THIS CHAPTER, YOU WILL BE ABLE TO:

- Explain why work in Canada is becoming more polarized into "good" and "bad" jobs.

- Contrast the way some workers get trapped in bad jobs with the way other workers protect access to good jobs.

- Identify how mobile communication devices are changing the way we work and blurring the boundaries between paid work, domestic work, and leisure time.

- Describe how management organizes work to reduce costs, increase productivity, and, in some cases, enhance worker empowerment.

- Analyze the determinants of job satisfaction and worker "alienation."

- Appreciate the important role social networks play in helping people find jobs.

AN INTRODUCTION TO WORK IN CANADA

WORKING IN RETAIL

Zainab Taiyeb worked for several months selling electricity and gas plans door to door in Toronto. Every day, her supervisor picked her up at a subway station and drove her to her assigned neighbourhood. One day, however, her supervisor took her to an office of Rogers Communications Inc. Although Zainab had been hired by a subcontractor, she received an ID card imprinted with the Rogers logo and was told she would now be selling high-speed Internet and cable services. Zainab, a recent immigrant from Pakistan, received no contract for her work at Rogers. She was also told she would have to wait for three weeks until she was paid. After Zainab had worked her first month, her employer owed her $1500.

Zainab worked in good faith and expected to see a paycheque. When she and her co-workers confronted their employer, he said he was a subcontractor and that he couldn't pay them because Rogers hadn't paid him. "When I demanded to be paid, along with the other workers, I was given $20. Can you imagine? I had worked for one month and was given $20. It was so insulting. I cried that day" (Berinstein, 2004).

Most of us assume we will be paid for our work. However, Zainab Taiyeb's experience shows that even today that is not always a safe assumption. What would you do if this happened to you? Would you chalk it up as a lesson learned about contract work and move on? Would you push back and fight? As a contract worker, Zainab did not have access to a union. So, to overcome their situation, she and her co-workers turned to the Toronto Organizing for Fair

How can workers have a job that pays a decent wage, treats them with respect, and offers some satisfaction?

SOURCE: © Getty Images/Jupiter Images.

Employment (TOFFE) and Workers Information Centre (now merged to form the Workers' Action Centre) to learn about their rights. They filed a complaint with the Ontario Labour Relations Board and launched a corporate campaign to pressure Rogers to "take responsibility and force the subcontractor to pay us" (Berinstein, 2004). It took two years, but eventually Zainab was able to collect the $1500 owed her. She also drew attention to a widespread practice: the unfair treatment of contract workers.

Zainab Taiyeb's work experience mirrors many of the issues facing people who are current and potential employees. She is part of the rising legion of service workers engaged in **nonstandard work**, which involves part-time, contractual, and seasonal work; the holding of multiple jobs; work secured through a temporary worker agency; and self-employment. As a woman and an immigrant, Zainab also personifies some of the key shifts in the Canadian workforce since the 1970s. Her concerns are ours: How can we have a job that pays a decent wage, treats us with respect, and offers some satisfaction?

This chapter will take you through many of the key issues facing workers today. I'll discuss what precarious employment means for our working lives, how employees and employers battle to gain the upper hand in determining what jobs will be like, what factors lead to "good" jobs and "bad" jobs, and what influences worker satisfaction in different kinds of jobs. Whether we look at an immigrant contract worker asking for her wages or doctors fighting provincial governments for the right to choose where they practise, the study of work and occupations is a study of the constraints and the struggles that occur daily in Canadian workplaces.

THE INDUSTRIAL REVOLUTION AND BEYOND

Zainab Taiyeb working as a contract worker represents the most recent phase in our economic development. To understand how we reached this phase, we need to review the development of the Canadian economy and occupational structure.

Most researchers think of changes in the economy and the world of work as "revolutions." The Industrial Revolution started in Great Britain in the late eighteenth century, completing the transition from feudalism to capitalism. Under feudalism, most people worked as peasant farmers, and a few skilled artisans made tools and a variety of goods. As a result of the growth of the textile industry and nonlocal markets for wool, Scottish landowners started to use their land for sheep grazing and other cash crops. Displaced by this shift in land use and in need of work, some peasant farmers migrated to Nova Scotia, but most moved to Glasgow and other urban areas in Great Britain, looking for jobs in the emerging factories and artisan shops.

The organization of work dramatically shifted during the Industrial Revolution. Under feudalism, most farmers produced enough to meet their own needs. There existed no clear separation between work and leisure. Agricultural labour had its own work rhythm, connected to the rising and the setting of the Sun and the passage of the seasons. However, the transition to capitalism transformed most peasant farmers into wage-earning factory workers. Now, workers' schedules were standardized and set by their bosses. The **division of labour** expanded; work previously done by skilled craftspeople was broken down into smaller components, so semiskilled workers, who were paid less than skilled craftspeople, could perform factory jobs. An urban capitalist class and a "blue-collar" working class emerged from these processes (Polanyi, 1957).

Canada went through its own industrial revolution, although it occurred later here than in Western Europe and the United States (Laxer, 1989). As late as the early twentieth century, 40 percent of the Canadian population worked in agriculture (Campbell, 1996). When industrialization began, activity centred on Canada's vast natural resources, such as lumber and minerals.

In the early twentieth century, the Second Industrial Revolution started. It was marked by the introduction of steel, petroleum, and electricity in the manufacturing process. Large corporations bought smaller companies engaged in similar lines of production. Henry Ford's assembly line and other mass-production technologies contributed to this expansion. Company owners increased their ability to dominate the market and control the activities of workers.

Simultaneously, an "administrative revolution" transformed office work (Lowe, 1987). Because of the vast amounts of information produced by companies, such as personnel and transaction records, management needed efficient systems to organize their offices. This circumstance led to the expansion of the "white-collar" job sector and the growth of bureaucratic organizations. All these changes amounted to an increased division of labour.

Now, managers managed, clerical workers handled paperwork, and production workers accomplished smaller and smaller parts of the production process.

So we can see that work as we know it in Canada and other capitalist economies is a new phenomenon. At the time of Confederation in 1867, most Canadians did not live in cities and work for employers in large bureaucratic organizations. Since then, we have moved from a society that depends heavily on agriculture to a society that depends heavily on manufacturing to a society that depends heavily on the provision of a wide variety of services.

The Canadian Labour Market in Context

Before discussing the shift to a service economy, it's useful to have some background information about the Canadian labour market. Since the 1970s, the labour force has changed dramatically. Some of the changes reflect demographic trends, such as the aging of the population. Some changes are due to a combination of economic and political factors, such as the increasing participation of women in the paid labour force. And some changes are the result of government policy to deal with predicted labour shortages, such as the increasing prominence of immigrants in the labour market.

So how exactly has the labour force changed? For one thing, Canada's population is more educated than it was in the 1970s. In 1971, 58 percent of Canadians in the paid force between the ages of 25 and 54 had not finished high school. In 2014, the figure was just over 7 percent. In contrast, just 18 percent of Canadians in the paid labour force between the ages of 25 and 54 had a college or university degree in 1971. In 2014, the figure was just over 69 percent (Laroche, and Mérette, 2000: 27; Statistics Canada, 2014a). The increased emphasis on education has made it more difficult for workers who have not completed high school to do well in the labour market. In 2013, just over half of Canadians between the ages of 25 and 44 with less than a Grade 9 education were employed. The comparable figure for Canadians with more than a bachelor's degree was nearly 86 percent (Statistics Canada, 2014b). So while the increased importance of education is a good news story for those who are well educated, it is a bad news story for those who are less well educated.

A second key change in the Canadian labour market is the growing reliance on immigration to meet the demand for skilled workers (Statistics Canada, 2003). In the 1980s, about 125 000 immigrants arrived in Canada annually. In recent years, the annual figure has been more than twice as high. Immigrant workers today, like Canadian-born workers, are more highly educated than those who arrived earlier. The rise in the educational status of immigrants is partly explained by the federal government's immigration policy. This policy emphasizes bringing skilled immigrants to Canada to "foster a strong and viable economy in all regions of Canada" (Statistics Canada, 2006a: 87). Recent immigrants are also more likely to be members of a "visible minority" compared with those arriving earlier. Recent arrivals face some difficulty in the labour market from discrimination and a lack of recognition of their educational credentials (see Chapter 9, Race and Ethnic Relations).

Women's participation in the labour force is the final important labour market change since the 1970s. Women now make up just under half of the paid workforce, compared with only 37 percent in 1976 (Statistics Canada, 2006b; Statistics Canada, 2011; see Chapter 8, Gender Inequality, for details).

The Canadian economy has experienced four big recessions since the 1970s—one in the mid-1970s, one in the early 1980s, one in the early 1990s, and one beginning in 2008. During each of these periods, the economy shrank and unemployment rose, particularly in the manufacturing sector. Young workers were particularly susceptible to layoffs because the last hired are usually the first fired when a company struggles in a difficult economy. Recovery from the 1991–92 recession was particularly sluggish. It was not until the end of that decade that the Canadian labour market began to fire on all cylinders. By 2008, the unemployment rate had dropped below 6 percent—a level not seen since the 1960s. Then, all hell broke loose. The housing and credit markets collapsed in the United States and the shock was soon felt globally. Manufacturers started shutting down factories. In Canada, the auto sector was particularly hard hit. By all accounts, Canada weathered the global recession better than other countries did, and by early 2011, the employment rate bounced back to where it was at the start of the 2008 recession (Gilmore and LaRochelle-Côté, 2011).

Keeping this overview in mind, we can now turn to an analysis of the rise of the service economy, what it means for where Canadians work, and the quality of the jobs they hold.

The Second Industrial Revolution started in the early twentieth century. It was marked by the introduction of steel and petroleum products in manufacturing, the spread of use of the assembly line and other mass-production technologies, and the growth of giant corporations.

SOURCE: Ellen Griesedieck, *Rouge Assembly Line*. Courtesy Gallery Henoch.

TIME FOR REVIEW

1. What were the main changes that the British labour force witnessed during the Industrial Revolution?
2. What are the main changes that the Canadian labour force has witnessed since the 1970s?

WORK IN THE SERVICE ECONOMY

Since 1976, Canada has experienced a shift away from goods-producing industries and a rapid growth in service industries (see Figure 12.1). Employment in services more than doubled, while employment in manufacturing increased less than 20 percent. Economic downturns affected employment in goods-producing industries more than in services; you can plainly see the big drops in manufacturing employment in the early 1980s, the early 1990s, and 2008–09, the three recessions covered by Figure 12.1. The effect of the recessions on service employment was much less pronounced. From 1976 to 2013, the percentage of Canadians employed in service industries grew from 65 to 78 percent (Statistics Canada, 2011a: 315; 2014c).

There are many reasons why Canada, like many industrialized countries, experienced massive growth in the service industry. Chief among them is that increased global competitiveness facilitated the movement of much manufacturing to low-wage, less-developed countries. Since the 1990s, free trade agreements with the United States and Mexico have facilitated the migration of manufacturing jobs out of Canada. Proportionately fewer manufacturing jobs mean proportionately more service jobs.

In 2013, the largest part of the economy in terms of the number of people employed was "trade," with 15.2 percent of all workers. Retail trade accounts for three-quarters of all trade. By far the largest category of retail trade is food and beverage stores, including grocery stores, specialty food stores, and beer, wine, and liquor stores. Lower-tier service jobs in such stores are characterized by low pay and nonstandard work hours: features of bad jobs (Presser, 2003). The second biggest part of the economy in terms of the number of people it employed was "health care and social assistance,' with 12.3 percent of all workers. Much of the growth in that sector is due to increased demand for healthcare by an aging population. From the early twentieth century until 1990, manufacturing industries employed more Canadians than did any other segment of the paid labour force. However, by 2013,

FIGURE 12.1 EMPLOYMENT IN GOODS AND SERVICES, CANADA, 1976–2013

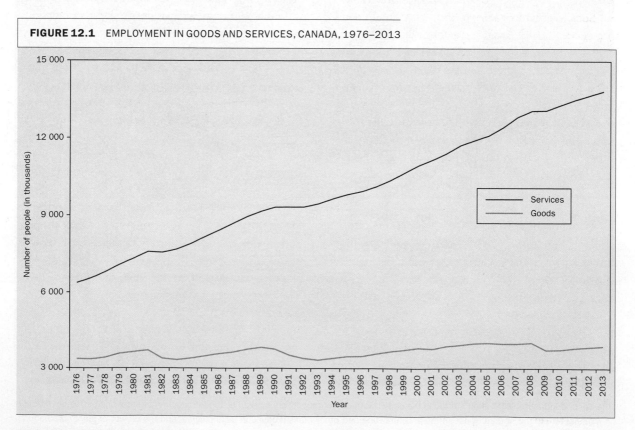

SOURCES: Statistics Canada (2012a, 2014c).

manufacturing industries employed just 9.8 percent of the paid labour force, making it the third biggest employment sector (Statistics Canada, 2014a).

Given that manufacturing is the third-largest employer of Canadian workers, you may wonder why there is so much concern about the decline of manufacturing. While manufacturing, along with retail and wholesale trade, and health and social services represent the largest categories of employment, they are not necessarily the industries experiencing the highest rate of growth. Professional, scientific, and technical services, along with business, building, and other support service industries, have experienced the highest rate of growth since the late 1980s. Manufacturing is far down the list in terms of growth, surpassing only the resource-based industries of forestry, fishing, mining, oil and gas, and agriculture.

Sociologists are concerned about the decline of jobs in manufacturing industries because jobs in this sector have long represented good jobs in terms of wages, benefits, and security. These jobs also represented the best opportunities for young workers, especially young men, with high school education or less. In 2013, wages were substantially higher in manufacturing industries (on average, $23.19 an hour) than in retail trade (on average, $15.94 per hour; Statistics Canada, 2014d).

Sociologists often refer to the shift from a goods- to a service-based economy as **deindustrialization**. Deindustrialization began in Canada and the United States in the 1970s and continues today. It reduced the number of unionized, well-paying, full-time manufacturing jobs and increased the number of "bad" jobs located in the lower-tier service industries. The process of deindustrialization also caused a host of long-term economic and labour market difficulties, such as a rise in unemployment and increasing income inequality.

GOOD JOBS OR BAD JOBS?

At the centre of our discussion of what the service economy means for Canadian workers is the question of whether more good or bad jobs are available for workers. At minimum, good jobs provide **extrinsic rewards**, such as high wages, good benefits, employment security, and opportunities for advancement. Good jobs can also provide **intrinsic rewards**, such as decision-making opportunities, challenging, nonrepetitive work, and autonomy that allows for self-direction and responsibility in carrying out tasks.

Debate revolves around changes in the skill level of jobs in the service economy. Conventional wisdom suggests that skill requirements are increasing because of technology (Spenner, 1983). As Daniel Bell (1973) and other postindustrialists propose, we should experience an upgrading of jobs in the economy as skill requirements increase. Postindustrialists also predict that job growth will occur in the higher-skilled occupations. In contrast, Harry Braverman (1974) and other postindustrial critics believe that skill levels are being downgraded. In this view, although some highly skilled professional and technical jobs are being created, most new jobs are lower-skilled industrial and service jobs.

So which is it? Are we moving to the postindustrial world of Bell or the downgraded world of Braverman? One way to answer this question is to look at which occupations are held by Canadians. About one in four men is employed in the construction trades and as transport and equipment operators. Another one in five men is employed in sales and service occupations. Just under one-third of all women work in sales and services. About one in four women work in business, finance, and administrative occupations. Hidden within these broad categories are important distinctions. For example, sales and service occupations include cashiers, food and beverage servers, police officers, and child-care workers. Business, finance, and administrative occupations include accountants, insurance agents, and clerical workers. As discussed in Chapter 8, Gender Inequality, significant gender segregation exists within these categories.

When we examine shifts in the Canadian occupational structure, we see a more complex picture than those sketched by Bell and Braverman. Blue-collar jobs in the middle have declined. Job growth is occurring at the top and the bottom of the occupational structure (see Figure 12.2). There is some evidence of a shift toward what Statistics Canada calls *knowledge occupations* in the Canadian labour market. Knowledge occupations are defined as those where a high proportion of workers have a university education. Some of the main knowledge occupations are in the health professions, science and engineering, and management. The percentage of Canadians in knowledge occupations increased from 14 to 25 percent between 1971 and 2001 (Baldwin and Beckstead, 2003). Statistical projections indicate that, between 2013 and 2022, the jobs that will grow most quickly in number (between 1.1 percent and 2.2 percent per year) will be in professional, scientific, and technical services; health care; mining, oil, and gas extraction; construction; and nonautomotive transportation equipment. The jobs

FIGURE 12.2 PROJECTED AVERAGE ANNUAL EMPLOYMENT GROWTH FOR 33 MAJOR INDUSTRIES, CANADA, 2013–2022 (PERCENTAGE)

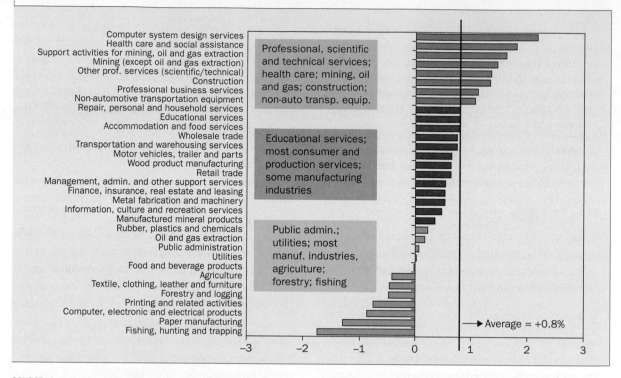

SOURCE: *Canadian Occupational Projection System 2013 Projections: Job Openings (2013-2022)*. URL: http://www23.hrsdc.gc.ca/l.3bd.2t.1ilshtml@-eng.jsp?lid=22&fid=1&lang=en. Employment and Social Development Canada, 2014. Reproduced with the permission of the Minister of Employment and Social Development Canada, 2015.

that will shrink most quickly in number (between –0.4 and –1.8 percent per year) will be in manufacturing, agriculture, forestry, and fishing) (see Figure 12.2).

As Figure 12.2 suggests, a service-based economy does not necessarily involve bad jobs for everyone. A misconception about the service economy is that the service sector creates only bad jobs and that the goods sector is the source of good jobs. This scenario assumes that all service jobs are alike. Instead, we should think of the service sector as having a lower tier made up of traditional services, such as retail trade, food, and personal services, and an upper tier consisting of other services, such as finance and business, utilities, health, education, and public administration. Whether you find yourself in a lower- or upper-tier service job has implications for your wages, job security, and the skill content of your work (Economic Council of Canada, 1991; Krahn, 1992).

However, these statistics are partly misleading. Statistics Canada points out that an increase in part-time work and self-employment is driving the growth in service occupations. So although business and other services have the potential to create good jobs, some of those jobs may not be full-time. The movement to a service economy has affected the types of jobs available in Canada. Some good jobs are created in financial services

and health services, while bad jobs with nonstandard hours are also created, primarily in sales and service. I now explore the issue of nonstandard work more fully.

NONSTANDARD JOBS

Twenty years ago, sociologists did not spend much time researching nonstandard jobs. That has changed with increasing numbers of temporary, part-time, contract, and self-employed workers. Nonstandard work is now a central part of the economy. Most of us know people who work in a nonstandard job. You may have a part-time job at a local retail store that helps you pay your tuition and other bills, while giving you (almost) enough time to study. One of your parents may have been laid off because of company restructuring, only to be hired back later as an independent contractor. One of your friends may have used a "temp" agency to find work when her other attempts didn't work out. You may know someone who works as a paid or unpaid intern (see the Critical Sociology: Protest and Policy box).

Part-time jobs, temporary jobs in which people are hired through a temporary agency, self-employment, contract work, outsourcing, and seasonal work are all considered nonstandard jobs. Some sociologists call

CRITICAL SOCIOLOGY: PROTEST AND POLICY   THE RISE OF THE UNPAID INTERN

Nicholas Smith landed a job right after he graduated from the University of Toronto with an ethics degree in 2013. A year later, he was working in his second job. The trouble is that both jobs were unpaid internships. "I used to do marketing and there are a couple of marketing companies that have marketing graduates working 50-hour weeks and overtime without pay, and if you refuse to work the OT you don't get a reference," he said (Canadian Press, 2014a).

Nobody knows how many Canadian internships are unpaid, but figures from the United States (where one-third of interns are unpaid) and Western Europe (where one-half are unpaid) may give a rough indication of the likely magnitude of the problem in this country (Library of Parliament, 2013). Anecdotal evidence suggests that unpaid internships first became widespread during the Great Recession of 2008–09. Many unpaid interns work at wealthy corporations, including Bell Media and Fairmont Hotels and Resorts.

Unpaid interns tend to be young and unable to find paid employment but they need job experience on their résumés so they work for nothing. Most interns who are unpaid or are receiving less than the minimum wage are women. Some are recent immigrants who need Canadian employment experience to land a paying job. At the *Huffington Post* in the United States, a few interns actually *pay* to work as unpaid interns. To become an unpaid intern, you must be able to afford it; typically, unpaid interns have savings, loans, or relatives who can support them while they work for nothing. The system can provide certain advantages—useful network ties, letters of reference, job experience—but it is mainly people from middle-class families who can afford to become unpaid interns (Cross, 2014).

In November 2014, Stephen Poloz, the governor of the Bank of Canada, was widely criticized for advising the 200 000 young Canadians who are out of work as follows: "If your parents are letting you live in the basement, you might as well go out and do something for free to put the experience on your CV" (Canadian Press, 2014b). Other outrages have sparked protests against unpaid internships. In 2011, a student DJ working for free died in a car accident after repeatedly being compelled to be on air all night at an Alberta radio station. In 2013, many Canadians were appalled when the Vancouver Fairmont Waterfront Hotel posted an ad for people to bus tables for free.

Some politicians in the New Democratic and Liberal parties are demanding laws to regulate internships fairly. The Canadian Intern Association was formed to advocate against the exploitation of interns and to improve the internship experience. People who have been abused by the system of unpaid internships have gone public with exposés of their exploitation. If such pressure persists, one may reasonably expect that, in the coming years, at least the more egregious forms of exploitation will be abolished.

Critical Thinking Questions

1. What are the potential advantages and disadvantages of unpaid internships?

2. Should internships be regulated and, if so, how? What potentially positive and negative outcomes might result from regulation?

SOURCES: Canadian Press (2014a, 2014b); Jessica Smith Cross (2014); and the Library of Parliament (2013).

them "precarious" jobs because they do not provide stable, long-term employment or adequate pay (Cranford, Vosko, and Zukewich, 2003). In most industrial countries, including Canada, one-quarter to one-third of all jobs are now nonstandard (Chaykowski, 2005; Cranford, Vosko, and Zukewich, 2003; Krahn, 1995).

It is not always clear what defines a job as nonstandard. Often, nonstandard jobs are defined in terms of what they are not: They are not jobs in which workers have a full-time, year-round job with one employer, located at the employers' premises, and under the supervision of that employer. In a standard job, workers also have a reasonable expectation that employment will continue indefinitely (Cranford, Vosko, and Zukewich, 2003: 459; Kalleberg, 2011; Kalleberg, Reskin, and Hudson, 2000).

In contrast, nonstandard jobs may lack some or all of the characteristics of a standard employment relationship. First, some nonstandard jobs lack an employer; self-employed workers do nonstandard work. They take on all the risk of their employment, including ensuring they make money, withhold taxes, and save for retirement. Second, in many nonstandard jobs, like contract and temporary work and some kinds of self-employment, workers are hired on short-term contracts and cannot assume their employment will continue indefinitely (Cranford, Vosko, and Zukewich, 2003; Kalleberg, Reskin, and Hudson, 2000). Third, many nonstandard jobs offer fewer than full-time hours.

Fourth, in many nonstandard jobs, the legal employer, who is responsible for hiring and paying the employee, is not the employer who oversees daily work.

This is the case for temporary help agency and contract jobs. For example, a worker hired by a temporary agency is legally employed by the agency but does not work for the agency (Kalleberg, 2011; Vosko, 2000). Rather, the temporary employee works for a client organization. When the job for which she is hired is completed, she must wait to receive payment and a new assignment from the temporary agency, not the company where she was working. This is similar to the experience of Zainab Taiyeb, whom we learned about at the beginning of this chapter. Although she was selling products for Rogers Cable, a Rogers subcontractor hired her and was responsible for paying her.

To understand nonstandard work, it is useful to look at part-time and temporary employment, two of the more common and widely discussed forms of nonstandard work. In 2013, just under 19 percent of Canadians worked in part-time jobs (Statistics Canada, 2014e). Since 1976, the part-time rate has more than doubled for young workers aged 15 to 24. Like women, young workers often prefer the flexibility of part-time work as a way to balance school attendance or family responsibilities. The part-time rate has also grown for workers over the age of 55. This increase may be due to older workers opting for part-time work as a step-ping stone to retirement (Pold, 2004). Alternatively, it could signal that older workers are unable to find full-time work to replace a full-time job they lost because of downsizing or corporate restructuring.

Employment in part-time work can indicate serious problems in the labour market. A sign of a poor labour market is having substantial numbers of people who would prefer full-time work but are working part-time. This phenomenon is called the *involuntary* part-time rate. Between 2000 and 2013, the number of part-time workers in Canada who said they would prefer to be working full-time fluctuated around 25 percent (OECD, 2014). They are involuntary part-time workers. Involuntary part-time jobs are especially common in the Atlantic provinces, where the unemployment rate is substantially higher than the national average (Statistics Canada, 2009).

To respond to changing demand for products and services, employers increasingly rely on temporary workers, ranging from clerical help to computer programmers, hired on contract or through temporary-employment agencies. Statistics Canada's data on temporary workers include seasonal labourers, contract workers, and those working for temporary-employment agencies. Nonstandard workers are usually hired for a predetermined period or until a project is completed. In 2011, 14 percent of Canadian workers were employed in temporary or contract positions (Statistics Canada, 2012b). Slightly more than one-third of these workers were between the ages of 15 and 24.

Immigrants who arrived in Canada within the past five years are twice as likely to work in temporary jobs as are the Canadian-born and immigrants who arrived more than 10 years ago (Gilmore, 2009). Temporary workers, who often work alongside full-time permanent workers, earn substantially less per hour than their full-time counterparts do. In 2014, the average hourly wage for a full-time worker was $26.41, compared with $19.97 for temporary workers (Statistics Canada, 2014f).

WHY THE RISE OF NONSTANDARD WORK?

Scholars link the increase in nonstandard work to the rise of the service economy, instability in the global economy, privatization of government services, and organizational restructuring that occurred in the late twentieth century (Vosko, 2000).

From an employer perspective, nonstandard work is attractive because it allows the creation of more flexible organizations. We can think about flexibility in two ways. First, there is **functional or internal flexibility** that allows employers to move workers from one job to another within an organization. However, it is a second type of flexibility—**numerical or external flexibility**—that drove employers to create nonstandard jobs. Numerical flexibility enables employers to adjust the size of their workforce by easily hiring and firing workers in response to fluctuations in labour demand (Kalleberg, 2003).

The downsizing of the 1980s and 1990s also drove the rise of nonstandard work—and not just in the private sector. In the 1990s, governments saddled with large deficits slashed jobs and privatized work previously carried out by government employees. Advances in telecommunications and information technology made it easier for private and public organizations to rely on outside suppliers and to quickly hire and fire temporary workers (Kalleberg, 2000). As well, some of the movement to nonstandard work is associated with the increased participation of women in the labour force. Some women, especially those with young children, prefer part-time and other non-standard work arrangements.

People commonly assume that because standard jobs now predominate they have been the most common form of work for centuries. In reality, the standard employment relationship as we know it arose after World War II (Fudge and Vosko, 2001). Insecure jobs, such as seasonal and casual labour, have always been a big part of the Canadian economy (Smith, 1999). In addition, linking the increase in nonstandard work only to the rise of the service economy overlooks the historic use of nonstandard work by manufacturing and other goods-producing industries. Automobile manufacturers have a long history of contracting out the production of auto parts. Agriculture has long relied on day labourers and seasonal employees (see the Critical Sociology: Globalization box). Thus, when discussing the rise of nonstandard work, we should remember that, historically, standard employment is unusual.

Most employers view the recent increase in nonstandard jobs positively. Employers reduce costs associated with full-time employees, such as costs associated with pensions and other benefits, and they gain flexibility in competitive markets. For employees, there are more downsides. Research documents increased job insecurity, loss of benefits, and wages that are too low to allow a decent standard of living.

ARE NONSTANDARD JOBS BAD JOBS?

Much of the early literature on nonstandard jobs referred to them as bad jobs. Evidence shows that nonstandard workers are worse off than are workers in standard employment relationships (Cranford, Vosko, and Zukewich, 2003; Kalleberg, Reskin, and Hudson, 2000). However, just how bad they are varies by type of nonstandard employment. Some nonstandard jobs are low-paid (e.g., jobs secured through a temporary worker agency) while others

---

CRITICAL SOCIOLOGY: GLOBALIZATION | **MIGRANT WORKERS**

In 2002 and again in 2006, Canada eased restrictions on temporary foreign workers entering the country. It is estimated that in 2016, there were nearly 810 000 non-permanent residents in the country—about 2 percent of the population (Statistics Canada, 2013). Most temporary foreign workers are agricultural labourers (mainly from Mexico) and live-in caregivers (mainly from the Philippines), but in recent years we have hired temporary foreign workers in a wider range of jobs, from fast-food work to engineering.

The business advantage of access to a pool of temporary foreign workers is clear. It helps to keeps labour costs low. So, until 2013, foreign workers in a given occupation were paid 15 percent less than the Canadian average wage in that occupation. The 15 percent rule took jobs away from Canadian citizens and permanent residents, increasing the unemployment rate and depressing wage levels, especially for unskilled workers (Gross, 2014). The federal government claims that temporary foreign workers are needed by business to ease labour shortages, particularly in western Canada, but most economists are skeptical about the existence of such shortages, especially in regions where the unemployment rate is relatively high. Anecdotal evidence supports their analyses—like the case of the Alberta First Nation reserve with a 70 percent unemployment rate, where a cafeteria owner hired temporary foreign workers to wash dishes and prepare food (Friesen, 2014).

Few temporary foreign workers enjoy a path to citizenship. (The main exceptions are live-in caregivers, who can become landed immigrants if they work for two years as nannies.) Few can bring family members into the country. Moreover, according to the Canadian Labour Congress, many migrant workers "are put in incredibly vulnerable situations where exploitation, abuse, [and] … unsafe working conditions are … often the norm" (Carletti and Davison, 2012).

In 2014, the federal government restricted the temporary foreign worker program, finally bowing to pressure from Canadians who understood the plight of migrant workers and the negative effect they have on wage levels. The view of many Canadians seems to be that if we truly need particular categories of workers, we should train residents or admit nonresidents as immigrants, not require that temporary foreign workers live the most precarious existence of all nonstandard workers in the country.

Critical Thinking Questions

1. Do you agree with the view that "if we truly need particular categories of workers, we should train residents or admit nonresidents as immigrants, not require that temporary foreign workers live the most precarious existence of all nonstandard workers in the country." Why, or why not?

2. How would you formulate criteria for deciding whether there is a need for particular categories of workers in Canada?

are not (e.g., independent technical contractors) (Houseman, Kalleberg, and Erickcek, 2003; Kunda, Barley, and Evans, 2002). The experience of nonstandard work is complicated and variable.

When we compare how nonstandard workers are treated by full-time employees, we find evidence for the negative evaluation of nonstandard jobs. Temporary workers placed by an agency in an organization for a short time often feel like "nonpersons" who are isolated from full-time employees (Rogers, 1995). As one temporary worker said,

> There was no Christmas present under the tree like the rest of the company would get [at the office party]. ... There were some places where it was just blatant, just terribly blatant. Whenever there was going to be a company party or something, the temps had to stay and work. You know, cover the phones so the regular people got to go. You could tell where the second-class citizenship started. (Quoted in Rogers, 1995: 150)

Compared with standard workers, nonstandard workers are at greater risk of experiencing alienation, isolation, and abuse.

In some European countries, strict regulations control the use of nonstandard workers. For example, in Norway, the use of fixed-term contracts and temporary help agencies is severely restricted (Olsen and Kalleberg, 2004). Some European Union countries have implemented the European Union's Framework Directive (EU Directive) on equality of treatment for part-time and fixed-term workers. This means that part-time and fixed-term workers in these countries should enjoy the same employment and working conditions, such as sick pay, pensions, and other benefits, as full-time workers receive. Although some countries limit the reach of the EU Directive (in Britain only 10 percent of part-time workers are covered), there is some hope that it will result in an increase in quality and stability for some forms of nonstandard work (Preisler, 2011).

WORK HOURS AND WORK ARRANGEMENTS

At the same time as nonstandard jobs are becoming more numerous, many workers are increasingly concerned with the number of hours they are working. Most of the focus is on overwork, with references to a "24-hour workday," needing to be available "24/7,"

and an "escalation in expectations" in terms of how many hours employees should be working (Epstein and Kalleberg, 2001: 6). The mass media, corporate executives, and students in my sociology of work course often discuss work–life balance and time for life outside work. Are we really working more than people did in previous generations, or has work changed in other ways?

To answer these questions, we first need to know how many hours per week Canadians are working. In 2012, Canadians worked 36.6 hours per week on average. In 1976, Canadians worked an average of 38.6 hours a week (Employment and Social Development Canada, 2014b; Usalcas, 2008). Contrary to the hype, Canadians are not working longer hours.

Canada is not alone in the decline in average hours worked per week. Most rich countries have experienced a decline in average work hours in recent decades. The rise of part-time work and reduction in the proportion of people working more than 50 hours per week account for most of the decline.

However, while on average Canadians today are no more overworked than their predecessors were, we are seeing another trend in work hours. As Figure 12.3 shows, a higher percentage of workers now work either longer or shorter hours compared with 30 years ago. While the 40-hour workweek was still the most common in 2011, the proportion of Canadians working a 40-hour week has declined since 1976. Proportionately more Canadians work fewer than 40 or more than 40 hours a week. Some analysts refer to this trend as the **polarization of working hours;** some workers are experiencing overwork while others have the opposite problem.

Many explanations exist for this polarization. Some have to do with choice. Certain groups of workers, such as students and those with young children, may choose to work fewer hours to balance competing demands. In addition, the rise of service industries has increased the number of people working nonstandard schedules and hours (Presser, 2003). Other explanations for the polarization of working hours point to the effect of economic restructuring and the increase in part-time, temporary, and other forms of nonstandard work.

According to sociologist Harriet Presser (1999, 2003, 2004), all the attention paid to changes in work hours has ignored the other way that work schedules have shifted. Presser says the issue is not just how many hours are worked, but *which* hours

FIGURE 12.3   DISTRIBUTION OF EMPLOYMENT BY HOURS WORKED PER WEEK, 1976 AND 2011

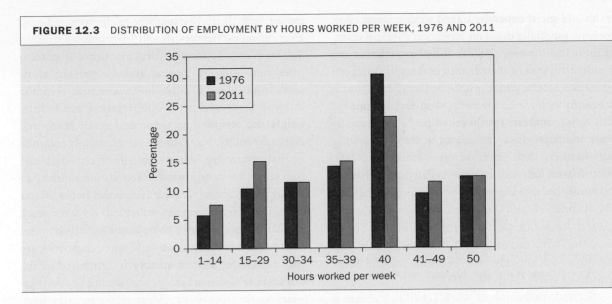

SOURCE: Statistics Canada (2012c).

of the day and days of the week are worked. She focuses on **nonstandard work schedules**, defined as either working nonstandard hours that fall outside the 9–to–5 workday (shift work) or working nonstandard days, such as Saturday and Sunday. Her research shows that nonstandard work schedules have increased because of three interrelated factors. First, the service sector demands nonstandard schedules to a much higher degree than manufacturing industries do. Linked to this is the increasing participation of women in the labour market. With more and more women working during the day, there is an increased demand for stores, restaurants, and other businesses to stay open later and on weekends.

Second, demographic changes such as the postponement of marriage and the rise in family income (mainly because of the increase in dual-earner couples) have increased the demand for recreation and leisure activities during the evenings and on weekends. The aging of the population has also increased demand for 24-hour services, especially in terms of the need for round-the-clock medical services. Third, technological changes and globalization processes have created a "24-hour economy" in which workers are on call at all hours. Email, fax machines, and cellphones enable workers to be connected at all times and allow companies to require their workers to stay connected. As well, the head office in one country may need to be in contact with branch offices in another. Working across time zones in the global economy increases the number of employees working nonstandard schedules.

In Canada, nearly 30 percent of people in the paid labour force work nonstandard hours (Williams, 2008). For example, shift work can consist of evening or late-night work, rotating shifts (where the time of shifts changes daily, weekly, or monthly), split shifts (working part of the day in the morning and part later in the day), and irregular shifts. Although women make up only about 37 percent of full-time shift workers, almost 70 percent of part-time shift workers are women (Williams, 2008). Women are also more likely than men are to work rotating shifts, evenings, and weekends, while men are more likely to work irregular shifts. Evidence suggests that nonstandard schedules have increased since 1991 (Shields, 2002).

Why do employees work nonstandard schedules? The great majority of Canadians working evening shifts—65 percent of men and 53 percent of women—say they do so because they have no choice or the hours are mandated by their employers (Shields, 2002: 17). Sixteen percent of men and 20 percent of women state they work evenings because of school demands. Caring for family is cited by 3 percent of men and 11 percent of women (Shields, 2002), with women more than men using nonstandard schedules to balance work and family needs (Presser, 2004). Thirteen percent of men and women state they work evenings because they like it. I conclude that most employees working nonstandard schedules are doing so because of the nature of their job, not by choice.

Why should we be concerned about people working nonstandard schedules? First, a variety of health and social issues are linked to shift work. Shift workers, especially those on night and rotating shifts, are more likely to experience disturbance of the natural circadian rhythm of their bodies as sleep is disrupted (Shields, 2002). Shift workers engage in more unhealthy behaviours, such as smoking, compared with other workers. Psychosocial problems, such as stress and depression, are also more common among shift workers than other workers (Shields, 2002). Shift workers can also become isolated from friends and family because their life is on a different schedule. The World Health Organization has conducted research showing that working the night shift is associated with increased risk of cancer—a finding that gives an entirely new meaning to the term "graveyard shift" (MSNBC, 2007).

Second, nonstandard work schedules create a hidden form of inequality (Presser, 2003; Shields, 2003). Workers who do not have a postsecondary degree are more likely to work nonstandard schedules. Nonstandard schedules are more common among women and men working fewer than 30 hours per week and among men working more than 40 hours per week. In the United States, black workers are more likely to work shifts compared with Hispanic and white workers. The workers most likely to work shifts are those that are already disadvantaged in the workplace—workers of colour, workers lacking higher education, and those working part-time or fewer than 40 hours per week. In Canada, shift work is more common among blue-collar and sales and service occupations than among professional and clerical jobs. Those most likely to work nonstandard schedules have some of the lowest-paying jobs, working as cashiers and salespeople.

We are also seeing other changes in work arrangements. Multiple-job holding, or "moonlighting," more than quadrupled between 1976 and 2011. In 1976, more than three-quarters of multiple-job holders were men. By 2011, more than half of multiple-job holders were women. It seems that to make ends meet, an increasing number of women have to cobble together more than one part-time job. While the growth in multiple-job holders may seem alarming, it's useful to keep in mind that moonlighters represented just around 6 percent of the paid labour force in 2011. The vast majority of Canadians continue to work one job.

Some changes to work schedules and arrangements are more positive. Evidence suggests that many employers are providing workers with more choice and flexibility, usually under the guise of creating more "family-friendly" workplaces. Half of Canadian employers offer part-time work, 45 percent offer flexible work hours, and 35 percent allow work from home. Flexible hours are most common in large firms and in the information and culture industries, business services, and retail trade and consumer industries. Flexible hours are less common in manufacturing, where individualized start and stop times are not possible. Men are more likely to report working flexible hours than women are. About 44 percent of university-educated workers work flexible hours (Statistics Canada, 2009, 2010). Thus, who works how many hours and when they work are part of the way that inequality is structured in the Canadian labour market.

THE IMPACT OF BLACKBERRYS, iPHONES, AND LAPTOPS

BlackBerrys, iPhones, laptops, and other Internet-connected mobile devices allow today's employee to work anywhere at any time. These devices can complement flexible work schedules and arrangements by making it possible to stay connected to work without being at the office. These devices have changed how we work and balance our work and nonwork time (Boswell and Olson-Buchanan, 2007).

We are starting to gain a better understanding of both the advantages and the disadvantages of using smart phones and from having nearly constant Internet access. Some studies point to increased productivity deriving from the use of smart phones (Mazmanian, Orlikowski, and Yates, 2005). Previously nonproductive time can now be productive—there is no need to stop working just because you've left the office. Smart phones also allow workers to stay connected with family throughout the workday and may help to balance family obligations. Sick kid? No worries. You can stay home and take care of your child while Skyping into meetings and communicating with co-workers over email.

However, the very advantages of mobile devices point to their disadvantages. Many users of these devices report a heightened need to stay connected and be responsive, adding to the pressure to be accessible at all times. As one BlackBerry user stated:

> The biggest advantage is far more frequent, rapid responses to largely business-related inquires and the ability to do that in a very

convenient way. Clearly the negative is there are some expectations. I know if my coworkers didn't get a response from me ... they'd be like, "Geez, what's he doing at 11:00 pm? Why isn't he responding to my emails? (Matusik and Mickel, 2011: 1016)

In this same study, workers reported that they were expected to respond quickly not only to co-workers and supervisors but also to family members who called during the workday.

The study found three types of mobile device users. *Enthusiastic users*, about 30 percent of the total, emphasized the personal and professional benefits of their devices. Because they perceived few downsides, they didn't feel the need to set firm boundaries between work and nonwork to limit the use of their mobile devices. *Balanced users*, also about 30 percent of the total, described the benefits and costs of their devices. They were most inclined to set boundaries limiting the negative effect of mobile communications devices on their daily lives. Finally, *tradeoff users*, about 40 percent of the total, claimed that both professional benefits and personal costs were associated with using their mobile devices, but they struggled to set boundaries between work and nonwork.

Based on such studies, sociologists have begun to question whether mobile devices really help most workers achieve work–life balance. What is emerging is a picture of blurred boundaries, where the line between work and the rest of life is disappearing (Olson-Buchanan and Boswell, 2006; Schieman and Glavin, 2008). As work permeates home life, concern grows about increased stress and conflict with family members. Recently, some companies have decided employees need help reining in their off-hour email time. Starting in late 2011, the servers at Volkswagen in Germany were prohibited from sending employees' email more than 30 minutes before or after work. It's not clear if other companies will follow suit. What is clear is that workers will continue to use their smart phones and other devices outside work and will need to learn to cope with the ongoing collision of work and nonwork time.

TIME FOR REVIEW

1. What are the main features of the Canadian service economy?
2. Why have nonstandard jobs become so widespread?
3. Are nonstandard jobs always bad jobs?
4. How have Canadians' work hours changed since the 1970s?
5. How do mobile devices affect the boundaries between work and nonwork?

LABOUR MARKET SEGMENTATION

You know from your study of social stratification that people with higher education and people from upper-class families are more likely than less-advantaged people are to end up in good jobs. Another factor that affects your life-chances is the structure of the labour market. Although some economists think of the labour market as a single, open competition in which people are rewarded in proportion to their education and skills (Becker, 1975), **labour market segmentation** theory offers a different perspective. Instead of assuming that we all have an equal chance of getting good jobs, labour market segmentation theory shows that *where* you enter the labour market may limit your chances of getting a different, better job.

Labour market segmentation theory emphasizes that jobs are divided according to their location in the "core" or "periphery" of the economy. A core industry is a group of companies in a relatively noncompetitive market, such as the automobile industry. Core industries tend to be capital-intensive, large, and unionized, and they tend to exert control over their environment—for example, by influencing governments to limit foreign competition. For a variety of reasons, such as the need to maintain skilled workers who can operate expensive equipment, and in response to the presence of unions, jobs in core industries tend to be stable and to offer good wages and access to benefits (Morissette, 1991).

The periphery, in contrast, is characterized by lower-tier service jobs and jobs in highly competitive markets. Firms in this sector tend to be smaller, labour-intensive, and nonunionized, and the employment they offer lacks security and pays low wages. Work is also characterized by high turnover rates, owing to product-demand fluctuations and seasonal work cycles, such as in the fisheries on the east and west coasts.

Your chance of finding a good job is determined not only by the sector of the economy you enter but also by the existence of **primary labour markets,** both external and internal to firms. Internal primary labour markets provide opportunities for advancement by providing the chance to climb up the job ladder as you gain skills and knowledge (Althauser, 1989). Secondary labour market jobs do not offer much of a job ladder. These jobs are sometimes referred to as "dead-end jobs" because of the lack of upward mobility associated with them. Workers at McDonald's may be able to move from being on the crew to assistant manager, but unless they buy their own franchise (which is rare), that is the extent of their mobility.

Employers often create primary labour markets for some employees but not for others. In a single firm, managers can have access to mobility through an internal labour market while their clerical, production, and maintenance staff may have little room to move up. In today's service economy, employers' increasing use of temporary and part-time workers is another way in which secondary labour markets are created within companies. Increasingly, these types of secondary markets are found outside the lower-tier service industries. At Canadian universities, departments have full-time professors to do research and teach. In addition, "sessional" instructors are hired to teach one or two classes. Substantial differences exist between these two groups in terms of pay, job security, and mobility opportunities. As a full-time, tenured professor, I have a long-term contract and may be promoted if I fulfill my job duties. My colleague, who is a part-time instructor, has no access to promotions or job security. Instead, she receives year-to-year contracts only if the department needs her to teach a specific course. Although having secondary labour market positions gives organizations the "flexibility" to unload employees when they are not needed, it increases the insecurity of these employees and decreases their chances of getting ahead, both in their jobs and in life.

Geography also plays a role in the chances of ending up in the primary or secondary labour market. Alberta, thanks to the oil and gas industry boom, has experienced lower than average unemployment rates in recent years. The Atlantic provinces have a high proportion of seasonal jobs, such as fishing and logging, and have a higher unemployment rate than the rest of Canada does (see Figure 12.4). Even if you are a highly skilled and motivated worker, you will have more trouble finding a good job in Newfoundland and Labrador than you would in Alberta because there are fewer jobs to go around. Those of us who live in urban and industrial areas are more likely to end up in a better job simply because there are more such jobs in the regional labour market (Statistics Canada, 2009).

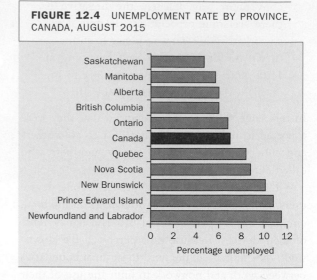

FIGURE 12.4   UNEMPLOYMENT RATE BY PROVINCE, CANADA, AUGUST 2015

SOURCE: Statistics Canada (2015).

JOB GHETTOS AND DISADVANTAGED GROUPS

Job ghettos are parts of the labour market that prevent certain groups of workers from experiencing upward mobility. Structural barriers based on stereotypes work to keep some individuals from entering the primary labour market and the best jobs. The labelling of occupations as "female" or "male" jobs is one such example. In the healthcare industry, women are still more likely to become nurses than doctors, and, as doctors, women are more likely to be found in pediatric and family medicine than in the higher-paying specialties of neurology and cardiology. Chapter 8, Gender Inequality, discusses how female job ghettos are formed through occupational sex segregation, sex typing, and other forms of discrimination.

Ethnic job ghettos exist throughout the world. For example, in Canada, between 1860 and 1960, black railway workers were restricted to sleeping-car porter jobs and were not allowed to compete for the higher-paid jobs of sleeping-car conductor and dining-car steward (Calliste, 1993). Today, employer prejudice can keep qualified minorities from being hired. Since many visible minorities are also recent immigrants, their ability to move into better jobs is constrained by this dual status, unless they are entrepreneurs. Often, employers will request "Canadian work experience" before hiring white-collar workers. Some professional occupations, like doctor and veterinarian, require additional training for professionals emigrating from certain countries. Highly educated members of visible minorities in these situations may

Geography affects a person's chance of finding work. For example, it is more difficult to find a good job in Atlantic Canada than in Saskatchewan.
SOURCE: David Blackwood, *For Edgar Glover: The Splitting Table Etching*, 1999. Courtesy the Edward Day Gallery.

find themselves forced to take low-level service jobs, such as taxi driver or restaurant worker. (For more on this topic, see Chapter 9, Race and Ethnic Relations).

People with disabilities face barriers to good jobs because of the inaccessibility of education and workplaces. In 2006, only 51 percent of Canadians with disabilities between the ages of 15 and 64 were employed, compared with 75 percent of those without disabilities (Collin, Lafontaine-Émond, and Pang, 2013). Lack of financial resources to attend school, inflexible workplace schedules, and lack of employers' commitment to hiring workers with disabilities are some of the reasons people with disabilities have trouble getting good jobs. Jamie Hunter, a 29-year-old with minimal control over his limbs because of a diving accident, experiences these barriers first-hand. Speaking about looking for work, he states,

> I recall one fellow, from the personnel department of a major corporation, who was so uncomfortable he couldn't even bring himself to take me to his office. So we sat in the lobby and he read me back my resume. "You're Jamie Hunter? You graduated from York University? You worked for a summer at Ontario Hydro?" Then he said thanks and left. That was it. The interview was over and I never heard from him again. (Quoted in McKay, 1993: 170)

Hiring workers who have disabilities is not as costly as some employers believe. Only a fifth of people with disabilities require changes to the physical accommodations of workplaces (Shain, 1995). Until more employers make the effort to hire people with disabilities, these workers will continue to face barriers to good jobs.

Indigenous people face formidable barriers in their search for employment. Living in remote areas limits both their job opportunities and their access to education and work training. Even when Indigenous people move to areas where jobs are more readily available, they often lack crucial work experience. Indigenous workers are especially vulnerable to the "bad-work syndrome" (Krahn and Lowe, 1998). Having access only to low-skill and part-time work gives individuals a spotty work history. They are then caught in a cycle where one low-skill job leads to another. For many, the "bad-work syndrome" makes it impossible to get better jobs.

Finally, the *youngest and oldest workers* may find themselves trapped in job ghettos based on age. Some employers view young workers as less serious and less interested in full-time jobs than more mature workers are. Because of downsizing and early retirement incentives, older workers may find themselves out of a job before they are ready to stop working. Access to better jobs is also limited by the prejudices of employers, who tend to view older workers as less productive and more resistant to new work methods. As the population of older Canadians grows, it is increasingly difficult to ignore the effects of age discrimination.

Labour market segmentation creates areas of better and worse jobs in the labour market. Although we would like to think that we all have an equal chance of getting good jobs, research shows that some groups of workers may be trapped in bad jobs. Moreover, as I show next, some workers are able to protect their good jobs through the labour market shelters of professional occupations and unions.

PROFESSIONS

The occupations of doctor, lawyer, and other professions are some of the most desirable jobs in the labour market. High pay, autonomy, and respect from the outside community are some of the advantages bestowed on members of professional occupations. Many of us consider these occupations to be different from other occupations. This special status has caught the attention of sociologists.

Early studies of professions attempted to delineate their general characteristics. First, all professional occupations control a unique body of knowledge. Second, professional occupations are autonomous. Third, professionals generally have authority over their clients and subordinates because of the special knowledge they possess. Finally, professional

Although most Canadian women in the paid labour force are segregated in jobs traditionally dominated by women, they are making advances in traditionally male-dominated jobs.
SOURCE: © iStockphoto.com/Lisa F. Young.

occupations are supposed to be altruistic because of their focus on helping clients.

Many sociologists believe that this description of professionals is an "idealized model that imperfectly describes reality" (Hodson and Sullivan, 1990: 266), and that it provides only a checklist for determining which occupations are more or less professional. Overlooked by this approach is how certain occupations became professions in the first place. To address this issue, we need to consider power and the contested nature of professions. Doing so will uncover how professions act as **labour market shelters**, protecting their members' access to good jobs.

Which occupations are viewed as legitimate professions changes historically. For example, nineteenth century Ontario had few dentists as we know them today. Many different occupations provided dental services. Itinerant "tramp dentists" travelled from town to town servicing most Ontarians. If citizens needed teeth pulled or false teeth constructed, they could go to their local blacksmith or gunsmith. When a patient came to visit, the blacksmith would "leave the forge, wipe his hands on his apron, get the old turnkey wrench, and his brawny arm would soon draw not only the sufferer's tooth, but often the screaming patient himself from the old kitchen chair" (Quoted in Adams, 2000: 22).

To get to where they are today, dentists, like people in other occupations, engaged in a *process* of professionalization, which involved establishing professional dominance and securing legitimacy from the public (Friedson, 1970; Pescosolido, Tuch, and Martin, 2001: 3). Professional dominance occurs when the government acknowledges an occupation's knowledge claims and expertise, and then grants an occupation the right to be the only (or one of a few) types of practitioners allowed to apply this body of knowledge. Professions also require public approval. If the public refuses to follow the instructions of members of the profession or views them as illegitimate or just one among many types of experts, then the profession will have difficulty establishing its authority.

Sometimes, battles between different professions erupt, with each profession claiming expertise over the same "turf" (Friedson, 1970). For example, until recently, only doctors had the authority to deliver babies in Canada. Doctors maintained their authority because of their monopoly over relevant knowledge. They used their national association to lobby provincial and federal governments to deny others the right to deliver babies. However, the public and other healthcare practitioners questioned whether doctors ought to be the only legitimate deliverers of babies. In recent decades, because of public demand for access to midwives and the development of professional midwifery schools, doctors have lost some control over the birthing process and have lost their monopoly over this body of professional knowledge.

Some occupations are continually striving for professional status. "Semi-professions" are occupations that have only some characteristics of a profession (Hodson and Sullivan, 1990). Examples include nurses, engineers, accountants, pharmacists, and teachers. Although we may call these occupations "professions" in our everyday use of the term, the sociological definition of professions requires us to view them as semi-professions. Often, semi-professions do not have full control over their body of knowledge, or their autonomy may be constrained by a more powerful profession, as is the case with nurses. Furthermore, female-dominated semi-professions, such as teachers and librarians, face additional barriers to professionalization because of occupational sex segregation.

Third parties, such as the government, can threaten professional power by intervening in the decisions of professional organizations. We become most aware of such threats when the government pays for part or all of the services received by clients, as is the case for the Canadian healthcare system. During the summer and fall of 1996, doctors in Ontario fought the provincial government over who had the right to decide where doctors work. Doctors wanted to maintain their professional autonomy to work and live where they choose, while the Ministry of Health believed it had the right to force doctors to work in underserviced areas. Some doctors did not accept new patients to protest what they saw as government interference with their autonomy. They made some gains in terms of their salaries and partly satisfied the government's demand for more doctors to work in northern areas of the province. How this battle continues to play out will determine who is the legitimate authority over doctors in this case: their own profession or the government of Ontario.

UNIONS

Like professions and their associations, unions also attempt to attain or maintain good jobs for their members. Workers have organized unions to gain respect, increase wages, reduce working hours, and gain more control over their working day. In fact, the presence of unions has helped all of us. Without union efforts,

we would not have such things as the eight-hour workday, child-labour laws, and occupational health and safety standards. I return to the state of unions in Canada and the role they play in the Canadian labour market when I discuss alienation later in this chapter.

Unions and professional associations are alike in a number of respects. They both shelter members from loss of jobs, pay cuts, and other employment-related risks. Legislation that mandates the hiring of union workers, such as exists on some construction sites, protects the jobs of union members. Likewise, when the professional association of lawyers restricts access to law school and the number of new lawyers, they too are protecting the jobs and incomes of existing members. Groups of workers who organize—whether it is a local union of flight attendants or a national association of doctors—increase their ability to keep their jobs.

TIME FOR REVIEW

1. What are the main arguments of labour market segmentation theory?
2. How do job ghettos operate?
3. How are professions and unions similar? How do they differ?

TECHNOLOGY AND WORK ORGANIZATION

The use of technology has long been a part of the employer–employee relationship. One of the most famous technologies, the assembly line, was used to control the pace of work (Edwards, 1979). In today's service economy, managers are more likely to invest in computers and information technology than other forms of work reorganization to improve their firms' productivity and efficiency (Osterman, 1995). Computerized office systems can reduce the time-consuming work of filing. Robots can do heavy and dangerous work. Advanced telecommunications systems make the globalization of work possible.

When employers introduce new technology in the workplace, skills are upgraded *and* downgraded. People must be trained to repair and maintain computer networks, but technology also simplifies some jobs, replaces workers, and allows work to be shifted to regions where labour is inexpensive. For example, automated bank machines not only made personal banking convenient but also sharply reduced the number of tellers while creating a small number of jobs for those who maintain the machines (Burman,

1997). More recently, Air Canada used computer and telecommunications technology to contract out the work of full-time Air Canada sales and service workers to private travel agency employees. This strategy had the effect of changing the "good" jobs at Air Canada into insecure, "bad" jobs (Shalla, 2002). New technologies often create a small number of skilled jobs but degrade or eliminate a larger number of jobs.

Technology also reduces geographic constraints as employers search for inexpensive labour or market expansion. Today, many companies have factories in Asia and product-development labs in the United States. For example, in recent decades, work in call centres grew quickly in bilingual, low-wage Moncton, New Brunswick, but growth slowed when call centres in even lower-wage India came online.

Although technology is changing the face of work, it does not mean that we have no control over what happens. Various social and techno-logical factors affect the way new technologies are implemented (Zuboff, 1988). For example, much depends on the outcomes management wants, the type of technology that companies can afford, and whether unions and workers have a say in techno-logical change (Shalla, 2002). According to Shoshana Zuboff (1988), management can design computer-based jobs either to increase or decrease the need for workers to use knowledge and judgment on the job. In her analysis of health insurance workers, she pro-vides examples of job enhancement in which man-agers gave workers the opportunity to use computers in complex ways. However, she also found that if management was interested only in productivity and efficiency, technology had detrimental effects on the quality of work.

THE ORGANIZATION OF WORK

Bureaucracies

We live and work in a bureaucratic society. According to Max Weber, bureaucracies are the most efficient and rational type of organization that people have created. In bureaucracies, written rules provide guidelines for handling routine situations. A com-plex division of labour ensures that workers know what is required of them and helps to identify who is responsible when something goes wrong. Weber also saw bureaucracies as a mechanism for overcoming arbitrary decisions and corruption. For example, by having written rules about how decisions should be made and having a hierarchy of authority that clari-fies who makes decisions, it is less likely that decision makers can decide to hire someone out of loyalty or obligation. Yet Weber was the first to admit that bureaucracies are not without their problems. Referring to bureaucracies as "the iron cage of the future," Weber was concerned about the potential for bureaucracies to limit creativity and initiative (Hodson and Sullivan, 1990: 184). Bureaucracies also can be rigid, tied down by "red tape," and lead to communication problems between managers and workers (Jones, 1996).

Weber believed that increased bureaucratization was the fate of modern society. Building on Weber, sociologist George Ritzer (1993) argues that society is now undergoing a new kind of rationalization process that he calls "McDonaldization." Today, writes Ritzer, the fast-food restaurant has surpassed bureaucracy as the organizational ideal. This means that our work-place, schools, leisure activities, and culture are taking on the characteristics of the fast-food restaurant.

There are four components to McDonaldization:

1. Creating the most *efficient* way to accomplish a task
2. Emphasizing things that can be *calculated*
3. Creating a *predictable* product and experience
4. Setting up systems of *control* to standardize the work of employees (Ritzer, 1993: 9–12)

Consider how we might apply Ritzer's ideas to universities. Ritzer would cite the textbook that you are reading as part of the drive for increased efficiency, predictability, and standardization. Chapters are written by experts in each area. Instead of one author taking years to learn all of sociology, the book can be produced quicker because, presumably, each expert knows his or her area inside-out (Ritzer, 1993: 57). Conversely, you could also argue that chapters are actually better because they are written by experts. If you are like my students at the University of Toronto, your introductory sociology class is probably a large class that uses multiple-choice exams. Gone are the days of inefficient and unpredict-able one-on-one examinations of students and, in many places, essay exams (Ritzer, 1993: 55). Multiple-choice exams take less time to mark compared with other ways of testing student's knowledge.

I would be doing my colleagues who are teaching you a disservice if I said that the only value of mul-tiple-choice exams is their efficiency over other testing

New technologies require job retraining, even for middle-aged and older workers.

SOURCE: © iStockphoto.com/Chris Schmidt.

methods; evidence shows that a well-written multiple-choice exam does a good job of capturing a student's knowledge. Still, Ritzer's thesis is correct in that, as universities have increased in size, faculty have been pushed to look for ways to increase the efficiency and the predictability of what they produce. This mimics some of the trends in the fast-food industry. Standardizing textbooks and exams are just two illustrations. If you look at other aspects of society, you will see other examples, such as vacationers who travel to other countries and stay at places like Sandals and Club Med, which offer a standard resort experience with little regard for the local culture.

If you look around at the organizations that touch your life, you will see evidence that Weber and Ritzer are correct. However, bureaucratic structure is not enough to ensure that organizations achieve their goals. As I discuss in the following section, management has also been developing strategies to organize how work is done by their employees.

Managerial Strategies for Organizing Work

Over the past century, several approaches to organizing work have come and gone. Some have endured (Braverman, 1974). Although early strategies were geared toward removing the need for workers to think on the job, more recent strategies have paid more attention to the ability and desire of workers to participate in workplace decisions.

Scientific management, also known as *Taylorism*, originated in the 1890s, when Frederick Taylor conducted studies that detailed the exact movements of factory workers and the time required to complete each of their tasks. Taylor then reconfigured factory work tasks to maximize efficiency, create standardized products, and thus generate higher profits. Workers no longer needed to think much about what they were doing, and management gained more control of the labour process. Taylorism allowed management to reduce reliance on skilled labour and hire inexpensive, unskilled workers to perform simplified tasks.

Henry Ford adopted the principles of scientific management in his company, where each worker stood in one place doing a repetitive job (the assembly line). Beginning in the early twentieth century, the principles of scientific management were applied to office work (Lowe, 1987). Scientific management is still around in many service industry jobs. Making hamburgers in a fast-food restaurant is broken down into small tasks, and telephone reservation agents for airlines are given scripts to follow when dealing with clients. Today, as in the past, workers complain about the limited opportunities for creativity and self-fulfillment when working under scientific management.

The **human relations school of management** approach to organizing work went beyond the view that workers are motivated only by the desire for their paycheques (Bendix, 1974; Jones, 1996). Instead, it emphasized that friendly supervision and attention to the social environment increase workers' cooperation and productivity. From this point of view, increasing worker job satisfaction yields productivity gains. Today, management strategies still incorporate elements of the human relations school. From suggestion boxes to workplace participation programs, organizations continue to try and find the right "human touch" to decrease worker resistance and increase productivity.

We see evidence of this continuity in such concepts as "total quality management" (TQM) and "Japanese management," ideas that were promoted in the 1990s as solutions for the productivity and quality problems of management. These programs emphasize quality control through communication and teamwork among management, workers, and customers. The rhetoric surrounding these programs promoted the potential for increased worker participation and workplace democratization.

Initial reactions to these programs were positive (Womack, Jones, and Roos, 1990). However, subsequent research suggested that many of these programs do little to promote worker empowerment because they tend to break down work tasks, much like scientific management and assembly line production did (Dassbach, 1996; Robertson et al., 1993). Some evidence from service industries shows that employee empowerment schemes can increase the development of workers' interpersonal and problem-solving skills because employees have to deal with customers' problems and requests (Smith, 2001). Whether these strategies will lead to increased empowerment on the part of workers depends on management's attitude. As long as these strategies are linked solely to management's desire for productivity increases and "the bottom line," their participatory potential will be limited. Alternatives, such as worker-owned companies, may bring us closer to real worker participation (Livingstone, 1993).

TIME FOR REVIEW

1. How does the McDonaldization thesis extend Weber's ideas about bureaucracy?

2. What are the main managerial strategies for organizing work?

"WILL I LIKE MY JOB?" JOB SATISFACTION AND ALIENATION

The service revolution has changed the structure of work in Canada and across the world. There are more part-time jobs and increased use of computer surveillance, as well as some increases in knowledge-based jobs. Given these changes, how do Canadians feel about their jobs? Surveys suggest that more than 90 percent of Canadians say they are satisfied with their jobs and that more Canadians like their jobs than the Dutch, the Americans, the British, the French, and the Germans do (*CBC News*, 2013; McKenzie, 2001). Surveys also show that getting respect from their bosses and feeling in control of their job mattered most to Canadian workers. Less important was the amount of money they made (see Figure 12.5). This finding reflects much of what we know about job satisfaction. To be satisfied at work, intrinsic rewards, such as autonomy and challenging work, are at least as important as extrinsic or material rewards.

Are the overwhelming majority of Canadians *really* satisfied with their jobs? What do sociologists

FIGURE 12.5   WHAT CANADIANS SAY IS VERY IMPORTANT IN A JOB

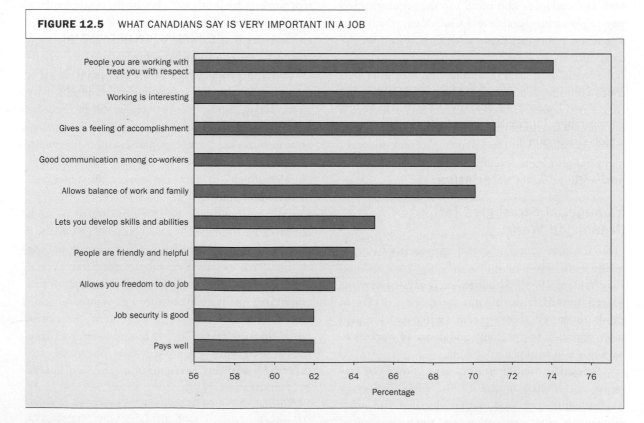

SOURCE: Canadian Policy Research Networks. "It's More than the Money—What Canadians Want in a Job." http://www.jobquality.ca/indicator_e/rew001. stm (Mar. 9, 2006). Reprinted with permission of Canadian Policy Research Networks.

mean by **job satisfaction**? These are important questions. Job satisfaction is usually determined by a survey question, such as "How satisfied are you with your job?" In many ways, the responses to job satisfaction questions are similar to replies to the question "How are you today?" (Krahn and Lowe, 1998: 408). Most of us would answer "Fine" to such a general question. Moreover, some analysts believe that most workers do not want to admit that they do not like their jobs.

One solution to this problem is to use more specific job satisfaction measures, especially measures that refer to behaviours or behavioural intentions (e.g., Hodson, 1991). For example, the 2001 survey found that 22 percent of Canadians interviewed said they planned to change their job in the near future (Canadian Press/Leger Marketing, 2001). When we discuss alienation, we will look more closely at workers' behaviours to understand workers' negative reactions to their job. For now, we'll spend a bit more time on job satisfaction. Even though it is a problematic measure, it is still used by management to gauge how happy and productive their workers are.

WHAT DETERMINES JOB SATISFACTION?

A multitude of factors affect how we feel about our jobs, ranging from our individual characteristics to the size of the firm we work in. To give you an idea of this range, I'll discuss some of the main predictors of job satisfaction.

Individual Characteristics

Based on what we know about job ghettos, it might be a safe bet to predict that women, older workers, and younger workers will be some of the least satisfied groups of workers. Although it is true that younger workers are some of the most dissatisfied workers (see Table 12.1), older workers—at least those who have stable jobs—are actually a relatively happy group (Krahn, 1992). The higher job satisfaction reported by older employed workers may be the result of reduced expectations about work, more meaningful lives outside of work, or past advancement in jobs (Krahn and Lowe, 1998).

When you consider occupational sex segregation and the differences in jobs held by women and men, you might expect women to be less satisfied

than men are. In most studies, though, women and men report similar levels of job satisfaction (see Table 12.1 and Krahn, 1992). However, when evaluating their feelings about their work, women tend to compare themselves with other women (Hodson and Sullivan, 1990). If women compared themselves with men, their reported level of satisfaction might be lower.

Job and Organizational Characteristics

Opportunities for autonomous and complex work are important predictors of job satisfaction: Satisfaction increases with autonomy and decreases with repetitive or automated work. For example, fast-food workers who repeat the same phrases every day and autoworkers who must do the same task repeatedly are less likely to be satisfied than people who do more creative work. Opportunities for participation and decision making can increase satisfaction. What occupation we are in also affects job satisfaction. Figure 12.6 shows that people employed in social science, government, education, and religion occupations are the most satisfied.

TABLE 12.1 JOB SATISFACTION OF CANADIANS

EMPLOYEE CHARACTERISTICS	PERCENTAGE WHO ARE "VERY SATISFIED" WITH THEIR JOB
All Canadians	28
Size of company	
Very small	30
Small	23
Medium	18
Large	26
Age	
18–25	22
26–45	26
45+	33
Gender	
Women	29
Men	27
Employment status	
Full-time	25
Self-employed	43

SOURCE: Canadian Policy Research Networks. "Job Satisfaction." http://www.jobquality.ca/indicator_e/rew002.stm (Mar. 9, 2006). Reprinted by permission of Canadian Policy Research Networks.

Organizational structure, such as technology and firm size, affects how happy we are at work. Blauner's (1964) classic study *Alienation and Freedom* shows how workers' alienation increased as technology shifted from craftwork to machine tending and assembly line work. In contrast, technology that requires the use of conceptual skills increases job satisfaction.

Employees in small companies experience a relatively high level of satisfaction. In 2000, 30 percent of Canadians who worked in very small companies were very satisfied, compared with 23 percent who worked in small companies and 18 percent who worked in medium-sized companies (refer back to Table 12.1). As company size increases, so do workers' feelings of isolation and powerlessness. However, large companies offer benefits and opportunities that boost job satisfaction almost to the level found in very small companies.

When I consider all the individual, job, and organizational factors that influence job satisfaction, I am struck by the realization that much of our satisfaction at work is determined by things over which we have little or no control. Our employers determine how much we are paid and how challenging and autonomous our jobs will be. And the chance to work in a small, locally owned company or a large national or multinational corporation has much to do with the employment opportunities where we live.

ALIENATION

If job satisfaction focuses on the individual worker's feelings about his or her job, alienation is linked to the lack of control or powerlessness an individual experiences in relation to his or her job. Originating in the work of Karl Marx, the concept of **alienation** examines how the structural conditions of work lead to workers' lack of power over their work and lives (Rinehart, 1996). For Marx, alienation is an "objective condition" that stems from capitalism. Marx argued that capitalism robs workers of control over the means of production and the products of their labour and puts control in the hands of owners.

According to Marx, alienation of workers under capitalism has four sources:

1. Workers are alienated from the products they produce. They do not own them, and they have no say over how they will be used. Rather, under capitalism, work is a means to an end—work provides a paycheque so workers can buy things they need, but few workers produce most of the things they themselves need, as was once the case.

2. Workers do not control the process of production. The advanced division of labour is indicative of this condition. Decisions about how fast to work, the order in which to complete tasks, and the use of equipment are made by someone other

FIGURE 12.6   WORK SATISFACTION BY OCCUPATION

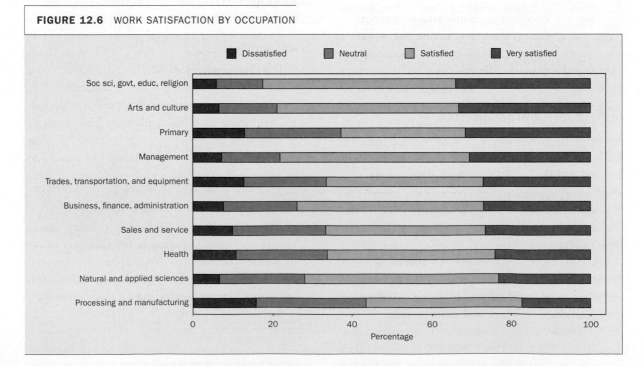

SOURCE: Canadian Policy Research Networks. "Satisfaction Most Common in Social Sciences, Arts/Culture and Management Occupations." http://www. jobquality.ca/indicator_e/rew002_1.stm#2 (Mar. 9, 2006). Reprinted by permission of Canadian Policy Research Networks.

than workers. Workers lose control over their daily work activity.

3. Workers are alienated from engaging in creative activity and thus from themselves.

4. Workers are alienated from others as they have fewer opportunities to talk and connect with co-workers. Also, work is not a collective process that can help the whole community. Overall, the division of labour under capitalism physically and emotionally isolates workers from one another.

Some sociologists conceptualize alienation as a way to think about how workers' psychological and emotional states are linked to the organization of work (Rogers, 1995). For example, when work is repetitive and does not allow for interaction between co-workers, workers may experience a high level of alienation. Some sociologists conceptualize alienation as a subjective state that arises from the reality of capitalist working conditions. Here the emphasis is on workers' feelings of powerlessness and lack of control or connection to their work and co-workers.

Fighting Alienation: Individual and Collective Responses to Work

To understand alienation, we also need to look at how workers resist it (Schmitt and Moody, 1994). Such analysis can shed light on their negative feelings toward work.

When a worker engages in sabotage or repeatedly skips work, management may define the worker as destructive or lazy. Yet, in the minds of workers, these seeming acts of insubordination may be an attempt to gain control over their job or reduce the amount of alienation they experience. To overcome a boring job where she was not assigned enough work, one temporary clerical worker stated, "I used to sleep there. Yes there's nothing to do. I always bring my book. When I get sick and tired of reading, I sleep. Sometimes, OK, you're not supposed to make phone calls, but what am I going to do with 8 hours?" (Rogers, 1995: 157). If management had provided enough work, this temporary worker might have exhibited good work habits.

When viewed as resistance to alienating conditions, the "misbehaviour" of workers appears in a different light. Some researchers argue that the alienating conditions of work lead some workers to "fight back" or react to these conditions (Edwards and Scullion, 1982; Rinehart, 1996). You may have had similar reactions to work, such as slacking off if you believed your supervisor required you to work too hard, or

turning your work into a game to make the time go faster. Engaging in these behaviours does not mean you are lazy or incompetent. Rather, they are typical reactions to alienating work.

To cope with poor working conditions, some workers quit their jobs. Those who cannot quit may respond passively by socializing with co-workers, playing games, or reducing their productivity (Burawoy, 1979). Management often devises strategies to prevent these types of behaviours. For example, scientific management was motivated in part by management's desire to reduce opportunities for workers to restrict their output.

For management, theft and destruction of company property is a particularly bothersome behaviour. But these criminal acts may be motivated by poor working conditions. A few years ago, an undergraduate student in my class confessed that, while working in a small T-shirt design factory, she purposely poked holes in some shirts. Because management had a policy of giving damaged T-shirts to employees, you might think she did this only to take advantage of her situation. As it turns out, though, employees were paid low wages and worked under conditions of extreme heat. This student saw her behaviour as a protest against the inadequate pay and difficult working conditions. Other workers engage in sabotage to gain concessions from management or to gain control over the work process. Factory workers may damage the assembly line to slow down the pace of work and clerical workers may hide files to reduce their workload (Hodson and Sullivan, 1990; Rinehart, 1996).

Do these individual acts of resistance change the amount of alienation workers experience? The answer to this question is complex. Many sociologists, beginning with Marx, illustrate how alienation is a condition of objective powerlessness that exists regardless of whether workers themselves consciously recognize it. Some workers become aware or conscious of the alienating conditions they experience at work. As predicted by Marx, these workers may respond to alienating conditions by forming unions, going on strike, or engaging in revolutionary behaviour focused on overthrowing capitalism. However, most workers do not develop "class-consciousness." Sociologists Harvey Krahn and Graham Lowe state, "In the absence of a well-defined alternative to the current economic system, we would not expect most workers to be able to clearly articulate their alienation and act on it. Apathy, or an attempt to forget about work as soon as one leaves it behind, are the common

Workers often resist alienating work conditions. Forms of resistance include striking, being absent, quitting, slacking off, and committing industrial sabotage.

SOURCE: Juan Manuel Sanchez. Courtesy of Nora Patrich and Juan Sanchez.

responses of many workers to a situation in which there is no viable alternative" (1998: 419).

This means that hiding files or poking holes in a shirt may make the worker feel better and thus make it possible to get through the day. These types of activities may reduce the subjective feeling of alienation: Workers may feel less powerless or may feel they have more control over their working conditions. But these types of individual strategies do not change the structural conditions of work. Collective responses to workplace conditions are more likely to lead to lasting changes in how work is organized. These collective responses, such as forming a union, may not "overthrow" the economic system, but they can improve working conditions. Although playing games and stealing may momentarily increase workers' feelings of control over their jobs, most researchers agree that, for lasting change to occur, collective responses are needed. Chapter 19, Politics and Social Movements, provides more details about the role of strikes in the Canadian labour movement's struggle for economic and social rights.

Unions play an important role in facilitating collective action by workers. In Canada today, about 30 percent of paid nonagricultural workers are union members (Canada Labour Program, 2013). Compared with some other countries, such as the United States and Australia, **union density**, or the percentage of nonagricultural paid workers who are unionized, has not significantly declined in Canada over the past 30 years (Adams and Welsh, 2008). However, over the past 150 years, the characteristics of unionized workers have shifted. During the late nineteenth century, craft workers organized; during the 1930s and 1940s, workers in the goods-producing sectors followed suit. Public-sector workers began to organize in the 1960s and 1970s. Public-sector industries now have the highest rate of unionization (Uppal, 2011). Contrary to the image of the male unionized factory worker, today's unionized worker is more likely to be a woman with postsecondary education working in education or healthcare (Uppal, 2011). Some union supporters warn that union density will stagnate if union organizing does not expand to cover new groups of workers, particularly young workers in service industries (White, 1993).

Whether the number of unionized workers in Canada will grow or decline depends on how unions deal with changes in the labour market and the economy. The rise of nonstandard work and the ease with which companies can move their businesses to other countries challenge union growth.

FINDING WORK

One of the buzzwords of twenty-first-century job seekers is *networking*. Networking is sometimes referred to as the "art of talking to as many people as you can without directly asking them for a job" (Flap and Boxman, 2001: 159). Potential job applicants are often advised to "network, network, network" (Ehrenreich, 2005).

This advice derives from the common belief that networking matters and is useful for finding a job, a belief with which sociologists concur. Sociologists define a **social network** as a bounded set of individuals linked by the exchange of material or emotional resources, everything from money to information to friendship. The patterns of exchange determine the boundaries of the network. Network members exchange resources more frequently with one another than with nonmembers. Individuals in a network think of themselves as network members. The people you know personally form the boundaries of your personal network.

One measure of the quality of a personal network is the number of ties or connections in the network. Someone with many ties has a "dense" network; he or she is connected to many people. Moreover, ties may be strong or weak. Frequency of interaction, emotional intensity, and reciprocity between individuals defines the strength of ties (Yakubovich, 2005). Strong ties exist between you and family members and close friends. You see such people regularly, care deeply about them, and would help them if they needed it. Weak ties exist between you and others in your personal network—say, the friend of a friend, someone you met via Facebook, or one of your parents' co-workers. You would not see such people often, nor would you count on them to help you in times of trouble.

In his study of professional, technical, and managerial workers in a Boston suburb, sociologist Mark Granovetter (1995 [1974]) discovered that 57 percent of his respondents found their job through personal contacts. Some 83 percent of these people said the contact who helped them get their job was someone they saw infrequently; they represented a weak tie. At the time his study was first published, Granovetter's finding was surprising and provocative. Common sense suggests that people to whom you are strongly tied would be most useful in helping you find a job because they are most motivated to help you. But it turns out what matters most in finding a job is good and unique information about jobs. Acquaintances who are one step removed from you are in a position to provide new (or nonredundant) information about jobs. These weak ties serve as "bridges" to "new parts of a social universe" or new parts of the labour market (Yakubovich, 2005: 410). In other words, the people you see frequently, such as your friends, probably have the same information about job openings that you do. But someone who is a weak tie in your network, such as your mom's best friend or your cousin's boss, may have information about job openings that your strong ties do not have. Because this information comes through personal contacts, it may not be readily available to the public, which decreases the amount of competition for the job opening. Thus, information from acquaintances or weak ties is most likely to lead to a new job. Granovetter calls this phenomenon "the strength of weak ties."

Since Granovetter's study, sociologists have continued to examine how personal contacts or networks help people find jobs. Recent studies emphasize the importance of social capital or resources in your personal network (Flap and Boxman, 2001). Having high-status contacts in your network improves your chances of finding a better job: "good networks help to get people good jobs" (Erickson, 2001: 156; Marsden and Hurlbert, 1988).

You might think that the biggest network of all—the Internet—would be especially useful in finding a job but evidence on this subject suggests otherwise. Internet job sites are widespread, but they often don't work as advertised. One sociologist posted her résumé on Monster.com and Hotjobs.com only to find that after two months she had yet to receive a legitimate inquiry, even from the health and biomedical companies she electronically "pelted." She concluded that the internet alone will not get you a job (Ehrenreich, 2005).

Using data from two American surveys, Fountain (2005) found that, in 1998, using the Internet increased searchers' chance of finding a job by 164 percent. By 2000, searchers using the Internet were 28 percent *less* likely to find a job than non-Internet searchers. Fountain offers two explanations for this dramatic shift. First, if only a small number of people are using the Internet, as was the case in 1998, then they have access to information about job openings that others, who are probably equally qualified, do not have. Second, when only a small number of workers apply through the Internet, employers may use this as a marker of the skill of workers, such as being more technologically savvy or resourceful than others are: useful information that may affect their hiring decision. But even two years later, by 2000, when the number of people using the Internet for job searches had doubled, these advantages disappeared. Fountain concludes that even though the Internet has changed the way people search for jobs, the change has been more about form than substance. The Internet may provide a new way for workers to find information about employers and vice versa, but it is unclear whether the information on the Internet is better than information obtained elsewhere.

TIME FOR REVIEW

1. What are the main determinants of job satisfaction?
2. What is alienation and how do workers respond to it?
3. What are the most effective strategies for finding a job?

THE FUTURE OF WORK

At the end of any discussion of work, one question remains for most students: "Where will the jobs be when I graduate?" While I do not have a crystal ball, it is possible to make some projections about future jobs.

Education and retirement play key roles in determining which job openings are growing and which are not. Almost three-quarters of the new jobs that will be created in the near future are expected to require some form of postsecondary education. They are in the fields of health, natural and applied sciences, education, social science, government service, and business and professional services. In the United States, 10 of the 20 fastest-growing occupations between now and 2018 will be related to healthcare, similar to the situation in Canada (U.S. Bureau of Labor Statistics, 2010). These projections also highlight that the economy will continue to generate both good and bad jobs: While many of these jobs, such as doctors and biomedical engineers require postsecondary education, others, such as home healthcare aides, require only short-term training.

Different forms of nonstandard work will continue to proliferate. One form of nonstandard work of particular interest to many undergraduates is self-employment, which will represent an ever-growing percentage of the labour force, partly because companies find outsourcing a good way to reduce labour costs. Although only about one-sixth of Canadian workers are self-employed, the growth rate of self-employment since the 1970s has outpaced that for workers in the public and private sectors (LaRochelle-Côté and Uppal, 2011; Statistics Canada, 2009). Even during economic downturns, self-employment grows. Some workers who lose jobs because of corporate restructuring are pushed into self-employment as their only employment option. Other workers are drawn to self-employment because of a desire to have more control over their work. Regardless of why people become self-employed, the future appears to involve an increase in self-employment.

In the immediate future, we can expect employers to continue looking for ways to reduce operating costs. As in the past, one focus will be on reducing the cost of labour. Employers continue to move factories to countries with the lowest labour costs. Along with labour-reducing uses of technology, this tendency may further the trend toward the use of temporary and contract employees. What one industrial manager said in 1994 still rings true for many current workers: "I'm here for the duration, five years or so" (quoted in Osterman, 1995: 72).

Two decades ago, analysts debated two divergent futures for work. On the one hand, optimists emphasized the "end of the job" as we know it and the rise of self-employed, autonomous entrepreneurs (Bridges, 1994). Part of the optimistic scenario is based on the hope that the service industry will continue to create good jobs in finance, medicine, and the like. Pessimists, on the other hand, predicted the "end of work." Based on an analysis of jobs in the United States, Jeremy Rifkin (1995) believed that as many as three-quarters of white- and blue-collar jobs could be automated, with no jobs to replace the ones lost to automation. In Rifkin's view, the unemployment level was going to rise and leave more of us scrambling for the few remaining jobs. By the middle of the twenty-first century, millions of workers could be left permanently idle, he said.

As I write this chapter, it is clear that neither prediction is completely right or wrong. As we discussed in this chapter, the service industry has created good jobs while also continuing to churn out lower-paid nonstandard ones. And while certain occupations, such as bank tellers and travel agents, have declined because of automation, we are far from reaching the end of work. As you've learned in this chapter, employers and employees have some control over whether technology creates good or bad jobs, reducing or increasing alienation. An important issue for the future of work is whether employers or employees will set the terms by which such changes will be judged. One thing is certain. The battle between workers and management will probably continue, as employees like Zainab Taiyeb try to organize their co-workers so they can improve their chances of having a say in what work looks like in the years to come.

TIME FOR REVIEW

Are you more likely to witness "the end of the job" or "the end of work?" Why?

SUMMARY

1. **How did the Industrial Revolution and the rise of the service economy affect the nature of jobs?**
   In the Industrial Revolution that began in Great Britain in the late eighteenth century, large segments of the population moved from being peasant farmers to being wage-earning factory workers living in urban areas. The rise of the service economy in the last third of the twentieth century witnessed the decline of manufacturing jobs and an increase in the proportion of nonmanual jobs. In recent decades, jobs in the service sector have become increasingly polarized into good jobs in upper-tier industries and bad jobs in lower-tier industries.

2. **What are nonstandard jobs?**
   Nonstandard jobs include part-time jobs, temporary jobs, contract work, seasonal work, and self-employment. The proportion of Canadians employed in nonstandard jobs has grown since the 1970s with the rise of the "24-hour economy," increased demand for consumer services, and the aging of the population. Young workers and older workers are overrepresented in some kinds of nonstandard jobs.

3. **Do Canadians work more than they used to?**
   On average, Canadians are not working longer hours than they were in the 1980s. The proportion of Canadians working a 40-hour work week has declined since then. However, work hours are becoming polarized, with more Canadians working fewer than 40 hours per week and more working more than 40 hours per week.

4. **How have mobile devices that connect to the Internet changed the way we work?**
   Such devices increase productivity but many users report downsides to these devices, such as a heightened need to be connected to work and the blurring of boundaries between work and nonwork time.

5. **In what sense is the labour market segmented?**
   Good jobs are located in core industries and firms with primary labour markets, while bad jobs may be found in peripheral industries and firms with secondary labour markets. Job ghettos are areas of the labour market that trap disadvantaged groups of workers. Labour market shelters, such as professional associations and unions, help their members maintain access to good jobs.

6. **What determines job satisfaction and alienation?**
   To be satisfied at work, intrinsic rewards, such as autonomy and challenging work, are at least as important as extrinsic or material rewards. Self-employed workers and workers in small companies who are 45 or older experience the most job satisfaction. Alienation is a structural condition of powerlessness that arises from the organization of work in capitalist economies.

QUESTIONS TO CONSIDER

1. Thinking about your own work experience, do you see evidence of the service economy creating good jobs or bad jobs? Do you see evidence of an increase in nonstandard work schedules?

2. Research points to three types of smart phone or mobile device users: "enthusiastic," "balanced," and "tradeoff users." What type of mobile device user are you? Have you experienced difficulty separating work from nonwork time?

3. What is the difference between job satisfaction and alienation? Is Marx's concept of alienation relevant for understanding work today? Why or why not? Have you ever engaged in workplace behaviour that could be interpreted as a reaction to alienating conditions? Did this behaviour change the alienating conditions? Why, or why not?

4. Think about how you or your friends have found jobs. What role have personal contacts played in your search for a job? What other ways have you or your friends found work?

GLOSSARY

In Marxist theory, **alienation** (p. 290) is a structural condition of "objective powerlessness." Workers do not have power or control over their work situation and are separated from the means of production. This situation is a characteristic of work in a capitalist economy.

Deindustrialization (p. 273) refers to the shift from a goods- to a service-based economy.

The **division of labour** (p. 270) refers to the specialized tasks performed by different categories of workers. The division of labour increases when work is broken down into smaller components.

Extrinsic rewards (p. 273) are the material benefits of working. Adequate pay, benefits, and opportunities for advancement are examples.

Functional or internal flexibility (p. 276) in nonstandard employment allows employers to move workers from one job to another within an organization.

The **human relations school of management** (p. 287) emphasizes the importance of the social aspects of work. Proponents argue that more satisfied workers are more productive workers.

Intrinsic rewards (p. 273) are the social-psychological benefits of working. They are derived from challenging work, nonrepetitive work, autonomy, and decision-making opportunities.

Job ghettos (p. 282) are parts of the labour market that prevent groups of workers from experiencing upward mobility.

Job satisfaction (p. 289) is determined by asking workers in a survey questions such as, "How satisfied are you with your job as a whole?"

Labour market segmentation (p. 281) involves the division of the labour market into sectors of good and bad jobs.

Labour market shelters (p. 284) are organizations that protect the jobs of certain groups of workers. Professional associations and unions are examples.

Nonstandard work schedules (p. 279) are characterized by either working nonstandard hours, which fall outside the 9–to–5 workday (shift work), or working nonstandard days, such as Saturday and Sunday.

Nonstandard work (p. 269) includes part-week employment, part-year employment, limited-term contract employment, employment through temporary-help agencies, self-employment, and multiple-job holding.

Numerical or external flexibility (p. 276) in nonstandard employment enables employers to adjust the size of their workforce by easily hiring and firing workers in response to fluctuations in labour demand.

Polarization of working hours (p. 278) occurs when many workers in the labour market are working either too many hours (overwork) or too few hours (underwork).

Primary labour markets (p. 281) are where most good jobs are found. Such markets have an internal labour market that provides a job ladder and the opportunity for upward mobility.

Scientific management (p. 287), also known as *Taylorism*, was developed by Frederick Taylor. This style of management breaks job tasks into their smallest components. Work is also separated into conceptual and manual tasks, removing the need for many workers to make decisions about their work.

A **social network** (p. 292) is a bounded set of individuals linked by the exchange of material or emotional resources, everything from money to information to friendship.

Union density (p. 292) is the percentage of paid workers in a country who are unionized.

CHAPTER 13

EDUCATION

Scott Davies
ONTARIO INSTITUTE FOR STUDIES IN EDUCATION
UNIVERSITY OF TORONTO

SOURCE: © REUTERS/Olivier Jean.

AFTER READING THIS CHAPTER, YOU WILL BE ABLE TO:

- Analyze how schools help to socialize students, how they affect the system of social stratification, and how they are socially organized.

- Summarize the main theories used by sociologists of education.

- Describe how social forces have shaped modern schooling.

- Understand how and why modern societies have to some degree become disenchanted with schooling.

INTRODUCTION

Go to the education section in any bookstore and you will see rows of titles declaring schools to be in crisis: *The Catastrophe in Public Education, Public Education: An Autopsy, Failing Our Kids: How We Are Ruining Our Public Schools, The University in Ruins*, and so on. Newspapers decry the quality of schooling with headlines like "Johnny Can't Read and He's in University." Such drama! Is it really that bad?

Not if you consider several facts about schools. Until quite recently higher education was deemed to be a waste for common people. Early in the twentieth century, most people did not complete high school. But the past half-century has brought a change in attitude. In Canada and elsewhere, advanced levels of education are seen to be not only suitable but also necessary for many people. Over 50 years, high-school attendance has become almost universal, and attaining a secondary-school diploma the norm. University enrolments have never been higher. Further, public opinion surveys show that most Canadians rate our public schools favourably and believe they are effective teachers of our youth (Canadian Council on Learning, 2007).

These facts highlight a key paradox. Modern schooling has been a success story in many respects,

having grown immensely, reshaped the lives of most Canadians, and received billions in government funds. Yet as schools become more central to society, they attract more and more criticism. This chapter will illuminate this paradox by exploring the transformation and changing connections between schools and Canadian society over the past century.

HOW SCHOOLS CONNECT TO SOCIETY: CLASSICAL AND CONTEMPORARY APPROACHES

Sociologists examine three main ways that schools connect to society. First, schools shape society by **selection**. Education systems have long channelled students into different types of schools and programs. This process creates stratification when programs are designated as "higher level" or "lower level" and link to better or worse job opportunities. The endless grading, judging, marking, and testing in schools sorts and certifies students with different "badges of ability." This may seem self-evident since

Schools *select* students to go into different programs and, eventually, they wind up in different occupations in a stratified social order. Schools *socialize* students into the ways of their society's culture. And schools help to *organize* society socially.
SOURCE: Newzulu – Layla Mashkoor/The Canadian Press.

we have all written hundreds of tests in our lives. But a sociological approach sets this process within a bigger picture: Schooling connects to societal-level inequality. In a society marked by disparities in wealth and income, and where more people go to school for longer periods, never before has the pursuit of educational credentials been as consequential for income, occupational success, and other life-chances. Sociologists ask *who* is selected for *what*, and *why?*

These kinds of questions can be traced back to the ideas of Karl Marx and the structural functionalists. Although Marx wrote little on schooling, his followers examined the role of schooling in maintaining patterns of economic inequality. They have argued that schools are stratified in ways that reflect workplace hierarchies, with basic forms of schooling teaching youth to be punctual and compliant, and with higher levels encouraging students to internalize orders and the expectations of authority figures. In contrast, structural functionalists see school selection as an increasingly meritorious process in which the brightest and hardest working are identified, rewarded, and selected for training in professional work and high-level management.

Second, schools shape society as they *socialize* people. They help prepare new adults, passing along values and knowledge. This too may seem glaringly obvious, but decisions on *which* values and knowledge are passed on can be contentious. When Émile Durkheim (1961 [1925]) was writing, industrialization and the rise of democracy were promoting individualism, and people began to feel free to develop their talents to their fullest extent. As individualism flourished, Durkheim sought to understand how modern societies could replace the binding and authoritative voice of religion, which had traditionally prescribed norms to guide people's thoughts and actions. What would now keep individuals from being self-centred and acting only in their own interest? Durkheim cared deeply about "moral education," the normative element of schooling that he hoped would become society's prime tool to combat the rising culture of individualism.

When Canada was more religious, schools imparted old-fashioned virtues and moral codes. But society has changed, so contemporary sociologists now ask these questions: Do schools still impart a clear set of values? Is socialization better understood as a series of unintended consequences that are beyond anyone's control? Just how successful are schools at socializing students? Do they treat everyone the same or does school socialization differ by class, gender, and race?

Third, education shapes society through *social organization*. Schools affect how we learn and help define different types of occupations. This was a core interest of another classical theorist, Max Weber, who was fascinated by "rationalization," supposedly the main "logic" of modern societies, embodied in bureaucratic organizations. For him, modern schooling was changing society by teaching knowledge in a systematic fashion and creating credentials to forge more formal pathways to labour markets. Why do employers seek and hire employees with school credentials? The conventional wisdom is that schools teach skills, employers hire the most skilled, and school credentials are signals of skills. But Weber's contemporary followers have questioned whether the school–labour market connection is so simple. They contend that most school content is only loosely connected to what is demanded in most jobs. They see schools as largely serving to distribute legitimate access to jobs.

Let us now examine in depth each of the three roles of education: selection, socialization, and social organization.

SELECTION

When Canada was an agricultural society, land was a prime economic resource, and affluent families strove to pass their property to their children. When manufacturing and commerce became the key economic activities, children from well-to-do families could inherit business fortunes. But today, most youth earn their living through employment and they need credentials. "Class reproduction," the passing of advantage from one generation to the next, does not operate through direct inheritance in education. No one can legally inherit his or her parents' law degree, medical licence, M.B.A., or teaching certificate. These things must be earned. Now that most positions of power and status require some sort of school credentials, how do the affluent pass on their advantages?

School selection occurs in two ways. First, schooling itself is structured in a stratified manner, although this structuring takes different forms across countries and over time. Second, within that structure, students from different backgrounds have unequal rates of success. Families navigate their way through this structure, searching for ways to boost their children's educational success for the most prized credentials. Most parents expect their children to receive a postsecondary education (Statistics Canada, 2002).

CHANGING SCHOOL STRUCTURE

In Canada, the traditional form of educational selection is known as "streaming." Streaming consists of splitting students into curricular groupings, one typically bound for postsecondary schooling, one headed for general training. Students in the upper tier are exposed to advanced mathematics and works of literature, while those in the lower tiers focus on the rudiments of literacy, numeracy, and practical workplace skills. Although Canada ranks near the top of the world in reading literacy (see Figure 13.1), most Canadian sociologists have long criticized streaming for limiting educational opportunity, particularly for students from working-class backgrounds. Streaming is seen to dampen their aspirations, manage their ambitions, and discourage them from moving on (Krahn and Taylor, 2007). To understand Canada's form of

educational stratification, we need to set streaming in an international context.

Compared with that in many European countries, Canadian education has actually been relatively open and flexible. For decades, schools in Britain, France, and Germany sorted students into entirely academic or entirely vocational schools at relatively young ages (Kerckhoff, 2002). European academic secondary schools were oriented to preparing elites and preserving a heritage of classic literature, philosophy, and rigorous exams. Excellence was equated with high culture. Until recently it was inconceivable for French secondary-school students to study "practical" electives, such as business or accounting. Stratification was rigid; once students entered a type of school, few moved out. If students failed an examination at age 15 or 16, they were effectively eliminated from further higher education.

To understand national differences, sociologists distinguish **sponsored mobility**, which takes place in educational systems that select relatively few youth early in their lives to enter elite universities, from **contest mobility**, which takes place in educational systems that group the bulk of youth

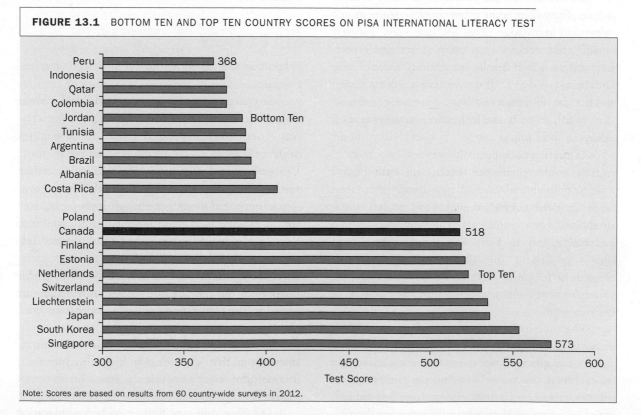

FIGURE 13.1 BOTTOM TEN AND TOP TEN COUNTRY SCORES ON PISA INTERNATIONAL LITERACY TEST

Note: Scores are based on results from 60 country-wide surveys in 2012.

SOURCE: Based on data from OECD (2014), PISA 2012 Results in Focus: What 15-year-olds know and what they can do with what they know http://www.oecd.org/pisa/keyfindings/pisa-2012-results-overview.pdf.

into the same school, expose them to the same curriculum, and send large numbers to higher education (Turner, 1960). Sponsored mobility uses highly structured streaming to restrict access to higher education, while contest mobility promotes more competition within a unitary structure. Canada is an example of a contest system, while many European countries have had sponsored systems. For most of the twentieth century, Canadian schooling did not sharply separate a "gifted" minority from the rest by creating separate schools. Academic curricula were instead given to almost everyone. From the 1960s until recently, proportionately more Canadian youth flowed into Canadian universities than European youth flowed into European universities, and even lower streams were not strongly vocational; little high-school content has been directly job-related in any stream. As a result, the high-school diploma lacks vocational meaning, and it does not guarantee any particular skill for any specific occupation. Canadian high schools channel many students to postsecondary levels and prepare few for any particular job.

This distinction may be changing, however, as nations expand their universities and colleges to take in more students (Wolf, 2002). As in Canada, European policymakers want more youth to study in university, claiming that more graduates will generate wealth and improve their nation's economic competitiveness. Most European nations are removing barriers, creating more alternative channels for youth, and moving toward a more streamlined contest model. As such, the form that inequality takes in education is changing.

As more youth enter higher education, competition shifts to higher levels, and stratification *within* universities and colleges becomes increasingly important. Higher education can be seen as stratified along two main dimensions: selectivity of institution and field of study (Davies and Guppy, 1997). Universities and colleges with the best reputations offer their graduates access to elite jobs, higher wages, contacts, and other advantages. In some countries, higher education institutions differ greatly in prestige. In Europe, ancient universities, such as Oxford, Cambridge, and the Sorbonne, have much more exclusive student bodies, and they more readily provide their students with access to elite positions. In Canada, universities are generally more selective and academically intensive than are community colleges, whose vocational mandates

Fields linked to powerful professions or commercial markets, such as medicine, law, engineering, and business, offer students pathways to lucrative job markets.
SOURCE: © Andresr/Shutterstock.

give them a subordinate position within higher education (Dennison, 1995).

Fields of study also differ in prestige, selectivity, access to resources, and payoffs for graduates. High prestige was once attached to humanistic fields such as philosophy and English that enjoyed elite patrons, but in recent decades this has changed. Fields linked to powerful professions or commercial markets, such as medicine, law, engineering, and business, have now gained the upper hand. These fields offer students pathways to lucrative job markets (Walters, 2004).

As colleges and universities are flooded with an unprecedented number of applicants, school selection moves upward to higher education. Students in different institutions and fields face unequal prospects. Universities and colleges sort these larger masses for vastly different occupational and social opportunities. Since there are simply not enough high-paying jobs for all graduates, entry into the most advantageous slots in higher education is becoming increasingly valuable. Required high-school grades—the prime currency for entrance to universities—have steadily risen over the past decade. Many universities are boosting their entrance standards and tuition fees, gaining repute not only by admitting top students but also by rejecting large numbers of qualified students. Institutions that were already highly exclusive are increasingly selective, while the less discriminating are expanding their enrolments.

The degree of stratification in higher education differs across nations. For instance, the American system is a mix of private-sector and public institutions that are arrayed on a steep prestige hierarchy. American higher education has famous Ivy League universities, elite liberal arts colleges, and flagship public universities that greatly overshadow less-renowned institutions. This steep, entrenched system makes the name of elite institutions important to employers.

Canadian higher education, in comparison, not only lacks a private sector but also lacks a steep institutional hierarchy (Davies and Zarifa, 2012). Until recently, Canadian governments have allowed only publicly funded universities. The resources allocated to these institutions have been fairly proportional to their size, while their American counterparts are much more unequal. Although the top American colleges and universities select from a national and international pool of applicants, only small numbers of Canadian undergraduates cross provincial or territorial borders, and most commute to their local institution. Canada has a relatively small national market for undergraduate credentials. Although degrees from top-ranked colleges in the United States can offer great opportunities there, few employers in Canada value the name of any one Canadian university over others.

Accordingly, Americans have long ranked their universities, but the practice is relatively new in Canada. The best-known Canadian rankings are compiled by *Maclean's* magazine. The magazine gives high scores to institutions with such attributes as large libraries, incoming students with top high-school grades, faculty with research awards, and small classes. Although popular, this ranking has been criticized for using questionable measures and for creating an artificial image of hierarchy and competition among our universities. However, university administrators take them seriously and strive to improve their relative position. In 2015, the top three "primarily undergraduate" universities according to *Maclean's* were Mount Allison University (Sackville, New Brunswick), the University of Northern British Columbia (Prince George, British Columbia), and the University of Lethbridge (Lethbridge, Alberta). The top "comprehensive" universities were Simon Fraser University (Burnaby, British Columbia), the University of Victoria (Victoria, British Columbia), and the University of Waterloo (Waterloo, Ontario). The top three "medical/doctoral" universities were McGill University (Montreal, Quebec), the University of

Toronto (Toronto, Ontario), and the University of British Columbia (Vancouver, British Columbia) (*Maclean's*, 2015).

Canada may be developing a more pronounced hierarchy in higher education. As our universities and colleges increasingly generate more of their own revenue, whether via large external research grants, corporate funds, alumni donations, or steeper tuition, some universities and colleges will likely enjoy advantages. If wealthier institutions are perceived by students and employers to offer a superior education, it may bring a steeper pecking order to Canadian higher education (see Davies, Maldonado, and Zarifa, 2014).

TIME FOR REVIEW

1. Why has modern schooling expanded over the past century?
2. In what ways has expansion necessitated a greater variety of accommodations among educators?
3. What social pressures are generated by rising demands for postsecondary credentials?

INEQUALITY AMONG STUDENTS

Within sociology, a debate has raged since the 1960s over whether schools create equal opportunity for all. Functionalists believed that schools were increasingly rewarding the best, allowing any bright students, regardless of their social backgrounds, to enter high-paying professional and managerial positions. In contrast, neo-Marxists contended that the very design of mass public schooling ensured that people who are born disadvantaged remain disadvantaged. In recent years, this claim has been extended to race and gender, with many analysts arguing that female students and those who are members of minority groups are treated poorly in school and are given little choice but to enter low-paying jobs in female and minority group "job ghettos." The claim here is that schools worsen existing inequalities by stereotyping disadvantaged youth, devaluing their cultures and skills, and steering them into lower streams. Sociologists have conducted research on this topic for decades. This research has consistently uncovered the following patterns.

First, educational attainment for youth from all class backgrounds has steadily risen over the past half-century. As Table 13.1 shows, more Canadians from all walks of life attend school for more years than did their fathers. Second, despite this expansion, student success has been found to be

TABLE 13.1   POSTSECONDARY PARTICIPATION OF 21-YEAR-OLD CANADIANS (PERCENTAGE)

	ATTENDED A POSTSECONDARY INSTITUTION	ATTENDED COMMUNITY COLLEGE OR CEGEP	ATTENDED UNIVERSITY
All Canadians	74.7	33.0	41.7
Family income			
Below $50 000	66.2	34.8	31.4
$50 000+	79.0	32.1	46.9
Indigenous status			
Indigenous	51.1	28.0	23.1
Non-Indigenous	75.4	33.2	42.2
Parents' education			
No postsecondary	60.9	36.6	24.3
Some postsecondary	80.7	31.5	49.2
Immigration status			
First generation	86.6	29.6	57.0
Second generation	83.0	30.0	53.0
Nonimmigrant	71.2	34.2	37.0

SOURCE: Adapted from Statistics Canada data in McMullen (2011).

consistently related to socioeconomic background. This has been true not only across time but also around the world, and, indeed, it is one of the "iron laws" in the sociology of education. Youth from less advantaged backgrounds are repeatedly over-represented in lower streams, get lower grades, drop out of school at higher rates, and are under-represented in higher education. Inequalities along socioeconomic lines were evident when such data were first collected and they have persisted ever since, (Anisef, 1974; Blossfeld and Shavit, 1993; De Broucker and Lavallée, 1998; Gamoran, 2001; Guppy and Arai, 1994; Knighton, 2002; Krahn, 2004; Porter, Porter, and Blishen, 1982; Ryan and Adams, 1999; Wanner, 2000).

To illustrate these inequalities, Table 13.1 shows the proportion of Canadians who were 21 years old in 2006 who had ever attended a postsecondary institution. The top row of Table 13.1 shows that 74.7 percent of Canadians of that age had attended a university, community college, or CEGEP. However, this percentage differs for different levels of parental schooling. For example, the likelihood of someone attaining a university degree was 24.3 percent if neither parent had any postsecondary education, but it rose to 49.2 percent if at least one parent had a

postsecondary education. We see a clear socioeconomic effect in Table 13.1—the likelihood of attaining a university degree more than doubles across levels of parental education. These findings are typical of dozens of studies on this topic.

However, a different picture emerges when we compare the school success of males and females. Males once had a virtual monopoly on higher education, but this imbalance began to change in the late 1950s. By the 1980s, more women than men were attending university. Females now drop out of high school in fewer numbers, graduate more often, enter universities in greater numbers, and score higher on many standardized tests (Frenette and Zeman, 2008). Today, women have surpassed men on most measures of educational attainment.

What explains this reversal? It partly reflects the success of the women's movement; partly the entry of women into traditionally male-dominated professions, such as law and medicine; and partly how some "female-dominated" occupations, such as teaching, nursing, and social work, not only grew but also demanded higher-level educational certificates. Men's attainment has not kept pace, partly because substantial numbers of men continue to work in blue-collar jobs, such as mining and construction, which rarely require postsecondary schooling (Guppy and Arai, 1994).

Although more women are going to university, they often enter different fields from their male counterparts. Figure 13.2 shows the distribution of university graduates by field of study in 2011. While most students in Canadian universities are female, women do not form the majority in fields that are related to math, computer science, or engineering. Of course, these numbers are *very* different from those of previous eras. For instance, in the early 1960s, about 25 percent of university graduates were women; in some fields, such as forestry, no women graduated, and several others, such as law, had only a handful of female graduates (Statistics Canada, 2001). But while this pattern has certainly changed, and while such fields as business, law, and medicine have seen dramatic change, women continue to be underrepresented in several dynamic and well-paying fields (DiPrete and Buchmann, 2013; see the Critical Sociology: Social Inequality box).

Patterns of educational attainment by Indigenous and immigration status show that on average, second- and especially first-generation immigrants exceed nonimmigrants in postsecondary participation, particularly in attending university (refer back to Table 13.1). Meanwhile, Indigenous Canadians have a much lower participation rate in postsecondary education and university attendance than do non-Indigenous Canadians. Other data show that Indigenous, black, and Hispanic Canadians have lower-than-average participation rates (Davies and Guppy, 2013). What accounts for these variations? An explanation must take three legacies into account: differences in socioeconomic status, colonization, and immigration policy.

The large variation among minority groups is partly a product of Canada's changed immigration policy. Whereas recruitment in previous eras targeted Europeans with relatively low levels of schooling, since the late 1960s, Canada has targeted Asians with advanced educational credentials. As a result, living conditions for immigrants vary widely. Some of them enter the country with profiles that typically promote educational success—high levels of parental education, comfortable incomes, urban residence—while others do not. Thus, Canada's educational rankings partly reflect the "inputs" from the immigration system as well

FIGURE 13.2   FIELDS OF STUDY FOR CANADIANS WITH B.A. OR HIGHER, 2011

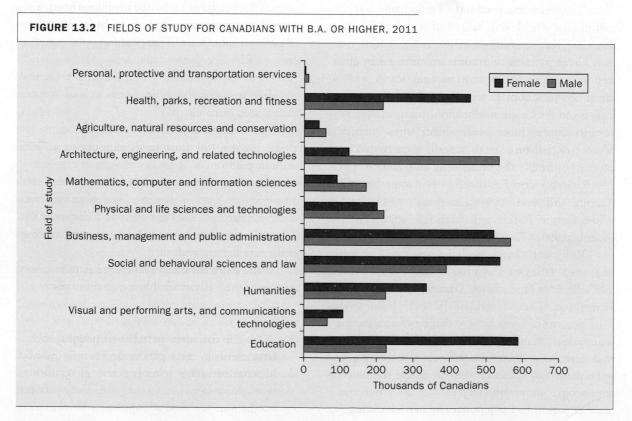

SOURCE: Adapted from Statistics Canada (2013).

In the 1970s and 1980s, many sociologists argued that schools caused gender segregation across fields of study. They claimed that educators reinforced gender traditionalism by discriminating against girls and not offering alternative role models. Since then, gender patterns in education have partially changed: Women now far outnumber men among university students and are making inroads in some fields that were formerly difficult for them to enter. The change is partly due to old gender norms being challenged in many formerly male preserves of employment, such as law, medicine, and business administration.

Beyond that, however, lies a more mundane story. Female-dominated fields such as teaching, nursing, social services, and secretarial work long ago moved their training into universities and colleges and upgraded their educational requirements. That move encouraged thousands of young women to get a postsecondary education, irrespective of whether they accepted traditional notions of femininity.

Meanwhile, there was no comparable increase in required credentials among male-dominated blue-collar occupations in mining, manufacturing, construction, and skilled trades—jobs that continue to offer good wages without requiring postsecondary degrees. This circumstance has allowed many males to avoid higher education without paying a hefty penalty in the labour market. So, paradoxically, the great gender reversal in school attainment has been partly fuelled by persistent patterns of treating women and men differently.

Critical Thinking Questions

1. Do you think that cultural change or continuing to treat women and men differently in education is more responsible for women's increasing university attendance and progress in entering previously restricted fields of study? On what do you base your opinion?

2. How would you design a sociological study to determine the relative influence of cultural change versus differential treatment of women and men in shaping change in women's fields of study?

as its own internal processes. Meanwhile, Indigenous Canadians are products of colonialism, segregation, and discrimination, which render them the most impoverished ethnic group in Canada.

These patterns of attainment raise a key question: Do schools ameliorate inequalities in society, maintain them, or make them worse? This question is difficult to settle empirically because almost everyone goes to school. If there were some groups or regions where youth didn't go to school, then researchers could see whether the presence of education worsens or improves rates of inequality. For something that resembles these conditions, sociologists have looked to the time of the year in which few students are in school: summer. This research has long been done in the United States and has been conducted recently in Canada (Alexander, Entwisle, and Steffel Olson, 2007; Burkam et al., 2004; Davies and Aurini, 2013; Downey, von Hippel, and Broh, 2004). Its basic logic runs like this: If schools gave superior treatment to middle-class children, then student learning gaps (as measured by standardized test scores) would grow over the school year and would either stagnate or shrink during the summer months. Alternatively, if such gaps grow in the summer and narrow during the school year, then schools probably do not disadvantage youth of lower socioeconomic standing and may even mitigate the effects of home and neighbourhood. This research is almost unanimous in its basic conclusion: Schooling *reduces* learning gaps along socioeconomic lines, while these gaps widen in the summer when students are not in school. Researchers conclude that schools indeed function as equalizers, at least in terms of measured learning.

The near-mountain of empirical research on school inequalities thus lends support to a more nuanced position. Schools can be seen as progressive institutions that offer opportunities for all youth but are limited in their power to eliminate inequalities. Contemporary schools have enjoyed some success in reducing inequality, but they have not come close to totally eliminating such disparities. Affluent children have many more advantages and fare better in school because of their advantaged home environments.

TIME FOR REVIEW

1. What are the main patterns of unequal school attainments by class, gender, and race in Canada?
2. In what ways are schools active generators of inequalities, and in what ways do they partially compensate for disparities generated in the larger society?

SOCIALIZATION

Contemporary sociologists offer different depictions of how schools socialize their students. According to structural-functionalist theory (Dreeben, 1967), schools teach modern values. As societies industrialize, urbanize, and become more cosmopolitan, schools provide a common culture to compensate for the declining influence of religion. Schools are said to transmit such values as universalism (which involves treating everyone as equal, rights-bearing individuals) and meritocracy (a system in which social rewards go to people with talent who exert effort in open competitions). But rather than teaching these new values overtly, the functionalists contend that schools teach them a **hidden curriculum**. Teachers do not repeatedly lecture students on universalism and meritocracy but instead teach these values by running schools in a universalistic and meritocratic fashion—students learn by doing. By treating all students equally according to common rules, schools are seen to embody the values of universalism, and by rewarding deserving students, they are seen to teach the value of meritocracy. Thus, modern schools teach core values by virtue of their very structure and practice.

Other sociologists see a darker side to school socialization. For instance, Marxists also claim that schools impose a hidden curriculum—but one that promotes obedience to authority, not cheery modern values (e.g., Bowles and Gintis, 1976; refer back to the Critical Sociology: Social Inequality box). They contend that public education is structured to support capitalism by creating a disciplined labour force. By organizing student learning in a competitive manner and having students vie for grades and rewards, schools are said to mirror capitalist competition and individualism. Likewise, feminists and many students of race claim that schools impose subordinate identities on their students. (This argument is elaborated below.)

To assess these theories, it is useful to think of school socialization as a continuum. At one extreme are boarding schools, where the institution regulates virtually all facets of life—not only lessons but also how and when students sleep, eat, dress, and play. The school becomes the student's entire social universe, resembling what sociologists call a *total institution*, an all-controlling organization that remakes people's identities, where people are isolated from the larger society and are strictly controlled by a specialized staff. In boarding schools, teachers become powerful socializing agents, forging identities and having an almost singular impact on how pupils speak, look, and act. At the other extreme of the continuum is online education. If a person's education consists solely of online courses taken at home, the school's position in that person's life can be marginal, something that merely appears on a computer screen, to be ignored at will. School becomes just one socializing force among many, like a television program that can be turned on or off.

Most Canadian students experience school socialization somewhere between these extremes. Few attend boarding schools or take only online courses from home. Most attend public schools full-time, Monday to Friday. Bearing this reality in mind, we next explore how schools socialize students, contrasting the ways socialization in schools has changed over the past 150 years. We then consider the ways in which schools treat different groups of students differently.

Functionalists claim that schools teach universalism and meritocracy, while Marxists assert that schools impose obedience to authority.

SOURCE: Michal Kowalski/Shutterstock.com.

CHANGING FORMS OF MORAL EDUCATION

The history of Canadian schools is one of declining religious influence and altered moral content. Canadian public schools were originally organized by churches, with Roman Catholics being granted separate schools in Ontario, and Protestants being granted separate schools in Quebec. Similar denomination-based arrangements were made in all provinces. In the mid-nineteenth century, few people questioned the proclaimed need for public schools to provide Christian teaching. The earliest schools were nominally secular, but their religious character was overt.

Egerton Ryerson, the father of public schooling in what is now Ontario, wanted schools to create literate, religious, and devoted citizens. He and other school promoters believed that religious schooling could curb an array of perceived problems, such as the rising incidence of youth crime and general ignorance (Prentice, 1977: 128). Christianity occupied a central place in public school missions for a century. Even in the 1950s, public authorities demanded strong religious influence in public schooling, with some calling for public schools to teach "cardinal virtues" and "Christian ideals" (Government of Ontario, 1950: 36–37). By the late 1960s, educators had very different ideas. Fewer educators saw their role as passing on religiously inspired wisdom, time-honoured truths, and a sense of moral duty. Instead, school socialization was to become more individualistic. Educators increasingly sought new ways of teaching for a new age. Consider this quotation from a 1968 provincial committee report:

> Learning by its very nature is a personal matter. There is virtually a metabolism of learning which is as unique to the individual as the metabolism of digestion. Parents and teachers may create conditions with learning in mind, but the actual learning experience is intimate and subjective, for each human being reaches out to the world in his own idiosyncratic way. (Ontario Department of Education, 1968: 49)

After the late 1960s, schools saw their role less as providing moral guidance and more as creating forums for thinking about moral issues. This created a different type of moral education, at least in emerging theories of pedagogy. Students were to be exposed to a fuller range of contemporary controversies, beliefs, and ideals than before. Teachers aimed to enable students to make informed choices, rather than have them accept moral edicts. Ideals from Christianity were replaced by ideals of critical thinking, science, and multiculturalism. Educators wanted less to tell students what was unambiguously true or false and more to nurture a deeper understanding of various subject matters, based on discovery rather than repetition. More educators saw their mission as taking a critical stance toward society, exposing injustices, and questioning established interpretations of history (Hurn, 1993: 191).

What has been the impact of these changing ideals? Although both functionalist and Marxist theories can be compelling, what do empirical studies tell us about *actual* socialization in current schools?

In partial support of functionalist theory, schooling does appear to make people more "progressive," in the sense of supporting civil liberties, tolerating minorities, appreciating social justice and ethnic diversity, and embracing nontraditional roles for women (Kingston et al., 2003; Pallas, 2000). However, schools do so in a relatively neutral and individualized manner, and they offer rather ambiguous moral messages. That is, although students are encouraged to identify with various progressive causes, such as protecting the environment, helping the homeless, fighting racism, and fundraising for overseas children, schools do this by having students relate their own experience and venture their own opinions. Classrooms increasingly have "feel-good" posters that exhort children to read and stay in school, a form of "bumper-sticker morality" containing catch phrases for quick consumption rather than deep discussion and reflection. Yet, in support of Marxist theory, schools spend most of their time on mundane matters of personal conduct, striving to get students to be orderly and task-oriented. Much of teachers' time is spent on urging students to be respectful of one another, to participate in class, and to be cooperative (e.g., Brint, Contreras, and Matthews, 2001; Jackson, Boostrom, and Hansen, 1998).

Although studies tend to support elements of both functionalist and Marxist theory, they also suggest that modes of shaping students are changing. Teachers now treat students in a more indulgent fashion than in previous eras. They see self-esteem as essential for learning and control their classes with a lighter touch than in the past. They increasingly rely on "token economies," giving small rewards to get

The diversification of Canadian society has influenced the way morality is taught in school.
SOURCE: wavebreakmedia/Shutterstock.com.

children to comply, rather than using overt authority. They use group projects, not just individual assignments, and especially in elementary schools, students work in rotating activity centres, freely moving around the classroom and choosing their tasks. Today's schools are making less use of classic styles of enforcing obedience. Further, teachers try to inspire *all* students. Whereas schools in the past would give up on those students deemed hopeless, whether too poor, too troubled, or too slow, today's schools work hard to engage the entire student body, even the least able performers. Indeed, the law demands that schools do so.

In some respects, the socializing power of Canadian education weakens as students progress from elementary and secondary to postsecondary levels. As Mullen (2010) notes, research comparing commuters to students who reside on campus concludes that university life has a far greater impact on the values, attitudes, and psychological growth of the latter. This is especially the case for students at elite universities in the United States. However, in Canada, most college and university students are commuters. They attend classes for 10 to 15 hours per week, so are not immersed in an intensive, all-encompassing educational environment. Further, Canadian higher education institutions are not arrayed on a steep prestige hierarchy, and so are less likely to breed social elites that are relatively homogeneous and cohesive, as American Ivy League colleges and England's Oxford and Cambridge do. Nevertheless, Canadian higher education influences students in more subtle ways by reshaping their social networks (Stevens, Armstrong, and Arum, 2008). Higher education can greatly alter the number, quality, and type of social ties students enjoy, and thereby influence their subsequent job, choice of marriage partner(s), and lifestyle opportunities.

To summarize, the morality taught in public schools has shifted from religious indoctrination to a more individualized and indulgent approach that encourages students to learn by reflecting, not reciting. This change reflects the diversification of Canadian society, where moral reference points are numerous and where stakeholders want schools to address social problems while not preaching a monolithic doctrine. Within this secular and individualized form of education, do schools treat everyone the same? That is the question to which we now turn.

CREATING IDENTITIES? GENDER AND RACE

Historically, Canadian education prepared girls and boys for different roles in adult society. Traditional school systems were premised on the notion that most young women should be homemakers or schooled for a narrow range of "nurturing" occupations, such as nursing and elementary-school teaching. Although boys and girls were mostly grouped together at lower ages, they were often segregated at older ages with the expectation that a select few boys would move to advanced studies (Prentice, 1977: 111–12). Although both sexes attended school, their experiences were dissimilar. Few people challenged gender traditionalism until the 1960s. Women's educational attainment has changed since then, matching and even outpacing male attainment in many areas. But despite this apparent change, critics continue to accuse schools of continuing to reinforce traditional gender roles (American Association of University Women Educational Foundation, 1998; Bennett DeMarrais and LeCompte, 1995; Kelly and Nihlen, 1982). They detect a hidden curriculum that quietly subordinates women, prepares them for a gendered division of labour, and sends messages about their inferiority. The explicit gender stereotyping of the late nineteenth century has only been masked, they argue, and they support their argument by pointing to several indicators beyond standard measures of school attainment.

First, feminist critics examine school staffing, noting that despite some change, most positions of power remain in the hands of men. Some observers have even called schools "academic harems." For instance, an elementary school can be staffed almost entirely by women, save for the most powerful position—the principal—who is often a man. While teaching positions in lower grades are held almost entirely by women, higher-level teaching and administrative positions are held by men. A second indicator of gender bias pertains to curriculum. For several decades, feminists have charged school textbooks with being loaded with sexist language, illustrations that depict most active characters as male, and stories that depict women in nurturing occupations and as stay-at-home moms. They also contend that high-school literature courses ignore female authors and that history textbooks disregard the contributions of women. Here there has been change, especially as most provincial governments have curriculum guidelines that monitor gender representation in most course material.

A third indicator of gender inequity is the fact that schools tolerate the conduct of male students that, in the adult world, would be considered sexual harassment. Feminist critics decry "hostile hallways" in which sexual comments, touching, jokes, and leers are deemed "normal" and "natural" and are therefore tacitly permitted. Schools are said to accept such behaviour when they rationalize such acts as "boys being boys." Such rationalizations are linked to inequities in extracurricular programs. Schools continue to be accused of considering it natural that men's sports teams should receive higher priority and more funding than women's teams do, an imbalance said to send a message of female inferiority. Finally, teachers stand accused of treating female students unfairly, directing girls toward stereotypical nurturing fields, such as teaching, nursing, and administrative studies. Others claim that girls' self-esteem is damaged in the classroom when teachers ignore them in favour of boys (this particular accusation has been controversial, since research suggests teachers give males more attention only for disciplinary reasons). The sum total of these inequities, it is argued, is a gendered "hidden curriculum" that alienates females from course material, dampens their aspirations, and ultimately reinforces gender inequality.

Similarly, some analysts argue that Canadian schools sometimes socialize minority students into racial identities. The historical episode of residential schools for Indigenous children is the most blatant. In the nineteenth and twentieth centuries, the Canadian government set out to mould Indigenous identities by sending up to half of all Indigenous children to these schools with the intent of making them "modern Indians" who would speak English or French, convert to Christianity, and learn skills for menial jobs. The residential school was a total institution that separated Indigenous children from their families and communities, interrupted the rhythms of their home lives, and implanted more regimented cultural norms. The legacy of this racism is felt in Indigenous communities to this day. Likewise, young black children in some cases were singled out for discriminatory treatment in the nineteenth and early twentieth century, labelled as "coloured," and segregated in black-only schools (Axelrod, 1997: 79).

Since the 1980s, Canadian schools have responded to such problems in two ways. First, they have reworked curricula to make them more multicultural and inclusive of minority groups. Policymakers have overseen the rewriting of history and literature textbooks to better reflect the experiences of immigrants and racial minorities, and have introduced anti-racist measures to encourage students to be more accepting of diversity. For multiculturalists, schools should also cultivate cosmopolitan citizens who identify more deeply with the global community and its concern with peace, ecological health, and the developing world's advancement, and see themselves not only as national citizens but also as members of the human race, with obligations to all people everywhere.

Although overt segregation laws have been long removed, and although multicultural curricula have been adopted in a variety of forms, some sociologists continue to charge Canadian schools with being insensitive to the needs of youth from minority groups (Dei, 2005). Schools, they contend, "racialize" children from minority groups by making them assume racial identities and experience themselves as "different." In this view, schools actively reinforce racial identities and inequalities. Students who are members of minority groups are seen to be ill-treated by school practices, particularly "colour-blind" policies that ignore the disadvantages of children from these groups. School multiculturalism, it is held, only superficially addresses historical legacies of racism, while white teachers are seen to be blind to experiences that are actually colour-coded and unwilling to challenge dominant understandings of race.

Partly in response to these changes, Canadian schools have attempted to accommodate minorities in a second and more controversial fashion: through greater school choice. "School choice" refers to the use of public funds that give parents more discretion in their children's education. It usually entails making available to parents a wider variety of educational options beyond a standard, local public school.

Each province has developed its own mix of support for religious and linguistic minority schools, and some sociologists support the move, reasoning that public schools have failed to meet the needs of minority youth (Dei, 2005). On these grounds, the Toronto District School Board has created two black-focus schools. These schools have received much attention over the past several years from educators and the public, not only because race is a hot-button issue in Canadian education, but also because they signal a key debate about school socialization. Underlying these schools is a more pluralist and less individualistic vision of nation building than currently exists.

Reformers see the nation as a community of communities, with schools playing a vital role in its construction. From their point of view, students' ethnicity, race, religion, and gender mediate their relationships to the national community, creating "unity through diversity." Accordingly, separate schools are needed to socialize minority groups into their own culture, defined by race, language, or religion. For opponents, however, pluralist schooling segregates students. Opponents favour multicultural education as a means of integrating all groups into society. At present, insufficient evidence exists to help settle the debate.

Schools on First Nations reserves are getting a lot of attention these days because of tensions between public funding and school governance. Many First Nations leaders are trying to balance their requests for more federal government funds with their desire to ensure that their schools remain autonomous and promote their cultures and languages. These debates over reserve schools should not deflect attention from the fact that most self-identified Indigenous people now live off-reserve, often in major urban centres. Consequently, educational advancements for First Nations peoples will occur largely in public schools. To this end, provincial ministries and school boards are developing Indigenous-sensitive pedagogies and curricula.

In recent years, perhaps no "equity category" has attracted as much attention as sexuality. Many people urge schools to recognize gay, lesbian, transgendered, and questioning youth and respond to the fact that they continue to be stigmatized, bullied, and harassed in many schools. Others, especially some religious conservatives, refuse to recognize sexual minorities. Educators thus face twin pressures to recognize and overlook student sexuality.

Sexual diversity is now institutionalized in human rights codes, workplace equity guidelines, and anti-discrimination policies. However, its recognition in schools still faces several roadblocks. For starters, sexual minorities are difficult to identify in schools, since they still face much risk by becoming visible. No other group has a comparable fear of being "outed." Further, since most youth are not sexually active until high school, younger students may be unsure about their sexual identity. Nor is students' sexual orientation officially recorded in school records, unlike student gender, age, or disability status. Sexual minorities are not a clinical population, unlike some mental health or criminal categories. Nonetheless, given ongoing evidence of bullying and harassment, school policies for sexual minorities are being developed in the form of teacher awareness training, new curricular material, revised codes of conduct, and specially tailored programs. In some respects, these curricular revisions echo those for gender in the 1970s and 1980s, and for race and multiculturalism in the 1990s (see the Critical Sociology: Protest and Policy box).

CRITICAL SOCIOLOGY: PROTEST AND POLICY   EQUITY CATEGORIES AND EQUITY POLICY

How do equity concerns from political arenas make their way into school policies? One subtle way is through the social categories by which education officials "see" students, count their enrolments, collect data, and tailor curricula to them.

Sociologists characterize groups' economic conditions (class), social expressions of biological sex (gender), ancestry (ethnicity and race), and so on. These characteristics have much social currency and a taken-for-granted quality that can capture real social divides in people's life-chances and experience. Ask someone to identify their gender or race, and most people can quickly give a definitive answer. Asking about their social class is more complicated. Most people claim to be "middle class" regardless of their income and wealth. Most people nonetheless "see" economic class.

Canadian schools have long sorted students by religion, language, and perceived ability, reasoning that each category is either part of a distinct community and/or cannot be educated by standard methods. However, many educators today are invoking the term *equity* to call for new reforms to Canadian schools. The term is not precise, but it is often used when people call for schools to recognize and address unique needs among different social categories of children. Equity categories are not static. Old ones are sometimes discarded if they are seen to be stigmatizing, as has happened with some older special-education labels. New categories can emerge through a two-step process.

In step one, new equity categories enter schools under pressure from social movements and political parties. These actors see public schools as crucial shapers of children's life-chances. They spotlight ill-treated groups, such as sexual minorities and students with mental health needs. They exercise organizational tactics ranging from protests to media campaigns, petitioning, lobbying, and writing about schools. They sometimes make schooling seem like a battleground, but they can make new equity categories soon seem routine and uncontroversial. Contentious politics urges educators to

recognize previously unseen groups and devise new pedagogical arrangements for them.

This process occurs in step two, when previously contentious categories become widely accepted and taken for granted. This happens when pressure is applied from the outside by politicians, from the inside by students, teachers, and parents, and from outsiders who become insiders, as new teachers and students bring with them new understandings of school goals and professional responsibility. Through these channels, new equity categories can take root. For instance, a Gay/Straight Alliance may initially be established through protests, lobbying efforts, media campaigns, and petitioning. However, after much pressure has been applied to change the culture of schooling, Gay/Straight Alliances may be widely adopted across many locales with relatively little effort because they are recognized as legitimate.

Once institutionalized, policies get reshaped by school routines. Most large school boards now hire credentialed specialists who interpret and enforce equity policies. Their efforts make formerly contentious equity categories seem normal and old terms appear stigmatizing. Think of a variety of shifts in terminology over the past few decades: from "coloured person" to "person of colour" to "race" to "racialized minority;" from "sex" to "gender;" from "homosexual" to "gay and lesbian" to "LGBQ" to "LGBTQ;" and from "Indian and Eskimo" to "Indigenous and First Nations" to "FNMI" (First Nations, Métis, and Inuit). These shifting terms mark the space where contentious politics get codified into standardized procedures.

Critical Thinking Questions

1. Can faith-based schools retain their religious mandates while also providing equity to sexual minorities? If so, what organizational strategies might they use?

2. Is special education more "equitable" now than it was in past? If so, how?

THE LIMITS OF SCHOOL SOCIALIZATION

Although claims that schools mould gender and racial identities are popular, one difficulty is that they assume that schools have a great deal of socializing power, rather than providing convincing evidence of their effects. It is conceivable that some educational

institutions, such as residential boarding schools, may wield great socializing power, but the average public school today is more limited in its reach. We need to recognize other socializing influences. Students clearly are influenced by forces well beyond the school—their families, neighbourhoods, workplaces, and, of course, peer groups (Looker and Thiessen, 1999).

Sociologists have long examined high-school peer groups, believing they set limits on schools' socializing sway, and how varying degrees of student autonomy may *hinder* school goals. Sociologists in the 1950s and 1960s became interested in peer cultures when they found student populations to be less deferential than in previous decades. Although most school deviance was mild, consisting of minor rule-breaking, irreverence, apathy, or truancy, it still subverted educational goals by disrupting classrooms and interrupting learning. James Coleman (1961) argued that, among adolescent peers, learning and achievement mattered less than popularity and looking good. Moreover, in the peer group, being a top student did little for a person's reputation. Coleman's ideas have since spawned a large body of research on the formation of student subcultures. This research has examined how the very structure of schooling encourages youth to respond in ways that can frustrate the socializing efforts of educators (Coleman, 1961; Tanner, 2009).

Specifically, over the decades, sociologists have interpreted youth's obsession with physical appearance, hairstyles, clothing brands, and cliques as no mere by-product of their relative immaturity. Instead, sociologists see them as responses to particular social conditions. Schools segregate youth by age, give youth little power, and require their attendance by law. Yet students do have some degree of autonomy. High school is not overly challenging for most youth. Most students have some disposable income. These conditions, sociologists argue, encourage youth to be status-conscious. Status groups emerge when social structures offer few alternative avenues for social mobility. Students become a status group because they lack power and authority but have enough autonomy to invent their own social realm within schools. By this logic, Murray Milner Jr. (2004) has likened high-school cliques to Indian castes. Castes emerged in traditional India when there was little democracy or economic mobility for people of low social rank. Upper castes obsessed about appearance, social ranking, and maintaining social distance from inferiors. They created elaborate rituals and pressures for conformity, especially for intimacies such as eating and romantic relationships.

So how are high-school cliques like castes? According to Milner, teens risk social demotion if they are seen eating with or dating someone with low status. They use small cruelties and put-downs to uphold their dominance. A jock pesters a nerd to maintain his own status at the nerd's expense. Status also explains why some teens are so concerned with conforming to brand-name clothing fashions. The isolated world of high school creates pressure for cliques to display their status through consumer commodities. Since teens are largely excluded from "producer" roles in prestigious workplaces but are freely granted "consumer" roles, the latter become their main source of reputation.

Sociologists have also traced a second, more antagonistic element of student subcultures to schools' very own selection function (Cohen, 1955; Stinchcombe, 1964). In this view, since schools reward only some students and deem others to be academically unfit, they create disincentives for unsuccessful students. Low-ranked students suffer an inglorious status and get labelled as "underachievers" and channelled into streams that lead neither to postsecondary education nor to useful job-training programs. These students suffer emotional injury in schools and hunger for a more positive self-image. Accordingly, low-achieving students form anti-school subcultures as an alternative source of social recognition. These subcultures invert the values that schools try to promote, rejecting students who are rule-abiding, obedient, and hardworking, and celebrating the rule-breaker, the insolent, and the hedonist. Among males, this rebellion is epitomized by confrontations with teachers, fighting, smoking, drinking, and sexual bravado. Among females, it is marked by a flaunting of their sexuality and a preoccupation with dating. In both cases, subcultures are seen to be a youthful expression of frustration with school selection processes that thwart upward mobility.

Since the 1980s, sociologists have argued that oppositional subcultures can also take racialized forms. Fordham and Ogbu (1986) claim that African Americans criticize their high-achieving peers for "acting white," that is, for adopting the culture and language of white America and being disloyal to their own community. Such pressures are said to discourage black students from identifying with schooling. The "acting white" thesis has become influential, but is it true? Several American sociologists have put it to the test, but most cast doubt on it. Some suggest that only a small portion of black students take oppositional stances to schools (Downey and Ainsworth-Darnell, 2002). Others argue that generic peer pressures are felt by *all* high-achieving students, regardless of race, and those who earn top grades are similarly labelled *geeks*, *nerds*, or *brainiacs*. Only in schools where student achievement is starkly unequal by race, they speculate, will this pressure take a racialized form (Tyson, Darity, and Castellino, 2005).

Studies of peer groups suggest that school selection provokes at least a mild form of antagonism from lower-achieving students and that this can frustrate the efforts of educators. However, the very existence of oppositional subcultures similarly suggests that some theories may exaggerate the extent to which schools mould gender and race identities. Students learn roles in their neighbourhoods, families, media, and places of employment (which can be highly segregated), and these are competing sources of socialization that may be partly counteracted by schools.

For instance, some feminists (Holland and Eisenhart, 1990; Weis, 1990) contend that peer groups, not school officials, divert female students toward established gender roles and discourage educational advancement. Some suggest that embracing a student role may actually erode gender traditionalism. In a field study of an English secondary school, Lynn Davies (1984) found that youth in university-bound streams were relatively more "androgynous" and less conforming to gender stereotypes. In contrast, girls who were about to drop out looked forward to motherhood rather than to careers, and would-be male dropouts were more traditionally masculine. Since new career opportunities for academically oriented males and females may weaken traditional conceptions of gender, it is not clear that schools continue to enforce gendered and racial identities. Although schools certainly treated females and minority students differently in the past, contemporary research shows that public schools promote more liberal and progressive views about gender and race. And schools have long been among the few places in society where boys and girls are grouped together to perform the same role.

These findings force us to think more about the *limits* of schools' socializing role. Paradoxically, as more people go to school for more years, the socializing impact of schooling may become *weaker*. More than in any previous era, schools now compete with other socializing agents. More youth are employed part-time, popular culture is everywhere, and today's parents are spending more time on developmental activities, hiring more tutors, and purchasing more extracurricular lessons for their children (Adler and Adler, 1994; Quirke, 2006; Sayer, Bianchi, and Robinson, 2004). Schools are losing their monopoly on structured lessons and developmental activities, at least among the middle class. The upshot is that their unique impact on students may be on the wane. Rather than being a total institution, schools are moving toward the weaker end of the socializing continuum, no longer imparting a cohesive ideology and now competing with more socializing agents than before.

TIME FOR REVIEW

1. In what ways has socialization through education changed over the past century?
2. In what ways are today's pedagogical philosophies more indulgent and less punitive than the pedagogical philosophies of previous eras?
3. What socializing agents compete with schools in contemporary societies?

SOCIAL ORGANIZATION

For Weber, modern schooling reflected the emergence of a rationalized worldview in the organizational form of bureaucracy. With schools being one of Canada's largest expenditures, costing at least $60 billion per year, they need to be seen as legitimate organizations that generate useful skills in a relatively efficient manner. Contemporary theorists offer widely differing accounts of whether schools are indeed efficiency-seeking organizations. Some see schools as converging with Weber's ideal type of bureaucracy; others do not.

THEORIES OF SCHOOL ORGANIZATION

The most straightforward account is offered by economists. **Human capital theory** asserts that the school's role is primarily economic: to generate needed job skills. The theory assumes that both individuals and governments "invest" their time and dollars in schools because they believe it will lead to prosperity. The costs of schooling—books, buildings, teacher salaries—are "inputs," and student learning is the "output" or product. Human capital theorists see schools as organized to maximize student skills. If the value of the output exceeds its cost, schooling becomes a worthwhile investment, such as when individuals' expenditures in schooling early in their life eventually raise their earnings or improve their health. Schooling is thus seen as a form of capital—*human* capital—since people cannot be separated from their knowledge and skills in the same way that they can be distinguished from their financial and physical assets (Becker, 1964).

Indeed, research consistently shows that education *does* pay. On average, people with more years of schooling earn higher wages and have better employment rates (Walters, 2004). School pays, but why? Although some analysts point directly to the skills that are generated through education, many sociologists question the extent to which schooling improves useful job-related skills and whether jobs use what schools teach.

"Credentialists" like Randall Collins (1979) are generally skeptical of human capital theory for at least two reasons. First, usually far fewer high-skilled jobs are available than there are graduates from high schools, colleges, and universities. Employees are often overqualified; available jobs often do not require their learned skills (Livingstone, 1998). Second, Collins sees weak connections between school content and the workplace. Much schooling—hours of essay writing, studying quadratic equations and periodic tables, practising the tuba—has little to do with most job realities. School curricula develop according to their own dynamics, he argues, and seldom in response to employers' demands. Further, employers rarely bother to look at student grades when hiring. With the exception of a few professions, merely possessing a diploma, certificate or degree will suffice. If school content were really connected tightly to the job market, Collins reasons, employers would surely use grades as vital indicators of a candidate's suitability. So why do employers seek graduates with credentials if little of their learning actually connects to job demands? Collins offers several answers.

One is **credential inflation**. Just as monetary inflation devalues money, modern education devalues credentials. Just as a dollar cannot purchase the same goods it could 50 years ago, a high-school diploma does not lead to the same job it did 50 years ago. Inflation results from intense competition in the labour market. When hiring, managers in large corporations and in government are often flooded with job applicants. The sheer number of candidates makes careful and personal consideration of each one impossible. Hence, managers need a bureaucratic screening device, a procedure to reduce the applicant pool that is seen to be fair and efficient. Over the past few decades, employers have increasingly used credentials for this purpose, even for jobs that are not complex or demanding. Hiring someone with credentials may not reflect a need for specific skills. Seeking a leg up on competitors, people comply by obtaining an educational credential. This inflation creates a growing gap between the competencies required in jobs and the level of education possessed by job occupants.

Another reason that employers seek graduates with credentials concerns **professionalization**. Professional associations, such as the Canadian Medical Association, control occupational standards by setting the educational requirements for their profession. By demanding higher levels of education, these occupations can limit the number of eligible competitors. Over the decades, many occupations have raised entry requirements—school teachers, nurses, accountants, and social workers, to name a few. Sociologists see this as part of a process of professionalization in which an occupation tries to raise its standing and command higher wages. Think of all the requirements that didn't exist 50 years ago: M.S.W., M.B.A., B.N., and so on. What fascinates Collins is that teaching, nursing, social work, and business easily survived in past generations without demanding these credentials, and little evidence suggests that the tasks of these occupations have become so much more complex as to necessitate these elevated school requirements.

Collins also contends that some employers prefer to hire employees with advanced credentials simply for their prestige. According to Collins, many employers hire university graduates for jobs to gain trust from clients and customers. Firms want to appear serious, businesslike, and trustworthy and not "fly-by-night." For Collins, well-educated employees are the human equivalent of a nice piece of office furniture: They signal that the firm is honourable. Advertising a workforce with many letters trailing their names (B.A., B.Sc., L.L.B., M.B.A, M.A., Ph.D., etc.) can be a mark of status in a world where business transactions can be highly uncertain and in which clients seek signals of high repute.

SCHOOL AUTHORITY: FROM TRADITION TO RATIONALITY TO MARKETS?

Premodern schools were typically small and informal, and educational authority was decentralized. Canada had thousands of school boards, most of which controlled only a few small schools. Each teacher had little formal training and enjoyed wide discretion over his or her classroom. Lessons were taught without many formal guidelines. There was little large-scale planning and there were few educational laws. Teachers had parental-like authority over students. They could discipline largely as they pleased, often resorting to corporal punishment, with little fear of reprisal. Curricula were justified in terms of passing on time-honoured doctrine and cultural traditions. Teachers were proclaimed to be moral trustees of society.

All this changed during the twentieth century. In Weber's terms, modern institutions like schools were rationalized. Public education was justified less in moral terms and more by its social utility. Canadian schools cut "irrelevant" subjects like ancient languages and adopted new ones, usually justified in terms of their necessity for daily living. Teachers were seen less as trustees of the common good and more as semi-professionals with skills and responsibilities.

Rationalization was accompanied by a change in organizational form. Schools grew and looked less like little red houses and more like office buildings. They were increasingly governed by general rules. Lines of control were formalized from top to bottom, with hierarchical chains of command and clearly defined responsibilities. Regulations delegated authority to credentialed officials in a more specialized division of labour, particularly at upper-grade levels. Personnel were selected for their advanced training rather than for personal ties to highly ranked officials. Public schools hired certified teachers with university diplomas. Curricula were standardized, approved by higher-ranking bodies, and arranged in uniform age-graded levels. Modern schools became bureaucracies.

After World War II, governments across Canada saw education as increasingly necessary for prosperity and the development of the citizenry. Consequently, they gave public high schools a new mandate: to retain as many youth for as many years as possible. Seeing only a few students as suitable for advanced education became passé. A new norm emerged: Virtually everyone ought to complete high school. Those who did not were to be deemed either deviant or proof of a failing system. The big challenge for schools was how to translate these new ideals into new realities.

The expanded mission for schooling transformed secondary schools within a generation. School officials interpreted their mandate as delivering a broadly comparable education to all students. They further standardized schooling, from physical plant, to teacher training, to curricula. Authority and power were increasingly wielded in distant hierarchies rather than in local communities, an approach that has been dubbed, somewhat derisively, as the "one best system" (Tyack, 1974), faulted for being indifferent to the needs of individual pupils. Critics commonly portrayed schools as resembling nineteenth-century industrial factories, a "one-size-fits-all" institution.

However, with a new mandate, schools needed to devise ways to motivate an increasingly wide range of students. That was not easy. In earlier times, high schools could steer students who were uninterested in academic work into jobs. But now schools were expected to retain the vast bulk of youth, including those with learning disabilities or little academic ambition. Since teachers encountered many youths who found academic work neither appealing nor absorbing, the big challenge for modern secondary schools was to accommodate a wider range of student aptitude, preparedness, abilities, and motivation than any high school had ever faced before. Again, that was not easy. Unlike the monetary incentives that some organizations offer their employees, the incentives that schools offer their students can be weak. Their most obvious reward is a grade—the prime currency for higher-education admissions. But for youth who do not seek studies beyond high school, grades can be nearly useless. Schools have other organizational constraints, too. Teachers would love to have students who enrol on a fully voluntary basis, but many students attend school only through compulsion. Many teachers want to deal individually with students, but current funding levels force most classes to consist of 20 to 30 students. As it stands, teachers face large classes of captive students with greatly varying abilities and levels of motivation.

This has been the core challenge for reformers. **Progressive pedagogy**, rooted in the ideas of John Dewey in the early twentieth century, has been a force in Canadian schools since the 1960s. Progressives do not want schooling to be merely utilitarian for students and aim instead to nurture intrinsic forms of motivation, to engage students and have them work voluntarily. Modern teachers want to entice students to do their work not just for grades or to evade sanction, but out of true curiosity. Dewey called for schools that catered to the interests of the learner. By having students direct their own learning, schools could unleash students' intrinsic motivation, he reasoned. Over the decades, many reforms have attempted to engage students within the parameters of schools' organizational constraints (Labaree, 2010).

Progressives reformed schools by destructuring classrooms, creating curricula with fewer rote and memory-based exercises, and relaxing discipline. Traditional classrooms strictly regulated student talk and movement by arraying student desks in straight rows. But in the 1970s, progressives saw such regimentation as stifling student imaginations. They encouraged more interaction and tolerated some chatting and freer movement in the classroom. They also decorated classrooms, adorning walls with student artwork and colourful posters, often next to traditional emblems like the flag. Corporal punishment was largely abandoned in favour of notions of student rights. The binding idea was that departures from traditional schooling were needed to motivate students.

After witnessing these changes, sociologists in the 1980s offered a different take on bureaucratic schools (Powell, Farrar, and Cohen, 1985). In their eyes, decades of reform had made schools more like "shopping malls" than factories. They were struck by the transformation of schools into human service organizations that strove to accommodate their students. Schools became mall-like, they argued, by differentiating courses by degree of difficulty and creating electives to cater to student choice. They created "specialty shops" for students with different abilities, whether "gifted," ESL, or specially able. Schools bolstered extracurricular activities and services to address a wide variety of social, physical, and emotional problems. Educators became sensitized to different kinds of learning styles, as proclaimed in theories of "multiple intelligences," which claim that student ability in, say, dance, should be valued as much as student ability in math (Gardner, 1999; see Table 13.2).

The theory of multiple intelligences was developed by Dr. Howard Gardner (1998), who contended that the traditional notion of intelligence based on IQ testing is an overly narrow model of human potential. Gardner instead proposed that there are eight different kinds of intelligence. Some Canadian schools have embraced this theory and are designing curricula to match each type of intelligence. By doing so, they illustrate how schools are attempting to accommodate a wide range of student needs.

Although secondary schools in the past openly promoted academic achievement, the shopping-mall high school eased expectations. Mastery of core subjects was no longer expected from all students. Students

TABLE 13.2   THE THEORY OF MULTIPLE INTELLIGENCES

INTELLIGENCE	END-STATES	CORE COMPONENTS
Logical, mathematical	Scientist, mathematician	Sensitivity to, and capacity to discern, logical or numerical patterns; ability to handle long chains of reasoning
Linguistic	Poet, journalist	Sensitivity to sounds, rhythms, and meanings of words; sensitivity to the different functions of language
Musical	Composer, violinist	Abilities to produce and appreciate rhythm, pitch, and timbre; appreciation of the forms of musical expressiveness
Spatial	Navigator, sculptor	Capacities to perceive the visual-spatial world accurately and to perform transformations on one's initial perceptions
Bodily kinesthetic	Dancer, athlete	Abilities to control one's body movements and to handle objects skillfully
Interpersonal	Therapist, salesperson	Capacities to discern and respond appropriately to the moods, temperaments, motivations, and desires of other people
Intrapersonal	Person with detailed, accurate self-knowledge	Access to one's own feelings and the ability to discriminate among them and draw on them to guide behaviour, knowledge of one's own strengths, weaknesses, desires, and intelligences
Naturalist	Biologist, naturalist	Abilities to recognize and categorize objects and processes in nature

SOURCE: Adapted from Howard Gardner and T. Hatch, "Multiple Intelligences Go to School: Educational Implications of the Theory of Multiple Intelligences," *Educational Researcher*, 18(8), 4–10. 1989. American Educational Research Association

who desired a more enriched curriculum could still find it, and lower-achieving students could pass from grade to grade in return for little more than orderly attendance. High schools had evolved unwritten rules about how tough certain courses should be. These informal rules unofficially designated elective courses to be easier than required math and science courses. Teachers in the latter subjects could legitimately demand much effort and time, but other teachers could face rebellion from students, parents, and even administrators if they dared to expect anything comparable.

The image of the shopping-mall high school in the mid-1980s accurately described new attempts to accommodate students. But policy priorities have since shifted. For the past two decades, educators have been stung by demands to raise standards and be "accountable." Canadian policymakers typically promote this agenda by using standardized performance indicators.

Some of these critics claim that public schools are too bureaucratic. For instance, Chubb and Moe (1990) see public bureaucracies as aloof and slow to change, and requiring a mechanism to inject quality-orienting dynamics. These reformers condemn public education as an inefficient monopoly that is unresponsive to its clients, and they hail "market" reforms for their potential to create competitive pressures, similar to those faced by for-profit businesses. Under the banner of "school choice," these reformers want to force schools to survive only by collecting funds directly from fee-paying clients. The imperative to attract clients, they contend, has many advantages. It can match the tastes of parents and educators. It can encourage new providers to enter the educational field, bringing innovation to schooling, and devising customized programs for their clients. And it can boost school performance in the form of standardized test scores, since market-based schools will presumably be motivated to raise their quality to attract customers (Ouchi, 2003).

School choice is indeed growing in Canada in at least two forms. One creates more choice within the public school system, expanding the menu of programs beyond standard school offerings. For instance, the City of Edmonton has largely reinvented its school system by offering a smorgasbord of pedagogical choice and offering a variety of special-theme schools, including those that specialize in sports, science, language, arts, intensive academics, alternative pedagogy, and multiple intelligences (Taylor and Woollard, 2003). Another Alberta initiative has been to create "charter schools," independently run but government-funded, each pursuing a

special theme, whether ESL, traditional academics, Suzuki music and philosophy, science and math, or programs aimed at gifted, Indigenous, female, or at-risk students (Bosetti, 2001).

The second type of choice is private schooling. The proportion of Canadian students enrolled in private schools is growing, particularly in affluent locales. For instance, in Toronto, 10 percent of students are enrolled in private schools, higher than the 7 percent national average (Davies and Quirke, 2007). Some of these schools attempt to appeal to their customers by developing specialty programs and small classes. Almost all offer some sort of specialty, creating an astonishing array of programs and philosophies of teaching, each seeking a niche in a competitive marketplace. Similarly, homeschooling is growing in Canada, as more parents are turning to themselves to provide educational options for their children (Arai, 2000; Davies and Aurini, 2011).

Are Canadian families embracing more competitive educational strategies? Traditionally, private education has been reserved either for elites or for members of religious minorities. But various forms of private education are now expanding. The proportion of Canadian students enrolled in private schools has grown (Davies and Aurini, 2011). The tutoring industry has also undergone a staggering transformation over the past 30 years, with great growth in major Canadian cities (Aurini, Davies, and Dierkes, 2013). In 2007, a third of Canadian parents reported

The campus of Upper Canada College in Toronto, one of Canada's premier private schools for boys. For the academic year 2015–16, the family of a new Canadian student entering Upper Canada College in Grade 12 and boarding at the school would have to pay $8700 in application and registration fees, $33 550 for tuition, and $23 960 for boarding fees: a total of $66 210 for the year. Among other amenities, the college has its own indoor, regulation-sized hockey rink.

SOURCE: © CharlineXia Ontario Canada Collection/Alamy Stock Photo

that they had hired tutors for their children (Canadian Council on Learning, 2007).

Although these private alternatives certainly create more variety in education, there is still no evidence that they offer higher-quality schooling than regular public schools do, taking into account the socioeconomic advantages of their students. Indeed, rather than being more academically intensive, many of these schools have strong "shopping-mall" and "progressive" elements, like those that have inspired public educators for decades. Proud of their customized offerings, they prize pedagogical freedom and intimate relations above all. Yet, as tuition-charging schools, they lack any mandate to ensure equal access. Despite good intentions, only wealthier families can afford them. These schools illustrate the tension between satisfying yearnings for choice and providing equity.

Indeed, a flip side of market reasoning is that the customer should pay. Such thinking has permitted Canadian universities to deregulate tuition fees for their professional schools, such as dentistry, law, medicine, and M.B.A. programs. Administrators of these professional programs believe student demand will not be deterred by soaring costs, since professional degrees often lead to high incomes. Accordingly, they have raised fees well above the Canadian average for undergraduates of $5959 in 2014–15 charging up to $73 333 in 2011–12 for a year's tuition in an executive M.B.A. program (Globe and Mail, 2012; Statistics Canada, 2014).

Although these fee hikes may not have discouraged student demand, they do appear to be influencing the composition of student bodies in these programs. A recent study suggests that when programs deregulate their fees, they become more likely to accept students who have highly educated parents and to have students from poorer backgrounds who are eligible for bursaries and scholarships. The losers in the process appear to be middle-class students, who lack advantageous family backgrounds yet are often ineligible for income-contingent loans and bursaries (Frenette, 2005).

These tuition trends reflect broad changes in the organizational form and governance of postsecondary schooling. In 1850, Canadian higher education consisted of a scattering of small and mostly religious institutions. Between 1850 and 1990, the system was expanded, secularized, socialized, rationalized, coordinated, and "massified." Since 1990, most provinces have significantly reduced per-student funding, while at the same time raising performance expectations. In response, universities and colleges have become more attuned to market and government forces. In finding ways to secure new revenue sources, they have transformed themselves. For instance, to attract and accommodate new kinds of students, colleges and universities have moved far beyond their conventional weekday timetables on their main campuses and are offering courses in evenings, on weekends, at branch campuses, and via online technologies—much as a business enterprise would change to pursue new customers.

To engage in large-scale fundraising, most universities and colleges now have large public relations offices that court would-be donors and corporate sponsors. To compete with rivals, some are even engaging in "image makeovers," using consultants to "rebrand" themselves, sometimes by replacing traditional coats of arms with corporate logos and slogans (Kirp, 2004). These activities signal the encroachment of traditional missions of teaching and research by new competitive pressures, a trend decried by some as "academic capitalism" (Slaughter and Rhoades, 2004).

At the same time, provinces are expecting colleges and universities to demonstrate their effective and efficient use of tax monies by participating in quality assurance programs. Politicians increasingly want closer links between these institutions and local industries and labour markets, and to justify their receipt of public funds by meeting "key performance indicators" that signal compliance with standards of hiring, course content, and graduate placement. Importantly, however, these "KPIs" do not include any measures of student learning, but instead consist of bureaucratic formalisms that are easily counted, such as ensuring that faculty have Ph.D.s or that courses fulfill required numbers of hours. British Columbia, Alberta, Ontario, and New Brunswick have also passed legislation allowing the opening of private degree-granting bodies, reasoning that market forces can help meet new demands for higher education.

These pressures are spawning greater organizational variety in higher education, one marked by private and for-profit universities, international branch campuses, transnational enrolments, corporate involvement, and online technologies. Venerable ideals of intellectual elites retreating in quiet contemplation are giving way to a new image of bustling "learning organizations" that can teach the masses by responding to ever-shifting market and political winds.

TIME FOR REVIEW

1. Have Canadian schools switched from wielding traditional authority to wielding legal-rational authority? Support your answer with examples.
2. How do "progressive pedagogues" attempt to nurture intrinsic forms of motivation among students?
3. What are some prime examples of schools becoming more "accountable" and "market-like?"

CONCLUSION

Canadian schooling has grown immensely. Almost all Canadians attend high school, most graduate, more than half now go on to postsecondary school, and many will return to some sort of educational institution later in life, as ideologies of "lifelong education" become reality. But what has been the impact of this monumental expansion? Schools partially compensate for pre-existing inequalities in student preparedness, but their selection role ensures that expansion does not bring greater equity, at least along socioeconomic lines. Further, the singular socializing power of schooling in our lives actually shrinks. School becomes a weaker socializing agent as it integrates into our lives, competing with many other agents. Some forms of schooling have become more competitive. Prestigious programs that offer the most recognition and best rewards are increasingly exclusive. Other programs are more accommodating, treating students in more progressive ways and offering more choice than ever before.

These trends remind us of the paradox discussed at the outset of this chapter. Canadian schools now serve unprecedented numbers of students for longer periods of their lives, yet they are a lightning rod for more and more criticism. This is a prime instance of "disenchantment" in Max Weber's definition: As schooling becomes ever more central to society in the modern era, it loses its "magical" quality to command deference. As all citizens attend school for most of their youth, more are familiar with schooling and have higher expectations for what schools should do for them. Education has become a "motherhood" issue that everyone supports in the abstract, yet in the process it loses its overtones of elite rituals, aristocratic cultures, and time-honoured pageantry. The caps and gowns, the great halls, and Latin-inscribed coats of arms have largely disappeared, replaced by rationalized bureaucracies that merely promise access to labour markets.

This disenchantment shouldn't cloud a sunnier accomplishment: School systems now offer unparalleled opportunities for individuals. Schooling helps extend human rights and literacy to even the poorest segments of society. Who today reminisces about bygone eras in which schooling was a privilege for the few? Such ideas now provoke a sense of outrage and are rightfully seen to deny basic rights. Schooling may be demystified, yet we cannot manage without it.

SUMMARY

1. **How has the process of school selection changed?**
   In past decades, secondary-level streaming played an important gate-keeping role, making an adolescent's performance in high school an important shaper of his or her eventual life-chances. However, as higher education expands, life-chances are determined increasingly by where a person graduates in a stratified structure of higher education.

2. **How does educational expansion affect the value of school credentials?**
   As more Canadians attain advanced levels of education, formerly valuable credentials, such as the high-school diploma, get devalued; this process generates demand for more schooling as people jockey for advantages in the labour market. Educational expansion and credential inflation tend to feed off each other.

3. **What are the key patterns of inequality in Canadian schooling?**
   Along social class lines, students from more affluent backgrounds continue to enjoy considerable advantages. In terms of gender, women now outpace men on many indicators, although much gender segregation remains in certain fields of study. The legacy of conquest for Indigenous peoples and their history of discrimination and segregation continue to be evident in schools, while changing immigration selection policies mean that, on average, immigrants have higher education levels than non-immigrants do.

4. **Has moral education changed?**
   Today, education is less religious and explicit than before. Schools now mostly aim to have students understand key social issues without a hard-edged, prescriptive tone. The hidden curriculum

continues to emphasize the orderly completion of tasks, punctuality, and neatness. Today's schools have a more indulgent quality than they did in the past, aiming to shore up students' self-esteem and elicit rather than command their interest.

5. **How has the organization of Canadian schools changed?**
   Schools have shifted from informal institutions that wielded traditional authority to legal-rational bureaucracies that attempt to cater to students in ever-more accommodating ways. In the 1970s, this process involved lessening teacher power in favour of students, although today, it increasingly involves the use of market-like mechanisms to treat students as if they are "customers."

QUESTIONS TO CONSIDER

1. Compare your schooling experience so far with that of one of your grandparents by using the themes of selection, accommodation, competition, and sponsored and contest mobility.

2. From what you have experienced in school, how would you motivate students to be effective learners? What organizational reforms might best inspire students? Give examples.

3. Observe an elementary-level public school classroom. Do you see socializing messages in operation? Cite examples. Sort out the socializing influences of schools from those of families, neighbourhoods, labour markets, and peer groups.

GLOSSARY

Contest mobility (p. 300) is a form of educational competition in which most youths are grouped into the same school and exposed to the same curriculum, and in which relatively large numbers are directed to higher education.

Credential inflation (p. 314) takes place when labour market competition encourages individuals to acquire schooling and employers raise required credential levels for reasons that are not connected to their needs for skilled employees.

Hidden curriculum (p. 306) comprises elements of school content, such as rules, procedures, structures, and norms that can shape students in covert ways.

Human capital theory (p. 313) emphasizes how schooling can enhance productive skills and thereby generate wealth for both individuals and society.

Professionalization (p. 314) is the process by which an occupation attempts to raise its social standing, often by creating formal educational credentials.

Progressive pedagogy (p.315) is an educational movement that emphasizes student-directed learning, less structured curricula, and inspiring intrinsic motivation among students.

Selection (p. 298) is the process by which the structure of schooling feeds into broader patterns of social stratification.

Sponsored mobility (p. 300) is a form of educational competition in which children are streamed in early grade levels and relatively few enter universities.

CHAPTER 14

RELIGION

Reginald W. Bibby
UNIVERSITY OF LETHBRIDGE

SOURCE: © Hugh Sitton/Corbis.

AFTER READING THIS CHAPTER, YOU WILL BE ABLE TO:

- Identify the key sociological theories of religion.

- Recognize that people display a wide range of levels of religious commitment, while groups and institutions play a major role in instilling and sustaining personal religiosity.

- Distinguish religion's influence on individuals from its role supporting social structure and culture in most societies.

- Explain why the future of religion in Canada and elsewhere is secure.

INTRODUCTION

Religion is very much alive today. In recent years, religion has received worldwide attention in such varied developments as the election of the new and controversial Pope Francis in 2013, the phenomenal sales of Dan Brown's *The Da Vinci Code*, and the exposure given to the so-called atheist books of such authors as Richard Dawkins, Sam Harris, and the late Christopher Hitchens. Religion's presence and importance is blatant in the conflict, terrorism, and peacemaking efforts in the Middle East. In 2006, it was centre stage in the clash of values and perhaps even civilizations as European countries and their leaders experienced the protests and threats of Muslims for allowing their newspapers to publish cartoon depictions of Muhammad (Ghafour, 2006). Even more daunting in light of September 11, 2001, was the 1998 directive of "fundamentalist"/"extremist" Osama bin Laden that "in compliance with God's order ... every Muslim who believes in God and wishes to be rewarded" is to "kill the Americans and plunder their money wherever and whenever they find it"—thinking that, in turn, has been widely condemned by most Muslim leaders.

In North America, religion's presence is also readily evident in the God-laced responses to such militancy on the part of U.S. political leaders, whose supporters frequently include large numbers of the so-called Christian Right. Apart from its links to global issues, religion in the United States is pervasive. Attendance at services is relatively high and the majority of people say that religion is very important to them. The organizational health of American religion can be seen in the emergence of a growing number of large and influential "megachurches," such as Joel Osteen's much-publicized Lakewood Church that occupies a 16 000-seat former basketball arena in Houston. Far from having only a local focus, many function as religious multinational corporations—spreading the message of "how to do ministry" to other parts of the world, including Canada. Spirituality has joined religion in going public and become part of pop culture, read about in books, such as Rhonda Byrne's *The Secret* and Eckhart Tolle's *A New Earth*.

In Canada, beyond such media offerings, the reality of religion is readily apparent in the tendency of the vast majority of people to continue to identify with a religious tradition; in the growing numbers of individuals identifying with faiths that include Islam, Hinduism, Sikhism, and Buddhism; in the widespread interest in spirituality; in debates about same-sex marriage and polygamy; in the ongoing efforts of Catholics and mainline Protestants to resolve problems relating to the legacy of residential schools; and in the national publicity given to Toronto's Catholic Archbishop, Thomas Collins, being elevated to the status of Cardinal in early 2012.

Many early social scientists were convinced that religion's days were numbered, that it would be just a short time before it was discarded in favour of science. Through the 1990s, the widespread consensus was that religion's influence was declining and that Canadians and people in most other technologically advanced countries were leaving religion behind—although the United States stood out as a puzzling anomaly.

We now know that such observers were wrong. In the early decades of the twenty-first century, religion lives on, embraced by large numbers of people in virtually all cultures, however "advanced" or "non-advanced." Moreover, interest in religion and spirituality is actually on the upswing in many parts of the world, including North America, Russia, and Asia. In many Islamic countries, it is not clear that the importance of religion has ever been in doubt. Today, religion is frequently associated with conflict and division. But it also continues to bring meaning, sustenance, and hope to billions of people.

I begin the chapter by taking a brief look at what some of the early and influential social scientists had to say about religion, and then discuss how sociologists go about studying religion in both its individual and group forms. After clarifying what sociologists mean by religion, I look at "how much of it" we have in Canada and proceed to examine its sources and consequences—what kinds of factors contribute to people being religious and the influence that religion has on both individuals and societies. In concluding the chapter, I reflect on the kinds of religious developments we can expect in the future.

I'll be giving particular attention to Canada, in large part because I have spent much of my life examining religious developments here and have some fairly unique research findings I can tell you about. However, while focusing on Canada, I will keep my eyes on the rest of the world, starting with the United States.

Contrary to the opinion of some people, religious belief is not disappearing in Canada. In fact, in urban areas, most people have many options for worship.
SOURCE: © Dick Hemingway.

SOCIOLOGY AND RELIGION

A number of years ago, an American evangelist who was holding services in Edmonton was asked by a fairly strident television interviewer, "How do you know there is a God?" The evangelist immediately responded, "Because I talked to Him five minutes ago." It was an interesting claim but one that a sociologist is not in a position to verify. A basic rule of science is that "what counts" as real is what we can detect through our senses—what we refer to as "empirical" knowledge. In contrast, proponents of religion have traditionally asserted that the world we know through the senses is only part of a greater reality that, because of the limitations of sense perception, can only be known through faith.

In principle, science and religion are compatible. Science limits itself to what is perceivable, and religion maintains that reality includes the nonperceivable. Conflict between the two should only arise when one oversteps its boundaries and invades the other's territory.

Still, for the most part, science is in the driver's seat. As Émile Durkheim (1965 [1912]: 479) pointed out many years ago, religion "can affirm nothing that [science] denies, deny nothing that it affirms." Try though it might, religion cannot overrule science in refuting basic evolutionary claims or dismissing sound medical diagnoses. At the same time, since science is limited to conclusions about the observable, it too can go only so far. Sociologists cannot address the evangelist's claim that he had actually spoken to God, any more than it can evaluate the claim that a person whose cancer has gone into remission was healed by God.

Sociology consequently suffers from one serious methodological limitation in studying religion: It cannot probe the supernatural claims that religion so often is about. Sociologists nonetheless can offer considerable insight into "the observable part" of religion. For example, they can examine the following:

- Who tends to think they have experienced God
- Who believes in life after death and what individuals think will happen when they die
- The extent to which people have spiritual needs, and what they mean by *spirituality*
- How many and what kinds of people are involved in religious groups
- The impact that religious involvement has on individuals and societies

In short, sociologists cannot address everything when it comes to religion, but they can address much without getting caught up in the issue of religion's ultimate truth or falsity. Max Weber summed up the focus of sociological explorations into religion this way: "The "essence" of religion is not even our concern," he wrote, "as we make it our task to study the conditions and effects of a particular type of social action" (1963 [1922]: 1). For our purposes, whether or not religious ideas are true is not as important as the fact they are often *believed* to be true. As W. I. Thomas and Dorothy Swaine Thomas noted in their classic theorem, if we define things as real, they are real in their consequences (Thomas and Znaniecki, 1918: 79). The very fact that religious ideas are held means they potentially can have an important impact on individuals and social life.

THEORETICAL TRADITIONS

Three early theorists—Karl Marx, Émile Durkheim, and Max Weber—have had a strong influence on the sociology of religion.

MARX AND CONFLICT

Karl Marx grew up in a Jewish environment but came to believe that religion is a human creation. Marx (1970 [1843]: 131) wrote, "Man makes religion; religion does not make man." He argued that man has "found only his own reflection in the fantastic reality of heaven, where he sought a supernatural being," and that being religious characterized "the self-consciousness and self-esteem of a man who has either not yet gained himself or has lost himself again."

We can resolve undesirable conditions by either changing them or reinterpreting them. Peasants, slaves, and the marginalized in our day theoretically can rise up and revolt; they also can minimize the importance of "this world" by looking heavenward, singing spirituals, and dreaming of walking streets of gold after they die. According to Marx, religion constitutes the latter response, resulting in people who are economically and politically deprived redefining reality, rather than changing their oppressive conditions. Religion, Marx wrote, soothes the disadvantaged like a narcotic—functioning as "the opium of the people" (Marx, 1970 [1843]: 131), in the process blinding them to the inequalities at hand and bottling up their creative energies. So it is that some observers today would argue that many socially and financially deprived individuals who are unable or unwilling to play an active role in altering social conditions or even their own lives substitute religious status for social status. A taxi driver by day is the head of a temple committee by night; the housekeeper in the hotel during the week is the star soloist in the church choir on the weekend. Religious status supplants social status; the next world supplants this world.

Marx did not see such a redefining of reality as a chance happening. On the contrary, he maintained that those who hold power encourage religious belief among the masses as a subtle tool in the process of exploiting and subjugating them. Aligned with the interests of the dominant few, religion serves to hold in check the potentially explosive tensions of a society. Consistent with his thinking, respected social historian H. Richard Niebuhr (1957 [1929]: 51) has been among those who have claimed, for example, that a widely held belief among nineteenth-century American slave owners was that religion helped African Americans to become "better" slaves. He cites one advocate of "negro missions" who asserted that "slaves well-instructed in the Christian faith were less likely to develop revolutionary inclinations than the half-educated, such as [revolt leader] Nat Turner."

Historically, said Marx, society and religion were so intertwined that attacks on feudalism, for example, were attacks on the church, while revolutionary social and political doctrines were simultaneously viewed as theological heresies (Marx and Engels, 1964: 132). We might argue that we see similar fusion between politics and religion today, not only in theocracies, such as Iran, but also in such a country as the United States, where the dominant religion, according to some observers, is "the American Way of Life," supported by the country's primary religious groups. We'll return to this issue shortly.

For Marx (1970 [1843]: 131), religion was an inadequate salve for a sick society—"the sigh of the oppressed creature, the heart of a heartless world and the soul of soulless conditions." When the sickness was remedied, there would be no need for the salve. Freed from the panacea of religion, individuals would be able "to think, act, and fashion their reality with illusions lost and reason regained" (Marx, 1970 [1843]: 132).

If you are someone who is personally religious, you understandably are not particularly excited to have Marx suggest that you may well be disadvantaged in some way and need to open your eyes and give your energies to changing your current situation. But before you reject his thinking altogether, it is worth noting that, at minimum, Marx seems to offer considerable insight, even today, into why some people join extreme religious groups that downplay the importance of this life—encouraging them to give up what possessions they have and, in some instances, give up their lives as well.

DURKHEIM AND COLLECTIVITY

Émile Durkheim was the son of a rabbi but was raised in a Catholic educational tradition. He himself was an atheist and an anti-cleric, who believed that a scientific understanding of society has the potential to raise the quality of social life.

In his classic work *The Elementary Forms of the Religious Life* (1965 [1912]), Durkheim argued that religion's origin is social. People who live in a community come to share common sentiments, and as a result a **collective conscience** is formed. When they gather together, they have a feeling of being in the presence of something beyond themselves that is experienced by each member, yet is greater than the sum of their individual consciences. The feeling is not unlike "the electricity in the air" we experience at an exciting playoff hockey game or a big rock concert, where that feeling "out there" seems to transcend the sum of individual emotions. Durkheim maintained that the experience is so vivid that people have felt the need to label it. In reality, Durkheim asserted, "God" is the group experiencing itself. The experience *is* real, he argues; it's just that it isn't what those involved think it is.

Once people experience such an alleged supernatural reality, they proceed to designate some related objects as **sacred** and others as **profane**. Christians have accorded special status to the cross, the Bible, and holy water, in contrast to almost everything else. Symbols of the sacred are many and diverse: Jews have assigned sacred status to the Torah and Star of David, Muslims to the Qur'an and the Saudi Arabian city of Mecca, Hindus to the Vedas and the sacred syllable "Aum" (or "Om"). In Durkheim's view, religious beliefs articulate the nature of the sacred and its symbols, and religious rites provide guidelines as to how people should act in the presence of the sacred. So it is that Muslims, for example, are expected to

In Durkheim's view, religious rites provide guidelines as to how people should act in the presence of the sacred. Muslims, for example, are expected to pray at specific times five times a day, facing Mecca, and to make a pilgrimage to Mecca at least once in their lifetimes.

SOURCE: © Shutterstock.

pray at specific times five times a day, facing Mecca, and to make a pilgrimage to Mecca at least once in their lifetimes; Hindus offer daily devotional prayers in the morning and evening, sometimes accompanied by ritual bathing. Sikhs, when they enter their temples, must cover their heads and remove their shoes, and, where the opportunity is provided, wash their hands and feet.

Because all groups feel the need to uphold and reaffirm their collective sentiments, people come together in what Durkheim refers to as a "church." According to Durkheim (1965 [1912]: 62–63), "the idea of religion is inseparable from that of the Church," since it is "an eminently collective thing." Even when religion seems to be entirely a matter of individual conscience, it still is nourished by social sources. Besides meeting needs at the individual level, he claimed, religion creates and reinforces social solidarity. Collective life is consequently both *the source* and *the product* of religion. Accordingly, Durkheim (1965 [1912]: 62) defined religion as "a unified system of beliefs and practices relative to sacred things ... which unite into one single moral community called a Church, all those who adhere to them."

Durkheim (1965 [1912]: 475–76) observed that "we are going through a stage of transition and moral mediocrity. The great things of the past which filled our fathers with enthusiasm do not excite the same ardour in us." He added poetically, "The gods are growing old or are already dead, and others are not yet born." But despite the problems of traditional Catholicism in particular, Durkheim didn't believe that religion would disappear: "There are no gospels which are immortal, but neither is there any reason for believing that humanity is incapable of inventing new ones." The dominant groups and forms of expression might change, but the social sources that give rise to religion obviously will remain and, with them, religion. Durkheim also contended that there would always be a place for religious explanations. The reason? Science is fragmentary and incomplete, advancing too slowly—life cannot wait. Religion will therefore continue to have an important "gap-filling" role.

Durkheim's legacy has been important. You don't have to agree with his assertion that the gods are socially created to realize that God and ethical conceptions, for example, frequently reflect social and individual characteristics. In fact, an age-old concern among people valuing faith has been the inclination of humans to create the gods in their own images. What's more, Durkheim's acknowledgment that science moves too slowly for many of us anticipated the ongoing "market" for alternative explanations on the part of religious leaders and just about anyone else, including—to use just one illustration—psychic phenomena. The vast market for explanations of the unknown is evident from the fact that in 2015, Google listed some 60 million entries for "psychic."

WEBER AND IDEAS

Max Weber was born in Germany. His grandparents were Protestants who had been refugees from Catholic persecution and eventually became successful in business. He was interested in religion from an early age but never shared the deep commitment of his Calvinist mother. His background was reflected in one of his most important works.

Weber's interest in the origin and nature of modern capitalism led him into extensive debate with Marx's ideas and stimulated much of his work in the sociology of religion. Unlike Marx and Durkheim, Weber had little interest in the question of whether religion is ultimately true or false. Rather, he maintained that religion, in addition to having a supernatural component, is largely oriented toward this world. As a result, religious ideas and behaviour should frequently be evident in everyday conduct. In *The Protestant Ethic and the Spirit of Capitalism* (1958 [1904–05]), for example, Weber examined the possibility that the moral tone that characterizes capitalism in the Western world—the *Protestant ethic*—can be traced back to the influence of the Protestant Reformation. His hope was that his work would contribute "to the understanding of the manner in which ideas become effective forces in history" (Weber, 1958 [1904–05]: 90).

Weber took the position that ideas, regardless of whether they are objectively true or false, represent a person's definition of reality and therefore have the potential to influence behaviour. Accordingly, he emphasized the need to interpret action by understanding the motives of the actor (a method he called *Verstehen*, or understanding). To achieve such awareness, he said, researchers should place themselves in the roles of those being studied.

Weber understood the need to study diverse societies, present and past, to examine culture's influence on religion. He therefore embarked on comparative and historical studies of religion and its relationship to social and economic life in China, India, and ancient Israel. A compilation of his writings, *Sociology of Religion* (1963 [1922]), illustrates the way that Weber approached religion. He noted that god-conceptions are strongly related to the economic, social, and political conditions in which people live. The gods of light and warmth and of rain and Earth have been closely related to practical economic needs; heavenly gods that rule the celestial order have been related to the more abstract problems of death and fate. In political conquest, the gods of the conquered are fused with the gods of the conqueror and reappear with revised characteristics. Furthermore, the growth of **monotheism** (belief in one god) is related to goals of political unification.

Beyond the social sources of the gods, Weber dealt with such major themes as the relationship between religion and social class, and the nature of religious organizations. He reflected on religious leadership and the important process whereby a personal following is transformed into a permanent congregation, which he referred to as "routinization." He noted that different groups in society vary in their inclination to be religious: Peasants are religious when they are threatened; the nobility find religion beneath their honour; the middle class sees religion largely in ethical terms; the working class supplants religion with other ideologies.

Over the years, I have found that students, whether religious or otherwise, appreciate the way in which Weber attempted to take religion seriously and not become embroiled in attacking it or dismissing it. His approach has become fairly typical in the contemporary study of religion. Some of the ideas of Marx and Durkheim have also remained insightful.

TIME FOR REVIEW

1. According to Marx, why does religion distort reality?
2. What did Durkheim mean when he held that the origin of religion is social?
3. Weber argued that social conditions can influence religious ideas while religious ideas can influence people's behaviour. Illustrate both processes.

THE NATURE OF RELIGION

Are you religious? If you are like many Canadians, you may promptly say, "Yes" or "No, I'm not," or indicate, "I'm spiritual but not religious." The term *religion* is widely used, but obviously people have different ideas in mind when they use it. Up to now, I have been assuming that we have a shared understanding of what we mean by "religion." But before we go much further, and particularly before we look at research on religion, we need to clarify what we actually mean by the term.

"Religion" can be a blurry concept. Many people use it in a functional sense: What people value most becomes their religion—money, career, family, sports. The problem with such functional definitions of religion, sociologist Peter Berger (1974: 129) once observed, is that they become like grey cats on a dark night. If religion is everything, then it is nothing.

In a pioneering work, Charles Glock and Rodney Stark (1965) offered some thoughts that remain helpful. They pointed out that, in defining religion for social scientific purposes, we should begin by recognizing that humans develop systems of meaning to interpret the world. Some systems—commonly referred to as **religions**, including Christianity, Judaism, and Islam—have a supernatural referent. Others, such as a science-based system (scientism) or political "isms" e.g., socialism do not. The latter systems, they suggested, might be viewed as human-centred or **humanist perspectives**, in contrast to *religious perspectives*, which are succinctly referred to here as *religions*.

The two types of perspectives differ on one critical point: Religion is concerned with discovering life's meaning, and humanist perspectives are concerned with making life meaningful. Philosopher Bertrand Russell stated the humanist position well: "I do not think that life in general has any purpose. It just happened. But individual human beings have purposes" (in Cogley, 1968: 171). Religious perspectives suggest that our existence has meaning, preceding that which we, as humans, decide to give it. In contrast, humanist perspectives assume that life has no "ultimate meaning" and therefore focus on giving it meaning.

The dichotomy is not perfect; some would say that such criteria might lead us to see Buddhism, for example, as a humanist perspective. Here I would simply defer to commonly understood thinking and place Buddhism in its familiar religion category for the sake of communication. However, for the most part, I think the religious perspectives/humanist perspectives approach is helpful.

PERSONAL RELIGIOSITY

Now that I've clarified things a bit, let's go back to the pointed question: How religious are you? And to be less pointed, how religious are Canadians as a whole?

Sociologists have not believed that the answers are arbitrary or simply subjective. They have given much effort to finding ways of defining and measuring what they have called **personal religiosity**.

Much of the early research used one of three basic indicators to determine the religiosity of a person. All three assumed group involvement: identification, membership, and attendance. In surveys, people were asked questions, such as "What is your religious preference?" "Do you belong to a religious congregation?" and "How often do you attend religious services?" People who indicated that they had a religious preference, belonged to a local religious group, or attended religious services with regularity were viewed as religious.

However, as you know well, simply knowing that someone is "Protestant" or "Hindu," "Jewish" or "Mennonite," tells us very little about a person's actual commitment to his or her faith. Similarly, people might be group members, but members may be active or inactive, committed or uncommitted. And service attendance, although measuring participation in a group, excludes people who could be very committed yet, for such reasons as age, health, work schedule, and geographical location, are not overly active in a religious organization.

Since the mid-1960s, social scientists have responded to the limitations of these three measures by viewing religious commitment as having a variety of dimensions. In one of the more helpful frameworks Stark and Glock (1968) suggested that the religions of the world typically expect their most devoted followers to hold key beliefs, engage in certain practices, have supernatural experiences, and be aware of the central tenets of their faiths. Stark and Glock refer to these belief, practice, experience, and knowledge components of commitment as **dimensions of religiosity**. It is not enough to believe *or* practise *or* experience *or* know; all four traits are expected of the committed.

My ongoing Project Canada national surveys, which to date span 1975 through 2015, provide comprehensive data on personal religiosity in this country. The surveys have found that Canadians continue to exhibit relatively high levels of religious belief, practice, experience, and knowledge (see Table 14.1). Indeed, some eight in ten say they believe in God, close to seven in ten maintain there is life after death, six in ten acknowledge that they pray privately at least once a month, and about five in ten think they have experienced the presence of God. Almost half also

TABLE 14.1   RELIGIOUS COMMITMENT ALONG FOUR DIMENSIONS, CANADA, 2015 (PERCENTAGE)

DIMENSION	RESPONSE	PERCENTAGE
Believe in God	Yes, I definitely do	41
	Yes, I think so	32
	No, I don't think so	14
	No, I definitely do not	13
Believe in life after death	Yes, I definitely do	29
	Yes, I think so	37
	No, I don't think so	22
	No, I definitely do not	12
Practise private prayer	Daily	22
	Several times a week to weekly	16
	Three times a month to monthly	10
	Less than once a month	8
	Hardly ever/never	44
Experience God	Yes, I definitely have	20
	Yes, I think so	27
	No, I don't think I have	30
	No, I definitely have not	23
Knowledge	The name of the sacred book of Islam (Qur'an)	58
	The first book in the Old Testament (Genesis)	42
	Who denied Jesus three times? (Peter)	31

SOURCE: Derived from Angus Reid and Reginald W. Bibby, *2015 Religion Survey*. Vancouver: Angus Reid Institute.

exhibit some basic knowledge of Islam, Judaism, and Christianity. On the surface, then, early twenty-first-century Canadians seem to be a fairly religious people.

COLLECTIVE RELIGIOSITY

How many times have you heard people say, "I don't have to go to church to be religious"? Increasingly the generalization has been expanded to include temples and synagogues as well. It may be a common argument, but it doesn't have much sociological support.

Most social scientists, beginning with Durkheim, have maintained that personal religiosity is highly dependent on **collective religiosity**, or group support of some kind. Such dependence is not unique to religion. It stems from a basic fact of life: The ideas we hold tend to come from our interaction with other people. However creative we might like to think we are, the fact is that most of the ideas we have in our heads right now can be traced back to the people with whom we have been in contact—family, friends, teachers, authors, journalists, and any number of

other so-called experts. Moreover, if we are to retain those ideas, they have to be continually endorsed by at least a few other people whose opinions we value. Ideas are sustained by relationships.

Consequently, it is not surprising that researchers find that evangelicals, for example, one of the most numerically vibrant "religious families" in the country, have learned that they need to "grow their own and keep their own." They have more children than members of most other groups do, provide them with positive church-life experiences from the time they hit the church nursery, make sure they have youth-friendly programs when they are teens, and encourage them to marry each other—or if worst comes to worst, marry an outsider and bring the partner into the group—and then continue to be part of young adult and adult activities. To fail at any of those three crucial points in the biography of their daughters and sons is to run the risk of seeing them abandon evangelical faith. People cannot hold ideas or commitment for long without a measure of social support.

Seem like a strong claim? Try it on your own biography.

The Church–Sect Typology

Those who have examined religious groups in predominantly Christian settings have recognized two major kinds of organizations. First, there are numerically dominant groupings—the Roman Catholic Church in medieval Europe, the Church of England, the so-called mainline denominations in Canada and the United States (Anglican, United, Presbyterian, Lutheran), and so on. Second, smaller groups have broken away from the dominant bodies. For example, in the sixteenth century, Protestant groups, including the Church of England, broke away from the Roman Catholic Church; but Methodists in turn broke away from the Church of England, and the Salvation Army emerged as a breakaway group from the Methodists. Today, additional emerging groups include an array of Baptist and Pentecostal denominations and non-denominational "grassroots" congregations that are found in virtually every North American city.

From this pattern of dominant groups and breakaway groups, sociologists who try to make sense of religious groups developed an analytical scheme known as the church–sect typology. This framework attempted to describe the central characteristics of these two types of organizations, as well as account for the origin and development of sects.

Although the church–sect typology has been used extensively, alternative ways of understanding religious groups have become increasingly popular.

Organizational Approaches

In sociological terms, religious organizations are no different from other social organizations. Therefore, there has been a growing tendency to analyze religious groups by making use of the same frameworks we use in studying social organizations in general.

Led by the work of respected American sociologist Rodney Stark and his associates (Finke and Stark, 1992; Stark and Bainbridge, 1985; Stark and Finke, 2000), a **market model** for understanding religion has become prominent in recent years. Religious groups are seen as "firms" or "companies" competing for "market share." Accordingly:

- Seen through such eyes, the Roman Catholic, Anglican, and Eastern Orthodox churches are part of multinational corporations; so is the Salvation Army.

- A number of groups, including the United Church and the Pentecostal Assemblies of Canada, are companies that are "Canadian-owned and -operated."

- Many smaller evangelical Protestant denominations have been "branch plant" operations of American groups—not unlike "Ford Canada" or "Walmart Canada"—that, over the years, have become increasingly autonomous. Some other groups, including Presbyterians and some Lutherans and Baptists, have similarly evolved from overseas operations.

- Despite the fact that Jews, Muslims, Hindus, Sikhs, and Buddhists all have worldwide roots and ongoing ties with those roots, none has developed official international or national structures that oversee their Canadian businesses. They have lobby groups and other organizations that address some common interests. But their "business outlets" are typically highly autonomous, with their synagogues, mosques, and temples owned and operated by their local congregations.

- Similarly, large numbers of other religious firms operate as privately owned companies. They are started by religious entrepreneurs who are convinced that a market exists for their particular product. The early days are often modest, with operations launched in homes, schools, and warehouses. Some are successful; many are not.

Apart from provocative marketing language and corporate analogies, a general organizational approach to religious groups sheds new light on basic features of religious groups, including (1) the nature and the sources of their members, (2) their formal and informal goals, (3) the norms and roles that are established to accomplish their purposes, (4) the sanctions that are used to ensure that norms are followed and roles are played, and (5) the degree of success that groups experience in pursuing their goals. Let me briefly illustrate.

Membership

When studying the membership of religious groups, it becomes readily apparent that the vast majority of those involved are following in parental footsteps. Canadian census data show that when two parents have the same faith, 95 percent of their children are also raised in that faith. As a result, new additions to almost any given congregation are primarily active members who are on the move geographically. These include people coming to Canada from other countries. For example, since the 1980s, immigrants have been the primary source of Hindu, Sikh, Muslim, and Buddhist growth. Given the extensive worldwide expansion of Roman Catholicism, Pentecostalism, and Islam, "immigration pipelines" are going to favour those traditions in the immediate future (Allen, 2009). Conversely, the "pipelines" have narrowed for members of the United and Presbyterian Churches (Bibby, 2011a: 30–31).

Congregations frequently compete with one another for members and staff, especially in urban areas where some "outlets" are larger and more affluent than others are. The more attractive congregations typically have the resources to search farther for their leaders and hold them longer. They also have better physical facilities. It's not just a Protestant or Catholic phenomenon: Muslims, Hindus, Sikhs, Buddhists, and Jews typically define their meeting places as important centres for social activity. Consequently, groups tend to build structures as lavish as their resources will permit.

In recent years, a number of Protestant "megachurches" have come into being in Canada and the United States. These "religious superstores" typically have seating for one thousand to four thousand people, are serviced by many full-time staff members, and have annual budgets in the millions of dollars. They are found in major cities, such as Toronto, Montreal, Winnipeg, Edmonton, Calgary, and Vancouver, but they also are appearing in smaller communities, such as Abbotsford, Red Deer, and St. Catharines. They typically co-opt

During the 1980s and 1990s, immigrants contributed most of the growth to Hindu, Sikh, Muslim, and Buddhist groups in Canada.
SOURCE: © iStockphoto.com/David P. Lewis.

technology and culture. PowerPoint and worship bands, cellphones and texting are part of services, with Starbucks coffee commonly found both outside and inside sanctuaries. These megachurches make it difficult for other congregations to compete. Catholics are showing signs of following suit, recognizing that one way of dealing with the priest shortage and the need for specialized ministries is to have larger, regional parishes.

Congregations, like secular businesses, also expand their services and personnel in keeping with their economic means. Some of the megachurches, for example, offer many of the typical worship and educational opportunities of more traditional, older groups. But they also have extensive programs aimed at children, teenagers, young adults, and seniors. The programs range from small but sophisticated groups studying in homes ("cell groups"), through well-developed music and drama programs, to multimedia education, entertainment, and elaborate Web activities that often include podcasts. A room in one well-known British Columbia megachurch resembles a 1950s diner—complete with a car front, jukeboxes, booths, and stools. As the church's head youth minister told me, "The young people love this room; but the seniors love it too." An obvious point of tension involves maintaining integrity while providing products that attract customers.

Goals

The conscious and unconscious goals of local religious groups vary by congregation and members. Like the goals of other social groupings, these conscious and unconscious goals commonly appear to be in conflict. For years observers have noted that the formal goals derived from religious doctrine, such as spiritual growth, frequently exist in tension with "survival goals" relating to numerical growth that translate into necessary human and financial resources (Metz, 1967).

Similarly, congregations frequently have difficulty in reconciling their pastoral or "comfort" function with their prophetical or "challenge" function (Glock, Ringer, and Babbie, 1967). For example, the national leadership of the United Church of Canada viewed itself as prophetic in its call during the mid-1980s to allow gays and lesbians to be eligible for ordination as ministers. In taking such a controversial position, the denomination lost a sizable number of dissenting members and, in some cases, entire congregations (O'Toole, Campbell, Hannigan, Beyer, and Simpson, 1993). Prophecy has its organizational price.

There is an additional point of tension: how to satisfy the needs of the existing clientele while reaching out to new people who are not involved yet have important needs themselves. For example, as the twenty-first century began, the most divisive issue in U.S. Protestant congregations was whether church music should be traditional and oriented toward *insiders* or contemporary and aimed at *outsiders*. It is a dilemma that congregations of virtually all religious stripes are not particularly adept at resolving, with obvious negative implications for growth.

Norms, Roles, and Sanctions

If groups, like companies, are to achieve their official and unofficial goals, they have to be able to establish norms for what has to be done and assign roles for their members to play. An examination of congregational roles reveals that most groups in Canada—led by Catholics, evangelicals, Muslims, Hindus, and Sikhs—often have a human resource problem for two main reasons. The first is that they are top-heavy with men and often inadequately tap the resources of women, a reality that has been variously met with acquiescence, resistance, and a measure of change (Dawson and Thiessen, 2014; Nason-Clark, 1993; Nesbitt, 1997; Speaker-Yuan, 2005; Stackhouse, 2005). The second problem is that groups typically rely on volunteers to carry out key roles. These are the same people whom congregational leaders have to work hard to recruit and retain—people on whom they depend for involvement and financial support. They are not hired and they can't be fired. It adds up to a situation in which religious groups are frequently fragile and inefficient companies (Bibby, 1993; Brannon, 1971; Monahan, 1999).

Success

In their studies of religion in Canada, researchers have tended to emphasize "the numerical bottom lines" of religious groups and to focus on such indicators of success as attendance, membership, and finances.

Through the early 1990s, the research news was not particularly good for organized religion. Overall, attendance and membership were down, with some groups feeling great hardship as a result of inadequate finances. The mainline Protestant groups—the United, Anglican, Presbyterian, and Lutheran churches—were the most severely hit, along with Roman Catholics in Quebec. Despite some attendance and membership losses, the Roman Catholic Church outside Quebec appeared to be relatively healthy. And although their numbers were not as large as many people think, conservative Protestant groups were at least able to hold their own and grow modestly—a significant accomplishment, given that they have represented only about 8 percent of the population since 1871 and could have readily been absorbed by larger competitors. Other faith groups, such as Hindus, Muslims, Sikhs, Jews, and Buddhists, were having a difficult time growing, primarily because they were having considerable difficulty holding on to their offspring, who all too frequently were marrying Catholics, Protestants, and people with no religion (Brym, Shaffir, and Weinfeld, 2010).

The size of a group is largely a function of immigration, birth, and mortality factors. What was disconcerting for religious leaders in Canada through the early 1990s was that most groups were top-heavy with older people, and many did not seem able to replace them with comparable numbers of younger people. As a result, it was estimated that, by 2015, weekly attendance would drop dramatically for mainline Protestants and Quebec Catholics, decline slightly for "Other World Faith" groups (Jews, Muslims, Sikhs, Hindus, and Buddhists), and remain fairly stable for conservative Protestants and Roman Catholics elsewhere in Canada (Bibby 1993: 103ff). There was a very real possibility that the dominant players on the Canadian religious scene would be Roman Catholics and evangelical Protestants.

Such projections are proving accurate. However, as we will see shortly, there is good reason to believe that the "old story" of *secularization* needs

Religious groups are increasingly recognizing the importance of connecting with culture. Here, Toronto Roman Catholic Archbishop Thomas Collins wears a Maple Leafs sweater in St. Peter's Square at the Vatican in February 2012, during the week when he was elevated to Cardinal.

SOURCE: Emanuel Pires/Archdiocese of Toronto.

to be replaced by a "new story" of polarization. **Religious polarization** refers to the growing tendency of some people in a given setting to embrace religion and the tendency of others to reject it. A solid and growing core of Canadians are choosing to live life without religion. Simultaneously, a solid and durable core continues to see faith as important. The ongoing significance of religion for many people appears to reflect the efforts of groups to be more effective in addressing the needs and interests of children, teenagers, and young adults (see the Critical Sociology: Protest and Policy box).

The Canadian Situation

Affiliation with religious groups has been widespread in Canada since the founding of this country. Close ties have always been apparent between Canadians of British descent and the Church of England, Methodism, and Presbyterianism; between the French and the Roman Catholic Church; and between other

---

CRITICAL SOCIOLOGY: PROTEST AND POLICY   **DOLLARS FOR DEITY: THE FUNDING OF RELIGIOUS EDUCATION**

An accurate reading of the Canadian religious situation today leads to the conclusion that we are a highly polarized country, as are most countries in the world.

Such a situation raises an important question: Can people with extremely diverse inclinations toward religion live in harmony? Over time, our much-heralded mosaic has been able to include tiles for pretty much everybody. But the emergence of religious polarization may put the resilience of the mosaic ideal to an unprecedented test.

For starters, we have seen growing dissension in Canada in recent years over the use of the term "God" in public speeches, prayers in public schools, and references to "Christmas" and "Easter." Invocations that used to launch graduation ceremonies have either been refurbished or abandoned altogether. However, things are just warming up. An issue in Canadian public life that undoubtedly will see intensified debate is the funding of religious schools.

To secure Quebec's agreement to enter Confederation in 1867, state support for both the Protestant and Roman Catholic school systems was enshrined. The Protestant system evolved into the public system but full funding for Catholic schools has continued through today in Ontario, Alberta, Saskatchewan, and the Territories. In addition, the four western provinces, along with Manitoba, Quebec, and the Territories, offer partial funding to religious schools of any faith that meet certain criteria. The Atlantic provinces stand alone in providing no funding for religious schools. Anomalously, Ontario stands alone in providing funding for Catholic schools only—full funding at that.

As would be expected, not everyone is happy with these varied funding rules, particularly in Ontario where a variety of religious groups have decried the current situation as both unfair and out of sync with the diversity of the twenty-first century. In 1999, the UN's Human Rights Committee ruled that the sole funding of the Catholic system was discriminatory, and that the public financial cupboard should either be open or closed to all religious schools. Others strongly disagree, sharing the view of the Ontario Public School Board Association that such an extension of funding would only contribute to fragmentation and division.

Some individuals and organizations say the time has come to end the funding of religious schools altogether. The Canada Secular Alliance, for example, takes the position that governments should not expend any public funds on religious schools since, among other things, faith-based education segregates students and increases prejudice and intergroup mistrust. All that is required to eliminate any constitutional obligations, it notes, is a simple, provincial–federal amendment.

Ontario Roman Catholic educators object. In 2013, the Catholic Trustees Association launched a province-wide campaign to clarify the role and value of Catholic schools and strengthen political and public support. Across the country, other religious groups maintain that public educational systems, rather than being ideologically neutral, promote secular humanism. In a pluralistic Canada, such groups argue, they should be able to receive public funding in the course of offering students an education that conforms to provincially prescribed core curricula which, they say, is enriched by their own emphases.

With growing religious polarization, this debate will only intensify.

Critical Thinking Questions

1. What is the rationale for the funding of religious schools by governments today?

2. Are there societal benefits to having religious schools?

3. Why not extend public funding to all schools in Ontario?

4. Should public funding of all religious schools in Canada be eliminated?

ethnic groups and the churches of their homelands (see, for example, Bramadat and Seljak, 2008). As noted earlier, Islam, Hindu, Sikh, and Buddhist growth in recent years has been directly related to the acceleration of immigration from Asia.

In the *2011 National Household Survey*, Canadians were asked to indicate their religion and the religion of people living in their households. Based on this information, Statistics Canada reported that 76 percent of Canadians have a religious preference. Some 67 percent of the population identify with Christian groups, led by Roman Catholicism (39 percent). Another 7 percent reported Other World Faith preferences, while the remaining 26 percent said they have no religion (Table 14.2).

In releasing the religion data, Statistics Canada (2013: 20-1) summarized the shift in religious identification by noting that Christianity remains the country's largest religion. Yet, consistent with changing immigration patterns, a growing proportion of the population is reporting religious affiliations other than Christian. Increases in the size of the Muslim, Hindu, Sikh, and Buddhist populations,

for example, have added considerable diversity and vitality to the Canadian religious scene. An impediment to their ongoing growth, however, is the tendency of many of their offspring to socialize with and marry people outside their groups—a reality and challenge well known, for example, to Canada's Jewish community. Christian groups continue to hold a large numerical advantage and are frequently the primary beneficiaries of such intermarital "religious defection" (Bibby, 2002: 82–85). Perhaps the pattern is changing. Time will fill out the story.

The Christian faith also continues to be pervasive in the United States, where the latest Gallup surveys show that about 75 percent of Americans identify with Christian groups (Newport, 2014), although those reporting they have no religion is now close to 20 percent (Pew 2012a; Zuckerman, 2012). However, the numerically dominant groups in the United States are not the same as those in Canada. While one in two Canadians is Catholic, the same is true of only one in four Americans. Furthermore, just one in ten Canadians identifies with conservative Protestant (evangelical) groups, in contrast to more

TABLE 14.2 RELIGIOUS IDENTIFICATION, CANADA AND THE PROVINCES AND TERRITORIES, 2011 (PERCENTAGE)

	CANADA	BC	AB	SK	MB	ON	QC	NB	NS	PEI	NL	YT	NT	NU
Christian	67	45	60	72	69	65	82	84	76	85	93	45	66	86
Roman Catholic	39	15	24	30	26	31	75	50	33	43	36	18	39	24
United	6	5	8	13	11	8	<1	7	12	15	15	4	3	1
Anglican	5	5	4	6	6	6	1	7	11	4	25	10	15	50
Baptist	2	2	2	2	2	2	<1	10	9	4	<1	1	1	<1
Orthodox	2	1	1	1	1	2	2	<1	<1	<1	<1	<1	<1	<1
Lutheran	1	2	3	6	4	1	<1	<1	1	<1	<1	1	1	<1
Pentecostal	1	1	2	2	2	2	<1	2	1	1	7	2	2	5
Presbyterian	1	1	1	1	1	3	<1	1	3	7	<1	<1	3	<1
Other	9	12	15	12	16	10	3	6	6	10	10	10	3	6
Other faiths	7	10	6	<1	3	9	4	<1	<1	<1	<1	1	2	<1
Muslim	3	2	3	1	1	5	3	<1	<1	<1	<1	<1	<1	<1
Jewish	1	<1	<1	<1	1	2	1	<1	1	<1	<1	<1	<1	<1
Hindu	1	1	1	<1	<1	<1	<1	<1	<1	<1	<1	<1	<1	<1
Buddhist	1	2	<1	<1	<1	<1	<1	<1	<1	<1	<1	<1	<1	<1
Sikh	1	5	1	<1	<1	1	<1	<1	<1	<1	<1	<1	<1	<1
Aboriginal Spirituality	<1	<1	<1	1	<1	<1	<1	<1	<1	<1	<1	1	1	<1
No religion	24	44	32	24	26	23	12	15	22	14	6	50	30	13

SOURCE: Computed from Statistics Canada (2013).

than three in ten Americans. A tipoff on the difference is that some 40 percent of Americans claim that they are "born again" (Gallup, 2015); the term itself is not even particularly common in Canadian religious group circles, even among many of today's evangelicals. In fact, 31 percent of Canadians told us a decade ago that if they were in the presence of someone they didn't know who was "born again," their immediate reaction would be to feel uncomfortable. They'd better not wander too far into the United States.

When Canadians are asked about actual *membership* in religious groups, as opposed to mere affiliation or identification, more people—about 30 percent—claim to belong to religious groups, higher than membership in any other single voluntary group. About one in four attends services at least once a month, and roughly the same proportion of parents with school-aged children expose their children to Sunday schools or similar kinds of religious instruction on a fairly frequent basis.

However, between approximately the 1940s and 2000, church attendance in Canada declined sharply, documented by Gallup poll findings summarized in Figure 14.1. Gallup had been asking Canadians if they attended a service "in the last seven days"— the phrasing of the inquiry adds sporadic attendees to those who claim they attend every week. Using such a measure, Gallup found that Protestant weekly attendance dropped from around 60 percent to about 30 percent between the 1940s and mid-1970s, rebounding to around 40 percent by the mid-1990s. The decline in Roman Catholic attendance appears to have started around 1965, dropping from roughly 85 percent to 40 percent by the late 1990s—led by

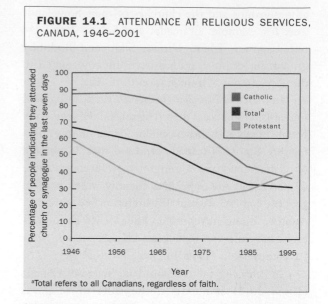

FIGURE 14.1 ATTENDANCE AT RELIGIOUS SERVICES, CANADA, 1946–2001

aTotal refers to all Canadians, regardless of faith.

SOURCES: Gallup Canada, Inc., surveys, 1946–1995. Gallup's national figure for 2001 is 31 percent, for 2010 26 percent; no Protestant-Catholic breakdowns are available. Reginald W. Bibby, *Beyond the Gods & Back: Religion's Rise and Demise and Why It Matters* (Lethbridge, AB: Project Canada Books, 2011).

low church-going in Quebec (for details, see Bibby, 2011b; Eagle, 2011). No such dramatic decline in attendance has taken place in the United States: Weekly attendance has remained remarkably steady at around 40 percent, dating back to the late 1930s when polling began (Newport, 2014; Newport, Moore, and Saad, 1999).

On the surface, evidence suggests that attendance has levelled off in Canada in recent years (Figure 14.2). In 1984, 23 percent of the country's 15- to 19-year-olds were attending services weekly. By 1992, the figure had dropped to 18 percent.

FIGURE 14.2 ATTENDANCE AT RELIGIOUS SERVICES IN CANADA, 1975–2012

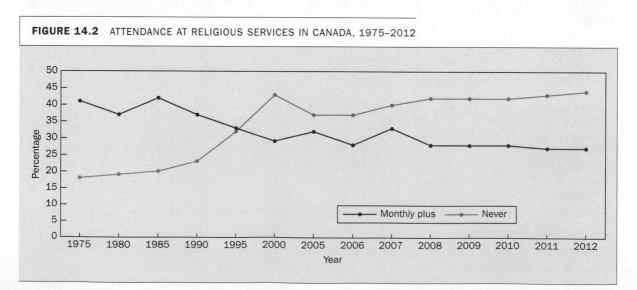

SOURCES: Reginald W. Bibby, *Project Canada Surveys*, 1975–1980; *General Social Surveys*, Statistics Canada, 1985–2012

Surprisingly, teenage attendance rebounded to 21 percent in 2000, remaining at around that level since (Bibby, 2009; *General Social Survey*, 2012). Close to the same proportion of adults—some one in five—say they attend religious services close to every week, and one in three, at least once a month. Both levels are down only slightly from around 1990 but have changed very little since 2005.

What can be missed when we look only at how often people attend is how many people never show up. The findings are very important. While the proportion of teenagers who were attending regularly changed little between 1984 and 2008 (23 percent to 21 percent), the segment who reported that they "never" attended services almost doubled, from 28 to 47 percent. Among adults, the "never" figure doubled from 20 to 40 percent between 1985 and 2007, and has changed little since then (Bibby, n.d. 2).

These attendance patterns point to an intriguing emerging religious situation in Canada: polarization. A fairly stable and durable segment of the population, comprised of both younger and older people, continue to value faith. However, for another growing segment, faith is unimportant. A significant proportion—like undecided voters—constitute something of an ambivalent middle who, in the longer run, "are up for grabs" (Bibby, 2011a: 51ff). Polarization, rather than secularization, captures the reality of these three important population components in Canada and elsewhere.

TIME FOR REVIEW

1. How do sociologists determine who is religious and who is not?
2. What are the main Canadian trends in participation in organized religion?
3. To what extent can you trace your religious inclinations or disinclinations to social sources?

THE SOURCES OF RELIGION

More than a few religious leaders over the years who have seen their best efforts to involve people come up empty have murmured, "There is only so much we can do." It's an insightful lament. The best programs and ministries in the world will not hit a responsive chord with everybody. Personal and societal factors also play critically important roles in determining who embraces religion and religious groups, and who does not.

Much of the early work in the scientific study of religion by people like Durkheim focused on preliterate cultures in which religion was pervasive. Everyone was religious, or so it seemed. Consequently, it's not surprising that observers gave considerable attention to the origin of religion itself, rather than examining variations in religious commitment.

However, individual differences in religion's importance in contemporary societies have called for explanations as to why some people are religious and others are not. The explanations tend to focus either on individuals or on social structure.

INDIVIDUAL-CENTRED EXPLANATIONS

At least three dominant "person-centred" explanations of religious commitment have emerged. See to what extent you see yourself and others in what the experts have had to say.

Reflection

The desire to comprehend reality is widespread among humans. In reflecting on the meaning of existence, people have commonly concluded that life has a supernatural, "transempirical" dimension. As Weber (1963 [1922]: 117) put it, religion is the product of an "inner compulsion to understand the world as a meaningful cosmos and take up a position toward it."

There is little doubt that Canadians, like people elsewhere, reflect on life's so-called big questions. Some 80 percent say they think about such issues as the origin and purpose of life, the meaning of suffering, and what happens after we die. Such questions take on particular urgency when people have to come to grips with such events as the attacks on September 11, 2001, or a devastating tsunami—or have to deal with the suicide of a friend or the loss of a parent. Still, although such times of reflection may provide religious groups with an opportunity to respond, reflection in itself does not usually lead to religious commitment and involvement. Fewer than one in three Canadians who often raise these meaning questions gives evidence of being religiously committed.

Socialization

A second person-centred explanation sees religious commitment as the product of learning—socialization factors that were the focus of Chapter 4. Freud (1962 [1928]) went so far as to say that religion is learned pretty much like the multiplication table. He may not have been exaggerating. I have never forgotten a high-school teacher who had played for the Edmonton Eskimos telling us that if we had grown up in India, we would all be Hindus. As Durkheim emphasized, personal religiosity has social origins and, consequently, will strongly reflect the social environments from which we come, beginning with our family.

Why is an Iraqi a Muslim, a Londoner Church of England, a Ute (as in Utah) a Mormon, a Quebecker a Catholic? The answers are obvious. What is less clear is why some of those four people take their religion more seriously than the others do. To address the question, we probably would start by looking at the commitment level of their parents. Beyond family, we would expect that individuals who are devout have been exposed to additional social sources that are positive toward religion—friends, an ethnic group, an institution, a community or region, perhaps an entire society. Religion is very much a learned phenomenon.

Accommodation to social pressures, notably those of primary groups, seems to be a related source of religious group involvement. For example, one marriage partner may become more active in response to the hopes and expectations of the other, friends in response to friends, parents in response to having young children, children in response to their parents. As John McEnroe of tennis fame once put it, "I can go to church once in a while, just for Mom." In small communities where religion is pervasive and normative, accommodation would be expected to be an important source of religious involvement.

It's important to keep in mind that socialization appears to be a *necessary* but not a *sufficient* cause of religiosity. That is to say, to the extent that Canadians are currently involved in religious groups, most had parents who also were involved. However, the fact that Canadians had parents who were involved does not ensure that their sons and daughters will follow suit. Although about eight in ten of today's weekly attendees had parents who attended weekly, only about three in ten Canadians whose fathers or mothers attended weekly have followed their example.

With a decreasing number of parents actively involved in religious groups in recent decades, fewer have been passing the experience of organized religion on to their children. For example, in 1975, some 35 percent of Canadians with school-aged children claimed that they and their children were attending services on a regular basis. By 2000, that figure had dropped to around 20 percent. Such a pattern, if it had continued, obviously would have had devastating

One of the strongest predictors of adult religiosity is childhood religious practice. When parents participate in religious observance with their children, the early socialization experience is often imprinted for life.

SOURCE: © iStockphoto.com/Sean Locke.

numerical consequences for organized religion. But as we have just seen, the pro-religious proportion of adults, including parents, has remained fairly stable in recent years. That finding points to religion continuing to be important for a significant core of people, at the same time as it is becoming less salient for others.

If religious involvement and commitment are to last a lifetime, they need to receive ongoing social support. Our surveys have found that the commitment level of a partner is strongly related both to personal involvement and to the importance placed on religion. In more than seven in ten cases, if one partner is a weekly attendee, so is the other. In fewer than three in ten cases does a person attend weekly or view religion as "very important" if the partner does not.

Deprivation

A third person-centred explanation of religious commitment is that the devout are drawn primarily from the ranks of society's deprived or disadvantaged. Religion provides them with compensation, sometimes in this life, sometimes later. The roots of such thinking, of course, are found in the work of Marx and Freud.

The deprivation argument was developed more fully by Glock and Stark (1965), whose work has been highly influential. They maintained that five types of deprivation are predominant in the rise and development of religious and secular movements: economic, social, organismic (that is, physical or mental), psychic, and ethical. The first three types of deprivation are self-explanatory. *Psychic deprivation* refers to the lack of a meaningful system of values, and *ethical deprivation* refers to having values that are in conflict with those dominant in a society.

Research in the 1970s and 1980s using objective indicators, such as income, health, and social relationships, did not find deprivation to be a particularly good predictor of broad religious participation in either the United States (Roof and Hoge, 1980) or Canada (Hobart, 1974). The learning perspective seems to have had far more applicability.

Since 2000, suicide bombing has received considerable world attention. Because such attacks are often religiously inspired, and because they are so violent, you might expect the attackers to be driven by extreme deprivation. And, in fact, some observers initially hypothesized that suicide bombers must be poor, unemployed, uneducated, unmarried, socially marginal young adults with little to lose. Analysts assumed that people with such characteristics could be relatively easily convinced to exchange their lives of suffering in the here-and-now for promises of glory and martyrdom in the hereafter.

Research has demonstrated, however, that the deprivation argument does not generally hold in the case of suicide bombers. For example, sociologists Robert Brym of the University of Toronto and Bader Araj of Birzeit University in Palestine note in their study of suicide bombings in Israel, the West Bank, and Gaza from 2000 to 2005 that suicide bombers typically come from working-class and middle-class backgrounds, and they are generally better educated than the populations from which they are drawn. The suicide bombers who were responsible for the attacks of September 11, 2001, were all well-educated, middle-class men (Brym and Araj, 2006).

Studies of extreme forms of religious participation thus lead us to the same conclusion as studies of general populations: Deprivation does not appear to be systematically associated with religious commitment. This leads us to look for additional explanations of religious commitment.

STRUCTURE-CENTRED EXPLANATIONS

Suicide bombers hardly exist in social isolation. On the contrary, they typically are members of political and military groups found in the Middle East and, in the case of the Tamil Tigers, Sri Lanka. The groups to which they belong in turn are committed to getting rid of occupying forces, overthrowing existing regimes in their own countries or, in the case of a group like Hamas—the largest Palestinian resistance movement—obliterating Israel and creating an Islamic theocracy. Structural conditions clearly play an important role in such "religio-political" organizations coming into being and in individuals being recruited as members.

Such realities remind us that, in addition to personal characteristics of the reflection, socialization, and deprivation variety, religious commitment is strongly influenced by the broader national, regional, and group contexts in which people find themselves. You might immediately think of a theocracy, such as Iran, where the president and legislature are subject to clerical supervision. However, in virtually every society, Canada included, history and culture combine to create milieux that, to varying degrees, do or do not support religion.

Those proclivities often vary not only along national lines but also by the region in which people live and the groups of which they are a part. Historically, Canada's "Bible Belt" has been viewed as Alberta, when by every conceivable measure it probably has actually been the Atlantic region (Bibby, 1987; Hiller, 1976). Regardless, in the past, to have grown up in either of these two regions resulted in being exposed to environments that were far more "pro-religious" than people experienced in a province like British Columbia. Social environments are important determinants of religious commitment and involvement.

Two early prominent Canadian sociologists, S. D. Clark (1948) and W. E. Mann (1962), argued that, historically, the emergence of sect-like groups, such as indigenous Baptists and Pentecostals, in Canada was tied to the existence of unstable conditions, which were produced by such factors as immigration and economic depression. With industrialization and increased prosperity and stability, some of these smaller, independent evangelical groups evolved into denominations—a process referred to as **denominationalism**.

A further example of the impact of societal factors on religion can be found in Quebec. Much of the drop-off in Roman Catholic attendance between 1965 and 1980 was related to the accelerated modernization of Quebec, including the Church's relinquishing of much of its important role in education and social services to the provincial government (Beyer, 1993, 1997; Rouleau, 1977).

The climate that present-day societies provide for religion is the subject of considerable debate. Some observers maintain that increasing industrialization and postindustrialization contribute to a decline in the pervasiveness and importance of religion. This widely held **secularization thesis** has been prominent in the social sciences, largely because of the influence of Durkheim, Marx, and Freud. It's a framework that seems particularly appropriate to developments in much of Protestant Europe. It also is the dominant explanatory framework the media and Statistics Canada use in making sense of religious developments in Canada (Catto, 2003; Statistics Canada, 2004a, 2004b; Valpy and Friesen, 2010).

But there is also another take on religious developments—what we might call the **persistence thesis**. Proponents of this position claim that religion—traditional or otherwise—persists in industrial and postindustrial or postmodern societies, continuing to address questions of meaning and purpose, and responding to widespread interest in spirituality (Bell, 1977; Stark and Bainbridge, 1985). Stark maintains that some religious groups or companies will fail, but because of ongoing market demand, new ones will emerge to pick up the slack. What is in doubt is not the persistence of religion, only the identity of the key players.

In Canada, we can readily explore the relationship between religious involvement and commitment and some of the correlates of social and cultural change, such as age, urbanization, education, and employment status. If the secularization thesis is correct, we would expect religiosity to be pretty low for everyone by this point in our history, particularly so for Canadians who are younger, are living in larger communities, are well educated, and are part of the paid work force. Conversely, if the persistence thesis is correct, we would expect some variations in the anticipated patterns.

Here are the main findings:

- Differences in religious group involvement are readily apparent, with attendance lowest among people under 35, somewhat higher for those 35 to 54, and highest among Canadians 55 and

older. But there is little support for the idea that secularization is more advanced in parts of Canada that were the first to experience extensive economic development. Bible belts have pretty much disappeared. What stands out is the relative secularity of Quebec and the less conventional religious and spirituality styles of British Columbia.

- Religious participation varies little by community size, education, and employment status, but there is a slight difference by gender. Moreover, full-time employment is associated with a noticeable decline in attendance for women, presumably related to time pressures. The post-1950s increase in dual-employed parents may, in fact, be largely responsible for the decline in mainline Protestant and Catholic attendance in Canada, the United States, and the United Kingdom in the last half of the twentieth century (Bibby, 2011a: 262; Brown, 2009; Putnam, 2000: 195). Religious groups needed to adapt by providing ministries that responded to changing family life. Few did.

- While just fewer than one in three Canadians currently attends services monthly or more, one in two people across the country says that he or she engages in personal religious practices or spiritual activities at least once a month, while almost two in three tell Statistics Canada that their religious or spiritual beliefs are either "very important" or "somewhat important" to how they live their lives. While there are variations by age, region, and gender, differences are minor by community size, education, and employment. Most Canadians in every demographic and social category report that their religious or spiritual beliefs significantly influence how they live.

Such findings about the ongoing personal importance of religion and/or spirituality are consistent with what observers from Durkheim to Stark have expected. Many Canadians are religious and spiritual, many are spiritual but not religious, but only a minority appears to be *neither* religious *nor* spiritual (Bibby, 2011a: 124–26). The data also point to the fact that an extensive market for religion and spirituality persists.

Research that I carried out in collaboration with Angus Reid in December 2013 further documents the religion–spirituality reality (Table 14.3; Bibby and Reid, 2013). In three national surveys of Canada, the

TABLE 14.3   RELIGIOUS AND SPIRITUAL SELF-DESCRIPTIONS, CANADA, THE UNITED STATES, AND THE UNITED KINGDOM, 2013

	CANADA	UNITED STATES	UNITED KINGDOM
Spiritual but not religious	41	33	27
Religious and spiritual	24	43	17
Religious but not spiritual	7	7	10
Neither spiritual nor religious	28	17	46
TOTALS	100	100	100

SOURCE: Reid and Bibby (2015). Copyright © Reginald Bibby.

United States, and the United Kingdom involving samples of 1500 people each, we found that the dominant inclination of Canadians is to view themselves as "spiritual but not religious." In contrast, the Americans are inclined to see themselves as "religious and spiritual," while residents of the United Kingdom lean toward "neither spiritual nor religious" self-images.

TIME FOR REVIEW

1. What are the main individual-centred explanations of religiosity?
2. What are the main structure-centred explanations of religiosity?
3. What is the evidence for and against the secularization thesis?

THE CONSEQUENCES OF RELIGION

In today's increasingly pragmatic world, Canadians face what seem like unlimited choices and limited resources. We need to sort out what is worth our time and what is not. Religion gets no exemption from such selective consumption.

Gone is the day when religious leaders could expect people to become involved in their groups because it's "their duty." Our 2005 national survey (Bibby, n.d.: 2) found that 61 percent of Canadians believed that their parents "felt they were supposed to go to church." Eighty-seven percent of respondents maintained that, today, "people who attend religious services should not go because they feel they have to but because they find it to be worthwhile."

Is religion "worthwhile"? On balance, does it enhance personal and social life?

PERSONAL CONSEQUENCES

Research findings on religion and what we might refer to generally as "mental health" are contradictory. Important early work carried out by social psychologist Milton Rokeach (1965: 2) led him to conclude, "We have found that people with formal religious affiliation are more anxious [than others are]. Believers, compared with non-believers, complain more often of working under great tension, sleeping fitfully, and similar symptoms." Yet research dating back to the 1970s has consistently found a negative relationship between religious commitment and *anomie*—valuelessness and rootlessness (Lee and Clyde, 1974). Over the years, a number of researchers have argued that involvement in groups, such as sects and cults, has contributed to upward mobility, providing an improved self-image and hope in the face

Canadians of every social and demographic stripe tend to acknowledge that they have spiritual needs.

SOURCE: © Shutterstock.

of economic and social deprivation (e.g., Johnson, 1961; Whyte, 1966). During the 1970s and 1980s, considerable literature emerged warning against the psychological and emotional damage that could be inflicted by the alleged "brainwashing" of cults (Dawson, 2006: 95ff).

Gale Frankel and W. E. Hewitt (1994) of the University of Western Ontario are among the researchers who have found a positive relationship between religious group involvement and good mental health. Research into the "Toronto Blessing" congregation even maintained that physical healing sometimes occurs (Poloma, 1997; Poloma and Hoelter, 1998). National denominational surveys that I have carried out for the United Church of Canada and the evangelical Christian and Missionary Alliance document a fairly predictable conclusion: People who are highly involved in established religious groups claim that their involvement significantly enriches their lives (Bibby, 2012; in the United States, Newport, 2007).

What seems apparent from all this is that some forms of religiosity are connected with well-being, while others are not. My own analyses of our survey data dating back to 2000 suggest that, overall, Canadians who exhibit religious commitment are slightly more inclined than others to claim a high level of happiness; to find life exciting; to express a high level of satisfaction with family, friends, and leisure activities (Bibby, 2004a: 128–29, 2011a: 98ff; Figure 14.3). However, when the impact of other factors, such as age, education, community size, and region, is taken into account, the apparently modest influence of commitment typically disappears.

In short, religious commitment by itself appears to have a fairly limited influence on valued personal characteristics. Moreover, it is often less important than age, education, and employment in predicting personal well-being.

An important word of caution: This "no difference" finding does not mean that faith is not adding something to the lives of people who value faith. Rather, in light of the high levels of happiness and contentment reported by Canadians generally, it suggests that large numbers of other people are finding alternative pathways to personal well-being. Religion is having an impact—but not necessarily a unique impact.

INTERPERSONAL CONSEQUENCES

One of the first attempts to examine the relationship between religious commitment and compassion was carried out by Clifford Kirkpatrick in Minnesota in

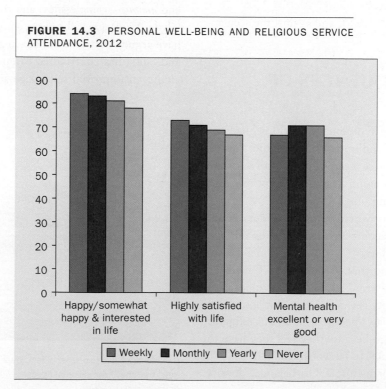

FIGURE 14.3 PERSONAL WELL-BEING AND RELIGIOUS SERVICE ATTENDANCE, 2012

SOURCE: *General Social Survey*, 2012.

1949. He found that religiously committed people were somewhat less humanitarian in their outlook than were others.

Some 20 years later, Rokeach (1969), drawing on U.S. national data, observed that religious commitment was *negatively* related to social compassion; in the case of Roman Catholics, no relationship—positive or negative—existed. Rokeach concluded that "the results seem compatible with the hypothesis that religious values serve more as standards for condemning others ... than as standards to judge oneself by or to guide one's own conduct" (Rokeach, 1969: 35).

These findings have not gone unchallenged. Research conducted on specific religious groups and in certain locales has found a positive relationship between commitment and compassion. In a more immediate relational sense, Wilcox (1998) has found that, although conservative Protestant parents were more likely than others were to use corporal punishment in disciplining their children, they also are more likely than other parents were to praise and hug their children. Extensive research on religion and racial prejudice, such as Smith's (1999) look at anti-Semitism and "the Religious Right," has yielded contradictory results.

However, some four decades ago, Richard Gorsuch and Daniel Aleshire claimed to have found the key reason for the discrepancies. Church members often appear to be more prejudiced than those who have never joined a church. But, they say, it is not because of religious involvement. On the contrary, when involvement level is taken into account, the people who turn out to be the most prejudiced are the "marginally involved" members. Gorsuch and Aleshire concluded, "The highly committed religious person is—along with the nonreligious person—one of the least prejudiced members of our society" (Gorsuch and Aleshire, 1974: 287). If this is the case, then, as with personal characteristics, religion may be making a difference interpersonally—but it is not a unique difference.

Ongoing analyses of Project Canada data have found that religiously committed people in this country do not differ significantly from others with respect to their interpersonal relationship attitudes (Bibby, 1987, 1995, 2004a). They hold a similar view of people, claim a comparable level of compassion, and appear to be no more or less tolerant of deviants, members of minority groups, and people of other religious faiths than are other Canadians. Furthermore, in contrast to the findings of Rokeach and Stark and Glock, no noteworthy differences appear in the interpersonal attitudes held by Roman Catholics and Protestants.

There is, however, one area in which religion still appears to speak with a fairly loud if not unique voice—the area of personal morality, notably sexuality. With few exceptions and with varying degrees of explicitness, religious groups tend to oppose "moral innovation." Examples include opposition to changing sexual standards, legal abortion, and distribution of pornographic materials.

That said, there is considerable variation in the position that religious groups take on many sex-related issues, as well as in the inclination of average people who identify with those groups to "follow the party line." Generally speaking, evangelical Protestants are the most likely to be opposed to changes in the sexual realm, Quebec Catholics—despite the official position of their Church—the most receptive, with their openness exceeded only by Canadians with no religion.

But this just in: Two recent analyses that I have carried out on adults and teens show that there is a consistent, positive relationship between holding clear-cut belief in God and endorsing interpersonal values that make for civility—such traits as honesty, concern for others, politeness, and the like. Canadians who "definitely believe in God" (theists) consistently differ from atheists (Bibby, 2009, 2011a; see Table 14.4). That's not to say that theists necessarily come through behaviourally, or that there is no social compassion, for example, among atheists. The findings do suggest, however, that belief in God is

TABLE 14.4 VALUES OF THEIST AND ATHEIST TEENS (PERCENTAGE INDICATING "VERY IMPORTANT")

	NATIONALLY	THEISTS	ATHEISTS
Trust	84	88	78
Honesty	81	86	75
Concern for others	65	72	54
Politeness	64	71	57
Forgiveness	60	72	44
Working hard	55	61	49
Patience	44	55	35

SOURCE: Reginald W. Bibby, *The Emerging Millennials* (Lethbridge, AB: Project Canada Books, 2009).

one, if only one, potential source of civility. To the extent that that is the case, there could be some significant social value in people believing in God. Recent atheist media blitzes in Canada and elsewhere—using such catch lines as, "There's probably no god. Now stop worrying and enjoy your life"—may, in the end, have limited interpersonal payoffs.

SOCIETAL CONSEQUENCES

So far, we've looked at some personal and interpersonal consequences of religious involvement and commitment. But what about the net consequences for societies more generally? On balance, is religion a plus or a minus—or simply irrelevant?

A cursory look at the historical evidence in Canada provides mixed reviews. Many would argue that religion has played and continues to play an important role in helping immigrants adjust to life in Canada, providing resources in the form of both personal faith and social support. Others would quickly add that many religious groups, notably the United, Anglican, and Roman Catholic churches, along with the Jewish community, have played important roles in helping to establish a just society, where diversity and inclusiveness today are valued on a level matched by few countries anywhere in the world. In addition, the claim can be made that religious groups are among the few organizations in Canada that explicitly attempt to instill morality, ethics, and compassion, thereby making an important contribution to civility.

Those things said, you hardly need me to remind you that other views of religious groups are not as charitable. For example:

- In the course of taking their place in the country, a number of Christian groups were anything but just and compassionate in their treatment of Indigenous peoples, including their complicity with government goals in running residential schools.
- The "Quiet Revolution" in Quebec in the 1960s that saw the province take over many services from the Catholic Church was not accompanied by an overt revolt. However, covertly, large numbers of Catholics had found the Church to be highly oppressive and began to stay away (Graham, 1990: 114ff).
- A variety of highly publicized sexual abuse cases that spanned the country—from the Mount Cashel orphanage in Newfoundland and Labrador, through the "Orphans of Duplessis" in Quebec and the Christian Brothers in Ontario, to the Catholic Diocese in Prince Rupert, B.C.—left many Canadians stunned and disenchanted with organized religion (see Bibby, 1993: 68ff).
- Catholics, Jews, and Muslims, along with smaller religious bodies, including Mennonites, Hutterites, Jehovah's Witnesses, Scientologists, and Doukhobors, have been on the receiving end of hostility and discrimination at various points in our nation's history.

Clearly the evidence to date is mixed. Religion adds to the quality of life in the country and sometimes subtracts. What does seem to contribute to a fairly unique religious situation in Canada is the entrenchment of pluralism. Religious groups here have to play by the rules of diversity, being respectful of one another—not making excessive claims of uniqueness, not being overly aggressive in raiding each other's ranks, not being exploitive of vulnerable categories, such as immigrants, children, and seniors. And they have to respect individual rights, in keeping with the Charter of Rights.

So contained, religious organizations that might otherwise have a detrimental effect on collective life in Canada are kept in check. We have no effective "Moral Majority," as the United States does. The same-sex marriage issue was not allowed to become an unrestrained and uncivil debate, and if someone tested the boundaries—as one Alberta bishop was tempted to do on occasion—public opinion tended to result in public relations retreats. This is not a country where Christians can call other people "heathen," but they also cannot be ridiculed as "bigoted Bible-thumpers." This is not a country where Muslims can call for the heads and hands of artists who draw caricatures of Mohammed, but it also is not a place where artists can insult and incite Muslims. Some groups don't always like the rules, but that's the way the religion game is played in Canada. So contained, religion—it seems to me—is positioned to contribute positively to our individual and collective life (see the Critical Sociology: Globalization box).

More than half a century ago, Peter Berger (1961) noted that Durkheim's assertion that religion functions primarily to integrate societies seems to offer a good description of religion in the United States. Religion, or at least the mainline segment of organized Christianity that historically has embraced the largest number of members, has tended to endorse American

CRITICAL SOCIOLOGY: GLOBALIZATION

WHY THE GLOBAL RAGE HASN'T ENGULFED CANADA: MULTICULTURALISM AND MEDIA LIKELY MUTED PROTESTS

Why haven't Muslims in Canada taken to the streets in large numbers to protest against cartoons of the Prophet Mohammed? It's not because everyone in Canada is so nice to each other, say Canadian Muslim leaders and Islamic scholars. It's because Canada's multiculturalism is complex.

They say Muslim immigration into Canada has been different. So has Muslim integration into Canadian society. And so has the political action of Canadian Muslim organizations around the highly sensitive issue of Islamic religious fundamentalism.

The difference is illustrated by events in France in 2004 and Canada in 2005, said Tarek Fatah, a leader of the Muslim Canadian Congress.

In France, few if any representative voices within the French Muslim community were heard in the news media speaking in favour of a law banning conspicuous religious symbols, such as the traditional Muslim head scarf, in public schools.

This was the case even though a significant percentage of French Muslims had no problem accepting the law within the cultural context of French secular society.

The powerful Muslim opposition that was heard, Fatah said, came from "the mosque structure" but "the mobilization of moderate Muslim voices never happened."

In contrast, in Canada in 2005, the news media pointedly reported that the most vociferous opposition to an Ontario law permitting Islamic religious tribunals to arbitrate family and marital disputes came from Muslim organizations themselves.

In Fatah's view, the mainstream Muslim community in Canada has recognized the need to take what he calls "ownership of the word Muslim." It has become actively involved in Canadian political life and not marginalized as is the case in many Western countries.

"It's a shift, for Canadian Muslims, that has not happened anywhere else."

Mohamed Elmasry, president of the Canadian Islamic Congress, said violent demonstrations simply aren't a fit with the Canadian Muslim community—which, because of Canada's immigration requirements, he said, is the most highly educated Muslim community in the world.

"They would find legal and peaceful means of protest far more productive," said Elmasry, an imam and professor at the University of Waterloo. "With demonstrations, you cannot have full control over who does what."

His organization, the largest Muslim umbrella group in Canada, has actively discouraged demonstrations over the cartoons and has spoken publicly against the violent protests—as has the Muslim Canadian Congress.

Earle Waugh, a University of Alberta Islamic scholar, said most Muslim immigrants to Canada do not feel sidelined, a factor significantly fuelling the protests in European countries.

"There is no sympathy within the Canadian Muslim community for a radical approach," he said. "No sympathy for the fundamentalists."

Canada has had no legacy of Muslim colonies like that of the British and French, and no history of migrant Muslim guest workers like that of Germany.

Critical Thinking Questions

1. A very small number of Canadian Muslims have been radicalized and gone to fight with extremist groups in Syria, Iraq, and elsewhere in the Middle East and North Africa. What do you think accounts for these few exceptions to the general rule that there is no sympathy for political extremism among Canadian Muslims?

2. Some observers think that different immigration policies account in part for differences between Canada and France in the degree to which Muslims have become radicalized. What do you think? Investigate these policies and come to your own conclusion.

SOURCE: Valpy, Michael, "Why the Global Rage Hasn't Engulfed Canada: Multiculturalism and Media likely muted protests." *The Globe and Mail*, February 08, 2006. Reprinted with permission from *The Globe and Mail* via iCopyright. License #3.8425-44168.

culture rather than to challenge it, to endorse the status quo rather than call for social transformation. So intense has been the bond between religion and American life that for some time observers such as Robert Bellah (1967) have described the phenomenon as American **civil religion**. In an influential book, *Protestant, Catholic, Jew*, Will Herberg (1960: 75) put it this way:

Americans, by and large, do have their "common religion" and that "religion" is the system familiarly known as the American Way of Life. ... By every realistic criterion the American Way of Life is the operative faith of the American people. ... To be a Protestant, a Catholic, or a Jew are today the alternative ways of being an American.

Canada, committed as it is to diversity and a downplaying of overt nationalism—except for the occasional international hockey championship—has no such civil religion. As the University of Regina's William Stahl (1986: 16) has colourfully put it, "Other than a few bands and firecrackers, Confederation was not attended by much emotional outpouring." And religious groups have done little to add fervour to our rather lifeless expressions of nationalism. Still, Harold Fallding (1978) reminds us that, historically, "Canadian Protestant churches have reflected the British position of legitimizing authority through supporting government, offering prayers, for example, for its success in securing order and justice." The fusion of Catholicism with life in Quebec, Anglicanism with the status quo in southern Ontario, and conservative Protestantism with political and social life in Alberta are obvious examples.

On occasion, of course, religion has challenged North American culture. The civil rights movement in the United States received much of its leadership and impetus from African American evangelical churches. American Catholic bishops and the National Council of Churches have frequently spoken out against perceived injustices, including poverty, racism, and war. Jerry Falwell's "Moral Majority," which peaked in the 1980s, contributed to a very vocal "Christian Right," committed to altering the nature of American life by influencing the country's major institutions.

In Canada, religious groups have had and continue to have the freedom to address governments. To varying degrees they have availed themselves of the opportunity—and responsibility. Protestant churches, for example, have received mixed reviews for their concern about the plight of Jews during World War II; some churches and individuals were silent, while others were not (Davies and Nefsky, 1997). In the 1940s, a radical effort was made by the Roman Catholic Church to support striking workers, a preview of the ongoing inclination of the Canadian Conference of Catholic Bishops to support average Canadians and to be vocal in criticizing the profit orientation of the nation's economy. Protestant groups, often led by the United Church, along with a growing number of ecumenical consortia and initiatives, and, more recently, evangelical churches, have been making concerted efforts to bring about social change (Crysdale, 1961; Lewis, 1993; Stiller, 1997). Religious coalitions, such as the national Citizens for Public Justice and, in Ontario, the broad-based Interfaith Social Assistance Reform Coalition (ISARC), have been among those

calling for greater and more effective attention being directed toward social programs, the environment, and Indigenous issues.

It is important to note that locally, nationally, and globally, religion clearly has the potential both to bring people together and to tear them apart. Religion's role in contributing to conflict, past and present, is well known. Globally, what seems like never-ending conflict in the Middle East and elsewhere provides further contemporary examples of religion playing a role in contributing to divisiveness. At times I—along with many others—wonder about the long-term outcome of what seems to be a deepening chasm between the West and the Muslim world.

Yet in the aftermath of both the September 11, 2001, attacks and the fury over the publishing of the Mohammed caricatures in 2006, significant numbers of Muslim leaders were among the first to decry violence and bloodshed, and to call on people worldwide to find peaceful means of resolving their differences. Therein lies the paradox of religion: It can both enrich and destroy social life.

TIME FOR REVIEW

1. What does research tell us about the impact of religion on personal happiness?
2. What influence, if any, does religion have in relation to sexual morality?
3. In Canada, is belief in God potentially a source of civility?

THE FUTURE OF RELIGION

One thing is certain: Religion is not going to disappear. Proponents of the secularization thesis expected religion to be replaced by science and reason as societies evolved. Opponents of the secularization thesis countered that humans have needs, notably the need to come to grips with death, that only religion can satisfy. It is noteworthy that one unique contribution religion brings to the Canadian religious and spiritual marketplace is hope in the face of death (Bibby, 2011a: 174–76). Consequently, even if secularization leads to the demise of some religious groups, new providers are bound to appear. Ironically, rather than signalling the end of religion, secularization stimulates innovation (Stark and Bainbridge, 1985).

Emerging religious forms will include sects—groups that break away from established religions, and new religious movements (**cults**) with origins outside of older religions. From this point of view,

INTRODUCTION

For much of our everyday lives, we take for granted that our routine activities will follow an orderly and predictable pattern. When we drive on the highway, we can rely on the fact that others will also be driving on the right-hand side of the road and will stop their vehicles at a red light. If they did not, the result would be chaos. Likewise, when we want our morning cup of coffee, we expect to join the lineup at Tim Hortons—and we don't like other patrons pushing in front of us. Everyday life depends on people following agreed-on rules, however unconsciously.

A good part of the sociological enterprise is concerned with explaining the orderliness of human behaviour (Giddens, 1991; Robertson, 1989). And yet just a moment's reflection will tell you that human behaviour is not always predictable, that the rules are not always obeyed, and that we don't always live up to other people's expectations. People do jump the queue and break the speed limit on the highway. They also do much worse things; they steal, cheat, rape, and murder. How and why people break rules—why they

deviate from the expectations of other people—is an important part of the subject matter of the sociology of crime and deviance.

We have a complicated relationship with crime and deviance. On the one hand, survey after survey confirms that deviance—particularly violent interpersonal crime—is one of the major discontents of our society. Many people, especially seniors, live in fear of crime. On the other hand, crime and deviance fascinate us. Crime stories constitute an important part of our entertainment culture. No new TV season would be complete without its roster of programs like *True Detective, Gotham, and Breaking Bad.* Movies, books, and newspapers also rely on crime and deviance for much of their content. In fact, this dependency seems to be increasing—crime coverage in the mass media has expanded substantially over the past decade or so (Greer and Reiner, 2012; Sacco, 2005: 80).

Real-life crime stories are no less likely to grip the public imagination. Indeed, few fictional representations can compare with the courtroom drama of Amanda Knox, the American student in Italy convicted, acquitted, re-tried, re-convicted, and definitively acquitted of the killing of her British female roommate in October 2011. Her various trials have attracted a global audience, captivated by a story of sexual intrigue involving attractive female protagonists, prosecutorial incompetence, and unreliable testimony and evidence. Her story has been told and retold in several books (including her own), TV documentaries, and made-for-TV movies, and is now the subject of a major international film. In this case, as with others, the line between fictional crime and factual crime has become blurred (Greer and Reiner, 2012). The very ambiguity of our feelings about crime and deviance makes it fertile ground for exercising the sociological imagination.

CONCEPTIONS OF CRIME AND DEVIANCE
CRIME AND DEVIANCE AS NORM-VIOLATING BEHAVIOUR

If I were to ask you what you consider examples of crime or deviance, you would probably include such acts as murder, rape, bank robbery, and theft, perhaps the occasional hockey riot in Vancouver, British Columbia, and disorder and protest in Ferguson, Missouri. You might also mention drug use, some

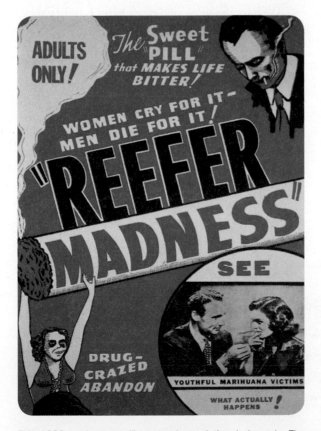

This 1936 movie poster illustrates how relative deviance is. The movie suggests that people go insane after smoking marijuana.
SOURCE: *Reefer Madness,* 1936. Directed by Louis Gasnier.

types of sexual behaviour, drunk driving, cyberbullying and a host of other acts of seemingly lesser importance: speeding on the highway, talking in theatres, jaywalking, and cigarette smoking in certain places.

These acts are all examples of rule-breaking behaviour. One way of conceptualizing crime or deviance is to emphasize its rule-breaking qualities, focusing in particular on its behavioural dimensions. Sociologists refer to the rules in question as **norms**, or generally accepted ways of doings things. The most important norms are written *laws*, or norms that the state enforces. **Deviance** involves breaking a norm. **Crime** involves breaking a law.

All human societies have norms about appropriate behaviour. Some norms have wide scope, applying to more or less everybody in the community—prescriptions against murder and armed robbery, for instance. Other norms may apply only to particular subgroups of society. For example, there are prohibitions on the behaviours of adolescents that do not apply to adults. They involve some types of sexual behaviour, for example, and alcohol use. In the United States, some jurisdictions have laws prohibiting young people from being in a public place after a certain time in the evening. Such curfew regulations (which some people would like to see introduced in Canada) do not apply to adults. Normative behaviour can be gendered, too. When I first visited Canada from the United Kingdom in 1970, I was surprised to find that women had to have a male escort if they wanted to enter a bar in Ontario.

Norms are enforced in many ways. The most important of them are laws, which are regulated by a **criminal justice system** that includes police, courts, prisons, and so on. The criminal justice system responds to law violators in legally prescribed ways, with the most grievous offences evoking the most severe sanctions. In Canada and all of Western Europe, life imprisonment is the most severe sanction afforded by the criminal code. In other parts of the world—the United States and China, for instance—capital punishment (the death penalty) remains the ultimate sanction.

Many of the norms that control everyday life do not require legal intervention. They are more likely to be enforced informally. People who insist on talking in a theatre are liable to be admonished by the people around them. Communal pressure is usually enough to regulate such behaviour.

How might we distinguish between diverse kinds of rule-breaking behaviour? One answer has been provided by John Hagan (1991), who suggests that norm violations can be differentiated by how serious they are, as gauged by three different measures of seriousness: (1) how harmful the act in question is deemed to be, (2) how much agreement there is that the behaviour in question is wrong, and (3) the severity of the sanction, or punishment, imposed on that behaviour (see Figure 15.1).

We have the sense that more harm is inflicted by, say, physical violence than soft drug use. The brutal murder of a small child grievously affects not just the victim but also her family, friends, and neighbours. In some high-profile cases—the alleged murder and dismemberment of a Chinese international student by sometime porn actor Luka Magnotta in 2012, for instance—the broader society shares a communal sense of horror and outrage. Sometimes the grief and condemnation is global: Recall the reaction to the mass killing of 20 elementary school students in Sandy Hook by a solitary gunman in December 2012.

FIGURE 15.1 TYPES OF DEVIANCE AND CRIME

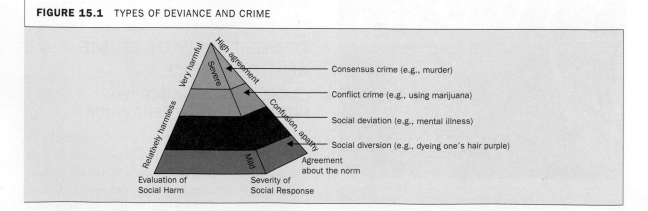

SOURCE: John Hagan (1991). Reprinted with permission from John Hagan.

Contrast these examples with the case of the person who occasionally uses marijuana. Many (although not all) people would say that marijuana has little or no harmful effects, and even if there are harmful effects, the only victims are the users themselves. Similarly, whereas most of us would agree that deliberately hurting somebody by physically assaulting him or her with a weapon is morally wrong, there is significant disagreement about how inherently wrong using marijuana is. Finally, we punish acts that we regard as very harmful and wrong more severely than those deemed less harmful and wrong. These days, convicted marijuana users are unlikely to receive a prison sentence (they are more likely to receive a fine or a probation order). By contrast, those convicted of physical assault with a weapon are likely to receive a lengthy prison term.

Hagan employs his conception of "seriousness" to identify different kinds of deviance. He designates a small group of offences as **consensus crime**—acts that are felt to be very harmful and wrong, and for which the harshest criminal sanctions are reserved. What he calls consensus crimes are referred to in legal philosophy as crimes *mala in se*—crimes that are evil in themselves. Homicide, attempted homicide, violent assault with a weapon, violent sexual assault, armed robbery, kidnapping, and theft are all examples of crimes *mala in se*.

A second group of illegal behaviours is what Hagan calls **conflict crime.** Here, "conflict" means not that they involve acts of interpersonal violence or aggression, but that members of the community disagree over whether the behaviours in question are harmful, wrong, or deserving of severe criminal sanction. In legal terminology, these acts are referred to as crimes *mala prohibita*—crimes wrong by definition. In the conflict crime category, we find such offences as euthanasia, gambling, prostitution, drug use, and public drunkenness—all examples of what are sometimes referred to as *morality offences*.

The important point about conflict crime is that its presence in the Criminal Code is loaded with controversy. A decade ago, much public debate surrounded the appropriateness of a lengthy prison term for Saskatchewan farmer Robert Latimer, who killed his daughter, who had severe disabilities, in what he regarded as an act of mercy. Some people regularly call for the decriminalization of marijuana use and assisted suicide or even of prostitution, much to the horror of other people.

The public is divided about how wrong, harmful, and deserving of strict punishment these offences are. With marijuana use, for example, we have a situation in which large numbers of people, particularly young people, have used it and believe that they, as well as other people, should be allowed to use it.

Not all norm-violating behaviour is illegal. While we may condemn the person who refuses to come to the assistance of somebody involved in a road accident, there is no law requiring that person to be a Good Samaritan (Siegel and McCormick, 2006: 6–7). Nor is it illegal to have a mental illness, be gay, be obese, be addicted to drugs, or attempt suicide. Nonetheless, people who have a mental illness, are gay or lesbian, are obese, or are alcohol- or drug-dependent are still subject to varying degrees of **social stigma**; they may be condemned, ostracized, and medicalized because of a marker that sets them off from others (Conrad and Schneider, 1992; Goffman, 1963; see the Critical Sociology: Social Inequality box). Research indicates that finding a job, somewhere to live, a circle of friends, or a marital partner is significantly more difficult for a person who is recognized as a "former mental patient" than it is for others (Link, 1982). The experience of "former mental patients" in this regard is not much different from that of ex-convicts. Hagan categorizes stigmatized, but legal, acts as "social deviations."

On occasion, victims of stigma fight back. Long-standing equal rights campaigns by gays and lesbians are one example; what have become known as "slut walks" are a more recent one—collective action against victim-blaming in support of survivors of sexual violence. Young women who fail to conform to dominant normative expectations about their sexual behaviour—who engage in casual sexual relationships, for example—risk condemnation and stigmatization as "sluts." For the most part, avoiding the slut identity requires individual commitment to a stable relationship leading to marriage and children (Dunn, 2008). Slut walks, however, represent a collective form of resistance.

In January 2011, a police officer speaking in a university classroom in Toronto proposed that "women should avoid dressing like sluts in order not to be victimized."

In response to this statement, a public slut walk was organized, with participants invited to dress in deliberately provocative clothing. After the Toronto event, slut walking went global, with other large cities around the world hosting similar protests.

CRITICAL SOCIOLOGY: SOCIAL INEQUALITY — THE CASE OF OBESITY

Most members of our society value thinness as an ideal body type. People who weigh more than average are often judged overweight or obese. The lower a person's income and level of education, the more likely he or she is to be obese. The overlap between obesity and social status is a principal source of its stigma (Goode, 2013).

Avoidance, exclusion, gossip, and ridicule are common responses to people who are defined as obese. Research shows that young men are reluctant to date heavy women, fearing ridicule from their peers, while heavy people feel that they are treated with less courtesy than other people are and receive poorer service in stores and restaurants. They are also hugely underrepresented as characters in movies and TV programs. When they are represented, they often lack a romantic partner. They are, however, likely to be shown eating.

What connects obesity to stigmatization is the conviction that body weight is something that individuals can control. Despite much medical evidence to the contrary, the view is widespread that obesity is entirely the fault of people who are overweight—a consequence only of overindulgence, laziness, or both. Public health advocates do well to emphasize the need to exercise and eat appropriate amounts of nutritious food, but they rarely mention the neurological and genetic determinants of body weight and the social constraints preventing many people from following their advice. (For instance, it is difficult to eat appropriate amounts of nutritious food if you earn little and live in a neighbourhood where you can't find affordable fruits and vegetables and restaurants serving healthy food. If the neighbourhood is dangerous, you are likely to avoid going out for a brisk walk in the evening.) Consequently, public health advocates reinforce the idea that obesity is a choice. Reality TV programs like *The Biggest Loser* do the same.

People who are physically handicapped typically evoke sympathy because we recognize that their condition is not of their making. However, we tend to define obesity as a self-made problem, so we stigmatize people we regard as obese, failing to recognize the degree to which obesity is a social construct.

Critical Thinking Questions

1. Why, in a chapter on crime and deviance, should we consider a physical condition such as obesity a form of deviance?

2. Why is obesity stigmatized?

3. Can you think of other physical conditions that might be similarly stigmatized?

What is it that slut walks do? First, by mocking the disreputable and demeaning label, they are draining it of its spoiling and hurtful effects. Second, they are a collective rejection of the inference that women invite their own sexual victimization.

Hagan reserves the term *social diversion* for minority heterosexual and same-sex activities—phone sex is a contemporary example—as well as forms of symbolic or expressive deviance involving adolescents. About the latter, the important point to remember is that young people often find themselves condemned as antisocial, threatening, or dangerous not because of what they do or don't do, but because of how they appear to others by virtue of the clothes they wear, the music that they listen to, and their hairstyles. It is not illegal to shave your head, colour your hair purple, cover your body in tattoos, have a stud in your nose, wear saggy pants, or listen to gangsta rap, but doing so often invites a censorious response from adults. Billie Joe Armstrong of the rock group Green Day, for instance, was thrown off his scheduled airline flight in August 2011 because he chose to wear saggy pants.

Particular clothing or hairstyles or musical choices are interpreted as signs of putative deviant or criminal behaviour. Before the rampage shooting at Columbine high school in April 1999, few people noted, or cared, that some adolescents wore long trench coats to school. After Columbine, trench coats were immediately banned from high schools across North America; students who wore them faced suspension (Tanner, 2015).

Generally speaking, the more serious the form of deviance, the less likely it is to occur. The most serious criminal acts—homicide and other violent interpersonal assaults—do not happen often. In 2013, homicide accounted for less than 1 percent of all violent crime in Canada (Boyce, Cotter, and Perreault, 2014). Conversely, other deviant acts occur routinely—so much so, in fact, that some commentators consider whether the behaviours in question (speeding on the highway, for instance) actually warrant characterization as deviant.

I must make one more point about Hagan's typology: It is subject to change. The acts, behaviours, and conditions that constitute his various categories vary over time. For instance, there was a time when drunk driving was not regarded as a serious offence, when it was inconsistently enforced and rarely punished with a prison sentence. Nowadays, we regard it as a more serious offence—indeed, it has become a consensus crime. In September 2011, Jack Tobin, the son of prominent Canadian politician Brian Tobin, was sentenced to three years imprisonment for the drunk driving death of his best friend. It is doubtful that he would have received a prison sentence 30 years ago. Violence against women is also treated more seriously than it was in the past.

One of the biggest changes in societal definitions of acceptable behaviour involves cigarettes. While it has long been known that smoking is addictive and dangerous to health, it is only relatively recently that legal restrictions have been placed on the practice. In the recent past, smoking was normative—socially acceptable behaviour—and in some quarters seen as a sign of adult sophistication and maturity. Change also works in the opposite direction. For example, abortion is no longer illegal in Canada. The law prohibiting abortion was repealed in 1988. In July 2008, the decision was made to award the Order of Canada to Dr. Henry Morgentaler, who started performing abortions in Canada in 1969, before it was legal. Likewise, while the use of marijuana has not been decriminalized, it is not the serious crime that it once was, and mental illness has become a medical problem rather than a criminal problem, with those affected by it treated, not punished.

We should note, however, that opinion is still divided about marijuana. While some academics now regard its use as a normalized feature of everyday youth culture (Aldridge, Measham, and Williams, 2011), the Canadian government recommends mandatory prison terms for those convicted of trafficking the drug.

CRIME AND DEVIANCE AS LABELS AND SOCIAL CONSTRUCTS

Labelling Theory

Because some acts that were once illegal are now legal, and vice versa, you should understand that while the study of crime and deviance is about rule-breaking behaviour, it is *not just* about rule-breaking behaviour. It is also about how members of society react to some behaviours. This understanding is the starting point for a second approach to the study of

deviance and crime, one that sees deviance and crime as a matter of definitions or labels that have been applied to some behaviours but not others. **Labelling theorists** believe that publicly recognizing somebody as criminal or deviant is an important cause in itself of criminal or deviant behaviour.

From a definitional perspective, crime and deviance are not distinctive types of human behaviour. We cannot divide human activity into its criminal and noncriminal variants based on behaviour alone (Becker, 1963). Few if any acts are viewed as wrong under all circumstances. On the one hand, all known human societies identify some activities as morally reprehensible and worthy of condemnation and punishment. In this sense, crime and deviance are universal. On the other hand, different human societies pronounce different acts and behaviours criminal or deviant. In other words, crime and deviance may be universal, but there are no universal forms of crime and deviance (Conrad and Schneider, 1992: 5–6).

That what counts as deviant or criminal behaviour varies by time and place is well illustrated by cases in which the argument about the universality of crime and deviance appears strongest. Take, for instance, the intentional killing of one person by another. You might think that murder would be universally acknowledged as a serious offence. However, intentional killing is not defined as murder in the context of war, when those doing the killing are our own soldiers, acting in the line of duty. Similarly, the fatal shooting of suspects by police officers rarely results in criminal charges. When the state (or government) kills on our behalf (in those nations that still have the death penalty, for instance), those doing the killing are not called murderers; they are public executioners.

Incest is another interesting example. While most societies have legal prohibitions against incest, significant variation exists regarding what counts as incest. Some jurisdictions forbid sexual relationships only between brothers and sisters, while others extend the ban to include third cousins (Conrad and Schneider, 1992: 5–6). Note too that while prostitution is legal in the state of Nevada in the United States and the city of Amsterdam, Holland, it is illegal in Canada. Similarly, while adult alcohol use is a legal and normal feature of Canadian lifestyles, in parts of the Middle East it is treated as a serious offence requiring a severe penalty—in some cases, corporal punishment.

Turning to drug use, we find that opiates have been illegal in Canada only since 1908. Before then, no legal prohibitions on their use existed. Opiate-based cough syrups and tonics were routinely prescribed by doctors and sold in pharmacies in a variety of forms. People who were dependent on opiate-based drugs were not stigmatized as criminal or deviant, nor was opiate dependency seen as a sign of mental illness.

Opiate drugs were also used for recreational purposes in smoking dens on Canada's West Coast. Their main users were Chinese immigrants who were brought to Canada to build the transcontinental railroad and received much lower wages than their European counterparts did. Public concern about the morality of recreational drug use served as a conduit for anti-Asian sentiment rooted in stiff competition for jobs after the Canadian Pacific Railroad was completed. The first Canadian anti-narcotics legislation introduced in 1908 targeted the opium dens, making the recreational usage of opiates a criminal offence for which there were heavy penalties. No such penalties accompanied the medicinal use of opiates (Cook, 1969).

Sociologists who study the social reaction to drug use conclude that the legality of a drug is determined as much by the status of its users as by the amount of harm done by the drug. The lower the status of the user, the more likely the drug will be criminalized (Becker, 1963). Consider that cocaine in its powdered form has been a drug of choice of sports stars and entertainment celebrities since the early 1970s. However, it became a significant social problem only when it became associated with poor, unemployed racial minorities in U.S. inner cities, who ingested it in small, precooked units as crack cocaine. Once cocaine travelled down from the Hollywood Hills to the inner city, it became a major crime problem, one measure of which is that penalties for crack cocaine convictions have been more severe in the United States than for other forms of cocaine use (Reinarman and Levine, 1989).

Social Constructionism

Treating crime and the evidence as norm-violating behaviour is a characteristic of "objectivist" (or "positivist") approaches to the subject matter. Such approaches assume that crime and deviance are easily identified categories of behaviour, the explanations for which are found in biological traits, psychological conditions, and social forces.

In contrast, **social constructionism** shares with labelling theory an emphasis on the *subjective* qualities of crime and deviance. It proposes that particular conditions are viewed as problematic because some

people—usually powerful ones—define them as such. Accordingly, social constructionists focus on the claims-making activities of interest groups, politicians, and investigative journalists, who draw our attention to conditions such as child abuse, prostitution, the disappearance and murder of Indigenous women, and cyberbullying. Social constructionists are more interested in what various claims makers say about these conditions than the conditions themselves.

They are also interested in how such conditions are described. Take the situation of many young people living on the streets of Canada's major cities. Is this a problem requiring the intervention of social welfare agencies or a law and order problem demanding a response from the criminal justice system? As this example illustrates, the same condition can be represented in different ways by different claims makers.

Social constructionists assert that so-called objective facts are not always responsible for the criminal or deviant status of a particular condition. They like to remind us that alcohol—a legal drug—is more damaging and harmful to individuals and society than some illegal drugs are. They point out that the number of deaths associated with tobacco and alcohol is much larger than the number stemming from the use of illegal drugs. They sometimes use such evidence to support the decriminalization of illegal drugs.

In some extreme cases, people have defined and reacted to social problems without showing that they exist. In the United States, satanic crime has received considerable media attention, even though not a shred of evidence supports repeated claims that it is a serious problem. Special crime units have been set up to tackle the problem. Parental advisory groups have been formed to prevent the spread of satanic imagery and, presumably, satanic values and lifestyles in popular music (Sacco, 2005). Based on such cases, constructionists argue that while objective conditions and agreed-on facts play a role in the designation of deviance, they are rarely the decisive determinants of whether a particular behaviour is defined as such.

Although not all social constructionists agree about the compatibility of objectivist and constructionist perspectives (Best, 1989), I believe it possible to study the same phenomena or condition and ask different but complementary questions about them. We could ask how and why hate crime has become a new crime problem (a constructionist question) and, at the same time, inquire about the characteristics of those who perpetrate hate crimes (an objectivist question). From an objectivist vantage point, you might ask, "Does listening to rap music cause crime and deviance?" From the constructionist perspective, the crucial question is, "Why are we so concerned about the violent content of rap music but pay so little attention to the violent content of country music?" Both are perfectly good research questions, and, in my judgment, a full understanding of crime and deviance requires both the norm-violation and labelling/constructionist approaches (Thio, 2010).

It is also often the case that objectivist and constructionist researchers study different kinds of crime and deviance. Objectivists tend to study serious, or consensual, crime—murder, sexual assault, armed robbery, and the like. Constructionists are more inclined to study noncriminal deviance—binge drinking, lap dancing, prescription drug abuse—or criminal activities, the criminal status of which is fiercely contested (prostitution, for example). They are also more interested in new or emerging forms of deviance, especially activities facilitated by the Internet and cyberspace, such as child pornography, telephone sex, or cyberbullying.

CRIME IN THE NEWS

How are crime and deviance represented in the news media and popular culture, and why does it matter? You may have heard the expression "If it bleeds, it leads." It's a good summary of the importance of crime to news organizations. The public has a big appetite for crime stories that the news media are happy to accommodate.

However, the media do not report all criminal incidents. Violent crime is reported more regularly than property or **white-collar crime**, defined as crime conducted by high-status individuals in the course of their occupation or profession. Research consistently shows that crimes of violence appear in news reports in numbers disproportionate to their incidence in official crime statistics (Greer and Reiner, 2012; Sacco, 2005).

The commonsense view about the relationship between the mass media and crime and deviance is that journalists simply record events as they happen. In this view, media accounts provide a more or less faithful reflection of objectively verifiable crime problems. However, news organizations do more than just record the facts. Whether they realize it or not, journalists shape how readers, viewers, and listeners feel and think about crime and deviance. Research on media institutions indicates that the news we consume is a result of a selection process (see Chapter 6, Communication and Mass Media). News items compete for time and space. Crime stories have an advantage in this competition because they are deemed highly newsworthy.

In his study of law and order reporting, British sociologist Steve Chibnall (1977) identified a number of informal criteria that are regularly used by journalists to select stories. Visible and spectacular incidents with political and sexual connotations rank highest. Similar rules determine how crime stories are presented—how many and which photographs will accompany a story, what headlines will be used, and so forth.

I am not suggesting that news organizations make up stories about crime or that crime problems would disappear if journalists chose to ignore them. My argument is that what we read in the newspapers and watch on TV is a result of a predictable selection process. The mass media typically exaggerate the nature and scope of crime, presenting rare cases as if they are typical or the start of a new and worrying trend.

How news organizations construct crime stories is of more than academic interest because it influences how citizens think about crime. For example, research shows that Canadians overestimate crime and **recidivism** (repeat offending) rates and underestimate the severity of criminal sanctions for crimes. Crucially, the same research also tells us that most people rely mainly on the mass media for their knowledge of crime (Roberts, 2004).

Sometimes those who report crime stories become the crime story themselves. In the United Kingdom, the news-gathering techniques of the tabloid newspaper, *News of the World*, has included the hacking of cellphones of politicians, celebrities, members of the British royal family, a missing teenager later found murdered, relatives of victims of the July 2012 bombings in London, and relatives of British soldiers killed in Afghanistan. Hacking is of course illegal, and the crime might be explained by the actions of a few errant journalists. More likely, though, phone hacking has become a routine practice of news organizations taking advantage of new technologies to bolster declining circulation (Downes and Morgan, 2012)

TIME FOR REVIEW

1. Are crime and deviance categories that are distinguishable by behaviour alone?
2. How does "seriousness" allow us to distinguish between different types of crime and deviance?

3. How do objectivist and social constructionist interpretations of crime and deviance differ?

4. How are crime and deviance represented in the news media and popular culture and why does it matter?

COUNTING CRIME AND DEVIANCE: NUMBERS AND MEANING

OFFICIAL STATISTICS

People naturally want to know about the amount of criminal and deviant activity in Canada, and whether or not it is increasing. One answer to these questions is provided by official statistics compiled by the government. Most accounts of crime and deviance are made persuasive by the use of data collected by the police, the courts, and other governmental agencies. Moreover, virtually every important theory of deviant behaviour, and especially criminal behaviour, relies on information about offences and offenders collected by or on behalf of the government. It is therefore important to know how these data are collected. For starters, note that the more serious the norm violation, the more comprehensive the data collection. Thus, we have considerably more information about crime and delinquency, and alcohol and drug use, than we do about the expressive or symbolic deviancy of adolescents (Tanner, 2015).

Since 1962, a system of uniform crime reports has provided the basic count of criminal infractions in Canada. According to an arrangement originally pioneered in the United States, police departments across the country file information on "crimes known to the police." The system is designed to produce consistent, comparable, nationwide crime statistics. For crime to become known to the police, one of two things must happen: Either members of the public experience or observe a criminal incident and pass that information on to the police, or the police themselves detect the incident.

One of the few undeniable facts about the official count of crime is that it underestimates the actual amount of crime occurring in any jurisdiction at any given time. This is not a comforting thought for people already concerned about the level of crime in society. There are well-documented reasons that citizens choose not to share their knowledge of some criminal events with the police. Sexual offences against women are notoriously underreported; lengthy and potentially humiliating court appearances are one deterrent, possible job loss another. Victims may also fear reprisals from offenders, particularly if they know them. They may feel that the incident is too trivial to bother the police. They may be too embarrassed to report the incident. They may mistakenly believe that stolen items were lost. Some crimes are never reported to the police because the crime in question is a commercial transaction between, say, a prostitute and her client or a drug dealer and a drug buyer. In each of these cases, neither party has an interest in reporting details of the deal to the police.

The public reports most of the crime that the police know about. No more than 10 percent of crime is discovered by the police in the course of their own patrols or investigations (Sacco and Kennedy, 2011). One of the difficulties that the police face is that many crimes are committed so as to avoid detection. Most burglars, for instance, do not break into houses when they know that the police are in the area or when residents are likely to be at home.

The number of criminal incidents that remain unknown to the police is often referred to as the **dark figure of crime.** It is a large figure. How large? In one of my studies, I found that just 33 percent of robberies, 23 percent of rapes, and 21 percent of assaults with a weapon were reported by young victims to the police (Tanner and Wortley, 2002). A more recent survey of Toronto high-school students found that less than half of all self-reported deviant acts had been discovered by parents, teachers, or the police (Savoie, 2006).

What happens if, for any reason, members of the public become more inclined to report crime to the police—if, say, it becomes easier for them to report crime because of the widespread use of cellphones or because the organizations they work for require them to report incidents that were previously dealt with informally? What happens if police departments are allowed to hire more police officers and acquire improved information technology? The answer, of course, is that we would start to see an increase in recorded crime, regardless of whether or not there had been any real change in criminal behaviour in the population. The important lesson here is that official statistics are affected by more than just the deviant motivations and behaviour of perpetrators (Liska and Messner, 1999).

In Canada in 2013, roughly 1.8 million crimes (excluding traffic offences) were reported to the police

(Boyce, Cotter, and Perrault, 2014). A large proportion of them were classified as property crimes. A substantially smaller proportion were classified as violent crime. Note, too, that violent crime includes everything from homicide and sexual assault to pushing and shoving ("common assault").

Figure 15.2 reveals that the total crime rate has been falling since its peak in 1991. In 2014, the total crime rate was at its lowest since 1969 (Statistics Canada, 2015). Why is the crime rate down—and why don't our perceptions of safety always match that decline?

Declining crime rates are easier to document than explain. While a number of factors have been suggested—more effective policing, increased imprisonment, early anti-gang interventions—there is little consensus about their impact on criminality. Most experts agree that demography is part of the explanation. Crime rates are higher when young people, young males in particular, represent a larger proportion of the population and lower when their numbers are fewer, as they have been for several decades.

Others see recent falling crime rates as having much deeper cultural roots. Over time, they argue, human societies have become less violent (Elias, 1969; Gurr, 1989; Pinker, 2011). By this larger standard, any change in the contemporary crime rate—up or down—is only a short-term fluctuation (Hough, quoted in Cobain, 2014).

Why then don't falling crime rates necessarily make us feel any safer? Again, a number of factors are probably at work. I would like to emphasize two. First, the growing preponderance of crime stories in news coverage probably increases fear of crime. Second, both the private security industry—Alarm Force, ADT, and so on—and law enforcement agencies benefit from public anxiety about crime (Wortley, 2011). The more anxious we are about crime, the more persuaded we are to buy home security devices and the more tolerant we are of expanding police budgets.

FIGURE 15.2 POLICE-REPORTED CRIMES, CANADA, 1963–2013

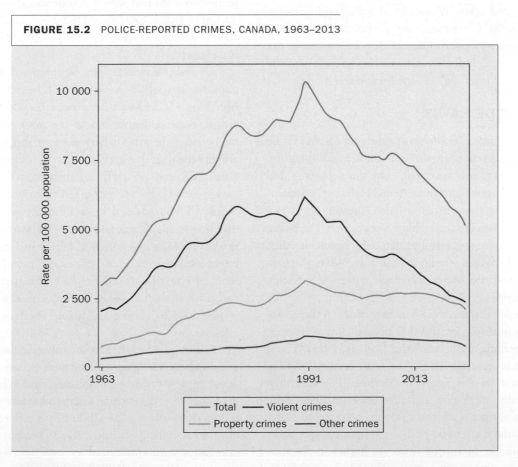

SOURCE: Statistics Canada (2014).

REGIONAL VARIATIONS IN CRIME RATES

Official crime figures reveal intriguing regional variations. Generally speaking, provinces and cities in the western part of the country have higher crime rates than those in the east. This pattern has existed for a long time and applies to both the overall crime rate and specific types of crime.

Why is the west more crime-prone? Tim Hartnagel (2004) offers a persuasive answer. He suggests that, like its American counterpart, western Canada encourages a "frontier mentality" favouring individualism, independence, and risk-taking. On occasion, risky behaviours lead to criminal ones. The western provinces have more migrants from the rest of Canada than any other part of the country does (see Chapter 16, Population and Urbanization). Migration loosens the social controls that prevent law-violating behaviour. It is easier to break rules as a stranger in town than in the community where you grew up, where everybody knows your name and where informal social control is stronger. In addition, the populations of the western provinces are relatively young, and crime is associated with youth. Finally, Indigenous Canadians are proportionately more numerous in western Canada than in the rest of the country, and Indigenous Canadians have especially high crime rates, for reasons I will discuss later.

HOMICIDE RATES

Homicide rates are the most valid and reliable crime indicator, partly because it is hard to hide bodies. Homicide is less susceptible to the reporting and detection problems described earlier. Consensus about the gravity of the offence means that it is a crime with exceptionally high report rates. The police are also more successful at detecting homicides than most other kinds of criminal offences. What, then, do official statistics tell us about the pattern of homicide in Canada?

In 2014, there were 516 homicides in Canada—1.45 homicides per 100 000 people (Boyce, Cotter, and Perrault, 2014; Statistics Canada, 2015). These figures represent both a short-term decrease and the continuation of a long-term decline. The Canadian homicide rate is now at its lowest level since 1966. As has always been the case, men are more likely than women are to be both victims and perpetrators of homicide. Homicide rates are higher in the west and the north, with western Canadian cities, such as Saskatoon and Regina, having higher rates than cities in the east (Boyce, Cotter, and Perrault, 2014). And Toronto, Canada's largest city? While Toronto had a larger number of homicides (79) than any other Canadian city in 2013, its homicide rate of 1.34 per 100 000 of the population is below the Canadian average and the lowest of all major metropolitan regions in the country (Boyce, Cotter, and Perrault, 2014). However, research suggests that the nature of homicide in the city is changing. Homicide victims in Toronto have become younger over time and are increasingly likely to be male and black. In addition, they are likely to be residents of particularly disadvantaged neighbourhoods (Gartner and Thompson, 2004).

Homicide in Toronto has also increasingly become a crime committed in public places, such as bars, city streets, and parks, rather than in private. For many people, the increasingly public nature of homicide is what makes it especially frightening; it suggests growing victimization of innocent bystanders in seemingly random acts of violence. Exemplifying these fears is the case of Jane Creba, a 15-year-old high-school student who was shot and killed outside Toronto's Eaton Centre on December 26, 2005. She was caught in the crossfire of a gun battle involving male youth.

Overall, however, the number of handgun murders in Canada is declining. Research—mostly American—indicates that, where they occur, gun murders are concentrated in the poorest parts of major cities, in areas where poverty and inequality are greatest, and where jobs are in short supply. Guns are used primarily by men from low status backgrounds who are estranged from conventional society. They are used to support criminal activity (the drug trade, break and enters), as instruments of threat, intimidation, and punishment in situations of interpersonal grievances ("disrespect"), and confer a sense of symbolic masculine power. Small automatic and semiautomatic handguns are the usual weapon of choice: easy to conceal, relatively cheap, extremely effective.

Sociologists of homicide are interested in the relationship between murderers and their victims. The frequent crime-story image of this relationship is one of a predatory killer dispatching victims otherwise unknown to him (it usually is a "him"). Reality is different. Most victims know their killer. In 2012, 84 percent of solved homicides were committed by someone familiar to the victim (Boyce and Cotter, 2013). Most stranger homicide occurs during the course of another criminal incident—during a robbery or as the culmination of a sexual assault, for instance. People we know as family members or acquaintances are a greater threat to our safety than strangers are. Acquaintances are responsible for just over one-third of homicide victims. Family members kill another 44 percent.

A familial relationship of particular interest involves husbands and wives, and common-law spouses. Women are significantly more likely to be victims of intimate partner homicide than men are. Likewise, women are at greater risk from the violent attentions of former spouses than are men. However, the rate of spousal homicide has been decreasing over the past three decades and in recent years has remained quite stable (Boyce and Cotter, 2013).

We can also compare Canada's homicide rate with those of other rich countries. Looking at Figure 15.3, you can see that in 2012 the rate of homicide in Canada was higher than in many European nations, but considerably lower than the U.S. rate. The homicide rate on this side of the border is roughly one–third of the rate on the other side,

with Chicago, of comparable size to Toronto, having a homicide rate more than five times higher than Toronto's (Boyce and Cotter, 2013).

Many people in Canada have easy access to American TV channels. Comparing Canadian and U.S. violent crime rates affords a splendid opportunity to examine one particularly popular explanation of violent crime, especially violent youth crime: that exposure to violent media contributes to real-life violence.

This is an argument with a long history. Beginning with dime store comics and continuing with movies, TV, and popular music—first, rock 'n' roll, now rap—popular culture has often been held responsible for crimes of violence. Many things are wrong with this argument. However, the point I want to concentrate on is that people in Canada watch much the same kind of entertainment and news programming as people in the United States do, yet there are big differences in patterns of violent crime, particularly homicide. While criminologists debate the factors responsible for cross-border differences, it is unlikely that media consumption has anything to do with them.

FIGURE 15.3 HOMICIDE RATE IN RICH COUNTRIES, 2012

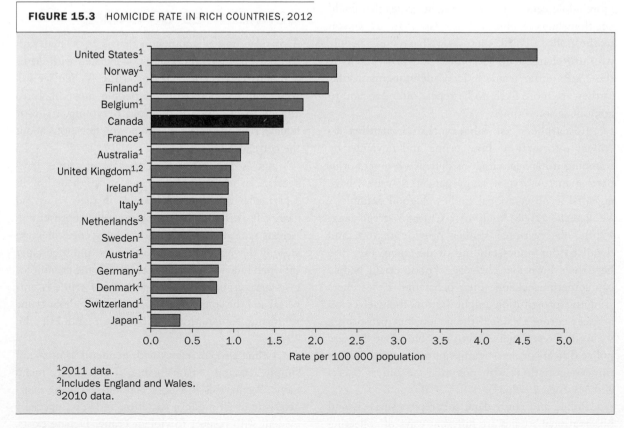

[1]2011 data.
[2]Includes England and Wales.
[3]2010 data.

SOURCE: Boyce and Cotter (2013).

OTHER DATA SOURCES: SELF-REPORT SURVEYS AND DIRECT OBSERVATION

Because of the shortcomings of official crime statistics, sociologists have developed additional information sources, the most important of which are self-report and observational studies. Sociologists use **self-report studies** mainly to conduct research on deviance among young people, particularly those in high school. They ask students about their deviant behaviour and, less often, their experiences of victimization. Respondents complete a questionnaire that asks them to report on their own deviant activities or experiences of victimization. Statistics Canada also conducts surveys of adult victimization periodically.

Self-report studies have their drawbacks. As with any survey on a sensitive subject, researchers must be careful to ensure that respondents give truthful answers to questions about criminal activity, drug use, and sexual assault. However, self-report studies have served sociologists well. First, they give a sense of the amount and type of crime and deviance that does not find its way into the official record. Second, their findings force us to abandon the idea that we can neatly divide the adolescent population into deviants and nondeviants—self-report studies show that many more adolescents are involved in activities that could get them into trouble with the law than are known to the police. Third, they show that young people who are charged by the police and prosecuted by the courts differ from "hidden" delinquents insofar as they are more likely to be repeat offenders and to commit serious crimes.

Researchers use **observational studies** to collect information about crime and deviance by watching it happen, either as outside observers or as participant observers. Many gang researchers have engaged in observational studies. A good example is Venkatesh's (2008) study of a Chicago street gang. While observational studies provide texture and detail to our understanding of deviance, they too have their downside. The very act of observing people can sometimes change their behaviour. Researchers studying prostitution might station themselves on a street corner to watch the action, but prostitutes, seeing the researchers, might conclude that they are police officers or investigative journalists and discontinue negotiations with potential customers (Liska and Messner, 1999: 24).

Police and court data, self-report surveys, and observational studies are different ways of collecting information about crime and deviance, but they are not necessarily alternative methods. Some investigations of crime and deviance combine different methods, gathering some information from surveys and official statistics, and additional information from observational or self-report research.

The overall profile of crime and deviance documented by the different sources is similar in many crucial respects. Students of crime and deviance are often interested in the characteristics of populations and individuals most involved with rule-breaking behaviour. Official police and court statistics and self-report studies often paint a roughly similar picture of these characteristics, as we will now see.

TIME FOR REVIEW

1. Why is the official count of crime and deviance always an underestimate?
2. What accounts for declining official crime rates in Canada since 1991?
3. How might crime rates be affected by factors other than the rule-breaking activity of criminals and deviants?
4. What are the main sources of crime data apart from official statistics?

CORRELATES OF CRIME

A correlate is a phenomenon that is associated with another phenomenon. Factors associated with criminal activity are correlates of crime. When we ask about the characteristics of people most likely to engage in crime—are they old or young, male or female, rich or poor?—we are posing questions about the correlates of crime.

Age is one important correlate of crime. Irrespective of whether crime rates are high or low in a particular time or place, people in their teens and early 20s will be disproportionately represented. Arrests typically begin in early adolescence, increase steadily throughout the teenage years, and then taper off when individuals reach their 20s. Some criminologists have argued that the age basis of crime is universal and the single most important fact about crime requiring explanation (Gottfredson and Hirschi, 1990).

Crime also correlates with gender. Crime is not simply a young person's game; it is a young man's game. Again, this is a universal and enduring characteristic of all modern societies, and it is especially evident with respect to violent crime. Debate exists, however, over the degree to which the gender gap in criminality may be narrowing.

Two other correlates of crime are mired in controversy. Official police, court, and prison data often indicate an inverse relationship between social class and criminality—that is, the lower people's social and economic standing, the more likely they are to be involved in crime. However, this relationship is considerably less likely to manifest itself in self-report studies, leading some experts to conclude that the relationship between class and crime is a myth and to recommend that class not be considered an explanation of crime.

This argument does not persuade everybody in the criminology community. Detractors suggest that self-report studies fail to find a connection between class and crime because they neglect to ask questions about serious crime—murder, armed robbery, and rape, for example. Instead, they pose questions about relatively minor offences. Moreover, self-report studies often focus on students, but the most disadvantaged and marginal people are the least likely to attend school. Crucially, they are also the people most likely to be involved in criminal behaviour. When surveys include both school and street populations, and contain measures of serious crime, class reemerges as a significant correlate of crime.

Significantly, which class is most involved with crime depends on what type of crime we are talking about. **Street crime**—robbery, burglary, and the like—involves mainly people from low-status backgrounds. White-collar or business crime is more likely to involve people from more privileged backgrounds. This observation stands as a corrective to the suggestion that only the poor and disadvantaged are criminals.

The second controversial correlate of crime is race. Unlike the United States, Canada does not officially record details about the racial characteristics of offenders or their victims. People who oppose the collection of race-related crime statistics argue that any evidence showing the overrepresentation of particular racial or ethnic groups in crime might result in increased public hostility toward those groups. People who support collecting race-based crime statistics argue that if racial and ethnic minorities are treated differently by the criminal justice system—if they are more likely to be stopped, searched, arrested, and charged by the police, and more harshly punished by the courts—then the only way such bias can be exposed and changed is by gathering racial data.

Indigenous people and blacks are overrepresented in Canada's prison population. Thus, Indigenous Canadians compose nearly a quarter of the federal inmate population but just 4 percent of the Canadian population. The rate of incarceration among Indigenous adults is about 10 times higher than for non-Indigenous adults. Blacks make up about 2.5 percent of Canada's population but nearly 10 percent of the federal inmate population. Between 2005 and 2013, the federal inmate population grew by 17.5 percent. Over the same period, the proportion of Indigenous people in federal prisons grew by more than 47 percent and the proportion of blacks grew by more than 75 percent (Office of the Correctional Investigator, 2013, 2014).

Do these facts mean that Indigenous and black Canadians are committing more crime than other Canadians or that they are more likely to come to the attention of the police and the courts? Research on Indigenous peoples in western Canada suggests both racial bias in the treatment of Indigenous offenders and greater criminal activity by Indigenous peoples. Sociologists typically explain high crime rates among Indigenous Canadians by the fact that Indigenous peoples were a subjugated, colonized people who suffered enforced cultural assimilation and abuse in residential schools. As a result, they now tend to experience relatively low levels of educational achievement, dysfunctional families, high rates of substance abuse, severe estrangement from Canadian society—and high crime rates (Grekul and LaBoucane-Benson, 2008).

Indigenous populations also suffer from disproportionately high rates of victimization, a condition largely unrecognized until the disappearance and subsequent murder of a young Indigenous woman, Tina Fontaine, in 2014 attracted national and international attention. According to the RCMP, 1122 Indigenous women were murdered or were missing under suspicious circumstances between 1980 and 2012 (Amnesty International, 2014). Criminal justice critics argue that colonialist institutions such as the reservation system and residential schools that created conditions inviting criminal and deviant behaviour also made Indigenous populations, women in particular, vulnerable to violent victimization. They also suggest that when young Indigenous women like Tina Fontaine go missing, criminal justice personnel act with less urgency than they do with other missing persons cases (Carlson, 2014a).

Research also indicates that, at least in some contexts, race is a correlate of crime because of the activities of police officers. One study found that young black males in Toronto reporting little or no deviant activity are more likely to be arrested by police officers than are their white counterparts (Wortley and Tanner, 2005). A more recent national study found a similar pattern when comparing the experiences of visible minority youth and white youth (Fitzgerald and Carrington, 2011). Such patterns are consistent with **racial profiling**, the selective enforcement of the law based on the racial or ethnic characteristics of those apprehended by police officers.

TIME FOR REVIEW

1. How are age, gender, class, and race correlated with crime?
2. Why is a correlate of crime not necessarily a cause of crime?

THEORIES OF CRIME AND DEVIANCE

When we hear about a criminal incident, especially a violent, dramatic one (a school rampage, for instance) the first question we usually ask is, Why did he do it? Sociological theories of crime and deviance drawn from the objectivist (norm violation) tradition are designed to answer these kinds of causal questions.

Sociologists are not alone in asking causal questions. Nor are they alone in answering them. Sociological explanations of crime compete with media accounts and biological and psychological explanations. A major difference between biological and psychological explanations of crime and deviance, on the one hand, and sociological explanations, on the other, is that sociologists are more interested in group-based variations in deviant and criminal activity. The psychologist will try to explain why particular individuals decided to end their lives, but sociologists, beginning with Émile Durkheim, will want to know why, for instance, Protestants are more inclined to commit suicide than Roman Catholics are, or why men are more likely to commit suicide than women are.

Different theories may explain the same deviant act. Do people steal because they have few other legitimate means of acquiring possessions or money? Because they have failed to develop strong social bonds to society? Because they pursue everyday routines that provide them with plentiful opportunities to do so with impunity? One of the tasks of sociological research is to determine which theory best explains the agreed-on facts.

Many theories of crime and deviance exist, and I will now introduce you to the most important ones.

STRAIN THEORY

Strain theory holds that crime and deviance are the result of societal pressures to break rules. We may trace the theory back to Durkheim's concept of anomie. (Recall from Chapter 1, Introducing Sociology, that, according to Durkheim, anomie exists when norms governing behaviour are vaguely defined.) Robert Merton (1938) modified the concept to explain patterns of crime and deviance in the twentieth-century United States.

All societies, wrote Merton, establish culturally approved goals for their members and socially approved means of achieving those goals. However, some societies, such as the United States, pay more attention to goals of wealth, power, and prestige than to appropriate ways of achieving them. The imbalance between goals and means creates stress for lower-class people. They want what all Americans want—a nice house, a big car, a steady job—but lack legitimate means of achieving them, notably school and work opportunities. Rebuffed, they respond in a variety of deviant ways to the resulting stress. One mode of adaptation (Merton called it "innovation") involves using criminal means to achieve economic success.

People involved in money-making criminal enterprises exemplify Merton's innovators. Gangsters like the fictional Tony Soprano or the real life Al Capone subscribed to the American dream. They believed in, and aspired to, power, wealth, and status. Where they differed from noncriminals is in their chosen means of achieving those goals. Instead of pursuing educational qualifications and legitimate careers, they opted for illegal strategies.

Merton's innovators have also made their appearance in the world of professional sports. International cycling has been rife with deviant behaviour—cheating—for years (Walsh, 2013). Its chief instigator has been Lance Armstrong.

Armstrong comes from a very poor background and learned very early on in his cycling career that the use of performance-enhancing drugs was the only way that he would achieve any success in his chosen occupation. He adopted a win-at-all-costs mentality.

Some analysts argue that sports had been primed for this kind of deviance because of its importance for large numbers of people because of the large amounts of sponsorship money poured into it and because it is difficult for sports administrators to monitor practices surrounding performance-enhancing drugs. Research confirms that the huge rewards associated with professional sports motivate the use of performance-enhancing drugs and cheating more generally (Stewart and Smith, 2008). While most athletes condemn the use of such drugs, many are nonetheless prepared to use them because of the importance of winning. Athletes also know that their careers are short—thereby providing more incentive to cheat. Finally, drug cheating is often rationalized or neutralized by offenders on the grounds that "Everybody does it."

Several studies add weight to strain theory by examining the relationship between income inequality and rates of homicide. They find that people in the lowest income group are most inclined to homicidal activity. This finding is consistent with the view that pressure to deviate is strongest among people with the fewest conventional opportunities. Moreover, the relationship is strongest in societies that most strongly emphasize success goals and where material inequalities are greatest (Krahn, Hartnagel, and Gartrell, 1986).

Other strain theories of crime and deviance focus on thwarted ambition and its criminal consequences among lower-class male youth. Albert Cohen (1955) saw delinquency among working-class boys as resulting from school experiences. Encouraged to strive for success, they find their ambitions blocked because the sort of socialization they have received at home prepares them poorly for success in school. Frustrated because of their inability to measure up to what Cohen calls the school's "middle-class measuring rod," they react against the school system by engaging in activities that directly counter those valued and sponsored by the school. Hence, they commit delinquent behaviour that appears to be without purpose, such as vandalism. According to Cohen, destructive behaviour is its own reward, a way of subverting the middle-class measuring rod.

A third variant of strain theory combines elements from both Merton and Cohen. According to Cloward and Ohlin (1960), deviant motivation, in the form of limited opportunity, is not enough to explain criminal behaviour. Frustrated adolescents also need access to deviant opportunities to become delinquent. Not all would-be delinquents have the opportunity to become criminal innovators, as Merton supposes. Low-status people become involved in different types of deviant subculture depending on the opportunities available to them. Those who have the opportunity to learn from adult thieves gravitate to criminal gangs. Those without those networks but in possession of the necessary physical attributes and combat skills may join fighting gangs. Those without conventional or criminal opportunities may end up in drug-based subcultures.

Some contemporary applications of strain theory document the social pressures that result in higher rates of deviance among socially disadvantaged groups. Other extensions of classic strain theory seek to explain the frustrations that drive some individuals to crime and deviance. An important and influential example of the latter is Robert Agnew's (1992) general strain theory, which focuses on the stresses that ensue from different social relationships, not just those that result from chasing inaccessible success goals. Agnew argues that negative relationships generate negative emotions, such as anxiety, fear, and anger, that, in turn, generate deviant responses. First, relationships with others may hinder the achievement of a valued goal. Adolescents might see parents or teachers as barriers to desired outcomes, such as spending leisure time with friends. Second, adolescents may lose or be threatened with losing something or someone of value to them—a job, say, or a parent through divorce. The third type of toxic relationship involves situations from which adolescents find it difficult or impossible to extricate themselves, such as the clutches of bullies at school or an abusive father at home. Agnew suggests that these myriad strains sour relationships with others and can lead to deviant and disreputable behaviour of various kinds. Much research supports Agnew's claims. Among young people who are experiencing the sorts of strains listed above, delinquency provides more relief than do non-deviant solutions (Vold, Bernard, and Snipes, 2002).

SOCIAL LEARNING THEORIES: EDWIN SUTHERLAND AND DIFFERENTIAL ASSOCIATION

The basic proposition of learning theories is that willingness to break rules is a consequence of the socialization experience to which individuals have been exposed. Some people are motivated to engage in crime because they have acquired favourable opinions about what others regard as deviant behaviour. The learning of antisocial conduct and practices takes place in a variety of settings, beginning with the family and continuing with the peer group and the neighbourhood. Within each of these contexts, people may see as normal what others regard as wrong, dangerous, harmful, and shameful.

The best-known proponent of the learning perspective is Edwin Sutherland (1947), who insisted that a process of **differential association** is primarily responsible for deviant or nondeviant behaviour. Specifically, if people experience more nondeviant than deviant associations as they grow up, they are likely to follow the straight and narrow. Otherwise, they are likely to become deviants. According to Sutherland, criminals need to learn the tricks of the trade—how to steal a car or rob a bank, for instance. No less importantly, they must also learn rationalizations that tell them that stealing other people's money or property is justifiable. More association with deviant than nondeviant lifestyles teaches people these two important sets of lessons. Moreover, learning continues later in life. For example, research that I conducted with Scot Wortley showed that ex-inmates often believe that their time in prison has been a learning experience. The ex-inmates we interviewed described how prison enabled them to become more immersed in gang culture, learn new skills, and develop additional reasons for hating the police (Wortley and Tanner, 2005).

CONTROL THEORY

Travis Hirschi (1969) pioneered **control theory.** Its basic argument is that a set of ties bind young people to the conventional world, and when those ties are weak, deviance and crime occur. No special motivation is required. According to Hirschi, we all have within us a natural inclination for rule-breaking that is kept in check only because we have developed *attachments* to family and friends, *commitments* to conventional ambitions and activities in school and at work, prosocial *values and beliefs* that we share with people who are important to us, and conventional *activities* at school and at work. Individuals not constrained by such ties are likely to become involved in crime and deviance.

Control theory has a solid reputation as a predictor of relatively minor and occasional deviance involving adolescents. However, when more serious crime and delinquency is involved, and when the deviant behaviour in question appears more motivated or has a political underpinning, it is less plausible In the summer of 2014, rioting in Ferguson, Missouri, broke out when a white police officer shot and killed an unarmed black youth. Explaining the riot and the rioters (like the victim, mainly black youth) by reference to weak ties alone obscures the racial politics involved–young black people taking to the streets to protest racial injustice (see the Critical Sociology: Protest and Policy box). Likewise, control theory fails to explain why members of disadvantaged groups fail to develop conventional attachments to society in the first place.

A more recent variant of control theory is the so-called general theory of crime, which argues that all deviance has a common cause in low self-control. Gottfredson and Hirschi (1990) propose that rule-breaking of all sorts shares common features. It is easy to execute, immediately satisfying, risky, exciting, produces few long-lasting rewards, and is harmful to others. The personality characteristics of individuals with low self-control include impulsivity, a taste for risk, an action orientation, and short-term thinking. Low self-control presumably originates in early socialization when parents are too busy or unconcerned to police their children's behaviour and unable or unwilling to teach them the difference between right and wrong. Canadian research finds that low self-control predicts driving under the influence of alcohol and school-related behavioural problems among high-school students (Keane, Maxim, and Teevan, 1993; Nakhaie, Silverman, and Lagrange, 2000).

ROUTINE ACTIVITIES THEORY

Routine activities theory, by locating the source of crime in the structuring of everyday life, also downplays the significance of criminal motivation. It argues that much criminal behaviour is not dependent on complex causation. The presence of a suitable target and the absence of capable guardians suffice. Bring these conditions together with motivated offenders, and deviance and crime are likely to result.

Cohen and Felson (1979; Felson and Boba, 2010) suggest that the development of expensive and highly valued consumer goods has encouraged property crime because items like iPods, computers, and cellphones are easy to steal and transport. They also reason that residential property is harder to protect because increased labour force participation means that fewer homeowners are around during the day to deter burglars, and that, compared with earlier eras, the amount of leisure time that teenagers have at their disposal provides them with the opportunity and motivation for delinquent episodes.

Routine activities theorists argue that crime rates vary not just because of the number of individuals in the population willing and prepared to commit crime, but also because of the presence or absence of capable guardians, and because of the daily routines that people follow. Research shows that some routines are more closely linked to criminal offending

CRITICAL SOCIOLOGY: PROTEST AND POLICY   BLURRED LINES: THE POLITICS OF CRIMINAL JUSTICE

In response to several government commissions and inquiries, Indigenous principles and practices have begun to be adopted in the administration of Canadian justice. Healing circles and restorative justice programs allow perpetrators to better understand the harm they have done, express their remorse to victims, and compensate them for their wrongdoing. In addition, police departments have created special hate crime units to counter high levels of Indigenous victimization. They have also mandated sensitivity training for police officers dealing with Indigenous communities and sought to recruit more Indigenous police officers on the grounds that police departments should reflect the racial and ethnic composition of the communities that they police (Carlson, 2014b; Minaker and Hogeveen, 2009:169–70; Stenning, 2003).

South of the border, the black—white divide has generated many of the same concerns with criminal justice that Indigenous people have in Canada. Ferguson, a primarily black suburb of St. Louis, Missouri, exemplifies the volatile character of the American criminal justice system, the lightning rod for which is black people's encounters with a police department that is overwhelmingly white and, like other American police forces, equipped with army surplus heavy weaponry, and highly militarized in its tactics.

The situation in Ferguson popularized a relatively cheap and easy measure for reducing the incidence of misused lethal force: mandatory body cameras. Like other people, if police officers know that their behaviours are being observed, they tend to behave differently. The only problem with this technological fix is that body cameras can be easily be turned off or broken, unintentionally or otherwise.

Both Ferguson and recent native protests in Canada, notably the Idle No More movement, demonstrate that it is not always easy to distinguish between criminal and political responses to

Riot in Ferguson, Missouri, 2014
SOURCE: © New York Daily News/James Keivom via Getty Images.

systemic inequality and discrimination. The Idle No More movement has been led for the most part by a university-educated generation of young Indigenous people, mostly women, who are longer prepared to put up with age-old inequities. The movement can be seen as the product of their rising expectations and frustrations with the slow pace of reform (Friesen, 2013). The same holds true for Ferguson, where events kindled a debate about the causes and consequences of racial inequality in the United States and the policies that could help deal with the problem. Surely, not all crime is tinged with political implications, but just as surely, some of it is. How then would you draw the line between crime that is generated by systemic inequality and discrimination and crime that is generated by other circumstances?

Critical Thinking Questions

1. How are crime and deviance different from political action?

2. How might the notion of resistance inform and enrich debates about crime and deviance?

and criminal victimization than others are. People who spend large stretches of time away from home each day at work and out on the town in the evening and on weekends report higher levels of victimization than those who live more home-centred lives. Teenagers who spend large stretches of time in unsupervised leisure activities with other teenagers are at particular risk of criminal victimization and offending.

A useful illustration of how daily routines structure deviant behaviour is Hagan and McCarthy's (1997) study of street youth and crime in Toronto. They demonstrate that a substantial amount of criminal activity by street youth is motivated by situational exigencies. Nothing very surprising about this observation, you might say—except for the fact that most theories of crime have looked to the past to explain the criminal present. Strain and learning theories identify the roots of crime in lack of opportunity and differential association; control theories explain deviance by the failure to develop pro-social bonds early on at home or in school. Hagan and McCarthy argue that while these theories do a good job of explaining why some young people leave home and are on the street in the first place, they are less useful for explaining patterns of crime that occur afterward. Crime on the streets has more immediate causes. Street life thus becomes a relatively independent influence on such activities as theft and prostitution.

TIME FOR REVIEW

1. What are the main differences among strain, social learning, social control, and routine activities theories of crime and deviance?

2. In what ways might crime and inequality be linked?

3. Why might control theories provide a good explanation of minor adolescent deviance but not the kind of race riots that occur frequently in the United States?

TYPES OF CRIME AND DEVIANCE

So far, we have looked at conceptions of deviance and crime, ways of measuring their incidence, and prominent theories of criminal deviance. I now turn to several subfields of the sociological study of crime and deviance.

GENDER AND CRIME

Sociological studies of female crime and deviance are a recent development. In the past, sociologists ignored female wrongdoers because they thought their numbers were small or assumed that all female deviants were prostitutes. They judged male deviance a law and order problem and female deviance a sexual problem. This sexualized view of female deviance derives from the criminal records of known offenders. Historically, most girls and women were arrested and incarcerated for prostitution or because they were suspected carriers of venereal disease.

Self-report studies have done much to dispel the notion of female offenders as sexual deviants. They show that girls and women are no strangers to deviant behaviour of all types. Official and unofficial measures of crime and deviance indicate that the major difference between males and females is largely one of volume. Males are more inclined than females to crime and deviance (especially violent crime), start their deviant activities earlier, and end them later.

Increasingly, however, some sociologists see female crime as a growing problem. Women and girls are becoming more violent, more involved in gang activity, and so on. High-profile cases, such as the murder in 1997 of 14-year-old Reena Virk in Victoria and the subsequent trials of one of the young females accused of the crime, have done much to consolidate this kind of argument.

The belief that we are witnessing shifting patterns of female crime and deviance has led to the development of theories that link these changes to the effects of changing gender roles in society. In the 1970s, sociologists proposed the "liberation hypothesis," suggesting that, as women less frequently perform traditional domestic roles as wives and mothers, and begin entering the paid labour force in larger numbers, their patterns of crime and deviance will come to resemble those of males (Adler, 1975; Simon, 1975). However, available evidence offers little support for the liberation hypothesis. Differences in male and female crime rates, particularly violent crime, are quite stable over time.

Recently, some sociologists have asserted that while young women may be less physically violent and aggressive than their male counterparts are, they are more likely to take part in psychological aggression directed against other girls, such as name

Should squeegee kids' actions be considered criminal, a nuisance, or a form of subsistence work?
SOURCE: © Fred Thornhill/Sun Media.

calling, spreading harmful gossip, and rumour mongering. This argument, too, has been challenged by research showing that psychological aggression is not the exclusive prerogative of "mean girls," and that girls who are victims of relational aggression are targeted by boys, too (Chesney-Lind, Morash, and Irwin, 2007).

Currently, two schools of thought exist about how to account for similarities and differences between the deviant activities of males and females. Some analysts think that female wrongdoing can be best explained by the same concepts and theories used to explain male wrongdoing. For example, Canadian research indicates that lower levels of deviance and criminality among young females than among young males can be explained by the concepts of control and opportunity (Hagan, Gillis, and Simpson, 1987).

Conversely, sociologists influenced by feminist ideas are more likely to argue for gender-specific theories of crime and deviance. They argue that it is unreasonable to suppose that theories devised with male behaviour in mind, and tested exclusively with information supplied by males, will prove equally applicable to female deviants. The idea that we might need different theories to explain male and female deviance receives partial support from a U.S. study. Researchers found that depression was a cause of female delinquency but not male delinquency. They also reported that playing sports increases male violence but not female violence (Daigle, Cullen, and Wright, 2007).

YOUTH, CRIME, AND DEVIANCE

Young people are at the heart of most people's concerns about crime and deviance (Tanner, 2015). It has been this way for a long time, with successive adult generations believing that the behaviour of young people has never been worse than it is. Media coverage encourages such views, preferring bad news stories to more uplifting ones, and focusing on high-profile and unrepresentative crimes of violence, rather than more typical shoplifting incidents, for example.

Moral panics are extreme reactions to deviance and crime, and social constructionists have examined them extensively. Episodes of moral panic are characterized by the conviction that the deviance or crime in question is sufficiently dangerous that it constitutes a threat to the core values and well-being of society. Politicians, newspaper editors, and prominent personages clamour for immediate action. They typically say that something has to be done right away or the situation will only get worse. Some examples of moral panic in Canada have focused on raves (Hier, 2002) and so-called squeegee kids (Parnaby, 2003).

In Summerville, South Carolina, Grade 9 student Alec Stone was arrested in 2014 just days into the new school year after writing a Facebook update about killing his neighbour's pet dinosaur with a gun. Police searched his book bag and locker, and school officials started questioning him about the comment. Stone said it was just a joke and then became irate. He was handcuffed, taken into custody, and suspended from school. Was the reaction on the part of school authorities and the police justified or did it reflect the moral panic surrounding school shootings in the United States?

Most moral panics involve young people for two main reasons. First, many adults view them as vulnerable to corrupting influences from "satanic" adults to violent movies, video games, and rap music. Second, young people represent the future. If bad influences corrupt them now, what will become of the nation when they reach adulthood?

How can we spot moral panics? Moral panics exist when the public reaction to deviance or crime is far out of proportion to the nature and scope of the problem—when, for instance, there is little or no factual basis to claims about increased levels of drug use among young people or incidents of lethal violence in schools (Ben-Yehuda, 1986; Lawrence and Mueller, 2003).

Youth Gangs

Youth gangs have emerged as a major crime problem in Canada over the past decade because of an apparent increase in gang activity in large cities. However, gang activity has attracted more media attention than academic research. Much of the research is several decades old and based on small samples of already-identified groups of young people in specific geographic locations—for instance, immigrant gangs in British Columbia (Gordon, 2000).

I conducted an investigation of youth gang activity in Toronto with Scot Wortley (Wortley and Tanner, 2004). We interviewed a sample of high-school students and street youth and learned that many of our respondents who reported past or present gang membership were not involved in criminal activities at all. Their gang membership had more to do with the pursuit of legitimate leisure activities than deviant ones. Membership in organizations involved with crime and deviance, such as drug trafficking and violent conflict with other gangs, was more common among street youth than among high-school students.

We also found that poverty, race and ethnicity, family structure, and living arrangements influence gang membership. These factors reflect the patterns of inequality, disadvantage, and discrimination to which strain theorists draw our attention. Other recent Canadian research tells a similar story. For example, disadvantaged Indigenous youth in the west are recruited into gangs who provide them with the status and the income (largely from the drug trade, where they work as low-level dealers) otherwise denied them in cities like Winnipeg and Regina or on the reserve. The larger American research literature documents the same pattern.

Serious and repetitive gang activity can result in incarceration for gang members. Evidence suggests that the prison system also functions as a recruiting ground for gang members. On occasion, gangs formed in prison extend their activities onto the street once members are released (Grekul and LaBoucane-Benson, 2008). American research has found a similar pattern with bike gangs and white supremacist groups.

NET EFFECTS: INTERNET DEVIANCE

The rapid development of computer technology—the Internet in particular—has significantly expanded opportunities for deviant and disreputable behaviour (Thio, 2010). The deviant purposes that computers have been used for include, but are not limited to, identity theft, cyberstalking, and the sale and distribution of pornography.

Identity theft has become the fastest-growing crime of the twenty-first century. Credit card, health card, and driving licence information is stolen and used to buy goods and services. It is easy to do and difficult to detect and is much more profitable than conventional property crime.

Pornography is not, of course, an invention of the Internet. The Internet has, however, made its consumption considerably easier, making it accessible to a wide range of buyers, including adolescents. Internet porn has the advantage of being a home-based activity, allowing users to indulge in it without surreptitious visits to adult bookstores and video stores that might reveal their disreputable tastes to others. The Internet has become a principal means by which the trade in child pornography has flourished (Jenkins, 2001).

The Internet has also become a medium by which people can target their dislike of, or hatred for, other people. In September 2010, an 18-year-old male student at Rutgers University in the United States used a webcam to secretly film his roommate kissing another male. The encounter was then streamed over the Internet. The roommate, Tyler Clementi, subsequently committed suicide—as did Rehtaeh Parsons and Amanda Todd, two young Canadian women, after each had been relentlessly cyberbullied. Cyberspace has also been used to send photos of Hollywood celebrities—nude and female—around the world.

On occasion, the Internet has been deployed not out of malice or for financial gain but for essentially political reasons. A case in point is the WikiLeaks phenomenon. Orchestrated by Internet activist Julian Assange, WikiLeaks is an organization that disseminates classified information over the Internet. It has been responsible for, among other activities, the downloading of secret military information detailing the Iraq war. While political and military leaders in Washington and London have portrayed such leaks as wildly outrageous criminal acts, Assange and his supporters prefer to see themselves as courageous defenders of freedom of information. (Crime fiction has similarly embraced the idea of the computer hacker as hero in the form of Lisbeth Sander, the heroine of *The Girl with the Dragon Tattoo* [Larsson, 2008]).

TIME FOR REVIEW

1. What are moral panics and why do they often involve young people?
2. How has the Internet allowed people to create new forms of crime and deviance and new ways of engaging in crime and deviance?

RESPONDING TO CRIME AND DEVIANCE

When sociologists study reactions to deviant behaviour, they are examining the ways in which societies try to prevent or control that behaviour.

INCARCERATION

The prison is the chief means by which we seek to control crime. Canada's first prison was Kingston Penitentiary, opened in 1835. Before then, convicted offenders received other forms of punishment, including hanging and deportation. Canada introduced prisons to incapacitate and punish offenders and discourage them (as well as other potential offenders) from committing additional crimes. Prisons were also expected to reform offenders, encouraging them to live law-abiding lives by teaching them work skills while serving time.

For more than a hundred years, Canada's prison population has varied very little in proportionate terms, fluctuating between 80 and 118 adults per 100 000 people (Brown, 2011; Walmsley, 2013). While the staggeringly high rate of incarceration in the United States and Russia is the main story told in Figure 15.4, it is worth noting that Canada is more likely to imprison offenders than are several Western European nations.

Prisons do a poor job of rehabilitating prisoners. Many studies show that the recidivism rate among ex-prisoners is high, with a large proportion of the prison population at any one time made up of people who have been there before—sometimes, several times before (Liebling and Crewe 2012).

Prison inmates suffer numerous deprivations They are denied their freedom, required to abide by other peoples' rules and schedules, not allowed to wear their own clothing, have limited contact with friends and family from the outside, and required to live in an overcrowded, dirty, smelly, and violent environment. The unpleasantness of prison life is not a problem for people who believe that prison's main purpose is to punish, deter, and incapacitate offenders. It is a problem for people who adhere to rehabilitative ideals.

Prisons fail to rehabilitate for three reasons. First, commitment to the rehabilitative ideal has never been strong to begin with, with few resources allocated to that goal. Second, in response to the harsh conditions that they encounter, prisoners have developed an inmate subculture with its own code of conduct that often challenges the regime imposed on them. Third, prisoners learn new criminal skills from other prisoners and learn how to justify the use of violence (Sykes, 1958). Given immersion in the prison subculture, prison time is more likely to lead to more prison time than to rehabilitation.

Prisons are the centrepiece of approaches to crime control that emphasize suppression. Calls for tougher law enforcement—more proactive policing, longer prison sentences for habitual criminals, mandatory minimum sentences for violent, gun, and gang-related crime—are all examples of suppressive strategies.

The "tough on crime" legislation proposed by the Conservative government is likely to increase the size of the prison population in Canada. Because crime rates are going down, this is a strange time for incarceration rates to be increasing; stranger still is that the rise will be a direct result of government policy that is unlikely to reduce the crime rate—an observation that brings us, appropriately, to deterrence theory.

FIGURE 15.4 PRISON POPULATION, SELECTED COUNTRIES, 2013

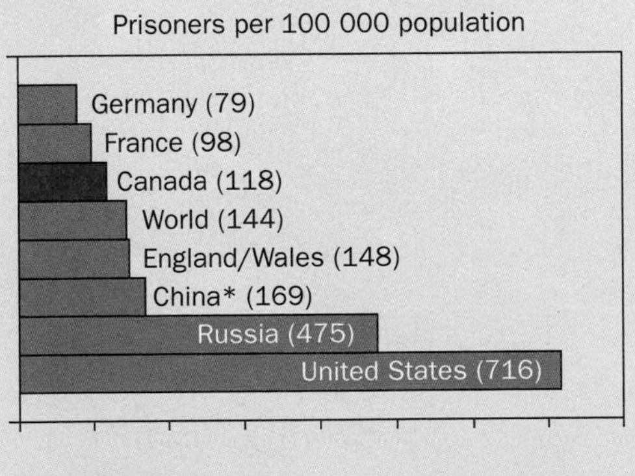

Prisoners per 100 000 population

Germany (79)
France (98)
Canada (118)
World (144)
England/Wales (148)
China* (169)
Russia (475)
United States (716)

* Includes 650 000 people in "administrative detention."

Share of Prisoners per Country		
Country	Percentage of World's Prisoners	Percentage of World's Prisoners/Percentage of World's Population
China*	20.8	1.1
United States	20.4	4.6
Russia	6.2	3.1
England/Wales	0.8	1.0
France	0.6	0.7
Germany	0.6	0.5
Canada	0.4	0.8
Other	50.2	0.7
Total	100.0	

SOURCE: Adapted from Roy Walmsley, *World Prison Population List,* 10th edition, 2013. http://www.prisonstudies.org/sites/prisonstudies.org/files/resources/downloads/wppl_10.pdf (accessed Dec. 15, 2014).

Deterrence theory holds that getting tough on crime will lead to its eradication or at least reduce the probability of offending. Deterrence can take one of two main forms. *General deterrence* is the process by which the punishment of some law violators discourages other potential law violators from breaking the law. *Specific deterrence* is the process by which an individual who has been caught and punished for an offence will find the experience sufficiently costly that he or she will not repeat the wrongdoing.

Deterrence, whether specific or general, has three elements. The first involves the severity of the penalty. Are offenders given jail time or just a fine? The second involves the certainty of punishment. When drivers consider the chance of getting caught speeding, they are considering the certainty of punishment. The final element is the speed of punishment. How long after law violators have been apprehended do they have to wait for punishment? Deterrence theory holds that law-violating behaviour will be low when severity, certainty, and speed of punishment are high.

Most practical applications of deterrence theory concentrate on the severity or harshness of legal sanctions. Hence, the advocacy of capital punishment, long prison terms, and boot camp. However, most research does not support the proposition that harsh punishment deters. Where it exists, the death penalty has not reduced homicide rates (Fuller and Wozniak, 2006: 266). Boot camp has been less effective than other means of dealing with young offenders (Doob and Cesaroni, 2004). Longer prison terms are no more effective in reducing recidivism than are shorter terms (Doob and Webster, 2003).

The problem with deterrence theory is its assumption that criminals are rational calculators, carefully calibrating the costs of crime against its rewards. However, most criminals have only an imprecise understanding of the punishment they might receive for a given offence. Moreover, many violent crimes are prefigured by anger, which works against rational calculation. More evidence supports the **certainty principle,** which holds that potential offenders are more often deterred by the thought of

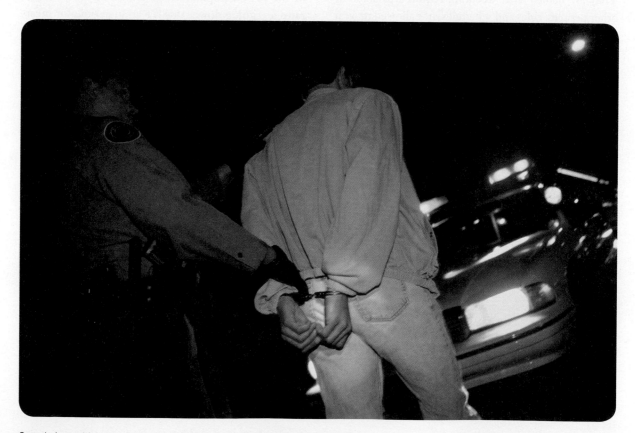

Canada has a higher incarceration rate than most Western European countries.
SOURCE: © Photodisc.

certain but moderate punishment than by the guarantee of severe punishment for an act they believe they can get away with (Ashworth and Roberts, 2012; Von Hirsch et al., 1999).

In addition to not necessarily producing lower crime rates, get-tough policies come with a high price tag. Keeping people in prison costs a lot. Mandatory minimum sentences mean that there will be more people in prison. More people in prison means that more people coming out of prison and trying to find a job and accommodation will be burdened with the stigma of being an ex-convict. In the United States, the "war on drugs" has resulted in the incarceration of bit players in the drug trade: addicted users and minor suppliers. The sheer expense of locking up minor criminals means that fewer tax dollars are available for other kinds of law enforcement and anti-crime policies that focus on prevention and intervention.

INTERVENTION

Many sociologists view community intervention on behalf of young offenders as an effective strategy for reducing crime. Interventionist policies assume that we can most effectively tackle crime by weakening motivations and minimizing opportunities for lawbreaking. Interventions include recreational programs for neighbourhood youth, counselling sessions, and the assignment of youth workers to neighbourhood street gangs. While programs of this sort have always commanded tremendous loyalty from their practitioners, they are expensive and have rarely been properly evaluated for their effectiveness.

PREVENTING CRIME

Too much of our thinking about crime focuses on catching and controlling offenders. Public policy debates about crime rarely discuss nonlegal solutions. Yet given what we know about the risk factors associated with serious and repetitive criminality among youth, one may reasonably suggest that expanded daycare, for example, might be a less costly and more effective investment of taxpayers' dollars than imprisonment is.

Evidence that some criminal justice policies do not work, or do not work as well as we would like them to, does not mean that they are going to be abandoned. Criminal justice policies are driven by political ideology, not criminological research (see the Critical Sociology: Protest and Policy box). This is particularly true for juvenile justice policy.

Much if not most of the controversy surrounding criminal justice policy in Canada centres on young people. Over the past century, young people in trouble with the law have fallen under the provisions of the Juvenile Delinquents Act of 1908, the Young Offenders Act of 1984, and the Youth Criminal Justice Act of 2003.

The Juvenile Delinquents Act was replaced by the Young Offenders Act in large measure because critics felt that it was failing to deter or prevent rising rates of juvenile crime. The Young Offenders Act was, in turn, replaced by the Youth Criminal Justice Act because critics felt that it was failing to deter or prevent rising rates of youth crime.

The current Youth Criminal Justice Act emphasizes getting tough on serious, repeat young offenders while adopting less punitive strategies for the far more numerous minor offenders, including warnings and community-based diversionary programs. The most recently available crime statistics indicate that since the introduction of the new legislation, the rate of youth crime, like the rate of adult crime, has declined. The facts notwithstanding, the present government has retained its tough-on-youth crime rhetoric, promising to impose longer sentences on violent and repeat offenders and make it less difficult to retain them in pre-trial detention.

BIG BROTHER IS WATCHING YOU: SURVEILLANCE IN EVERYDAY LIFE

Prisons and incarceration are not the only means by which authorities seek to constrain the behaviour of citizens. Nor are lawbreakers their only concern. Today, public and private institutions increasingly seek to monitor and control the behaviour of ordinary law-abiding citizens as well as recognized deviants (Staples, 2008).

Consider the following facts: Convicted offenders under house arrest are required to wear electronic bracelets, tracking their movements. Some job seekers are required to comply with obligatory drug tests as a condition of employment. Store owners use video cameras to observe customers and employees. Companies routinely trace the online purchasing habits of Internet users. These examples illustrate eroding differences between the criminal justice system's way of doing things and the ordinary, everyday culture of surveillance. Their common goal is to regulate everyday behaviour and establish conformity.

Everyday surveillance is distinguished from more formal kinds of social control, first, by its scope. The closed circuit television (CCTV) camera scans everybody—not just the suspicious-looking shoppers in high-end stores and not just the teenagers lurking in the parking lot. Second, our behaviour is controlled less by the threat of punishment than by the certain knowledge that we are being watched. Third, surveillance is everywhere. Whereas, historically, criminals were confined to prisons, and those with mental illnesses to asylums, ordinary citizens are regulated, and encouraged to self-regulate, by the omnipresence of the all-seeing CCTV camera, the threat of random drug tests, and compulsory ID tags.

The perception of high crime rates and the resultant fear has persuaded many people that crime is a problem that the state and its criminal justice apparatus cannot do much about. Specifically, many people believe crime cannot be easily contained and controlled by rehabilitative policies. In their place, new forms of social control have emerged, particularly among those who can afford elaborate private security arrangements—gated communities patrolled by private security guards, extensive home security systems, and the like (Garland, 2001).

Much of the expansion and growing intrusiveness of surveillance is also a response to international terrorism—Al-Qaeda after 9/11, ISIS currently. Hence, more border controls at airports and ports cities (and reality TV programs devoted to security operations at airports). We have had to learn to accept increased airline surveillance, including full body scans, as a reasonable price for safer flying. At the same time, some analysts are growing increasingly concerned about governmental surveillance of the citizenry. They draw attention not just to the growing use of CCTV cameras in shopping malls, workplaces, hospitals and schools, but also to the electronic compilation of vast amounts of information from banking transactions, credit cards, driver's licences, and so on.

Since 2001, the federal government has introduced anti-terrorist legislation requiring, among other things, that telephone companies make available to law enforcement agencies the personal details of those who subscribe to their services—names, street and e-mail addresses, telephone numbers, mobile phone identification numbers and SIM card numbers. The murder of two members of the Canadian Armed Forces by self-styled ISIS supporters in October 2014 will undoubtedly harden the resolve for tighter security measures.

The concern expressed by civil liberties watchdogs is that these measures will not just be used against terrorists but will also target other individuals and groups whose values and interests do not necessarily coincide with governmental and corporate interests, such as environmental groups, activists opposed to big oil, and the Occupy movement (Downes, Rock, and McCormick, 2011).

The heart of the problem is that surveillance policies and practices that successfully balance reasonable public safety concerns with the rights of ordinary citizens are difficult to design. Tracking people's Internet activity or scrutinizing their bank records may not be as obviously intrusive as an electronic bracelet on your ankle—but the intent is the same (see the Critical Sociology: Globalization box).

TIME FOR REVIEW

1. What are the main societal responses to crime? What are their strengths and weaknesses?
2. How is it possible to reconcile the need for national security with respect for citizens' rights and civil liberties?

CRITICAL SOCIOLOGY: GLOBALIZATION   THE EDWARD SNOWDEN AFFAIR

The global scope of governmental surveillance was graphically highlighted in 2013, when Edward Snowden leaked classified information from the U.S. National Security Agency to various news agencies. The documents in question exposed details of military operations and plans. It also revealed government interest in the private activities of its own citizens, such as the online sexual activity of individuals deemed by governments to be radicals—information that could be used to discredit them.

Edward Snowden.
SOURCE. © Barton Gellman/Getty Images.

Governments were not just spying on their own citizens. The leaked documents also revealed that the United States was spying on a number of its erstwhile allies—the leaders of Britain, Germany, and Spain among them. Nor was the data gathering restricted to national security matters. The German electronics company Siemens was electronically robbed of confidential information, an act of industrial espionage.

Considerable debate has taken place concerning how Snowden's activities should be judged. Is he a traitor, as the American authorities argue? Or is he a courageous whistleblower who has legitimately drawn attention to the wrongful and harmful activities of governments? Global reaction is mixed. Were he to be apprehended, charged, and convicted by the American government, he would be liable to a 30-year prison sentence. On the other hand, he has also been awarded a number of international humanitarian awards. What do you think?

Critical Thinking Questions

1. Is Edward Snowden a hero or a villain?

2. Should governments surveil their citizens? If so, for what reasons? How intrusive should this surveillance be?

SUMMARY

1. **Are any societies free of crime and deviance?**
   No, criminal and deviant behaviour exists in all human societies. However, what counts as crime and deviance varies by time and place. Crime and deviance also vary by how serious they are judged to be. The more serious the offence, the more severe the punishment.

2. **How do sociologists study crime and deviance?**
   Crime and deviance can be studied as objective behaviours and as social constructs. Objectivist and constructionist perspectives tend to ask different, although not necessarily competing, questions about crime and deviance.

3. **How much crime and deviance is there?**
   Much more than most of us think! Official counts of crime and deviance underestimate the amount of crime and deviance occurring in society. There is an inverse relationship between the seriousness of crime and deviance and the frequency of

their occurrence. The homicide rate is generally regarded as the most valid and reliable measure of criminal activity.

4. **What factors predict criminal behaviour?**
   Age, gender, class, and race are the most important predictors. However, correlation does not necessarily imply causation. Sociological theories of crime and deviance are designed to answer questions about causation.

5. **Are some groups of people the source of greater concern than others are with regard to their criminal and deviant activity?**
   Since at least the end of the nineteenth century, young people have figured prominently in people's worries about crime and deviance. Sociologists are interested in why this is so (a constructionist question) and in the determinants of their deviant and criminal behaviour (an objectivist issue).

6. **How has Canadian society responded to crime and deviance?**
Imprisonment and other deterrence-based policies have been mainstays of the societal response to criminal behaviour. Research suggests that they are not very effective in reducing crime levels. Other anti-crime strategies focus on prevention. Increasingly, governments have sought to control the behaviour of their citizens with a variety of surveillance strategies.

QUESTIONS TO CONSIDER

1. When studying crime and deviance, must we choose between objectivist and constructionist approaches?

2. How are criminal statistics social constructions?

3. Why are crime rates falling?

4. What is a moral panic? Why do moral panics often involve young people?

5. How has cyberspace changed crime and deviance and reactions to crime and deviance?

6. Why is studying reaction to crime and deviance often as important as studying criminal and deviant behaviour itself?

7. How do the mass media influence criminal and deviant behaviour?

8. What are the most important causes of crime?

GLOSSARY

The **certainty principle** (p. 372) is a component of deterrence theory that argues that it is the probability of punishment, rather than its severity, that dissuades potential offenders from breaking the law.

Conflict crime (p. 353) involves criminal acts that are subject to disagreement about the amount of harm they cause, how wrong they are, and how severely they should be punished.

Consensus crime (p. 353) involves criminal acts that are generally agreed to be seriously harmful, wrong, and deserving of severe penalty.

Control theory (p. 366) argues that crime and deviance are likely to occur when internal and external controls are weak or absent.

Crime (p. 352) is a breach of the criminal law that is liable to prosecution and punishment.

The **criminal justice system** (p. 352) comprises the social institutions charged with the task of apprehending, prosecuting, and punishing known offenders.

The **dark figure of crime** (p. 358) is the number of criminal incidents that take place but are unknown to the police.

Deterrence theory (p. 372) argues that the threat of punishment discourages criminal violation.

Deviance (p. 352) is the breaking of a norm.

Differential association (p. 366) theory proposes that criminal behaviour is learned through contact with other individuals and groups.

Labelling theorists (p. 355) believe that public identification of individuals as criminal or deviant leads to more crime or deviance by those individuals.

Moral panics (p. 369) are extreme reactions to crime and deviance.

Norms (p. 352) are rules that prescribe standards of everyday behaviour.

In **observational studies** (p. 362), information about crime and deviance is collected by observing them.

Racial profiling (p. 364) is a selective enforcement of the law based on racial or ethnic characteristics of those apprehended by police officers.

Recidivism (p. 357) is repeat offending, particularly following punishment or rehabilitation.

Routine activities theory (p. 366) argues that in addition to a motivated offender, criminal events require a suitable target and the absence of a capable guardian.

In **self-report studies** (p. 362), respondents report about their involvements with crime and deviance as offenders and victims.

Social constructionism (p. 356) emphasizes the subjective qualities of crime and deviance, proposing that particular conditions are viewed as problematic only because some people—usually powerful ones—define them as such.

Social stigma (p. 353) is severe social disapproval of a person because of a particular trait that indicates their deviance from social norms. A damaged reputation or reduced social status is usually a result.

Strain theory (p. 364) argues that people are pressured into breaking rules because they have few opportunities to succeed in life by legitimate means.

Street crime (p. 363) refers to conventional violent and property crime. It is often contrasted with white-collar crime.

White-collar crime (p. 357) is crime committed by high-status people in the course of their careers.

CHAPTER 16

POPULATION AND URBANIZATION

John Hannigan
UNIVERSITY OF TORONTO

SOURCE: © Hindustan Times/Sakib Ali via Getty Images.

AFTER READING THIS CHAPTER, YOU WILL BE ABLE TO:

- Trace the evolution of cities from preindustrial times through the Industrial Revolution to the current era.

- Identify the distinctive patterns and challenges of rapid urban growth in the cities of the southern hemisphere.

- Describe how the theme of rural-urban differences has influenced how we think about cities.

- Explain how urban growth is influenced by broader demographic (population) factors.

- Recognize the widening polarization between the gentrified, privatized, and fortified city of the middle class and the imprisoning city of the urban disadvantaged.

INTRODUCTION

A few years ago, *Toronto Life* magazine published a cover story entitled "The New Suburbanites" about why some "diehard downtowners" are giving up on the city and moving to small towns within a 150-kilometre radius of Toronto (Preville, 2011). Profiled are Carrie Low, a corporate lawyer, Brian Porter, a firefighter, and their two daughters. Life in Toronto's east-end neighbourhood, the Beaches, had become too stressful and "over-engineered" given the demands of two careers and a never-ending shuttle of kid dropoffs and pickups to lessons, play dates, and birthday parties. The couple felt like runners in a relay race, always passing the baton. They decided that the problem wasn't each other, or their careers, or their children, "but the city itself." Living in Toronto, Carrie and Brian concluded, "required too many contortions," so they "decided to divorce it." Their solution was to purchase a 2700-square-foot detached house in Cobourg, 118 kilometres east of Toronto along Lake Ontario.

Nineteenth-century towns like Cobourg have delivered everything these escapees from the city are seeking. Carrie, who commutes to Toronto several days a week, contrasts her current Via train ride back to Cobourg, where "those of us who make that commute all know one another" to riding to work on Toronto's transit system, where "everyone is in their own bubble, no one makes eye contact, and even if you ride with the same people every day you never say hi to them." Simon Heath, a writer who moved to Creemore, 123 kilometres north of Toronto, reports that he and his wife, Lily, feel absolutely comfortable allowing their children to wander off at the local farmers' market, something they would never have done in the big city. "Outside the city," Heath says, "everyone knows who you are and what you're up to."

This profile of small-town life highlights a theme that has resounded through the discipline of sociology since its founding in the nineteenth century. Urban life, it is said, is qualitatively different from a rural or small-town existence: meaner, more stressful, more alienating. Obsessed as they are with efficiency and making money, urbanites are said to have no time for relating to others in a more holistic and humane way. Increasing population size and density bring with them a host of urban problems, from traffic gridlock and pollution to family breakdown and crime.

The tale of Carrie, Brian, and their daughters illustrates one of the most influential ways of looking at residential settings. Termed **environmental-opportunity**

theory (Michelson, 1973), it posits that people actively choose where they want to live depending on the extent to which a particular place either meshes with or constrains their preferred lifestyle. Not all of us, of course, get to choose our community freely, but people will always strive to match their choices with their needs.

A second lens through which urban life can be viewed is that of *demography*—the study of populations: their size, distribution, and composition. As you will learn later in this chapter, in the preindustrial city, significant growth was constrained by a high birth rate and a high death rate. Only when the death rate began to fall because of advances in hygiene, nutrition, medical knowledge, and public health did the industrial city thrive, bringing with it a distinctive spatial organization and way of life. Today, the social organization and character of cities are being powerfully influenced by flows of highly diverse groups of immigrants. This has resulted in the re-urbanization of the central city, the growth of the multiethnic city, and other urban changes.

A third approach asserts that the urban experience is constrained not just by the nature of the physical environment or by demographic forces, but also by the changing configuration of international, national, and local economic arrangements. In recent years, the emergence of a globalized economy has had profound implications for North American cities, changing both their physical form and their social-class patterns. In particular, it has resulted in an increasing polarization between rich and poor, affecting the homeless person sleeping in the park, the highly paid professional eating in the chic urban restaurant, and the suburban homeowner

Is urban life meaner, more stressful, more alienating than small-town life?

SOURCE: © akg-images.

shopping in a "big-box" megastore on the fringes of the city (Kleniewski, 1997: 135).

Similarly, resource towns and farming communities have been hard hit by international trade agreements and a harsher rural–urban division of labour in the global economy. In this changing climate, the countryside comes to serve two new and very different purposes: vacation playground and toxic dumping ground. Thus, while towns in the British Columbia interior and the Alberta foothills are transformed into ski and golfing resorts linked to global tourism, other communities are forced to "grasp at environmentally dubious schemes like hazardous waste treatment, strawboard manufacture, tire incineration and mega-hog barns" (Epp and Whitson, 2001: xv).

In this chapter, I will look at this three-pronged influence of environment and structure on city life over the past century. In the course of the discussion, you will encounter three main types of cities: the industrial city, the corporate city, and the **postmodern city.** The industrial city originated in the nineteenth century and reached its zenith in the 1920s and 1930s, the corporate city arose after World War II and dominated during the 1950s and 1960s, and the postmodern city dates from the 1970s up to the present.

TIME FOR REVIEW

1. What are the three lenses through which urban experience can be viewed?
2. Which of these lenses do you think is most influential in shaping the nature of cities in the early twenty-first century?

EARLY CITIES

Cities are "relatively large, dense, permanent settlements in which the majority of the residents do not produce their own food" (McGahan, 1995: 1). By most accounts, the city as a distinct form dates back five thousand or six thousand years to 3000–4000 BCE, when it first appeared in Mesopotamia (now southern Iraq) and Egypt. Three elements of prime importance characterized these preindustrial cities: the existence of a food surplus in fertile valleys, which permitted the specialization of labour in zones of dense settlement; the achievement of literacy among scribes, priests, and other elite members of society, which allowed for the keeping of financial and other records; and technological innovations, notably metallurgy, agricultural irrigation, and the harnessing of wind and water power for sailing and grain milling.

Although preindustrial cities were important as centres of commerce, knowledge, and art, they never contained much more than a small fraction of the overall population. Even at their height, ancient and medieval cities were incapable of supporting urban populations of more than 5 or 10 percent of society, primarily because such societies could not generate a sufficiently large agricultural surplus to feed a huge urban populace. When the cities did begin to swell, periodic outbreaks of the bubonic plague (the notorious "Black Death"), spread by fleas from infected rats, killed as many as half the people in Europe's cities. Thus, by 1800, of the roughly 900 million people in the world, only about 3 percent lived in urban places of 5000 or more inhabitants (Hauser, 1965: 7). And despite significant changes in architectural styles and building materials, the physical layout of the communities in which they lived had not changed all that much from antiquity to the eighteenth century—they were still built up within protective walls and organized around a central market square and places of worship, such as cathedrals, temples, or mosques (Abu-Lughod, 1991: 49–50).

TIME FOR REVIEW

1. What are the three distinguishing characteristics of preindustrial cities?
2. What accounts for the failure of early cities to support human populations of significant size?

POPULATION ISSUES AND URBAN GROWTH

Urban growth is a product not only of technological progress and social invention but also of the broader patterns of population growth that shape a society. These demographic forces operate in conjunction with other social and economic factors to create a slow-moving but powerful current that relentlessly moves us in certain directions (McQuillan, 1994: 229).

THE DEMOGRAPHIC TRANSITION

For much of human history, societies hovered in a steady state in which both birth rates and death rates were high. As a result, the overall size of the population remained more or less stable from decade to decade.

In the absence of any effective form of birth control, women in preindustrial societies were destined to bear a large number of children. This was deemed necessary for several reasons. Infant and childhood mortality rates were high; routinely, only about half of the children born survived to adulthood. Thus, it was necessary to have large families in the hope that some would escape the Grim Reaper. Furthermore, in traditional societies, offspring were viewed as having considerable economic value, especially in the poorer classes where children were expected to help with the farm work or were sent off to work as servants in the homes of the rich. In the absence of pension plans or retirement funds, parents fortunate enough to reach old age depended on their children to care for them.

The human lifespan was much shorter than it is today. For example, in 1867, the year Canada officially became a country, the average life expectancy at birth was 42 years as compared with 80.9 years for those born between 2006 and 2008 (Beaujot, 2004: 446; Statistics Canada, 2011a). Even the most learned medical authorities did not understand the causes of and proper treatments for illnesses, attributing them to intangibles, such as "vapours" and the like. Those who fell ill were "bled" by leeches and subjected to other such treatments.

Beginning in the eighteenth century, this pattern began to change dramatically with breakthroughs in hygiene, public health, nutrition, and medical knowledge. Once it was understood that often-fatal maladies, such as cholera, were preventable by establishing a clean water supply, the death rate declined significantly. Now the causes of death were more likely to be degenerative diseases, such as cancer and heart disease. Especially important strides were made in reducing infant mortality. Note, for example, the declining infant mortality rate in Canada: In 1831, 1 in 6 children did not survive his or her first year; in 1931, it was 1 in 14; and by 1999, this dropped to 1 in 190 (Beaujot, 2004: 446). In 2008, infant mortality declined further to approximately 1 in 200 (Statistics Canada, 2011b).

While death rates plunged, birth rates, at first, remained relatively high. Deeply ingrained cultural traditions and beliefs remained stubbornly embedded. Large families remained the norm and the use of birth control was outlawed. The result was a period of rapid population growth, especially in urban areas.

Eventually, however, birth rates also began to fall. Contributing to the decline was a series of changes associated with increasing modernization, industrialization, and urbanization. One crucial factor was the offloading of responsibilities formerly attached to the family onto the state. Children now were required to remain in school until they were adolescents; consequently, child

rearing became more costly. Primary care for seniors began to shift from adult children to government-operated programs and institutions. The change from high to low birth and death rates is known as the **demographic transition** (see Figure 16.1). Initially, the change was most characteristic of cities in Western Europe and North America, but ultimately it spread to rural districts as new health technologies and medical treatments expanded beyond city limits.

From the mid-1960s, wealthier nations in the developed world entered a new demographic era that differs in several ways from that associated with the demographic processes outlined above. First, fertility plunged below 2.1 births per woman—the **replacement level** at which births and deaths balance and the population level remains stationary, ignoring population inflows from other countries (immigration) and population outflows to other countries (emigration). This situation reflects a fundamental shift in contemporary values, especially among the middle class. Whereas previously the pressure to raise a family was paramount, now the emphasis shifted to equality of opportunity and freedom of choice. Increasingly, women entered the paid labour force on a full-time basis, not just out of economic necessity but also in pursuit of self-fulfillment. With declining fertility rates, the population as a whole is becoming older, especially in countries where immigration has concurrently slowed. Some analysts have described this as the "second demographic transition" (Champion, 1993; Van de Kaa, 1987).

Malthus versus Marx

As the initial demographic transition loomed, fears arose over the possibility of overpopulation. Alarm was first sounded by the British clergyman and political economist Thomas Malthus. Under normal

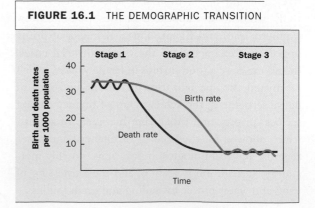

FIGURE 16.1   THE DEMOGRAPHIC TRANSITION

With declining fertility rates, the population as a whole is becoming older.

SOURCE: © Jupiter Images.

conditions, Malthus (1798) believed, there exists a natural "urge to reproduce" that flows from the attraction between the sexes. The resulting population growth is potentially limited by two checks. "Positive checks" are related to mortality: famine, epidemics, wars, and plagues, such as the Black Death. Positive checks are generally beyond human control. In contrast, "preventive checks" are related to fertility. Since Malthus condemned the use of contraception as immoral, the only remaining remedy was for couples to exercise "moral constraint." For all practical purposes, this meant postponing marriages as long as possible.

Of greater interest today are Malthus's comments about the relationship between population growth and resource (especially food) depletion. Malthus argued that population, if left unchecked, would increase geometrically or exponentially (as in the series 2, 4, 8, 16). Meanwhile, food supply would increase only arithmetically (as in the series 2, 4, 6, 8). Eventually, population would outstrip the food supply, resulting in widespread poverty, hunger, and misery. Malthus concluded that only grinding poverty would ultimately succeed in discouraging people from marrying early and raising large, healthy families.

Karl Marx was one of Malthus's most outspoken critics (Meek, 1971). According to Marx, Malthus was blind to the real cause of excess population: the capitalist economic system. Capitalism, Marx insisted, is organized to keep the working class in a perpetual state of poverty and unemployment. That is because it is to the financial advantage of capitalists to have more workers than jobs. The excess supply of workers

allowed factory and mill owners to keep wages low and easily replace workers who created trouble. Furthermore, it facilitated the maintenance of a "reserve army of labour" that could be expanded or shrunk depending on whether the economy was expanding or in recession. Rapid population growth, then, was less a result of a mismatch between population and resources and more a case of deeply flawed social and economic arrangements.

The contrasting views of Malthus and Marx have reappeared in today's environmental debate. In the 1960s, several authors became widely known for their doomsday scenarios concerning overpopulation and dwindling resources. In the spirit of Malthus, conservation biologist Paul Ehrlich warned in his provocatively titled *The Population Bomb* (1968) that world population was expanding out of control, especially in Asia and Africa. At the same time, he held the unchecked consumption habits of people in the world's rich countries were depleting supplies of food, oil, and water. The result will be catastrophic, Ehrlich predicted. One notable critic of this viewpoint is economist Julian Simon. Simon notes that the price of most resources has been dropping, cities are becoming less polluted, and humans can be counted on to cope with population pressures through their technological ingenuity (Simon and Kahn, 1984).

THE INDUSTRIAL CITY

By the end of the eighteenth century, a new type of city had begun to emerge, first in England and later in continental Europe and America. The *industrial city* was larger, more complex, and more dynamic than any urban settlement that had preceded it. In 1800, more than 50 percent of the population of England and Wales lived in places with 20 000 or more people, compared with only 17 percent in 1700 (Weber, 1963 [1899]: 47). England, however, was the first country to industrialize. Fewer than 10 percent of the world's population lived in urban areas in 1900. In 1950, the figure was about 20 percent (Davis, 1955: 430). After that, the world's urban population exploded (see Figure 16.2).

What contributed to the growth of industrial cities? One popular theory emphasizes advances in transportation and agricultural technology, inasmuch as these factors contributed to the production and movement of agricultural surpluses from farm to city. Among the innovations were better methods of land drainage, the use of fertilizers, methods of seed selection, techniques

FIGURE 16.2   PERCENTAGE URBAN AND CITY SIZE, 1970 AND 2030

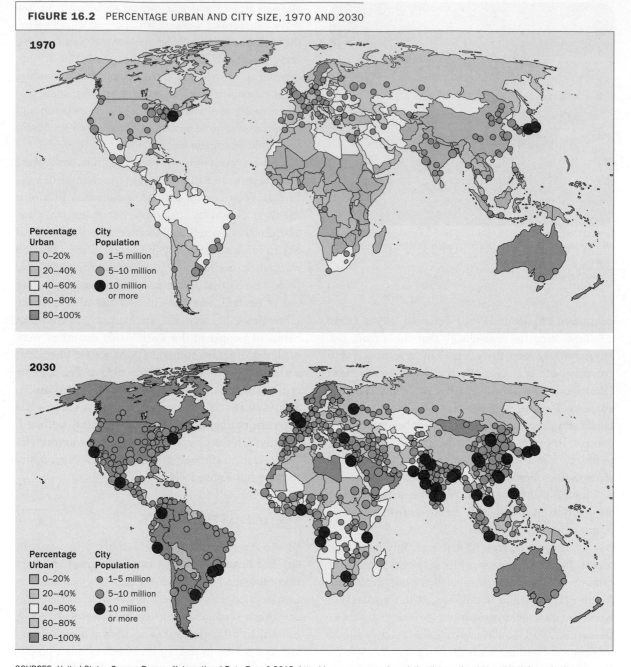

SOURCES: United States Census Bureau, "International Data Base." 2013. http://www.census.gov/population/international/data/idb/informationGateway.php; United Nations, "Percentage Urban and Urban Agglomerations by Size Class." 2014. http://esa.un.org/unpd/wup/Maps/CityDistribution/CityPopulation/CityPop.aspx (accessed Sept. 25, 2015).

of animal breeding, toll-road building, and the application of steam power to farm machinery and rail transport. Other scholars emphasize a boom in trade and commerce, which provided a powerful inducement to greater investment, technological improvements, and, ultimately, increased agricultural productivity.

Another key factor appears to have been a shift in the sources of capital accumulation—that is, how factory owners raised the investment money needed to build and improve their manufacturing facilities. In

England after 1850, capital investment was facilitated by the creation of the joint stock company, a business structure that pooled the capital of many investors and that enjoyed limited liability (the shareholders could not be held personally responsible for enterprises that failed).

Finally, urban growth has been linked to the invention of the factory. Previously, under the "putting-out" system, piecework was done in village or rural cottages and collected at regular intervals by the agents of merchant entrepreneurs. With the advent of the factory system, workers were required to work in a central location. Initially, factories had to be located next to rivers to run directly on water power. Then, as steam-powered machines became the standard, factories concentrated in cities because steam power could not be distributed economically over a wide grid, as electrical systems can be today.

THE DEVELOPMENT OF AN URBAN-INDUSTRIAL ECONOMY IN CANADA

As the twentieth century dawned, Canada had a population of just more than five million, with two-thirds of these people living in rural areas and dependent for their livelihood on farming and the farm economy (Kremarik, 2000: 19). Soon, however, industrial cities began to emerge. Although Toronto and Montreal were the largest industrial centres, factory towns also grew up elsewhere in Ontario, chief among them Windsor, because of its proximity to industry and markets in Detroit, and to Hamilton, because of its port and strategic location on the Great Lakes.

In addition to strategic location, the availability of investment capital played a significant role in directing where industry was established. The Canada Bank Act of 1871 was instrumental in concentrating economic power in a few national metropolitan centres, notably Toronto and Montreal. The act adopted the British model of a branch-banking system wherein a handful of major banks each established a network of branches. In contrast, under the U.S. unit-banking system, many more banks are independent. Investment capital was thus concentrated in a handful of urban centres rather than being widely dispersed across the country (Nader, 1975: 215).

Through various interventions by the federal government—the building of the transcontinental railroad, the imposition of a protective tariff system to encourage domestic manufacturing, a vigorous immigration policy that encouraged agriculture on the Prairies—a system of national economic markets was eventually established. In particular, at the turn of the twentieth century, these interventions found form in the expansion of wheat production for export. With cash from wheat sales jingling in their pockets, Prairie grain farmers were able to purchase manufactured goods from the factories of Ontario and Quebec, thus stimulating a marked upsurge in Canadian urbanization from 1891 to 1911 (Stone, 1967: 20–21). By 1911, four cities had populations exceeding 100 000: Montreal (470 480), Toronto (376 538), Winnipeg (136 035), and Vancouver (100 401). However, the formation of a national market led to the deindustrialization of the Maritime provinces (Brym, 1986).

As the twentieth century progressed, the proportion of the Canadian population classified as "urban" increased dramatically, crossing the 50 percent mark before 1931 and reaching 70 percent in 1961. By 2011, 81 percent of the Canadian population was living in towns and cities (see Figure 16.3).

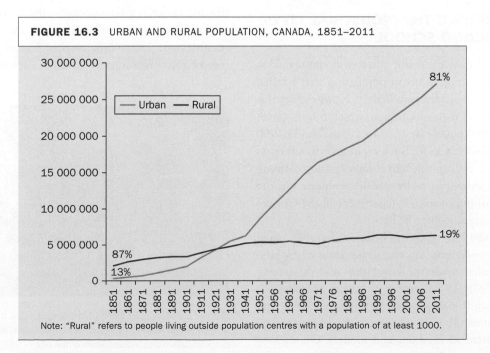

FIGURE 16.3 URBAN AND RURAL POPULATION, CANADA, 1851–2011

Note: "Rural" refers to people living outside population centres with a population of at least 1000.

SOURCE: Adapted from Statistics Canada (2011c).

A handful of large urban regions account for most of the increase in urbanization in recent decades. As of 2011, more than one Canadian in three (35.0 percent) was living in one of the three largest census metropolitan areas (CMAs)—Toronto, Montreal, and Vancouver—and these areas were growing at a faster rate (7.9 percent between 2006 and 2011) than were Canada's other 33 CMAs over the same period. Immigration was largely responsible for this growth pattern (Statistics Canada, 2012a).

A historical analysis of census data reveals interesting differences in the way Canada's largest cities grew at the end of the twentieth century. Net international migration (immigrants minus emigrants) has been the single biggest source of population increase in Toronto: 85 percent of the total between 1991 and 1997, compared with 68 percent in Vancouver. By contrast, migrants from the rest of Canada accounted for 29 percent of Vancouver's growth, whereas Toronto actually lost people to other provinces (2 percent of the city's population). Calgary fired on all cylinders, with natural increase (births minus deaths) accounting for 43 percent, net international immigration for 31 percent, and interprovincial migration for 22 percent of growth (Little, 1999). The last figures reflected the strong growth of Alberta's natural resources sector, coupled with a continuing decline in manufacturing in central Canada.

RESEARCHING THE INDUSTRIAL CITY: THE CHICAGO SCHOOL

By the final quarter of the nineteenth century, U.S. cities were seeing jumps in population that rivalled and even surpassed those in Britain. Nowhere was this more dramatic than in Chicago, which mushroomed from 122 000 people in 1860 to 1.7 million in 1900 and 3.4 million in 1930. Such rapid growth left in its wake social dislocation and human misery. Among those who sought to address these problems was the chairman of the sociology department of the University of Chicago, Robert E. Park.

Park and his colleagues believed that they could improve conditions for the disadvantaged by discovering what made the city "tick" and then using this knowledge to help solve its "social pathologies": crime, juvenile delinquency, family breakdown, and mental illness. To carry out this task, they employed an assortment of methods and models. On the one hand, Park argued that researchers should consider themselves urban anthropologists who would venture out into the field and study the natives and their customs, beliefs, and practices. This inspired a rich ethnographic tradition of urban research in which Park's colleagues and students rendered finely detailed, first-hand accounts of homeless men, gangs, "taxi-dance halls," and so on.

At the same time, Park also urged his students to consider the city of Chicago as a kind of social laboratory in which various natural processes took place. One way of documenting these processes was through the development of urban-growth models (discussed in the next section) by which the changing social and spatial structure of the city could be depicted visually. Another was to use "ecological spot maps" in which differences in the rate of various deviant behaviours, such as juvenile delinquency and schizophrenia, could be plotted geographically to discover underlying patterns. Some of the most memorable work to come out of the Chicago School tradition drew on personal documents and other biographical materials (Zorbaugh, 1929).

To put this mountain of data into some kind of theoretical order, Park and his colleagues used several approaches. First, they tapped into a long tradition of exploring the contrast between rural and urban life. In the latter part of the nineteenth century, German social philosopher Ferdinand Tönnies (1957 [1887]) had attempted to depict the difference between traditional and modern societies by introducing a distinction between a *Gemeinschaft*—the "community of feeling" that exists in villages, tribes, and small communities—and *Gesellschaft*—the characteristic feature of social relations in the city. Tönnies favoured

German philosopher Ferdinand Tönnies contrasted the community of feeling that exists in villages and small communities with the commercialism and individualism of the city.

SOURCE: Sheila Maloney, *Zephyr Ontario*. Courtesy Nancy Poole's Studio.

Gemeinschaft and saw its decline as a loss of all that is natural and satisfying about small-town life. In contrast, he wrote, *Gesellschaft* denotes a lifestyle based on money, commercial contracts, individual interest, and class antagonism. Although he was more positive about the possibilities for individual freedom in modern urban life, German sociologist Georg Simmel (1950) used the same rural–urban contrast to interpret the shift to an urban society.

The rural–urban dichotomy runs through much of Chicago School theorizing. Thomas and Znaniecki (1918–20), for example, depict the city as being responsible for destroying the traditional institutions of peasant life—family, neighbourhood, church—and substituting nothing but an empty well of social disorganization. Freed from the ties that formerly bound the community together, marriages dissolve, teenagers run wild, and even murder is not uncommon.

In his modification of Simmel's social-psychological profile of urban life, Louis Wirth (1938) proposed that the city is characterized by the concurrent trends of increasing size, density, and heterogeneity. In his view, the city creates a distinct way of life—**urbanism**—that is economically efficient but socially destructive. Wirth's list of urban characteristics includes the decline of the family, the disappearance of the neighbourhood, and the undermining of traditional bases of social solidarity. Urbanites are said to be superficial, unable to step outside their narrow occupational roles to relate to people in a holistic and meaningful way, and guided by an all-consuming drive for success and money.

A century later, the rural–urban typology is still pervasive in the popular imagination. In the final weeks of December 2008, the Canadian media featured several stories from the British Columbia interior that accented small-town altruism and solidarity. One of these stories cast the people of McBride, a village hard-hit by mill closings and job losses, as heroes for fighting freezing cold to dig a kilometre-long passageway through massive snowfalls to rescue two trapped and starving horses. In a second, more tragic case, residents of Sparwood, a coal-mining town 300 kilometres southwest of Calgary, came together at a candlelight vigil to remember seven local men who perished in an avalanche during a snowmobile ride in the backcountry. "Each and every one of us know them," Sparwood's mayor told the hundreds of mourners at the vigil (Montgomery, 2008).

By contrast, a 28-year-old man was found dead on Christmas morning in the east Toronto district of Scarborough. According to one press report, no one seemed acquainted with the victim, although a couple of people had heard loud arguments coming from his apartment. The 11-storey block of community housing units where he resided was described as "not a place where tenants know their neighbours" ("Slain Man Mystery to Tenants," 2008).

ECOLOGY OF THE INDUSTRIAL CITY

Industrial cities were also unique in their ecology— that is, their spatial layout, physical structure, and population distribution. To depict the spatial or ecological patterns of the city, a group of sociologists and geographers from the University of Chicago devised a set of urban-growth models in the 1920s and 1930s.

Burgess's **concentric-zone model** conceptualized the expansion of cities as a succession of concentric rings, each of which contained a distinct resident population and type of land use (Burgess, 1961). This concentric model of urban growth identified five zones (see Figure 16.4).

Zone 1, the central business district (CBD), is the commercial pulse of the city. It is the site of the major department stores, live theatres, hotels, banks,

FIGURE 16.4 BURGESS'S CONCENTRIC ZONE MODEL APPLIED TO CHICAGO

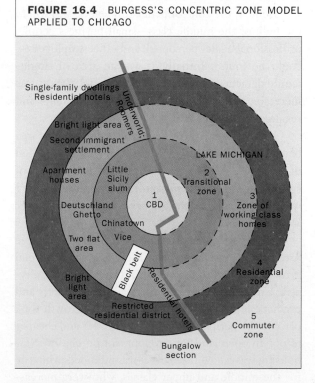

SOURCE: Redrawn from Ernest W. Burgess, "The Growth of the City: An Introduction to a Research Project," in George A. Theodorson, ed., *Studies in Human Ecology* (Evanston, IL: Row, Peterson, 1961), p. 41.

and office space. The land is the most valuable in the city, which means that residential and low-rent commercial uses are inevitably displaced in favour of big-money commercial enterprises.

Zone 2 is called the *zone in transition*. In the 1920s, large parcels of land in Chicago's transitional zone were being held by speculators who expected that the CBD would push outward, making them millionaires. In the meantime, Zone 2 stood as an area of cheap housing that became the initial resting point for each new wave of immigrants who took jobs in the nearby factories. Also located there were a variety of marginal businesses—pawn shops, tattoo parlours, second-hand stores—that could not afford the high rents of the city centre. The transitional zone also attracted a raft of illegal commercial activities—gambling, prostitution, drug dealing—that needed to be accessible to clientele in the CBD but that were considered socially unacceptable in the high-profile heart of the downtown area.

Zone 3, the zone of working-class homes, denotes the area settled by second-generation immigrants and rural migrants. In Burgess's time, Zone 3 was a neighbourhood of semi-detached, two-family homes where fathers still worked in inner-city factories but from which the upwardly mobile children aspired to escape into the middle-class suburban zones.

Zone 4, the zone of better residences, was where the bulk of the middle class—small-business people, professionals, sales personnel, and office employees—could be found. Initially, it was an area of single-family detached houses, but by the mid-1920s, it was increasingly characterized by apartment buildings and residential hotels.

Finally, Zone 5, the commuter zone, was an area beyond the political boundaries of the city composed of satellite towns and suburbs. With the growth of commuter railroads and automobile travel, Zone 5 was a precursor of the suburbs that boomed after World War II.

Burgess's concentric-zone model made three interrelated assumptions. First, all commercial growth was said to emanate from the dominant city-centre nucleus and proceed outward in an orderly and predictable manner. Second, residential growth took place at the periphery, where it was easier and cheaper to obtain open land for development purchases. New housing was added here, but it was intended primarily for the middle and upper classes, who were increasingly able to take advantage of newly constructed commuter rail lines and, later, expressways. Third,

the model was dynamic in that it assumed a sort of filtering-down process. As housing aged, it deteriorated, became less desirable, and was abandoned by better-off citizens, who moved into newer housing farther away from the city centre. The homes they left behind, some of them mansions, were subdivided into rooming houses, flats, and dormitories for artists and students. In recent years, many of these have been restored to a measure of their former glory, either by residential "gentrifiers" or by commercial users, such as restaurateurs or hair stylists. Furthermore, Burgess assumed that, as immigrant newcomers to the industrial city found their balance and began to prosper, they would want to upgrade their housing. For example, the second generation of "white ethnics"—the acculturated sons and daughters of those who had come as part of the Polish, Italian, German, and other European immigration around the turn of the twentieth century—could be expected to settle in the zone of working-class homes, which possessed superior housing to that occupied by their parents in the transitional zone.

Burgess's urban-growth model appears to have fitted Chicago in the 1920s reasonably well but, as a scheme for understanding all cities in different places and times, it is not as successful. First, the notion of a single growth nucleus has not held up. Such cities as Calgary and Edmonton, which developed later in the century and which were shaped largely by the automobile, are more likely to possess more than one nucleus or growth centre. Similarly, Los Angeles is widely known as "the city without a downtown." This was first recognized in the 1940s by geographers Chauncey Harris and Edward Ullman (1945), who proposed a **multiple-nuclei model** of urban growth in which were located a series of growth centres—retail, wholesale, residential—each representing the concentration of a specific function or activity within the urban economy.

Second, Burgess seems to have underestimated the importance of transportation corridors as magnets for urban growth. Geographer Homer Hoyt (1939) developed a **sector model** of urban growth after studying 142 U.S. cities during the Depression years. He argued that cities grew not in concentric circles but in sectors or wedges along major transportation arteries, extending like the tentacles of an octopus from the CBD. Within each sector, the social character of the residential housing would remain constant. For example, upper-income groups would follow a northward progression, and working-class groups a southward path, thereby producing a distinct sectoral pattern to the developing city. Montreal and Vancouver seem to fit this sector model, because their populations tended to spread out along the natural shorelines of the bodies of water on which they are located (Driedger, 1991: 90).

Third, Burgess failed to appreciate that some resident groups would develop strong residential attachments to their neighbourhoods and refuse to move on, even in the face of an aging housing stock. This was first pointed out by Walter Firey (1947) in his study of Boston. Firey gives several examples that span the socioeconomic spectrum, from Beacon Hill, an elite area near the city centre, to the North End, a blue-collar Italian area where the residents chose to remain in their old neighbourhoods because the places were cherished as symbols of the residents' family connections, traditions, and culture.

URBANIZATION OF THE DEVELOPING WORLD

A century ago, most urban growth was concentrated in the rapidly industrializing countries of Europe and North America. Today, nearly two-thirds of the world's urban population resides in the less developed regions of Asia, Oceania, Africa, Latin America, and the Caribbean (Gugler, 1996: vii). In the southern hemisphere, the demographic transition is moving faster and with far greater numbers than those experienced in the past (Ness and Low, 2000). Over the next three decades, cities in the global south are expected to double in size to about 4 billion people, with 19 cities reaching a population of more than 10 million by 2015 (see Figure 16.5).

Cities of the south are often described as victims of **overurbanization.** This means that the population of urban areas is growing faster than the urban economy, services, and resources can absorb it. This creates an underclass of residents who live in illegal squatter settlements and employ themselves in marginal trades, such as selling food and lottery tickets on street corners (Flanagan, 1995: 153). Canadian cities have recently had a taste of this in the form of growing numbers of panhandlers, "squeegee kids," and other homeless urban people, but the numbers in southern cities such as those shown in Figure 16.5 are much larger. With public housing scarce, "squatter settlements" are common. In such settlements, people occupy urban land without legal title, frequently organizing "invasions" at set times and places. Once they have staked out their plots, the squatters put up makeshift shelters and establish basic public services, such as water supply and sewage disposal. Some squatter settlements remain poor, but others significantly upgrade their housing and eventually persuade municipal governments to extend utilities and health and sanitation services into the area.

FIGURE 16.5 MEGACITY GROWTH

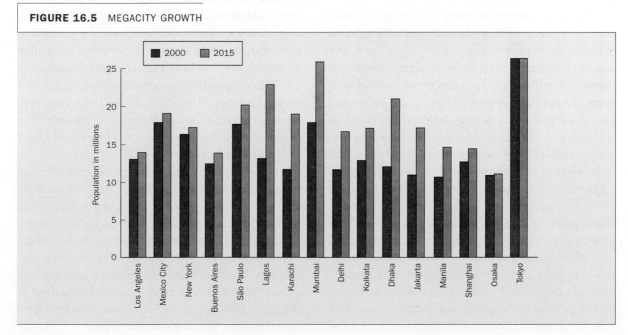

SOURCE: Reprinted by kind permission of the *New Internationalist*. Copyright New Internationalist, www.newint.org.

The concept of overurbanization has provoked debate among social scientists. Some claim that overurbanization is the single most important factor leading to the generation and intensification of serious social problems in southern cities: grinding poverty, mass unemployment, inadequate services, social unrest, increasing crime, and political instability (Smith, 1996: 148). Others claim that it is misleading to isolate the mismatch between demographic growth and employment opportunities, arguing that it makes more sense to look to larger structural factors, such as undue reliance on foreign multinational corporations and continued deep inequality between an urban-based elite and the urban and rural masses.

Finally, sociologists who study urbanization in the south have been much concerned with urban bias, that is, uneven investment and development that favour urban over rural areas. Despite the problems generated by overurbanization, landless migrants continue to flow into cities, which they see as their best chance to improve their lot in life. Economic growth strategies focus primarily on these rapidly growing cities, while the rural hinterland is overlooked. Thus, for the two decades following independence (the 1960s and 1970s), many of Africa's first-generation political leaders penalized agriculture through their monetary and tax policies to obtain resources to finance industrial development in the cities. In addition, public services were concentrated in the large cities, especially national capitals (Lofchie, 1997: 24–25).

Although poverty statistics are not always reliable, data from 2006–07 (ECLAC, 2008, cited in Winchester and Szalachman, 2009: 29) suggest that absolute poverty in rural areas continues to outstrip that found in the cities. For example, in Brazil, where there are notoriously poor slums in Rio de Janeiro and São Paulo, 45.6 percent of the population in rural areas continues to live below the poverty line versus 26.9 percent in the cities. In Mexico, the figures follow the same pattern (40.1 percent in rural areas versus 26.8 percent in cities). Much the same holds for most African nations. India, by contrast, shows more or less comparable levels of poverty in urban and rural areas (Drakakis-Smith, 1988).

While many explanatory factors are the same across urban and rural areas, some key specific attributes of poverty can be found only in cities. In particular, high rates of inequality and unemployment may lead to increases in crime and other forms of social and political conflict, especially for young men. High rates of violence make mobility within the community dangerous, especially in neighbourhoods where gang activity is prevalent (Winchester and Szalachman, 2009: 11).

TIME FOR REVIEW

1. What is the demographic transition?
2. What factors contributed to the rapid growth of industrial cities in the nineteenth and early twentieth centuries?
3. How did Canada's largest cities differ from each other in their pattern of population growth at the end of the twentieth century?
4. What main theoretical and methodological approaches did Robert Park and his colleagues take to study urban life and structures in Chicago in the 1920s and 1930s?
5. How useful is the classic Burgess model in describing historical growth patterns and the present-day shape of the city in which you currently reside or attend university?
6. Why are patterns of urbanization in cities of the southern hemisphere different from those that described industrial cities in Western Europe and North America in the nineteenth and twentieth centuries?

THE CORPORATE CITY

Although the industrial city continued to exist in North America into the 1970s, it began to lose ground after 1945 to a new urban form—the corporate city. Simply defined, the **corporate city** denotes the perception and organization of the city as a vehicle for capital accumulation—that is, as a money-making machine.

The corporate city comprises five major elements (Lorimer, 1978; Reid, 1991): (1) the corporate suburb, (2) the shopping centre, (3) the suburban industrial park, (4) the downtown office tower, and (5) the high-rise apartment building.

Each of these five elements has evolved over the years. Some of the central features have recently changed. Facing the spectre of shopper boredom and increased competition from revitalized downtown retail districts and exurban big-box stores (Home Depot, Costco, Walmart, and the like), shopping centres have been undergoing a redesign that includes a more diverse mix of retail tenants. In the face of changing demographics, suburban developments have also been forced to include a greater variety of housing types, including more townhouses and row houses and such innovations as "granny flats" (separate quarters for aged parents). After years of being half-empty, some downtown office buildings have begun to convert to condominiums. Nevertheless, the process by which the corporate city has been assembled and maintained remains much the same and stands in marked contrast to that which undergirds the building of the industrial city. Nowhere has this been more evident than in the corporate suburb.

THE CORPORATE SUBURB

Before World War II, North American cities such as Toronto were configured in a grid system, with residential avenues crossing long commercial streets at right angles. Since most urban residents lived within a few blocks of neighbourhood stores and services, pedestrian traffic constantly moved up and down the streets. This spawned a lively "front-yard culture" in which passersby regularly interacted with porch sitters, since front yards and families faced the street rather than the house itself (Fowler, 1992: 205).

When cities expanded, they did so incrementally, often a dozen houses at a time. The cost of extending sewers, water lines, and other city services was assumed by the municipality and paid for over 20 or 30 years through tax increases or special bonds. Lots were narrow and houses were two or three storeys high. Parking space was mostly on the street and, as auto ownership spread rapidly, increasingly scarce.

In the early 1950s, all this changed with the building of Don Mills, Canada's first mass suburb, on the northern fringe of Toronto. Don Mills emphasized a system of short curving roads in the form of circles and crescents. Initially, this layout was probably meant to convey a sense of privileged exclusivity, although over time it also came to reflect a desire to shield children from the perceived danger of through-traffic. In any case, it made public transit difficult, consigning buses to main arterial roads on the perimeter of the housing subdivision. Don Mills houses were placed on wider lots with larger setbacks from the streets. With no sidewalks, small front porches, and minimal pedestrian traffic (most residents drove to the nearby Don Mills Plaza to shop), the social action shifted to the fenced-in backyards, which were, in any case, favoured by parents, who appreciated being able to keep an eye on their toddlers from the kitchen window.

Don Mills was one of the first residential areas in Canada to be planned completely from scratch and built all at once. In contrast to the development pattern in the central city, almost all the servicing costs, including that of a sewage treatment plant along the Don River, were assumed by the developer, E. P. Taylor. By doing so, Taylor changed the rules of urban development, relegating the municipality to a more passive role and introducing corporate success as a major planning consideration (Sewell, 1993: 95).

With the triumph of Don Mills, the corporate suburb spread rapidly across Canada and the United States. (The United States had already introduced its own early prototype of a planned, mass-produced suburb in Levittown, Long Island, 32 kilometres from New York City.) Although there were local differences, these first-generation postwar suburbs shared five main characteristics: a peripheral location, relatively low population densities, architectural similarity, a relatively low purchase price for houses, and a fairly high degree of economic and racial homogeneity (Jackson, 1985: 238–43).

Suburbanism as a Way of Life

In the 1950s, the suburbs were routinely disparaged as being sterile social and cultural wastelands where conformity ruled and individual taste and thought were stifled. This notion was given wide exposure in the 1956 best-seller *The Organization Man*, a study of Park Forest, Illinois, 48 kilometres south of Chicago (Whyte, 1956). Suburban dwellers were invariably depicted as living in mass-produced housing that was uniform in design and decoration. This image is bitingly evoked in folk singer Malvina Reynolds's 1950s ditty, "Little Boxes" (Reynolds, 1964: 28):

> Little Boxes on the hillside
> Little Boxes made of ticky tacky,
> Little Boxes on the hillside,
> Little Boxes all the same.

Not only was the physical appearance of suburban areas said to be homogeneous, but life there was also said to revolve around a "dry-martini culture." During the workweek, fathers commuted in car pools or by rail to jobs at IBM, General Motors, and other corporate giants, while mothers ferried the children around in the family station wagon and socialized at coffee parties. On the weekend, the husbands washed the cars and tended well-manicured lawns, while the wives shopped for groceries at nearby plazas. At night, couples socialized in one another's homes, around the pool or the barbecue.

For sociological researchers, **suburbanism** represented an important trend. In a much-quoted 1956 article, "Suburbanism as a Way of Life," Sylvia Fava did a take on Louis Wirth's classic 1938 essay, "Urbanism as a Way of Life." Fava claimed that suburbanites were far more likely than their counterparts in the central city were to be both sociable and socially active. Similarly, in a much-cited before-and-after study of middle-class couples in Toronto who chose to relocate during the early 1970s, Michelson (1973) found that suburban movers increased their involvement with neighbours, while city relocators increased interactions with friends and relatives.

Another key feature of the suburban lifestyle was its emphasis on children and the family. Perhaps the most influential study with regard to the importance of children in suburban communities was that by Seeley and Loosley (1956) in *Crestwood Heights*, a profile of the affluent community of Forest Hill Village in 1950s Toronto. Although Crestwood Heights was more a neighbourhood on the northern edge of the city, its organization around the needs of its children (schools, camps, counselling) was said to be typical of the developing suburbs of the time.

Suburbanism was further depicted as a lifestyle choice rather than a strictly economic decision. City dwellers who packed up and left the central city were said to be embracing a new, family-oriented way of life, seduced by advertisements in the real estate section of the Saturday newspaper promising "bourgeois utopias" (Fishman, 1987). Not all residents, however, embraced this lifestyle with equal enthusiasm. Women in the suburbs frequently felt cut off from the social and cultural stimulation of the central city with its theatres, art galleries, restaurants, and shopping streets. Sociability in the corporate suburb was restricted to private gatherings in the home or the backyard with neighbours. Not surprisingly, a number of researchers found that women were less satisfied than their husbands were with their choice of residence, often having a sense of stagnation and isolation despite relatively frequent visiting and entertaining (Michelson, 1973).

Significantly, this lifestyle did not appear to be replicated in working-class suburbs, where people's values and social behaviours remained firmly anchored in blue-collar culture. Berger (1960) refers to the myth of suburbia, by which he means a standardized and stereotyped view of the suburbs as uniformly middle-class, homogeneous, conformist, child-centred, female-dominated hotbeds of sociability.

It is possible to discern three alternative interpretations of the relationship between suburban residence and lifestyle patterns (McGahan, 1995: 232–36).

According to the *structural* interpretation, the environmental and demographic characteristics of the suburb encourage a distinct style of life. For example, by excluding stores and services, such as restaurants, bars, and movie theatres, from residential neighbourhoods and by discouraging public transit, the Don Mills model promoted greater reliance on private sociability, as evidenced by the weekday morning coffee klatches and weekend pool parties that came to be identified with suburban life in the 1950s and 1960s.

In contrast, the *selective migration* interpretation denies that the suburban environment exercises any independent effect on behaviour patterns. Rather, it is suggested that those who chose to move to the corporate suburbs after World War II were already primed to embrace **familism**—a lifestyle that places a high value on family living, marriage at a young age, a brief period of childlessness after marriage, and child-centredness of the type that Seeley and his colleagues observed in Crestwood Heights (Bell, 1968: 147).

Finally, the *class and life-cycle* interpretation proposes that what Berger had branded the "suburban myth" was nothing more than a snapshot of middle-class life at mid-century. Today, many of the same characteristics—child-centredness, commuting, backyard culture—can be observed in the second wave of gentrification in the central city. As the corporate suburb matured, it changed appreciably, with a new set of social activities replacing those that had prevailed at an earlier stage in the life cycle of both the suburb and the families who settled there. Whether it was the Don Mills-style suburb or downtown office towers, the corporate city did not just happen. It was the deliberate product of an alliance between government and business interests.

Logan and Molotch (1987) have termed this alliance an **urban-growth machine**, a loosely structured coalition of local economic and political interest groups with a commitment to sustained growth and development. Urban-growth machines can include an extensive cast of players: businesses, property owners, investors and developers, politicians and planners, the media, utilities, cultural institutions (museums, theatres), professional sports teams, labour unions, and even universities. Growth machines pursue a narrow band of interests, sacrificing the sentimental and symbolic value of places—which is associated with jobs, neighbourhood, hometown, and community—in favour of a strict emphasis on land use as an investment and commodity to be bought and sold (Palen, 1995: 20) Although government and business may honestly believe that local communities thrive only if they continue to expand economically, it could also be said that the structure that growth machines impose on urban living gives people a minimum of freedom to live their lives in the corporate city as they choose (Lorimer, 1978: 220).

TIME FOR REVIEW

1. What are the five major elements that together comprise the corporate city?
2. What are the key features of the suburban lifestyle as it developed in the 1950s and 1960s?
3. What are the three alternative interpretations of the relationships between suburban residence and lifestyle patterns? Which of these is most convincing?
4. How are the suburbs today different from the corporate suburbs described in this section? In what ways are they similar?

THE POSTMODERN CITY

In recent years, a new kind of urban form has appeared on the global landscape: the postmodern city. Although there is some debate over what exactly is meant by this term, several aspects seem clear.

First, the postmodern city is the product of the simultaneous operation of the forces of re-urbanization and counter-urbanization. Counter-urbanization occurs when people move from central cities and inner suburbs into the surrounding rural hinterland (Berry and Gillard, 1977). Writing a quarter-century ago, respected Canadian urban planner Hans Blumenfeld (1982, 1983) ventured that, if sustained, counter-urbanization might well result in a new urban form—the exurb. A decade later, exurbs in Canada and the United States were already home to nearly 60 million people, making them the fastest-growing component of the continental landscape (Davis, Nelson, and Dueher, 1994). Initially entirely residential, exurbs today are increasingly likely to take the form of edge cities that include significant commercial, leisure, and entertainment components.

At the same time, the central city has been staging a comeback from the dismal days of the 1960s and 1970s, an era in which it was effectively abandoned by middle-class families who moved in large numbers to the corporate suburbs. In part this re-urbanization of inner city districts reflects the continuing gentrification of older neighbourhoods. Additionally, however, it has been powered by the migration of immigrants from around the world (Fishman, 2005).

Second, cities are becoming multiethnic, with many ethnic neighbourhoods in the largest cities becoming home to visible minority groups. This development is generating racial and ethnic residential and commercial patterns that stand in marked contrast to the ecology of the industrial city. These new urban settlers can be found both in suburban subdivisions and in inner-city precincts. In Toronto, most of the recent growth in the foreign-born population has occurred in the "905" area—the ring of satellite towns and cities, named after the telephone area code, that surrounds the urban core. For example, Brampton to the northwest of Toronto, once a symbol of small-town Ontario conservatism, attracted 42 900 immigrants between 2001 and 2006, roughly a tenth of all newcomers to the Toronto metropolitan area. Two-thirds of the new residents came from three countries: India, Pakistan, and the Philippines. In Vancouver, many recent immigrants headed for the suburban municipalities of Richmond, Burnaby, and Surrey. In Richmond, foreign-born people, about half from the People's Republic of China, made up 57.4 percent of the population in 2006, the highest proportion of those born elsewhere in all of Canada's municipalities (Statistics Canada, 2008).

Third, the postmodern city is characteristically fragmented, even chaotic. Elizabeth Wilson (1991: 136) describes it as resembling "a split screen flickering with competing beliefs, cultures and 'stories.'" Geographically and socially split, the postmodern city does not have a single "way of life" of the sort identified by Wirth for the industrial city and Fava for the corporate suburb.

Finally, the postmodern city is characterized by the privatization of publicly owned space. Privatization occurs across a wide spectrum of settings, from downtown malls and festival marketplaces to private, gated communities on the fringes of the city. Although suburban dwellers have always put a premium on private space, from the enclosed backyard to the car in the drive-in theatre, this value is now washing over the city as a whole and, in the process, drastically reducing the number of publicly owned places where people can come together to shop or socialize (Goldberger, 1996: 139).

While some urban observers have applauded the changing contours of the postmodern city, especially those associated with re-urbanization, others have expressed serious reservations. In particular, they have displayed considerable unease over the escalating "suburbanization" of the inner city.

The postmodern city is characterized by the privatization of public space, as shown in this mall scene.

SOURCE: © Norman Chan/Shutterstock.

We next examine three overlapping components of the postmodern city: the edge city, the multiethnic city, and the dual city. Although each component has real-life spatial and demographic components, none exists in pure form. Instead, they are constructs, formulated by academic researchers or journalists, that help us visualize an important dimension of the globalized, privatized, and fragmented postmodern city.

THE EDGE CITY

Although they differed significantly in their patterns of housing, transportation, and shopping, the industrial city and the corporate city displayed more or less the same spatial configuration: an urban core containing the bulk of the office space, cultural institutions, factories, and a ring of suburbs where much of the more affluent middle class resided. Even with the growth of shopping centres and industrial parks in the 1950s and 1960s, the lion's share of jobs and services remained within the city itself, and suburbanites were daily commuters.

During the past quarter-century, however, this traditional pattern has been turned inside out with the rapid growth of **edge cities** (Garreau, 1991). Situated in exurbia—the rural residential area around the suburbs within commuting range of the city—edge cities have no dominant single core or definable set of boundaries; they are typically "clusters of malls, office developments and entertainment complexes that rise where major highways cross or converge" (Fishman, 1990: 18). Some edge cities are expansions of existing satellite cities, but others sprout up in unincorporated townships, lacking clearly definable borders and legal status as places (Palen, 1995: 187).

What has led to the growth of edge cities? Leinberger and Lockwood (1986) offer five reasons for edge cities' recent emergence. First, there has been a major shift in North American economies from manufacturing to a service and knowledge base. One result of this shift is that middle-class employees are now more willing to live near where they work than they used to be when jobs were located in factories that were dirty, noisy, and unattractive. An example of the older pattern can be found in Ontario's steel industry, where the managers and executives at Stelco and Dofasco traditionally settled on the other side of the Skyway Bridge in Burlington, while the mill workers remained in Hamilton. In contrast, Kanata, the outer suburban location of Ottawa's microchip computer industry, is solidly middle class.

Second, there have been significant changes in transportation patterns that favour trucks and cars over subways, streetcars, and trains. As a result, urban facilities have scattered over the exurban landscape, unfettered by the requirement of locating along established transportation corridors.

Third, recent advances in telecommunications technology have reduced the necessity for offices to locate downtown in close physical proximity. Some types of businesses—stock brokerages, banks—still prefer to be close to one another and to central city services. However, the tremendous growth of technology, such as fax machines, cellular phones, and email, has geographically freed many employees whose linkages to the workplace are now activated on the road or from home offices.

Fourth, as it has become increasingly expensive to operate in the city, offices, industries, and professional practitioners (lawyers, accountants, and so on) have pulled up their roots and moved to less expensive locations. Among other things, parking is more plentiful and less expensive out of the city.

Fifth, the coming of age of dual-income, baby-boom families with one or two children has meant that people's lives are increasingly governed by considerations of time, convenience, and efficiency. The

The tremendous growth of technology, such as fax machines, cellphones, and email, has geographically freed many employees whose linkages to the workplace are now activated on the road or from home offices.
SOURCE: © Jupiter Images.

clustering of offices, shopping centres, and recreational facilities at the juncture of exurban highways meets the needs of this subpopulation, the members of which have little time in their lives to commute downtown to shop, eat, or be entertained.

These changes have shown up in new patterns of commuting to work in large urban areas. In Canada, census data from 1996 and 2001 already pointed to several significant trends (Heisz and LaRochelle-Coté, 2005: 16). First, the number of workers who commute within a suburb or across the city from suburb to suburb has risen appreciably. Second, the growth of "reverse commuters" (those who travel from the city centre to the suburbs) has uniformly outstripped that of traditional commuters (those who travel from outside to inside the city centre).

Edge cities have been of particular interest to urban sociologists because they are neither suburbs nor centralized cities but a hybrid that incorporates elements of each. Unlike the typical suburb, which is primarily residential, edge cities contain many of the functions of the traditional city: shopping, office space, housing, entertainment facilities. Also, in contrast to suburbanites, who commute to work in the central city by rail or car, edge-city residents are inclined to live and work in the same geographic area. Commuting now means driving to an adjoining suburb or exurb rather than heading downtown. This can be seen in the "905" belt surrounding Metro Toronto, where a number of areas now function as "magnets." That is, more people travel to jobs there each day than journey out of the community to jobs elsewhere in the Greater Toronto Area. Finally, in

contrast to the typical suburb, which lacks a well-developed infrastructure of sports, entertainment, and cultural facilities, the edge city is increasingly the site of a burgeoning number of performing arts centres, sports arenas, and entertainment complexes.

Nevertheless, it would be wrong to think that there are no real differences between edge cities and older cities. Unlike the industrial city, the edge city lacks a single centre. In the former, it was always possible to start downtown and eventually reach the outer boundaries of the city. In contrast, the spatial logic of the edge city dictates that centres and boundaries are not needed. Instead, the edge city is made up of three overlapping types of socioeconomic networks: household networks, networks of consumption, and networks of production. Each of these runs on the guiding principle of convenience. Two-income families with children, who make up the largest demographic segment of the edge-city population, are increasingly pressed for time and, as a result, frequently create their own "personal cities" out of the destinations they can reach within a manageable time (Fishman, 1990).

THE MULTIETHNIC CITY

According to Statistics Canada's population projections, by 2031, 31 percent of Canada's population is likely to consist of visible minority group members (Statistics Canada, 2010). This contrasts with 13 percent in 2001 and less than 5 percent in 1981 (Bélanger and Malenfant, 2005). Just over 71 percent of visible minority people are expected to reside in the CMAs of Montreal, Toronto, and Vancouver. By 2031, it is estimated that the visible minority population will account for 63 percent of Toronto's population, up from 43 percent in 2006. In Vancouver, this figure will reach a comparable level (nearly 60 percent). In Montreal, visible minorities will constitute a lower proportion of the urban population (31 percent), although this is still nearly double the 2006 number (16 percent; see Table 16.1). This new demographic makeup has important implications for our understanding of contemporary urban structures and processes (Fong and Shibuya, 2005).

In particular, we are likely to witness the growth of a new generation of residentially segregated neighbourhoods (Fong, 1996; Fong and Wilkes, 1999). Whereas newcomers from Northern and Western European nations tended to blend in residentially with Canadians from the charter groups (British and French), members of most Asian ethnic groups are likely to cluster together, apart from other groups.

TABLE 16.1 PROPORTION OF FOREIGN-BORN AND VISIBLE MINORITY POPULATIONS BY CENSUS METROPOLITAN AREA, 2006 AND 2031 (SELECTED CANADIAN CITIES)

	FOREIGN-BORN (PERCENTAGE OF TOTAL POPULATION)		VISIBLE MINORITY (PERCENTAGE OF TOTAL POPULATION)	
	2006	2031	2006	2031
Canada	20	26	16	31
Census metropolitan area				
Toronto	46	50	43	63
Vancouver	40	44	42	59
Montreal	21	30	16	31
Ottawa-Gatineau (Ottawa part)	22	29	19	36
Calgary	24	30	22	38
Edmonton	19	22	17	29
Hamilton	24	27	12	25
Winnipeg	18	24	15	27
Windsor	23	28	16	33
Kitchener	23	28	14	28

SOURCE: Adapted from Statistics Canada (2010).

The evidence so far indicates that these visible minority neighbourhoods are formed when residents who are not visible minority members move out as large numbers of a visible minority group move into the neighbourhood (Hou and Picot, 2004). (See the Critical Sociology: Globalization box.)

THE DUAL CITY

With the edge city increasingly becoming the occupational, residential, and commercial centre for the middle classes, what has become of urban downtowns? The central city, some analysts suggest, has become polarized between two starkly different realities that are spatially discrete and have only the name of the city and some public places in common. Situated just blocks or streets away from one another, the city of despair and squalor and the city of hope and splendour are light years apart. This split reality has been called the *dual city*. The term **dual city** has come to refer to the urban expression of two increasingly divergent streams in the global economy. On the one

hand, there is an information-based, formal economy rooted in financial services, telecommunications, and the microchip. Typically, those who are part of this upper-tier informational city live in a world of computer software, fax machines, cellphones, and Internet surfing. Residentially, they can be found in "gentrified" niches of the inner city (gentrification is discussed below) or in exclusive suburbs, where they isolate themselves both socially and geographically from the rest of the city. These spaces constitute a microsociety with their own separate circuit of leisure, lifestyle, and services (Castells, 1989).

On the other hand, juxtaposed to the informational city is an "informal economy" that has been excluded from the main loop. Residents here rely not on high-technology communications but on face-to-face social networks, usually established on the basis of shared race and ethnicity. People are engaged in a wide range of activities, from labouring in immigrant sweatshops in the clothing trade to offering such services as furniture making, home renovation, and auto repairs (Gordon and Sassen, 1992). Although this informal

CRITICAL SOCIOLOGY: GLOBALIZATION   **MULTIETHNIC IMMIGRANT NEIGHBOURHOODS IN CANADIAN SUBURBS**

Contrary to the classic urban-growth model proposed by the Chicago School's human ecologists, the postmodern city doesn't exhibit a simple pattern of first-generation immigrant settlement in the zone of transition adjacent to the commercial core. Using data from New York and Los Angeles, sociologists have distinguished between two very different types of ethnic communities: the traditional immigrant enclave with dense concentrations of immigrants and high levels of poverty and other urban problems, and the more desirable ethnic neighbourhood whose residents are much better endowed both financially and socially (Logan, Alba, and Zhang, 2002). This dual pattern is especially evident in suburban neighbourhoods in major Canadian cities.

Whereas some groups, notably the Chinese, settle in suburban neighbourhoods to take advantage of a more plentiful supply of new owner-occupied housing, others with fewer resources come for affordable subsidized social housing (Bourne, 1996). What is less well understood is the nature of social relations among multiple minority groups in a multiethnic context and how these relationships shape urban structures and processes between minority groups and members of charter groups (Fong and Shibuya, 2005). One thing we do know is that relatively little overlap exists in the minority neighbourhoods of different groups. In 2001, for example, among the 135 visible minority neighbourhoods in Toronto, only in three did both Chinese and South Asians combined represent at least 30 percent of the neighbourhood population (Hou and Picot, 2004: 11).

Critical Thinking Question

How does the dual pattern of immigrant settlement undercut the classic Chicago School ecological model, which predicted that each newly arrived ethnic group would eventually be brought into the wider society as group members established themselves economically and socially?

economy cannot be equated with urban poverty per se, its participants stand relatively little chance of ever penetrating the upper-tier information economy.

Gentrification

In the 1970s and 1980s, considerable attention was paid by urban researchers to the phenomenon of **gentrification** in the dual city. By gentrification, I mean the transformation of working-class housing into fashionable downtown neighbourhoods by middle- and upper-income newcomers. Gentrification is neither anticipated nor accounted for by the ecological growth models discussed previously. Similarly, it runs counter to predictions about mass flight to the suburbs that dominated urban sociology in the 1950s and 1960s. A comparison of the suburban lifestyle and the postmodern urban lifestyle as typified by gentrification is set out in Table 16.2.

TABLE 16.2 COMPARISON OF SUBURBAN AND POSTMODERN URBAN LIFESTYLES

	SUBURBAN	POSTMODERN GENTRIFIED URBAN
Neighbourhood social involvement	Deliberate and sustained	Incidental
Lifestyle focus	Family	Consumerism
Typical activities	Home activities (gardening, entertaining)	Dining out, shopping
Typical occupation of resident	Middle manager	Architect, corporate lawyer, etc.
Housing type	Split-level, detached	Victorian, semi-detached
Social composition	Class-exclusive	Socially and culturally diverse
Ideology	Anti-urban	Pro-urban

SOURCE: John A. Hannigan, *Current Sociology* (43, 1), pp. 173–182, copyright © 1995 by SAGE. Reprinted by Permission of SAGE.

Four primary explanations for gentrification have been advanced (Ley, 1991: 182–85). First, demographic changes led to gentrification in the 1970s and 1980s. At the time, baby boomers who were born and raised in the suburbs began to look for housing of their own. Facing high demand and short supply, they turned to inner-city housing, which was inexpensive but in dire need of rehabilitation. They opposed demolition, favoured by urban-renewal advocates.

Unlike suburban settlers in the previous period, many of these urban migrants were childless and career-oriented. This meant that schools, playgrounds, and parks were not their major concerns and they were happy with smaller housing units lacking the big backyards and basement recreation rooms that were characteristic of Don Mills-type housing. Since many of these young professionals worked downtown, they were willing to trade space for proximity to their places of employment and to downtown cultural and entertainment facilities.

Second, gentrification may be accounted for by economic changes related to the flow of capital in and out of the housing market. In this view, gentrification functions as a "back to the city movement by capital, not people" (Smith, 1979). As you have seen, in the 1950s and 1960s, financial capital flowed into the building of the suburbs under the guidance of governments that viewed the construction of large-scale projects by development companies as the fastest, most efficient way of coping with the pressures created by the baby boom. Developers were encouraged by an array of incentives: tax breaks, government-backed mortgages, guarantees, and insurance with low premiums. By the 1970s, the profit levels in suburban building had begun to shrink, and capital flow switched back to the urban centre to take advantage of the rent gap—that is, the difference between the current value of land in its "depressed" state and the value that could be charged given a better land use (Smith and LeFaivre, 1984).

Third, middle-class newcomers to the central city arrived in search of a lifestyle that was more distinctive and cosmopolitan than that available within the constraints of suburban conformity. In the central city, they could express a distinctive aesthetic and style of consumption, characterized by a dislike of mass-produced goods and a penchant for objects and buildings from a bygone era, notably the Victorian age (Filion, 1991: 554). This new lifestyle also extended to the surrounding neighbourhood, which filled up with wine bars, California-style restaurants, franchise coffee outlets, and trendy boutiques.

A fourth explanation of gentrification looks to the kinds of changes in the urban economy that were described at the beginning of the section on the dual city. With the tremendous boom in jobs in advanced service industries, such as those connected to the "globalized information economy," there has been a dramatic increase in the number of well-paying occupations located downtown. This growth has, in turn, produced a pool of middle-class workers interested in trying the experience of inner-city living.

It should be emphasized that the image of gentrifiers as returning from the suburbs is false; gentrification is, in fact, a "stay in the city" rather than a "back to the city" movement (Wittberg, 1992: 27). Ley (1991: 186) cites data from Canadian cities that indicate that only 2 to 3 percent of a sample of households moving into Toronto's Don Vale neighbourhood between 1966 and 1976 originated in the suburbs. Similarly, a high percentage of those in Ottawa's Centretown (55 percent); Vancouver's False Creek (78 percent); and Montreal's Milton-Parc, Plateau Mont-Royal, and Papineau (79 percent) neighbourhoods had previous addresses in the central city. This research suggests that gentrifiers are devoted to an inner-city lifestyle, even when they have reached a stage in the life cycle where they might have predictably moved to the suburbs.

Among those most likely to settle in gentrified areas of the inner city are women. Summarizing the evidence available from these studies, Warde (1991: 228) lists the following as typical of gentrified enclaves:

> ... a female population increasing faster than the male population; an unusually high proportion of young and single women; very high proportions of women in professional and technical occupations; high levels of academic credentials; a high proportion of dual-earner households, but few nuclear families; presence of young professional women; and the postponement of marriage and childbearing.

Why do gentrified neighbourhoods appeal to the women described by Warde? One explanation is that inner-city communities help to relieve some of the pressures of women's dual roles as both members of the paid labour force and mothers of young children. The advantages include relatively cheap housing, public transit, and readily available child-care and social-support systems. Travel time is an especially important consideration. Female gentrifiers tend to have jobs in downtown office buildings, so inner-city housing allows them to lead their lives on a tight schedule, with such services as shopping, schools, day-care, and medical clinics located nearby. In contrast, suburban residence requires long daily commutes, especially when the weather is bad, as well as the devotion of a good share of leisure time to travelling to widely scattered stores and services. Gentrification thus represents an environmental solution to a potential set of social problems (Rose, 1984: 66).

At the same time, gentrification produces its own set of social problems. By definition, gentrification involves the displacement of existing working-class residents by middle-class "settlers" (see the Critical Sociology: Social Inequality box).

Private Communities

In recent years, another phenomenon—the rise of private communities—has been embraced by an even greater number of middle-class homeowners than has gentrification. Located in the newer suburbs and in edge cities, private communities compete with central

---

CRITICAL SOCIOLOGY: SOCIAL INEQUALITY   THE WALLS WERE THEIRS TO WRITE ON

This article appeared in the *Toronto Star* in November 2014.

On the morning of the last day, with belongings packed up and stowed away, Yvette stood in her home and wondered how to say goodbye.

Her daughter had the answer.

"Why don't we write something on the walls?"

Their building, a Toronto Community Housing Corporation [TCHC] townhouse unit in Regent Park, was set to be torn down as part of the "revitalization" of the neighbourhood. They had lived in the row of homes at 44 Wyatt since around 2001. Surely the walls were theirs to write on.

"Go for it," Yvette told her daughter. Then she grabbed a marker too.

The building has since been demolished, with nothing left but the pits of the basements where their home once stood.

But at first, just the walls of the structure had been ripped off, leaving a jagged, half-standing hulk near River St. and Dundas St. E.

And the messages left by Yvette and her family were visible from the street.

"Love this house." Yvette's youngest daughters wrote on their pink bedroom wall.

Yvette herself, in her own room, scrawled: "May God bless us all in our new home." She drew a smiley face for punctuation.

"I moved here when I was expecting my second child," said Yvette, who has three kids of her own and two step-kids.

"My girls, they know no other home than this home."

After 13 years in their four-bedroom low-income townhouse in the east-side downtown neighbourhood, the family was forced to pack up and leave when the TCHC turned over the property to a developer working on the latest phase of the decades-long Regent Park Revitalization project. Dilapidated buildings are gradually being razed and replaced by mixed-income housing, new space for businesses, a community centre, pool and athletic facilities, all connected fully to the city's normal street grid. ...

But like many of the 7,500 TCHC tenants who lived in the old Regent Park, Yvette and her family had to relocate, at least for a while, to new digs elsewhere in the city, which the housing agency co-ordinated through a lottery system.

"I liked living (in Regent Park)," Yvette told the *Star*.

"It was a neighbourhood that could be extremely dangerous, but at the same time, us as neighbours, we took care of each other." ...

Critical Thinking Questions

1. Are the losses incurred by "revitalizing" neighbourhoods like Regent Park outweighed by what is gained?

2. If you were Yvette, what would you have written on the walls of your home at 44 Wyatt before leaving forever?

cities for residents, offering as incentives a homogeneous middle-class population, physical security, stable housing values, local control, and freedom from exposure to the social problems of the inner city. In the United States, nearly 4 million residents are estimated to live in access-controlled developments (Sanchez, Lang, and Dhavale, 2005), and another 28 million in areas governed by private community associations. In Canada, although there are some gated communities around Toronto and cities in British Columbia's Okanagan Valley, the majority can be found in rural areas, usually in vacation, resort, or retirement sites. Only a small percentage of these are equipped with the guards and video surveillance that are more standard in gated projects in the United States (Grant, 2005).

In her detailed case studies of 10 gated communities in British Columbia, Ontario, and Nova Scotia, Grant (2005) found that the residents were less likely than their equivalents in other countries, such as the United States and Brazil, to cite security concerns as the major reason for moving there. Rather, they were in search of a privileged enclave where they could separate themselves from younger generations (many were seniors and empty nesters) and those who are less well off. The gates, Grant concludes, "function to secure homogeneity within a wider context of urban diversity" (p. 309).

The Fortress City

At the same time as middle-class homeowners are barricading themselves in private gated communities, the public–private partnerships that increasingly dictate what happens to postmodern cities are said to be systematically privatizing and militarizing public space to secure it against the homeless and the poor. Emerging from such alliances is the "fortress city" in which the urban disadvantaged are isolated socially and spatially from office workers, tourists, and suburban day trippers.

The fortress city has been described in *City of Quartz*, Mike Davis's (1990) sweeping examination of present–day Los Angeles. Los Angeles, Davis notes, is a city obsessed with urban security. What passes for a downtown, a series of billion-dollar, block-square megastructures around Bunker Hill, has been insulated by removing almost all pedestrian linkages to the poor immigrant neighbourhoods that surround it on every side. To make public facilities and spaces as unlivable as possible for the homeless and the poor, the city is engaged in a virtual war against them. Tactics and defences include the establishment of barrel-shaped, "bum-proof" bus benches that make sleep impossible, the random deployment of outdoor overhead

sprinklers in Skid Row Park to discourage overnight camping, and the removal of public toilets and washrooms in areas patronized by vagrants. To secure its garbage, one popular seafood restaurant has spent $12 000 to build a "bag-lady-proof trash cage" out of three-quarter-inch steel rods with alloy locks and vicious curved spikes. To cope with a burgeoning inmate population, law-enforcement agencies are building downtown jails and prisons designed by celebrity architects to look like hotels, convention centres, or office buildings, thus camouflaging their real purpose.

Nor is the fortress city restricted to Los Angeles. In the late 1970s, Henry Ford II persuaded the heads of 50 large corporations in Detroit to put equity capital into the Renaissance Center, a $357-million megaproject along the Detroit River opposite Windsor, Ontario. Poorly planned, the hotel–office venture resembles a castle with virtually invisible pedestrian entrances. It is cut off from downtown Detroit by a wide road and railroad tracks. It stands as a "symbol of isolation: an extreme case of a self-contained, inward-facing complex, surrounded by fortress-like two-story walls covering the heating and ventilating equipment" (Frieden and Sagalyn, 1989: 222). In 1996, General Motors purchased the Renaissance Center and moved its corporate headquarters there. Over the next decade, GM completed an extensive renovation that cost $1 billion. On the Jefferson Avenue side, the concrete berms that cut off the buildings from the sidewalk were removed, and a more pedestrian-friendly glass entryway installed. Most of the changes, however, were on the Detroit River side, where a five-storey Wintergarden atrium and the Detroit Riverwalk were constructed.

TIME FOR REVIEW

1. What are the four identifying characteristics of the postmodern city?
2. What led to the growth of edge cities and how did they turn inside out the traditional spatial patterns associated with both the industrial and the corporate city?
3. How do the different realities of the dual city represent the urban expression of two divergent streams in the contemporary global economy?
4. How do the suburban and the postmodern gentrified urban lifestyles differ?
5. What are the four primary explanations for the process of gentrification?
6. In what ways are the urban disadvantaged isolated socially and spatially from the middle-class in the fortress city?

A homeless person carrying her cat is evicted from her dwelling in the shantytown near Toronto's waterfront on September 24, 2002. Home Depot, the company that owns the land, requested that police remove the squatters. (See the Critical Sociology: Protest and Policy box.)
SOURCE: © The Canadian Press/Paul Chiasson.

CRITICAL SOCIOLOGY: PROTEST AND POLICY   TENT CITY EVICTION

The clash between the guardians of the fortress city and the urban poor was highlighted in the "Tent City Eviction" in Toronto. Tent City was a two-hectare plot of polluted, abandoned industrial land near the shore of Lake Ontario. For five years, as many as 110 residents had been squatting on the waterfront property owned by big-box building supplies store Home Depot, making it Canada's largest homeless community. After a high-profile story in the *New York Times* described the site, which seemed to be increasingly hosting prostitution and drug-dealing activities, Home Depot abandoned any further pursuit of plans to erect safe, affordable housing and, in September 2002, sent in private security guards accompanied by police to evict the squatters. Guards were posted and the former residents were given 72 hours to retrieve their belongings.

Supporters of the eviction cited the public health risks associated with the site: contaminated soil, an insufficient number of portable toilets, and inconsistent garbage collection and water supply. Yet, as Marybeth McTeague observed, "Contrary to suggestions by its detractors, Tent City was not a shantytown constructed to promote a political agenda nor a place for partying dropouts. However makeshift, it was a community, a neighbourhood, a collection of homes assembled by people with nowhere else to go" (McTeague, 2002).

Critical Thinking Questions

1. Do you think the risks associated with the Tent City site justified shutting it down and evicting the residents?

2. How does the Tent City case in Toronto compare to the squatter settlements that are common in cities of the southern hemisphere?

SUMMARY

1. **What do many sociologists consider to be the main differences between urban and rural or small-town life?**
Many sociologists claim that urban life is more impersonal, stressful, and alienating than rural life is. They describe urban dwellers as more preoccupied with efficiency, making money, and getting ahead.

2. **What are the three lenses through which sociologists have viewed urban life?**
Sociologists have viewed urban life through environmental opportunity theory (which holds that people choose where to live consistent with their preferred life styles); through demography (which looks at the size, distribution, and composition of human populations); and through an examination of the effects on cities of extra-local economic arrangements, notably the emergence of a globalized economy.

3. **Why were cities incapable of supporting more than 5 per cent of a societal population before the nineteenth century? How did this change during the Industrial Revolution?**
Agricultural surpluses in preindustrial cities were not large enough to feed an urban population of significant size. Additionally, high mortality rates, especially among infants and children, depressed population growth. In the first stages of industrialization, death rates fell due to advances in sanitation, public health, and medicine. The discovery and practical application of steam power facilitated the creation of food surpluses, the building of railroads, and the introduction of new manufacturing methods, notably the factory system.

4. **How did Thomas Malthus and Karl Marx differ in their explanations of human overpopulation?**
Malthus argued that while food supplies increase slowly, populations grow quickly. Because of this presumed natural law, only war, pestilence, and famine can keep human population growth in check. In contrast, Marx argued that overpopulation is not a problem of too many people. Instead, it is a problem of too much poverty. Marx said that if the exploitation of workers under capitalism is ended, poverty will disappear along with the overpopulation problem.

5. **How does the contrast between rural and urban life described in the first answer in this summary inform much of the theory and research of the Chicago School of urban sociology?**
In key contributions by Park, Thomas and Zaniecki, and Wirth, the city is held responsible for destroying the traditional institutions of family, neighbourhood, and church, substituting a distinct way of life, urbanism, that is economically efficient but socially destructive. Park and his colleagues thought that by understanding what made the city run, people could act to combat social disorganization and rebuild urban society.

6. **How do the megacities of the southern hemisphere differ from the industrial cities of the West that emerged in the late nineteenth and early twentieth centuries?**
In contrast to the rise of the city in Western Europe and North America, cities of the south have grown at a much faster pace than the industrial economy. The resulting "overurbanization" has accelerated problems of poverty and unemployment, which are rooted in uneven development and inequality.

7. **What did the corporate city of the 1950s and 1960s look like?**
The corporate city of the 1950s and 1960s was the product of an urban-growth machine in which a coalition of politicians, planners, real-estate developers, business people, and other interest groups joined forces to engineer economic development and progress. The main products of this alliance were corporate suburbs, shopping centres, suburban industrial parks, downtown office towers, and high-rise apartment buildings.

8. **How have urban sociologists accounted for the distinct character of suburban life in the mid-twentieth century?**
Three theories—structural, selective migration, and class and life-cycle stage—have been proposed to explain the relationship between suburban residence and lifestyle patterns. Although all three have merit, the suburban way of life observed by many researchers in the 1950s and 1960s appears to have been a unique product of a particular time and place.

9. **What are the defining characteristics of the postmodern city?**
The postmodern city is a product of the simultaneous operation of counter-urbanization (resulting in edge cities) and re-urbanization (as characterized by gentrified downtown neighbourhoods. It is multiethnic, socially fragmented, and dominated by the privatization of public space, notably by gated residential communities.

QUESTIONS TO CONSIDER

1. Map out your own "personal city" by keeping a record for a full week of all the trips you take to work, school, shopping, medical and dental appointments, friends' houses, restaurants and night clubs, and so on. What proportion of these trips occurs within your neighbourhood? Within the community in which you live? Across the wider metropolitan area?

2. To what extent does the big city in which you live or that you live closest to constitute a dual city?

3. How has suburban life been depicted in the mass media? Think, for example, of popular television series, such as *Desperate Housewives, Weeds,* and *The Simpsons.* To what extent do these depictions support the "myth of suburbia"?

4. Visit Statistics Canada's website (www.statcan. gc.ca). What kinds of questions about cities could you answer by using this data source?

GLOSSARY

Cities (p. 379) are relatively large, dense, permanent settlements in which few if any of the residents produce their own food.

The **concentric-zone model** (p. 385) is the classic urban-growth model proposed by Ernest Burgess in which the expansion of cities is visualized as a successive series of concentric rings, each of which contains a distinct resident population and type of land use. As social groups become more established and prosperous, they move farther away from the city centre.

The perception and organization of the city as a vehicle for capital accumulation create a **corporate city** (p. 388). The corporate city contains five major elements: the corporate suburb, high-rise apartments, suburban industrial parks, downtown office towers, and shopping malls.

The **demographic transition** (p. 380) is the change from high to low birth and death rates that characterized modernization, industrialization, and urbanization.

The juxtaposition and mutual isolation of an upper-tier information city and a lower-tier city creates a **dual city** (p. 394). Members of the upper tier work in jobs related to financial services, telecommunications, and high technology, and live in gentrified neighbourhoods and private communities on the edge of the city. A lower tier of people work in informal and low-technology jobs, and live in ethnic or racial ghettos.

Edge cities (p. 392) include self-contained entertainment, shopping, and office areas and have emerged in formerly suburban areas or just beyond the fringe of suburbia.

The **environmental-opportunity theory** (p. 378) proposes that people choose where they want to live depending on the extent to which a particular place meshes with or constrains their preferred lifestyle.

Familism (p. 390) is a lifestyle that places a high value on family living, marriage at a young age, a brief period of childlessness after marriage, and child-centredness.

In **gentrification** (p. 395), working-class houses are transformed into fashionable downtown dwellings by middle- and upper-income migrants.

The **multiple-nuclei model** (p. 386) is a model of urban growth characterized by a series of growth centres—retail, wholesale, residential—each representing the concentration of a specific function or activity within the urban economy.

Overurbanization (p. 387) is the process whereby the population of urban areas is growing faster than the urban economy, services, and resources can absorb. It is especially evident in large cities in the southern hemisphere.

The **postmodern city** (p. 379) is a new urban form that is more privatized and more socially and culturally fragmented and globalized than the corporate city.

The **replacement level** (p. 380) is the number of children that each woman must have on average to sustain the size of a population, ignoring immigration and emigration. The replacement level is 2.1 children.

The **sector model** (p. 386) of urban growth proposes that the city expands outward from the centre in a series of sectors or wedges along major transportation arteries, such as highways and railroad lines.

Suburbanism (p. 389) is a way of life outside city centres that is organized mainly around the needs of children and involves higher levels of conformity and sociability than does life in the central city.

The **urban-growth machine** (p. 390) is a loosely structured coalition of local economic and political interest groups that hold in common a commitment to sustained growth and development.

Urbanism (p. 385) is a way of life that involves increased tolerance but also emotional withdrawal and specialized, impersonal, and self-interested interaction.

CHAPTER 17

SOCIOLOGY AND THE ENVIRONMENT

S. Harris Ali
YORK UNIVERSITY

SOURCE: © Frank Röder/Westend61/Corbis.

AFTER READING THIS CHAPTER, YOU WILL BE ABLE TO:

- Understand how environmental problems are not just biophysical issues but social issues as well.

- Analyze the complex relationship among industry, government, the media, science, and citizens in raising awareness of environmental issues and responding to environmental problems.

- Describe how environmental concerns and the environmental movement have developed over time.

- Explain how strategies to manage and govern the environment are based on regulatory approaches shaped by differences in the power and influence of social groups.

- Explain how environmental health risks come to be unevenly distributed in society, with a disproportionate share falling on the socially and economically marginalized people.

INTRODUCTION
THE EARTH IN DANGER

Sometimes small, seemingly trivial changes make huge differences. For instance, very small changes in the temperature of our planet—just a few degrees—may suddenly trigger an avalanche of large-scale environmental changes with enormous consequences for life on Earth. This example highlights our vulnerability to "tipping points." A **tipping point** is a critical threshold (Gladwell, 2002). When a slow and gradual process reaches a tipping point, it will, with little or no warning, rapidly accelerate, causing dramatic change. Current scientific evidence indicates that the world's ecological systems are coming dangerously close to just such a tipping point. When that tipping point is reached, Earth's environmental system will change dramatically. Our planet will no longer be able to provide all of the natural resources we depend on.

Global climate change is one example of how environmental problems may develop incrementally and almost imperceptibly until a tipping point is reached. Scientists have found that intensified industrial activity over the last century has added huge amounts of carbon dioxide and other greenhouse gases to the atmosphere. These gases trap heat, gradually warming the Earth. However, once we reach a critical temperature increase, global warming will occur far more rapidly. Accelerated warming will, in turn, lead to the rapid onset of many environmental changes that have serious consequences, including greater frequency of hurricanes and storms, record flooding, reduced biodiversity, extensive droughts, shrinking river flows, extensive bush fires, the diffusion of bacteria and viruses to new areas, the scarcity of many natural resources, and the creation of large numbers of environmental refugees and large weather-related insurance losses that can destabilize global financial markets.

Greater understanding of the role tipping points play in environmental problems has led to the realization that we need to act fast to prevent catastrophe. Sociologists can contribute to these efforts because many environmental problems originate in the relationship between nature and society. For example, the industrial and consumer activities that contribute to climate change are based on collective decisions about how we should structure social institutions and policies. We have the capacity to change them if we want.

In this chapter, I begin by examining how environmental issues and problems are linked to the way societies are organized. I then address some of the chief questions environmental sociologists investigate. First, how do members of society think, feel, and act in relation to environmental issues? Which social factors influence their thoughts, feelings, and actions? Second, how do different social groups affect various strategies for addressing environmental problems? Third, why are environmental risks unevenly distributed in society? What are the implications of the uneven distribution of risk for our health and well-being?

INCORPORATING THE ENVIRONMENT INTO SOCIOLOGICAL ANALYSIS

Biology and geography were used in the nineteenth century to "explain" and thereby justify the superiority of certain classes, races, and civilizations. Sociology developed partly as a critique of conventional wisdom and an attempt to demonstrate the superiority of *social* explanations of such inequalities. Accordingly, sociologists were reluctant to consider the biophysical environment in their analyses until recently. The emergence of urgent environmental problems in the 1970s led them to reevaluate their bias. They came to appreciate that environmental problems have social *and* biophysical bases. Much of environmental sociology focuses on the relationships among industry, the state, and the environmental movement, including the role the mass media play in these relationships. To help understand these matters, it is useful to introduce a sociological perspective known as the "the tragedy of the commons" (Hardin, 1968).

The Tragedy of the Commons

The environmental commons consists of the natural resources that we share and depend on, such as the air, water, and soil. Tragedy arises when people try to maximize their personal economic gain by exploiting the commons. For example, industrial pollutants may enter the air and contaminate it. Currently, the cost of cleaning up the air falls not to the private company that caused the pollution but to the party responsible for taking care of the commons, namely the state (and, by extension, taxpayers and society at large). In this sense, the private company enjoys a "free ride." It profits from increased production but does not have to pay the costs associated with air pollution because all members of society share them.

We refer to the pollution as an **externality** because its cost is externalized from the private company to the state and society. The tragedy of the commons grows when many companies engage in detrimental environmental pursuits. Motivated by profit, they all look for a free ride. If this practice is sufficiently widespread and enduring, the commons will be destroyed. Everyone will breathe foul air and pay the environmental and health consequences. Today, threats to the global commons are widespread.

TIME FOR REVIEW

1. How do environmental problems originate in the relationship between nature and society?
2. What is the tragedy of the commons? How can global climate change be understood as a tragedy of the commons?

THE DEVELOPMENT OF ENVIRONMENTAL AWARENESS AND CONCERN

Although environmental issues have always existed, they did not become prominent until the 1970s. Until then, analysts emphasized protecting natural resources. They did not question the industrial processes that threatened them. Their outlook began to change when Rachel Carson published *Silent Spring* (1962). Carson documented how chemicals in the environment could transform a world full of life and the sounds of the wilderness into a world shrouded in silence. She focused in particular on the effects of the pesticide DDT on the food chain. DDT was used indiscriminately after World War II. Its pervasiveness, combined with strong evidence of its dangers, made the silent spring scenario feasible and frightening. A movement sprang up to protect the environment from chemical contamination and demand more government regulation of industrial activity. In response, the chemical industry mobilized resources to counter the movement's claims. The confrontation became a dispute that politicians could not ignore. (See the Critical Sociology: Protest and Policy box).

In 1968, the environmental movement gained impetus when a group of European industrialists, business advisers, and civil servants known as the Club of Rome became convinced that governments' environmental policies were short-sighted and dangerous. They commissioned researchers to develop computer models to extrapolate the effects of continued industrialization, technological development, natural resource depletion, pollution, food production, and population growth to 2010 based on existing trends. Published in 1972, the Club of Rome report painted a picture of total societal collapse because of inadequate food, too much pollution, and insufficient natural resources (Meadows et al., 1972). These findings reinforced the idea that industrial growth had to be curbed to prevent catastrophe.

In 1973, war broke out between Israel and its neighbouring Arab states. Because the West supported Israel, the Arab states stopped the flow of oil to the West, causing a crisis that drove home the environmental movement's message: Many natural resources are in short supply. In the following years, governments in Canada and abroad established new environmental laws and agencies in response to this message.

During the 1980s, governments and societies grappled with two environmental problems of global proportions: ozone depletion and climate change. A decade earlier, scientists had predicted that chlorofluorocarbons (CFCs), a class of chemicals used as a refrigerant and a solvent for cleaning metals, could rapidly destroy Earth's ozone layer. The ozone layer filters out ultraviolet radiation from sunlight and thereby protects us from such ailments as skin cancer, immune system disorders, snow blindness, retinal damage, and cataracts. In 1985, scientists verified the earlier prediction. They found an enormous hole in the ozone layer over the Antarctic. Action was swift. Coordinated international efforts led to the banning of CFCs in 1987.

During the same period, some people raised concern about other chemicals arising from industrial activity, namely carbon dioxide and methane, and the ensuing problem of global climate change.

In light of the magnitude of environmental problems, the United Nations World Commission on Environment and Development published *Our Common Future* in 1987. It introduced the idea of **sustainable development**. As an industrial strategy, sustainable development recognizes the dual needs of protecting the environment and allowing economic growth. The idea was to adopt industrial strategies that meet the needs of the present generation without compromising the ability of future generations to meet their own needs. Many of the policies and actions that are needed to move sustainable development forward can happen only if there is buy-in from the public. For this reason, it is important to

CRITICAL SOCIOLOGY: PROTEST AND POLICY   ENVIRONMENTAL GOVERNANCE

Environmental governance refers to attempts by those in power to regulate and alleviate environmental problems (Davidson and Frickel, 2004). Students of environmental governance explore how environmental policies are developed and implemented, and how government interacts with industry, social movements, and consumers in addressing environmental issues.

The capacity of a state to regulate activities that have environmental consequences depends partly on its sovereign power—its ability to rule without external interference. However, many environmental threats are not confined to a particular locality or jurisdiction; they are international in scope. Cooperation among states is required to address them. For instance, the need to regulate the emission of greenhouse gases on the part of each country led to heated disputes about sovereignty rights at the United Nations Framework Convention on Climate Change in Kyoto, and the 2011–15 follow-up conferences in Copenhagen, Lima, and Paris. Some countries, including the United States, Canada, and Saudi Arabia, strongly oppose the imposition of regulations that would limit the extent to which their domestic industries are able emit greenhouse gases.

Another example of this type of dispute occurred in 2008 when the Canadian government lobbied against proposed American legislation that would ban the United States from buying oil from the Alberta tar sands because extracting and refining it releases more pollutants than conventional petroleum production does. The Canadian lobby wanted to ensure a market for the oil despite its harsh environmental consequences (Nikiforuk, 2010).

Opposing such market-driven lobbying efforts is the environmental movement. Although originally concerned with preserving the natural beauty of wilderness areas at the turn of the twentieth century, the first wave of the modern environmental movement was born with the publication of *Silent Spring* in 1962. It took a somewhat anti-industrial perspective. By the mid-1980s, a second wave of environmentalism was unfolding. It was less apocalyptic and

more pragmatic and professional in tone, more willing to work with business and government in dealing with issues such as acid rain. In Canada, business–government–environmentalist round tables were established. The shift from an adversarial to a cooperative stance may have reflected broader changes in society, including aging members in the first wave of environmentalists, who now had families to raise and mortgages to pay; a growing number of second-wave members who had graduated from university programs in environmental studies; and recognition by business and government that environmentalism was not just a passing fad (Paehlke, 2009).

By the early twenty-first century, global climate change was at the top of the political agenda, signalling the rise of a third wave of environmentalism. Addressing climate change requires large-scale alterations in the way society is organized. For this reason, the issue subsumes other types of environmental issues, such as increasing energy efficiency in manufacturing, building design, and transportation; switching to renewable energy sources; significantly increasing the recycling and reuse of materials; and adopting more effective forest and other resource management strategies. This third wave of environmentalism was also characterized by the emergence of the federal Green Party. In every election since 2004, the Greens have been able to run a candidate in all federal ridings. So far, they have elected just one MP, but their presence on the national stage has forced the other political parties to give greater prominence to environmental issues—if only to prevent supporters from being attracted to the Green Party (Paehlke, 2009).

Critical Thinking Questions

1. Do you think environmental issues will become more prominent in the near future? Why, or why not?

2. Do you think environmental concerns will vary according to age, gender, and race/ethnicity? How so, and why?

determine the degree to which environmental attitudes and behaviours are changing in the direction of environmental sustainability.

ENVIRONMENTAL CONCERN

Environmental Attitudes

According to sociologist Ulrich Beck's (1992) **risk society thesis**, in the optimistic decades immediately

preceding World War II, the developing welfare states of the Western world were preoccupied with issues related to the production and distribution of social goods, including wealth, educational opportunities, consumer goods, income, and property. In contrast, over the last few decades, we have become preoccupied with issues related to the distribution of social "bads," chief among them the environmental risks and externalities produced by industry. For Beck, this switch has prompted individuals and institutions to start questioning the industrial basis of people's relationship to the environment. Previously, the environment was not widely perceived as an issue because any risks that were produced were simply dismissed as the "price of progress" and ignored. In the risk society, we ignore such issues as global warming and ozone depletion at our peril.

Environmental concern has been on the upswing in Canada in recent decades. Canadians now regard it as the third most important issue facing the country (see Figure 17.1) Environmental concern appears to follow an **economic contingency** logic (Buttel, 1975). That is, a larger proportion of the population considers environmental issues important during good economic times, while a smaller proportion considers environmental issues important during times of economic hardship. Still, many Canadians regard environmental problems as important even in the worst of economic times: In one poll taken during the height of the 2008-09 recession, 74 percent of Canadians agreed that the current focus on the environment in our society is not going far enough (Harris/Decima, 2009). The realization persists that we need to confront environmental issues no matter what.

Environmental Behaviour

Although surveys show that many people are sympathetic to environmental issues, they do not necessarily modify their behaviour accordingly. What accounts for inconsistency between environmental attitudes and behaviour? Sociologists have proposed several explanations.

Anthony Giddens (2009) argues that environmental issues are back-of-the-mind because many environmental dangers, no matter how frightening they may appear, are not tangible, immediate, or visible in day-to-day life. Environmental issues are also kept on the back burner because of a psychological tendency known as **future discounting**. People find it difficult to give the same amount of consideration and thought to the future as they do to the present. Present reality hits home more than future possibilities do. The future is therefore discounted. As such, a small reward offered now will normally be taken in preference to a much larger one offered at an undetermined later point. Future discounting has big implications for how people act in response to environmental problems. It means that many people are not inclined to change environmentally destructive practices because of the current benefits they receive from it.

The inconsistency between environmental attitudes and behaviour is further complicated by the influence of **Jevon's paradox**—as we become more efficient in the use of a natural resource, the cost of using it falls and we then use more of it (Cato, 2011: 153). Environmental savings are thus soon lost. For instance, people may switch to low-energy light bulbs but they may soon realize that using them saves money, so they leave their lights on longer. The same may happen with the introduction of more fuel-efficient cars. People save money on gas by purchasing such vehicles, so they feel justified in going on more frequent or longer trips. Consequently, the rate of gas consumption remains high.

The **framing** of an environmental problem also influences the relationship between attitudes and behaviour. Framing refers to the way people interpret and give meaning to events and things in their social settings. When people enter a social setting, they frame it by asking themselves, in effect, "What's going on here?" (Goffman, 1974:8). Framing changes what would otherwise be meaningless into something that we take into account when interacting. How something is framed therefore influences how people act. If people regard an environmental problem as significant, they may act on it. Otherwise they may not. For social constructionists, such considerations form the basis for analyzing environmental issues.

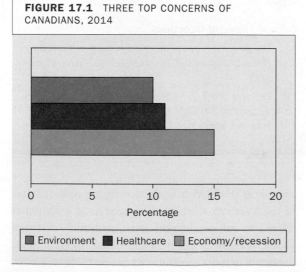

FIGURE 17.1 THREE TOP CONCERNS OF CANADIANS, 2014

Percentage

■ Environment ■ Healthcare ■ Economy/recession

SOURCE: Adapted from Indra Das, "Survey Suggests Canadians Displeased with Government's Balancing of Economy and Environment," *DeSmog Canada* (2014). http://www.desmog.ca/2014/01/09/survey-suggests-canadians-displeased-government-s-balancing-economy-and-environment (retrieved Jan. 2, 2015).

TIME FOR REVIEW

1. What are the main historical events that contributed to heightened environmental awareness and concern?
2. What are some of the social and environmental advantages and disadvantages of adopting the strategy of sustainable development? What are some of the reasons that strategy has not been adopted?
3. What accounts for the discrepancy between being concerned about the environment and not being willing to do anything to protect it?

THE SOCIAL CONSTRUCTION OF ENVIRONMENTAL ISSUES

How is a problem transformed from a nonissue to an issue that attracts public attention and political interest? The social constructionist perspective focuses on the three-stage social process through which this happens (Hannigan, 2014).

In the first stage, people assemble a claim or complaint about an environmental problem. Scientists typically assemble claims based on their technical research but a scientific claim can be influenced by political decisions relating to the funding of particular lines of research. For example, a Canadian archeologist who discovered evidence of contact between Indigenous and Norse explorers on Baffin Island a thousand years ago had her government funding cut (CBC, "Silence of the Labs"). She claimed that this happened because her research did not support the finding the British had first contact with Indigenous people in the Arctic, thereby weakening Canada's claim to sovereignty rights.

Second, the claim must be presented, that is, brought to people's attention. Typically, the mass media serve as the platform for publicizing claims. Not all claims-makers have equal access to the media. Similar to the first stage, the presentation of claims may also be influenced by political processes. For instance, some state-employed scientists have complained that speaking directly to the media has become difficult because of the recent introduction of bureaucratic hurdles (CBC, "Silence of the Labs"). They contend that they encounter media access problems if their research runs counter to government policies on matters related to environmental protection, tar sands development, and climate change.

Popularizers, such as David Suzuki, and celebrities, such as Leonardo DiCaprio, often play an important role in publicizing environmental claims because their fame allows them to grab the media spotlight. Environmental activists may also try to lure the mass media by drawing on dramatic visual images—for example, the widespread ruin of the countryside caused by the development of the Alberta tar sands. Coverage of high-profile events, such as the awarding of the 2007 Nobel Peace Prize to the Intergovernmental Panel on Climate Change and former U.S. vice-president Al Gore, serve the same purpose.

In the third stage of the social construction of environmental issues, claims are contested as claims-makers' positions clash in the public spotlight.

CONTESTING CLIMATE CHANGE

People often contest claims about environmental problems, especially if the claims have wide-ranging political and economic implications. Consider climate change. Reducing the emission of greenhouse gases requires massive change in the way industry and government operate, as well as the lifestyles we will be able to pursue. Conflict has been fierce between those calling for action on climate change and those denying its existence. Many of the latter have backing from powerful corporations.

Evidence for climate change has been accumulating for some time. The Intergovernmental Panel on Climate Change (IPCC) was established by the United Nations and the World Meteorological Organization to collect and summarize relevant evidence. The IPCC consists of thousands of scientists who interpret tens of thousands of climate studies. Based on levels of carbon dioxide accumulating in tree rings, coral reefs, and ice core columns from the Arctic, the IPCC concluded that scientific evidence clearly indicates a dramatic rise in greenhouse gas since the time of industrialization. This in turn is linked to increased surface temperature (see Figure 17.2).

Much is at stake if actions are taken to curb climate change by reducing fossil fuel use. Because fossil-fuel-intensive industry represents the largest contributor to climate change, it has a particularly strong responsibility to curb fossil fuel extraction and use. However, fossil-fuel-intensive industries have organized to discredit scientific research on climate change, sow doubt among the public by claiming that the research is erroneous or a hoax, and influence politicians to avoid passing meaningful environmental legislation. Oil industry interests in particular have organized themselves through front operations, such as the Global

FIGURE 17.2 VARIATIONS OF THE EARTH'S SURFACE TEMPERATURE

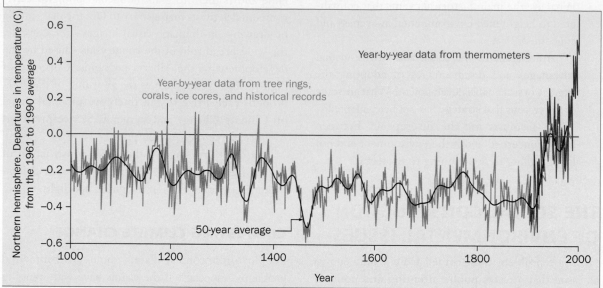

SOURCE: Fred Pearce (2010). Copyright Guardian News & Media Ltd. 2010.

Climate Coalition and the World Climate Council (McCright and Dunlap, 2010).

The competing claims of those acknowledging climate change and the skeptics highlight the difference between popular and scientific truth (Derber, 2010). Popular truth refers to knowledge that most people in a society believe to be true. Scientific truth refers to knowledge established by scientific methods and on which the great majority of scientists agree. It is clear that the phenomenon of climate change, as confirmed by the IPCC, is an established scientific truth. Yet powerful corporate interests, by deliberately creating doubt, seek to influence popular truth, often through the mass media.

Media, Culture, and the Environment

Popular culture plays an important role in influencing people's environmental attitudes and behaviours. In the decades following the energy crisis of the mid-1970s, depictions of a dark environmental future proliferated in Western popular culture. Such films as *Blade Runner*, *Total Recall*, and *The Day After Tomorrow* painted a picture of a time when Earth's environment is ruined. Misery, poverty, oppression, violence, disease, scarcity, and pollution are everywhere. The popularity of such films raised environmental consciousness among the public (Buell, 2004). More recently, *Avatar*, the highest-grossing film ever, had a strong environmental theme. Set in 2154, the film tells the story of a powerful corporation mining a faraway planet for a

valuable mineral. In the process, the corporation seeks to eradicate the Indigenous people and the natural environment. Events now taking place in northern Alberta's tar sands region apparently inspired the movie.

The news media also play a significant role in framing environmental issues. They often cover environmental problems and issues precisely because the controversy associated with them is filled with dramatic moments. Environmental movements sometimes deliberately employ sensationalistic techniques to draw media attention (Hannigan, 2014). For instance, they may stage "morality plays" in which environmental group members present themselves as the idealistic and morally good protectors of the environment, challenging whalers, loggers, and nuclear operators who are depicted as villains in a David-versus-Goliath confrontation. For their part, journalists may themselves be involved in the framing process by covering environmental issues in ways they know will resonate with a larger audience. Thus, the coverage of an environmental issue might, for example, be framed in terms of health and safety, bureaucratic bungling, or good citizenship.

TIME FOR REVIEW

1. What are the three stages in the social construction of environmental issues?

2. What role do popular culture and the news media play in the social construction of environmental issues?

NATURAL RESOURCES

NONRENEWABLE RESOURCES

We can classify natural resources according to their quantity and their ability to regenerate. Nonrenewable resources are finite in quantity and therefore exhaustible since they can only be used once. Oil is an example. The finite quantity of nonrenewable resources has significant economic implications because resource scarcity results in high prices for the commodity in question. For instance, oil extraction has become problematic because sources that are more difficult and expensive to exploit must now be tapped. Some analysts believe that, if we factor in externalities paid by taxpayers, the cost of extraction will soon be higher than the price we pay for oil from the Alberta tar sands. The technical difficulties involved in extracting oil from the tar sands means that tar sands oil generates three times the greenhouse gas emissions of normal oil extraction while consuming huge amounts of water and energy (Nikiforuk, 2010: 3).

Oil extraction from other sources will also prove challenging in the future if we are forced to explore increasingly remote, inaccessible, and inhospitable environments such as the deep sea and the Arctic (Davidson, Andrews, and Pauly, 2014). Such prospects have the potential to be environmentally destructive, as illustrated, for instance, by the Mobile Oil Ocean Ranger disaster off the coast of Newfoundland in 1982, and the BP Deepwater Horizon oil spill disaster in the Gulf of Mexico in 2010.

The Great Canadian Pipeline Debate

One of the great challenges that Canada has always faced is how to transport natural resources to market over the wide expanse of our country. Today, it is recognized that transportation infrastructure has tremendous environmental implications.

To transport oil extracted from the Alberta oil sands, various proposals have been put forth to build or expand pipelines. They include the TransCanada Keystone XL Canada–U.S. pipeline leading to the huge oil refineries of Louisiana and the open waters of the Gulf of Mexico; the Enbridge Northern Gateway Alberta–BC pipeline leading to the coast of British Columbia; and the "Energy East" pipeline from Alberta to the large oil refinery on New Brunswick's Bay of Fundy, which opens onto the Atlantic Ocean.

Like the climate change issue, the pipelines have mobilized numerous claims-makers who have tried to animate or bury the issue. Each group vies for better visibility of their respective position. In particular, the oil and pipeline industries and some politicians argue that the pipelines are needed to grow the economy, while environmentalists and other politicians argue that the process of extracting oil from the oil sands has negative environmental consequences, including an increased reliance on a nonrenewable resource, increased greenhouse gas emissions, forest clear-cuts, water and land contamination, and the displacement and endangerment of First Nations peoples. Popularizers, such as Leonardo DiCaprio, Neil Young, and a group of 10 Nobel Peace Prize laureates, have brought attention to the debates by publically expressing their opposition to the pipelines. Furthermore, since the construction of pipeline infrastructure is so extensive, politicians and claims-makers from various jurisdictions have entered the debate, including U.S. President Barrack Obama, Prime Minister Stephen Harper, the provincial premiers, and international environmental groups.

RENEWABLE NATURAL RESOURCES

In contrast to fossil fuels, forests are renewable if we take care to ensure that new trees replace those that are harvested. In practice, renewal may not occur as quickly as needed. Some types of trees, such as those in the old-growth forests of British Columbia, take centuries to grow. Similarly, overfishing may not allow fish stocks to replenish, as was the case with the cod fishery in Newfoundland in the early 1990s.

Greenpeace activists confronting whaling ships.
SOURCE: Photo by Rex Weyler.

The government had to impose a moratorium on cod fishing in 1992 to give the cod an opportunity to replenish, and only recently has hope been expressed that commercial fishing may soon resume. Some renewable natural resources—sunlight, gravity, wind power, and tidal wave power—are inexhaustible for all practical purposes. Such inexhaustible resources are widely considered to be critically important for sustainable development.

Canada is a country of vast natural resources but abundance may not translate into wealth for all. Why not? To answer this question, we must understand how profits generated from resource extraction are unequally distributed across society and why this is allowed to occur.

THE RESOURCE CURSE

In Canada, natural resources are owned by provincial governments. Governments issue a licence for a private corporation to extract natural resources and are paid royalties for this right. Usually, the royalty is a percentage of the revenue obtained through its use. In absolute terms, royalty rates for certain natural resources are very low. For example, at 39 percent of gross revenue, Alberta has one of the lowest royalty rates for oil extraction in the world (see Figure 17.3). Nevertheless, the amount of revenue generated from oil royalties enables Alberta to forgo imposing a provincial sales tax on its citizens and to collect income tax at a comparatively low rate. In fact, the province collects more revenue from oil than it does from taxpayers. This situation has significant social and political consequences.

One consequence is that the public is less likely to scrutinize how the government spends public funds than would be the case if they were taxed at a higher rate. Taxation strengthens democracy but the government of Alberta is less inclined to feel that it has to answer to the public because relatively little of its revenue comes from taxes. This is seen, for instance, in the Alberta government's failure to measure oil production data and report oil royalties accurately

FIGURE 17.3   GOVERNMENT SHARE OF INDUSTRY OIL REVENUES COLLECTED THROUGH ROYALTIES

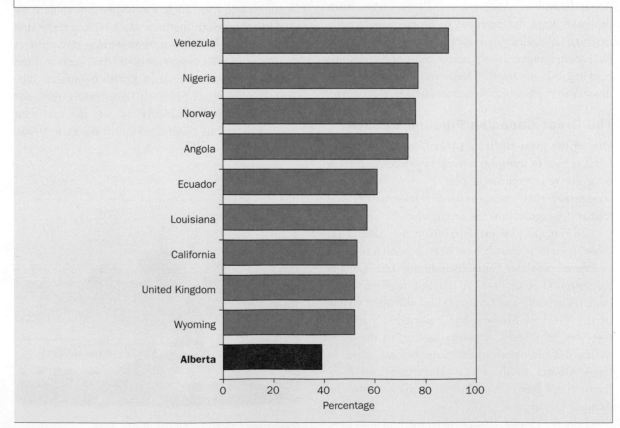

SOURCE: United States Government Accountability Office. Based on data supplied to the Alaska State Legislature, 2006. (GAO-07-676R).

(Alberta Royalty Review Panel, 2007). At the same time, heavy dependence on resource royalties obliges the government to please the petroleum industry. For example, not wanting to bite the hand that feeds it, the government is disinclined to strictly regulate the environmental impact of the petroleum sector (Nikiforuk, 2010).

Such situations as those just described have led sociologists to conclude that ownership and licensing arrangements used to govern natural resources in resource-rich countries amount to a **resource curse** that hampers democracy, increases corruption, and creates injustice (Friedman, 2006). In extreme cases, including those in Saudi Arabia and the other oil-rich Gulf states, autocratic government becomes firmly entrenched.

TIME FOR REVIEW

1. What are the differences between renewable and nonrenewable resources? Why are renewable resources better for the environment?
2. What is meant by the "resource curse?" How is Canada affected by the resource curse?

INDUSTRY, ECONOMY, AND THE ENVIRONMENT

From an environmental point of view, the material basis of our economy is organized in a linear fashion. This means that raw natural resources are first extracted from the earth, processed and refined into purer form, and used to manufacture commodities. The commodities are then transported to retailers, where consumers buy them. Once they no longer satisfy consumer needs, the commodities are discarded. Waste products end up in landfills.

Each stage of this linear economy—resource extraction, processing, commodity transport, wholesale and retail sale, consumption, and postconsumption—has its own environmental impacts. For example, with resource extraction, such materials as fossil fuels and iron ore are taken from the environment but farmland or forested areas may be destroyed in the process. During other stages, environmental impacts usually take the form of solid, liquid, and gas emissions. Governments direct much regulatory attention to controlling or limiting these emissions. Clearly, the environment and the economy are intimately linked.

The regulatory approach of fining or taxing industrial organizations for exceeding specified environmental impacts is based on the **polluter-pays principle**. According to this principle, the party producing an environmental pollutant should not be able to get a free ride by externalizing associated costs. Instead, the polluter must pay the costs. The idea is that a fine or a tax serves as a disincentive, causing the industry to reduce or eliminate the environmental impact of its activities. However, critics argue that this approach is too coercive. They say that industry complies only reluctantly with regulations to avoid legal liability, taxation, or insurance claims. More recently, other approaches have been suggested, one of which proposes creating a market for buying and selling "pollution permits." This approach serves as the foundation for the Kyoto Protocol, aimed at curbing greenhouse gas emissions (see the Critical Sociology: Globalization box).

CRITICAL SOCIOLOGY: GLOBALIZATION   **GLOBAL CLIMATE CHANGE AND THE KYOTO PROTOCOL**

Generally speaking, industry and nation states have tended to oppose **command-and-control approaches** to regulating their activities for the purpose of environmental protection. Such approaches are based on the government issuing commands to industry to adopt environmentally protective practices and to control environmentally harmful emissions by adhering to certain regulations. One of the objections to this approach is that it fails to give industry any room to adopt environmentally better practices on their own terms. That is, if industry is to implement changes to their practices, they want to do so according to their own schedule and capacity. In theory, marketable pollution permit schemes—also called "cap-and-trade"—allow such flexibility.

Here is how cap-and-trade works in principle: National or international governmental bodies set an absolute limit on the total amount of a certain pollutant that can be emitted. This limit (or cap) is to be reached by a certain date. For example, the target of the Kyoto Protocol was to reduce overall

(continued)

(continued)

global emissions of greenhouse gases by at least 5.2 percent below 1990 levels by 2012 (Giddens, 2009: 186). To reach such a cap, each country would have had to cut emissions by a certain amount. Each country would be allowed to pollute, but at a level significantly lower than before. Under cap-and-trade, the right to pollute would have to be purchased in the form of a permit from the national or international agency running the newly created market. In the case of the 1997 Kyoto Protocol, this body would be an agency of the United Nations. The total number of pollution permits issued would be fixed to ensure that the pollution cap is not exceeded.

Some countries may find it difficult for their domestic industries to change their ways and emit less. Consequently, these countries would be forced to buy more pollution permits from countries that are successful in reducing their emissions. Since these other countries would have reduced their emissions, they would no longer need all of their pollution permits. In this way, pollution permits would be bought and sold in a market. Since the buying and selling would occur within the overall pollution cap limit, some analysts think it would eventually lead to the desired overall reduction in emissions.

There are many problems with cap-and-trade schemes. One is well illustrated by the attempt to implement the Kyoto Protocol. It is related once again to the issue of sovereignty—trying to make independent nation states conform to international agreements. There is no worldwide sovereign to impose sanctions if individual countries violate regulations or do not agree to participate in the scheme. Thus, in 2001, United States President Bush withdrew his country from the Kyoto Protocol (CBC, "Kyoto and Beyond"). Differences within a nation state may also make it difficult to ratify the protocol. For example, in Canada, politicians from oil-rich Alberta strongly opposed it, while Quebec was a strong supporter since that province draws mainly on hydroelectric power. Manitoba supported it because of the potential devastation that global climate change may wreak on agriculture in that province (Mitchell, 2010: 4). In the end, Canada did not commit to the agreement (see Figure 17.4)

Critical Thinking Questions

1. Why do industry and the environmental movement disagree on the use of market-based schemes to control climate change?

2. Compare and contrast the positions of the countries of the Global North and the Global South on the Kyoto Protocol. Why is there such great disagreement?

FIGURE 17.4   GREENHOUSE GAS EMISSIONS, CANADA, 1990–2012

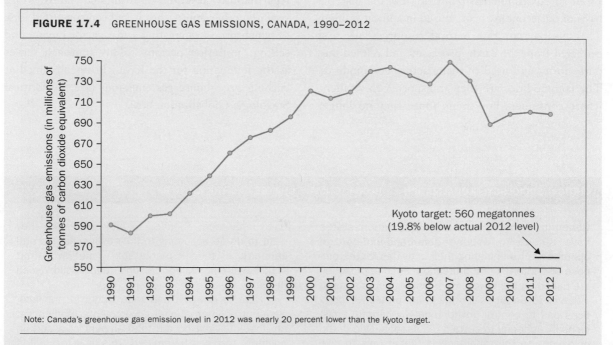

Note: Canada's greenhouse gas emission level in 2012 was nearly 20 percent lower than the Kyoto target.

SOURCE: Environment Canada (2014a). © Her Majesty The Queen in Right of Canada, Environment Canada, 2014. Reproduced with the permission of the Minister of Public Works and Government Services Canada.

CORPORATE SOCIAL RESPONSIBILITY AND ECO-STANDARDS

Increasing public concern about the environment has forced industry to make concessions. Today, for instance, some companies say they exercise corporate social responsibility by ensuring that their practices are ethically and environmentally sound and in the public interest. The problem is that such measures are voluntary, so they may not be effective. In some cases, companies even claim they are engaged in environmentally protective practices when they are not. They promote a "green" image merely as a public relations ploy to attract more business—a practice sometimes called "corporate greenwashing."

People would be able to identify instances of corporate greenwashing more easily if the environmental practices of companies were made transparent to the public. One attempt to do this is with eco-standards and eco-labels (Bostrom and Klintman, 2011). A company that conforms to established environmental standards for production and manufacturing would be able to apply for certification stating that its product or practice is environmentally friendly. The environmental standards themselves would be developed by another agency or sometimes by the government. An external auditor would ensure that the company complies with the standards and procedures, and issue a certificate on the basis of the assessment. The agency and auditor would therefore operate as watchdogs for the public, vouching for the company and ensuring it is not making false claims. The issued certificate could take different forms, such as the company or product being included in official green shopping guides or green mutual fund portfolios or through the issuing of environmental stewardship certificates that can be displayed publicly in the storefront or factory. In addition, eco-labels could be displayed on products so consumers could see they conform to a standard before deciding whether to buy them.

The eco-standards approach has been used for a variety of products and processes, including organic food labelling, labelling of genetically modified food, energy efficiency certification, and marine certification and seafood labelling (to certify that only sustainable yields are being caught). But can these eco-labels be trusted? Toilet paper produced by J. D. Irving Limited of New Brunswick carries the Sustainable Forestry Initiative (SFI) eco-label, yet investigation by CBC journalists found that forestry practices involved in manufacturing it violates important principles that the general population associates with sustainable forestry, including clear-cutting, herbicide use, lack of recycled material in the manufacturing process, and the replanting of just one tree species, which threatens the long-term survivability of the replanted forest (CBC, "Toilet Paper Chase"). To address such false environmental claims, such groups as Greenpeace and CorpWatch have established websites and blogs to investigate and then inform the public of specific cases of greenwashing. This is just one sort of activity with which environmental movement groups are involved.

TIME FOR REVIEW

1. How do marketable pollution permit schemes work? How effective are such strategies in protecting the environment?
2. What are two ways businesses incorporate social and environmental concerns into their practices? What are the limitations of such strategies?

THE ENVIRONMENT AND FOOD

The quantity and quality of food available to us is dependent on the state of the natural environment. Food issues are therefore an important research area for environmental sociologists. One issue they research is food insecurity: the inability or uncertainty that one will be able to acquire an adequate level of nutrition in socially acceptable ways (Koc, Sumner, Winson, 2012). The rise of food insecurity may be accounted for in several ways (see also Chapter 20, Globalization). The first involves the competing functions of the environment. That is, the environment must serve three functions for society: as a supply depot for our natural resources (including food), the provision of space for living (including housing, infrastructure, and transportation), and as a waste repository to accept pollution, sewage and garbage (Dunlap and Catton, 2002). If, for example, a given area is dedicated to the growth of biofuel for cars, or for housing developments, roads and pipelines, it cannot be used for growing food.

Second, it has been argued that the availability of food is the not the problem, rather it is access to food (Sen, 1981). Through the postwar Green Revolution based on the transfer of Western agricultural techniques, knowledge, and equipment, it was thought that food yields would rise dramatically, thereby putting an end to world hunger. Although food production increased, it did so mainly for export crops. The food did not always go toward the feeding of people in the area where it was grown. It should not be thought that food insecurity is only a problem for the developing world, however. Accessibility to nutritious food is also an issue for Canadians.

FOOD DESERTS

Food deserts are residential areas where people have little or no access to affordable and healthy food. Supermarkets tend to carry fresh produce and healthier foods in comparison to variety stores, which tend to mainly have packaged foods high in sodium, sugar, and trans fat. Supermarkets also have lower food prices. Yet, in some inner-city neighbourhoods, supermarkets are not within reasonable walking distance, forcing residents to obtain their food from variety stores and rendering their areas food deserts. Larsen and Gilliland (2009) noted that food deserts exist in Canadian neighbourhoods that have many renters, single parents, Indigenous Canadians, seniors with mobility issues, low-income families, and people dependent on public transportation (which limits the amount of groceries that can be carried). Such neighbourhoods also tend to have a higher proportion of fast-food outlets.

Food deserts are associated with a high incidence of obesity, anemia, diabetes, heart disease, hypertension, and depression, as well as the stress associated with the daily struggle to feed, clothe, and care for a family (Health Canada, 2007). Food insecurity issues such as these are especially prevalent in the First Nations communities of Canada's far north, where transportation of food products is difficult and costly: 32 percent of Nunavut residents (56 percent of children) live in food-insecure households (Statistics Canada, 2006), as do 12 percent of adults in the Northwest Territories and Yukon (Howard and Edge, 2013). By comparison, only 6 percent of Albertans are food insecure.

ORGANIC FOODS

Organic agriculture refers to farming practices that cause relatively little harm to the environment. Since the 1990s, there has been a noticeable increase in the popularity of organic food in Canada (Wallace and Brklacich, 2010). Part of the impetus has come from farmers themselves, who are increasingly worried about the environmental impact of industrialized monoculture (the growing of single crops rather than a diversity of foodstuffs) and the ethical issues around factory farming. *Industrialized monoculture* refers to the large-scale cultivation of one crop based on the extensive input of pesticides and herbicides. *Factory farming* refers to intensified livestock operations where large numbers of animals are kept in close and confined conditions (Ali, 2004). Such livestock often become stressed and ill. To counter illness, they are given large quantities of antibiotics and hormones to promote quick growth. These chemicals pose a threat to human health and the environment when they enter the food chain. In addition to concerns about antibiotics, consumers have raised concerns about other harmful aspects of conventional agriculture, including pesticide residues on fruits and vegetables, the decreased nutritional value of processed foods, and ethical concerns regarding the treatment of animals.

Organic agriculture addresses these concerns by abandoning chemical inputs, refusing to use genetically modified organisms, avoiding animal confinement, and adopting natural biological processes in growing food. However, the organic farming sector faces challenges. One of the main issues is the high cost of locally grown organic foods. The price is driven up by not having the economy of scale enjoyed by large-scale conventional agricultural operations. As a result, organic farmers face higher labour costs, government policies that favour conventional agriculture, and higher rates for crop insurance, all of which increase organic food prices (Wallace and Brklacich, 2010).

TIME FOR REVIEW

1. What is food insecurity and what causes it?
2. What are food deserts and how are they related to food insecurity?

THE ENVIRONMENT AND HEALTH

You are what you eat—and what you touch and breathe. If the air, water, food, and physical surroundings in which we carry on our daily activities are contaminated, we too become contaminated. Environmental and health issues are thus intimately connected. All human beings alive today have some level of **body burden**—the sum of dangerous chemicals that accumulate in the human body over a given period. Human decision making and the resulting organization of society shape the way chemicals enter the human body.

For example, in the mid-1960s, the Ontario Department of Lands and Forests (now the Ministry of Natural Resources) and private timber companies collaborated to spray the chemical Agent Orange on northern Ontario forests (Zlomislic, 2011). Agent Orange killed shrubs and birch, maple, and poplar tress so that profitable spruce trees would be free to grow without competition. We now know that Agent Orange causes cancer, but in the mid-1960s, workers involved in the spraying program, many of them university students, were unaware of the risks. They mixed chemicals with little protection and stood in fields holding red, helium-filled balloons on fishing lines while low-flying planes flew over them and sprayed the chemical. Decades later, these workers are experiencing serious health effects.

The Agent Orange case is one of acute exposure, that is, high-dose exposure in a short period. Other examples of acute exposure include explosions at chemical factories and industrial accidents. However, many environmental health risks are chronic, involving low-dose exposure over an extended period. One example involves bisphenol A, which is found in many clear, hard plastic products, such as CDs and DVDs, water and baby bottles, eyeglass lenses, and hockey helmet visors. It is also used in epoxy resins and the lining of tin cans containing food. It is one of the most common chemicals in the world (Smith and Lourie, 2009). Consequently, most people are in contact with bisphenol A every day for most of their lives.

With bisphenol A (and other chemicals that disrupt the body's hormonal system), low doses lead to potent health effects. Hence, low levels of such chemicals in the environment are of particular concern. Low levels of bisphenol A have been associated with a range of illnesses, including prostate and breast cancer, uro-genital abnormalities in male babies, declining sperm quality in men, early onset of puberty in girls, insulin-resistant diabetes, obesity, and attention deficit hyperactivity disorder (Smith and Lourie, 2009). Because of such concerns, in 2008, Canada became the first country to ban bisphenol A from baby bottles. There are, however, many other harmful chemicals that pervade the environment. How are these regulated? To address these questions we need to understand the process of risk management.

In 2008, Canada became the first country to ban bisphenol A from baby bottles.
SOURCE: Maxine Hicks/The New York Times/Redux.

RISK MANAGEMENT

Body burden is influenced by how a country regulates chemicals in the environment. The state does this through **risk management**—the process by which a regulatory agency establishes the levels of chemicals that are allowed to enter the environment. Risk management uses information from animal experiments to help determine safe levels of exposure. This technical information is combined with environmental information to come up with a specific regulation (Ali, 2008). However, the terms of the regulation are subject to political pressure. It may be that the strict regulation of a chemical emission will be costly to industry. Industry will therefore lobby for a laxer and less costly regulation. The environmental lobby, in contrast, may call for stricter regulation. As such, risk management is hardly a politically neutral, technical exercise.

In North America, risk management works on the principle that a chemical is assumed to be harmless until it is proven dangerous. Until then, the chemical will still be produced and allowed to enter the environment. This pro-industry orientation has been challenged by environmentalists calling for the adoption of the precautionary principle.

THE PRECAUTIONARY PRINCIPLE

The essence of the scientific method and the experimental approach is to establish the existence of cause–effect relationships. With respect to environmental health issues, this involves showing that exposure to a certain amount of a chemical in the environment (the cause) leads to a particular illness (the effect). In practice, causality is difficult to prove because environmental exposures take place while many compounding factors impinge on a given dose-response interaction. Laboratory experiments remove these confounding factors by manipulating the physical setting (see Chapter 2, Research Methods). However, researchers cannot remove compounding factors in the real world, where the cause of a disease may be due to many factors. Cancer, for instance, may result from several causes acting at different points in life, such as exposure to factory smoke during childhood, cigarette smoke during youth, and radon gas during adulthood. Ambiguity exists about what causes cancer; it may be one thing, or it may be several. The tobacco industry argued for decades that cigarette smoking might not be a cause of cancer because cigarette smokers tend to be overweight, have poor diets, live in polluted neighbourhoods, and so on—and all these factors are causes of cancer. (Only in recent decades did researchers show how exposure to tobacco smoke turns cells carcinogenic, thus silencing this particular line of defence.)

Similarly, defenders of polluting industries have argued that just because a disease is found in laboratory animals exposed to a particular contaminant, this does not necessarily mean that it will lead to the disease in humans. In the end, polluting industries often argue that insufficient evidence proves conclusively the existence of a cause–effect relationship between a pollutant and a disease, so regulating or banning a pollutant is not justified. Chemicals are innocent until proven guilty beyond doubt in Canada and the United States.

In Western Europe, regulatory agencies take a different approach. They do not allow the introduction of a new chemical if statistical evidence shows a correlation between its use and a dangerous health effect. Underlying this approach is the precautionary principle—the view that, under conditions of uncertainty, it is better to err on the side of safety. Some researchers argue that the logic of the precautionary principle should be applied not just to the regulation of chemicals but also to other regulatory issues, including the use of genetically modified food, genetic engineering, nanotechnologies, global warming, and activities that lead to the loss of biodiversity (Raffensperger and Tickner, 1999).

Because of the inadequacies of risk management, environmental health risks persist. However, sociologists have found that these risks do not affect everyone in society equally. Some individuals and groups are disproportionately affected by these risks,

depending on their race/ethnicity, social class, and place of residence. In other words, inequality exists in the distribution of risk. Certain organizations in the environmental movement have mobilized to address issues related to the unequal distribution of risk (see the Critical Sociology: Social Inequality box). Other organizations emphasize that certain groups are situated so as to be especially sensitive to environmental risk, as we shall now see.

TIME FOR REVIEW

1. How does the organization of society influence the amount and type of chemicals that enter our body?
2. What is the precautionary principle and how can it lead to improved risk management?
3. How is social inequality related to exposure to environmental risk?

GENDER AND THE ENVIRONMENT

The fundamental insight of ecofeminism is that patriarchy has environmental implications. Ecofeminism explores the linkages between the domination of women and the domination of the environment. Several streams of ecofeminism exist (Bell, 1998).

Essentialist ecofeminists argue that women are inherently more in tune with nature because of their intimate connection to life, including giving birth and nurturing the young. Accordingly, women are supposedly in a better position than men are to protect the natural environment. In contrast, men are more closely associated with the domination of nature and technologies that led to the environmental crisis in the first place. It follows that, to deal with the environmental crisis, attributes associated with women must be given greater prominence while those associated with men should be given less prominence.

Essentialist ecofeminists perpetuate traditional, biologically based stereotypes of men and women (see Chapter 5, Gender and Sexualities). In response, *cultural ecofeminists* argue that women have a particular affinity with the natural world because, like the natural world, they are exploited by men. From this point of view, social norms that define masculinity influence men to think and act in ways that encourage both the domination of women and environmental degradation. Cultural ecofeminists argue that the appropriate response to the ecological crisis is therefore a change in norms and behaviour related to gender.

Environmental inequality focuses on the relationship between social inequality and environmental quality. That is, how do patterns of social inequality based on income, race/ethnicity, gender, and age influence the type of environment in which people find themselves?

Generally, people in subordinate positions are more exposed to environmental risk than are people in superordinate or dominant positions. Recognition of this fact spurred the **environmental justice movement**. The initial impetus for the movement was the work of sociologist Robert Bullard (1993). Based on quantitative evidence and mapping, his research showed that toxic waste sites were located disproportionately in African American and Hispanic neighbourhoods in the United States. For example,

he discovered that about 60 percent of African Americans live near toxic waste sites. Similarly, in Canada, a strong correlation exists between race and class, on the one hand, and exposure to environmental hazards, on the other. Thus, in Toronto, the poorest neighbourhoods tend to be those with the most air pollution while the richest neighbourhoods tend to have the cleanest air (see Figure 17.5). In Canada as a whole, the Indigenous population seems to be particularly highly exposed to environmental dangers (see Figure 17.6).

Today, many workers, members of racial minority groups, and women have been drawn into environmental justice organizations. They tend to engage in local campaigns focusing on the survival needs of the poor, in contrast to some national

FIGURE 17.5   LOW INCOME AND HIGH INDUSTRIAL POLLUTION IN TORONTO

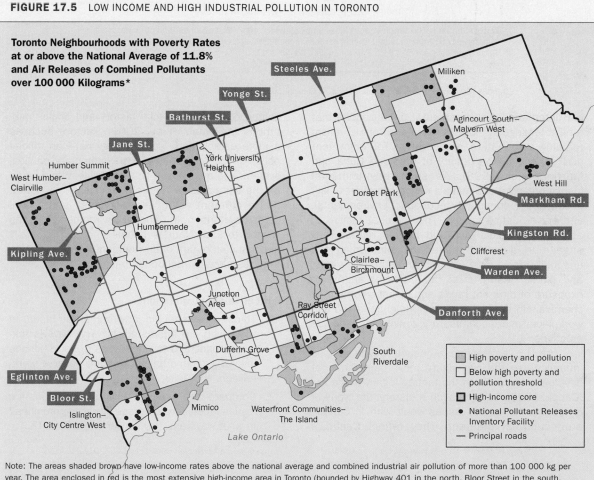

Note: The areas shaded brown have low-income rates above the national average and combined industrial air pollution of more than 100 000 kg per year. The area enclosed in red is the most extensive high-income area in Toronto (bounded by Highway 401 in the north, Bloor Street in the south, Bathurst Street in the west, and Leslie Street in the east). Circles indicate sources of industrial pollution monitored by the federal government. Note the virtual absence of industrial polluters in the high-income core and the abundance of industrial polluters in low-income areas.

SOURCE: Adapted from Canadian Environmental Law Association, *Pollution Watch Fact Sheet* (November 2008), p. 13, http://www1.toronto.ca/city_of _toronto/social_development_finance__administration/files/pdf/pollutionwatch_toronto_fact_sheet.pdf (accessed July 9, 2015).

(continued)

(continued)

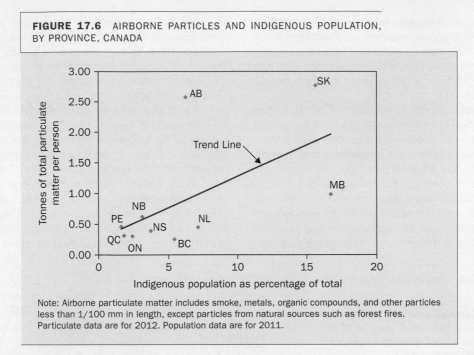

FIGURE 17.6   AIRBORNE PARTICLES AND INDIGENOUS POPULATION, BY PROVINCE, CANADA

Note: Airborne particulate matter includes smoke, metals, organic compounds, and other particles less than 1/100 mm in length, except particles from natural sources such as forest fires. Particulate data are for 2012. Population data are for 2011.

SOURCES: Environment Canada (2014b); Statistics Canada (2013, 2014).

and international environmental organizations that tend to engage in "full-stomach" environmentalism (dealing with nature preservation for enjoyment and enhancing the quality of life; see Guha and Martinez-Alier, 1998). As such, environmental justice organizations make a concerted effort to link occupational, community, economic, environmental, and social justice issues. They combat racism by asserting people's civil and human rights. They engage in activities aimed at eliminating the unequal enforcement of environmental, civil rights, and public health laws; the different degree of exposure of different races and classes to harmful chemicals in the home, school, neighbourhood and workplace; and discriminatory zoning and land-use practices.

The U.S. environmental justice movement was influenced by the civil rights movement that that developed to deal with the lasting legacy of slavery (Capek, 1993). Lacking such a history, the types of environmental justice issues dealt with in Canada are somewhat different. They reflect Canada's unique colonial and racial history and social institutions (Agyeman et al., 2009). Factors such as a more established "social safety net," an official policy of multiculturalism, a parliamentary political system, and a particular type of development based on the extraction of natural resources have meant that a different set of environmental justice concerns have arisen. In Canada, environmental issues related to First Nations people and the regionally unequal distribution of environmental contamination from resource extraction loom large.

Critical Thinking Questions

1. Think of a specific environmental issue in which you are interested. In what ways is this issue connected to other types of social issues involving race/ethnicity, gender, poverty, work, religion, and aging?

2. Compare the type of environmental justice issues faced in rural versus urban communities? In what ways are they similar and different?

Finally, *anticolonial ecofeminists* locate the source of the environmental crisis not in biology or in culture but in the existence of hierarchical social structures based on nation, race, and gender. Proponents of this viewpoint hold that colonization, largely by white men from rich, northern countries, locked most of the Global south into poverty for centuries (see Chapter 10, Development and Underdevelopment). It also imposed unsustainable agricultural practices such as monoculture on the Global south, practices that are ecologically destructive and reinforce the domination of colonized people, especially women (Shiva, 1993).

ENVIRONMENTAL JUSTICE AND CANADA'S FIRST NATIONS

First Nations peoples in Canada face the environmental consequences of colonization and inequality (Agyeman et al., 2009). For example, the rural area in the Sarnia–Windsor–London triangle of southern Ontario is home to eight First Nations territories (Mascarenhas, 2009). It also hosts many harmful industries, including a regional landfill, numerous smaller landfills, a sewage treatment plant processing 15 million litres a day, and the country's largest concentration of heavy industry, much of it related to petrochemicals. From 1974 to 1986, this area experienced 32 major chemical spills and 300 smaller ones that poured about 9 metric tonnes of pollutants into the St. Clair River, which runs through the area (Walpole Island First Nation, n.d.). The waterways in the region are so polluted that they have been designated as "areas of concern" by the International Joint Commission (Environment Canada, 2010).

The Aamjiwnaang First Nations Reserve is located in Chemical Valley. Epidemiological studies of this community show that, over the past decade, a statistically significantly lower number of boys than girls have been born. The imbalance has been attributed to environmental endocrine disruptors present in the toxic chemicals emitted by area industry (Mackenzie, Lockridge, and Keith, 2005).

Many of the issues that environmental justice groups deal with in the United States relate to the urban setting. In contrast, the environmental justice issues many First Nations people face involve the distribution of environmental risks in more remote settings, such as mercury contamination in northern Ontario (Erikson, 1995), water quality problems on reserves (Indian and Northern Affairs Canada, 2003), contamination from radioactive materials from uranium mining at Great Bear Lake in the Northwest Territories (Blow, 1999), and chemical contamination in the Mohawk territory of Akwesasne in eastern Ontario and western Quebec (Tarbell and Arquette, 2000).

Issues of environmental justice are dealt with even by people in some of the most remote parts of

A sign warning of toxic substances in Talfourd Creek on the Aamjiwnaang First Nation reserve near Sarnia, Ontario.
SOURCE: © AP Photo-Carlos Osorio/The Canadian Press.

the country, such as Inuit in Nunavik. Since some dangerous chemicals found in the environment are fat-soluble, they contribute to the body burden of women more than men. Mother's milk in particular is high in fat. Analysis of Inuit mothers' milk has shown that it contains five times as much polychlorinated biphenyl (PCB), a cancer-causing agent, than that of southern Canadian white women. In some cases, the concentration was even higher (Milly and Leiss, 1997). It is not permissible to feed cow's milk with this much PCB to infants.

PCB belongs to a set of chemicals known as persistent organic pollutants (POPs). POPs do not break down in the environment, even after centuries. They are produced for various industrial purposes in the southern areas of world. Over time, POPs are carried through wind currents to the northern regions, where they bioaccumulate in the fat of living things. Living things in the Arctic region are therefore threatened by environmental health risks they had no role in producing and from which they did not benefit. Such facts raise once again issues of inequality and injustice.

TIME FOR REVIEW

1. How is gender related to environmental inequality? How do the three main variants of ecofeminism differ?
2. What are some of the environmental justice issues faced by First Nations peoples in Canada?

SUMMARY

1. **What is the tragedy of the commons?**

   The *commons* refers to the environment we hold collectively, including the air, water, and soil that we all rely on to survive. As such, all environmental problems have a biophysical or material basis. But they also have a social basis insofar as the commons is used by people who decide how to manage and regulate the environment. Until recently, Western industrial societies encouraged the overexploitation of nature in a way that benefited the privileged few while externalizing the costs of environmentally destructive actions to everyone else. This is the tragedy of the commons. Today, society has to confront the tragedy of the commons by implementing policies based on the polluter-pays principle, the precautionary principle, and sustainable development.

2. **What are the key events that have contributed to increased environmental awareness and concern since the 1960s?**

   Public awareness of environmental issues increased from the 1960s onward, starting with the publication of *Silent Spring* and the *Limits to Growth Report*, the establishment of the environmental movement, and the oil crisis of 1973. In the 1980s, the discovery of two global environmental problems further reinforced the public's environmental concern: ozone depletion and global climate change. During that period, the influential notion of sustainable development was proposed by the international community as a way to manage environmental impacts without derailing economic growth. Since the 1990s, several high-profile international conferences have sought to coordinate efforts to combat global environmental problems.

3. **How are environmental issues socially constructed?**

   The social construction of environmental issues involves three stages: assembling, presenting, and contesting different claims or positions on an environmental issue. Claims-makers typically include scientists, celebrities, members of industry, politicians, social movement members, and journalists. Assembling evidence for the existence of an environmental problem usually relies on the work of scientists. The claim that the problem exists is then taken up by those involved in publicizing the issue. Different claims about the particularities and/or seriousness of the issue are then debated.

4. **What are the implications for the economy and society of using renewable versus nonrenewable natural resources?**

   To reduce environmental impacts, the use of renewable resources should be emphasized. Yet, because of the way our society has evolved since the industrial era, we appear to be locked into a way of life that depends on using environmentally destructive, nonrenewable resources. Thus, in Canada, the government receives revenue from the extraction of natural resources in the form of royalties from industry. Governments often argue that this is good for the economy. Yet this practice may not necessarily be good for society and the environment. The government may offer industry concessions in terms of environmental regulations so government can secure financial benefits. Such circumstances may enhance the opportunity for increased corruption, less democracy, and greater injustice. This situation is referred to as the "resource curse."

5. **What is the relationship between health and the environment? How is that relationship regulated by the state?**

   A polluted and contaminated environment in which we live, work, and play has negative impacts on human health—an unhealthy physical surrounding means an unhealthy person. Exposure to substances that cause us harm is subject to regulatory control based on risk management. Risk management is the process through which state agencies analyze data from animal experiments and epidemiological studies to come up with environmental regulations. These regulations set a legal limit to the amount of toxic chemicals that a company may emit. Industry often lobbies for less stringent regulation to save costs, while environmentalists call for stricter regulations to protect people. Thus, risk management is not just a technical exercise but is also a political debate.

6. **How is the environment relevant to issues of inequality and injustice?**

   People who are economically and socially disadvantaged are more likely to work and live in areas that are polluted or are otherwise hazardous to their health. Inequality is therefore linked to the unequal distribution of environmental risks, with relatively low status groups tending to shoulder a disproportionately large share of them. This pattern of unequal distribution is the result of political and economic decisions of dominant groups in society. Environmental justice groups have been created to raise awareness of such injustice and demand a fair response.

QUESTIONS TO CONSIDER

1. Sociologist Ulrich Beck (1995: 140) wrote that "the environmental problem is by no means a problem [only] of our surroundings. It is a crisis of industrial society itself, reaching deeply into the foundations of institutions; risks are produced industrially, externalized economically, legitimized scientifically, and minimized politically." Take an example of any environmental problem and construct an argument that supports or challenges the above statement.

2. Select an environmental issue and explain how it is socially constructed. Consider the different claims made by government officials, environmental movement actors, scientists, and industry officials. How did media coverage of the environmental issue you selected represent the various claims expressed? Was equal coverage given to all involved?

3. Search the Web to analyze the controversies that arose at the United Nations Climate Change Conference held in Lima, Peru, in 2014. What sort of issues arose and how can they be understood sociologically in terms of such concepts as the tragedy of the commons, sovereignty rights, environmental inequality and injustice, power relations, economic contingency, and framing?

GLOSSARY

Body burden (p. 414) refers to the sum of all foreign chemicals that accumulate in the human body over a given period.

Command-and-control approaches (p. 411) to environmental management are top–down government strategies that involve issuing regulations to control the environmental impact of industry.

The **economic contingency** (p. 406) thesis holds that public environmental concern depends on the state of the economy. In good economic times, more attention is given to environmental issues, while in bad times, environmental concerns lessen.

The **environmental justice movement** (p. 417) is a social movement that seeks to address issues associated with the unequal distribution of environmental risks caused by discrimination.

An **externality** (p. 404) is an environmental impact that is produced by one party (such as an industry) that does not take responsibility for the consequences of the environmental impact. Rather, the consequences are addressed by the state or the general public, which bears the cost of the environmental impact.

Food deserts (p. 414) refer to socially and economically distressed neighbourhoods that have sharply restricted access to healthy and nutritious foods.

Framing (p. 406) refers to the process of how events and issues are interpreted based on how they are presented.

Future discounting (p. 406) refers to the psychological tendency to forgo future benefits in favour of immediate benefits.

Jevon's paradox (p. 406) refers to a situation in which gains in the efficiency of natural resource use lead to greater overall consumer use of that resource. The paradox implies that increased efficiency yields no net benefit for the environment.

The **polluter-pays principle** (p. 411) addresses the externality problem by charging fines or taxes to force a corporation or country that causes pollution to pay the cost of environmental cleanup and protection.

A **resource curse** (p. 411) arises in regions where valuable natural resources are especially abundant. Such abundance discourages democracy because privately owned natural resource industries provide government with most of its revenue, allowing industry to exert excessive political influence and rendering government insufficiently politically accountable to taxpayers.

Risk management (p. 415) is the process of establishing regulations for protecting the environment and health. Risk management is not a narrow, technical field as much as a political process.

The **risk society thesis** (p. 405) states that contemporary societies have become preoccupied with issues related to the distribution of social "bads," chief among them the environmental risks and externalities produced by industry.

Sustainable development (p. 404) is an industrialization strategy that attempts to address economic, social, and environmental concerns in a balanced way by meeting the needs of the present generation without jeopardizing the ability of future generations to meet their needs.

A **tipping point** (p. 403) is a threshold beyond which a system unexpectedly, rapidly, and dramatically changes.

CHAPTER 18

HEALTH AND AGING

Margaret J. Penning **Neena L. Chappell**
UNIVERSITY OF VICTORIA

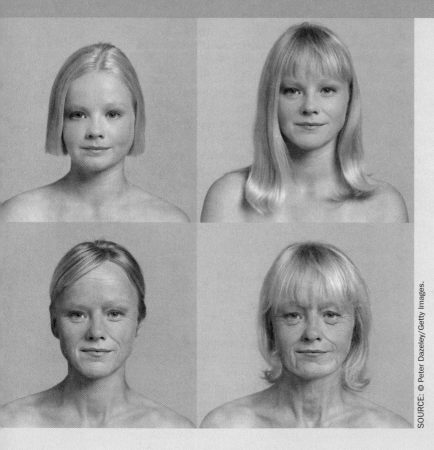

SOURCE: © Peter Dazeley/Getty Images.

AFTER READING THIS CHAPTER, YOU WILL BE ABLE TO:

- Challenge common misconceptions about health and aging.

- Recognize discrimination based on age and its implications.

- Understand how social inequalities associated with age, gender, social class, Indigenous status, and other factors influence health.

- Assess the importance of self-care; informal or unpaid care by family members and friends; and formal medical and nonmedical healthcare services for the provision of healthcare in later life.

- Evaluate claims regarding the benefits of public versus private provision of healthcare.

CHALLENGING COMMONSENSE BELIEFS ABOUT HEALTH AND AGING

Jean was born in 1925 on a small farm, one of seven children of a Swedish immigrant mother and a Métis father. She graduated from high school, finished a year of teacher's college, and returned home to marry John, whom she had met a few years earlier. John had been forced to quit school after Grade 8 to work on the family farm. Together, they settled on a small farm across the road from his parents. John dreamed of the day when he could buy more land and make a good living for himself and his family. Until then, he worked in the local steel mill, tending to the farm during the evening and on weekends. Meanwhile, Jean supported him in his work, taking care of their children and his parents, and doing various chores on the farm when she had time.

In 1953, John developed polio and spent the next year and a half in bed. Throughout his ordeal, Jean nursed him and cared for his parents. To make ends meet, she also worked the night shift as a nurse's aide at a local nursing home. Money was tight and there were numerous mouths to feed. With five children and another on the way, they were overjoyed when, after 12 years on the farm, they were able to add indoor plumbing. No more hand-washed diapers and no more running to the outhouse in the middle of winter! Living on a farm meant that although they could not afford much beyond necessities, there was always plenty to eat.

Over the years, economic circumstances improved as the children grew older and were able to help. Yet the years of poverty, hard work, and deprivation had left their mark. In 1991, at the age of 68, John died of a brain tumour. Although no one was sure, family members speculated about whether it had anything to do with the years spent working in the steel foundry and breathing in the chemical sprays that kept the weeds at bay on the farm. The pension that John earned at the steel mill did not provide Jean with an income, so she was forced to sell the family farm and rent an old house close to one of her daughters, whose children she cared for as her daughter worked. However, helping became increasingly difficult as Jean's health declined. Although she had quit smoking as soon as she heard about the problems it caused, she had developed a cough that would not go away. It left her winded, and she was unable to walk very far. For several years, she had also battled weight problems and was eventually diagnosed with diabetes. A year after moving, Jean suffered a stroke and died before she could get to the hospital. She was 69—old from the point of view of someone in his or her 20s but not in terms of the average life expectancy of women in Canada at the time. (**Life expectancy** is the number of years that the average person can expect to live.)

Jean's life story points to the many complexities we encounter when thinking about aging, health, and healthcare. When Jean died, people wondered why she hadn't taken better care of herself. Why did she let her weight go? Why hadn't she quit smoking before it became such a problem? Why had she opted to live in an area far from health services? After all, she was a bright and capable woman; if any woman could look after herself, it was Jean.

The assumption that Jean should have been able to make choices that would have been more beneficial to her health ignores the complex role of social-structural factors, such as social class, gender, age, ethnicity, and rural—urban residence, in defining the available range of choices and their implications for health and longevity. During and after the Depression and World War II, living and working conditions were often harsh. Gender also played an important role. At the time Jean and John were married, family fortunes were generally tied to men's occupations and income levels. The fact that Jean's work was largely unpaid and that she assumed responsibility for the care of other family members, continually placing their needs (including their health) above her own, was typical of the experience of women at the time. As a Métis woman, Jean may also have experienced additional barriers in her ability to gain access to employment, healthcare, and other resources. By the time John died, Jean was experiencing the accumulated health effects of her earlier life circumstances. However, old age and its associated low status also appear to have played a role, possibly undermining her health further by limiting access to economic resources, affordable housing, and appropriate healthcare.

Sociology offers a lens through which to examine the social factors linked to people's health and longevity as they age. This chapter discusses these issues.

It brings together two areas of sociology often considered separately—the sociology of aging and the sociology of health and illness (also known as *medical sociology*). We can easily connect the two: Aging tends to be equated with, and defined in terms of, ill health. Health tends to be a major problem in later life, and older adults account for much of the illness, disability, and healthcare use in any society. (By "older adults" we follow convention and refer to people over the age of 64.)

We begin by focusing on individual and population aging and the role of social factors in influencing how people age. Next, we address health as people age, including the relations among social inequalities, health, healthcare, and aging. Finally, we examine health-related issues in Canada in the context of international and global trends in healthcare.

At Confederation, average life expectancy in Canada was 42 years. In 2008, it approached 81 years. The number of people over the age of 64 has increased because of improved hygiene, sanitation, and nutrition, as well as healthcare.
SOURCE: © Monkey Business Images/Shutterstock.

INDIVIDUAL AND POPULATION AGING

In 1920, Canadian men lived to around 60 (see Table 18.1). People can now expect to live more than 20 years longer than if they had been born in 1920. Once they reach age 65, they can expect to live even longer. The fact that almost everyone can expect to live to old age distinguishes our era from earlier historical periods. In the past, some individuals lived as long as people live today, but never before has the vast majority lived to old age. With most of us now living to old age, it will not surprise you that older adults represent an increasing proportion of the Canadian population. In 1921, just over 5 percent of the population was age 65 and over. In 2014, this cohort represented almost 16 percent of the Canadian population. It is projected to constitute one-quarter of the population by 2036 (Statistics Canada, 2012a).

The main reason for the increasing proportion of older adults in the population is decreasing fertility from around four children per woman on average in the mid-1950s, to about one and two-thirds children per woman on average today. With declines in the number and proportion of children in the population, the proportion of older people necessarily increases. Moreover, declines in the **mortality rate** (deaths per 1000 people in a population) are now concentrated in older age cohorts (Chappell, McDonald, and Stones, 2008), resulting in relatively larger older age groups and thus contributing more to population aging.

We now live much of our lives assuming that an extended future lies before us. Consequently, forward thinking has become realistic. Most of us now are members of multigenerational families. Unlike in the past, young people today often know their grandparents and even their great-grandparents. Increased longevity also means that the illnesses and disabilities accompanying old age are more prominent and that different demands are placed on the healthcare system than was the case when fewer people lived to old age. Longer life expectancy results in more healthcare and service jobs for the younger generation. It affects when people retire and what they do after they retire. Now that mandatory retirement has disappeared from nearly all Canadian provinces and territories, more people will likely continue to be employed into their 70s and even their 80s (see Figure 18.1).

TABLE 18.1 LIFE EXPECTANCY BY BIRTH COHORT, CANADA, 1920–2009

YEAR	LIFE EXPECTANCY AT …					
	BIRTH FOR WOMEN	**65 FOR WOMEN**	**BIRTH FOR MEN**	**65 FOR MEN**	**BIRTH FOR POPULATION**	**65 FOR POPULATION**
1920	61	77	59	76	60	76.5
1930	62	78	60	77	61	77.5
1940	66	79.7	63	77.7	64.5	78.7
1950	71	80	66	78	68.5	79
1960	74	80.5	68	78	71	79.3
1970	76	81.5	69	78	72.5	79.8
1980	79	82.5	72	78.5	75.5	80.5
1990	81	81.5	75	81.5	78	81.5
2000	82	85.6	76.9	82.2	79.3	84.1
2007–09	83.3	86.6	78.8	83.5	81.1	85.2

SOURCES: Human Resources and Skills Development Canada (2009); Munroe (2003); Organisation for Economic Co-operation and Development (2009); Statistics Canada (2003a, 2006, 2011a, 2012b).

The social construction of old age—how society views older adults and the opportunities and constraints that they face—influences how older adults experience life. In contemporary Western societies, we tend to stereotype older people, a tendency referred to as **ageism**. We are inclined to see older adults as poor; frail; having no interest in, or capacity for, sexual relations; being socially isolated and lonely; and lacking a full range of abilities in the workplace. Researchers have documented ageism in younger people's attitudes toward older people, healthcare treatment, literary and dramatic portrayals, humour, and legal processes (Chappell, McDonald, and Stones, 2008). Some have called it a "quiet epidemic" that contributes to indifference (Stones and Stones, 1997). However, ageism speaks to our treatment of older people as a social category and not necessarily to interpersonal antagonism. Thus, we may treat our grandmothers well while also referring to and treating other older adults with indifference or even contempt.

Ageism exists for several reasons. Some analysts point to the importance of structural factors, such as the segregation of young and old age cohorts

and the fact that most older adults in Canada are not in the paid labour force and are therefore considered to be nonproductive members of society. Segregation can also result in a lack of knowledge about, and interaction with, older people. That also contributes to ageism (Hagestad and Uhlenberg, 2005). Thus, people who have had positive interactions with older people and those who have learned about aging tend to have fewer negative attitudes toward older adults (Ferraro et al., 2008). Finally, ageism is attributable in part to people's fear of their own future. Old age is associated with declining health, both physical and mental, and death. Old age has been "medicalized," so aging tends to be equated with disease.

Medicalization refers to the process whereby more and more areas of life come under the control of medicine (Zola, 1983). Families and the clergy used to deal with various forms of deviance, including alcoholism and mental health problems, that are now the province of medical authorities. The same holds for aging. Once considered a natural process, the effects of which could be eased only by social and spiritual support, aging is now treated largely as a

FIGURE 18.1   CANADIAN POPULATION AGE STRUCTURE, 1901–2050 (POPULATION IN THOUSANDS)

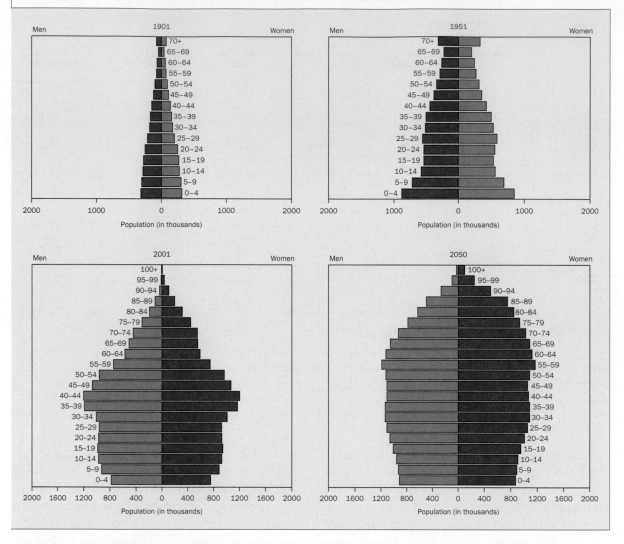

SOURCES: BCStats, "Population Estimates." 2014. http://www.bcstats.gov.bc.ca/StatisticsBySubject/Demography/PopulationEstimates.aspx (accessed Dec. 9, 2014); United States Census Bureau, "International Data Base." 2013. http://www.census.gov/population/international/data/idb/informationGateway.php (accessed Dec. 9, 2014).

disease requiring medical intervention (Estes, 1979; see Figure 18.2). Of course, medicine still cannot cure much of what happens during old age—a cure does not exist for Alzheimer's disease, and treatments for cancer are often ineffective—but we invest the bulk of our energies on finding medical cures for these and other ailments, often neglecting ways in which social and spiritual support can help older people as they face disease and death.

TIME FOR REVIEW

1. How is an aging population reflected in the changing shape of population pyramids over time (see Figure 18.1)?

2. In what sense is an aging society an achievement to be celebrated?

3. In what sense is an aging society a social problem requiring solution?

4. What is medicalization and how does it influence our attitudes toward, and treatment of, old age?

HEALTH AND OLD AGE

Old age tends to be associated with declining health. However, contrary to popular belief, most older adults are not in poor health. Nor do psychological and emotional health and social well-being necessarily deteriorate in step with deteriorating physical health.

FIGURE 18.2 HOW OFTEN THE TERMS *FEMALE SEXUAL DYSFUNCTION* AND *ERECTILE DYSFUNCTION* ARE MENTIONED IN THE PROQUEST DATABASE, 1990–2014

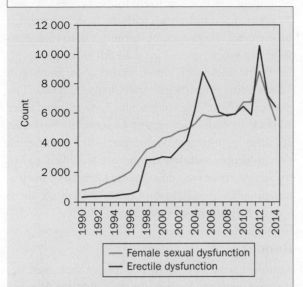

Note: Declining interest in sexual activity and ability to engage in sexual intercourse were considered normal aspects of aging until the 1990s, when female sexual dysfunction and erectile dysfunction became medicalized, that is, the subject of intense and growing medical and pharmaceutical interest. Viagra was first marketed in 1998 and the search for a female equivalent continues today. The pharmaceutical industry had to invest many millions of dollars on advertising to turn what was thought to be a natural problem into what is now widely regarded as a medical issue. This graph traces the transformation by showing how many times the medical phrases *female sexual dysfunction* and *erectile dysfunction* were mentioned in the ProQuest database every year from 1990 through 2014. The database contains the full text of 22 049 different newspapers, magazines, and academic journals in the sciences, social sciences, and humanities. Data for 2014 were collected on December 4 and extrapolated to December 31. That is, with 7.4 percent of 2014 not included in the count, the figures for 2014 were increased by 7.4 percent (ProQuest, 2014).

The probability of having one or more long-term health condition increases with age. Sixty percent of Canadians between the ages of 45 and 64, and 89 percent of Canadians over the age of 64 have at least one chronic condition (Public Health Agency of Canada, 2010). The most common conditions experienced in later life include high blood pressure, arthritis, back problems, eye problems (such as cataracts), and heart disease (Canadian Institute for Health Information, 2011).

However, these conditions do not necessarily interfere with day-to-day functioning. **Functional disability** exists when a health problem interferes with day-to-day functioning. For the most part, older Canadians consider themselves to be in good functional health based on levels of vision, hearing, speech, mobility, dexterity, feelings, cognition, and pain. In 2005, 62 percent of Canadians over the age of 64 reported having very good or excellent functional health (Public Health Agency of Canada, 2010).

Mental health is "the capacity of each of us to feel, think and act in ways that enhance our ability to enjoy life and deal with the challenges we face" (Public Health Agency of Canada, 2010). Mental health and physical health are related. People in good physical health tend to enjoy good mental health. Therefore, as people age and their physical health declines, we would expect their mental health to decline as well. However, research suggests that people's overall happiness tends to decrease after age 24, reaching a low among 35- to 44-year-olds, and then increases again so that 55- to 64-year-olds are as happy as 18- to 24-year-olds. People over the age of 64 are even happier (Helliwell, 2003). In 2008, fully 79 percent of older women and 77 percent of older men said they were happy (Milan and Vézina, 2011). In addition, over 90 percent of older adults reported being satisfied with their lives compared to 84 percent of 15- to 24-year-olds (Statistics Canada, 2005).

Self-esteem and feelings of mastery or control also seem to improve with age, peaking in middle age, followed by a modest decline in later life (Statistics Canada, 2001, 2007a). It is unclear why older adults often have such good mental and emotional health. Part of the answer may involve selection bias: surveys necessarily exclude people who died prematurely because of ill health, a disproportionately large number of whom may have been unhappy. Moreover, the older people who participate in surveys may have learned to cope with the exigencies of life or to compare themselves with those who are worse off, including those who have died. Perhaps the importance of material and physical matters wanes over time.

Although older adults generally enjoy good mental health, some experience mental disorders such as depression and cognitive impairment. These ailments tend to be linked to abuse and poverty early in life and increasing grief, poor physical health, institutionalization, isolation, and loneliness in the later years (Public Health Agency of Canada, 2010). Mental disorders often have physical causes. Dementia, or loss of cognitive function, is one example. In Canada, about one in eleven adults over the age of 64 has some form of dementia, including Alzheimer's disease (Canadian Institute for Health Information, 2011). About three-quarters of older adults with dementia live in long-term-care facilities. These rates increase with age (Dubois and Hébert, 2006).

In general, however, the social life of older adults is characterized by social integration, not social isolation. A minority of older adults, particularly those who are poor, very old, or physically frail, are vulnerable to social isolation. However, most older adults are embedded in **modified extended family** networks (Litwak, 1960) characterized by mutual and close intergenerational ties, responsible filial behaviour, and contact between generations. Sociological research conducted over the past three decades has debunked the notion that families abandon their older members. Most older adults enjoy extensive social contacts, live close to at least one of their children, and have close friends and confidantes (Antonucci, 1990).

Evidence that an increasing proportion of older adults is enjoying good health has led sociologists to introduce the **compression of morbidity hypothesis**, which holds that, in the future, we will be able to postpone the onset of chronic disability to the point where most people will be able to live relatively healthy lives until very shortly before death, when they will experience rapid deterioration (Fries, 1983). Recent research suggests that although we are far from a dependency-free old age, many Canadians are experiencing a later age of onset of functional limitations. This is good news, especially if the trend continues. Unfortunately, however, the vagaries of old age are not evenly distributed, as we will now see.

INEQUALITY, HEALTH, AND AGING

Research suggests that in recent decades the declining death rate has been steeper in some segments of the population than in others (Schalick et al., 2000). In general, people with more education, income, and wealth live longer than others do. They also tend to spend a greater proportion of their lives in good health.

Education

People with more education are able to avoid or postpone disability to a greater extent than are those with less education, although education may be less beneficial once disability is present (Huisman et al., 2005). People with a university degree often feel healthy and function well late into their 60s, 70s, and 80s, whereas those with less education do not (Ross and Wu, 1996). A recent Canadian study focused on changes in health over a three-year period among adults aged 50 and over, all of whom were in good health in the first year. It found that the likelihood of remaining in good health was greater among men and women in the highest educational groups (Buckley et al., 2005).

Income

Income is also important to health. One report shows that men with the lowest 5 percent of earnings before retirement are twice as likely to die between 65 and 70 years of age as are men with the highest 5 percent of earnings. High-income earners experience considerably more years of good health than those with lower incomes, with some reporting as much as a 12-year difference (Segall and Chappell, 2000). The pattern holds among older adults. Low-income, older adults with disabilities tend to be more disabled than are their high-income counterparts. As a result, even though people with low income are less likely to live to old age, those who do are more likely to be institutionalized in long-term-care facilities than are those with higher incomes (Trottier et al., 2000).

Gender

Although women tend to live longer than men do, they are generally less healthy than men are. Women report more multiple health problems associated with chronic conditions, such as arthritis and rheumatism, high blood pressure, back problems, and allergies (Chappell, McDonald, and Stones, 2008). Men are more likely to have heart disease, diabetes, cancer, and Alzheimer's disease (DesMeules, Turner, and Cho, 2004; Gilmour and Park, 2005).

One study found that 85 percent of older women report one or more chronic condition, compared with 78 percent of older men. Although the likelihood of disability increases with age for both men and women, women are more likely to report limitations in activities of daily living or disability in later life than men are (Gilmour and Park, 2005). Women also report more severe disability than men do. That is, although men have lower life expectancy, they live a greater proportion of their lives without disabling conditions. While evidence suggests that men and women experience similar levels of mental health problems, they may manifest them differently—for example, as depression in women and as alcohol and drug abuse and suicidal behaviour in men (Simon, 2000).

Indigenous Status

In Canada, big differences exist between Indigenous and non-Indigenous adults in terms of health and well-being. Although the gap appears to have decreased somewhat in recent years, the life expectancy of Indigenous Canadians currently remains six years less than that of non-Indigenous Canadians (Cooke et al., 2007). Differences are also evident

FIGURE 18.3 ABORIGINAL AND NON-ABORIGINAL CANADIANS' LIFE EXPECTANCY AT BIRTH BY SEX, 1991, 2001, AND 2017 (PROJECTED)

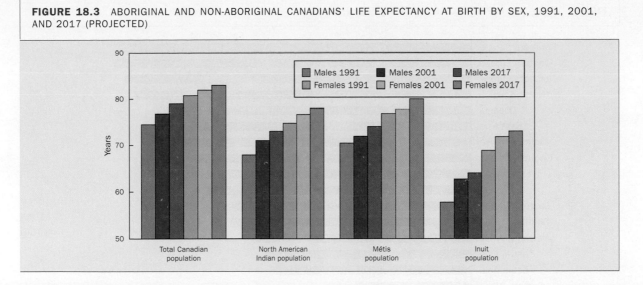

SOURCE: Statistics Canada (2007b; 2010).

within the Indigenous population (see Figure 18.3). Indigenous populations suffer from more chronic illnesses, including heart disease and diabetes, than non-Indigenous populations do (Anand et al., 2001). They also have higher disability levels. In 2001, 70 percent of Indigenous adults ages 65 and over living off-reserve reported one or more disabilities, including difficulties hearing, seeing, walking, climbing stairs, bending, and doing various other activities, nearly twice the rate for non-Indigenous people of the same age (Statistics Canada, 2007b). Although most older Canadian adults rate their health as excellent or very good, fewer than half of non-reserve Indigenous adults over the age of 64 report having excellent or very good health.

Reasons for these differences in health and life expectancy are numerous. In Indigenous populations, death from infectious and parasitic diseases is associated with inadequate housing and unsanitary conditions.

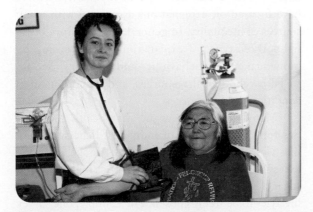

The life expectancy of Indigenous Canadians is about six years shorter than that of non-Indigenous Canadians.
SOURCE: © Photodisc.

According to one government report, 75 percent of Indigenous community water systems pose a high or medium risk to water quality (Indian and Northern Affairs Canada, 2003). Suicide rates are also high, as are death rates from drowning, fire, homicide, and motor vehicle accidents (Allard, Wilkins, and Berthelot, 2004). Racism and discrimination increase the risk of psychological distress, depression, and unemployment, and lack of access to opportunities and resources is conducive to poor health (Noh et al., 1999).

Race, Ethnicity, and Immigration Status

Health inequities are also evident when we compare other racial, ethnic and immigrant groups. Health and longevity vary widely from one country to the next (see Figure 18.4). Less than one-quarter of Canadians aged 65 and over who were born in Canada, the United States, Europe, Australia, and Asia report fair or poor health. This percentage is considerably higher (about 33 percent) among those born in Central and South America and Africa (Chappell, McDonald, and Stones, 2008). Interestingly, however, immigrants, especially recent arrivals, generally enjoy better health than their Canadian-born counterparts do, a pattern observed to varying degrees for such health outcomes as chronic diseases, disability, dependency, life expectancy, and disability-free life expectancy (Chen, Ng, and Wilkins, 1996).

This **healthy immigrant effect** may seem surprising at first glance. However, it likely reflects the Canadian government requirement that potential immigrants meet a minimum standard of health before being admitted to the country.

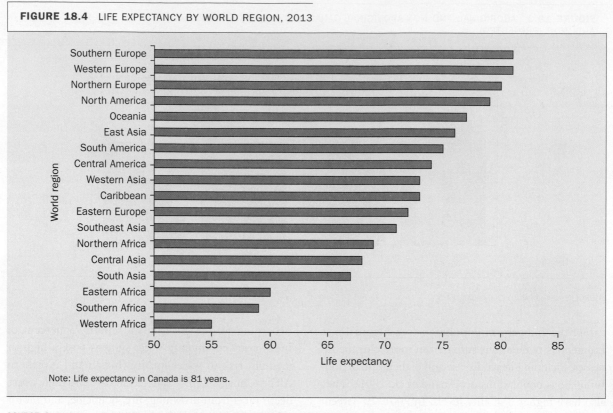

FIGURE 18.4 LIFE EXPECTANCY BY WORLD REGION, 2013

Note: Life expectancy in Canada is 81 years.

SOURCE: Carl Haub and Toshiko Kaneda, *2014, World Population Data Sheet* (Washington: Population Reference Bureau, 2014). http://www.prb.org/pdf14/2014-world-population-data-sheet_eng.pdf (accessed Dec. 6, 2014).

Immigrants who have lived in Canada for a long period do not have a similar advantage. Does this mean that immigrants' health tends to decline after immigration? In fact, this seems to be what is taking place (Pérez, 2002). The search is on for explanations of this phenomenon. Most analysts focus on the negative health implications of changes in diet and activity levels, discrimination, declines in income and other resources, and difficulties in accessing healthcare services in the years immediately following immigration (Gee, Kobayashi, and Prus, 2004).

EXPLAINING SOCIAL INEQUALITIES IN HEALTH

What exactly is it about age, gender, Indigenous status, ethnicity, race, social class, and other inequalities that result in poorer health? Early research focused on biological explanations and on differences associated with health services use, including differences in the likelihood that people would follow doctors' orders and inequalities in access to healthcare services. Indeed, the view that creating an equitable healthcare system would eliminate or at least reduce health inequalities was a major argument for the creation of a universal healthcare system in this country. More recently, evidence that inequalities in health and longevity have persisted despite the introduction of a universal healthcare system has led to renewed attempts to account for such differences. Some researchers have offered explanations that are specific to one or another type of inequality. Others have focused on explanations associated with many sources of inequality. In general, the literature highlights three types of explanations: one focusing on individual health behaviours and lifestyles, one on social psychological resources, and one on material conditions and resources.

Many researchers argue that health inequalities reflect the impact of individual behaviours and lifestyles, including whether people smoke, consume excessive amounts of alcohol, eat foods high in fat and sugar, and lack regular exercise. People often consider lifestyles to be freely chosen. For example, one survey asked Canadians what the major determinants of health are. The most common responses referred to

When surveyed, Canadians identified a person's smoking, eating, weight, experience of stress, and exercise habits as the major determinants of health.

SOURCE: © Neil Roy Johnson/Shutterstock.

such factors as those just listed (Canadian Institute for Health Information, 2005).

Although research finds a link between social location and lifestyle factors, sociologists often criticize such explanations because they ignore how social inequalities can trump individual decisions in determining health outcomes (see the Critical Sociology: Social Inequality box). Thus, studies comparing the importance of individual decisions against social factors, such as income adequacy, often find that the latter are more important (House, 2001; Williamson, 2000). Moreover, when researchers focus on individual decision making, they often neglect the fact that people rarely make choices freely from a full range of possible options. We can criticize low-income earners for failing to exercise more, but only if we ignore that they may live in neighbourhoods where an evening jog is dangerous, affordable recreational facilities don't exist, and lack of child-care options means they have little time for such pursuits in any event. As this example shows, social inequalities structure choices. Attending only to individual decision making often amounts to blaming victims for structured inequalities.

A second explanation for how social location generates health inequalities draws attention to the role of stress and other psychosocial factors, including depression and perceptions of relative deprivation. From this perspective, inequality and lack of access to economic and other resources generate stress, leading to poor health. In addition,

some analysts argue that more than poverty is at work here. They note that if poverty were the only problem, we would expect to find substantial differences in health between the poor and the nonpoor, but little or no difference between those who are only moderately well off versus those who are wealthy. Yet this is not the case. Instead, each increment in income brings additional health advantages.

This finding suggests that it is not just poverty but the *perception* or *awareness* of inequality that leads to bad health. This is the **hierarchy stress perspective**, which suggests that when people compare their situation with that of others and see their situation negatively, they experience stress and their health declines (Link and Phelan, 2000). In addition to causing poor health, stress can operate indirectly by leading people to smoke tobacco, consume too much alcohol, eat too much or too little, sleep too little, and take dangerous drugs—all of which eventually have a negative impact on health in their own right (Link and Phelan, 2000).

Finally, some explanations emphasize resources and material conditions as the mechanisms linking people's social location to health outcomes. Such arguments hold that people's social class, age, gender, race, and ethnicity contribute to differential access to a range of resources that contribute to good or poor health. These resources include enough income to buy nutritious food, enough education to be aware of health issues (such as what constitutes a nutritious diet), access to means of illness prevention, the ability to avoid risk factors (such as living in environments where dangerous chemicals are present), and so on (Link and Phelan, 2000). Some researchers operating in this tradition insist that we should focus less on the resources that contribute to good or poor health and more on the way social class, age, gender, race, and ethnicity directly contribute to "systematic material, social, cultural, and political exclusion from mainstream society" (Raphael, 2005: 4). These structural factors are therefore considered to be fundamental causes of health status, influencing access to health-related resources, which, in turn, influence health (Link and Phelan, 2000; see the Critical Sociology: Protest and Policy box).

Debate continues regarding whether individual behaviours and lifestyle characteristics, stress and other psychosocial factors, or material conditions and resources are more important for understanding inequalities in health. The answer may well be "all of

Governments, health associations, and health workers pepper the public with health tips. They almost always focus on individual decision making and assume that people are free to decide what to do with their lives. They fail to take into account the important role of social inequality in structuring health choices. In contrast, social inequality lies at the centre of sociological studies of health choices. From a sociological point of view, while people are free to choose what to do with their lives, their ability to make healthy choices is constrained by their social location. Table 18.2 contrasts the two approaches.

Critical Thinking Questions

1. Compare and contrast individualistic and sociological approaches to explaining the impact of diet and exercise on health.

2. How has social location influenced your ability to make healthy choices?

TABLE 18.2   INDIVIDUALISTIC AND SOCIOLOGICAL HEALTH TIPS COMPARED

INDIVIDUALISTIC HEALTH TIPS	SOCIOLOGICAL HEALTH TIPS
Don't smoke. If you can, stop. If you can't, cut down.	Don't be poor. If you can, stop. If you can't, try not to be poor for long.
Eat a balanced diet with plenty of fruits and vegetables.	Don't have poor parents.
Keep physically active.	Own a car.
Manage stress by, for example, talking things through and making time to relax.	Don't have a stressful, low-paid manual job.
If you drink alcohol, do so in moderation.	Don't live in a damp, dilapidated dwelling.
Cover up in the sun, and protect children from sunburn.	Be able to afford to go on a holiday.
Practise safe sex.	Don't become unemployed. If you must become unemployed, don't remain unemployed for long.
Get screened for cancer regularly.	Use all of the benefits you are entitled to if you are unemployed, retired, or sick, or if you have a disability.
Be safe on the roads.	Don't live next to a busy road or near a polluting factory.
Learn first aid.	Learn how to fill out complex social housing application forms before you become destitute and homeless.

SOURCE: Townsend Centre for International Poverty Research, "Health Inequalities: Alternative Tips." http://www.bristol.ac.uk/poverty/healthinequalities.html (accessed Sept. 25, 2015). Adapted courtesy of David Gordon; Liam Donaldson, "Ten Tips for Better Health," *Saving Lives: Our Healthier Nation* (London: The Stationery Office, 1999).

the above." As one study notes, "material conditions are intimately tied to psychological states, health behaviors, and social circumstances that also influence health," and we can see "these psychosocial states and health behaviors ... as responses to adverse conditions imposed by broader social and economic structures" (Lynch and Kaplan, 2000: 25).

INTERSECTING INEQUALITIES AND HEALTH OVER THE LIFE COURSE

Increasingly, sociologists are interested in the effects of multiple statuses or inequalities on health outcomes. For example, the **age as leveller hypothesis** argues that age effects cut across all other statuses, in effect levelling inequalities from earlier in life. The

Genes by themselves are responsible for just 5 to 10 percent of all cancers and a substantially smaller percentage of cancers in people over the age of 25. In other words, although genetic mutations cause all cancers, environmental factors cause more than 90 percent of the genetic mutations leading to cancer. "Environment" in this context means anything that people interact with, including exposures resulting from what we eat, drink, or smoke; natural and medical radiation; drugs; socioeconomic factors that affect exposures and susceptibility; and substances in air, water, and soil.

If environmental carcinogens cause more than 90 percent of the genetic mutations resulting in cancer, it follows that we can win the war on cancer by eliminating the offending substances or at least drastically reducing their prevalence and our contact with them. Unfortunately, the structure of our society makes it difficult for us to take preventive measures, partly because many people lack the resources that would allow them to, partly because industry and government resist change. This is the cancer paradox: although we know how to reduce the cancer incidence rate drastically, we have not been able to do so.

For example, tobacco consumption and poor diet (especially consuming too much red meat, animal fat, salt, sugar, and alcohol) cause more than 60 percent of cancers. Environmental pollution and exposure to hazardous substances at work account for another 10 percent or so. However, people who avoid these hazards tend to be comparatively well educated and well to do.

Even when low-income and less educated people know about the need to stop smoking and improve their diets, urging them to do so tends to have little effect. That is because the conditions of their existence conspire against them. At work, they are more likely to experience little control and high stress than higher-income and better-educated people are. At home, they are more likely to face marital stress and divorce because of money problems. They are therefore more likely to turn to tobacco and alcohol to help them feel better in the short term.

They are also more likely than better-educated and higher-income people are to be exposed to carcinogens at work. Miners, construction workers, people who work with asbestos, welders, petroleum refinery workers, rubber industry workers, textile industry workers, footwear production and repair workers, hairdressers, farmers, paint manufacturing workers, house painters, furniture and cabinet makers, machine shop workers, and garage mechanics all have elevated cancer incidence rates. In their neighbourhoods, they tend to suffer relatively high exposure to air and water pollutants that contribute to cancer risk because on average they live closer to dirty industries and industrial waste sites than others do. Because of their low income, they often find unhealthy foods within their budget and healthy foods too expensive. The notion that people in such circumstances are free to lower their cancer risk is naive to say the least.

Given the situation just described, you might think that governments and voluntary associations concerned with cancer would be investing heavily in research on how disadvantaged people can gain the educational, organizational, and political resources needed to change health, environmental, industrial, and social policy in a way that would lower their exposure to cancer risk. However, if we break down the $402 million that the Canadian government and voluntary associations spent in 2007 on cancer research, we find nothing of the kind. Some 55.1 percent of this sum went to investigating the biological causes of the disease. Another 43.1 percent went to research on detection, diagnosis, prognosis, treatment, and related efforts. Just 1.8 percent—$7 million—was allocated to work on prevention. These sums refer just to research budgets. If we added the medical costs of dealing with cancer, the imbalance between the massive effort aimed at cure versus the paltry effort aimed at prevention would be even more glaring.

Funding priorities remain what they are because powerful industrial interests, governments, and segments of the population benefit economically from a bias toward finding cures rather than taking preventive action. A reorientation of policy would cause them financial harm. For example, cleaning up cancer "hot spots," such as Windsor and Sarnia, Ontario; Fort Chipewyan, Alberta; and Sydney, Nova Scotia would involve massive expense and industrial dislocation on the part of major petrochemical and other companies. Or consider the cost of creating a string of "wellness centres" in low-income neighbourhoods across Canada to equalize opportunities across classes for good health and longevity. Such neighbourhood institutions could offer tasty and healthy meals for the same price as a Big Mac, medium fries, and a Coke, with menus formulated to suit the ethnic tastes of area residents. They could offer free nicotine patches and support groups for people wanting to quit smoking; free on-site cancer screening facilities; free counselling services for people facing marital or work-related stress; free competitive and instructional basketball, soccer, dance, and swimming activities for all age groups; and ads everywhere (multilingual where necessary) featuring famous role models promoting the new centres. How would McDonald's respond to the

(continued)

(continued)

competition? How would taxpayers (most of them middle-, upper-middle, and upper-class) respond to the required expense?

Critical Thinking Questions

1. Why is it that those with lower education or income levels are less likely to take steps to reduce their cancer risk?

2. What are some things that you can do to minimize your risk of cancer?

3. Anti-smoking policies would seem to represent an area where governmental and powerful industrial interests differ. Why is it that governments have introduced policies detrimental to industry's interests in this area but not in others?

SOURCE: From BRYM. *Sociology as a Life or Death Issue*, 2E. © 2012 Nelson Education Ltd. Reproduced by permission. www.cengage.com/permissions

competing **multiple jeopardy hypothesis** argues that the effects of membership in multiple low-status groups are cumulative. Thus, being female and old has more negative consequences than being either female *or* old (Markides, 1983).

More recently, researchers have argued that statuses cannot simply be added together to judge their effects. Instead, the **intersectionality hypothesis** argues that health inequities result from the intersection of different social locations (Hankivsky, 2009; McMullin, 2004). For example, annual income influences health but does so differently for men and women. Living in poverty has a stronger negative effect on women's health than on men's health (Prus and Gee, 2002). As a result, the greatest differences in life expectancy between men and women occur in the poorest areas of the country (DesMeules, Manuel, and Cho, 2004). Thus, in this example, health inequity results from the intersection of annual income and gender. Similarly, Indigenous status and age intersect so that the gap in health status between Indigenous people and the rest of the Canadian population widens in older age groups (Statistics Canada, 2003b).

Conversely, some factors shrink health inequalities later in life. For example, the gap between upper- and lower-income groups increases as people reach their middle years (40s, 50, and 60s) and declines thereafter (Martel, Bélanger, Berthelot, and Carrière, 2005). Does this mean that socioeconomic inequalities in health diminish with age? This seems unlikely because many poor people die before reaching old age, a fact that comparisons of the health status of survivors ignores.

Finally, we note that, as a person ages, the social and economic factors that influence health change. According to the **life course perspective**, the circumstances experienced at all stages of life (including infancy, childhood, adolescence, young adulthood,

and later adulthood) combine to influence what happens in later life. Some events and circumstances experienced earlier in life (for example, a car accident that leaves a person unable to walk) will affect that person's health for life regardless of what else happens later on. However, the impact of other events or circumstances is likely to accumulate gradually over the life course. Over time, a person may experience a number of events or situations (such as a car accident, subsequent unemployment, and the death of a spouse) that may have a negative impact on health. These events may be unrelated to one another. However, it is common for adverse exposures to be related. Children born into poor social and economic circumstances are more likely to have low birth weights, be exposed to poor diets, experience passive smoke exposure, and have below-average educational opportunities. These early life experiences are likely to continue in adulthood. Longevity and health in later life is likely to be a product of all these factors.

TIME FOR REVIEW

1. What are the implications of gender, social class, and ethnic differences for health in later life?

2. Assess the importance of individual health behaviours or lifestyles, social psychological factors, and material conditions and resources for an understanding of social inequalities in health.

3. Compare and contrast the multiple jeopardy and intersectionality hypotheses for understanding differences in the health of Indigenous and non-Indigenous men and women in later life.

HEALTHCARE

How we view the causes of health problems influences how we deal with them. If we see the health problems of older adults as the result of what happens only in later life, we will target interventions to older adults. If we adopt a life course perspective and conclude that many of the health problems of older adults have their roots in lifelong experiences, we will want to address what happens early in life as well. If we attribute health problems to freely chosen personal behaviours, we will consider older adults responsible for their own health problems and will likely implement solutions aimed at educating people to make better choices in the future or we will demand that people deal with the problems they themselves have created. If we attribute health inequalities to perceptions of stress, we may focus on altering how people view their circumstances rather than changing the circumstances themselves. If we see the organization of society and the distribution of economic and social resources as the main determinants of health, we will see economic and social policies as a means of improving health (Raphael, 2005). How then do Canadians deal with healthcare?

SELF-CARE AND INFORMAL CARE

Most people care for themselves most of the time; **self-care** is the primary form of care even when health declines and we require help from others and the healthcare system. We wash our hands, exercise, choose what to eat, establish any number of lifestyle practices, try to have a positive outlook on life, and when we feel ill, go to bed or take over-the-counter drugs.

Except in emergencies, when we turn to others for help, we generally turn first to family members and friends. This is just as true in old age as when we are young. Indeed, throughout history, family members and friends have been the first resources for care. Despite what you may hear about modern, Western societies such as Canada being individualistic, youth-oriented, and dismissive of older adults, the fact is that we continue to care for older family members in need. In virtually all developed societies, about three-quarters of all care to older adults comes from family members and, to a lesser degree, from friends and neighbours (Cranswick, 2003; Kane, 1990). Typically, the spouse is the first to provide care when the health of the other spouse fails; typically, the wife provides care for her husband.

After the husband's death, the wife may enjoy a few more years of good health before she needs assistance. Her children, usually her daughters,

Regardless of the resources that the healthcare system makes available, most older adults first turn to family members for care.
SOURCE: © Shutterstock.

provide most of the care before her death. Notice that informal caring comes primarily from wives and daughters. Sons provide mainly financial assistance and advice, while daughters provide mainly emotional support and hands-on care. However, if no daughter is available and a son is close by, then the son usually provides the necessary care (Keating, Fast, Frederick, Cranswick, and Perrier, 1999). This is possible because the great majority of older adults live close to at least one child.

Usually, families readily assume responsibility for the care of their older members. Research has put to rest the myth that families in contemporary Western societies abandon older members (Montgomery, Borgatta, and Borgatta, 2000). Despite what we have been hearing for many years about changing family forms, more women working in the paid labour force, fewer children being available to provide help, and greater geographic mobility, there is no indication that families are decreasing their involvement in the care of their older family members.

FORMAL MEDICAL AND HOME CARE

Often, family members cannot provide all the care loved ones need. Sometimes care calls for specialized knowledge, skills, medicine, and equipment that only physicians or other healthcare personnel can provide. Sometimes the sheer amount of time and effort required exceeds the family's capabilities. In such cases, people turn to the formal healthcare system. Canada's publicly funded healthcare system, like the healthcare systems of other wealthy countries (the United States excepted), offers universal access to physician and acute care hospital services for its citizens based on need rather than the ability to pay. In Canada, this system is known as Medicare.

A Brief History of Medicare

Before the establishment of Medicare, people needing healthcare were required to pay for it or do without. This situation was especially problematic for poor people whose health needs were often great—among them a disproportionately large number of older adults, the unemployed, and those with chronic disabilities. Gaps in access to healthcare were particularly apparent in the years following World War I and the Depression of the 1930s. With Tommy Douglas, the leader of the Cooperative Commonwealth Federation (CCF) party and premier of Saskatchewan, leading the way, Canada gradually introduced legislation to address these needs. In 1957, the Hospital Insurance and Diagnostic Services Act led to hospital care coverage for the entire population. In 1966, the Medical Care Act laid the groundwork for universal health insurance for physician services. By 1972, all Canadian provinces and territories had joined the program, with the federal government sharing physician and hospital services costs on a 50/50 basis with the provinces and territories.

From the outset, healthcare in Canada was structured as a provincial and territorial responsibility. The federal government develops policy and assists with funding, but each province and territory is responsible for delivering services. Through Medicare, every province and territory offers publicly funded physician and acute care hospital services. This does not mean that we have "socialized medicine." Rather, a third party (the government) pays for most services on our behalf. Most physicians in Canada operate as private entrepreneurs; governments pay them for the services they decide are necessary and that they render. In other words, we publicly finance healthcare but physicians provide it privately, with payment guaranteed by the government. The more services physicians provide, the more they earn. They hold this privileged position because of the importance our society attaches to their expertise, which makes them the gatekeepers to our healthcare system. Only physicians can certify that we are sick, order medical tests and prescription drugs, and admit us to hospital.

Historically, we defined health as the absence of disease, thereby excluding from coverage preventative measures and other therapies based on a broad, holistic view of health. We did not cover many types of healthcare, such as dentistry, home care, nursing homes, physiotherapy, counselling, podiatry, drugs prescribed outside the hospital, chiropractic services, midwifery, and massage therapy. As a result, coverage for such services varies across provinces and territories. Some jurisdictions provide some of these services as part of their healthcare system at no cost to the user. Others provide them at minimal cost or on a means-tested basis whereby people's finances are assessed. If they can afford a required service, they pay for it. Otherwise, government subsidizes the cost. Access to such services also varies. For example, some places require physician referral while others permit self-referral.

Home Care Services in an Aging Society

Although different healthcare services are important to different people at different times, one type of healthcare service that has become especially important in an aging society is home care. It brings services into people's homes, where they prefer to live, rather than requiring them to move to a seniors' residence or a nursing home. It is also much less expensive than nursing home care (Chappell and Hollander, 2011).

Typically, home care includes personal care, nursing, and physiotherapy services. It can also include housekeeping, meal preparation, transportation, and respite services. Home care is not primarily about providing medical care. Instead, it offers care for social roles or activities that a medical condition prevents us from providing for ourselves, such as housekeeping, grocery shopping, and seeking the company of others. For many older adults, staying in their own homes requires not only home care but also the presence of an unpaid caregiver. Despite its importance, home care accounts for less than 5 percent of public healthcare expenditures (Conference Board of Canada, 2012). Today, most provinces are moving to more private, for-profit provision of home care, particularly for nonmedical services.

HEALTHCARE SYSTEM CHANGE AND REFORM

In the years following the establishment of Medicare, the cost of healthcare rose steadily. As a result, by the 1980s, the federal government had shifted away from earlier agreements to share the costs of healthcare equally with the provinces and territories to a form of block funding, giving provinces and territories a set amount of money to cover healthcare services. In response, the provinces and territories began experimenting with user fees and extra billing to offset federal funding cuts. In 1984, the federal government passed the Canada Health Act requiring the provinces and territories to maintain universal coverage, reasonable access to services, portability of benefits across provinces and territories, comprehensive services, and nonprofit administration by a public agency. It also banned user fees and extra billing.

However, fiscal concerns remained. In the late 1980s and 1990s, the provinces, territories, and federal government further restricted healthcare spending and appointed commissions to review the system. Public debate erupted around the viability of a publicly funded healthcare system and, within government, the discussion broadened from concerns over financing to whether we need a different type of healthcare system. For the first time since the introduction of Medicare, Canadian citizens and governments began to ask whether the right providers were providing the right services to the right people.

Without denying the importance of medical care by physicians, nearly all government reviews reached the same conclusion: We need to shift away from a system that is almost entirely biomedical and concerned only with the treatment and cure of disease, and acknowledge that health is "a state of complete physical, mental, and social well-being and not merely the absence of disease or infirmity" (World Health Organization, 1948). This definition implies a broad conception of care that incorporates health promotion, disease prevention, and attention to the social and environmental determinants of health. Deinstitutionalizing health services and providing more care outside hospitals was also recommended as more appropriate and cost-effective.

Major reforms followed. Most provinces regionalized healthcare services, fewer people received acute and extended care, hospital admissions fell, length of hospital stays dropped, and many surgical treatments moved to outpatient settings (Brownell, Roos, and Roos, 2001; Canadian Institute for Health Information, 2007; Carriere, Roos, and Dover, 2000). At the same time, people increased their use of healthcare services not usually considered part of conventional medicine. This included various forms of complementary and alternative medicine (CAM), such as aromatherapy, naturopathic medicine, chiropractic care, acupuncture, yoga and massage therapy (Chappell and Penning, 2009). Those who were the most likely to use CAM were women, middle-aged adults, people with higher education and income levels, people residing in urban areas, certain ethnic groups, and people with a chronic health problem (Esmail, 2007; Metcalfe et al., 2010; Park, 2004). Their reasons for using CAM included dissatisfaction with conventional medicine, a belief in CAM's more holistic philosophy, and a desire for more involvement and control over their health and healthcare (Penning and Votova, 2008).

Despite these shifts, a new vision for a publicly funded healthcare system that is more holistic and incorporates health promotion, disease prevention, CAM, and attention to the social and environmental determinants of health, did not occur (Lewis et al., 2001). To date, there is little evidence of an expanded focus on health promotion and disease prevention. Nor has attention shifted toward dealing with the social and environmental determinants of health, including poverty and inequality. For the most part, CAM services still receive only limited coverage under Medicare or other healthcare plans. Increases to home care budgets are being directed mainly to short-term, post-hospital and nursing care, reinforcing a medical focus, rather than meeting the long-term chronic care needs of older adults (Penning, Brackley, and Allan, 2006). Indeed, healthcare reform is now narrowing the scope back to medical care. Why?

PRIVATIZATION AND PROFITIZATION

Some health care reformers emphasize the need for privatization and profitization. **Privatization** involves a shift in the production of goods and services from the public (government or state) sector to the private sector (Starr, 1988). It includes selling publicly owned or controlled organizations or services to businesses or other nongovernmental entities. **Profitization** involves turning institutions into profit-making organizations. Privatization and profitization expand the money-making opportunities available to big businesses and their owners but render individual citizens, particularly those with low-income, less well protected.

Recent changes in Canada's healthcare system, including shortened hospital stays and the decline in long-term home care services, allow increasing profitization (Williams et al., 2001). Citizens, as consumers, are being asked to seek services privately that were once provided by the public sector. Private funding accounts for an increasing share of Canada's healthcare budget, including CAM and home care expenses (Armstrong, Armstrong, and Coburn, 2001). Of particular concern is that the terms of the North American Free Trade Agreement (NAFTA) can be interpreted as meaning that once the Canadian government allows businesses to enter an area previously in the public sector, returning it to the public sector is permissible only if the government compensates for-profit firms for lost future profits—practically an impossibility. That is why a 2002 Royal Commission devoted an entire chapter of its report to arguing that Canada must state publicly and at every opportunity that our healthcare services are not to be included in NAFTA (Commission on the Future of Health Care in Canada, 2002). Government has failed to do so.

For-profit healthcare tends to be more expensive than universal public programs. For-profit healthcare costs governments less, but people who use the services pay more. Much of the increased cost comes from administrative overhead charges (Marmor and Sullivan, 2000; see Figure 18.5). A for-profit system also leaves many citizens without any health insurance. In the United States, one-sixth of the population lacked health insurance and another one-sixth lacked adequate coverage before President Obama's 2010 healthcare reform (DeNavas-Walt, Proctor, and Smith, 2010). In the period 2010–2014, health insurance coverage broadened, although tens of millions of Americans remained uninsured or underinsured after 2014—most of them poor, illegal immigrants, or both. Canada's Medicare system provides basic care to all people in need although some research suggests this is not the case for specialist services (Dunlop, Coyte, and McIsaac, 2000). People who earn low income, the older population, and women receive more services because their needs tend to be greater.

The risk is that as more of our healthcare services are profitized, more people with healthcare needs will be disadvantaged. Access to needed care will increasingly vary by class, gender, and racial and

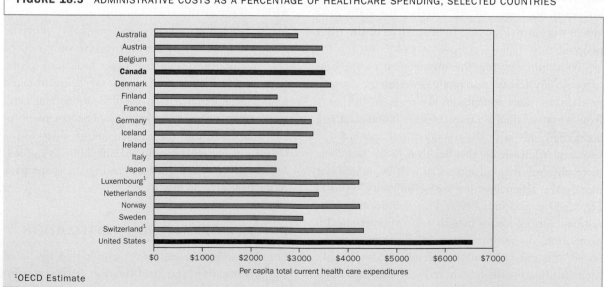

FIGURE 18.5   ADMINISTRATIVE COSTS AS A PERCENTAGE OF HEALTHCARE SPENDING, SELECTED COUNTRIES

[1]OECD Estimate

SOURCE: Based on data from OECD (2011), *Health at a Glance 2011: OECD Indicators*, OECD Publishing. http://dx.doi.org/10.1787/health_glance-2011-en

ethnic inequalities. With fewer healthcare options available, people lacking economic resources will do without healthcare services or rely only on self-care or care from family and friends (Arber and Ginn, 1991).

For this reason, many sociologists argue that privatization and profitization do not support the type of healthcare system that is appropriate for an aging society—a system that combines medical care and a strong long-term home care program, including social services for older adults. Instead, privatization and profitization are resulting in the dismantling of many existing services, adding new inequalities in access to healthcare services to existing inequalities in healthcare needs. Disadvantaged older adults and their families are feeling most of the resulting pressure. It can be different, but whether Canada's citizens will demand greater equity in healthcare, and whether governments will listen, remains to be seen.

TIME FOR REVIEW

1. How important are self-care, informal or unpaid care from family members and friends, and formal medical and other services for the provision of health care in later life?

2. Canada's Medicare system is sometimes referred to as "socialized." How accurate is this view?

3. In recent decades, healthcare in Canada has been subject to widespread debate and reform. What direction has reform taken?

SUMMARY

1. **What is health and how does health vary by age?**
Health is about physical, social, and psychological well-being, not just the absence of disease. Not all aspects of health status decline as we age. Older adults generally assess their health in positive terms and have good mental health and social well-being.

2. **What are the main sources of variation in health status in Canada?**
Despite the overall picture of good health in old age in Canada, significant inequalities in health exist. They are associated with such factors as socioeconomic position, gender, Indigenous status, race, and ethnicity. Past increases in health and longevity have been concentrated in more advantaged social groups. Indigenous and immigrant seniors, older women, and the poor continue to experience major health disadvantages.

3. **What are the main causes of health-related inequalities?**
Health-related inequalities have been attributed to individual health behaviours and lifestyle factors; psychosocial factors, such as stress; and material conditions and resources. Research findings suggest that economic circumstances, living conditions, and other material factors contribute much to health-related inequalities, and that health-related lifestyles and stress levels largely reflect these conditions.

4. **What are the main forms of healthcare?**
We tend to equate healthcare with medical care provided by physicians in clinics or hospitals. However, the most common forms of healthcare are self-care and informal care by family members. When it comes to formal healthcare services, home care is particularly important to the health and well-being of older adults, yet it is not included in Canada's nationally insured healthcare system.

5. **What effects has the recent emphasis on privatization and profit-making in Canada's healthcare system had on health inequality?**
In recent years, increased emphasis has been placed on privatization and profit-making in Canada's healthcare system, particularly when it comes to services that are most important to older adults. As a result, people who are most in need of care have the least access to it and are the most likely to have to rely on themselves and family members for care.

QUESTIONS TO CONSIDER

1. What are the major myths about old age? How does the reality of old age in Canada compare with these myths?

2. How can we best account for inequalities in health among senior Canadians?

3. How well does Canada's healthcare system currently meet the healthcare needs of its senior population?

4. What are some of the consequences of privatization and profitization for Canada's healthcare system?

GLOSSARY

The **age as leveller hypothesis** (p. 432) holds that aging renders everyone disadvantaged, regardless of their other statuses.

Ageism (p. 425) is stereotyping or discrimination based on age.

The **compression of morbidity hypothesis** (p. 428) holds that, in the future, we will be able to postpone the onset of chronic disability to the point where most people will be able to live relatively healthy lives until shortly before death, when they will experience rapid deterioration.

Functional disability (p. 427) is long-term restriction or lack of ability to perform various activities of daily living (such as personal care and housework) because of a health problem.

The **healthy immigrant effect** (p. 429) refers to the tendency for recent immigrants to enjoy better health than do their Canadian-born counterparts. The effect dissipates over time.

The **hierarchy stress perspective** (p. 431) is an approach to understanding health inequality that emphasizes the stress associated with occupying a lower position in the social hierarchy and its negative impact on health.

The **intersectionality hypothesis** (p. 434) holds that health inequities result from the intersection of different social locations.

The **life course perspective** (p. 434) draws attention to the interplay between individual life course change and larger societal changes.

Life expectancy (p. 423) is the number of years that the average person can expect to live.

Medicalization (p. 425) refers to a process whereby more and more areas of life come under the control of medical professionals.

The **modified extended family** (p. 428) is characterized by mutual and close intergenerational ties, responsible behaviour on the part of adult children, and contact between generations.

The **mortality rate** (p. 424) is the number of deaths per thousand people in a population.

The **multiple jeopardy hypothesis** (p. 434) holds that the effect of occupying multiple low statuses is cumulative.

Privatization (p. 437) involves shifting the production of goods and services from the public (government or state) sector to the private sector.

Profitization (p. 438) involves turning institutions into profit-making organizations.

Self-care (p. 435) is the range of activities that individuals undertake to enhance health, prevent disease, and restore health. Individuals may engage in these activities on their own or in conjunction with health professionals.

CHAPTER 19

POLITICS AND SOCIAL MOVEMENTS

Robert Brym
UNIVERSITY OF TORONTO

SOURCE: rmnoa357/Shutterstock.com

AFTER READING THIS CHAPTER, YOU WILL BE ABLE TO:

- Analyze the relationship between the level of democracy in society and the capacity of citizens to influence the state through their support of political parties and social movements.

- Describe the connection between the way power is distributed in society and the success of particular kinds of parties and policies.

- Explain how and why people sometimes riot, strike, and take other forms of collective action to correct perceived injustices.

- Recognize the history of democracy as a struggle for the acquisition of constantly broadening citizenship rights.

INTRODUCTION

I almost caused a small riot once. It happened in Grade 11, shortly after I learned that water combined with sulfur dioxide produces sulfurous acid. The news shocked me. To understand why, you have to know where I lived: in Saint John, New Brunswick, about 100 metres downwind of one of the larger pulp and paper mills in Canada. Acrid waves of sulfur dioxide billowed day and night from the mill's imposing smokestacks. The town's pervasive rotten-egg smell was a longstanding complaint in the area. But, for me, disgust turned to upset when I realized the fumes were toxic. Suddenly it was clear why many people I knew—especially people living near the mill—woke up in the morning with a kind of "smoker's cough." By the simple act of breathing, we were causing the gas to mix with the moisture in our bodies and form an acid that our lungs tried to expunge, with only partial success.

Twenty years later, I read the results of a medical research report showing that residents of that New Brunswick area suffer from rates of lung disease, including emphysema and lung cancer, significantly above the national average. However, even in 1968 it was evident a serious problem was brewing in my hometown. I therefore hatched a plan. Our high school was about to hold its annual model parliament. The event was notoriously boring, partly because, year in, year out, virtually everyone voted for the same party, the Conservatives. But here was an issue, I thought, that could turn things around. The pulp and paper mill was owned by K. C. Irving, an industrialist so powerful that his companies were said to control 40 percent of New Brunswick's economic output. *Forbes* magazine in the United States annually ranked Irving among the wealthiest men in the world. I figured that once I told my fellow students the political implications of the fact that water combined with sulfur dioxide produces sulfurous acid, they would quickly demand the closure of the mill until Irving guaranteed a clean operation.

Was *I* naive. As head of the tiny Liberal Party, I had to address the entire student body during assembly on election day to outline the party platform and mobilize votes. When I got to the part of my speech explaining why K. C. Irving was our enemy, the murmuring in the audience, which had been growing like the sound of a hungry animal about

The year 1968 was one of student rebellion worldwide. Here students run from police in Paris, France.
SOURCE: © Bettmann/Corbis.

to pounce on its prey, erupted into loud "boos." A couple of students rushed the stage. The principal suddenly appeared from the wings and commanded the student body to settle down. He then took me by the arm and informed me that, for my own safety, my speech was finished. So, I discovered on election day, was our high school's Liberal Party. And so, it emerged, was my high school political career.

This incident troubled me for many years, less because of the embarrassment it caused me than because of the puzzles it presented. Why did I almost cause a small riot? Why didn't my fellow students rebel in the way I thought they would? Why did they continue to support an arrangement that was enriching one man at the cost of a community's health? Why weren't they enraged? Couldn't they see the injustice? Other people did. The year 1968 was not just the year of my political failure at Saint John High School. It was also the year that student riots in France nearly caused the fall of the government of Charles de Gaulle. It was the year in which the suppression of student strikes by the Mexican government left dozens of students dead. It was the year in which American students at Berkeley, Michigan, and other universities fought with unprecedented vigour for free speech on their campuses, an end to American involvement in the war in Vietnam, increased civil rights for American blacks, and an expanded role for women in public affairs.

I didn't know it at the time, but by asking why students in Paris, Mexico City, and Berkeley rebelled while my fellow students did not, I was raising the main question that animates the sociological study of politics and social movements. Why are some groups more successful than others in formulating their demands and getting them carried out? In other words, who gets what and under what social circumstances? That is the main issue addressed by this chapter.

Power is the ability of an individual or a group to impose its will on others, even if they resist (Weber, 1946 [1922]: 180). In the first section of this chapter, you will learn that the power of a group may be widely recognized as legitimate or valid under some circumstances. If it is, raw power becomes legitimate **authority**. The people who occupy the command posts of institutions are then generally seen as **authorities**. Under other circumstances, however, power flows to nonauthorities. This situation undermines the legitimacy of authority. In this case, nonauthorities form **social movements**, or collective attempts to change part or all of the social order.

They may riot, petition, strike, demonstrate, and establish pressure groups, unions, and **political parties** (organizations that seek to control state power) to achieve their aims.

The terms defined above allow us to distinguish between "normal politics" and "politics beyond the rules." Normal politics is politics as it is practised when authorities are firmly in power. Politics beyond the rules is politics as it is practised when the legitimacy of authority grows weak. Sociologists have proposed various theories to explain the two types of politics. In the second and third sections of this chapter, I evaluate these theories using mainly Canadian data.

Finally, in the chapter's concluding section, I place our discussion in historical context. How has politics developed over the past 300 years? What developments can we reasonably expect in the near future? This section will help you to better understand your political options in coming years.

TIME FOR REVIEW

1. What is the difference between power and authority?
2. What is the difference between political parties and social movements?

POWER FROM ABOVE: NORMAL POLITICS

In 2010, government delegates from the world's 20 biggest economies met for a summit in downtown Toronto to discuss the state of the world economy. Protesters gathered to protest growing inequality and poverty, among other issues. At its height, about 20 000 security personnel and 10 000 protesters faced each other. The demonstrations were largely peaceful. However, vandalism causing $750 000 in damage sparked police brutality, the use of sound cannons, and the arrest of about 1000 protesters. During and after the summit, security forces were widely criticized for using excessive force and violating human rights.

Paradoxically, the use of **force** or coercive power by authorities is a sign of their weakness: If authorities are truly in a position of strength, their rule will be widely recognized as legitimate. They will not need to use force to impose their will because most people agree with their policies. Here, politics will be routine, nonviolent, or "normal." To be sure, minor outbursts of violence occur even under normal politics. However, such events are unusual in Canada today.

Demonstration in Toronto during the G-20 summit, 2010.
SOURCE: arindambanerjee/Shutterstock.com.

They rarely result in fatalities. For the most part, Canadian politics today is normal politics.

Power is exercised in all social settings, from the family to the classroom to the workplace. However, the ultimate seat of power in society is the state. The **state** is a set of institutions that formulate and carry out a country's laws, policies, and binding regulations. Why is the state's power "ultimate?" Because its authority stands above all others, and if the state needs to use force to maintain order or protect its borders, most people will regard its actions as legitimate.

In democratic countries, such as Canada, the government is formed by the elected members of the political party that wins the most seats in a general election (see Figure 19.1). It comprises the head of the party, who becomes prime minister, and the cabinet ministers whom the prime minister selects to advise him or her. It is the job of the government to initiate policies, propose laws, and see that they are enforced. That is why the government is also called the *executive* branch of the state. Proposed laws are turned into operating statutes by the *legislature*, which consists of all the people elected to Parliament. It is the responsibility of the *judiciary* or court system to interpret laws and regulations, that is, to figure out whether and how particular laws and regulations apply in disputed cases. The state's *administrative apparatus or bureaucracy* undertakes enforcement of laws. If laws are broken or the state's security is jeopardized, it is the role of the *coercive apparatus*—the police and military—to enforce the law and protect the state.

The state, then, is a set of institutions that exercise control over society. However, individuals in **civil society**, the private sphere of life, also exercise control over the state through a variety of organizations and institutions. We have already noted how social movements may influence the state. In addition, the mass media are supposed to keep a watchful and critical eye on the state and help to keep the public informed about the quality of government. Pressure groups or "lobbies" are formed by trade unions, manufacturers' associations, ethnic groups, and other organizations to advise politicians of their members' desires. Lobbies also remind politicians how much their members' votes and campaign contributions matter. Finally, political parties regularly seek to mobilize voters as they compete for control of government.

FIGURE 19.1 THE INSTITUTIONS OF STATE AND CIVIL SOCIETY

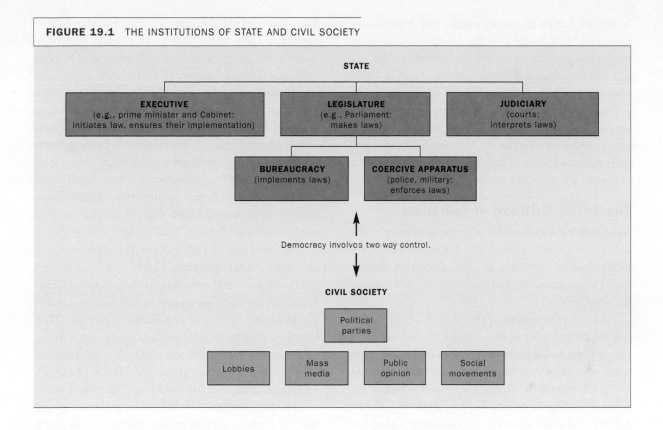

How democratic is the Canadian state? Does the interaction between state and civil society ensure that every citizen has a roughly equal say in the determination of laws and policies? Or, as George Orwell asked in *Animal Farm*, are some citizens more equal than others? Do we, as Abraham Lincoln claimed for the Americans, enjoy "government of the people, by the people, for the people?" Or is it more accurate to say, in the words of one wit, that we are subjected to "government of the people, by the lawyers, for the business owners"? These are among the chief questions asked by sociologists who study the state and its operations. It is now time to consider them in detail.

PLURALIST THEORY

Pluralist theory is one interpretation of the relationship between state and civil society (Dahl, 1961; Polsby, 1959). According to pluralists, we live in a heterogeneous society with many competing interests and centres of power. For example, the interests of parents with school-aged children may differ from the interests of pensioners. Parents may want school budgets to grow. Pensioners may want them to shrink. Because of such heterogeneity, no one group can control politics, according to the pluralists. They argue that, over time, all voters and interest groups influence the political

process almost equally. Sometimes one category of voters wins a political battle, sometimes another. Most often, however, politics involves negotiation and compromise among competing groups. According to the pluralists, because no one group of people is always able to control the political agenda or the outcome of political conflict, democracy is guaranteed.

ELITE THEORY

Elite theorists, C. Wright Mills (1956) foremost among them, sharply disagree with the pluralist account. According to **elite theory**, *elites* are small groups that occupy the command posts of a society's institutions. In the United States, the country that Mills studied, the most powerful elites are the people who run the country's several hundred biggest corporations, the executive branch of government, and the military. Mills wrote that the people who control these institutions (they are almost all men) make the important decisions that profoundly affect members of society. Moreover, they do so without much regard for elections or public opinion.

Mills showed how the corporate, state, and military elites are interconnected. People move from one elite to another over their careers. Their children intermarry. They maintain close social contact. They tend to be recruited from the upper-middle and upper classes. However, Mills denied that these similarities and interconnections turn the three elites into a **ruling class**, that is, a self-conscious and cohesive group of people, led by corporate executives and owners of big business, who act to advance their common interests. The three elites are independent of each other, Mills insisted. They may see eye to eye on many issues, but each has its own jealously guarded sphere of influence, and conflict between elite groups is therefore common (Mills, 1956: 277).

The Elitist Critique of Pluralism

Most political sociologists today question the pluralist account of democratic politics because research has established the existence of large, persistent, wealth-based inequalities in political influence and political participation.

John Porter's classic, *The Vertical Mosaic* (1965), was the first in a series of Canadian studies that demonstrate the weaknesses of pluralism and corroborate some aspects of elite theory (Brym, 1989; Clement, 1975; Olsen, 1980). These studies show that a disproportionately large number of people in Canada's political and other elites come from upper- and upper-middle-class families. For example, about 40 percent of Canadian prime ministers, premiers, and Cabinet ministers were born into the richest 10 percent of families in the country (Olsen, 1980: 129). In their youth, members of Canada's elites are likely to have attended expensive private schools. As adults, they tend to marry the offspring of other elite members and belong to exclusive private clubs. In the course of their careers, they often move from one elite to another. Arguably, people with this sort of background cannot act dispassionately on behalf of all Canadians, rich and poor.

Controversy persists over whether Canada's elites form a ruling class. Porter (1965), like Mills (1956), noted frequent conflict among elites. He argued against the view that a ruling class controls Canada. His top students disagreed. They argued that the interests of large corporations dominate Canadian political life (Clement, 1975; Olsen, 1980). However, both Porter and his students agreed on one point: Contrary to pluralist claims, Canada's well-to-do consistently exercise disproportionate influence over political life in this country.

Studies of political participation in Canada add weight to the elitist view (Blais et al., 1997; Frank, 1994; Mishler, 1979: 88–97). Many surveys show that political involvement decreases with social class. For example, the likelihood of voting falls with a person's class position.

The likelihood of phoning or writing a member of Parliament, helping a candidate in an election campaign, and running for office declines even more steeply as we move down the socioeconomic hierarchy.

In addition, well-to-do Canadians contribute much more money to political parties than other Canadians do—and in 2015, the relative importance of private contributions increased substantially because government subsidies to political parties were eliminated. Private contributions are especially beneficial to the Conservative Party, which receives more money in the form of private contributions than do all other political parties combined (Jansen, Thomas, and Young, 2012).

As intensity of political participation declines, so does political influence. Consequently, although political apathy and cynicism are high among Canadians, the poorest Canadians are the most politically apathetic and cynical of any income category. They have less interest in politics than do the well-to-do, and they are more likely to think that government does not care what they think (see Figure 19.2). As a leading political sociologist wrote, "The combination of a low vote and a relative lack of organization among the lower-status groups means that they will suffer

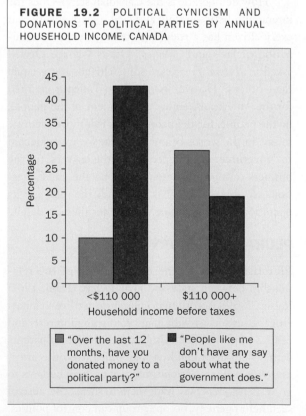

FIGURE 19.2 POLITICAL CYNICISM AND DONATIONS TO POLITICAL PARTIES BY ANNUAL HOUSEHOLD INCOME, CANADA

SOURCE: Adapted from Patrick Fournier, Fred Cutler, Stuart Soroka, and Deitland Stolle, *Canadian National Election Study* (2011). http://www.queensu.ca/cora/ces.html (accessed Nov. 2, 2014).

from neglect by the politicians who will be receptive to the wishes of the more privileged, participating, and organized strata" (Lipset, 1981: 226–27).

The Marxist Critique of Elite Theory

Although compelling in some respects, elite theory has its critics, Marxists foremost among them. Some Marxists, known as "instrumentalists," deny that elites enjoy more or less equal power. Actually, they say, elites form a ruling class dominated by big business. From their point of view, the state is an arm (or "instrument") of the business elite. Big business gains control of the state in three main ways. First, members of wealthy families occupy important state positions in highly disproportionate numbers. Second, government officials rely mainly on the representatives of big business for advice. Third, political parties rely mainly on big business for financial support. According to some Marxists, members of different elites may disagree about specific issues. However, as a result of the three control mechanisms listed above, they always agree about one issue: the need to maintain the health of the capitalist system (Miliband, 1973 [1969]).

A second group of Marxists, known as "stucturalists" offers a somewhat different interpretation of why the state in capitalist society is necessarily biased in favour of big business. For the structuralists, it is not so much the social origins of high government officials or the social ties linking them with big business that encourages the state to act with a pro-capitalist bias. Rather, they argue, the capitalist state acts as an arm of big business because it is constrained to do so by the nature of the capitalist system itself. For example, if the Canadian government doubled the corporate tax rate, investment would be redirected to countries with regimes that are kinder to company profits. Such a move would cost Canada jobs and prosperity. It would be highly unpopular. The government could easily fall. Fearing such outcomes, governments in capitalist societies find their field of action restricted to policies that ensure the well-being of big business. According to the structuralists, it is the very fact that the state is embedded in a capitalist system that forces it to act in this way (Poulantzas, 1975 [1968]).

It follows from both the instrumentalist and the structuralist positions that ordinary citizens, and especially members of the working class, rarely have much influence over state policy. According to Marxists, true democracy can emerge only if members of the working class and their supporters overthrow

Karl Marx predicted that capitalism would create a large mass of impoverished workers who would eventually take over the state, eliminate private property, and forge a communist society. After the revolution of 1917, the Soviet Union became the first self-proclaimed communist society. This early May Day poster reads: "Workers of all countries unite. The 1st of May work holiday. Long live the international unity of the proletariat!"
SOURCE: © CORBIS.

capitalism and establish a socialist system in which economic differences between people are eliminated or at least substantially reduced.

POWER-BALANCE THEORY

Pluralists assume that all major groups in society enjoy approximately equal power. Elitists assume that members of the upper class enjoy the most power. Both approaches, however, assume that the distribution of power in society does not change much over time, except in those rare instances when revolutions take place.

In contrast, power-balance theorists argue that the distribution of power in society changes significantly more frequently. **Power-balance theory** allows that power is usually concentrated in the hands

The peak year of strike activity in Canada was 1919. In that year, 17.3 strikes took place for every 100 000 nonagricultural workers in the country. This photo was taken on "Bloody Saturday," June 21, 1919, during the Winnipeg General Strike. It shows a violent confrontation between rioters and Mounties and special police.
SOURCE: LAC C-33392.

of the wealthy. However, adherents of this approach also note that other classes sometimes gain power. This has big implications for political life. Among other things, the distribution of power determines how democratic a society is.

To make their case, power-balance theorists first measure variations in the social distribution of power. They then show how those variations are reflected in the successes and failures of different political parties and the rejection and adoption of different state policies. Along with the pluralists, they recognize that society is truly democratic only when power is widely distributed. Along with the elitists, they recognize that society is not very democratic when power is highly concentrated in the hands of a few wealthy citizens. However, by treating the distribution of power as a variable, they improve our understanding of the relationship between power and democracy.

We can better understand power-balance theory by examining Canadian politics in comparative perspective. We first note that a group's power is partly determined by the degree to which it forms organizations to further its interests. For example, unionized blue-collar and white-collar workers are more powerful than their nonunionized counterparts are.

That is because unions allow workers to speak with one voice. They enable workers to bargain effectively with employers and governments for improved wages, working conditions, and social policies. Moreover, if bargaining fails, they can go out on strike to try to force the issue.

If level of unionization increases working-class power, that should be reflected in the political behaviour of citizens and the policies adopted by governments. And, in fact, it is. Compare Sweden and Canada (Casper, McLanahan, and Garfinkle, 1994; Korpi, 1983; Myles, 1989; O'Connor, 1996; O'Connor and Brym, 1988; O'Connor and Olsen, 1998; Olsen, 2002; Olsen and Brym, 1996). In Sweden, more than three-quarters of blue- and white-collar workers are union members. In Canada, about three in ten nonagricultural workers are members of unions. Several consequences follow:

- About 68 percent of Canadians voted in the 2015 federal election, compared with 83.3 percent of Swedes in the 2014 Swedish federal election (International Institute for Democracy and Electoral Assistance, 2014; CBC News, 2015). The difference is largely due to the fact that working-class Swedes are more likely to vote than working-class Canadians are.

- The Swedish socialist party has formed the government almost continuously since World War II. In contrast, Canada's socialist party, the NDP, has never formed the federal government or even had a representative in the federal cabinet. The parties that have formed Canada's federal governments (Liberals, and Conservatives) are those that are most strongly supported by business; see Figure 19.3).

- Swedish governments have acted more vigorously than Canadian governments have to eradicate poverty and equalize incomes. Thus, fewer than 4 percent of Swedes are classified as living below the poverty line (as defined by the low income cutoff; see Chapter 7, Social Stratification). The comparable figure for Canadians is about 15 percent. In Sweden, about 20 percent of all income goes to the top 10 percent of income earners. The comparable figure for Canada is about 30 percent of all income. And in Sweden, a broader range of retired people receive more generous pensions and more frequent cost-of-living adjustments than do pensioners in Canada.

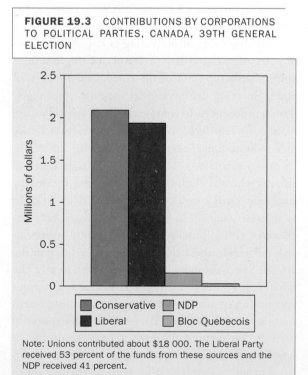

FIGURE 19.3 CONTRIBUTIONS BY CORPORATIONS TO POLITICAL PARTIES, CANADA, 39TH GENERAL ELECTION

Note: Unions contributed about $18 000. The Liberal Party received 53 percent of the funds from these sources and the NDP received 41 percent.

SOURCE: Elections Canada (2014). This reproduction is a copy of the version available at www.elections.ca. Reproduced with the permission of Elections Canada.

- Since women are disproportionately concentrated in low-income, low-status jobs (see Chapter 8, Gender Inequality), they benefit more than men do when the working class is more powerful. As a result, the ratio of women's to men's earnings is about 80 percent in Sweden and 67 percent in Canada. (These figures are based on full-time and part-time workers.) Moreover, in Sweden, the ratio of women to men who live below the poverty line is just above 90 percent, while in Canada the comparable figure is nearly 130 percent. Finally, parental benefits are superior in Sweden and child-care facilities are more widely available and affordable.

We thus see that elections matter a great deal in the lives of ordinary people. Elections determine the types of parties that get elected. Elected parties, in turn, shape government policies. The outcome of any particular election depends on the appeal of party leaders, their effectiveness in presenting issues to the public, and myriad other short-term factors (Clarke, Jenson, Le Duc, and Pammett, 1996; see Figure 19.4). However, when considering the types of parties that get elected over several decades, as we did previously, we see that the distribution of power between classes and other groups shapes the character of politics in a country.

The preceding analysis also implies that Sweden is more democratic than Canada is. True, citizens of both countries are legally free to vote and influence their governments. But because the working class is more powerful in Sweden, Swedes' legal right to vote and influence governments has been turned into real political influence on a wider scale. In general, only if more citizens wield more clout can society become more democratic.

STATE-CENTRED THEORY

Power-balance theory suggests that democratic politics is a contest among various classes and other groups to control the state for their own advantage. When power is substantially redistributed—when, for example, a major class gets better organized while another major class becomes less socially organized—old ruling parties usually fall and new ones take office.

Note, however, that a winner-take-all strategy would be nothing short of foolish. If winning parties monopolized the spoils of office, passing laws that benefited only their supporters, they might cause massive outrage and even violent opposition. Yet allowing

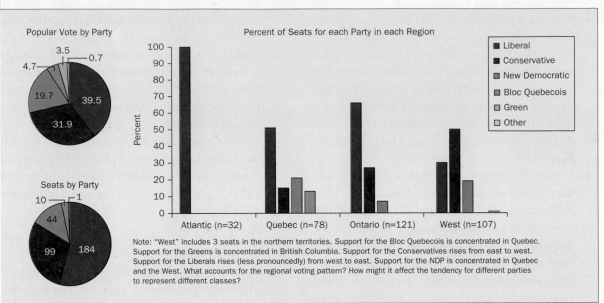

FIGURE 19.4   RESULTS OF 2015 CANADIAN FEDERAL ELECTION

Popular Vote by Party

Seats by Party

Percent of Seats for each Party in each Region

Legend:
- Liberal
- Conservative
- New Democratic
- Bloc Quebecois
- Green
- Other

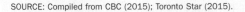

Note: "West" includes 3 seats in the northern territories. Support for the Bloc Quebecois is concentrated in Quebec. Support for the Greens is concentrated in British Columbia. Support for the Conservatives rises from east to west. Support for the Liberals rises (less pronouncedly) from west to east. Support for the NDP is concentrated in Quebec and the West. What accounts for the regional voting pattern? How might it affect the tendency for different parties to represent different classes?

SOURCE: Compiled from CBC (2015); Toronto Star (2015).

opponents to become angry, organized, and resolute would be counterproductive. After all, winners want more than just a moment of glory. They want to be able to enjoy the spoils of office in a stable political environment over the long haul. To achieve such stability, it is crucial that people who *lose* elections are given a say in government. To a degree, the party in power must attend to the wants of losing minorities. That way, even determined opponents are likely to recognize the legitimacy of the government and its right to rule. Pluralists thus make a good point when they say that democratic politics is about accommodation and compromise; they only lose sight of the fact that accommodation and compromise typically give more advantages to some than to others, as both elite theorists and power-balance theorists stress.

There is, however, more to the story of politics than conflict between classes and between other groups. Theda Skocpol and other **state-centred theorists** have shown how the state itself can structure political life independently of the way power is distributed among classes and other groups at a given time (Block, 1979; Evans, Rueschemeyer, and Skocpol, 1985; Skocpol, 1979). Their argument is a valuable supplement to power-balance theory.

To illustrate how state structures shape politics, consider the problem of nonvoting in the United States. In presidential elections, voter turnout fell more or less steadily between the end of World War II

and 1996, when it stood at just 48 percent of the voting age population. Turnout increased to 57.5 percent by 2012, but the United States still has one of the lowest voter turnouts of any rich democracy in the world (Piven and Cloward, 1989: 5). How can we explain this fact?

The high rate of nonvoting is largely a product of voter registration law—a feature of the American political structure, not of the current distribution of power. In every democracy, laws specify voter registration procedures. In some countries, such as France, citizens are registered to vote automatically once they receive state-issued identity cards at the age of 18. In other countries, such as Canada, a database of citizens who are eligible to vote was first created by state-employed canvassers who went door to door to register voters. The database is updated between elections with information supplied mainly by provincial, territorial, and federal data sources. Only in the United States do individual citizens have to take the initiative to go out and register themselves in voter registration centres. In some states, they must present state-issued ID (a driver's licence or a passport) to register. Yet many American citizens are unable or unwilling to register. As a result, the United States has a proportionately smaller pool of eligible voters than the other democracies do. Only about 65 percent of American citizens are registered to vote (Piven and Cloward, 1989: 256–59).

Apart from shrinking the pool of eligible voters, American voter registration law has a second important consequence. Because some *types* of people are less able and inclined than others to register, a strong bias is introduced into the political system. Specifically, the poor are less likely to register than the better-off are. People without much formal education are less likely to register than the better educated are. Members of disadvantaged racial minority groups, especially African Americans, are less likely to register than whites are. Such people are less likely than others are to have the knowledge, time, and money needed to register, let alone a driver's licence or a passport. Thus, American voter registration law is a pathway to democracy for some but a barrier to democracy for others. The American political system is less responsive than other rich democracies are to the needs of the disadvantaged. That is partly because, as state-centred theory suggests, the law requires citizen-initiated voter registration. As a result, many disadvantaged people are effectively disenfranchised.[1]

Big shocks sometimes rock state structures. In general, however, they are resistant to change. The foundations of state structures are anchored by constitutions, which can be altered only by large majorities of federally elected representatives and state- or provincial-level legislatures. Their upper storeys are girded by laws, regulations, and policies, some of which help to keep potentially disruptive social forces at bay. American voter registration law is a case in point.[2] And then there are the many ideological reinforcements. All states create anthems, flags, ceremonies, celebrations, sporting events, and school curricula that stimulate patriotism and serve in part to justify existing political arrangements.

In sum, each school of thought reviewed above makes a useful contribution to our appreciation of normal democratic politics (see Table 19.1). Pluralists teach us that normal democratic politics is about compromise and the accommodation of all group interests. Elite theorists teach us that, despite compromise and accommodation, power is concentrated in the hands of higher-status groups, whose interests the political system therefore serves best. Power-balance theorists teach us that, despite the concentration of power in society, substantial shifts in the distribution of power often occur, and they have discernible effects on voting patterns and public policies. Marxists highlight the rare occasions when political power is rapidly redistributed by revolutionary upheavals. And state-centred theorists teach us that, despite the influence of the distribution of power on political life, state structures exert an important independent effect on politics, too.

TIME FOR REVIEW

1. Describe the functions of the institutions comprising the state and the relationship of those institutions to civil society.
2. Outline the strengths and weaknesses of pluralist theory, elite theory, Marxist theory, power-balance theory, and state-centred theory.

TABLE 19.1   FIVE SOCIOLOGICAL THEORIES OF DEMOCRACY COMPARED

	PLURALIST	ELITE	MARXIST	POWER BALANCE	STATE-CENTRED
How is power distributed?	dispersed	concentrated	concentrated	concentrated	concentrated
Who are the main power holders?	various groups	elites	ruling class	upper class	state officials
On what is their power based?	holding political office	controlling major institutions	owning substantial capital	owning substantial capital	holding political office
What is the main basis of public policy?	the will of all citizens	the interests of major elites	capitalist interests	the balance of power between classes, etc.	the influence of state structures
Do lower classes have much influence on politics?	yes	no	rarely	sometimes	sometimes

POWER FROM BELOW: POLITICS BEYOND THE RULES

RELATIVE-DEPRIVATION THEORY

All five theories of democracy reviewed above focus on normal politics. However, we know that politics is sometimes anything but normal. Routine political processes can break down. Social movements can form. Large-scale political violence can erupt. As Vladimir Lenin, the leader of the Russian revolution of 1917, said, people sometimes "vote with their feet." In Canada, evidence suggests that normal politics is increasingly unpopular, especially among younger people, while participating in demonstrations is an increasingly popular form of political expression (see Figure 3.2 in Chapter 3).

Until about 1970, many sociologists argued that social movements tend to emerge when people experience **relative deprivation**. People feel relatively deprived when they experience an intolerable gap between the social rewards they think they deserve and the social rewards they expect to receive. (Social rewards are widely valued goods, including money, education, security, prestige, and so on.) Accordingly, people are most likely to rebel against authority when rising expectations (brought on by, say, rapid economic growth and migration) are met by a sudden decline in social rewards (perhaps because of economic recession or war; Davies, 1969). In addition, until about 1970, many sociologists held that the people who lead and first join social movements are likely to be outsiders who lack strong social ties to their communities.

A large body of research has now discredited these ideas. For example, we now know that the leaders and early joiners of social movements are usually well-integrated members of their communities, not socially marginal newcomers. In the 1930s, for example, Saskatchewan farmers and workers formed the Cooperative Commonwealth Federation (CCF) to protest federal government policy toward the West in general and Western agriculture in particular. The movement's leaders and early recruits were not outsiders. The workers were mainly local trade union activists. The farmers had been involved in the establishment of community-owned retail stores, credit unions, and marketing cooperatives (Lipset, 1971).

Much research also calls into question the idea that relative deprivation leads to the formation of social movements. For example, sociologists have compared measures of relative deprivation with the frequency of demonstrations, strikes, and acts of collective violence in France, Italy, Germany, and England. They have found that, in general, outbreaks of collective unrest do not increase with mounting relative deprivation (Lodhi and Tilly, 1973; Snyder and Tilly, 1972; Tilly, 1979a; Tilly, Tilly, and Tilly, 1975).

RESOURCE MOBILIZATION THEORY

Because of the inadequacies of relative deprivation theory noted above, an alternative approach to the study of social movements gained popularity. **Resource mobilization theory** is based on the idea that social movements emerge only when disadvantaged people can marshal the means necessary to challenge authority (Jenkins, 1983; McCarthy and Zald, 1977; Oberschall, 1973; Tilly, 1978). Foremost among the resources they need to challenge authority is the capacity to forge strong social ties among themselves. Other important resources that allow disadvantaged people to challenge authority include jobs, money, arms, and access to means of spreading their ideas.

You can appreciate the significance of resource mobilization theory by considering patterns of strike activity in Canada. When blue-collar and white-collar workers go out on strike, they are withholding their labour to extract concessions from employers or governments in the form of higher wages and improved social welfare benefits. When are workers most inclined to challenge the authority of employers and governments in this way? Research shows that in Canada since World War II, strike activity has been high when (1) unemployment is low, (2) union membership is high, and (3) governments have been relatively generous in their provision of social welfare benefits. Low unemployment indicates a strong economy. Workers are inclined to strike when business activity is robust because they know employers and governments can afford to make concessions. (Employers make bigger profits and governments collect more taxes during economic booms.) A high level of unionization is also conducive to more strike activity because unions provide workers with leadership, strike funds, and coordination. Thus, as resource mobilization theory predicts, strong social ties among workers (as indicated by a high level of unionization) and access to jobs and money (as indicated by a booming economy) increase challenges to authority (as indicated by strikes).[3]

FIGURE 19.5   FREQUENCY OF STRIKES, CANADA 1946–2013

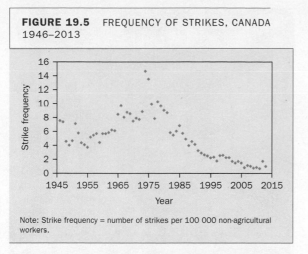

Note: Strike frequency = number of strikes per 100 000 non-agricultural workers.

SOURCES: Brym, Birdsell Bauer, and McIvor (2013); Government of Canada, Labour Program (2014a, 2014b).

Figure 19.5 shows the pattern of strike activity in post-World War II Canada. It supports the arguments of resource mobilization theory. Until 1974, the trend in strike activity was upward. (In the 1970s, Canada was, in fact, one of the most strike-prone countries in the world.) This was a period of growing prosperity, low unemployment, expanding state benefits, and increasing unionization. With increasing access to organizational and material resources, workers often challenged authority in the three decades after World War II. In 1973, however, economic crisis struck. Oil prices tripled, and then tripled again at the end of the decade. Inflation increased and unemployment rose. Soon, the government was strapped for funds

and had to borrow heavily to maintain social welfare programs. Eventually, the debt burden was so heavy that the government felt obliged to cut various social welfare programs.

Unionization reached a peak in 1978, stabilized, and then began to fall (see Figure 19.6). Thus, in the post-1973 climate, the organizational and material resources of workers fell. As a result, strike activity plummeted. In 1974, nearly 16 strikes took place for every 100 000 Canadian workers. By 2013, that figure had fallen to less than one (Brym, 2008; Brym, Birdsell Bauer, and McIvor, 2013).

FRAMING DISCONTENT

As you have seen, resource mobilization theory is a useful approach to the study of social movements, such as the strike movement in Canada. Even so, the emergence of a social movement sometimes takes sociologists by surprise. In addition, the failure of an aggrieved group to press its claim is sometimes equally unexpected. And movements that do emerge are successful to varying degrees. It seems, therefore, that something lies between (1) the capacity of disadvantaged people to mobilize resources for collective action and (2) the recruitment of a substantial number of movement members. Sociologists call that "something" **frame alignment** (Goffman, 1974; Snow, Rochford, Worden, and Benford, 1986). Frame alignment is the process by which individual interests, beliefs, and values either become congruent and

FIGURE 19.6   PERCENTAGE OF NONAGRICULTURAL WORKERS UNIONIZED, CANADA AND THE UNITED STATES, 1925–2013

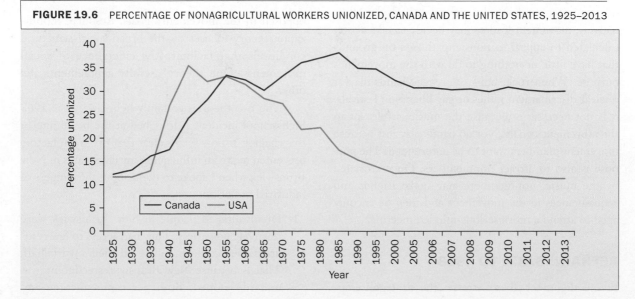

SOURCES: Bureau of Labor Statistics (2012, 2014); Canada Department of Labour (1973); Government of Canada, Labour Program (2014a); Human Resources Development Canada (1995, 1998); Human Resources and Skills Development Canada (2011); Mayer (2004); Statistics Canada (2008).

complementary with the activities, ideas, and goals of the movement or fail to do so. Thanks to the efforts of scholars operating mainly in the symbolic interactionist tradition (see Chapter 1, Introducing Sociology), frame alignment has recently become the subject of sustained sociological investigation.

Frame alignment can be encouraged in several ways. Social movement leaders can reach out to other organizations that, they believe, include people who may be sympathetic to the social movement's cause. For example, an anti-nuclear movement may use the mass media, telephone campaigns, and direct mail to appeal to feminist, anti-racist, and environmental organizations on the assumption they are likely to have members who would agree at least in general terms with the anti-nuclear platform. In addition, social movements can emphasize attractive values that have so far not featured prominently in the thinking of potential recruits.

Social movements can also elevate the importance of positive beliefs about the movement and what it stands for. For example, in trying to win new recruits, movement members might emphasize the seriousness of the social movement's purpose. They might analyze in a clear and compelling manner the causes of the problem the movement is trying to solve. Or they might stress the likelihood of the movement's success. By doing so they might increase the movement's appeal to potential recruits and win them over to the cause. Social movements can also stretch their objectives and activities to win recruits who are not initially sympathetic to the movement's original aims. This may involve watering down the movement's ideals. Alternatively, movement leaders may decide to take action calculated to appeal to nonsympathizers on grounds that have little or nothing to do with the movement's purpose. When rock, punk, or reggae bands play at nuclear disarmament rallies or gay liberation festivals, it is not necessarily because the music is relevant to the movement's goals. Nor do bands play just because movement members want to be entertained. The purpose is also to attract nonmembers. Once attracted by the music, nonmembers may make friends and acquaintances in the movement and then be encouraged to attend a more serious-minded meeting.

REFRAIN: BACK TO 1968

Frame alignment theory stresses the strategies employed by movement members to recruit nonmembers who are like-minded, apathetic, or even initially

The Assembly of First Nations, which represents 633 Indigenous groups, demands that Indigenous Canadians have the right to formulate their own laws and reject some Canadian laws. Here, Indigenous peoples protest certain taxes outside a government office.
SOURCE: © Dick Hemingway.

opposed to the movement's goals. Resource mobilization theory focuses on the broad social-structural conditions that facilitate the emergence of social movements. One theory usefully supplements the other.

The two theories certainly help clarify the 1968 high-school incident I described at the beginning of this chapter. It now seems clear that two main factors prevented me from influencing my classmates in New Brunswick when I spoke to them about the dangers of industrial pollution:

1. Disadvantaged people in New Brunswick were relatively powerless. They had access to few resources they could mobilize on their own behalf. That is because New Brunswick's economy was underdeveloped. Both per capita income and the level of unionization were among the lowest in the country. The unemployment rate was

among the highest. In contrast, K. C. Irving, who owned the pulp and paper mill against which I railed, was so powerful that most New Brunswickers could not even conceive of the need to rebel against the conditions of life that he helped to create for them. He owned most of the industrial establishments in the province—the oil refinery and a network of gas stations, the dry docks, the pulp mills, the mines, and the logging operations. Every daily newspaper, most of the weeklies, all of the TV stations, and most of the radio stations were his, too. Little wonder we rarely heard a critical word about his operations. Many people also believed that Irving could make or break provincial governments single-handedly. Should I therefore have been surprised that mere high-school students refused to take him on? In their conservatism, my schoolmates were only mimicking their parents, who, on the whole, were as powerless as Irving was mighty (Brym, 1979).

2. Many of my classmates did not share my sense of injustice. Most of them regarded K. C. Irving as the great provider. They thought his pulp and paper mill, as well as his myriad other industrial establishments, gave many New Brunswickers jobs. They regarded that fact as more important for their lives and the lives of their families than the pollution problem I raised. Frame-alignment theory suggests I needed to figure out ways of building bridges between their understanding and mine. I did not. I therefore received an unsympathetic hearing.

TIME FOR REVIEW

Analyze the strengths and weaknesses of relative deprivation theory, resource mobilization theory, and framing theory.

THE HISTORY AND FUTURE OF SOCIAL MOVEMENTS

I. THE RICH COUNTRIES

Three hundred years ago, social movements were typically small, localized, and violent. In Europe, poor residents of a particular city might riot against public officials in reaction to a rise in bread prices or taxes. Peasants on a particular estate might burn their landowner's barns (or their landowner) in response to his demand for a larger share of the crop. Then the reach of the state grew, soon encompassing most aspects of life. The state taxed nearly all its citizens at higher and higher rates as government services expanded. It imposed a uniform language and a common curriculum in a compulsory education system. It drafted most young men for army service. It instilled in its citizens all the ideological trappings of modern nationalism, from anthems to flags to historical myths. And in the process, social movements changed. They became national in scope, typically directing themselves against central governments rather than local targets. They grew in size, partly because potential recruits were now literate and could communicate using the printed word, partly because big new social settings—factories, offices, densely populated urban neighbourhoods—could serve as recruitment bases. And, in most cases, social movements became less violent. Their size and organization often allowed them to stabilize, bureaucratize, and become sufficiently powerful to get their way without frequent resort to extreme measures (Tilly, 1978, 1979a, 1979b; Tilly, Tilly, and Tilly, 1975).

Social movements often used their power to expand the rights of citizens. We can identify four stages in this process. In Britain, for example, rich property owners struggled against the king in the eighteenth century for **civil citizenship:** the right to free speech, freedom of religion, and justice before the law. The male middle class and the more prosperous strata of the working class struggled against rich property owners in the nineteenth century for **political citizenship:** the right to vote and run for office. In early twentieth-century Britain, women and poorer workers succeeded in achieving these same rights despite the opposition of well-to-do men in particular. During the remainder of the century, blue- and white-collar workers struggled against the well-to-do for **social citizenship:** the right to a certain level of economic security and full participation in the social life of the country by means of the creation of the modern welfare state (Marshall, 1965).

In the last third of the twentieth century, the struggle to broaden citizenship rights entered a new phase, which we now examine in greater detail. The broadening of the struggle for citizenship rights was signalled by the emergence of so-called **new social movements** in the 1960s and 1970s (Melucci, 1980, 1995). What is new about new social movements is the breadth of their goals, the kinds of people they attract, and their potential for going global. I will consider each of these issues in turn.

Goals

Some new social movements, such as the peace movement, the environmental movement, and the human rights movement, promote the rights not of specific groups but of humanity as a whole to peace, security, and a clean environment. Other new social movements, such as the women's movement and the gay rights movement, promote the rights of particular groups that have been excluded from full social participation. Accordingly, gay rights groups have fought for laws that eliminate all forms of discrimination based on sexual orientation. They have also fought for the repeal of laws that discriminate on the basis of sexual orientation, such as anti-sodomy laws and laws that negatively affect parental custody of children (Adam, Duyvendak, and Krouwel, 1999).

Since the 1960s, the women's movement has succeeded in getting admission practices altered in professional schools, winning more freedom of reproductive choice for women, and opening up opportunities for women in the political, religious, military, educational, medical, and business systems (Adamson, Briskin, and McPhail, 1988; see the Critical Sociology: Protest and Policy box).

CRITICAL SOCIOLOGY: PROTEST AND POLICY   THE WOMEN'S MOVEMENT AND ELECTORAL POLITICS

The women's movement was the first new social movement.

At the beginning of the twentieth century, women began to play a smaller role in domestic and farm work and started to enter the paid labour force in significant numbers. Owning more of their own economic resources, they became more independent-minded. They began to realize they might free themselves of oppressive authority in the home. They also started to understand there was nothing inevitable about their receiving less pay and working in worse conditions than men with comparable jobs did (Strong-Boag, 1986: 179).

Formulating a program for social change requires such resources as time, money, and education. Not surprisingly, therefore, the "first wave" of the women's movement comprised highly educated professionals. A group of women with just that social profile established the Toronto Women's Suffrage Association in Toronto in 1883. By demonstrating, petitioning, and gaining the support of influential liberal-minded men, women won the right to vote federally in 1918, in all provinces and territories except Quebec and the Northwest Territories by 1925, in Quebec in 1940, and in the Northwest Territories in 1951.

Along with the right to vote, women won the right to run for public office. They immediately exercised that right, running mainly on the CCF and Liberal tickets. A woman was first elected to provincial office in Alberta in 1917 and to the federal Parliament in 1921.

In provincial and territorial legislatures and the federal Parliament, women sought institutional reform through government action. Specifically, they pursued equitable pay for women, easier access to higher education, protection from domestic violence, and a fair share of family assets and child support in case of divorce or desertion. However, progress was slow on all these fronts. That was partly because women's representation in the country's legislatures remained meagre. In 2015, women composed just 25 percent of federal MPs (Bashevkin, 1986; "Women in National Parliaments," 2015). Moreover, some female MPs were hardly advocates of women's rights.

Involvement in electoral politics requires time and money. Women are disadvantaged in this regard. On average, they have lower socioeconomic status than men do, and they are saddled with more domestic responsibilities. These factors prevent many women from running for office.

Public policy analysts note that female political participation can increase if such barriers are removed (Boyd, 2011: 175–76; Brodie, 1991). For example, laws could be passed that would allow candidates to take unpaid leave from their jobs to contest nominations and elections, set spending limits for nomination and election campaigns, make contributions for nomination campaigns tax-deductible, treat child-care and housekeeping costs as reimbursable campaign expenses, and so on. Additionally, laws could be enacted that make government subsidies to political party campaigns dependent on the proportion of their elected candidates that are women. In such a system, party subsidies would increase with the proportion of women elected.

Despite the existence of viable ideas for increasing women's participation in electoral politics, progress has been slow. Therefore, many feminists have developed a strategy that is oriented less toward established political institutions and more toward grassroots action. The new strategy sought to achieve change not just "from above," by means

(continued)

(continued)

of party politics, but also "from below," by creating a whole network of new organizations, such as study groups, consciousness-raising circles, women's bookstores, rape crisis centres, abortion clinics, shelters for battered women, and opportunities to publicize the importance of feminist aims, such as International Women's Day marches.

It was not only slow progress on the established political front that led women to create this network of new organizations. Many "second-wave" feminists were deeply involved in the student movement of the 1960s and 1970s. They were appalled to discover that, despite much rhetoric about liberation and equality, men controlled the student movement and often refused to allow feminist issues to become part of their agenda. To pursue their aims, they felt it was necessary to create new organizations run by women.

Today, the women's movement operates both at the grassroots level and within established political organizations to achieve its aims. It is internally differentiated. *Liberal feminists* believe that women can participate fully in society if they achieve equality of opportunity with men. They therefore advocate policies aimed at pay equity and the elimination of gender discrimination in the workplace. *Radical feminists* hold that male domination is rooted in the family. They champion free and safe contraception and abortion, an equitable division of domestic labour, and the like. *Socialist feminists* maintain that legal equality is not enough to ensure that women can participate fully in society. In addition, they argue, the state should provide affordable and accessible daycare facilities and other services. These services, they say, could alleviate the economic burdens that prevent most women, especially those from the working class, from taking full advantage of available opportunities for education and employment. *Anti-racist and postmodernist feminists* have criticized liberal, socialist, and radical feminists for generalizing from the experience of white women and failing to see how women's lives are rooted in particular historical and racial experiences. These new currents have done much to extend the relevance of feminism to previously marginalized groups. Thus, despite their different emphases, the various types of feminism share a strong desire to see members of a previously marginal group expand their citizenship rights and become full participants in society.

Critical Thinking Questions

1. Canada is in many respects a socially and economically advanced country. However, when it comes to women's representation in Parliament we lag badly. Just 25 percent of Canada's parliamentarians are women, placing us in 47th place out of 140 countries as of May 1, 2015. The United Kingdom is in 58th place (23 percent women) and the United States is in 72nd (19 percent women). Leading the list is Rwanda, where 64 percent of parliamentarians are women, followed by Bolivia at 53 percent and Cuba at 49 percent ("Women in National Parliaments," 2015). Clearly, a country's prosperity is not decisive in determining women's representation in Parliament. What factors are decisive?

2. Does the percentage of female parliamentarians matter? If so, how? If not, why not?

The emergence of the peace, environmental, human rights, gay rights, and women's movements marked the beginning of a fourth stage in the history of social movements. This fourth stage involves the promotion of **universal citizenship**, or the extension of citizenship rights to all adult members of society and to society as a whole (Roche, 1995; Turner, 1986: 85–105).

Membership

New social movements are also novel in that they attract a disproportionately large number of highly educated, well-to-do people from the social, educational, and cultural fields—teachers, professors, journalists, social workers, artists, actors, writers—and student apprentices to these occupations. Such people are predisposed to participate in new social movements for several reasons. Their higher education exposes them to radical ideas and makes those ideas appealing. They tend to hold jobs outside the business community, which often opposes their values. And they often get personally involved in the problems of their clients and audiences, sometimes even becoming their advocates (Brint, 1984; Rootes, 1995).

Globalization Potential

Finally, new social movements possess more potential for globalization than old social movements did. In the 1960s, social movements were typically *national* in scope. That is why, for example, the intensity and frequency of urban race riots in the United States in the 1960s did not depend on such local conditions as the degree of black–white inequality in a given city (Spilerman, 1970, 1976). Instead, congressional and presidential action (and lack of action) on civil rights issues, national TV coverage of race issues, and growing black consciousness and solidarity helped to create the view among African Americans that racial problems are nationwide and can be solved only by the federal government.

Many new social movements that gained force in the 1970s increased the scope of protest still further. For example, members of the nuclear disarmament and environmental movements viewed federal legislation as a necessary but insufficient solution to the issues that troubled them. Once they recognized that, say, the condition of the Brazilian rainforest affects climatic conditions worldwide and that the spread of weapons of mass destruction can easily destroy all of humanity, movement activists pressed for international agreements binding all countries to stop environmental destruction and nuclear proliferation. Social movements went global.

The globalization of social movements was facilitated by the ease with which people in various national movements could travel and communicate with like-minded activists from other countries. In the age of CNN, inexpensive jet transportation, fax machines, and email, it is possible not only to see the connection between apparently local problems and their global sources but also to act locally and globally. Greenpeace, for instance, is a highly successful environmental movement that originated in Vancouver in the mid-1970s and now has offices in 41 countries, with its international office in Amsterdam. A more recent global initiative with roots in Vancouver is the Occupy Movement.

On July 13, 2011, Kalle Lasn, editor of the Vancouver-based anti-consumerist magazine *Adbusters*, created a hashtag on Twitter, #OCCUPYWALL-STREET, and designed a poster of a ballerina dancing on the back of the bronze sculpture of a bull (symbolic of a profitable market) racing up Wall Street in Manhattan (Yardley, 2011). The poster called for people to go to the centre of the financial world and protest the growing wealth and greed of the richest 1 percent of society and their role in causing the world financial crisis of 2008–09. Thousands did, and within days, demonstrations and encampments were sprouting in cities around the world. It was the most remarkable evidence of the globalization of social movements ever observed. Although nearly all of the protests had died down by the end of 2011 (St. John's, Newfoundland and Labrador, was the last Canadian holdout), the

A poster of the Occupy movement.

SOURCE: © Monica E/Occupy Together/www.occupytogether.org.

movement succeeded in influencing global political discourse. One poll found that two-thirds of Americans surveyed in December 2011 believed that conflict between the rich and the poor was the main conflict in society—an increase of 19 percent since 2009 (Pew Research Center, 2012). The Occupy Movement helped to put class conflict back on the political agenda of the United States and other countries.

The globalization of social movements can be further illustrated by coming full circle and returning to the anecdote with which I began this chapter. In 1991, I visited my hometown. I had not been back in years. As I entered the city, I vaguely sensed that something was different. I could not define the change precisely until I reached the Irving pulp and paper mill. Suddenly, it became obvious: The rotten-egg smell was virtually gone. I subsequently discovered that in the 1970s a local woman whose son developed a serious case of asthma took legal action against the mill and eventually won. The mill owner was required by law to install a "scrubber" in the main smokestack to remove most of the sulfur dioxide emissions. Soon, the federal government was putting pressure on the mill owner to purify the polluted water that poured out of the plant and into the St. John River and the Bay of Fundy. Apparently, local citizens and the environmental movement had caused a change in the climate of opinion, influencing the government to force the mill owner to spend millions of dollars on a cleanup. It took decades, but what was political heresy in 1968 eventually became established practice because environmental concerns had been amplified by the voice of a movement that had grown to global proportions. In general, as this case illustrates, globalization helps to ensure that many new social movements transcend local and national boundaries and that many of them—but, as you will now learn, not all—promote universalistic goals.

II. THE OTHER 85 PERCENT

With variations, the pattern of social movement evolution sketched previously applies to the 20 or so rich countries of North America, Western Europe, Oceania, and Japan. As we have seen, social movements in these rich countries typically sought to broaden democracy through the expansion of citizenship rights. In contrast, social movements in the other 85 percent of the world (by population) developed differently. They focused less on broadening the bases of democracy than on ensuring more elemental human rights, notably freedom from colonial rule and freedom to create the conditions for independent economic growth.

The "other 85 percent" of the world is relatively weak economically, politically, and militarily because it began substantial industrialization only after World War I and in some cases after World War II. This circumstance allowed the early industrializers (Britain, France, Japan, Russia, the United States, and so on) to carve up most of Asia, Africa, and South America into colonies, protectorates, mandates, spheres of influence, and other administrative forms of subjugation. The nineteenth century was the age of imperialism. The early industrializers used the rest of the world as a captive market for their manufactured goods and a source of inexpensive raw materials and labour. They enriched themselves even as they limited economic growth and well-being in the less-developed countries (see Chapter 10, Development and Underdevelopment).

The Muslim World

Because events in the Muslim world were in many respects typical, they illustrate the problem well (Hourani, 1991: 265–349). Already by the 1830s, the armed forces of France had taken control of part of Algeria, those of Britain had taken control of part of the Arabian Peninsula, and those of Russia had taken over the Muslim lands of the Caucasus. A century later, almost the entire Middle East and North Africa were under British and French control. Egyptian cotton fed the looms of Lancashire. Iraqi oil supplied half of France's needs. British and French ships brought European machinery and textiles to the region. British and French financiers profited handsomely from their control of local banking. Some indigenous merchants and landowners benefited from the new economic relations too. However, the growing number of peasants and urban workers remained poor and almost powerless.

In the world's rich countries, an affluent and politically powerful class of merchants, industrialists, and financiers did much to promote the growth of democracy in its early stages (Moore, 1967). In contrast, in the Muslim countries and the rest of the less economically developed world, the bourgeoisie was small, weak, and dependent on imperial interests. Consequently, democratic ideals had little chance to sink deep roots. Where democratic movements emerged in less-developed countries, they often resisted imperial control, in which case rich imperial powers opposed them, sometimes militarily. Thus, European and (especially after World War II) American domination of less-developed countries bred much resentment, resistance, and revolt. Peasants, urban workers, intellectuals, and military officers were increasingly attracted to anti-imperialist independence movements based on various forms and mixes of socialism and nationalism (Brym, 1980: 50–53; Wolf, 1999 [1969]).

In the Muslim world, Islam was an additional source of anti-imperialist sentiment. In 1928, the Society of the Muslim Brothers was formed in Egypt ("Muslim Brotherhood Movement," 2002). It served as a prototype for other, similar groups. The Muslim Brotherhood argued against Western values and imperialist domination. It called for a return to the teaching of the Qur'an, strictly interpreted, and demanded that Egypt become an Islamic state based on religious law (*shari'a*). This type of thinking became popular in Egypt and throughout the Muslim world in the twentieth century, gaining impetus especially in Iran from the 1960s on and then spreading to Algeria and as far afield as Afghanistan and Sudan by the end of the century.

Growing popularity did not translate into widespread political ascendance until recent times. After World War II, almost all Middle Eastern and North

African countries were authoritarian regimes that suppressed the Muslim Brotherhood and forced it underground. There, it branched into two streams—an extremist current exemplified by al Qaeda and a more liberal current exemplified by political parties that a plurality of Tunisians, Moroccans, and Egyptians supported in national elections held in 2011 and 2012. Let us consider each of these currents in turn.

Extremist Political Islam: From al Qaeda to ISIL

A clear line of intellectual influence leads from the early Muslim Brothers to the assassins of Egypt's President Anwar Sadat in 1981 after he made peace with Israel to Osama bin Laden and al Qaeda (Worth, 2001). Al Qaeda's chief aims are to remove all Western influence from areas with Muslim majorities, create in their place societies based on a fundamentalist interpretation of Islamic law, and destroy Israel as a Jewish state.

It is noteworthy that, however much al Qaeda is influenced by ideas dating back to the 1920s, it is every inch a global movement that relies on modern technology for its successes. Al Qaeda has operatives in as many as 60 countries. It finances itself through a complex international network of legitimate businesses, charitable and relief organizations, private donors, and opium trafficking operations (Shahar, 2001). Bin Laden communicated with his operatives via satellite telephone until U.S. law enforcement authorities inexplicably revealed they were tapping calls from his base in Afghanistan. Once he learned of these taps, he increased his use of another, more effective means of global communication—sending messages that are easily encrypted but difficult to decode via the Internet (Kelley, 2001; McCullogh, 2000). Some analysts think such messages were used to help plan and coordinate the complex, virtually simultaneous jet hijackings that resulted in the crash of an airliner in Pennsylvania and the destruction of the World Trade Center and part of the Pentagon on September 11, 2001, killing some 3000 people.

In the summer of 2014, a still more violent and extreme offshoot of al Qaeda known as the Islamic State in the Levant (ISIL) emerged on the international scene. Well financed, heavily armed, and well trained, it had already taken over large parts of Syria, which was in the midst of a civil war. It now raced across eastern and northern Iraq, shooting, raping, torturing, beheading, and crucifying Christians, Muslims, and others—in fact, anyone who was not prepared to convert to its extremist views.

Liberal Political Islam: From Arab Spring to Arab Winter

In late 2010, Mohamed Bouazizi, a 27-year-old Tunisian street vendor, set himself on fire to protest harassment and humiliation by local officials. His action catalyzed widespread and often violent anti-regime, pro-democracy demonstrations that first overthrew the Tunisian government and then spread with similar results to Egypt, Libya, and Yemen while also rocking other governments throughout the region. Bouazizi and those inspired by him objected to the authoritarianism, corruption, economic stagnation, unemployment, and poverty that characterizes most of the Middle East and North Africa. They initiated a pro-democratic movement that was soon dubbed the "Arab Spring" (see the Critical Sociology: Globalization box).

Although the prospects for democracy in the region at first seemed bright, things did not work out as widely expected. Four distinct political patterns emerged:

1. *Monarchical steadfastness.* Eight countries containing 24 percent of the Arabs in the Middle East and North Africa are authoritarian monarchies (Bahrain, Jordan, Kuwait, Morocco, Oman, Qatar, Saudi Arabia, and the United Arab Emirates). Although some of these regimes found it necessary to use their security forces to suppress pro-democracy protests, the most powerful anti-democratic weapon that most of them enjoy is oil wealth. Most of the monarchies have, in effect, been able to stay in power by buying off their populations with heavily subsidized food and fuel and relatively high incomes.

2. *Civil war.* Another 24 percent of the region's Arabs live in Iraq, Libya, Syria, and Yemen. Beginning in 2011, these countries descended into civil wars that, as of this writing (fall 2015), are ongoing. Democratic, authoritarian, and Islamist forces, some affiliated with al Qaeda or ISIL, are contending for power in these countries.

3. *Reform and reaction.* In a free and fair vote in 2012, the people of Egypt, representing 23 percent of the region's Arabs, elected a political party associated with the Muslim Brotherhood. The party was unlike anything most Westerners had ever seen. On the one hand, it was suspicious of Western intentions and insisted that Islam should form the basis of politics and law. On the other hand, it repeatedly proclaimed support for democratic

CRITICAL SOCIOLOGY: GLOBALIZATION   WILL THE REVOLUTION BE TWEETED?

Some observers claim that Twitter and Facebook made the Arab Spring possible because they allowed Arab protesters not just to express their grievances locally, regionally, and globally, but also to coordinate their actions. In this view, social media enabled movement members to develop their ideas, inspire others, mobilize political and financial support, organize demonstrations, and warn comrades of imminent danger at the neighbourhood level, all at low cost. Parallels are sometimes drawn between the Arab Spring and other new social movements that have used social media to good effect. For example, in 2011–12, a widespread demand for greater economic equality was championed by the Occupy Movement. The idea for the movement originated in Vancouver. Its first occupation and demonstration took place in New York. Protests then spread quickly to 951 cities in 82 countries, aided by social media.

Despite the advantages of using social media to mobilize protest, one must be careful not to exaggerate their benefits. For example, survey research among a representative sample of Egyptian Arab Spring activists paints a more subtle picture. While using new electronic communications media was associated with being a demonstrator, other factors were more important in distinguishing demonstrators from mere sympathetic onlookers. Protesters tended to be people with stronger grievances over unemployment, poverty, and corruption. They were more available for protest activities than others were because they tended to be unmarried men living in cities. And they tended to have more and stronger pre-existing ties than others did to various charities, political groups, and other civic associations. The use of new electronic communications media was less important than were strong grievances, high availability, and dense social connections in distinguishing demonstrators from sympathetic onlookers (Brym et al., 2014).

A protester in Tahrir Square, Cairo, Egypt, in 2011, helping to overthrow the authoritarian regime of President Hosni Mubarak.
SOURCE: © Patrick Baz/Getty Images.

Critical Thinking Question

Some analysts claim that social media weaken social movements insofar as they (a) give government opponents increased opportunities to surveil and repress activists and (b) allow potential recruits to feel politically involved while actually doing little in practice (for example, merely joining a Facebook group or contributing a dollar to a cause). On balance, do you think social media weaken or strengthen social movements?

---

elections and tolerance of religious and ethnic minorities. In practice, the Islamist tendencies of the party won out, and many liberal, secular, and Christian Egyptians took to the streets to protest. The country's powerful military soon stepped in and took over the government, thus returning Egypt to its political condition before the Arab Spring.

4. *The Tunisian model.* Tunisia is a North African country with a population of less than 11 million, representing just 4 percent of the region's Arabs.

In 2011, Tunisians elected to office a party affiliated with the Muslim Brotherhood. Less Islamist and more democratic than its Egyptian counterpart, the party was defeated by a more liberal and secular party in the 2014 election. In Tunisia, the Arab Spring lives. In the rest of the region, it has become the Arab Winter.

As recent events in the Middle East and North Africa illustrate, a wide range of reactions against Western power and influence now grips much of the developing world. In its extreme forms, the anti-Western reaction has no respect for minority rights, multiculturalism, elections, relatively open markets, and many of the other freedoms we enjoy and often take for granted in the West. In its more moderate forms, it shares many of the West's fundamental values. Yet regardless of its orientation, the anti-Western reaction is everywhere based on the desire of people to restore the independence and dignity they lost when the industrialized world showed up on their doorstep uninvited. One of the great tasks the West faces in the twenty-first century is to defend itself against violence while doing its utmost to remove the ultimate source of that violence: the gap between rich and poor countries that opened up at the time of the Industrial Revolution and that has widened ever since. Whether we are up to the task is anyone's guess.

TIME FOR REVIEW

1. How and why have social movements changed over the past three centuries?
2. What are the main differences between social movements in rich and developing societies?

SUMMARY

1. **What is democracy and what determines the level of democracy in a society?**
   Democracy involves a two-way process of control between the state (the set of institutions that formulate and carry out a country's law, policies, and binding regulations) and civil society (the private sphere, consisting of social movements, political parties, and so on). The level of democracy in a society depends on the capacity of civil society to influence the state through citizen support of social movements, political parties, and other groups. That capacity increases as power becomes more widely distributed in society.

2. **What are the main ideas and criticisms of pluralists, elite theorists, Marxists, power-balance theorists, and state-centred theorists?**
   Although pluralists correctly note that democratic politics is about negotiation and compromise, they fail to appreciate how advantaged groups tend to have more political influence than others do. Although elite theorists are right to note that power is concentrated in the hands of advantaged groups, they fail to appreciate how variations in the distribution of power influence political behaviour and public policy. Marxists assert that, in capitalist societies, elites always form a ruling class, but power-balance theorists focus on the political effects of *changes* in the distribution of power in society. However, power-balance theorists fail to appreciate that state institutions and laws also affect political behaviour and public policy, as state-centred theorists emphasize.

3. **How does the distribution of power in society affect the success of particular political parties?**
   The degree to which power is widely distributed influences the success of particular kinds of parties and policies. Widely distributed power is associated with the success of labour parties and policies that redistribute wealth.

4. **Under what circumstances do people rebel against established authority?**
   Research does not support the view that social movements emerge when relative deprivation spreads. Research suggests that people are more inclined to rebel against the status quo when they are bound by close social ties to many other people who feel similarly wronged and when they have the money and other resources needed to protest.

5. **What is frame alignment?**
   For social movements to grow, members must engage in frame alignment, making the activities, goals, and ideology of the movement congruent with the interests, beliefs, and values of potential new recruits.

6. **How can the history of democracy be characterized in terms of citizenship rights?**
   The history of democracy is a struggle for the acquisition of constantly broadening citizenship rights—first the right to free speech, freedom of religion, and justice before the law, then the right to vote and run for office, then the right to a certain level of economic security and full participation in the life of society, and finally the right of marginal groups to full citizenship and the right of humanity as a whole to peace and security.

7. **What is the chief focus of social movements in the developing world?**
   In the developing world, social movements have focused less on broadening the bases of democracy than on ensuring more elemental human rights, notably freedom from colonial rule and freedom to create the conditions for independent economic growth. In some cases, these movements have taken extreme, anti-democratic forms.

QUESTIONS TO CONSIDER

1. Have you ever participated in a social movement or been actively involved in a political party? If so, explain how your political choices (which party you joined, your level of participation, the timing of your recruitment) were influenced by the sociological factors discussed in this chapter. If you have never participated in a social movement or been actively involved in a political party, explain how the sociological factors discussed in this chapter influence you to remain politically inactive.

2. How would you achieve a political goal? Map out a detailed strategy for reaching a clearly defined aim, such as a reduction in income tax or an increase in university funding. Who would you try to recruit to help you achieve your goal? Why? What collective actions do you think would be most successful? Why? To whose attention would these actions be directed? Why? Write a manifesto that frames your argument in a way that is culturally appealing to potential recruits.

3. Do you think that social movements will be more or less widespread in the twenty-first century than they were in the twentieth century? Why, or why not? What kinds of social movements are likely to predominate?

4. Do you think that the twenty-first century will be more or less democratic than the twentieth? Why, or why not?

GLOSSARY

Authorities (p. 443) are people who occupy the command posts of legitimized power structures.

Authority (p. 443) is power that is widely viewed as legitimate.

Civil citizenship (p. 455) recognizes the right to free speech, freedom of religion, and justice before the law.

Civil society (p. 444) is the private (nonstate) sphere of social life.

Elite theory (p. 445) maintains that well-to-do people consistently have more political influence than people who are less well-to-do have and that society is therefore not as democratic as it is often portrayed.

Force (p. 443) is coercive power.

Frame alignment (p. 453) is the process by which individual interests, beliefs, and values become congruent and complementary with the activities, goals, and ideology of a social movement.

New social movements (p. 455) are post-1950s movements that attract a disproportionately large number of highly educated people in the social, educational, and cultural fields and universalize the struggle for citizenship.

Pluralist theory (p. 445) holds that society has many competing interests and centres of power and that no one interest or power centre predominates in the long run.

Political citizenship (p. 455) recognizes the right to run for office and vote.

Political parties (p. 443) are organizations that seek to control state power.

Power (p. 443) is the ability of an individual or a group to impose its will on others, even if they resist.

Power-balance theory (p. 447) suggests that social movement formation and success depend on how powerful authorities are, compared with partisans of change. It also holds that societies with widely distributed power are more democratic and more egalitarian than are societies with narrowly held power.

Relative deprivation (p. 452) is an intolerable gap between the social rewards people feel they deserve and the social rewards they expect to receive.

Resource mobilization theory (p. 452) holds that social movements crystallize and succeed in achieving their goals to the degree that they have access to scarce resources, such as money and effective communication facilities.

A **ruling class** (p. 446) is a self-conscious and cohesive group of people, led by corporate executives and owners of big business, who act to advance their common interests.

Social citizenship (p. 455) recognizes the right to a certain level of economic security and full participation in social life.

Social movements (p. 443) are enduring collective attempts to change part or all of the social order by means of rioting, petitioning, striking, demonstrating, and establishing pressure groups, unions, and political parties.

The **state** (p. 444) is a set of institutions that formulate and implement a country's laws, policies, and binding regulations. It consists of an executive branch (which initiates laws), a legislative branch (which makes laws), a judicial branch (which interprets laws), and an administrative and coercive apparatus (which enforces laws and protects state security).

State-centred theory (p. 450) shows how the state structures political life independently of the way power is distributed among classes and other groups at a given time.

Universal citizenship (p. 457) recognizes the right of marginal groups and the rights of humanity as a whole to full citizenship.

NOTES

1. In addition, less than 11 percent of the American working class is unionized, making it the least organized working class in any of the world's rich countries.

2. For example, in the 1890s, a coalition of white and black southern farmers threatened the established American political parties. It was precisely for this reason that American electoral laws were made more restrictive.

3. Some of these generalizations do not apply to countries with a long tradition of labour government. For example, since World War II, Sweden has experienced high levels of unionization and low strike rates. That is because Swedish workers and their representatives are involved in government policymaking. Decisions about wages and benefits tend to be made in negotiations among unions, employer associations, and governments rather than on the picket line.

CHAPTER 20

GLOBALIZATION

Josée Johnston
UNIVERSITY OF TORONTO

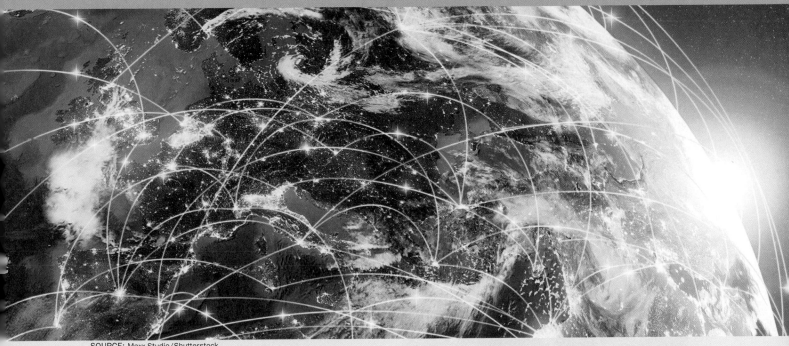

SOURCE: Maxx-Studio/Shutterstock.

AFTER READING THIS CHAPTER YOU WILL BE ABLE TO:

- Define globalization and identify its key elements.

- See how globalization influences your everyday life as a consumer, a worker, and a citizen.

- Explain why globalization provokes a reaction against itself.

- Compare different perspectives on globalization. In particular, you will be able to compare the "top–down" forces of globalization that promote the expansion of global markets with the "bottom–up" forces demanding greater democracy, social justice, and sustainability in the global system.

THE BURGER AND FRIES GO GLOBAL

Think about the average fast-food meal: a burger, fries, and a pop. This is the food of North America— simple, greasy, fast, and familiar. Maybe fast food has something to do with the sociology of health or the sociology of food, but what does it have to do with the sociology of globalization?

It turns out that globalization has a lot to do with everyday events like eating fast food. The average North American meal travels more than 1600 kilometres to reach your dinner table, so there is a good chance that your burger and fries have been *globalized*.

Let's start with the burger. Although Canadian ranchers pride themselves on their cattle exports, at least 30 percent of the beef eaten in Canada is imported from the United States, Australia, New Zealand, and Uruguay. Even if the beef in your burger did originate in Canada, the process of transforming a cow into your hamburger was deeply affected by globalization processes. Because of global market competition, the meat-packing industry in Canada was restructured in recent decades to cut costs by centralizing production and finding cheaper labour supplies.

Ronald McDonald in China.
SOURCE: © Dwight Cendrowski/Alamy.

Cargill Meat Solutions and JBS Food Canada account for about 90 percent of Canada's beef-slaughtering capacity. JBS Food Canada owns Lakeside Packers, situated in the small town of Brooks, Alberta. Thousands of people immigrated to work at Lakeside, and many languages are spoken inside the factory walls, including Arabic, French, Spanish, Tagalog, Chinese, and Cambodian. JBS USA, a subsidiary of Brazilian multinational JBS SA, purchased Lakeside from another company in 2013 after *E. coli* bacteria were discovered in beef from the plant (Cargill, 2014; Graveland, 2013). The restructuring of ownership and labour in the meat-packing industry is an illustration of what globalization means.

Even a vegetarian's fast-food choices are affected by globalization. In 2001, six vegetarians from British Columbia working with an American lawyer sued McDonald's after it was revealed that McDonald's French fries use beef fat for "flavouring." After hearing the announcement, vegetarian activists in India held demonstrations and attacked a McDonald's in Bombay, demanding that McDonald's leave the country ("McDonald's Apologizes," 2001). McDonald's settled the lawsuit in 2002 by agreeing to donate $10 million dollars to Hindu and consumer groups.

If our fast food is influenced by global forces, North American fast food also influences global eating. North American markets became relatively saturated with fast-food outlets in the 1980s, so McDonald's made a push in the 1990s for international expansion. The number of countries with a McDonald's grew from 59 in 1991 to 119 in 2014 (McDonald's, 2014). Today, McDonald's operates more than 35 000 restaurants, more than half outside the United States, including 1400 in Canada (McDonald's Canada, 2013; McDonald's Corporation, 2014). McDonald's opens about four new restaurants a day (McDonald's Corporation, 2013). Ronald McDonald is the second most recognized figure in the world, next to Santa Claus (Brownell and Horgen, 2004: 58). By 2013, sales in the United States accounted for only 31 percent of McDonald's revenue (McDonald's Corporation, 2013). For these reasons, scholars now believe we should be studying not only the globalization of fast food but also the globalization of obesity (Sobal, 2001). A recent study estimated that over 2.1 billion people, nearly 30 percent of the global population, are overweight or obese (Dobbs et al., 2014; OECD, 2014a).

It turns out, then, that everyday activities—like eating a hamburger and fries—have a lot do to with globalization. In an obvious way, the resources and labour that make up a fast-food meal originate from locations all around the globe. But even when the ingredients come from close to home, the food itself can be affected by global events, such as international trade agreements, European social movements, international labour migration, and faraway protests against McDonald's.

GLOBALIZATION OR "GLOBALONEY"?

Before going any farther, let's raise perhaps our most difficult question in this chapter: What do we mean by *globalization*? It is a frequently heard buzzword, yet there is no consensus on its meaning. The term was coined in the late 1970s, and today there are thousands of globalization books, conferences, university courses, and references in newspapers and magazines, many of which contradict each other. This confusion has led some academics to dismiss the term altogether as a confused mixture of globalization and baloney—what some crankily refer to as "globaloney."

While it is hard to find agreement on a definition of globalization, you don't have to look hard to find controversy about whether globalization is good or bad. A common tendency on both the left and the right of the political spectrum is to depict globalization in simplistic terms. For right-wing free-marketers, globalization represents the welcome spread of capitalism throughout the world. For many left-wing social activists and politicians, globalization is more like a Death Star. In the words of the former executive director of *Global Business* magazine,

> Globalization is many things, and much has been written about it and said. But throw all the tomes and studies and placards into a giant try-works, and you'll render two simple arguments:
>
> 1. Globalization is good because it spreads what is good in America, such as a liberal approach to business, and McDonald's.
> 2. Globalization is bad because it spreads what is worst about America, such as a liberal approach to business, and McDonald's. (Lynn, 2002: 34)

A primary objective of this chapter is to get beyond this kind of simplistic thinking and gain a more sophisticated sense of what exactly is meant by globalization. The objective is not to provide the ultimate definition of globalization that will ring true for all people until the end of time, but to understand how different political and economic interests struggle to promote their own brand of globalization.

DEFINING GLOBALIZATION

While figuring out exactly what we mean by globalization is a primary objective of the chapter, we need a neutral definition to get us started: **Globalization** is a social, economic, and political process that makes it easier for people, goods, ideas, and capital to travel around the world at an unprecedented pace (Waters, 1995: 3). Globalization makes the world look and feel smaller.

Of course, the world is not shrinking literally. What is instead occurring is that people, money, corporations, and ideas are travelling across the globe more quickly and efficiently than ever before. Distance no longer seems as relevant, and time lags that used to characterize our social relations are diminished. We no longer think it's crazy to have a romantic relationship with somebody across the country or even on the other side of the world. We can now communicate instantly through telephone, email, instant messenger, or a web-camera. If we want to see our girlfriend or boyfriend in person, we can take a relatively inexpensive plane trip rather than waiting for an ocean-going vessel to take us for a week-long journey across the seas. If our beloved is broke and needs money, we can transfer money instantly through electronic banking networks. And if you are single, you can systematically search the world for love through the thousands of online dating sites, some of which are devoted just to vegetarians, tattoo artists, and cat lovers.

One term for this shrinking world phenomenon is **time–space compression**, which suggests that we are no longer slowed down by long distances and time differences (Harvey, 1990: 284). Not only do we feel less constrained by time and distance, but some global phenomena also seem to transcend the idea of physical space altogether. The Internet has facilitated the creation of **virtual communities**, in which people can meet, share ideas, play games, and build relationships across borders without ever meeting face to face. Use of the Internet has not only increased dramatically but has also changed the patterns of our daily lives and interactions. In a survey of college graduates in 14 countries, including Canada, 40 percent felt that the Internet is more important to daily life than is music, dating, or spending time with friends (Cisco, 2011).

While the Internet may seem indispensable to many readers of this textbook, it is important to note that just 39 percent of the world's population is connected to it (see Table 20.1).

There are many examples of time–space compression but there are also many instances in which time still passes slowly and the limits of geography are still relevant. People may be more "wired" in the global age, but they are often connecting with friends and family in their city—not necessarily making new friends around the world (Ghemawat, 2007). In fact, fewer than 2 percent of phone calls and less than 20 percent of data transmitted over the Internet cross national borders (Ghemawat, 2011). In addition, not all people and ideas have access to channels of globalization, such as the Internet or even the telephone. Inequality of access to means of communication is commonly called the **digital divide** (see the Critical Sociology: Social Inequality box).

There is a lot of academic debate about how recent globalization is. We won't venture far into this contested territory, but it is important to note that the world has been shrinking for a long time. Time–space

compression can be traced back at least to the fifteenth century, with the beginning of transoceanic European exploration. The world became smaller with the invention of the steamship and the locomotive—two technologies that connected distant populations at a rate unimagined by previous generations. Colonial relationships in the eighteenth and nineteenth centuries moved millions of people and shiploads of wealth around the world.

The current phase of time–space compression is not radically different in form, but its pace has grown especially quickly since the 1980s. The intensification of space–time compression in recent decades has had enormous consequences for all areas of life, from entertainment to political protest.

HOW GLOBALIZATION SPREADS UNREST

In December 2010, an incident in Tunisia ignited a protest movement that quickly spread throughout the Middle East and North Africa. Mohamed Bouazizi, 27, could not find a job, so he began selling fruit and

TABLE 20.1 WORLD INTERNET USERS AND POPULATION

WORLD REGION	POPULATION IN MILLIONS (2014)	INTERNET USERS IN MILLIONS	% USAGE GROWTH (2000–14)	INTERNET USERS AS % OF POPULATION	% OF WORLD USERS	FACEBOOK USERS IN MILLIONS (2012)
Africa	1125.7	240.1	5219.6	21.3	8.6	51.6
Asia	3996.4	1265.1	1006.8	31.7	45.1	254.3
Europe	825.8	566.3	438.8	68.6	20.2	250.9
Middle East	231.1	103.8	3060.9	44.9	3.7	23.8
North America	353.9	300.3	177.8	84.9	10.7	182.4
Latin America/ Caribbean	612.3	302	1571.4	9.3	10.8	198
Oceania/ Australia	36.7	24.8	225.5	67.5	0.9	14.8
World total	7181.9	2802.5	6676.3	39	100	975.9

SOURCE: Adapted from Internet World Stats (2014a, 2014b, 2014c, 2014d, 2014e, 2014f, 2014g).

CRITICAL SOCIOLOGY: SOCIAL INEQUALITY   HOW INEQUALITY LIMITS GLOBALIZATION

Various means of electronic communication compress space and time, allowing information of various sorts to be transmitted almost instantly across vast distances. However, economic inequality greatly limits the global flow of information, as Table 20.2 shows.

Critical Thinking Questions

1. What are the major technological devices that connect *you* to people and ideas from around the globe? What faraway ideas or events or issues do you currently know about, thanks to the space–time compression of globalization-era technologies?

2. Think about a spectrum of space–time compression. On one end are people who are the *least* mobile, and at the other end are people with *extreme* global mobility. Where do you place yourself on this spectrum?

TABLE 20.2   INEQUALITY LIMITS GLOBAL INFORMATION FLOW

MEANS OF COMMUNICATION	HOW IT COMPRESSES SPACE AND TIME	HOW INEQUALITY LIMITS GLOBALIZATION
Telephone	Telephones make person-to-person communication possible across oceans and almost all national boundaries.	Many people in poor regions lack telephone access. In sub-Saharan Africa, there is only 1 fixed telephone line per 100 inhabitants while in Canada there are 50 (World Bank, 2014a). Mobile telephony has greatly increased, but there are still big regional differences: Eurozone consumers enjoy 122 mobile lines per 100 inhabitants but sub-Saharan Africa has just 66 mobile lines per 100 inhabitants (World Bank, 2014a).
Internet	The Internet allows images, videos, music, and text to be transmitted almost instantly around the world.	Globally, Internet access is even more limited than access to the telephone is (see Table 20.1.)
Satellite TV	Satellites allow transmission of TV programming from multiple points of production around the world.	Ownership of TV sets is concentrated in wealthy countries, television production is controlled by a small number of media monopolies centred in the industrialized north, and television content globally is fairly homogeneous and linked to consumer capitalism (McKibben, 1993).
Electronic money markets	Electronic banking allows capital to flow across national borders almost instantly.	About 2.5 billion people do not have access to formal financial services, including bank accounts, let alone access to electronic money markets (World Bank, 2013).

vegetables to make ends meet. When the authorities humiliated him and confiscated his produce because he did not have a licence, Bouazizi set himself on fire out of desperation and rage. In the weeks that followed, protests escalated across the country as Tunisians decried the bleak future they faced. In mid-January 2011, after a month of unrest, they overthrew Tunisia's dictator. By late January, similar rumblings had spread to neighbouring Egypt. Thousands of people gathered in Cairo's central square to protest the regime of the country's dictator. Egyptians rallied against difficult living conditions, high unemployment, corruption, and stagnation. They, too, overthrew their regime. In the months that followed, similar uprisings took place in Libya, Bahrain, Yemen, and Syria for similar reasons ("Egypt Protests," 2011; "Egypt Uprising," 2011; "Tahrir Square's Place," 2011; Whitaker, 2010).

The "Arab Spring," as it came to be called, was greatly aided by globalized electronic communications media, including satellite TV, cellphones, and the Internet. Apart from spreading the news about the effect that widespread protests could have on corrupt dictatorships, social media in particular enabled activists to mobilize support from abroad, organize demonstrations, and warn of impending danger. Although the effect of global communications media has been exaggerated by some analysts, there is no question that they facilitated the mobilization and spread of the Arab Spring (Brym et al., 2014).

Similarly, in 2011 the Occupy Wall Street movement was proposed in Vancouver, first mobilized in New York, and quickly spread to Toronto, Tokyo, Tel Aviv, Paris, and scores of other cities, thanks in part to the effective use of social media (see Figure 20.1). The members of the Occupy movement criticized the inequalities generated by capitalism. However, unlike demonstrators in the Middle East and North Africa, they did not seek to overthrow their leaders. They focused instead on glaring contrasts in the global economy: CEOs earn millions of dollars a year while middle-class families struggle to keep their homes. The movement resonated even among people who did not protest. Former Canadian prime minister Paul Martin noted that he "[had] yet to talk to anyone who says [the protesters] aren't reflecting a disquiet that they themselves feel," and added, "the powerful thing is that Occupy Wall Street has hit a chord that really is touching the middle class—the middle class in Canada, the middle class in the United States, the middle class right around the world—and I think that makes it ... very, very powerful" (Freeland, 2011).

TOP–DOWN VERSUS BOTTOM–UP GLOBALIZATION

Questions of equality, security, and social justice are critical in the ongoing debate about globalization and will be explored in the rest of this chapter. These debates can be understood as part of the tension between top–down and bottom–up globalization. **Top–down globalization** involves the actions of groups promoting globalized capitalism and free trade. The term *globalization* was first widely used by the American Express credit card company, which boasted in the 1970s that its card was accepted worldwide (Harvey, 1990: 13). The term was then taken up in financial and business circles, where it

---

FIGURE 20.1   OCCUPY PROTESTS AROUND THE WORLD OCTOBER 2011

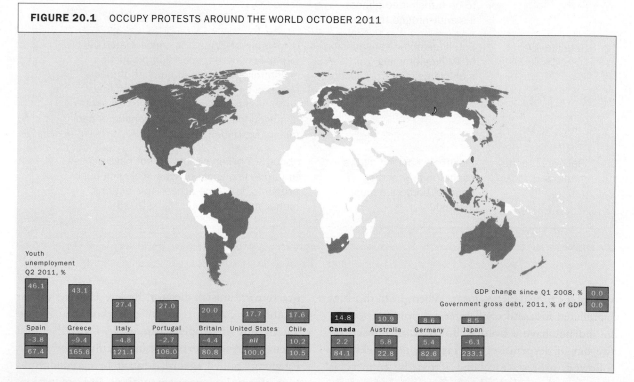

Youth unemployment Q2 2011, %										
46.1	43.1	27.4	27.0	20.0	17.7	17.6	14.8	10.9	8.6	8.5
Spain	Greece	Italy	Portugal	Britain	United States	Chile	**Canada**	Australia	Germany	Japan
-3.8	-9.4	-4.8	-2.7	-4.4	*nil*	10.2	2.2	5.8	5.4	-6.1
67.4	165.6	121.1	106.0	80.8	100.0	10.5	84.1	22.8	82.6	233.1

GDP change since Q1 2008, % [0.0]
Government gross debt, 2011, % of GDP [0.0]

Note: Data unavailable for countries shaded white.
SOURCE: © The Economist Newspaper Limited, London (Nov. 2, 2011).

came to represent hope for a world where capital could flow freely, uninhibited by national boundaries or governments insisting on national regulations and taxation.

Top–down globalization has been dominated by neoliberal economic policies, which have become prevalent in both rich and poor countries since the 1980s. **Neoliberalism** is associated with a retreat from state spending and regulation, a focus on individual responsibility for one's own welfare, less protection for labour and the environment, privatization of state resources, and faith in the power of the market and the profit motive to create wealth (see Chapter 10, Development and Underdevelopment). Top–down globalization is also strongly associated with the United States because of its role in promoting neoliberal policies globally through such institutions as the International Monetary Fund (IMF) and the World Bank, headquartered in Washington, DC. For this reason, top–down globalization has also been referred to as the "Washington consensus." In addition, the United States is often perceived as an exemplar of neoliberal policy domestically, even though it seems to deviate on such key matters as a balanced budget (in part because of high levels of U.S. military spending).

Globalization from below describes the actions of groups that criticize the injustices that result from globalization processes, and in particular, the expansion of global markets. The mass media frequently describe these groups as being opposed to globalization. That is inaccurate. Many groups that criticize the injustices resulting from globalization actually support particular types of globalization, such as the spread of international human rights and global labour standards. Moreover, they use technologies, like the Internet, to help them organize and communicate internationally.

In general, groups that support globalization from below advocate more democracy, environmental protection, and social justice in the global system. Bottom–up globalizers are against the neoliberal forms of globalization that put capital mobility, markets, and profits before people's basic needs, and they criticize the powerful economic, political, and military influence of transnational corporations and the United States government.

Top–down globalization has been targeted by environmentalists, peasant organizations, and farmers' unions, but it has also been criticized by capitalist insiders, such as world-famous economist and policy adviser Jeffrey Sachs, international financier George Soros, and Joseph Stiglitz, Nobel Prize winner and former chief economist and vice-president of the World Bank (Sachs, 2005; Soros, 1998; Stiglitz, 2003).

While everyone from rock stars to prime ministers demands greater justice in the global system, how to achieve it is not clear. There is no consensus on whether moderate capitalist reforms are sufficient, whether trade liberalization will help the poor, or whether the answer lies in partial or total withdrawal from global markets. Because of these differences, globalization from below should be understood less as a cohesive movement and more as a broad framework that encompasses multiple perspectives, including moderate critiques of neoliberalism, radical anti-capitalist positions, various forms of anarchism, armed peasant uprisings, and fair trade coffee projects.

How then do the forces of globalization operate in our daily lives? People are involved with globalization processes as capitalists, consumers, workers, and citizens (Robbins, 2005: 2–4). In the remainder of this chapter, we explore the profound influence of time–space compression in each of these realms.

TIME FOR REVIEW

1. Globalization is a complex process that involves the compression of space and time, making everyday events, people, and ideas often feel close to home. How do your connections to remote events, people, and ideas differ from those of your parents?
2. Globalization relies on, and reproduces, inequalities. What kind of global inequalities are embedded in your cellphone? Your running shoes? Are any protest movements connected to the globalization inequalities embedded in these products?

CAPITALISTS GO GLOBAL
THE RISE OF FINANCIAL CAPITAL

In economic terms, money used for investment, currency trading, and so forth is "financial capital." In the globalized economy, financial capital has grown much faster than production and trade. More than US$1.5 trillion flows through electronic financial channels every day, and an estimated 98 percent of these flows are purely speculative, meaning they are unrelated to the buying and selling of physical goods but involve short-term trading of such things as foreign currencies. In 2013, the value of world merchandise and commercial service exports was $23.4 trillion. While this seems an impressive number, it is equal to only four days' worth of trade on foreign exchange markets (Schäfer, Ross, and Strauss, 2013; WTO, 2014). Using a fully computerized global financial system, traders can move around billions of dollars to profit from minuscule changes in currency rates.

The rise of financial capital has been labelled "casino capitalism" since financial speculators, like casino gamblers, stand to make or lose millions of dollars in short periods (Strange, 1986). The rise of casino capitalism has been facilitated by the financial deregulation that has occurred under neoliberal regimes since the 1980s as governments gave up regulatory powers. The danger with casino capitalism is that investor speculation (a process akin to placing a bet) makes financial systems unstable. Money floods into markets during periods of optimism, creating a financial "bubble" that drives markets up. The bubble bursts when investors realize that the market is overpriced relative to the value of real assets. This causes a period of panic involving an outflow of capital and, in due course, economic recession.

A snowball of financial panic is precisely what the world witnessed during the 1997 Asian financial crisis, which started in Thailand and went on to affect the currencies, stock markets, and asset prices of a host of Asian countries, including Indonesia, South Korea, and Hong Kong as well as the financial systems of Brazil and Russia.

In 2008–09, a similar crisis occurred when the real estate market collapsed in the United States. Initially, inexpensive mortgages lured millions of Americans into the housing market. All was well while house prices rose. People felt richer, and they borrowed more and more money against the value of their homes. When people had to renew their mortgages at higher interest rates, many of them could not afford it. Foreclosures increased. With more houses on the market, house prices began to fall. The spiral of falling house prices and skyrocketing foreclosures soon put some large financial institutions in a position of not having enough cash on hand to continue operations. Some of them went bankrupt while others sought government assistance to stay in business.

Because financial institutions around the world had invested heavily in U.S. debt, the financial crisis was global, not simply American. Some institutions, such as Iceland's three biggest private banks and Lehman Brothers, the fourth-largest investment bank in the United States, went bankrupt, while governments had to lend money to keep other financial institutions afloat. Among other things, the crisis demonstrated how porous global financial borders are. In the words of the chief European economist at Deutsche Bank, "In this day and age, a bank run spreads around the world, not around the block" (Landler, 2008).

Canada's banking regulations and low level of involvement in inexpensive mortgage lending relative to the U.S. tempered the impact of the financial crisis, so that Canadian banks needed no financial support from the government. Nonetheless, the recession weakened Canadian exports and further undermined the manufacturing sector, which accounted for more than half of the net decline in employment between October 2008 and October 2009 (Statistics Canada, 2010). Moreover, the federal and Ontario governments contributed $13.7 billion to sustain General Motors and Chrysler during the crisis, on top of the $66 billion bailout from the U.S. government (Owram, 2014).

Global economic growth has inched steadily upward since the 2008 financial crisis, although the European and Japanese recovery continues to lag (Fischer, 2014). Despite recovering the 8.7 million jobs lost during the recession as of 2014, American job creation has not kept up with population growth and labour force participation rates in the U.S. remain lower than usual (Center on Budget and Policy Priorities, 2014).

OVERCAPACITY AND CENTRALIZATION

The growth of casino capitalism is also linked to overcapacity in the economy of goods and services. Put simply, global corporations are able to produce more things than the world's consumers can afford to purchase—a problem clearly related to global inequality. Justin Lin, chief economist at the World Bank, noted in 2009 that, "unless we deal with excess capacity, it will wreak havoc on all countries," thus acknowledging the connection between recent economic downturns and the tendency toward overproduction (Evans-Pritchard, 2009). While financial markets boomed throughout the early 2000s, and wealth appeared to be growing exponentially for some people, a number of economists worried that excess capacity in the productive economy—accompanied by growing inequality and global poverty, which erode the worldwide consumption base—meant that a global recession was in the works (Bello, 2002).

The 2008–09 financial crisis demonstrated the overcapacity problem, the importance of consumer demand for global growth, and the interpenetration of global financial markets. For example, the Indian high-tech and outsourcing industries, which rely heavily on business from the U.S. financial sector, began to freeze wages and announce layoffs for software programmers and workers in call centres in 2008. Growth and hiring levels in India's information technology sector remained low into 2014 (Bundhun, 2014; Kahn, 2008).

Canadian industries are facing their own challenges. For example, Canadian steel production and productive capacity utilization have diminished in the wake of the global overproduction of steel, while the manufacture of solar panels and cells in Canada has slowed because of a global glut of solar products that isn't matched by sufficient demand (Blackwell, 2011; Canadian Steel Producers Association, 2013).

Besides creating complex webs of interdependence among national economies, the creation of a global economy has changed the way corporations look and operate. In short, these conditions have made corporations leaner, meaner, bigger, more diverse in terms of the goods they produce, and more

involved in complex financial dealings and investments throughout the world.

To survive problems of overcapacity and economic slowdown, corporations have merged to trim operating costs. The Chinese automaker Geely bought Volvo from Ford (Nicholson, 2010). Renault took over Nissan, and Chrysler teamed up with Daimler-Benz (briefly), and then with Fiat. Chasing the high profits found in the financial sector, traditional corporations have gotten into the money-lending business, while banks have become involved in new kinds of businesses, such as securities trading. Today, transnational corporations find it hard to survive without diversifying into multiple goods in many countries, and this explains why the last decades have witnessed the greatest rate of mergers and consolidation in history (Institute of Mergers, Acquisitions, and Alliances, 2014; see Figure 20.2). It also helps explain why the same handful of corporations can be found almost everywhere, offering a similar range of products in the world's shopping malls and airports. These giant corporations trade with one another, but they also trade goods and services internally. The European Commission (2013) estimates that a third or more of all global trade involves transfers among different branches of the same corporation.

FIGURE 20.2   MERGERS AND ACQUISITIONS WORLDWIDE: 1985–2014

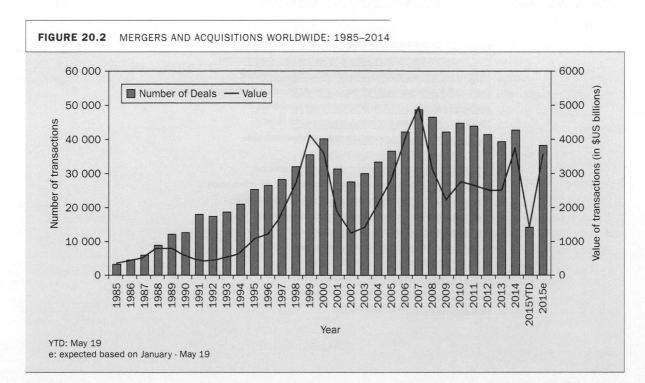

YTD: May 19
e: expected based on January - May 19

SOURCE: Institute of Mergers, Acquisitions and Alliances (IMAA), "M&A Activity: Number & Value of Announced Transactions, Worldwide," *Statistics*. http://www.imaa-institute.org/statistics-mergers-acquisitions.html#MergersAcquisitions_Worldwide (accessed Nov. 5, 2014).

GROWTH OF THE CORPORATE GIANTS

Corporations have become extremely big and powerful. In fact, many are bigger and more powerful than many national governments (Trivett, 2011). Consider just these two facts:

1. Of the largest 200 economic entities in the world, 131 (65.5 percent) are corporations (measured by revenue), and 69 are countries (measured by gross domestic product) (World Bank, 2014b).
2. The world's biggest corporation, Walmart, generated revenue in 2013 in excess of the GDP of Venezuela (27th on the World Bank's list of 192 countries by GDP), and greater than the GDPs of Portugal and Ireland (47th and 48th) combined ("Global 500," 2014).

It will perhaps surprise you to learn that big corporations do not necessarily pay big taxes. In fact, corporations are paying less in taxes today than in the 1990s. Companies regularly play nation-states against one another, pressuring governments to lower tax rates by threatening to move production to a more favourable location. The resulting decline in corporate taxes can be observed across all developed countries in the last two decades, as mobile individuals and corporations increasingly take advantage of global tax shelters, forcing governments to rely on taxes paid by less mobile individuals and small businesses (Figure 20.3).

Recent trends in several countries show that tax rates for corporations are being maintained, and even lowered. In the midst of the economic crash in 2008 (and again in 2009, 2010, and 2011), Ireland hiked tax rates to individuals, but maintained its corporate tax rate—one of the lowest among the wealthy countries at 12.5 percent (KPMG, 2014a, 2014b). Corporate tax rates were cut in all regions between 2006 and 2014, but Asia has seen the largest decline in average rates, from 29 percent to 22 percent, followed by North America's 5 percent decline (KPMG, 2014a). A study of 288 of America's largest corporations revealed that 41 percent paid less than half the statutory corporate tax rate for the 2008–12 period, 38.5 percent paid no taxes or received tax rebates for at least one of those years, and 20 percent enjoyed multiple no-tax years in that period (McIntyre, Gardner, and Phillips, 2014). These corporate tax breaks have taken place in spite of relatively high government debt.

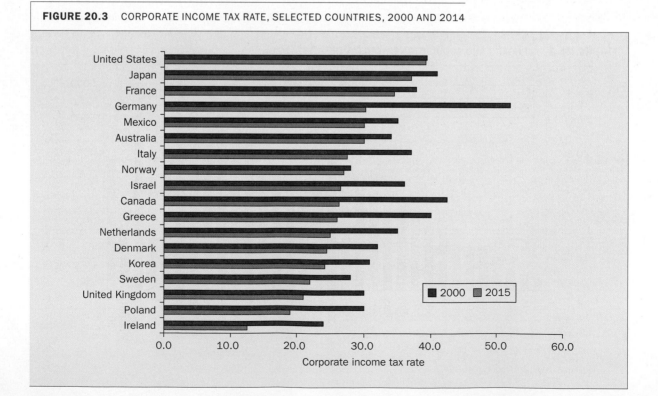

FIGURE 20.3   CORPORATE INCOME TAX RATE, SELECTED COUNTRIES, 2000 AND 2014

Canadian corporations have also enjoyed big tax breaks, which they justify by their need to compete with the United States. Reductions in corporate taxes decreased the Canadian government's federal revenues by an estimated $13 billion in 2012–13 (Canadian Labour Congress, 2014:14). Canada's own corporate tax rate was reduced from 50 percent in the early 1980s to just 26.5 percent in 2014 (KPMG, 2014a). These corporate tax breaks have significant implications for income inequality, as they lessen the ability of the state to redistribute wealth (Grant, 2011). Before the mid-1990s, Canada's tax-benefit system was able to offset 70 percent of income inequality, with a redistributive effect similar to that of some Scandinavian countries. Recently, this number has fallen to less than 40 percent (Grant, 2011).

The problems caused by tax imbalances because of corporate tax cuts and growing inequality in the redistribution of wealth have not gone unnoticed, even by Warren Buffett, one of the richest businessmen in the world. In 2011, Buffett wrote an op-ed in *The New York Times* stating that he paid taxes at around half the rate of anyone else in his office, including ordinary secretaries, and urging Congress to raise taxes on households earning in excess of $1 million a year. President Obama has taken up the challenge and developed the "Buffett rule," a proposal seeking a minimum 30 percent tax rate on all incomes over $1 million (Kaufman, 2014).

CRITICS OF CORPORATE POWER

Bottom–up globalizers have reacted to the growth of global corporations in various ways (Bello, 2002; Starr, 1999). For example, the 1990s saw the emergence of an anti-sweatshop movement in North America after poor working conditions in the garment industry were exposed (Ross, 1997). Of particular importance was the 1996 Kathie Lee Gifford controversy, which revealed that her Walmart clothing line was produced by child labour and involved human rights abuses.

In 2000, Naomi Klein's *No Logo* became an international bestseller. She argued that large corporate brands are vulnerable to a backlash against corporate power (Klein, 2000: 338). Klein's prediction has had some truth to it, although many firms have gone on the offensive, developing outreach programs and websites to sell themselves as responsible and even charitable organizations. Still, many corporations have been criticized on issues including labour practices, environmental sustainability, animal welfare, and relationships with the military–industrial complex (see, for example, Oxfam 2014).

Corporate tax avoidance has attracted much critical attention, with media, civil society groups, and the public increasingly naming and shaming companies. For example, Starbucks paid no corporate tax in the United Kingdom in 2012, despite boasting sales of £400 million. Similarly, Amazon paid just £1.8 million in taxes despite generating sales of over £3 billion in 2011 (Barford and Holt, 2013). Calls to curb corporate tax avoidance have gained momentum in the United States, with the Obama administration revising the tax code in 2014 to make it harder for American companies to merge with a foreign business and reincorporate abroad to take advantage of lower corporate tax rates (Bogiasky, 2014). Corporations responded to this wave of anti-corporate criticism in various ways. Starbucks responded to tax shaming efforts in the United Kingdom by forgoing tax deductions and accepting a £10 million tax liability for 2013, making its first corporate tax payments in four years (BBC, 2013).

Another way that global corporations are attempting to stem the tide of bad press is through a growing movement for corporate social responsibility, in which corporations voluntarily try to introduce best practices for labour and the environment. For instance, the Molson Coors Brewing Company converts brewing by-products into fuel-grade ethanol, while Tim Hortons restaurants use only wood certified by the Forest Stewardship Council in construction (Maclean's, 2013).

While many corporations are aggressively promoting themselves as good citizens, there is definitely room for improvement. This is particularly evident in the case of the clothing and textile industry. Have you ever wondered why clothing can be sold for such low prices? Part of the answer is low-cost globalized labour. The International Labour Organization reports that workers in the garment sector are especially vulnerable to poor working conditions (ILO, 2014). More than 100 workers perished in the November 2012 Tazreen Fashions factory fire in Bangladesh while producing clothing for Walmart and other companies in a facility without proper fire exits or evacuation procedures (Canadian Labour Congress, 2012). On April 24, 2013, the collapse of the Bangladeshi Rana Plaza building (declared structurally unsound the previous day) killed over 1000 garment workers.

While some corporate users of the factory, like Canada's Loblaw Companies Limited (owners of Joe Fresh) acknowledged their connection with the factory, others, like Walmart, promptly issued a denial of any association (Motlagh, 2014). Since the disaster, more than 150 countries have adopted the Accord on Fire and Building Safety in Bangladesh, a five-year, legally binding commitment to independent factory inspections and corporate funding of safety upgrades. Some American companies, like Walmart, Gap, and Target, signed onto a similar, but less binding, plan, the Alliance for Bangladesh Worker Safety. However, progress on a proposed $40 million compensation fund for workers and their families has been slow, and many corporations continue to purchase clothing from suppliers who threaten or fire employees seeking to unionize in order to challenge low wages and physical and sexual abuse in the workplace (Institute for Global Labour and Human Rights, 2014; Motlagh, 2014).

The growing power of corporations has not emerged in a political vacuum. As corporations have grown in strength, some governments have lost ground, both to corporate power and to international institutions, such as the World Trade Organization. This change has led many analysts to wonder if the age of globalization means the end of the state system.

TIME FOR REVIEW

1. What implications do casino capitalism and industrial overcapacity have for the stability of the global economy?
2. What are the key criticisms of large corporations? How have corporations responded to these critiques? Can you think of a corporate marketing campaign that works to portray the firm as a responsible global citizen?

ARE STATES RELEVANT IN A GLOBAL WORLD?

Critics of neoliberal policies have wondered about the extent to which states continue to be the main instrument of democratic governance. Has the state been replaced by a kind of "global governance?" Does real power rests in the hands of unelected officials in the world's three biggest international financial institutions: the International Monetary Fund (IMF), the World Bank, and World Trade Organization (WTO), sometimes called "the three sisters"? Because of pressure to meet the demands of these three powerful international financial institutions, some critics argue that states have become less oriented toward meeting the demands of citizens. The result is a **democratic deficit** in which ordinary citizens

are disenfranchised from the process of governance. Let's look briefly at how the three sisters challenge the capacity of states to make democratic decisions for average citizens.

THE THREE SISTERS

The IMF was established after World War II. Its official role was to maintain the stability of the international monetary system. Since the 1980s, the IMF has come to serve a different yet important role as the gatekeeper of the institutional financial system. IMF loans are conditional on the lending government following a package of reforms of known as "structural adjustment programmes" (renamed "poverty reduction strategies" in 1999; Brym et al., 2005; Woodroffe and Ellis-Jones, 2000). IMF reforms typically require countries to deregulate capital markets, remove price subsidies, decrease social spending, orient the economy toward exports, and privatize state-run industries. If a country refuses to adopt the reform package, it can find itself shut out of international lending circles and unable to service its debt.

Joseph Stiglitz, former senior vice-president and chief economist at the World Bank and Nobel Prize laureate, is no stranger to the inner circles of international finance. Yet he is also one of the IMF's harshest critics, which he describes as imprisoned in "market fundamentalism" and as staffed by "third-rate economists from first-rate universities" (Denny, 2002). For Stiglitz, decisions made by the IMF to solve various financial crises show that "the IMF is not particularly interested in hearing the thoughts of its 'client countries' on such topics as development strategy or fiscal austerity," and that "[all] too often, the Fund's approach to developing countries has the feel of a colonial ruler" (Stiglitz, 2003: 40). Many poor countries have witnessed massive protests against the IMF.

Like the IMF, the World Bank was also established after World War II, and its job was to make loans to help postwar reconstruction. Most World Bank loans were made to poor countries and were often tied to large development projects, such as hydroelectric dams. As a condition of receiving loans, the World Bank required that certain structural adjustment criteria be met. Like the IMF, the World Bank has had its share of critics, both external and internal (Chapter 10, Development and Underdevelopment). In response, the World Bank increased its collaboration with local nongovernmental organizations (NGOs). While some observers applaud these efforts as part of the Bank's self-help approach to social problems, others argue that the Bank's NGO collaborations do not change its fundamentally undemocratic nature or the severity of its structural adjustment reforms.

The WTO emerged in 1995. The WTO's job is to lower trade barriers, thereby increasing international trade and, presumably, prosperity. The WTO became known to many North Americans with the famous "Battle of Seattle" in 1999. WTO meetings in that city were met by huge, disruptive street protests. Every major meeting of the WTO since then has elicited protests, often from citizens of poor countries who charge that international trade works only to the benefit of the rich and ignores the unfair protection of corporate agribusiness at the expense of farmers. While some globalization-from-below organizations argue that trade liberalization will help the poor (e.g., Oxfam and Live 8 organizers), others argue that it will not and that entry to the WTO forces countries to comply to a set of trade rules written by wealthy countries for their own benefit (Bivens and Hersh, 2003).

EMPIRE U.S.A.?

While the IMF, World Bank, and WTO influence state policies throughout the world, not all states are equally affected by these institutions. Some observers note that the age of globalization is also an age of more power for some states and relative powerlessness for states at the bottom of the global hierarchy. Critics of the United States sometimes accuse it of acting like an empire. Neoconservative thinkers in Washington acknowledge that the United States acts like an empire, although they argue that it uses its power benevolently to promote peace and democracy throughout the world.

Analysts debate whether the United States is a modern empire or a fading superpower (Ferguson, 2004; Wallerstein, 2002). The United States still enjoys enough political, economic, and military power to make unilateral foreign policy decisions (such as invading Iraq, which it did without United Nations endorsement), maintain a substantial global military presence (see Figure 20.4), and adopt unorthodox

FIGURE 20.4   U.S. MILITARY FOOTPRINT ON THE WORLD

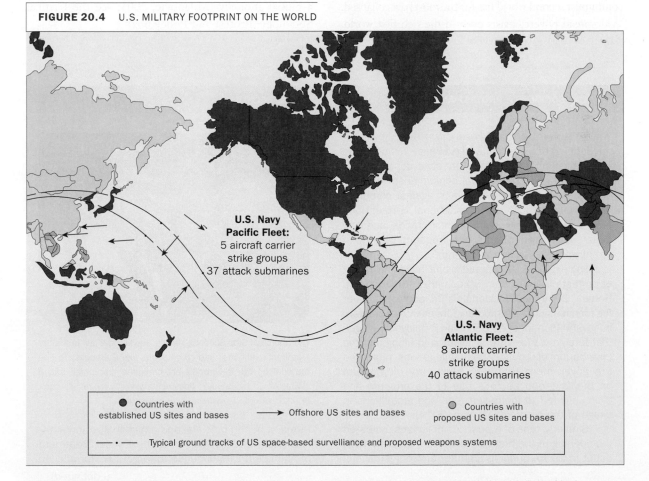

SOURCE: U.S. Department of Defense, *Base Structure Report* (2008). http://combatingglobalization.com/articles/combating_globalization4.html (accessed Aug. 12, 2012)

economic policies (like running huge fiscal deficits). Do these policies indicate the *decline* of U.S. hegemony? The United States is the world's biggest debtor, with a debt load of over $17 trillion dollars in 2014 (U.S. Treasury, 2014). Especially after the 2008–09 financial crisis hit, some analysts argued that the power of the United States was waning relative to that of the countries that own its debt holdings, notably China (Fallows, 2008).

GLOBAL INEQUALITY AND THE "FOURTH WORLD"

Another feature of the global state system is a widening power gap between and within states. In the 1970s, analysts often divided the world into three parts. The "first world" comprised the wealthy capitalist countries. The "second world" comprised the countries of the communist bloc. The "third world" comprised all the rest. This division is now inaccurate. The old third world now comprises a disparate assortment of nations that don't necessarily share common traits, the communist second world has for the most part collapsed. Widespread poverty exists even in the rich first world,

while some citizens in third world countries live middle-class lives or lives of wealth and luxury.

To capture asymmetries among the world's countries meaningfully, analysts sometimes refer to the division between the "Global North" and the "Global South" or between developed and developing countries. Another useful terminological distinction is between the "majority world," which is generally poor and lacks basic social goods like housing, food, employment, and education, and the "minority world," which is generally well educated and has access to good jobs and public goods like healthcare.

People from the privileged minority world may live in wealthy countries like Canada, but they can also live in Mexico City or Hong Kong. Similarly, people from the majority world can be homeless and searching for adequate food and shelter in downtown Toronto. The majority world–minority world distinction serves as a valuable reminder that state borders do not always indicate who benefits and who suffers in a globalized economic system and that the high living standard of the Canadian middle class is a global anomaly (Milanovic, 2005; see the Critical Sociology: Protest and Policy box).

CRITICAL SOCIOLOGY: PROTEST AND POLICY   THE GLOBAL BRAND BACKLASH

While the term *cultural imperialism* may drown out the subtlety of global cultural exchange, visible signs of antagonism toward Western-style consumerism remain. One way that global consumerism is being contested is through a backlash against corporate brand names. Just as transnational corporations have spread globally, so have their brands, and now many well-known brands are frequent targets of street protests around the world.

For example, McDonald's has been the target of protests in more than 50 countries (Brownell and Horgen, 2004: 61). McDonald's Canada came under fire for misusing the temporary foreign worker program in several locations, as Canadian employees alleged that foreign workers were favoured in hiring and the distribution of hours. These allegations prompted the government to put a temporary moratorium on the fast-food sector's use of the program and eventually led to increased fees and restrictions in usage of the program (Morgan, 2014).

Similarly, tens of thousands of Indians protested the opening of the first Kentucky Fried Chicken (KFC) outlet in 1995, bringing together environmentalists,

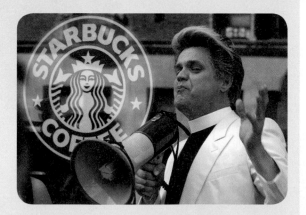

The Church of Stop Shopping, led by "Reverend Billy," promotes "retail interventions" into corporations like Starbucks. To see material on the Reverend's anti-consumer campaign and a "What Would Jesus Buy?" documentary, visit www.revbilly.com.

SOURCE: Reprinted by permission of Reverend Billy.

farmers, health officials, and anti-globalization activists (Wall, 2000). People for the Ethical Treatment of Animals (PETA) continue to target KFC for alleged

(continued)

(continued)

mistreatment of chickens among its suppliers, and these critiques have led to protests in the United States and India.

A global-brand backlash has also inspired greater attention to Coca-Cola's corporate practices throughout the world (Campaign to Stop Killer Coke; Nestle, 2011). In some instances, consumption of Coke has dropped off in favour of domestic soft drinks, leading Coke to retool its sales strategy by focusing on specialized local drinks (Hays, 2000).

Finally, Apple faced intense criticism when it was revealed that 15 workers at Foxconn, the Taiwanese company that produces parts for its products, killed themselves in the years before 2012. Another 150 workers threatened to jump from the roof of a factory in protest over lack of safety, inadequate wages, and unpaid overtime. In response, Apple agreed to join the Fair Labour Association, a monitoring group, which found numerous labour law violations in Foxconn's 13 factories (Sanchez and Blackden, 2012).

The idea that corporate globalization can be effectively fought by protesting against branded products is controversial. Many people argue that global corporations are geniuses at using social dissent to sell new consumer products (Frank, 1997; Heath and Potter, 2004). Just as 1960s radicals wore tie-dyed T-shirts and drove around in Boogie Vans, people today can purchase consumer products that express their opposition to the global capitalist system. You can wear a Che Guevara T-shirt while listening to anti-establishment rap music on your Dr. Dre earphones. While certain styles of cultural consumption can *feel* rebellious, the extent to which countercultural consumption disrupts global flows of wealth and circuits of power is unclear. Marketing gurus are well aware of such consumer tendencies and advise global corporations to advance their brand by using anti-establishment messages to sell products to young people around the world (Lindstrom, 2003: 132).

Critical Thinking Questions

1. How might you change your consumption patterns to reflect sensitivity to economic inequality and environmental degradation? What products and brands might you consume or avoid consuming?

2. How do certain products, brands, or marketing campaigns convey a sense of rebellion, or youthful dissent, or environmental protection? For example, how do Apple marketing campaigns convey a sense of being "different," radical, or rebelling against the mainstream? What is the purpose of conveying such ideas?

The following facts illustrate the extent of economic inequality in the world:

- In 2014, the world's 1645 billionaires (0.00000023 percent of the world's population) were worth $6.4 trillion. The richest man in the world in 2014 was Microsoft founder Bill Gates (worth $76 billion), and the second richest was Mexican telecommunications titan, Carlos Slim Helu (worth $72 billion) (Forbes, 2014c).

- Thirty-two Canadians are among the world's 1645 billionaires, the richest being David Thomson (who controls Thomson Reuters) in 27th place, followed by Loblaws owner Galen Weston in 153rd place.

- Canada's top 10 percent of earners make almost triple the national median income, while the top 1 percent of earners make more than 13 times the average income (Statistics Canada, 2014a).

- Half the world lives on less than US $2.50 a day (UNDP, 2014).

While the global economy has made part of the world's population wealthy, a large proportion of the world's people (at least 50 percent) may be considered poor. The global economy operates independently of large populations and geographical areas, which are seen as irrelevant for its functioning. These marginalized populations and regions are sometimes called the **Fourth World** (Cardoso, 1993; Castells, 1998; Hoogvelt, 1997: 66, 162). The Fourth World exists as a result of the new economic and technological paradigm of global competitiveness, where only a portion of the world's states and inhabitants are competitive in the global economy.

Recognizing that time–space compression and the global economy affect people differently allows our understanding of globalization to become more nuanced. Globalization does involve a number of intense connections within the core of the global system, as people in the minority world travel more, hold global investments, and integrate the Internet into their daily lives. At the same time, globalization also involves a process of *peripheralization* that marginalizes certain groups. Some people in rich countries like Canada—Indigenous peoples, homeless populations, unemployed workers—are subject to exclusionary processes like those that affect people in parts of Africa, Asia, and Latin America (Hoogvelt, 1997: 129).

TIME FOR REVIEW

1. The power of states in the global economy remains important but has been challenged by other actors. What international actors challenge the power of states? Which states have the most power in the global system?
2. The old division between first, second, and third worlds is now considered archaic. What new concepts describe global inequality? Have you seen evidence of the "Fourth World" in places you have lived in or visited?

THE GLOBAL CONSUMER

Maybe you have yet to be convinced that globalization has anything to do with you. But have you gone shopping lately? If you consume commodities—meaning goods purchased in the marketplace rather than made from your own labour—then you are inevitably part of globalization. The tags on your clothing are more likely to read "Made in China" or "Made in Bangladesh" than "Made in Canada."

A **global commodity chain** is "a [worldwide] network of labor and production processes, whose end result is a finished commodity" (Hopkins and Wallerstein, 1986: 159). Global commodity chains are not transparent to the casual consumer. When you eat a tomato on a fast-food hamburger, you usually don't know whether it has been shipped from Mexico or a local greenhouse. When you buy a pair of running shoes, the price tag doesn't tell you much about the workers who made the shoes or the company's environmental track record. In this section, we will learn about the critical role consumption plays in the global economy, as well as some of the social and environmental critiques of globalized consumerism.

GLOBALIZATION OF CONSUMPTION

While consumers don't always understand the complexity of global commodity chains, consumption plays a critical role in driving growth in the global economy. High consumer spending increases economic growth, while a lack of consumer confidence is associated with economic slowdown and recession. Because North American and European markets are relatively saturated consumer markets, many corporations see expansion into global markets as essential for growth. **Consumerism**—a way of life in which a person's identity and purpose is oriented primarily toward the purchase and consumption of material goods—is currently being exported to the world's middle and working classes.

As noted earlier, the global economy suffers from a problem of overcapacity that makes finding new consumer markets essential. In particular, many corporations are looking to expand sales to China, the world's most populous country, to solve the problem. So far, Chinese production has been focused mainly on export markets, thereby worsening the problem of global overproduction (Bello, 2002). This situation is beginning to change. In 2013, China overtook Japan to become the second-largest consumer market, behind the United States (*Economist*, 2014).

CULTURE AS COMMODITY?

Another characteristic of globalized consumerism is the tendency to treat culture like any other commodity. The United States has been instrumental in advancing this viewpoint—not surprisingly, given the tremendous size and power of the culture/entertainment industry in the United States. The biggest U.S. export consists of mass-produced products of popular culture (Barlow, 2001). While many countries have a tradition of protecting cultural products, the United States has used the WTO to prohibit states from using subsidies and quotas to protect domestic cultural products, such as films, music, magazines, books, and music. For example, in 1997, the WTO supported a U.S. complaint and ruled that the Canadian government's usage of preferential tax and postal rates to protect the domestic magazine industry was unlawful. (U.S. magazines make up 85 percent of the magazines found on Canadian newsstands.)

Or consider a more recent example: In 2007, the United States submitted a partially successful complaint to the WTO, claiming that China unfairly restricted the rights and ability of businesses to import and distribute films, sound recordings, and reading materials. Although the WTO adjudicating bodies agreed with China's stance that cultural goods and services have a unique character and warrant protection, China was urged to loosen its restrictions surrounding the sale and distribution of cultural products like books and movies (WTO, 2009).

A growing movement to resist the interpretation of culture as simply another global commodity is centred on a 2005 UN treaty: the United Nations Educational, Scientific, and Cultural Organization's (UNESCO) Convention on Cultural Diversity (CCD). The UNESCO Convention was vehemently opposed by the United States, since the treaty allows states to exclude cultural policies from free trade deals. As with most treaties, the devil will ultimately lie in the legal details, yet the CCD opens up the possibility for states legally to protect domestic cultural industries from the rules of trade. The convention clearly states that culture is *not* merely a commodity: "cultural activities, goods and services have both an economic and a cultural nature, because they convey identities, values and meanings, and must therefore not be treated as solely having commercial value." Today, the treaty has over 130 signatories (excluding the United States) who have committed to collect and share data on policies to facilitate diverse forms of cultural expression. Moreover, under the treaty's banner, 70 projects in 122 developing countries are in place to promote sustainable development and reduce poverty by fostering the development and strength of local cultural sectors (UNESCO, 2013).

CULTURAL IMPERIALISM?

The global spread of consumerism has been criticized as form of **cultural imperialism** (Barlow, 2001). From this viewpoint, global corporations, bolstered by sophisticated advertising tools, media monopolies, and declining trade barriers, are exporting a Western way of life throughout the world (Tomlinson, 1991). Cultural imperialism is often associated with liberal values around sexuality, feminism, and secularism.

Of course, people are not passive recipients of Western cultural products, which can be taken up in unique ways. A Japanese game shows like *The Iron Chef*, for instance, represents a unique cultural hybrid that combines an American game-show format with Japanese cultural and culinary mores. When it was first shown in the United States, it was unlike any show made by American television producers, yet it was a huge hit on the American-based Food Network and inspired *Iron Chef America*, a highly successful English-language spinoff of the original Japanese show.

Western cultural products are transformed as they are consumed by different global cultures. However, this does not mean that the world's cultural products

compete as equals. Free trade favours large economies and big economic actors. Canadians are more likely to eat in a McDonald's than they are to eat in a Jollibee, the leading fast-food restaurant in the Philippines. Because of the tremendous economic power of Hollywood, filmgoers in Canada are much more likely to watch an American movie than we are to watch a film made in Denmark or even a film made in Canada (see Table 20.3). French political figures, such as former president Jacques Chirac, have been particularly vocal in criticizing the cultural power of Hollywood. He used the French state to protect and promote the French film industry. Chirac warned of a "catastrophe" for global diversity if U.S. cultural dominance goes unchallenged (Agence France-Presse, 2004).

Although tremendous economic and cultural power is centred in the corporate culture of the United States and Europe, a backlash is evident in many parts of the world (refer back to the Critical Sociology: Protest and Policy box). The al-Jazeera television network counters the global prevalence of CNN, offering an Arab alternative to U.S.-produced news. An English-language channel of al-Jazeera went on air in 2006, making al-Jazeera's presence felt even more widely. The largest producer of movies in the world is not Hollywood, but Bollywood—the film industry based in Mumbai (formerly Bombay), India, which produces more than a thousand films a year and attracts more than 10 million Indians to the cinema every day. Bollywood films are seen in Russia, the Middle East, Africa, and Indian immigrant communities around the world. The cultural pervasiveness Bollywood films is so great that smaller Asian countries, like Bangladesh, have reacted against the perceived domination of Indian movies, which crowd out Bangladeshi films. In addition to Bollywood, the Nigerian film industry produces films with actors and themes that are wildly popular with African viewers, and which some Nigerians believe have "eliminated the cultural stranglehold of Hollywood" (Kennedy, 2004).

CONSUMER ALTERNATIVES: FAIR TRADE

Subverting corporate logos is not the only tactic used to disrupt global commodity chains. Bottom–up globalizers also focus on developing consumer products that are environmentally sustainable and produced by relatively well-paid workers. The fair-trade movement is one of the main proponents of this approach, arguing that producers should be paid a fair price rather than the free market price (Figure 20.5).

TABLE 20.3   TOP 20 FILMS WORLDWIDE BY GROSS BOX OFFICE, 2013

RANK	TITLE	COUNTRY OF ORIGIN	STUDIO
1	*Iron Man 3*	US/China	Walt Disney
2	*Despicable Me 2*	US	Universal Pictures
3	*The Hunger Games: Catching Fire**	US	Lionsgate
4	*Furious 6*	US/Spain	Universal Pictures
5	*The Hobbit: The Desolation of Smaug**	US/New Zealand	Warner Bros.
6	*Monsters University*	US	Walt Disney
7	*Gravity**	US/UK	Warner Bros.
8	*Man of Steel*	US/Canada/UK	Warner Bros.
9	*Frozen**	US	Walt Disney
10	*Thor: The Dark World*	US	Walt Disney

*Still in release when ranked.

SOURCE: Adapted from European Audiovisual Observatory, *Focus 2014: World Film Market Trends* (Cannes: Marché du film, 2015, p. 13). http://issuu.com/marchedufilm/docs/focus_2014

The fair-trade movement has paid special attention to coffee. Around the turn of the twenty-first century, the market for coffee plummeted to a 30-year low, leaving coffee prices below the cost of production for many farmers and causing heightened levels of poverty and debt for 25 million coffee-producing families worldwide (Oxfam, 2002). According to its proponents, fair-trade coffee is an important solution to the "sweatshops in the field" that characterize contemporary coffee production. Fair-trade coffee allows producers to earn a living wage and offer a guaranteed price that protects farmers against wild

FIGURE 20.5   FAIR TRADE GLOBAL SNAPSHOT

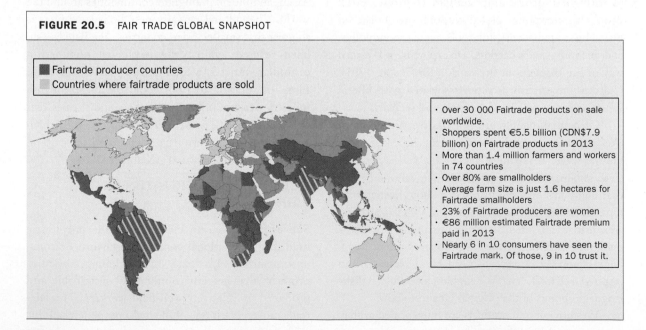

■ Fairtrade producer countries
■ Countries where fairtrade products are sold

- Over 30 000 Fairtrade products on sale worldwide.
- Shoppers spent €5.5 billion (CDN$7.9 billion) on Fairtrade products in 2013
- More than 1.4 million farmers and workers in 74 countries
- Over 80% are smallholders
- Average farm size is just 1.6 hectares for Fairtrade smallholders
- 23% of Fairtrade producers are women
- €86 million estimated Fairtrade premium paid in 2013
- Nearly 6 in 10 consumers have seen the Fairtrade mark. Of those, 9 in 10 trust it.

SOURCE: Adapted from Fairtrade Label South Africa, "Fairtrade Global Snapshot 2013" (2014). http://www.fairtradelabel.org.za/news/fairtrade-delivering-change-annual-sales-figures-2013-14.191.html (Dec. 27, 2014).

price fluctuations (see Figure 20.5). Fair trade also promises to protect the environment since most fair-trade coffee is "shade-grown" (that is, grown alongside trees that support wildlife and biodiversity).

While the market for fair-trade coffee is growing, it represents only a small fraction of the total coffee market. An estimated 8 percent of the coffee sold at Starbucks is fair-trade, and about 4 percent of all the coffee sold in the United States is fair-trade certified (Haight, 2011; Hickman, 2008; Howard and Jaffee, 2013). Fair-trade coffee organizations must convince consumers to pay more for their coffee—a choice that goes against the socialization of most consumers to shop for the best deal.

ECOLOGICAL CONSEQUENCES OF CONSUMERISM

Global consumerism has also been criticized for being based on a Western high-consumption lifestyle that is ecologically unsustainable. On an average day, an inhabitant of North America consumes around 90 kilograms of resources, a resident of Europe uses 45 kilograms, and a person living in Africa consumes only around 10 kilograms (Friends of the Earth Europe, 2009). Canada uses approximately 3.7 times its share of the Earth's annual productivity relative to its population, and had the 11th largest per capita ecological footprint of 130 countries included in a recent study (World Wildlife Fund, 2014). What would be the implications if everyone consumed at the rate of wealthy Europeans and North Americans?

While some analysts believe that the solution to this problem is to become more efficient and find more resources, most experts believe that the world does not have enough reserves to sustain this level of consumption. Moreover, the current level of fossil fuel consumption is linked to global climate change. Sustainable consumption probably lies somewhere between the world's two extremes of overconsumers and underconsumers—at levels maintained by the roughly 3.3 billion people who eat moderate amounts of food (especially meat), rely primarily on sustainable modes of transportation, such as walking and public transportation, and consume minimal amounts of raw materials in their daily lives (Durning, 1992; see Figure 20.6).

While proponents of top–down globalization hope to turn the global middle-income stratum into overconsumers, the ecological challenge is to extend middle-income consumption habits to the world's poor

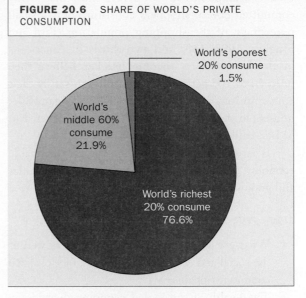

FIGURE 20.6   SHARE OF WORLD'S PRIVATE CONSUMPTION

World's poorest 20% consume 1.5%

World's middle 60% consume 21.9%

World's richest 20% consume 76.6%

SOURCE: World Bank, "World Bank Development Indicators" (2008). © World Bank. http://www.rrojasdatabank.info/wdi2008toc.htm (accessed Aug. 19, 2009).

underconsumers and the world's elite overconsumers. This will not be an easy political feat given the push to expand global consumption to address the problem of overcapacity in global production. The global economic system is currently organized around, and requires, high levels of consumption. In addition, it seems that members of the world's consumer class are often more interested in maximizing their consumption possibilities than they are in curbing

Some observers think that a Western, high-consumption lifestyle is ecologically unsustainable if it is adopted by people around the world. For example, each passenger taking a round trip from Toronto to Vancouver on Air Canada (economy class) is responsible for putting nearly 533 kilograms of carbon dioxide into the atmosphere. What happens when hundreds of millions of additional people take to the skies?

SOURCE: © iStockphoto.com/EGDigital.

their consumption habits. Surveys show that totally committed ethical shoppers constitute only a small percentage of the shopping population (Bird and Hughes, 1997: 160) and two-thirds of Americans in the US$75 000+ income bracket believe they need 50 to 100 percent more income to satisfy their consumption desires (Schor, 1998). Meanwhile, household debt in the United States skyrocketed to $11.52 trillion in 2014 (Frizell, 2014).

It is unclear how to build a more sustainable economy that also provides economic opportunities and good jobs—a topic to which I now turn.

TIME FOR REVIEW

1. What are some of the key benefits, as well as the social and ecological criticisms, of globalized commodity chains?

2. The health of the global economy depends on high demand for consumer items. What would happen if growing inequality or environmental problems constrained consumption?

GLOBAL WORKERS

Karl Marx and Friedrich Engels (1972 [1848]) ended the *Manifesto of the Communist Party* with the now famous phrase, "Proletarians [workers] of all countries, unite." The political unification of working people across national borders is, however, relatively rare. Capitalists, in contrast, have proven adept at global planning and organization. Global capitalists have used numerous organizations and venues to formulate economic policy and interact with government policymakers, like the World Economic Forum held annually in Davos, Switzerland.

Global workers are relatively immobile and politically fragmented. Some of them cross international borders, but working abroad is constrained by international travel restrictions, work permits, and passports. When workers do move abroad to work, they are not always able to take their families with them and may be separated from loved ones for years at a time. Labour unions are struggling to protect workers in the competitive, footloose business environment of neoliberalism. While capital can move across borders with relative ease, unions are organized primarily within rather than across states. There have been attempts to increase the level of transnational union organization and solidarity, but most unions are oriented mainly to protecting domestic workers and wages against competition from foreign workers. In addition,

many workers who travel abroad work in sectors that are relatively nonunionized and underregulated (e.g., nannying, the sex trade, agricultural workers), leaving them vulnerable to exploitation. While serious obstacles to organizing global workers remain, globalization processes have increased public awareness of sweatshop exploitation in factories around the world, leading some companies to ban the use of sweatshop labour. This section details some of the opportunities and challenges that globalization presents for global workers.

WAGE LABOUR AND WAGE INEQUALITY

The world of global labour might seem relatively mundane compared with the branded world of transnational corporations and global consumer goods. Yet without a global labour force there would be no goods for consumers to consume and no profits for capitalists. Most people exchange their labour for a wage, which they then use to pay their rent, buy groceries, and so forth.

Throughout the world, however, there is still a sizable section of the population for which the concept of wage labour is new. These people gain access to food, water, and shelter directly through their own work rather than receiving a wage and purchasing needed commodities. Many of the world's people still make a living off the land and subsist mainly on what they produce themselves; a little less than half the world's population lives in rural areas (World Bank, 2011).

As urbanization increases and the use of wage labour spreads across the globe, so does the *segmentation* of labour markets. Women, people of colour, rural workers, and the people from the developing world in general are overrepresented at the bottom of the wage hierarchy.

While income inequality in the United States is the most extreme among the world's rich countries, income and wealth inequality is a problem that worsened in Canada in the late 1990s (Picot and Myles, 2005). In 2012, the average CEO earned $7.96 million, 171 times the average Canadian worker's earnings of $46 000 (Canadian Centre for Policy Alternatives, 2014). Disparities in the Canadian labour market are based on class, as well as on race and country of birth.

Are low wages an age-old problem, or are they a unique result of globalization? The historical record shows that the search for cheap labour has been going on for hundreds of years. Indentured workers were brought from China to construct the North American railway system, while impoverished Irish immigrants competed with freed African American slaves for unskilled work in nineteenth-century North America. But globalization has heightened corporate competition for cheap labour. Firms use the threat of relocation as a way of keeping wages low. In effect, workers from different parts of the world compete against one another to attract foreign investment, driving wages down (see Chapter 7, Social Stratification; Chapter 10, Development and Underdevelopment; and Chapter 12, Work and Occupations, for details on the effects of this competition).

SEARCHING FOR CHEAP LABOUR: "THE RACE TO THE BOTTOM"

Governments have reacted in different ways to the global competition to create jobs and attract corporate investment. In the less developed countries, some states have set up **export processing zones (EPZs)** where special financial deals—tax holidays, preferential rates for electricity and telecommunications, special exemptions from national labour laws, and the like—are used to lure corporations to set up shop and provide jobs. The most famous EPZ in North America is the *maquiladora* region in northern Mexico. *Maquiladoras* are factories that allow companies to assemble goods for export by using low-cost Mexican labour and imported high-tech machinery and parts.

Maquiladoras employ low-cost labour compared with the United States and Canada, but since 2001 hundreds of thousands of *maquiladora* workers have been laid off, threatened with layoffs, paid lower wages, and compelled to work in worse conditions. Why? Mexican labour is cheap, but not cheap enough in a global marketplace where transnational firms try to find the world's least expensive, least regulated, and least unionized labour supply. Although Mexican wages are a bargain by Canadian standards, low-cost manufacturing has increasingly moved to Indonesia, Vietnam, and China, where labour is even cheaper; the Chinese legal monthly minimum wage is around US$176 ("Seven Countries," 2011). Wage competition pits workers against one another in a "race to the bottom." Globalization has placed Mexico in a difficult position: Wages are too low to alleviate poverty rates yet too high to continue to attract more low-cost manufacturing.

Although working conditions in the factories of the developing countries are often wretched, some members of the world's labour force suffer in conditions that resemble slavery in the literal sense of the word. An estimated 30 million people worldwide are enslaved—more than at any other time in our history—and forced labour generates approximately $150 billion in revenue a year (ILO, 2014; UNGIFT, 2014). We are connected to this extreme form of labour exploitation through global commodity chains. In the words of an authority on global slavery:

> Slaves in Pakistan may have made the shoes you are wearing and the carpet you stand on. Slaves in the Caribbean may have put sugar in your kitchen and toys in the hands of your children. In India they may have sewn the shirt on your back and polished the ring on your finger. They are paid nothing. ... Your investment portfolio and your mutual fund pension own stock in companies using labor in the developing world. Slaves keep your costs low and returns on your investments high. (Bales, 1999: 3–4)

The injustices of the global labour system have not gone unnoticed or uncontested, even though serious obstacles lie ahead for unions and workers.

In Canada, unionized workers as a percentage of nonagricultural workers fell from a high of 38 percent in 1981 to 30 percent in 2013 (Labour Program, 2014), while the American unionization rate fell to just 11.3 percent in 2013 (U.S. Bureau of Labor Statistics, 2014b). Historically, unionism arose in large capitalist factories, yet globalized firms often decentralize and subcontract work to small, independent firms, making unionization and labour regulation more difficult. Unions have responded by developing new strategies that include cross-border organization, transnational solidarity campaigns emphasizing the importance of good wages for all working people (not just union members), and drives to organize service-sector workers, such as janitors, hotel workers, and security guards (Babson, 2000; Frundt, 2000; Milkman, 2000; Nissen, 2000).

The anti-sweatshop movement of the 1990s also raised awareness of labour exploitation by transnational firms (A. Ross, 1997; R. Ross, 2004). Today, prominent retail corporations like Nike and Gap must at least appear to take global labour issues seriously (reports suggest that working conditions are still abysmal in Nike's subcontracted operations; R. Ross, 2004: 42).

Although it was unimaginable to promote a "sweatshop-free" clothing line in the early 1990s, the popular label American Apparel has proven that it is possible (albeit difficult) to run a successful business without the use of sweatshop labour. Although American Apparel rejects unions and does not consider itself an "altruistic company," it produces all of its garments and shoes in Los Angeles and pays its workers more than California's minimum wage (R. Ross, 2004: 1).

American Apparel has also become vocal about the fight to legalize undocumented workers in Los Angeles, launching the "Legalize LA" campaign. In a letter that introduced this campaign, Dov Charney, founder and CEO of American Apparel, says that "[American Apparel's] dream for Los Angeles is that the over 1 million undocumented migrant workers who live here, and contribute to the city economically, culturally, and socially will have the opportunity to become legal residents of the city, and the United States" (American Apparel, 2008.). American Apparel (2013) joined in the 2012 and 2013 May Day rallies to show support for immigration reform that would prevent employee exploitation and improve wages and working conditions. Other clothing lines, such as No Sweat, use unionized labour in North America *and* developing countries. According to the No Sweat website, "We believe that the only viable response to globalization is a global labor movement" (No Sweat, 2005).

TIME FOR REVIEW

1. What is the "race to the bottom?" How do globalization processes make it more difficult to find a job that is stable, unionized, and well paid?
2. Who benefits and who loses from outsourcing? Who should be responsible for regulating the working conditions of labourers vulnerable to exploitation in foreign countries?

GLOBAL ECOLOGY

Consumers, workers, citizens, and nations all play critical roles in the globalization processes we have outlined. In turn, all these actors fit together in a larger global ecology that connects people, resources, and commodities. To better understand these ecological connections, we now examine the globalized food system.

GLOBAL FOOD

Global trade in agriculture allows relatively prosperous people to consume a wide variety of exotic fruits, imported bottled water, and distant marine life, such as shrimp and fresh tuna. Although the global trade in food products is a boon for discriminating eaters, critics of industrialized global agriculture question its environmental costs. Trade experts and environmental groups warn that agriculture is the largest contributor of greenhouse gas when food production and distribution chains are taken into account, and suggest that the global food system represents the biggest environmental challenge facing humanity (Clay, 2004; Shrybman, 2000).

One of the major environmental problems with the world's agricultural system is the immense amount of fossil fuel required to produce, package, and transport food. Fossil fuel consumption generates greenhouse gases, such as carbon dioxide, which is linked to global climate change. But why is food so closely linked with carbon dioxide emissions? The first and simplest answer is transportation. Today, most Europeans and North Americans eat foods that have travelled a long distance to get to their plate. Food's travel time is captured in the concept of "food miles," a measure of the distance food travels from production to consumption and an indicator of the amount of fossil fuels burned in the process. A Toronto study compared the distance travelled by conventional agricultural products purchased at a discount supermarket with the distance travelled by the same basket of goods purchased at a nearby farmers' market (Bentley, 2004). While the supermarket food travelled 5734 kilometres on average, the same farmers' market produce travelled an average of only 101 kilometres to get to the consumer (Bentley, 2004: 7).

Food transported from far away might add variety to our diet, but it frequently involves an unsustainable and irrational energy tradeoff. For a head of iceberg lettuce transported from California to the United Kingdom, 127 calories of nonrenewable fossil fuel energy are required to produce 1 calorie of food energy (Sustain/Elm Farm Research Centre, 2001: 1). The way that most of our foods are produced and packaged also relies heavily on fossil fuels. The food processing industry uses 10 calories of fossil fuel energy to produce 1 calorie of food energy. Intensive livestock operations are even more wasteful: 1 calorie of beef requires 35 calories of fossil fuel, and 1 calorie of pork requires 68 calories of fossil fuel. Because of these energy-intensive production techniques, food scholars estimate that if the entire world adopted North American food habits, fossil fuel reserves would be gone in just seven years (Manning, 2004: 42, 44).

Just as consumers in India and China move toward a meat-intensive diet, increasing demand for both animal feed and oil calls into question the stability of global food supplies. Despite short-term fluctuations, demand for oil is increasing while supply is just about stagnant. As a result, the price of oil increases, and agricultural crops, such as corn, are increasingly turned into biofuel to offset oil supply problems. However, the diversion of food crops into biofuel production causes food prices to rise. In 2007–08, news headlines reported food riots by poor people in many developing countries, ignited by sharply rising food prices (Walt, 2008).

Soil, Water, and Genetic Engineering

Besides relying heavily on fossil fuel, industrial methods of food production are associated with global environmental problems like deforestation, soil erosion, and declining water tables. In the past 40 years, soil degradation has caused farmers around the world to abandon about 430 million hectares of arable land. This area amounts to one-third of all cropland (Kindall and Pimentel, 1994; see Figure 20.7). Every year, 130 000 square kilometres of forest, an area four times the size of Switzerland, are destroyed to make way for agriculture. Between 2004 and 2020, an estimated 22 million hectares of savannah and forest,

an area as large as the United Kingdom, will have been cut down in South America to meet global demand for soya, a crop that is used largely for livestock feed and vegetable oil (World Wildlife Fund, 2004).

Even when adequate land can be found to grow crops, water is also needed. Seventy percent of world water usage is for irrigation, and food analysts worry about an emerging water deficit (Brown, 2005: 10). Underground aquifers refill slowly and are currently being pumped at rates that are unsustainable. In Northern China, for instance, groundwater levels are falling by at least one metre a year, while aquifers in the United States are being pumped at a pace that vastly exceeds replacement rates (Pimentel and Wilson, 2004).

Some scientists believe that global agriculture problems can be addressed by switching to genetically modified or genetically engineered (GE) crops that have been designed to be drought- and pest-resistant by reengineering the plant's genetic structure. This technological solution is opposed by many environmentalists who worry about the long-term health and ecological impact of GE crops, particularly the negative impact on biodiversity, since GE crops tend to out-compete and contaminate related species. GE canola has already infected organic canola in western Canada to such an extent that it is impossible for organic farmers to grow and market GE-free

FIGURE 20.7   THE HEALTH OF OUR FORESTS

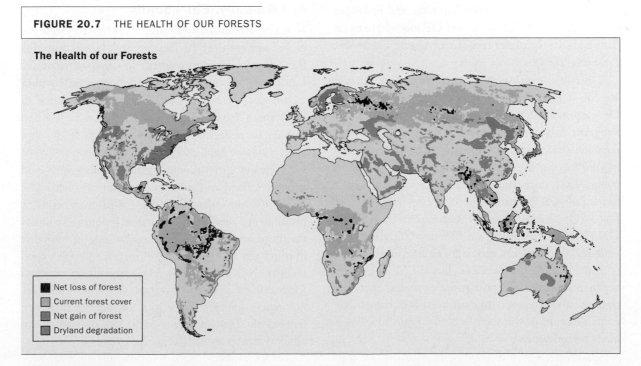

The Health of our Forests

Net loss of forest
Current forest cover
Net gain of forest
Dryland degradation

SOURCE: GRID-Arendal. http://www.grida.no/graphicslib/detail/the-health-of-our-forests_a7f0 (accessed Sept. 28, 2015).

organic canola. Saskatchewan farmer Percy Schmeiser launched a lawsuit against seed giant Monsanto, suing for damages, and was awarded an out-of-court settlement. Activists in less developed countries are concerned that GE crops will permit large corporations to consolidate their control over agriculture and erode traditions of seed saving and innovation by farmers.

Although many of the world's genetically engineered crops have been grown in North America, their usage in the Global South has expanded considerably—by 2013, developing countries were growing 54 percent of the world's GE crops (ISAAA, 2014). In 2013, GE crops were grown in 27 countries by 18 million farmers, most of whom ran relatively small operations. Canada itself grew 10.8 million hectares of GE crops that year—almost enough to cover the surface of Newfoundland (ISSA, 2014).

Because of the huge capital investment in these technologies, multinational bioscience companies would like to expand adoption rates globally (currently 10 percent of crop land globally is planted with GE crops). One way this may be occurring is through food aid, which contains genetically engineered crops. This issue made headlines in 2001–02, when southern Africa experienced a famine and was given genetically modified maize by the United States. African leaders protested, not only for health and safety reasons but for fear that the GE corn would contaminate their own supplies (assuming that people would save some of the corn to plant in future harvests), and endanger export markets in Europe, where GE foods have faced bans and stiff consumer resistance (African Centre for Biosafety, 2005).

In 2005, scientists discovered that grain donated by the United States Agency for International Development (USAID) through the World Food Program (WFP) to Central American and Caribbean countries was heavily contaminated with genetically modified corn. Eighty percent of the samples tested included GE corn, including "StarLink," corn that is not authorized for human consumption in the United States (Organic Consumers Association, 2005). The UN Cartagena Protocol on Biosafety stipulates that genetically engineered crops can enter countries only with prior informed consent, but the WFP's heavy reliance on USAID grain supplies means that this right is currently not being enforced and that genetic contamination of the world's global grain supplies is likely to continue.

Global Hunger amid Plenty

The world grows enough grain to provide nearly 3000 calories per person per day (FAO, 2009), yet the number of undernourished people in the world has risen since the early 1980s, totalling at least 867 million people (FAO, 2013). World grain production is a general measure of global food security. Although the 1.5 percent annual increases in world grain production between 2008 and 2014 represent an improvement over falling per capita grain production levels between 1984 and 1995, and flat overall production between 1996 and 2003, demand increases will likely more than match these production gains (Brown, 2005: 4; International Grains Council 2013).

It is especially troubling to consider these numbers in the context of widespread soil erosion, loss of crop land to urbanization, rising global temperatures, and shrinking water supplies—all of which will have a negative impact on the capacity of global grain production (Brown, 2005: 7). With the population rising to an estimated 9 billion people by 2050 and the low likelihood of expanding global grain supplies much further, grain prices will likely rise in the future. For affluent consumers, this would make food supplies, particularly meat, more expensive. For the world's malnourished people this situation will make it increasingly difficult to access the basic food staples needed for survival.

Act Globally, Eat Locally

Is there an alternative to the current system of global agriculture? In Europe and North America there is a growing movement to eat foods that are locally grown and produced with organic farming techniques. Researchers in Britain estimate that if all farms there became organic, an estimated $1.1 billion in environmental costs would be saved (Lang and Pretty, 2005; Lappé and Lappé, 2002).

The move to promote organic, locally grown food is not confined to the affluent minority world. The Navdanya movement in India, for instance, aims to promote indigenous agricultural techniques to counter the presence of multinational agribusiness in ways that improve the environment and increase people's food security (Navdanya, 2005). Many organic farmers and food activists believe that organic farming techniques, not genetic engineering or food aid, are the answer to famines and food shortages (Hall, 2005), although not all food experts agree (Paarlberg, 2010).

The tension between local and global food represents the challenge and the paradox of bottom–up globalization. It is a challenge because most small-scale activists and food producers, like most of the world's workers, are rooted where they grow food and are not nearly as globalized as corporate agribusiness and its CEOs. It is a paradox because peasant and small farmer movements want to encourage *local* food consumption, defend *local* agricultural ecosystems, and, at the same time, use *global* networks to fight these battles. Their motto could be "act globally, eat locally."

Cuba: An Island's Isolation and Innovation

What would happen if globalization processes were reversed, and a country suddenly found itself isolated, without the ability to trade for food in global markets? Cuba provides a real-life answer to that question. It is literally an island, but is also a metaphorical island in that it is largely isolated from the major ebbs and flows of global food trade. The United States refused to trade with Cuba between 1960, a year after the Cuban revolution, and 2015. After the collapse of the Soviet Union in 1989, Cuba lost access to an extremely important source of food supplies and fossil fuels. Suddenly, the nation was hungry. Calorie consumption per person per day fell from 3000 in 1989 to 1600 four years later.

Without fossil fuels or cheap grain supplies, Cuba's agriculture had to change, and change it did. Cuban agronomists began experimenting with more sustainable, low-input agriculture that used crop rotation to provide natural fertilization. They developed large urban gardens to feed and employ thousands of Cubans. Farmers began using oxen instead of tractors, saving fossil fuel. Today, almost completely cut off from global agricultural trade, Havana feeds itself from gardens within city limits. There are still problems ensuring adequate supplies of milk and meat, yet Cuban agriculture is remarkably successful, leading some analysts to suggest that the Cuban model is a possible future scenario for what agriculture could look like when fossil fuel supplies become scarce and the environmental consequences of globalized industrial agriculture become too onerous to ignore (McKibben, 2005: 69).

In an article profiling the costs and benefits of the Cuban agricultural experiment, environmental journalist Bill McKibben concludes with a provocative and difficult question that we would do well to ponder—a question that applies not only to Cuban agriculture, but to globalization more generally:

> Is it also possible … that there's something inherently destructive about a globalized free-market society—that the eternal race for efficiency, when raised to a planetary scale, damages the environment, and perhaps the community, and perhaps even the taste of a carrot? Is it possible that markets, at least for food, may work better when they're smaller and more isolated? The next few decades may be about answering that question. (McKibben, 2005: 69)

TIME FOR REVIEW

1. How is a globalized food system vulnerable to environmental limits and extreme weather events linked to climate change?
2. What are main lessons of the Cuban food experiment, post-1989?

SUMMARY

1. **What is "globalization"?**
   Globalization effectively shrinks the world. Workers, commodities, ideas, and capital cross distances more quickly in a globalized world. Sociologists use the term "time–space compression" to describe this process.

2. **Is globalization straightforwardly good or bad?**
   No. Globalization processes have generated contradictory outcomes that benefit some groups but have also been linked to poverty, economic marginalization, democratic deficits, and the digital divide for other groups.

3. **How is globalization related to the changing character of financial markets?**
   Developments in information technology have facilitated the economic integration of financial markets. Consequently, global flows of financial capital are much bigger than global flows of tangible goods and productive capital. Globalization processes also foster a sense of growing competitiveness. Corporations in the global era have become much bigger and are under pressure to become more competitive in the global marketplace. Local and even national

competitiveness are no longer seen as sufficient for economic survival.

4. **What are the political dimensions of globalization processes?**
Politically, the globalization era has witnessed the creation of new international institutions of governance like the International Monetary Fund, the World Bank, and the World Trade Organization, which have diminished the power and sovereignty of some states.

5. **What is globalization from below?**
Globalization processes have allowed communities around the world to gain knowledge of the injustice and suffering inflicted by the global economy. Such awareness has inspired efforts to increase social justice in the global system.

6. **How do everyday goods connect consumers to globalization processes?**
Most of the goods we consume connect us to workers and production processes thousands of kilometres away. The globalization process is almost impossible to escape given the extent of global commodity chains.

7. **What impact does globalization have on work?**
Globalization is associated with a shift in manufacturing employment out of the more developed countries. Competitive pressure is driving corporations to seek the lowest wages possible (the "race to the bottom"), which increases the trend toward greater inequality, as exemplified in the growing ratio of CEO income to average worker income.

8. **Are global environmental issues connected to global economic issues?**
Yes. The connection between these domains resides mainly in the fact that the economy depends on natural resources and produces environmental pollutants. Global ecological connections are intimately shaped by, and connected to, the actions of citizens, consumer habits, worker opportunities, and state regulations.

QUESTIONS TO CONSIDER

1. How do you benefit from globalization processes? What are the negative consequences of these processes? Consider your role as a worker, consumer, and citizen.

2. Has globalization caused the Canadian state to lose sovereignty? Do you think Canadians suffer from a democratic deficit?

3. Are consumer activism and social movement campaigns like the anti-sweatshop campaign an effective way of making global commodity chains more equitable? Does the corporate movement for social responsibility offer a more promising avenue for change? Is voluntary corporate action sufficient or are governments needed to pass legislation and enforce corporate responsibility?

GLOSSARY

Consumerism (p. 480) is a way of life focusing on the purchase and acquisition of commodities. While traditionally thought of as a problem for North America and Europe, consumerism is also a cultural and ecological issue among affluent populations in the less developed countries.

Cultural imperialism (p. 481) is a controversial theory of cultural domination, according to which powerful economic and political actors (primarily Euro-American) are thought to impose their values, norms, and lifestyles on other populations. *Cultural imperialism* often refers to the export of certain Euro-American cultural practices, such as materialism, consumerism, and sexual liberalism through the media of television, music, and film.

A **democratic deficit** (p. 476) involves the disenfranchisement of ordinary citizens from the decisions and process of governments. Democratic deficits are often attributed to the influence of corporate actors and international financial institutions on governments and the transfer of governance to institutions such as the IMF and WTO, which do not permit average citizens to vote or influence decisions.

The **digital divide** (p. 468) is the gap between people who are easily able to access communication technologies, such as the Internet and cellular phones, and people who lack the material resources, education, or infrastructure to access these technologies.

Export processing zones (EPZs) (p. 485) are manufacturing areas in which government programs provide special incentives to help promote export-oriented manufacturing. Sometimes EPZs are territorial zones demarcated by fences and borders, while in other cases they are programs that apply to all industries in a country. For instance, in 1991, Sri Lanka declared the entire country an EPZ.

The **Fourth World** (p. 479) comprises marginalized populations and regions that are not competitive in the global economy.

A **global commodity chain** (p. 480) is a worldwide network of labour and production processes, the end result of which is a finished commodity.

Globalization (p. 467) is a social, economic, and political process that facilitates the movement of people, goods, ideas, and capital around the globe. With globalization, the world appears to shrink, although the ability to cross borders varies tremendously depending on one's position in the global economy.

Globalization from below (p. 471) is a short-hand way of describing a diverse range of projects seeking greater democracy, equality, and sustainability in globalization processes. These projects are generally opposed to neoliberal policies and U.S. hegemony in the global system.

Neoliberalism (p. 471) refers to economic policies that became prominent in the late 1970s in both developed and developing countries. Neoliberalism is associated with a retreat from state intervention and regulation, greater focus on individual responsibility, less protection for labour and the environment, privatization of state resources, and faith in the power of the market and the profit motive to provide the greatest good for the greatest number.

Time–space compression (p. 467) refers to the diminished importance of geography and time lags due to globalization.

Top–down globalization (p. 470) refers to the extension of capitalism globally, particularly as a result of the neoliberal policies and programs authorized by international financial authorities, such as the IMF and World Bank, and implemented by national governments. Top–down globalization is organized by elites in governments, corporations, and international institutions with little democratic input.

Virtual communities (p. 467) are groups whose members share interests and meet primarily on the Internet.

EPILOGUE

THE FUTURE OF SOCIOLOGY

Michael Burawoy
UNIVERSITY OF CALIFORNIA, BERKELEY

MARKETIZATION

A wave of marketization is sweeping the world. Entities that used to be embedded in human bodies, communities, and nature are being ripped out of their habitats, appropriated by new classes of merchants, and sold in chains of markets that stretch around the globe. This is not the first wave of marketization; it is not the first time markets have expanded their reach by turning common goods and public services into new commodities. The Industrial Revolution of the nineteenth century worked through a similar global expansion in the marketization of labour and its products. The financial revolution of the twentieth century turned money into a full-blown commodity, eventually threatening the very viability of markets. The ecological transformation that now besets us digs even deeper, making land, water, air, and genes the subject of market exchange, thereby threatening human existence.

So far, each wave of marketization has set in motion a counter-movement, erecting institutions to regulate, channel, and contain commodification. Yet each wave also swept away the ramparts erected against the previous wave. Under demolition today are rights won by Western labour movements against the marketization of the nineteenth century (such as the right to form unions) and the social rights guaranteed by states against the marketization of the twentieth century (the provision of minimum standards of economic security). In the end, nothing seems immune to the third wave of marketization. Will there be a counter-movement strong enough to contain its destructive powers?

Behind the third wave are classes colluding with nation-states and sometimes also with multilateral agencies, such as the World Bank and the International Monetary Fund, imposing their will on the desperate and the destitute, on workers, students, farmers, and the middle class. The last holdout against this economic storm is society itself, or more precisely civil society, composed of *associations* with a measure of collective self-regulation, *movements* forged out of a collective will, and *publics* of mutual recognition and communication. Will society measure up to the challenge? What role can sociology play in meeting it?

SOCIOLOGY VERSUS THE MARKET

If there is a common thread to sociology's diverse traditions, it is opposition to the reduction of society to a market. Whether it is Marx's critique of capitalism, Durkheim's critique of the abnormal forms of the division of labour, Weber's critique of rationalism, or Parsons's critique of utilitarianism, each tradition opposes market reductionism, albeit from different viewpoints. Today, it is even more important for sociology to continue its tradition of opposing market reductionism as commodification threatens to destroy society and, with it, human existence. In meeting this challenge, sociologists can join one of four groups of practitioners:

1. *Policy sociologists* help to formulate policies that side with the state against the market, using what remains of state autonomy to help regulate market forces. In Northern European countries with a continuing legacy of social democratic politics or welfare provision, this approach might make sense.

2. *Professional sociologists* argue that their discipline must be based on firm scientific foundations before it can be of any practical use. From this point of view, by wading into stormy seas prematurely, we will discover only that we cannot swim. Professional sociologists may understand the dangers of rampant marketization, but they sit tight waiting for the storm to pass, hoping that it will not sweep them up with the rest of society.

3. *Critical sociologists* agitate against the first two groups, writing tracts against their moral bankruptcy, complaining about those who collude with state and market, and also about those who busy themselves writing scientific papers. Critical sociologists are a shrinking band. Like the professionals, they live in insulated communities, seeking to preserve the power of critique, acting as if their words have the power to hold the storm at bay. Yet their message is often incomprehensible and few are listening.

4. *Public sociologists* refuse to collaborate with the market and the state. They say that science without politics is blind and that critique without intervention is empty. They engage directly with communities, institutions, and social movements, listening and speaking, observing and participating, learning and writing in order to defend society against rampant marketization. Third-wave marketization calls forth the age of public sociology.

There may be a need for public sociology, but it can move forward only on the legs of policy, professional, and critical sociologies. Without the kind of sociological knowledge accumulated in our discipline and presented in this book, public sociology cannot exist.

Public sociology also depends on critical knowledge that keeps professional science honest, steering it away from irrelevance and self-referentiality. At the same time, critical knowledge infuses public sociology with the values and direction that motivate its engagement with publics. Public sociology is nothing if it cannot help to bring about social change. It cannot, therefore, dismiss policy science. It can examine it from without, pushing it in appropriate directions, opposing the temptations of serving power. Public sociology must be the conscience of policy sociology.

Together, public, professional, critical, and policy sociologists form a discipline that takes civil society as its standpoint—as opposed to political scientists, who take the standpoint of the state, and economists, who take the standpoint of the market. Sociology's existence depends on the health of civil society, thereby declaring its commitment to the future of humanity that is currently threatened by the collusion of state and market. Here is the paradox: Sociology has never been so important, yet its foundations have never been more precarious.

THE GREAT TRANSFORMATION

To appreciate the future of sociology, we must understand the context of third-wave marketization, within which it is forced to operate. For that, I draw on Karl Polanyi's classic, *The Great Transformation* (1944).

Polanyi (who, incidentally, lived outside Toronto from the early 1950s until his death in 1964) devoted himself to understanding the dangers and potentialities of the market. He showed that markets that advance too far cause a social counter-movement. This was the "great transformation"—not the rise of the market, but the *reaction* to its rise.

Perhaps Polanyi's most important but least developed idea was that of "fictitious commodities"—entities that lose their value when subject to unrestricted exchange, unrestricted commodification. For Polanyi, there were three fictitious commodities: labour, money, and land.

When *labour* is overly commodified, people lose their capacity to work. For example, in a perfectly free labour market, where only supply and demand determine the cost of labour, the absence of laws governing minimum wages, child labour, safety standards, and the length of the working day allows some workers to die prematurely because of accidents, ill health, or starvation. Typically, when the New Poor Law was passed in England in 1834, revoking certain forms of labour protection and poor relief, the ensuing desperation forged a spontaneous reaction in the form of social movements, such as the factory movement to restrict the length of the working day, and associations, such as burial societies, trade unions, cooperatives, and experiments in creating utopian communities. The nineteenth-century commodification of labour led to the spontaneous self-reconstitution of society.

Similarly, when *money* is overly commodified, it loses the capacity to facilitate exchange. The full commodification of money began in the early twentieth century and continues today. Thus, before the global financial crisis that began in 2008, important American laws regulating financial institutions were scrapped, encouraging banks to invest ordinary people's money in extraordinarily risky ways. In the process, the richest 1 percent of Americans multiplied their wealth many times over. However, when mortgages and other credit vehicles began to fail, millions of ordinary Americans lost their homes. Soon, the Occupy Wall Street movement emerged to protest growing economic inequality.

Finally, when *land* is overly commodified, it loses its capacity to deliver human subsistence. When land is enclosed and sold as real estate, as is happening in many parts of the world, the livelihood of small farmers is threatened. However, it is not just land but other elements of nature that are being commodified. For instance, in Bolivia in the mid-1990s, the government decided to sell water supplies and delivery systems to a private company. The company soon set water prices higher than many poor Bolivians could afford. Water's availability—its human value as a source of life—fell as the cost of commodified water skyrocketed. Poor Bolivians naturally rebelled to protest the untenable conditions of their existence.

Polanyi (1944) wrote about the first two waves of marketization and the reactions to them— the nineteenth-century marketization of labour (and the ensuing rise of workers' rights) and the twentieth-century marketization of money (which led to the Great Depression of 1929–39 and the ensuing rise of the New Deal in the United States, Nazism in Germany, and Stalinism in the Soviet Union). Polanyi believed that, after the horrors of World War II, most people would come to understand the importance of regulating markets. He was wrong. In the mid-1970s, a third wave of marketization began, whose distinctive feature would be the commodification of nature as well as labour and money. How, more specifically, should we characterize the third wave of marketization? What societal reactions to it can we observe?

THIRD-WAVE MARKETIZATION

First-wave marketization generated a counter-movement against the commodification of labour. Second-wave marketization generated a counter-movement against the commodification of money. Third-wave marketization is generating a counter-movement against the commodification of land or, more broadly, of nature. Of course, land began to be commodified before the third wave. However, the commodification of nature as a whole did not yet threaten the devastation of the planet. Today it does. Squatters and shack dwellers now defend themselves against local governments trying to clear them out of cities. Middle-class city residents oppose high-rise developers. Indigenous peoples refuse to give up their land so large commercial plantations can take their place. Farmers battle against dams that threaten their existence. Activists struggle for clean air, against the dumping of toxic waste, and against privatization of water and electricity. The list goes on. The commodifications of labour and of money, of course, continue to be important, generating their own counter-movements, but the reaction to the commodification of nature will define the reaction to third-wave marketization and, thus, the future of humanity.

A second way to characterize the third-wave marketization is by its scale, which is global in its causes and ramifications. The response to the commodification of labour under first-wave marketization was mainly local, although it eventually aspired to become national (through the creation of national trade unions and political parties, for instance). The response to the commodification of money under second-wave marketization was mainly at the level of the nation-state (through central banks) but eventually aspired to be global (through the creation of the International Monetary Fund and the World Bank, for instance). The response to the commodification of nature under third-wave marketization has to be initiated by society—first at the local level but then rising almost immediately to the global level. Because the effects of climate change, nuclear accidents, water privatization, and the spread of contagious diseases are global, so the response to third-wave marketization must ultimately assume a global scale.

A third way of characterizing successive waves of marketization is in terms of the destruction of the defences people have erected against marketization.

Second-wave marketization destroyed the trenches defended by labour before it generated a counter-movement to build new trenches of state social protection (the welfare state). Third-wave marketization is rolling back labour and social rights. We see this almost everywhere as trade unions decline, the real wages of workers stagnate or fall, and budgets for social security, pensions, and welfare contract. On what foundation will the next round of defences be built—defences that will fend off the degradation of nature but also recover labour and social rights? The deeper the challenge to humanity and community, the deeper the reaction must be. In response to third-wave marketization, we will need to develop the defence of human rights—the defence of a community of mutual recognition as human beings—that will necessarily incorporate labour and social rights, too.

Of course, human rights may be appropriated and narrowed to suit particular interests. For instance, electoral democracy has become a human right that, for some people, can justify invasion, killing, and subjugation abroad. Similarly, markets have been promoted in the name of the human right to freedom of choice and the protection of private property, ignoring what this means to those who cannot choose and who lack property. Human rights that are universal, and that therefore include labour rights and social rights, must aim for the protection of the human community as a whole, which involves first recognizing and treating each other as ends rather than means. Human rights, then, present a complex terrain of struggle in which groups stake their claim on the basis of their own interests, but ultimately human rights are about the protection of humanity with the potential to galvanize struggles of global proportions against third-wave marketization. Now that I have described the major characteristics of third-wave marketization and its counter-movement, what is their significance for sociology?

THREE WAVES OF SOCIOLOGY

A distinctive sociology emerges with each wave of marketization. Sociology grew up in the nineteenth century together with civil society, itself a response to first-wave marketization. Thus, sociology began as a moral enterprise defending society against the market, especially the destruction of community, as newly proletarianized, destitute, and degraded populations made the city their home. It was foremost a critical enterprise, but it was also utopian. Sociology imagined life outside the market. For example, Marx and Engels postulated communism, which they expected

to arise out of the ashes of capitalism. Comte imagined a familial order led by sociologists. Durkheim envisaged an organic solidarity built on corporatist organization. In English Canada, the religious principles of the social gospel movement influenced sociology in its early stages.

Comte, Marx, Durkheim, and other early sociologists would object to my characterization. They saw themselves as scientists, committed to what is and what could be by virtue of the laws of society. Still, from today's standpoint, for all the scientific breakthroughs they brought to the study of society, their science was partly speculative, especially regarding the future, and strongly imbued with moral concerns aimed at reversing the degradation brought about by nineteenth-century capitalism. At the heart of their utopianism lay the critique of the division of labour and its transformation.

Second-wave marketization, which took off following World War I, challenged the rights that labour had won through trade unions and political parties. As Polanyi (1944) argued, the ravages of international trade and exchange threatened the conditions of capital accumulation and prompted protectionist reactions by the state. In countries that reacted to second-wave marketization with authoritarian regimes, notably Germany and the Soviet Union, sociology was eclipsed, but in countries that reacted with some form of social democracy, a new type of sociology emerged. It collaborated with the state to defend society against the market. In the United Kingdom, the United States, Sweden, Canada, and elsewhere, a policy-oriented sociology developed. Even in the colonies, there was a policy science, although there it was called *anthropology*. This was the golden era of state-funded research into social problems.

Where sociology remained relatively divorced from the state, as in the United States, it also developed a strong professional branch, committed to the expansion of specific research programs chiefly concerned with social stability. There, stratification studies highlighted achievement-based mobility up the occupational hierarchy. Family studies emphasized the benefits of the smoothly functioning nuclear family. Studies of crime and deviance focused on regulation and control. Industrial sociology was chiefly concerned with pacifying labour and maximizing the extraction of value from it. Political sociology underscored the social bases of electoral democracy and the containment of extremism. The overarching theoretical framework was summed up by structural functionalism—the delineation of the functional prerequisites needed to keep any social system in equilibrium and the mechanisms allowing social institutions to meet those prerequisites. During this period, sociologists gave detailed attention to empirical research, new methods of data collection and analysis, and the elaboration of "middle-range" theories that nestled in the scaffolding of structural functionalism. This approach was a reaction against the earlier, more speculative traditions that were propelled by the desire for moral reform. It wanted to expunge moral questions from sociology.

If the first wave of sociology invented utopias, the second wave of policy-oriented and professional sociology opposed utopian thinking, in effect claiming that utopia was almost within reach, or even already at hand. Indeed, in the United States and the Soviet Union, structural-functionalism and Marxism-Leninism, respectively, mistook utopia for reality. These were sociological traditions that were riveted to the present, concerned only with ironing out its small irrationalities. A critical sociology developed in reaction to these presuppositions of harmony and consensus, restoring an interest in struggle and conflict, but also in imagining a world beyond capitalism.

What sort of sociology marks the response to third-wave marketization? As we have seen, the third wave rolls back the statist defence of society, taking the offensive against labour and social rights. Unlike the second wave, which provoked an anti-market reaction from the state—variously involving protectionism, economic planning, wage guarantees, the welfare state, and public ownership of the means of production—third-wave marketization is promoted by the state. Still a regulatory state, it is nonetheless regulation *for* rather than *against* the market. It undoes all that was achieved against second-wave marketization. Society is thus under a double assault from economy and state. Unable to gain much leverage in the state or from the market, the fate of sociology rests with society. In other words, sociology's self-interest lies in the constitution of civil society where it barely exists and in its protection where it is in retreat—hence the claim we are living in the age of public sociology.

Today, sociology cannot limit its engagement to local or national publics, but must be concerned with knitting together a global civil society. Moreover, the third wave of sociology calls for a science quite different from the speculative science of the nineteenth century and the policy-oriented professional science of the mid-twentieth century—one that seeks to combine scientific rigour with the development of alternative values. We no longer strive for a single paradigmatic science but a discipline made up of multiple intersecting research programs, founded on the values of different publics, working out theoretical frameworks through engaging their anomalies and contradictions. I call this a *reflexive science*, a science that is not frightened of reflecting on its value foundations or of articulating them publicly, but a science nonetheless (see Table 1).

As sociology becomes more global, borrowings across national lines become more feasible and important. For example, after its 1974 anti-authoritarian revolution, Portugal drew on critical and professional traditions in American and French sociologies, harnessing them to a vibrant civil society. This small country is one of the leaders in public sociology,

TABLE 1   SOCIOLOGY VERSUS THE MARKET

	FIRST-WAVE MARKETIZATION	SECOND-WAVE MARKETIZATION	THIRD-WAVE MARKETIZATION
Dominant "fictitious commodity"	labour	money	land ("nature")
Dominant locus of response	local	national	global
Dominant rights protected	labour	social	human
Dominant orientation of sociology	utopian and critical	policy and professional	public
Dominant thrust of sociological science	speculative	positivist	reflexive

connected to policy, critical, and professional sociologies. Public sociology has flourished in other countries, such as Brazil, South Africa, and India, based on selectively imported North American or European professional sociology but reshaped in anti-authoritarian or anti-colonial struggles.

Global borrowings present dangers as well as possibilities. Notably, the domination of the United States' professional sociology can constrain the responsiveness of national sociologies to local concerns. Facing the dilemma of having the United States on its doorstep in the late 1960s and early 1970s, many Canadian sociologists led an attack on the Americanization of academic life. Farther afield, the dilemma can be even deeper. Pressures to write in English for remote professional audiences not only disadvantage peripheralized sociologists, but inevitably threaten the vitality of local public sociology. Writing of the Middle East, Sari Hanafi (2011) has expressed the dilemma as follows: publish globally and perish locally or publish locally and perish globally. Are there ways to transcend this chasm, to constitute a public sociology that is not isolationist but globally connected? That remains our challenge.

CONCLUSION

I have argued that sociology is taking a public turn in response to third-wave marketization. Sociology lives and dies with society. When society is threatened, so is sociology. We can no longer rely on the state to contain the market, so sociologists have to forge their own connections to society, that is, to develop public sociologies. We have to do more than serve society passively. We must conserve and constitute society. In this, sociology has many potential allies and partners as they too come under increasing assault from state and market. That is the broader contemporaneous context within which public sociology can be a guiding spirit and directing force.

However, we cannot think of the contemporary context outside of its past. We cannot compartmentalize the three waves of marketization and the corresponding configurations of sociology as three separate periods. Each wave deposits its legacy in the next wave. The waves of commodification deepen as they move *regressively* from labour to money to nature, each wave incorporating the commodification of the previous period, just as the counter-movement leads *progressively* from labour rights to social rights (which includes labour rights)

and then aspires to human rights that include all three.

The development of sociology is different. Policy and professional sociology, with their value-neutral, scientific approach, are a reaction against utopian and critical sociology, with their speculations and moral infusions. Public sociology tries to synthesize the value commitment of the first period with the scientific advances of the second. However, even here we should be careful not to think in terms of discrete sociologies, but rather reconfigurations of the four elements of sociology, in which the weights of professional, policy, critical, and public sociologies shift over time. Indeed, a public sociology cannot really take off in a sustained manner unless it is impelled by critical sociology and grounded in professional sociology.

The rhythm and spacing of the waves of sociological development vary from country to country. For the advanced capitalist world today, the waves are more clearly separated in time, whereas for such countries as Russia, India, and China, the waves are compressed, with the commodification of labour, money, and nature occurring almost simultaneously in recent decades. National variation notwithstanding, we can still identify the present era as one in which the commodification of nature concentrates within itself the cumulative impact of the commodification of labour and money. In its subsumption of all commodification, the commodification of nature becomes the planet's most pressing problem, generating social movements that are held together by the principle of human rights.

It is unclear whether these movements can reverse third-wave marketization and whether the result will be to expand or narrow the confines of human freedom. It is possible that sociology itself will succumb to commodification—the commodification of the production of knowledge in the university and elsewhere, the commodification of the distribution of knowledge by the mass media, and the commodification of the consumption of knowledge as student fees continue their upward trajectory. Conversely, there may be a place for public sociology to participate in the knitting together of organizations, movements, and publics around the globe, helping to fortify a civil society beyond the control of market and state. The world needs public sociology engaging publics across the globe: one that rests on the shoulders of a dynamic professional sociology that is inspired by a vital critical sociology, while holding policy sociology to account.

REFERENCES

CHAPTER 1

Babbie, Earl. (1992). *The Practice of Social Research*, 6th ed. Belmont, CA: Wadsworth Publishing.

Bell, Daniel. (1976). *The Coming of Post-Industrial Society: A Venture in Social Forecasting*. New York: Basic Books.

Berger, Peter L. and Thomas Luckmann. (1966). *The Social Construction of Reality: A Treatise in the Sociology of Knowledge*. Garden City, NY: Doubleday.

Briggs, Jean. (1970). *Never in Anger: Portrait of an Eskimo Family*. Cambridge MA: Harvard University Press.

Carole, Melissa. (2011). "Mental Illness? Yes, But Also Homophobia." *Globe and Mail* 7 October: A21.

Clark, S. D. (1968). *The Developing Canadian Community*, 2nd ed. Toronto: University of Toronto Press.

Coleman, James S. (1961). *The Adolescent Society*. New York: Free Press.

Derrida, Jacques. (2004). *Positions*, Alan Bass, trans. London: Continuum.

Douglas, Jack D. (1967). *The Social Meanings of Suicide*. Princeton, NJ: Princeton University Press.

Durkheim, Émile. (1951 [1897]). *Suicide: A Study in Sociology*, G. Simpson, ed., J. Spaulding and G. Simpson, trans. New York: Free Press.

Edel, Abraham. (1965). "Social Science and Value: A Study in Interrelations." In Irving Louis Horowitz, ed., *The New Sociology: Essays in Social Science and Social Theory in Honor of C. Wright Mills* (pp. 218–38). New York: Oxford University Press.

Eichler, Margrit. (1987). *Nonsexist Research Methods*. Boston: Allen and Unwin.

Eichler, Margrit. (1988). *Families in Canada Today*, 2nd ed. Toronto: Gage.

Foucault, Michael. (1973). *The Birth of the Clinic: An Archaeology of Medical Perception*, A. M. Sheridan, trans. London UK: Routledge.

Foucault, Michel. (1977). *Discipline and Punish: The Birth of the Prison*, Alan Sheridan, trans. New York: Vintage.

Foucault, Michael. (1988). *Madness and Civilization: A History of Insanity in the Age of Reason*, Richard Howard, trans. New York: Random House.

Fukuyama, Francis. (1992). *The End of History and the Last Man*. New York: HarperCollins.

Garfinkel, Harold. (1967). *Studies in Ethnomethodology*. Englewood Cliffs, NJ: Prentice-Hall.

Giddens, Anthony. (1982). *Sociology: A Brief but Critical Introduction*. New York: Harcourt Brace Jovanovich.

Giddens, Anthony. (1990). *The Consequences of Modernity*. Stanford, CA: Stanford University Press.

Goffman, Erving. (1959). *The Presentation of Self in Everyday Life*. Garden City, NY: Anchor.

Gramsci, Antonio. (1957). *The Modern Prince and Other Writings*. L. Marks, trans. New York: International Publishers.

Gramsci, Antonio. (1971). *Selections from the Prison Notebooks*, Q. Hoare and G. Smith, eds. London UK: Lawrence & Wishart.

Granovetter, Mark. (1973). "The Strength of Weak Ties." *American Sociological Review, 78* (6), 1360–80.

Guillén, Mauro F. (2001). "Is Globalization Civilizing, Destructive or Feeble? A Critique of Five Key Debates in the Social Science Literature." *Annual Review of Sociology, 27.* On the World Wide Web at http://knowledge.wharton.upenn.edu/PDFs/938 pdf (retrieved 6 February 2003).

Guppy, Neil et al. (2014). *Opportunities in Sociology*. Department of Sociology, University of British Columbia, and Canadian Sociological Association.

Hamlin, Cynthia Lins and Robert Brym. (2006). "The Return of the Native: A Cultural and Social-Psychological Critique of Durkheim's *Suicide* Based on the Guarani-Kaiowá of South-Western Brazil." *Sociological Theory 24*, 42–57.

Hersch, Patricia. (1998). *A Tribe Apart: A Journey into the Heart of American Adolescence*. New York: Ballantine Books.

Hochschild, Arlie and Anne Machung. (1989). *The Second Shift: Working Parents and the Revolution at Home*. New York: Viking.

Jubilee Debt Campaign. (2010). "Getting into Debt." On the World Wide Web at http://www.jubileedebtcapmaign.org.uk /Getting%20into%20Debt+6281.twl (retrieved 20 December 2011).

Kuhn, Thomas. (1970). *The Structure of Scientific Revolutions*, 2nd ed. Chicago: University of Chicago Press.

Marx, Karl. (1904 [1859]). *A Contribution to the Critique of Political Economy*, N. Stone, trans. Chicago: Charles H. Kerr.

Marx, Karl and Friedrich Engels. (1972 [1848]). "Manifesto of the Communist Party." In R. Tucker, ed., *The Marx-Engels Reader* (pp. 331–62). New York: Norton.

Merton, Robert K. (1968 [1949]). *Social Theory and Social Structure*. New York: Free Press.

Mills, C. Wright. (1956). *The Power Elite*. New York: Oxford University Press.

Mills, C. Wright. (1959). *The Sociological Imagination*. New York: Oxford University Press.

Moore, Oliver. (2010). "Smuggled Alcohol Recalls Tragedy of Davis Inlet." *Globe and Mail* 2 October: A6.

Organisation for Economic Cooperation and Development. (2008). "Aid Targets Slipping Out of Reach." On the World Wide Web at http://www.oecd.org/dataoecd/47/25/41724314.pdf (retrieved 20 December 2011).

Ornstein, Michael D. (1983). "The Development of Class in Canada." In J. Paul Grayson, ed., *Introduction to Sociology: An Alternate Approach* (pp. 224–66). Toronto: Gage.

Parsons, Talcott. (1951). *The Social System*. Glencoe, IL: Free Press.

Porter, John. (1965). *The Vertical Mosaic: An Analysis of Social Class and Power in Canada*. Toronto: University of Toronto Press.

Russett, Cynthia Eagle. (1966). *The Concept of Equilibrium in American Social Thought*. New Haven, CT: Yale University Press.

Samson, Colin, James Wilson, and Jonathan Mazower. (1999). *Canada's Tibet: The Killing of the Innu*. London, UK: Survival International. On the World Wide Web at http://assets.survivalinternational.org/static/files/books/InnuReport.pdf (retrieved 8 August 2014).

Statistics Canada. (2014a). "Suicides and Suicide Rate, by Sex and by Age Group (Both sexes rate)." On the World Wide Web at http://www.statcan.gc.ca/tables-tableaux/sum-som/l01/cst01/hlth66d-eng.htm (retrieved 8 August 2014).

Statistics Canada. (2014b). "Labour Force Survey, July 2014." On the World Wide Web at http://www.statcan.gc.ca/daily-quotidien/140808/dq140808a-eng.htm (retrieved 8 August 2014).

Thompson, Kenneth, ed. (1975). *Auguste Comte: The Foundation of Sociology.* New York: Wiley.

Tierney, John. (1997). "Our Oldest Computer, Upgraded." *New York Times Magazine* 28 September: pp. 46–49, 97, 100, 104–05.

Tillyard, E. M. W. (1943). *The Elizabethan World Picture.* London, UK: Chatto and Windus.

Toffler, Alvin. (1990). *Powershift: Knowledge, Wealth, and Violence at the Edge of the 21st Century.* New York: Bantam.

Weber, Max. (1946). *From Max Weber: Essays in Sociology.* Hans Gerth and C. Wright Mills, eds. and trans. New York: Oxford University Press.

Weber, Max. (1958 [1904–05]). *The Protestant Ethnic and the Spirit of Capitalism.* New York: Scribner.

West, Candace and Don Zimmerman. (1987). "Doing Gender." *Gender and Society 1,* 125–51.

World Health Organization. (2011). "Suicide Rates per 100,000 by Country, Year and Sex (Table): Most Recent Year Available, as of 2011." On the World Wide Web at http://www.who.int/mental_health/prevention/suicide_rates/en/ (retrieved 20 December 2011).

Yates, Gayle Graham, ed. (1985). *Harriet Martineau on Women.* New Brunswick, NJ: Rutgers University Press.

CHAPTER 2

Baumann, S. and L. Ho. (2014). "Cultural Schemas for Racial Identity in Canadian Television Advertising." *Canadian Review of Sociology, 51* (2), 152–69.

Boyd, J. (2014). "Performing "East Van": Spatial Identifications and Class Anxieties." *Journal of Contemporary Ethnography, 44* (1), (November 12).

Brym, R. (1978). *The Jewish Intelligentsia and Russian Marxism: A Sociological Study of Intellectual Radicalism and Ideological Divergence.* London: MacMillan.

Brym, R. (2014). *2011 Census Update: A Critical Interpretation.* Toronto, ON: Nelson Education.

Brym, R. and R. L. Lenton. (2001). *Love Online: A Report on Digital Dating in Canada.* Toronto: MSN.CA.

Cresswell, J. W. (1998). *Qualitative Inquiry and Research Design: Choosing among Five Traditions.* Thousand Oaks, CA: Sage.

Davies, Scott and Neil Guppy. (2014). *The Schooled Society: An Introduction to the Sociology of Education.* 3rd ed. Toronto: Oxford University Press.

DeVault, Marjorie. (1996) "Talking Back to Sociology: Distinctive Contributions of Feminist Methodology." *Annual Review of Sociology, 22,* 29–50.

Douglas, J. (1970). "Understanding Everyday Life." In J. Douglas, ed., *Understanding Everyday Life* (pp. 3–44). Chicago: Aldine.

Fisher, R. A. (1966 [1936]). "Has Mendel's Work Been Rediscovered?" In C. Stern and E. Sherwood, eds., *Origin of Genetics: A Mendel Sourcebook* (pp. 139–72). San Francisco: W. H. Freeman.

Foshci, Martha and Jerilee Valenzuela (2008). "Selecting Job Applicants: Effects from Gender, Self-Presentation and Decision Type." *Social Science Research, 37* (3), 1022–38.

Gabor, T. (2004). "Inflammatory Rhetoric on Racial Profiling Can Undermine Police Services." *Canadian Journal of Criminology and Criminal Justice, 46* (3), 457–66.

Galarneau, D. and E. Fecteau. (2014). "The Ups and Downs of Minimum Wage." *Insights on Canadian Society.* Ottawa: Statistics Canada, Catalogue No. 75-006-X.

Goffman, E. (1961). *Asylums: Essays on the Social Situations of Mental Patients and Other Inmates.* New York: Doubleday/Anchor.

Gold, A. D. (1998). "President's Report." *Criminal Lawyers' Newsletter, 19* (2). On the World Wide Web at http://www.criminallawyers.ca/newslett/19–2/gold.html (retrieved 3 November 2000).

Green, D. and K. Milligan. (2010). "The Importance of the Long Form Census to Canada" *Canadian Public Policy—Analyse de Politiques, XXXVI* (3), 383–88.

Gross, N. (2009). "A Pragmatist Theory of Social Mechanisms." *American Sociological Review, 74,* 358–79.

Guppy, N. and K. Beck. (2015) *On Distinction in Academic Circles: The Social Distribution of Merit among Undergraduate Students.* Working paper, Sociology, University of British Columbia.

Guppy, N. and S. Davies. (2009). "School's Out for the Summer: Should It Be?" In E. Grabb and N. Guppy, eds., *Social Inequality in Canada: Patterns, Problems, and Policies* (pp. 429–31). Toronto: Pearson Prentice Hall.

Guppy, N. and G. Gray. (2008). *Successful Surveys: Research Methods and Practice,* 4th ed. Toronto: Thomson Nelson.

Haggerty, K. D. (2001). *Making Crime Count.* Toronto: University of Toronto Press.

Haggerty, K. D. (2004). "Ethics Creep: Governing Social Science Research in the Name of Ethics." *Qualitative Sociology, 24* (4), 391–414.

Houshmand, M., M. Seidel, and D. Ma. (2014). "Beneficial 'Child Labor': The Impact of Adolescent Work on Future Professional Outcomes." *Research in the Sociology of Work,* 25: 191–220.

Kelly, Dierdre, Shauna Pomerantz, and Dawn H. Currie. (2005). "Skater Girlhood and Emphasized Femininity: 'You can't land an ollie properly in heels,'" *Gender and Education, 17* (3), 229–48.

Kleppner, D. and R. Jackiw. (2000). "One Hundred Years of Quantum Physics." *Science, 289* (August), 893–98. On the World Wide Web at http://vega.bac.pku.edu.cn/,rxxu/teach/qp100.htm (retrieved 21 September 2000).

Kuhn, T. S. (1962). *The Structure of Scientific Revolutions.* Chicago: University of Chicago Press.

Lauster, Nathan and Adam Easterbrook. (2011). "No Room for New Families? A Field Experiment Measuring Rental Discrimination against Same-Sex Couples and Single Parents." *Social Problems, 58* (3), 389–409.

Masuda, J., C. Teelucksingh, T. Zupancic, A. Crabtree, R. Haber, E. Skinner, B. Poland, J. Frankish, and M. Fridell. (2012). "Out of Our Inner City Backyards: Re-Scaling Urban Environmental Health Inequity Assessment." *Social Science & Medicine, 75* (7), 1244–53.

Mawani, Renisa. (2003). "Imperial Legacies and Postcolonial Identities: Law, Space, and the Making of Stanley Park, 1859–2001." *Law/Text/Culture, 7,* 98–141.

Mosby, Ian. (2013). "Administering Colonial Science: Nutrition Research and Human Biomedical Experimentation in Aboriginal Communities and Residential Schools, 1942–1952." *Social History, 46* (91), 145–72.

Park, R. (2000). *Voodoo Science: The Road from Foolishness to Fraud.* New York: Oxford University Press.

Pineo, P. and J. Porter. (1967). "Occupational Prestige in Canada." *Canadian Review of Anthropology and Sociology, 4,* 24–40.

Popper, Karl. (1977 [1934]). *The Logic of Scientific Discovery,* 14th ed. New York: Harper.

Ragin, C. and L. Amoroso. (2011). *Constructing Social Research,* 2nd edition. Thousand Oaks, CA: Pine Forge Press.

Riga, L. (2008). "The Ethnic Roots of Class Universalism: Rethinking the 'Russian' Revolutionary Elite." *American Journal of Sociology, 114,* 649–705.

Roethlisberger, F. J. and D. W. Dickson. (1939). *Management and the Worker.* Cambridge, MA: Harvard University Press.

Scarce, R. (2000). *Fishy Business: Salmon, Biology, and the Social Construction of Nature.* Philadelphia, PA: Temple University Press.

Schieman, S. and A. Naridada. (2014). "In Control or Fatalistically Ruled? The Sense of Mastery among Working Canadians." *Canadian Review of Sociology, 51*(4), 343–74.

Smith, Dorothy. (2005). *Institutional Ethnography: A Sociology for People.* Lanham, MD: Rowman AltaMira.

Statistics Canada. (2015). *National Graduates Survey:* Public Use Microdata File, 2013. http://www5.statcan.gc.ca/olc-cel/olc.action?ObjId=81M0011X2015001&ObjType=46&lang=en (retrieved 8 July 2015).

Stoddart, M., H. Ramos, and D. Tindall. (2015). "Environmentalists' Mediawork for Jumbo Pass and the Tobeatic Wilderness, Canada: Combining Text-Centred and Activist-Centred Approaches to New Media and Social Movements" *Social Movement Studies, 14* (1), 75–91.

Weber, M. (1949 [1904]). *The Methodology of the Social Sciences.* Glencoe, IL: Free Press.

Wortley, S. and J. Tanner (2003). "Data, Denials, and Confusion: The Racial Profiling Debate in Toronto." *Canadian Journal of Criminology and Criminal Justice, 45* (3), 367–89.

Wortley, S. and J. Tanner (2005). "Inflammatory Rhetoric? Baseless Accusations? A Response to Gabor's Critique of Racial Profiling Research in Canada" *Canadian Journal of Criminology and Criminal Justice, 47* (3), 581–609.

CHAPTER 3

Adams, Michael. (1997). *Sex in the Snow: Canadian Social Values at the End of the Millennium.* Toronto: Penguin.

Akwagyiram, Alexis. (2009). "Hip Hop Comes of Age." *BBC News* 12 October. On the World Wide Web at http://news.bbc.co.uk/2/hi/8286310.stm (retrieved 11 January 2011).

Albas, Daniel and Cheryl Albas. (1989). "Modern Magic: The Case of Examinations." *The Sociological Quarterly, 30,* 603–13.

Baudrillard, Jean. (1988 [1986]). *America,* Chris Turner, trans. London: Verso.

Bibby, Reginald W. (1987). *Fragmented Gods: The Poverty and Potential of Religion in Canada.* Toronto: Irwin.

Bierstedt, Robert. (1963). *The Social Order.* New York: McGraw-Hill.

Bissoondath, Neil. (2002). *Selling Illusions: The Cult of Multiculturalism in Canada,* rev. ed. Toronto: Penguin.

Boroditsky, Lera. (2010). "Lost in Translation." *Wall Street Journal* 23 July. On the World Wide Web at http://online.wsj.com/article/SB10001424052748703467304575383131592767868.html (retrieved 14 March 2012).

Brym, Robert (2009). *Canadian Society and the 2006 Census.* Toronto: Nelson.

Brym, Robert (2014). "Hip Hop from Caps to Bling." In R. Brym, ed., *Sociology as a Life or Death Issue,* 3rd Canadian ed. (pp. 12–31). Toronto: Nelson.

Brym, Robert with Bonnie J. Fox. (1989). *From Culture to Power: The Sociology of English Canada.* Toronto: Oxford University Press.

Cardozo, Andrew and Ravi Pendakur. (n.d.). "Canada's Visible Minorities: 1967–2017." On the World Wide Web at http://aix1.uottawa.ca/~pendakur/pdf%20docs/VisMin_1967–2017.pdf (retrieved 16 March 2012).

Carpenter, Dave. (2003). "McDonald's High-Tech with Kitchen, Kiosks." KioskCom. On the World Wide Web at http://www.redorbit.com/news/technology/12629/mcdonalds_hightech_with_kitchen_kiosks (retrieved 23 October 2003).

Citizenship and Immigration Canada. (2014). *Facts and Figures 2012—Immigration Overview: Permanent and Temporary Residents.* On the World Wide Web at http://www.cic.gc.ca/english/resources/statistics/facts2012/permanent/10.asp (retrived 12 August 2014).

Clarke, Harold D., Jane Jenson, Lawrence LeDuc, and Jon H. Pammett. (1996). *Absent Mandate: Canadian Electoral Politics in an Era of Restructuring,* 3rd ed. Toronto: Gage.

Damisch, Lysann, Barbara Stoberock, and Thomas Mussweiler. (2010). "Keep Your Fingers Crossed! How Superstition Improves Performance." *Psychological Science, 21,* 1014–20.

Davis, Mike. (1990). *City of Quartz: Excavating the Future in Los Angeles.* New York: Verso.

Delmos, Monika. (2002). "Mangled Words Divide Generations in Japan." *Globe and Mail* 24 August: A14.

Deutscher, Guy. (2010). "Does Your Language Shape How You Think?" *New York Times* 26 August. On the World Wide Web at http://www.nytimes.com/2010/08/29/magazine/29language-t.html?pagewanted=all (retrieved 14 March 2012).

Durkheim, Émile. (1976 [1915]). *The Elementary Forms of the Religious Life,* Joseph Ward Swain, trans. New York: Free Press.

Elections Canada. (2013). "Voter Turnout at Federal Elections and Referendums." On the World Wide Web at http://www.elections.ca/content.aspx?dir=turn&document=index&lang=e&section=ele (retrieved 3 November 2014).

Fleras, Augie and Jean Leonard Elliott. (2002). *Engaging Diversity: Multiculturalism in Canada.* Toronto: Nelson.

Forman, Murray. (2001). "It Ain't All About the Benjamins: Summit on Social Responsibility in the Hip-Hop Industry." *Journal of Popular Music Studies, 13,* 117–23.

Frank, Thomas and Matt Weiland, eds. (1997). *Commodify Your Dissent: Salvos from the Baffler.* New York: Norton.

Gap.com. (1999). On the World Wide Web at http://www.gap.com/onlinestore/gap/advertising/khakitv.asp (retrieved 14 September 1999).

Ghosh, Bobby. (2011). "Rage, Rap, and Revolution: Inside the Arab Youth Quake." *Time.com* 17 February. On the World Wide Web at http://www.time.com/time/world/article/0,8599,2049808,00.html (retrieved 17 February 2011).

Gleick, James. (2000). *Faster: The Acceleration of Just About Everything.* New York: Vintage.

Harris, Kathleen. (2015). "Voter turnout spikes after long, unpredictable campaign." CBC News. On the World Wide Web at http://www.cbc.ca/news/politics/canada-election-2015-voting-polls-turnout-1.3278838 (retrieved 20 October 2015).

Harris, Marvin. (1974). *Cows, Pigs, Wars and Witches: The Riddles of Culture*. New York, Random House.

Ignatieff, Michael. (2000). *The Rights Revolution*. Toronto: Anansi.

Kristof, Nicholas D. (1997). "With Stateside Lingo, Valley Girl Goes Japanese." *New York Times* 19 October: Sections 1, 3.

Art History Archive. Feminist Art: Barbara Kruger, (1987). On the Worldwide Web at http://www.arthistoryarchive.com/arthistory/feminist/Barbara-Kruger.html (retrieved June 29, 2015).

Lipset, Seymour Martin. (1963) "Value Differences, Absolute or Relative: The English-Speaking Democracies." In *The First New Nation: The United States in Historical Perspective* (pp. 248–73). New York: Basic Books.

Lurie, Allison. (1981). *The Language of Clothes*. New York: Random House.

McConaghy, Nathaniel. (1999). "Unresolved Issues in Scientific Sexology." *Archives of Sexual Behavior* 28, 4, 285–318.

McCrum, Robert, William Cran, and Robert MacNeil. (1992). *The Story of English*, new and rev. eds. London, UK: Faber and Faber.

McLuhan, Marshall. (1964). *Understanding Media: The Extensions of Man*. New York: McGraw-Hill.

Mealey, Linda. (2010). "The Sociobiology of Sociopathy: An Integrated Evolutionary Model." *Behavioral and Brain Sciences* 18 (3), 523–41.

Neal, Mark Anthony. (1999). *What the Music Said: Black Popular Music and Black Public Culture*. New York: Routledge.

Nevitte, Neil. (1996). *The Decline of Deference: Canadian Value Change in Cross-National Perspective*. Peterborough, ON: Broadview Press.

Neuberg, S. L., D. T. Kenrick, and M. Schaller. (2010). "Evolutionary Social Psychology." In S. T. Fiske, D. T. Gilbert, and G. Lindzey, eds., *Handbook of Social Psychology*, Vol. 2, 5th ed. (pp. 761–96). John Wiley & Sons.

Ontario Human Rights Commission. (2009). "Policy on Female Genital Mutilation (FGM)." On the World Wide Web at http://www.ohrc.on.ca/en/policy-female-genital-mutilation-fgm (retrieved 12 August 2014).

Peters, Russell. (2009). "Russell Peters: Canadian East Indian Comedian." On the World Wide Web at http://thebookmarketingnetwork.com/video/russell-peter-canadian-east (retrieved 16 March 2012).

Pinker, Steven. (1994). "Apes—Lost for Words." *New Statesman and Society*, 15 April: 30–31.

Piven, Frances Fox and Richard A. Cloward. (1977). *Poor People's Movements: Why They Succeed, How They Fail*. New York: Vintage.

Ritzer, George. (1993). *The McDonaldization of Society: An Investigation into the Changing Character of Contemporary Social Life*. Thousand Oaks, CA: Pine Forge Press.

Ritzer, George. (1996). "The McDonaldization Thesis: Is Expansion Inevitable?" *International Sociology*, 11, 291–308.

Schlosser, Eric. (2002). *Fast Food Nation: The Dark Side of the All-American Meal*. New York: Perennial.

Schor, Juliet B. (1992). *The Overworked American: The Unexpected Decline of Leisure*. New York: Basic Books.

Scott, James C. (1998). *Seeing Like a State: How Certain Schemes to Improve the Human Condition Have Failed*. New Haven, CT: Yale University Press.

Statistics Canada. (2012). "Labour Force Survey Estimates (LFS), Employees Working Overtime (Weekly) by National Occupational Classification for Statistics (NOC-S), Sex and Age Group Annually." CANSIM Table 2820082. On the World Wide Web at http://dc2.chass.utoronto.ca.myaccess.library.utoronto.ca/cgi-bin/cansimdim/c2_getArrayDim.pl (retrieved 16 March 2012).

Statistics Canada. (2014). "Ethnic Origin (264), Single and Multiple Ethnic Origin Responses (3), Generation Status (4), Age Groups (10) and Sex (3) for the Population in Private Households of Canada, Provinces, Territories, Census Metropolitan Areas and Census Agglomerations, 2011 National Household Survey." On the World Wide Web at http://www12.statcan.gc.ca/nhs-enm/2011/dp-pd/dt-td/Rp-eng.cfm?LANG=E&APATH=3&DETAIL=0&DIM=0&FL=A&FREE=0&GC=0&GID=0&GK=0&GRP=1&PID=105396&PRID=0&PTYPE=105277&S=0&SHOWALL=0&SUB=0&Temporal=2013&THEME=95&VID=0&VNAMEE&VNAMEF (retrieved 12 August 2014).

Thompson, E. P. (1967). "Time, Work Discipline and Industrial Capitalism." *Past and Present*, 3, 59–67.

UNICEF. (2013). "Female Genital Mutilation/Cutting: A Statistical Overview and Exploration of the Dynamics of Change." On the World Wide Web at http://www.unicef.org/esaro/FGCM_Lo_res.pdf (retrieved 12 August 2014).

United Nations. (1998). "Universal Declaration of Human Rights." On the World Wide Web at http://www.un.org/Overview/rights.html (retrieved 29 August 2002).

Veblen, Thorstein. (1899). *The Theory of the Leisure Class*. On the World Wide Web at http://www.gutenberg.org/files/833/833-h/833-h.htm (retrieved 12 August 2014).

Weber, Max. (1958 [1904–05]). *The Protestant Ethic and the Spirit of Capitalism*. New York: Scribner. On the World Wide Web at https://www.marxists.org/reference/archive/weber/protestant-ethic/ch05.htm (retrieved 8 July 2015).

Whorf, Benjamin Lee. (1956). In John B. Carroll, ed., *Language, Thought, and Reality*. Cambridge, MA: MIT Press.

Wilson, William Julius. (1987). *The Truly Disadvantaged: The Inner City, the Underclass and Public Policy*. Chicago: University of Chicago Press.

Woodbury, Anthony. (2003). "Endangered Languages." Linguistic Society of America. On the World Wide Web at http://www.lsadc.org/web2/endangeredlgs.htm (retrieved 19 July 2003).

World Health Organization. (2014). "Female Genital Mutilation." On the World Wide Web at http://www.who.int/mediacentre/factsheets/fs241/en/ (retrieved 12 August 2014).

World Values Survey. (2012). "Online Data Analysis." On the World Wide Web at http://www.wvsevsdb.com/wvs/WVSAnalize.jsp (retrieved 16 March 2012).

CHAPTER 4

Adler, Patricia A. and Peter Adler. (1998). *Peer Power: Preadolescent Culture and Identity*. New Brunswick, NJ: Rutgers University Press.

Ariès, Phillipe. (1962 [1960]). *Centuries of Childhood: A Social History of Family Life*, Robert Baldick, trans. New York: Knopf.

Becker, Dominik. (2013). "The Impact of Teachers' Expectations on Students' Educational Opportunities in the Life Course: An Empirical Test of a Subjective Expected Utility Explanation." *Rationality and Society* 25 (4), 422–69.

Benzaquen, Adriana S. (2006). *Encounters with Wild Children: Temptations and Disappointment in the Study of Human Nature*. Montreal, QC: McGill-Queen's University Press.

Bibby, Reginald W. 2001. *Canada's Teens: Today, Yesterday, and Tomorrow*. Toronto: Stoddart.

Brym, Robert and Rhonda Lenton. (2001). "Love Online: A Report on Digital Dating in Canada." Toronto: MSN.CA. On the World Wide Web at http://projects.chass.utoronto.ca/brym/loveonline.pdf (retrieved 8 July 2015).

Cohen, I. Glenn. (2013). "Transplant Tourism: The Ethics and Regulation of International Markets for Organs." *Journal of Law, Medicine and Ethics 41* (1), 269–85.

Cooley, Charles Horton. (1902). *Human Nature and the Social Order.* New York: Scribner's.

Coupland, Douglas. (1991). *Generation X: Tales for an Accelerated Culture.* New York: St. Martin's Press.

Crosnoe, Robert and Monica Kirkpatrick Johnson. (2011). Research on Adolescence in the Twenty-First Century." *Annual Review of Sociology 37,* 439–60.

Eagley, Alice H. and Wendy Wood. (1999). "The Origins of Sex Differences in Human Behavior. Evolved Dispositions versus Social Roles." *American Psychologist 54,* 412–13.

Eisenstadt, S. N. (1956). *From Generation to Generation.* New York: Free Press.

Freud, Sigmund. (1962 [1930]). *Civilization and Its Discontents.* James Strachey, trans. New York: Norton.

Freud, Sigmund. (1973 [1915–17]). *Introductory Lectures on Psychoanalysis.* James Strachey, trans., James Strachey and Angela Richards, eds. Harmondsworth, UK: Penguin.

Fried, Martha Nemes and Morton H. Fried. (1980). *Transitions: Four Rituals in Eight Cultures.* New York: Norton.

Gillies, Val. (2005). "Raising the 'Meritocracy': Parenting and the Individualization of Social Class." *Sociology, 39* (5), 835–53.

Gillis, John R. (1981). *Youth and History: Tradition and Change in European Age Relations, 1770–Present.* Expanded student ed. New York: Academic Press.

Goffman, Erving. (1961). *Asylums: Essays on the Social Situation of Mental Patients and Other Inmates.* Garden City, NY: Anchor Books.

Gordinier, Jeff. (2008). *X Saves the World: How Generation X Got the Shaft but Can Still Keep Everything from Sucking.* New York: Viking.

Haney, Craig, W. Curtis Banks, and Philip G. Zimbardo. (1973). "Interpersonal Dynamics in a Simulated Prison." *International Journal of Criminology and Penology 1,* 69–97.

Haythornthwaite, Caroline and Barry Wellman. (2002). "The Internet in Everyday Life: An Introduction." In B. Wellman and C. Haythornthwaite, eds., *The Internet in Everyday Life* (pp. 3–41). Oxford: Blackwell.

Higgs, Paul and Chris Gilleard. (2010). Generational Conflict, Consumption and the Ageing Welfare State in the United Kingdom. *Aging and Society 30* (8): 1439–51.

Howe, Neil and William Strauss. (2009). *Millennials Rising: The Next Great Generation.* New York: Vintage Books.

Interactive Advertising Bureau of Canada. (2014). "2014: Internet in the Media Garden." On the World Wide Web at http://iabcanada.com/wp-content/uploads/2014/12/V2-Total-Canada-2014-CMUST-Exec-Summary-Nov-18-2014.pdf (retrieved 6 January 2015).

Internet World Stats. (2015). *Internet World Stats: Usage and Population Statistics.* On the World Wide Web at http://www.internetworldstats.com/stats.htm (retrieved 6 January 2015.

Jackson, Phillip W. (1990 [1968]). *Life in Classrooms.* New York: Teachers College Press.

Lane, Harlan. 1976. *The wild boy of Aveyron.* Cambridge, MA: Harvard University Press.

Lareau, Annette. (2003). *Unequal Childhoods: Class, Race and Family Life.* Berkeley, CA: University of California Press.

Le Mare, Lucy and Karyn Audet. (2006). "A Longitudinal Study of the Physical Growth and Health of Postinstitutionalized Romanian Adoptees." *Paediatrics and Child Health 11,* 1, 85–91. On the World Wide Web at http://www.ncbi.nlm.nih.gov/pmc/articles/PMC2435332 (retrieved 8 July 2015).

Mannheim, Karl. (1952). "The Problem of Generations." In Paul Kecskemeti, ed., *Essays on the Sociology of Knowledge* (pp. 276–320). New York: Oxford University Press.

Mead, George Herbert. (1934). *Mind, Self and Society.* Chicago: University of Chicago Press.

Nelson, Charles, A., Nathan A. Fox, and Charles H. Zeanah. (2014). *Romania's Abandoned Children: Deprivation, Brain Development and the Struggle for Recovery.* Cambridge, MA: Harvard University Press.

Pew Research Center. (2014). *Millennials in Adulthood: Detached from Institutions, Networked with Friends.* Washington, DC: Author.

Riley, Matilda White, Anne Foner, and Joan Waring. (1988). "Sociology of Age." In Neil Smelser, ed., *Handbook of Sociology* (pp. 243–90). Newbury Park, CA: Sage.

Rosenthal, Robert and Lenore Jacobson. (1968). *Pygmalion in the Classroom: Teacher Expectation and Pupils' Intellectual Development.* New York: Holt, Rinehart, and Winston.

Rubie-Davis, Christine, John Hattie and Richard Hamilton. (2006). "Expecting the Best for Students: Teacher Expectations and Academic Outcomes." *British Journal of Educational Psychology 76,* 429–44.

Sanchez, F. J. P. and M. D. S. Roda. (2003). Relationships between Self-Concept and Academic Achievement in Primary Students." *Electronic Journal of Research in Educational Psychology and Psychopedagogy 1,* 1, 95–120.

Shanahan, Michael J. and Ross Macmillan. (2008). *Biography and the Sociological Imagination: Contexts and Contingencies.* New York: W. W. Norton and Company.

Statistics Canada. (2011). "Canadian Vital Statistics, Marriage Database and Demography Division (population estimates)," Ottawa: author.

Statistics Canada. (2012). "Generations in Canada: Age and Sex, 2011 Census." Catalogue No. 98-311-X2011003. Ottawa, ON: Minister of Industry.

Statistics Canada. (2015a). "Family Life—Marriage." On the World Wide Web at http://well-being.esdc.gc.ca/misme-iowb/.3ndic.1t.4r@-eng.jsp?iid=78 (retrieved 1 July 2015).

Statistics Canada. (2015b). "Table 282-0004: Labour Force Survey Estimates (LFS), by Educational Attainment, Sex and Age Group, Annual (Persons Unless Otherwise Noted)," CANSIM (database). On the World Wide Web at http://www5.statcan.gc.ca/cansim/a26?lang=eng&id=2820004 (retrieved 24 January 2015).

Strohschein, Lisa, Anne H. Gauthier, Rachel Campbell, & Clay Kleparchuk. (2008). Parenting as a dynamic process: A test of the resource dilution hypothesis. *Journal of Marriage and Family,* 70(3), 670-83.

Tach, L. (2015). "Social Mobility in an Era of Family Instability and Complexity." *The Annals of the American Academy of Political and Social Science, 675,* 83–96.

Television Bureau of Canada. (2014). *TV Basics, 2013–14.* Toronto, ON: Author.

Thomas, William Isaac. (1966 [1931]). "The Relation of Research to the Social Process." In Morris Janowitz, ed. *W.I. Thomas on Social Organization and Social Personality* (pp. 289–305). Chicago: University of Chicago Press.

Torche, Florencia. (2015). An Analysis of Intergenerational Mobility: An Interdisciplinary Review. *Annals of the Academy of Political and Social Science, 675*, 37–62.

Turkle, Sherry. (1995). *Life on the Screen: Identity in the Age of the Internet.* New York: Simon & Schuster.

Turkle, Sherry. (2011). *Alone Together: Why We Expect More from Technology and Less from Each Other.* New York: Basic Books.

Watson, Elwood. (2013). *Generation X: Professor Speak.* Plymouth, UK: Scarecrow Press.

Willis, Paul. (1990). *Common Culture: Symbolic Work at Play in the Everyday Cultures of the Young.* Milton Keynes: Open University Press.

Winograd, Morley, and Michael D. Hais. (2011). *Millennial Momentum: How a New Generation Is Remaking America.* New Jersey: Rutgers University Press.

Zimbardo, Philip (1972). "Pathology of Imprisonment." *Society 9,* 6, 4–8.

Zimbardo, Philip. (2008). *The Lucifer Effect: Understanding How Good People Turn Evil.* New York: Random House.

CHAPTER 5

Anderssen, Erin. (2014). "Sex on Campus: How No Means No Became Yes Means Yes." *Globe and Mail* 15 November. On the World Wide Web at http://www.theglobeandmail.com/life/relationships/sex-on-campus-how-no-means-no-became-yes-means-yes/article21598708/ (retrieved 15 November 2014).

Averett, Susan and Sanders Korenman. (1996). "The Economic Reality of the Beauty Myth." *The Journal of Human Resources, 31* (2), 304–30.

Bagley, Christopher and Kathleen King. (1990). *Child Sexual Abuse: The Search for Healing.* London, UK: Tavistock/Routledge.

Berch, D. B. and B. G. Bender. (1987). "Margins of Sexuality." *Psychology Today* December: 54–57.

Bergen, D. J. and J. E. Williams. (1991). "Sex Stereotypes in the United States Revisited: 1972–1988." *Sex Roles, 24,* 413–23.

Bibby, Reginald W. (1995). *The Bibby Report: Social Trends Canadian Style.* Toronto: Stoddart.

Bibby, Reginald W. (2006). *The Boomer Factor.* Toronto: Bastian Books.

Bibby, Reginald W., with Sarah Russell and Ron Rolheiser. (2009). *The Emerging Millenials.* Lethbridge, AB: Project Canada Books.

Bleier, Ruth. (1984). *Science and Gender: A Critique of Biology and Its Theories on Women.* New York: Pergamon.

Blum, Deborah. (1997). *Sex on the Brain: The Biological Differences between Men and Women.* New York: Penguin Books.

Broverman, I. K., S. R. Vogel, D. M. Broverman, F. E. Clarkson, and P. S. Rosenkratz. (1972). "Sex-Role Stereotypes: A Current Appraisal." *Journal of Social Issues, 28,* 59–78.

Brym, Robert. (2014). "Gender Risk." In Robert Brym, *Sociology as a Life or Death Issue,* 3rd Canadian ed. (pp. 107–27 Toronto: Nelson.

Buss, D. M. (1994). *The Evolution of Desire.* New York: Basic Books.

Buss, D. M. (1995a). "Evolutionary Psychology: A New Paradigm for Psychological Science." *Psychological Inquiry, 6,* 1–30.

Buss, D. M. (1995b). "Psychological Sex Differences: Origins through Sexual Selection." *American Psychologist, 50,* 164–68.

Buss, D. M. (1998). "The Psychology of Human Mate Selection: Exploring the Complexity of the Strategic Repertoire." In C. Crawford and D. L. Krebs, eds., *Handbook of Evolutionary Psychology: Ideas, Issues and Applications* (pp. 405–29). Mahwah, NJ: Erlbaum.

Buss, D. M., M. Abbott, A. Angleitner, A. Asherian, A. Biaggio, A. Blanco-Villasenor, et al. (1990). "International Perspectives in Selecting Mates: A Study of 37 Cultures." *Journal of Cross-Cultural Psychology, 21* (1), 5–47.

"Canadian Public Opinion Polls on Same-Sex Marriage: 2005-Jan-01 to the Present." (2005). On the World Wide Web at http://www.religioustolerance.org/homssmpoll05.htm (retrieved 10 December 2005).

Campbell, James R. and Jeffrey S. Beaudry. (1998). "Gender Gap Linked to Differential Socialization for High-Achieving Senior Mathematics Students." *Educational Research 91,* 140–47.

Caplan, Paula J. and Jeremy B. Caplan. (1999). *Thinking Critically about Research on Sex and Gender,* 2nd ed. New York: Longman.

Carrigan, Tim, Bob Connell, and John Lee. (1985). "Toward a New Sociology of Masculinity." *Theory and Society 14,* 551–604

CBC News. (2014). "Dalhousie University Probes Misogynistic Student 'Gentlemen's Club.'" *CBC News*: Nova Scotia 15 December. On the World Wide Web at http://www.cbc.ca/news/canada/nova-scotia/dalhousie-university-probes-misogynistic-student-gentlemen-s-club-1.2873918 (retrieved 23 December 2014).

Chodorow, Nancy. (1997). "The Psychodynamics of the Family." In Linda Nicholson, ed., *The Second Wave: A Reader in Feminist Theory* (pp. 181–97). New York: Routledge.

Colapinto, John. (1997). "The True Story of John/Joan." *Rolling Stone* 11 December: 54–73, 92–97.

Colapinto, John. (2001). *As Nature Made Him: The Boy Who Was Raised as a Girl.* New York: Perennial.

Condry, J. and S. Condry. (1976). "Sex Differences: A Study of the Eye of the Beholder." *Child Development, 47,* 812–19.

Coontz, Stephanie and Peta Henderson, eds. (1986). *Women's Work, Men's Property: The Origins of Gender and Class.* London: Verso.

Coubrough, Jill. (2014). "Misogyny Complaints Emerge from Manitoba Dentistry Program." *CBC News*: Manitoba, 22 December. On the World Wide Web at http://www.cbc.ca/news/canada/manitoba/misogyny-complaints-emerge-from-manitoba-dentistry-program-1.2880987 (retrieved 23 December 2014).

Creighton, Sarah and Catherine Minto. (2001). "Managing Intersex." *British Medical Journal, 323* (7324), 1264–65.

Davis, Simon. (1990). "Men as Success Objects and Women as Sex Objects: A Study of Personal Advertisements." *Sex Roles, 23,* 43–50.

Davis, T., G. Peck, and J. Stormant. (1993). "Acquaintance Rape and the High School Student." *Journal of Adolescent Health, 14,* 220–24.

Dawkins, Richard. (1976). *The Selfish Gene.* London: Oxford University Press.

DeKeseredy, Walter S. and M. D. Schwartz. (1998). *Woman Abuse on Campus: Results from the Canadian National Survey.* Thousand Oaks, CA: Sage.

Duffy, Ann. (1998). "The Feminist Challenge: Knowing and Ending the Violence." In Nancy Mandell, ed., *Feminist Issues:*

Race, Class, and Sexuality (pp. 132–59). Scarborough, ON: Prentice Hall Allyn & Bacon Canada.

Durex. (2005). "Give and Receive: 2005 Global Sex Survey Results." On the World Wide Web at http://www.durex.com/cm/gss2005result.pdf (retrieved 10 December 2005).

Durex. (2012). "Sexual Well-Being Global Survey, 07/08." On the World Wide Web at http://www.durex.com/en-CA/SexualWellbeingSurvey/pages/default.aspx (retrieved 20 February 2012).

Dworkin, Andrea. (1981). *Pornography: Men Possessing Women*. New York: Penguin.

Dworkin, Andrea. (1987). "Intercourse." Chapter 7 in *Occupation/Collaboration*. On the World Wide Web at http://www.nostatusquo.com/ACLU/dworkin/IntercourseI.html (retrieved 9 December 2011).

Eagley, Alice H. and Wendy Wood. (1999). "The Origins of Sex Differences in Human Behavior. Evolved Dispositions versus Social Roles." *American Psychologist, 54*, 408–23.

Eccles, J. S., J. E. Jacobs, and R. D. Harold. (1990). "Gender-Role Stereotypes, Expectancy Effects and Parents' Socialization of Gender Differences." *Journal of Social Issues, 46*, 183–201.

Eisler, Riane. (1987). *The Chalice and the Blade*. New York: HarperCollins.

Elkin, F. and G. Handel. (1989). *The Child and Society: The Process of Socialization*, 5th ed. New York: Random House.

Ellis, Lee, Brian Robb, and Donald Burke. (2005). "Sexual Orientation in United States and Canadian College Students." *Archives of Sexual Behavior, 34*, 569–81.

Equality Now. (2014). "Global Sex Trafficking Fact Sheet." On the World Wide Web at http://www.equalitynow.org/node/1010 (retrieved 11 November 2014).

Fausto-Sterling, Anne. (2000). "The five sexes, revisited." *The Sciences* 40: 18–23.

Feiring, C. and M. Lewis. (1979). "Sex and Age Differences in Young Children's Reactions to Frustration: A Further Look at the Goldberg and Lewis Subjects." *Child Development, 50*, 848–53.

Fischtein, Dayna S., Edward S. Herold, and Serge Desmarais. (2007). "How Much Does Gender Explain in Sexual Attitudes and Behaviors? A Survey of Canadian Adults." *Archives of Sexual Behavior, 36*, 451–61.

Freud, Sigmund. (1977 [1905]). *On Sexuality*, James Strachey, trans., Angela Richards, ed., Vol. 7, Pelican Freud Library. Harmondsworth, UK: Penguin Books.

Gammon, Katherine. (2009). "Infoporn: Today's Playmates Are More Like Anime Figures than Real Humans." *Wired 17*, 2. On the World Wide Web at http://archive.wired.com/special_multimedia/2009/st_infoporn_1702 (retrieved 14 January 2013).

Garner, David M. (1997). "The 1997 Body Image Survey Results." *Psychology Today, 30* (January/February): 30–44, 74–80, 84.

Gates, Gary J. (2011). "How many people are lesbian, gay, bisexual, and transgender?" *The Williams Institute* April. http://williamsinstitute.law.ucla.edu/wp-content/uploads/Gates-How-Many-People-LGBT-Apr-2011.pdf (retrieved 17 September 2015).

Goldberg, S. and M. Lewis. (1969). "Play Behavior in the Year-Old Infant: Early Sex Differences." *Child Development, 40*, 21–31.

Goldie, Terry. 2001. *In a Queer Country: Gay & Lesbian Studies in the Canadian Context*. Vancouver: Arsenal Pulp Press

Green, Adam Isaiah. (2007). "Queer Theory and Sociology: Locating the Subject and the Self in Sexuality Studies." *Sociological Theory 25*, 26–45.

Gruber, J. E. (1997). "An Epidemiology of Sexual Harassment: Evidence from North America and Europe." In W. O'Donohue, ed., *Sexual Harassment: Theory, Research and Treatment* (pp. 84–98). Boston: Allyn and Bacon.

Gunderson, Elizabeth A., Gerardo Ramirez, Susan C. Levine, and Sian L. Beilock. (2012). "The Role of Parents and Teachers in the Development of Gender-Related Math Attitudes." *Sex Roles, 66*, 153–66.

Hesse-Biber, Sharlene. (1996). *Am I Thin Enough Yet? The Cult of Thinness and the Commercialization of Identity*. New York: Oxford University Press.

Hird, Myra J. (2005). *Sex, Gender and Science*. London: Palgrave Macmillan.

Hobart, Charles. (1996). "Intimacy and Family Life: Sexuality, Cohabitation, and Marriage." In Maureen Baker, ed., *Families: Changing Trends in Canada* (pp. 143–73). Toronto: McGraw-Hill Ryerson.

Hughes, Fergus P. (1995). *Children, Play, and Development*, 2nd ed. Boston: Allyn and Bacon.

Human Rights Watch. (1995). *The Human Rights Watch Global Report on Women's Human Rights*. New York: Human Rights Watch.

Internet Movie Database. (2014). On the World Wide Web at http://www.imdb.com/name/nm0000123/?ref_=fn_al_nm_1

Jeffreys, Sheila. (1990). "Heterosexuality and the Desire for Gender." In Diane Richardson, ed., *Theorising Heterosexuality* (pp. 75–90). Buckingham, UK: Open University Press.

Jensen, Margaret Ann. (1984). *Love's Sweet Return: The Harlequin Story*. Toronto: Women's Press.

Kerig, Patricia K., Philip A. Cowan, and Carolyn Pape Cowan. (1993). "Marital Quality and Gender Differences in Parent–Child Interaction." *Developmental Psychology, 29*, 931–39.

Kimmel, Michael and Tristan Bridges. 2011. "Masculinity." *Oxford Bibliographies*. On the World Wide Web at http://www.oxfordbibliographies.com/view/document/obo-9780199756384/obo-9780199756384-0033.xml (retrieved 14 November 2014).

Kinkartz, L., K. Wells, and A. Hillyard. (2013). *Safe Spaces Campus Climate Survey Report: Gauging the Environment for Sexual and Gender Minorities at the University of Alberta*. Edmonton: Institute for Sexual Minority Studies and Service.

Kinsey, Alfred C., Wardell B. Pomeroy, and Clyde E. Martin. 1948. *Sexual Behavior in the Human Male*. Philadelphia: W. B. Saunders.

Kinsey, Alfred C., Wardell B. Pomeroy, Clyde E. Martin, and Paul H. Gebhard. (1953). *Sexual Behavior in the Human Female*. Philadelphia: W. B. Saunders

Kitzinger, Celia and Sue Wilkinson. (1994). "Problematizing Pleasure: Radical Feminist Deconstructions of Sexuality and Power." In H. L. Radtke and H. J. Stam, eds., *Power/Gender: Social Relations in Theory and Practice*. London: Sage.

Knight, Luis F. Morales and Deborah A. Hope. (2012). "Correlates of Same-Sex Attractions and Behaviors Among Self-Identified Heterosexual University Students." *Archives of Sexual Behavior 41*, 1199–1208.

Lenton, Rhonda, Michael D. Smith, John Fox, and Norman Morra. (1999). "Sexual Harassment in Public Places: Experiences of Canadian Women." *Canadian Review of Sociology and Anthropology, 36*, 517–40.

Lightfoot-Klein, Hanny, Cheryl Chase, Tim Hammond, and Ronald Goldman. (2000). "Genital Surgery on Children below the Age of Consent." In Lenore T. Szuchman and Frank

Muscarella, eds., *Psychological Perspectives on Human Sexuality*, (pp. 440–49). New York: John Wiley and Sons.

Lips, Hilary M. (2014). *Gender: The Basics.* London UK: Routledge.

Lisak, David. (1992). "Sexual Aggression, Masculinity, and Fathers." *Signs, 16*, 238–62.

MacDonald, K. and R. D. Parke. (1986). "Parent-Child Physical Play: The Effects of Sex and Age on Children and Parents." *Sex Roles, 15*, 367–78.

Mackay, Judith. (2000). *The Penguin Atlas of Human Sexual Behavior.* New York: Penguin.

Mackinnon, Catharine A. (1997). "Sexuality." In Linda Nicholson, ed., *The Second Wave: A Reader in Feminist Theory* (pp. 158–80). New York and London: Routledge.

Matrix, C. ed. (1996). *Tales from the Clit.* Edinburgh, UK: AK Press.

McCarthy, B., C. Benoit, and M. Jansson. (2014). "Sex Work: A Comparative Study." *Archives of Sexual Behavior 43* (7), 1379–90.

Mead, Margaret. (1935). *Sex and Temperament in Three Primitive Societies.* New York: Dell.

Michael, Robert T., John H. Gagnon, Edward O. Laumann, and Gina Kolata. (1994). *Sex in America: A Survey.* Boston: Little, Brown.

Milligan, Shelly. (2011). "Criminal Harassment in Canada, 2009." *Juristat 3* (March). On the World Wide Web at http://www.statcan.gc.ca/pub/85-005-x/2011001/article/11407-eng.pdf (retrieved 20 February 2012).

Nelson, E. D. and Barrie W. Robinson. (1999). *Gender in Canada.* Scarborough, ON: Prentice Hall Allyn & Bacon Canada.

O'Donnell, Vivian and Susan Wallace. (2011). "First Nations, Métis and Inuit Women." Statistics Canada. On the World Wide Web at http://www.statcan.gc.ca/pub/89-503-x/2010001/article/11442-eng.pdf (retrieved 11 November 2014).

Paek, H. J., M. R. Nelson, A. M. Vilela. (2010). "Examination of Gender-Role Portrayals in Television Advertising across Seven Countries." *Sex Roles 64* (3–4), 192–207.

Pipher, M. (1994). *Reviving Ophelia: Saving the Selves of Adolescent Girls.* New York: Ballantine.

Power, Nina. (2009). *One-Dimensional Woman.* Winchester, UK: Zero Books.

Pryor, John B., J. L. Giedd, and K. B. Williams. (1995). "A Social Psychological Model for Predicting Sexual Harassment." *Journal of Social Issues, 51*, 69–84.

Raag, Tarja and Christine L. Rackliff. (1998). "Preschoolers' Awareness of Social Expectations of Gender: Relationships to Toy Choices." *Sex Roles, 38*, 685–700.

Rao, Smriti and Christina Presenti. (2012). "Understanding Human Trafficking Origin: A Cross-Country Empirical Analysis." *Feminist Economics 18*, 231–63.

Reiss, I. (1986). *Journey into Sexuality: An Exploratory Voyage.* Englewood Cliffs, NJ: Prentice Hall.

Rotermann, Michele. (2008). "Trends in Teen Sexual Behavior and Condom Use." *Health Reports, 19* (3), 1–5.

Rubin, Gayle. (1993). "Thinking Sex: Notes for a Radical Theory of the Politics of Sexuality." In Henry Abelove, Michèle Aina Barale, and David M. Halperin, eds., *The Lesbian and Gay Studies Reader* (pp. 3–34). London: Routledge.

Rubin, J. Z., F. J. Provenzano, and Z. Lurra. (1974). "The Eye of the Beholder." *American Journal of Orthopsychiatry, 44*, 512–19.

Ryan, Kathryn M. and Jeanne Kanjorski. (1998). "The Enjoyment of Sexist Humor, Rape Attitudes and Relationship Aggression in College Students." *Sex Roles, 38*, 743–56.

"Same-Sex Marriage in Canada: Public Opinion Polls from 2006 to Now." (2008). On the World Wide Web at http://www.religioustolerance.org/homssmpoll06.htm (retrieved 6 December 2008).

Sanday, Peggy. (1981). *Female Power and Male Dominance.* Cambridge, UK: Cambridge University Press.

Saxton, Lloyd. (1990). *The Individual, Marriage, and the Family*, 7th ed. Belmont, CA: Wadsworth.

Schrock, David and Michael Schwalbe. (2009). "Men, Masculinity, and Manhood Acts." *Annual Review of Sociology 35*, 277–95.}

Schwartz, Daniel. 2014. "Pornography, Kids and Sex Education: What to Do?" *Globe and Mail* 17 November. On the World Wide Web at http://www.cbc.ca/news/health/pornography-kids-and-sex-education-what-to-do-1.2836021.

Sinha, Maire. 2013. "Measuring Violence against Women: Statistical Trends." *Juristat 25* (February). On the World Wide Web at http://www.statcan.gc.ca/pub/85-002-x/2013001/article/11766-eng.pdf (retrieved 10 November 2014).

Smith, Jeff. (2012). "Normalizing Male Dominance: Gender Representation in 2012 Films." Grand Rapids Institute for Information Democracy. On the World Wide Web at http://griid.org/2013/02/12/normalizing-male-dominance-gender-representation-in-2012-films/ (retrieved 8 July 2015).

Smith, Kara. 2005. "Prebirth Gender Talk: A Case Study in Prenatal Socialization." *Women and Language 28*, 49–53.

Smith, Michael. (1990). "Patriarchal Ideology and Wife Beating: A Test of a Feminist Hypothesis." *Violence and Victims 5*, 257–73.

Statistics Canada. (2006). "Prevalence and Severity of Violence against Women." On the World Wide Web at http://www.statcan.gc.ca/pub/85-570-x/2006001/findings resultats/4144393-eng.htm (retrieved 6 December 2008).

Statistics Canada. (2011). "Family Violence in Canada: A Statistical Profile." On the World Wide Web at http://www.statcan.gc.ca/pub/85-224-x/85-224-x2010000-eng.pdf (retrieved 20 February 2012).

Statistics Canada. (2013a). "Sexual Behavior and Condom Use of 15- to 24-Year-Olds in 2003 and 2009/2010." On the World Wide Web at http://www.statcan.gc.ca/pub/82-003-x/2012001/article/11632-eng.htm (retrieved 10 November 2011).

Statistics Canada. (2013b). "Police-Reported Crime for Selected Offences, 2010 and 2011." On the World Wide Web at http://www.statcan.gc.ca/pub/85-002-x/2012001/article/11692/tbl/tbl04-eng.htm (retrieved 10 November 2014).

Statistics Canada. 2014. "Same-Sex Couples and Sexual Orientation … by the Numbers." On the World Wide Web at http://www.statcan.gc.ca/dai-quo/smr08/2014/smr08_189_2014-eng.htm (retrieved 10 November 2014).

Statistics Canada. (2015). *Family Violence in Canada: A Statistical Profile, 2013.* (Ottawa: Canadian Centre for Justice Statistics.) http://www.statcan.gc.ca/pub/85-002-x/2014001/article/14114-eng.pdf (retrieved 17 September 2015).

Steinem, G. (1994). *Moving beyond Words.* New York: Simon and Schuster.

Straus, Murray. (1995). "Trends in Cultural Norms and Rates of Partner Violence." In Sandra M. Stith and Murray A. Straus, eds., *Understanding Partner Violence: Prevalence, Causes, Consequences and Solutions* (pp. 30–33). Minneapolis, MN: National Council on Family Relations.

Sutfin, Erin L., Megan Fulcher, Ryan P. Bowles, and Charlotte J. Patterson. (2008). "How Lesbian and Heterosexual Parents

Convey Attitudes about Gender to Their Children: The Role of Gendered Environments." *Sex Roles* 58, 501–13.

Tavris, Carol. (1992). *The Mismeasure of Woman: Why Women Are Not the Better Sex, the Inferior Sex or the Opposite Sex.* New York: Touchstone.

Tjepkema, Michael. (2008). "Health Care Use among Gay, Lesbian and Bisexual Canadians." *Health Reports* 19 (1): 53–64.

Tjepkema, Michael. n.d. "Measured Obesity: Adult Obesity in Canada: Measured Height and Weight." Statistics Canada. On the World Wide Web at http://www.aboutmen.ca/application/www.aboutmen.ca/asset/upload/tiny_mce/page/link/Adult-Obesity-in-Canada.pdf (retrieved 14 January 2013).

Twenge, Jean M. (1997). "Changes in Masculine and Feminine Traits over Time: A Meta-analysis." *Sex Roles, 36,* 305–25.

Udry, J. R. (1971). *The Social Context of Marriage,* 2nd ed. Philadelphia, PA: J. B. Lippincott.

Vasey, Paul L. and Miranda Abild. (2013). "A Billion Wicked Thoughts: What the Internet Tells Us about Sexual Relationships." *Archives of Sexual Behavior 42,* 1101–03

Vrangalova, Zhana and Ritch C. Savin-Williams. (2012). "Mostly Heterosexual and Mostly Gay/Lesbian: Evidence for New Sexual Orientation Identities." *Archives of Sexual Behavior.* On the World Wide Web at http://rd.springer.com/article/10.1007/s10508-012-9921-y#page-1 (retrieved 20 February 2012).

Walters, Vivienne. (1992). "Women's Views of Their Main Health Problems." *Canadian Journal of Public Health, 83* (5), 371–74.

Weeks, Jeffrey. (1986). *Sexuality.* London: Routledge.

Welsh, Sandy. (1999). "Gender and Sexual Harassment." *Annual Review of Sociology, 25,* 169–90.

Welsh, Sandy and A. Nierobisz. (1997). "How Prevalent Is Sexual Harassment? A Research Note on Measuring Sexual Harassment in Canada." *Canadian Journal of Sociology, 22,* 505–22.

Wilson, Edward O. (1975). *Sociobiology.* Cambridge, MA: Harvard University Press.

Wilson, Edward O. (1978). *On Human Nature.* Cambridge, MA: Harvard University Press.

Wilson, Margo and Martin Daly. (1998). "Lethal and Nonlethal Violence against Wives and the Evolutionary Psychology of Male Sexual Proprietariness." In R. Emerson Dobash and Russell P. Dobash, eds., *Rethinking Violence against Women* (pp. 199–230). Thousand Oaks, CA: Sage Publications.

Wingfield, Nick. (2014). "Feminist Critics of Video Games Facing Threats in 'GamerGate' Campaign." *New York Times* 15 October.

Zayer, Linda Tuncay, Katherine Sredl, Marie Agnes Parmentier, and Catherine Coleman. (2012). "Consumption and Gender Identity in Popular Media: Discourses of Domesticity, Sexuality and Authenticity." *Consumption, Markets & Culture* 15 (4), 333–57

CHAPTER 6

ALS Association. (2014). "Ice Bucket Donations Continue to Rise: $94.3 Million since July 29." *ALS Association* 27 August. On the World Wide Web at http://www.alsa.org/news/media/press-releases/ice-bucket-challenge-082714.html (retrieved 11 September, 2014).

Anderson, B. (1989). *Imagined Communities.* London: Verso.

Arvidsson, A. (2006). *Brands: Meaning and Value in Media Culture.* London: Routledge.

BCE. (2014). "2013 Annual Report." On the World Wide Web at http://www.bce.ca/assets/investors/AR_2013/BCE_2013_Annual_Report.pdf (retrieved 20 November 2014).

Bradshaw, J. (2014). "Five Things to Know about the Postmedia-Quebecor Deal." *Globe and Mail* 6 October. On the World Wide Web at http://www.theglobeandmail.com/report-on-business/five-things-to-know-about-the-postmedia-quebecor-deal/article20941478/ (retrieved October 10, 2014).

Brodock, Katharine. (2010). "Economic and Social Factors: The Digital (Activism) Divide." In Mary Joyce, ed., *Digital Activism Decoded: The New Mechanics of Change* (pp. 71–84). New York: International Debate Education Association.

Byers, M. (2008). "*Canadian Idol* and the Myth of National Identity." In Z. Druick and A. Kotsopoulos, eds., *Programming Reality: Perspectives on English-Canadian Television* (pp. 69–84). Waterloo: Wilfred Laurier University Press.

Canadian Press [The]. (2014a). "Leonardo DiCaprio Nominates Stephen Harper to Do Ice Bucket Challenge." *CTV News* 26 August. On the World Wide Web at http://www.ctvnews.ca/entertainment/leonardo-dicaprio-nominates-stephen-harper-to-do-ice-bucket-challenge-1.1976345 (retrieved 10 September 2014).

Canadian Press [The]. (2014b). "DiCaprio Challenges Harper." *Winnipeg Free Press* 27 August, C11.

CBC. (2014). "Annual Report—2013–2014." On the World Wide Web at http://www.cbc.radio-canada.ca/_files/cbcrc/documents/annual-report/2013-2014/cbc-radio-canada-annual-report-2013-2014.pdf (retrieved 20 November 2014).

CBC News. (2013). "9 Questions about Idle No More" 5 January. On the World Wide Web at http://www.cbc.ca/news/canada/9-questions-about-idle-no-more-1.1301843 (retrieved October 20, 2014).

Chen, T., F. Law, and N. Purnell. (2014). "Apps Speed Up, and Often Muddle, Hong Kong Protesters' Messages." *Wall Street Journal* 9 October. On the World Wide Web at http://online.wsj.com/articles/whatsapp-key-to-quickly-rallying-protesters-in-hong-kong-but-groups-struggle-to-stay-on-message-1412878808 (retrieved October 20, 2014).

CRTC. (1999). *Building on Success – A Policy Framework for Canadian Television* CRTC 1999-97. On the World Wide Web at http://www.crtc.gc.ca/eng/archive/1999/PB99-97.HTM (retrieved October 5, 2014).

CRTC. (2011). "Amendment to the Television Broadcasting Regulations, 1987—Broadcast of Canadian Programs." Broadcasting Regulatory Policy CRTC 2011-288. On the World Wide Web at http://www.crtc.gc.ca/eng/archive/2011/2011-288.htm (retrieved October 5, 2014).

de Souza e Silva, A. and J. Frith. (2012). *Mobile Interfaces in Public Spaces.* New York: Routledge.

Dewing, Michael. (2010a). *Social Media: 1. An Introduction* (background paper). No. 2010-03-E. Ottawa: Library of Parliament.

Dewing, Michael. (2010b). *Social Media: 2. Who Uses Them?* (background paper). No. 2010-05-E. Ottawa: Library of Parliament.

DiCaprio, L. (2014). Post on Leonardo DiCaprio's Facebook page. 25 August. On the World Wide Web at https://www.facebook.com/LeonardoDiCaprio (retrieved 10 September 2014).

Fleras, A. (2003). *Mass Media Communication in Canada.* Toronto: Nelson.

Fleras, A. and J. L. Kunz. (2001). *Media and Minorities: Representing Diversity in a Multicultural Canada*. Toronto: Thompson Educational Publishing.

Flew, T. and T. Smith. (2011). *New Media: An Introduction*. Canadian edition. Toronto: Oxford University Press.

"FP 500: 2014." *Financial Post*. On the World Wide Web at http://www.financialpost.com/news/fp500/2014/index.html (retrieved 19 November 2014).

Gillespie, M. (1995). *Television, Ethnicity and Cultural Change*. London: Routledge.

Government of Canada. (1991). Broadcasting Act (S.C. 1991, c. 11). On the World Wide Web at http://laws-lois.justice.gc.ca/eng/acts/B-9.01/ (retrieved October 20, 2014).

Greenberg, A. 2013. "Startup Palantir Denies Its 'Prism' Software Is the NSA's 'PRISM' Surveillance System." http://www.forbes.com/sites/andygreenberg/2013/06/07/startup-palantir-denies-its-prism-software-is-the-nsas-prism-surveillance-system/ (retrieved November 25, 2014).

Greenberg, J. and Gilberds, H. (2011). "Alternative Media." In W. Straw, S. Gabriele, and I. Wagman, eds., *Intersections of Media and Communications: Concepts and Critical Frameworks* (pp. 197–216). Toronto: Emond Montgomery Publications.

Hall, S. (1980). "Encoding/Decoding." In S. Hall, D. Hobson, A. Love, and P. Willis, eds., *Culture, Media, Language* (pp. 128–38). London: Hutchinson.

Hall, S. (2013). "The Work of Representation." In S. Hall, J. Evans and S. Nixon, eds., *Representation* (pp. 1–56). Second ed. London: Sage.

Hampton, K. (2010). "Social Ties and Community in Urban Places." In H, Hiller, ed., *Urban Canada*. 2nd ed. (pp. 86–107). Toronto: Oxford University Press.

Harlow, Summer. (2011). "Social Media and Social Movements: Facebook and an Online Guatemalan Justice Movement that Moved Offline." *New Media & Society* (August 5, online), 1–19.

Herman, E. and N. Chomsky (2006). "A Propaganda Model." In M.G. Durham and D. Kellner, eds., *Media and Cultural Studies*. Revised ed. (pp. 257–94). Oxford: Blackwell Publishing.

Herman, E. and R. McChesney (1997). *The Global Media*. London: Cassell.

Hesmondalgh, D. (2013). *The Cultural Industries*. 3rd ed. London: Sage.

Hjarvard, S. (2013). *The Mediatization of Culture and Society*. New York: Routledge.

Horkheimer, M. and T. Adorno. (2006). "The Culture Industry: Enlightenment as Mass Deception." In M. G. Durham and D. Kellner, eds., *Media and Cultural Studies*. Revised ed. (pp. 41–72). Oxford: Blackwell Publishing.

Idle No More. (2014a). "The Story." On the World Wide Web at http://www.idlenomore.ca/story (retrieved October 21, 2014).

Idle No More. (2014b). "Calls for Change." On the World Wide Web at http://www.idlenomore.ca/calls_for_change (retrieved October 21, 2014).

Innis, Harold. 1951. *The Bias of Communication*. Toronto: University of Toronto Press.

International Telecommunication Union. (2015). "ICT Facts and Figures - The World in 2015." http://www.itu.int/en/ITU-D/Statistics/Pages/facts/default.aspx (retrieved 10 September 2015).

Internet World Stats. (2014). "Internet Users in the World." On the World Wide Web at http://www.internetworldstats.com/stats.htm (retrieved 8 July 2015).

Internet World Stats. (2014.) On the World Wide Web at www.internetworldstats.com. Copyright © 2001–2015, Miniwatts Marketing Group. All rights reserved worldwide.

Ipsos Reid. (2012). *The Ipsos Canadian inter@ctive Reid Report 2012 Fact Guide*. On the World Wide Web at http://www.ipsos.ca/common/dl/pdf/Ipsos_InteractiveReidReport_FactGuide_2012.pdf

ITU. 2014. "Statistics." On the World Wide Web at http://www.itu.int/en/ITU-D/Statistics/Pages/stat/default.aspx (retrieved 25 November 2014).

Kaplan, A.M. (2012). "If You Love Something, Let It Go Mobile: Mobile Marketing and Mobile Social Media 4x4." *Business Horizons*, 55 (2), 129–39.

Kaplan, A. M. and M. Haenlein. (2010). "Users of the World, Unite! The Challenges and Opportunities of Social Media." *Business Horizons*, 53, 59–68.

Le, V. (2014). "Global 2000: The World's Largest Media Companies of 2014." *Forbes Magazine* 5 July. On the World Wide Web at http://www.forbes.com/sites/vannale/2014/05/07/global-2000-the-worlds-largest-media-companies-of-2014/ (retrieved 19 November, 2014).

Lievrouw, Leah. (2011). *Alternative and Activist New Media*. Cambridge: Polity Press.

Lorimer, R., Gasher, M., and D. Skinner. (2008). *Mass Communication in Canada*. 6th ed. Toronto: Oxford University Press.

Madrid, I. (2014). "12 Times Leslie Knope Totally Nailed Being a Feminist." *GOOD* 23 September. On the World Wide Web at http://magazine.good.is/articles/leslie-knope-feminism (retrieved October 14, 2014).

McFall, L. (2004). *Advertising: A Cultural Economy*. London: Sage.

McLuhan, M. (1964). *Understanding Media: The Extensions of Man*. New York: Mentor Books.

Morozov, E. 2011. *The Net Delusion: The Dark Side of Internet Freedom*. New York: Public Affairs.

Mosco, V. (2009). *The Political Economy of Communication*. 2nd ed. London: Sage.

Newspapers Canada. (2014). "2014 Ownership Groups—Canadian Daily Newspapers." 6 May. On the World Wide Web at http://www.newspaperscanada.ca/sites/default/files/2014OwnershipofCanadianDailyNewspapers05062014.pdf (retrieved November 23, 2014).

O'Shaughnessy, M. and J. Stadler. (2005). *Media and Society*. Third ed. South Melbourne, Australia: Oxford University Press.

O'Shaughnessy, M. and J. Stadler. (2012). *Media and Society*. 5th ed. South Melbourne, Australia: Oxford University Press.

"Palantir 101." https://www.youtube.com/watch?v=f86VKjFSMJE (retrieved November 25, 2014).

Pew Research Center. (2014). "Emerging Nations Embrace Internet, Mobile Technology." *Pew Research Global Attitudes Project* 13 February. On the World Wide Web at http://www.pewglobal.org/2014/02/13/emerging-nations-embrace-internet-mobile-technology/ (retrieved October 21, 2014).

Raboy, M. and D. Taras. (2007). "On Life Support: The CBC and the Future of Public Broadcasting in Canada." In D. Taras, M. Bakardjieva, and F. Pannekoek, eds., *How Canadians Communicate II: Media, Globalization and Identity* (pp. 83–103). Calgary: University of Calgary Press.

Ramakrishnan, S. (2013). "Twitter to be Available on Mobile Phones without Internet." Reuters 5 December. On the World

Wide Web at http://www.reuters.com/article/2013/12/05/us-twitter-partnership-u2opia-idUSBRE9B413M20131205 (retrieved October 19, 2014).

Rheingold, Howard. (1993). *The Virtual Community: Finding Connection in a Computerized World*. London: Secker & Warburg.

Ritzer, G., P. Dean, and N. Jurgenson. (2012). "The Coming of Age of the Prosumer." *American Behavioral Scientist*, *56* (4), 379–98.

Robertson, R. (1995). "Glocalization: Time–Space and Homegeneity–Heterogeneity." In M. Featherston, S. Lash, and R. Robertson, eds., *Global Modernities* (pp. 25–44). London: Sage.

Roth, L. (2014). "Canadian First Peoples' Mediascapes: Reframing a Snapshot with Three Corners." In L. R. Shade, ed., *Mediascapes: New Patterns in Canadian Communication*. 4th ed. (pp. 364–89). Toronto: Nelson Education.

Science & Society Picture Library. (1874). On the World Wide Web at http://www.ssplprints.com/image.php?imgref=10300112.

Schiller, H. (1976). *Communication and Cultural Domination*. White Plains, NY: International Arts and Sciences Press.

Skinner, David and Mike Gasher. (2005). "So Much by So Few: Media Policy and Ownership in Canada." In David Skinner, James Compton, and Mike Gasher, eds., *Converging Media, Diverging Politics: A Political Economy of News in the United States and Canada* (pp. 51–76). Lanham MD: Lexington Books.

Statistics Canada. (2011). "Canadian Internet Use Survey." *The Daily* 25 May. On the World Wide Web at http://www.statcan.gc.ca/daily-quotidien/110525/dq110525b-eng.htm (retrieved October 15, 2014).

Straw, W., S. Gabriele, and I. Wagman. (2011). "The Political Economy of the Media." In W. Straw, S. Gabriele, and I. Wagman, eds., *Intersections of Media and Communications: Concepts and Critical Frameworks* (pp. 135–50). Toronto: Emond Montgomery Publications.

Sturken, M. and L. Cartwright. (2009). *Practices of Looking: An Introduction to Visual Culture*. New York: Oxford University Press.

Theckedath, D. and Thomas, T. (2012). *Media Ownership and Convergence in Canada (In Brief)*. Publication No. 2012-17-E. Ottawa: Library of Parliament. On the World Wide Web at http://www.parl.gc.ca/content/lop/researchpublications/2012-17-e.pdf (retrieved 19 November 2014).

Turkle, S. (2011). *Alone Together: Why We Expect More from Technology and Less from Each Other*. New York: Basic Books.

Utz, S. (2010). "Show Me Your Friends and I Will Tell You What Type of Person You Are: How One's Profile, Number of Friends, and Type of Friends Influence Impression Formation on Social Network Sites." *Journal of Computer-Mediated Communication*, *15*, 314–35.

Vegh, S. (2003). "Classifying Forms of Online Activism: The Case of Cyperprotests Against the World Bank." In M. McCaughey and M. Ayers, eds., *Cyberactivism: Online Activism in Theory and Practice* (pp. 71–96). London: Routledge.

Werbin, K. (2014). "Social Media, Commodification, and Surveillance." In L. R. Shade, ed., *Mediascapes: New Patterns in Canadian Communication*. 4th ed. (pp. 258–77). Toronto: Nelson Education.

CHAPTER 7

Aboriginal Affairs and Northern Development Canada. (2013). "Fact Sheet—*2011 National Household Survey* Aboriginal Demographics, Educational Attainment and Labour Market Outcomes." Ottawa: Aboriginal Affairs and Northern Development Canada. On the World Wide Web at http://www.aadnc-aandc.gc.ca/eng/1376329205785/1376329233875 (retrieved 5 January 2015).

Tweddle, Anne, Ken Battle and Sherri Torjman. (2013). *Welfare in Canada 2012*. Ottawa: Caledon Institute. On the World Wide Web at http://www.caledoninst.org/publications/pdf/1031eng.pdf

Alexander, Craig and Francis Fong. (2014). *TD Economics Special Report: The Case for Leaning Against Income Inequality in Canada*. On the World Wide Web at http://www.td.com/document/PDF/economics/special/income_inequality.pdf (retrieved 8 January 2015)

Blatchford, Andy. (2015). "Top CEO Pay Rises at Twice Average Rate." *Edmonton Journal 2* January: B1.

Bourdieu, Pierre. (1986). "The Forms of Capital." In J. C. Richardson, ed., *Handbook of Theory and Research for the Sociology of Education*. New York: Greenwood Press.

Brym, Robert (1979). "Political Conservatism in Atlantic Canada." In Robert Brym and R. James Sacouman, eds., *Underdevelopment and Social Movements in Atlantic Canada* (pp. 59–79). Toronto: New Hogtown Press.

Brym, Robert, Louise Birdsell Bauer, and Mitch McIvor. (2013). "Is Industrial Unrest Reviving in Canada? Strike Duration in the Early 21st Century." *Canadian Review of Sociology 50* (3) 222–33.

Byl, Yessy and Jason Foster. (2014). "Creating an Underclass of Disposable Workers." *Edmonton Journal 2* December: A19.

Calliste, Agnes. (1987). "Sleeping Car Porters in Canada: An Ethnically Submerged Split Labour Market." *Canadian Ethnic Studies*, *19*, 1–20.

Camfield, David. (2011). "The 'Great Recession,' the Employers' Offensive, and Canadian Public Sector Unions." *Socialist Studies*, *7* (1/2), 95–115.

Canadian Centre for Policy Alternatives (CCPA). (2015). "All in a Day's Work: CEO vs Average Pay in Canada." On the World Wide Web at https://www.policyalternatives.ca/ceo (retrieved 2 January 2015)

Canadian Press. (2014). "Call for Probe into Racism in Health Care Rejected." *Edmonton Journal* 13 December: A19.

Cavanagh, John and Chuck Collins. (2008). "The Rich and the Rest of Us." *The Nation* 30 June. On the World Wide Web at http://www.thenation.com/doc/20080630/cavanagh_collins (retrieved 12 July 2009).

Charbonneau, Léo. (2013). "Why No Quebec-style Student Protests in the Rest of Canada?" *University Affairs/Affaires universitaires*. (29 January, 2013). On the World Wide Web at http://www.universityaffairs.ca/opinion/margin-notes/why-no-quebec-style-student-protests-in-the-rest-of-canada

Conference Board of Canada. (2011). *World Income Inequality: Is the World Becoming More Unequal?* On the World Wide Web at http://www.conferenceboard.ca/files/hcp/pdfs/hot-topics/worldinequality.pdf (retrieved 8 January 2015).

Davies, Scott and Neil Guppy (2006). *The Schooled Society: An Introduction to the Sociology of Education*. Toronto: Oxford University Press.

Davis, Kingsley and Wilbert E. Moore. (1945). "Some Principles of Stratification." *American Sociological Review*, *10*, 242–49.

Dorling, Daniel, J. Rigby, B. Wheeler, D. Ballas, B. Thomas, E. Fahmy, D. Gordon, and R. Lupton. (2007). *Poverty, Wealth, and Place in Britain—1968 to 2005*. Bristol, UK: Policy Press.

Edmonton Journal. (2014). "On Giving Tuesday, Think of the Needy." *Edmonton Journal*, 2 December: A6.

Yakabuski, Konrad. (2014). "Fighting Inequality Is Not a Job for Toronto's New Mayor." *Globe and Mail*, 4 December: A19.

Employment and Social Development Canada. (2015). "Indicators of Well-Being in Canada: Financial Security—Low Income Incidence." On the World Wide Web at http://www4.hrsdc .gc.ca/.3ndic.1t.4r@-eng.jsp?iid=23 (retrieved 5 January 2015).

Esping-Andersen, Gøsta. (1990). *Three Worlds of Welfare Capitalism*. Princeton, NJ: Princeton University Press.

Everett, Jeffrey (2002). "Organizational Research and the Praxeology of Pierre Bourdieu." *Organizational Research Methods*, 5: 56–80.

Fitzgerald, Robin T. and Peter J. Carrington. (2008). "The Neighbourhood Context of Urban Aboriginal Crime." *Canadian Journal of Criminology and Criminal Justice*, 50 (5), 523–57.

Forbes Magazine. (2014) "The World's Billionaires." On the World Wide Web at http://www.forbes.com/billionaires/list/ (retrieved 4 January 2015).

Fuller, Sylvia and Leah F. Vosko. (2008). "Temporary Employment and Social Inequality in Canada: Exploring Intersections of Gender, Race and Immigration Status." *Social Indicators Research*, 88, 31–50.

Gougeon, Philippe. (2009). "Shifting Pensions." *Perspectives on Labour and Income*. (Summer), 43–51.

Grabb, Edward G. (2007). *Theories of Social Inequality*, 5th ed. Toronto: Harcourt Canada.

Grenfell, Michael. Ed. (2008). *Pierre Bourdieu: Key Concepts*. Durham, UK: Acumen.

King, Douglas E. and John A. Winterdyk. (2010). *Diversity, Inequality, and Canadian Justice*. Whitby, ON: de Sitter Publications.

Krahn, Harvey, Karen Hughes, and Graham S. Lowe. (2015). *Work, Industry and Canadian Society*, 7th ed. Toronto: Nelson Education.

Krugman, Paul. (1994). "Long-Term Riches, Short-Term Pain." *New York Times* September: F9.

Lehmann, Wolfgang. (2012). "Extra-Credential Experiences and Social Closure: Working-Class Students at University." *British Educational Research Journal*, 38 (2), 203–18.

Lenski, Gerhard. (1966). *Power and Privilege: A Theory of Social Stratification*. New York: McGraw-Hill.

Li, Peter. (1982). "Chinese Immigrants on the Canadian Prairie, 1919–47." *Canadian Review of Sociology and Anthropology*, 19, 527–40.

Luong, May. (2011). "The Wealth and Finances of Employed Low-income Families." *Perspectives on Labour and Income, 23* (Autumn), 29–38.

Macdonald, David. (2014). "Outrageous Fortune: Documenting Canada's Wealth Gap." Ottawa: Canadian Centre for Policy Alternatives. On the World Wide Web at https://www .policyalternatives.ca/outrageous-fortune (retrieved 5 January 2015).

Marglin, Stephen A. and Juliet B. Schor, eds. (1990). *The Golden Age of Capitalism: Re-interpreting the Postwar Experience*. Oxford, UK: Clarendon.

Mason, Gary. (2013). "University Students: Another Day Smarter, but Deeper in Debt." *Globe and Mail*, 6 September, 2013.

On the World Wide Web at http://www.theglobeandmail .com/globe-debate/another-day-smarter-but-deeper-in-debt/ article14157421

Marx, Karl. (1904 [1859]). *A Contribution to the Critique of Political Economy*, N. Stone, trans. Chicago: Charles H. Kerr.

Marx, Karl and Friedrich Engels. (1972 [1848]). "Manifesto of the Communist Party." In R. Tucker, ed., *The Marx-Engels Reader* (pp. 331–62). New York: Norton.

Milan, Anne and Kelly Tran. (2004) "Blacks in Canada: A Long History." *Canadian Social Trends* (Spring), 2–7.

Morissette, René and Xuelin Zhang. (2007). "Revisiting Wealth Inequality." *Perspectives on Labour and Income* (Spring), 6–17.

Myles, John and Adnan Turegun. (1994). "Comparative Studies in Class Structure." *Annual Review of Sociology, 20*, 103–24.

National Council of Welfare. (2008). *Poverty Profile, 2004*. Ottawa.

National Council of Welfare. (2010). *Welfare Incomes 2009*. Ottawa.

O'Neill, Jeff. (1991). "Changing Occupational Structure." *Canadian Social Trends* (Winter), 10.

OECD (Organisation for Economic Co-operation and Development). (2011). *Divided We Stand: Why Inequality Keeps Rising*. On the World Wide Web at http://www.oecd.org/docu ment/51/0,3746,en_2649_33933_49147827_1_1_1_1,00.html (retrieved 14 January 2012).

Ortiz, David G. (2007). "Confronting Oppression with Violence: Inequality, Military Infrastructure and Dissident Repression." *Mobilization: An International Quarterly, 12* (3): 219–38.

Palmer, Bryan. (1986). *The Character of Class Struggle: Essays in Canadian Working Class History, 1850–1985*. Toronto: McClelland and Stewart.

Parkin, Frank. (1972). *Class Inequality and Political Order*. London: Paladin.

Parkin, Frank. (1979). *Marxism and Class Theory: A Bourgeois Critique*. London: Tavistock.

Piketty, Thomas. (2014). *Capital in the Twenty-First Century*. Cambridge, MA: Harvard University Press.

Pratt, Sheila. (2014). "Rate of Kids in Poverty Still High, Says Report." *Edmonton Journal* 25 November: A3.

Raphael, Dennis. (2011). *Poverty and Policy in Canada: Implications for Health and Quality of Life*, 2nd ed. Toronto: Canadian Scholars' Press.

Remington, Thomas F. (2011). *The Politics of Inequality in Russia*. Cambridge: Cambridge University Press.

Sauvé, Roger and Nathan Battams. (2013). *The Current State of Canadian Family Finances*. Ottawa: Vanier Institute of the Family. On the World Wide Web at http://www.vanierinstitute .ca/include/get.php?nodeid=3301 (retrieved 4 January 2014).

Shaker, Erika and David Macdonald, with Nigel Wodrich. (2013). *Degrees of Uncertainty: Navigating the Changing Terrain of University Finance*. Ottawa: Canadian Centre for Policy Alternatives. On the World Wide Web at https://www.policyalternatives.ca/degrees-of -uncertainty (retrieved 9 January 2015).

Sharpe, Andrew and Evan Capeluck. (2012). *The Impact of Redistribution on Income Inequality in Canada and the Provinces, 1981–2010*. Ottawa: Centre for the Study of Living Standards. CSLS Research Report 2012-08.

Statistics Canada. (2005). *Income in Canada*. Catalogue No. 75-202-XIE. Ottawa: Minister of Industry.

Statistics Canada. (2011). "2011 *National Household Survey*, Employment Income Statistics in 2010 by National Occupational Classification." Catalogue No. 99-014-X2011042.

On the World Wide Web at http://www12.statcan.gc.ca/nhs
-enm/2011/dp-pd/dt-td/Av-eng.cfm?LANG=E&APATH
=5&DETAIL=0&DIM=5&FL=A&FREE=0&GC=61&GID
=0&GK=1&GRP=0&PID=106738&PRID=0&PTYPE
=105277&S=0&SHOWALL=0&SUB=0&Temporal
=2013&THEME=98&VID=22816&VNAMEE=&VNAMEF
= (retrieved 5 January 2015).

Statistics Canada. (2013). "2011 National Household Survey: Data
Tables." Catalogue No. 99-012-X2011033. On the World Wide
Web at http://www12.statcan.gc.ca/nhs-enm/2011/dp-pd/dt-td/
Lp-eng.cfm?LANG=E&APATH=3&DETAIL=0&
DIM=0&FL=A&FREE=0&GC=0&GID=0&GK=0&GRP=0
&PID=0&PRID=0&PTYPE=105277&S=0&SHOWALL
=1&SUB=0&Temporal=2013&THEME=96&VID=0&VNAME
E=&VNAMEF= (retrieved 4 January 2015).

Statistics Canada. (2014a). "2011 National Household Survey:
Data Tables." Catalogue No. 99-014-X2011042. On the World
Wide Web at http://www12.statcan.gc.ca/nhs-enm/2011/
dp-pd/dt-td/Rp-eng.cfm?LANG=E&APATH=3&DETAIL
=0&DIM=0&FL=A&FREE=0&GC=0&GID=0&GK=0
&GRP=1&PID=106738&PRID=0&PTYPE=105277&S=0&S
HOWALL=0&SUB=0&Temporal=2013&THEME=98&VID
=0&VNAMEE=&VNAMEF= (retrieved 5 January 2015).

Statistics Canada. (2014b). "Low Income Lines, 2012–2013."
Catalogue No. 75F0002M—No. 003. On the World Wide Web
at http://www.statcan.gc.ca/pub/75f0002m/75f0002m2014003
-eng.htm (retrieved 5 January 2015).

Statistics Canada. (2015). "Summary Statistics: Labour—
Employment and Unemployment." On the World Wide Web
at http://www5.statcan.gc.ca/subject-sujet/result-resultat?
pid=2621&id=1803&lang=eng&type=CST&sortType=1&pag
eNum=2 (retrieved 5 January 2014).

Swanson, Jean. (2001). *Poor-Bashing: The Politics of Exclusion.*
Toronto: Between the Lines.

Tanner, Julian, Harvey Krahn, and Timothy F. Hartnagel. (1995).
*Fractured Transitions from School to Work: Revisiting the Dropout
Problem.* Toronto: Oxford University Press.

Taylor, Alison and Harvey Krahn. (2009). "Streaming in/for the
New Economy." In Cynthia Levine-Raskyed ed., *Canadian
Perspectives on the Sociology of Education* (pp. 103–23). Toronto:
Oxford University Press.

Toneguzzi, Mario. (2014). "Alberta Home to Top Earners."
Edmonton Journal 19 November: B3.

Turcotte, Martin. (2011). "Intergenerational Education Mobility:
University Completion in Relation to Parents' Education
Level." *Canadian Social Trends* (Winter): 38–44.

Tweddle, Anne, Ken Battle, and Sherri Torjman. (2013). *Welfare
in Canada 2012*, Tables 3 and 6. Ottawa: Caledon Institute of
Social Policy.

Wallis, Maria A. and Siuming Kwok (2008). *Daily Struggles: The
Deepening Racialization and Feminization of Poverty in Canada.*
Toronto: Canadian Scholars' Press.

Wanner, Richard A. (2009). "Social Mobility in Canada: Concepts,
Patterns, and Trends." In Edward Grabb and Neil Guppy, eds.,
Social Inequality in Canada: Patterns, Problems, Policies, 5th ed.
(pp. 116–32). Toronto: Pearson.

Weber, Max. (1948 [1922]). *Max Weber: Essays in Sociology.*
H. H. Gerth and C. W. Mills, eds., and trans. London:
Routledge & Kegan Paul.

Westergaard, John. (1995). *Who Gets What? The Hardening of Class
Inequality in the Late Twentieth Century.* Cambridge, UK: Polity
Press.

Whyte, Martin King. (2010). *Myth of the Social Volcano: Perceptions
of Inequality and Distributive Injustice in Contemporary China.*
Stanford, CA: Stanford University Press.

Wilkinson, Richard and Kate Pickett. (2010). *The Spirit Level:
Why Equality is Better for Everyone.* London: Penguin
Books.

Wolff, Edward N. (1991). "The Distribution of Household Wealth:
Methodological Issues, Time Trends, and Cross-sectional
Comparisons." In Lars Osberg, ed., *Economic Inequality and
Poverty: International Perspectives* (pp. 92–133). Armonk, NY:
Sharpe.

Wolfson, Michael, Mike Veall, and Neil Brooks. (2014). *Piercing the
Veil—Private Corporations and the Income of the Affluent.* On the
World Wide Web at https://uwaterloo.ca/school-of-accounting
-and-finance/sites/ca.school-of-accounting-and-finance/files/
uploads/files/wolfson-brooks-veall_-_incomes_of_affluent.pdf
(retrieved 5 January 2015).

Wright, Erik Olin. (1985). *Classes.* London: Verso Books.

Yalnizyan, Armine. (2010). *The Rise of Canada's Richest 1%.* Ottawa:
Canadian Centre for Policy Alternatives.

Zeitlin, Irving M. with Robert Brym. (1991). *The Social Condition of
Humanity.* Toronto: Oxford University Press.

CHAPTER 8

Acker, Joan. (1990). "Hierarchies, Jobs, Bodies: A Theory of
Gendered Organizations." *Gender & Society, 4* (2), 139–58.

Aumann, Kerstin, Ellen Galinsky, and Kenneth Matos. (2011). *The
New Male Mystique.* Families and Work Institute. On the World
Wide Web at http://familiesandwork.org/site/research/reports/
newmalemystique.pdf (retrieved 12 November 2013).

Balkissoon, Denise. (2013). "Working Dads Push for More Family-
Friendly Policies, Making Life Better for Working Moms."
On the World Wide Web at http://www.canadianbusiness.com/
economy/working-dads-push-for-more-family-friendly
-policies-making-life-better-for-working-moms/ (retrieved
5 September 2014).

Baxter, Janeen. (2000). "The Joys and Justice of Housework."
Sociology, 34, 609–31.

Beaujot, Roderic and Andersen, Robert. (2007). "Time-crunch:
Impact of Time Spent in Paid and Unpaid Work, and its Division
in Families." *Canadian Journal of Sociology, 32* (3), 295–315.

Becker, Gary. (1993). "Nobel Lecture: The Economic Way of
Looking at Behavior." *The Journal of Political Economy, 101* (3),
385–409.

Belkin, Lisa. (2003). "The Opt-Out Revolution." *The New York
Times.* On the World Wide Web at http://irasilver.org/wp
-content/uploads/2011/08/Reading-Opt-out-revolution
-Belkin.pdf (retrieved 20 January 2013).

Bellavia, Gina and Michael Frone. (2003). "Work–Family
Conflict." In Julian Barling, Kevin Kelloway and Michael
Frone, eds., *Handbook of Work Stress* (pp. 113–48). Thousand
Oaks, CA: Sage.

Berdahl, Jennifer L., and Sue H. Moon. (2013). "Workplace
Mistreatment of Middle Class Workers Based on Sex,
Parenthood, and Caregiving." *Journal of Social Issues, 69* (2),
341–66.

Berk, Sarah Fenstermaker. (1985). *The Gender Factory: The Appointment of Work in American Households*. New York: Plenum Press.

Bianchi, Suzanne M. and Melissa A. Milkie. (2010). "Work and Family Research in the First Decade of the 21st Century." *Journal of Marriage and Family, 72* (3), 705–25.

Bianchi, Suzanne M., Melissa A. Milkie, Liana C. Sayer, and John P. Robinson. (2000). "Is Anyone Doing the Housework? Trends in the Gender Division of Household Labor." *Social Forces, 79* (1), 191–228.

Bianchi, Suzanne M., John Robinson, and Melissa A. Milkie. (2006). *The Changing Rhythm of American Family Life*. New York: Russell Sage Foundation.

Bianchi, Suzanne M., Liana C. Sayer, Melissa A. Milkie, John. P. Robinson. (2012). "Housework: Who Did, Does or Will Do It, and How Much Does it Matter?" *Social Forces, 91* (1), 55–63.

Bielby, William and James Baron. (1986). "Men and Women at Work: Sex Segregation and Statistical Discrimination." *American Journal of Sociology, 91* (4),759–99.

Bird, Chloe, E. and Patricia Rieker. (1999). "Gender Matters: An Integrated Model for Understanding Men's and Women's Health." *Social Science and Medicine, 48* (6),745–55.

Blair-Loy, Mary. (2003). *Competing Devotions*. Cambridge: Harvard University Press.

Blau, Francine and Jed DeVaro. (2007). "New Evidence on Gender Differences in Promotion Rates: An Empirical Analysis of a Sample of New Hires." *NBER Working Paper Series*.

Boyd, Monica. (2014). "Gender Inequality: Economic and Political Aspects." In Robert Brym, ed., *New Society*, 7th Canadian ed. (pp. 156–81). Toronto: Nelson.

Brines, Julie. (1994). "Economic Dependency, Gender, and the Division of Labor at Home." *American Journal of Sociology, 100*, 652–88.

Browne, Irene and Joya Misra. (2003). "The Intersection of Gender and Race in the Labor Market." *Annual Review of Sociology, 29* (1), 487–513.

Canada's Top 100 Employers. (2014). Canada's Top Family-Friendly Employers. On the World Wide Web at http://canadastop100.com/family/ (retrieved 5 June 2014).

Canadian Medical Association. (2012). "Statistical Information on Canadian Physicians." On the World Wide Web at http://www.cma.ca/statistical-info-canadian-physicians (retrieved 20 January 2014).

Carriero, R. (2011). "Perceived Fairness and Satisfaction with the Division of Housework among Dual-Earner Couples in Italy." *Marriage & Family Review, 47*, 436–58.

Ceci, Stephen J. and Wendy M. Williams. (2010). *The Mathematics of Sex: How Biology and Society Conspire to Limit Talented Women and Girls*. New York, NY: Oxford University Press.

Clement, Wallace and John Myles. (1994). *Relations of Ruling: Class and Gender in Postindustrial Societies*. Montreal: McGill-Queen's University Press.

Cohen, Philip N. and Matt L. Huffman. (2003). "Occupational Segregation and the Devaluation of Women's Work across U.S. Labor Markets." *Social Forces, 81* (3), 881–908.

Craig, Lyn. (2006). "Parental Education, Time in Paid Work and Time with Children: An Australian Time-Diary Analysis." *The British Journal of Sociology, 57* (4), 553–75.

Creese, Gillian and Daiva Stasiulis. (1996). "Introduction: Intersections of Gender, Race, Class, and Sexuality." *Studies in Political Economy, 51* (1), 5–14

Doucet, Andrea. (2006). *Do Men Mother? Fathering, Care, and Domestic Responsibility*. Toronto: University of Toronto Press.

Duffy, Ann and Norene Pupo. (1992). *Part-time Paradox: Connecting Gender, Work & Family*. Toronto, ON: McClelland & Stewart.

Eccles, Jacquelynne S., Robert Roeser, Allan Wigfield, and Carol Freedman-Doen. (1999). "Academic and Motivational Pathways through Middle Childhood." In L. Balter, ed., *Child Psychology* (pp. 287–377). Philadelphia, PA: Psychology Press.

Eichler, Leah. (2013a). "When Men Take Paternity Leave, the Whole Family Wins." On the World Wide Web at http://www.huffingtonpost.ca/leah-eichler/paternity-leave-quota_b_3411237.html (retrieved 4 June 2014).

Eichler, Leah. (2013b). "Would More Men Take a 'Use It Or Lose It' Paternity Leave?" *Globe and Mail*. On the World Wide Web at http://www.theglobeandmail.com/report-on-business/careers/career-advice/life-at-work/would-more-men-take-a-use-it-or-lose-it-paternity-leave/article11156542 (retrieved 20 January 2014).

England, Paula. (2005). "Gender Inequality in Labor Markets: The Role of Motherhood and Segregation." *Social Politics: International Studies in Gender, State and Society, 12* (2), 264–88.

Fast, Janet E., and Norah C. Keating. (2000). "Family Caregiving and Consequences for Carers: Toward a Policy Research Agenda." (CPRN Discussion Paper #F/10). Ottawa, ON: Canadian Policy Research Networks.

Feenstra, Nicole. (2014). "WestJet Passenger Leaves Sexist Note on Plane for Female Pilot." *Canoe*. On the World Wide Web at http://blogs.canoe.ca/travel/what-the/westjet-passenger-leaves-sexist-note-on-plane-for-female-pilot (retrieved 20 May 2014).

Ferrao, Vincent. (2010). "Paid Work." *Women in Canada: A Gender-Based Statistical Report*. Statistics Canada. Catalogue No. 89-503-X.

Ferree, Myra Marx. (1991). "The Gender Division of Labor in Two-Earner Marriages: Dimensions of Variability and Change." *Journal of Family Issues, 12* (2), 158–80.

Fortin, Nicole and Michael Huberman. (2002). "Occupational Gender Segregation and Women's Wages in Canada: An Historical Perspective." *Canadian Public Policy, 28* (Supplement), S11-S39.

Frone, Michael R., John K. Yardley, and Karen S. Markel. (1997). "Developing and Testing an Integrative Model of the Work-Family Interface." *Journal of Vocational Behavior, 50* (2), 145-67.

Gorman, Elizabeth. (2005). "Gender Stereotypes, Same-Gender Preferences, and Organizational Variation in the Hiring of Women: Evidence from Law Firms." *American Sociological Review, 70* (4), 702–28.

Gorodzeisky, Anastasia and Moshe Semyonov. (2005). "Labor Migration, Remittances and Household Income: A Comparison between Filipino and Filipina Overseas Workers." *International Migration Review, 39* (1), 45–68.

Greenhaus, Jeffery H. and Nadine Beutell. (1985). "Sources of Conflict between Work and Family Roles." *The Academy of Management Review, 10* (1), 76–88.

Hays, Sharon. (1996). *The Cultural Contradictions of Motherhood*. New Haven, CT: Yale University Press.

Jain, Harish C., John J. Lawler, Bing Bai, and Eun Kyung Lee. (2010). "Effectiveness of Canada's Employment Equity Legislation for Women (1997–2004): Implications for Policy

Makers." *Relations industrielles/Industrial Relations, 65* (3), 304–29.

Jarman, Jennifer, Robert Blackburn, and Girts Racko. (2012). "The Dimensions of Occupational Gender Segregation in Industrial Countries." *British Journal of Sociology, 46* (6),1003–19.

Kaufman, Robert L. (2002). "Assessing Alternative Perspectives on Race and Sex Employment Segregation." *American Sociological Review, 67* (4), 547–72.

Kay, Fiona M. and Joan Brockman. (2000). "Barriers to Gender Equality in the Canadian Legal Establishment." *Feminist Legal Studies, 8* (2),169–98.

Kay, Fiona and John Hagan. (1998). "Raising the Bar: The Gender Stratification of Law-Firm Capital." *American Sociological Review, 63* (5), 728–43.

King, Deborah. (1988). "Multiple Consciousness: The Context of a Black Feminist Ideology." *Signs, 14* (1), 42–72.

Lennon, Mary Clare and Sarah Rosenfield. (1994). "Relative Fairness and the Division of Housework: The Importance of Options." *American Journal of Sociology, 100* (2), 506–31.

Licuanan, Patricia. (1994). "The Socio-Economic Impact of Domestic Worker Migration: Individual, Family, Community, Country." In N. Heyzer, G. Lycklama à Nijeholt, and N. Weerakoon, eds., *The Trade in Domestic Workers: Causes, Mechanisms, and Consequences of International Migration* (pp. 103–15). London: Zed.

Livingston, Gretchen and Kim Parker. (2011). "A Tale of Two Fathers." *Pew Research Social and Demographic Trends.* On the World Wide Web at http://www.pewsocialtrends .org/2011/06/15/a-tale-of-two-fathers (retrieved 20 January 2014).

Marshall, Katherine. (2009). "The Family Work Week." *Perspectives on Labour and Income.* Statistics Canada. Catalogue No. 75-001-X.

Marshall, Katherine. (2011). "Paid and Unpaid Work over Three Generations." *Perspectives on Labour and Income.* Statistics Canada.

McFarland, Janet. (2013). "Female MBA Grads Earn Less at Career Outset, Struggle to Catch Up: Study." *Globe and Mail.* On the World Wide Web at http://www.theglobeandmail.com/ report-on-business/careers/business-education/female-mba -grads-earn-less-at-career-outset-struggle-to-catch-up-study/ article15734154 (retrieved 5 June 2014).

Meerman, Marije. (2000). *The Care Chain* (Amsterdam: VPRO-TV).

Mincer, Jacob and Solomon Polachek. (1974). "Family Investments in Human Capital: Earnings of Women." *The Journal of Political Economy, 82* (2), S76–S108.

Morissette, Rene, Garnett Picot and Yuqian Lu. (2013). "The Evolution of Canadian Wages over the Last Three Decades." *Analytical Studies Branch Research Paper Series.* Statistics Canada. Catalogue No. 11F0019M-347. On the World Wide Web at http://www.statcan.gc.ca/pub/11f0019m/11f0019m2013347 -eng.pdf.

Nash, June C. and Patricia Fernandez-Kelly, eds. (1985). *Women, Men and the International Division of Labor.* Albany, NY: State University of New York Press.

O'Campo, Pat and Blair Wheaton. (2011). "Neighbourhood Effects on Health and Well-Being." Toronto: Department of Sociology, University of Toronto. Data set.

O'Kane, Josh. (2013) "Paternity-Leave Dads Seen as 'Not Man Enough.' " *Globe and Mail.* On the World Wide Web at http://

www.theglobeandmail.com/report-on-business/careers/ business-education/paternity-leave-dads-seen-as-not-man -enough/article13821961 (retrieved 20 January 2014).

Ontario Ministry of Labour. (2013). "Equal Work for Equal Pay." On the World Wide Web at http://www.labour.gov.on.ca/ english/es/pubs/guide/equalpay.php (retrieved 10 June 2014).

Ornstein, Michael. (2010). "Racialization and Gender of Lawyers in Ontario: A Report for the Law Society of Upper Canada." *The Law Society of Upper Canada.* On the World Wide Web at http://www.lsuc.on.ca/media/convapril10_ornstein.pdf (retrieved 20 January 2014).

Padavic, Irene and Barbara F. Reskin. (2002). *Women and Men at Work.* 2nd ed. Thousand Oaks, CA: Pine Forge Press.

Pampel, Fred. (2010). "Cohort Changes in the Socio-demographic Determinants of Gender Egalitarianism." *Social Forces, 86* (3), 961–82.

Parrenas, Rhacel S. (2000). "Migrant Filipina Domestic Workers and the International Division of Reproductive Labor." *Gender and Society, 14* (4), 560–80.

Pinchbeck, Ivy. (1930). *Women Workers and the Industrial Revolution, 1750–1850.* London: George Routledge.

Reskin, Barbara F. (2002). "Rethinking Employment Discrimination and its Remedies." In M. F. Guillen, R. Collins, P. England, and M. Meyer, eds., *The New Economic Sociology: Developments in an Emerging Field* (pp. 218–39). New York: Russell Sage Foundation.

Reskin, Barbara F. and Heidi Hartmann. (1986). *Women's Work, Men's Work: Sex Segregation on the Job.* Washington, DC: National Academy Press.

Reskin, Barbara F. and Patricia Roos. (1990). *Job Queues, Gender Queues: Explaining Women's Inroads into Male Occupations.* Philadelphia: Temple University Press.

Rosenfield, Sarah. (1999). "Splitting the Difference: Gender, the Self, and Mental Health." In C. S. Aneshensel and J. Phelan, eds., *The Handbook of the Sociology of Mental Health,* (pp. 209–24). New York: Kluwer Academic.

Schieman, Scott, Markus Schafer, and Mitch McIvor. (2013). "The Rewards of Authority in the Workplace: Do Gender and Age Matter?" *Sociological Perspectives, 56* (1), 75–96.

Schieman, Scott, Marisa Young, and Paul Glavin. (Forthcoming, 2014). *A Brief Description of the Canadian Workforce: Findings from the 2012–2014 Canadian Work, Stress and Health Study.* Toronto, ON: University of Toronto.

Schroeder, K. A., L. L Blood, and D. Maluso. (1993). "Gender Differences and Similarities between Male and Female Undergraduate Students Regarding Expectations for Career and Family Roles." *College Student Journal, 27* (1), 237–49.

Simon, Robin W. (1995). "Gender, Multiple Roles, Role Meaning, and Mental Health." *Journal of Health and Social Behavior, 36* (2), 182–94.

Slaughter, Anne-Marie. (2012). "Why Women Still Can't Have It All." *The Atlantic.* On the World Wide Web at http://www .theatlantic.com/magazine/archive/2012/07/why-women-still -cant-have-it-all/309020 (retrieved 20 January 2014).

Statistics Canada. (2006). *Census of Canada: National Household Survey.* On the World Wide Web at http://www12.statcan .gc.ca/census-recensement/2006/index-eng.cfm

Statistics Canada. (2008). "*Labour Force Survey*, CANSIM Tables 282-0002 and 282-0014." On the World Wide Web at http://www .statcan.gc.ca/pub/71-222-x/2008001/sectiong/g-involuntary -involontaire-eng.htm (retrieved 4 September 2014).

Statistics Canada. (2011). *Census of Canada: National Household Survey*. On the World Wide Web at http://www12.statcan.gc.ca /census-recensement/index-eng.cfm (retrieved 1 January 2014).

Statistics Canada (2012). Table 282-0002: *Labour Force Survey (LFS) Estimates, by Sex and Detailed Age Group, Annual (Persons Unless Otherwise Noted)*, CANSIM (database). On the World Wide Web at http://well-being.esdc.gc.ca/misme -iowb/.3ndic.1t.4r@-eng.jsp?iid=13.

Statistics Canada. 2014a. "*Labour Force Survey*, CANSIM Table 2820087." On the World Wide Web at http://dc2.chass .utoronto.ca.myaccess.library.utoronto.ca/cgi-bin/cansimdim/ c2_getArrayDim.pl (retrieved 5 October 2014).

Statistics Canada. 2014b. "Historical Statistics of Canada: Section D: The Labour Force." http://www.statcan.gc.ca/pub/11-516-x/ sectiond/4057750-eng.htm (retrieved 5 October 2014).

Stichman, A. J., K. D. Hassell, C. A. Archbold. (2010). "Strength in Numbers? A Test of Kanter's Theory of Tokenism." *Journal of Criminal Justice, 38* (4), 633–39

Stone, Pamela. (2007). *Opting Out? Why Women Really Quit Careers and Head Home*. Berkeley, CA: University of California Press.

Truitt, Jos. (2011). "Closing the Gender Wage Gap at the Federal Level." *Feministing*. On the World Wide Web at http://feministing .com/2011/08/18/closing-the-federal-gender-wage-gap.

Wallace, Jean and Marisa Young. (2008). "Parenthood and Productivity: A Study of Demands, Resources, and Family-Friendly Firms." *Journal of Vocational Behavior, 72* (1), 110–22.

Williams, Joan C. (2000). *Unbending Gender: Why Family and Work Conflict and What to Do About It*. New York, NY: Oxford University Press.

Williams, Joan C. and Heather Boushey. (2010). *The Three Faces of Work–Family Conflict: The Poor, the Professionals, and the Missing Middle*. Washington, DC, and San Francisco: Center for American Progress and Center for Work Life Law.

Women in Canada. (2000). "The Facts about Women and Poverty." On the World Wide Web at http://www.canadianwomen.org/ facts-about-poverty (retrieved 5 September 2014).

World Economic Forum. (2013). *The Global Gender Gap Report 2013*. On the World Wide Web at http://www3.weforum.org/docs/ WEF_GenderGap_Report_2013.pdf (retrieved 4 June 2014).

Young, Marisa. (2010). "Gender Differences in Precarious Work." *Relations Industrielles/Industrial Relations, 65* (1), 74–97.

Young, Marisa and Scott Schieman. (2014). "Gender Differences in Employment Trade-offs to Reduce Work-Family Conflict." Presented at the annual *Canadian Sociological Association Meetings*, Brock University, St. Catharines Ontario.

Young, Marisa, Scott Schieman, and Melissa Milkie. (2014). "Spouse's Work-to-Family Conflict, Family Stressors, and Mental Health among Dual-Earner Mothers and Fathers." *Society & Mental Health, 4* (1), 1–20

Young, Marisa, Jean Wallace, and Alicia Polachek. (2013). "Gender Differences in Perceived Domestic Equity: A Study of Professionals." *Journal of Family Issues* (November 21).

Young, Marisa and Blair Wheaton. (2013). "The Impact of Neighborhood Social Composition on Work–Family Conflict and Distress." *Journal of Health and Social Behavior, 54* (4), 481–97.

CHAPTER 9

Abella, Irving, and Harold Troper. (1982). *None Is Too Many: Canada and the Jews of Europe, 1933–1948*. Toronto: Lester and Orpen Dennys.

Aboriginal Affairs and Northern Development Canada. (2013). "Aboriginal Demographics and Well-Being." Ottawa: Aboriginal Affairs and Northern Development Canada. On the World Wide Web at http://www.aadnc-aandc.gc.ca/ eng/1358878601807/1358878656346#ch2_2 (retrieved 21 November 2014).

Adeyanju, Charles. (2010). *Deadly Fever: Racism, Disease and a Media Panic*. Halifax: Fernwood Publishing.

Alfred, Taiaiake. (1999). *Peace, Power and Righteousness: An Indigenous Manifesto*. Toronto: Oxford University Press.

Anderson, Benedict. (1983). *Imagined Communities: Reflections on the Origin and Spread of Nationalism*. London: Verso.

Angus Reid Group. (1991). *Multiculturalism and Canadians: National Attitude Study 1991*. Ottawa: Multiculturalism and Citizenship Canada.

Avery, Donald. (1995). *Reluctant Host: Canada's Response to Immigrant Workers*. Toronto: McClelland and Stewart.

Balthazar, Louis. (1993). "The Faces of Quebec Nationalism." In Alain-G. Gagnon, ed., *Quebec: State and Society*, 2nd ed. (pp. 2–17). Scarborough, ON: Nelson.

Barkan, Elazar. (1992). *The Retreat of Scientific Racism*. Cambridge, UK: Cambridge University Press.

Barker, Martin. (1981). *The New Racism: Conservatives and the Ideology of the Tribe*. London: Junction Books.

Basran, Gurcharn, and Li Zong. (1998). "Devaluation of Foreign Credentials as Perceived by Non–white Professional Immigrants." *Canadian Ethnic Studies, 30*, 6–23. Bissoondath, Neil. (1994). *Selling Illusions: The Cult of Multiculturalism*. Toronto: Stoddart.

Bolaria, B. Singh, and Peter Li (1988) *Racial Oppression in Canada* Toronto: Garamond.

Boldt, Menno. (1993). *Surviving as Indians: The Challenge of Self–Government*. Toronto: University of Toronto Press.

Bonacich, Edna. (1972). "A Theory of Ethnic Antagonism: The Split Labor Market." *American Sociological Review, 37*, 547–59.

Bonacich, Edna. (1979). "The Past, Present and Future of Split Labor Market Theory." *Research in Race and Ethnic Relations, 1*, 17–64.

Bonacich, Edna. (1980). "Class Approaches to Ethnicity and Race." *Insurgent Sociologist, 10*, 9–23.

Bouchard, Gérard, and Charles Taylor. (2008). *Building the Future: A Time for Reconciliation*. On the World Wide Web at http:// www.accommodements.qc.ca/documentation/rapports/rapport –final–integral–en.pdf (16 July 2009).

Bourgeault, Ron. (1988). "The South African Connection." *Canadian Dimension, 21*, 6–10.

Brown, Louise, and Brett Popplewell. (2008). "Board Okays Black-Focused School." *Toronto Star* 30 January. On the World Wide Web at http://www.thestar.com/News/article/298714 (retrieved 15 July 2009).

Brym, Robert, with Bonnie Fox. (1989). *From Culture to Power: The Sociology of English Canada*. Toronto: Oxford University Press.

Brym, Robert, and Rhonda Lenton. (1993). "The Distribution of Anti–Semitism in Canada in 1984." In Robert Brym, William Shaffir, and Morton Weinfeld, eds., *The Jews in Canada* (pp. 112–19). Toronto: Oxford University Press.

Castles, Stephen, and Godula Kosack. (1984). *Immigrant Workers and Class Structure in Western Europe*. London: Oxford University Press.

Citizenship and Immigration Canada. (1996). *You Asked About ... Immigration and Citizenship.* Ottawa: Supply and Services Canada.

Citizenship and Immigration Canada. (2002). "Family-Class Immigration." On the World Wide Web at http://www.cis.gc.ca/english/sponsor/index.html (retrieved 10 September 2003).

Citizenship and Immigration Canada. (2012). "Facts and Figures 2012: Immigration Overview—Permanent and Temporary Residents." On the World Wide Web at http://www.cic.gc.ca/english/resources/statistics/menu-fact.asp (retrieved 13 November 2014).

Citizenship and Immigration Canada. (2014). "Six Selection Factors—Federal Skilled Workers." On the World Wide Web at http://www.cic.gc.ca/english/immigrate/skilled/apply-factors.asp.

Clement, Wallace. (1975). *The Canadian Corporate Elite.* Toronto: McClelland and Stewart.

Cole, Douglas, and Ira Chaikin. (1990). *An Iron Hand upon the People: The Law against the Potlatch on the Northwest Coast.* Vancouver: Douglas and McIntyre.

Collins, Jock. (1988). *Migrant Hands in a Distant Land: Australia's Post–war Immigration.* Sydney: Pluto Press.

Congress of Aboriginal Peoples. (2008). "The Forgotten People and the Indian Act." On the World Wide Web at http://www.abo-peoples.org/about/Indian_Act.html (retrieved 15 July 2009).

Daenzer, Pat. (1993). *Regulating Class Privilege.* Toronto: Canadian Scholars' Press.

Darroch, Gordon. (1979). "Another Look at Ethnicity Stratification and Social Mobility in Canada." *Canadian Journal of Sociology, 4,* 1–25.

Doob, Christopher. (1996). *Racism: An American Cauldron.* New York: HarperCollins. "A Dream That Does Not Fade" (Quebec's Sovereignty)." (2005). *The Economist* 3 December: 8.

Economic Council of Canada. (1991). *Economic and Social Impacts of Immigration.* Ottawa: Supply and Services Canada.

Farmer, Nathan. (2005). "Kingston Police Chief Apologizes for Force's Systemic Racism." On the World Wide Web at http://friendsofgrassynarrows.com/item.php.?427F (retrieved 12 November 2005).

Fiske, Jo-Anne. (1996). "The Womb Is to the Nation as the Heart Is to the Body: Ethnopolitical Discourses of the Canadian Indigenous Women's Movement." *Studies in Political Economy 51,* 65–96.

Fleras, Augie. (2012). *Unequal Relations: An Introduction to Race, Ethnic, and Aboriginal Dynamics in Canada,* 7th ed. Toronto: Pearson.

Fleras, Augie and Jean Leonard Elliott. (1996). *Unequal Relations: An Introduction to Race, Ethnic and Aboriginal Dynamics in Canada.* Scarborough ON: Prentice-Hall Canada.

Fournier, Marcel, Michael Rosenberg, and Deena White. (1997). *Quebec Society: Critical Issues.* Scarborough, ON: Prentice Hall.

Frideres, James, and René Gadacz. (2012). *Aboriginal People in Canada,* 9th ed. Toronto: Pearson.

Gerber, Linda. (1990). "Multiple Jeopardy: A Socioeconomic Comparison of Men and Women among the Indian, Métis and Inuit Peoples of Canada." *Canadian Ethnic Studies, 22,* 69–84.

Gibbins, Roger and J. Rick Ponting. (1986). "Historical Background and Overview." In J. Rick Ponting, ed., *Arduouf Journey* (pp. 18–56). Toronto: McClelland and Stewart.

Government of Canada. 2014. "2014 Annual Report to Parliament on Immigration." http://www.cic.gc.ca/english/resources/publications/annual-report-2014/ (retrieved 20 September 2015).

Government of Canada. (2015). "Six selection factors – Federal skilled workers." http://www.cic.gc.ca/english/immigrate/skilled/apply-factors.asp (retrieved 20 September 2015).

Granatstein, Jack. (2007). *Whose War Is It? How Canada Can Survive in the Post-9/11 World.* Toronto. HarperCollins.

Groupe de recherche ethnicité et societé (GRES). (1997). "Immigration and Ethnic Relations in Quebec: Pluralism in the Making." In Marcel Fournier, Michael Rosenberg, and Deena White, eds., *Quebec Society: Critical Issues* (pp. 95–112). Scarborough, ON: Prentice Hall.

Ha, Tu Thanh. (1995). "The PQ's Narrow Ethnic Vision." *Globe and Mail* 11 November: D1.

Hawkins, Freda. (1989). *Critical Years in Immigration: Canada and Australia Compared.* Montreal and Kingston, ON: McGill–Queen's University Press.

Henry, Frances. (1989). *Who Gets the Work in 1989?* (background paper). Ottawa: Economic Council of Canada.

Henry, Frances, and Effie Ginsberg. (1985). *Who Gets the Work: A Test of Racial Discrimination in Employment.* Toronto: Urban Alliance on Race Relations and the Social Planning Directorate.

Henry, Frances, and Carol Tator. (2006). *The Colour of Democracy: Racism in Canadian Society,* 3rd ed. Toronto: Thomson Nelson.

Herberg, Edward. (1990). "The Ethno–racial Socioeconomic Hierarchy in Canada: Theory and Analysis in the New Vertical Mosaic." *International Journal of Comparative Sociology, 31,* 206–21.

Holton, Robert, and Michael Lanphier. (1994). "Public Opinion, Immigration and Refugees." In Howard Adelman, Allan Borowski, Meyer Burstein, and Lois Foster, eds., *Immigration and Refugee Policy: Australia and Canada Compared,* Vol. 1. Toronto: University of Toronto Press.

Hou, Feng and Simon Coulombe. (2010). "Earnings Gaps for Canadian-Born Visible Minorities in the Public and Private Sectors." *Canadian Public Policy, 36* (1), 29–43.

House of Commons. (2014). *Invisible Women: A Call to Action: A Report on Missing and Murdered Indigenous Women in Canada.* On the World Wide Web at http://www.acatcanada.org/download/XC2-411-2-1-1-eng.pdf (retrieved 8 July 2015).

Howard, Rhoda. (1998). "Being Canadian: Citizenship in Canada." *Citizenship Studies, 2,* 133–52.

Howard–Hassmann, Rhoda. (1999). "Canadian as an Ethnic Category: Implications for Multiculturalism and National Unity." *Canadian Public Policy, 25* (4), 523–37.

Human Rights Watch. (2013). *Those Who Take Us Away: Abusive Policing and Failures in Protection of Indigenous Women and Girls in Northern British Columbia, Canada.* New York: Human Rights Watch.

Iacovetta, Franca. (1992). *Such Hardworking People: Italian Immigrants in Postwar Toronto.* Montreal and Kingston, ON: McGill-Queen's University Press.

Idle No More. (2113). "The Manifesto." On the World Wide Web at http://www.idlenomore.ca/manifesto (retrieved 12 December 2014).

Immen, Wallace. (2011). "How an Ethnic Sounding Name May Affect the Job Hunt." *Globe and Mail,* November 18, B21.

Isajiw, Wsevolod. (1999). *Understanding Diversity: Ethnicity and Race in the Canadian Context.* Toronto: Thompson Educational Publishing.

Jenson, Jane. (1993). "Naming Nations: Making Nationalist Claims in Canadian Public Discourse." *Canadian Review of Sociology and Anthropology, 30,* 337–58.

Kazemipur, Abdolmohammad, and Shiva Halli. (2000). *The New Poverty in Canada.* Toronto: Thompson Educational Publishers.

Krosenbrink-Gelissen, Ernestine. (1994). "The Native Women's Association of Canada." In James Frideres, ed., *Native Peoples in Canada* (pp. 335–64). Scarborough, ON: Prentice Hall.

Laforest, Guy. (2005). "Can Canada Win Back the Children of Bill 101? YES: Canada Can Woo Back Quebeckers—by Admitting Past Insults and Decentralizing, Says a Former ADQ Leader, Guy Laforest." *Globe and Mail* 20 December: A25.

Latouche, Daniel. (1993). "'Quebec: See under Canada': Quebec Nationalism in the New Global Age." In Alain-G. Gagnon, ed., *Quebec: State and Society*, 2nd ed. (pp. 40–51). Scarborough, ON: Nelson.

Leger Marketing. (2007). *Sun Media: Racial Tolerance Report.* On the World Wide Web at www.legermarketing.com/documents/SPCLM/070119ENG.pdf (retrieved 15 July 2009).

Lewis, Oscar. (1961). *The Children of Sanchez.* New York: Random House.

Li, Peter. (1988). *The Chinese in Canada.* Toronto: Oxford University Press.

Li, Peter. (2003). *Destination Canada: Immigration Debates and Issues.* Toronto: Oxford University Press.

Li, Peter. (2012). "Differences in Employment Income of University Professors." *Canadian Ethnic Studies, 44* (2): 39–48 at 43.

Lieberson, Stanley. (1991). "A New Ethnic Group in the United States." In Norman Yetman, ed., *Majority and Minority* (pp. 444–56). New York: Allyn and Bacon.

Macmillan, David. (1985). "Scottish Enterprise and Influences in Canada, 1620–1900." In R.A. Cage, ed., *The Scots Abroad: Labour, Capital and Enterprise, 1750–1914* (pp. 46–79). London: Croom Helm.

Manpower and Immigration. (1967). *Immigration Statistics, 1966.* Ottawa: Queen's Printer.

Marger, Martin. (1997). *Race and Ethnic Relations: American and Global Perspectives,* 4th ed. New York: Wadsworth.

Marx, Karl. (1967 [1867]). *Capital,* Vol. 1. New York: International Publishers. McMillan, Alan. (1988). *Native Peoples and Cultures of Canada.* Vancouver: Douglas and McIntyre.

Métis National Council. (1983). *A Brief to the Standing Committee on Legal and Constitutional Affairs.* Ottawa: Author.

Miles, Robert. (1982). *Racism and Migrant Labour.* London: Routledge.

Miles, Robert, and Malcolm Brown. (2003). *Racism,* 2nd ed. London: Routledge.

Milner, Henry, and Sheilagh Hodgins Milner. (1973). *The Decolonization of Quebec.* Toronto: McClelland and Stewart.

Mitchell, Marybelle. (1996). *From Talking Chiefs to a Native Corporate Elite.* Montreal and Kingston, ON: McGill-Queen's University Press.

Montagu, Ashley. (1972). *Statement on Race.* London: Oxford University Press.

Nagler, Mark. (1972). "Minority Values and Economic Achievement: The Case of the North American Indian." In Mark Nagler, ed., *Perspectives on the North American Indian* (pp. 131–42). Toronto: McClelland and Stewart.

Nakhaie, M. Reza. (2006). "A Comparison of the Earnings of the Canadian Native–Born and Immigrants, 2001," *Canadian Ethnic Studies, 38* (2), 19–46.

Nikolinakos, Marios. (1973). "Notes towards an Economic Theory of Racism." *Race, 14,* 365–81.

Omi, Michael, and Howard Winant. (1986). *Racial Formation in the United States: From the 1960s to the 1980s.* New York Routledge and Kegan Paul.

Oreopoulos, Phillip and Diane Dechief (2011). *Why Do Some Employers Prefer to Interview Matthew, but Not Samir? New Evidence from Toronto, Montreal and Vancouver.* Vancouver: Metropolis British Columbia, Centre of Excellence for Research on Immigration and Diversity, Working Paper No. 11-13.

Pentland, H. Clare. (1981). *Labour and Capital in Canada, 1650–1860.* Toronto: Lorimer.

Pettipas, Katherine. (1995). *Severing the Ties That Bind.* Winnipeg: University of Manitoba Press.

Pineo, Peter, and John Porter. (1985). "Ethnic Origin and Occupational Attainment." In Monica Boyd, John Goyder, Frank Jones, Hugh McRoberts, Peter Pineo, and John Porter, eds., *Ascription and Achievement: Studies in Mobility and Status Attainment in Canada* (pp. 357–93). Ottawa: Carleton University Press.

Porter, John. (1965). *The Vertical Mosaic.* Toronto: University of Toronto Press.

Presse Canadienne. (2015). "Support for PQ, sovereignty rising: poll." 19 May. http://montrealgazette.com/news/quebec/support-for-sovereignty-increasing-new-leger-poll-suggests (retrieved 20 September 2015).

Ramirez, Bruno. (1991). *On the Move: French–Canadian and Italian Migrants in the North Atlantic Economy 1860–1914.* Toronto: McClelland and Stewart.

Reitz, Jeffrey. (2011). "Tapping Immigrants' Skills." In Robert Brym, ed., *Society in Question,* 6th ed., 178–93. Toronto: Nelson.

Rex, John, and David Mason, eds. (1986). *Theories of Race and Ethnic Relations.* Cambridge: Cambridge University Press.

Roy, Patricia. (1989). *A White Man's Province.* Vancouver: University of British Columbia Press.

Royal Commission on Aboriginal Peoples. (1996). *Report.* Ottawa: Supply and Services Canada.

Royal Canadian Mounted Police. (2014). *Missing and Murdered Aboriginal Women: A National Operative Overview.* On the World Wide Web at http://www.rcmp-grc.gc.ca/pubs/mmaw-faapd-eng.htm.

Satzewich, Vic. (1991). *Racism and the Incorporation of Foreign Labour.* London: Routledge.

Satzewich, Vic, and Linda Mahood. (1994). "Indian Affairs and Band Governance: Deposing Indian Chiefs in Western Canada, 1896–1911." *Canadian Ethnic Studies, 26,* 40–58.

Satzewich, Vic, and William Shaffir. (2009). "Racism versus Professionalism: Claims and Counter-clams about Racial Profiling." *Canadian Journal of Criminology and Criminal Justice,* 51 (2): 199–226.

Satzewich, Vic, and Lloyd Wong. (2003). "Immigration, Ethnicity and Race: The Transformation of Transnationalism, Localism and Identities." In Wallace Clement and Leah Vosko, eds., *Changing Canada: Political Economy as Transformation.* Montreal and Kingston: McGill–Queen's University Press.

Satzewich, Vic, and Terry Wotherspoon. (2001). *First Nations: Race, Class and Gender Relations.* Regina: Canadian Plains Research Centre.

Scott, George. (1990). "A Resynthesis of the Primordial and Circumstantial Approaches to Ethnic Group Solidarity: Towards an Explanatory Model." *Ethnic and Racial Studies, 13,* 147–71.

Somerville, Kara. (2008). "Transnational Belonging among Second Generation Youth: Identity in a Globalized World." *Journal of Social Sciences*, Special Volume, No. 10: 23–33.

Soroka, Stuart, and Sarah Roberton (2010). *A Literature Review of Public Opinion Research on Canadian Attitudes Towards Multiculturalism and Immigration, 2006–2009.* Ottawa: Citizenship and Immigration Canada. On the World Wide Web at http://www.cic.gc.ca/english/pdf/research-stats/2012 -por-multi-imm-eng.pdf (retrieved 21 November 2014).

Special Committee on the Participation of Visible Minorities in Canadian Society [Special Committee]. (1984). *Equality Now!* Ottawa: Supply and Services Canada.

Statistics Canada. (2011). "Immigration and Ethnocultural Diversity: *National Household Survey, 2011.*" Ottawa: Minister of Industry. Catalogue number 99-010x2011001.

Statistics Canada. (2014a). "Ethnic Origin (264), Single and Multiple Ethnic Origin responses (3), Generation Status (4), Age Groups (10) and Sex (3) for the Population in Private Households in Canada, Provinces, Territories, Census Metropolitan Areas and Census Agglomerations, *2011 National Household Survey*. Catalogue No. 99-010-X2011028.

Statistics Canada (2014b). "The Educational Attainment of Aboriginal Peoples in Canada." On the World Wide Web at http://www12.statcan.gc.ca/nhs-enm/2011/as-sa/99-012-x/ 99-012-x2011003_3-eng.cfm (retrieved 12 December 2014).

Steckley John. (2003). *Aboriginal Voices and the Politics of Representation in Canadian Introductory Sociology Textbooks.* Toronto: Canadian Scholars' Press.

Steinberg, Stephen. (1981). *The Ethnic Myth.* New York: Knopf.

Stoffman, Daniel. (2002). *Who Gets In: What's Wrong with Canada's Immigration Program—and How to Fix It.* Toronto: Macfarlane Walter and Ross.

Thomas, W. I., and Florian Znaniecki. (1918). *The Polish Peasant in Europe and America.* New York: Knopf.

Titley, Brian. (1986). *A Narrow Vision: Duncan Campbell Scott and the Administration of Indian Affairs in Canada.* Vancouver: University of British Columbia Press.

Turp, Daniel. (2005). "Can Canada Win Back the Children of Bill 101? No: Canada Isn't First in the Hearts of Young Quebeckers, Regardless of Their First Language, says PQ MNA Daniel Turp." *The Globe and Mail* 20 December: A25.

van den Berghe, Pierre. (1986). "Ethnicity and the Sociobiology Debate." In John Rex and David Mason, eds., *Theories of Race and Ethnic Relations* (pp. 246–63). Cambridge, UK: Cambridge University Press.

Voyageur, Cora. (2008). *Firekeepers of the Twenty-First Century: First Nations Women Chiefs.* Montreal and Kingston: McGill-Queen's University Press.

Whitaker, Reginald. (1987). *Double Standard: The Secret History of Canadian Immigration.* Toronto: Lester and Orpen Dennys.

Whitaker, Reginald. (1993). "From the Quebec Cauldron to the Canadian Cauldron." In Alain-G. Gagnon, ed., *Quebec: State and Society*, 2nd ed. (pp. 18–39). Scarborough, ON: Nelson.

White, Pamela. (1992). "Challenges in Measuring Canada's Ethnic Diversity." In Stella Hryniuk, ed., *20 Years of Multiculturalism: Success and Failure* (pp. 163–82). Winnipeg: St. John's College Press.

Widdowson, Frances, and Albert Howard. (2008). *Disrobing the Aboriginal Industry: The Deception behind Indigenous Cultural Preservation.* Montreal and Kingston: McGill-Queen's University Press.

Wiley, Norbert. (1967). "Ethnic Mobility and Stratification Theory." *Social Problems*, 15, 147–59.

Wilkes, Rima, Neil Guppy and Lily Farris. (2008). "'No Thanks, We're Full': Individual Attitudes, National Context, and Changing Attitudes toward Immigration." *International Migration Review*, 42 (2), 303–28.

Williams, Eric. (1964). *Capitalism and Slavery.* London: Andre Deutsch.

Wilson, Edward. (1978). *On Human Nature.* New York: Vintage.

Woodsworth, J. S. (1972). *Strangers within Our Gates.* Toronto: University of Toronto Press.

Wortley, Scot. (2005). *Bias Free Policing: The Kingston Data Collection Project, Preliminary Results.* Toronto: Centre of Criminology, University of Toronto and the Centre of Excellence for Research on Immigration and Settlement (CERIS).

Wotherspoon, Terry. (2012). "Education and Class Relations: Canada's Indigenous People and the Knowledge Society," *International Journal of Arts and Sciences*, 5, (6), 415–35.

Xu, Li. (2012). "Who Drives a Taxi in Canada?" Ottawa: Citizenship and Immigration Canada. On the World Wide Web at http://www.cic.gc.ca/english/resources/research/taxi/ index.asp (retrieved 27 November 2014).

York, Geoffrey (1989). *The Dispossessed.* Toronto: Lester and Orpen Dennys.

CHAPTER 10

Acheson, T. W. (1972). "The National Policy and the Industrialization of the Maritimes, 1880–1910." *Acadiensis*, 1 (Spring), 3–28.

Alexander, David. (1978). "Economic Growth in the Atlantic Region, 1880–1940." *Acadiensis*, 8 (1), 47–76.

Antonenko, Oksana. (2001). "Russia's Military Involvement in the Middle East." *Middle East Review of International Affairs*, 5 (1). On the World Wide Web at http://meria.idc.ac.il/journal/2001/ issue1/jv5n1a3.html (retrieved 18 March 2009).

Arrighi, Giovanni. (1970). "Labour Supplies in Historical Perspective: A Study of the Proletarianization of the African Peasantry in Rhodesia." *Journal of Development Studies*, 6 (3), 197–234.

Bairoch, Paul. (1982). "International Industrialization Levels from 1750 to 1980." *Journal of European Economic History*, 11, 269–331.

Blaut, James M. (2000). *Eight Eurocentric Historians.* New York: Guilford Press.

Bluestone, B. and B. Harrison, eds. (1982). *The De-Industrialization of America: Plant Closings, Community Abandonment and the Dismantling of Basic Industries.* New York: Basic Books.

Bluestone, B. and B. Harrison. (1988). *The Great U-Turn: Corporate Restructuring and the Polarizing of America.* New York: Basic Books.

Bornschier, Volker. (2002). "Changing Income Inequality in the 2nd Half of the 20th Century: Preliminary Findings and Propositions for Explanation." *Journal of World Systems Research*, 8, 100–127.

Borras, Saturnino. (2008). "Contemporary Land Policies and Land Struggles." In *Critical Development Studies: Readings for Change.* Zacatecas, Mexico: Global Capital and Alternative

Development Unit, Doctorate in Development Studies, Universidad Autónoma de Zacatecas and CDS Network.

Braun, D. (1997). *The Rich Get Richer: The Rise of Income Inequality in the United States and the World.* Chicago: Nelson-Hall Publishers.

Brenner, Robert. (1977). "The Origins of Capitalist Development: A Critique of Neo-Smithian Marxism." *New Left Review, 104* (July/August), 25–92.

Brown, Lester. (2003). *Plan B: Rescuing a Planet under Stress and a Civilization in Trouble.* New York: Norton.

Brym, Robert, Stephanie Chung, Sarah Dulmage, Christian Farahat, Mark Greenberg, Manki Ho, Khadra Housein, Dina Kulik, Matthew Lau, Olivia Maginley, Armen Nercessian, Emilio Reyes Le Blanc, Adrian Sacher, Nadia Sachewsky, Alex Sadovsky, Stephen Singh, Shankar Sivananthan, Nick Toller, Sara Vossoughi, Krista Weger, and Tommy Wu. (2005). "In Faint Praise of the World Bank's Gender Development Policy." *Canadian Journal of Sociology, 30,* 95–100. On the World Wide Web at http://www.cjsonline.ca /articles/brymetal05.html (retrieved 7 March 2009).

Brym, Robert, Lance Roberts, John Lie, and Steven Rytina. (2012). *Sociology: Your Compass for a New World,* 4th Canadian ed. Toronto: Nelson.

Cardoso, Fernando Henrique and Enzo Faletto. (1979). *Dependency and Development in Latin America.* Berkeley, CA: University of California Press.

"Chavez: Venezuela Aiding Latin America." (2007). *Miami Herald* 15 March.

Chesnais, François. (2004). "Globalisation against Development. Liberalisation, Deregulation, Privatisation and the Contemporary Performance of the International Economy." On the World Wide Web at http://www.nadir.org/nadir/initiativ/agp/free/wsf/mumbai2004/0117chesnais.htm (retrieved 7 March 2009).

Diamond, Jared. (1999). *Guns, Germs and Steel: The Fates of Human Societies.* New York: Norton.

Ellis, Frank. (1983). *Las Transnacionales del Banano en Centroamérica [Banana Transnationals in Central America].* San Jose, CA: EDUCA.

Falla, Ricardo. (1994). *Massacres in the Jungle: Ixcan, Guatemala 1975–1982.* Boulder, CO: Westview.

Frank, Andre Gunder. (1966). *Capitalism and Underdevelopment in Latin America: Historical Studies of Chile and Brazil.* New York: Monthly Review Press.

Gareau, Frederick H. (2004). *State Terrorism and the United States.* Atlanta: Clarity Press.

Handy, Jim. (1985). *A Gift of the Devil: A History of Guatemala.* Toronto: Between the Lines.

Happy Planet Index. (2015). On the World Wide Web at http://www.happyplanetindex.org/data.

Hochschild, Adam. (1999). *King Leopold's Ghost: A Story of Greed, Terror, and Heroism in Colonial Africa.* New York: Mariner Books.

Inkeles, Alex and David H. Smith. (1976). *Becoming Modern: Individual Change in Six Developing Countries.* Cambridge, MA: Harvard University Press.

Leiva, Fernando Ignacio. (2008). "Toward a Critique of Latin American Neostructuralism," *Latin American Politics and Society, 50,* 4,1–25.

Marchak, Patricia. (1999). *God's Assassins: State Terrorism in Argentina in the 1970s.* Montreal, QC, and Kingston, ON: McGill-Queen's University Press.

Marshall, Jonathan, Peter Dale Scott, and Jane Hunter. (1987). *The Iran-Contra Connection.* Montreal: Black Rose Books.

McClelland, David. (1961). *The Achieving Society.* Princeton, NJ: Van Nostrand.

Milanovic, Branko. (2005). "Global Income Inequality: What It Is and Why It Matters?" (UN Department of Economic and Social Affairs [DESA] Working Paper No. 26). On the World Wide Web at http://www.un.org/esa/desa/papers/2006/wp26_2006.pdf (retrieved 7 March 2009).

Milanovic, Branko. (2008). "An Even Higher Global Inequality Than Previously Thought: A Note on Global Inequality Calculations Using the 2005 International Comparison Program Results." *International Journal of Health Services, 38,* 421–29.

Milanovic, Branko. (2009). "Developing Countries Worse Off Than Once Thought." Washington: Carnegie Endowment for International Peace. On the World Wide Web at http://www.carnegieendowment.org/publications/index.cfm?fa=view&id=19907 (retrieved 12 July 2009).

Milanovic, Branko. 2012. *The Haves and the Have-Nots: A Brief and Idiosyncratic History of Global Inequality.* New York: Basic Books.

Murmis, Miguel and Juan Carlos Portantiero. (1969). *Estudios Sobre Los Orígenes del Peronismo.* Buenos Aires: Siglo XXI.

Neilsen, François. (2007). "Income Inequality in the Global Economy: The Myth of Rising World Inequality." *Harvard College Economics Review, 1* (2), 23–26.

"Occupy Protests Around the World." (2011) *Guardian* October 17. On the World Wide Web at http://www.guardian.co.uk/news/datablog/2011/oct/17/occupy-protests-world-list-map (retrieved 19 January 2012).

OXFAM. (2015). "Richest 1% will own more than all the rest by 2016." On the World Wide Web at http://www.oxfam.org/en/pressroom/pressreleases/2015-01-19/richest-1-will-own-more-all-rest-2016 .

Parpart, Jane and Henry Veltmeyer. (2003). "The Dynamics of Development Theory and Practice: A Review of Its Shifting Dynamics." *Canadian Journal of Development Studies, 25* (1).

Pickover, Clifford. (1997). "Why Did Human History Evolve Differently on Different Continents for the Last 13,000 Years?" Edge Foundation. On the World Wide Web at http://www.edge.org/discourse/diamond_evolution.html (retrieved 7 March 2009).

Richards, Alan. (1976). "The Political Economy of Gutswirtschaft: A Comparative Analysis of East-Elbian Germany, Egypt, and Chile." *Comparative Studies in Society and History, 21* (3), 483–518.

Rodney, Walter. (1972). *How Europe Underdeveloped Africa.* London: Bogle-L'Ouverture Publications.

Rodriguez Gomez, Guadalupe and Gabriel Torres. (1996). "El Barzón y la Comagro: La Resistencia de los Agricultores a la Politica Neoliberal." In Hubert Carton Grammont and Héctor Tejera Gaona, eds., *La Sociedad Rural Mexicana Frente al Nuevo Milenio.* Mexico City: Plaza y Valdez Editores.

Rostow, W. W. (1960). *The Stages of Economic Growth: A Non-communist Manifesto.* Cambridge, UK: Cambridge University Press.

Shiva, Vandana. (1993). "GATT, Agriculture and Third World Women." In Maria Mies and Vandana Shiva, eds., *Ecofeminism* (pp. 241–45). Halifax: Fernwood Books.

Stiglitz, Joseph. (2003). *Globalization and Its Discontents.* New York: Norton.

Stone, Samuel. (1975). *La Dinastia de los Conquistadores.* San Jose, Costa Rica: EDUCA.

Sutcliffe, Robert. (2005). "Interview with Bob Sutcliffe: Measuring Global Inequality." Amherst: University of Massachusetts, Political Economy Research Institute, February 23. On the World Wide Web at http://www.peri.umass.edu/338/ (retrieved 12 July 2009).

United Nations. (2009). "Indicators on Income and Economic Activity." *Social Indicators.* On the World Wide Web at http://unstats.un.org/unsd/demographic/products/socind/inc-eco.htm (retrieved 12 July 2009).

United Nations. (2013). *Human Development Report.* On the World Wide Web at http://hdr.undp.org/sites/default/files/reports/14/hdr2013_en_complete.pdf.

United National Development Programme. (2014). "Human Development Index (HDI)." On the World Wide Web at http://hdr.undp.org/en/content/human-development-index-hdi.

Vilas, Carlos. (1986). *The Sandinista Revolution.* New York: Monthly Review Press.

Waldman, Carl. (2005). "Teotihuacán." *Microsoft Encarta 2006* [CD]. Redmond, WA: Microsoft.

Winson, Anthony. (1983). "The Formation of Capitalist Agriculture in Latin America and Its Relationship to Political Power and the State." *Comparative Studies in Society and History,* 25, 83–104.

Winson, Anthony. (1985). "The Uneven Development of Canadian Agriculture: Farming in the Maritimes and Ontario." *The Canadian Journal of Sociology,* 10 (4), 411–38.

Winson, Anthony. (1989). *Coffee and Democracy in Modern Costa Rica.* London: Macmillan.

Winson, Anthony and Belinda Leach. (2002). *Contingent Work, Disrupted Lives: Labour and Community in the New Rural Economy.* Toronto: University of Toronto Press.

Wittman, Hannah, Annette Desmarais, and Nettie Wiebe. (2010). "The Origins and Potential of Food Sovereignty." In H. Wittman, A. Desmarais, and N. Wiebe, eds., *Food Sovereignty: Reconnecting Food, Nature and Community.* Halifax: Fernwood Publishing.

World Bank. (2013). *World Development Indicators* (data for 2011). On the World Wide Web at http://data.worldbank.org/data-catalog/world-development-indicators/wdi-2013.

World Bank. 2015. "Poverty Headcount Ratio at $1.25 a Day (PPP) (% of Population)."On the World Wide Web at http://data.worldbank.org/indicator/SI.POV.DDAY/countries?display=default.

World Social Forum. (2009). "World Social Forum Charter of Principles." On the World Wide Web at http://www.forumsocialmundial.org.br/main.php?id_menu=4&cd_language=2 (retrieved 20 March 2009).

CHAPTER 11

Abbott, Elizabeth. (2010). *A History of Marriage.* Toronto: Penguin Canada.

Adams, Mary Louise. (1997). *The Trouble with Normal: Postwar Youth and the Making of Heterosexuality.* Toronto: University of Toronto Press.

Ambert, Anne-Marie. (2012) *Changing Families: Relationships in Context,* 2nd Canadian ed. Toronto: Pearson Education Canada.

Arat-Koc, Sedef. (2001) *Caregivers Break the Silence.* A Participatory Action Research on the Abuse and Violence, Including the Impact of Family Separation Experienced by Women in the Live-in Caregiver Program. Toronto: INTERCEDE.

Baker, Maureen. (2009a). "Introduction to Family Sociology." In Maureen Baker, ed., *Families: Changing Trends in Canada,* 6th ed. (pp. 1–25) Toronto: McGraw-Hill Ryerson.

Baker, Maureen. (2009b). "Strengthening Families? The State and Family Policies." In Maureen Baker, ed., *Families: Changing Trends in Canada,* 6th ed. (pp. 206–24) Toronto: McGraw-Hill Ryerson.

Basten, Stuart. (2009). *Voluntary Childlessness and being Childfree. The Future of Human Reproduction.* Working Paper No. 5: University of Oxford. On the World Wide Web at http://www.spi.ox.ac.uk/fileadmin/documents/pdf /Childlessness_-_Number_5.pdf (retrieved 30 July 2012).

Bradbury, Bettina. (1993). *Working Families: Age, Gender, and Daily Survival in Industrializing Montreal.* Toronto: McLelland and Stewart.

Burgoyne, C. B. and V. Morison. (1997). "Money in Remarriage: Keeping Things Simple—and Separate." *The Sociological Review,* 45 (3), 363–95.

Calliste, Agnes. (2001). "Black Families in Canada: Exploring the Interconnections of Race, Class, and Gender." In Bonnie Fox, ed., *Family Patterns, Gender Relations,* 2nd ed. Toronto: Oxford University Press.

Carroll, Laura. (2000). *Families of Two: Interviews with Happily Married Couples without Children by Choice.* Bloomington, IN: Xllibris.

Colavecchia, Sandra. (2009). "Moneywork: Caregiving and the Management of Family Finances." In Bonnie Fox, ed., *Family Patterns: Gender Relations,* 3rd ed. (pp. 417–27). Toronto: Oxford University Press.

Coontz, Stephanie. (1992). *The Way We Never Were: American Families and the Nostalgia Trap.* New York: Basic Books.

Coontz, Stephanie. (2005). *Marriage, a History: From Obedience to Intimacy or How Love Conquered Marriage.* New York: Viking.

Cory, Jill and Karen McAndless-Davis. (2008). *When Love Hurts: A Women's Guide to Understanding Abuse in Relationships.* New Westminister, BC: WomanKind Press.

Cott, Nancy. (2009). "Domesticity." In Bonnie Fox, ed., *Family Patterns, Gender Relations,* 3rd ed. (pp. 111–17). Toronto: Oxford University Press.

DeVault, M. (1991). *Feeding the Family.* Berkeley, CA: University of California Press.

DeVault, M. (1999). *Liberating Method: Feminism and Social Research.* Philadelphia, PA: Temple University Press.

Dunne, Gillian. (2000). "Opting into Motherhood: Lesbians Blurring the Boundaries and Transforming the Meaning of Parenthood and Kinship." *Gender and Society,* 14, 11–35.

"Editorial: Canada Is Leading the Pack in Mixed Unions." Macleans.ca 29 July 2014. http://www.macleans.ca/society/there-is-no-better-index-of-racial-and-cultural-integration-than-mixed-unions-and-canada-is-leading-the-pack/ (retrieved 13 January 2015).

Eichler, Margrit. (1983). *Families in Canada Today: Recent Changes and Their Policy Consequences*. Toronto: Gage.

Engels, Friedrich. (1972). *The Origin of the Family, Private Property and the State*. New York: International Publishers.

Fetner, Tina. (2008). *How the Religious Right Shaped Lesbian and Gay Activism*. Minneapolis, MN: University of Minnesota Press.

Fox, Bonnie. (2009). *When Couples Become Parents: The Creation of Gender in the Transition to Parenthood*. Toronto: University of Toronto Press.

Fox, Bonnie and Meg Luxton. (2001). "Conceptualizing Family." In Bonnie Fox, ed., *Family Patterns, Gender Relations*, 2nd ed. Toronto: Oxford University Press.

Furstenberg, Frank and Andrew Cherlin. (1991). *Divided Families: What Happens to Children When Parents Part*. Cambridge, MA: Harvard University Press.

Gartner, Rosemary, M. Dawson, and M. Crawford. (2001). "Women Killing: Intimate Femicide in Ontario, 1874–1994." In D. E. H. Russell and R. A. Harmes, eds., *Femicide in Global Perspective* (pp. 147–65). New York: Teachers College Press.

Gerson, Kathleen. (1985). *Hard Choices: How Women Decide about Work, Career, and Motherhood*. Berkeley and Los Angeles: University of California Press.

Green, Adam Isaiah. (2011). "The Changing Face of Matrimony: Same-Sex Civil Marriage in the Twenty-First Century." In Robert Brym, ed., *Society in Question*, 6th ed. Toronto: Nelson.

Hochschild, Arlie Russell. (1989). *The Second Shift: Working Parents and the Revolution at Home*. New York: Viking.

Javed, N. (2008). "GTA's Secret World of Polygamy." *Toronto Star*, 24 May: A10.

Juby, H., N. Marcil-Gratton, and C. Le Bourdais. (2004). *When Parents Separate: Further Findings from the National Longitudinal Survey of Children and Youth*. Ottawa: Department of Justice.

Luxton, Meg. (1980). *More than a Labour of Love*. Toronto: Women's Press.

Margolis, Nancy. (2009). "Putting Mothers on the Pedestal." In Bonnie Fox, ed., *Family Patterns, Gender Relations*, 3rd ed. (pp. 118–34) Toronto: Oxford University Press.

McGill Institute for Health and Social Policy. (2012). "Raising the Global Floor." On the World Wide Web at http://raisingtheglobalfloor.org/index.php (retrieved 30 July 2012).

Mojtehedzadeh, Sara. (2014). "GTA Child-Care Costs Tops in National Study." *Toronto Star* 10 November 2014. On the World Wide Web at http://www.thestar.com/news/gta/2014/11/10/gta_childcare_costs_tops_in_national_study.html (retrieved 13 January 2015).

Murdock, George Peter. (1949). *Social Structure*. New York: Macmillan.

Nelson, Fiona. (1996). *Lesbian Motherhood: An Exploration of Canadian Lesbian Families*. Toronto: University of Toronto Press.

Oakley, Ann. (1975). *The Sociology of Housework*. New York: Pantheon Books.

Organisation for Economic Co-operation and Development. (2011). "Key Characteristics of Parental Leave Systems." Available on the World Wide Web at http://www.oecd.org/dataoecd/45/26/37864482.pdf (retrieved 30 July 2012).

Pagliaro, Jennifer. (2014). "Ontario Falling Behind Its Own Poverty Reduction Goals."

Toronto Star 24 November 2014. On the World Wide Web at http://www.thestar.com/news/gta/2014/11/24/ontario_falling_behind_its_own_poverty_reduction_goals.html (retrieved 13 January 2015).

Parsons, T. (1951). *The Social System*. New York: Free Press.

Phipps, Shelley A. (2009). "Lessons from Europe: Policy Options to Enhance the Economic Security of Canadian Families." In Bonnie Fox, ed., *Family Patterns: Gender Relations*, 3rd ed. (pp. 552–73). Toronto: Oxford University Press.

Popenoe, David. (1993). "American Family Decline: 1960–1990: A Review and Appraisal." *Journal of Marriage and the Family*, 55, 527–55.

Richards, John. (2010). "Reducing Lone-Parent Poverty: A Canadian Success Story." *C.D. Howe Institute Commentary*. On the World Wide Web at http://www.cdhowe.org/reducing-lone-parent-poverty-a-canadian-success-story/4425 (retrieved 30 July 2012).

Sev'er, Aysan. (1992). *Women and Divorce in Canada*. Toronto: Canadian Scholars' Press.

Stacey, Judith. (2011). *Unhitched: Love, Marriage, and Family Values from West Hollywood to Western China*. New York: New York University Press.

Stacey, Judith and Timothy Biblarz. (2001). "How Does the Sexual Orientation of Parents Matter?" *American Sociological Review*, 66 (2), 159–83.

Statistics Canada. (2005). "Divorces." *The Daily 9*, 2–5.

Statistics Canada. 2011. "Living Arrangements of Young Adults Aged 20 to 29." On the World Wide Web at http://www12.statcan.gc.ca/census-recensement/2011/as-sa/98-312-x/98 312 x2011003_3-eng.pdf (retrieved 12 January 2015).

Statistics Canada. (2013). "Conjugal Status, Opposite/Same-sex Status and Presence of Children for the Couple Census Families in Private Households of Canada, Provinces, Territories and Census Metropolitan Areas, 2011 Census." On the World Wide Web at http://www12.statcan.gc.ca/census-recensement/2011/dp-pd/tbt-tt/Rp-eng.cfm?LANG=E&APATH=7&DETAIL=0&DIM=0&FL=C&FREE=0&GC=0&GID=0&GK=0&GRP=1&PID=102659&PRID=0&PTYPE=101955&S=0&SHOWALL=0&SUB=0&Temporal=2011&THEME=0&VID=0&VNAMEE=Conjugal%20status%20%283%29&VNA (retrieved 12 January 2015).

Statistics Canada. 2014. "Young Adults in the Parental Home for the Population Aged 20 to 29 in Private Households, Percentage Distribution (2011), for Both Sexes, 20 to 24 years, for Canada, Provinces, and Territories." On the World Wide Web at http://www12.statcan.gc.ca/census-recensement/2011/dp-pd/hlt-fst/fam/Pages/highlight.cfm?TabID=1&Lang=E&Asc=1&PRCode=01&OrderBy=999&Sex=1&Age=2&View=2&tableID=305&queryID=1 (retrieved 12 January 2014).

Sudarkasa, N. (1993). "Female-Headed African American Households: Some Neglected Dimensions." In H. P. McAdoo, ed., *Family Ethnicity: Strength in Diversity*. Newbury Park, CA: Sage.

Vanier Institute of the Family. (2010). "Forming Unions—Again." *Fascinating Families*, 30 (September 15). On the World Wide Web at http://www.vanierinstitute.ca/include/get.php?nodeid=371.

Walzer, Susan. (1998). *Thinking about the Baby: Gender and Transitions into Parenthood*. Philadelphia, PA: Temple University Press.

West, Candace and Don Zimmerman. (1987). "Doing Gender." *Gender and Society, 1* (2) 125–51.

Wilson, Sue. (2009). "Partnering, Cohabitation, and Marriage." In Maureen Baker, ed., *Families: Changing Trends in Canada*, 6th ed. (pp.68–90). Toronto: McGraw-Hill Ryerson.

Wilson, W. J. (1987). *The Truly Disadvantaged: The Inner City, the Underclass, and Public Policy*. Chicago: University of Chicago Press.

Wu, Zheng and Christoph Schimmele. (2009). "Divorce and Repartnering." In Maureen Baker, ed., *Families: Changing Trends in Canada*, 6th ed. (pp.1–25) Toronto: McGraw-Hill Ryerson.

CHAPTER 12

Adams, Tracey and Sandy Welsh. (2008). *The Organization and Experience of Work*. Toronto: Nelson.

Adams, Tracey L. (2000). *A Gentleman and a Dentist: Gender and the Rise of Dentistry in Ontario*. Toronto: University of Toronto Press.

Althauser, Robert. (1989). "Internal Labor Markets." *Annual Review of Sociology, 15,* 143–61.

Baldwin, John R. and Desmond Beckstead. (2003). "Knowledge Workers in Canada's Economy, 1971–2001." Statistics Canada, Catalogue No. 11-624-MIE, Research Paper No. 004. Ottawa: Ministry of Industry.

Becker, Gary S. (1975). *Human Capital: A Theoretical and Empirical Analysis with Special Reference to Education*, 3rd ed. Chicago: University of Chicago Press.

Bell, Daniel. (1973). *The Coming of Post-Industrial Society*. New York: Basic Books.

Bendix, Reinhard. (1974). *Work and Authority in Industry*. Berkeley, CA: University of California Press.

Berinstein, Juana. (2004). "Temp Workers and Deadbeat Bosses." *Our Times* (October/November).

Blauner, Robert. (1964). *Alienation and Freedom*. Chicago: University of Chicago Press.

Boswell, W. R. and J. B. Olsen-Buchanan. (2007). "The Use of Communication Technologies after Hours: The Role of Work Attitudes and Work-Life Conflict." *Journal of Management 33,* 592–610.

Braverman, Harry. (1974). *Labor and Monopoly Capital: The Degradation of Work in the Twentieth Century*. New York: Monthly Review Press.

Bridges, William. (1994). *Job Shift: How to Prosper in a Workplace without Jobs*. Don Mills, ON: Addison-Wesley.

Burawoy Michael. (1979). *Manufacturing Consent: Changes in the Labour Process under Monopoly Capitalism*. Chicago: University of Chicago Press.

Burman, Patrick. (1997). "Changes in the Patterns of Unemployment: The New Realities of Joblessness." In Ann Duffy, Daniel Glenday, and Norene Pupo, eds., *Good Jobs, Bad Jobs, No Jobs: The Transformation of Work in the 21st Century* (pp. 190–216). Toronto: Harcourt Brace.

Calliste, Agnes. (1993). "Sleeping Car Porters in Canada: An Ethnically Submerged Split Labour Market." In Graham S. Lowe and Harvey Krahn, eds., *Work in Canada: Readings in the Sociology of Work and Industry* (pp. 139–53). Toronto: Nelson.

Campbell, Andrew. (1996). "From Shop Floor to Computer Room." *Globe and Mail* 30 December: A1, A8.

Canada Labour Program. 2013. "Union Coverage in Canada, 2013." On the World Wide Web at http://www.labour.gc.ca/ eng/resources/info/publications/union_coverage/union _coverage.shtml (retrieved 23 October 2014).

Canadian Policy Research Networks. (2006a). "It's More Than the Money—What Canadians Want in a Job." On the World Wide Web at http://www.jobquality.ca/indicator_e/rew001 .stm (retrieved 9 March 2006). Reprinted with permission of Canadian Policy Research Networks.

Canadian Policy Research Networks. (2006b). "Job Satisfaction." On the World Wide Web at http://www.jobquality.ca /indicators/ rewards/rew2.shtml (retrieved 9 March 2006). Reprinted with permission of Canadian Policy Research Networks.

Canadian Policy Research Networks. (2006c). "Satisfaction Most Common in Social Sciences, Arts/Culture and Management Occupations." On the World Wide Web at http://www .jobquality.ca/indicator_e/rew002_1.stm#2 (9 March 2006). Reprinted with permission.

Canadian Press. (2014a). "Unpaid Internships Focus of Growing Backlash." *CBC News* 2 March 2014. On the World Wide Web at http://www.cbc.ca/m/touch/news/story/1.2556977 (retrieved 25 October 2014).

Canadian Press. (2014b). "Stephen Poloz Comments on Unpaid Work Raise Ire of Youth Groups." *CBC News* 5 November 2014. On the World Wide Web at http://www.cbc.ca/news/ business/stephen-poloz-comments-on-unpaid-work-raise-ire -of-youth-groups-1.2824388 (retrieved 5 November 2014).

Canadian Press/Leger Marketing. (2001). *How Much Importance Canadians Place on Their Work*. Montreal.

Carletti, Fabiola and Janet Davison. (2012). "Who's Looking Out for Tim Hortons' Temporary Foreign Workers?" *CBC Hamilton* 13 December. On the World Wide Web at http:// www.cbc.ca/news/canada/hamilton/news/who-s-looking -out-for-tim-hortons-temporary-foreign-workers-1.1282019 (retrieved 25 October 2014),

CBC News. 2013. "Canadians Top Job Satisfaction Survey." On the World Wide Web at http://www.cbc.ca/news/business/ canadians-top-job-satisfaction-survey-1.2430864 (retrieved 23 October 2014).

Chaykowski, Richard. (2005). *Non-Standard Work and Economic Vulnerability*, Vulnerable Workers Series, No. 3. Ottawa: CPRN.

Collin, Chantal, Isabelle Lafontaine-Émond, and Melissa Pang. 2013. "Persons with Disabilities in the Canadian Labour Market: An Overlooked Talent Pool." *Parliament of Canada* 29 March. On the World Wide Web at http://www.parl .gc.ca/Content/LOP/ResearchPublications/2013-17-e.htm#a3 (retrieved 23 October 2014).

Cranford, Cynthia, Leah Vosko, and Nancy Zukewich. (2003). "The Gender of Precarious Employment in Canada." *Relations Industrielles/Industrial Relations, 58* (3), 454–79.

Cross, Jessica Smith. (2014). "Unpaid Intern Study Reveals Inequity, Researcher Says." *Metro News* 21 May. On the World Wide Web at http://metronews.ca/news/canada/1040684/ unpaid-intern-study-reveals-inequity-researcher-says/ (retrieved 25 October 2015).

Dassbach, Carl H. A. (1996). "Lean Production, Labor Control, and Post-Fordism in the Japanese Automobile Industry." In William C. Green and Ernest J. Yanarella, eds., *North American Auto Unions in Crisis: Lean Production as Contested Terrain* (pp. 19–40). Albany, NY: SUNY Press.

Economic Council of Canada. (1991). *Good Jobs, Bad Jobs: Employment in the Service Economy*. Ottawa: Supply and Services Canada.

Edwards, P. K. and Hugh Scullion. (1982). *The Social Organization of Industrial Conflict*. Oxford: Blackwell.

Edwards, Richard. (1979). *Contested Terrain: The Transformation of the Workplace in the Twentieth Century*. New York: Basic Books.

Ehrenreich, Barbara. (2005). *Bait and Switch: The (Futile) Pursuit of the American Dream*. New York: Metropolitan Books.

Employment and Social Development Canada. (2014a). "Job Openings (2013–2022)." On the World Wide Web at http://www23.hrsdc.gc.ca/l.3bd.2t.1ilshtml@-eng.jsp?lid=22&fid=1&lang=en (retrieved 23 October 2014).

Employment and Social Development Canada. (2014b). "Work—Weekly Hours Worked." On the World Wide Web at http://www4.hrsdc.gc.ca/.3ndic.1t.4r@-eng.jsp?iid=19 (retrieved 23 October 2014).

Epstein, Cynthia Fuchs and Arne Kalleberg. (2001). "Time and the Sociology of Work: Issues and Implications." *Work and Occupations, 28* (1), 5–16.

Erickson, Bonnie. (2001). "Good Networks and Good Jobs: The Value of Social Capital to Employers and Employees." In Nan Lin, Karen Cook, and Ronald Burt, eds., *Social Capital: Theory and Research* (pp. 127–58). New York: Aldine de Gruyter.

Flap, Henk and Ed Boxman. (2001) "Getting Started: The Influence of Social Capital on the Start of the Occupational Career." In Nan Lin, Karen Cook, and Ronald Burt, eds., *Social Capital: Theory and Research* (pp. 159–81). New York: Aldine de Gruyter.

Fountain, Christine M. (2005). "Finding a Job in the Internet Age." *Social Forces, 83* (3), 1235–62.

Friedson, Eliot. (1970). *The Profession of Medicine: A Study in the Sociology of Applied Knowledge*. New York: Harper and Row.

Friesen, Joe. (2014). "Numbers of Low-Skilled Temporary Foreign Workers Rose Despite Push to Curtail Program." *Globe and Mail* 27 October.

Fudge, J. and L. F. Vosko. (2001). "By Whose Standards? Re-Regulating the Canadian Labour Market." *Economic and Industrial Democracy, 22* (3), 327.

Gilmore, Jason. (2009). "The 2008 Canadian Immigrant Labour Market: Analysis of Quality Employment." (November), 1–39. Statistics Canada. Catalogue No. 71-606-X.

Gilmore, Jason and Sébastien LaRochelle-Côté. (2011). "Inside the Labour Market Downturn." *Perspectives on Labour Market and Income* (Spring), pp. 3–14. Statistics Canada. Catalogue No. 75-001-X.

Government of Canada. 2013. "Facts and Figures 2012 – Immigration Overview: Permanent and Temporary Residents." On the World Wide Web at http://www.cic.gc.ca/english/resources/statistics/facts2012/permanent/01.asp (retrieved 25 October 2014).

Granovetter, Mark. (1995 [1974]). *Getting a Job: A Study of Contacts and Careers,* 2nd ed. Cambridge, MA: Harvard.

Gross, Dominique M. (2014). "Temporary Foreign Workers in Canada: Are They Really Filling Labour Shortages?" Toronto: C.D. Howe Institute. On the World Wide Web at http://www.cdhowe.org/pdf/commentary_407.pdf (retrieved 25 October 2014).

Hodson, Randy. (1991). "The Active Worker: Compliance and Autonomy at the Workplace." *Contemporary Ethnography, 20* (April), 271–90.

Hodson, Randy and Teresa Sullivan. (1990). *The Social Organization of Work*. Belmont, CA: Wadsworth.

Houseman, Susan, Arne Kalleberg, and George Erickcek. (2003). "The Role of Temporary Agency Employment in Tight Labour Markets." *Industrial and Labor Relations Review, 57* (1), 105–27.

Jones, Frank E. (1996). *Understanding Organizations: A Sociological Perspective*. Cooksville, ON: Copp Clark.

Kalleberg, Arne. (2000). "Nonstandard Employment Relations: Part-time, Temporary and Contract Work." *Annual Review of Sociology, 26,* 341–65.

Kalleberg, Arne. (2003). "Flexible Firms and Labor Market Segmentation: Effects of Workplace Restructuring on Jobs and Workers." *Work & Occupations, 30* (2), 154–75.

Kalleberg, Arne (2011). *Good Jobs, Bad Jobs: The Rise of Polarized and Precarious Employment Systems in the United States, 1970s–2000s*. New York: Russell Sage Foundation, American Sociological Association Rose Series in Sociology.

Kalleberg, Arne L., Barbara F. Reskin, and Ken Hudson. (2000). "Bad Jobs in America: Standard and Nonstandard Employment Relations and Job Quality in the United States." *American Sociological Review, 65,* 256–78.

Krahn, Harvey J. (1992). *Quality of Work in the Service Economy*. General Social Survey Analysis Series 6. Ottawa: Statistics Canada. Catalogue No. 11-612E.

Krahn, Harvey J. (1995). "Nonstandard Work on the Rise." *Perspectives on Labour and Income* (Winter), 35–42.

Krahn, Harvey J. and Graham S. Lowe. (1998). *Work, Industry and Canadian Society,* 3rd ed. Toronto: ITP Nelson.

Kunda, Gideon, Stephen R. Barley, and James Evans. (2002). "Why Do Contractors Contract? The Experience of Highly Skilled Technical Professionals in a Contingent Labor Market." *Industrial and Labor Relations Review, 55* (2), 234–61.

Laroche, Mireille and Mérette, Marcel. 2000. "Measuring Human Capital in Canada." Department of Finance, Government of Canada. http://www.fin.gc.ca/pub/pdfs/wp2000-05e.pdf (retrieved 23 October 2014)

LaRochelle-Côté, Sébastien and Sharanjit Uppal. (2011). "The Financial Well-being of the Self-Employed." *Perspectives on Labour Market and Income* (Winter). Statistics Canada. Catalogue No. 75-001-X. pp. 3–15.

Laxer, Gordon. (1989). *Open for Business: The Roots of Foreign Ownership in Canada*. Toronto: Oxford University Press.

Library of Parliament. (2013). Untitled. On the World Wide Web at http://www.internassociation.ca/wp-content/uploads/2013/05/Library-of-Parliament1.pdf (retrieved 25 October 2015).

Livingstone, D. W (1993). "Conclusion: Aging Dinosaurs or All-Round Workers?" In June Corman, Meg Luxton, D. W Livingstone, and Wally Secombe, eds., *Recasting Steel Labour: The Stelco Story* (pp. 145–55). Halifax, NS: Fernwood.

Lowe, Graham S. (1987). *Women in the Administrative Revolution: The Feminization of Clerical Work*. Toronto: University of Toronto Press.

Marsden, Peter and J. Hurlbert. (1988). "Social Resources and Mobility Outcomes." *Social Forces, 66,* 1038–59.

Matusik, Sharon F. and Amy E. Mickel. (2011). "Embracing or Embattled by Converged Mobile Devices? Users' Experiences with a Contemporary Connectivity Technology." *Human Relations 64* (8), 1001–1030.

Mazmanian, Melissa, Wanda J. Orlikowski, and JoAnne Yates. (2005). CrackBerrys: Exploring the Social Implications of Ubiquitous Wireless Email Devices. In *Proceedings of the IFIP 8.2 Working Conference on Ubiquitous Computing*, Cleveland, OH.

McKay, Shona. (1993). "Willing and Able." In Graham S. Lowe and Harvey Krahn, eds., *Work in Canada: Readings in the Sociology of Work and Industry* (pp. 166–71). Toronto: Nelson.

McKenzie, Donald. (2001). "Poll: 90% Satisfied with Their Jobs, 70% Happy with Salary." *Financial Post* 31 December: FP3.

Morissette, René. (1991). "Are Jobs in Large Firms Better?" *Perspectives on Labour and Income* (Autumn), 40–50.

MSNBC. (2007). "Graveyard Shift Linked to Cancer Risk." On the World Wide Web at http://www.msnbc.msn.com/id/22026660/ (retrieved 26 March 2009).

OECD. (2014). "Incidence of involuntary part time workers." On the World Wide Web at http://stats.oecd.org/Index.aspx?DataSetCode=INVPT_I (retrieved 23 October 2014).

Olsen, Karen M. and Arne Kalleberg. (2004). "Nonstandard Work in Two Different Employment Regimes: Norway and the United States." *Work, Employment and Society, 18* (2), 321–48.

Olson-Buchanan, J. B. and W. R. Boswell (2006). "Blurring Boundaries: Correlates of Integration and Segmentation between Work and Non-Work. *Journal of Vocational Behavior 68*, 432–45.

Osterman, Paul. (1995). "The Transformation of Work in the United States: What the Evidence Shows." In Bryan Downie and Mary Lou Coates, eds., *Managing Human Resources in the 1990s and Beyond* (pp. 71–92). Kingston, ON: Industrial Relations Centre Press.

Pescosolido, Bernice, Steven Tuch, and Jack Martin. (2001). "The Profession of Medicine and the Public: Examining Americans' Changing Confidence in Physician Authority from the Beginning of the 'Health Care Crisis' to the Era of Health Care Reform." *Journal of Health and Social Behavior, 42* (March), 1–16.

Polanyi, Karl. (1957). *The Great Transformation*. Boston: Beacon Press.

Pold, Henry. (2004). "Duration of Nonstandard Employment" *Perspectives on Labour and Income, 5* (12).

Preisler, Marie. (2011). "EU Directive on Temporary Agency Work Could Reduce Social Dumping." *Nordic Labour Journal*. April. On the World Wide Web at http://www.nordiclabourjournal.org/i-fokus/in-focus-2011/temporary-workers/article.2011-04-01.4693831011 (retrieved 30 July 2012).

Presser, Harriet. (1999). "Toward a 24-Hour Economy." *Science, 284* (June 11), 1778–89.

Presser, Harriet. (2003). "Race, Ethnic, and Gender Differences in Nonstandard Work Shifts." *Work & Occupations, 30* (4), 412–39.

Presser, Harriet. (2004). *Employment in a 24/7 Economy: Challenges for American Families*. New York: Russell Sage.

Rifkin, Jeremy. (1995). *The End of Work: The Decline of the Global Labor Force and the Dawn of the Post-Market Era*. New York: G. P. Putnam.

Rinehart, James. (1996). *The Tyranny of Work: Alienation and the Labour Process*, 3rd ed. Toronto: Harcourt Brace.

Ritzer, George. (1993). *The McDonaldization of Society*. Newbury Park, CA: Pine Forge.

Robertson, David, James Rinehart, Christopher Huxley, Jeff Wareham, Herman Rosenfeld, Alan McGough, and Steve Benedict. (1993). *The CAMI Report: Lean Production in a Unionized Auto Plant*. North York, ON: CAW Research.

Rogers, Jackie Krasas. (1995). "Just a Temp: Experience and Structure of Alienation in Temporary Clerical Employment." *Work and Occupations, 22* (2), 137–66.

Schieman, S. and P. Glavin. (2008) "Trouble at the Border? Gender, Flexibility at Work, and the Work–Home Interface. "*Social Problems 55* (4), 590–611.

Schmitt, R. and T. E. Moody. (1994). *Alienation and Social Criticism*. Atlantic Highlands, NJ: Humanities Press.

Shain, Alan. (1995). "Employment of People with Disabilities." *Canadian Social Trends* (Autumn), 8–13.

Shalla, Vivian. (2002). "Jettisoned by Design? The Truncated Employment Relationship of Customer Sales and Service Agents under Airline Restructuring." *Canadian Review of Sociology and Anthropology, 27* (1), 1–32.

Shields, Margot. (2002). "Shift Work and Health." *Health Reports, 13* (4), 11–33. Statistics Canada. Catalogue No. 82–003.

Shields, Margot. (2003). "The Health of Canada's Shift Workers. *Canadian Social Trends* (Summer), 21–25. Statistics Canada. Catalogue No. 11–008.

Smith, Michael. (1999). "Insecurity in the Labour Market: The Case of Canada since the Second World War." *Canadian Journal of Sociology, 24* (2), 193–224.

Smith, Vicki. (2001). *Crossing the Great Divide: Worker Risk and Opportunity in the New Economy*. Ithaca and Cornell, NY: IRL Press.

Spenner, Kenneth. (1983). "Deciphering Prometheus: Temporal Change in the Skill Level of Work." *American Sociological Review, 48* (6), 824–37.

Statistics Canada. (2003). "The Changing Profile of Canada's Labour Force." *2001 Census: Analysis Series*. Ottawa: Ministry of Industry. Catalogue No. 96F0030XIE2001009.

Statistics Canada. (2006a). "The Canadian Labour Market at a Glance, 2005." Ottawa: Industry Canada. Catalogue No. 71-222-XIE.

Statistics Canada. (2006b). "Latest Release from the Labour Force Survey." *The Daily* August 4. On the World Wide Web at http://www.statcan.ca/english/Subjects/Labour/LFS/lfs-en.htm (retrieved 22 September 2006).

Statistics Canada. (2009). "The Canadian Labour Market at a Glance, 2007." Ottawa: Industry Canada. Catalogue No. 71-222-X.

Statistics Canada. 2010. "Percentage of Employers Offering Flexible Work Arrangements and Percent of Older Workers Who Would Use Them." On the World Wide Web at http://www.statcan.gc.ca/pub/89-646-x/2010001/c-g/c-ga4.2-eng.htm (retrieved 23 October 2014).

Statistics Canada. (2011). *Canada Year Book 2011* (pp. 302–325). Statistics Canada. Catalogue No. 11-402-X.

Statistics Canada. (2012a). "Labour Force Survey, July 2012. *The Daily* August 10. On the World Wide Web at http://www.statcan.gc.ca/daily-quotidien/120810/dq120810a-eng.htm (retrieved 2 September 2012).

Statistics Canada. (2012b). Table 282–0079 (CANSIM). "Labour Force Survey Estimates (LFS), Employees by Job Permanency, North American Industry Classification System (NAICS), Sex and Age Group, Unadjusted for Seasonality."

On the World Wide Web at http://www5.statcan.gc.ca/cansim/pick-choisir?lang=eng&p2=33&id=2820079 (retrieved 1 March 2012).

Statistics Canada. (2012c). Table 282–0008 (CANSIM). "Labour Force Survey Estimates (LFS), by North American Industry Classification System (NAICS), Sex and Age Group." On the World Wide Web at http://www5.statcan.gc.ca/cansim/pick-choisir?lang=eng&p2=33&id=2820008 (retrieved 15 February 2012).

Statistics Canada. (2014a). "People Employed, by Educational Attainment." On the World Wide Web at http://www.statcan.gc.ca/tables-tableaux/sum-som/l01/cst01/labor62-eng.htm (retrieved 23 October 2014).

Statistics Canada. (2014b). "Labour Force Survey Estimates (LFS), by Immigrant Status, Educational Attainment, Sex and Age Group, Canada, 3 Month Moving Average, Unadjusted For Seasonality." On the World Wide Web at http://data.gc.ca/data/en/dataset/d97fe711-48bc-478d-85a2-18de2cdaf89b (retrieved 23 October 2014).

Statistics Canada. (2014c). "Employment by Industry and Sex." On the World Wide Web at http://www.statcan.gc.ca/tables-tableaux/sum-som/l01/cst01/labor10a-eng.htm (retrieved 23 October 2014).

Statistics Canada. (2014d). "Earnings, Average Hourly for Hourly Paid Employees, by Industry." On the World Wide Web at http://www.statcan.gc.ca/tables-tableaux/sum-som/l01/cst01/labr74a-eng.htm (retrieved 23 October 2014).

Statistics Canada. (2014e). "Full-Time and Part-Time Employment by Sex and Age Group." On the World Wide Web at http://www.statcan.gc.ca/tables-tableaux/sum-som/l01/cst01/labor12-eng.htm (retrieved 23 October 2014).

Statistics Canada. (2014f). "Average Hourly Wages of Employees by Selected Characteristics and Occupation, Unadjusted Data, by Province." On the World Wide Web at http://www.statcan.gc.ca/tables-tableaux/sum-som/l01/cst01/labr69a-eng.htm (retrieved 23 October 2014).

Statistics Canada. 2015. "Labour force characteristics, seasonally adjusted, by province (monthly)." http://www.statcan.gc.ca/tables-tableaux/sum-som/l01/cst01/lfss01a-eng.htm (retrieved 22 September 2015).

U.S. Bureau of Labor Statistics. (2010). "Occupational Outlook Handbook, 2010–11 Edition." On the World Wide Web at http://www.bls.gov/oco (retrieved 30 July 2012).

Uppal, Sharanjit. (2011). "Unionization 2001. Inside the Labour Market Downturn." *Perspectives on Labour Market and Income* (Winter), 3–12. Statistics Canada. Catalogue No. 75-001-X.

Usalcas, Jeannine. (2008). "Hours Polarization Revisited." In *Perspectives on Labour Market and Income* (March), 5–15. Statistics Canada. Catalogue No. 75-001X.

Vosko, Leah. (2000). *Temporary Work: The Gendered Rise of a Precarious Employment Relationship.* Toronto: University of Toronto Press.

White, Julie. (1993). "Patterns of Unionization." In Linda Briskin and Patricia McDermott, eds., *Women Challenging Unions: Feminism, Democracy, and Militancy* (pp. 191–206). Toronto: University of Toronto Press.

Williams, Cara. (2008). "Work–Life Balance of Shift Workers." *Perspectives on Labour and Income, 9* (8), 5–16. Statistics Canada. Catalogue No. 75-001-X.

Womack, J., D. Jones, and D. Roos. (1990). *The Machine That Changed the World.* New York: Rawson and Associates.

Yakubovich, Valery (2005). "Weak Ties, Information and Influence: How Workers Find Jobs in a Local Russian Labor Market." *American Sociological Review, 70* (3), 408–21.

Zuboff, Shoshana. (1988). *In the Age of the Smart Machine: The Future of Work and Power.* New York: Basic Books.

CHAPTER 13

Adler, Patricia A. and Peter Adler. (1994). "Reproduction of the Corporate Other: The Institutionalization of After-School Activities." *Sociological Quarterly, 35* (2), 309–28.

Alexander, Karl L., Doris Entwisle, and Linda Steffel Olsen. (2007). "Lasting Consequence of the Summer Learning Gap." *American Sociological Review, 72,* 167–80.

American Association of University Women Educational Foundation. (1998). *Gender Gaps: Where Schools Still Fail Our Children.* American Institutes of Research. Washington, DC: AAUW Educational Foundation.

Anisef, P. (1974). *The Critical Juncture.* Toronto: Ministry of Colleges and Universities.

Arai, A. Bruce. (2000). "Changing Motivations for Homeschooling in Canada." *Canadian Journal of Education, 25* (3), 204–17.

Aurini, Janice, Scott Davies, and Julian Dierkes, eds. (2013). *Out of the Shadows: The Global Intensification of Supplementary Education.* Emerald.

Axelrod, Paul. (1997). *The Promise of Schooling: Education in Canada 1800–1914.* Toronto: University of Toronto Press.

Becker, Gary. (1964). *Human Capital,* 2nd ed. New York: Columbia University Press.

Bennett DeMarrais, Kathleen and Margaret D. LeCompte. (1995). *The Way Schools Work: A Sociological Analysis of Education,* 2nd ed. White Plains, NY: Longman.

Blossfeld, H. P. and Y. Shavit. (1993). "Persisting Barriers: Changes in Educational Opportunities in Thirteen Countries." In Y. Shavit and H. P. Blossfeld, eds., *Persistent Inequality: Changing Educational Attainment in Thirteen Countries.* Boulder,CO: Westview.

Bosetti, Lynn. (2001). "The Alberta Charter School Experience." In Claudia R. Hepburn, ed. *Can the Market Save Our Schools?* (pp. 101–20). Vancouver: The Fraser Institute.

Bowles, Samuel, and Herbert Gintis. (1976). *Schooling in Capitalist America: Educational Reform and the Contradictions of Economic Life.* New York: Basic Books.

Brint, Steven, M. F. Contreras, and M. T. Matthews. (2001). "Socialization Messages in Primary Schools: An Organizational Analysis." *Sociology of Education, 74,* 157–80.

Burkam, David, Douglas Ready, Valerie Lee, and Laura LoGerfo. (2004). "Social Class Differences in Summer Learning between Kindergarten and First Grade: Model Specification and Estimation" *Sociology of Education, 77,* 1–31.

Canadian Council on Learning. (2007). *2007 Survey of Canadians' Attitudes Toward Learning: Results for Elementary and Secondary Learning.* Ottawa: Author.

Chubb, John E. and Terry M. Moe. (1990). *Politics, Markets and America's Schools.* Washington, DC: The Brookings Institution.

Cohen, Albert. (1955). *Delinquent Boys: The Culture of the Gang.* Glencoe, IL: Free Press.

Coleman, James. (1961). *The Adolescent Society.* New York: Free Press.

Collins, R. (1979). *The Credential Society*. New York: Academic Press.

Davies, Lynn. (1984). *Pupil Power: Deviance and Gender in School*. London: Falmer Press.

Davies, Scott and Janice Aurini. (2011). "School Choice in Canada: Who Chooses What and Why?" *Canadian Public Policy*, 37 (4), 459–77.

Davies, Scott and Janice Aurini. (2013). "Summer Learning Inequality in Ontario." *Canadian Public Policy*, 39 (2), 287–307.

Davies, Scott and Neil Guppy. (1997). "Fields of Study, College Selectivity, and Student Inequalities." *Social Forces*, 73 (4), 131–51.

Davies, Scott and Neil Guppy. (2013). *The Schooled Society: An Introduction to the Sociology of Education*, 3rd ed. Toronto: Oxford University Press.

Davies, Scott, Vicky Maldonado, and David Zarifa. (2014). "Effectively Maintaining Inequality in Toronto: Predicting University Destinations of Toronto District School Board Graduates." *Canadian Review of Sociology*, 51 (1), 22–53.

Davies, Scott and Linda Quirke. (2007). "The Impact of Sector on School Organizations: The Logics of Markets and Institutions." *Sociology of Education*, 80 (1), 66–89.

Davies, Scott and David Zarifa. (2012). "The Stratification of Universities: Structural Inequality in Canadian and American Higher Education." *Research in Social Stratification and Mobility*, 30 (2): 143–58.

De Broucker, Patrice and Laval Lavallée. (1998). "Getting Ahead in Life: Does Your Parents' Education Count?" *Education Quarterly Review*, 5 (1), 22–28.

Dei, George. (2005). "The Case for Black Schools." *Toronto Star* 4 February.

Dennison, John D. (1995). Ed., *Canada's Community Colleges at the Crossroads*. Vancouver: UBC Press.

DiPrete, Thomas and Claudia Buchmann. (2013). *The Rise of Women: The Growing Gender Gap in Education and What It Means for American Schools*. New York: Russell Sage.

Downey, Douglas and James Ainsworth–Darnell. (2002). "The Search for Oppositional Culture among Black Students." *American Sociological Review*, 67, 156–64.

Downey, Douglas B., Paul T. von Hippel, and Beckett A. Broh. (2004). "Are Schools the Great Equalizer? Cognitive Inequality during the Summer Months and the School Year." *American Sociological Review*, 69 (5), 613–35.

Dreeben, Robert. (1967). *On What Is Learned in School*. Reading, MA: Addison–Wesley

Durkheim, Émile. (1961 [1925]). *Moral Education: A Study in the Theory and Application of the Sociology of Education*. New York: Free Press.

Fordham, Signithia and John Ogbu. (1986). "Black Students' School Success: Coping with the 'Burden' of 'Acting White.'" *The Urban Review*, 18, 176–206.

Frenette, Marc. (2005). "The Impact of Tuition Fees on University Access: Evidence from a Large-Scale Price Deregulation in Professional Programs." Ottawa: Statistics Canada. Catalogue No. 11F00119MIE.

Frenette, Marc and Klarka Zeman. (2008). "Why Are the Majority of University Students Women?" *Education Matters*, 5 (1).

Gamoran, Adam. (2001). "American Schooling and Educational Inequality: A Forecast for the 21st Century." *Sociology of Education* (extra issue), 135–53.

Gardner, Howard. (1998). "A Multiplicity of Intelligences." [Special Issue]. *Scientific American 9* (4), 18–23.

Gardner, Howard. (1999). *Intelligence Reframed: Multiple Intelligences for the 21st Century*. New York: Basic Books.

Gardner, Howard and T. Hatch. (1989). "Multiple Intelligences Go to School: Educational Implications of the Theory of Multiple Intelligences." *Educational Researcher*, 18 (8), 4–10.

Globe and Mail. "Which Canadian EMBA schools cost the most?" (2012). *Globe and Mail* 31 August. http://www.theglobeandmail.com/report-on-business/careers/business-education/which-canadian-emba-schools-cost-the-most/article4508437/ (retrieved 24 September 2015).

Government of Ontario. (1950). *Aims of Education: Report of the Royal Commission on Education in Ontario (The Hope Report)*. Toronto: The King's Printer.

Guppy, Neil and Bruce Arai. (1994). "Teaching Sociology: Comparing Undergraduate Curricula in the United States and Canada." *Teaching Sociology*, 22, 217–30.

Holland, D. C. and M. Eisenhart. (1990). *Educated in Romance: Women, Achievement, and College Culture*. Chicago: University of Chicago Press.

Hurn, C. J. (1993). *The Limits and Possibilities of Schooling: An Introduction to the Sociology of Education*. Boston: Allyn and Bacon.

Jackson, Philip W., Robert E. Boostrom, and David T Hansen. (1998). *The Moral Life of Schools*. San Francisco: John Wiley and Sons.

Kelly, Gail and Ann Nihlen. (1982). "Schooling and the Reproduction of Patriarchy: Unequal Workloads, Unequal Rewards." In Michael Apple, ed., *Cultural and Economic Reproduction in American Education: Essays in Class, Ideology, and the State* (pp. 162–80). London, UK: Routledge.

Kerckhoff, Alan C. (2002). "The Transition from School to Work." In Jeylan Mortimer and Reed W Larson (eds.), *The Changing Adolescent Experience* (pp. 52–87). New York: Cambridge University Press.

Kingston, P. W, R. Hubbard, B. Lapp, P. Schroeder, and J. Wilson. (2003). "Why Education Matters." *Sociology of Education*, 76 (1), 53–70.

Kirp, David. L. (2004). *Shakespeare, Einstein and the Bottom Line: The Marketing of Higher Education*. Cambridge MA: Harvard University Press.

Knighton, T. (2002). "Postsecondary Participation: The Effects of Parents' Education and Household Income." *Education Quarterly Review*, 8 (3), 25–31.

Krahn, Harvey. (2004). "Social Class, Postsecondary Education, and Occupational Outcomes: Choose Your Parents Well." In James E. Curtis, E. E. Grabb, and N. Guppy, eds., *Social Inequality in Canada: Patterns, Problems, Policies*, 4th ed. (pp. 187–203). Scarborough, ON: Pearson Prentice–Hall.

Krahn, Harvey and Alison Taylor. (2007). "Streaming in the 10th Grade in Four Canadian Provinces in 2000." *Education Matters*, 4 (2).

Labaree, David. (2010). *Someone Has to Fail*. Cambridge MA: Harvard University Press.

Livingstone, David W. (1998). *The Education–Jobs Gap: Underemployment or Economic Democracy*. Boulder, CO: Westview Press.

Looker, Diane and Victor Thiessen. (1999). "Images of Work: Women's Work, Men's Work, Housework." *Canadian Journal of Sociology*, 24 (2), 225–51.

Maclean's. 2015. "Rankings." http://www.macleans.ca/education/unirankings/ (retrieved 23 September 2015).

Milner, Murray, Jr. (2004). *Freaks, Geeks, and Cool Kids: American Teenagers, Schools, and the Culture of Consumption.* London, UK: Routledge.

McMullen, Kathryn. (2011). "Postsecondary Education Participation among Underrepresented and Minority Groups." Statistics Canada table: *"Youth in Transition Survey.* Cohort A. Cycle 4." On the World Wide Web at http://www.statcan.gc.ca/pub/81-004-x/2011004/article/11595-eng.htm.

Mullen, Ann. (2010). *Degrees of Inequality: Culture, Class and Gender in American Higher Education.* Baltimore: Johns Hopkins University Press.

OECD. (2014). "Snapshot of performance in mathematics, reading and science." *PISA 2012 Results in Focus.* On the World Wide Web at http://www.oecd.org/pisa/keyfindings/pisa-2012-results-overview.pdf.

Ontario Department of Education. (1968). *Living and Learning: The Report of the Provincial Committee on the Aims and Objectives of Education in the Schools of Ontario.* Toronto: Author.

Ouchi, William. (2003). *Making Schools Work: A Revolutionary Plan to Get Your Children the Education They Need.* New York: Simon and Schuster.

Pallas, A. (2000). "The Effects of Schooling on Individual Lives. In M. T. Hallinan, ed., *Handbook of the Sociology of Education* (pp. 499–525). New York: Kluwer Academic/Plenum Publishers.

Porter, J., M. Porter, and B. Blishen. (1982). *Stations and Callings: Making It through the School System.* Toronto: Methuen.

Powell, A. G., E. Farrar, and D. K. Cohen. (1985). *The Shopping Mall High School: Winners and Losers in the Educational Marketplace.* Boston: Houghton Mifflin.

Prentice, A. (1977). *The School Promoters.* Toronto: McClelland and Stewart.

Quirke, Linda. (2006). "'Keeping Young Minds Sharp': Children's Cognitive Stimulation and the Rise of Parenting Magazines, 1959–2003." *Canadian Review of Sociology, 43* (4), 387–406.

Ryan, B. A. and G. R. Adams. (1999). "How Do Families Affect Children's Success in School?" *Education Quarterly Review, 6* (1), 30–43.

Sayer, L. C, S. M. Bianchi, and J. P. Robinson. (2004). "Are Parents Investing Less in Children? Trends in Mothers' and Fathers' Time with Children." *American Journal of Sociology, 107,* 1–43.

Slaughter, Sheila and Gary Rhoades. (2004). *Academic Capitalism and the New Economy.* Baltimore: Johns Hopkins University Press.

Statistics Canada. (2001). *Education in Canada, 2000.* Ottawa: Ministry of Industry.

Statistics Canada. (2002). *Survey of Approaches to Educational Planning.* Public Use Microdata File.

Statistics Canada. (2013). "Major Field of Study—Classification of Instructional Programs (CIP) 2000 (425), Highest Certificate, Diploma or Degree (7), Age Groups (8B) and Sex (3) for the Population Aged 15 Years and Over, in Private Households of Canada, Provinces, Territories, Census Metropolitan Areas and Census Agglomerations, *2011 National Household Survey.*" On the World Wide Web at http://www12.statcan.gc.ca/nhs-enm/2011/dp-pd/dt-td/Rp-eng.cfm?LANG=E&APATH=3&DETAIL=0&DIM=0&FL=A&FREE=0&GC=0&GID=0&GK=0&GRP=1&PID=107754&PRID=0&PTYPE=105277&S=0&SHOWALL=0&SUB=0&Temporal=2013&THEME=96&VID=0&VNAMEE=&VNAMEF=.

Statistics Canada. (2014). "Undergraduate tuition fees for full time Canadian students, by discipline, by province (Canada)." http://www.statcan.gc.ca/tables-tableaux/sum-som/l01/cst01/educ50a-eng.htm (retrieved 24 September 2015).

Stevens, Mitchell L., Elizabeth A. Armstrong, and Richard Arum. (2008). "Sieve, Incubator, Temple, Hub: Empirical and Theoretical Advances in the Sociology of Higher Education." *Annual Review of Sociology, 34,* 127–51.

Stinchcombe, Arthur. (1964). *Rebellion in a High School.* Chicago: Quadrangle Books.

Tanner, Julian. (2009). *Teenage Troubles: Youth and Deviance in Canada,* 3rd ed. Toronto: Nelson Thomson Learning.

Taylor, A. and L. Woollard. (2003). "The Risky Business of Choosing a High School." *Journal of Education Policy 18* (6), 617–35.

Turner, Ralph H. (1960). "Sponsored and Contest Mobility and the School System." *American Sociological Review, 25,* 855–67.

Tyack, David B. (1974). *The One Best System: A History of American Urban Education.* Cambridge, MA: Harvard University Press.

Tyson, Karolyn, William Darity Jr., and Domini Castellino. (2005). "It's Not a Black Thing: Understanding the Burden of Acting White and Other Dilemmas of High Achievement." *American Sociological Review, 70* (4), 582–605.

Walters, David. (2004). "'Recycling': The Economic Implications of Obtaining Additional Postsecondary Credentials at Lower or Equivalent Levels." *Canadian Review of Sociology and Anthropology, 40* (4), 463–77.

Wanner, Richard. (2000). "Expansion and Ascription: Trends in Educational Opportunity in Canada 1920–1994." *Canadian Review of Sociology and Anthropology, 36* (3), 409–43.

Weis, L. (1990). *Working Class without Work: High School Students in a De–industrializing Economy.* New York: Routledge.

Wolf, Alison. (2002). *Does Education Matter? Myths about Education and Economic Growth.* London: Penguin.

CHAPTER 14

Allen, John L., Jr. (2009). *The Future Church.* New York: Doubleday.

Bell, Daniel. (1977). "The Return of the Sacred: The Argument on the Future of Religion." *British Journal of Sociology, 28,* 419–49.

Bellah, Robert. (1967). "Civil Religion in America." *Daedalus, 96* (1), 1–21.

Berger, Peter. (1961). *The Noise of Solemn Assemblies.* New York: Doubleday.

Berger, Peter L. (1974). "Some Second Thoughts on Substantive versus Functional Definitions of Religion. *Journal for the Scientific Study of Religion, 13,* 125–33.

Beyer, Peter. (1993). "Roman Catholicism in Contemporary Quebec." In W. E. Hewitt, ed., *The Sociology of Religion: A Canadian Focus* (pp. 133–55). Toronto: Butterworths.

Beyer, Peter. (1997). "Religious Vitality in Canada: The Complementarity of Religious Market and Secularization Perspectives." *Journal for the Scientific Study of Religion, 36,* 272–88.

Bibby, Reginald W. (n.d. 1). *Project Canada Surveys,* 1975–1980.

Bibby, Reginald W. (n.d. 2). *General Social Survey,* Statistics Canada, 1985–2012.

Bibby, Reginald W. (1987). *Fragmented Gods: The Poverty and Potential of Religion in Canada.* Toronto: Stoddart.

Bibby, Reginald W. (1993). *Unknown Gods: The Ongoing Story of Religion in Canada.* Toronto: Stoddart.

Bibby, Reginald W. (1995). *The Bibby Report: Social Trends Canadian Style*. Toronto: Stoddart.

Bibby, Reginald. (2002). *Restless Gods: The Renaissance of Religion in Canada*. Toronto: Stoddart.

Bibby, Reginald W. (2004a). *Restless Gods: The Renaissance of Religion in Canada*, 2nd ed. Ottawa: Novalis.

Bibby, Reginald W. (2004b). *Restless Churches: How Canada's Churches Can Contribute to the Emerging Religious Renaissance*. Ottawa: Novalis.

Bibby, Reginald W. (2009). *The Emerging Millennials*. Lethbridge, AB: Project Canada Books.

Bibby, Reginald W. (2011a). *Beyond the Gods & Back: Religion's Rise and Demise and Why It Matters*. Lethbridge, AB: Project Canada Books.

Bibby, Reginald W. (2011b). "Continuing the Conversation on Canada: Changing Patterns of Religious Service Attendance." *Journal for the Scientific Study of Religion, 50* (4), 831–39.

Bibby, Reginald W. (2012). "Why Bother with Organized Religion?" *Canadian Review of Sociology, 49* (1), 91–101.

Bibby, Reginald and Angus Reid. (2013). "We'll Be Home for 'Christmas,' However It's Celebrated." *Globe and Mail*, 24 December.

Bramadat, Paul and David Seljak. (2008). "Charting the New Terrain: Christianity and Ethnicity in Canada." In Paul Bramadat and David Seljak, eds., *Christianity and Ethnicity in Canada* (pp. 3–48). Toronto: University of Toronto Press.

Brannon, Robert. (1971). "Organizational Vulnerability in Modern Religious Organizations." *Journal for the Scientific Study of Religion, 10*, 27–32.

Brown, Callum. (2009). *The Death of Christian Britain*, 2nd ed. London: Routledge.

Brym, Robert and Bader Araj. (2006). "Suicide Bombing as Strategy and Interaction: The Case of the Second Intifada." *Social Forces, 84*, 1965–82.

Brym, Robert, William Shaffir, and Morton Weinfeld, eds. (2010). *The Jews in Canada*. Toronto: Oxford University Press.

Catto, Susan. (2003). "In Search of the Spiritual." *Time* 24 November: 72–80.

Clark, S. D. (1948). *Church and Sect in Canada*. Toronto: University of Toronto Press.

Cogley, John. (1968). *Religion in a Secular Age*. New York: New American Library.

Cox, Harvey. (2009). *The Future of Faith*. New York: Harper One.

Crysdale, Stewart. (1961). *The Industrial Struggle and Protestant Ethics in Canada*. Toronto: Ryerson Press.

Davies, Alan and Marilyn F. Nefsky. (1997). *How Silent Were the Churches? Canadian Protestantism and the Jewish Plight during the Nazi Era*. Waterloo, ON: Wilfrid Laurier University Press.

Dawson, Lorne L. (2006). *Comprehending Cults: The Sociology of New Religious Movements*. Toronto: Oxford University Press.

Dawson, Lorne L. and Joel Thiessen. (2014). *The Sociology of Religion*. Toronto: Oxford University Press.

Durkheim, Émile. (1965 [1912]). *The Elementary Forms of the Religious Life*. New York: Free Press.

Eagle, David E. (2011). "Changing Patterns of Attendance at Religious Services in Canada, 1986–2008." *Journal for the Scientific Study of Religion, 50* (1), 187–200.

Fallding, Harold. (1978). "Mainline Protestantism in Canada and the United States: An Overview." *Canadian Journal of Sociology 2*, 141–60.

Finke, Roger and Rodney Stark. (1992). *The Churching of America, 1776–1990*. New Brunswick, NJ: Rutgers University Press.

Frankel, B. Gail and W. E. Hewitt. (1994). "Religion and Well-Being among Canadian University Students." *Journal for the Scientific Study of Religion, 33*, 62–73.

Freud, Sigmund. (1962 [1928]). *The Future of an Illusion*. New York: Doubleday.

Gallup. (2015). *Religion*. On the World Wide Web at http://www.gallup.com/poll/1690/Religion.aspx (retrieved 05 January 2015).

General Social Survey. (2012). "Caregiving and Care Receiving (Cycle 26)." Statistics Canada.

Ghafour, Hamida. (2006). "Muslim Fury over Cartoons Hits Britain." *Globe and Mail* 4 February.

Glock, Charles Y., Benjamin Ringer, and Earl Babbie. (1967). *To Comfort and to Challenge*. Berkeley, CA: University of California Press.

Glock, Charles Y. and Rodney Stark. (1965). *Religion and Society in Tension*. Chicago: Rand-McNally.

Gorsuch, Richard and Daniel Aleshire. (1974). "Christian Faith and Ethnic Prejudice: A Review and Interpretation of Research." *Journal for the Scientific Study of Religion, 13*, 281–307.

Graham, Ron. (1990). *God's Dominion: A Sceptic's Quest*. Toronto: McClelland and Stewart.

Herberg, Will. (1960). *Protestant, Catholic, Jew*, rev. ed. New York: Doubleday.

Hiller, Harry H. (1976). "Alberta and the Bible Belt Stereo type." In Stewart Crysdale and Les Wheatcroft, eds., *Religion in Canadian Society* (pp. 372–83). Toronto: Macmillan.

Hobart, Charles. (1974). "Church Involvement and the Comfort Thesis." *Journal for the Scientific Study of Religion, 13*, 463–70.

Johnson, Benton. (1961). "Do Holiness Sects Socialize in Dominant Values?" *Social Forces, 39*, 309–16.

Kirkpatrick, Clifford. (1949). "Religion and Humanitarianism: A Study of Institutional Implications." *Psychological Monographs 63* (9).

Lee, Gary and Robert Clyde. (1974). "Religion, Socioeconomic Status and Anomie." *Journal for the Scientific Study of Religion, 13*, 35–47.

Lewis, David L. (1993). "Canada's Native Peoples and the Churches." In W. E. Hewitt, ed., *The Sociology of Religion: A Canadian Focus* (pp. 235–51). Toronto: Butterworths.

Lim, Chaeyoon, Carol Ann MacGregor and Robert Putnam. (2010). "Secular and Liminal: Discovering Heterogeneity among Religious Nones." *Journal for the Scientific Study of Religion 49* (4): 596–618.

Mann, W. E. (1962). *Sect, Cult and Church in Alberta*. Toronto: University of Toronto Press.

Marx, Karl. (1970 [1843]). *Critique of Hegel's "Philosophy of Right,"* Annette Jolin and Joseph O'Malley, trans. Cambridge, MA: Harvard University Press.

Marx, Karl and Friedrich Engels. (1964). *On Religion*. New York: Schocken Books.

Mead, Walter Russell. (2010). "Pentecostal Power." A blog in *The American Interest*, May 28.

Metz, Donald. (1967). *New Congregations: Security and Mission in Conflict.* Philadelphia, PA: Westminster Press.

Monahan, Susanne C. (1999) "Who Controls Church Work? Organizational Effects on Jurisdictional Boundaries and Disputes in Churches." *Journal for the Scientific Study of Religion, 38,* 370–85.

Nason-Clark, N. (1993). "Gender Relations in Contemporary Christian Organizations." In W. E. Hewitt, ed., *The Sociology of Religion* (pp. 215–34). Toronto: Butterworth.

Nesbitt, P. D. (1997). *The Feminization of the Clergy in America.* New York: Oxford University Press.

Newport, Frank. (2007). "Just Why Do Americans Attend Church?" April 6. On the World Wide Web at http://www .gallup.com/poll/27124/just-why-americans-attend-church .aspx (retrieved 30 July 2012).

Newport, Frank. (2014). "Three-Quarters of Americans Identify as Christian." Gallup 24 December. On the World Wide Web http://www.gallup.com/poll/180347/three-quarters-americans -identify-christian.aspx (retrieved 5 January 2015).

Newport, Frank, David W. Moore, and Lydia Saad. (1999). "Long-Term Gallup Poll Trends: A Portrait of American Public Opinion through the Century." 20 December. On the World Wide Web at http://www.gallup.com/poll/3400/longterm -gallup-poll-trends-portrait-american-public-opinion.aspx (retrieved 30 July 2012).

Niebuhr, H. Richard. (1957 [1929]). *The Social Sources of Denominationalism.* New York: Henry Holt and Co.

O'Toole, Roger, Douglas F. Campbell, John A. Hannigan, Peter Beyer, and John H. Simpson. (1993). "The United Church in Crisis." In W.E. Hewitt, ed., *The Sociology of Religion: A Canadian Focus* (pp. 273–87). Toronto: Butterworths.

Pew Research (2012a). "'Nones' on the Rise." 9 October. On the World Wide Web http://www.pewforum.org/2012/10/09/ nones-on-the-rise (retrieved 05 January 2015).

Pew Research. (2012b). "The Global Religious Landscape." December 18. On the World Wide Web http://www.pewforum. org/2012/12/18/global-religious-landscape-exec (retrieved 04 January 2015).

Poloma, Margaret M. (1997). "The 'Toronto Blessing': Charisma, Institutionalization and *Revival.*" *Journal for the Scientific Study of Religion, 36,* 257–71.

Poloma, Margaret M. and Lynette F. Hoelter. (1998). "The 'Toronto Blessing': A Holistic Model of Healing." *Journal for the Scientific Study of Religion, 37,* 257–72.

Putnam, Robert. (2000). *Bowling Alone: The Collapse and Revival of American Community.* New York: Simon and Schuster.

Reid, Angus and Reginald W. Bibby. (2015). *2015 Religion Survey.* Vancouver: Angus Reid Institute. Copyright © Reginald Bibby

Reynolds, Neil. (2011). "The Globalization of God in the 21st Century." *Globe and Mail* 10 January.

Rokeach, Milton. (1965). *Paradoxes of Religious Belief.* Information Service, National Council of Churches, 1–2.

Rokeach, Milton. (1969). "Religious Values and Social Compassion." *Review of Religious Research, 11,* 3–23.

Roof, Wade Clark and Dean R. Hoge. (1980). "Church Involvement in America: Social Factors Affecting Membership and Participation." *Review of Religious Research, 21,* 405–26.

Rouleau, Jean-Paul. (1977). "Religion in Quebec: Present and Future." *Pro Mundi Vita: Dossiers, 3* (November/December).

Smith, Tom W. (1999). "The Religious Right and Anti-Semitism." *Review of Religious Research, 99,* 244–58.

Speaker-Yuan, Margaret, ed. (2005). *Women in Islam.* Detroit: Greenhaven Press/Thomson Gale.

Stackhouse, John G., Jr. (2005). *Finally Feminist: A Pragmatic Christian Understanding of Gender.* Grand Rapids, MI: Baker Academic.

Stahl, William. (1986). "The Land That God Gave Cain: Nature and Civil Religion in Canada." Presented at the Annual Meeting of the Society for the Scientific Study of Religion, Washington, DC, November.

Stark, Rodney and Charles Y. Glock. (1968). *American Piety.* Berkeley, CA: University of California Press.

Stark, Rodney and William Sims Bainbridge. (1985). *The Future of Religion.* Berkeley, CA: University of California Press.

Stark, Rodney and Roger Finke. (2000). *Acts of Faith: Explaining the Human Side of Religion.* Berkeley, CA: University of California Press.

Statistics Canada. (2004a). "General Social Survey: Social Engagement." *The Daily* 6 July.

Statistics Canada. (2004b). "National Survey of Non-Profit and Voluntary Organizations." *The Daily* 20 September.

Statistics Canada. (2013). *2011 National Household Survey*: Data Tables, Catalogue No. 99-010-X2011032.

Stiller, Brian. (1997). *From the Tower of Babel to Parliament Hill.* Toronto: HarperCollins.

Thomas, Scott M. (2010). "A Globalized God." *Foreign Affairs* (November/December) *89,* 93–101.

Thomas, W. I. and Florian Znaniecki. (1918). *The Polish Peasant in Europe and America.* New York: Knopf.

Valpy, Michael. (2006). "Why the Global Rage Hasn't Engulfed Canada: Multiculturalism and Media Likely Muted Protests," *Globe and Mail* 8 February: p. A14. Reprinted with permission from *The Globe and Mail.*

Valpy, Michael and Joe Friesen. (2010). "Canada Marching from Religion to Secularization." *Globe and Mail* 11 December.

Weber, Max. (1958 [1904–05]). *The Protestant Ethic and the Spirit of Capitalism.* New York: Scribner's.

Weber, Max. (1963 [1922]). *The Sociology of Religion,* Ephraim Fischoff, trans. Boston: Beacon Press.

Whyte, Donald. (1966). "Religion and the Rural Church." In M. A. Tremblay and W. J. Anderson, eds., *Rural Canada in Transition* (pp. 79–92). Ottawa: Agricultural Economics Research Council of Canada.

Wilcox, W. Bradford. (1998). "Conservative Protestant Childrearing: Authoritarian or Authoritative?" *American Sociological Review, 63,* 796–809.

Zuckerman, Phil. (2012). *Faith No More: Why People Reject Religion.* New York: Oxford University Press.

CHAPTER 15

Adler, Freda. (1975). *Sisters in Crime.* New York: McGraw-Hill.

Agnew, Robert. (1992). "Foundation for a General Theory of Crime and Delinquency." *Criminology, 30,* 47–87.

Aldridge, Judith, Fiona Measham, and Lisa Williams. (2011). *Illegal Leisure Revisited.* London: Routledge.

Amnesty International. (2014). "The Need for Accurate and Comprehensive Statistics on Missing and Murdered Indigenous Women and Girls." On the World Wide Web at http://www.amnesty.ca/blog/the-need-for-accurate-and

-comprehensive-statistics-on-missing-and-murdered
-indigenous-women-and (retrieved 14 July 2015).

Ashworth, Andrew and Julian Roberts. (2012). "Sentencing: Theory, Principle and Practice." In Mike McGuire, Rod Morgan, and Robert Reiner, eds., *The Oxford Handbook of Criminology*, 5th ed. (pp. 866–894). New York: Oxford University press

Becker, Howard. (1963). *Outsiders: Studies in the Sociology of Deviance*. New York: Free Press.

Ben-Yehuda, Nachman. (1986). "The Sociology of Moral Panics: Toward a New Synthesis." *Sociological Quarterly, 4*, 495–513.

Best, J. (1989). *Images of Issues: Typifying Contemporary Social Problems*. New York: Aldine de Gruyter.

Boyce, Jillian and Adam Cotter. (2013). "Homicide in Canada, 2012." *Juristat, 2013*. Statistics Canada. Catalogue No. 85–002-x.

Boyce, Jillian, Adam Cotter and Samuel Perreaut (2014). "Police-Recorded Crime Statistics in Canada, 2013." *Juristat*. Statistics Canada Catalogue No. 85-002-x.

Brown, Ian. (2011). "Unlocking the Crime Conundrum." *Globe and Mail* April: F1, F5.

Carlson, Kathryn Blaze. (2014a). "Fontaine death shows 'there's so far to go.'" *Globe and Mail* 30 September: A3.

Carlson, Kathryn Blaze (2014b.). "Police Work to Build Trust with First Nations." *Globe and Mail* 4 October: A3.

Chesney-Lind, Meda, Merry Morash, and Katherine Irwin. (2007). "Policing Girlhood? Relational Aggression and Violence Prevention." *Youth Violence and Juvenile Justice, 5* (3), 328–45.

Chibnall, Steve. (1977). *Law and Order News*. London: Tavistock.

Cloward, Richard and Lloyd Ohlin. (1960). *Delinquency and Opportunity: A Theory of Delinquent Gangs*. New York: Free Press.

Cobain, Ian. (2014). "Tough Case to Crack: The Mystery of Britain's Falling Crime Rate." *Guardian* 31 August.

Cohen, Albert. (1955). *Delinquent Boys*. Chicago: Free Press.

Cohen, Lawrence and Marcus Felson. (1979). "Social Change and Crime Rate Trends: A Routine Activity Approach." *American Sociological Review, 44* (August), 588–608.

Conrad, Peter and Joseph Schneider. (1992). *Deviance and Medicalization*. Philadelphia, PA: Temple University Press.

Cook, Shirley. (1969). "Canadian Narcotics Legislation, 1880–1923: A Conflict Model Interpretation." *Canadian Review of Sociology and Anthropology, 6*, 36–46.

Daigle, Leah, Francis Cullen, and John Paul Wright. (2007). "Gender Differences in the Predictors of Juvenile Delinquency: Assessing the Generality-Specificity Debate." *Youth Violence and Juvenile Justice, 5*, 254–86.

Doob, Anthony and Carla Cesaroni. (2004). *Responding to Youth Crime in Canada*. Toronto: University of Toronto Press.

Doob, Anthony and Cheryl Webster. (2003). "Sentence Severity and Crime: Accepting the Null Hypothesis." In Michael Tonry, ed., *Crime and Justice: a Review of Research. 30*, 143–95.

Downes, David and Rod Morgan. (2012). "Overtaking on the Left? The Politics of Law and Order in the 'Big Society.'" In Mike McGuire, Rod Morgan, and Robert Reiner, eds., *The Oxford Handbook of Criminology*, 5th ed. (pp. 182–205). New York: Oxford University Press.

Downes, David, Paul Rock, and Chris McCormick. (2013). *Understanding Deviance*, 2nd Canadian ed. New York: Oxford University press.

Dunn, Jennifer (2008). "Everyone Knows Who the Sluts Are: How Young Women Get around the Stigma." In Alex Thio, Thomas C. Calhoun, and Aadrain Conyers, eds., *Readings in Deviant Behavior*, 5th ed. (pp. 226–29). New York: Pearson.

Elias, Norbert. (1969). *The Civilising Process*. Oxford: Blackwell.

Felson, Marcus and Rachel Boba. (2010). *Crime and Everyday Life*, 4th ed. Thousand Oaks, CA: Pine Forge Press.

Fitzgerald, R. and P. Carrington. (2011). "Disproportionate Minority Contact in Canada: Police and Visible Minority Youth." *Canadian Journal of Criminology and Criminal Justice, 53* (4), 449–86.

Friesen, Joe. (2013). "What's Behind the Explosion of Native Activism? Young People." *Globe and Mail* 18 January.

Fuller, John and John Wozniak. (2006). "Peacemaking Criminology: Part, Present and Future." In Francis Cullen, John Paul Wright, and Kristie Blevins, eds., *Taking Stock* (pp. 251–73). New Brunswick, NJ: Transaction.

Garland, David. (2001). *The Culture of Control: Crime and Social Order in Contemporary Society*. Chicago: University of Chicago Press.

Gartner, Rosemary and Sarah Thompson. (2004). "Trends in Homicide in Toronto." In Bruce Kidd and Jim Phillips, eds., *Research on Community Safety* (pp. 28–41). Toronto: The Centre of Criminology, University of Toronto.

Giddens, Anthony. (1991). *Introduction to Sociology*. New York: Norton.

Goffman, Erving. (1963). *Stigma: Notes on the Management of Spoiled Identity*. Englewood Cliffs, NJ: Prentice Hall.

Goode, Erich. (2013). "The Stigma of Obesity." In Alex Thio, Thomas Calhoun, and Addrain Conyers, eds., *Deviance Today*, (pp. 221–29). New York: Pearson.

Gordon, Robert. (2000). "Criminal Business Organizations, Street Gangs, and Wannabe Groups: A Vancouver Perspective." *Canadian Journal of Criminology, 42* (1), 39–60.

Gottfredson, Michael and Travis Hirschi. (1990). *A General Theory of Crime*. Palo Alto, CA: Stanford University Press.

Greer, Chris and Robert Reiner. (2012). "Mediated Mayhem: Media, Crime, Criminal Justice." In Mike McGuire, Rod Morgan, and Robert Reiner, eds., *The Oxford Handbook of Criminology*, 5th ed. (pp. 206–78). New York: Oxford University Press.

Grekul, Jana and Patti LaBoucane-Benson. (2008). "Aboriginal Gangs and Their (Dis)placement: Contextualizing Recruitment, Membership, and Status." *Canadian Journal of Criminology and Criminal Justice, 50* (1), 59–82.

Gurr, Ted. (1989). "Historical Trends in Violent Crime: Europe and the United States." In Ted Gurr, ed., *Violence in America*. Newbury Park, CA: Sage.

Hagan, John. (1991). *The Disreputable Pleasures: Crime and Deviance in Canada*, 3rd ed. Toronto: McGraw-Hill Ryerson.

Hagan, John, Ron Gillis, and John Simpson. (1987). "Class in the Household: A Power-Control Theory of Gender and Delinquency." *American Journal of Sociology, 92*, 788–816.

Hagan, John and Bill McCarthy (1997). *Mean Streets*. Cambridge, UK: Cambridge University Press.

Hartnagel, Timothy. (2004). "Correlates of Criminal Behavior." In R. Linden, ed., *Criminology: A Canadian Perspective*, 5th ed. (pp. 120–63). Toronto: Harcourt Brace.

Hier, Sean. (2002). "Raves, Risks and Ecstasy Panic: A Case Study in the Subversive Nature of Moral Regulation." *Canadian Journal of Sociology, 27* (1), 33–57.

Hirschi, Travis. (1969). *Causes of Delinquency*. Berkeley, CA: University of California Press.

Jenkins, P. (2001). *Beyond Tolerance: Child Pornography on the Internet*. New York: New York University Press.

Keane, Carl, Paul Maxim, and James Teevan. (1993). "Drinking and Driving, Self-Control and Gender: Testing the General Theory of Crime." *Journal of Research in Crime and Delinquency, 30*, 30–46.

Krahn, Harvey, Tim Hartnagel, and John Gartrell. (1986). "Income Inequality and Homicide Rates: Cross-National Data and Criminological Theories." *Criminology, 24*, 269–95.

Larsson, Stieg. (2008). *The Girl with the Dragon Tattoo*. Toronto: Viking.

Lawrence, Richard and David Mueller. (2003). "School Shootings and the Man Bites Dog Criterion of Newsworthiness." *Youth Violence and Youth Justice, 1* (4), 330–45.

Liebling, Alison and Ben Crewe. (2012). "Prison Life, Penal Power, and Prison Effects." In Mike McGuire, Rod Morgan, and Robert Reiner, eds., *The Oxford Handbook of Criminology*, 5th ed. (pp. 895–927). New York: Oxford University Press

Link, Bruce. (1982). "Mental Patient Status, Work, and Income: An Examination of the Effects of a Psychiatric Label." *American Sociological Review, 47*, 202–15.

Liska, Allen and Steven Messner. (1999). *Perspectives on Deviance*, 3rd ed. Englewood Cliffs, NJ: Prentice-Hall.

Merton, Robert. (1938). "Social Structure and Anomie." *American Sociological Review, 3*, 672–87.

Minaker, J. and B. Hogaveen. (2009) *Youth, Crime and Society: Issues of Power and Justice*. Pearson Canada.

Nakhaie, Reza, Robert Silverman, and Teresa LaGrange. (2000). "Self-Control and Resistance to School." *Canadian Review of Sociology and Anthropology, 37* (4), 444–60.

Office of the Correctional Investigator. (2013). "Backgrounder: Aboriginal Offenders—A Critical Situation." On the World Wide Web at http://www.oci-bec.gc.ca/cnt/rpt/oth-aut/oth-aut20121022info-eng.aspx (retrieved 15 December 2015).

Office of the Correctional Investigator. (2014). "Annual Report: 2013–2014." On the World Wide Web at http://www.oci-bec.gc.ca/cnt/rpt/pdf/annrpt/annrpt20132014-eng.pdf (retrieved 15 December 2014).

Parnaby, Patrick. (2003). "Disaster through Dirty Windshields: Law, Order and Toronto's Squeegee Kids." *Canadian Journal of Sociology, 28* (3), 281–307.

Pinker, Steven. (2011). *The Better Angels of Our Nature*. Viking Books.

Reinarman, Craig and Harry Levine. (1989). "The Crack Attack: Politics and Media in America's Latest Drug Scare." In J. Best, ed., *Images of Issues: Typifying Contemporary Social Problems* (pp. 147–90). New York: Aldine De Gruyter.

Roberts, Julian. (2004). "Public Opinion and the Evolution of Juvenile Justice Policy in Western Nations." In Michael Tonry and Anthony Doob, eds., *Youth Crime and Youth Justice: Comparative and Cross-National Perspectives* (pp. 495–542). Chicago: University of Chicago Press.

Robertson, Ian. (1989). *Society: A Brief Introduction*. New York: Worth.

Sacco, Vince. (2005). *When Crime Waves*. Thousand Oaks, CA: Sage.

Sacco, Vince and Les Kennedy. (2011). *The Criminal Event: An Introduction to Criminology in Canada*, 5th ed. Toronto: Nelson.

Savoie, Josée. (2006). "Youth Self-Reported Delinquency. Toronto." *Juristat, 27* (6).

Siegel, Larry and Chris McCormick. (2006). *Criminology in Canada*. Toronto: Nelson.

Simon, Ruth. (1975). *Women and Crime*. Lexington, MA: Lexington Books.

Staples, William G. (2008). "Everyday Surveillance in Postmodern Society." In Alex

Statistics Canada (2014). "Police-Reported Crime Statistics, 2013." On the World Wide Web at http://www.statcan.gc.ca/daily-quotidien/140723/dq140723b-eng.htm (retrieved 15 December 2014).

Statistics Canada. (2015). "Police-reported crime statistics, 2014." *The Daily* 22 July. http://www.statcan.gc.ca/daily-quotidien/150722/dq150722a-eng.htm (retrieved 25 September 2015).

Stenning, Philip. (2003). "Policing the Cultural Kaleidoscope: Recent Canadian Experience." *Police and Society, 7* (1), 21–87.

Stewart, Bob and Aaron Smith. (2008). "Drug Use in Sport: Applications for Public Policy." *Journal of Sport and Social Issues* (August), *32*, (3), 278–98.

Sutherland, E. H. (1947). *Principles of Criminology*, 4th ed. Chicago: Lippincott.

Sykes, Gresham. (1958). *Society of Captives: A Study of a Maximum Security Institution*. Princeton: Princeton University Press.

Tanner, J. (2015). *Teenage Troubles: Youth and Deviance in Canada*, 4th ed. Toronto: Oxford.

Tanner, Julian and Scot Wortley. (2002). *The Toronto Youth Crime and Victimization Survey*. Toronto: Centre of Criminology, University of Toronto.

Thio, Alex. (2010). *Deviant Behavior*, 10th ed. Boston: Allyn and Bacon.

Venkatesh, S. (2008). *Gang Leader for a Day: A Rogue Sociologist Takes to the Streets*. New York: Penguin.

Vold, George, Thomas Bernard, and Jeffrey Snipes. (2002). *Theoretical Criminology*, 5th ed. New York: Oxford University Press.

Von Hirsch, Andrew, Anthony Bottoms, Elizabeth Burney, and Per-Olöf Wikstrom. (1999). *Criminal Deterrence: An Analysis of Recent Research*. Oxford, UK: Hart Publishing

Walmsley, Roy. 2013. *World Prison Population List*, 10th ed. On the World Wide Web at http://www.prisonstudies.org/sites/prisonstudies.org/files/resources/downloads/wppl_10.pdf (retrieved 15 December 2014).

Walsh, David. (2013). *Seven Deadly Sins: My Pursuit of Lance Armstrong*. Altria Books.

Wortley, Scot. (2011). "Interview with." *University of Toronto Bulletin*, 11 November.

Wortley, Scot and Julian Tanner. (2004). "Social Groups or Criminal Organizations? The Extent and Nature of Youth Gang Activity in Toronto." In B. Kidd and J. Phillips, eds., *Research on Community Safety*. Toronto: Centre of Criminology, University of Toronto.

Wortley, Scot and Julian Tanner. (2005). "Inflammatory Rhetoric? Baseless Accusations? A Response to Gabor's Critique of Racial Profiling Research in Canada." *Canadian Journal of Criminology and Criminal Justice, 47* (3), 581–614.

CHAPTER 16

Abu-Lughod, Janet L. (1991). *Changing Cities: Urban Sociology*. New York: HarperCollins.

Ballingal, Alex. (2014). "Regent Park Tenants Move On." *Toronto Star* 14 November: 6. On the World Wide Web at http://www.thestar.com/news/gta/2014/11/25/departing_regent_park_tenants_leave_goodbye_messages_behind.html.

Beaujot, Roderic. (2004) "Population, Aging, and Health." In Robert Brym, ed., *New Society: Sociology for the 21st Century*, 4th ed. (pp. 431–64). Toronto: Nelson.

Bélanger, Alain and Éric Caron Malenfant. (2005). "Ethnocultural Diversity in Canada: Prospects for 2017." *Canadian Social Trends*, 79, 18–21.

Bell, Wendell. (1968). "The City, the Suburbs and a Theory of Social Choice." In Scott Greer, Dennis McElrath, David W. Minar, and Peter Orleans, eds., *The New Urbanization* (pp. 132–68). New York: St. Martin's Press.

Berger, Bennett. (1960). *Working Class Suburb*. Berkeley, CA: University of California Press.

Berry, Brian J. L. and Quentin Gillard. (1977). *The Changing Shape of Metropolitan America*. Cambridge, MA: Ballinger Publishing Co.

Blumenfeld, Hans. (1982). *Have the Secular Trends of Population Distribution Been Reversed?* Research paper 137. Toronto: Centre of Urban and Community Studies.

Blumenfeld, Hans. (1983). "Metropolis Extended." *Journal of the American Planning Association*, 52 (3), 346–48.

Bourne, L. S. (1996). "Reinventing the Suburbs: Old Myths and New Realities." *Progress in Planning*, 46, 163–84.

Brym, Robert. (1986). "An Introduction to the Regional Question in Canada." In Robert Brym, ed., *Regionalism in Canada* (pp. 1–45). Toronto: Irwin.

Burgess, Ernest W. (1961). "The Growth of the City: An Introduction to a Research Project." In George A. Theodorson, ed., *Studies in Human Ecology* (pp. 37–44). Evanston, IL: Row, Peterson and Co.

Castells, Manuel. (1989). *The Informational City: Information, Technology, Economic Restructuring and the Urban-Regional Process*. Oxford and Cambridge, MA: Blackwell.

Champion, A. G. (1993). "Urban and Regional Demographic Trends: The Developed World." In Ronan Paddison, Bill Lever, and John Money, eds., *International Perspectives in Urban Studies 1* (pp. 136–59). London and Philadelphia, PA: Jessica Kingsley.

Davis, Judy S., Arthur C. Nelson, and Kenneth J. Dueher. (1994). "The New 'Burbs': The Exurbs and their Implications for Planning Policy." *Journal of the American Planning Association*, 60, 45–59.

Davis, Kingsley. (1955). "The Origin and Growth of Urbanization in the World," *American Journal of Sociology*, 60, 430.

Davis, Mike. (1990). *City of Quartz: Excavating the Future in Los Angeles*. London and New York: Verso.

Drakakis-Smith, David. (1988). "Third World Cities: Sustainable Urban Development II—Population, Labor, and Poverty." In R. Paddison and B. Lever, eds., *International Perspectives in Urban Studies 5* (pp. 70–101). London and Bristol, UK: Jessica Kingsley.

Driedger, Leo. (1991). *The Urban Factor: Sociology of Canadian Cities*. Toronto: Oxford University Press.

ECLAC. (2008) *Panorama social de América Latina 2008*. Economic Commission for Latin America and the Caribbean. December, United Nations: Santiago.

Ehrlich, Paul R. (1968). *The Population Bomb*. New York: Ballantine Books.

Epp, Roger and Dave Whitson. (2001). "Writing Off Rural Communities." In R. Epp and D. Whitson, eds., *Writing Off the Rural West* (pp. xii–xxxv). Edmonton: The University of Alberta Press/Parkland Institute.

Fava, Sylvia Fleis. (1956). "Suburbanism as a Way of Life." *American Sociological Review*, 21, 34–37.

Filion, Pierre. (1991). "The Gentrification-Social Structure Dialectic: A Toronto Case Study." *International Journal of Urban and Regional Research*, 15, 553–74.

Firey, Walter. (1947). *Land Use in Central Boston*. Cambridge, MA: Harvard University Press.

Fishman, Robert. (1987). *Bourgeois Utopias: The Rise and Fall of Suburbia*. New York: Basic Books.

Fishman, Robert. (1990). "Megalopolis Unbound." *The Wilson Quarterly* (Winter), 25–45.

Fishman, Robert. (2005). "Longer View: The Fifth Migration." *Journal of the American Planning Association*, 71, 357–66.

Flanagan, William G. (1995). *Urban Sociology: Images and Structure*. Boston: Allyn and Bacon.

Fong, Eric. (1996). "A Comparative Perspective of Racial Residential Segregation: American and Canadian Experiences." *The Sociological Quarterly*, 37, 501–28.

Fong, Eric and Kumiko Shibuya. (2005). "Multiethnic Cities in North America." *Annual Review of Sociology*, 31, 258–304.

Fong, Eric and Rima Wilkes. (1999). "The Spatial Assimilation Model Re-examined: An Assessment by Canadian Data." *International Migration Review*, 33, 594–620.

Fowler, Edmund P. (1992). *Building Cities That Work*. Montreal and Kingston, ON: McGill-Queen's University Press.

Frieden, Bernard J. and Lynne B. Sagalyn. (1989). *Downtown, Inc.: How America Rebuilds Cities*. Cambridge, MA: MIT Press.

Garreau, Joel. (1991). *Edge City: Life on the New Frontier*. New York: Doubleday.

Goldberger, Paul. (1996). "The Rise of the Private City." In Julia Vitullo-Martin, ed., *Breaking Away: The Future of Cities* (pp. 135–47). New York: Twentieth Century Fund zPress.

Gordon, Ian and Saskia Sassen. (1992). "Restructuring the Urban Labor Markets." In Susan S. Fainstein, Ian Gordon, and Michael Harloe, eds., *Divided Cities: New York and London in the Contemporary World* (pp. 105–28). Oxford and Cambridge, MA: Blackwell.

Grant, Jill. (2005). "The Function of the Gates: The Social Construction of Security in Gated Developments." *Town Planning Review*, 76, 291–313.

Gugler, Josef. (1996). "Preface." In J. Gugler, ed., *The Urban Transformation of the Developing World*. Oxford: Oxford University Press.

Hannigan, John A. (1995). "The Postmodern City: A New Urbanization?" *Current Sociology*, 43 (1), 180.

Harris, Chauncey and Edward Ullman. (1945). "The Nature of Cities." *Annals of the American Academy of Political and Social Science*, 242 (November), 7–17.

Hauser, Philip M. (1965). "Urbanization: An Overview." In Philip M. Hauser and Leo F. Schnore, eds., *The Study of Urbanization*. New York: Wiley.

Heisz, Andrew and Sébastien LaRochelle-Coté. (2005). "Getting to Work." *Canadian Social Trends*, 79 (Winter), 16.

Hou, Feng and Garnett Picot. (2004). "Visible Minority Neighbourhoods in Toronto, Montréal and Vancouver." *Canadian Social Trends*, 72, 8–13.

Hoyt, Homer. (1939). *The Structure and Growth of Residential Neighborhoods in American Cities.* Washington, DC: Federal Housing Authority.

Jackson, Kenneth T. (1985). *Crabgrass Frontier: The Suburbanization of the United States.* New York: Oxford University Press.

Kleniewski, Nancy. (1997). *Cities, Change and Conflict: A Political Economy of Urban Life.* Belmont, CA: Wadsworth.

Kremarik, Frances. (2000). "Urban Development." *Canadian Social Trends, 59,* 18–22.

Leinberger, Christopher B. and Charles Lockwood. (1986). "How Business Is Reshaping America." *The Atlantic Monthly* (October): 43–52.

Ley, David. (1991). "Gentrification." In Kent Gerecke, ed., *The Canadian City* (pp. 181–96). Montreal: Black Rose Books.

Little, Bruce. (1999). "Tale of Three Canadian Cities: What Makes Them Grow So Big." *Globe and Mail* 20 September: A20.

Lofchie, Michael F. (1997). "The Rise and Demise of Urban-Biased Developmental Policies in Africa." In Josef Gugler, ed., *Cities in the Developing World: Issues, Theory and Policy* (pp. 23–39). Oxford: Oxford University Press.

Logan, John R., Richard D. Alba, and Wenquan Zhang. (2002). "Immigrant Enclaves and Ethnic Communities in New York and Los Angeles." *American Sociological Review, 67,* 299–322.

Logan, John R. and Harvey L. Molotch. (1987). *Urban Fortunes: The Political Economy of Place.* Berkeley, CA: University of California Press.

Lorimer, James. (1978). *The Developers.* Toronto: Lorimer.

Malthus, T. R. (1798). *An Essay on the Principle of Population, as It Affects the Future Improvement of Society. With Remarks on the Speculations of Mr. Godwin, M. Condorcet and Other Writers.* London: J. Johnson.

McGahan, Peter. (1995). *Urban Sociology in Canada,* 3rd ed. Toronto: Harcourt Brace.

McQuillan, Kevin. (1994). "Population." In Robert Hagedorn, ed., *Sociology,* 5th ed. Toronto: Harcourt Brace.

McTeague, Marybeth. (2002). "Breaking Camp at Tent City." *Canadian Architect,* November, 62.

Meek, Ronald L., ed. (1971). *Marx and Engels on the Population Bomb: Selections from the Writings of Marx and Engels Dealing with the Theories of Thomas Robert Malthus.* Dorothea L. Meek and Ronald L. Meek, trans. Berkeley, CA: Ramparts Press.

Michelson, William D. (1973). *Environmental Change.* Research Paper No. 60. Centre for Urban and Community Studies: University of Toronto.

Montgomery, Shannon. (2008). "Avalanche Survivors Devastated by 7 Deaths." *Toronto Star* 30 December: A1, A4.

Nader, George A. (1975). *Cities of Canada, Volume One: Theoretical, Historical and Planning Perspectives.* Toronto: Macmillan.

Ness, Gayl D. and Michael M. Low. (2000). *Modelling Asian Urban Population—Environment Dynamics.* Singapore: Oxford University Press.

Palen, J. John. (1995). *The Suburbs.* New York: McGraw-Hill.

Preville, Philip. (2011) "The New Suburbanites." *Toronto Life* September: 34–44.

Reid, Barton. (1991). "A Primer on the Corporate City." In Kent Gerecke, ed., *The Canadian City* (pp. 63–78). Montreal: Black Rose.

Reynolds, Malvina. (1964). *Little Boxes and Other Handmade Songs.* New York: Oak.

Rose, D. (1984). "Rethinking Gentrification: Beyond the Uneven Development of Marxist Urban Theory." *Environment and Planning D: Society and Space, 2* (1), 47–74.

Sanchez, T. W., R. E. Lang, and D. M. Dhavale. (2005). "Security versus Status? A First Look at the Census's Gated Community Data." *Journal of Planning Education and Research, 24,* 281–91.

Seeley, R. A. Sim and E. W. Loosley. (1956). *Crestwood Heights: A Study of the Culture of Suburban Life.* New York: Wiley.

Sewell, John. (1993). *The Shape of the City: Toronto Struggles with Modern Planning.* Toronto: University of Toronto Press.

Simmel, Georg. (1950). "The Metropolis and Mental Life." In Kurt H. Wolff, ed. and trans., *The Sociology of Georg Simmel* (pp. 409–24). Glencoe, IL: Free Press.

Simon, Julian L. and Herman Kahn. (1984) *The Resourceful Earth: A Response to Global 2000.* Oxford: Blackwell.

"Slain Man Mystery to Tenants." (2004). *Metro* (Toronto) 29 December: 4.

Smith, David A. (1996). *Third World Cities in Global Perspective: The Political Economy of Uneven Urbanization.* Boulder, CO: Westview Press.

Smith, Neil. (1979). "Toward a Theory of Gentrification." *Journal of the American Planning Association, 45,* 538–48.

Smith, Neil and Michael LeFaivre. (1984). "A Class Analysis of Gentrification." In John J. Palen and Brian London, eds., *Gentrification, Displacement and Neighborhood Revitalization* (pp. 43–64). Albany, NY: SUNY Press.

Statistics Canada. (2008). "Census Snapshot—Immigration in Canada: A Portrait of the Foreign-Born Population, 2006 Census." *Canadian Social Trends, 85* (Summer), 46–53. Statistics Canada. Catalogue No. 11-008-X.

Statistics Canada. (2010). "Study: Projections of the Diversity of the Canadian Population: Table 1: Proportion of Foreign-Born and Visible Minority Populations by Census Metropolitan Area, 2006 and 2031." *The Daily* 9 March. On the World Wide Web at http://www.statcan.gc.ca/daily-quotidien/100309/t100309a1-eng.htm (retrieved 9 March 2011).

Statistics Canada. (2011a). "Deaths: Table 1: Life Expectancy at Birth and at Age 65 by Sex, Canada, Provinces and Territories, 2006–2008." *The Daily* 27 September. On the World Wide Web at http://www.statcan.gc.ca/daily-quotidien/110927/t110927a1-eng.htm (retrieved 30 July 2012).

Statistics Canada. (2011b). "Infant Mortality Rates by Province and Territory (Both Sexes)." On the World Wide Web at http://www.statcan.gc.ca/tables-tableaux/sum-som/l01/cst01/health21a-eng.htm (retrieved 30 July 2012).

Statistics Canada. 2011c. "Population, Urban and Rural, by Province and Territory (Canada)." On the World Wide Web at http://www.statcan.gc.ca/tables-tableaux/sum-som/l01/cst01/demo62a-eng.htm.

Statistics Canada. (2012a). "The Canadian Population in 2011: Population Counts and Growth— Part 3: Portrait of Metropolitan and Non-Metropolitan Canada." On the World Wide Web at http://www.statcan.gc.ca (retrieved 8 February 2012).

Stone, Leroy O. (1967). *Urban Development in Canada.* Ottawa: Dominion Bureau of Statistics.

Thomas, William I. and Florian Znaniecki. (1918–20). *The Polish Peasant in Europe and America,* 5 vols. Chicago: University of Chicago Press.

Tönnies, Ferdinand. (1957 [1887]). *Community and Society,* Charles Loomis, trans. East Lansing, MI: Michigan State University Press.

United Nations. (2014). "Percentage Urban and Urban Agglomerations by Size Class." On the World Wide Web at http://esa.un.org/unpd/wup/Maps/CityDistribution/CityPopulation/CityPop.aspx.

United States Census Bureau. (2013). "International Data Base." On the World Wide Web at http://www.census.gov/population/international/data/idb/informationGateway.php.

Van de Kaa, Dirk. (1987). "Europe's Second Demographic Transition." *Population Bulletin, 42* (1), 1–58.

Warde, Alan. (1991). "Gentrification as Consumption: Issues of Class and Gender." *Environment and Planning D: Society and Space, 9* (2), 223–32.

Weber, A. F. (1963 [1899]). *The Growth of Cities in the Nineteenth Century.* Ithaca, NY: Cornell University Press.

Whyte, William H. (1956). *The Organization Man.* New York: Simon and Schuster.

Wilson, Elizabeth. (1991). *The Sphinx in the City: Urban Life, the Control of Disorder and Women.* London: Virago Press.

Winchester, Lucy and Raquel Szalachman. (2009). "The Urban Poor's Vulnerability to the Impacts of Climate Change in Latin America and the Caribbean: A Policy Agenda." Fifth Urban Research Symposium: Cities and Climate Change. Expert Group Meeting on Population Dynamics and Climate Change. London, June 24–25.

Wirth, Louis. (1938). "Urbanism as a Way of Life." In *American Journal of Sociology, 44,* 1–24.

Wittberg, Patricia. (1992). "Perspectives on Gentrification: A Comparative Review of the Literature." *Research in Urban Sociology, 2,* 17–46.

Zorbaugh, Harvey. (1929). *The Gold Coast and the Slum.* Chicago: University of Chicago Press.

CHAPTER 17

Agyeman, Julian, Peter Cole, Randolph Haluza-DeLay, and Pat O'Riley. (2009). *Speaking for Ourselves: Environmental Justice in Canada.* Vancouver, BC: UBC Press.

Alberta Royalty Review Panel. (2007). *Our Fair Share* (September). Edmonton: Alberta Government.

Ali, S. Harris. (2004). "A Socio-Ecological Autopsy of the E. coli O157:H7 Outbreak in Walkerton, Ontario, Canada." *Social Science and Medicine 58* (12), 2601–12

Ali, S. Harris. (2008). "Environmental Health and Society." In B. Singh Bolaria and Harley D. Dickinson, eds., *Health, Illness, and Health Care in Canada,* 4th ed. (pp. 370–87). Toronto: Nelson.

Beck, Ulrich. (1992). *Risk Society: Towards a New Modernity,* Mark Ritter, trans. London: Sage.

Beck, Ulrich. (1995). *Ecological Enlightenment: Essays on the Politics of the Risk Society,* M. Ritter, trans. Atlantic Highlands, NJ: Humanities Press.

Bell, Michael M. (1998) *An Invitation to Environmental Sociology.* Thousand Oaks: Pine Forge Press.

Blow, P. (Director). (1999). *The Village of Widows: The Story of the Sahtu Dene and the Atomic Bomb* [videorecording]. Peterborough, ON: Lindum Films.

Bostrom, M. and M. Klintman. (2011). *Eco-standards, Product Labelling and Green Consumerism.* NY: Palgrave Macmillan.

Buell, Frederick. (2004). From *Apocalypse to Way of Life: Environmental Crisis in the American Century.* New York: Routledge.

Bullard, Robert. (1993). *Confronting Environmental Racism: Voices from the Grassroots.* Boston: South End Press.

Buttel, Fred. (1975). "The Environmental Movement: Consensus, Conflict and Change." *Journal of Environmental Education, 7,* 53–63.

Capek, S. M. (1993). "The Environmental Justice Frame: A Conceptual Discussion and an Application." *Social Problems, 40,* 5–24.

Carson, Rachel. (1962). *Silent Spring.* Boston: Houghton Mifflin.

Cato, Molly Scott. (2011). *Environment and Economy.* New York: Routledge.

CBC. (2007). "Kyoto and Beyond." On the World Wide Web at http://www.cbc.ca/news/background/kyoto/#s5 (retrieved 30 July 2012).

CBC. (2012). "The Toilet Paper Chase." *Marketplace.* On the World Wide Web at http://www.cbc.ca/marketplace/2012/thetoiletpaperchase/ (retrieved 30 July 2012).

CBC. (2014). "Silence of the Labs." *The Fifth Estate.* On the World Wide Web at http://www.cbc.ca/fifth/episodes/2013-2014/the-silence-of-the-labs (retrieved 22 December 2014).

City of Toronto. (2008). "Median Household Income Couple Families, 2006." On the World Wide Web at http://www1.toronto.ca/city_of_toronto/social_development_finance__administration/files/pdf/ct06_income_private_households_median.pdf (retrieved 3 January 2015).

Das, Indra. (2014). "Survey Suggests Canadians Displeased with Government's Balancing of Economy and Environment." On the World Wide Web at http://www.desmog.ca/2014/01/09/survey-suggests-canadians-displeased-government-s-balancing-economy-and-environment (retrieved 2 January 2015).]]

Davidson, Debra J. and Scott Frickel. (2004). "Understanding Environmental Governance: A Critical Review." *Organization and Environment, 17* (4), 471–92.

Davidson, Debra J., Jeffrey Andrews, and Daniel Pauly. (2014). "The Effort Factor: Evaluating the Increasing Marginal Impact of Resource Extraction over Time." *Global Environmental Change 25,* 63–68.

Derber, Charles. (2010). *Greed to Green: Solving Climate Change and Remaking the Economy.* Boulder, CO: Paradigm Publishers.

Dunlap, Riley E. and William R. Catton, Jr. (2002). "Which Functions of the Environment Do We Study? A Comparison of Environmental and Natural Resource Sociology." *Society and Natural Resources 14,* 239–49.

Environment Canada. (2010). "Areas of Concern in the Great Lakes–St. Lawrence River Basin." On the World Wide Web at http://www.ec.gc.ca/raps-pas (retrieved 30 July 2012).

Environment Canada (2014a). "Greenhouse Gas Emission Data." On the World Wide Web at http://www.ec.gc.ca/indicateurs-indicators/default.asp?lang=en&n=BFB1B398-1#ghg1 (retrieved 2 January 2014).

Environment Canada. (2014b). "2012 Total Air Pollutant Emissions for Canada." On the World Wide Web at http://www.ec.gc.ca/inrp-npri/default.asp?lang=en&n=0EC58C98-1#Emission_Summaries (retrieved 2 January 2015).

Erikson, K. (1995). *A New Species of Trouble: The Human Experience of Modern Disaster.* New York: Norton.

Freidman, Thomas. (2006). "The First Law of Petropolitics." *Foreign Policy* (May/June).

Giddens, Anthony. (2009). *The Politics of Climate Change.* Cambridge, UK: Polity Press.

Gladwell, Malcom. (2002). *The Tipping Point*. New York: Back Bay Books.

Goffman, Erving. (1974). *Frame Analysis: An Essay on the Organization of Experience*. Boston: Northeastern University Press.

Guha, Ramachandra and Juan Martinez-Alier. (1998). *Varieties of Environmentalism: Essays North and South*. New Delhi: Oxford.

Hannigan, John. (2014). *Environmental Sociology*, 3rd ed. New York: Routledge.

Hardin, Garrett. (1968). "The Tragedy of the Commons." *Science*, *162* (3859), 1243–48.

Harris/Decima. (2009). *In Spite of Recession, Environment Remains a High Priority*. On the World Wide Web at http://www .harrisdecima.ca/news/releases/200908/275-spite-recession -environment-remains-high-priority (retrieved 13 February 2012).

Health Canada. (2007). "Nutrition and Healthy Eating." On the World Wide Web at http://www.hc-sc.gc.ca/fnan/nutrition/ index_e.htmlS (retrieved 20 November 2007).

Howard, Alison and Jessica Edge. (2013). "Enough for All: Household Food Security in Canada." Conference Board of Canada. On the World Wide Web at http://www .conferenceboard.ca/cfic/research/2013/enoughforall.aspx (retrieved 20 December 2014).

Indian and Northern Affairs Canada. (2003). *National Assessment of Water and Wastewater Systems in First Nations Communities*. Ottawa: Government of Canada.

Koc, Mustafa, Jennifer Sumner, and Tony Winson. (2012). *Critical Perspectives in Food Studies*. Oxford: Oxford University Press.

Larsen, Kristian and Jason Gilliland. (2009). "A Farmers' Market in a Food Desert: Evaluating Impacts on the Price and Availability of Healthy Food." *Health & Place 15*, 1158–62.

Mackenzie, Constanze A., Ada Lockridge, and Margaret Keith. (2005). "Declining Sex Ratio in a First Nation Community." *Environmental Health Perspectives, 113* (10). On the World Wide Web at http://ehp03.niehs.nih.gov/article/info:doi/10.1289/ ehp.8479 (retrieved 4 August 2012).

Mascarenhas, Michael. (2009). "Environmental Inequality and Environmental Justice." In Kenneth A. Gould and Tammy L. Lewis, eds., *Twenty Lessons in Environmental Sociology* (pp. 127–141). Toronto: Oxford University Press.

McCright, Aaron and Riley Dunlap. (2010). "Anti-Reflexivity: The American Conservative Movement's Success in Undermining Climate Science and Policy." *Theory, Culture & Society*, 27 (2/3), 100–33.

Meadows, Donella H., Dennis L. Meadows, Jørgen Randers, and William W. Behrens III. (1972). *Limits to Growth: A Report for the Club of Rome's Project on the Predicament of Mankind*. New York: Universe Books.

Milly, Pascal and William Leiss. (1997). "Mother's Milk: Communicating the Risks of PCBs in Canada and the Far North." In Douglas Powell and William Leiss, eds., *Mad Cows and Mother's Milk: The Perils of Poor Risk Communication* (pp. 184–209). Montreal: McGill-Queen's University Press.

Mitchell, Bruce. (2010). *Resource and Environmental Management in Canada*. Toronto: Oxford.

Nikiforuk, Andrew. (2010). *Tar Sands: Dirty Oil and the Future of a Continent*. Vancouver, BC: Greystone Books.

Paehlke, Robert. (2009). "The Environmental Movement in Canada." In Debora L. VanNijnatten and Robert Boardman, eds., *Canadian Environmental Policy and Politics: Prospects for Leadership and Innovation*, 3rd ed. (pp. 1–13). Toronto: Oxford University Press.

Pearce, Fred. (2010). "Controversy behind Climate Science's 'Hockey Stick' Graph." On the World Wide Web at http:// www.guardian.co.uk/environment/2010/feb/02/hockey -stick -graph-climate-change (retrieved 11 February 2012). Copyright Guardian News & Media Ltd. 2010.

Pollution Watch. (2008). "An Examination of Pollution and Poverty in the City of Toronto." On the World Wide Web at http://www.pollutionwatch.org/pressroom/factSheetData/ PW_Toronto_Fact_Sheet.pdf (retrieved 3 January 2015).

Raffensperger, Carolyn and Joel Tickner. (1999). *Protecting Public Health and the Environment: Implementing the Precautionary Principle*. Washington, DC: Island Press.

Sen, Amartya. (1981). *Poverty and Famines: An Essay on Entitlement and Deprivation*. NY: Oxford University Press.

Shiva, Vandana. (1993). "GATT, Agriculture and Third World Women." In Maria Mies and Vandana Shiva, eds., *Ecofeminism* (pp. 241–45). Halifax: Fernwood Books.

Smith, Rick and Bruce Lourie. (2009). *Slow Death by Rubber Duck: How the Toxic Chemistry of Everyday Life Affects Our Health*. Toronto: Alfred A. Knopf.

Statistics Canada. (2006). *Aboriginal Peoples Survey, 2006: Inuit Health and Social Conditions*. On the World Wide Web at http:// www.statcan.gc.ca/pub/89-637-x/89-637-x2008001-eng.htm (retrieved 20 December 2014).

Statistics Canada. (2013). "Table 2: Number and Distribution of the Population Reporting an Aboriginal Identity and Percentage of Aboriginal People in the Population, Canada, Provinces and Territories, 2011." On the World Wide Web at https://www12.statcan.gc.ca/nhs-enm/2011/as-sa/99- 011-x/2011001/tbl/tbl02-eng.cfm (retrieved 2 January 2015).

Statistics Canada. (2014). "Population and Dwelling Counts, for Canada, Provinces and Territories, 2011 and 2006 Censuses." On the World Wide Web at http://www12.statcan.gc.ca/ census-recensement/2011/dp-pd/hlt-fst/pd-pl/Table-tableau .cfm?LANG=Eng&T=101&S=50&O=A (retrieved 2 January 2015).

Tarbell, Alice and Mary Arquette. (2000). "Akwesasne: A Native American Community's Resistance to Cultural and Environmental Damage." In Richard Hofrichter, ed., *Reclaiming the Environmental Debate: The Politics of Health in a Toxic Culture* (pp. 93–111). Cambridge, MA: MIT Press.

United Nations World Commission on Environment and Development. (1987). *Our Common Future*. Oxford, UK: Oxford University Press

Wallace, Iain and Mike Brklacich. (2010). "Agriculture and Rural Resources." In Bruce Mitchell, ed. *Resource and Environmental Management in Canada*, 4th ed. Toronto: Oxford.

Walpole Island First Nation. (n.d.). "Walpole Island First Nation, Canada." On the World Wide Web at http://www .iisd.org/50comm/commdb/desc/d09.htm (retrieved 17 February 2012).

Zlomislic, Diana. (2011). "Ontario Teens Doused with Agent Orange while Helping with Northern Ontario Forestry Spraying Programs." *Toronto Star*. On the World Wide Web at http://www.thestar.com/news/canada/article/940243--star -exclusive-agent-orange-soaked-ontario-teens (retrieved 18 February 2012).

CHAPTER 18

Allard, Y. E., R. Wilkins and J.-M. Berthelot. (2004). Premature Mortality in Health Regions with High Aboriginal Populations. *Health Reports, 15* (1), 51–60.

Anand, S. S., S. Yusuf, R. Jacobs, A. D. Davis, Q. Yi, H. Gerstein, P.A. Montague, and E. Lonn. (2001). "Risk Factors, Atherosclerosis, and Cardiovascular Disease among Aboriginal People in Canada: The Study of Health Assessment and Risk Evaluation in Aboriginal peoples (SHARE-AP)." *The Lancet, 358,* 1147–53.

Antonucci, T. C. (1990). "Social Supports and Social Relationships." In R. H. Binstock and L. K. George, eds., *Handbook of Aging and the Social Sciences,* 3rd ed. (pp. 205–44). New York: Academic Press.

Arber, S. and J. Ginn. (1991). *Gender and Later Life.* London: Sage Publications.

Armstrong, P., H. Armstrong, and D. Coburn. (2001). *Unhealthy Times: Political Economy Perspectives on Health and Care in Canada.* Toronto: Oxford University Press.

BC Stats. (2014). "Population Estimates." On the World Wide Web at http://www.bcstats.gov.bc.ca/StatisticsBySubject/Demography/PopulationEstimates.aspx (retrieved 9 December 2014).

Brownell M. D., N. P. Roos, and L. L. Roos. (2001). "Monitoring Health Reform: A Report Card Approach." *Social Science Medicine, 52,* 657–70.

Brym, Robert et al. (2012). "The Social Bases of Cancer." In R. Brym, ed., *Sociology as a Life or Death Issue,* 2nd Canadian ed. (pp. 81–102). Toronto: Nelson.

Buckley, N. J., F. T Denton, A. L. Robb, and B. G. Spencer. (2005). "Healthy Aging at Older Ages: Are Income and Education Important?" *Canadian Journal on Aging, 23* (Suppl. 1), S155–S169.

Canadian Institute for Health Information. (2005). *Select Highlights on Public Views of the Determinants of Health. Canadian Population Health Initiative.* Ottawa: Author.

Canadian Institute for Health Information. (2007). Released 10 January. *Significant 10-Year Increase in the Number of Surgeries Performed in Canadian Hospitals.*

Canadian Institute for Health Information. (2011). *Health Care in Canada, 2011: A Focus on Seniors and Aging.* Ottawa: Canadian Institute for Health Information.

Carriere, K. C, L. L. Roos, and D. C. Dover. (2000). "Across Time and Space: Variations in Hospital Use during Canadian Health Reform." *Health Services Research, 35* (2), 467–87.

Chappell, N. L. and M. J. Hollander. (2011). *Evidence-Based Policy Prescription for an Aging Population. Invited Essay. HealthcarePapers, 11* (1), 8–18. The volume includes 11 commentaries by diverse experts. The authors' responses, 86–91.

Chappell, N. L., L. MacDonald, and M. Stones. (2008). Aging in *Contemporary Canada,* 2nd ed. Toronto: Pearson.

Chappell, N. L. and M. J. Penning. (2009). *Understanding Health, Health Care, and Health Policy in Canada.* Don Mills, ON: Oxford.

Chen J., E. Ng, and R. Wilkins. (1996). "The Health of Canada's Immigrants in 1994–95." *Health Reports, 7* (4), 33–45.

Commission on the Future of Health Care in Canada. (2002). *Building on Values: The Future of Health Care in Canada—Final Report.* Ottawa: National Library of Canada. Catalogue No. CP32-85/2002E-IN.

Conference Board of Canada (2012). *Home and Community Care in Canada: An Economic Footprint.* Ottawa, Ontario. On the World Wide Web at http://carewatchtoronto.org/wp-content/uploads/2012/05/12-306_HomeandCommunityCare_PRT.pdf (retrieved 19 November 2014).

Cooke, M., F. Mitrou, D. Lawrence, E. Guimond, and D. Beavon. (2007). "Indigenous Well-being in Four Countries: An Application of the UNDP's Human Development Index to Indigenous Peoples in Australia, Canada, New Zealand, and the United States." *BMC International Health and Human Rights, 7,* 9.

Cranswick, K. (2003). *General Social Survey, Cycle 16: Caring for an Aging Society.* Ottawa: Statistics Canada.

DeNavas-Walt, C., B. D. Proctor, and Jessica C. Smith. (2010). "U.S. Census Bureau—Current *Population* Reports." In *Income, Poverty, and Health Insurance Coverage in the United States: 2009* (pp. 60–238). Washington: U.S. Government Printing Office.

DesMeules, M., D. Manuel, and R. Cho. (2004). "Mortality: Life and Health Expectancy of Canadian Women." *BMC Women's Health, 4* (Suppl. 1), S1–S9.

DesMeules, M., L. Turner, and R. Cho. (2004). "Morbidity Experiences and Disability among Canadian Women." *BMC Women's Health, 4* (Suppl. 1), S10.

Dubois, M-F. and R. Hébert. (2006). "Cognitive-Impairment-Free Life Expectancy for Canadian Seniors." *Dementia and Geriatric Cognitive Disorders, 22,* 327–33.

Dunlop, S., P. C. Coyte, and W. McIsaac. (2000). "Socio-economic Status and the Utilization of Physician's Services: Results from the Canadian National Population Health Survey." *Social Science & Medicine, 51,* 123–33.

Esmail, N. (2007). Complementary and Alternative Medicine in Canada: Trends in Use and Public Attitudes, 1997–2006. *Public Policy Sources, 87,* 1–53.

Estes, C. L. (1979). *The Aging Enterprise.* San Francisco: Jossey-Bass.

Ferraro, C. G., F. J. Freeman, G. Nellett, and J. Sheel. (2008). Changing Nursing Students' Attitudes about Aging: An Argument for the Successful Aging Paradigm. *Educational Gerontology, 34* (1), 51–66.

Fries, J. F (1983). "Compression of Morbidity." *Milbank Memorial Fund Quarterly, 61,* 397–419.

Gee, E. M., K. M. Kobayashi, and S. G. Prus. (2004). "Examining the Healthy Immigrant Effect in Mid-to-Later life: Findings from the Canadian Community Health Survey." *Canadian Journal on Aging* (Supplement), S55–S63.

Gilmour, H. and J. Park. (2005). "Dependency, Chronic Conditions and Pain in Seniors." *Health Reports, 16* (Supplement), 21–31.

Hagestad, G. and P. Uhlenberg. (2005). "The Social Separation of Old and Young: A Root of Ageism." *Journal of Social Issues, 61,* 343–60.

Hankivsky, O. and R. Cormier. (2009). *Intersectionality: Moving Women's Health Research and Policy Forward. Vancouver: Women's Health Research Network.*

Helliwell, J. F. (2003). "How's Life? Combining Individual and National Variables to Explain Subjective Well-Being." *Economic Modelling, 20,* 331–60.

House, J. S. (2001). "Understanding Social Factors and Inequalities in Health: 20th Century Progress and 21st Century Prospects." *Journal of Health and Social Behavior, 43* (125), 2–4.

Huisman, M., A. Kunst, D. Deeg, F. Grigoletto, W. Nusselder, and J. Mackenbach. (2005). "Educational Inequalities in the Prevalence and Incidence of Disability in Italy and the

Netherlands Were Observed." *Journal of Clinical Epidemiology, 58*, 1058–65.

Human Resources and Skills Development Canada. (2009). "Indicators of Well-being in Canada." On the World Wide Web at http://www4.hrsdc.gc.ca/indicator .jsp?lang+eng&indicatorid=3 (retrieved 19 August 2009).

Kane, R. L. (1990). "Introduction." In R. L. Kane, J. G. Evans, and D. MacFadyen, eds., *Improving the Health of Older People: A World View* (pp. 15–18). New York: Oxford University Press.

Keating, N., J. Fast, J. Frederick, K. Cranswick, and C. Perrier. (1999). *Elder Care in Canada: Context, Content, and Consequences.* Ottawa: Statistics Canada, Housing, Family and Social Statistics Division. Catalogue No. 89-570-XPE.

Lewis, S., C. Donaldson, C. Mitton, and G. Currie. (2001). "The Future of Health Care in Canada." *British Medical Journal, 323*, 926–29.

Link, B. G. and J. C. Phelan. (2000). "Evaluating the Fundamental Cause Explanation for Social Disparities in Health." In C. E. Bird, P. Conrad, and A. M. Fremont, eds., *Handbook of Medical Sociology*, 5th ed. (pp. 33–46). Upper Saddle River, NJ: Prentice Hall.

Litwak, E. (1960). "Geographic Mobility and Extended Family Cohesion." *American Sociological Review, 25*, 385–94.

Lynch, J. and G. Kaplan. (2000). "Socioeconomic Position." In L. F. Berkman and I. Kawachi, eds., *Social Epidemiology* (pp. 13–35). New York: Oxford University Press.

Markides, K. S. (1983). "Minority Aging." In M. W. Riley, B. B. Hess, and K. Bond, eds., *Aging in Society: Reviews of Recent Literature.* Hillsdale, NJ: Lawrence Erlbaum Associates.

Marmor, T. R. and K. Sullivan. (2000). "Canada's Burning! Media Myths about Universal Health Coverage." *Washington Monthly* (July/August). On the World Wide Web at http://www.washingtonmonthlycom/features/2000/0007.marmorsul .html#byline (retrieved 21 November 2006).

Martel, L., A. Bélanger, J.-M. Berthelot, and Y. Carrière. (2005). *Health Aging.* Ottawa: Statistics Canada. Catalogue No. 82-618- MWE2005004.

McMullin, J. (2004). *Understanding Social Inequality: Intersections of Class, Age, Gender, Ethnicity and Race in Canada.* Toronto: Oxford University Press.

Metcalfe, A., J. Williams, J. McChesney, S. B. Patten, and N. Jetté. (2010). "Use of Complementary and Alternative Medicine by Those with a Chronic Disease and the General Population—Results of a National Population Based Survey." *BMC Complementary and Alternative Medicine, 10* (58), doi:10.1186/1472-6882-10-58.

Milan, A. and M. Vézina. (2011). "Table 5: Characteristics of Social Networks and Senior Women's and Men's Feeling about Life as a Whole by Age Group, 2008." In *Women in Canada: A Gender-Based Statistical Report* (p. 14). Component of Statistics Canada. Catalogue No. 89-503-X.

Metcalfe, A., J. Williams, J. McChesney, S. B. Patten, and N. Jetté. (2010). Use of Complementary And Alternative Medicine by Those with a Chronic Disease and the General Population—Results of a National Population Based Survey. *BMC Complementary and Alternative Medicine, 10*, 58, doi:10.1186/1472-6882-10-58.

Montgomery, R. J. V, E. F. Borgatta, and M. L. Borgatta. (2000). "Societal and Family Change in the Burden of Care." In

William T. Liu and Hal Kendig, eds., *Who Should Care for the Elderly?: An East–West Value Divide* (pp. 27–54). Singapore: Singapore University Press, National University of Singapore, and World Scientific Publishing.

Munroe, S. (2003). "2003 Canadian Life and Death Statistics—Life Expectancy and Statistics on Deaths in Canada." On the World Wide Web at http://canadaonline.about.com/od /statistics/a/ deathstats2003.htm (retrieved 19 August 2009).

Noh, S., M. Beiser, V. Kaspar, F. Hou, and J. Rummens. (1999). "Perceived Racial Discrimination, Depression, and Coping: A Study of Southeast Asian Refugees in Canada." *Journal of Health and Social Behavior, 40* (3), 193–207.

Organisation for Economic Co-operation and Development. (2009). "Health Data 2008: Statistics and Indicators for 30 Countries." On the World Wide Web at http://www.ecosante.org/ OCDEENG/111000.html (retrieved 19 August 2009).

Organisation for Economic Co-operation and Development. (2011). "Health at a Glance 2011: OECD Indicators." OECD Publishing. On the World Wide Web at http://dx.doi.org/ 10.1787/health_glance-2011-en.

Park, J. (2004). "Use of alternative health care." *Health Reports, 16* (2), 39–42. Ottawa: Statistics Canada. Catalogue No. 82-0103-XIE.

Penning, M. J., M. Brackley, and D. E. Allen. (2006). "Home Care and Health Reform: Changes in Home Care Utilization in One Canadian Province, 1990–2000." *The Gerontologist, 46* (6), 744–58.

Penning M .J. and K. Votova. (2008). "Aging, Health and Health Care: From Hospital and Residential Care to Home and Community Care." In S. Bolaria and H. D. Dickinson, eds., *Health, Illness and Health Care in Canada*, 4th ed. Toronto: Harcourt.

Pérez, C. E. (2002). "Health Status and Health Behaviour among Immigrants." *Health Reports, 13*, 1–12.

Population Reference Bureau. (2014). "2014 World Population Data Sheet." On the Wide World Web at http://www.prb.org/ pdf14/2014-world-population-data-sheet_eng.pdf (retrieved 6 December 2014).

ProQuest (2014). "Advanced Search." On the World Wide Web at http://search.proquest.com.myaccess.library.utoronto.ca/ advanced (retrieved 5 December 2014).

Prus, S. G. and E. Gee. (2002). *Gender Differences in the Influence of Economic, Lifestyle and Psychosocial Factors on Later-Life Health.* Hamilton. ON: Program for Research on Social and Economic Dimensions of an Aging Population, McMaster University.

Public Health Agency of Canada. (2010). *The Chief Public Health Officer's Report on the State of Public Health in Canada 2010.* On the World Wide Web at http://www.phac-aspc.gc.ca/ cphorsphc-respcacsp/2010/fr-rc/cphorsphc-respcacsp-06-eng .php (retrieved 19 November 2014).

Raphael, D. (2005). "Introduction to the Social Determinants of Health." In D. Raphael, ed., *Social Determinants of Health: Canadian Perspectives* (pp. 1–19). Toronto: Canadian Scholars' Press Inc. Reprinted by permission of Canadian Scholars' Press Inc.

Ross, C.E. and C. Wu. (1996). "Education, Age, and the Cumulative Advantage in Health." *Journal of Health and Social Behavior, 37*, 104–20.

Schalick, L. M., W. C. Hadden, E. Pamuk, V. Navarro, and G. Pappas. (2000). "The Widening Gap in Death Rates among

Income Groups in the United States from 1967 to 1986." *International Journal of Health Services, 30,* 13–26.

Segall, A. and N. L. Chappell. (2000). *Health and Health Care in Canada.* Toronto: Pearson Education Canada.

Simon, R. (2000). "The Importance of Culture in Sociological Theory and Research on Stress and Mental Health. A Missing Link?" In C. E. Bird, P. Conrad, and A. M. Fremont, eds., *Handbook of Medical Sociology,* 5th ed. Englewood Cliffs, NJ: Prentice-Hall.

Starr, P. (1988). "The Meaning of Privatization." *Yale Law and Policy Review, 6,* 6–41.

Statistics Canada. (2001). Self-Esteem by Age Group and Sex, Household Population Aged 12 and over, Canada Excluding Territories, *1994/95.* Ottawa: Author. Catalogue No. 82-221-XIE.

Statistics Canada. (2003a). Annual Demographic Statistics, 2003. Ottawa: Author. Catalogue No. 91-213-XIB/XPB.

Statistics Canada. (2003b). Aboriginal Peoples Survey 2001— Initial Findings: Well-being of the Non-Reserve Aboriginal Population. Ottawa: Author. Catalogue No. 89-589-XIE.

Statistics Canada. (2005). Canadian Community Health Survey, 2004. Ottawa: Author.

Statistics Canada. (2006). "Life Tables, Canada, Provinces and Territories, 2000 to 2002." On the World Wide Web at http://www.statcan.gc.ca/pub/ 84–537-x/4064441-eng.htm (retrieved 10 October 2006).

Statistics Canada. (2007a). "2006 Census: Immigration, Citizenship, Language, Mobility and Migration." On the World Wide Web at http://www.statcan.gc.ca/daily-quotidien/071204/dq071204a -eng.htm (retrieved 4 January 2012).

Statistics Canada. (2007b). A Portrait of Seniors in Canada, 2006. Ottawa: Author. Catalogue No. 89-519-XIE.

Statistics Canada. (2010). "Projected life expectancy at birth by sex, by Aboriginal identity, 2017." http://www.statcan.gc.ca/ pub/89-645-x/2010001/c-g/c-g013-eng.htm (retrieved 29 September 2015).

Statistics Canada. (2011a). "Life Expectancy at Birth and at Age 65 by Sex and by Province and Territory." CANSIM, Table 102–0512. On the World Wide Web at http://www.statcan .gc.ca/tables-tableaux/sum-som/l01/cst01/health72a-eng.htm (retrieved 3 August 2012).

Statistics Canada. (2012a). Annual Demographic Estimates: Canada, Provinces and Territories, 2012. Ottawa: Author. Catalogue No. 91-215-X.

Statistics Canada. (2012b). "Life Expectancy at Birth and at Age 65 by Sex and by Province and Territory." CANSIM, Table 102–0512. On the World Wide Web at http://www.statcan .gc.ca/tables-tableaux/sum-som/l01/cst01/health72a-eng.htm (retrieved 19 November 2014).

Statistics Canada (2013a). "Table 202-0802: Persons in low income families, annual." CANSIM (database). On the World Wide Web at http://www5.statcan.gc.ca/cansim/ a26?lang=eng&id=2020802 (retrieved 19 November 2014).

Stones, M. J. and L. Stones. (1997). "Ageism: The Quiet Epidemic." *Canadian Journal of Public Health, 88* (5), 293–94.

Trottier, H, L. Martel, C. Houle, J.-M. Berthelot, and J. Légaré. (2000). "Living at Home or in an Institution: What Makes the Differences for Seniors?" *Health Reports, 11,* 49–59.

United States Census Bureau. (2013). "International Data Base." On the World Wide Web at http://www.census.gov/ population/international/data/idb/informationGateway.php (retrieved 9 December 2014).

Williams, A. P., R. Deber, P. Baranek, and A. Gildiner. (2001). "From Medicare to Home Care: Globalization, State Retrenchment and the Profitization of Canada's Health Care System." In P. Armstrong, H. Armstrong, and D. Coburn, eds., *Unhealthy Times: Political Economy Perspectives on Health and Care in Canada* (pp. 7–30). New York: Oxford University Press.

Williamson, D. J. (2000). "Health Behaviors and Health: Evidence That the Relationship Is Not Conditional on Income Adequacy." *Social Science and Medicine, 51* (12), 1741–54.

World Health Organization. (1948). *Official Records of the World Health Organization, No. 2.* New York: WHO Interim Commission, UN.

Zola, I. K. (1983). *Socio-Medical Inquiries.* Philadelphia, PA: Temple University Press.

CHAPTER 19

Adam, Barry, Jan Willem Duyvendak, and André Krouwel. (1999). *The Global Emergence of Gay and Lesbian Politics.* Philadelphia, PA: Temple University Press.

Adamson, Nancy, Linda Briskin, and Margaret McPhail. (1988). *Feminist Organizing for Change: The Contemporary Women's Movement in Canada.* Toronto: Oxford University Press.

Bashevkin, Sylvia. (1986). "Independence versus Partisanship: Dilemmas in the Political History of Women in English Canada." In V. Strong-Boag and A. Fellman, eds., *Rethinking Canada: The Promise of Women's History* (pp. 246–75). Toronto: Copp Clark Pitman.

Blais, André, Elisabeth Gidengil, Richard Nadeau, and Neil Nevitte. (1997). *1997 Canadian Election Survey.* On the World Wide Web at http://prod.library.utoronto.ca/datalib/ codebooks/utm/elections/1997 (retrieved 20 June 2002).

Block, Fred. (1979). "The Ruling Class Does Not Rule." In R. Quinney, ed., *Capitalist Society* (pp. 128–40). Homewood, IL: Dorsey Press.

Boyd, Monica. (2011). "Gender Inequality: Economic and Political Aspects." In Robert Brym, ed., *New Society,* 6th ed. (pp. 154–78). Toronto: Nelson.

Brint, Stephen. (1984). "'New-Class' and Cumulative Trend Explanations of the Liberal Political Attitudes of Professionals." *American Journal of Sociology, 90,* 30–71.

Brodie, Janine. (1991). "Women and the Electoral Process in Canada." In Kathy Megyery, ed., *Women in Canadian Politics: Toward Equity in Representation* (pp. 3–59). Toronto: Dundurn Press.

Brym, Robert. (1979). "Political Conservatism in Atlantic Canada." In Robert Brym and R. James Sacouman, eds., *Underdevelopment and Social Movements in Atlantic Canada* (pp. 59–79). Toronto: New Hogtown Press.

Brym, Robert. (1980). *Intellectuals and Politics.* London, UK: Allen and Unwin.

Brym, Robert. (1989). "Canada." In Tom Bottomore and Robert Brym, eds., *The Capitalist Class: An International Study* (pp. 177–206). New York: New York University Press.

Brym, Robert. (2008). "Affluence, Power and Strikes in Canada, 1973–2000." In Edward Grabb and Neil Guppy, eds., *Social*

Inequality in Canada: Patterns, Problems, Policies, 6th ed. (pp. 55–68) Scarborough, ON: Prentice-Hall Canada.

Brym, Robert, Louise Birdsell Bauer, and Mitch McIvor. (2013). "Is Industrial Unrest Reviving in Canada? Strike Duration in the Early 21st Century." *Canadian Review of Sociology 50, 2,* 227–38.

Brym, Robert, Melissa Godbout, Andreas Hoffbauer, Gabe Menard, and Tony Huiquan Zhang. (2014). "Social Media in the 2011 Egyptian Uprising." *British Journal of Sociology 65, 2,* 266–92.

Bureau of Labor Statistics, U.S. Department of Labor. (2012). "Table 1. Union Affiliation of Employed Wage and Salary Workers by Selected Characteristics." On the World Wide Web at http://www.bls.gov/webapps/legacy/cpslutab1.htm (retrieved 21 January 2012).

Bureau of Labor Statistics, U.S. Department of Labor. (2014). "Union Members Summary." On the World Wide Web at http://www.bls.gov/news.release/union2.nr0.htm (retrieved 2 November 2014).

Canada Department of Labour. (1973). *Labour Organizations in Canada, 1972.* Ottawa: Economics and Research Branch, Canada Department of Labour. Catalogue No. L2-2-1972.

Casper, L. M., S. S. McLanahan, and I. Garfinkel. (1994). "The Gender-Poverty Gap: What Can We Learn from Other Countries?" *American Sociological Review, 59,* 594–605.

CBC News. (2015). "Justin Trudeau's Liberals to form majority government." On the World Wide Web at http://www.cbc.ca/news2/interactives/results-2015/ (retrieved 20 October 2015).

Clarke, Harold D., Jane Jenson, Lawrence LeDuc, and Jon H. Pammett. (1996). *Absent Mandate: Canadian Electoral Politics in an Era of Restructuring,* 3rd ed. Toronto: Gage.

Clement, Wallace. (1975). *The Canadian Corporate Elite: An Analysis of Economic Power.* Toronto: McClelland and Stewart.

Dahl, Robert A. (1961). *Who Governs?* New Haven, CT: Yale University Press.

Davies, James C. (1969). "Toward a Theory of Revolution." In Barry McLaughlin, ed., *Studies in Social Movements: A Social Psychological Perspective* (pp. 85–108). New York: Free Press.

Elections Canada. (2013). "Voter Turnout at Federal Elections and Referendums." On the World Wide Web at http://www.elections.ca/content.aspx?dir=turn&document=index&lang=e&section=ele (retrieved 3 November 2014).

Elections Canada. (2014). "Candidate's Electoral Campaign Return." On the World Wide Web at http://www.elections.ca/WPAPPS/WPF/EN/CC/SelectContributions?act=C24&eventid=25&returntype=1&option=4 (retrieved 3 November 2014).

Evans, Peter B., Dietrich Rueschemeyer, and Theda Skocpol. (1985). *Bringing the State Back In.* Cambridge, UK: Cambridge University Press.

Fournier, Patrick, Fred Cutler, Stuart Soroka, and Deitland Stolle. (2011). *Canadian National Election Study* [dataset]. On the World Wide Web at http://www.queensu.ca/cora/ces.html (retrieved 2 November 2014).

Frank, Jeffrey. (1994). "Voting and Contributing: Political Participation in Canada." In *Canadian Social Trends* (pp. 333–37). Toronto: Thompson Educational Publishers.

Goffman, Erving. (1974). *Frame Analysis.* Cambridge, MA: Harvard University Press.

Government of Canada, Labour Program. (2014a). "Union Coverage in Canada, 2013." On the World Wide Web at http://www.labour.gc.ca/eng/resources/info/publications/union_coverage/union_coverage.shtml (2 November 2014).

Government of Canada, Labour Program. (2014b). "Work Stoppages by Jurisdiction and Year." On the World Wide Web at http://www.labour.gc.ca/eng/resources/info/datas/work_stoppages/work_stoppages_year_jurisdiction.shtml (retrieved 2 November 2014).

Hourani, Albert. (1991). *A History of the Arab Peoples.* New York: Warner Books.

Human Resources Development Canada. (1995). *1994–1995 Directory of Labour Organizations in Canada.* Ottawa: Minister of Supply and Services Canada. Catalogue No. L2-2-1995.

Human Resources Development Canada. (1998). *1998 Directory of Labour Organizations in Canada.* Ottawa: Workplace Information Directorate.

Human Resources and Skills Development Canada. (2011). "Union Membership in Canada, 2010." On the World Wide Web at http://www.hrsdc.gc.ca/eng/labour/labour_relations/info_analysis/union_membership/2010 /unionmembership2010.shtml (retrieved 21 January 2012).

International Institute for Democracy and Electoral Assistance. (2014). "Voter Turnout Data for Sweden." On the World Wide Web at http://www.idea.int/vt/countryview.cfm?id=197 (retrieved 2 November 2014).

Jansen, Harold J., Melanee Thomas, and Lisa Young. (2012). "Who Donates to Canada's Political Parties?" Paper presented to the Annual Meeting of the Canadian Political Science Association, Edmonton. On the World Wide Web at http://www.cpsa-acsp.ca/papers-2012/Jansen-Thomas-Young.pdf (retrieved 2 November 2014).

Jenkins, J. Craig. (1983). "Resource Mobilization Theory and the Study of Social Movements." *Annual Review of Sociology, 9,* 527–53.

Kelley, Jack. (2001). "Terror Groups Hide Behind Web Encryption." *USA Today* 19 June. On the World Wide Web at http://www.usatoday.com/life/cyber/tech/2001-02-05-binladen.htm (retrieved 13 September 2001).

Korpi, Walter. (1983). *The Democratic Class Struggle.* London: Routledge and Kegan Paul.

Lipset, Seymour Martin. (1971). *Agrarian Socialism: The Cooperative Commonwealth Federation in Saskatchewan,* rev. ed. Berkeley, CA: University of California Press.

Lipset, Seymour Martin. (1981). *Political Man: The Social Bases of Politics,* 2nd ed. Baltimore: Johns Hopkins University Press.

Lodhi, Abdul Qaiyum and Charles Tilly. (1973). "Urbanization, Crime and Collective Violence in 19th Century France." *American Journal of Sociology, 79,* 296–318.

Marshall, T. H. (1965). "Citizenship and Social Class." In T. H. Marshall, ed., *Class, Citizenship, and Social Development: Essays by T. H. Marshall* (pp. 71–134). Garden City, NY: Anchor.

Mayer, Gerald. (2004). "Union Membership Trends in the United States." *Federal Publications,* Paper 174. On the World Wide Web at http://digitalcommons.ilr.cornell.edu /key_workplace/174 (retrieved 21 January 2012).

McCarthy, John D. and Mayer N. Zald. (1977). "Resource Mobilization and Social Movements: A Partial Theory." *American Journal of Sociology, 82,* 1212–41.

McCullagh, Declan. (2000). "Bin Laden: Steganography Master?" *Wired* 7 February. On the World Wide Web at http://www

.wired.com/news/print/0.1294.41658.00.html (retrieved 13 September 2001).

Melucci, Alberto. (1980). "The New Social Movements: A Theoretical Approach." *Social Science Information, 19*, 199–226.

Melucci, Alberto. (1995). "The New Social Movements Revisited: Reflections on a Sociological Misunderstanding." In Louis Maheu, ed., *Social Classes and Social Movements: The Future of Collective Action* (pp. 107–19). London: Sage.

Miliband, Ralph. (1973 [1969]). *The State in Capitalist Society*. London: Fontana.

Mills, C. Wright. (1956). *The Power Elite*. New York: Oxford University Press.

Mishler, William. (1979). *Political Participation in Canada: Prospects for Democratic Citizenship*. Toronto: Macmillan.

Moore, Barrington, Jr. (1967). *Social Origins of Dictatorship and Democracy: Lord and Peasant in the Making of the Modern World*. Boston: Beacon Press.

"Muslim Brotherhood Movement Homepage." (2002). On the World Wide Web at http://www.ummah.org.uk/ikhwan (retrieved 7 May 2003).

Myles, John. (1989). *Old Age in the Welfare State: The Political Economy of Public Pensions*, rev. ed. Lawrence, KS: University Press of Kansas.

Oberschall, Anthony. (1973). *Social Conflict and Social Movements*. Englewood Cliffs, NJ: Prentice-Hall.

O'Connor, Julia S. (1996). "From Women in the Welfare State to Gendering Welfare State Regimes." *Current Sociology, 44* (2), 1–130.

O'Connor, Julia S. and Robert Brym. (1988). "Public Welfare Expenditure in OECD Countries: Towards a Reconciliation of Inconsistent Findings." *British Journal of Sociology, 39*, 47–68.

O'Connor, Julia S. and Gregg M. Olsen, eds. (1998). *Power Resources Theory and the Welfare State: A Critical Approach*. Toronto: University of Toronto Press.

Occupy Together (2012). On the World Wide Web at http://www.occupytogether.org/downloadable-posters (retrieved 21 January 2012).

Olsen, Dennis. (1980). *The State Elite*. Toronto: McClelland and Stewart.

Olsen, Gregg. (2002). *The Politics of the Welfare State: Canada, Sweden and the United States*. Toronto: Oxford University Press.

Olsen, Gregg and Robert Brym. (1996). "Between American Exceptionalism and Swedish Social Democracy: Public and Private Pensions in Canada." In Michael Shalev, ed., *The Privatization of Social Policy? Occupational Welfare and the Welfare State in America, Scandinavia and Japan* (pp. 261–79). London: Macmillan.

Pew Research Center. (2012). "Rising Share of Americans See Conflict between Rich and Poor." On the World Wide Web at http://www.pewsocialtrends.org/files/2012/01/Rich-vs-Poor .pdf (retrieved 21 January 2012).

Piven, Frances Fox and Richard A. Cloward. (1989). *Why Americans Don't Vote*. New York: Pantheon.

Polsby, Nelson W. (1959). "Three Problems in the Analysis of Community Power." *American Sociological Review, 24*, 796–803.

Porter, John. (1965). *The Vertical Mosaic: An Analysis of Social Class and Power in Canada*. Toronto: University of Toronto Press.

Poulantzas, Nicos. (1975 [1968]). *Political Power and Social Classes*. T. O'Hagan, trans. London: New Left Books.

Roche, Maurice. (1995). "Rethinking Citizenship and Social Movements: Themes in Contemporary Sociology and Neoconservative Ideology." In Louis Maheu, ed., *Social Classes and Social Movements: The Future of Collective Action* (pp.186–219). London: Sage.

Rootes, Chris. (1995). "A New Class? The Higher Educated and the New Politics." In Louis Maheu, ed., *Social Classes and Social Movements: The Future of Collective Action* (pp. 220–35). London: Sage.

Shahar, Yael. (2001). "Tracing bin Laden's Money: Easier Said Than Done." International Policy Institute for Counter-Terrorism. On the World Wide Web at http://www.ict.org.il/articles/articledet.cfm?articleid=387 (retrieved 30 July 2002).

Skocpol, Theda. (1979). *States and Revolutions: A Comparative Analysis of France, Russia and China*. Cambridge, UK: Cambridge University Press.

Snow, David A., E. Burke Rochford, Steven K. Worden, and Robert D. Benford. (1986). "Frame Alignment Processes, Micromobiization and Movement Participation." *American Sociological Review, 51*, 464–81.

Snyder, David and Charles Tilly. (1972). "Hardship and Collective Violence in France, 1830–1960." *American Sociological Review, 37*, 520–32.

Spilerman, Seymour. (1970). "The Causes of Racial Disturbances: A Comparison of Alternative Explanations." *American Sociological Review, 35*, 627–49.

Spilerman, Seymour. (1976). "Structural Characteristics of Cities and the Severity of Racial Disorders." *American Sociological Review, 41*, 771–93.

Statistics Canada. (2008). "Table E175–177: Union Membership in Canada, in Total and as a Percentage of Non-Agricultural Paid Workers and Union Members with International Affiliation, 1911–1975." On the World Wide Web at http://www.statcan.gc.ca/pub/11–516-x/sectione/4147438-eng .htm#6 (retrieved 23 January 2011).

Strong-Boag, Veronica. (1986). "Ever a Crusader: Nellie McClung, First-Wave Feminist." In V. Strong-Boag and A. Fellman, eds., *Rethinking Canada: The Promise of Women's History* (pp. 178–90). Toronto: Copp Clark Pitman.

Tilly, Charles. (1978). *From Mobilization to Revolution*. Reading, MA: Addison-Wesley.

Tilly, Charles. (1979a). "Collective Violence in European Perspective." In H. Graham and T. Gurr, eds., *Violence in America: Historical and Comparative Perspective*, 2nd ed. (pp. 83–118). Beverly Hills, CA: Sage.

Tilly, Charles. (1979b). "Repertoires of Contention in America and Britain, 1750–1830." In Mayer N. Zald and John D. McCarthy eds., *The Dynamics of Social Movements: Resource Mobilization, Social Control and Tactics* (pp. 126–55). Cambridge, MA: Winthrop.

Tilly, Charles, Louise Tilly, and Richard Tilly. (1975). *The Rebellious Century, 1830–1930*. Cambridge, MA: Harvard University Press.

Toronto Star. (2015). "How the parties performed in each province." *Toronto Star* 19 October. On the World Wide Web at http://www.thestar.com/news/federal-election/2015/10/19/how-the-parties-performed-in-each-province.html (retrieved 20 October 2015).

Turner, Bryan S. (1986). *Citizenship and Capitalism: The Debate over Reformism*. London: Allen and Unwin.

Weber, Max. (1946 [1922]). "Class, Status, Party." In H. H. Gerth and C. Wright Mills, eds. and trans., *From Max Weber: Essays in Sociology* (pp. 180–95). New York: Oxford University Press.

Wolf, Eric. (1999 [1969]). *Peasant Wars of the 20th Century*. Norman, OK: Oklahoma University Press.

"Women in National Parliaments."(2015). On the World Wide Web at http://www.ipu.org/wmn-e/classif.htm (retrieved 26 May 2015).

World Values Survey. (2014). On the World Wide Web at http://www.worldvaluessurvey.org/WVSOnline.jsp (retrieved 3 November 2014).

Worth, Robert. (2001). "The Deep Intellectual Roots of Islamic Terror." On the World Wide Web at http://www.nytimes.com (retrieved 13 October 2002).

Yardley, William. (2011). "The Branding of the Occupy Movement." *New York Times* 27 November. On the World Wide Web at http://www.nytimes.com (retrieved 21 January 2012).

CHAPTER 20

African Centre for Biosafety. (2005). On the World Wide Web at http://www.biosafetyafrica.net/index.htm (retrieved 7 March 2005).

Agence France-Presse. (2004). "Chirac Lashes Out against US Cultural Domination." *Free Republic.* 7 October. On the World Wide Web at http://www.freerepublic.com/focus/f-news/1237687/posts (retrieved 16 August 2012).

American Apparel. (2008). "Legalize LA." On the World Wide Web at http://www.americanapparel.net/contact/legalizela/Legalize_LA.pdf (retrieved 14 December 2011).

American Apparel. (2013). *Facebook*. On the World Wide Web at https://www.facebook.com/AmericanApparel (retrieved 25 November 2014).

Babson, Steve. (2000). "Cross-Border Trade with Mexico and the Prospect for Worker Solidarity: The Case of Mexico." *Critical Sociology*, 26 (1, 2), 13–35.

Bales, Kevin. (1999). *Disposable People: New Slavery in the Global Economy*. Los Angeles: University of California Press.

Barford, Vanessa and Gerry Holt. (2013). "Google, Amazon, Starbucks: The Rise of 'Tax Shaming.'" *BBC* May 21. On the World Wide Web at http://www.bbc.com/news/maga-zine-20560359 (retrieved 18 November 2014).

Barlow, Maude. (2001). "The Global Monoculture: 'Free Trade' versus Culture and Democracy." *Earth Island Journal*, 16, 3. On the World Wide Web at http://www.earthisland.org/eijournal/new_articles.cfm?articleID=270&journalID=48 (retrieved 22 November 2006).

BBC. (2013). "Starbucks pays UK corporation tax for first time since 2009." *BBC* June 23. On the World Wide Web at http://www.bbc.com/news/uk-politics-23019514 (retrieved 18 November 2014).

Bello, Walden. (2002). "Drop Till We Shop?" *The Nation Online.* On the World Wide Web at http://www.thenation.com/doc.mhtml?i520021021andc51ands5bello (retrieved 3 October 2002).

Bentley Stephen. (2004). "Fighting Global Warming at the Farmers' Market. The Role of Local Food Systems in Reducing Greenhouse Gas Emissions." *A FoodShare Research in Action Report*. On the World Wide Web at http://www.foodshare.net/resource/files/ACF230.pdf (retrieved 9 January 2004).

Bird, Kate and David Hughes. (1997). "Ethical Consumerism: The Case of 'Fairly-Trade' Coffee." *Business Ethics. A European Review*, 6, 159–67.

Bivens, Lyle J. and Adam Hersh. (2003). "A Rough Row." *Global Policy Forum.* On the World Wide Web at http://wwwglobalpolicy.org/socecon/bwi-wto/wto/2003/0909rough.htm (retrieved 9 September 2003).

Blackwell, Richard. (2011). "Solar Power Boom Hits a Wall." *Globe and Mail* 6 November. On the World Wide Web at http://www.theglobeandmail.com/report-on-business/industry-news/energy-and-resources/solar-power-boom-hits-a-wall/article4180337 (retrieved 9 September 2014).

Bogiasky, Jeremy. (2014). "Obama Administration Moves to Crack Down on Tax Inversions." *Forbes* 22 September. On the World Wide Web at http://www.forbes.com/sites/jeremybogaisky/2014/09/22/obama-administration-moves-to-crack-down-on-tax-inversions (retrieved 18 November 2014).

Brown, Lester. (2005). *Outgrowing the Earth: The Food Security Challenge in an Age of Falling Water Tables and Rising Temperatures*. Washington, DC: Earth Policy Institute.

Brownell, Kelly and Katherine Battle Horgen. (2004). *Food Fight. The Inside Story of the Food Industry, America's Obesity Crisis, and What We Can Do About It*. Toronto: Contemporary Books.

Brym, Robert et al. (2005). "In Faint Praise of the World Bank's Gender Development Policy." *Canadian Journal of Sociology*, 30, 95–111.

Brym, Robert, Melissa Godbout, Andreas Hoffbauer, Gabe Menard, and Tony Huiquan Zhang. (2014). "Social Media in the 2011 Egyptian Uprising." *British Journal of Sociology* 65, 2, 266–92.

Bundhun, Rebecca. (2014). "Back Office Bid to Stay in Front in Indian IT." *The National* November 15. On the World Wide Web at http://www.thenational.ae/business/economy/back-office-bid-to-stay-in-front-in-indian-it#page2 (retrieved 25 November 2014).

Campaign to Stop Killer Coke, www.http://killercoke.org.

Canadian Centre for Policy Alternatives. (2014). "CEO vs Average Pay in Canada: All in a Day's Work?" On the World Wide Web at https://www.policyalternatives.ca/ceo (retrieved 29 October 2014).

Canadian Labour Congress. (2012). "Day of Mourning for Bangladeshi Garment Fire Victims." On the World Wide Web at http://www.canadianlabour.ca/news-room/statements/day-mourning-bangladeshi-garment-fire-victims (retrieved 21 November 2014).

Canadian Labour Congress. (2014). "What Did Corporate Tax Cuts Deliver? A Background Report for Corporate Tax Freedom Day, 2014." On the World Wide Web at http://www.canadianlabour.ca/news-room/publications/what-did-corporate-tax-cuts-deliver-background-report-corporate-tax-freedom-d (retrieved 18 November 2014).

Canadian Steel Producers Association. (2013). "Canadian Steel Matters." On the World Wide Web at canadiansteel.ca/wp-content/.../02/CanadianSteelMatters_Winter1.pdf (retrieved 9 September 2014).

Cardoso, Fernando Henrique. (1993). "The Challenges of Social Democracy in Latin America." In Menno Vellinga, ed., *Social*

Democracy in Latin America: Prospects for Change. Boulder, CO: Westview Press.

Cargill. (2014). "Meat Processing." On the World Wide Web at http://www.cargill.ca/en/products-services/meat-processing/ (retrieved 29 September 2014).

Castells, Manuel. (1998). *The Information Age: Economy, Society, and Culture: Vol. 3, End of the Millennium.* Malden, MA: Blackwell.

Center on Budget and Policy Priorities. (2014). "Chart Book: The Legacy of the Great Recession." On the World Wide Web at http://www.cbpp.org/cms/index.cfm?fa=view&id=3252 (retrieved 21 November 2014).

Cisco Systems Inc. (2011). *Cisco Connected World Technology Report.* On the World Wide Web at http://www.cisco.com/en/US/netsol/ns1120/index.html (retrieved November 8 2011).

Clay, Jason. (2004). *World Agriculture and the Environment: A Commodity-by-Commodity Guide to Impacts and Practices.* Washington, DC: Island Press.

Denny, Charlotte. (2002). "The Contented Malcontent." *Guardian* 6 July. On the World Wide Web at http://www.guardian.co.uk/business/2002/jul/06/globalisation (retrieved 13 December 2011).

Dobbs, Richard, Corinne Sawers, Fraser Thompson, James Manyika, Jonathan Woetzel, Peter Child, Sorcha McKenna, and Angela Spatharou. (2014). *Overcoming Obesity: An Initial Economic Analysis.* McKinsey Global Institute. On the World Wide Web at http://www.mckinsey.com/insights/economic_studies/how_the_world_could_better_fight_obesity (retrieved 15 November 2014).

Durning, Alan. (1992). *How Much Is Enough? The Consumer Society and the Fate of the Earth.* New York: Norton.

Economist [The]. (2014). "The World's Second Biggest Consumer." *Economist* 18 February. On the World Wide Web at http://www.economist.com/blogs/analects/2014/02/chinas-economy (retrieved 17 September 2014).

"Egypt Protests: Q and A." (2011). *Telegraph* 27 January. On the World Wide Web at http://www.telegraph.co.uk/news/worldnews/africaandindianocean/egypt/8286864/Egypt-protests-Q-and-A.html (retrieved 13 December 2011).

"Egypt Uprising: Timeline." (2011). *Telegraph* 22 November. On the World Wide Web at http://www.telegraph.co.uk/news/worldnews/africaandindianocean/egypt/8907227/Egypt-uprising-timeline.html (retrieved 13 December 2011).

European Commission. (2013). *Global Value Chains: Investment and Trade for Development Chapter IV.* On the World Wide Web at trade.ec.europa.eu/doclib/html/151922.htm (retrieved 26 November 2014).

Evans-Pritchard, Ambrose. (2009). "There's No Quick Fix to the Global Economy's Excess Capacity." *Telegraph* 15 August. On the World Wide Web at http://www.telegraph.co.uk/finance/comment/ambroseevans_pritchard/6035300/Theres-no-quick-fix-to-the-global-economys-excess-capacity.html (retrieved 16 November 2011).

Fairtrade Label South Africa. (2014). "Fairtrade Global Snapshot 2013." On the World Wide Web at http://www.fairtradelabel.org.za/news/fairtrade-delivering-change-annual-sales-figures-2013-14.191.html (retrieved 27 December 2014).

Fallows, James. (2008). "'Be Nice to the Countries that Lend You Money.' An Interview with Gao Xiqing." *Atlantic Monthly, 302* (December), 62–65.

FAO. (2009). *How to Feed the World in 2050.* Rome: Food and Agriculture Organization of the United Nations.

FAO. (2013). *FAO Statistical Yearbook 2013: World food and Agriculture.* Rome: Food and Agriculture Organization of the United Nations.

Ferguson, Niall. (2004). *Colossus: The Rise and Fall of the American Empire.* New York: Penguin Books.

Fischer, Stanley. (2014). "The Great Recession: Moving Ahead." Presented at *The Great Recession—Moving Ahead Conference,* August 11.

Forbes. 2014c. "The World's Billionaires." On the World Wide Web at http://www.forbes.com/billionaires (retrieved 27 December 2014).

Frank, Thomas. (1997). *The Conquest of Cool.* Chicago: University of Chicago Press.

Freeland, Chrystia. (2011). "Protesters Should Get Occupied with Economic Solutions." *Globe and Mail* 4 November: B2.

Friends of the Earth Europe. (2009). "Overconsumption? Our Use of the World's Natural Resources." On the World Wide Web at www.foe.co.uk/sites/default/files/downloads/overconsumption.pdf (retrieved 5 November 2014).

Frizell, Sam. (2014). "Americans Are Taking on Debt at Scary High Rates." *Time* February 19. On the World Wide Web at http://time.com/8740/federal-reserve-debt-bankrate-consumers-credit-card (retrieved 5 November 2014).

Frundt, Henry. (2000). "Models of Cross-Border Organizing in the Maquila Industries." *Critical Sociology, 26* (1–2), 36–55.

Ghemawat, Pankaj. (2007). "Why the World Isn't Flat." *Foreign Policy.* (March/April 2007), 54–60.

Ghemawat, Pankaj. (2011). "Implications of a Borderless World—Interview with Pankaj Ghemawat." *Process Excellence Network.* July 20. On the World Wide Web at http://www.processexcellencenetwork.com/change-management/articles/the-temptation-of-a-borderless-world-interview-wit (retrieved 7 November 2011).

"Global 500." (2014). *Fortune* November 25. On the World Wide Web at http://fortune.com/global500/wal-mart-stores-1 (retrieved 25 November 2014).

Grant, Tavia. (2011). "Canada's Wage Gap at a Record High: OECD." *Globe and Mail* December 5. On the World Wide Web at http://www.theglobeandmail.com/report-on-business/economy/canadas-wage-gap-at-record-high-oecd/article4099041 (retrieved 13 December 2011).

Graveland, Bill. (2013). "One Year Later: Beef Industry Bounces Back After Massive XL Foods Recall." *CTV News* September 8. On the World Wide Web at http://www.ctvnews.ca/business/one-year-later-beef-industry-bounces-back-after-massive-xl-foods-recall-1.1445299 (retrieved 29 September 2014).

Haight, Colleen. (2011). "The Problem with Fair Trade Coffee." *Stanford Social Innovation Review* Summer. On the World Wide Web at http://www.ssireview.org/articles/entry/the_problem_with_fair_trade_coffee (retrieved 14 December 2011).

Hall, Sally. (2005). "Hungry for an Alternative." *Independent* (UK) 28 June.

Harvey, David. (1990). *The Condition of Postmodernity.* Cambridge, MA: Blackwell.

Hays, Constance. (2000). "Learning to Think Smaller at Coke." *New York Times* 6 February: Business Section.

Heath, Andrew and Joseph Potter. (2004). *The Rebel Sell: Why the Culture Can't Be Jammed.* Toronto: Harper Collins.

Hickman, Martin. (2008). "All Starbucks' Coffee to be Fairtrade." *Independent* November 26. On the World Wide Web at http://www.independent.co.uk/life-style/food-and-drink/news/all-starbucks-coffee-to-be-fairtrade-1035162.html (retrieved 14 December 2011).

Hoogvelt, Ankie. (1997). *Globalization and the Postcolonial World.* Baltimore, MD: Johns Hopkins University Press.

Hopkins, Terrence and Immanuel Wallerstein. (1986). "Commodity Chains in the World Economy Prior to 1800." *Review* (a Journal of the Fernand Braudel Center), *10* (1), 157–70.

Howard, Philip H. and Daniel Jaffee. (2013). "Tensions Between Firm Size and Sustainability Goals: Fair Trade Coffee in the United States" *Sustainability 5* (1), 72–89.

ILO *(International Labour Organization).* (2014). "Profits and Poverty: The Economics of Forced Labour." On the World Wide Web at http://www.ilo.org/global/topics/forced-labour/publications/WCMS_243391/lang--en/index.htm (retrieved 10 October 2014).

Institute for Global Labour and Human Rights. (2014). "Rana Plaza: A Look Back, and Forward." On the World Wide Web at http://www.globallabourrights.org/alerts/rana-plaza-bangladesh-anniversary-a-look-back-and-forward (retrieved 21 November 2014).

Institute of Mergers, Acquisitions, and Alliances. (2014). "Announced Mergers & Acquisitions: Worldwide, 1985–2014e." Thomson Financial, Institute of Mergers, Acquisitions and Alliances. On the World Wide Web at http://www.imaa-institute.org/statistics-mergers-acquisitions.html#TopMergersAcquisitions_Worldwide (retrieved 25 November 2014).

International Grains Council. (2013). *Five-Year Global Supply and Demand Projections.* On the World Wide Web at www.igc.int/en/downloads/grainsupdate/igc_5yrprojections.pdf (retrieved 12 September 2014).

Internet World Stats. (2014a). "Internet Usage and Population in Oceania" On the World Wide Web at http://www.internetworldstats.com/stats6.htm (retrieved 29 October 2014).

Internet World Stats. (2014b). "Internet Usage Statistics for Africa." On the World Wide Web at http://www.internetworldstats.com/stats1.htm (retrieved 29 October 2014).

Internet World Stats. (2014c). "Internet Usage Statistics for all the Americas" On the World Wide Web at http://www.internetworldstats.com/stats2.htm (retrieved 29 October 2014).

Internet World Stats. (2014d). "Internet Usage in Asia" On the World Wide Web at http://www.internetworldstats.com/stats3.htm (retrieved 29 October 2014).

Internet World Stats. (2014e). "Internet Usage in Europe" On the World Wide Web at http://www.internetworldstats.com/stats4.htm (retrieved 29 October 2014).

Internet World Stats. (2014f). "Internet Usage in the Middle East" On the World Wide Web at http://www.internetworldstats.com/stats5.htm (retrieved 29 October 2014).

Internet World Stats. (2014g). "Internet Usage Statistics: The Internet Big Picture, World Internet Users and Population Stats." On the World Wide Web at http://www.internetworldstats.com/stats.htm (retrieved 29 October 2014).

ISAAA (International Service for the Acquisition of Agri-biotech Applications). (2013). "ISAAA Brief 46-2013: Executive Summary: Global Status of Commercialized Biotech/GM Crops: 2013" On the World Wide Web at http://www.isaaa.org/resources/publications/briefs/46/executivesummary (retrieved 20 November 2014).

Kahn, Jeremy. (2008). "Recession Trickles to India." *New York Times* 3 December. On the World Wide Web at http://www.nytimes.com/2008/12/04/business/worldbusiness/04rupee.html (retrieved 19 August 2009).

Kaufman, Alexander C. (2014). "Warren Buffett: U.S. Never Followed Through on That Whole 'Tax the Rich' Thing." *Huffington Post* 8 October. On the World Wide Web at http://www.huffingtonpost.com/2014/10/08/warren-buffett-taxes_n_5952776.html (retrieved 18 November 2014).

Kennedy, Dawn. (2004). "Nollywood Thinks Outside the Box." *Sunday Independent.* On the World Wide Web at http://www.sundayindependent.co.za/index.php?fSectionId51083andfArticleId52324573 (retrieved 28 November 2004).

Kindall, Henry and David Pimentel. (1994). "Constraints on the Expansion of the Global Food Supply," *Ambio, 23,* 3.

Klein, Naomi. (2000). *No Logo.* Toronto: Knopf Canada.

KPMG. (2014a). "Corporate tax rates table." On the World Wide Web at http://www.kpmg.com/global/en/services/tax/tax-tools-and-resources/pages/corporate-tax-rates-table.aspx (retrieved 18 November 2014).

KPMG. (2014b). "Individual income tax rates table." On the World Wide Web at http://www.kpmg.com/global/en/services/tax/tax-tools-and-resources/pages/individual-income-tax-rates-table.aspx (retrieved 18 November 2014).

Labor Program. (2014). "Union Coverage in Canada, 2013." *Government of Canada.* On the World Wide Web at http://www.labour.gc.ca/eng/resources/info/publications/union_coverage/union_coverage.shtml (retrieved 11 October 2014).

Landler, Mark. (2008). "The US Financial Crisis Is Spreading to Europe." *New York Times* September. On the World Wide Web at http://www.nytimes.com/2008/10/01/business/worldbusiness/01global.html?partner=rssnyt&emc=rss (retrieved 19 August 2009).

Lang, Tim and Jules Pretty. (2005). "Farm Costs and Food Miles: An Assessment of the Full Cost of the UK Weekly Food Basket." *Food Policy, 30* (1).

Lappé, Anna and Frances Moore Lappé. (2002). *Hope's Edge: The Next Diet for a Small Planet.* New York: Tarcher/Penguin.

Lindstrom, Martin. (2003). *Brand Child. Remarkable Insights into the Minds of Today's Global Kids and Their Relationships with Brands.* Sterling, VA: Millward Brown.

Lynn, Barry. (2002). "Unmade in America. The True Cost of the Global Assembly Line." *Harper's Magazine, 304* (1825), 34–41.

Maclean's. (2013). "The Top 50: Best in Class." *Macleans* On the World Wide Web at http://www.macleans.ca/canada-top-50-socially-responsible-corporations-2013/ (retrieved 21 November 2014).

Manning, Richard. (2004). "The Oil We Eat: Following the Food Chain Back To Iraq." *Harper's Magazine* (February). On the World Wide Web at http://www.harpers.org/TheOilWeEat.html (retrieved 15 October 2006).

Marché du film. (2004). European Audiovisual Observatory. *Focus 2014: World Film Market Trends* http://issuu.com/marchedufilm/docs/focus_2014.

Marx, Karl and Friedrich Engels. (1972 [1848]). "Manifesto of the Communist Party." In R. Tucker, ed., *The Marx-Engels Reader* (pp. 331–62). New York: Norton.

"McDonald's Apologizes for Beefy Fries." (2001). *CBC News.* On the World Wide Web at http://www.cbc.ca/news/

canada/story/2001/05/24/fries_010524.html (retrieved 25 May 2001).

McDonald's Corporation. (2013). *2013 Annual Report*. On the World Wide Web at http://www.aboutmcdonalds.com/mcd/investors/annual_reports.html (retrieved 29 September 2014).

McDonald's Canada. (2014). "Frequently Asked Questions." On the World Wide Web at http://www.mcdonalds.ca/ca/en/contact_us/faq.html (retrieved 29 September 2014).

McIntyre, Robert S., Matthew Gardner, and Richard Phillips. (2014). "The Sorry State of Corporate Taxes." *Citizens for Tax Justice*. On the World Wide Web at http://www.ctj.org/corporatetaxdodgers/sorrystateofcorptaxes.php#Whos Paying and Whos Note (retrieved 18 November 2014).

McKibben, Bill. (1993). *The Age of Missing Information.* New York: Plumb.

McKibben, Bill. (2005). "The Cuba Diet: What Will You Be Eating When the Revolution Comes?" *Harper's Magazine* (April). On the World Wide Web at http://www.harpers.org/TheCubaDiet.html (retrieved 15 October 2006).

Milanovic, Branko. (2005). "Global Income Inequality: What It Is and Why It Matters?" DESA Working Paper No. 26. On the World Wide Web at http://www.un.org/esa/desa/papers/2006/wp26_2006.pdf (retrieved 7 March 2009).

Milkman, Ruth. (2000). "Immigrant Organizing and the New Labor Movement in Los Angeles." *Critical Sociology, 26* (1/2), 59–81.

Morgan, Gwyn. (2014). "Temporary Foreign Workers Perform Critical Jobs." *The Globe and Mail August* 17. On the World Wide Web at http://www.theglobeandmail.com/report-on-business/temporary-foreign-workers-perform-critical-jobs/article20088968/ (retrieved 22 November 2014).

Motlagh, Jason. (2014). "The Ghosts of Rana Plaza." *The Virginia Quarterly Review 90*, 2, 44–89.

Navdanya. (2005). Homepage. On the World Wide Web at http://www.navdanya.org/ (retrieved 1 October 2006).

Nestle, Marion. (2011). "Coke's New Buddy: Oxfam Helps Coca-Cola Reduce Poverty." *Atlantic Monthly*. On the World Wide Web at http://www.theatlantic.com/health/archive/2011/04/cokes-new-buddy-oxfam-helps-coca-cola-reduce-poverty/237666 (retrieved 21 April 2011).

Nicholson, Chris V. (2010). "Chinese Carmaker Geely Completes Acquisition of Volvo from Ford." *New York Times* 2 August. On the World Wide Web at http://www.nytimes.com/2010/08/03/business/global/03volvo.html (retrieved 16 November 2011).

Nissen, Bruce. (2000). "Editor's Introduction: The Labor Movement in a New Globalized Environment." *Critical Sociology, 26* (1/2), 3–8.

No Sweat. (2005). "Changing an Industry." On the World Wide Web at http://www.nosweatapparel.com (retrieved 1 October 2006).

OECD. (2014a). "Obesity Update." On the World Wide Web at www.oecd.org/els/health-systems/Obesity-Update-2014.pdf (retrieved 15 November 2014).

OECD. (2014b). "Foreign Direct Investment (FDI) Statistics-OECD Data, Analysis and Forecasts." On the World Wide Web at http://www.imaa-institute.org/images/figure_announced%20mergers%20&%20acquisitions%20%28worldwide%29.jpg (retrieved 22 June 2015).

OECD. (2014c). Tax database. On the World Wide Web at http://www.oecd.org/tax/tax-policy/tax-database.htm#C_CorporateCapital (retrieved 27 December 2014).

Organic Consumers Association. (2005). "Prohibited Gene-Altered Corn Found in Latin American & Caribbean Food Aid Shipments. Source: Environmental News Service. On the World Wide Web at http://www.organicconsumers.org/ge/caribbean21705.cfm (retrieved 16 February 2005).

Owram, Kristine. (2014). "Canada's $9-Billion Auto Sector Bailout Lacked Proper Oversight, says Auditor General." *National Post* November 25. On the World Wide Web at http://business.financialpost.com/2014/11/25/canadas-9-billion-auto-sector-bailout-lacked-proper-oversight-says-auditor-general (retrieved 25 November 2014).

Oxfam. (2002). "Mugged: Poverty in Your Coffee Cup." (Research paper). On the World Wide Web at http://www.oxfamamerica.org/newsandpublications/publications/research_reports/mugged (retrieved September 2002).

Oxfam. (2014). "Behind the Brands." On the World Wide Web at http://www.oxfam.org/en/campaigns/behind-brands (retrieved November 8th, 2014).

Paarlberg, Robert. (2010). *Food Politics: What Everybody Needs to Know*. New York: Oxford University Press.

Picot, Garnett and John Myles. (2005). "Income Inequality and Low Income in Canada: An International Perspective." Statistics Canada Research Paper. On the World Wide Web at http://www.statcan.ca/english/research/11F0019MIE/11F0019MIE2005240.pdf (retrieved 10 February 2005).

Pimentel, David and Anne Wilson. (2004). "World Population, Agriculture and Nutrition." *World Watch Magazine*, September/October. *Energy Bulletin*. On the World Wide Web at http://www.energybulletin.net/3834.html (retrieved 5 January 2005).

Robbins, Richard H. (2005). *Global Problems and the Culture of Capitalism*, 3rd ed. Boston: Pearson.

Ross, Andrew, ed. (1997). *No Sweat: Fashion, Free Trade and the Rights of Garment Workers*. New York: Verso.

Ross, Robert J. S. (2004). *Slaves to Fashion: Poverty and Abuse in the New Sweatshops*. Ann Arbor, MI: University of Michigan Press.

Sachs, Jeffrey D. (2005). *The End of Poverty: Economic Possibilities for Our Time*. New York: Penguin.

Sanchez, Raf and Richard Blackden. (2012). "Apple Supplier Foxconn Promises to Improve Following Scathing Report into Working Conditions." *The Telegraph* 29 March. On the World Wide Web at http://www.telegraph.co.uk/technology/apple/9175077/Apple-supplier-Foxconn-promises-to-improve-following-scathing-report-into-working-conditions.html (retrieved 22 November 2014).

Schäfer, Daniel, Alice Ross, and Delphine Strauss. (2013). "Foreign Exchange: The Big Fix." *Financial Times* November 12. On the World Wide Web at http://www.ft.com/cms/s/2/7a9b85b4-4af8-11e3-8c4c-00144feabdc0.html#axzz2l5tqPv7V (retrieved 25 October 2014).

Schor, J. B. (1998). *The Overspent American*. New York: Basic Books.

"Seven Countries Raising The Minimum Wage." (2011). *Financial Edge*. 21 January. On the World Wide Web at http://financialedge.investopedia.com/financial-edge/0111/7-Countries-Raising-The-Minimum-Wage.aspx#axzz1f8DCs6uE (retrieved 29 November 2011).

Shrybman, Steven. (2000). *Trade, Agriculture and Climate Change: How Agricultural Trade Policies Fuel Climate Change*. Institute for Agriculture and Trade Policy. On the World Wide Web at http://www.iatp.org (retrieved 3 November 2000).

Sobal, Jeffrey. (2001). "Commentary: Globalization and the Epidemiology of Obesity." *International Journal of Epidemiology, 30* (5), 1136–37.

Soros, George. (1998). *The Crisis of Global Capitalism: Open Society Endangered*. New York: Public Affairs

Starr, Amory. (1999). *Naming the Enemy: Anti-Corporate Movements Confront Globalization*. London: Zed Books.

Statistics Canada. (2010). "Canada's Employment Downturn." On the World Wide Web at http://www.statcan.gc.ca/pub/75-001-x/2009112/article/11048-eng.htm (retrieved 25 September 2014).

Statistics Canada. (2014a). "Education and Occupation of High-Income Canadians." On the World Wide Web at http://www12.statcan.gc.ca/nhs-enm/2011/as-sa/99-014-x/99-014-x2011003_2-eng.cfm (retrieved 21 November 2014).

Stiglitz, Joseph. (2003). *Globalization and Its Discontents*. New York: W. W. Norton.

Strange, Susan. (1986). *Casino Capitalism*. London: Blackwell Books.

Sustain/Elm Farm Research Centre Report. (2001). "Eating Oil: Food in a Changing Climate." On the World Wide Web at http://www.sustainweb.org/pdf/eatoil_sumary.pdf (retrieved 15 December 2001).

"Tahrir Square's Place in Egypt's History." (2011). *BBC News*, 22 November. On the World Wide Web at http://www.bbc.co.uk/news/world-middle-east-12332601 (retrieved 13 December 2011).

Tomlinson, John. (1991). *Cultural Imperialism: A Critical Introduction*. Baltimore, MD: John Hopkins University Press.

Trivett, Vincent. (2011). "25 US Mega Corporations: Where They Rank if They Were Countries." *Business Insider* June 27. On the World Wide Web at http://www.businessinsider.com/25-corporations-bigger-tan-countries-2011-6?op=1 (retrieved 25 October 2014).

UNDP. (2014). *Human Development Report 2014*. New York: UNDP.

UNEP-FAO. *Vital Forest Graphics*. (2009). In GRID-Arendal (2012). "The Health of Our Forests" UNEP/GRID-Arendal Maps and Graphics Library. On the World Wide Web at http://www.grida.no/graphicslib/detail/the-health-of-our-forests_a7f0 (retrieved 28 October 2014).

UNESCO. (2013). "Diversity of Cultural Expressions." On the World Wide Web at https://en.unesco.org/creativity (retrieved 24 November 2014).

UNGIFT. (2014). "Survey: 30 Million People Enslaved Around the World Today." *United Nations Global Initiative to Fight Human Trafficking*. On the World Wide Web at http://www.ungift.org/knowledgehub/stories/October2013/survey_-30-million-people-enslaved-around-the-world-today.html (retrieved 9 October 2014).

U.S. Bureau of Labor Statistics. (2014b). "Union Members—2013." On the World Wide Web at www.bls.gov/news.release/pdf/union2.pdf (retrieved 11 October 2014).

U.S. Department of Defense. (2008) *Base Structure Report, 2008*. On the World Wide Web at http://combatingglobalization.com/articles/combating_globalization4.html (retrieved 12 August 2012).]]

U.S. Treasury. (2014). "The Debt to the Penny and Who Holds it." *Treasury Direct*. On the World Wide Web at http://www.treasurydirect.gov/NP/debt/current (retrieved 22 September 2014).

Wall, Melissa. (2000). "KFC into India: A Case Study of Resistance to Globalization Discourse." In Robin Andersen and Lance Strate, eds., *Critical Studies in Media Commercialism* (pp. 291–309). Oxford: Oxford University Press.

Wallerstein, Immanuel. (2002). "The Eagle Has Crash Landed." *Foreign Policy, 131* (July/August), 60–68.

Walt, Vivienne. (2008). "The World's Growing Food-Price Crisis." *Time* 27 February. On the World Wide Web at http://www.time.com/time/world/article/0,8599,1717572-2,00.html (27 February 2008).

Waters, Malcolm. (1995). *Globalization*. New York: Routledge.

Whitaker, Brian. (2010). "How a Man Setting Fire to Himself Sparked an Uprising in Tunisia." *Guardian* 28 December. On the World Wide Web at http://www.guardian.co.uk/commentisfree/2010/dec/28/tunisia-ben-ali (retrieved 13 December 2011).

Woodroffe, Jessica and Mark Ellis-Jones. (2000). "States of Unrest: Resistance to IMF Policies in Poor Countries." *World Development Movement Report* (Global Policy Forum). On the World Wide Web at http://www.globalpolicy.org/socecon/bwi-wto/imf/2000/protest.htm (retrieved 8 September 2000).

World Bank. (2008). "World Bank Development Indicators." © World Bank. On the World Wide Web at http://www.rrojasdatabank.info/wdi2008toc.htm (retrieved 19 August 2009). License: Creative Commons Attribution CC BY 3.0.

World Bank. (2013). "Microfinance and Financial Inclusion." On the World Wide Web at http://web.worldbank.org/WBSITE/EXTERNAL/NEWS/0,,contentMDK:20433592~menuPK:34480~pagePK:64257043~piPK:437376~theSitePK:4607,00.html (retrieved 29 October 2014).

World Bank. (2014a). "5.11 World Development Indicators: Power and Communications." On the World Wide Web at http://wdi.worldbank.org/table/5.11 (retrieved 29 October 2014).

World Bank. (2014b). "Gross Domestic Product 2014." On the World Wide Web at databank.worldbank.org/data/download/GDP.pdf (retrieved 5 October 2014).

World Wildlife Fund. (2004). "Soy Boom: Doom or Boon for South America's Forests and Savannah?" On the World Wide Web at http://www.wwf.org.uk/news/scotland/n_0000001332.asp (retrieved 2 September 2004).

World Wildlife Fund. (2014). "Living Planet Report 2014." On the World Wide Web at http://www.wwf.ca/newsroom/reports/living_planet_report_2014.cfm (retrieved 5 November 2014).

WTO. (2009). *China—Measures Affecting Trading Rights and Distribution Services for Certain Publications and Audiovisual Entertainment Products, AB-2009-3: Report of the Appellate Body*. World Trade Organization. WT/DS363/AB/R 21 December 2009 (09-6642).

WTO. (2014). "Modest Trade Growth Anticipated for 2014 and 2015 Following Two Year Slump." On the World Wide Web at http://www.wto.org/english/news_e/pres14_e/pr721_e.htm (retrieved 25 October 2014).

EPILOGUE

Hanafi, Sari. (2011). "University Systems in the Arab East: Publish Globally and Perish Locally vs. Publish Locally and Perish Globally." *Current Sociology, 59* (3), 291–309.

Polanyi, Karl. (1944). *The Great Transformation*. New York: Farrar & Rinehart.

INDEX

Bold numbers indicate pages on which a key term appears bolded; numbers starting with "21-" refer to Online Chapter 21.